THE OXFORD HANDBOOK OF

ISLAMIC LAW

THE OXFORD HANDBOOK OF

ISLAMIC LAW

Edited by

ANVER M. EMON

RUMEE AHMED

OXFORD
UNIVERSITY PRESS

OXFORD
UNIVERSITY PRESS

Great Clarendon Street, Oxford, OX2 6DP,
United Kingdom

Oxford University Press is a department of the University of Oxford.
It furthers the University's objective of excellence in research, scholarship,
and education by publishing worldwide. Oxford is a registered trade mark of
Oxford University Press in the UK and in certain other countries

First Edition published in 2018
Impression: 1

Published in the United States of America by Oxford University Press
198 Madison Avenue, New York, NY 10016, United States of America

British Library Cataloguing in Publication Data
Data available

Library of Congress Control Number: 2018943673

ISBN 978–0–19–967901–0

Printed and bound by
CPI Group (UK) Ltd, Croydon, CR0 4YY

Contents

PART I DISCIPLINE AND CRITIQUE

A. ISLAMIC LEGAL STUDIES: DISCIPLINE AND CRITIQUE

B. ISLAMIC LEGAL STUDIES: DISCIPLINARY APPROACHES

PART II LEGAL THEORY AND INSTITUTIONS

A. LEGAL THEORY

B. INSTITUTIONS

PART III ORIGINS, EMPIRES, AND STATES

A. HISTORICAL STUDIES

B. MUSLIM MINORITIES

PART V SUBSTANTIVE LEGAL AREAS

A. CASE STUDIES

Editors' Introduction

The idea for this project took root many years ago. As scholars based in the North American academy, we regularly confront artificial limits imposed by the disciplinary formation(s) of Islamic legal studies. Those limits not only affect the kind and range of debates possible within the academy, but also constitute the outer boundaries of what others (e.g. journalists, politicians, and pundits) represent Islamic law to be. Of course, these limits are not unique to Islamic legal studies; rather they are found in the study of Islam broadly. We focus on Islamic legal studies both because of our specialization and because of the way it captures myriad Islamic legal fantasies, some of which would be utterly humorous if it were not for the fact that they inform actual state policies that target the civil liberties of Muslim citizens across the North American continent, Europe, and elsewhere. The spate of bills across states in the USA that, for instance, seek to "ban Sharīʿa," are but one example; there are others across Europe and elsewhere whose formulation reveals the limits in the imagination and scope of Islamic legal scholarship. While humanities scholars are often loath to discuss what their scholarship is "for," we strenuously hold that our small subsection of the humanities and social science scholarly community can no longer thumb our noses at the larger world to which our scholarly legacy directly or indirectly contributes. It is time that those of us in Islamic legal studies take stock of the scholarship on Islamic law, mark the limitations of its disciplinary formation(s), and identify the interstices, gaps, and ambiguities that remain fertile sites for further inquiry and scholarship. This is not only an academic need given the fast-evolving state of the field, but a moral imperative given the immediate political implications and uses of our academic work.

We are of course not alone in this aspiration. In recent years, scholars of Islamic studies more broadly have carved out spaces for more reflective analyses of what Islamic studies are or might yet be. There is a sense among many scholars, in particular those who both demand greater scholarly positionality and value interdisciplinarity, that a turning point has come where the long-standing paradigms that have informed Islamic studies generally, and Islamic legal studies specifically, can no longer occupy an unaccounted for, uncritiqued, or unchallenged privileged status. Of course, not all of those in the field of Islamic legal studies will agree with our assessment. Indeed, for many in the field, the status quo of disciplinary formation has been more than beneficial. We respect those who have built their careers on the long-standing disciplinary approaches that inform so much of Islamic legal studies. Nevertheless, we draw upon the aggregate disciplinary perspectives of the contributors to this volume to illustrate that the dominant approaches to the study of Islamic law in the academy are inadequate. They preserve the ghettoized state of Islamic legal studies in the academy at a time when the study of Islamic law can offer a range of disciplinary vantage points to interrogate the pieties that have too long informed the humanities and social sciences, broadly construed.

Method and Discipline

This *Handbook* is not designed to offer readers extended encyclopedia entries on key topics in Islamic law. Other books and handbooks already do that. As editors, we expressly encouraged our authors—and likewise encourage our readers—to examine and appreciate the contests over what Islamic law "is" or is "supposed to be." The scholarly literature can be quite cantankerous; sadly, this is not unusual in academia. But our aim is to take stock of the contests, fights, and animosities that animate the field of Islamic legal studies to understand what is or was at stake in a particular view of Islamic law in one period of study, or according to one disciplinary perspective, as opposed to others. In short, the *Handbook* is meant to offer a self-reflective moment for the field at large. We believe this kind of endeavor signals the maturity of a field that is moving away from positivist accounts of a particular object of study (for instance, Islamic law), and gives us greater appreciation of the implicit—and even explicit—politics in the scholarly construction of a positivist account of Islamic law. We are grateful to the contributors to this volume for taking this journey with us. It was not always easy; for some, thinking along these lines meant prioritizing secondary literature over findings unearthed in primary sources; and in other cases, it meant standing back from a scholarly context in which the contributor was and remains an active participant. We are fortunate to have many luminaries in the field participating in this experiment, and are pleased with the outcome.

At the same time, there are areas in which we struggled, and in which we hope to do better in the future. When soliciting authors, we consciously searched for those who would bring diverse perspectives to the study of Islamic law, expressly aiming to recalibrate excellence by calling to account parochial scholarly tendencies that tend to accompany the homogenization of expertise. We were concerned about privileging historically overrepresented voices in what is a heterogeneous field of differently positioned scholarly voices. To that end, we sought out women, racialized minorities, and scholars working outside of the western academy. Yet, despite our efforts toward gender parity, only a little over one-third of the scholars writing in this volume are women. Such imbalances do more than reflect the current male dominance of our field; they serve to reinforce it, and to legitimize prevailing assumptions about what counts as excellence in the study of Islamic law. To address this shortcoming, we encouraged our authors to pay attention to gender dynamics in their work and to cite female scholars of Islamic law, to varying degrees of success.

We did only marginally better at including racialized scholars. With respect to those working outside of the western academy, we fell woefully short, including only a handful of such scholars. Through this process, we learned about the need to be mindful about diversity early on in a project's lifecycle, about the overburdening that women and minorities experience as they are tokenized and regularly called upon to provide a "diversity voice" in otherwise homogeneous fields, and about the need for editors to take extraordinary measures to ensure diverse representation in order to achieve a more robust understanding of excellence, rather than enable the further provincialization of our field.

Despite our shortcomings, we hope that this volume still represents progress toward broadening the conversation about Islamic law, in bringing marginalized voices to the fore, and in complicating our notions of excellence in scholarly production. We hope that our contributors as well as readers will find the *Handbook* a valuable contribution to Islamic studies in the early years of the twenty-first century.

Organization

The *Handbook* is organized in five parts, beginning with a methodological section that brings a range of disciplinary questions and interrogations to the study of Islamic law. We begin with this section in order to emphasize the self-reflective mode this *Handbook* aims to inspire, and to acknowledge that there is no single way to approach the study of Islamic law. Depending on discipline, audience, and intellectual starting points, the study of Islamic law might be primarily textual (Anver M. Emon, chapter 2), stylized by the life experiences of Muslim interlocutors (Saadia Yacoob, chapter 3, and John R. Bowen, chapter 5), or a manifestation of broader inquiries into the nature of God or the good life (Rumee Ahmed, chapter 4, and Andrew F. March, chapter 6). As Ayesha S. Chaudhry's piece (chapter 1) provocatively suggests, the study of Islamic law may be marked by implicit racial politics that hide behind particular methodological pieties. The interrogations in this first part help us think about how the study of Islamic law can and should intersect across a range of disciplines in the humanities and social sciences, and about how insights gained through the study of Islam and Islamic law can illuminate those disciplines.

The *Handbook* continues thereafter to address a wide range of subjects that both inform and problematize contemporary studies of Islamic law. Our aim was not to be comprehensive across the wide range of possible topics. Such an endeavor would have been more appropriate for an encyclopedia, and not suitable to the kind of intervention this *Handbook* aims to make. Rather, each chapter in the *Handbook* historiographically addresses a narrowly defined topic within the study of Islamic law, and illuminates for a range of readers the highly provocative spaces within which the scholar of Islamic law intervenes with a proof text, an argument, or a conclusion about the nature and/or content of Islamic law. The subjects vary across a wide range of topics, which include: legal theory and institutions (Part II); the historiography of Islamic law from its origins to its place in the modern state (Part III); the various manifestations of Islamic law in the Muslim-majority world and in states where Muslims live as minorities (Part IV); and the Islamic legal approach to various legal subject matters of interest inside and outside the academy (Part V). The range of subjects is vast, but the contents are not designed to be comprehensive. Rather they are illustrations of the overall aim of the *Handbook*, namely to interrogate the study of Islamic law in the hope that twenty-first-century scholars in the powerful knowledge centers of North America and Europe consider and perhaps recast the imagined reality of Islamic law.

The editors would like to thank Professor Kristen Stilt, who served as an editor in the early stages of this project. We would also like to thank the academic law division at Oxford University Press—especially Jamie Berezin, Alex Flach, Natasha Flemming, William Richards, and Elinor Shields—for affording us the space to produce a volume that, though imperfectly and incompletely, breaks with the dominant forms of academic historiography, and that, we hope, will signal new possibilities for the study of Islam and Islamic law.

Anver M. Emon and Rumee Ahmed
February 2018

Notes on the Contributors

Rula Jurdi Abisaab is Associate Professor of Islamic History at the Institute of Islamic Studies at McGill University.

Rumee Ahmed is Associate Dean in the Faculty of Arts and Associate Professor of Islamic Law at the University of British Columbia.

Natasha Bakht is Associate Professor at the University of Ottawa.

John R. Bowen is the Dunbar-Van Cleve Professor in Arts and Sciences at Washington University in St. Louis.

Nathan J. Brown is Professor of Political Science and International Affairs and the Director of the Institute for Middle East Studies at Elliott School of International Affairs.

Ayesha S. Chaudhry is Associate Professor of Islamic Studies and Gender Studies at the University of British Columbia, and is the Canada Research Chair of Religion, Law, and Social Justice.

Melissa Crouch is Senior Lecturer at the Law Faculty at the University of New South Wales, Sydney.

Shannon Dunn is Associate Professor of Religious Studies at Gonzaga University.

Anver M. Emon is Professor of Law and History, and director of the Institute of Islamic Studies at the University of Toronto. He is also the general editor of the Oxford Islamic Legal Studies Series.

Mohammad Fadel is Associate Professor at the University of Toronto and Canada Research Chair for the Law and Economics of Islamic Law.

Antonia Fraser Fujinaga is a translator and independent scholar. She holds a Ph.D. in Islamic law from the University of Edinburgh.

Haim Gerber is Professor of Islamic and Middle Eastern Studies at Hebrew University.

Robert Gleave is Professor of Arabic Studies and Director of the Centre for the Study of Islam at the University of Exeter.

Syed Adnan Hussain is Associate Professor of Religious Studies at Saint Mary's University, Halifax.

Matthew B. Ingalls is Associate Professor of Middle Eastern Studies at the American University of Dubai.

Benjamin Jokisch is a researcher at the Free University of Berlin.

Marion Katz is Professor of Middle Eastern and Islamic Studies at New York University.

Andrew F. March is a Berggruen Fellow at the Edmond J. Safra Center for Ethics, Harvard University.

Ruth A. Miller is Professor of History at the College of Liberal Arts, University of Massachusetts, Boston.

M. Reza Pirbhai is Associate Professor at Georgetown University's School of Foreign Service in Qatar.

Jeff Redding is Associate Professor at Melbourne Law School.

Mara Revkin is a Ph.D. candidate in the Political Science Department at Yale University and an Islamic Law and Civilization Research Fellow of Yale Law School.

Mathias Rohe is Professor and Director of the Department of Civil Law and Civil Procedure at the University of Erlangen-Nuremberg.

Abdullah Saeed is the Sultan of Oman Professor of Arab and Islamic Studies and the Director of the National Centre of Excellence for Islamic Studies at the University of Melbourne.

M. Safa Saraçoğlu is Associate Professor of History at Bloomsburg University of Pennsylvania.

Ayman Shabana is Associate Research Professor at Georgetown University's School of Foreign Service in Qatar.

Ahmed El Shamsy is Associate Professor of Islamic Thought in the Department of Near Eastern Languages and Civilizations at the University of Chicago.

Mariam Sheibani is a Ph.D. candidate in the Near Eastern Languages and Civilizations Department at the University of Chicago.

Youcef Soufi is a Lecturer of Islamic and Religious Studies at the University of British Columbia.

Kristen Stilt is Professor of Law at Harvard Law School. She is the Faculty Director of the Animal Law and Policy Program and Director of the Islamic Legal Studies Program.

Mairaj U. Syed is Associate Professor at the University of California, Davis.

Mathieu Tillier is Professor of History of Medieval Islam at the Université Paris-Sorbonne.

Amir Toft is a research scholar in the Department of Law and an Islamic Law and Civilization Research Fellow at Yale Law School, as well as a Ph.D. candidate in the Department of Near Eastern Languages and Civilizations at the University of Chicago.

Lynn Welchman is Professor of Law at the School of African and Oriental Studies, University of London.

Leonard Wood is an attorney at Sidley Austin LLP and a former research fellow at the Islamic Legal Studies Program of Harvard Law School.

Saadia Yacoob is Assistant Professor of Religion at Williams College.

PART I

DISCIPLINE AND CRITIQUE

A

ISLAMIC LEGAL STUDIES: DISCIPLINE AND CRITIQUE

CHAPTER 1

ISLAMIC LEGAL STUDIES

A CRITICAL HISTORIOGRAPHY

AYESHA S. CHAUDHRY*

We have fought hard and long for integration, as I believe we should have, and I know that we will win. But I've come to believe we're integrating into a burning house.

Martin Luther King, Jr.

I.

Is the Qur'an a book of law? Is Islamic law rooted first and foremost in the Qur'an? What is the relationship between the Qur'an and Islamic law? These are questions that are asked of Muslims the world over, and at their root, the questions that are

* I would like to thank two Institutes for Advanced Study for supporting me during the thinking and writing of this chapter, the Radcliffe Institute for Advanced Study at Harvard University, and the Peter Wall Institute for Advanced Study at the University of British Columbia. I am grateful to the Rainbow Coalition at RIAS, for planting the seeds that grew into this project, for helping me cultivate the persistent and disciplined practice of self-trust, self-care, and courage necessary to listen and hear my own voice. I am thankful to Ross A. Gay for listening to the entirety of this paper, out loud, and for being a careful interlocutor. Finally, I am indebted to the editors of this volume, Rumee Ahmed and Anver Emon for their intellectual and moral support, which was indispensible for the writing of this chapter.

really being asked are these: Where is Islamic Law? Where can we find it? Where is it located? The answers to these questions, which are variations of the same question, differ based on who is asking and answering them. And with a religion that belongs to 1.6 billion living Muslims, it is not surprising that the answers to these questions are varied. Is the Qur'an a book of law? Yes and no. Is Islamic law rooted in the Qur'an? No and yes. What is the relationship between the Qur'an and Islamic law? It's complicated. The answers to these questions do not tell us very much, and the fact that we learn so little from them probably means that they are not the right questions.

So, then we should wonder, who is asking these questions? And why? After all, these questions are not leveled at other scriptures in the same way; such as, is the Bible a book of law? This alerts us to the fact that questions are asked and answered in a complex political and social web of power. The ability to ask questions and demand answers is usually a function of power. And asking questions, especially questions that feel irrelevant and unimportant, is a performance of power that ought to be evaluated. If most Muslims do not care about, nor are animated by these questions, then these questions do not center Muslims, and in fact, they de-center Muslims. If Muslims are de-centered by these questions, then who is being centered? Whose questions about Muslims and Islam matter more than the questions of Muslims themselves?

The answer to this question—who do these questions center as the primary audience for the production and consumption of scholarship on Islam and Muslims—helps us uncover the roots and operating assumptions of Islamic studies as conceived of in western countries, where these questions are incessantly repeated and are considered to facilitate legitimate scholarly inquiry. By western countries, I mean countries that systematically and institutionally enshrine whiteness and white subjectivities as privileged. In this chapter, I'd like to consider the topic of the Qur'an and Islamic law as a lens through which to discuss the politics of knowledge production in the field of Islamic studies, of which Islamic Legal Studies is a subset.

II.

On a typically rainy and grey November morning in Vancouver, I made the tough decision to skip my Saturday morning boot camp class, which I love, to attend an Islamic law conference. I made the decision to support a bright young scholar, woman of color, who was presenting on a panel that morning. I had met her the night before and wanted to hear her paper. On the panel with her was a South Asian, Muslim American man, presenting on his lengthy pre-circulated paper. He was discussing the case of *rajm* laws in Pakistan in the 1980s. *Rajm* is the law of stoning to death. In the classical conception of Islamic law, illicit sex is prohibited and punishable corporally. The Qur'anic text delineates the punishment for *zina*, interpreted variously as fornication and/or adultery, with 100 lashes for both the male and female:

Al-zaniyatu wa-l-zani fa-l-jliduu ihdahuma mi'ata jilda.
[The female who commits *zina* and the male who commits *zina*, whip each of them 100 stripes.]

But precolonial legal scholars distinguished between the marital subjectivity of the person engaging in illicit sex. If the "culprit" was unmarried, they applied the punishment found in the Qur'anic text—100 lashes. But if s/he was married, then they thought the punishment ought to be more severe. So, relying on a prophetic report of dubious strength, they argued that married "culprits" ought to be stoned to death. *Rajm*. If the application of this punishment seemed too gruesome to those executing it, legal scholars countered with the Qur'anic verse,

Wa-la ta'khudhkum bi-hima ra'fatan ...
[Do not let compassion for the two sway you ...]

Qur'anic and extra-Qur'anic sources were interpreted to create laws around illicit sex, creating a loop that moved from personal interpretation to the Qur'an and back again. Personal interpretation, based in social, historical, political, and philosophical reasoning, was mixed in with readings of various Qur'anic verses to create laws on illicit sex. Take, for example, the way that precolonial legal scholars defined "illict" sex, or *zina*. *Zina* is used in a gender neutral way in the Qur'anic verse, both the crime and its punishment treat the genders with parity. But precolonial scholars turned *zina* into a gendered crime. They defined *zina* in the case of women as sex with anyone other than a woman's own husband. But for men, *zina* was defined as sex with anyone other than one of his four wives or unlimited concubines. Consent was not a relevant category for licit sex. Nor was age; sex with minors was considered licit.

Precolonial legal scholars felt that this definition of "licit" sex should be the determining factor for corporal punishment, and argued that those who have access to "licit" sex should be punished differently than those without. So they defined the "*zani*" mentioned in the Qur'anic verse narrowly as a "fornicator" rather than "adulterer," even though there is no philological basis for this interpretation. This restricted definition of the *zani* as fornicator created space for a different, extra-Qur'anic, non-Qur'anic punishment—*rajm*—for the adulterer, which is anchored in contested prophetic reports. You can see through this example, I hope, why the question, "Is the Qur'an a book of law?" is pointless. As long as law is created by humans and scripture is interpreted by humans, there can never be a straightforward answer to this question.

At any rate, the American Muslim South Asian male scholar was discussing the permutation of the *rajm* debate in the 1980s, in the postcolonial, self-identifying Muslim nation-state of Pakistan; which, incidentally, means "Land of the Pure." You can imagine that this might be a fascinating paper—the topic allows us to see how Muslims with vastly different moral and social compasses reckon with historical laws in the contemporary world. And since no Pakistani has ever been sentenced to death by *rajm*, despite *rajm* being formally adopted as part of Pakistani Law, the case of *rajm* can help us see the kind of discretionary power that Pakistan's Federal Shariʿa Court wields in determining what is "Islamic" in the face of the country's shariʿa source laws. However, the paper entirely ignored these fascinating questions and instead focussed on the minute details of a very narrow debate about *rajm* among male Pakistani *ulama*, without taking into account even their own political and social context. I sat there, somewhat agitated and surprised at this familiar form of scholarship in Islamic Legal Studies. I was disappointed because I expected better from this Muslim South Asian American scholar, for whom, presumably the stakes of this debate are higher. Or should be higher. And as I listened to him, I noticed that all the people he was referencing in his paper were either Muslim men or white men (and a few white women), writing about Islam and Muslims and Pakistan and sex.

So, here was a South Asian, American, Muslim man, a postcolonial subject, writing about a postcolonial nation-state—Pakistan. Pakistan, whose borders were drawn by a white man named Cyril Radcliffe over lunch (!). Pakistan, the creation of which entailed the massacre of millions, and the rape and displacement of millions more. And this South Asian scholar was using only patriarchal and white colonialist frames to theorize about laws related to sexuality in Pakistan, despite the fact that Pakistani Muslim women had participated vigorously in the national debate on this exact topic. The paradoxes being performed in that room that Saturday morning were stunning. Whose voices were being erased in this performance of patriarchal and colonialist scholarship? Muslim women's voices, the erasure of which is unconscionable, especially since Muslim women's voices are finally part of the production of Islamic knowledge after centuries of silence through erasure. And this topic—on the laws around sexuality—not only concerns Muslim women but affects them disproportionately and detrimentally. This young scholar was erasing the voices of the very people whose voices should have been the center of the debate. And I wondered, how are we accountable for using patriarchal and colonialist frames for thinking about Islam in a postcolonial context, for studying colonized people through colonialist perspectives as postcolonial subjects?

What was equally fascinating to me, having started to ask these questions, was watching the white male scholar who responded to this paper. He kept qualifying his questions and comments by identifying himself as an "anthropologist." He'd start sentences with "as an anthropologist . . . ." Not as a white, elite, male, outsider, but as an "anthropologist." It occurred to me that whiteness is rarely discussed, or even mentioned, in Islamic Studies, even though the field is dominated by white scholars; perhaps *because* the field is dominated by white scholars. Even though brown Muslims are regularly asked to demonstrate, to prove their objectivity in the face of whiteness that sets the standard for objectivity. And it also occurred to me that in Islamic Studies, the two voices that dominate the field, that created it, are the seminal voices in it, that set the form and standards of excellence in Islamic Studies are either a small, white, male elite, or a small, Muslim, male elite. I'm using the word seminal here intentionally; "seminal" comes from the word "semen," assuming that semen is the foundation for life, as opposed to an ovum. And while this assumption is incorrect about life, it is appropriate for the description of Islamic Studies, founded as it is by a small group of elite men.

Islamic Studies in the western academy finds its roots in the colonialist project, which was, at its core, a white supremacist project. Colonialism championed the ideology that whites ought to rule the world and in the hierarchy of human races, whites ranked above all other colors. In this ideology, they are the chosen people. God (and/or "nature," and/or social Darwinism, and/or whomever) chose them and made them better. This thinking privileges whites above all other races, is white supremacist without regard to its intentionality. In the same way that patriarchal thinking privileges men over women; it does not matter if a patriarchal thinker means to be patriarchal or not. Similarly, it does not matter if white supremacist thinking means to be white supremacist, if it privileges whites and whiteness de facto, then it is white supremacist. The French and German colonialists studied Muslims in the lands they colonized, along with the animals, and vegetation, and architecture. There is a reason that Islamic Studies doctoral programs require language competency in German and French, rather than other living Muslim languages. The Study of Islam in the western academy follows the frames of these early colonialist scholars, where white scholars can presume to master and speak authoritatively about Islam and Muslims. They can presume to know them better than they know themselves, to "correct" their knowledge about their own religion and traditions, based on "arm's length," "objective" study, treating their distance as an asset rather than as a weakness and shortcoming. In what other discipline is intimate knowledge of a subject, knowing too much about a subject, a drawback? Only in disciplines constructed around the imagined "other," for instance in race studies. It never ceases to amaze me that whites presume themselves to be in an ideal position to study, examine, and judge racism, when they are uniquely unqualified for such study given that they have never experienced racism.

And from this position of superiority, the colonialist, the white supremacist study of Islam decides which Muslim voices are more valuable, more authentic, more reflective of "true" Islam than others. Colonialist Islamic studies, which is to say, white supremacist Islam Studies designates above all else, precolonial, medieval male Muslim voices, as captured in precolonial texts as the most important, and authentic expression of Islam and Muslims eternally. So, a small, male, Muslim elite comes to speak for Muslims universally and eternally. Thus, a living religion—an evolving and vibrant religion—is treated like a dead religion, captured only in medieval texts. Even when discussing urgent contemporary debates, the standards of excellence in the field demand that we ignore contemporary Muslim voices, that we confine ourselves to historical, textual study, because that is what "good" scholarship looks like.

And thus, the colonialist study of Islam finds a fruitful alliance with the patriarchal study of Islam, because the patriarchal study of Islam is also birthed during the period of colonialism to serve the interest of the colonialist and later the postcolonialist nation-state. For its own reasons, the patriarchal study of Islam would also rather center the voices of precolonial male Muslim scholars, that is to say, dead Muslim scholars, rather than respond to the pressing moral needs of living Muslim communities, especially with respect to legal studies. As its name suggests, Patriarchal Islamic Legal Studies assumes a gendered rather than racial hierarchy, where men are the chosen people. Again, God (and/or "nature," and/or social Darwinism, and/or whomever) said so. He made them better.

The main challenger to both these forms of Islamic Studies is a new and burgeoning form of Islamic study, Intersectional Islamic Studies. Intersectional Islamic Studies raises the ire of both White Supremacist Islamic Studies and Patriarchal Islamic Legal Studies because it challenges the definition of Islam and Muslims posited by both; it asks questions about the political nature of the Study of Islam; it names and challenges existing white supremacist and patriarchal power structures; and it breaks the very form of Islamic Studies in these two modes, using subjectivities as a way to make scholarship accountable. Feminist Islamic Studies is a subset of Intersectional Islamic Studies, but, given the racially violent history of feminism, with its willingness to serve as cover for white supremacy, feminism alone is insufficient for challenging these two dominant modes of thought in Islamic Studies. Intersectional Islamic Study goes further and centers social justice as its main axis. Drawing on Kimberlé Crenshaw's term "intersectionality," Intersectional Islamic Studies considers the various intersecting layers of multiple identities that compound the privileges and oppressions that influence scholars and their scholarship.

In this chapter, I will discuss these forms of Islamic Studies: White Supremacist Islamic Studies (WhiSIS), Patriarchal Islamic Legal Studies (PILS), and Intersectional Islamic Studies (IIS), focusing on the study of the Qur'an, to think broadly about the future of Islamic Studies.

III.

Let's begin with White Supremacist Islamic Studies (WhiSIS), which traces its roots to the western university. Universities are often thought of as forward thinking, progressive establishments, as liberal bastions where the future of the world is designed and planned. Describing a university scholar as "ahead of their time" is a compliment. And sometimes university scholars are indeed ahead of their time. However, universities as a whole are often also backward looking, conservative bastions, protectors of the status quo, where conversations are stuck decades behind the evolving social issues at hand, just barely catching up to current political and social developments, rather than predicting and leading them. This is certainly true for the field of Islamic Studies in the western academy, which is one of the last bastions where old school colonialism remains respectable.

White men are the foundational figures and central voices of authority of the western university, as they are in White Supremacist Islamic Studies. White women have recently joined the ranks of white men, so that, despite increasing gender diversity, whites still dominate the field. Religion has been used as a diversion to avoid discussing this white hegemony in Islamic Studies. Muslim scholars are often made to feel that their belief in Islam, their identity as Muslims, somehow compromises their intellectual integrity and objectivity. Belief hurts good scholarship, we are taught, in a million (not so) subtle ways. White Muslims are an exception to this rule. White Muslims—converts or born Muslims—both male and female, do quite well in the field. Their Islam becomes an asset to their scholarship, but not so with Muslims of color. The conversion of white scholars to Islam is read in the field as a magical story, a story of falling in love with one's subject matter, which deepens the insights of their scholarship. In contrast, for Muslims of color who are born into Islam, their Islam is read as baggage that can never be fully purged, that eternally threatens to color their vision and compromise their scholarly rigor. For white Muslims, their religion is part of their capital; they can choose to reveal their Islam or not in various contexts depending on whether this will increase or decrease their authority. They can speak *as* Muslims about Islam while also being able to claim distance and objectivity when necessary. In the case of converts, white Muslims can write books under their born western name, or their adopted Muslim name, or a hybrid western and Muslim name. However, Muslims of color with Muslim names, even if secular, must perform a distance from their identities and their traditions to demonstrate that they are capable of intellectual rigor, to demonstrate that their faith isn't getting in the way of their reason.

Another diversion from discussing race in WhiSIS is the terminology of "descriptive" vs. "prescriptive" scholarship; religiosity is coded this way. WhiSIS considers itself to produce "descriptive" scholarship, in which scholars "objectively" describe what they find in texts or in observations of communities, that are then examined, read, filtered through white colonialist frames and theories. This kind of scholarship is by no means "prescriptive." That kind of "scholarship" ("can you even call it 'scholarship'?," they will ask) is for the seminary, not the academic study of Religion. "We're better than that here!" And this view isn't implicit either. In every interview with academic institutions, from graduate school and through two academic jobs, I've been asked, "Do you intend to do prescriptive or descriptive work?" And I've been asked to explain how I would keep my beliefs out of the classroom. But this heightened binary of religious vs. non-religious Muslims, which detrimentally affects Muslims of color isn't applied to other religions in Religious Studies. Jewish and Christian Studies scholars are allowed to be Jewish and Christian in their scholarship. They are allowed to use the word "we" in their writings and mean their religious communities rather than the scholarly community. And they are allowed to produce openly prescriptive scholarship, theologies of grace and citizenship, which is to say, they are allowed to speak to their own communities in their scholarship.

WhiSIS fundamentally de-centers Muslims from the Study of Islam, which is an inevitable and necessary result of centering whiteness in the Study of Islam. As such, in the case of Islamic Legal Studies, the study becomes preoccupied with precolonial texts. Muslims are reduced to texts as if they are not living, not alive. So, when a prominent news reporter asks an Islamic Studies scholar at a prestigious university, "Is ISIS Islamic?," which is a form of the question, "Is the Qur'an a book of law?," the scholar says, "Yes, yes it is Islamic" because a few of the views espoused by the group can be found in medieval legal texts. Rather than complicating the civic discourse about Islam and Muslims; rather than draw our attention to the political, social, and economic nature of ISIS, which can only exist in a postcolonial, modern, and globalized world, the scholar confirms the worst stereotypes of Muslims and Islam. Perhaps he does this without even meaning to, but it doesn't matter, does it? The damage is done. The article is written. This is akin to a scholar arguing that slavery is "American" because despite the amendment abolishing slavery, slavery is accommodated in the constitution. Or because Christian religious language was a key tool for justifying slavery, that slavery is a quintessentially Christian practice. We might even say it is more Christian than Islamic, because Christianity predates Islam by several centuries. Islam was just copying Christianity in sanctioning slavery. If you're cringing, that's the point.

Despite the methodological problems with finding the "true" meaning of Islam in medieval texts, WhiSIS designates precolonial, medieval texts as "real" Islam. The reasons for this are multiple and pragmatic. For one thing, "Islam" can be mastered as a subject if you can master some of these texts. So, it is a cheat of sorts. It allows claims of mastery over a subject that cannot be mastered. Since most of the medieval texts on Islam were written in Arabic, the WhiSIS scholar is required to learn only one language, Arabic. And even then, only reading knowledge of Arabic is required. The scholar learns *fusha* Arabic, which is not a spoken language, it is only a written language. Many Arabic language textbooks are written entirely in English. I studied Arabic at university from a white man who did not speak any Arabic, using a slim red textbook with only the occasional Arabic word, and lots of archaic English grammatical terms, like subjunctive, jussive, and pluperfect. I had to learn English grammar to study Arabic grammar. Needless to say, I did not learn much Arabic in the years of Arabic courses I enrolled in, despite earning high grades. In the end, it took extended visits to Syria and Yemen, learning Arabic from Arabic speaking teachers for me to learn Arabic.

Okay, so you master reading knowledge of Arabic to master "Islam." A language, mind you, that the vast majority of Muslims do not speak, read or write. Arabs make up barely 20 percent of the Muslim population. But many medieval texts are written in Arabic. Most of these texts are printed, so they are easily accessible. Many are digitized now. This makes the study of obscure texts that no one has ever heard of earn a scholar bonus points, even if it might make their research more obscure and irrelevant. Importantly, these are a finite, limited set of texts, they are a defined body of texts, so they can be mastered. Those words, "master" and "mastery," seem especially apt here. Because, if WhiSIS can locate "real" Islam in a delineated body of texts, then someone who only studies these texts can claim expertise on Islam and Muslims, making calls about who is (or isn't) "Muslim" and what is (or isn't) authentically "Islamic," when, in fact, such a scholar has no business, no expertise, no authority to be making such calls. This is akin to someone who studies constitutional law in the 1800s feigning expertise on Black Lives Matter. Limiting the definition of "real" Islam to texts frees WhiSIS scholars from learning about and keeping up with current and evolving debates about the topics they study in the contemporary world.

And because Muslims are de-centered in WhiSIS, WhiSIS engages in painstaking, in-depth research on subjects that are irrelevant and uninteresting to Muslims. Asking and answering questions Muslims would not ask, ignoring what might interest Muslims. Much of WhiSIS is about examining Islam and Muslims through the lens of Christianity and Judaism.

> "The Qur'an is an apocalyptic text."
> "Islamic Law is *halakha*."
> "*Tafsir* is like *midrash*."
> "What does Islamic history look like if we dismiss all Islamic sources? Because Muslims are biased and polemical and unable to record events as they happened."
> "What if we reconstruct Islamic history through Aramaic sources?"
> "What if we read the Qur'an as it might have sounded in Syriac?"

WhiSIS is a conversation about Islam and Muslims amongst white scholars. They are talking *about* Islam and Muslims to each other. Islam and Muslims are the object, never the subject of study.

> "What do *they* think about *rajm*?"
> "How do *they* engage in global finance?"
> "How do *they* structure political authority?"
> "What are *their* ritual purity laws?"

And because WhiSIS scholars mostly speak to themselves, they rarely engage Muslim voices beyond texts from the past. WhiSIS scholars often come to the study of Islam with faulty assumptions, asking questions the answers to which would be self-evident to Muslims. For example, one of the recent "important" developments in Islamic Legal Studies is that the study of Islamic legal texts and

Qur'an commentaries ought to be intertwined because the two disciplines, hitherto treated as discrete, are actually connected. Well, that is not news to Muslims. Of course the two are connected. Legal texts regularly cite Qur'anic verses and *tafsir* texts engage in extended legal discussions. Many of the scholars who wrote legal texts also wrote Qur'an commentaries and vice versa. Islam is a *religion*. What you believe and what you do is connected. Theology and law build on each other. To treat *fiqh* and *tafsir* as discrete bodies of literature is to miss the point entirely. As a Muslim scholar, it is embarrassing to see this as the "cutting edge" discovery in my field of study. We have far to go!

Apart from the topics that are considered "legitimate" and "serious inquiries" into the field, one of the things that WhiSIS is able to do, actually demand that "serious," "real" scholars do, is suspend moral judgment when studying a topic. WhiSIS takes all topics, no matter how relevant or urgent, and turns them into obscure study, making sure to avoid any moral voice. An absence of a moral voice is praiseworthy in WhiSIS. Should scholars engage a topic as if it had moral relevance, taking seriously the moral accountability of scholarship itself, they risk slipping away from descriptive to prescriptive scholarship. Which is to say, they risk losing their objectivity, slipping from objective scholarship into polemical rants. So, a study about women-led prayer can focus solely on what medieval texts say about women-led prayer, examining only what dead elite Muslim men wrote to each other—another insular world! It can ignore completely the dramatic debate about women-led prayer in the world today. Such studies can uncover and highlight patriarchal arguments that catalog in intricate detail the mental, physical, and spiritual unworthiness of women, describing the arguments as "elegant," without a word about how these ideas are contested by living Muslims. The marriage of minors can be dispassionately studied, while dismissing Muslim moral objections to the practice, often by describing these objections as "western influenced critiques" because white, Christian polemicist writings also criticized the marriage of minors in their jeremiads against Islam. WhiSIS scholars can study stories that include vivid depictions of non-consensual sex and theorize about their bearing on the law, describing the stories as "titillating," without mentioning the word "rape."

WhiSIS defends what it sees as a morally neutral stance, or an amoral gaze, in service to objective, descriptive scholarship. They criticize those who break rank as guilty of anachronism, imposing new moral perspectives on the past, holding dead Muslim scholars to moral standards that they could not have conceived. To make this argument, WhiSIS must posit its own scholars write in a social, political, and historical vacuum; writing from and into a vacuum. But there is no such vacuum, since scholarship is always political, produced in history, and morally accountable. And failing to wrestle with morality when studying religious topics is a moral failure. Failing to have a moral voice is an abnegation of responsibility. Not speaking morally, not making moral judgments condones what is immoral. It acquiesces to and legitimates a patriarchal version of Islam because all of its privileged texts were written by men in patriarchal social and historical contexts. These topics and this study affect real people, in tangible ways, because Muslims are alive. This is our religion. And it is contested. There is no such thing as value neutral scholarship on Islam.

What I am saying is that when scholars avoid "anachronism" while reducing a living religion to its historical texts, they accept and re-instantiate the misogyny, racism, and elitism of the texts they are studying, texts that were written by a small male elite closely connected to power. Studying medieval texts without considering the various contemporary permutations of the topics under study is a moral failure. I am saying that there is no such thing as "anachronism" in the study of a living religion like Islam. The charge of "anachronism" creates an artificial binary between the past and the present that does not exist in the religious framework. The past is always relevant and present. As is the future. The metaphysical past and future are immanent, urgently present, requiring moral action in the present, here and now. In religious reasoning, there is no past separate, cut off from the present. So, by definition, you cannot be anachronistic in your study of a living religious tradition. The past is present, making moral demands on believers, who negotiate ways to live with the past in the present. And so, anachronism is only a relevant category in WhiSIS, which treats Islam like a dead religion, a religion whose essential truths are already determined, a long time ago, captured in static, unchanging texts. The truth of Islam, according to WhiSIS can only be recovered by reading ancient texts, rather than accessed by speaking to living Muslims. But, Islam is a *living* tradition. It is not dead.

The insularity of WhiSIS is reflected in its form as well as content. WhiSIS is difficult to read, as if its primary purpose was not communication. Its sentences are long and unwieldy. Good WhiSIS scholarship is filled with specialized jargon that only a few can follow. In this way, language is turned into a tool of exclusivity, creating a fence around an elite community of knowledge, rather than a bridge that connects various communities to each other. The more footnotes a piece of scholarship has, the better it is. And the footnotes are self-referential, filled with names of white scholars. WhiSIS constructs authority as a tautology. It is authoritative because it keeps referencing itself as authoritative. A great deal of energy is spent in mastering correct transliteration technique. So, we can show off, not just by listing every source consulted but also by demonstrating our mastery over Arabic. That WhiSIS is inaccessible, its form bewildering, even alienating to most Muslims is not an accident. It is strange to read your own religious tradition treated in this foreign and unfamiliar way. What is even more painful as a Muslim scholar of color is learning to speak in this way about Islam and Muslims, mastering this jargon; it is defeat masquerading as mastery.

This brings me to the Muslim scholar of color who writes and speaks the language of WhiSIS. You will not be hard-pressed to find a Muslim scholar of color writing in the tradition of WhiSIS, replicating white supremacist scholarship. They are often compelled to do this in order to be part of the conversation, because the gatekeepers to WhiSIS are largely white. Remember that question I was asked—"Do you intend to do descriptive or prescriptive scholarship?" I was accepted into the graduate program where I was asked that question, so you can guess that I answered correctly. "Descriptive!" I piped up, too quickly, too eagerly. Studying Islam and Muslims in this way means we must de-center ourselves from our own scholarship about our own religious tradition. We must silence our moral voice. Change our primary questions. Speak in a foreign language that feels uncomfortable, alien on our tongues, painful to our hearts.

Why do this then? Because this is the only way we can play in the game of the academic Study of Islam in western countries, where WhiSIS dominates. Since the terms, the rules of engagement are set by WhiSIS, Muslim scholars of color have no choice but to contort themselves out of shape to play the game. But playing the game like this, on these terms, that demand we de-center ourselves and write as if we do not care about our subject matter, when the only reason we are here is because we care deeply, means that even if we get to play the game, we can never win. Which is to say, we always lose.

IV.

If the central tenet of WhiSIS is a hierarchy of human races where whites enjoy pride of place, then a central tenet of Patriarchal Islamic Legal Studies (PILS) is that men rank above women in the hierarchy of genders. This means that men are better than women, they are more intelligent, more objective, more reasonable, closer to God, and thus have better access to "Truth." PILS is first and foremost a discourse about Islam amongst a small male elite that largely ignores the voices of mainstream Muslims. PILS is conducted around the world, from the Indian subcontinent to Africa, from South East Asia to the Middle East, from Europe to North America. Some proponents of PILS are based in the western academy. PILS is populated by Muslim men who create a hierarchal ranking, not just between men and women but also between races, where Arab voices are the most legitimate representations of "true" Islam. Like WhiSIS, PILS is a form of scholarship that emerged during the colonial period. As a result, PILS has a complicated love-hate relationship with colonialism. Colonialism dismantled traditional forms of Islamic scholarship and this scholarship re-configured itself anew to first serve the demands of the colonial empires, and then anti-colonialist movements, and finally the interests of contemporary nation-states.

PILS is carried out in various settings—in secular and religious universities, in *madrasas* and in governments, in NGOs, and think tanks. PILS portrays itself as representing the beliefs and practices of Muslims and Islam, with Muslims and Islam defined narrowly and flatly, without complexity, much like WhiSIS. Medieval texts are a central source for authority and authenticity for PILS, too. During colonialism, the *ulama*, a key component of PILS, provided the colonialists with specific legal texts that would be applied in Muslim civil codes, turning dialectic texts into stagnant and reified laws. And in the postcolonial period, PILS uses medieval texts to inform, derive, and sometimes import wholesale "Islamic" laws into the personal, civil, and criminal legal codes in countries that adhere to shari'a source laws. PILS scholars include those who sit on federal councils in Muslim majority countries where they make calls about the "Islamic" nature of various legal proposals.

PILS has a complicated relationship with colonialism because, while colonialists undermined and destroyed traditional legal guilds and forms of religious knowledge production, they also recognized PILS as authoritative and relied on PILS scholars to represent Muslims when determining "Islamic" law. PILS was created by colonialism, it is the product of colonialism. And there can be an easy and comfortable alliance between the patriarchal interests of colonialism found in WhiSIS and PILS. The best demonstration of this alliance is the white male convert who advocates for and is championed by PILS. Hence, although PILS dreams of a return to a time before colonialism when Muslims dominated the globe, before colonialism ravaged Muslim lands, before problems like Islamic feminism emerged, destroying the patriarchal family, PILS is also a product, a child of colonialism. It owes its very existence to colonialism.

Whereas WhiSIS posits whiteness and distance from one's subject matter as the standards of excellence in Islamic Studies, PILS posits maleness and adherence to a particular patriarchal performance of faith as the key to true knowledge of Islam. In PILS, knowledge is demonstrated through a patriarchal performance of piety. For PILS, the male Muslim is the normative subject and Muslim women are fundamentally de-centered. They are the objects of study rather than producers of knowledge. Muslim male scholars speak to each other about women, ignoring their voices, erasing their substantive contributions to scholarship, much like WhiSIS scholars speak to each other about living Muslims, ignoring and erasing their voices.

Faith is essential to "good" scholarship in PILS, which is described as "sincere" scholarship. This means that, in PILS, judging a scholar's faith is a legitimate way to judge the quality of their scholarship. So, the way that faith is expressed is important. Faith is expressed in many ways, in ways big and small. It is expressed through the use of proper respectful language when referring to the Prophet Muhammad, peace be upon him (*pbuh*); or his wives, the Mothers of the Believers, may God be pleased with them; or his family, the *ahl al-bayt*, may God be pleased with them; or his Companions, the *Sahaba*, may God be pleased with them; or his Successors, the *tabi'n*, may God have mercy on them; or the *ulama*, Shaykh so-and-so and Imam so-and-so, may God have mercy on them. It is demonstrated through extensive knowledge of Muslim rituals, the correct prayers to utter throughout one's daily life, the correct level of modesty and humility, praying before and throughout a project with appeals for guidance from Allah, "please do not allow me to be led astray and then lead others astray"—because then the sin of everyone will lie with the scholar. Faith is expressed by praying five times a day, undertaking supererogatory prayers, fasting, avoiding pork and alcohol. Good character and good scholarship are closely connected. And the inverse of this is true, too; bad character, defined in this narrow performance of a patriarchal religiosity, must lead to bad scholarship.

Faith is also expressed through a performance of adherence to the luminous scholars of the past. PILS takes as a fundamental precept that history is in a state of decline. The best time, the best historical moment, and the best generation to ever exist was the Prophet's generation. This generation ought to be emulated as closely as possible. The second best generation is the generation of the Successors, and then their successors, and so on and so forth until we get to us, today, birthed by the ugliness of colonialism, tainted, impure, unworthy inheritors of this great and luminous religious tradition whose light dims and falters in the darkness of our present. By definition then, we cannot have insights about Islam that escaped or stand in contradiction to the predecessors, the "real" Islamic legal scholars, who preceded colonialism. In this framework, innovation, creativity, new ideas are not only discouraged, they are bad, they demonstrate arrogance, hubris, and delusion. Who are you to think you know something about Islam that every preceding generation of better men and better scholars missed? Of course, to remain current, relevant, and to serve the interests of vastly different political and social interests, PILS has to evolve, change, adapt to new norms and values. PILS does this by rooting, anchoring itself in precolonial Islamic legal texts, cherry picking some texts over others, sometimes falsely attributing its positions to previous scholars, changing laws, creating new laws all the while claiming adherence and allegiance to precolonial Islam to maintain authority.

This means that PILS can reform laws around Islamic finance, making permissible, *halal*, the use of *riba*, interest, usury, the taking of which is described in the Qur'an as waging war against God herself while at the same time holding onto domestic violence as divinely sanctioned in the Qur'anic text, resisting any attempt to criminalize it by insisting that this would contravene God's law. In the case of Islamic finance, PILS scholars will make the argument that they are following the tradition by defining *riba* anew. But in the case of domestic violence, they accuse those proposing reform as subverting God's law with innovation, they say, "an unworthy generation's new ideas can only ever be corrupt." PILS is willing to reform, revive Islamic law on any topic unless it challenges male supremacy, which is to say unless it improves women's rights such that they are treated on par with men, as the normative subjects of Islamic Law. So, reform of laws related to family law is strongly resisted. As are laws regarding corporal punishment for illicit sex, laws that control women's sexuality. But there is a great deal of reform on corporal punishment for theft, for instance—most Muslim majority countries claiming to follow Islamic law do not apply the punishment of chopping off the hand of the thief based on legal reasoning produced by PILS that reinterprets the Qur'anic prescription of cutting off the hand of the thief:

> *al-sariqatu wa-l-sariqu fa-l-qta'u aydiyahuma.*
> [The female thief and the male thief, cut off each of their hands.] (Q. 5:38)

Ever wonder why the Qur'anic text mentions the female counterpart to the male especially in discussions of corporal punishment? The *sariqa*, the *zaniya*, the female thief, the female fornicator? This is a question that does not arise for PILS.

Similarly, in the case of the punishment for drinking alcohol, many Muslim majority countries claiming adherence to Islamic law do not apply the traditional punishment of eighty stripes. The Federal Shari'a Court of Pakistan ruled in 2015 that drinking alcohol should not elicit the punishment of eighty lashes prescribed in classical Islamic legal texts. These reforms are read as "Islamic," however, PILS strongly resists reform of sexual punishments for "crimes" like fornication and adultery, claiming such reforms to be "un-Islamic." In the *maqasid* approach, for instance, the idea of reforming Islamic law to protect the *maqasid* while accommodating change is not extended to gender equality. Questioning the patriarchal nature of the *maqasid* in which at least one *maqsad, nasl* (lineage), is devoted to controlling women's sexuality in order to ensure patrilineal descent, is seen as an insidious, feminist—read colonialist—attempt to destroy Islam from within.

"Islam" means "submission" and submission is a highly valued quality, so a performance of submission—whether or not the submission is actual or imagined—is important. Submission is also performed in PILS through regular criticism of others who do not submit enough, who do not adhere enough, who are arrogant enough to embrace innovation and critical thinking as ideals of scholarship. Criticizing the faith and/or the sincerity of Muslim feminists allows PILS scholars to ignore substantive arguments in favor of attacks on moral rectitude. Hence, I often find my faith questioned in scholarly contexts. For example, when I was in graduate school, still wearing the hijab and loose, long sleeved shirts and long skirts, I presented a paper on the moral dilemma that a violent reading of Q. 4:34, a verse that has been read as prescribing physical violence against women as a means for resolving marital discord, creates for the believer. A male Muslim co-panelist who embodies PILS while based in a WhiSIS academic context asked me, "what does your questioning and argument say about your *iman* (faith)?" Implying, not so subtly, that if I had faith, I wouldn't be researching this topic at all. My faith, real faith, if I had it, would magically remove all ethical and moral concerns this verse raised for me as a believer. So, rather than reading my struggle, my engagement with the moral issues raised for me by patriarchal scholarship on Q. 4:34 as a believer, as a sign of faith—why would I care about these issues otherwise?—he saw my scholarship as a demonstration of my lack of faith. I was only willing to ask these questions because I did not have any faith. And in this way, he could discredit all my research, thinking, my intellectual engagement in one fell swoop, not taking my thought seriously, refusing to intellectually and morally engage my work. The irony is that I was clad in Muslim garb at this conference, living in America, suffering the casual Islamophobia of Americans on a daily basis because I looked identifiably Muslim, while he was dressed in western garb, without any sign of his Islam on display, avoiding the relentless Islamophobia that followed closely on my heels wherever I went. And yet, I was the one with weak faith, because I was asking the wrong questions.

This brings me to the relationship between "good" scholarship and garb. You might think these two things are unrelated, why should what you wear affect the judgment of your scholarship? Yet, in both WhiSIS and PILS, what you wear matters, because what you wear communicates your religious subjectivity vis-à-vis your scholarship. In WhiSIS, a lack of faith, and an internalization of whiteness as a standard of excellence is demonstrated through the donning of western clothing. If you're wearing a kufi, or a non-western shirt, or a hijab, or a *jilbab*, or even if you are a male of color with a beard, you have to overcome assumptions about being a partisan and weak scholar. This works in strange and complex ways. Sometimes people—scholars of Islamic Studies—cannot hear the words coming out of your mouth because of decisions they have made about you, because of how they interpret your identity based on what you are wearing. When I was wearing hijab, scholars in the tradition of WhiSIS regularly read my scholarship as apologetic of PILS, even when I was deeply critical of it. They were consistently shocked that I could speak English, despite the numerous Islamic Studies scholars who wear hijab and speak flawless English.

Similarly, since faith is connected to sincere—and therefore good—scholarship in PILS, an expression of piety and religiosity through clothing is a performance of authority. Insofar as faith can be expressed through clothing, scholars in PILS express their religiosity through various physical markers. Unsurprisingly, these expressions of faith through clothing function differently for men than for women. Men can express their religiosity through beards, kufis, imamas, jilbabs, tasbihs (rosaries), etc. But Muslim men are not restricted to physical markers of religiosity. Plenty of PILS scholars sport short, fashionable beards or no beards at all, hipster or business outfits without compromising their scholarly standing.

Muslim women, on the other hand, are not afforded this fluidity in sartorial choice. In the framework of PILS, women, by virtue of their gender are disadvantaged. They cannot access the highest levels of education, they are largely kept out of gender exclusive and gender segregated spaces of learning. Even when there are alternative, so-called "parallel" institutions of female scholarship, like the Qubaysiyyat of Damascus, Syria or Dar al-Zahra in Tarim, Yemen, the highest ranked female shaykhs ranks lower than the male shaykhs. And they are usually related to the male shaykhs through familial bonds, such as the daughter, sister, aunt, or wife of a shaykh, where they have special access to learning otherwise denied to Muslim women. So, Dar al-Zahra in Tarim is the parallel Baʿalawi institution to Dar al-Mustafa, but Habib Umar is the grand shaykh of the Baʿalawi's, and whereas men can study with him, women who are not related to him, can only access him through a closed circuit TV or speaker system. Similarly, when earning an *ijaza* in *tajwid* (Qur'an recitation) from the Qubaysiyyat, ultimately, I found that it was only the late Shaykh al-Kurdi who could confer an *ijaza* upon me. He was one of three shaykhs in Damascus who could confer an *ijaza*, but the only one who was willing to confer an *ijaza* upon women. So, it was up to the individual whims, beliefs, mercy of a male shaykh as to whether women could formally participate in PILS.

And in order to be worthy of PILS, there is enormous pressure on women to hyper-perform an idealized patriarchal femininity, expressed in part through covering, for a chance to participate in PILS. This is much like the scholar of color in WhiSIS, who must hyper-perform at once a kind of whiteness—speak the correct jargon and dress appropriately—and also a kind of fetishized brownness or blackness, a Muslimness, that fulfills the expectations WhiSIS scholars have for scholars of color. Similarly, in PILS Muslim women must at once overcome their gender and also fully embrace it, not act above it while also being exceptional to their gender. The Qubaysiyyat, for example, wear long loose-fitting *mantos* and color-coded hijabs. The women of Dar al-Zahra cover their entire bodies, including their faces and even their eyes. Muslim women ought to at least wear a hijab and loose fitting long sleeved shirts and skirts, or loose pants in order to be taken seriously as scholars of Islam. Even a scarf around the neck is better than nothing.

A few years ago, I found myself on a panel in Morocco, organized by a Muslim NGO that promotes gender equality in Muslim majority countries. The NGO was trying to build broad based support for its goals, so they invited—and paid for the travel and accommodation—of a progressive shaykh from al-Azhar to attend the conference. The shaykh arrived garbed in a kufi, a beard, a robe, and a *sibha* (rosary), a dramatic performance of his sincerity and devotion. Everything was meant to make him look the part of a traditional Islamic scholar. I sat next to him, in an Ann Taylor pant suit, my hair uncovered and down, wearing red lipstick. After a decade of wearing *niqab* and a lifetime of wearing hijab (ever since I was five years old), I was trying to dissociate my scholarship from my sartorial choices. My book was just coming out from Oxford University Press and I felt confident in myself as a scholar of Islam. Though I'd packed a hijab, I didn't want to wear it to look more "Muslim," to be taken seriously. I wanted to be taken seriously on the merit of my scholarship. When I showed up to the room where the panel was to take place, I saw other women who did not wear hijab otherwise, wearing hijabs or shawls. We all play this game in various, changing ways.

As I sat next to the shaykh, I could sense his agitation. He didn't smile at me or return my *salam*. Though we were talking about Q. 4:34 on the panel and the challenges that patriarchal interpretations of the verse pose for criminalizing domestic violence in Muslim majority countries in which the physical discipline of wives is protected by law, and though I'd just written a book tracing the intellectual history of Q. 4:34 from the ninth to the twenty-first century, he did not recognize me as a scholar. He bristled at the fact that there was a time limit on how long he could speak, that another panelist—a *hijabi* woman—spoke before him, that he was being asked to be a conversation partner rather than a venerated shaykh at whose feet we ought to be sitting, collecting pearls of wisdom. He quoted Q. 4:59:

> *Ya ayyuha-l-adhina amanu ati'u-l-aha wa ati'u-l-rasula wa ulu-l-amri minkum.*
>
> [O you who believe, obey Allah and obey the Messenger and those in authority over you.]

This shaykh saw himself in authority over us, as the only real scholar in the room, and he wondered why he was not being treated this way. And when I disagreed with him about some of his representations of the Islamic tradition and said, "In this room, we are all *ulu-l-amr*, 'those in authority' because we all have expertise in Islamic studies," he lost his temper. Becoming a caricature of an Arab man yelling and screaming at everyone in the room—we were primarily women—he accused us of disrespecting him. He asked, "How could you have any expertise in Islam, you are not even dressed modestly, you're not wearing hijab!" His critique was a prime example of PILS; dismissing our—my—scholarship based on my refusal to perform the kind of piety patriarchal Islam demands of me.

This is to say, in PILS, not only do faith, sincerity, race, and gender matter greatly, in terms of who has authority to speak on the subject of Islam and Muslims, but the performance of these identities matters greatly too; how are you Muslim or not, white or not, Arab or not, male or not. And I want to say, these identities matter as much as the content of your scholarship, if you are a scholar of Islamic Studies. But, actually, that is not entirely true. In both WhiSIS and PILS, these identities and their performances matter *more* than the content of your scholarship. So that, no matter how rigorous your scholarship is, if you're the wrong color, the wrong gender, the wrong race, or wear the wrong clothes (which is to say, you're the wrong combination of race, gender, and religion, or if you perform that combination in the wrong way) then your argument is irrelevant because you are already disqualified from making an argument. Your scholarship couldn't possibly be sincere, or excellent, because you are Muslim or not Muslim, or a woman, or too western or not western enough. The gatekeepers of WhiSIS and PILS, that is to say white and Muslim men for the most part, judge our subjectivities and performances to decide if we are legitimate participants in Islamic Studies, if our voices could possibly have anything to add to Islamic Studies.

As in WhiSIS, education in PILS is highly unregulated and dramatically variable. In WhiSIS, you can become an "expert" in Islamic law even if you didn't study Islamic law formally in graduate school. You can earn a degree in Islamic Studies in graduate programs that are three to six years long, you can graduate with a degree in Islamic Studies even if there isn't an Islamic Studies program at your university, if there isn't even an Islamic Studies scholar on your advisory committee. And a degree that combines some amount of Islamic Studies with western law is seen as somehow translating into expertise in Islamic law. Similarly, madrasas and universities in Muslim countries produce Islamic legal experts who may have formal or informal training in Islamic Studies that might span a few or many years. Or, you can be trained in engineering or medicine or political science or another subject altogether and still become an authoritative scholar in Islamic law through self-study.

PILS, like WhiSIS, exalts and holds precolonial texts written by Muslim male scholars as representative of "true" Islam. But while WhiSIS performs a hyper-skepticism in relation to these texts, seemingly questioning everything about them while also accepting them to be representative of universal and eternal Muslim thought, PILS performs a submissiveness to these texts, while cherry picking the parts they will adhere to, discarding and abandoning inconvenient texts. Since PILS scholars are living Muslims, they treat the texts in the manner of living communities. They realize that adherence to these texts affords them authority, so reform must be proposed in the language of submission. Whereas WhiSIS celebrates a morally neutral gaze when approaching precolonial texts, PILS takes as a given that precolonial texts are morally praiseworthy. This means that if contemporary readers encounter something morally reprehensible in those texts, their own moral compass is askew, corrupt, tainted. Because, by definition, contemporary scholars cannot be more morally righteous than precolonial scholars, whose scholarship we inherit, unworthy though we may be.

PILS takes the male as its normative subject. This means that PILS scholarship is gender-blind and thus, serves the interests of patriarchy. Women's issues are treated in special sections of legal manuals, like in chapters on ritual purity. And because women's voices are absent from the selected texts that form the "Islamic Tradition" as defined by PILS, discussions about women and their bodies can be wildly inaccurate without this inaccuracy compromising the scholarly integrity and standing of the scholar in question. So, although these texts describe women as being pregnant for five years, or include treatises that promote virginity testing (a thing that cannot be tested), they remain authoritative for deriving ritual, civil, and criminal laws concerning women. In this framework, when the contemporary reader encounters a flaw, a moral problem with a precolonial text, the contemporary reader is likely wrong: we've misunderstood the text, maybe the violence is more limited than we think, or we need to distinguish between beating and battery, and definitely, we do not want to be anachronistic, because then we'd be applying corrupt moral standards to a tradition that represents pristine, excellent morality.

In PILS, morally reprehensible things like violence against wives, or a hierarchy between men and women, are upheld as representations of God's will. In this way, all moral responsibility is evaded. God said it. And He created us. He knows better. As a Sunni Arab scholar prince once said to me in conversation, defending discrimination against Shiʿas, "I'm not saying this. This is what God says!" Maintaining the elitist, racist, misogynist elements of the Islamic tradition, defined by PILS as captured in precolonial legal texts, does violence anew. Especially when these texts are absorbed into the legislation of nation-states, wherein minimum marriage age is rejected, or virginity testing is a formal state exam, or where domestic violence is a protected right afforded to husbands. Thus, PILS morally sanctions what WhiSIS encourages us to suspend our moral judgment about—in both cases, for fear of anachronism. Anachronism, which can only exist if we accept the artificial separation between the religious past and the present. Anachronism, the theoretical tool used to silence morally engaged scholarship, when moral engagement is necessary to protect living humans from the elitism, racism, and misogyny of precolonial legal texts, to protect living, believing women from the violence these texts sanction against them.

PILS maintains a discourse of male supremacy by ignoring, erasing, and silencing Muslim women's voices unless they conform to a PILS worldview, and in so doing PILS recreates a precolonial male patriarchy as essential to its definition of Islam. This discourse is as self-referential as WhiSIS, where male Muslim scholars reference themselves exclusively, creating an isolated and insular discourse about Islam and Muslims that is disconnected from evolving Muslim concerns. Despite the sometimes antagonistic relationship between PILS and WhiSIS, PILS scholars are more likely to cite WhiSIS scholars in their discourse than they are to cite Muslim feminist scholars, whose scholarship is seen as pernicious, because it admittedly seeks to undermine the patriarchy that is the characteristic feature of PILS.

It is painful to read the texts celebrated in WhiSIS and PILS, the texts that you are told make up your legal tradition, only to find that they are cold, cruel, and uncaring about you because of your gender, and race, and class. That they think of you as less intelligent, less faithful, less worthy than men, then Arabs, then the nobility. That they sanction shocking levels of violence against you. To find that these texts you grew up loving do not love you back. And then, to watch men you admire, respect, and love defend, apologize for, ignore the violence of these texts and the pain they inflict on your heart and mind, your psyche. That hurts too. And though Muslim women participate in PILS, they must accept the assumptions that PILS makes about them in order to participate. They must "overcome" their gender, which automatically puts them at a disadvantage. It is strange to participate in a discourse in which you are treated so poorly, unwelcomed, silenced, reprimanded for immodesty, reduced to a sexual object, described as less than—to withstand all of this, to withstand the loss of your dignity in order to speak in a conversation from which you were meant to be excluded. And yet, this is the only way to participate in the discourse, to be taken seriously; we must play by the rules of a game designed by and for elite men, and of which elite men are the gatekeepers. But to play the game, we must de-center ourselves, our concerns, our questions, and accept caricatures of ourselves as our most accurate representations. That is to say, we cannot play this game and win. Again, we lose.

V.

Let us now turn to the third form of Islamic Studies—Intersectional Islamic Studies. This is the youngest form of Islamic Studies, the newest, the least entrenched, and it has emerged and developed in response to the inadequacies and moral failings of WhiSIS and PILS. Whereas WhiSIS and PILS emerged in the colonial period, were created by colonialism itself, are the children—by design—of colonialism, and so are deeply entrenched in that period, IIS emerged in the postcolonial period. IIS is the result of significant and unprecedented postcolonial developments. Scholarship on Islam has become diversified so that its domain no longer belongs to a small, male, powerful elite. The printing press, increased literacy, and the internet have made it possible for many more people of different races, ethnicities, genders, and socio-economic classes and political leanings to access and produce knowledge, knowledge that can be disseminated and consumed widely. Islamic scholarship is now produced in different languages, by people formally trained in Islamic studies at traditional institutions, and also by Muslims trained through informal self-study and study circles. Increased literacy has allowed Muslims once on the margins of Islamic scholarship, about whose lives and fate Islamic Studies pondered from a distance, to now speak for themselves. Muslim women have become producers of Islamic knowledge and scholarship for the first time in Muslim history. Whereas we have little to no access to texts about Islam written by women in their own voices before the sixteenth century, by the twentieth century, we have plenty of texts written by women. Muslim women are active participants in discussing, teaching, learning, and producing Islamic knowledge. So, they can now speak for themselves, ask questions that concern them, study topics they care about.

IIS takes as an essential truth that racial and gender hierarchies are oppressive frames for the study of Islam. The theory of intersectionality, posited by the African American scholar Kimbelé Crenshaw, argues that humans operate at the nexus of various converging and constantly shifting subjectivities that compound and complicate privilege and oppression. Gender, race, class, sexuality, religion—to mention a few subjectivities—must be taken into account together when thinking about the politics of scholarship. Centering this theoretical framework means that anyone committed to social justice from an intersectional framework is an IIS scholar, no matter their race, gender, class, etc. In much the same manner that scholars of color and women can engage in WhiSIS and PILS, IIS scholars can be white and male. An intersectional view of social justice is crucial to avoid replicating some forms of oppression while fighting against others. A good example of this is that adherents of PILS might be anti-colonialist scholars who at once support patriarchy while opposing colonialism. Or feminist scholars can engage in racist discourses, supporting white supremacy while fighting for gender equality. Intersectionality calls us to think harder, be more thoughtful, to interrogate our assumptions as we engage in social justice work. IIS seeks to engage in a form of Islamic studies that does not replicate racist, misogynist, classist structures of inequality in its scholarship.

IIS comes with its own logic, which breaks from the dominant ways in which Islamic Studies are carried out in WhiSIS and PILS. There are five underlying principles that animate IIS' approach to Islamic Studies. First and foremost, IIS takes seriously the claim that Islam is committed to social justice. The purpose of IIS is to further the cause of social justice while at the same time ensuring that it doesn't promote discourses of inequality and oppression. Social justice is understood as equality for all of humanity, without consideration of race, gender, class, sexuality, religion, etc., as measures for ranking some over others. IIS follows the Qur'anic edict that God created distinctions between peoples, distinctions such as tribes and ethnicities, not as a means for creating hierarchies between people, but rather as a way for humans to know themselves better. IIS adheres to the prophetic call for treating people as equal, "as the teeth of a comb," as captured in the idea of the pilgrimage, the *hajj*, where humanity stands before God's house, without distinctions (in theory, anyways), dressed exactly the same.

Second, and related to this, is the principle that subjectivity and positionality in scholarship matters a great deal. In this principle, IIS seems to follow the model of WhiSIS and PILS. But whereas WhiSIS and PILS posit whiteness, a patriarchal religiosity, and maleness as crucial subjectivities, as the criterion itself for producing good scholarship, IIS undermines these narrow subjectivities as the standards for producing good scholarship. Rather, by thinking about subjectivities through the lens of intersectionality, IIS connects subjectivities to power and asks scholars to interrogate the ways they produce scholarship, to wonder about the questions they take for granted, the concerns they ignore as irrelevant, and the dimensions of their scholarship that are invisible to them because their privilege blinds them to the concerns of those who are marginalized. Privilege is like a blind spot for the driver, so that awareness of it does not erase the blind spot. Blind spots are fluid, always moving, never static, never defined. You must always turn your head and look behind you to make sure you're not plowing into another driver just because you feel like changing lanes. You have to turn your head and look, even when you don't want to, even when you don't feel like it, even when it is annoying, even when you're pretty sure no one is there, so that no one will be hurt.

A presupposition of IIS is that the subjectivity of the scholar is crucial for understanding their scholarship. No one writes from a vacuum of subjectivity. So, while WhiSIS calls for historicizing Islamic texts in order to produce good scholarship, IIS calls for historicizing the scholar producing the scholarship. Why stop with precolonial religious texts, when scholars exist and live and produce knowledge in history, too? The scholars' subjectivity affects the nature of their scholarship. Once we accept this, we can ask, how does a scholar's whiteness or maleness affect their scholarship? What blinders do these privileges produce? In WhiSIS and PILS scholarship, these questions are only leveled in a discriminatory way against scholars of color and women. But IIS calls for them to be applied to everyone, to white scholars and male scholars too. So, when someone says, "I study gender and Islam in India," and she is a white scholar, we can ask, "Why?" The answer to this question is relevant to the scholarship this scholar produces. Insofar as all study is autobiographical, we can ask, why do white people study Islam? What is at stake for them? The answers to these questions make visible what is hidden, what must otherwise be deduced, what can easily be masked under the guise of objectivity.

Third, a consequence of presupposing that subjectivities influence and shape scholarship is that the myth of objectivity is busted. There is no such thing as an objective scholar. Everyone comes to their area of expertise with a set of subjectivities that influence the questions they ask, where they look for answers, who they write to, and how they lay claim to authority. Distance from one's subject matter is not an "advantage," it does not make one more "objective." Specific performances of religiosity, your race, your gender, do not necessarily make your scholarship better or worse. Moreover, if there is no objective truth in scholarship, then we can see that all scholarship is political. IIS holds that scholarship is always produced in a nexus of power, and serves various political interests, even when it claims not to do so—*especially* when it claims not to do so. Being up front about a scholar's subjectivities and the political interests that the scholar means to serve is important because it locates the scholar and their scholarship in its proper context. Scholarship can be more honest and less disingenuous. And it can be morally accountable for the discourses it promotes, the inequalities it reinforces or undermines.

Moral accountability in scholarship is the fourth principle of IIS. Scholarship on Islam and Muslims ought to be morally accountable. If objectivity is a myth, then morally neutral scholarship is a farce. Scholarship that expounds, explains, and clarifies racist, misogynist, elitist discourses without taking into account their bearing on living communities and without accounting for the influence of the scholarship itself, the voices it exalts and the ones it eliminates and erases—is not morally ambivalent. Such scholarship commits the violence of racism, misogyny, and elitism anew.

Finally, IIS demands that the Qur'an be treated as the meaning-generating text that it is, a text that belongs to living communities around the globe. This means that any study of the Qur'an and Islamic law must be embodied. Pure textual study of any topic related to the Qur'an and Islamic law is by definition shallow, incomplete, and inaccurate. The Qur'anic text has no meaning independent of the communities interacting with it. There is no plain-sense or literal meaning of the text, because this meaning is always created by people reading and speaking for the text. And Muslims decide, variously, when or how the text relates to law. This means that good scholarship engages Muslim voices, it centers Muslims in the study of Islam, and it speaks to Muslims, engaging Muslim communities in both forming and answering the main questions of the discipline. And because Islam is a living religion, the experience of living Muslims is a source of expertise and knowledge about Islam. Closeness to one's subject matter, speaking about one's topic without being burdened by jargon—these enhance rather than compromise good scholarship. Intellectual expertise should help scholars engage in civic conversation rather than isolate us in an insular, self-contained world.

Together, these five principles form the ideal of IIS. And they form the major contributions of IIS to the study of Islam and Islamic law. Given that IIS breaks radically from WhiSIS and PILS, and contains in its very principles a critique of these two discourses that currently dominate the study of Islam and Islamic law, it is subjected to a contemptuous and harsh critique from both. The main criticism that WhiSIS levels against IIS is that it is not "real" scholarship and, as such, IIS scholarship is dismissed by WhiSIS scholars, mostly ignored, even when they adopt some of IIS' conclusions. So, when a white, male scholar writes an extended section on domestic violence and Islam in a book about the Prophet, he draws heavily from IIS scholarship while barely mentioning any of the robust and important scholarship produced by IIS scholars on this topic in the last decade. He thereby builds on IIS scholarship while also erasing it, by not referencing it, claiming for himself insights that are not his. And the major criticism leveled against IIS by PILS is that IIS is "insidious," a trojan horse sent by the neo-colonialists to destroy Islam from within. This, despite the fact that PILS scholars are likely to see WhiSIS scholarship as more authoritative than IIS scholarship, citing scholars from WhiSIS respectfully, with admiration, seeking their approval, while disparaging IIS scholars. The fact that WhiSIS and PILS agree with each other in their critique of IIS brings to light their shared lineage as siblings, children of colonialism that they are. Despite the rivalry between the two, they are united in their contempt for IIS.

Here are some of the criticisms that WhiSIS and PILS level against IIS:

1. IIS is not rigorous enough. Because IIS breaks the form of these two types of scholarship, it does not reference the same body of texts as authoritative. It breaks the loop of authority as tautology created by WhiSIS and PILS. By centering Muslims, especially Muslim women's scholarly voices, to critique both WhiSIS and PILS, IIS is seen as de-sacralizing the study of Islam. IIS scholars ask different questions, speak to Muslims, take Muslim experience as an authoritative source of knowledge, write accessibly, are engaged with Muslim communities—in all these ways they are seen as compromised. But the real reason they are seen as compromised scholars is because they are not willing to contort themselves out of shape to fit the uncomfortable molds demanded by WhiSIS and PILS in order to produce "legitimate" scholarship. IIS scholars are changing the game, playing by different rules, rules by which they can actually win. What if their color, their gender, their religion gave them special insights into Islamic Studies rather than counting against them?

2. IIS scholars are accused of being "too western" by both WhiSIS and PILS, because both see, for example, gender equality, a demand for equal rights for women based on the idea of universal human rights, as essentially western. As if the west owns feminism, which it doesn't. As if Muslims aren't western, which they are. As if Islam is essentially patriarchal, which it isn't. As if scholars don't have multiple subjectivities, which they do. As if identities are not complex and fluid, which they are.
3. IIS scholars are accused of being anachronistic because they treat Islam like the living religion that it is, refusing to confine its study to precolonial texts. This way, a moral voice on scholarship is seen as weakening scholarship, rather than strengthening it. And evading moral responsibility by positing a mythical morally neutral gaze, or by pleading submission, becomes an act of "rigorous" scholarship, rather than morally failed and irrelevant scholarship that supports structural inequalities.
4. IIS scholars are often criticized for not mastering the Arabic language before writing about Islam and Muslims. But because IIS centers Muslims in the study of Islam and Muslims, there is no reason that Arabic should be a necessary prerequisite for scholarship on Islam and Muslims. Most Muslims do not speak Arabic, nor see the Qur'an as an authoritative legal text, nor live lives structured by Islamic laws, or what they believe to be Islamic laws. Why should Arabic be a prerequisite for how Muslims, for example in South Asia, think about Islamic law and the Qur'an?
5. IIS is accused of being methodologically unsound. A male, South Asian, Muslim scholar at a conference at Yale University, critiquing IIS said, "Justice is not a methodology!" Why not? And yet this same scholar saw WhiSIS and PILS as methodologically sound. So, white supremacy and patriarchy are fine methodologies?

Of course, the standards of IIS are so high, and this form of study so new, there are few works that achieve these standards, but many that aspire to them. It is difficult to shift one's perspective about scholarship on Islam and Muslims so that we think of Islam not as defined by scholars sitting around and thinking about it, but rather as defined by Muslims living and practicing the religion. Such that even Muslim women of color, trying to write in the newly emerging tradition of IIS can find themselves slipping into WhiSIS and PILS frames of thought, which are so much more entrenched and can be especially compelling for the authority and power that their approval guarantees. They may even use the language and logic of WhiSIS and PILS to critique each other. Recently a Muslim woman of color critiqued foundational Islamic feminist scholarship in the tradition of IIS. She argued that Muslim feminists might be making the Qur'an say something it doesn't say, that it may not be as gender egalitarian as they are claiming. Which is to say, she said, that the

Qur'an might not actually say what Muslims said it did. That reading the Qur'an as a feminist text is not a "fair" reading of the text. What struck me about this Muslim woman of color's critique was that it is a critique in the tradition and form of WhiSIS and PILS—claiming that the text has a meaning independent of and overriding contemporary Muslim interpretation and engagement with the text. This isn't a fair reading for whom? By what metric?

I recently heard an interview with Joe McNeil, one of the Greensboro Four, who changed America, who rejected its racial segregation, by insisting on the right to sit at a Woolworths lunch counter in 1960. American racism in the form of white supremacy segregated public spaces racially, so that black people were not allowed to even sit at a lunch counter reserved for white people, let alone order and be served lunch. When the Greensboro Four rejected this law of the land in North Carolina, a nationwide struggle ensued, in which black people were beaten and abused and harassed by white civilians and cops policing racial segregation. Finally, after great national uproar, the Greensboro Four prevailed and Woolworths was forced to desegregate, and black people were allowed to enter the Woolworths, sit at the lunch counter, order food, and be served. Following Woolworths' desegregation, McNeil went to the lunch counter to place an order and eat something—something he'd not yet done, something that until now he was forbidden from doing. He ordered coffee and apple pie. About the coffee, he said, "it was bad." And the apple pie—"it sucked."

Many scholars of color and Muslim women find their experience of WhiSIS and PILS similar to McNeil's experience of the coffee and apple pie at the Woolworths lunch counter. After decades of fighting, resisting, just trying to get in, have a seat at the table and be permitted to speak, we arrive, look around and think, "That's it?" Time to create the field anew.

VI.

A fact that people with privilege are reluctant to confront is that there is no morally neutral, no innocent position of privilege. I have found that when people are made aware of their racial, gendered, class privilege, they usually ask, in a whiny tone, what am I supposed to do about my privilege? Should I hate myself for my privilege? I'm not responsible for the system that privileges me, it is not *my* fault. I didn't create it. I'm as much trapped in this system as those who are uniquely discriminated by it. And besides, my life is hard too.

And the answer I have for this is that those who are systematically privileged based on their race, gender, class, religion, etc., the onus is greatest on them to divest from their privilege, to use their privilege, after acknowledging and seeing their privilege for what it is—unearned and unjust—in order to lose it. Use it to lose it.

Just as privilege is bestowed upon people in a million ways, in ways big and small, it must be divested from in those ways, in ways big and small. And it is the responsibility of the privileged, the ones with the most power—both soft and hard—in a system that bestows power unequally, where they enjoy advantages denied to others, to figure out how they should divest from their privilege. Certainly, this will involve listening, and seeing, and learning from marginalized and disempowered groups. But the onus cannot be on marginalized groups to come up with ways for the privileged to divest from their privilege. Such divestment will involve a commitment of resources, time, thought, creative energy, the investment of one's soul, a setting aside of the ego, experiencing discomfort and remaining steadfast in that discomfort, to continuously, consistently, persistently divest. As long as you have unearned privilege on the back of another, you have a responsibility to resist the system that grants you privilege, to fight for those who are discriminated against and abused by the same system, to use your privilege to lose it. Forever, eternally. Or until we remove the systematic inequalities that privilege us. And if it feels exhausting, unbearable, like it will never end, and you will fail; if it feels hopeless, just imagine what it feels like to be on the other side, to be the one without privilege, to be the one hurt, abused, humiliated by the system that exalts your own subjectivity. You can never imagine, or get what it's like to be on the other side, but your knowledge of the limitation of your imagination, of the terrible consequences of the structural inequalities of a system that privileges you, should be motivation enough; motivation to continue fighting to remove structural inequalities, so that others are not discriminated against, and so that you no longer enjoy privileges de facto, due to your race, gender, class, religion, etc. It doesn't matter how nice or well-intentioned you are, as long as you enjoy unearned privilege, you participate in and reinforce structural inequality. That is the burden of privilege.

Intersectionality is a useful theoretical tool for us here, because it posits privilege as fluid, as not fixed, and brings to light, for example, my privilege. As a woman of color, I am often on the bottom rung of both WhiSIS and PILS. I'm a person of color (POC) and a woman. This compounds the disadvantages, the discrimination I experience. However, as an educated middle class woman born in the Global North, as a scholar employed at a prestigious university, I also enjoy special privileges denied to others. I have a book published by Oxford University Press. I am the Canada Research Chair of Religion, Law, and Social Justice. I have been elected to the Board of Governors at the University of British Columbia. I wield influence from these positions of power and authority—at the same time, I endured racism and sexism and Islamophobia throughout my academic career to get to this place, and I continue to experience racism and sexism and Islamophobia. Remember, privilege isn't fixed, you don't get to a place and now you can feel comfortable and become untouchable. It increases and decreases in various contexts. I will always be a woman of color, and my color and gender will continue to count against me in various, and compounding ways. But I also have a Ph.D., I come from the Global North, I am heterosexual, I speak English, so I also enjoy privileges of social and economic class, of able-bodiedness, of sexuality.

In this chapter, I've been performing thus far a kind of divestment from power by speaking the names of power, describing how structural inequality is expressed, preserved and protected in the Study of Islam, and how it is resisted. I want to go a step further and turn this critical gaze on my own scholarship, to speak self-critically. How does my own scholarship fit the molds of WhiSIS and PILS, how has it been shaped and influenced by these forms? How can I do better?

I'm going to address these questions by examining my book, *Domestic Violence and the Islamic Tradition: Ethics, Law and the Muslim Discourse on Gender*, published by Oxford University Press. The book emerged out of my dissertation, building on it in crucial ways, and still rooted in it in significant ways. In the first few years of its publication, the book received over sixteen reviews, mostly excellent, all of them positive, by prestigious journals in Religious Studies, Islamic Studies, Feminist Studies, and it has been reviewed by Muslims and non-Muslims alike. And I am grateful for the positive reviews and attention the book has received. But I am also troubled by the overwhelmingly positive attention, because, why? Did the book so thoroughly serve the status quo as to not rock the boat at all? As to upset no one? That disappoints me.

Looking back at the book now, I am struck by several things. It is clearly a pre-tenure project, rooted in a dissertation. The relationship of scholarship to power influences the nature and content of the scholarship itself. For example, this chapter, which dares to critique the field of Islamic Studies, can only be written from a position of relative security provided by tenure. Projects produced in the service of tenure, writing produced in service of a Ph.D. and tenure are characterized by their powerlessness. The positionality of a graduate student or assistant professor coupled with race and gender—a South Asian woman who at various points was too Muslim or not Muslim enough, too western or not western enough—means that I was well aware, I was *made* well aware that I needed the approval of WhiSIS and PILS to be perceived as a legitimate scholar, worthy of a Ph.D., worthy of tenure. And since my very subjectivities placed me at a constant disadvantage vis-à-vis PILS and WhiSIS, I had to master myself, overcome my own subjectivities, learn to speak in a foreign language about my own tradition, accept lightly a denial of my human dignity and worth, as necessary collateral damage in order to produce scholarship that would be judged worthy of the field, that would be worth merit, that would prove I deserved first a Ph.D., and then tenure, both of which I would be granted, but only reluctantly, grudgingly, like I was weaseling my way into a guild I didn't actually deserve to be in.

When I started writing my dissertation I knew only that I wanted to please the gatekeepers of WhiSIS and PILS, which, at the time, I saw as the authoritative embodiments of the western academy and of Muslim scholarship on Islam. That is to say, I wanted a Ph.D. from a western academic institution, and still be able to speak to Muslims. I'd seen how the scholarship of Muslim feminists, scholarship that shaped my life and my intellectual trajectory, scholarship that saved my faith, was harshly criticized by both WhiSIS and PILS. I wanted to produce scholarship that contributed to a feminist Islamic discourse while avoiding all of the critiques, all of the pitfalls associated with Islamic feminism. I wanted my work to be "rigorous," based on extensive medieval Arabic and contemporary white, western sources, methodologically sound, rooted in theory; which is to say, I wanted to excel by the standards of excellence set by the myth of whiteness as objectivity, and maleness as the model of sincerity. As a Muslim woman of color, it is clear to me now that I was doomed to failure before I even began, but back then, when I started the project some fifteen years ago, I was hopeful, and naïve, and clueless.

In the dissertation, following the standards of WhiSIS and PILS, I focussed exclusively on precolonial Islamic texts, which I called "premodern" texts in the dissertation. WhiSIS designates the precolonial period as "premodern," thereby directing our gaze away from white supremacist colonialism, which ravaged Muslim lands and birthed WhiSIS. Ignoring colonialism allows WhiSIS to forget its moral responsibility to its subject of study, born as it was in the service of violence; it depoliticizes a political subject matter, allowing the WhiSIS scholar to study their subject as an object, from and into a historical, social, and political vacuum. The term "precolonial" reminds WhiSIS of its roots, of the white supremacy entrenched in its study of Islam. The move from medieval to contemporary is not smooth and uneventful; the modern is birthed by the devastating effects of colonialism and its aftermath. Since I was seeking the approval of WhiSIS in the dissertation, I used the correct nomenclature, "premodern" rather than "precolonial." Truth be told, I was so deeply caught in the desperate need of approval from WhiSIS, I could not even imagine, consider, think of the "premodern" as the "precolonial."

And in exclusively studying precolonial texts on domestic violence, I treated Islam like the dead religion it is not. Instead of treating the Qur'an as a meaning-generating text with a present and future as well as a past, I only focussed on a specific history. I traced the intellectual history of a Qur'anic verse, Q. 4:34, as it was interpreted by elite, male, Muslim scholars in Qur'an commentaries and Islamic legal works. My work was "cutting edge" in that I examined precolonial Islamic texts over the course of centuries, from the ninth to the sixteenth, but also across disciplines, examining both Qur'an commentary and Islamic law, *tafsir* and *fiqh*. I cleverly described my examination of these sources as "diachronic and synchronic," which seems silly to me now because it was work that was historical but also stubbornly pretending to be in a vacuum, which is not a good way to study religious texts.

Writing the dissertation, the research and writing were deeply painful and disappointing for me, because I was learning through my research that every luminous, great, admired, beautiful, authoritative Muslim scholar of *tafsir* and *fiqh* condoned rather extreme forms of violence against women based on culturally contingent, essentialist theories of gender hierarchy. Men were better than women, according to these male scholars because they were stronger, smarter, better at archery, grew facial hair, could have several wives, their testimony was worth the testimony of two women, because God favored them. Men's general social privileges over women translated into the heteronormative and patriarchal marriage in which husbands were responsible for the moral rectitude of their subordinates—their wives, their children, their enslaved humans. To keep their wives straight, husbands could discipline them, through verbal council, abandonment, and physical violence short of broken bones and open wounds.

Imagine learning this about your tradition as you're writing a dissertation. I wrote my dissertation in a state of heartbreak. How could these men I loved so much care for me so little, think of me as so inferior, so unworthy? How could I belong to a religious tradition that rejected me so? The words of these scholars were like a thousand arrows to my heart. Why didn't anyone, not even one of them, see how wrong they were, speak up for the women—the poor oppressed in the texts—as the Qur'an calls them to: "What is wrong with you that you do not fight for the poor, the oppressed of the earth?" Did none of them love women? Did none of them know brilliant, intelligent women to challenge the belief that men were better than women? Did none of them want to protect women from violence in patriarchal societies, where women were already disadvantaged and marginalized? My heart bled and broke in silence, in obscurity, because in the dissertation I knew, was *made* to know, that I must write as a dispassionate scholar, as someone at arm's length, at a distance from her subject of study, in the tradition of white men, where the standards of excellence are set and measured by white scholars, as someone who didn't care. And so that is how I wrote the dissertation, performing a lack of moral compass, focusing on texts alone. Acting like these texts were not killing me, asking the correct questions, which were not my questions. All of this is to say, my dissertation was not my own. It could not be my own.

In my book then, rooted as it is in the dissertation, I missed out on the chance to have a robust moral voice. For fear of critique, I appealed to certain kinds of authority—white supremacist and patriarchal—for an important structural reason. I still needed the approval of the academy, my scholarship had to be respectable and respected for me to earn tenure. I was traumatized by the process of dissertation writing, so I took some time away from the book, even though I had a contract to write it. Under the mentorship of a supportive editor (one of the greatest gifts for a writer!), I re-wrote the entire book, virtually every sentence. I tried to bring more of myself into the book. In a new Introduction, I shared a bit about my relationship with Q. 4:34, growing up with this verse swirling around me: how did I learn of it, how did discussions about it unfold around me? I wrote about the politics of writing such a book that might be seen as airing dirty laundry, the cost of sanitizing Islam for the external gaze, what does this cost Muslims? I had to say explicitly that I was not writing for "small minded bigots."

I expanded my research to examine postcolonial and contemporary Muslim positions on Q. 4:34—treating Islam like the living religion that it is, and the Qur'an like the meaning-generating text that it is. To treat the Qur'an as a meaning-generating text is never to treat it as if its meanings are foreclosed, predetermined, static, but rather as if the meanings of the Qur'an are dynamic, unfolding, its self-disclosure eternal. I expanded the texts that I studied by looking at those written by Muslims in Urdu, alongside English and Arabic. I expanded the sources I used from written to audio-visual and web-based sources. I used that word, "precolonial," rather than "premodern." I treated contemporary positions and claims about the Qur'an with as much authority as precolonial sources. The myth of a pristine, perfect precolonial Islam had been dead for me for a few years by the time I was writing the book.

When the book came out, I received many emails of congratulations. One of the messages I most cherished was from a respected male, South Asian scholar of Islam. He said, "You get the award for the most intimidating footnotes in recent memory." I was so proud of my footnotes. They were a shroud for my insecurity. I kept saying through them, "Look, I know what I'm talking about!" and "I'm not making this up!" I wanted to be as intimidating as some of the white, male founders of WhiSIS, the footnotes were in their tradition, but written for PILS scholars who might reject my scholarship out of hand on account of poor, unrigorous scholarship, on account of poor methodology. At least they couldn't dismiss my scholarship because I hadn't researched my subject area enough, because I hadn't considered this or that source.

But who was I writing for? I should have been writing for the Muslim reader first, this is our tradition, and we should be centered in research and writing about our religious tradition. Here's what I wish: I wish I'd centered myself and Muslims in the book to a greater degree. I'm amazed, for example, that in reviews of my book, people have speculated as to which postcolonial position I align myself with, whether traditionalist, neo-traditionalist, progressive or reformist, and they came to different conclusions! I was so thoroughly de-centered from my own scholarship, so committed to performing, demonstrating my arm's-length distance, my remove from my writing, lest I be accused of allowing emotional and personal connections to my subject matter debilitate my intellectual treatment of my subject, that I didn't even say which approach I was championing in the book that I wrote! And just to be clear now, I was championing the Reformist approach; that is the direction I'd like to see us go.

I wish I'd included more female voices in my book—as it stands, it is dominated by male scholarship. I wish I'd engaged in moral as well as intellectual critique of the scholars featured in the book. Domestic violence is a moral subject, to treat it only as an intellectual topic without regard to its moral implications for living humans is a moral failure. In my book, I speak about a "plain-sense" meaning of Q. 4:34, as if there is a standalone, plain-sense meaning independent of communities of interpreters. Although I wrote that we needed to have a performative relationship with the Qur'an, that the Qur'an has no meaning apart from its communities of interpreters, I still treated the text of Q. 4:34 has if it had an essential meaning. I wish I'd not done that, I wish I'd treated Q. 4:34 in the way I was calling for it to be read, as a text whose meanings are only ever disclosed in relationship with Muslim communities. There is a complete absence of the category of race in my book, which is inexcusable, when this topic is also a racial topic. A white, male convert defending the right of husbands to hit their wives, as he speaks to a primarily brown audience of South Asians and Arabs is racial. His using characterizations of Arabs as "an angry people" who would not have abided a Qur'anic ruling prohibiting domestic violence is all out racist. I should have said that. I notice now how I mention the race of brown and black scholars—as in, "this African American scholar," or "this South Asian activist," but I do not mention the race of white people, instead saying, "this American convert to Islam," writing American as white, as if American stands for white, which it absolutely does not. I wish I'd connected precolonial religious texts on Q. 4:34 with the tangible implications of those texts in the personal status, civil, and penal codes of contemporary Muslim majority countries. And finally, I wish there had been an ethnographic element of the book that connected textual discussions of Q. 4:34 by scholars and activists to the beliefs of living Muslims.

I know no book can do everything, but paying attention to the power structures of the field in which I was writing would have improved my scholarship and contributions to the study of Islam and Muslims, perhaps challenging the status quo, upsetting a few people along the way, and also supporting others who may have needed it. Even though I worked hard to make my book my own, my attempt to appeal to both WhiSIS and PILS hurt my scholarship, I was intellectually contorted out of shape, not speaking of the texts I was writing about as if they were mine, as if they belonged to me. I ceded authority to white scholars and Muslim male scholars, trusting them more than I trusted my own instincts based on my own experience of lived and embodied Islam. And pragmatically, in terms of my career, it worked. The book has been extensively and well-reviewed, and I received tenure and a few other awards. The academy sets up mechanisms so that you are always at the mercy of your peers' approval in order to advance, to progress, to be nominated for an award, to publish an article, to publish a book, you always need letters of reference, reviewers for your file. All of these mechanisms amount to regulations that maintain the status quo, that constrict the kind of writing you can or cannot do, what you can or cannot say, what you can or cannot imagine. I am acutely aware of this as I write this chapter. What will this cost me? But I've learned from the experience of writing my dissertation and book, earning a Ph.D. and tenure, succeeding in the confines of a religious discourse dominated by WhiSIS and PILS. Ultimately, the entire experience has been deeply dissatisfying.

If trying to center myself by mentioning my subjectivities in the Introduction had not been an act of courage, if being myself and trying not to be ashamed for being brown and a woman wasn't an act of bravery, imagine the book I could have written. When I read passages from the book now, I cringe a little—I was so scared to say what I thought! I'm so uncomfortable on those pages. I am contorted out of shape. I don't fit. And is it any surprise? I am playing a game designed to exclude me, writing in traditions in which my voice is not welcome, elbowing my way through resistant crowds, claiming authority that is at best grudgingly bestowed, and at worst rejected.

"You are brown."
"You are not white."
"You are a woman."
"You are too Muslim."
"You are not Muslim enough."
"You are too western."
"You are too (un)covered."

I know now what I didn't know back then. I'm the perfect set of subjectivities, perfect combination of brown, Muslim, South Asian, western, woman to write my book. Imagine if I had known that then, if I'd trusted myself when writing a book on the topic on which I am an expert. I no longer want to be the exception that proves the rule, the one who is allowed to enter, despite all her shortcomings, despite her color, despite her religion, despite her gender, despite her class. The price of such entrance is too high; the admission is not worth the price.

VII.

Some books have an afterlife, and in the afterlife of my book, I have developed my research in various ways. I've started paying attention to the role Q. 4:34 plays in the excuses that nation-states give for justifying gender inequality—patriarchy—in family law and for not criminalizing domestic violence. To this end, I have spoken, written about, and consulted on a civil case involving the United Arab Emirates (UAE), specifically regarding their reservations to Article 16 of the Convention on the Elimination of all Forms of Discrimination Against Women (CEDAW).

I also conducted surveys of about 200 Muslims in Toronto, Canada, and Kuala Lumpur, Malaysia, at sites of religious education—including mosques and academies—with conservative, moderate, and progressive leanings. These surveys reveal the importance of connecting textual Islamic Legal Studies with practice, confirming the need for a sustained interdisciplinary approach in Islamic Legal Studies. This study helped me to see that it is not only important to break the forms of excellence set by WhiSIS and PILS by writing in a morally responsible way, but also to break the forms of our disciplines to produce truly interdisciplinary scholarship where theoretical scholarship on Islam and Muslims is connected to the actual lived, embodied experiences of Islam and Muslims.

One of the reasons I decided to conduct the surveys was to find out if Muslims recognized Q. 4:34 as a text that permits the physical discipline of wives. When presenting on my book, people often asked me how this verse relates to domestic violence in Muslim communities. I know that domestic violence is prevalent in every human society irrespective of religion, but religious discourses contribute to domestic violence in important ways, both sanctioning it and prohibiting it. In my conversations with Muslim scholars, I found that views on whether Muslims knew about this verse were anecdotal, based on our own experiences with our own communities. "Most Muslims know about this verse," "Most Muslims have never heard of it before," "Most Muslims don't see this verse as permitting domestic violence." So I decided to survey Muslims in two diverse cities, one in which Muslims are a minority—Toronto—and one in which Muslims form a majority—Kuala Lumpur.

In Toronto, I surveyed mosque-going Muslims in the month of Ramadan, which expanded the sample size of Muslims, because more Muslims go to the mosque in Ramadan than would otherwise. I surveyed Muslims in three mosques; a conservative mosque that was patriarchally structured, where all positions of authority were occupied by men; a more moderate mosque, where women held some positions of authority, sometimes spoke to mixed gendered audiences and held seats on the mosque board; and a progressive mosque, where women held positions of religious and ritual authority. The racial make-up of these mosques was diverse, peopled mostly by brown and black Muslims (South Asian, Arab, African).

In Kuala Lumpur, the Muslims surveyed were mostly Malay, but they included South Asians and Africans. And instead of surveying in mosques, which have a different function in Kuala Lumpur than they do in Toronto, I conducted my surveys in three settings of Islamic teaching and learning. These included a conservative academic setting that champions a patriarchal version of Islam, a think tank that produces reformist Islamic scholarship, and a progressive NGO that promotes a gender equal vision of Islam. There was strong representation of women in each of these three institutions.

The first question of the survey scrambled six patriarchal verses from the three Abrahamic scriptures; two verses each from the Hebrew Bible, the Gospels, and the Qur'an. I removed identifying characteristics from the verses, like any mentions of Allah or the Church, referring to them instead as God or house of worship. A translation of Q. 4:34 that permitted physical violence was one of the verses in the mix. I asked participants to identify the Qur'anic verses. Then, after a series of questions about marriage and life partners, I asked, "Is it ever okay for a husband to hit his wife to correct her behavior?" I wanted to see how many Muslims answered "yes" to this question, and whether there was any correlation between the level of structural patriarchy in an institution and its members' acceptance or rejection of domestic violence. I also wanted to know if there was any correlation between a participant's recognition of Q. 4:34 as a Qur'anic verse and the answer to the final question; i.e. did recognizing Q. 4:34 mean that participants believed that husbands could hit their wives?

Here's what I found.

A significant minority of participants in both cities recognized Q. 4:34 as a Qur'anic verse; 44 percent in Toronto and 35 percent in Kuala Lumpur. The majority of Muslims surveyed answered the question, "Is it ever okay for a husband to hit his wife to correct her behavior?" with a "No"; 87.7 percent in Toronto and 59.8 percent in Kuala Lumpur. A minority of participants believed that husbands had the right to hit their wives to correct their behavior; 12.3 percent in Toronto, and 25.6 percent in Kuala Lumpur, with 14.6 percent of all surveyed declining to answer the question altogether.

As I had suspected, there was a correlation between the sites where the surveys were conducted and survey responses. In Toronto, the mosque with the most patriarchal structures of authority had the strongest levels of tolerance for domestic violence. Nearly half of the respondents at that mosque recognized Q. 4:34 as a Qur'anic verse (47 percent), and 20 percent of respondents said that husbands could hit their wives to correct their behavior. In the more moderate mosque, where women held positions of limited authority, 42 percent of the participants recognized Q. 4:34, but only 10.5 percent were willing to concede that husbands could hit their wives. Most interestingly, the mosque in which women had ritual authority had zero tolerance for domestic violence. 100 percent of the participants of that mosque said that, no, husbands can never hit their wives. This mosque demonstrated the largest Qur'anic literacy, with 50 percent recognizing Q. 4:34 as a Qur'anic verse.

Similarly, in Kuala Lumpur, the survey responses differed based on institutions' commitment to patriarchal Islam. At the most conservative institution, in which patriarchal Islam is seen as ideal, 43 percent of respondents believed that husbands could hit their wives, while 38 percent believed husbands couldn't hit their wives. 19 percent abstained from answering the question. At the think tank that promotes proscribed Islamic legal reform, preserving some forms of patriarchy while challenging others, 65.6 percent of respondents believed that husbands could never hit their wives, while a third (31.2 percent) responded to that question affirmatively. And finally, at the NGO that promotes women's rights and is headed by women, a majority of the participants did not believe that husbands could hit their wives (69 percent), while only 7 percent thought that hitting wives was acceptable. Interestingly, this group had the largest abstentions, with 24 percent not answering the question at all.

These surveys bring to light the correlation between structures of authority and tolerance for domestic violence, which is important: structural change must accompany social justice rhetoric. There is also a strong correlation between the desired idealized religious cosmology and attitudes toward domestic violence. The more beholden a community is to interpretations of precolonial texts that were unabashedly patriarchal, the more likely they are to justify domestic violence.

What do these surveys tell us about Muslims and their relationship to the Qur'an and their view of Islamic law? What do they tell us about the relationship between recognizing Q. 4:34 as Qur'anic and beliefs about domestic violence? There was a strong correlation between not recognizing Q. 4:34 and zero tolerance for domestic violence; that is to say, the majority (just over a half) of people surveyed both did not recognize Q. 4:34 and believed that husbands could not hit their wives. The second strongest correlation (28 percent) was between people who recognized Q. 4:34 and answered that husbands could not hit their wives. This means, they knew that Q. 4:34 was a part of the Qur'an, but did not think that it justified domestic violence. There was a significant but weaker correlation between people who recognized Q. 4:34 as Qur'anic and who believed that husbands could hit their wives, just under 12 percent. Finally, a minority of people did not recognize Q. 4:34 as Qur'anic and thought that husbands could hit their wives, less than 1 percent.

The majority of people surveyed did not recognize Q. 4:34 as Qur'anic, and further, most participants did not believe that husbands could hit their wives regardless of whether they recognized Q. 4:34 as Qur'anic or not. This means that, for these participants, Qur'anic verses did not function as legal verses without the mediation of other factors.

What should be largely unsurprising, except to the scholar who ignores Muslims in his study of Islam, is that there is at best a tenuous and highly contested connection between precolonial interpretations of the Qur'anic text and what Muslims believe is "Islamic." And surely, Muslims ought to decide what is Islamic about Islam, no? Seen in light of these surveys, it makes little sense to ask questions like, "Is the Qur'an a book of law?" or "Is ISIS Islamic?," much less to answer these questions as if they are legitimate.

Looking back at my book, I see that the most interesting discussions about domestic violence were happening in the contemporary period. And, certainly, it was important for me to patiently, methodically, and painstakingly (and it was painful!) lay bare the violence against women and wives sanctioned in precolonial texts in order to counter the rhetoric of plurality and diversity and beauty of these same texts. Though precolonial texts might be described in those ways on other topics, they are devoid of such qualities in discussions of violence against wives. Still, even though I said in the book that the most interesting conversations about domestic violence and Islam were happening now, I acted as if the most important conversations had happened in the past, devoting three chapters to the precolonial period, and only two to the postcolonial period, and even less to the voices of living Muslims. This is something I hope to correct in my research going forward, because research on Islam that ignores living Muslims is not just irrelevant and obsolete. It is bad scholarship.

VIII.

If we return to the question this chapter started with, "Is the Qur'an a book of law?" we can now see that the three forms of Islamic studies recounted above answer this question differently. The question is produced by WhiSIS and the answer of WhiSIS to this question is as simplistic as the question itself. The answer is "yes." The Qur'an is a book of law, and Muslims adhere to Islam by following the laws in the Qur'an. So, corporal punishments mentioned in the Qur'an are "Islamic." Never mind that most Muslims don't speak Arabic, that corporal punishment isn't applied in most Muslim majority countries, and most Muslims do not even know that corporal punishments are mentioned in the Qur'an. If precolonial texts understood the punishment for illicit sex in the Qur'an as 100 lashes, then even though most Muslims majority countries reject this historical interpretation and do not apply this law, the law is "Islamic" because it is found in precolonial texts. Muslims who interpret the Qur'anic text differently, and do not apply this law are less "Islamic," because precolonial texts are seen as representing, reflecting Islam more than the practice of living Muslims.

When living Muslims offer new and creative interpretations of Islamic law, they are seen by WhiSIS as breaking from the tradition, rather than in a dialectic relationship with their tradition, a tradition that is still evolving and developing on account of its being alive, which is to say, not dead. In fact, when Muslims argue that the Qur'an ought to be interpreted anew so that illicit sex is not punished corporally, or that the very definition of illicit sex should be re-examined, they are seen as following "western" precedent, as acting under the influence of the "west." Hence, living Muslims are portrayed as brainless creatures that either submit uncritically to precolonial texts or live under the influence of western moral standards. They are incapable of fresh, creative religious insights into an evolving religious tradition in which they are active participants.

The question "Is the Qur'an a book of law?" is less relevant to a PILS framework. The answer is, "partly, yes." For PILS, Islamic law is a form of spiritual practice; rather than an orthodoxy, Islam is an orthopraxy. Faith is expressed through action, and so even the definition of law is broad rather than narrow. Islamic law is concerned with the law of the land, including political, civil, and personal law, but it is so much more than that. The laws of ritual purity, for example, are also part of Islamic law. The laws around menstruation, obedience to parents, which foot you use to step into the bathroom (left), which hand you eat with (right), this is all part of Islamic law. Islamic law is about the relationship between the believer and God, and submission characterizes this relationship. In this context, the emphasis on devotion, a performance of piety, submission, and sincerity in the production of scholarship in PILS makes a good deal of sense. PILS looks back to the prophetic and precolonial past to live by its standards of piety in the present, which it does through adherence to a patriarchal conception of Islam law.

And this past is mediated through particular, designated living scholars. These scholars interpret which aspects of the past, of the tradition, of prophetic practice are relevant and which are to be disregarded. So, for example, though Muhammad facilitated the conditions for a female Companion (Umm Waraqa) to lead mixed-gendered prayers, assigning her a *mu'azzin* (one who makes the Call to Prayer), these scholars argue that despite these reports, Muslim women today cannot lead mix-gendered prayers. Or, for example, though the Qur'an forbids *riba* (usury) categorically, this prohibition isn't categorical and various kinds of usury can be considered "Islamic."

In the framework of IIS, the question, "Is the Qur'an a book of law" is distracting and entirely irrelevant. For IIS, the Qur'an is a book of liberation—universally and eternally. Instead of looking backwards and following the model of emulation, IIS scholars look around now and ask "How can the Qur'an help the marginalized here and now?" Law derived from the Qur'an that is not liberatory, or that leads to tyranny and oppression violates the ethos, the intent of the Qur'anic message. IIS posits that if the Qur'an is a universal text that speaks to Muslims regardless of time period and geographic location, subjectivity, etc., then Muslims should be able to receive the text as they are, with their subjectivities intact, without shame about being Muslim and western, without shame of believing in gender equality, of being anti-colonial, or feminist. Muslims can demand the Qur'an speak to them where they are, as they are, without them having to contort themselves out of shape, become people they are not, in order to receive its message of liberation.

So, if WhiSIS and PILS scholars hold that Islam is captured in precolonial texts, however narrowly and selectively defined, IIS scholars claim that Islam is what Muslims aspire to, what they hope to see in the world, what they are trying to create. IIS asks, what kind of worlds do Muslims aspire toward, how do they envision the ideal relationship between God and humans, what is their idealized cosmology? Is the world that Muslims aspire to patriarchal or egalitarian? Does it reinforce the status quo or challenge it? Is it committed to social justice or does it condemn any challenge to authority as *fitna* (sedition)? Does the ideal world reinforce or eliminate hierarchies—racial, gendered, sexual, religious, ethnic? The answers to these questions help us understand the kind of worlds Muslims see their Islam fashioning, imagining, dreaming.

Domestic violence is a powerful lens through which to think about the contributions of these three forms of Islamic Studies. Moving away from the abstract question, "Is the Qur'an a book of law?," let's ask a more useful question, "Does Islamic law allow domestic violence?" WhiSIS, consulting only precolonial Islamic texts will answer this question with a resounding "yes," as in "yes, Islamic law allows domestic violence." This is because the small, male cadre of elite scholars who wrote the precolonial Islamic texts that we now have access to were very comfortable with violence against women. Across the board, they assumed a gendered hierarchy between men and women, and held that men had divinely sanctioned disciplinary privileges over their subordinates including wives, children, and enslaved humans. So, WhiSIS answers this question with a "yes."

PILS scholars, who are committed to protecting, preserving, and maintaining the superiority of men over women, in a bid to adhere to the positions of the great, luminous scholars of the past, will also answer this question with a "yes, Islam allows domestic violence, but. . . ." Since PILS scholars are interested in remaining relevant and speaking to Muslims, they emphasize the limitations on permissible hitting. Men can hit their wives, but they can't break bones, they can't leave bruises, they can "hit" but not "beat" their wives. PILS scholars worry about the optics of their positions; if Islam looks bad, they look bad. They have more skin in the game, there is more at stake for them. Still, they base their authority in the same precolonial texts as WhiSIS.

But are these positions correct? Does Islam allow domestic violence? Well, if Islam died before colonialism, then WhiSIS and PILS are correct. But it did not die then; Islam and Muslims continue to live today, and Muslims disagree strongly with precolonial interpretations of the Qur'an that permitted violence against wives to the extent that the entire conversation has shifted. Precolonial legal scholars wondered, if he causes broken bones, open wounds, or death, should a husband be held liable for beating his wife? If so, how much, or how little? Contemporary Muslims reject this entire line of inquiry. Though some still justify and protect the right of husbands to physically discipline their wives, most do not see the Qur'an as permitting domestic violence in any way, shape, or form. So, if we treat Islam like a living tradition and the Qur'an as a meaning-generating text, this creates space to answer the question, "Does Islamic law permit domestic violence?" differently. We may well answer the question with "no, absolutely not." And this position is no less "Islamic" than that of a Muslim who answers this question with a "yes" just because that answer has roots in a misogynist, historical text.

IIS takes the "no" of a contemporary Muslim as authentically Muslim, as Islamic, and as a reflection of their Islamic view. And it goes further than that by developing a framework for answering that question in the negative, so that Islamic law cannot be read as permitting violence against women, so that Islamic law derived from the Qur'an protects women from violence. IIS is creative, it is forward looking, it is literally refreshing, it is developing the Islamic legal tradition so that it remains relevant and interesting and appealing to Muslims. So that it doesn't become stagnant and die under the weight of its own history, so that it is permitted to evolve and change and regenerate. IIS sees Islam as more than its history. It sees Islam as alive, developing, evolving into a better future.

[Editors' Note]: The editors wish to acknowledge the absence of footnotes and proper names in this chapter. This decision was made for two reasons. First, it models the kind of breaking of received academic form that is being advocated for in the article. Second, it ensures that the substantive structural critiques found therein are not mistaken for criticism of individual institutions or persons.

CHAPTER 2

ON READING FIQH

ANVER M. EMON

I. Introduction

Fiqh is a curious term of art, let alone genre of literature, in Islamic legal history. In the *Encyclopaedia of Islam*, second edition, *fiqh* is initially defined as "understanding, knowledge, intelligence," but is later specified for its technical legal use to mean "jurisprudence," specifically the legal doctrinal jurisprudence of Islamic law. Its scope is wide: "[i]n addition to the laws regulating ritual and religious observances (*ʿibadat*), containing orders and prohibitions, it includes the whole field of family law, the law of inheritance, of property and contracts and obligations, in a word provisions for all the legal questions that arise in social life (*muʿamalat*); it also includes criminal law and procedure, and finally constitutional law and laws regulating the administration of the state and the conduct of war."[1] Often the terms *fiqh* and *furuʿ* (branches) are used to refer to the same doctrinal corpus; in fact, the *EI2* entry for *furuʿ* directs the reader to the entry for "*fikh*."[2] This conflation is problematic from the perspective of debates on *ijtihad*, where *furuʿ* stands in contrast to *usul* to signify not so much specific legal doctrines, but rather as a proxy for particularizations of more general, if not universal, truth claims (see, chapter 7 *Ijtihad* in this volume).

This chapter will survey Islamic legal scholarship that focuses on the production and analysis of *fiqh*. In doing so, the treatment of *fiqh* studies will be

[1] J. Schacht and I. Goldziher, *Encyclopedia of Islam*, second edition, *sv* "*Fikh*."

[2] *Encyclopedia of Islam*, second edition, *sv* "*Furūʿ*."

analyzed from competing disciplinary angles to showcase the different implications each analytic approach brings to the study of *fiqh* as both doctrine and literary genre. Before getting into a detailed analysis of *fiqh* studies, Section II will outline what is not included in this study; namely, those approaches to *fiqh* that try to fill the legal lacunae that some scholars perceive between historical *fiqh* and the needs of the modern world. Those approaches fall broadly under the rubric of *fiqh al-waqi'*, and concern areas of human activity that are novel and have yet to be *fiqh*-ized, so to speak. Section III concerns philology as a disciplinary frame, examining the limits of that approach and the implications for when those limits are not appropriately heeded. The segregation of philology from what follows is in large part due to its formative role in the enterprise of Islamic legal scholarship, as well as its interpretive limits, as highlighted in Section IV. Section IV turns to studies of *fiqh* sources using more interpretive disciplinary approaches, often alongside, but sometimes in contrast to, the philological tendencies that initiated the field. Section IV concludes with a set of studies concerning what might be called "critique"; they will be addressed in light of the insights they provide when *fiqh* both provides the vantage point of analysis, and is the object of critique. The chapter will then conclude with a set of suggestions for future research.

II. *Fiqh*, Reform, and Contemporary Issues: "*Fiqh*" as Lacuna

The field of *fiqh* has been the genre in which debates about legal reform in the context of "modernity" have taken place. This can take the form of outright reformist ideologies and epistemologies that cast premodern *fiqh* as outdated, outmoded, and antiquated.[3] For others, *fiqh* is read in light of *usul al-fiqh* theories of *ijtihad* to render historical *fiqh* doctrines vulnerable to human fallibility, and thereby create an epistemic opening for legal change and reform.[4] On the other hand, historical *fiqh* may be claimed as the legal site for asserting what is authentically Islamic, and

[3] Abdullahi Ahmed An-Na'im, *Toward an Islamic Reformation: Civil Liberties, Human Rights, and International Law* (Syracuse: Syracuse University Press, 1990); Ziba Mir-Hosseini, "The Construction of Gender in Islamic Legal Thought and Strategies for Reform," *Hawwa* 1, no. 1 (2003): 1–31.

[4] Anver M. Emon, *Religious Pluralism and Islamic Law: Dhimmis and Others in the Empire of Law* (Oxford: Oxford University Press, 2012), 7–12; Anver M. Emon, "To Most Likely Know the Law: Objectivity, Authority, and Interpretation in Islamic Law," *Hebraic Political Studies* 4, no. 4 (2009): 415–440. For an illustrative example, see Ziba Mir-Hosseini, "The Construction of Gender in Islamic Legal Thought and Strategies for Reform," *Hawwa* 1, no. 1 (2003): 1–28.

thereby imputing authority to the claimant to represent what is and is not Islamic law. These sorts of debates about *fiqh* were especially well-trodden throughout the twentieth century and will not be fully examined here.

A more recent development in *fiqh* debates concerns the implication of "modernity" on the need for new *fiqh*. Broadly, this topic is invoked as *fiqh al-waqi'*, which is a terminological placeholder for the absence of *fiqh* in a context that is radically different than the reality from which premodern Muslim jurists wrote.[5] A sub-category of this concern with *fiqh* as lacuna is the vibrant topic of the *fiqh* of Muslim minorities (*fiqh al-mustaqilla*). This is a more recent development that scholars have addressed given both conversion to Islam in Europe and North America, and immigration to these regions in the latter half of the twentieth century.[6] Both topics provide conceptual sites for compelling debates on orthopraxy for and in Muslim communities in the modern world where (a) the speed of technological development (e.g. migration, labor, internet, etc.) changes the experience of living in the world, and (b) Muslims are dispersed across borders, living in varying political, economic, and social circumstances as minorities or majorities of particular nation-states. However, such topics and conceptual approaches are less about the disciplinary uses of *fiqh* sources and more about the underlying approaches to ongoing, present forms and modes of legal reasoning in the language of *fiqh*. These are of course important debates, but lie outside the scope of this chapter. Rather this chapter focuses on more recent developments in the utilization of *fiqh* sources, and therefore approaches *fiqh* not as legal lacuna, but instead as content-laden literary genre.

III. Philology and the Art of Reading (In) Slowly

Key to the study of *fiqh* are the texts themselves. Published *fiqh* collections are the end-product of editorial work (*tahqiq*) that pieces together a single text from extant manuscripts (*makhtuta*) held in different libraries. Edited collections of *fiqh* may start with a preface by the editor (*muhaqqiq*), who introduces the text and the author, as well as outlining the process of producing what may amount to dozens of volumes of a single, encyclopedic *fiqh* compendium. For instance, the editor of

[5] Ronald A.T. Judy, "Sayyid Qutb's fiqh al-waqiʿi, or New Realist Science," *Boundary 2* 31, no. 2 (2004): 113–148.

[6] Alexander Caeiro, "The Power of European Fatwas: The Minority *Fiqh* Project and the Making of an Islamic Counterpublic," *International Journal of Middle East Studies* 42 (2010): 435–449.

al-Muqaddimat al-Mumahhidat, Muhammad Hujji, remarked in his preface (*al-tamhid*) how he transcribed the final version from various manuscripts (eight in total) preserved in libraries in Fez, Meknes, Rabbat, Tunis, and Cairo.[7] Each manuscript, he wrote, suffered defects in the "beginning, middle or end," but he was nonetheless able to piece together (*talfiq*) a complete copy from them all.[8] After listing each manuscript, their qualities, and limitations, he briefly described the slow, painstaking process of juxtaposing each manuscript, section by section, to authenticate (*ithbat*) the correct text.[9] To do so, Hujji identified the version of the text that all manuscripts (or at least most) agreed upon, or alternatively the version he preferred (*ma rajjahnahu*) where the meaning across the manuscripts was obscure or murky.[10] He does not elaborate on what he meant by preferred or how he resolved obscure passages. This ought to raise concerns, given what Suzanne Marchand reminded us about the implicit interpretivism of philology: "texts and artifacts do not interpret themselves."[11] Editors regularly use footnotes to explain where the manuscripts suffered defects or ambiguities, and to identify Qur'anic verses and hadith mentioned in the text.[12] Some editors, though not Hujji, provide facsimiles of the original manuscripts in their prefaces, as did Muhammad Faris, the editor of al-Sarakhsi's *Sharh Kitab al-Siyar al-Kabir*.[13] The philological work required to produce such texts is both immense and painstaking; and indeed it is a *sine qua non* of research in Islamic legal studies. Those published monographs find their way to university libraries, and the hands of scholars who benefit from them without having to travel far and wide to locate and identify extant sources.

The place of philology in Islamic legal history can be traced back to the development and salience of grammar in premodern *madrasa* settings, but in the academy it harkens back to academic practices in the European university. As Marchand explained in her masterful study on German orientalists, the philologist engages in an "internalist source criticism, perfecting its attempts to take texts apart from the inside, and to determine their authenticity, date, and authorship. Combined with 'external' testimony ... these findings could be, if one dared, used to recreate lost worlds."[14] The implicit historical positivism of the philological enterprise, Marchand recalled, was also the reason for the presumed beauty of such

[7] Abu Walid Ibn Rushd, *al-Muqaddimat al-Mumahhidat*, ed. Muhammad Hujji (Beirut: Dar al-Gharb al-Islami, 1988), 7.

[8] Ibn Rushd, *al-Muqaddimat al-Mumahhidat*, 7 Ibid.

[9] Ibid.

[10] Ibid., 8.

[11] Suzanne L. Marchand, *German Orientalism in the Age of Empire: Religion, Race and Scholarship* (Cambridge: Cambridge University Press, 2009), 159.

[12] Ibn Rushd, *al-Muqaddimat al-Mumahhidat*, 8.

[13] Muhammad b. Ahmed al-Sarakhsi, *Sharh Kitab al-Siyar al-Kabir*, ed. Muhammad Hasan Muhammad Hasan Ismail al-Shafi'i [aka Muhammad Faris] (Beirut: Dar al-Kutub al-'Ilmiyya, 1997), iii–xvi.

[14] Marchand, *German Orientalism*, 160.

a disciplinary commitment: "the lasting beauty of it was that at least in principle, one listened to the texts themselves, speaking in their own tongues, and even sometimes trusted their testimony over and against that of traditional authorities" such as those assuming canonical status in European academe.[15]

A. Philology and History: Between the Past and the Present

A classic study that places philology in conversation with history is Patricia Crone's *Roman, Provincial and Islamic Law*.[16] Her study is narrowly directed at establishing the cultural origins of Islamic law as residing, at least potentially, in provincial law—the "non-Roman law practiced in the provinces of the Roman empire, especially the provinces formerly ruled by Greeks."[17] Particularly, she was interested in the distinction between collective notions of *mawali* that relationally linked non-Arabs to Arab tribes, and the particular legal device of *wala'* that relationally linked a freed slave to his former master as patron.

To analyze her *fiqh*-related intervention requires first appreciating how her study was meant as an antidote to, or at least an at-times-scathing critique of, the professionalization and compartmentalization in the modern university. According to Crone, the limits of the modern university were apparent in how Islamicists emphasized the Roman law origins of Islamic law, despite the fact that their classicist colleagues of ancient Greece and Rome had long known that Roman law was not uniformly applied across the Roman Empire at the rise of Islam in the seventh century.[18] The failure to account for the work of other scholars in different departments echoes contemporary concerns about the silo-mentality in the modern university.

But her critique of the university was not merely about compartmentalization. It was also about a politics that devalued the kind of historical positivism that is characteristic of philology. Crone's own interest in the origins of Islam was premised upon a conviction that Islamic law could not have arisen "parthenogenetically," as if out of nothing. But as she lamented, the study of origins was less fashionable in the academy at the time she wrote her study. For Crone, the reason Islamicists dropped this line of research had to do with a complex set of factors associated with the

[15] Marchand, *German Orientalism*, 160. See also Eckehard Simon, "The Case for Medieval Philology," *Comparative Literature Studies* 27, no. 1 (1990): 16–20, 18, who recounts one view of philology as "having the capacity to retrieve the experiences of the past, of lost cultures, through close study of the written record."

[16] Patricia Crone, *Roman, Provincial, and Islamic Law: The Origins of the Islamic Patronate*, (Cambridge: Cambridge University Press, 1987).

[17] Ibid., 1.

[18] Ibid., 4.

organization and production of knowledge at the turn of the twentieth century, and in particular after the First World War.

> All branches of the arts suffered from professionalization, or in other words from the transfer of scholarship to universities, where standard syllabi, departmental divisions and academic career structures led to loss of depth and range alike. It was not just Islamic studies that went into Splendid Isolation at that time. In the case of legal studies, the change was all the more drastic in that Germany and Italy, the leading countries as regards the study of Roman and provincial law, had begun to exchange Roman law for national codes about the turn of the century, thereby depriving Roman legal studies of their practical importance. But for Islamicists a political factor was also at work. As the era of the colony gave way to that of the mandate and eventually to that of independence, Islamicists increasingly preferred to study Islam as an autonomous system developing internally in response to its own needs and by the use of its own resources. At the same time the Russian revolution helped to redirect attention from cultural origins to socio-economic problems.[19]

These factors did not require one to turn away from a study of cultural origins; however, her critique stems from the implication of these political factors on the pursuit of knowledge and advanced research.

Appreciating her critique of the university, both for its compartmentalization and knowledge politics, puts the stakes implicit in her study on Islamic law into stark relief. Her study argued that Islamic law's origins lie in the Greek and provincial cultural context in which Arabs found themselves when they conquered lands beyond the Arabian peninsula. Her claim rests on her analysis of clientage in Islam, specifically on the term *mawali*. But one cannot fully appreciate the tenor and tone of her study without reckoning with the overwhelming historical positivism that characterizes her research endeavor, and her own tragic, if not politically naïve, sense that such positivism is no longer fashionable. Indeed, in an unmistakable tone of resignation, if not resentment, Crone wrote: "in practice an interest in genetic links has long come to be regarded as old-fashioned—philological as opposed to sociological, diffusionist as opposed to structuralist. Worse still, it is now considered ethnocentric and offensive to Islam."[20]

Whatever one may think of Crone's actual study—and many have disputed its findings[21]—it nonetheless reflects a historically positivist approach to the field that understands the study of Islamic law as a study of origins. Her study may very well be ethnocentric for rendering the "Islamic" as a variable, while treating Roman and Provincial law as constants; though that may have less to do with ethnocentrism, and more to do (ironically) with Crone's own compartmentalized approach to her field of study. Whether her study can be counted as "sociological" depends

[19] Crone, *Roman, Provincial and Islamic Law*, 6.

[20] Ibid.

[21] See, for instance, Wael B. Hallaq, "Review: The Use and Abuse of Evidence: The Question of Provincial and Roman Influences on Early Islamic Law," *Journal of the American Oriental Society* 110, no. 1 (1990): 79–91.

on whether one accepts her method of reading early Islamic texts on *mawali* in light of nineteenth- and twentieth-century anthropological literature on Bedouin practices of clientage in the underdeveloped regions of the Arab peninsula. As she stated: "The information on Arabia in the last century before it was transformed by the inroads of modern government and oil industry provides a reasonably full and intelligible picture of the position of the outsider. This picture is not of course in itself evidence for pre-Islamic conditions; but in its light the fragmentary pre-Islamic evidence becomes more informative than when it is taken on its own."[22] It seems strange that she turned to more recent anthropological accounts to inform her reading of the premodern literary tradition. But in a sense, that is exactly what she did. One might characterize this as part of the more sociological dimension to the philology of German university culture, as Marchand has described.[23] This curious leap between late antique and early medieval texts, and nineteenth- and twentieth-century anthropological accounts might be methodologically plausible if one appreciates philology as a study of culture, akin to, if not a sub-branch of, anthropology.[24] From a legal perspective, Crone's juxtaposition implicitly reads texts (in this case, legal texts) as a mirror of society, though in this case a backward projection of society to corroborate her analysis of a much earlier set of texts. Whether or not law can be read as a "mirror" of society is itself a suspect claim, given recent scholarship in the field of law and society.[25] But regardless of one's approach to anthropology or law and society, we cannot ignore the politics implicit in Crone's turn to anthropology, namely a turn in the service of her unabated historical positivism. Her approach, in other words, never departed from the narrow positivism that marks (for better or worse) the philological enterprise.

The hegemony of her positivism is also felt in the way she characterizes the very genre of interest here, namely the corpus of *fiqh* literature. Crone considered *fiqh* literature "the single most important corpus of information on the nature of legal practice in the Roman Near East."[26] But in saying this, she collapsed legal doctrine and legal practice. Moreover, her historical positivism in the service of her inquiry into origins explains why she maintained *fiqh* as relatively consistent across centuries. "Though the law was perhaps not quite so unchanging as it was supposed to be, it certainly did not change very much before the impact of the West ... In practical terms, this means that any legal work composed between 800 and 1800 may be cited as evidence of classical doctrine."[27] Crone's failure to appreciate the

[22] Crone, *Roman, Provincial, and Islamic Law*, 44.

[23] Marchand, *German Orientalism*, 160.

[24] Calvert Watkins, "What is Philology?" *Comparative Literature Studies* 27, no. 1 (1990): 21–25, 23.

[25] Brian Z. Tamanaha, *A General Jurisprudence of Law and Society*, Oxford Socio-Legal Studies (Oxford: Oxford University Press, 2001), esp. ch. 5, which critiques what Tamanaha calls "the mirror thesis."

[26] Crone, *Roman, Provicial and Islamic Law*, 15.

[27] Ibid., 19.

discourse of law as its own subject matter, outside the historical positivism of her philological search for origins, blinded her to what later historians have observed as distinct changes across *fiqh* as a genre.

For instance, in an important study on peasant land holding, tax, and rent, Baber Johansen reviews Hanafi doctrines on land tax and rent to counter a common historiographic narrative that the *fiqh* after the tenth century CE was an "unchanging structure of legal ordinances."[28] On the contrary, Johansen argued, based on an analysis of Hanafi sources that "the whole history of Islamic law may be studied as a slow process of accumulating legal opinions which diverge from the old doctrine"[29] thus allowing him to characterize Hanafi doctrine as both classical and late Hanafi.

Methodologically, Johansen shared Crone's philological orientation, though his focus on legal doctrine and development as opposed to origins left him asking different questions. Johansen suggested that Islamic law ought to be studied by reference to the different literary layers of Islamic law, which would allow "us to see wide-ranging changes at certain levels of the legal literature" and to appreciate how "Near Eastern society reconciled its awareness of change with its preservation of a normative tradition."[30] It should be noted that Johansen's study was a preliminary one, and he acknowledged the limited historical context in his study of the law.[31] In light of that qualification, it is nonetheless surprising to read his presumption that a textual analysis might offer a window into the extra-textual world of "Near Eastern society."

No such window comes without an interpretive frame of analysis, and Johansen revealed one frame when he addressed the contract of tenancy. For Johansen, a key feature of the historical notion of "property" was that it was a fungible good subject to exchange. What was more precarious was the value of labor, or use of property for purposes of farming and agricultural production. Johansen remarked that jurists often refused to see productive use of land as a commodity that could be valued in the form of a price point. Citing the work of anthropologist Abdellah Hammoudi, he wrote that the "religious opposition to considering the productive use of land as a commodity resulted from a social and economic order, in which ... the ownership or the use of land and water was a 'relationship' and not a 'substance.'"[32] However, the work of Hammoudi, as Johansen rightly notes, concerned the irrigation system in nineteenth- and twentieth-century Morocco, in particular the importance of cultural norms of hierarchy and status in managing water distribution. Nonetheless, Johansen asserted that "the results which Hammoudi obtains from his analysis shed light on the way in which the Eastern Muslim world of the preclassical and

[28] Baber Johansen, *The Islamic Law on Land Tax and Rent* (London: Croom Helm, 1988), 124.
[29] Ibid., 124.
[30] Ibid., 125.
[31] Ibid., vii.
[32] Ibid., 28.

classical periods of Hanafite law perceived the productive use of land."[33] This turn to an anthropological frame of reference coincides with Crone's turn to anthropology to distinguish the collective practice of patronage/clientage from *wala'* as an individualized relationship of dependency.

However, his turn to anthropology is no less troubling than Crone's, whether from the analytic vantage point of anthropology or law and society. Moreover, Johansen's anthropological turn is situated in what is throughout an economically (if not Marxist) informed analysis of property, labor, and production. He peppered his study with phrases like "productive use,"[34] "commodity value,"[35] "commodity exchange,"[36] and "means of production."[37] Given this broadly materialist, narrowly economic, standpoint (which we can assume Crone would have decried as the result of the Russian revolution), it is curious that he did not see a correlation between the "religious" concern about valuing labor as property, and the arguments of Adam Smith for a valuation of labor in dollars and cents in his *The Wealth of Nations*.[38] Indeed, one might even find greater affinity between the Hanafi contract of tenancy, which allows labor to be commodified, and the measure of wage determination Smith offers in his seminal work. The paradox that affected Crone's historical positivism also affects Johansen's analysis of land tax and rent in Hanafi law. On the one hand, he sought to infer from these Hanafi texts sensibilities about Near Eastern society at the time the texts were written; in other words, he implicitly used these texts in the service of social history. On the other hand, his resort to after-the-fact anthropological analysis of societies services the historical positivism about the material conditions of premodern Near Eastern society as expressed in the legal texts of that time.

B. Whither Philology or to Weather Philology?

While philology continues to play an important role in the historical account of language, in particular Arabic with respect to *fiqh* sources, many in the humanities share Crone's concern about the demise of philology in the British and North American academy, and insist on its centrality to the humanistic endeavor.[39] But as demonstrated above, philology evinces a historical positivism that runs against (consciously or

[33] Ibid., 28.
[34] Ibid., 29.
[35] Ibid., 31.
[36] Ibid., 91.
[37] Ibid., 57, 58.
[38] Adam Smith, *The Wealth of Nations*, ed. Edwin Cannan (New York: The Modern Library, 2000), 73–99.
[39] James Turner, *Philology: The Forgotten Origins of the Modern Humanities* (Princeton: Princeton University Press, 2014).

otherwise) the interpretive turn in the human sciences, and in particular literary studies. The journal *Comparative Literature Studies* published papers from a conference held at Harvard University in a special issue devoted to the topic "What is Philology?"[40] Introducing the special issue, Latinist and medievalist Jan Ziolkowski recognized the polarizing effect of the term "philology" across various departments. For some, philology is "belittled as being a set of basic tools or data rather than as an approach valid in its own right."[41] For its defenders, philology represents a discipline of "refined techniques acquired through centuries of learned enterprise" whereas its detractors are worried that philologists are unable or unwilling to "test their own presuppositions and to ask new questions" leading to studies that are little more than "stale and irrelevant."[42] At the very least, philology may best be appreciated as a "slow reading that aims at establishing and commenting upon documents."[43] At its most aspirational, it "involves restoring to words as much of their original life and nuances as we can imagine."[44] Whether a mere set of techniques or a historical positivism through the study of language and documents, philology offers either a great deal or very little depending on the question being asked.

The problem, however, is that this rather arm's length approach to the controversy does not fully capture the stakes involved in the claims for and against philology. Drawing upon the polemical essays of William Arrowsmith and Paul de Man, Barbara Johnson articulated in stark terms the underlying stakes concerning philology *after* the literary turn. Arrowsmith's attack on philology comes by way of his discussion of Nietzsche's writings on classics and classicists. Specifically, Arrowsmith takes issue with Wilamowitz-Moellendorff's critique of Nietzsche's philological exactitude in the latter's readings from the Greek classics when writing *The Birth of Tragedy.* Nietzsche, Arrowsmith reminded us, was a philologist at first, though one who was skeptical about its disciplinary vision. His *Birth of Tragedy* shocked his colleagues in philology for its departure from the confines of the philological toward the philosophical mode for which he is remembered. Arrowsmith's polemic is particularly strident in his derision of philology:

> Classicists, of course, have unanimously preferred to believe that Wilamowitz—who caught Nietzsche in several factual errors—had the best of it. But in point of fact none of Wilamowitz' arguments disproves or even seriously damages Nietzsche's thesis; for the notion, particularly dear to philologists, that a thesis (or interpretation, translation, etc.) is only as good as its author's philological expertise—the *ad scientatum* argument—is clearly a fallacy. For although sorites of rigorous argument and proofs may be relevant to strict philological work ... a thesis like Nietzsche's—a large, intuitive, esthetic insight addressed finally

[40] *Comparative Literature Studies* 27, no. 1 (1990).
[41] Jan Ziolkowsky, "'What is Philology': Introduction," *Comparative Literature Studies* 27, no. 1 (1990): 1–12, 2.
[42] Ibid., 3.
[43] Ibid., 6.
[44] Ibid., 7.

to esthetic experience—cannot be defeated by showing errors in fact in the argument. And to think that it could be is the kind of crude category-mistake to which philologists, in so far as they are primarily technicians, are professionally susceptible.[45]

It is not that factual accuracy was unimportant to Arrowsmith. Rather it was the "apparently boundless" pretentions of philologists that he found objectionable.[46] Paul de Man, on the other hand, embraced philology as a response to those who found the theoretical emphasis in literary theory overbearing and unhelpful. For de Man "[a]ttention to the philological or rhetorical devices of language is not the same as aesthetic appreciation, although the latter can be a way of access to the former. Perhaps the most difficult thing for students and teachers of literature to realize is that their appreciation is measured by the analytic rigor of their own discourse about literature, a criterion that is not primarily or exclusively aesthetic."[47] Admittedly, Arrowsmith and de Man are responding to two different sorts of attacks, and so it may not be fair to situate them as opponents: they are not writing about philology in the same way, for the same reasons, or the same audience. Arrowsmith was troubled by the hegemony or hubris of the philologist who substitutes technique for substance, while de Man sought to constrain a sometimes highfalutin, jargonistic literary theory with the rigor of the slow reading that is characteristic of the philological enterprise.

Islamic legal studies have witnessed their fair share of philological hegemony, linking in compelling ways the travails of Nietzsche with innovative scholars in Islamic legal studies. Perhaps the most recent and well-known account involves a review of Wael Hallaq's *The Origins and Evolution of Islamic Law*, written by Mohammad Akram Nadwi in the *Journal of Islamic Studies*. Nadwi began the review ominously, with a hope that this book would not be influential given its "gross failings," which for Nadwi amounted to "not checking simple facts"; "not checking original sources"; and "a quite incredible indifference to the meaning of Arabic terms."[48] As if channelling Wilamowitz on *The Birth of Tragedy*, Nadwi remarked that such errors "are symptomatic of indifference to accuracy and fair-minded commentary."[49] In a fiery and indignant response, Hallaq retorted that Nadwi "combed the book" to find "miniscule technicalities" without actually engaging the interpretive framework of the book.[50] Moreover, Hallaq noted that in Nadwi's six-page

45 William Arrowsmith, "Nietzsche on Classics and Classicists (Part II)," *Arion: A Journal of the Humanities and the Classics* 2, no. 2 (Summer 1963): 5–27, 8–10.

46 Arrowsmith, "Nietzsche," 9 n. 3.

47 Paul de Man, "The Return to Philology," *The Resistance to Theory*, Theory and History of Literature vol. 33 (Minneapolis: University of Minnesota Press, 1986), 24.

48 Mohammad Akram Nadwi, "[Review] The Origins and Evolution of Islamic Law," *Journal of Islamic Studies* 19, no. 1 (2008): 109–115, 109, 110.

49 Nadwi, "[Review]," 109.

50 Wael Hallaq, "*The Origins and Evolution of Islamic Law*: A Response," *Journal of Islamic Studies* 19, no. 3 (2008): 456–466, 457.

review, "[t]here is absolutely no review of five out of the eight chapters making up the book."[51]

The language used by Nadwi and Hallaq against each other's texts could be easily mapped onto the debate within the humanities more broadly about the nature and hegemonic potential of philology.[52] One should not see their exchange as positing a choice between exactitude and interpretation. Rather, going forward, Islamic law scholars would do well to heed Johnson's harmonizing approach:

> What is at stake, then, is clearly the nature of reading; the question is not whether to be or not to be philological but how to read in such a way as to break through preconceived notions of meaning in order to encounter unexpected otherness—in order to learn something one doesn't already know—in order to encounter the other.

To read, then, is to read openly and freely but with attention to the text and its limits. But to draw upon Arrowsmith, the text should not be read with the hegemonic hoof of philology—or whatever it is proxying for—stamping one's back.

IV. *Fiqh* and the Social Sciences

This section considers the way in which *fiqh* as a genre of legal literature has informed (or been informed by) academic disciplinary approaches to law, meaning, and value. Consequently, whereas Section II explored how the notion of "*fiqh*" has been employed as a placeholder for an absence or lacuna in the law, and Section III addressed the limits of a philological analysis of *fiqh* sources, this section considers *fiqh* as a substantively rich genre of legal literature that informs interpretive approaches in the social sciences. The literature in this area is extensive, and this chapter does not pretend to capture the full range of discussions at the intersection of *fiqh* and the interpretive social sciences. For the purpose of this chapter, a range of issues drawn from the social sciences will be examined to illustrate the kinds of questions asked of *fiqh* sources, the range of answers provided, and the limits implicit in each approach.

[51] Hallaq, "A Response," 456 (italics in original).

[52] Incidentally, this author's own book, *Islamic Natural Law Theories* (Oxford: Oxford University Press, 2010), has been the victim of such philological hegemony by a hungry ingénue publishing in a student journal for which he served as editor. Rami Koujah, "A Critical Review Essay of Anver M. Emon's *Islamic Natural Law Theories*," *UCLA Journal of Islamic and Near Eastern Law* 14, no. 1 (2015): 1–28.

A. *Fiqh*, Ritual, and Politics: Law and Anthropology

Increasingly, the field of Islamic legal studies has been approached from an anthropological vantage point. There is a larger field of law and anthropology, within which the Islamic law and anthropology literature fits. The chapter by John Bowen in this *Handbook* offers a more sustained examination of how anthropology has influenced and informed a wide range of studies in Islamic legal studies. Of particular interest for this chapter are those studies that focus on narrow aspects of *fiqh* from an anthropological vantage point. As such, we shift from the historical positivism of philology, and to an interpretive approach to culture, meaning, and value. In articulating an interpretive approach for the social sciences broadly, Clifford Geertz explained: "Interpretive explanation—and it is a form of explanation, not just exalted glossography—trains its attention on what institutions, actions, images, utterances, events, customs, all the usual objects of social-scientific interest, mean to those whose institutions, actions, customs, and so on they are."[53]

From the range of anthropological approaches to *fiqh*, ritual offers an illuminating example for the purpose of this chapter. Catherine Bell, in her *Ritual Theory, Ritual Practice*, offers an impressive survey of competing approaches to the study of ritual. Ritual appears variously as a "strategic way of acting,"[54] or as a "window" on the "cultural dynamics by which people make and remake their worlds."[55] It is a "type of critical juncture wherein some pair of opposing social or cultural forces comes together."[56] For Bell, much of the theoretical reflection on ritual is "highly structured by the differentiation and subsequent reintegration of two particular categories of human experience: thought and action."[57] The turn to ritual permits reflection on a range of social relations that traverse the boundaries of the religious and the secular; the rite and the social practice—and instead casts a conceptual shadow over the invention and imagination of traditions more generally understood.[58] This is not the place to survey the literature on ritual; the literature is vast, and others have provided impressive surveys of both the debates on ritual[59] and its limits from different disciplinary perspectives.[60]

[53] Clifford Geertz, "Blurred Genres: The Refiguration of Social Thought," *The American Scholar* 49, no. 2 (1980): 165–179, 167.

[54] Catherine Bell, *Ritual Theory, Ritual Practice*, Kindle edition (Oxford: Oxford University Press, 1992), 7–8.

[55] Ibid., 3. [56] Ibid., 16. [57] Ibid.

[58] Eric Hobsbawm, "Introduction," in *The Invention of Tradition*, eds. Eric Hobsbawm and Terence Ranger (1983; reprint, Cambridge: Cambridge University Press, 1999), 3–4; Adam Seligman et al., *Ritual and its Consequences: An Essay on the Limits of Sincerity* (Oxford: Oxford University Press, 2008), 10–11.

[59] See, e.g., Bell, *Ritual Theory, Ritual Practice*.

[60] Seligman et al., *Ritual and its Consequences*; Geoffrey Koziol, "Review Article: The Dangers of Polemic: Is Ritual Still an Interesting Topic of Historical Study?" *Early Medieval Europe* 11, no. 4 (2002): 367–388.

Those who are familiar with the tradition of Islamic law are all too aware of how the word "law"—with its more secular, statist assumptions—does not fully capture the scope of what counts as law in the Islamic legal tradition.[61] A review of indexes in *fiqh* manuals across the centuries will reveal that nearly all of them start with chapters on purity and purification rituals (*wudu'*, *ṭahara*), prayer and supplication (*salat*), and the lesser and greater pilgrimage (*hajj*) to Mecca. These subjects of ritual worship and practice are points of entry into the genre of *fiqh*. The formality, invariant, non-instrumental nature[62] of the rituals described by these rules lend them to a ritualizing analysis.

A formidable scholar of Islamic law who applies a ritualizing frame of analysis to *fiqh* is Marion H. Katz. Her study of ritual purity rules, for instance, couples a search for historical origins with an inquiry into the construction of meaningfulness. As such, her study reflects the philological influence in Islamic studies *and* an expansive engagement with the interpretive turn in her analysis of *fiqh*;[63] in particular she draws upon Mary Douglas' important study *Purity and Danger* to reflect on the meaning of purity rituals in Islamic law. To start with Katz' discussion of purity will illuminate the relative merits, strengths, and limits of the philological and anthropologically informed ones, and how attentiveness to both enrich the study of Islamic law.

From a historical perspective, Katz argued that the Islamic regime of ritual purity has a pre-Islamic heritage connected to, among others, Zoroastrian purity rituals. But as she noted, "Muslims were always perfectly aware of basic commonalities between their own purity practices and those of their neighbors ... Some medieval authors thus argued that *wudu'* had not originated with the [sic] own community, but was part of the broader monotheistic heritage."[64] This acceptance of a shared ritual heritage, though, had its limits. Katz noted how Muslim jurists were keen to distinguish Islamic practices from Zoroastrian ones, for reasons having to do with Islamic supersessionist claims to which Zoroastrianism was irrelevant. "Zoroastrianism, unlike Judaism and Christianity, had no such role in Islamic salvation history ... [C]onscious memory of the Zoroastrian example had nothing to contribute to the theological self-understanding of the Muslim community"[65]—a self-understanding implicit in the regime of ritual purity rules.

[61] Wael B. Hallaq, *Sharia: Theory, Practice, Transformations* (Cambridge: Cambridge University Press, 2009).

[62] On the salience of these and other characteristics to the definition of ritual, see Roy A. Rapoport, *Ritual and Religion in the Making of Humanity*, Cambridge Studies in Social and Cultural Anthropology, Kindle edition (1999; reprint, Cambridge: Cambridge University Press, 2000), ch. 21.

[63] For another example of Katz' deployment of an interpretive turn, see Marion Holmes Katz, *Prayer in Islamic Thought and Practice* (Cambridge: Cambridge University Press, 2013), esp. ch. 3.

[64] Marion H. Katz, *Body of Text: The Emergence of the Sunni Law of Ritual Purity* (Albany: SUNY Press, 2002), 9.

[65] Katz, *Body of Text*, 11.

Identifying this distinction as theologically motivated, Katz moved from the historical positivism of philology to the symbolic meaning of an anthropological approach to appreciate the purity rules as a discursive activity. Drawing on the seminal study by Kevin Reinhart,[66] Katz tested the limits of Douglas' principal idea of purity rules as a control mechanism, where constructions of purity and impurity were ordering devices, and where dirt was cast as disorder.[67] Importantly, Katz showed that Douglas' thesis of controllability is not workable across different traditions of ritual, specifically Islamic purity rules. "[D]ifferent systems of purity often present contradictory evaluations of the same bodily functions, and unless divergent attitudes toward the degree of control involved in these functions can be demonstrated, an identical criterion (controllability) must be manipulated to explain mutually contradictory data."[68]

Ze'ev Maghen echoes Katz' critique of ritual law as a means of control, while arguing that the regulating function of law can make certain aspects of life possible. Rituals as regulating, restricting, and ordering, give effect to what can be an otherwise unruly passionate life. His study on passion and purity in Islamic law juxtaposes early Islamic literature on love, passion, and sex with Islamic purification rules pertaining to touching a member of the opposite sex (*mulamasa*).[69] He showed that the "regimented elements of religion allow for the fuller appreciation of and exploitation of the unregimented elements of life. Both sexuality and spirituality are largely exercises in unruliness; the *shari'a* delimits each of them and thereby makes them possible."[70] Or in other words, "[d]iscipline allows for enjoyment."[71]

To shift from a principle of control to one of discipline (and the imagination it makes possible) is to move beyond Douglas and see in the *fiqh* a politics of human relation. David Friedenreich impressively illuminated this politics in his remarkable study, *Foreigners and their Food*.[72] Cheekily framing his analysis of Jewish, Christian, and Islamic dietary rites by reference to good fences and good neighbors, he argued that dietary rules have political implications for the scope of affection and community one can and should also enjoy. Dietary rules, like good fences, make good neighbors because they implicitly "express particular systems of classifying insiders and outsiders."[73] Drawing on Benedict Anderson's seminal study *Imagined Communities*,[74] Friedenreich showed how rules regulating

[66] A. Kevin Reinhart, "Impurity/No Danger," *History of Religions* 30, no. 1 (1990): 1–24.

[67] Katz, *Body of Text*, 18, 19.

[68] Ibid., 22.

[69] Ze'ev Maghen, *Virtues of the Flesh: Passion and Purity in Early Islamic Jurisprudence*, Studies in Islamic Law and Society (Leiden: Brill Publications, 2005).

[70] Maghen, *Virtues of the Flesh*, 282.

[71] Ibid.

[72] David M. Freidenreich, *Foreigners and Their Food: Constructing Otherness in Jewish, Christian, and Islamic Law* (Berkeley: University of California Press, 2011).

[73] Ibid., 3, 8.

[74] Benedict Anderson, *Imagined Communities: Reflections on the Origin and Spread of Nationalism* (rev. edn. New York: Verso Books, 1998).

diet implicitly "reveal the ways in which their participants imagine their own communities, other religious communities in their midst, and the broader social order in which these communities are embedded."[75] For instance, in his analysis of Islamic legal restrictions on meat consumption, Freidenreich illustrated how insiders and outsiders were not subject to a zero-sum game but rather to a more complex analysis that situated Muslims, People of the Book, and idolaters in relation to each other by reference to a principle of moderation or what Freidenreich calls a "golden mean." Though there are shared restrictions among the three monotheistic faiths, the "discourse about food restrictions furthers the goal of establishing a new, emphatically monotheistic, community distinct and preferable to Judaism" and in stark contrast to the error of idolatry.[76] In fact, as Freidenreich later stated, "the Qur'an establishes proper food practices as a divinely ordained golden mean between two undesirable extremes, the former being false [i.e. idolatry] and the latter excessively rigorous [i.e. Judaism]."[77]

B. Theory and Practice: *Fiqh* versus *Fatwa*

Alongside the more recent literature on Islamic law and anthropology lies the *fatwa* as a site of legal practice, in contrast to the *fiqh*, which is assumed to be doctrinal, and thereby static.[78] As Muhammad Khalid Masud, Brinkley Messick, and David S. Powers describe: "While the more theoretical aspect of the shari'a is embodied in the literatures dealing with the 'branches' of substantive law (*furu' al-fiqh*) and with the 'roots' of legal methodology and jurisprudence (*usul al-fiqh*), its more practical aspect is embodied in fatwas issued by muftis in response to questions posed by individuals in connection with ongoing human affairs."[79] Elsewhere, Messick characterized *fiqh* as a "doctrinal corpus,"[80] or "body of knowledge" that certainly "pertained to history . . . to societies of rifts and hierarchies"[81]—in other words, to a history external to the text itself. Yet when he addressed the historical tradition of Islamic law (e.g. *fiqh*), the picture he created was "nevertheless relatively timeless."[82]

75 Freidenreich, *Foreigners and Their Food*, 8.

76 Ibid., 133, 134.

77 Ibid., 135.

78 Other approaches to legal practice include the invocation of the American Legal Realist movement with its attendant focus to what judges do in fact. On this turn, see Kristen Stilt, *Islamic Law in Action: Authority, Discretion, and Everyday Experiences in Mamluk Egypt* (Oxford: Oxford University Press, 2011).

79 Muhammad Khalid Masud, Brinkley Messick, and David S. Powers, eds., *Islamic Legal Interpretation: Muftis and Their Fatwas* (Cambridge, MA: Harvard University Press, 1996), 4.

80 Brinkley Messick, *The Calligraphic State: Textual Domination and History in a Muslim Society* (Berkeley: University of California Press, 1993), 5.

81 Ibid., 17.

82 Messick, *The Caligraphic State*, 6.

The view of *fiqh* as theory, doctrine, or ahistorical knowledge is not uncommon; but it has the effect of under-theorizing *fiqh* as an epistemic practice that is in history; it is shaped by and may even shape a history outside the four corners of the *fiqh* text. However, an under-theorized *fiqh* genre in part explains the turn to the *fatwa* as more conducive to interdisciplinary analysis across the social sciences. For Masud, Messick, and Powers, the *fatwa*, by revealing legal argument in a particular factual setting, can raise "issues of an interdisciplinary and comparative nature concerning law, society, and history."[83]

It is not that *fiqh* and *fatwa* are mutually exclusive categories; indeed, *fatwa*s draw upon *fiqh* in order to resolve legal disputes, and may even inform future developments and changes in the prevailing *fiqh* of a school of law. As Powers has adeptly shown elsewhere, *muftis* often intervened in judicial disputes by bringing (or being asked to bring) their expertise on legal doctrine (*fiqh*) to bear upon complex factual scenarios.[84] Wael Hallaq has also shown how compendia of *fatwas* later informed the development of a legal school's *fiqh*, thus casting the *fatwa* as a vehicle for legal change.[85] But even as *fatwa*s draw upon and contribute to *fiqh* as a doctrinal corpus, *fiqh* has remained for scholars a doctrinal repository. *Fatwas*, in other words, become the textual proxy for agency in the law, while *fiqh* is the textual proxy for a structure that highlights—given its relative stasis in the moment of the *fatwa*—the agency of/in/through the *fatwa*.[86]

Arguably, the turn to the *fatwa*, with all that it implies for what *fiqh* is or may be, coincides with the development of "Law and Society" as a distinct field of legal scholarship, with its internal plurality of approach and subject matter. The scope of Law and Society scholarship is broad, ranging from a "law in context" approach, to a "decentered" approach to law as both inside and outside formal state institutions, or a "global" approach, where law is imagined transnationally, "outside its traditional moorings to nation states."[87] Tracing itself back to American Legal Realism, Law and Society scholars contest and critique assumptions about law as a mirror of society and an instrument of social order.[88] The "mirror thesis," as it is called, holds

[83] Masud, Messick, and Powers, eds., *Islamic Legal Interpretation*, ix.

[84] David Powers, *Law, Society and Culture in the Maghrib, 1300–1500* (Cambridge: Cambridge University Press, 2002).

[85] Wael B. Hallaq, *Authority, Continuity and Change in Islamic Law* (Cambridge: Cambridge University Press, 2005). See also Messick, *The Calligraphic State*, 147, who also considered the genre of *fatwa* as a vehicle of legal change and development over time.

[86] On "structure" as resource-rich, and as enabling and constraining action, see William Sewell, "A Theory of Structure: Duality Agency, and Transformation," *American Journal of Sociology* 98, no. 1 (1992): 1–29.

[87] Calvin Morrill and Kelsey Mayo, "Charting the 'Classics' in Law and Society: The Development of the Field Over the Past Half-Century," in *The Handbook of Law and Society*, eds. Austin Sarat and Patrica Ewick, 18–36 (San Francisco: Wiley-Blackwell, 2015) 19.

[88] This critique of the "mirror" thesis would also undercut the inference implicit in Crone's and Johansen's turn to anthropology, as discussed in Section III of this chapter.

that law is a reflection of society; as Brian Z. Tamanaha has described, the "mirror thesis" is "one of the most powerful and pervasively applied metaphors of the last two thousand years, central in philosophy ... in literature and art ... and in the social sciences. In law, its predominant use has been to provide a reassuring representation of the place that law holds in society."[89] And while Tamanaha offered various reasons to doubt the "mirror thesis," it is important to recognize the *fatwa*-turn in Islamic legal studies as part of this larger presumption about law in the social sciences and humanities. In a more affective strain, Alexandre Caeiro suggested that attention to the *fatwa* of contemporary European Muslims offers insight into "the projects, desires, and fears of Muslim individuals and communities living in specific contexts."[90]

But the turn to *fatwa* negatively reveals the ambiguity about how best to describe, understand, appreciate, and analyze *fiqh*. Labels become challenging in this regard, as various ones are used to describe *fiqh*: doctrine, positive law, substantive law, formal law, jurists' law. Moreover, to view *fatwa* as a form of legal practice situates the *fatwa* in history, and concomitantly places *fiqh* out of time or even *ex nihilo*, *pace* philologists such as Crone. Messick's admission that his characterization of *fiqh* and associated doctrinal materials as "timeless" is symptomatic of this analytic ambiguity about *fiqh* when viewed outside the more traditionally philological frame of analysis. Of course, some like Johansen would disagree that this ambiguity is as pervasive as I suggest, given the earlier analysis of Johansen's work on Hanafi land tax and rent in which he discerned a diachronic development in legal doctrine; his use of "early Hanafi" and "late Hanafi" are meant to capture this sort of development and change though without reference to the *fatwa* as the mechanism for this change, *pace* Hallaq and Messick. But for the purpose of this chapter, the distinction reveals the limited approaches to reflecting about *fiqh* in time.

C. *Fiqh* and Legal Theory

Related to an interest in legal practice are studies that examine *fiqh* to infer more general theories of legal reasoning and, indeed, law-making. In Islamic legal studies, the interest in legal reasoning is often located in studies of the *uṣul al-fiqh* genre, which is the subject of Youcef Soufi's essay in this *Handbook*. The *fiqh*

[89] Tamanaha, *A General Jurisprudence*, 2.

[90] Alexandre Caeiro, "The Making of the Fatwa: The Production of Islamic Expertise in Europe," *Archives de Sciences Sociales des Religions* 155 (July–September 2011): 81–100, 81. From a different affective perspective, Hussein Agrama explained the rise of academic literature on the *fatwa* as a symptom of "a felt sense of crisis, a perceived confrontation between modern ideals and a seemingly tenacious religious tradition, and an intensified concern over Islam's capacities for modern reform." Hussein Agrama, "Ethics, Tradition, Authority: Toward an Anthropology of the Fatwa," *American Ethnologist* 37, no. 1 (2010): 2–18.

literary genre, though, need not be viewed merely as an endpoint in a presumably deductive interpretive process framed by a canon of interpretive principles; rather, the *fiqh* rules themselves may provide insight into particular forms of legal logic that, in their piecemeal or systemic approach, are not easily included within the confines of *usul al-fiqh*.

For instance, Behnam Sadeghi's *The Logic of Law Making in Islam*[91] examines the *fiqh* of women and prayer to gain insight about the underlying legal logic of this *fiqh* subject matter. For Sadeghi, *fiqh* is not the deductive product of an Islamic epistemic theoretical framework. Rather, it is the site of post-hoc justifications for doctrines that have already long existed. His work, like Katz' on purity, blends a philological analysis of historical origins with a sensitivity to the concepts, methods, and techniques of legal reasoning to render *fiqh* a historically subjunctive site for a presentist legal discipline. In other words, the techniques of legal reasoning collapse time to cover the historical origins of law with a timeless sense of rational justification that is subsequently used to inform later generations of jurists on what the law is and why. Moreover, the genre reflects a juristic practice of writing and reflection for other jurists primarily, and thereby contributes to the disciplinary formation of law and legal education.

By accounting for how *fiqh* operates, Sadeghi also uncovered a curious legal logic that runs contrary to assumptions that inform and underlie the genre of *usul al-fiqh* and those writing about it. Sadeghi's study shows that juristic reasoning about *fiqh* was not a deductive process from source texts to legal rule, but rather the opposite. The reasoning jurists offered was meant to justify a rule they already knew and accepted. Rather than moving from source texts to legal doctrine as outlined in *usul al-fiqh* sources, jurists began with a legal doctrine they already knew and accepted, and worked backward to source texts to create a legitimating "scaffolding" for their legal analysis. Drawing on Sherman Jackson's helpful image of "scaffolding" in the law,[92] Sadeghi illuminated how a close analysis of technical legal doctrines, debates, and disputes reveals the *fiqh* genre as a site for theoretical reflection on legal analysis, interpretation, and development.

If *fiqh* is not merely the product of an *usul al-fiqh* logical process, then what is it? In some sense, it can reflect a wide range of theoretical interventions, and thereby pose a rich trove of legal materials for further analysis and explanation. For instance, Anver M. Emon's article on *huquq Allah* and *huquq al-'ibad* examines a range of *fiqh* debates across the Sunni schools of law to reflect on these two concepts as hermeneutics.[93] The approach is "theoretical" in that the close reading of *fiqh*

[91] Behnam Sadeghi, *The Logic of Law Making in Islam: Women and Prayer in the Legal Tradition* (Cambridge: Cambridge University Press, 2015).

[92] Sherman Jackson, "Fiction and Formalism: Toward a Functional Analysis of *usul al-fiqh*," in *Studies in Islamic Legal Theory*, ed. Bernard Weiss (Leiden: E.J. Brill, 2002), 177–201.

[93] Anver M. Emon, "Huquq Allah and Huquq al-'Ibad: A Legal Heuristic for a Natural Rights Regime," *Islamic Law and Society* 13, no. 3 (2006): 325–391.

debates is meant to better capture how premodern jurists used *fiqh* debates to explain what these heuristics were designed to do prospectively, such as in cases with no legal precedent. The article frames the heuristics in terms of a natural rights heuristic; admittedly, a more conceptually appealing approach might draw upon Wesley Newcombe Hohfeld's taxonomy of jural composites that, in the aggregate, help explain rights debates and analyses.[94] For instance, Hohfeld held that rights and duties are mutually constitutive and correlated with each other, but that not every claim or interest is easily understood in the abstract sense of "right." Hohfeldian frameworks of rights, claims, and legal reasoning help inform how different rules on sexual slander (*qadfh*), theft (*sariqa*), and other *hudud* penalties reflect the sometimes competing interests between individuals (whether claimant or wrongdoer), and between individuals and the ruling authority (e.g. deterrence, retribution, compensation, social standing, and reputation). For instance, the Maliki grant of standing to witnesses of *qadfh* to file a claim with the authorities reflects a public commitment to combat certain social ills, even if it means subjecting the victim's reputation to public scrutiny. As another example, Shafi'is and Hanbalis allowed a theft victim to seek compensation (*haqq al- 'abd*) and permit the ruling authority to amputate the thief's hand (*haqq Allah*). Hanafis, however, only permitted one or the other, while the Malikis only allowed for both depending on the financial ability of the thief to pay compensation. These different approaches reflected different legal balances between the interests of victims, defendants, and the ruling authority in service of a presumed public order.

Of course, to infer an approach to legal theory from an analysis of *fiqh* need not be limited only to examining the *fiqh* genre. Incorporating close attention to *fiqh* with scrutiny of extensive judicial archives of Ottoman Egypt, Ahmed Fekry Ibrahim has shown the importance of pragmatic decision-making to judicial practice, despite the jurisprudential shadow of presumably determinate doctrines of *fiqh*.[95] His analysis challenges a normative claim in the Islamic legal studies field that such pragmatism, or more polemically utilitarianism, runs counter to the ethical and moral content of the Islamic legal tradition. Certainly, one cannot help but appreciate the significance of utilitarianism (e.g. *maslaha*) in the writings of legal reformists. On this normative account, legal utilitarianism is intimately (and ideologically) associated with reform in the shadow of European colonialism, the imposition of the modern state in European form, and the project of modernity in the Muslim world. In contrast, Ibrahim has expertly argued that such pragmatism was present in judicial practice in courts in Mamluk Egypt, well before the onset of colonialism. On his reading, pragmatism is better conceived as part of, if not endemic to, the very

[94] Wesley Newcomb Hohfeld, *Fundamental Legal Conceptions as Applied in Judicial Reasoning, and Other Legal Essays*, ed. Walter Wheeler Cook (1919; reprint, New Haven: Yale University Press, 1920).

[95] Ahmed Fekry Ibrahim, *Pragmatism in Islamic Law: A Social and Intellectual History* (Syracuse: Syracuse University Press, 2015).

enterprise of law and legal decision-making. To suggest otherwise would render Islamic law outside law more broadly construed.

D. Critical *Fiqh*; Critique of *Fiqh*

The above analysis has positioned *fiqh* as a genre of primary source that can serve certain methodological ends, whether the historical positivism of philology or the interpretive analysis of an anthropological approach to law. In some cases, the *fiqh* genre offers a useful vantage point from which to critique how Islamic legal knowledge is produced. It is also a central object against which many critique its operation, whether from a gender egalitarian, anti-domination, or other analytic standpoint. Together, both approaches raise questions not only about how *fiqh* doctrine is created and construed (e.g. by whom, for whom, and under what circumstances), but also how *fiqh* operates (whether in fact or imagination) on the bodies of those who are considered or consider themselves its legal subjects.

1. *Critical* fiqh

An appreciation of the *fiqh* genre, with its various strands of texts and intertextual encounters, provides a standpoint from which to examine the underlying politics implicit in how subsequent scholarship or judicial decisions select their relevant archive of *fiqh* sources. Such selections may be conditioned by colonial frustrations in management and regulation, or by the limits of institutional competencies. But in the examples below, what becomes painfully apparent is how *fiqh* is made determinate (if not hyper-determinate) in the service of the colonial or state project.

For instance, David S. Powers directed Edward Said's critique Orientalism at French scholars who deemed Algerian practices of the *waqf* to be Islamically inauthentic. Powers located the production of French scholarship on Islamic law squarely within the French colonial endeavor in Algeria:

> Specifically, the colonization of Algeria created an inevitable conflict between Islamic law and the *colons* (French settlers). Efforts by the latter to purchase land were repeatedly frustrated by the fact that much of the land in Algeria had been designated as religious endowments and therefore could not legally be bought or sold on the open market. The colonial administration endeavoured to gain control over the endowment institution through a series of legislative enactments and *was assisted by French orientalists who campaigned to discredit the institution among the Algerians themselves.*[96]

[96] David S. Powers, "Orientalism, Colonialism, and Legal History: The Attack on the Muslim Family Endowments in Algeria and India," *Comparative Studies in Society and History* 31, no. 3 (1989): 535–571, 535–536.

Examining the French scholarship on the *waqf*, and in particular the "family *waqf*" (*waqf ahli*), Powers showed how French scholars of Islamic law aided the colonial enterprise of managing, regulating, and transacting across the (legal) landscape of Algeria. Powers' appreciation of the *fiqh* literature on the *waqf* across the relevant legal schools offered a *fiqh* vantage point from which he unmasked the underlying politics animating the much later French scholarly intervention.

This *fiqh* vantage point is no less pertinent when reflecting on how colonial translation of *fiqh* texts gives *fiqh* a hyper-determinism at the expense of a robust understanding of the genre itself. As Emon has shown, the translation of certain Islamic legal texts into English to adjudicate Anglo-Mohammadan law presented a problem for British judges on the Privy Council when they had to review decisions by Muslim judges who were trained both in the common law and in Islamic law. For instance, the 1903 case *Baker Ali Khan v. Anjuman Ara* involved a testatrix who created a charitable trust (*waqf*) by a will (*wasiyya*).[97] The underlying issue is whether the testatrix could create a *waqf* by will, which further turned on whether Shiʿa law governed the matter or not. The relevant precedent on this issue was the 1892 decision by Mahmood J. of the Allahabad High Court in *Agha Ali Khan v. Altaf Hasan Khan*, in which the learned Muslim justice held that, though valid in Hanafi law, one cannot create a *waqf* under Shiʿa law through a bequesting instrument like the *wasiyya*.[98] As part of his analysis, Mahmood J. examined a range of Shiʿa *fiqh* sources, many of which were commentaries on Muhaqqiq al-Hilli's *Sharʾiʿ al-Islam*, only the latter of which had been translated into English.

For the Privy Council, recourse to this untranslated archive of material undermined the determinacy of the law and could not be relied upon for purposes of judicial decision. In his opinion for the Judicial Committee, Wilson J. noted that Mahmood J.'s decision was not based on "any positive statement by any of the recognized authorities on Shiah law, but in the reasoning of Mahmood, J. upon a number of more or less ambiguous texts."[99] For the justices of the Judicial Committee, while Mahmood J. was indeed a well-respected jurist and expert on Islamic law, his analysis relied on ancient texts that presented far too much indeterminacy in the law and should not have been consulted. It did not matter that the sources themselves were (and still are) significant within the Shiʿa tradition, or that they reflected a general agreement on the conception of a *waqf* as a contract requiring offer, acceptance, and an *inter vivos* transfer. Despite Mahmood J.'s argument, translation of texts, and inclusion of the original Arabic in the footnotes, the British judges argued that citing

[97] *Baker Ali Khan v. Anjuman Ara* (1903) 30 IA 94, in *Cases in the Muhammadan Law of India, Pakistan and Bangladesh*, Asaf A.A. Fyzee, ed. Tahir Mahmood, 2nd edn. (New Delhi: Oxford University Press, 2005), 4–16.

[98] *Agha Ali Khan and another (Plaintiffs) v. Altaf Hasan Khan and another (Defendants)*, ILR 14 All. 429–497 (1892). For those not familiar with legal citation, the reporter is the Indian Law Reports, Allahabad Series.

[99] *Baker Ali Khan*, at 14.

the untranslated sources led to more ambiguities than determinate answers. But as Emon suggested, the ambiguity was not so much in what the *fiqh* sources said, but rather in how selective translation allowed aspects of Islamic law not only to be legible[100] for purposes of adjudication, but even hyper-determinate, given how the broader *fiqh* tradition was rendered illegible for purposes of legal consideration.

Hyperdeterminacy, of course, need not be a function of translation or of the colonial enterprise. Certainly one could argue that codification of Islamic law has a tendency toward hyperdeterminacy in the service of the modern state, as many have argued in the Islamic legal studies field.[101] But it would be a mistake to associate hyperdeterminacy with the onset of an imposed modernity on the Muslim majority world. Mohammad Fadel's seminal article on the *mukhtasar*, a sub-genre within the broader genre of *fiqh* literature, reminds us that modes of hyperdeterminacy in the law are not merely in the service of modern state projects, but rather of governance more broadly construed, whether diachronically or across different political associations.[102] Fadel takes issue with the scholarship on Islamic law that emphasizes *ijithad* to the detriment of *taqlid*. *Ijtihad* offers a conceptual vehicle to reflect on change and development but also discounts the salience of precedent, determinacy, and stability as equally important features of a legal system. He recounted how the plurality of opinions within a school of law meant that "indeterminacy was also a serious problem within a *madhhab*."[103] However, he also showed that over time, "the various opinions found within a school were evaluated, and only one came to be considered the rule of a school. These rules, moreover, beginning in the 7th/13th century, were compiled into works known as *mukhtaṣars*, 'abridgements.' "[104] Fadel analyzed the *mukhtasar* as a literary genre that reconciled *ijithad* and *taqlid* by providing a buoy of determinacy in a sea of plurality, or as he called it a "codified common law."[105]

2. *Critique of* fiqh

Adopting *fiqh* as a vantage point will often presume *fiqh* as a constant in order to observe how and why it is managed, applied, and even manipulated in different contexts and in varying forms. But to presume it as a constant does not preclude critique of it as the output of a set of other variables that are often hidden by the disciplinary vocabulary of *fiqh*. In other words, the more one appreciates *fiqh* as object of critique, the more one recognizes it as a legal mask covering a range of factors

[100] My use of "legibility" owes a debt to James C. Scott, *Seeing Like a State: How Certain Schemes to Improve the Human Condition Have Failed* (New Haven: Yale University Press, 1999).

[101] Wael Hallaq, *The Impossible State: Islam, Politics and Modernity's Moral Predicament* (New York: Columbia University Press, 2012).

[102] Mohammad Fadel, "The Social Logic of *Taqlīd* and the Rise of the *Mukhtaṣar*," *Islamic Law and Society* 3, no. 2 (1996): 193–233.

[103] Ibid., 197. [104] Ibid. [105] Ibid., 198.

that go into the construction of the law, thereby opening *fiqh* to a range of critical approaches and methods (e.g. socio-legal, gender egalitarian). Perhaps no area of *fiqh* is more subject to critique than those affecting gender equality (e.g. marriage, divorce, inheritance, child custody). It is not merely an ideological commitment to gender egalitarianism that contributes to the robustness of this area of literature. Rather, Islamic family law remains one of the few areas of the historical *fiqh* tradition that remains vibrant in codified formats across Muslim majority states whose personal status laws (*al-ahwal al-shakhsiyya*) are based on or informed by the historical *fiqh* tradition on marriage, divorce, and child custody (*nikah, talaq, hidana*). The literature in this field is vast, and this is not the place to offer an examination of this subject area. The examples below are merely meant to illustrate different approaches to the critique of *fiqh*. Other chapters in this volume will take up the sub-field of Islamic family law and feminist critiques.

To appreciate the critique of *fiqh* is to recognize that it reflects a standpoint that transforms *fiqh* from a constant to a variable, or at least a potential variable whose concretization reflects a disciplinary endeavor that informs, if not constitutes, the political project of Islamic law. Indeed, to suggest that *fiqh* is not political or somehow pre-political is to flatten law's differentiating and regulatory capacity and power.

The work of Kecia Ali is significant for showcasing how a gendered reading of *fiqh* offers a productive approach to critique. Drawing on the insights of earlier scholars of Islam and gender (e.g. Leila Ahmed, Fatima Mernissi, Amina Wadud, and Asma Barlas) Ali's *Sexual Ethics and Islam* was first published in 2006, and republished in revised and edited form on its tenth anniversary in 2016.[106] Acknowledging the deeply polemical nature of debates on Islam and gender, Ali nonetheless recognized that "[s]ystemic injustices call for comparative treatment of hierarchical and gendered domination across geographic, chronological and cultural boundaries."[107] Of course, her focus on Islamic texts (legal and otherwise) might not be an obvious focus of analysis since people's social lives do not "neatly follow the patterns set out in legal manuals, and have never done so."[108] Nonetheless, she insisted on the salience of her analysis of the literary tradition because "there is a relationship between ideal and reality and there is a certain coherence to premodern prescriptive models of Muslim womanhood and sexual relations."[109] Indeed, as she forcefully remarked, "[i]t is precisely in the area of sexual ethics where normative Islamic texts and thought have been, and continue to be, most influential."[110] Ali's analysis of legal issues from an anti-hierarchical and gender egalitarian standpoint spread across

[106] Kecia Ali, *Sexual Ethics and Islam: Feminist Reflections on Qur'an, Hadith, and Jurisprudence*, 2nd edn. (Oxford: Oneworld Publications, 2016).

[107] Ibid., xxvi (footnote omitted).

[108] Ibid., xxviii (footnote omitted).

[109] Ibid., xviii (footnote omitted).

[110] Ibid., xviii.

a range of legal issues, including marriage and money, divorce, concubinage, and modes of sexual regulation. *Sexual Ethics*, in other words, offers a sustained critique of a range of *fiqh* areas that involve or inform gender and sexual relations.

Ali expanded this analysis in her later study, *Marriage and Slavery in Early Islam*.[111] In this second book, the *fiqh* on sexual relations is illuminated by reference to the *fiqh* on slaves, slave-owning, and manumission of slaves. Ali recognized that in the laws on sexual relations and ethics, a husband exercised *milk*, dominion, over his wife's sexual and reproductive capacity. But that same Arabic term was used to refer to the scope of ownership one exercised over a slave.[112] According to Ali, pre-modern jurists would have unremarkably read marriage and divorce rules along-side slavery rules. Indeed, as Ali quite rightly pointed out, "[t]he omnipresence of slaves in legal texts owes not only to their social presence but also to their utility in legal discussions: slaves are useful to think with."[113] What makes her analysis critical has more to do with presentist abhorrence to slavery, and the presumed discomfort her readers will have upon recognizing the logic of slavery *fiqh* as informing the *fiqh* of marital relations, especially since the latter continues to inform contemporary debates in the Muslim world about regulating sexual relations.

Ziba Mir-Hosseini likewise has brought a gender egalitarian perspective to the study of *fiqh* throughout her vast scholarly corpus. Her work, however, has a critical edge that is not merely directed at *fiqh* as an object, but also at how one construes a vantage point from which to critique *fiqh*. Recognizing the power of both human rights and feminism as vehicles of critiques, she nonetheless takes aim at both for their sometimes-unabashed service to colonialism and neo-imperial policies. Writing in her capacity as both scholar and founding member of *Musawah*, an Islamic feminist advocacy organization, she forcefully stated:

> To achieve sustainable and deep-rooted change, dialogue and consensus are needed; we knew that we must show the injustices that arise from patriarchal customs and laws based on the classical *fiqh* notion of marriage; and in this case, we must offer defensible and comprehensible alternatives within a framework that recognizes equality and justice in Islam. It was only then that we could free ourselves from an apparent choice between the devil of those who want to impose patriarchal interpretations on Islam's sacred texts, and the deep blue sea of those who pursue a neo-colonialist hegemonic global project in the name of human rights and feminism.[114]

Mir-Hosseini and *Musawah* assumed the possibility of gender egalitarianism as a vantage point of critique; for them, the problem was to critique classical *fiqh* for

[111] Kecia Ali, *Marriage and Slavery in Early Islam* (Cambridge, MA: Harvard University Press, 2010).
[112] Ibid., 6. [113] Ibid., 7.
[114] Ziba Mir-Hosseini, "Women in Search of Common Ground: Between Islamic and International Human Rights Law," in *Islamic Law and International Human Rights Law: Searching for Common Ground?*, eds. Anver M. Emon, Mark Ellis, and Benjamin Glahn (Oxford: Oxford University Press, 2012), 291–303, 299.

the patriarchy it codified in its stark, disciplinary vocabulary. At the same time, her approach involved a critique of other vantage points, such as feminism and human rights, which have their own disciplinary vocabulary that can operate in no less dominating a fashion as patriarchy has on the minds and bodies of Muslim women.

The analysis of Ali and Mir-Hosseini, however, should not be understood as reflecting the lived experience of Muslims the world over. As Ali noted, an analysis of texts does not (and indeed, cannot) capture the full complexity of lived experience, whether past or present. Yossef Rapoport's impressive study of Mamluk Egypt is an important reminder of how the ideational patriarchy implicit in *fiqh* rules can come undone as the framework they uphold as default is also the target of sophisticated and complex negotiations between parties.[115] Rapoport began with a query about the implication of divorce rates for the pre-eminence of patriarchy as both ideal and real. Noting the contemporary Euro-centric concern about high divorce rates, he noted that high divorce rates are really nothing new. Rather, one finds high divorce rates across a range of time periods and regions, including the Mamluk period of Egypt. In a society in which *fiqh* rules on marriage and divorce gave voice to an ideal of patriarchy, high rates of divorce undercut the effect, let alone primacy, of patriarchy on society. "Though inscribed in Islamic law as a patriarchal privilege, divorce undermines the patriarchal social order by destabilizing households, increasing the number of female-headed households, and debating the ideal of marriage."[116] With the shadow of *fiqh* hovering over his inquiry, Rapoport showed through analyses of court records and other documentary evidence that "divorce was rarely a one-sided affair. Some women (or their families) manipulated patriarchal ideals in order to initiate divorce, or used their financial leverage power in order to force a husband to grant them a divorce. In most accounts of individual cases divorce appears as a balanced affair, in which women very often had their say."[117]

Thinking with Ali, Mir-Hosseini, and Rapoport on the critique of *fiqh*, one can appreciate the importance of the *fiqh* as representing an ideational backdrop that frames and informs a complex agency that operates within and through the mechanisms of law. Law, on this reading, is merely one vehicle of social ordering, and not always dispositive of the reasons people act as they did, do, or will. In this regard, it is worth reminding ourselves of Naomi Davidson's *Only Muslim*, where she examined the French constructions of Islam and the Muslim for purposes of regulating both in the service of France's statutory commitment to laicité.[118] Davidson critiqued the French government for "saturating" Muslims with a Muslimness that was derived from sources like *fiqh* texts, which the government viewed as robustly

115 Yossef Rapoport, *Marriage, Money and Divorce in Medieval Islamic Society* (Cambridge: Cambridge University Press, 2005).

116 Ibid., 4.

117 Ibid., 70.

118 Naomi Davidson, *Only Muslim: Embodying Islam in Twentieth-Century France* (Ithaca, NY: Cornell University Press, 2012).

(if not hyper-determinatively) constituting what is and is not Islam, Muslim belief, and Muslim practice. *Fiqh* as an ideational site is of course an important one that demands scrutiny for reasons that Ali and Mir-Hosseini, as well as others make plain. But it is no less important to recognize that the operation and experience of the *fiqh* was and remains a mediated one. To read and think with *fiqh* requires a commitment to intersectionality in any analysis of *fiqh*, if one is to study *fiqh* in various sites of practice, whether of the judge, the jurist-consult, or the litigant seeking a legal advantage against a rival party.

V. Conclusion: Considerations for Future Research

The above analysis of *fiqh* reflects different approaches to the genre of *fiqh* as a source of legal, historical, and critical analyses. The different disciplinary postures reveal the underlying assumptions that animate distinct methodological preferences, and the implications of those preferences on how *fiqh* can be understood amid the range of genres that constitute the Islamic legal literary tradition. Future studies of *fiqh* may want to dwell on aspects of the above interventions that remain open for inquiry and further analysis. For instance, one may want to explore how an anthropologically informed approach to law might give greater nuance to the study of *fiqh* as a site for reflecting relationally on the construction of meaning among groups of people, and between people and animals, or even between people and the earth.[119]

Of particular interest, however, is how a robust appreciation of *fiqh* in disciplinary and historical terms might inform future prospects for *fiqh* as a source and genre of Islamic law. Teemu Ruskola's important study on US legal perceptions of law in China provides a glimpse into how one might recognize and perhaps even overcome the limits inherent to how Islamic legal scholars understand what *fiqh* is, and importantly, how it construes those who are its legal subjects. Ruskola was keenly interested in how an American ideal of legality informed judgments about the absence of law in China—its law-lessness—given an unchecked presumption of America's legal tradition as full of law, and appropriately so—its law-fullness so to speak. Titling his study *Legal Orientalism*, his study examines "the ways in which 'the

[119] See, for instance, Beth Berkowitz and Marion H. Katz, "The Cowering Calf and the Thirsty Dog: Narrating and Legislating Kindness to Animals in Jewish and Islamic Texts," in *Islamic and Jewish Legal Reasoning: Encountering Our Legal Other*, ed. Anver M. Emon (Oxford: Oneworld Publications, 2016), 61–112.

Orient,' as well as the Euro-American 'West,' have been produced through discourses of law."[120] He explained how his use of "Orientalism" referred to law as both "ideational and material practices, which are ultimately indissociable from each other. While the world always and necessarily exceeds discourse, discourse always has a worldly existence and material effects."[121] In other words, law consists of both epistemic and material practices. As an epistemological practice, law covers questions about its key assumptions and the construction of knowledge about the object of legal discourse, whether of China, the US, or the very notion of law. Epistemically, Legal Orientalism examines "how Western observers of Chinese law—especially but not exclusively within the academic field of comparative legal scholarship—have viewed the object of their study."[122] Materially, Legal Orientalism investigates "some of the uneven effects produced by the global circulation of ideas of perverse Chinese legality."[123] Ruskola's is not so much a project of correcting mistakes about Chinese law, but rather to appreciate the productivity of such mistakes, in particular how and why mistakes perpetuated particular (and particularist) understandings of Chinese law, and a universalist casting of American law as a global index of legality.

In some sense, Ruskola's approach to Chinese law reflects some of the critical analysis of/from *fiqh* addressed above. But his approach to law as both epistemic and material practices allows us to ask a wide range of questions about the *fiqh* genre that may also inform broader debates about law in the academy. For instance, how might we understand *fiqh* as a practice of legal writing? In one sense, compendia of *fiqh* represent the law as always present. Jurists may be dead for centuries, yet their pronouncements speak as if they were present with us in the room. While socio-legal scholars of *fiqh* may want to analyze *fiqh* in time, it may be useful to think of *fiqh* (and perhaps law more broadly) as having an internal, collapsed sense of time: *fiqh*-time so to speak, or a grammar of the present. For instance, section 10 of Canada's Federal Interpretation Act states: "The law shall be considered as always speaking ..." If the law is always speaking, it must be speaking in the present tense. Certainly, to speak in the present tense is to collapse time and expel history or historicism from the legal discursive project. But why? What are the disciplinary and institutional implications of speaking law in the present tense always and at all times? Arguably, the moment law speaks in the past tense is the moment when that law is overruled, rejected, or repudiated. The grammar of time functions as a matrix of authority. To think of *fiqh* and time as *fiqh*-time is to envision the *fiqh* as the product of a discipline that is reinstantiated each time we ask what the law *is*, expecting an answer in the present tense.

[120] Teemu Ruskola, *Legal Orientalism: China, the United States and Modern Law* (Cambridge, MA: Harvard University Press, 2013), 5.

[121] Ibid., 10. [122] Ibid. [123] Ibid.

One may also examine different aspects of *fiqh* to better appreciate the underlying political assumptions that made the *fiqh* rules intelligible, or *fiqh* as representing a set of material practices that take shape institutionally, politically, and so on. For instance, this author's analysis of the *dhimmi* rules regulating non-Muslim permanent residents under Islamic suzerainty provided a vehicle for critiquing the historiography of "tolerance" that both hovered over prior studies of this legal doctrine, and currently informs deliberations across the Atlantic Ocean about political liberalism, constitutional law, and increasing forms of militant democracy (or illiberal liberalism).[124] But it also revealed a set of assumptions within *fiqh* about political order, governance structures, and the place of the "outsider" in that political matrix. To understand the *dhimmi* rules requires an appreciation of empire as the political logic informing jurists of the past. To abandon an imperial vision (i.e. to adopt the international state order in place of Islamic Empire) undercuts the rationalizing force that an imperial assumption once provided to the *dhimmi* rules. Ruskola's approach to legal discourse as epistemological and material practices is useful both to better appreciate the motivations of different critical approaches to Islamic law, and to understand why the power of law to construct the legal subject plays out the way it does.

[124] Anver M. Emon, *Religious Pluralism and Islamic Law: Dhimmis and Others in the Empire of Law* (Oxford: Oxford University Press, 2012).

CHAPTER 3

ISLAMIC LAW AND GENDER

SAADIA YACOOB[1]

ONE of the joys of teaching at a liberal arts college is the interdisciplinarity accorded to me in my teaching. With this in mind, I decided to cross-list my Islamic law course not only with the History and with the Arabic Studies departments, but also with the Women's, Gender, and Sexuality Studies program. The course was a pedagogical experiment that introduced students to the study of Islamic law through a gendered lens. My primary concern in structuring the course in this manner was my frustration with the pervasive model in Islamic legal studies of designating a session or week as the one time in the semester to deliberate on gender.[2] Such an approach functions to isolate and marginalize scholarship on gender and Islamic law, relegating it to a footnote in the story we tell our students about Islamic law.

The critique that scholarship on gender (and scholarship by female scholars) is relegated to the peripheries of the field is certainly not new. Kecia Ali has noted that many scholars of Islam, in particular male scholars, continue to publish without taking scholarship on gender into consideration. Her brief survey of books by a few prominent male scholars revealed that they largely failed to consider or mention even significant works on gender.[3] In his chapter in this *Handbook*, Rumee Ahmed

[1] I would like to thank Rumee Ahmed for his insightful comments and helpful edits on multiple drafts of this chapter.

[2] This marginalization of gender is not unique to Islamic legal studies but is in fact quite prevalent in the academy at large.

[3] Kecia Ali, "The Omnipresent Male Scholar," *Critical Muslim* (2013): 61–73.

has similarly pointed out that Muslim feminist critiques are often dismissed both inside and outside the academy.[4] As a gender scholar, I am painfully aware of this dynamic and wanted to give my students a different account of the history of Islamic law. I thus constructed a syllabus in which I incorporated scholarship on gender and Islamic law into the central driving narrative I presented to my students.

The scholarship on Islamic law and gender is extensive, spanning different geographical regions and historical periods and encompassing varied methodological and disciplinary approaches, such as history, anthropology, religion, and feminist studies. It also tackles different fields of inquiry, from historical court records and legal opinions, to contemporary court proceedings and feminist engagements with legal discourse (*fiqh, usul al-fiqh,* and *fatawa*). The depth and diversity of the field cannot be captured comprehensively, and so for this chapter I analyze three major developments in the field. These developments have challenged orientalist narratives about the law's oppression of Muslim women and urged us to consider the methodologies and categories that are employed in the study of Islamic law.

In the first section of this chapter, I highlight how gender scholars turned to legal practice, taking a social historical approach to challenge orientalist narratives. In doing so, they focussed on the agency of non-legal actors in negotiating the law. While much attention has been given to legal discourse and to jurists as producers of the law, a gendered analysis of legal practice urges us to think of law not simply as the realm of jurists but also as the product of a dialectical relationship between legal and non-legal actors. In placing the judge and *mufti* in a local milieu, these studies demonstrate extra-legal concerns that were at play in adjudicating legal matters and the agency of non-legal actors, and women in particular, as they accessed and negotiated the law.

The second section moves to discuss a parallel body of scholarship that provides a feminist critique of legal discourse. These works critically examine the development of premodern substantive law (*fiqh*) and legal theory by interrogating the gendered assumptions and "idealized cosmology"[5] that informed and shaped premodern legal discourse. In historically situating the development of early legal discourse, these scholars bring our attention to the cultural and social milieu that constrained interpretive possibilities and shaped the meaning that jurists derived from sacred texts as they developed their legal thought. Critically engaging with the gendered

[4] Rumee Ahmed, "Islamic Law and Theology," in *Oxford Handbook of Islamic Law*, ed. Anver Emon and Rumee Ahmed (Oxford: Oxford University Press, 2018).

[5] I am borrowing here Ayesha Chaudhry's term from her book on the historical and contemporary discourses around verse 4:34 in the Qur'an. Chaudhry describes "idealized cosmology" as the normative and idealized vision of the world that orders society and configures social relations. This idealized cosmology is critical to how the God-human relationship is imagined and plays a determinative role in the assumptions that exegetes and jurists brought to their sources. This, in turn, shaped the limits and possibilities of interpretation. Ayesha Chaudhry, *Domestic Violence and the Islamic Tradition* (Oxford: Oxford University Press, 2014), 12.

logic of legal discourse also prompted scholars to investigate the gendered construction of legal subjecthood. In doing so, these scholars have encouraged the field to interrogate the very categories that it brings to the study of Islamic law.

I. Social and legal histories on women and Islamic law

That the study of Islamic law and gender in the Western academy has an orientalist legacy should come as no surprise. As such, early research in this field took a primarily textual approach, focusing on substantive legal texts as the source for ascertaining the legal realities of Muslim women and determiningfamily relations. Drawing on textual sources, they characterized Islamic law as rigidly patriarchal and unchanging.[6]

Until the mid-twentieth century, many scholars of Islamic law unquestionably presumed the oppressive and patriarchal nature of the law. This narrative was powerful in framing and dismissing evidence that might contradict it. Gabriel Baer's work on women and endowments is an illustrative example of this paradigm. Having described in significant detail women's involvement in the establishment and administration of endowments, Baer argues that women primarily endowed their wealth to protect their income and property from the male members of their families. He further concludes that despite these efforts, women would lose their wealth since the endowed property would eventually fall into the hands of males who gradually became beneficiaries and managers of the endowments. For Baer, endowments served to weaken women's economic positions as their domination was unavoidable and any attempt to circumvent their position was futile.[7]

[6] Annelise Moors characterizes the orientalist method as a textual approach to the study of Islamic law that "considered family relations as the outcome of the provisions of Islamic law. Concentrating heavily on the classical texts of the leaders of the major law schools on the one hand, and on the texts of the newly codified twentieth-century laws on the other, they constructed an Islamic family that remained monolithic, static, and rigidly patriarchal until the promulgation of the twentieth-century legal reforms." Annelies Moors, "Debating Islamic Family Law," in *Social History of Women and Gender in the Modern Middle East*, ed. M. Meriwether and J. Tucker (Boulder: Westview, 1999), 142.

[7] See for example Gabriel Baer, "Women and Waqf: An Analysis of the Istanbul Tahrīr of 1546,"*Asian and African Studies* 17 (1983): 27. Baer's conclusion was eventually challenged by Margaret L. Meriwether in her study of endowments in Aleppo. She argued against Baer's assertions that women invested their wealth in endowments to protect their properties from their male family members concluding instead that, at least in the case of Aleppo, women's endowments were similar to those of men and these properties did not eventually return to male ownership. See Margaret Meriwether, "Women and Waqf Revisited: The Case of Aleppo, 1770–1840," in *Women in the Ottoman Empire*, ed. M. Zelfi (Leiden: Brill, 1997), 128–152.

Such narrative tropes and the textual approach of Orientalists have come increasingly under critique since the late 1970s. As a growing number of historians and anthropologists engaged the study of Islamic law, they introduced the methodological concerns and research questions predominant in their disciplines.[8] Feminist historiography and the growing interest in women's histories also contributed significantly to this shift in the field. In her 1985 book, *Women in Nineteenth-Century Egypt*,[9] Judith Tucker critiqued the orientalist heritage for bequeathing "a specifically 'Islamic' definition of history and culture, promoting an idealist epistemology in which much of Middle East history was perceived as the embodiment of the Islamic spirit, rather than the outcome of the complex interaction of material forces and ideological formations."[10] She argued that whereas scholars like Gabriel Baer challenged this orientalist approach by shifting focus from texts to social and economic histories, they largely ignored women. Tucker pushed against the field's methodological constraints and argued instead for taking more seriously women's activities as a field of inquiry and to study their activities in relation to broader social formations.[11]

This shift in the 1970s led to one of the most prominent methodological approaches to the study of gender in Islamic law: a focus on legal practice. Scholarship in this vein takes both a historical and ethnographic approach. While historians like Judith Tucker and Leslie Peirce employ court records and legal opinions as sources, anthropologists like Ziba Mir-Hosseini and Susan Hirsch turn to contemporary Islamic courts as ethnographic sites. Both these scholarly inquiries help us understand the legal realities of women and the mechanisms they employed in negotiating Islamic legal institutions and actors. Legal opinions coupled with court records also provide a strong contrast to the substantive legal texts that had been the primary subject of most orientalist literature on Muslim women.

Lynn Welchman's chapter on Islamic family law and John Bowen's chapter on anthropology and Islamic law in this *Handbook* both deal extensively with this body of literature. Thus, in this section I will focus specifically on select historical studies and offer an account for their efficacy in broadening our understanding of law in practice.

In her book, *In the House of Law*,[12] Judith Tucker employs legal opinions and court records from seventeenth- and eighteenth-century Syria and Palestine to investigate the role of *muftis* as legal actors in the construction of gender. Each chapter of her book deals with a particular aspect of family relations—from marriage and

[8] Moors, "Debating Islamic Family Law," 142.

[9] Judith Tucker, *Women in nineteenth-century Egypt* (Cambridge: Cambridge University Press, 1985).

[10] Ibid., 3.

[11] Judith Tucker, "Problems in the historiography of women in the Middle East: The case of nineteenth-century Egypt," *International Journal of Middle East Studies* 15, no. 3 (1983): 323.

[12] Judith Tucker, *In the House of Law: Gender and Islamic Law in Ottoman Syria and Palestine*, (Berkeley: University of California Press, 1998).

divorce to parenting, sexuality, and reproduction—where competing claims of male and female members of the family were subject to legal adjudication. Legal records indicate that women often approached *muftis* and courts to demand their rights, with the expectation that the court would accommodate their requests.[13] These legal actors in turn responded to this expectation, upholding the legal rights of women and acting to ameliorate some of the legal, social, and cultural disparities between women and men.

While women's demand for legal protection was met by *muftis* and judges who acted as benevolent patriarchs, Tucker is careful to point out that we should not interpret this attitude as an attempt to subvert male authority. *Muftis* and judges, she argues, were responsible for maintaining male authority, as established in the substantive legal texts.[14] As such, they protected male prerogatives and maintained a patriarchal familial system in which women were subordinate to male members of the family. They were, however, attentive to the excesses of male authority and worked to temper it, ensuring that men fulfilled their legal and financial obligations. Divorce is an instructive example for demonstrating this careful balance of male authority and female protection. While the courts upheld men's privilege to unilateral repudiation in divorce, judges were nevertheless careful about women's entitlements to dower and financial support and ensured that these rights were not violated.[15] In matters of annulment initiated by women, the court accommodated their needs by accepting and adopting more flexible rulings from among the different legal schools.[16] For Tucker, flexibility was an important feature of Islamic law in the premodern period that was motivated by a desire to serve the needs of the community and prioritize social harmony and stability.

[13] Tucker's observation regarding the gendered dynamic of Ottoman courts has been corroborated by other legal histories as well. See for example an earlier work by Ronald Jennings. Jennings' work concentrated on the legal position of women in the Ottoman city of Kayseri in the sixteenth century. Among his results was the finding that the women of Kayseri frequently approached the court with their problem. He concluded that judges often played a protective role, and women depended on them to uphold their rights granted under Islamic law. Ronald Jennings, "The Legal Position of Women in Kayseri, a Large Ottoman City, 1590–1630," in *Studies on Ottoman Social History in the Sixteenth and Seventeenth Centuries*, ed. Ronald Jennings (Istanbul: ISIS Press, 1999), 120. See also Yvonne J. Seng, "Standing at the Gates of Justice: Women in the Law Courts of Sixteenth-Century Uskudar, Istanbul," in *Contested States: Law, Hegemony, and Resistance*, ed. Mindie Lazarus-Black and Susan F. Hirsch (New York: Routledge, 1994).

[14] Tucker, *In the House of Law*, 183.

[15] Judges did not always actively curtail the excesses of male authority. Several gender historians have observed that in *khul* proceedings (wife-initiated divorce), women not only returned the dower in exchange for the husband's consent but often also relinquished financial support due to them or child support, if they wanted to keep custody of the children. Men also often extracted a good sum of money from wealthy women in exchange for consent to divorce. See Iris Agmon, *Family and Court: Legal Culture and Modernity in Late Ottoman Palestine* (Syracuse: Syracuse University Press, 2006).

[16] Tucker, *In the House of Law*, 180.

Leslie Peirce's microhistory of the city of Aintab in the sixteenth century represents another such analysis of court records.[17] While Tucker's book focuses on legal actors (the *muftis* and judges), Peirce turns her attention to the non-legal actors who brought their cases to court and thus functioned as negotiators and interpreters of the law. Gendered narratives and the language strategies employed by men and women in the court is one of the key ways in which Peirce demonstrates how women negotiated legal institutions and actors. Men, she points out, spoke with anger and indignation, often taking an accusatory tone. Women, on the other hand, did not have a predictable pattern in their linguistic strategies. At times, they appealed to the emotional sensibility of the listener and employed a strategy of appeal and protest to gain leverage. They also had a tendency to avoid narrative coherence, which was most apparent in situations where they were liable or vulnerable. Given the structural and procedural disadvantages faced by women in the court and their position within the social hierarchy, they found humility and ambiguity advantageous as linguistic strategies for negotiating legal discourse and appeal to the varied social protections granted to them.[18]

Despite their different investigative approaches, both Tucker and Peirce arrive at several similar conclusions regarding the role of the court and disposition of legal actors. Like Tucker, Peirce too illustrates that despite the fact that the court upheld social hierarchies, women approached the court in significant numbers as arbiters of their rights. In shifting focus from legal texts to legal practice, these historians demonstrate that the gendered hierarchy so clearly delineated in substantive law was ameliorated in legal practice, granting women greater latitude and additional mechanisms to negotiate male authority.

Anthropologists of Islamic law have made similar observations about courts and judges in their ethnographic studies. Works such as Ziba Mir-Hosseini's *Marriage on Trial: A Study of Islamic Family Law* and Susan Hirsch, *Pronouncing and Persevering: Gender and the Discourses of Disputing in an African Islamic Court* have similarly focussed on women's use of the court systems to negotiate their rights. Using the social and legal histories mentioned previously, many scholars in this field have also offered critiques of the modern Islamization projects. Amira Sonbol argues that the historical transformations over the past two centuries have greatly restricted the flexibility of the court systems and the possibilities of maneuverability for women. She argues further that it is an erroneous belief that the current *sharia* codes are a

[17] Leslie Peirce, *Morality Tales: Law and Gender in the Ottoman Court of Aintab* (Berkeley: University of California Press, 2003).

[18] Peirce's attention to gendered narratives also serves to complicate a simple association of gender with biological sex. She is careful to point out that the divergence between masculine and feminine registers cannot be reduced to biological sex but instead to the legal agency of those who were marginalized within the legal system. In fact, a female register was utilized by male subjects whose maleness was compromised by social or mental factors. Peirce gives the example of a male slave who used the female idiom of protestation and plea to gain credibility for his claims. Ibid., 202.

continuation of a centuries-old legal tradition. What these modern nation states are attempting to do instead "is the institution of new customs labeled as 'shariah' that deny previous freedoms while emphasizing earlier discriminations."[19] Asifa Quraishi-Landes' work on the *Hudood* Ordinance in Pakistan has employed a similar critique. She argues that these modern ordinances are in fact discordant with the premodern legal tradition, which offers possibilities of reform that would lead to more gender-egalitarian laws.[20]

In contrast to previous works that portrayed a monolithic image of the oppressed Muslim woman, these studies present a complex and nuanced gendered analysis of Islamic law. Despite the methodological, geographic, and temporal variances between these different studies, they share an approach that treats Muslim women as agential subjects. Far from presenting a picture of women as mere objects of the law, these studies center Muslim women's legal claims and the gendered strategies they deployed to negotiate and navigate the constraints of a legal system that maintained and enforced a gender hierarchy. By applying a gendered lens to legal practice, these studies situate *sharia* courts as spaces wherein legal discourse was contested and negotiated between not only men and women (albeit within an asymmetrical power dynamic) but also between legal actors and individuals who approached the court.

By focusing on legal practice, these studies give us a different picture of the position of women in the law than what is evident in legal discourse. The contribution of these studies, however, is far more extensive than this alone. In approaching law as process, these studies challenge us to think about Islamic law not simply as the purview of legal actors but also as the product of engagement and negotiation between legal texts, legal actors, and non-legal actors. If we take seriously that gender is constituted through legal interactions, then the law is similarly formulated and reformulated through these interactions.

II. Feminist engagements with legal discourse

A second prominent methodological approach to the study of Islamic law and gender, partially resulting from increased numbers of female Muslim scholars

[19] Amira El Azhary Sonbol, *Women, the Family, and Divorce Laws in Islamic History* (Syracuse, NY: Syracuse University Press, 1996), 11.

[20] Asifa Quraishi, "Her Honor: An Islamic Critique of the Rape Laws of Pakistan from a Woman-Sensitive Perspective," in *Windows of Faith: Muslim Women Scholar-Activists in North America*, ed. Gisela Webb (Syracuse: Syracuse University Press, 2000), 102–135.

entering the field in the 1980s and 1990s, brought a feminist analysis to substantive legal texts (*fiqh*). While Muslim women scholars carried out many of the studies that I discuss below, several prominent studies were produced by scholars who are not Muslim. I mention here the religious identity of the scholars only to give context to this turn towards an engagement with legal texts. The legal histories that I discussed in the previous section (many of which were produced concurrently with the studies in this genre) juxtaposed their methodological approach (i.e. the focus on legal practice) to previous scholarship that focussed solely on legal texts. However, the turn to substantive legal texts in the 1980s and 1990s was not a vestige of orientalist approaches that had already come under critique. This turn emerged, instead, due to the rise of Islamism in the 1970s and the demands for *sharia* implementation under the purview of the state.[21] These calls made more urgent a critical engagement with the patriarchal elements of the legal tradition, pushing for a return to the legal texts that were touted as repositories forthe law.[22]

There were three different modes of feminist engagements with Islamic law that developed from the 1990s onwards. The first approach develops a narrative about the patriarchal nature of Islamic law and the increasing decline of women's rights throughout Islamic history. The second approach takes a more constructive approach to the legal texts while the third approach historically contextualizes the development of substantive law and interrogates its gendered assumptions.

The first perspective is best represented by Leila Ahmed in her 1992 book *Women and Gender in Islam*.[23] Contrary to popular apologist narratives about the rise of Islam bringing about a radical change in the position of women, Ahmed argues that Islam continued and reinforced an increasingly patriarchal shift that was already under way due to the Greek, Roman, and Christian periods that preceded Islam.[24]

[21] Ziba Mir-Hosseini provides a similar historiography for these scholarly developments in the '80s and '90s arguing that the Islamist agenda of *sharia* implementation not only provoked scholarly criticism and activism but also brought the premodern legal texts into the public arena. Mir-Hosseini makes a compelling argument that this movement, which has been termed Islamic feminism, is the "'unwanted child' of political Islam." While political Islam certainly did not offer an egalitarian understanding of Islam, Mir-Hosseini argues, it gave Muslim women "the language to sustain a critique of the gender biases of Muslim family laws in ways that were previously impossible, which opened a space, an arena, for an internal critique of patriarchal readings of the Shari'a that was unprecedented in Muslim history." Ziba Mir-Hosseini, "Beyond 'Islam' vs. 'Feminism,'" *IDS Bulletin* 42, no. 1 (2011): 6. See also Ziba Mir-Hosseini, "Islamic law and Feminism: The story of a relationship," *Yearbook of Islamic and Middle Eastern Law* 9, no. 1 (2002): 32–42.

[22] It is for this reason that much of the feminist engagements with Islamic law have focussed primarily on issues of marriage and divorce (and, more recently, sexual violence). The application of Islamic law in most modern nation states has been reduced primarily to matters pertaining to the family, most centrally marriage and marital disputes.

[23] Leila Ahmed, *Women and Gender in Islam: Historical roots of a modern debate* (New Haven: Yale University Press, 1992).

[24] Ibid., 33. As Fatima Seedat points out, the normative narrative about the advent of Islam characterizes the situation of women in pre-Islamic Arabia as particularly dire. Islam, these narratives argued, radically shifted the position of women, granting them spiritual equality with men and curbing

Ahmed's historical account, which has been highly influential in the field, insisted on a tension between what she saw as the ethical impulse in Islam that was "stubbornly egalitarian"[25] and the developing orthodoxy that was not only hierarchical but also decidedly patriarchal. Speaking of the development of the law in particular, she argued:

> orthodox Islam, on the contrary, gave paramountcy, as it elaborated its understanding of Islam into laws, to the practices and regulations Islam had enunciated, paying little heed in elaborating laws regarding women to the religion's ethical teachings, particularly its emphasis on the spiritual equality of women and men and its injunctions to treat women fairly. As a result, the religion's emphasis on equality and the equal justice to which women were entitled has left little trace on the law as developed in the Abbasid age.[26]

For Ahmed, the status and autonomy of women was increasingly restricted as Islamic law developed and matured as an intellectual tradition.

One of Ahmed's key contributions to the study of Islamic law and gender was not only her description of the tension between egalitarian and patriarchal impulses, but also her observation that legal interpretation was not simply an intellectual enterprise. She called for scholars to recognize the influence of the intellectual, cultural, and political context within which Islamic law developed that not only informed the subjectivity of the jurists but also defined the parameters and frameworks within which interpretation took place.

The second approach takes a constructive approach to Islamic law, turning to the vast corpus of legal discourse as a space from within which to articulate women's rights. Female Muslim scholars taking this approach did not presume that Islamic law was necessarily patriarchal.They argue instead that while particular aspects or legal rulings were indeed patriarchal, other legal rulings could be reclaimed to support women's rights, particularly within marriage. For these scholars, Islamic law serves as a framework within which they make ethical and legal claims, and can be interpreted to support gender equality. Their strategy for dealing with patriarchal legal rulings is to particularize them, chalking them up to the individual bias of jurists. As Asifa Quraishi-Landes argues in her critical assessment of the legal dismissal of women's testimony in cases involving illicit sexual intercourse: "although the principle that reasonable doubt should negate convictions of violent crimes is a laudable one, the reasoning leading to it appears to stem from a condescending patriarchal view of women."[27] This patriarchal bias stands in stark contrast to the

male authority and dominance. Ahmed's argument that I mention above seems to be an implicit response to these prevailing narratives. Seedat, "When Islam and Feminism Converge," *The Muslim World* 103, no. 3 (2013): 405.

25 Ahmed, *Women and Gender in Islam*, 63. 26 Ibid., 88.

27 Asifa Quraishi, "Her Honor: An Islamic Critique of the Rape Laws of Pakistan From a Woman-Sensitive Perspective," in *Windows of Faith: Muslim Women Scholar-Activists in North America*, ed. Gisela Webb (Syracuse: Syracuse University Press, 2000), 120. See also Azizah al-Hibri who argues that the patriarchal elements in legal discourse are largely because jurists, as interpreters of the law, were influenced by the patriarchal society within which they were located. Azizah Y. Al-Hibri, "An

Qur'an, which makes no such distinction, thus confirming that the restriction was a product of jurisprudential interpretation rather than a Qur'anic injunction.[28]

For scholars who take a constructivist approach, we might ask how they are able to maintain simultaneously that the law is patriarchal while also insisting that Islamic law can indeed support gender equality. In order to understand their reasoning, it is important to consider a distinction that they make between the terms *sharia* and *fiqh*. For them, *sharia* refers not to a body of legal rulings but instead to an idealized divine law. *Sharia*, in this understanding, stands as an aspiration and *fiqh* as the actualization of a human endeavor to live out divine law. Both Asifa Quraishi-Landes and Azizah al-Hibri term this "human endeavor" (*ijtihad*) or "juristic reasoning." *Ijtihad* is a necessary tool for making *sharia* concrete, yet is also the means through which the individual bias (here, patriarchy) seeps into legal rulings. Noting this bias, Azizah al-Hibri states emphatically that the "oppression of women is the result of Satanic logic infiltrating Muslim laws and distorting Muslim beliefs. For this reason I find patriarchal interpretations (*ijtihads)* unacceptable to the extent they are based on Satanic logic and conflict with *tawhid*."[29] The distinction created by these scholars between *sharia* and *fiqh*, and *ijtihad* as the intervening human element between them, allows for a claim that the *sharia* is essentially egalitarian while arguing that the historical legal tradition at times reflected this egalitarianism and at other times erroneously adopted patriarchal norms. With this understanding of the historical legal tradition, these scholars take a piecemeal approach to substantive law, rejecting certain legal rulings as the product of the individual jurists' patriarchal bias while adopting other legal rulings that support women's rights, whether taken from historical rulings from the various Sunni legal schools or from modern legal reforms.

While both Azizah al-Hibri and Asifa Quraishi-Landes uphold the distinction between an idealized divine law and its earthly, human manifestation, their articulation of the rights granted to women in Islamic law does not always follow such a neat differentiation. As Kecia Ali notes in her critique of their approach, these scholars often move back and forth between different normative frameworks in making

Introduction to Muslim Women's Rights," in *Windows of Faith: Muslim Women Scholar-Activists in North America*, ed. Gisela Webb (Syracuse: Syracuse University Press, 2000), 51.

[28] As Kecia Ali points out, such a position often fails to distinguish the different sources of authority from which claims about women's rights are being made (i.e. the historical legal tradition, the Qur'an, prophetic traditions, etc). In this example, Quraishi moves between Islamic law and the Qur'an in making claims regarding the validity of women's testimony. Kecia Ali, "Progressive Muslims and Islamic Jurisprudence: The Necessity for Critical Engagement with Marriage and Divorce Law," in *Progressive Muslims: On Justice, Gender, and Pluralism*, ed. Omid Safi (Oxford: Oneworld, 2003), 166.

[29] Al-Hibri, "An Introduction to Muslim Women's Rights," 54. Raga' El-Nimr makes a similar argument for *sharia* as the foundation for making moral judgments and *fiqh* as the body of jurisprudential rulings. Raga' El-Nimr, "Women in Islamic Law" in *Feminism and Islam: Legal and Literary Perspectives*, ed. Mai Yamani (Washington Square: New York University Press, 1996), 88.

their claims. Azizah al-Hibri, for example, moves between substantive legal rulings and her interpretation of Qur'anic passages. While she draws on the legal tradition to argue that Muslim women are not required to perform domestic services as part of their marital duties, at other times she turns to the Qur'an to challenge patriarchal legal rulings, asserting the centrality of the Qur'an in formulating Islamic law.[30] Islamic law, as understood and formulated by these scholars, is an amalgamation of the historical legal tradition, their interpretation of Qur'anic passages, prophetic traditions, and modern legal reforms.[31]

The early 2000s saw another shift in the gendered analysis of substantive law. This third approach steps away from substantive law as a space for reclaiming the rights of Muslim women and argues instead for historically contextualizing the development of the law. Kecia Ali's 2003 article, "Progressive Muslims and Islamic jurisprudence: The necessity for critical engagement with marriage and divorce law" was a methodological turning point in the field. In her article, she engaged extensively with the scholarship mentioned previously, arguing that it fails to recognize the internal functioning logic of the law, particularly concerning marriage. For Ali such an approach not only risks further entrenching the authority of the historical legal tradition but also accepts its framing of different legal constructs (particularly marriage) that adversely affect women. Rather than critiquing the very gendered assumptions embedded in substantive law, she argues, such an approach only limits its critique to blatant gendered disparities.[32]

Ali's methodological intervention pushed the field to interrogate and critically engage the internal logic of substantive law and its foundational assumptions regarding gender. In doing so, she pushed for an approach to legal discourse that situates legal texts and jurists within the cultural milieus that produce them. In taking this methodological approach in her own scholarship on marriage and divorce in early Islamic law, Ali concludes that the laws on marriage and divorce are in need of a radical rethinking in order to argue for a gender egalitarian marriage from within a legal framework.[33]

Ali's scholarship has been an important intervention in the field and a catalyst for the expansion of methodological approaches in the field. In response to Ali's provocation, Quraishi-Landes proposed an alternative model for the marriage contract from within the legal framework. While she agrees with Ali about the problematic analogy between a sales contract and the marriage contract in early Islamic law, she offers partnership as an alternative contractual model for marriage. This approach,

[30] Al-Hibri, "An Introduction to Muslim Women's Rights," 53.

[31] Kecia Ali makes this observation as well, arguing that it is often not clear how Islamic law or Islam is defined as it could be based on a whole host of different sources and norms. She also critiques these scholars for treating the law as a single body, failing to distinguish between the minority and majority opinions or changes in legal rulings over time. See Ali, "Progressive Muslims and Islamic Jurisprudence," 166.

[32] Ibid., 165. [33] Ibid., 181.

she argues, would allow for a more equitable framing of marriage, equalize divorce, and center mutuality in the relationship while remaining within the pre-existing legal framework. Even though Quraishi-Landes' proposed alternative for framing the marriage contract still functions from within the parameters of the premodern legal system, it is a creative response to Ali's provocation and pushes beyond the limitations of the constructive approach that Ali previously critiqued. Shifting the marriage contract from a contract of sale to a contract of partnership radically re-orients and reconfigures the legal construction of marriage, making possible the articulation of an equitable marriage while remaining within the framework of the premodern legal paradigm. However, as Quraishi-Landes herself acknowledges, it remains to be seen whether such a reorientation can gain traction.[34]

The turn in the field to interrogate the foundational assumptions and internal logic of substantive law has made critical contributions to Islamic legal studies. In the two sub-sections that follow, I will discuss two important contributions of this body of scholarship to our understanding of the development of legal discourse. In the first section, I will discuss the historical contextualization of substantive law in the scholarship of Kecia Ali and Hina Azam, focusing on the way in which this contextualization challenges an account of legal interpretation as the sole interpretive mode through which legal rulings were produced. These scholars attune us to the gendered assumptions embedded in legal texts that were external to formal interpretive frameworks. Their scholarship pushes us to consider that cultural norms and conceptual frameworks begin to influence the interpretative enterprise of jurists prior to the very act of legal interpretation. In the second section, I will examine the scholarly investigation of gendered legal subjecthood in the work of Judith Tucker, Kecia Ali, Marion Katz, and Fatima Seedat. Their scholarship raises fundamental questions regarding the legal conception of the human and the gendering of humans in legal discourse. Their conclusions complicate not only our idea that there is a singular legal subject in the law but also pushes the field to consider the very category of 'woman' that is applied in the study of Islamic law.

A. Historically Contextualizing Legal Discourse

One of the driving motivations for employing gender in the study of the premodern legal texts has been to investigate the gendered assumptions embedded in the law.The subsequent scholarship that emerged from this inquiry has provided us with an archeology of fundamental assumptions in these texts about the

[34] Asifa Quraishi-Landes, "A Meditation on *Mahr*, Modernity, and Muslim Marriage Contract Law," in *Feminism, Law, and Religion*, eds. Marie A. Failinger, Elizabeth R. Schiltz, and Susan J. Stabile (England: Ashgate, 2013).

gendered body, sexuality, and constructions of masculinity and femininity. They have also demonstrated how the early development of legal structures were shaped by these gendered assumptions. For this subsection, I will discuss the scholarship of Kecia Ali, Hina Azam, and Marion Katz as it allows us to focus on the nexus of the body, sexuality, and commodity in substantive law. In reading their scholarship comparatively we can observe how this nexus shaped legal interpretation on issues pertaining to marriage and sexuality.

In her book, *Marriage and Slavery in Early Islam,* Kecia Ali traces the development of the marital contract in early Islamic law, demonstrating the vital link between enslavement and femaleness. Despite the claims by modern Muslim neo-traditionalists that the "Islamic" marriage upholds the principle of gender complementarity, early Muslim jurists constructed marriage as a relationship of male control and dominion over the wife.[35] Marital claims were understood and articulated within this gendered hierarchy where the husband provided financial maintenance to the wife in exchange for sexual access and control of the wife's mobility.[36] Ali argues that the solidification of marriage as a transactional and hierarchical relationship is best understood if we situate the development of early Islamic law within a world where the institution of slavery was a norm. She compellingly demonstrates that claims of male slave owners over their female slaves structured the way juristsconceived of marriage and divorce. In this analogical framework between marriage and slavery, marriage conferred a form of dominion to the husband in exchange for the dower, which in turn allowed for licit sexual intercourse between the two.[37]

Male dominion and authority in the marriage relationship was not only critical to the structure of the marriage contract but also impacted legal interpretation. In her article, "'The best of you will not strike': Al-Shafi'i on Qur'an, Sunnah, and Wife-Beating," Ali demonstrates that the eminent ninth-century jurist Muhammad b. Idris al-Shafi'i departed from his own stated legal methodology in the interest of establishing and enforcing the authority of a husband over his wife. While al-Shafi'i held that rules must be supported through scriptural sources, he also came to the extra-textual conclusion that defiant wives lost entitlement to financial maintenance from their husbands. While verse Q. 4:34 prescribes various disciplinary techniques that a husband may employ to establish his authority over his rebellious wife, withholding financial support is not one of them. Ali thus concludes that while there are many potential explanations for why al-Shafi'i moved away from his stated methodology, one of the reasons was the transactional model of marriage that had

[35] Kecia Ali speaks briefly in the introduction of her book regarding the discontinuity between the juridical construction of marriage in early Islam and the model of gender complementarity upheld by neo-traditionalists. For a thorough and compelling account of this dissonance see Chaudhry, *Domestic Violence,* Chapter 4.

[36] Ibid., 189.

[37] Kecia Ali, *Marriage and Slavery in Early Islam* (Cambridge, MA: Harvard University Press, 2010), 6.

already gained currency in early substantive law and tied a wife's sexual availability and obedience to monetary exchange.[38]

Other scholars of legal discourse have also observed how jurists instinctually preserved husbands' authority. In her recent book, *Women in the Mosque: A History of Legal Thought and Social Practice,* Marion Katz provides a longitudinal study of Sunni legal discourse[39] regarding women's access to the mosque. While her book makes several important observations regarding legal change, the relationship between substantive law and social practice, and the shifting conceptions of gender,[40] I am most interested here in the first chapter where she details how jurists wrestled with a prophetic tradition prohibiting men from hindering women's mosque attendance. Her detailed analysis of substantive law shows how concerns for maintaining husbands' authority made jurists uncomfortable with the full implications of the prophetic tradition.

The prophetic tradition reads: "Do not forbid the maidservants of God from [going to] the mosques of God."[41] While a plain sense reading of this statement would support women's unlimited access to the mosque, none of the four Sunni legal schools interpreted it so expansively. Similar to Ali's observation regarding his stance on withdrawing financial support from a rebellious wife, Katz too notes that for al-Shafiʿi the range of interpretive possibilities was already constrained by the need to maintain husbands' authority. What is perhaps most intriguing is that al-Shafiʿi authorized his move away from the apparent meaning of the prophetic tradition by referring to scholarly consensus on the right of a husband to control his wife's mobility. Citing this scholarly consensus, al-Shafiʿi's interpretation of the prophetic tradition reduced a seeming blanket permission for women's mosque attendance to only prohibiting a husband from preventing his wife from making the *Hajj* pilgrimage once in her lifetime.[42]

Hina Azam's book, *Sexual Violation in Islamic Law,*[43] also demonstrates the close linkages between sexuality, property, and the female body and the ways in which the assumptions about them framed the development of substantive law. Azam's book places the development of legal conversations on sexual violation within the

[38] Kecia Ali, "'The best of you will not strike': al-Shafiʿi on Qur'an, Sunnah, and Wife-Beating," *Comparative Islamic Studies* 2, no. 2 (2006): 143–55.

[39] In addition to the four Sunni legal schools she does provide a brief survey of the Ẓāhirī legal school as well.

[40] I will discuss this aspect of Katz's book later, in the next sub-section. While I did not mention Katz's book in the previous section on legal practice, her comparative framework in this study places legal discourse alongside a history of social practice, challenging the assumption of a one-to-one correlation between substantive law and social practice.

[41] Marion Katz, *Women in the Mosque: A History of Legal Thought and Social Practice* (New York: Columbia University Press, 2014), 18.

[42] Ibid., 48.

[43] Hina Azam, *Sexual Violation in Islamic Law: Substance, Evidence, and Procedure* (Cambridge: Cambridge University Press, 2015), 9.

context of the broader late antique and medieval world which, she argues, is necessary in order to understand that legal rulings did not emerge from interpretation of sacred sources alone but also arose from the broader religious, cultural, and legal systems that preceded Islam. Her book documents the divergent legal conception of sexual violation between the Maliki and Hanafi legal schools, providing a genealogy for the concept as it emerged through a tension between a theocentric and proprietary sexual ethic in late antiquity.[44]

Describing this tension, Azam argues that prior to the emergence of Islam, there were two conceptions of female sexuality prevalent in the late antique world. The first was a proprietary ethic where female sexuality was commodified and sexual violation classified as a property crime. This ethical framing of sexual violation largely rendered irrelevant the legal agency and subjectivity of women, as their coercion was of little consequence. What was paramount instead was the usurpation of her sexual commodity, which belonged to a male kin. The second view infused sexuality with moral import, introducing the element of a transcendent deity into determinations of sexual morality. With the emergence of Islam, Azam argues, the Qur'an and the Prophet configured sexuality primarily within theocentric terms where licitness of sexual activity was determined foremost by God's command.[45] The woman, in this conception of sexual morality, was granted autonomy as a legal subject, as her will and volition acquired legal recognition and significance.[46]

This continued tension, with an increased tendency toward a theocentric ethic, influenced the development of early legal rulings on sexual violation. Early jurists, Azam argues, were in agreement that consensual illicit sex was to be punished as a crime against God and the rape of slave women as a property crime. It was the sexual violation of a free woman, however, that remained a matter of legal discussion. With the maturation of the legal tradition, two positions solidified on the sexual violation of the free woman. The Maliki legal school held both the proprietary and theocentric ethic in equal regard, instituting a dual punishment in cases of sexual violation where the man received the prescribed punishment for illicit sexual intercourse and was also obligated to pay monetary compensation to the woman. The Hanafi legal tradition, on the other hand, leaned heavily toward the theocentric ethic, prosecuting the crime as illicit sexual intercourse, rejecting any monetary compensation in sexual violation.[47]

[44] Ibid., 24.

[45] Azam is quick to point out that this theocentric ethic, however, did not fully replace the proprietary ethic as the Qur'an and Prophet maintained the commodification of female sexuality in some form. Ibid., 62.

[46] Ibid., 24–25.

[47] Azam's comparative study demonstrates that the theocentric ethic of the Hanafis functioned to sideline the volition of the woman in cases of sexual violation, as Hanafi jurists were far more concerned with the legal categorization of the act. While the proprietary approach of the Maliki legal school is rather distasteful for modern readers, it was far more equitable in adjudicating cases of sexual violation. Ibid., 240.

Reading Kecia Ali, Hina Azam, and Marion Katz in conversation with one another attunes us to the jurists' assumptions about the body as a commodity, notions of ownership, and a hierarchical social orderthat were embedded in their construction of legal subjecthood and legal agency. These fundamental assumptions were also gendered in ways that affected the position of women as legal subjects, particularly within the family. The contributions of these scholars are crucial for the study of Islamic law not only in their observations concerning the gendered assumptions embedded in legal texts but also for their theorization of the nature of legal interpretation. Their studies complicate any simple conception of legal interpretation as a largely textual exercise, bringing our attention to the extra-textual influences that shape legal interpretation anddemonstrating the gendered politics of meaning-making.

B. Gender and Legal Subjecthood

One of the most valuable insights and contributions of the gendered readings of Islamic law has been an investigation into the construction of legal subjecthood. Focusing on legal subjecthood is important as it allows us to observe how the law acts upon individuals and construes them as accountable before the law. Fundamentally, questions of legal subjecthood address how the law imagines and constructs humanness. The studies I will discuss here reveal that women's legal subjecthood was complicated by the intersection of gender with other social factors, particularly enslavement. The interrogation into women's legal subjecthood thus raises critical questions in the field about the category of gender and how it is employed by scholars in the study of Islamic law.

In her discussion on the legal construction of the marriage contract, Kecia Ali argues that gender is a fundamental framing device for the legal construction of subjecthood. She states emphatically:

> Gender was, then, the most enduring aspect of legal personality. Both slavery and minority were legal disabilities of a sort, as was – in a different respect – being non-Muslim. However, only femaleness permanently limited a person's legal capacity. A slave might be manumitted, a non-Muslim could convert, a child would reach maturity. A woman, however, would remain female, with the "whiff of disability" attached to her legal capacity.[48]

To substantiate her claim, Ali offers the legal incapacity of the female slave owner to marry off her female slave. In Islamic law, slaves may marry with the permission of their slave owner thus requiring the consent even of a female slave owner in order for her slaves to marry. This necessity raised the question, however, as to whether a free woman may contract the marriage of her female slave. Whereas Abu Hanifa

[48] Ali, *Marriage and Slavery in Early Islam*, 47.

allowed a female slave owner to marry off both her male and female slaves, this was not the only opinion on the matter.[49] Malik held that the female slave owner had to delegate the contracting of the marriage to an adult male Muslim as she herself was incapable of doing so. Al-Shafiʿi, on the other hand, argued that only the male guardian of a female slave owner could contract the marriage. For both Malik and al-Shafiʿi, gender influenced the legal capacity of the slave owner. Femaleness not only curtailed the legal capacity of women in contracting their own marriages but also transferred that capacity to slave owners.[50] Gender, Ali concludes, was the most crucial distinction between individuals in Islamic law, as femaleness was the only permanent impediment to an individual's legal capacity.[51]

Judith Tucker, on the other hand, observed that women's legal agency was hampered only in her capacity as a member of the family. This is particularly evident in the curtailment of women's legal agency in matters pertaining to marriage and divorce. In other aspects of the law, particularly those related to property rights, women exercised full legal autonomy.[52] Thus, while a woman could contract commercial transactions on her own behalf and dispose of her property as she wished, she did not possess the unrestricted right to contract a marriage or a unilateral right to divorce. Tucker concludes that "Woman as family member (whose marriage will affect her male relatives and therefore must be vetted by them) and Woman as part of patriarchal society (whose behavior must be policed and restricted, thereby limiting her knowledge of and activity in the public sphere) trump the Woman as equal legal subject."[53]

Marion Katz pushes Tucker's observation about the shifting legal agency of the woman further by bringing into question the very category of "woman" in the law. In tracing the development of Sunni legal thought on the question of women's mosque attendance, she argues that in the first two centuries of Islam, "woman" was not a homogenous category. At this early moment in the development of substantive law, the category of "woman" always intersected with other factors such as age

[49] Of the four Sunni legal schools, only the Hanafis allow a virgin woman to contract her own marriage. However, the father of a virgin woman retains the right to contest the marriage if he finds the match to be incompatible. For more information see Mona Siddiqui, "Law and Desire or Social Control: An Insight into the Hanafi Concept of *Kafaʾa* with Reference to the Fatawa ʿAlamgiri," in *Feminism and Islam: Legal and Literary Perspectives*, ed. Mai Yamani (New York: New York University Press, 1996), 49–68.

[50] In addition to this legal case, Ali also offers as an example the inability of the female slave owner to take her male slave as a concubine. While the law granted the male slave owner the sexual use of his female slave, the female slave owner was not granted a similar use of her male slave. Ali, *Marriage and Slavery in Early Islam*, 178.

[51] Ali, *Marriage and Slavery in Early Islam*, 47.

[52] While Tucker is quite accurate in noting that property ownership was not gender differentiated, my previous discussion of Ali's work does indicate that there were particular instances where femaleness did serve as an impediment to legal capacity even in commercial matters.

[53] Judith Tucker, *Women, Family, and Gender in Islamic Law* (New York: Cambridge University Press, 2008), 173.

and enslavement. "Early jurists universally presumed," she argues, "that women of different ages or statuses were subject to significantly different standards of behavior; there was no assumption that a consistent rule could be applied to "women" as a group."[54] By the thirteenth century, however, this category became increasingly monolithic as women across the board came to be associated with sexual temptation.[55] This growing cohesion, however, was fractured by the emerging concern in post-eleventh century legal texts with sultry youth.[56] Katz observes that legal texts after this period were greatly concerned with forbidding desirous gazes upon young boys and with their presence in homo-social male spaces. Just as the rising concern with sexual chaos was constructing women into a monolithic category in the law, the figure of the sultry youth fractured the binary distinction between male and female by making certain categories of males desirable to other men.[57]

The picture of gendered legal subjecthood that we receive from this scholarship raises critical questions in the field about the diverse and multiple constructions of gender in Islamic law. Their observations urge us to consider the intersection of other systems of distinction with gender that might at times displace gender as the primary means of differentiation. Such an intersectional approach pushes for a critical reflection on the category of gender as it is utilized in the study of Islamic law. What are the different possibilities that emerge if we begin to analyze masculinity and femininity as internally fractured concepts?

In my own research on the eleventh century Hanafi jurist, Muhammad b. Ahmad al-Sarakhsi, I demonstrate the intimate link between the law's assumptions regarding gender and the process of law-making.[58] I have argued, in particular, that al-Sarakhsi constructs gendered subjects along the active/passive binary in which men are constructed as active and desiring and women as passive and desirable. This binary construction, however, breaks down when gender intersects with other social facts such as slavery.

To illustrate, let me offer a legal case in al-Sarakhsi's substantive legal text, *al-Mabsuṭ*,[59] where he delineates the appropriate parameters of interaction between a slave woman and men who are unrelated to her. In considering the parameters of the male gaze on a slave woman, al-Sarakhsi argues that a man may look at her in the same manner that he looks at female relatives (i.e. those female relatives who are prohibited to him in marriage). Thus, a man may look at and touch all parts of the slave woman's body except for her torso, upper thighs, and genitals. Earlier in the text, al-Sarakhsi asserted adamantly that the entirety of the female body is a cause

54 Katz, *Women in the Mosque*, 3. 55 Ibid., 104–105.

56 The sultry youth was understood to be an adolescent boy whose beard had just begun to emerge and was an object of male desire.

57 Ibid., 106.

58 Saadia Yacoob, "Hermeneutics of Desire: Ontologies of Gender and Desire in Early Hanafi Law," Ph.D. diss., Duke University, Durham, 2016.

59 Al-Sarakhsī, Muḥammad ibn Aḥmad, *Al-Mabṣūṭ* (Beirūt: Dār al-Maʿrifa, 1993).

of temptation and must remain hidden from sight.[60] Given this, he must justify why the law permits such significant exposure of the slave woman's body. In justification, he argues that since a slave woman must often emerge in public to serve the needs of her slave owner, to enforce extensive covering of her body would impose undue restrictions on her mobility.[61]

The difference between the free and slave woman is not restricted to covering alone but also pertains to sight and touch. As a slave was considered a commodity that was bought and sold on the market, the slave's body was stripped of the bodily autonomy granted to free individuals and was exposed to look and touch.[62] This permission, however, comes with a caveat. Al-Sarakhsi insists that if a man experiences desire he must not avail himself of the allowance to touch the body.[63]

In al-Sarakhsi's discussion on the appropriateness of the male gaze and touch in relation to slave women, his assumptions regarding the desiring male subject are intriguing in their contradictory nature. While he holds that women are a cause of temptation and no woman is beyond desirability, he simultaneously assumes that a man can look upon the exposed body of a slave woman and control his desire.

In order to understand these competing claims about male desire, we must attend to the way in which gender is not the sole determinative social marker in legal discourse, but rather functions alongside and intersects with other systems of distinction and social identity. In the case of the slave woman, we see that a general categorical statement about the nature of women and male desire is then followed by an engagement with details of particular scenarios that complicate or belie this general representation.

In al-Sarakhsi's account of slave and free women as objects of the male gaze, the gender binary intersects with the binary distinction of master/slave to produce different configurations of desire and desirability. The same male subject is construed as desiring and undesiring in different circumstances and in relation to different female subjects. Male and female subjects in al-Sarakhsi's legal thought are not singular, consistent legal subjects.The shifting position of the gender binary in al-Sarakhsi's legal text led me to interrogate my own assumptions about gender and its salience as a category of analysis in the study of Islamic law.

Feminist historian Jeanne Boydston cautions that gender as a category often functions as a set of universalized premises, flattening complex historical processes

[60] "*Al-mar'a min qarnihāilāqadamihā 'awrah.*" Al-Sarakhsī supports his claim by citing a prophetic tradition to the effect that a woman's very being is to be concealed. Al-Sarakhsī, *Al-Mabsūṭ*, 10:145.

[61] Ibid., 10:151. [62] Ibid., 10:151.

[63] He may, however, still look upon her body, even if it is animated by desire. Al-Sarakhsī states explicitly that if a man wishes to purchase a slave woman, he may look upon her body even if he experiences desire as financial matters necessitate the assessment of the appropriate value of a commodity. Touching with desire, however, is not always necessary to ascertain the monetary value of the slave woman and is thus prohibited. Ibid., 10:160.

and meanings.[64] She argues that feminist historiography has treated gender as "non-historically-contingent – that is, as unfolding in much the same way and in much the same terms in all societies."[65] Such historical accounts disregard the very local character of the concept, instead universalizing what was particular to the United States and Western Europe.

Afsaneh Najmabadi, also pushes against the ethnocentricity of gender as a category of historical analysis. She reflects on her own work on gender in the formation of Iranian modernity and her realization that she needed to break free of the narrative implicit in the category of gender. This was necessary in order to show how thinking of gender as the binary construction of man/woman was a production of early modernity and not reflective of the cultural logic of gender in premodern Iran. There was a shift, she argues, from a premodern logic in which "all gender categories were defined in relation to adult manhood, to a view in which woman and man became opposite and complementary, to the exclusion of other categories that would not fit."[66]

In taking on Boydston's and Najmabadi's theoretical critique, I do not wish to argue that gender is not a salient category for Islamic law. Indeed, I take seriously al-Sarakhsi's claim that gender is a fundamental distinguishing factor for human beings. Al-Sarakhsi himself routinely employs the terms 'male/man' and 'female/woman' as general categories regardless of the distinctions between different types of men and women.

However, despite these observations regarding the efficacy of the gender binary in legal discourse, the categories of "man" and "woman" are disrupted and displaced when they intersect with other systems of differentiation. Enslavement both binds the slave woman to femaleness (in that she, unlike the male slave, can be used as a concubine) and yet displaces it as well. At times, the master/slave binary trumps gender as a system of differentiation.

While the scholarship I have discussed above has offered a compelling critique of the gendered politics of legal interpretation it has mostly focussed on court records, legal opinions, and positive law, while largely leaving untouched the genre of jurisprudential methodology. To date, Fatima Seedat's dissertation is the only study that has investigated the gendered assumptions in legal subjecthood as constructed in legal theory (*usul al-fiqh*) works.[67] Seedat's work is a rich, multilayered comparative analysis of gendered legal subjecthood that reads both legal theory and substantive

[64] Jeanne Boydston, "Gender as a Question of Historical Analysis," *Gender & History*, 20, no. 3 (2008): 560.

[65] Ibid., 559.

[66] Afsaneh Najmabadi, "Beyond the Americas: Are Gender and Sexuality Useful Categories of Analysis?" *Journal of Women's History* 18, no. 1 (2006): 13–14.

[67] Fatima Seedat, "Sex and the Legal Subject: Women and Legal Capacity in *Ḥanafī* Law" Ph.D. diss., McGill University, Montreal, 2013.

legal texts together and covers the classical to contemporary periods. She argues that while classical legal theory did not make gender a distinctive category in establishing legal capacity, this was contradicted in the substantive legal texts where female legal subjects were subject to inequities, particularly within marriage. This tension between "presence" and "lack" of gender as a distinctive category, Seedat concludes, suggests that female legal subjecthood in classical Islamic law was varied and situational:[68]

> ... the female legal subject of Islamic law is not a simply or singularly constituted legal subject that moves in time with the legal identity 'woman.' The evidence supports a notion of subjectivity that is multiple and changing even if the biological female person holding the differing legal subjectivity is constant.[69]

In contrast to the premodern Islamic legal discourse, contemporary legal theoretical texts demonstrate a more essentialized notion of gender. This shift is most evident in the emergence of gender as a distinguishing category in discussions on legal capacity and the determination of contemporary Islamic legal theorists that women inhabit an imperfect legal capacity. Seedat argues that this shift not only categorizes women as a distinct legal subject but also leads to greater rigidity around legal constructions of femaleness. The contrast between the classical and contemporary constructions of the legal subject in Seedat's study is particularly illustrative of the importance of historicizing and particularizing the category of gender as it is employed in the study of Islamic law.

III. Conclusion

The introduction of feminist methods to the study of Islamic law since the 1970s has made significant contributions to our understanding of Islamic law. Despite its importance, however, the engagement with gender theory and feminist studies has yet to be taken as a norm in the field. As I mentioned in the introduction to this chapter, gendered analyses of Islamic law are often marginalized and their methods and conclusions are not considered more broadly for the field. It is my hope that this chapter has made a compelling case for how scholars of Islamic law can incorporate a gendered analysis of Islamic law into their scholarship and pedagogy on Islamic law.

As I end this chapter, I want to return to the issue of categories that are employed by scholars in the study of Islamic law. As I discussed in the last

[68] Ibid., 245. [69] Ibid.

section, a critical reflection on the category of gender has crucial implications for the field. If we take the methods and conclusions of these gender scholars as a scholarly model, then we must also reflect on other categories (in particular the category of law) that we employ in the study of Islamic law. Some of this work has already begun,with prominent Muslim feminist scholars and activists posing a challenge to prevalent conceptions of "law" in the field. Amina Wadud's theorization of lived experience, for example, centers justice in women's lived experiences of the law. Such an approach challenges the assumption of orientalists and religious authorities alike that law and legal interpretation are a discursive exercise produced by a disembodied subject. She argues instead that justice must be rooted in the lived experiences of those who are subject to the law. One cannot claim that a gendered legal ruling is just if women do not experience it as such. Following Wadud's provocation, *Musawah*, a transnational Muslim feminist organization launched their Global Life Stories research project aimed at documenting the experiences of Muslim women with Islamic law and its enforcement of male authority in the family.

The work done by *Musawah* and Wadud's turn to lived experience confronts our assumptions about the category of "law," assumptions that function to restrict what the field considers legitimate objects of study. I mention their work here to argue that *Musawah* and Wadud are in fact engaged in the process of law-making. In theorizing lived experience, Wadud places moral authority in lived life rather than the text.[70] Such an approach proposes an epistemological shift in conventional notions of law and legal interpretation. To assess the legitimacy of a legal ruling on how it manifests in the lives of those affected by it, grants lived experience primacy over legal interpretation. The implication of such an approach would be to establish lived experience as a critical source for deriving legal rulings, radically redefining how we conceptualize law and knowledge production. Zainah Anwar, Director of *Musawah*, makes this reconception most clear when she states: "We believe that in this way the knowledge produced will be grounded in the lived realities of women and men, such realities then informing the approach to the text and the questions to be asked."[71] The theoretical contributions and scholarly self-reflexivity that has emerged from a gendered analysis of Islamic law is a model for critically examining the legacy of orientalism that continues to haunt the field.

[70] Shadaab Rahemtulla make a similar argument noting that Wadud's centering of lived experience broadens our conception of knowledge, thus challenging the idea that authority lies in religious texts alone. Shadaab Rahemtullah, *Qur'an of the Oppressed: Liberation Theology and Gender Justice in Islam* (Oxford: Oxford University Press, 2017), 107.

[71] Ziba Mir-Hosseini, Mulki Al-Sharmani, and Jana Rumminger eds., *Men in Charge? Rethinking Authority in Muslim Legal Tradition* (London: Oneworld, 2015), viii.

References

Abou El-Fadl, Khaled, "Legal and Jurisprudential Literature: 9th to 15th Century," in Joseph Suad (ed.) *Encyclopedia of Women and Islamic Culture* vol. 1 (Leiden: Brill, 2003) 37–41.

Abou El-Fadl, Khaled, *Speaking in God's Name: Islamic Law, Authority and Women* (Oxford: Oneworld Publications, 2001).

Abou Bakr, Omaima, "Teaching the Words of the Prophet: Women Instructors of Hadith (Fourteenth and Fifteenth Centuries)." *Hawwa* 1.3 (2003): 306–328.

Abou Bakr, Omaima, "Teaching the Words of the Prophet: Women Instructors of Hadith (Fourteenth and Fifteenth Centuries)." *Hawwa* 1.3 (2003): 306–328.

Agmon, Iris, *Family and Court: Legal Culture and Modernity in Late Ottoman Palestine* (Syracuse: Syracuse University Press, 2006).

Agmon, Iris, "Women's History and Ottoman Sharia Court Records: Shifting Perspectives in Social History." *Hawwa* 2.2 (2004): 172–209.

Ahmed, Leila, *Women and Gender in Islam: Historical Roots of a Modern Debate* (New Haven: Yale University Press, 1992).

Ahmed, Rumee, "Islamic Law and Theology," in Anver Emon and Rumee Ahmed (eds.) *Oxford Handbook of Islamic Law* (Oxford: Oxford University Press, 2018): 105–132.

Al-Faruqi, Maysam, "Women's Self-Identity in the Qur'an and Islamic Law," in Gisela Webb (ed.) *Windows of Faith: Muslim Women Scholar-Activists in North America* (Syracuse: Syracuse University Press, 2000) 72–101.

Al-Hibri, Azizah Y., "Islamic Law and Muslim Women in America," in Marjorie Garber, and Rebecca L. Walkowitz (eds.) *One Nation Under God? Religion and American Culture* (New York and London: Routledge, 1999).

Al-Hibri, Azizah Y., "An Introduction to Muslim Women's Rights," in Gisela Webb (ed.) *Windows of Faith: Muslim Women Scholar-Activists in North America* (Syracuse: Syracuse University Press, 2000) 51–71.

Al-Hibri, Azizah Y., "Muslim Women's Rights in the Global Village: Challenges and Opportunities." *Journal of Law and Religion*, 15, Vol. 1/2, (2000): 37–66.

Al-Hibri, Azizah Y., "An Islamic Perspective on domestic violence." *Fordham International Law Journal*, 27: 1, (2003): 195.

Al-Sarakhsī, Muḥammad ibn Aḥmad. Al-Mabṣūṭ (Beirūt: Dār al-Maʿrifah, 1993).

Ali, Kecia, "Progressive Muslims and Islamic Jurisprudence: The Necessity for Critical Engagement with Marriage and Divorce Law," in Omid Safi (ed.) *Progressive Muslims: On Justice, Gender, and Pluralism* (Oxford: OneworldPublications, 2003) 163–189.

Ali, Kecia, "'The best of you will not strike:' Al-Shafiʿi on Qur'an, *Sunnah*, and Wife-Beating." *Journal of Comparative Islamic Studies*, 2, Vol. 2 (2006): 143–155.

Ali, Kecia, *Marriage and Slavery in Early Islam* (Cambridge, MA: Harvard University Press, 2010).

Ali, Kecia, "The Omniprescent Male Scholar." *Critical Muslim* (2013): 61–73.

Ali, Kecia, *Sexual Ethics and Islam: Feminist Reflections on Qur'an, Hadith, and Jurisprudence* (expanded and revised edn. Oxford: Oneworld Publications, 2016).

Ali, Kecia, "Concubinage and Consent."*International Journal of Middle East Studies* 49, no. 1 (2017): 148–52.

Amien, Waheeda, Overcoming the Conflict between the Right to Freedom of Religion and Women's Rights to Equality: A South African Case Study of Muslim Marriages." *Human Rights Quarterly* 9, no. 3 (2006): 729–754.

Antonio, Isabelita, *The Shari'a courts in the Philippines: Women, Men, and Personal Laws* (Davao City: Pilipina Legal Resources Center, 2003).
Anderson, J.N.D., "The Eclipse of the Patriarchal Family in Contemporary Islamic Law," in J.N.D. Anderson (ed.) *Family Law in Asia and Africa* (London: Allen and Unwin, 1968) 221–234.
Aslan, Ednan, Marcia Hermansen, and Elif Medeni, *Muslima Theology The Voices of Muslim Women Theologians.*Wiener IslamstudienMuslima Theology (Frankfurt: Peter Lang GmbH, InternationalerVerlag Der Wissenschaften, 2014).
Awde, Nicholas, trans. and ed. *Women in Islam: An Anthology From the Qur'an and Hadiths* (New York: St.Martin's Press, 2000).
Azam, Hina, *Sexual Violation in Islamic Law: Substance, Evidence, and Procedure* (New York: Cambridge University Press, 2015).
Azam, Hina,"Rape as a Variant of Fornication (*Zinā*) in Islamic Law: An Examination of the Early Legal Reports." *Journal of Law and Religion*, 28, no. 2 (2013): 441–466.
Azam, Hina,"Competing Approaches to Rape in Islamic Law," in Marie A. Failinger, Elizabeth R. Schiltz, and Susan J. Stabile (eds.) *Feminism, Law, and Religion* (Ashgate Press, 2013) 327–341.
Azam, Hina, "The Exclusion of Women's Testimony in the Ḥudūd: Toward a Rethinking," in Kecia Ali, Juliane Hammer, and Laury Silvers (eds.) *A Jihad for Justice: Honoring the Work and Life of Amina Wadud* (48HrBooks, 2012) 135–147.
Baer, Gabriel, "Women and Waqf: An Analysis of the Istanbul Tahrir of 1546."*Asian and African Studies* 17 (1983): 9–27.
Baugh, Carolyn, "An Exploration of the Juristic Consensus (Ijmāʿ) on Compulsion in the Marriage of Minors." *Comparative Islamic Studies* 5, vol. 1, (2011): 33.
Baugh, Carolyn, "Ibn Taymiyya's Feminism?Imprisonment and the Divorce Fatwas," in Ednan Aslan, Marcia Hermansen, and Elif Medeni (eds.) *Muslima Theology: The voices of Muslim women theologians.* Wiener IslamstudienMuslima Theology (Frankfurt: Peter Lang GmbH, InternationalerVerlag Der Wissenschaften, 2014) 181–196.
Baugh, Carolyn, *Minor Marriage in early Islamic law* (Leiden: Brill, 2017).
Baxamusa, Ramala M., *A Historic Perspective on Muslim Personal Law in India* (Bombay: SNDT Women's University, 1984).
Baugh, Carolyn, *The Legal Status of Muslim Women: An Appraisal of Muslim Personal Law in India.* Rcws Gender Series. Gender & Law Bk 3 (Mumbai: Research Centre for Women's Studies, S.N.D.T. Women's University, 1998).
Boydston, Jeanne, "Gender as a Question of Historical Analysis." *Gender & History* 20, no. 3 (2008)
Chaudhry, Ayesha, *Domestic Violence and the Islamic Tradition* (Oxford: Oxford University Press, 2014).
El-Nimr, Raga', "Women in Islamic Law," in Mai Yamani (ed.) *Feminism and Islam: Legal and Literary Perspectives* (Washington Square: New York University Press, 1996) 88.
Fazaeli, Roja, *Islamic feminisms: rights and interpretation across generations in Iran* (London: Taylor and Francis Group, 2017).
Gani, H. A., *Reform of Muslim Personal Law: the Shah Bano Controversy and the Muslim Women (Protection of Rights on Divorce) Act, 1986* (New Delhi: Deep & Deep Publications, 1988).
Gerber, Haim, "Social and Economic Position of Women in an Ottoman City, Bursa, 1600–1700." *International Journal of Middle East Studies* 12.3 (1980): 231–244.

Hanne, Eric, "Women, Power, and the Eleventh and Twelfth Century Abbasid Court." *Hawwa* 3.1 (2005): 80–110.

Hamzic, Vanja, *Sexual and Gender diversity in the Muslim world: History, law, and vernacular language* (London: I.B. Tauris, 2016).

Haeri, Shahla, "The Politics of Dishonor: Rape and Power in Pakistan," in Mahnaz Afkhami (ed.) *Faith and Freedom: Women's Human Rights in the Muslim World* (Syracuse, NY: Syracuse University Press, 1995).

Haeri, Shahla, *Law of Desire : Temporary Marriage in Shi'i Iran*. Contemporary Issues in the Middle East 1st edn. (Syracuse, NY: Syracuse University Press, 1989).

Hirsch, Susan, *Pronouncing &Persevering : gender and the discourses of disputing in an African Islamic court* (Chicago: Chicago University Press, 1998).

Hoodfar, Homa, ed. *Shifting Boundaries in Marriage and Divorce in Muslim Communities* (Montpellier, France: Women Living Under Muslim Laws, 1996).

Jennings, Ronald, "The Legal Position of Women in Kayseri, a Large Ottoman City, 1590–1630," *Studies on Ottoman Social History in the Sixteenth and Seventeenth Centuries* (Istanbul: ISIS Press, 1999) 115–41.

Katz, Marion, *Women in the Mosque: A History of Legal Thought and Social Practice* (New York: Columbia University Press, 2014).

Korteweg, Anna and Jennifer A. Sleby, *Debating Sharia: Islam, gender politics, and family law* (Buffalo: University of Toronto Press, 2012).

Kamaruddin, Zaleha, "Protecting Muslim Women against Abuse of Polygamy in Malaysia: Legal Perspective." *Hawwa* 6.2 (2008): 176–201.

Layish, Aharon, *Divorce in the Libyan Family: a Study Based on the Sijjls of the Shari'a Courts of Ajdabiyya* (London and New York: I.B. Tauris & Co., 1993).

Lutfi, Huda, "Manners and Customs of Fourteenth Century Cairene Women: Female Anarchy Versus Male Shar'i Order in Muslim Perspective Treatises," in N. Keddie (ed.) *Women in Middle Eastern History: Shifting Boundaries in Sex and Gender* (New Haven: Yale University Press, 1991) 99–121.

Meriwether, Margaret, "Women and Waqf Revisited: The Case of Aleppo, 1770–1840," in M. Zelfie (ed.) *Women in the Ottoman Empire* (Leiden: Brill, 1997) 128–52.

Mir-Hosseini, Ziba. *Marriage on Trial: A Study of Islamic Family Law, Iran and Morocco Compared* (New York: I.B. Tauris, 2000).

Mir-Hosseini, Ziba, *Islam and Gender: The Religious Debate in Contemporary Iran*, Princeton Studies in Muslim Politics (Princeton, NJ: Princeton University Press, 1999).

Mir-Hosseini, Ziba, "The Construction of Gender in Islamic Legal Thought and Strategies for Reform." *Hawwa* 1.1 (2003): 1–28.

Mir-Hosseini, Ziba, "Islamic law and Feminism: The story of a relationship," *Yearbook of Islamic and Middle Eastern Law* 9, no. 1 (2002): 32–42.

Mir-Hosseini, Ziba, "Beyond 'Islam' vs. 'Feminism'" *IDS Bulletin* 42, vol. 1 (2011): 67–77.

Mir-Hosseini, Ziba, ed. *Gender and Equality in Muslim Family Law: Justice and Ethics in the Islamic Legal Tradition*. Library of Islamic Law; 5 (London and New York, NY: I.B. Tauris; US, Canada: Palgrave Macmillan Distributed in the United States and Canada by Palgrave Macmillan, 2013) 5.

Mir-Hosseini, Ziba, "Muslim legal tradition and the challenge of gender equality," in Mir-Hosseini, Ziba, Al-Sharmani, Mulki, and Rumminger, Jana (eds.) *Men in charge? Rethinking authority in Muslim legal tradition* (London, England: Oneworld, 2015) 13–43.

Mir-Hosseini, Ziba, ed. *Men in Charge? Rethinking Authority in Muslim Legal Tradition* (London, England: Oneworld, 2015).

Moors, Annelies, "Debating Islamic Family Law." in M. Meriwether and J. Tucker (eds.) *Social History of Women and Gender in the Modern Middle East* (Boulder: Westview, 1999) 141–172.

Najmabadi, Afsaneh, "Beyond the Americas: Are Gender and Sexuality Useful Categories of Analysis?" *Journal of Women's History* 18, no. 1 (2006).

Olivia, Remie, "Her Day in Court: Women's Property Rights in Fifteenth-Century Granada." *Islamic law and society* 16.1 (2009): 98–100.

Peirce, Leslie, *The Imperial Harem: Women and Sovereignty in the Ottoman Empire* (New York: Oxford University Press, 1993).

Peirce, Leslie, *Morality Tales: Law and Gender in the Ottoman Court of Aintab* (Berkeley: University of California Press, 2003).

Quraishi, Asifa, "Her Honor: An Islamic Critique of the Rape Laws of Pakistan from a Woman-Sensitive Perspective" in Gisela Webb (ed.) *Windows of Faith: Muslim Women Scholar-Activists in North America* (Syracuse: Syracuse University Press, 2000) 102–135.

Quraishi, Asifa, ed. *The Islamic Marriage Contract: Case Studies in Islamic Family Law*, Harvard Series in Islamic Law (Cambridge, MA: Islamic Legal Studies Program Distributed by Harvard University Press, 2008).

Quraishi-Landes, Asifa, "A Meditation on *Mahr*, Modernity, and Muslim Marriage Contract Law" in Marie A. Failinger, Elizabeth R. Schiltz, and Susan J. Stabile (eds.) *Feminism, Law, and Religion* (Ashgate Press, 2013) 327–341.

Rahemtullah, Shadaab, *Qur'an of the Oppressed: Liberation Theology and Gender Justice in Islam* (Oxford: Oxford University Press, 2017).

Rapoport, Youssef, *Marriage, Money and Divorce in Medieval Islamic Society* (Cambridge: Cambridge University Press, 2005).

Seedat, Fatima, "When Islam and Feminism Converge." *The Muslim World* 103, no. 3 (2013).

Seedat, Fatima, "Sex and the Legal Subject: Women and Legal Capacity in *Ḥanafī* Law." Ph.D. diss., McGill University, 2013.

Serrano, Delfina, "Rape in Maliki Legal Doctrine and Practice (8th-15th Centuries C.E.)" *Hawwa* 5.2–3 (2007): 166–207.

Seng, Y.J., "Standing at the Gates of Justice: Women in the Law Courts of Sixteenth-Century Uskudar, Istanbul" in M. Lazarus-Black and S.F. Hirsch (eds.) *Contested States: Law, Hegemony, and Resistance* (New York: Routledge, 1994) 184–203.

Shatzmiller, Maya, *Her Day in Court: Women's Property Rights in Fifteenth-Century Granada* (Cambridge, MA: Harvard University Press, 2007).

Shaham, Ron, *Family and the Courts in Modern Egypt: A Study Based on Decisions by the Shari'a Courts, 1900–1955* (Leiden and New York: E.J. Brill, 1997).

Shaham, Ron, "A Woman's Place: A Confrontation With Bedouin Custom in the Sharia Court." *The Journal of the American Oriental Society* 113, no. 2 (1993).

Shaikh, Sa'diyya, "In Search of "Al-Insān": Sufism, Islamic Law, and Gender." *Journal of American Academy of Religion* 77, no. 4 (2009): 781–822.

Shaikh, Sa'diyya, *Sufi Narratives of Intimacy: Ibn 'Arabī, gender, and sexuality* (Chapel Hill: University of North Carolina Press, 2012).

Siddiqui, Mona, "*Mahr*: Legal Obligation or Rightful Demand?" *Journal of Islamic Studies*, 6, no. 1 (1995): 14–24.

Siddiqui, Mona, "Law and the Desire for Social Control: An Insight into the Hanafi Concept of *Kafa'a* with Reference to the Fatawa 'AlamgiriAlamgiri" in Mai Yamani (ed.) *Feminism in Islam: Legal and Literary Perspectives* (New York: New York University Press, 1996), 49–68.

Siddiqui, Mona, "The Defective Marriage in Classical Hanafi Law: Issues of Form and Validity" in G.R. Hawting, J.A. Mojaddedi, and A. Samely (eds.) *Studies in Middle Eastern Texts and Traditions in Memory of Norman Calder* (Oxford: Oxford University Press (on behalf of the University of Manchester), 2000).

Sonneveld, Nadia and Monika Lindbekk, *Women judges in the Muslim world: a comparative study of discourse and practice* (Leiden: Brill, 2017).

Sonbol, Amira El Azhary, *Women, the Family, and Divorce Laws in Islamic History*. Contemporary Issues in the Middle East (1st edn. Syracuse, NY: Syracuse University Press, 1996).

Spectorsky, Susan A., *Women in Classical Islamic Law : A Survey of the Sources*, Themes in Islamic Studies (Leiden; Boston: Brill, 2010).

Spectorsky, Susan A., *Chapters on Marriage and Divorce: Responses of Ibn Hanbal and Ibn Rahwayh*. [Selections from *Masa'il Ahmad ibn Hanbal*] (Austin: University of Texas Press, 1992).

Stockreiter, Elke, *Islamic law, gender, and social change in post-abolition Zanzibar* (New York: Cambridge University Press, 2015).

Stowasser, Barbara, "Legal Codes and Contemporary Fatawa: Muslim Women and Contesting Paradigms." *Hawwa* 6.1 (2008): 32–51.

Tillier, Mathieu, "Women before the Qādī under the Abbasids." *Islamic law and society* 16.3–4 (2009): 280–301.

Tucker, Judith E., "Problems in the historiography of women in the Middle, East: The case of nineteenth-century Egypt." *International Journal of Middle East Studies* 15, no. 3 (1983): 323.

Tucker, Judith E. *Women in nineteenth-century Egypt* (Cambridge: Cambridge University Press, 1985).

Tucker, Judith E., *In the House of Law Gender and Islamic Law in Ottoman Syria and Palestine* (Berkeley: University of California Press, 1998).

Tucker, Judith E., *Women, Family, and Gender in Islamic Law*. Themes in Islamic Law (Cambridge, UK and New York: Cambridge University Press, 2008).

Welchman, Lynn, "The Development of Islamic Family Law in the Legal System of Jordan." *International and Comparative Law Quarterly* 37 (1988): 868–886.

Welchman, Lynn, "Honour and Violence Against Women in a Modern Shar'i Discourse." *Hawwa* 5.2–3 (2007): 139–165.

Webb, Gisela, *Windows of Faith: Muslim Women Scholar-Activists in North America*. Women and Gender in North American Religions (Syracuse, NY: Syracuse University Press, 2000).

Yacoob, Saadia, "Hermeneutics of Desire: Ontologies of Gender and Desire in Early Hanafi Law." Ph.D. diss., Duke University, Durham, 2016.

Zilfi, Madeline, "Servants, Slaves, and the domestic order in the Ottoman Middle East." *Hawwa* 2.1 (2004): 1–33.

B

ISLAMIC LEGAL STUDIES: DISCIPLINARY APPROACHES

CHAPTER 4

ISLAMIC LAW AND THEOLOGY

RUMEE AHMED

I once traveled to Germany for a conference on Islamic law, and when I got to the train station a young German approached me and asked, "Are you here for a theology conference?" I answered, "No, I'm here for a law conference," and then watched as he took another look around the station, then got in his car, and drove away. I spent the next thirty minutes futilely waiting for my ride, before eventually giving up and catching a cab to the conference site, only to find that same young German greeting me at the door. In Germany, I belatedly learned, Islamic law is considered a sub-field of Islamic theology. This was strange to my North American ears, where Islamic law is seen as an independent social science, not to be confused with the more fanciful abstractions of theology. When I explained this to my hosts, they were incensed at such an odd, and in their view unnecessary, bifurcation. Debate ensued, and passions flared, as they sometimes do at conferences such as this.

This whole exchange might seem quaint; what difference does it make if Islamic law and theology are independent sciences, or if one is a sub-field of another? And why did we have such visceral reactions to one another? The answer lies in the fact that what seems like a mere academic debate reveals latent, deep-seated prejudices about who Muslims are, how Islam functions in their lives, and whether and/or how Islamic law evolves in response to changing circumstances. Positing a relationship between Islamic law and Islamic theology is a thoroughly political act that has direct implications for contemporary Islamic studies, whether that study is rooted in text or practice. That is because before positing a relationship between law and theology in Islamic thought, one must first construct a narrative of the Muslim community and its evolution. Such an enterprise necessarily speaks to the relationship that Muslims have with law and theology, and the presumed (in)ability for that relationship to change or evolve.

It should be no surprise, then, that the relationship between Islamic law and Islamic theology has been hotly debated amongst Islamic Studies scholars over the last century. Some scholars vociferously argue that Islamic law is the core of Islam, that theology is only a political tool, and that both ceased development after the year 900 CE. Others insist that the two sciences started out as equal and interconnected, and that they are meant to work together, but that law came to supersede theology over time, leading to intellectual stagnation. Theology, therefore, has to be "recovered" if Muslims are to practice their religious law in its fullness. Yet another camp contends that law and theology cannot be separated, that law and theology change together, and that the two are always extensions, one of another, as Muslim scholars continuously adapt to changing circumstances. Each of these camps relies on narratives of the Muslim community in which law and theology help shape and/or hinder social and intellectual growth and development.

In this chapter, I discuss three major approaches to this issue in Islamic Studies scholarship, which I am calling "Orientalist," "Revisionist," and "Pragmatist." This grouping reflects differing methods for reading Islamic source texts, and corresponds to different beliefs about those texts' relationship to the Muslim community. I describe the overarching narratives that each constructs to explain the historical relationship between law and theology. I then highlight the relationship of those narratives to contemporary attempts to reform Islamic law in order to demonstrate both the very real implications of the debate in the political sphere, and how those implications shape scholarship on the subject. I conclude by highlighting some of the gaps in research on this topic, and suggest avenues for further research.

I. Key Terms

There are two terms that should be clarified prior to engaging with the historiographical narratives of Islamic law and theology. The first is "law," which could mean several things. This chapter uses the term "law" in a very specific way, namely as *fiqh* (normative jurisprudence). *Fiqh* refers to injunctions enumerated in legal manuals that provide rulings for believers on myriad aspects of daily and ritual life on the personal, interpersonal, and state levels. These injunctions have normative descriptions attached to them, like "mandatory," "forbidden," "recommended," "reprehensible," or "permissible," depending on the personal opinion, method, and affiliation of the jurist who authors the legal manual. What these manuals represented and continue to represent in the lives of ordinary Muslims is a subject of debate, as will be discussed later.

The term "law" is not meant in the sense of "*shari'a*," which, though literally meaning "the way," practically came to be understood as the all-encompassing code of conduct that Muslims are meant to follow. The term "*shari'a*" is nebulous, and was historically used more as a rhetorical device than as a technical term.[1] "Law" is also not meant in the sense of "*qanun*," which refers to the state policies of certain postclassical Muslim empires, such as the Ottoman Empire. *Qanun* was often the purview of the ruling class, rather than that of the religious scholarly elite. It should be kept in mind that in this chapter, "law" refers only to *fiqh*, and though "law" is an inexact term of art in this case, it reflects the way that *fiqh* has been discussed by Islamic Studies scholars over the last 200 years.

The second term that requires definition is "theology." There is no exact cognate for "theology" in classical Islamic scholarly works. The closest two terms are *'ilm al-kalam* and *'aqida*. *'Ilm al-kalam* refers to works of dialectical theology, in which authors argue for particular views of God, creation, the intellect, revelation, prophethood, and the like; essentially providing "an authentic explanation of the world."[2] These treatises were usually less constructive and more defensive, protecting the doctrinal views of the author against heresies of all types. The second term, *'aqida*, refers to creedal works, in which Muslim scholars enumerated—usually in bullet point format—doctrines to which all Muslims must adhere if they are to be considered part of the believing community. Different authors would enumerate different doctrinal points, but creeds generally coalesced around major schools of thought. The term "theology" refers to some amalgamation of *'ilm al-kalam* and *'aqida*; again, this is inexact, but it is how Islamic Studies scholars have used the term.

With these definitions in mind, we can engage with the narratives promoted by three major historiographical approaches to Islamic law and theology. The first is that of the "Orientalists,"[3] characterized by a highly suspicious approach to Islamic religious texts, and a privileging of Enlightenment ideals. The second approach,

[1] See Ahmad Atif Ahmad, *The Fatigue of the Shari'a* (New York: Palgrave MacMillan, 2012), 51–54; Anver Emon, *Religious Pluralism and Islamic Law: Dhimmīs and Others in the Empire of Law* (Oxford: Oxford University Press, 2013), 176–204; Bernard Weiss, *The Spirit of Islamic Law* (Athens, GA: University of Georgia Press, 2006), 17–20.

[2] Josef van Ess, *The Flowering of Muslim Theology* (Cambridge, MA: Harvard University Press, 2006), 2.

[3] Though the term has now taken on pejorative overtones, this is the term that scholars in this group used to describe themselves. It is used in this chapter as an identity-marker, rather than as a critique. As a descriptor, the term "Essentialist" used by Frank Griffel is apropos; "Introduction," in *Shari'a*, A. Amanat and F. Griffel, eds., (Stanford: Stanford University Press, 2007), 7.

dubbed "Revisionist" in this chapter, attempts to free Islamic Studies from western preconceptions, and to re-read Islamic sources on their own terms. The final approach, called "Pragmatist," takes a critical look at Islamic texts, but tries to do so without over-determining that critique to fit within either Orientalist or Revisionist narratives of the Muslim community. As we will see, each approach has political implications for contemporary Islamic Studies, and makes bold claims about the nature of Islam and the structure and function of law and theology amongst believers.

II. Orientalists

As the reader will no doubt observe in other chapters in this volume, most academic discussions on the Islamic religious sciences trace back to the late nineteenth and early twentieth centuries, and certain names stand out from this time. Regularly cited are Ignác Goldziher, C. Snouck Hurgronje, D.S. Margoliouth, Louis Massignon, and especially Joseph Schacht. There is good reason to start any historiographical conversation about Islamic studies, especially Islamic legal studies, with these academic giants. They not only introduced the western academy to the depth of the Islamic intellectual tradition, often without overt evangelical overtones, but also described how and why Islamic thought developed within the historical Muslim community. They linked the intellectual tradition to historical events so as to provide an overarching narrative for the development of Islamic thought. This narrative was, of course, conjectural and based on the texts available to these scholars. Yet, it made a kind of holistic sense, and captured the imagination of Islamic studies scholars the world over. The narrative affected the way that scholars thereafter conceived of the Islamic sciences, and the relationship and hierarchy amongst them.

The Orientalist story begins with Muhammad, who was both prophet and statesman, and the embodied source of both law and theology. Muhammad fused the two, representing an ideal form of religiosity. His legal pronouncements changed over time to reflect his changing circumstances, and his theological discourses evolved to meet the growing curiosity and sophistication of his followers. In Muhammad's time, therefore, both law and theology were expressed through a kind of casuistry, meaning that context was the primary driver of doctrine. Whenever circumstance demanded a certain law or theological doctrine, Muhammad responded with revelation that addressed that circumstance.[4] These laws and theologies were

[4] Duncan MacDonald, *Development of Muslim Theology, Jurisprudence and Constitutional Theory* (New York: Russell and Russell, 1965), 70–71. Orientalists debated the reasons for this casuistry, with Hurgronje arguing that it was due to Muhammad's self-consciously weak judicial qualifications,

not readily forthcoming; Orientalists described Muhammad as hesitant in making strong pronouncements on either law or theology, preferring broad, flowery statements to hard details, providing detail only when pushed by necessity. Even then, his detailed pronouncements concerned only trifling matters; on most major issues, Muhammad gave his fledgling community precious little to go on. Lammens, capturing the Orientalist view of Muhammad, wrote,

> Forced by circumstances to legislate, he did so, sometimes with astonishing prolixity, and on questions of secondary importance, such as wills and inheritance. On the other hand, the Caliphate and the hierarchical organization of Islam are never touched upon. In the matter of religious legislation properly so-called, and of devotional life, the Medina *Suras* have forseen and solved only an insignificant number of problems … Naturally a temporalizer, [Muhammad] seems to have been afraid of using his authority …[5]

All of this presents a picture of Muhammad as a religious leader who relied mostly on personal charisma to guide his community, rather than on systematic beliefs and rules.

It is unsurprising, then, that when Muhammad died, there was a crisis regarding his succession. He left behind a personal legacy that included charismatic political authority and casuistic prophecy. A gifted diplomat could certainly emulate his example as a statesman, but there was debate over whether and how anyone could emulate his example as a prophet. In the first generation after Muhammad's death, and not without controversy, four of his companions came to rule in succession. They each adopted the title of "Caliph," or, "representative" of Muhammad. These Caliphs had the sanction of broad swaths of the Muslim community, and, as respected companions of Muhammad, they also had charismatic authority. Apart from the political power vested in them through the office of the Caliph, they "ruled by persuasion and force of personality."[6] The Caliphs themselves combined law and theology in their casuistic decrees, continuing the casuistic legacy of Muhammad. Law and theology might change, therefore, depending on context and the temperament of the Caliph. For instance, the second Caliph, 'Umar, was depicted as promoting a fatalistic, Arabo-centric God who favored the Arabs as His chosen people, much as He had earlier chosen the Children of Israel. The legal result of 'Umar's theological belief was that he actively discouraged non-Arabs from converting to Islam, and Arabs and non-Arabs had different rights and obligations under his rule;

whereas Wellhausen suggests that it is because Muhammad assumed Jewish and Christian norms, and only articulated new laws when either Judeo-Christian norms did not address the new situation, or if Muhammad wanted to contravene those norms to differentiate his new Arab religion; C. Snouck Hurgronje, *Mohammedanism: Lectures on its Origins its Religious and Political Growth* (New York: G.P. Putnam and Sons, 1916), 60; Julius Wellhausen, *The Arab Kingdom and Its Fall* (London: Routledge, 2000), 18–19.

[5] Henri Lammens, *Islam: Beliefs and Institutions* (London: Frank Cass & Co., 1968), 67.

[6] A.S. Tritton, *Islam: Beliefs and Practices* (London: Hutchinson's University Library, 1951), 109.

including extra taxes, special clothing, and limited political roles. In contrast, the fourth Caliph, 'Ali, was depicted as promoting a more justice-oriented, ethnically-egalitarian God; thus 'Ali accorded non-Arabs more legal rights than did 'Umar. In this example and in many others, the sheer authority of the Caliph in the eyes of the Muslim community allowed Caliphs to change laws and theological principles depending on circumstance and predilection.

The first four Caliphs claimed personal mandates from the community, and purported to represent Muhammad's interests after his demise. They claimed that, as close companions to Muhammad—and in each case, relatives of some sort—they were best suited to do so. This mandate was severed, however, when a sizable army, headed by the Umayyad clan, challenged 'Ali's right to rule. Over the course of several years, Ummayad partisans and 'Ali's partisans—both of whom included companions and relatives of Muhammad—fought against one another. When the Umayyads won the day, they established a hereditary dynasty that ruled for almost 100 years. Within the context of dynasty, though, no ruler could claim a similar charismatic authority or personal mandate to that of the first four Caliphs. That is primarily because dynastic succession precludes any communal sanction for the next leader. The ruler simply appoints one of his sons to succeed him, and that succeeding son does the same, and so on in perpetuity until the empire's demise. Such a process might make for smooth successions and dynastic stability, but it meant that the succeeding ruler did not have expressed communal sanction. Nor could these successive leaders, after the first generation, claim that they were companions of Muhammad, or that they had intimate knowledge of Muhammad's views and preferences. Thus, unlike the Prophet and the first four Caliphs, the Umayyad ruler was unable to embody the casuistic fusion of law and theology in his person. This meant that the Umayyad ruler could not claim the same religious and political authority that was so easily wielded by Muhammad and his four successors.

To address this problem, the Umayyads embarked on a conscious effort to set up official institutions that would create rules, regulations, and doctrines that responded to the context of their empire.[7] These institutions were stocked with state-sponsored scholars who articulated laws and theologies that justified state practices. Those laws happened to accord with whatever the state was doing at the time, and the accompanying theology was a fatalistic one that supported dynastic rule. In such a fatalist view, God determines all things, so that everything that comes to pass is with God's implicit sanction. Thus, the Umayyads were in power because God willed them to be, and God approved of their normative practice, else God would have replaced them. Based on this fatalistic theology, questioning Umayyad rule became akin to questioning God. The Umayyads had an interest in promoting such a theology because it both encouraged obedience and discouraged

[7] MacDonald, *Development*, 89, 124; Ignác Goldziher, *Muslim Studies* (London: Allen & Unwin, 1967–71), 2:38–29; Wellhausen, *The Arab Kingdom and Its Fall*, 26ff.

rebellion. By replacing Muhammad and the Caliphs with these political institutions, the Umayyad's normative practice itself became Islamic law, and the theologies articulated by the state-sponsored scholars became official Islamic theology.[8]

It is here that Orientalists placed the beginnings of an independent Islamic theology, describing it as a highly political enterprise, whether conducted by state or non-state actors.[9] The Umayyads, for their part, used their institutional authority to fill in the many theological gaps left by Muhammad, who, as Tritton characteristically stated, "was a preacher, not a theologian."[10] Since the Umayyads used a fatalistic theology to justify their rule, any religious resistance movement would have to articulate a counter-theology that both rejected the authoritativeness of Umayyad practice and justified rebellion against the ruling class.[11] One of these movements, described as the proto-Shi'i sect, staunchly rejected the fatalism of the Umayyads and insisted that the community must be led by a charismatic authority descended from Muhammad himself.[12] They argued that God was committed to justice, not fatalism, and that the normative practice of Muhammad and his descendants was authoritative, rather than the normative practice of the Umayyads. They developed a rebellious attitude toward the Umayyads, culminating in the Abbasid revolution.[13]

Another group, described as the proto-Sunni sect, argued that rulers needed the approval of the Muslim community for legitimacy.[14] In addition to their complaints against the blatant Arabism of the Umayyads, proto-Sunnis argued against fatalism, saying instead that, although God knows all things before they happen, God does not cause them to be so.[15] Humans choose to act in certain ways, and though God knows how they will act, God does not compel their action, nor does God approve of all actions. This theological move, known as the doctrine of *iktisab*, had two major consequences. The first is that though God may not compel present and future action, all past action was fully within God's knowledge and occurred by God's will. This absolved historical persons from worldly judgment without giving sanction

[8] See especially Joseph Schacht, *The Origins of Muhammadan Jurisprudence* (Oxford: Clarendon Press, 1967), 190ff.

[9] D.S. Margoliouth, *The Early Development of Mohammedenism* (New York: C. Scribner's Sons, 1914), 229.

[10] Tritton, *Islam*, 36.

[11] Orientalists had a deep interest in the Umayyad use and construction of *hadith*, which was the subject of great debate in the Muslim community, but since Orientalists did not directly link it to the development of law and theology, I have not discussed it here. For similar reasons, I do not discuss the Khariji/Murji'i movements.

[12] Wellhausen, *Religio-Political Factions in Early Islam* (New York: American Elsevier Pub. Co., 1975), 151–152.

[13] Wellhausen, *The Arab Kingdom and Its Fall*, 62ff. Wellhausen also credits failed Shi'i revolts with the Abbasid revolution, the latter of whom capitalized on the damage these revolts inflicted on the Umayyads, *Religio-Political Factions in Early Islam*, 165.

[14] Goldziher, *Muslim Studies*, 1:97–98; Wellhausen, *The Arab Kingdom and Its Fall*, 498.

[15] See Joseph Schacht, "New Sources for the History of Muhammadan Theology," *Studia Islamica* 1 (1953): 29–33.

to the present and future actions of a person or regime. The second, related consequence of *iktisab* is that, if God does not approve of all actions, then God does not *de facto* approve of the normative practice of the Umayyads. That meant that proto-Sunni Muslims had to find some new authority upon which to base normative practice.

The proto-Sunni community split into two factions based on two divergent sources of normative practice.[16] The first faction, known as the *ahl al-ra'y*, believed that Muslims should apply their intellect to the indubitable sources of law—specifically the Qur'an and well-attested *hadith*—to develop normative laws that address multiple contexts in which Muslims might find themselves. This conception of Islamic law was one that allowed for strong disagreement, and in which Islamic law could change based on circumstance. The second faction, known as the *ahl al-hadith*, was suspicious of the intellect, and advocated relying on reported sayings of Muhammad over and above speculation when deriving normative law. This conception of Islamic law demanded strict adherence to *hadith*, and allowed for much less disagreement than did the *ahl al-ra'y*.

After the fall of the Umayyads in the year 750, these proto-Sunni groups jostled for authority under the Abbasids, the latter of whom sometimes favored the *ahl al-ra'y* and sometimes the *ahl al-hadith*, and would variously apply the laws of one or another in state courts. State patronage put pressure on both groups to develop unified laws and legal theories, so that they could be applied at a state level and thus gain power.[17] By the late ninth century, major scholarly figures from both groups had articulated "official" laws through methods of argumentation characterized by different forms of casuistry.[18] These scholars formed sub-groups, and about ten of them were renowned for having formed legal "schools" that passed on their laws to future generations. In a short amount of time, these ten schools further consolidated into five, and then ultimately four. The normative laws that these four schools put forth in the ninth century were considered authoritative in perpetuity; they would not be modified or added to except in exceptional circumstances.[19]

In this conception of events, theology played a minimal role once the schools of law had reified.[20] Scholars were preoccupied with creating laws that would garner

[16] Goldziher, *Muslim Studies*, 2:78–82.

[17] Ibid., 1:72; Hurgronje, *Mohammedanism*, 109–110.

[18] Lammens describes the casuistry as follows, "These collections of quibbles, subterfuges and evasions that the jurisconsult recommends to his clients introduced a whole tradition of hypocritical laxity into the Sunni law: they permit believers to respect the letter in order the better to betray the spirit"; Lammens, *Islam*, 91.

[19] Noel J. Coulson, *Conflicts and Tensions in Islamic Jurisprudence* (Chicago: University of Chicago Press, 1969), 41–44; Joseph Schacht, *Islam* (Oxford: Oxford University Press, 1974), 394; Tritton, *Islam*, 64.

[20] According to Schacht, "The connexion of fact which exists between the other [non-Hanbali] schools of religious law and the schools of theology is rather of a personal and adventitious character." Schacht, "New Sources for the History of Muhammadan Theology," 39.

state patronage, and had no real concern for theology. Once the "official" schools of law were reified and laws were set, there was no need to reflect on the law, only to follow it. There were, to be sure, theologians who wrote expansive treatises on dialectical theology, and dogmatists who composed concise creeds, but these were peripheral to daily life and—apart from a cynical dalliance with theology on the state level in the ninth century—to the workings of empire.[21] Muslims had "immutable"[22] laws that regulated all aspects of their daily lives, and thus had no need for theology. Law, therefore, was more than just the crown jewel of the Islamic sciences; it was, according to Joseph Schacht, the "corn and kernel of Islam itself."[23] Anyone interested in studying how Muslims lived and thought ought to study law, and avoid all the other distracting, vanity sciences.

The preceding Orientalist story is powerful in that it provides a coherent narrative that starts with Muhammad and continues seamlessly to the modern day. Muslims, in this telling, are hostage to a law that reified in the ninth century, and have no theological tools to reconceive of their religion or the relation of law to the divine. The core of Muslim practice is to act and obey, not to reflect and reform; and so the process of legal reification was "natural and almost inevitable."[24] In the Orientalist narrative, reform movements are antithetical to the spirit of Islam, and though reformers have cropped up now and again, they are exceptional in their defiance of Islamic norms.[25] It is therefore no wonder, Orientalists explain, that Muslims have a difficult time adapting to modern, western values, and that they valorize adherence to an historical law, rather than derivation of new and relevant laws.[26]

Needless to say, this narrative paints a rather unflattering picture of historical Muslim thought. The early community, which Orientalists defined as Muslims prior to the ninth century when the law reified, is portrayed as cynically motivated by political casuistry as opposed to religious piety. Muslim thought after the ninth century is characterized as stagnant, uncreative, and irremediable. The complete lack of theological sophistication and legal development led Orientalists like Margoliouth to write that "Islam is far more a political system than a religious system."[27] According

[21] MacDonald, *Development*, 135; Tritton, *Islam*, 41.

[22] J.N.D. Anderson, *Islamic Law in the Modern World* (New York: New York University Press, 1959), 3.

[23] Schacht, *Islam*, 392. See also, Gotthelf Bergstrasser, *Grundzüge des islamischen Rechts* (Leipzig: W. de Gruyter, 1935), 1.

[24] Joseph Schacht, "Modernism and Traditionalism in a History of Islamic Law," *Middle Eastern Studies* 1, no. 4 (1965): 390.

[25] Lammens, *Islam*, 179; Joseph Schacht, *The Legacy of Islam* (Oxford: Clarendon Press, 1974), 400. Massignon believed that reform only began with Jamal al-Din al-Afghani, and he equated/limited reform groups to the emerging Salafiyya movement, in which he placed great hope. Yet, Massignon still believed that any theological change the Salafis might effect would be slow, if at all; Louis Massignon, "What Moslems Expect: An Introductory Study of Moslem Demands," *The Muslim World* 12, no. 1 (1922): 20–21.

[26] Hurgronje, *Mohammedanism*, 118–119, 133.

[27] D.S. Margoliouth, *The Early Development of Mohammedanism*, 229.

to Orientalists, this politically-centered heritage has given modern Muslims few religious tools at their disposal to reform and rethink their religion.

In the mid-twentieth century, however, Islamic Studies scholars revisited historical texts in an explicit attempt to view them on their own terms. They read the texts without assuming a latent political agenda, and tried to uncover their internal logic without reducing them to their accordance with or opposition to Enlightenment values. At the same time, Muslim Islamic Studies scholars entered the conversation, presenting a different narrative of historical events. This new narrative was difficult to dismiss out of hand since they relied on the same sources as did the Orientalists. A number of Islamic Studies scholars began to rethink, or, "revise" the grand narrative, and to suggest that the historical development of the Islamic tradition—especially as related to law and theology—was more complicated than the Orientalists would have us believe. A sizable group, including Wilfred Cantwell-Smith, H.A.R. Gibb, Fazlur Rahman, Annemarie Schimmel, and Montgomery Watt retold the grand narrative with respect to new empirical findings and a growing scholarly interest in the subaltern. Their reimagining of the origins of Islamic law and theology influenced a generation of Islamic Studies scholars, and continues to influence modern thought related to Islam and Muslims.

III. Revisionists

In this new narrative, Muhammad was less of a casuistic tribal chief and more of a religious revivalist and social justice advocate. He and his early community were animated by a core message embedded in the Qur'an that traced its origins back to Abraham. This message was one of radical monotheism, accountability in a life to come, and social justice. In bursting, eloquent poetry and prose, the early Qur'an spoke of a just God who commands obedience and ethical conduct. Those in Mecca who believed in this message formed a dedicated community of believers reflecting that ethos. This community was given a chance to institutionalize their values and demonstrate both their obedience to God and their ethical character in the context of the nascent city-state of Medina. There, they attempted to institute a polity that would reflect God's wisdom and justice.

The Qur'anic verses revealed in Medina also discussed theology and ethical conduct, but often did so in the language of the mundane. Mixed in with grand calls to establish justice and engage in fair dealings were quotidian rules of conduct, ranging from guest etiquette to inheritance divisions to terms of warfare. These rules reflected the divine intention, and the spirit animating the Medinan verses was a just God guiding a pious community as it grew and evolved, not of a prophet making ad hoc decisions. Amidst these quotidian rules were a handful of punitive laws that were the minority, rather than the focus, of Medinan verses.

Thus, a picture of the early Muslim community emerged with God at the center, and in which religiosity is irreducible to any one descriptor, like "legal" or "theological." Instead, this community was concerned with right conduct; they were, to use Marshall Hodgson's term, "piety-minded."[28] Being part of this religious community did not require expertise in either law or theology, but rather "knowledge" (*ʿilm*).[29] The science of *ʿilm* concerned how one should conduct oneself so as to be obedient to God, and be an upright member of society; *ʿilm* was about far more than the particularities of law, it was about the religion as a whole. According to Gibb, "for the early Muslims, there was little or no distinction between 'legal' and 'religious.'"[30]

The community continued in this vein through the first four Caliphs, after which there was a rupture with the emergence of the Umayyad Empire. The Umayyads introduced an important innovation that would change the face of the community. This was not a theological innovation; certainly, the Umayyads promoted a fatalistic, Arabo-centric theology, but it was relatively unsuccessful in gaining adherents. As a doctrine, fatalism had to compete with many other theologies that arose in the wake of the first Muslim civil war decades earlier,[31] and proved far less popular than doctrines promoted by the likes of al-Hasan al-Basri (d. 728), who tried to mediate between predestination and freewill.[32] Rather, the Umayyads' important innovation was a centralized system of judges (*qadis*) who would represent the Caliphate. The judges would pronounce on matters of law and law alone, giving sanction to certain rulings over others. Their judicial rulings did not constitute a precedent, nor were they rooted in a codified source, but they demonstrated a certain bias toward existing Umayyad policies. Thus, the most visible and most tangible manifestation of the empire was the court system, which dispensed legal rulings in favor of the empire.

In contrast to the court-appointed judges arose a piety-minded class of scholars who were experts in *ʿilm*, and therefore called "*ʿulama*" (people of knowledge), and who developed normative systems of law based on their understanding of the Qur'an and the practices of Muhammad.[33] They might have applied their own modes of reasoning to these sources, thus mitigating claims to objectivity, but at least they

[28] Marshall Hodgson, *The Venture of Islam* (Chicago: University of Chicago Press, 1977), 1:250ff.

[29] Fazlur Rahman, *Islam*, 2nd edn. (Chicago: University of Chicago Press, 2002), 101–102.

[30] H.A.R. Gibb, *Islam: A Historical Survey* (Oxford: Oxford University Press, 1969), 61. Rahman stated, "Indeed, at this stage, law can hardly be separated or even distinguished from administration."; Gibb, *Islam*, 79. See also Franz Rosenthal, *Knowledge Triumphant: The Concepts of Knowledge in Medieval Islam* (Brill: Leiden, 2007), 19ff.

[31] Montgomery Watt, *Islamic Philosophy and Theology: An Extended Survey* (Edinburgh: University of Edinburgh Press, 1985), 2.

[32] Watt, *Islamic Philosophy and Theology*, 27–28.

[33] Rahman, *Islam*, 80.

could argue that they derived law without any predisposition toward state policy. The *'ulama* had many and varied approaches to law that reflected their various contexts and predilections. Whereas Orientalists place the beginnings of formalized law and theology with the Umayyad regime's machinations, Revisionists credit the *'ulama* with fleshing out law and theology independently from the state.[34] It is true, Revisionists concede, that the Umayyads sometimes poached members of the scholarly class to serve as judges, but most scholars were not affiliated with the state, and prided themselves on that fact. These scholars in the late-Umayyad period were primarily concerned with *'ilm*,[35] but it was their pronouncements on normative law that comprised the clearest declarations of independence from the perceived injustice and Arabo-centrism of the Umayyads and their judiciary.

It is no surprise, then, that political opponents of the Umayyads found a natural ally in the *'ulama*. The former seized on the legal opinions of the *'ulama* and presented them in contradistinction to the policies of the Umayyads. If the Umayyads were overthrown, the opposition claimed, then the law of the *'ulama* could be implemented through the offices of both the Caliph and the *qadi*, and justice would be established on earth. As a result of linking social justice to the application of just laws—and not to a just theology—the opposition reduced the *'ilm* of the scholars to *fiqh*. The piety-minded became known for their adherence to the law, and thereafter piety-mindedness was equated with shari'a-mindedness.[36]

The shari'a-minded opposition to the Umayyads culminated in the Abbasid revolution. Both the *'ulama* and the Muslim masses expected a reversal of Umayyad policies in the wake of the revolution, but the Abbasid leadership betrayed the revolutionaries and re-instantiated many Umayyad political structures and policies. The shari'a-minded *'ulama* retreated to their private study circles and set about explaining normative law in ever more detailed and systematic ways, free from direct political influence.[37] The Abbasids tried to co-opt them through judgeships and seminary positions, but most *'ulama* were already ensconced in complex systems of patronage that involved ruling tribes and local communities, and were able to eschew official Abbasid patronage. Within their circles of study, the *'ulama* coalesced into legal schools (*madhhab*s), vying with one another to best articulate laws that captured God's will.

Elite groups of shari'a-minded scholars thereafter debated about the law within and amongst *madhhab*s. The reality of the lived community was often peripheral to these debates. Since *'ulama* were not directly involved in the workings of the state, except sometimes as judges, they primarily concerned themselves with articulating

[34] Gibb argued that Medina was a particularly fecund site for Islamic theology to develop precisely because it did not have strong state intervention; Gibb, *Islam*, 74–75.

[35] W.C. Smith, in fact, states that the shari'a was not a central concern and was not intended to mean "law" at all, but rather "morality"; Smith, *On Understanding Islam* (Mouton: The Hague, 1981), 97–109.

[36] Hodgson, *The Venture of Islam*, 1:315ff.

[37] H.A.R. Gibb, "An Interpretation of Islamic History—I," *The Muslim World* 45, no. 1 (1955): 11–12.

an ideal, rarified law. Muslims were neither bound to act according to this law nor did the law reflect Muslim practice. That is partly because jurists were not involved in day-to-day affairs of local governance; and although judges affiliated with legal schools adjudicated everyday matters, the ultimate legal authority was always with the local sultan and his administration. Thus, Islamic legal discussions were highly theoretical, and addressed legal situations that might never have occurred, coming to conclusions that had no necessary correlate in communal practice.

By the tenth century, legal schools had grown in size and stature, and their leadership began to insist that their laws were fixed and inviolable. The *'ulama* became more interested in promoting the positions of their schools than in providing practical guidance. In Hodgson's words, "the kerygmatic force of Shari'ah-minded piety had been reduced in favour of a greater degree of ritualistic 'paradigm-tracing' piety; that is, Muslims were more inclined to articulate the patterns of proper Shar'i life into an enduring, almost natural cosmos, in which the Qur'anic message was an eternal datum almost as much as it was a challenging event."[38] Islamic law became a good in and of itself, and jurists were more concerned with its internal logic than its role in the promotion of justice and *'ilm*. Thereafter, Islam became a religion characterized by "orthopraxy, not orthodoxy."[39] As they fleshed out more and more of the legal system and adopted official positions for their legal schools, jurists had decreasing leeway to revise and reform earlier laws, and could only accommodate minor changes to the law, especially those that dealt with novel or extreme circumstances.

Once Islamic law became more or less reified, *'ulama* started devoting their energy toward more theoretical reflections on law in a genre known as *usul al-fiqh* (legal theory), which George Makdisi called "juridical theology."[40] Starting in the ninth century with al-Shafi'i, and then with increasing frequency in the eleventh century, jurists wrote detailed legal theory manuals, seeking to explain the theoretical and theological underpinnings of the law. Revisionists, following the lead of some classical *'ulama*, categorized these writings into one of two methodologies.[41] The first method was "the way of the theologians," in which jurists enumerated theoretical principles according to which all law should be derived. These principles were to serve as the basis for deriving new laws and abandoning any old laws that might no longer serve higher principles, allowing independent legal reasoning (*ijtihad*) once again to play a role in articulating the law. The second method was "the way of the jurists," in which theoretical principles were induced to explain the

[38] Hodgson, *The Venture of Islam*, 2:179.

[39] Montgomery Watt, "The Future of Islam," in *Religion and Culture in Medieval Islam*, eds. Hovannisian and Sabagh (Cambridge: Cambridge University Press, 1999), 28.

[40] George Makdisi, "Classical Islam and the Christian West," in *Religion and Culture in Medieval Islam*, eds. Hovannisian and Sabagh (Cambridge: Cambridge University Press, 1999), 7.

[41] George Makdisi, "The Juridical Theology of Shâfi'î: Origins and Significance of Uṣûl al-Fiqh," *Studia Islamica* 59 (1984): 26.

laws that were already derived. In the first method, the law is subject to higher principles, and in the second, principles are only valid inasmuch as they agree with existing laws.

As might be surmised, theology was front and center in "the way of the theologians." Jurists writing according to this method deliberated on how issues like free will and the nature of God's speech affected the human obligation to act according to God's law and the ability for God's speech to command obedience in perpetuity. But as shari'a-mindedness grew amongst the *ulama*, there was less appetite to discuss such theological matters, and scholars chose instead to focus on the particularities of the law.[42] Thus, though the "way of the theologians" was initially ascendant, the "way of the jurists" enjoyed dominance from the eleventh century onwards.[43] Eventually, legal theory, too, began to reify, and with the fall of the 'Abbasids, according to Revisionists, "the gate of *ijtihad* was closed."[44]

Thereafter, theology was a side issue that never regained its earlier prominence. By the fourteenth century it was practically dormant, with some citing Ibn Taymiyya (d. 1328) as the last true Muslim jurist–theologian.[45] State functionaries on occasion used theology to justify the ruling structure and promote a kind of political quietism that would lead believers to focus more on the details of the law than on revolution.[46] As a science of its own, however, theology was more akin to philosophy, which was seen as the fanciful abstractions of the educated elite.[47] According to Izutsu, some scholars might have devised "elaborate systems of theology," but those were "nothing but a theocratic treatment of the basic problem of what a 'true believer' should believe in, what kind of attitude he should take towards God, and how he should act according to the dictates of his belief."[48] Theology had no practical function, neither in legal discourse nor in the life of the Muslim community.

[42] Gibb states that *'ilm* began to be associated with theology, and *fiqh* with shari'a; *Islam*, 61.

[43] Baber Johansen, *Contingency in a Sacred Law: Legal and Ethical Norms in Muslim Fiqh* (Leiden: Brill, 1999), 32.

[44] Gibb, *Islam*, 66. This is a common trope to be found throughout revisionist writing; for its specific use with relation to law and theology, see Mawil Izzi Dien, *Islamic Law: From Historical Foundations to Contemporary Practice* (Edinburgh: Edinburgh University Press, 2004), 27–29.

[45] Rahman, *Islam*, 113–114. William Shepard, *Introducing Islam* (London: Routledge, 2009), 140.

[46] Fazlur Rahman, "The Post-Formative Developments in Islam," *Islamic Studies* 1, no. 4 (1962): 8.

[47] In fact, writers in this group explicitly linked theology to philosophy. See, for instance, chapter headings like "Philosophy and Kalam" in books on Islam and the Islamic Sciences, or chapters on theology that discuss philosophy, and vice versa. Richard C. Taylor chalks their differences up to education setting, "*kalam* and *falsafa* existed as parallel discourses … with *kalam* having a place inside religious institutions such as schools and mosques, while *falsafa* was taught separately as a secular science espoused by Muslims, Christians, Jews and others outside the confines of their religious confessions"; "Philosophy," in *The New Cambridge History of Islam, Volume 4*, ed. Robert Irwin (Cambridge: Cambridge University Press, 2010), 533. See also, e.g., Rahman, *Islam*, 94–99; Annemarie Schimmel, *Islam: An Introduction* (Albany, NY: State University Press New York, 1992), 73ff.

[48] Toshiko Izutsu, *Ethico-Religious Concepts in the Qur'an* (Montreal, Que.: McGill University Press, 2002), 3.

The Revisionist narrative of Islamic law and theology gained prominence in the mid-twentieth century, and coincided with the rise of self-determination and anti-colonial sentiments in the western and Muslim worlds. Many anti-colonial activists adopted the Revisionist story of Islamic law wholesale and touted Islam as a holistic system that would create a just society through both its theological principles and its legal injunctions. Rather than being the product of unguided casuistry, Islamic law and theology grew out of a core spirit of piety that animated the early Muslim community.[49] In line with Revisionist thinking, anti-colonial activists saw this early community as having a multifaceted vision of Islam in which law and theology were interwoven in the science of *'ilm*, and both reflected an inner devotion to God. It was only when the shari'a-minded opposition to the Umayyads co-opted the language of law that was embedded within pietistic discourse that law became detached from its theological moorings. Law was thereafter seen as a good unto itself, and its practical quality made it attractive to scholars and laypersons alike. It is therefore unsurprising that Orientalists viewed Islamic law as the most authentic expression of Islam, given that they were reading works by post-Umayyad, shari'a-minded *'ulama*. However, if Muslims were to return to the original *'ilm* that was prominent in the time of Muhammad and amongst the early *'ulama*, they could create a just society that would correct the wrongs committed by medieval Muslim empires, shari'a-minded *'ulama*, and colonial powers. Such a vision of Islam's true spirit was popular amongst Islamic revivalists and self-determination movements alike.

The Revisionist retelling also points out an important aspect of Islamic law that was previously overlooked; namely, that legal discourse was the exclusive purview of the educated elite. Legal works did not reflect social reality; instead they presented arguments for what Muslims were *supposed* to do.[50] In this rarified discourse, Muslim jurists were more interested in the coherence of their doctrines than in their impact on Muslim communities. Yet, jurists were not merely conjecturing about law in the abstract; rather, jurists were part of a complex web of interrelations—which included colleagues within one's legal school, historical precedent, local customs, state actors, political/personal rivals, and patrons—and developed law within that complex. In response to these factors, they sometimes changed minor points of law to reflect evolving circumstances, even if they resisted change in general. Expressions of Islamic law amongst shari'a-minded *'ulama*, then, were contextually-bound

[49] Ebrahim Moosa notes that, for Fazlur Rahman, the idea of subjectivity was therefore problematic; there must be some objective core spirit of Islam that can be scientifically retrieved; Fazlur Rahman, *Revival and Reform in Islam* (Oxford: Oneworld, 2000), 19–20. Rahman was particularly influential in his argument that the core message of the Qur'an animated the early community's piety, in works like "Some Key Ethical Concepts of the Qur'an," *Journal of Religious Ethics* 11, no. 2 (1983): 170–185; "Islamization of Knowledge: A Response," *Islamic Studies* no. 3/4 (2011): 449–457; and *Major Themes of the Qur'an* (Minneapolis, MN: Bibliotheca Islamica, 1980).

[50] W.C. Smith, *Islam in the Modern World* (Princeton: Princeton University Press, 1957), 19–20.

abstractions; they did not capture the reality of Muslim societies, nor were they inevitable conclusions to which all Muslims are forever bound.

Revisionists are agreed that theology was eventually pushed out of all legal and ethical conversations.[51] Islamic law may have started out as a theological enterprise within an *ʿilm*-based discourse, but eventually shariʿa-mindedness denuded *ʿilm* of all but legal concerns. The same was to happen to *usul al-fiqh*, which was an explicit project of the "theologians" but was co-opted by the "jurists." The underlying theme is that Islam began as a coherent theologico-legal movement that was embodied by a pietistic community. Over time, however, the focus on *ʿilm* shifted to a focus on law, and law became the highest source for legitimation. This was only an historical accident,[52] and though law came to represent one of the highest levels of Islamic scholarly discourse, it is by no means the true "corn and kernel of Islam itself," as the Orientalists believed.[53]

There are tangible implications resulting from this Revisionist retelling for both scholars of Islam and contemporary Muslims. "True Islam"[54] is portrayed as a highly theological enterprise,[55] and if Muslims wish to return to their historical roots, they must re-engage with theology.[56] This might mean approaching Islam from a primarily philosophical or theological viewpoint, and demonstrating the relevance of Islam to all contexts on a theoretical level.[57] It might also mean returning to "the way of the theologians" in *usul al-fiqh*, and outlining the ethical legal principles (*maqasid al-shariʿa*) that should underlie the derivation of Islamic law.[58] By doing so, contemporary Muslims can cut through centuries of irrelevant positive law and derive new laws that accord to a theology of justice and promote modern values.[59]

[51] Kevin Reinhart, "Islamic Law as Islamic Ethics," *Journal of Religious Ethics* 11, no. 2 (1983): 186–187.

[52] George Makdisi, "The Significance of the Sunni Schools of Law in Islamic Religious History," *International Journal of Middle East History* 10, no. 1 (1979): 6.

[53] Smith, *On Understanding Islam*, 108–109.

[54] Whether or not scholars in this mold called this core spirit "true Islam" or not, it was an implicit assumption in their analysis. Hodgson, for instance, was roundly criticized for advocating for "true Islam," despite his attempts to skirt that criticism; see Earle Waugh, "An Evasive Vision," *History of Religions* 18, no. 2 (November 1978): 197; John Wansbrough, "[Review] The Venture of Islam: Conscience and History in a World Civilization by Marshall G.S. Hodgson," *Bulletin of the School of Oriental and African Studies, University of London*, 40, no. 1 (1977): 170.

[55] Smith, *Islam in the Modern World*, 3–9.

[56] Nasr Hamid Abu Zayd, *Reformation of Islamic Thought* (Amsterdam: Amsterdam University Press, 2006), 15.

[57] Hasan Hanafi, *Dirasat Islamiyya* (Cairo: Maktabat al-Anghlu al-Misriyya, 1981), 7ff.

[58] Muhammad Abduh, "Laws Should Change in Accordance with the Conditions of Nations and the Theology of Unity," in *Modernist Islam 1840–1940: A Sourcebook*, ed. Charlez Kurzman (New York: Oxford University Press USA, 2002), 53; Jasser Auda, "A Maqaṣidi Approach to Contemporary Application of the Shariʿah," *Intellectual Discourse* 19, no. 2 (2011), 193–215; Abdulaziz Sachedina, *The Islamic Roots of Democratic Pluralism* (New York: Oxford University Press, 2001), 45.

[59] See, for instance, Mohammad Hashim Kamali, "Law and Ethics in Islam—The Role of the Maqaṣid," in *New Directions in Islamic Thought*, eds. K. Vogt, L. Larsen, and C. Moe (New York: I.B. Tauris, 2009), 23–46.

The Revisionists have been highly successful in influencing thought in the academy and beyond.[60] By advocating a "return to theology," they offer a method for recapturing the original spirit of Islam, and for articulating Islamic law so that it responds to contemporary concerns.[61] This fueled a surge of interest in Islamic philosophy and in theoretical discussions that identify unchanging principles that should underlie Islamic law.

However, starting in the mid-1990s, many scholars—whom we will call "Pragmatists" for their attention to the socio-political implications of law and theology—began to question the narrative presented by Revisionists. Pragmatists suggest that theology was not as peripheral to the development of Islamic jurisprudence after the tenth century as Revisionists would claim.

In fact, the Pragmatists argue, theology was always of central import in the articulation of Islamic law, not only in *usul al-fiqh*, but in *fiqh* itself. Pragmatists hold that theological concerns permeated legal discussions throughout the medieval period, and continue to do so in the modern day. That is because law and theology are always politically-inflected attempts to understand how God and humans relate to one another in the world, and are thus inextricably bound. Islamic law is always a statement about theology; theology is always a statement about law; and both are always related to one's socio-political context. Sometimes the theological and political concerns in law are explicit, but more often they are implicit, expressing themselves in subtle, but far-reaching ways.

IV. Pragmatists

The re-conceived narrative promoted by Pragmatists is informed by two major developments: one in theology and one in law. In theology, Josef van Ess provided a new and exquisitely detailed picture of the early community's theological character in his landmark *Theologie und Gesellschaft im 2. und 3. Jahrhundert Hidschra.*[62] In six volumes, published between 1991 and 1997, van Ess carefully reconstructed the theological thought of Muslim figures in the eighth and ninth centuries, and

[60] R. Michael Feener, "Cross-Cultural Contexts of Modern Muslim Intellectualism," *Die Welt des Islams* 47, no. 3/4 (2007): 274ff.

[61] Jeffry Halverson, *Theology and Creed in Sunni Islam: the Muslim Brotherhood, Ash'arism, and Political Sunnism* (New York: Palgrave Macmillan, 2010), 56; Peter Mandaville, "When Meaning Travels: Muslim Translocality and the Politics of 'Authenticity'," in *Meaning and International Relations*, eds. P. Mandaville and A. Williams (London: Routledge, 2003), 132–133.

[62] Josef van Ess, *Theologie und Gesellschat im 2. Und 3. Jahrhudert Hidschra (Band 1–6)* (Berlin: DeGruyter, 1991–97).

his reconstruction suggests a vibrant theological diversity. Theologically-inclined persons and small groups cropped up across Muslim lands throughout Umayyad and early Abbasid rule,[63] usually in the form of loose organizations, with nothing so formal as a creed. These groups were largely political, and the theology that they espoused reflected political grievances and aspirations. They, in turn, inspired rival theologies that were also politically-inflected, so that theological debates were often proxies for political arguments.[64] That is not to say that theology was merely a vehicle for the piety-minded to express their political concerns, but that the link between theology and politics was self-conscious and inescapable.[65]

In the field of law, Pragmatist scholars described a similarly diverse—or chaotic, depending on one's point of view—situation. In contrast to Orientalist scholars who described the early community as coalescing around major pious figures in the eighth and ninth centuries, Pragmatist scholars characterize the early community as engaging in regular and sustained debate amongst the *'ulama*.[66] Within any given city or township, there might have been several strands of legal thought and practice, each championed by different *'ulama* with their own conceptions of law and theology. Some might have been more shari'a-minded, and some might have been less so; there was no clear dichotomy between law and theology, nor was there a clear consensus amongst the *'ulama* on most issues. This means that there were no major legal schools with set principles and legal positions in the first couple of centuries of Islam,[67] nor were there distinct theological groups.[68]

Instead, there were individual *'ulama* and study groups that might gravitate toward what we would now associate with discrete legal and theological schools. Over time, these individuals formed associations based on shared teachers and ideas. By the ninth century, these associations began to reverse-attribute their legal and theological opinions back in time to prominent historical persons and particular locales.[69] This was done for the purpose of giving the association a sense of history, continuity, and consensus. As these associations gained a sense of self-identity, they became full-fledged "schools of thought" (*madhhabs*), with distinct theological and legal positions. Their theological positions informed how they *applied* law rather

[63] R. Stephen Humphreys, "Syria," in *The New Cambridge History of Islam: Volume 1*, ed. Chase F. Robinson (Cambridge: Cambridge University Press, 2010), 525.

[64] Muhammad Qasim Zaman, *Religion and Politics Under the Early Abbasids* (Leiden: Brill, 1997), 63.

[65] Josef van Ess, "The Beginnings of Islamic Theology," in *The Cultural Context of Medieval Learning*, eds. J.E. Murdoch and E.D. Sylla (Dordrecht, Holland: D. Reidel, 1975), 101.

[66] O. Arabi, D. Powers, and S. Spectorsky, eds. "Introduction," in *Islamic Legal Thought: A Compendium of Muslim Jurists* (Brill: Leiden, 2013), 2.

[67] Christopher Melchert, "How Hanafism Came to Originate in Kufa and Traditionalism in Medina," *Islamic Law and Society* 6, no. 3 (1999): 346.

[68] Pragmatists believe this to be true even of schools that rely heavily on the legal and theological positions of its founders, such as the Zaydi school; see Muhammad Ali Aziz, *Religion and Mysticism in Early Islam* (London: I.B. Tauris, 2011), 20.

[69] Leor Halevi, *Muhammad's Grave* (New York: Columbia University Press, 2007), 239.

than how they *derived* law. If a school held, for instance, that God commanded complete conformity to a single jurisprudence, then law should be applied with little consideration for changing circumstances. If, on the other hand, God only intended for humans to live by moral principles, then law could look different when applied in different contexts.

By the tenth century, *'ulama* began to fully identify with particular schools of law, and started to separate out their legal, theoretical, and theological expositions into distinct genres of writing that represented their school. *Fiqh* captured the legal dictates held by a single school, *usul al-fiqh* described how those dictates were to be applied, and *'aqida* outlined the logic that informs the application of law as a salvific practice. Pragmatists argue that although these were separate genres, they informed one another, and one did not make sense in practice without the other.[70] After all, what can be done with jurisprudence when one does not know how to apply it, and how can one know how to apply the law without knowing what God expects from believers? Each legal injunction, therefore, has connected, or, "concomitant" positions in legal theory and theology that inform how that injunction is to be understood and applied. This means that texts were not divided into distinct approaches, like "the way of the theologians" or "the way of the jurists," but that they were all legal, theological, and political at the same time. [71]

Pragmatist scholars also call into question the previous narratives in which law ceased development after the tenth century, and theology ceased development after the fourteenth century. Wael Hallaq demonstrated that medieval scholars did not themselves think that "the gate of *ijtihad* has closed," so modern scholars have little cause to claim it to be so.[72] The only reason that scholars assumed that law and theology were stagnant was because texts from the medieval period tend to look very similar, with similar premises and similar conclusions. However, as Baber Johansen and many after him have shown, this similarity is superficial. In fact, legal positions changed with startling regularity, as did the theological and legal theory positions concomitant to those laws.[73] One needs to know how to read the sources

[70] Weiss, *The Spirit of Islamic Law*, 25. Weiss captures the interrelated nature of the genres in an endnote, "The grounding (*tawaqquf, istimdad*) of jurisprudence in theology was customarily established in the opening sections of the works on usul al-fiqh" (191).

[71] Anver Emon, *Islamic Natural Law Theories* (Oxford: Oxford University Press, 2010), 191–193. Hallaq said of legal theory that it "presupposed theology for the foundational premises upon which it was squarely based"; Wael Hallaq, *A History of Islamic Legal Theories* (Cambridge: Cambridge University Press, 1997), 256.

[72] Wael Hallaq, "Was the Gate of Ijtihad Closed?" *International Journal of Middle East Studies* 16, no. 1 (1984): 3ff.

[73] For studies on how and why these changes occurred, see Rumee Ahmed, "The Ethics of Prophetic Disobedience," *Journal of Religious Ethics* 39, no. 4 (2011); Najam Haider, "Contesting Intoxication: Early Juristic Debates over the Lawfulness of Alcoholic Beverages," *Islamic Law and Society* 20, no. 1–2 (2012), 48–89; Baber Johansen, *The Islamic Law on Land Tax and Rent* (London: Croom Helm, 1988); Judith Tucker, *In the House of the Law: Gender and Islamic Law in Ottoman Syria and Palestine* (Berkeley, CA: University of California Press, 1998), especially 11ff.

to understand how to identify and measure those changes, but they are indeed present and persistent.[74]

As Muslim empires rose and fell, state-sponsored *'ulama* were able to manipulate law and theology to serve the purposes of empire. They worked within the system of concomitance to change laws to suit their needs, and they adopted theologies that encouraged applications of law that might best promote the positions of the ruling elite.[75] Resistance movements and dissident *'ulama*, for their part, would espouse laws and theologies that questioned the legitimacy of the ruling elite, and argued for political ideals that countered the existing setup. Both state-sponsored *'ulama* and dissident *'ulama* would argue for political ends through the language of law and theology,[76] which sometimes involved resurrecting minority opinions and presenting them as normative[77]; sometimes concocting new laws and characterizing them as ancient[78]; and sometimes developing new laws and suggesting that they are natural extensions of historical laws.[79] In all cases, theological ideals, whether expressed or not, worked hand-in-hand with laws to buttress a religious and political vision of a just society,[80] whether seen from above or below.[81]

All of this calls into question the Revisionist view of the early community as a piety-minded, *'ilm*-centered movement that devolved into shari'a-mindedness. Instead, Pragmatists argue that theology and law started out responding to local politics and that some of these trends became ascendant over time due to their success in gaining adherents and their efficacy in changing with the changing fortunes of both empire and judiciary. However, law and theology were always interrelated

[74] Norman Calder, "Islamic Law," in *A History of Islamic Philosophy*, eds. S.H. Nasr and O. Leaman (London: Routledge, 1996), 2:986.

[75] Rudolph Peters, "What Does it Mean to be an Official Madhhab?" in *The Islamic School of Law: Evolution, Devolution, and Progress*, eds. P. Bearman, R. Peters, and F. Vogel (Cambridge, MA: Harvard University Press, 2005), 157–158.

[76] The use of law and theology for political ends was certainly not limited to dissidents and ruling elites. Seemingly apolitical Sufi works have been shown to be heavily political. It is being argued that the works of Muslim philosophers, usually seen to be purely theoretical, were actually better understood as political theology; Rumee Ahmed, "Jurisprudence and Islamic Philosophy," in *Routledge Companion to Islamic Philosophy* (London: Routledge, 2015); Massimo Campanini, "Alfarabi and the Foundation of Political Theology in Islam," in *Islam, the State, and Political Authority: Medieval Issues and Modern Concerns*, ed. Asma Afsaruddin (New York: Palgrave MacMillan, 2011), 35–52.

[77] Jon E. Mandaville, "Usurious Piety: The Cash Waqf Controversy in the Ottoman Empire," *International Journal of Middle East Studies* 10, no. 3 (1979): 298–300.

[78] Amira E. Sonbol, "Adults and Minors in Ottoman Shari'a Courts and Modern Law," in *Women, the Family, and Divorce Laws in Islamic History*, ed. Amira E. Sonbol (Syracuse: Syracuse University Press, 1996), 256; for several examples in the South Asian context, see Muhammad Qasim Zaman, *The Ulama in Contemporary Islam* (Princeton: Princeton University Press, 2002).

[79] Guy Burak, "The Second Formation of Islamic Law: The Post-Mongol Context of the Ottoman Adoption of a School of Law," *Comparative Studies in Society and History* 55, no. 3 (2013): 589–594.

[80] Rumee Ahmed, *Narratives of Islamic Legal Theory* (Oxford: Oxford University Press, 2012), 151–153.

[81] Mariam al-Attar, *Islamic Ethics: Divine Command Theory in Arabo-Islamic Thought* (New York: Routledge, 2010), xvi.

expressions of *'ilm*, both expressed according to the political circumstances of the time.

If we assume the Pragmatist narrative of the precolonial past, then the colonial and postcolonial present seems like less of a dramatic rupture. Dissident groups continue to use law and theology to argue for political ideals against the ruling elite, whether these groups have primarily societal[82] or spiritual[83] ends in mind. Ruling classes continue to use law to demonstrate their legitimacy to the masses, again primarily through a system of courts.[84] The one major difference is that modern governments do not overtly utilize theological language, instead relying almost exclusively on the language of law.[85] Yet, by doing so, they admit an unspoken theology: that the state legislates on behalf of God, and that obedience to state law is obedience to God.

Everyone, then, whether purportedly working on the side of traditionalism or reform, or trying not to take sides, has theological presuppositions that underpin their approach to jurisprudence and legal theory, whether explicitly or not. Those theological presuppositions drive individual approaches to law and its application. Conversely, reforming Islamic law requires contending with the underlying theologies presumed by certain applications of law.

Just as the Revisionist retelling of the story of Islamic law and theology was spurred by self-determination and anti-colonial movements, so is the Pragmatist retelling strongly influenced by Islamic feminism, whether acknowledged or (more likely) not. Feminist scholarship is animated by a "view from the bottom," which focuses on those who are affected by law, especially in adverse ways, and addresses their concerns.[86] Feminist scholars trying to reform Islamic law on myriad

[82] Several recent studies have pointed out the regular use of theology to support larger claims about law, order, and appropriate governance. Such studies include, Natana Delong-Bas, *Wahhabi Islam: From Revival and Reform to Global Jihad* (New York: Oxford University Press, 2004); Halverson, *Theology and Creed in Sunni Islam*; Daviel Lav, *Radical Islam and the Revival of Medieval Theology* (Cambridge: Cambridge University Press, 2012).

[83] See, for instance, the case of the mystic Abu al-Wafa al-Taftazani (d. 1994), whose attempt to reconcile mystical thought with *'ilm al-kalam* was with the expressed purpose of restoring Egypt to its Abbasid-era power; Andreas Christmann, "Reconciling Sufism with Theology: Abū al-Wafa al-Taftazani and the Construct of 'al-Taṣawwuf al-Islami' in Modern Egypt," in *Sufism and Theology*, ed. Ayman Shihadeh (Edinburgh: Edinburgh University Press, 2007), 191.

[84] Clark Lombardi, "Constitutional Provisions Making Sharia 'A' or 'The' Chief Source of Legislation: Where Did They Come From? What Do They Mean? Do They Matter?" *American University International Law Review* 28, no. 3 (2013): 772.

[85] Frank Griffel, "Introduction," in *Shari'a*, eds. A. Amanat and F. Griffel (Stanford: Stanford University Press, 2007), 7–8.

[86] The "view from the bottom" has undergone immense and sophisticated transformations through modern feminism, moving from the relatively simplistic approaches of Marx and Weber to one that considers intersectionality as a fundamental concern; see Susan Hekman, "Truth and Method: Feminist Standpoint Theory Revisited," *Signs* 22, no. 2 (Winter 1997): 341–365. Feminist concerns have permeated the larger academic discourse, and can be seen in different forms in Islamic Studies scholarly works, especially those described here as "pragmatists." For an explicit link between the rise of re-investigations

issues—whether to grant women equal status in the law, guarantee sexual freedoms, or delegitimize patriarchal laws—are confounded by legal arguments from Muslim scholars that appear more theological than legal.[87] That is, though feminists may offer traditionally grounded legal alternatives to patriarchal, hetero-normative laws, they nonetheless face resistance from scholars espousing patriarchal, hetero-normative theologies, based on which reform is rebuffed.[88] Some feminists have concluded, as a result, that theology informs any and all understandings of law and legal application. And whereas many scholars argue that the Islamic tradition provides the necessary theological tools to reform law from a feminist perspective,[89] others have argued that an entirely new theology—in Jerusha Lamptey's words, a "Muslima theology"—is required.[90]

The feminist concern that theology and theological reform be conducted alongside, or prior to, legal reform comes partly out of frustration with the ubiquitous patriarchy that frames juristic discussions on Islamic law. It is clear that, with a few recent exceptions, the *'ulama* do not take feminist critiques seriously, nor do they hold gender egalitarianism to be a virtuous ideal. It would appear that this scorn for gender egalitarianism has deep historical roots. The *'ulama* historically promoted, and for the most part continue to promote, a hierarchical model of gender relations in which men are accorded "a degree" over women in terms of rights and responsibilities.[91] This hierarchy is what Ayesha S. Chaudhry calls an "idealized cosmology,"[92] and it describes the theological presuppositions about the God–human relationship that informs how law is created and discussed. So long as jurists presume a patriarchal idealized cosmology, in which men and women are fundamentally unequal, gender-egalitarian Islamic legal reforms will be stymied.

of Islamic law and feminism, see Ziba Mir-Hosseini, "Muslim Women's Quest for Equality: Between Islamic Law and Feminism," *Critical Inquiry* 32, no. 4 (Summer 2006): 638ff.

[87] Kecia Ali, *Sexual Ethics in Islam* (Oxford: Oneworld, 2006), 78.

[88] Mir-Hosseini, "Muslim Women's Quest for Equality," 642–643.

[89] See the way that feminists—specifically Khaled Abou El Fadl, Kecia Ali, and Amina Wadud—have built upon one another's ideas to describe how this works in Aysha Hidayatullah, *Feminist Edges of the Qur'an* (New York: Oxford University Press, 2014), 139ff.

[90] Jerusha Lamptey, *Never Wholly Other* (New York: Oxford University Press, 2014), 10–11. It is important to note that this is a shift from the Qur'an-first approach promoted by many Revisionists. Wadud, for instance, is calling for a *tawhidic* paradigm through which the Qur'an should be read to glean new interpretations, whereas Revisionists might argue that the Qur'an already contains latent principles that can be unearthed without any preconceived theological ideals; Hidayatullah, *Feminist Edges*, 89 . Lamptey, likewise, does not argue for a Qur'an-first or Qur'an-only approach. Rather, she argues that reading the Qur'an through Muslima theology is the first step toward reforming other sciences, including law.

[91] For an in-depth discussion on how and why this model was implemented across the early Muslim empire, see Halevi, *Muhammad's Grave.*

[92] Ayesha Chaudhry, *Domestic Violence and the Islamic Tradition* (Oxford: Oxford University Press, 2013), 222–223. Chaudhry points out that Muslim jurists had different "idealized cosmologies" that led them to privilege men over women. Asma Barlas discusses the role of "theological patriarchy" in *Believing Women in Islam* (Austin, TX: University of Texas Press, 2002), 99–100; Amina Wadud, *Inside the Gender Jihad: Women's Reform in Islam* (Oxford: Oneworld, 2006), 50.

By attending to the theological presuppositions that come to light when discussing Islamic laws related to gender, Islamic feminists opened up new avenues of inquiry that helped shape Pragmatist research on Islamic law and theology. For instance, Islamic feminist scholarship encouraged scholars to ask, if the *ʿulama*, when they wrote treatises on Islamic law, were not speaking to women, to whom were they speaking? Who else was excluded from the discourse apart from women? What patriarchal socio-historical context were the *ʿulama* assuming, and how did their theological presuppositions affect their articulations of Islamic law? What other theological and political presuppositions did they have, and how did they express them in the language of law?

All of these questions humanize the *ʿulama*, and place the focus on understanding their personal and socio-historical contexts in order to grasp their individual conceptions of law and overall worldview.[93] Theology—what jurists thought about God and the God–human relationship—must have always been a foundational part of jurists' worldview, and so helps determine how they intended their law to be *applied*. Indeed, when Pragmatist scholars look back on jurisprudence—informed by the findings of van Ess and Hallaq, and animated by the feminist critique—they find that jurists argued along a spectrum of theological beliefs in their legal writings, and their arguments cannot be reduced to a rubric provided by a handful of legal and theological "schools." Pragmatists see these diverse theologies reflected in all works of jurisprudence, whether written in the medieval, colonial, or contemporary period. Theology's relationship to law, then, was not severed with Ibn Taymiyya, or even with the advent of colonialism, but it lives on in different forms. This was a key finding of Islamic feminists, and it is surely no accident that the Pragmatist approach emerged shortly after the rise of Islamic feminism.[94]

According to the Pragmatist view of law and theology, the current state of affairs is not the result of Muslim piety devolving into legalism. There is no need for reformers to recover the language of theology or to get back to a holistic view of the religion. Rather, Islamic law and theology are and always have been inextricably bound up with political concerns, and their relationship is expressed in different ways in response to different political situations. Far from being mere casuistry, as David Vishanoff notes, this is part of the "genius" of Islamic thought: that it can express new ways of thinking and relating to the world through a discourse that appears ancient and unchanging.[95] The task for reformers, in the Pragmatist conception, is to use the already existing relationship between law, theology, and politics, and to reform that relationship in a way that reflects modern concerns.

[93] For an example of such an approach, see Knut Vikor, *Between God and Sultan: A History of Islamic Law* (New York: Oxford University Press, 2005), 140ff.

[94] On the rise of Islamic feminism and its attendant politics, see Fatima Seedat, "Islam, Feminism, and Islamic Feminism: Between Inadequacy and Inevitability," *Journal of Feminist Studies in Religion* 29, no. 2 (Fall 2013): 25–45.

[95] David Vishanoff, *The Formation of Islamic Hermeneutics* (New Haven, CT: American Oriental Society), 278.

V. Conclusion

I chose to discuss the historiographical relationship between Islamic law and theology in terms of narrative and the contemporary implications for reform because that is the underlying political reality of Islamic studies, both historically and contemporaneously. Islam is a living tradition and one cannot escape the major questions that drive funding and interest in its academic study. Whether one is studying the early community or modern Muslims, these studies have political implications resulting from the narratives they perpetuate. It would be a disservice to pretend that a topic like "law and theology" can be studied in an apolitical vacuum, and it explains why the subject is hotly contested.[96] When one argues about whether law and theology are separate or somehow intertwined, one is making an argument about the historical Muslim community's narrative, and also about the way that the contemporary community functions with respect to its tradition.

That makes the study much more difficult, for it can never be divorced from the concerns of the day. It also highlights the fact that there is much work to be done to separate historical realities from modern anachronisms, whether those anachronisms are due to naïveté or optimism or cynicism or something else. It means that describing the interplay between theology and law in Muslim history requires the scholar to move beyond textual analysis, and examine historical, political, economic, social, and other concerns to fully appreciate the stakes involved in articulating Islamic law. Finally, conscientious scholars must take a moment to consider the contemporary implications of their study, for such implications exist, and affect individuals and societies in substantive and abiding ways.

References

Abduh, Muhammad, "Laws Should Change in Accordance with the Conditions of Nations and the Theology of Unity," in Charles Kurzman (ed.) *Modernist Islam 1840–1940: A Sourcebook* (New York: Oxford University Press, 2002) 50–60.

Ahmad, Ahmad Atif, *The Fatigue of the Shari'a* (New York: Palgrave MacMillan, 2012).

Ahmed, Rumee, "The Ethics of Prophetic Disobedience." *Journal of Religious Ethics* 39, no. 4 (2011): 440–457.

Ahmed, Rumee, *Narratives of Islamic Legal Theory* (Oxford: Oxford University Press, 2012).

[96] For a review of some of the historical, social, and practical impediments to studying Islamic history, let alone law and theology, see Fred Donner, "Modern Approaches to Early Islamic History," in *The New Cambridge History of Islam: Volume 1*, ed. Chase F. Robinson (Cambridge: Cambridge University Press, 2010), 625–647.

Ahmed, Rumee, "Jurisprudence and Islamic Philosophy in Islam," in R. Taylor and L. Farjeat (eds.) *Routledge Companion to Islamic Philosophy* (London: Routledge, 2016).

al-Attar, Mariam, *Islamic Ethics: Divine Command Theory in Arabo-Islamic Thought* (New York: Routledge, 2010).

Ali, Kecia, *Sexual Ethics in Islam* (Oxford: Oneworld, 2006).

Amanat, A. and Griffel, F., eds. *Shari'a* (Stanford: Stanford University Press, 2007).

Anderson, J.N.D, *Islamic Law in the Modern World* (New York: New York University Press, 1959).

Arabi, O., Powers, D., and Spectorsky, S., eds. "Introduction." In *Islamic Legal Thought: A Compendium of Mulsim Jurists*, 2 (Brill: Leiden, 2013).

Auda, Jasser, "A Maqaṣidi Approach to Contemporary Application of the Shari'ah." *Intellectual Discourse* 19, no. 2 (2011): 193–218.

Aziz, Muhammad Ali, *Religion and Mysticism in Early Islam* (London: I.B. Tauris, 2011).

Barlas, Asma, *Believing Women in Islam* (Austin, TX: University of Texas Press, 2002).

Bergstrasser, Gotthelf, *Grundzüge des islamischen Rechts* (Leipzig: W. de Gruyter, 1935).

Burak, Guy, "The Second Formation of Islamic Law: The Post-Mongol Context of the Ottoman Adoption of a School of Law." *Comparative Studies in Society and History* 55, no. 3 (2013): 589–594.

Calder, Norman, "Islamic Law" in S.H. Nasr and O.Leaman (eds.) *A History of Islamic Philosophy* (London: Routledge, 1996), 2:979–998.

Campanini, Massimo, "Alfarabi and the Foundation of Political Theology in Islam" in Asma Afsaruddin (ed.) *Islam, the State, and Political Authority: Medieval Issues and Modern Concerns* (New York: Palgrave Macmillan, 2011) 35–52.

Cantwell Smith, Wilfred, *Islam in the Modern World* (Princeton: Princeton University Press, 1957).

Cantwell Smith, Wilfred, *On Understanding Islam* (The Hague: Mouton, 1981).

Chaudhry, Ayesha, *Domestic Violence and the Islamic Tradition* (Oxford: Oxford University Press, 2013).

Christmann, Andreas, "Reconciling Sufism with Theology: Abū al-Wafa al-Taftazani and the Construct of 'al-Taṣawwuf al-Islami' in Modern Egypt," in Ayman Shihadeh (ed.) *Sufism and Theology* (Edinburgh: Edinburgh University Press, 2007) 177–193.

Coulson, Noel J., *Conflicts and Tensions in Islamic Jurisprudence* (Chicago: University of Chicago Press, 1969).

Delong-Bas, Natana, *Wahhabi Islam: From Revival and Reform to Global Jihad* (New York: Oxford University Press, 2004).

Dien, Mawil Izzi, *Islamic Law: From Historical Foundations to Contemporary Practice* (Edinburgh: Edinburgh University Press, 2004).

Donner, Fred, "Modern Approaches to Early Islamic History," in Chase F. Robinson (ed.) *The New Cambridge History of Islam: Volume 1* (Cambridge: Cambridge University Press, 2010) 625–647.

Emon, Anver, *Islamic Natural Law Theories* (Oxford: Oxford University Press, 2010).

Emon, Anver, *Religious Pluralism and Islamic Law: Dhimmīs and Others in the Empire of Law* (Oxford: Oxford University Press, 2013).

Ess, Josef van, *Theologie und Gesellschat im 2. Und 3. Jahrhudert Hidschra (Band 1-6)* (Berlin: DeGruyter, 1991–97).

Ess, Josef van, *The Flowering of Muslim Theology* (Cambridge, MA: Harvard University Press, 2006).

Ess, Josef van, "The Beginnings of Islamic Theology," in J.E. Murdoch and E.D. Sylla (eds.) *The Cultural Context of Medieval Learning* (Dordrecht, Holland: Reidel, 1975) 87–103.

Feener, R. Michael, "Cross-Cultural Contexts of Modern Muslim Intellectualism." *Die Welt des Islams* 47, no. 3/4 (2007): 264–282.

Gibb, H.A.R., "An Interpretation of Islamic History—I," *The Muslim World* 45, no. 1 (1955): 4–15.

Gibb, H.A.R., *Islam: A Historical Survey* (Oxford: Oxford University Press, 1969).

Goldziher, Ignác, *Muslim Studies* (London: Allen & Unwin, 1967–1971).

Griffel, Frank, "Introduction" in A. Amanat and F. Griffel (eds.) *Sharīʿa*, 1–19 (Stanford: Stanford University Press, 2007) 1–19.

Haider, Najam, "Contesting Intoxication: Early Juristic Debates over the Lawfulness of Alcoholic Beverages." *Islamic Law and Society* 20, no. 1–2 (2013): 48–89.

Hallaq, Wael, "Was the Gate of Ijtihad Closed?" *International Journal of Middle East Studies* 16, no. 1 (1984): 3–41.

Hallaq, Wael, *A History of Islamic Legal Theories* (Cambridge: Cambridge University Press, 1997).

Halevi, Leor, *Muhammad's Grave* (New York: Columbia University Press, 2007).

Halverson, Jeffry, *Theology and Creed in Sunni Islam: the Muslim Brotherhood, Ash'arism, and Political Sunnism* (New York: Palgrave MacMillan, 2010).

Hanafi, Hasan, *Dirasat Islamiyya* (Cairo: Maktabat al-Anghlu al-Misriyya, 1981).

Hekman, Susan. "Truth and Method: Feminist Standpoint Theory Revisited." *Signs* 22, no. 2 (Winter 1997): 341–365.

Hidayatullah, Aysha, *Feminist Edges of the Qur'an* (New York: Oxford University Press, 2014).

Hodgson, Marshall, *The Venture of Islam* (Chicago: University of Chicago Press, 1977).

Humphreys, R. Stephen, "Syria," in Chase F. Robinson (ed.) *The New Cambridge History of Islam: Volume 1.* (Cambridge: Cambridge University Press, 2010) 506–540.

Hurgronje, C. Snouck, *Mohammedanism: Lectures on its Origins its Religious and Political Growth* (New York: G. P. Putnam and Sons, 1916).

Izutsu, Toshiko, *Ethico-Religious Concepts in the Qur'an* (Montreal: McGill University Press, 2002).

Johansen, Baber, *The Islamic Law on Land Tax and Rent* (London: Croom Helm, 1988).

Johansen, Baber, *Contingency in a Sacred Law: Legal and Ethical Norms in Muslim Fiqh* (Leiden: Brill, 1999).

Kamali, Mohammad Hashim, "Law and Ethics in Islam—The Role of the Maqaṣid," in K. Vogt, L. Larsen, and C. Moe (eds.) *New Directions in Islamic Thought* (New York: I.B. Tauris, 2009) 23–46.

Lammens, Henri, *Islam: Beliefs and Institutions* (London: Frank Cass & Co., 1968).

Lamptey, Jerusha, *Never Wholly Other* (New York: Oxford University Press, 2014).

Lav, Daviel, *Radical Islam and the Revival of Medieval Theology* (Cambridge: Cambridge University Press, 2012).

Lombardi, Clark, "Constitutional Provisions Making Sharia 'A' or 'The' Chief Source of Legislation: Where Did They Come From? What Do They Mean? Do They Matter?" *American University International Law Review* 28, no. 3 (2013): 733–774.

MacDonald, Duncan, *Development of Muslim Theology, Jurisprudence and Constitutional Theory* (New York: Russell and Russell, 1965).

Makdisi, George, "The Significance of the Sunni Schools of Law in Islamic Religious History." *International Journal of Middle East History* 10, no. 1 (1979): 1–8.

Makdisi, George, "The Juridical Theology of Shâfi'î: Origins and Significance of Uṣûl al-Fiqh." *Studia Islamica* 59 (1984): 5–48.
Makdisi, George, "Classical Islam and the Christian West" in R. Hovannisian and G. Sabagh (eds.) *Religion and Culture in Medieval Islam* (Cambridge: Cambridge University Press, 1999) 3–23.
Mandaville, Jon E., "Usurious Piety: The Cash Waqf Controversy in the Ottoman Empire." *International Journal of Middle East Studies* 10, no. 3 (1979): 289–308.
Mandaville, Peter, "When Meaning Travels: Muslim Translocality and the Politics of 'Authenticity,'" in P. Mandaville and A. Williams (eds.) *Meaning and International Relations* (London: Routledge, 2003) 117–138.
Massignon, Louis, "What Moslems Expect: An Introductory Study of Moslem Demands." *The Muslim World* 12, no. 1 (1922): 7–24.
Melchert, Christopher, "How Hanafism Came to Originate in Kufa and Traditionalism in Medina." *Islamic Law and Society* 6, no. 3 (1999): 318–347.
Mir-Hosseini, Ziba, "Muslim Women's Quest for Equality: Between Islamic Law and Feminism." *Critical Inquiry* 32, no. 4 (Summer 2006): 629–645.
Peters, Rudolph, "What Does it Mean to be an Official Madhhab?," in P. Bearman, R. Peters, and F. Vogel (eds.) *The Islamic School of Law: Evolution, Devolution, and Progress* (Cambridge, MA: Harvard University Press, 2005) 147–158.
Rahman, Fazlur, "The Post-Formative Developments in Islam." *Islamic Studies* 1, no. 4 (1962): 1–21.
Rahman, Fazlur, *Major Themes of the Qur'an* (Minneapolis, MN: Bibliotheca Islamica, 1980).
Rahman, Fazlur, "Some Key Ethical Concepts of the Qur'an." *Journal of Religious Ethics* 11, no. 2 (1983): 170–185.
Rahman, Fazlur, *Revival and Reform in Islam* (Oxford: Oneworld, 2000).
Rahman, Fazlur, "Islamization of Knowledge: A Response." *Islamic Studies* No. 3/4 (2011): 449–457.
Reinhart, Kevin, "Islamic Law as Islamic Ethics." *Journal of Religious Ethics* 11, no. 2 (1983): 186–203.
Rosenthal, Franz, *Knowledge Triumphant: The Concepts of Knowledge in Medieval Islam* (Brill: Leiden, 2007).
Sachedina, Abdulaziz, *The Islamic Roots of Democratic Pluralism* (New York: Oxford University Press, 2001).
Schacht, Joseph, "New Sources for the History of Muhammadan Theology." *Studia Islamica* 1 (1953): 23–42.
Schacht, Joseph, "Modernism and Traditionalism in a History of Islamic Law." *Middle Eastern Studies* 1, no. 4 (1965): 388–400.
Schacht, Joseph, *The Origins of Muhammadan Jurisprudence* (Oxford: Clarendon Press, 1967).
Schacht, Joseph, *Islam* (Oxford: Oxford University Press, 1974).
Schacht, Joseph, *The Legacy of Islam* (Oxford: Clarendon Press, 1974).
Schimmel, Annemarie, *Islam: An Introduction* (Albany, NY: State University Press New York, 1992).
Seedat, Fatima, "Islam, Feminism, and Islamic Feminism: Between Inadequacy and Inevitability." *Journal of Feminist Studies in Religion* 29, no. 2 (Fall 2013): 25–45.
Shepard, William, *Introducing Islam* (London: Routledge, 2009).

Sonbol, Amira E., "Adults and Minors in Ottoman Shari'a Courts and Modern Law" in Amira E. Sonbol (ed.) *Women, the Family, and Divorce Laws in Islamic History* (Syracuse: Syracuse University Press, 1996) 236–258.
Taylor, Richard C, "Philosophy" in Robert Irwin (ed.) *The New Cambridge History of Islam, Volume 4* (Cambridge: Cambridge University Press, 2010) 532–563.
Tritton, A. S., *Islam: Beliefs and Practices* (London: Hutchinson's University Library, 1951).
Tucker, Judith, *In the House of the Law: Gender and Islamic Law in Ottoman Syria and Palestine* (Berkeley, CA: University of California Press, 1998).
Vikor, Knut, *Between God and Sultan: A History of Islamic Law* (New York: Oxford University Press, 2005).
Vishanoff, David, *The Formation of Islamic Hermeneutics* (New Haven, CT: American Oriental Society, 2011).
Wadud, Amina, *Inside the Gender Jihad: Women's Reform in Islam* (Oxford, UK: Oneworld, 2006).
Watt, Montgomery, *Islamic Philosophy and Theology: An Extended Survey* (Edinburgh: University of Edinburgh Press, 1985).
Watt, Montgomery, "The Future of Islam" in R. Hovannisian and G. Sabagh (eds.) *Religion and Culture in Medieval Islam* (Cambridge: Cambridge University Press, 1999) 24–35.
Wansbrough, John, "[Review] The Venture of Islam: Conscience and History in a World Civilization by Marshall G. S. Hodgson." *Bulletin of the School of Oriental and African Studies, University of London* 40, no. 1 (1977): 169–170.
Waugh, Earle, "An Evasive Vision." *History of Religions* 18, no. 2 (November 1978): 192–197.
Wellhausen, Julius, *The Arab Kingdom and Its Fall* (London: Routledge, 2000).
Weiss, Bernard, *The Spirit of Islamic Law* (Athens, GA: University of Georgia Press, 2006).
Zaman, Muhammad Qasim, *Religion and Politics Under the Early Abbasids* (Leiden: Brill, 1997).
Zaman, Muhammad Qasim, *The Ulama in Contemporary Islam* (Princeton: Princeton University Press, 2002).
Zayd, Nasr Hamid Abu, *Reformation of Islamic Thought* (Amsterdam: Amsterdam University Press, 2006).

CHAPTER 5

ANTHROPOLOGY AND ISLAMIC LAW

JOHN R. BOWEN

THE anthropology of Islamic law is concerned centrally with observing and analyzing practices governed by explicit norms that are given Islamic justification, from commercial transactions to marriage and divorce to rituals of worship. Such governance may or may not involve state-empowered courts or judges. Two key questions underlie much of the divergence and debate in this field: one about "Islamic law," the other about anthropology.

The English word "law," even in its extended anthropological usages, is used to denote a narrow range of phenomena, whereas the relevant Islamic terms—shari'a, *fiqh*, *hukm*—refer both to the widest sphere of normativity—all that God commands—and to specific practices. If *fiqh* is close to the Anglo-American sense of case-law or jurisprudence, it depends on the ultimately unknowable pathway for humans in all their affairs, or shari'a. Consequently, a much wider range of activities than are normally denoted by "law" (or other European cognates) are subject to vigorous debates in Islamic contexts about their conformity to shari'a, as humans can discern it through *fiqh*. Rituals of worship, sacrifice, and pilgrimage are most clearly subject to this "legal" scrutiny, but so are everyday acts of greeting or dressing. Rarely, however, are these matters the subject of state-law proceedings; they are, however, central to anthropology.

The conceptual gap between "law," on the one hand, and shari'a/*fiqh*/*hukm* on the other, means that different topics fit more or less comfortably into Islamic studies or into legal studies. As we move from formal proceedings in courts or councils toward normative but extra-institutional reflections and debates about everyday activities, we move further from the usual sense of "law." Less evidently, but quite importantly, is the effect of state codification on Islamic discussions: as we move from ritual, ethics, and religious topics and toward the practices more frequently regulated by courts, such as marriage and divorce or property transactions, we often (depending on the legal regime) move away from a domain of debate governed by the texts and traditions of Islam, and toward the application of positive law, meaning state statutes and jurisprudence. In one sense, then, "law" and "Islamic" are at opposite ends of a chiastic structure: the more state law, the less Islam.[1]

How then do anthropologists frame and analyze processes such as those listed above? Has the anthropological effort to extend the reach of "law" to include non-state processes and institutions resolved the issue? The second question concerns precisely the problems of such an extension within anthropology. The discipline of social or cultural anthropology focuses on dimensions of society and culture, conceived of as structures, networks, or conceptual worlds that link across domains, cohere internally, and differ from other societies or cultures. It has highlighted distinctions across spatial units, rather than continuities of supra-local traditions. How, then, does anthropology approach a field of specialized, text-based knowledge such as Islamic law, where the normative ground is based on claims of continuity and universality?

I. Historiography

The most influential early analyses of Islamic law that resembled anthropological studies were undertaken under colonial regimes as part of efforts to dominate Muslim societies. When tasked to advise the Dutch government on its efforts to suppress resistance in Aceh, the Islamicist Christiaan Snouck Hurgronje (1857–1936) recommended that Islam's legal and political dimensions be suppressed but that its spiritual dimensions be allowed. In any case, he argued, the fixed rules of classical Islamic jurisprudence had little to do with shaping how Muslims actually practice their religion. Rather, local scholars accommodated local usages and ideas by baptizing them as "Islamic," as when local ideas about spirits, *jinn*, and *aulia*,

[1] Baudouin Dupret, *Au nom de quel droit* (Paris: Maison des Sciences de l'Homme, 2000); Wael B. Hallaq, *Sharī'a: Theory, Practice, Transformations* (Cambridge: Cambridge University Press, 2009), 357–370.

were drawn on to allow people to make extensive petitionary prayers to saints. For Snouck, doctrine was irrelevant to everyday life, but the practical judgments of scholars (*ulama*) did conform to "human needs."[2]

A similar distinction between enunciated norms and practical resolutions of conflicts underlies the modern anthropology of law, which was inspired by the fieldwork carried out by Bronislaw Malinowski (1884–1942) in the Trobriand Islands. Malinowski used field observations to castigate Europeans for their generalizations about "primitives," including those made about "primitive law." His argument, here as on other topics, was that humans work out their lives in strikingly similar ways, starting from different funds of knowledge. They resolve disputes in ways that everyone can recognize as law-like. Malinowski's attention to social process and social structure, as well as to psychology and to ways of speaking, left a strong influence on what was to develop in the anthropology of law, through such key figures as Max Gluckman and Sally Falk Moore, to most of today's practitioners of that field.[3]

Early social anthropology focussed on politics and social structure lying outside the state, initially as part of the colonizing mission and later in recognition of all that was left unstudied by jurists and political scientists. Insofar as they concerned Muslim peoples, anthropologists were rarely concerned with issues of *fiqh* or shari'a but focused on local mechanisms of dispute settlement, such as in E. E. Evans-Pritchard's studies in Cyrenaica.[4] This concern with finding local sources of authority led British social anthropology toward an interest in the interrelationships among tribal structures, men of learning (*ulama*), and Sufi lodges in North Africa. Insofar as *ulama* pronounced on legal matters, this concern with political authority created the potential for explorations in Islamic law, but did not lead to direct engagement with the Islamic legal tradition.[5]

Nor did the Boasian lineage of American cultural anthropology exhibit much interest in the matter, in part because American anthropologists prior to the Second World War rarely worked in Muslim societies. Things changed somewhat with the postwar turn to studies of large-scale religious traditions in "new nations," starting with South Asia, and, by the 1960s, to symbols and interpretations, now in an awkward Parsonian dance with the norms and structures that remained the province of sociologists. Nevertheless, the discipline remained perhaps overly respectful of a division of labor between the Islamicists' study of the "Great Tradition" of urban, literate religious scholars and anthropologists' focus on smaller-scale societies or nicely-bounded Sufi cults, with little attention to ways in which adepts of those

[2] C. Snouck Hurgronje, *The Acehnese*, trans. A.W.S. O'Sullivan (Leiden: Brill, 1906), 1: 271–288.

[3] For an overview of the anthropology of law, see the annotated reader: Sally Falk Moore, ed., *Law and Anthropology: A Reader* (Malden, MA: Blackwell, 2005).

[4] E.E. Evans-Pritchard, *The Sanusi of Cyrenaica* (Oxford: Clarendon Press, 1949).

[5] See Michael Gilsenan, *Recognizing Islam* (New York: Pantheon, 1982); Ernest Gellner, *Saints of the Atlas* (Chicago: University of Chicago Press, 1969).

"Little Traditions" tied their practices back to scripture, legal schools, and literary works.[6]

Things changed on the American side when Clifford Geertz and his students ventured into the territory of Islamic law in Morocco, with studies of courts and judges.[7] Dale Eickelman (a student of W. Cantwell Smith as well as of Geertz) traced changes in Islamic traditions of law and learning by working with an Islamic judge, while Clifford Geertz contrasted the Islamic idiom of *haqq* ("right, just") with its Indic and Indonesian counterparts to describe a Muslim culture of law and justice. Islamic law remained, however, peripheral to their projects. Lawrence Rosen, by contrast, endeavored to trace the articulation of Moroccan culture, Islamic legal practices, and law as a comparative domain, and was in this respect the first to construct a cultural anthropology of Islamic law.

Rosen (and Geertz) asked to what extent is what we see in Islamic legal settings the rendering of key cultural idioms in Islamic terms. This question—more explicitly posed by Rosen, less so by Geertz (for whom *haqq* somewhat confusingly stood for both Islamic and Arabic ways of seeing the world)—opened up Islamic law to anthropology.

This move, however, also created a tension between two potential starting points for an eventual anthropology of Islamic law. One such point was the Islamic tradition, which local actors understand and appropriate in locally specific ways. Across Muslim societies, people marry, divorce, pray, and so on, and some of them, *ulama* or not, specify the textual referents for these practices: how do they do these things and justify them in *this* place? This direction of anthropological inquiry facilitated exchanges with textual scholars trained in the older philological approach to the tradition, even though, by privileging the local, it was for a while seen by some of philologically-oriented scholars as a kind of shariʿatic slumming. Today it makes possible close collaboration between anthropologists, historians, and legal scholars.[8]

The other starting point was a particular cultural order, which shapes local practices. In this society, people see the world in a certain way, and this shapes how they navigate their economic, religious, and artistic worlds; how does *this* worldview shape how they discuss Islam? This direction of inquiry facilitated exchanges with anthropologists not particularly interested in Islam, because it privileged the cultural links between law and other domains in any particular society. For example, Rosen shows how ideas about relationships and credibility pervade domains

[6] See Richard T. Antoun, *Muslim Preacher in the Modern World* (Princeton: Princeton University Press, 1989), 3–44.

[7] Clifford Geertz, "Local Knowledge: Fact and Law in Comparative Perspective," in *Local Knowledge*, ed. Clifford Geertz (New York: Basic Books, 1983), 167–234; Dale F. Eickelman, *Knowledge and Power in Morocco* (Princeton: Princeton University Press, 1992); Lawrence Rosen, *The Anthropology of Justice: Law as Culture in Islamic Society* (Cambridge: Cambridge University Press, 1989).

[8] Evidenced in volumes such as Muhammad Khalid Masud, Rudolph Peters, and David S. Powers, eds., *Dispensing Justice in Islam: Qadis and their Judgments* (Leiden: Brill, 2006).

of Islamic law and market transactions in a Moroccan town.[9] This focus left in the background the debates among people in any one society over textual interpretation, however, and thus was less open to comparative treatments across societies wherein authorities referred to Islamic law. In this regard, Geertz's famous Morocco/Java study provided a *contrast* of completely different cultural types, rather than a *comparison* of alternative interpretations of a shared tradition.[10] Paradoxically, this latter approach, which came to be called "interpretive anthropology," turned out to be particularly ill-suited for studying interpretations in domains (such as Islamic law) where members of the same society arrive at quite different judgments and do so drawing on authorities from times and places distant.

One can see ensuing debates and expansions in anthropology as gradually narrowing the gap between these two directions of inquiry. By the 1990s, a growing number of anthropologists were framing the question in terms of how local legal actors interpret and practice elements of the Islamic tradition in a context that included positive law, competing understandings of *fiqh*, cultural ideas and social norms, and practical assessments of competing statements. Within the anthropology of law, this way of posing the question was banal, echoing rather classic anthropological approaches to dispute resolution as practiced by Malinowski or Gluckman. Within the anthropology of Islam, however, this framing meant that fieldworkers now paid attention to practices of justification found on multiple levels: in village forums and local mosques, by judges in courtrooms, and by muftis and scholars in national debates. Now anthropologists studied not only how people resolved a dispute, but also how people justified what they did and how they invoked multiple traditions, including that of classical Islamic jurisprudence.

II. Judges and Courts

Even in ethnographic studies of courts and judges, we find the division between the two starting points, Islam or culture, operating in fractal fashion. Some anthropologists place Islamic tradition in the foreground, while others emphasize cultural ideas and processes. Two studies of East African courts illustrate this distinction. Susan Hirsch, working in Muslim Kenya, highlights the gendered quality of courtroom narratives. She bases her analysis on local (Swahili) categories to best capture the understanding

[9] Clifford Geertz, Hildred Geertz, and Lawrence Rosen, *Meaning and Order in Moroccan Society: Three Essays in Cultural Analysis* (New York: Cambridge University Press, 1979).

[10] Clifford Geertz, *Islam Observed: Religious Development in Morocco and Indonesia* (Chicago: University of Chicago Press, 1968).

that ordinary men and women bring to the courtroom experience. She places in the background scholarly knowledge or the sources and reasoning used by judges. By contrast, Erin Stiles, studying in a Zanzibar divorce court, highlights how judges dispense justice, justify their decisions, and respond to varied claims and complaints. The links between courtroom narratives and Islamic law are placed in the foreground.[11] These choices of framing make for different sets of references: Hirsch mainly to works in law and language; Stiles to scholars working in Islamic legal studies.

Both Hirsch and Stiles take note of the pluralistic legal context in which their judges operate. "Legal pluralism" has become a phrase operating as a distinct frame for studies in the anthropology of law, particularly when pursued by scholars whose initial training was in law. This approach is exemplified by the work of Franz and Keebet von Benda-Beckmann.[12] Pioneers in empirical analyses of pluralistic legal orders, the von Benda-Beckmanns highlighted the internal social logics of two or more legal orders, most prominently in West Sumatran inheritance cases, where customary *adat* law and Islamic law had provided competing normative grounds for law and social life since the early nineteenth century. By starting from these legal orders, they pay particular attention to links between social institutions and normative orders—links also pursued by other students of Sumatran history and religion. In this Weberian type of analysis, scholars show how traders supported reformist Islamic ideas and opposed *adat* law in favor of Islamic law. By the same token, these authors background the ways that judges make references to multiple types of normative or legal sources in the same courtroom. By contrast, my own work in Sumatra on similar issues examines ways that Islamic court judges have changed their tendencies to follow Islamic or *adat* law judgments over time, not because of changes in available legal repertoires but because of shifts in local power and resources. The unit of analysis thereby becomes the judge and his or her multiple sets of references and justifications, not one or more distinct legal orders.[13]

One finds similarly diverse analytical frames in studies of courtrooms elsewhere. Working in Iran and Morocco, Ziba Mir-Hosseini emphasizes the ways litigants strategically represent their divorce demands and the ways judges seek to bring about the outcomes they personally prefer. She shows all actors working strategically within the constraints of statutes and of the authoritative opinions (*fatwas*) of scholars. The result of her framing is that these actors appear very much like their strategizing counterparts in non-Islamic environments. Mir-Hosseini's work indeed strikes a balance in framing, showcasing a working judicial system in a classical

[11] Susan F. Hirsch, *Pronouncing and Persevering: Gender and the Discourses of Disputing in an African Islamic Court* (Chicago: University of Chicago Press, 1998); Erin E. Stiles, *An Islamic Court in Context: An Ethnographic Study of Judicial Reasoning* (London: Palgrave Macmillan, 2009).

[12] See, e.g., Franz von Benda-Beckmann, *Property in Social Continuity: Continuity and Change in the Maintenance of Property Relationships through Time in Minangkabau, West Sumatra* (The Hague: M. Nijhoff, 1979).

[13] John R. Bowen, *Islam, Law, and Equality in Indonesia: An Anthropology of Public Reasoning* (Cambridge: Cambridge University Press, 2003), 89–122.

social anthropological way, as a set of mechanisms within which people work to achieve ends, but also emphasizing the Islamic repertoire as interpreted by judges, *muftis*, and litigants. Arzoo Osanloo (trained as a jurist) visits similar courtrooms but as part of a study of rights discourses. She shows how women's claims to be rights-bearers are nourished in Qur'anic study groups but also by the codification of Iranian civil law that makes explicit individual rights; the framing is thus in terms of multiple pathways to asserting rights, rather than the strategic manipulation of references in the courtrooms.[14]

At the same time that we observe different framing effects in works by different anthropologists, we can also draw on these works to construct a comparative matrix of Islamic courts, with particular attention to the very different structures within which they function. The "Kadhi courts" of Kenya studied by Hirsch are used by an ethno-religious minority outside the state civil law system, whereas the Iranian courts studied by Mir-Hosseini and Osanloo are regulated by precisely such a state system, a difference that opens up a wider and more consequential domain-specific but yet public sphere for Iranian women seeking to demand rights. In such contexts, statutes may have a liberating judicial effect vis-à-vis a conservative religious establishment.

If the above studies start from the courtroom setting and then ask how judges and litigants act in that setting, another set of studies focuses on categories of Islamic law and how they are applied in those settings. Rosen and Brinkley Messick both examined the importance of "intention" (*niyya*) in courts, and the differences in their approaches returns us to the distinct starting points described earlier.[15] For Rosen, Moroccan (and more broadly Arabic) ideas of the person do not consider intentions to be unreadable because private, but readable because tightly tied to their actions and their social relationships. This idea does not derive from Islamic jurisprudence but from Arabic culture, as it underlies actions in other areas of life as well. For Messick, Islamic writings stress the difficulties of knowing intention but also the crucial role of assessing intention for judging the effects of an act, including a speech act; beyond that, scholars have developed diverging and contrasting opinions, in some cases influenced by the desire to model Islamic law on European commercial law, where intention can be sufficient to enforce a contract. Although Messick limits his textual exploration to the Zaydi legal school, issues raised therein surface across the Muslim world, for example, concerning whether the correct expression of a husband's divorce pronouncement (for example, *anti taliq*, "you are divorced"), or the correct intention (as opposed to speaking in jest), or both, are

[14] Ziba Mir-Hosseini, *Marriage on Trial: A Study of Islamic Family Law* (London: I.B. Tauris, 2001); Arzoo Osanloo, *The Politics of Women's Rights in Iran* (Princeton: Princeton University Press, 2009). See also Ziba Mir-Hosseini, *Islam and Gender: The Religious Debate in Contemporary Iran* (Princeton: Princeton University Press, 1999); Léon Buskens, *Islamitisch recht en familiebetrekkingen in Marokko* [Islamic Law and Family Relationships in Morocco] (Amsterdam: Bulaaq, 1999).

[15] Rosen, *Anthropology of Justice*, 51–53; Brinkley Messick, "Indexing the Self: Intent and Expression in Islamic Legal Acts," *Islamic Law and Society* 8, no. 2 (2001): 151–178.

required for the pronouncement to take effect. This area of the felicity conditions for an Islamic speech is understudied but central to the anthropology of Islamic law. As we shall see below, *niyya* is a central concept in judging the successful performance of a ritual obligation as well.

As we have assembled a greater number of ethnographies of courtrooms we have become better able to show the variation across traditions and sometimes among judges on these issues. For example, Clarke shows that Lebanese Sunni judges hold that they *cannot* know a person's intentions, and therefore on the matter of a divorce pronouncement cannot invalidate it on grounds of incorrect intention. And yet sometimes a judge will sense that the general good is best served by finding another way, which some of them do by urging the couple to halt the legal proceeding (where the outcome is certain) and seek a more accommodating *fatwa* from a jurisconsult (*mufti*).[16]

Because "family law" is the legal domain most likely to be labeled as "Islamic" in Muslim societies today, marriage contracts deserve particular attention—and because they are sometimes cited as the solution to unequal treatment of women under Islamic family law. The Saudi case is particularly illuminating because of the importance of religious jurists' interpretations for legal practices. Lisa Wynn shows how Saudi brides' mothers insist on including conditional clauses (*shurut*) in the marriage contracts, mainly to ensure the right to complete higher education or to work outside the home (the proceeds of which would remain their own assets). They could, but rarely do, add a clause to guarantee the right to a divorce in case the husband took a second wife. Wynn also shows how the large investment by the husband in the marriage provides a disincentive to pronounce a *talaq*. Ever since the pioneering studies by Annelies Moors and Mir-Hosseini, the ways in which *mahr*, either paid or promised, strengthens women's bargaining power has become an important empirical contribution.[17]

III. Normativity and Property

Islamic law (at least as studied in anthropology) is not limited to the settings of state courtrooms, but includes other settings where actors refer to Islamic normative writings (scriptures, texts of *fiqh* or *fatwas*) to justify actions.

16 Morgan Clarke, "The Judge as Tragic Hero: Judicial Ethics in Lebanon's Shari'a Courts," *American Ethnologist* 39, no. 1 (2012): 106–121.

17 Lisa Wynn, "Marriage Contracts and Women's Rights in Saudi Arabia: Mahr, Shurût, and Knowledge Distribution," in *The Islamic Marriage Contract: Case Studies in Islamic Family Law*, ed. Asifa Quraishi and Frank E. Vogel (Cambridge, MA: Harvard University Press, 2008), 200–214. Mir-Hosseini, *Marriage on Trial*; Annelies Moors, *Women, Property and Islam: Palestinian Experiences, 1920–1990* (Cambridge: Cambridge University Press, 1995).

The next most "state-like" settings are Islamic councils and *fatwa* bodies. The former developed in the British Indies in parallel to unsuccessful efforts to create Islamic courts, beginning in Bihar in 1921 with the creation of the *Imarat-i Shari'ah*, sponsored by the Jamiatul Ulema-e Hind. Today these *dar ul qazi* bring together moral and shari' concerns to hear cases of family conflicts and sometimes award a judicial divorce. They have no enforcement powers, and base judgments on their readings of *fiqh* rather than on the state personal law applied in the courts. The relationship between the shari'a councils (relying on *fiqh*) and the state courts (relying on law codes) illustrates the conceptual tension between "law" and "Islam" mentioned at the beginning of this chapter. It also shows the advantage for women in approaching an institution where their moral arguments are given considerable weight.[18] However, here as elsewhere, these two kinds of institutions do not exist in different worlds: a judge might send a case to a *dar ul qazi* precisely in order to move it from one framework for judgment to another, for example away from a dispute with criminal implications toward an effort to restore harmony (even if by divorcing the couple).

British shari'a councils are transplanted, and somewhat transformed, versions of the Indian institutions, with altered terms of trade with courts and a more international set of scholars and clients, as are their North American counterparts. In those courts the law/Islam tension becomes not a *de facto* division of labor between institutions, as in India, but a division internal to the shari'a councils. If traditional *fiqh* allows the wife to initiate a divorce by making an incentive payment to her husband, and limits the capacity of a judge to dissolve the marriage without the husband's consent, most Islamic state legal regimes include the possibility of a judicial divorce. In Western Europe and North America there are no Islamic judges. A shari'a council has no enforcement power, and is not a college of *qadis*. Muslim wives have nowhere else to turn to obtain a divorce, however. Councils find themselves in an uncertain and sometimes difficult quandary, which they attempt to overcome by inducing the husband to give a *talaq*, or to not object to their action in dissolving the marriage. In much of Europe and North America, some scholars try to avoid this quandary by encouraging prenuptial contracts, or by arguing (in *de facto fatwas*) that civil divorce counts as Islamic.[19]

In nearly all anthropological studies of judges and courts, including those already mentioned, attention is also directed to extra-judicial ways of resolving disputes and regulating property transmission. Here careful ethnographic work has shown that a rule or category, such as those regarding women's rights to inheritance shares, conceals a multi-dimensional space of power and resources. Important here was the

[18] Katherine Lemons, *At the Margins of the Law: Adjudicating Muslim Families in Contemporary Delhi* (Ph.D. dissertation, University of California, Berkeley, 2010).

[19] John R. Bowen, *On British Islam: Religion, Law and Everyday Practice in Shari'a Councils* (Princeton: Princeton University Press, 2016).

study of Palestinian women carried out by Annelies Moors, who showed that when a woman inherits property this inheritance could be a mark of her social status, that she is of a wealthy, high-status family, or it could happen because she is in a weak situation and must try to claim property to survive—but even then is likely to find herself subsequently deprived of the property by more powerful brothers or cousins. Moors's study adds ethnographic substance to Pierre Bourdieu's well-known argument that "following rules" explains little of the political economy of marriage or transfers of property.[20]

IV. LAW AND ETHICS

In the early 2000s, anthropologists writing on Islam and Christianity began to underscore the analytical importance of ethical practices in religious traditions. Talal Asad had argued earlier, and in the context of a rebuttal of Clifford Geertz's symbolic approach to religion, that for some important religious thinkers (St. Augustine principal among them) as for ordinary practitioners, religious practices and religious discipline are seen as means to instill faith and character, both seen as part of a tradition. This intervention coincided with the turn to considering Aristotelian virtue ethics and the rise of communitarian political philosophy.[21]

Since that intervention, and subsequent ethnographic studies on prayer and sermons by students of Asad,[22] other studies have sought to disentangle ethical from legal dimensions of judgments about shari'a. Hussein Ali Agrama argues that the *fatwa* should be seen as a way of "caring for the self"—an ethical discourse—at least as much as a way of judging doctrinal matters or adapting to changing contexts.[23] Advice-giving (to invoke a category perhaps broader than *ifta'*) surely seeks to apply a broad range of knowledge to a particular case. A religious leader north of Paris once described to me the way in which he distinguished between the scholarly consensus on abortion, which he saw as a blanket condemnation, and his response to a

[20] Moors, *Women, Property*, 48–76; Pierre Bourdieu, *Outline of a Theory of Practice* (Cambridge: Cambridge University Press, 1977); See also Martha Mundy, *Domestic Government: Kinship, Community and Policy in North Yemen* (London: I.B. Tauris, 1996).

[21] Talal Asad, *Genealogies of Religion: Disciplines and Reasons of Power in Christianity and Islam* (Baltimore: Johns Hopkins University Press, 1993); Alasdair MacIntyre, *After Virtue* (Notre Dame: University of Notre Dame Press, 1981).

[22] Saba Mahmood, *Politics of Piety: The Islamic Revival and the Feminist Subject* (Princeton: Princeton University Press, 2005); Charles Hirschkind, *The Ethical Soundscape: Cassette Sermons and Islamic Counterpublics* (New York: Columbia University Press, 2009).

[23] Hussein Ali Agrama, "Ethics, Tradition, Authority: Toward an Anthropology of the Fatwa," *American Ethnologist* 37 (2010): 2–18.

particular woman seeking advice, in which he gauges her needs and capacities, and gives advice accordingly. This scholar described the difference in terms of general principles, on the one hand, and looking to ensure the welfare of the individual, on the other, not far from the Foucauldian "care of the self."[24]

Are the activities of judges so different? As Clarke points out, some judges adopt more than one discursive stance, changing from a non-legal to a legal modality as they move into the courtroom setting.[25] But does this mean that we need to distinguish "ethics" and "rules" as two distinct ways judges (and other scholars) approach ordinary Muslims and their questions? An alternative is to study the way individuals providing judgments (*muftis*, judges, scholars, or *imams*) combine distinct types of considerations and distinct kinds of justifications, in a single case. In studying the Islamic appellate court in Aceh, Indonesia in 2012, I found judges deciding a *talaq* case discussing the moral quality of a husband's or wife's behavior, the husband's likely ability to pay, and rules in *Shafi'i fiqh*, before setting the level of payments due the wife. In their written decisions, however, they justified their awards solely in terms of statutes and Supreme Court circulars. Only through fieldwork could the difference be discerned between the multiple forms of moral and legal reasoning shaping the judgment, on the one hand, and the written, and legalistic, formal justification, on the other.

A. Medical Ethics

By the 2000s, the fast-developing field of anthropology of biotechnology had turned to the shifting relationships between reproductive technology and Islamic jurisprudence and ethics. Abdulaziz Sachedina provided an overall analysis of the issues for Islam, and Marcia Inhorn and others studied ways in which these issues were debated and decided locally.[26] Inhorn worked in Egypt and Lebanon; she contrasts official Sunni and Shi'a *fatwas* on the question of in vitro fertilization (IVF). The position enunciated by Egypt's al-Azhar and followed thereafter permits fertilization using the wife's egg and the husband's sperm, because these techniques respect marriage as a contract between the husband and wife. By the same token, use of surrogates or another man's sperm is disallowed. By contrast, some Shi'a scholars have permitted the use of donated eggs or sperm, with the proviso that the child

[24] John R. Bowen, *Can Islam Be French? Pluralism and Pragmatism in a Secularist State* (Princeton: Princeton University Press, 2009), 83–84.

[25] Clarke, "The Judge as Tragic Hero."

[26] Abdulaziz Sachedina, *Islamic Biomedical Ethics: Principles and Application* (Oxford: Oxford University Press, 2011); Marcia Inhorn, "Making Muslim Babies: IVF and Gamete Donation in Sunni versus Shi'a Islam," *Culture, Medicine and Psychiatry* 30, no. 4 (2006): 427–450; Morgan Clarke, *Islam and New Kinship: Reproductive Technology and the Shariah in Lebanon* (New York: Bergahn Books, 2009).

born through such technologies inherit from the donor, as the biological parent; other scholars require that a man conduct a temporary (*mut'a*) marriage with an egg donor (the issue being whether *zina* occurs only with physical intercourse) and forbid sperm donation. For some of these latter scholars, embryo donation is allowed, as it comes from one married couple to another. Inhorn finds, however, that despite the variation in scholarly views, most Shi'a and Sunni Muslims reject the possibility of donating sperm or eggs, because it would confuse issues of kinship and inheritance, and is a form of adultery. And yet some couples do engage in all these practices, and find ways to register babies so as to conform to the public rulings.[27] Here we find a divergence among practices, popular opinion, and formal religious positions.

In the most in-depth treatment of Islamic law and medical ethics and practices to date, Sherine Hamdy explores the progression of positions and debates concerning organ transplantation in Egypt.[28] She notes that in the cross-currents of official *fatwas* on the matter, one could miss the way a prominent television personality and preacher (*da'iya*), M. Sha'rawi, framed the issue for most Egyptians through his introduction of the phrase "our body belongs to God." Subsequent debates on all levels can be seen as a series of meditations on what that phrase means for the ethics of particular medical practices. Sha'rawi, although dismissed or reviled by many scholars, reasoned from clear principles to an outright rejection of organ transplantation. In the debate that ensued, those in official positions took pains to emphasize that his statement was not a *fatwa*, because he did not engage in the proper legal reasoning and was not a recognized *mufti*. But his followers did publish his statements as *fatwas*, in the broader sense of *ifta'* or responses to questions. They led the grand *mufti*, at the time Shaykh Tantawi, to issue a rebuttal. He started from Sha'rawi's premises, but used them to prohibit only selling organs, arguing that under conditions of necessity (*darura*) human need permits donating organs. For Tantawi, as for most other scholars, the benefit (*maslaha*) achieved through organ transplantation justified its use. As Hamdy points out, medical doctors were critical of this reasoning, having as it does the potential to justify any action that benefits someone. In the gap between Sha'rawi and Tantawi we can see the division between traditionalist and pragmatist forms of Islamic reasoning.

This contrast shows how, alongside official forms of *ifta'* are other modes of dispensing advice, which some may refer to as *ifta'*, but which follow different genre conventions. Sha'rawi's particular education, medium, and ways of arguing

[27] Morgan Clarke, "New Kinship, Islam, and the Liberal Tradition: Sexual Morality and New Reproductive Technology in Lebanon," *Journal of the Royal Anthropological Institute* (N.S.) 14 (2008): 153–169.

[28] Sherine Hamdy, *Our Bodies Belong to God: Organ Transplants, Islam, and the Struggle for Human Dignity in Egypt* (Berkeley: University of California Press, 2012).

may have placed him outside "official *ifta*" circles, but many Egyptians nonetheless followed his advice.

V. Norms of 'Ibadat

Although less often involving judges and courts, the core rituals of Islam (including worship, pilgrimage, fasting, and sacrifice) are subject to similar processes of normative scrutiny and judgment. Here the Islam/culture division reappears, even as anthropologists are able to emphasize the creative dimensions of what seem at first blush to be the most scripted actions: the formulaic practices of ritual prayer (*salat*).

Although social anthropologists might label prayer as "ritual" as distinguished from the "legal" act of divorcing, both have tightly scripted and highly debated "felicity conditions," or the conditions under which an act counts as accomplishing a divorce or as satisfying the requirements for prayer. These conditions are set out in similar fashion in books of *fiqh*, and justified by pointing to *hadith* attributed to the Prophet. The Prophet's actions, including his responses to questions, provide grounds for specifying how to divorce, worship, perform the pilgrimage, or carry out a wide range of other actions. Divine retribution and reward follow proper or improper carrying out of these obligations, and so from an Islamic perspective they are all governed by law, whether or not states choose to enact statutes regarding one or another such action.

We could perhaps think (in a very non-Weberian fashion) of the opposition law/non-law as one of analytical framework rather than one that distinguishes among types of action. Viewing the question in this way helps to sort out differences among anthropologists regarding ritual. For example, prayer or *salat* can be studied for ways in which practitioners evaluate the correctness of performance. Unlike prototypical rituals in anthropology, practitioners of prayer emphasize its felicity conditions. Muslims' disputes about *salat* concerned, for example, how to hold the arms in the correct fashion, or to formulate the right intention (*niyya*) while in prayer. Viewed from a normative Islamic perspective, in terms of its law-like properties, one could emphasize the criteria for correct performance. Because the basic ritual template is fixed, attention often is focussed on minute variations in performance, allowing these variations to take on a great deal of social significance, indexing differences in theology, idea of community, or ethnic affiliation.[29] Other anthropologists have emphasized other dimensions of the performance; Saba Mahmood analyzes *salat* as

[29] John R. Bowen, "Salat in Indonesia: The Social Meanings of an Islamic Ritual," *Man* (N.S.) 24 (1989): 299–318; Mahmood, *Politics of Piety*.

performance of certain ethical dispositions, which are developed through repeated prayer. In other words, Mahmood investigates the interrelationship between self-discipline and ritual performance, whereas I focussed on the social–performative implications of such a tightly scripted practice. My analysis situated *salat* in the domain of *fiqh*; Mahmood in the domain of worship (*'ibadat*).

VI. Conclusions

The advances made since the 1990s concern a rapprochement between anthropology and Islamic studies. The main elements of that change has been the willingness of Islamicists to consider seriously the interpretations and practices of the unlettered, and the corresponding willingness of anthropologists to trace derivations and adaptations of textual elements in specific social and cultural contexts.[30] Many convergences have resulted, for example about how judges and courts work in a number of contexts. This convergence is, of course, partial, as each discipline formats and evaluates work in distinct ways: anthropologists still focus on social processes and cultural ideas. But the finding that Muslims approach questions of law and religion in a wide range of ways, some more grounded in the written tradition than others, does not threaten that tradition but displays its versatility.

Anthropology is expanding its reach and, as it does so, it is adjusting its conceptual and methodological toolkits. What appear at one point to be quarrels—What is a *fatwa*? What is prayer?—will turn out to be different questions asked of the same, complex object. Fine-grained analyses of practices, interactions, and emotions allow anthropologists to, for example, appreciate the different modalities of ways a judge might speak (in and out of the courtroom, at different moments), the changes and variations in emotional dimensions of prayer (at different stages of personal development, in different circles), and the multiplicity of ways that an inheritance rule is realized in social life (by social status, wealth, and region).

This more sophisticated rendering of anthropology's conception of what it is doing—meta-theory of what an approach is and what an object is—should be accompanied by the further expansion of empirical study into areas currently only dimly illuminated: the varieties in *ifta'*, the complexities of non-state shari'a councils, the mechanisms generating different levels of *mahr*—among many others. Recursively these two movements—better grasp of variation and better appreciation of pluralism in approach and frameworks—ought to enrich and clarify how we think about "law," "Islam," and anthropology.

[30] An early example is Brinkley Messick, *The Calligraphic State. Textual Domination and History in a Muslim Society* (Berkeley: University of California Press, 1993).

References

Agrama, Hussein Ali, "Ethics, Tradition, Authority: Toward an Anthropology of the Fatwa." *American Ethnologist* 37 (2010): 2–18.

Antoun, Richard T., *Muslim Preacher in the Modern World* (Princeton: Princeton University Press, 1989).

Asad, Talal, *Genealogies of Religion: Disciplines and Reasons of Power in Christianity and Islam* (Baltimore: Johns Hopkins University Press, 1993).

Bourdieu, Pierre, *Outline of a Theory of Practice* (Cambridge: Cambridge University Press, 1977).

Bowen, John R., "Salat in Indonesia: The Social Meanings of An Islamic Ritual." *Man* (N.S.) 24 (1989): 299–318.

Bowen, John R., *Islam, Law, and Equality in Indonesia: An Anthropology of Public Reasoning* (Cambridge: Cambridge University Press, 2003).

Bowen, John R., *Can Islam Be French? Pluralism and Pragmatism in a Secularist State* (Princeton: Princeton University Press, 2009).

Bowen, John R., *On British Islam: Religion, Law and Everyday Practice in Sharīʿa Councils* (Princeton: Princeton University Press, 2016).

Buskens, Léon, *Islamitisch recht en familiebetrekkingen in Marokko* [Islamic Law and Family Relationships in Morocco] (Amsterdam: Bulaaq, 1999).

Clarke, Morgan, "New Kinship, Islam, and the Liberal Tradition: Sexual Morality and New Reproductive Technology in Lebanon." *Journal of the Royal Anthropological Institute* (N.S.) 14 (2008): 153–169.

Clarke, Morgan, *Islam and New Kinship: Reproductive Technology and the Shariah in Lebanon* (New York: Bergahn Books, 2009).

Clarke, Morgan, "The Judge as Tragic Hero: Judicial Ethics in Lebanon's Sharīʿa Courts." *American Ethnologist* 39, no. 1 (2012): 106–121.

Dupret, Baudouin, *Au nom de quel droit* (Paris: Maison des Sciences de l'Homme, 2000).

Eickelman, Dale F., *Knowledge and Power in Morocco* (Princeton: Princeton University Press, 1992).

Evans-Pritchard, E. E., *The Sanusi of Cyrenaica* (Oxford: Clarendon Press, 1949).

Geertz, Clifford, *Islam Observed: Religious Development in Morocco and Indonesia* (Chicago: University of Chicago Press, 1968).

Geertz, Clifford, "Local Knowledge: Fact and Law in Comparative Perspective" in Clifford Geertz (ed.) *Local Knowledge* (New York: Basic Books, 1983) 167–234.

Geertz, Clifford, Geertz, Hildred, and Rosen, Lawrence, *Meaning and Order in Moroccan Society: Three Essays in Cultural Analysis* (New York: Cambridge University Press, 1979).

Gellner, Ernest, *Saints of the Atlas* (Chicago: University of Chicago Press, 1969).

Gilsenan, Michael, *Recognizing Islam* (New York: Pantheon, 1982).

Hallaq, Wael B., *Sharīʿa: Theory, Practice, Transformations* (Cambridge: Cambridge University Press, 2009).

Hamdy, Sherine, *Our Bodies Belong to God: Organ Transplants, Islam, and the Struggle for Human Dignity in Egypt* (Berkeley: University of California Press, 2012).

Hirsch, Susan F., *Pronouncing and Persevering: Gender and the Discourses of Disputing in an African Islamic Court* (Chicago: University of Chicago Press, 1998).

Hirschkind, Charles, *The Ethical Soundscape: Cassette Sermons and Islamic Counterpublics* (New York: Columbia University Press, 2009).

Hurgronje, C. Snouck, *The Acehnese* Translated by A.W.S. O'Sullivan (Leiden: Brill, 1906).
Inhorn, Marcia, "Making Muslim Babies: IVF and Gamete Donation in Sunni versus Shi'a Islam." *Culture, Medicine and Psychiatry* 30, no. 4 (2006): 427–450.
Lemons, Katherine, *At the Margins of the Law: Adjudicating Muslim Families in Contemporary Delhi*. Ph.D. dissertation, University of California, Berkeley, 2010.
MacIntyre, Alasdair, *After Virtue* (Notre Dame: University of Notre Dame Press, 1981).
Mahmood, Saba, *Politics of Piety: The Islamic Revival and the Feminist Subject* (Princeton: Princeton University Press, 2005).
Masud, Muhammad Khalid, Peters, Rudolph, and Powers, David S., eds. *Dispensing Justice in Islam: Qadis and their Judgments* (Leiden: Brill, 2006).
Messick, Brinkley, *The Calligraphic State. Textual Domination and History in a Muslim Society* (Berkeley: University of California Press, 1993).
Messick, Brinkley, "Indexing the Self: Intent and Expression in Islamic Legal Acts." *Islamic Law and Society* 8, no. 2 (2001): 151–178.
Mir-Hosseini, Ziba, *Islam and Gender: The Religious Debate in Contemporary Iran* (Princeton: Princeton University Press, 1999).
Mir-Hosseini, Ziba, *Marriage on Trial: A Study of Islamic Family Law* (London: I.B. Tauris, 2001).
Moore, Sally Falk, ed. *Law and Anthropology: A Reader* (Malden, MA: Blackwell, 2005).
Moors, Annelies, *Women, Property and Islam: Palestinian Experiences, 1920–1990* (Cambridge: Cambridge University Press, 1995).
Mundy, Martha, *Domestic Government: Kinship, Community and Policy in North Yemen* (London: I.B. Tauris, 1996).
Osanloo, Arzoo, *The Politics of Women's Rights in Iran* (Princeton: Princeton University Press, 2009).
Rosen, Lawrence, *The Anthropology of Justice: Law as Culture in Islamic Society* (Cambridge: Cambridge University Press, 1989).
Sachedina, Abdulaziz, *Islamic Biomedical Ethics: Principles and Application* (Oxford: Oxford University Press, 2011).
Stiles, Erin E., *An Islamic Court in Context: An Ethnographic Study of Judicial Reasoning* (London: Palgrave Macmillan, 2009).
Von Benda-Beckmann, Franz, *Property in Social Continuity: Continuity and Change in the Maintenance of Property Relationships through Time in Minangkabau, West Sumatra* (The Hague: M. Nijhoff, 1979).
Wynn, Lisa, "Marriage Contracts and Women's Rights in Saudi Arabia: Mahr, Shurût, and Knowledge Distribution" in Asifa Quraishi and Frank E. Vogel (eds.) *The Islamic Marriage Contract: Case Studies in Islamic Family Law* (Cambridge, MA: Harvard University Press, 2008) 200–214.

CHAPTER 6

FALSAFA AND LAW

ANDREW F. MARCH

I. Introduction: *Falsafa*, Political Philosophy, and Law

In classical Islamic civilization, "philosophy" (*falsafa*) was a practice that began with the translation of Greek philosophy into Arabic.[1] *Falsafa* developed in the form of summaries and commentaries on the "Ancients," as well as in the form of treatises that addressed philosophical problems to a large extent received from the Greeks.[2] As with the Greeks, the entry to political topics in *falsafa* was often philosophical anthropology: the discussion of the human soul in its various parts leads to an account of reason, habit, and desire, which leads to treatments of human happiness, perfection, and the potential for immortality, all of which demand an account of how humans are to live best in this world. Recognizable assumptions of Greek political philosophy that permeate Islamic writings are that the highest

[1] See Dimitri Gutas, *Greek Thought, Arabic Culture: The Graeco-Arabic Translation Movement in Baghdad and Early ʿAbbāsid society (2nd–4th/8th–10th centuries)* (New York: Routledge, 1998).

[2] For general historical and thematic introductions to the philosophical tradition in "Islamicate" civilization, see Peter Adamson and Richard C. Taylor, eds., *The Cambridge Companion to Arabic Philosophy* (Cambridge, UK: Cambridge University Press, 2005); Seyyed Hossein Nasr and Oliver Leaman, *History of Islamic Philosophy* (New York: Routledge, 1996); and Majid Fakhry, *A History of Islamic Philosophy*, 3rd edn. (New York: Columbia University Press, 2004). For anthologies of *falsafa* in translation, see above all: John McGinnis and David C. Reisman, *Classical Arabic Philosophy: An Anthology of Sources* (Indianapolis: Hackett, 2007). Translations of works related to political and legal philosophy are cited in the notes that follow.

aspiration of human life is to attain true theoretical knowledge about the world and to order one's behavior in line with practical virtue, and that humans are naturally unequal in their capacities for reason and perfection (and even in their prospects for immortality).

However, the Islamic context also brought a new set of political problems to address or to reconcile with philosophy.[3] Chief among these were the questions of prophecy and the status of revealed law.[4] The latter is the particular focus of this chapter, although it cannot be elucidated in isolation from a wider survey of the doctrines advanced by Muslim philosophers. Indeed, problems such as God's justice, the nature of the soul, and the meaning of resurrection in the afterlife are not without political implications.

The relationship of the Muslim philosophers to orthodox religion has traditionally been one of the primary foci for western scholars of Arabic philosophy, particularly those following the teachings of Leo Strauss, who stressed the radical incompatibility of philosophy and theology and invited students to see esoteric meanings in both the explicit statements and the silences used by philosophers attempting to present their writings as harmonious (enough) with orthodox religion.[5] However, political philosophy was largely a derivative topic for the philosophers of the Islamic world themselves. One indication of this is that the *falsafa* tradition did not produce a coherent philosophy of law that would concern itself with the meaning, essence, source, and forms of "law" as such.[6] There is no clear analogue in the *falsafa* tradition to, for example, Aquinas's discussion in the *Summa* I–II, QQ. 90–105. Thus,

[3] For introductions to the political aspects of the Islamic philosophical tradition, see Hans Daiber, "Political Philosophy," in *History of Islamic Philosophy*, ed. Nasr and Leaman; Patricia Crone, Ch. 14, "The Greek Tradition and 'Political Science" in *God's Rule: Six Centuries of Medieval Islamic Political Thought* (New York: Columbia University Press, 2004), and Charles Butterworth, "Ethical and Political Philosophy," in *The Cambridge Companion to Arabic Philosophy*, eds. Adamson and Taylor. Somewhat more advanced are the essays in *The Political Aspects of Islamic Philosophy*, ed. Charles Butterworth (Cambridge, MA: Harvard University Press, 1992) and E. Gannagé et al., eds., *The Greek Strand in Islamic Political Thought*, special issue of *Mélanges de l'Université Saint-Joseph* 62 (2004). Works on specific thinkers or topics are cited in the notes that follow.

[4] See Frank Griffel, "Muslim Philosophers' Rationalist Explanation of Muhammad's Prophecy," in *The Cambridge Companion to Muhammad*, ed. Jonathan E. Brockopp (Cambridge, UK: Cambridge University Press, 2010), 158–179 and "Philosophy and Prophecy" in *The Routledge Companion to Islamic Philosophy*, eds. Richard C. Taylor and Luis Xavier López-Farjeat (New York: Routledge, 2016), 385–398.

[5] See Leo Strauss, "How Fārābī read Plato's *Laws*," in *What is Political Philosophy? And Other Studies* (Chicago: University of Chicago Press, 1988) and *Persecution and the Art of Writing* (Chicago: University of Chicago Press, 1980). See also Muhsin Mahdi, *Alfarabi and the Foundation of Islamic Political Philosophy* (Chicago: University of Chicago Press, 2001).

[6] See Charles E. Butterworth, "Philosophy of Law in Medieval Judaism and Islam," in *A History of the Philosophy of Law from the Ancient Greeks to the Scholastics*, ed. Fred D. Miller Jr. (vol. 6 of *A Treatise of Legal Philosophy and General Jurisprudence*; Dordrecht: Springer, 2007), 219. See also Rémi Brague, *The Law of God: The Philosophical History of an Idea*, trans. Lydia G. Cochrane (Chicago: University of Chicago Press, 2007), 161–162.

answering this question "What is the place of law in the *falsafa* tradition?" will require cobbling together remarks on law found within treatments of quite distinct moral and theoretical problems in the writings of a number of important philosophers in the Islamic tradition.

II. Farabi

The philosopher in the Islamic tradition most prominently associated with political philosophy is undoubtedly Abu Nasr al-Farabi (d. 339/950-1). While it is far from true that apart from Farabi "there is no other philosopher who with any stretch of the imagination can be said to have been a 'political philosopher',"[7] Farabi discussed political problems more explicitly and extensively over a greater number of texts than any other Muslim thinker until Ibn Khaldun.[8] These texts include *The Principles of the Opinions of the Citizens of the Virtuous City*,[9] *Political Governance*,[10]

[7] Dimitri Gutas, "The Study of Arabic Philosophy in the Twentieth Century: An Essay on the Historiography of Arabic Philosophy," *British Journal of Middle Eastern Studies* (2002): 23.

[8] For a general introduction to Farabi, see David C. Reisman, "Al-Fārābī and the Philosophical Curriculum," in *The Cambridge Companion to Arabic Philosophy* eds. Adamson and Taylor. The secondary literature on Farabi's political philosophy is quite substantial. Book length studies include (in addition to Mahdi) Miriam Galston, *Politics and Excellence: The Political Philosophy of Alfarabi* (Princeton, NJ: Princeton University Press, 1990); Hans Daiber, *The Ruler as Philosopher: A New Interpretation of al-Fārābī's View* (Amsterdam: North-Holland Pub. Co., 1986); and Christopher A. Colmo, *Breaking with Athens: Alfarabi as Founder* (Lexington Books, 2005). Other important studies of Farabi's political philosophy include Patricia Crone, "Al-Fārābī's Imperfect Constitutions"; Dimitri Gutas, "The Meaning of *madanī* in al-Fārābī's 'Political' Philosophy"; and Nelly Lahoud, "Al-Fārābī: On Religion and Philosophy" (all three in Gannagé et al., eds, *The Greek Strand in Islamic Political Thought*) as well as Fauzi M. Najjar, "al-Fārābī and Political Science," *The Muslim World* 48, no. 2 (1958): 94–103. If there is a single point of contention in scholarship on Farabi, it is between the view (advanced by Straussians) that for Farabi politics was the primary science that conditioned his metaphysical and cosmological doctrines and the contrary view (advanced by most non-Straussian Islamicists) that metaphysics and logic were primary for Farabi, and his political philosophy was derivative of his metaphysically informed psychology.

[9] Abu Nasr al-Farabi, *On the Perfect State (Mabadi' ara' ahl al-madina al-fadila)*, Richard Walzer, ed. and trans. (Chicago, IL: Kazi Publications, 1988) (henceforth: *Virtuous City*.) For a revisionist interpretation of the structure of this work, arguing that it should be read as an answer to orthodox works outlining the principles of theology and creed in Islam, see Ulrich Rudolph, "Reflections on al-Fārābī's, *Mabādi' ārā' ahl al-madīna al-fāḍila*," in *In The Age of Al-Fārābī: Arabic Philosophy in The Fourth-Tenth Century*, ed. Peter Adamson (London: Warburg Institute, 2008), 1–14.

[10] *Al-Siyasa al-madaniyya*. Translated as "The Political Regime" by Charles Butterworth in *Medieval Political Philosophy: A Sourcebook*, ed. Joshua Parens and Joseph C. Macfarland, 2nd edn. (Ithaca, NY: Cornell University Press, 2011) and in Alfarabi, *The Political Writings, Volume II: "Political Regime" and "Summary of Plato's Laws"* (Ithaca, NY: Cornell University Press, 2015) (henceforth: *Regime*).

The Attainment of Happiness,[11] *Selected Aphorisms (of the Statesman)*,[12] *Enumeration of the Sciences*,[13] *Book of Religion*,[14] *The Harmonization of the Two Opinions of the Two Sages: Plato the Divine and Aristotle*,[15] and *Summary of Plato's Laws*.[16]

For Farabi, "political science" (*al-ʿilm al-madani*) is the investigation into voluntary (as opposed to innate) actions, character traits, dispositions, and ways of life that are conducive to true happiness in this life and the next, in particular the two faculties comprising the craft of rulership: (a) the faculty for setting down universal rules, and (b) the faculty of practical experience and judgment (*phronesis; taʿaqqul*) acquired through lengthy experience and long observation of public affairs.[17] However, political philosophy for Farabi is not a free-standing discipline with its own autonomous logic and concerns (as it would become, arguably, in Ibn Khaldun) but a branch of one integral, harmonious philosophical teaching that begins with ontology ("the first cause"), proceeds to cosmology (from "the world above the moon" to "sublunar bodies"), and eventually to psychology.

For Farabi, man is distinguished from other creatures by the possession of a rational faculty capable both of governing the lower faculties (appetitive, deliberative) and of attaining theoretical (that is, scientific and metaphysical) knowledge.[18] Many "intelligibles" arise in man's rational faculty naturally due to the presence of the Active Intellect (*al-ʿaql al-faʿal;*), a divine-like presence at the bottom of a descendent order of beings beginning with the First Cause, which Farabi suggests impacts the intellect in a way comparable (following Aristotle in *De anima* 3.5) to the role of light in making sight possible. Some "first intelligibles" impress themselves on the intellect immediately through the Active Intellect, including logical

[11] *Tahsil al-saʿada*. English translation in *Alfarabi, Philosophy of Plato and Aristotle*, trans. Muhsin Mahdi (Ithaca, NY: Cornell University Press, 2001), 13–50 (henceforth: *Attainment*).

[12] *Fusul muntazaʿa*. English translation in *Alfarabi, The Political Writings: "Selected Aphorisms" and Other Texts*, Charles Butterworth, trans. (Ithaca, NY: Cornell University Press, 2001), 1–67 (henceforth: *Aphorisms*).

[13] *Ihsaʾ al-ʿulum*. English translation in *Alfarabi, The Political Writings*, 76–84 (henceforth: *Enumeration*).

[14] *Kitab al-milla*. English translation in *Alfarabi, The Political Writings*, 93–113 (henceforth: *Religion*).

[15] *Kitab al-jamʿ bayn raʾyay al-hakimayn, Aflatun al-Ilahi wa Aristutalis*. English translation in *Alfarabi: The Political Writings*, 125–167 (henceforth: *Harmonization*). For doubts on al-Farabi's authorship of this text, see Marwan Rashed, "On the Authorship of the Treatise *On the Harmonization of the Opinions of the Two Sages* attributed to al-Fārābī," *Arabic Sciences and Philosophy* 19, no. 1 (2009): 43–82.

[16] *Jawamiʿ Kitab al-nawamis li-Aflatun*. Extract translated by Muhsin Mahdi in *Medieval Political Philosophy: A Sourcebook*, ed. Ralph Lerner and Muhsin Mahdi, 1st edn. (Ithaca, NY: Cornell University Press, 1972), 83–94. A complete translation of the work, edited and revised by Charles Butterworth, is now published in *Alfarabi, The Political Writings, Volume II: "Political Regime" and "Summary of Plato's Laws,"* Charles Butterworth trans. and ed. (Ithaca, NY: Cornell University Press, 2015) (henceforth: *Plato's Laws*). For a somewhat controversial book-length interpretation of this text, in the tradition of Strauss' "How Fārābī Read Plato's Laws," see Joshua Parens, *Metaphysics as Rhetoric: Alfarabi's Summary of Plato's "Laws"* (Albany, NY: SUNY Press, 1995).

[17] *Enumeration*, §1, 76–77.

[18] See *Virtuous City*, Ch. 13, 197–211 for the present two paragraphs.

truths (e.g. the whole is greater than the part) and knowledge of what is good and evil in human actions. Man's ultimate goal, the goal that is pursued for its own sake and never for the sake of something else, is happiness or felicity (*eudaimonia, sa'ada*), which consists in true knowledge of the cosmos and man's place in it, as well as the voluntary performance of those "beautiful deeds" (*al-af'al al-jamila*) which help in attaining felicity.

It is the goal of philosophy to teach men not only the concept of happiness or true beliefs about the world, but also how to train the will (the appetitive faculty) to desire happiness and to develop the deliberative faculty so that it can correctly identify the actions that lead to happiness. Those dispositions (*hay'at*) and habits (*malakat*) from which such actions proceed are the virtues (*fada'il*). In sum, for happiness to be attained: it must bc known by the rational faculty; it must be desired by the appetitive faculty; the actions that lead to it must be discerned by the deliberative faculty; and the virtues that result in sound dispositions and habits must be firmly developed in the rational man. Ultimately the goal is the purification of the soul to such an extent that it can subsist without matter and survive eternally after the death of the body.[19]

From these metaphysical and psychological premises Farabi derives his political philosophy. As in Aristotle, man cannot provide for all of his needs alone and cannot attain "the perfection for the sake of which his inborn nature (*fitra*) has been given to him, unless many people who co-operate come together."[20] Many forms of human association might provide for a number of the natural needs that individuals cannot satisfy alone, but only "the city in which people aim through association at co-operating for the things by which felicity in its real and true sense can be attained is the excellent city."[21] Farabi's excellent city is necessarily inegalitarian; citizens' qualities, predispositions, talents, and ranks are all of unequal quality and worth, and are given to persons as part of their nature and inborn character (*fitra*).[22] It is a large part of the task of the political and kingly craft to cultivate the habits appropriate to citizens' innate dispositions. As justice in the individual consists in the parts of the soul being ordered and governed rationally, justice in the city consists in the performance of "voluntary" (*ikhtiyariyya*) actions and roles according to one's proper place in a harmonious, hierarchically ordered, organic whole.

Atop the city sits the ruler (*ra'is*), who is its most perfect part and embodies the best of everything found within it. Farabi's ruler is not only a sovereign over whom no other human can have any authority whatsoever, but an archetypical founder: "the ruler must come to be in the first instance, and will subsequently be the cause of the rise of the city and its parts and of their arrangement in the ranks proper to them."[23] Thus, the polis is analogized not only to the body or the soul, but to the cosmos, and the political ruler not only to the ruling organ of the body (for

[19] *Regime*, §83, 43. [20] *Virtuous City*, Ch. 15, 229. [21] *Virtuous City*, Ch. 15, 231.
[22] *Regime*, §§73–77, 40–41. [23] *Virtuous City*, Ch. 15, 235.

Farabi, the heart) or the soul (reason) but to God, the First Cause: "the relation of the First Cause to the other existents is like the relation of the king of the excellent city to its other parts . . . The excellent city ought to be arranged in the same way: all its parts ought to imitate in their actions the aim of their first ruler according to their rank."[24]

Farabi's true ruler is a philosopher who has attained perfection in all aspects of his humanity (theoretical and practical). He is, in fact, a demigod:[25] a man who has become "actually intellect" and actually "being thought" (intelligized) by the absolute perfection of his representative faculty.[26] Farabi of course intends this description to invoke associations with the Prophet and, more ambiguously, with Shiʿa notions of the Imams after Muhammad:[27] "the idea of Philosopher, Supreme Ruler, Prince, Legislator and Imam is but a single idea."[28] Farabi gives a naturalistic account of prophecy, which was to be profoundly influential on subsequent philosophers, particularly Ibn Sina: "When [perfection] occurs in both parts of his rational faculty, namely the theoretical and the practical rational faculties, and also in his representative faculty, then it is this man who receives Divine Revelation, and God Almighty grants him Revelation through the mediation of the Active Intellect, so that the emanation from God Almighty to the Active Intellect is passed on to his Passive Intellect through the mediation of the Acquired Intellect, and then to the faculty of representation."[29]

The ruler is thus distinguished in the first order by the union of his soul with the Active Intellect and his perfect knowledge of every action by which happiness is attained. However, his perfection as a philosopher must be joined with the political and deliberative arts,[30] including exceptional skills of oration and rhetoric that allow him to rouse the imaginations of those not able to be led to virtue through reason and demonstration. The true ruler—who has a thoroughly personal political sovereignty in that he is the cause of the happiness of his city's inhabitants (rather than the law, or the system)—would possess a full panoply of twelve natural qualities (*khisal*) of moral, intellectual, and physical excellence. Farabi's listing, which parallels Islamic juridical discussions of the legal qualifications for supreme authority (*shurut al-Imama*), describes the natural ruler not only of a virtuous city but also of a universal civilization (*al-maʿmura kulluha; oikumene*) organized around the collective pursuit of true felicity.

[24] *Virtuous City*, Ch. 15, 237–239.

[25] Farabi notes in *Aphorisms* that the Ancients referred to the person disposed by nature for both the theoretical and the practical virtues and who perfected them through habit as divine (*Aphorisms*, §12, 18).

[26] *Regime*, §§79–80, 42.

[27] On Farabi as having Twelver Shiʿa sympathies, see Fauzi M. Najjar, "Fārābī's Political Philosophy and Shīʿism," *Studia Islamica* (1961): 57–72.

[28] *Attainment*, §57, 47.

[29] *Virtuous City*, Ch. 15, 245.

[30] *Attainment*, §54, 43–44.

But such men are rare. Farabi thus introduces a descending hierarchy of next-best options. First is a man who displays many of the qualities of the true philosopher-Imam but not all of them. Such a man can exercise sovereignty even without the attribute of prophecy. Farabi's view is thus that prophecy—the essential quality in determining the authority of law in traditional religion—is, in fact, a dispensable attribute of a lawgiver if he is a philosopher and possesses the most important moral, intellectual, and physical attributes.

But even these near-perfect rulers are not always available. However, if "there was previously an unbroken succession of sovereigns of this kind, the laws and the customs [*shara'i' wa sunan*] which were introduced will be adopted and eventually firmly established."[31] Later rulers without exceptional qualities of philosophical knowledge and political skill are advised to faithfully execute and follow the laws (*sunan*) of their forbearers that the city has come to accept as authoritative.[32] This seems to be something of a philosophical allegory of the formation of law in early Muslim society, with the actions and rulings of the Prophet and the earliest Rightly Guided Caliphs (or, possibly, the 'Alid Imams) being recognized as authoritative precedent, but only contingently because of the rupture in right guidance by true rulers.

At any point a new sovereign ruler can appear and be regarded as the successor of the first ones. However, his nomothetic qualities, while exalted, appear somewhat diminished from those of the original first ruler. Farabi speaks of a philosopher (*hakim*) possessing the qualities of rulership by nature who, however, appears bound in his sovereign will by the past. Such a ruler will *know and remember* the laws and customs with which the first rulers had governed the city, conforming in all his action to theirs; his legislative authority consists mostly in his excellence at deducing (*istinbat*) new laws by analogy where no law had been recorded, following the principles laid down by the first Imams.[33] Such successors complete the law based on their judgment of what is good for their time and place.[34]

The echoes here of orthodox Islamic legal theory and public law are obvious. The classical works of Islamic public law (composed around the time, or shortly after, Farabi wrote) required that the Imam or Caliph be qualified in Islamic law to *mujtahid* level, and the notion of law-making here seems to track developed notions of extending the revealed law into new areas through a disciplined use of *qiyas* based on the original rules and principles enshrined in the law. Farabi also declares that the ruler will have great powers of deliberation (*ru'yya*) and will be able to make decisions based on the common good (*salah*) where the founders could not have laid down any precedent. This, of course, overlaps with both the principle of allowing for legal rules based on *maslaha mursala* as well as constitutional theories in Islam

[31] *Virtuous City*, Ch. 15, 251. [32] *Regime*, §82, 43; *Religion*, §9, 99–100.
[33] *Virtuous City*, Ch. 15, 251; *Aphorisms*, §58, 38. [34] *Religion*, §8, 99.

that allow for temporarily binding decisions by the ruler if they are motivated by considerations of the common good.

Farabi also considers the scenario when no single man possessing all the qualifications of rulership can be found (a concern that the jurists shared from an early period as well). His proposal of a condominium of power between two men—one a philosopher and another who possesses the remaining qualifications—is reminiscent of the ancient Roman consulship during the republican era. But it—admittedly with a leap of the imagination—can be analogized to the practical condominium of authority that developed in classical Islam between the symbolic reigning Caliph and the executive Sultan. One might even compare it to the arrangement whereby the "secular" executive apparatus (whether downgraded Caliph or sultanic strongman) deferred to the religious scholars at large on matters of law and creed. For his part, Farabi was even able to imagine a ruling council of six different men, each of whom possessed one of the necessary qualifications for a just ruler. What he was not able to countenance was that philosophy might have no share in government at all.

With this brief sketch of Farabi's overall political philosophical project, it is possible to appreciate how the revealed law of Islam (the shari'a) and its practical science (*fiqh*) appear marginalized and diminished. Farabi never hides his quite provocative view that "religion" (usually: *milla*) is at best a public representation through symbolic and affective language of philosophical truth: "the determined opinions in the virtuous religion are either the truth or a likeness of the truth."[35] But even if a virtuous religion asserts opinions that approximate the truth, there is "no link or true congruence between one who has received revelation and who is perfect in theoretical knowledge, and one who has received revelation without having become perfect in theoretical knowledge."[36] Religion is a local attempt to direct the multitude (*jumhur*) to a close enough simulacrum of what can be authentically known only by the few through philosophical demonstration (*burhan*).[37]

The purpose of exposing the many to the kinds of images and metaphors that approximate philosophical truth is largely political. It is important for their good that they be ruled in accordance with truth, but it is equally important that they form opinions that induce them to accept their place within a harmoniously organized polis. "The descriptions of the things comprised by the opinions of religion ought to be such as to bring the citizens to imagine everything in the city ... so that what is described will be likenesses the citizens will follow in their ranks and actions."[38] There can be many religions that each approximate truth in different ways appropriate for different nations,[39] but only one unchanging philosophical truth. In both aspects of religion—its regulation of opinions and of actions—it is subordinate to philosophy.[40]

[35] *Religion*, §4, 97. [36] *Religion*, §4, 97.
[37] *Virtuous City*, ch. 17, 279; *Harmonization*, §61, 159; *Regime*, §90, 45; *Attainment*, §50, 41.
[38] *Religion*, §2, 95. [39] *Attainment*, §45, 39. [40] *Religion*, §5, 97.

The religious sciences are downgraded, without quite being degraded. While there is no path to true virtue and perfection except through theoretical philosophy, the revealed law can be regarded as an acceptable shortcut to the rules one ought to follow: "Another way [other than the true philosophical path] is for someone to be given the practical part by a revelation that directs him toward a determination of each thing that he ought to prefer or avoid."[41] Farabi regards looking to *fiqh* for practical guidance as a kind of heteronomous rule-following for those incapable of achieving genuine practical virtue.

Elsewhere, Farabi suggests that religious law, at its highest, is a locally acceptable way of working out particulars that are undetermined by philosophical universals: "the practical things in religion are those universals made determinate by stipulations restricting them … all virtuous laws are subordinate to the universals of practical philosophy."[42] He describes jurisprudence (*fiqh*) as "that by which a human being is able to infer, from the things the lawgiver declared specifically and determinately, the determination of each of the things he did not specifically declare. And he is able to aspire to a verification of that on the basis of the purpose of the lawgiver in the religion he legislated with respect to the nation for which it was legislated."[43]

Farabi's language here invokes core concepts from Islamic legal theory: the use of analogy (*qiyas*) to derive new rules and reference to the "purposes of the lawgiver" (*maqasid al-shari'a*). But note that, unlike classical *usul al-fiqh*, Farabi seems to limit *fiqh* to the extraction of new rulings for areas where the revealed law is silent. For the classical jurists, this was only a limited (and controversial) part of their practice; revelation itself demanded painstaking efforts at interpretation and the extraction of rulings. Also, Farabi's reference to jurisprudence as relative to a specific nation recapitulates his view of religion as a local practice of which there can be many (unlike philosophy). Moreover, Farabi at times suggests that jurisprudence is a practice to be pursued in ordinary times when an enlightened philosopher–ruler is not present to freely lay down new law or creatively reinterpret the law of the founder.[44]

Farabi's works also contain scattered philosophical prescriptions that mirror certain provisions within positive Islamic law (*fiqh*). A section of the *Selected Aphorisms* discusses different views of governors concerning crimes against individual persons, which may be excused by the harmed individuals, and crimes against the public sphere that may not be excused. Such categories might be thought analogous to *fiqhi* distinctions between the rights of persons (*huquq al-'ibad*) and the rights of God (*huquq Allah*).[45] Elsewhere, Farabi outlines the various purposes of just wars, one of which might be thought a philosophical translation of the Islamic expansionary jihad. In *The Attainment of Happiness*, for instance, Farabi speaks of

[41] *Aphorisms*, §94, 63. [42] *Religion*, §5, 97. [43] *Enumeration*, §4, 80.
[44] *Religion*, §9, 99–100. [45] *Aphorisms*, §63, 42.

war (*harb*, not *jihad*) as part of a *mission civilisatrice*: "conquering the nations and cities that do not submit to doing what will procure them that happiness for whose acquisition man is made.... the art of war that pursues this purpose is the just and virtuous art of war."[46] To give a final example, when Farabi writes that a "virtuous person is forbidden to reside in the corrupt regimes, and it is obligatory for him to emigrate to the virtuous cities if any exist in actuality at his time,"[47] this invites comparison to the Islamic notion of *hijra* and the view (particularly in the Maliki school) that all Muslims are obliged to migrate from non-Muslim lands to the *dar al-Islam*.

III. Ibn Sina

Farabi's successor Ibn Sina (Avicenna, d. 428/1037) was the greatest philosopher in the Islamic tradition.[48] Ibn Sina devoted much less attention to political issues than did Farabi.[49] Apart from a brief, but suggestive, discussion on practical philosophy in his *Epistle on the Divisions of the Rational Sciences* (*Risala fi aqsam al-'ulum al-'aqliyya*), the major source for Ibn Sina's political views is Book 10 of the section (*jumla*) on Metaphysics, or Theology (*Ilahiyyat*), of his massive philosophical *summa, al-Shifa'* (*The Healing*).[50] In the relatively brief treatment to be found in the *Shifa'* there are both clear debts to Farabi as well as intriguing differences where

[46] On the place of *jihad* in the philosophical tradition, see Joel L. Kraemer, "The *Jihād* of the *Falāsifa*," *Jerusalem Studies in Arabic and Islam* 10 (1987): 288–324. Kraemer does not see Farabi's discussions here as amounting to providing a philosophical underpinning to Islamic *jihad* doctrines. My claim is only that Farabi's views can plausibly be read as philosophical *analogues* to the theological and juridical treatments, not that they are full-fledged philosophical *allegories* (as I will suggest later with regard to Ibn Sina).

[47] *Aphorisms*, §93, 60–61.

[48] For general studies of Avicenna's philosophy, see Dimitri Gutas, *Avicenna and the Aristotelian Tradition: Introduction to Reading Avicenna's Philosophical Works* (Leiden: Brill, 1988); Jon McGinnis, *Avicenna* (Oxford: Oxford University Press, 2010); and Robert Wisnovsky, "Avicenna and the Avicennan Tradition," in Adamson and Taylor, *The Cambridge Companion to Arabic Philosophy*, 91–136.

[49] Accordingly, literature on Avicenna's political philosophy is quite sparse. But see Miriam Galston, "Realism and Idealism in Avicenna's Political Philosophy," *The Review of Politics* 41, no. 4 (1979): 561–577, James W. Morris, "The Philosopher–Prophet in Avicenna's Political Philosophy," in *The Political Aspects of Islamic Philosophy*, ed. Charles E. Butterworth, "The Political Teaching of Avicenna," *Topoi* 19 (2000): 35–44. For a study of Avicenna's impact on later political, ethical, and legal philosophy, see M. Cüneyt Kaya, "In the Shadow of 'Prophetic Legislation': The Venture of Practical Philosophy after Avicenna," *Arabic Sciences and Philosophy* 24, no. 2 (September 2014): 269–296.

[50] Avicenna, *The Metaphysics of* The Healing, trans. Michael E. Marmura (Provo, UT: Brigham Young University Press, 2005) (henceforth: *Metaphysics*).

Ibn Sina articulates political doctrines somewhat less at odds with orthodox Islamic sensibilities.

Ibn Sina shares with Farabi the view that the highest form of human existence consists in intellectual and spiritual perfection,[51] which is a preparation for the eternal existence of the soul free from the needs, desires, and imperfections of the body. The notion, found in much philosophy taking its inspiration from Plato and Aristotle, that ultimate happiness is simply not a realistic aspiration for all humans because of their innate intellectual inequalities, quite unabashedly articulated in Farabi, is one of the primary tensions between philosophy and orthodox religion. However, in the *Metaphysics* (Book Ten, Chapter Three, §5) Ibn Sina stresses moral and spiritual virtue over theoretical contemplation and intellectual perfection, without ever abandoning the idea that contemplation is associated with the highest form of human achievement. Unlike theoretical virtue, moral and spiritual virtues are, in principle, available to all humans even those without exceptional intellectual capacities, and cognitive excellence alone is not necessarily a morally relevant distinction between humans.

Ibn Sina's account of perfection and immortality for this reason appears somewhat more congenial to popular religion than Farabi's. When he writes that "moral states and positive dispositions are acquired by acts whose task is to turn the soul away from the body and the senses and to make continuous its remembrance of its true element,"[52] he is referring to the kinds of acts prescribed by religious law as worship and devotion. A person might alight on such soul-purifying acts alone without believing them to be commanded by God (as the Ancients might have), although action inspired by belief is preferable.[53] Moreover, Ibn Sina speculates that even persons of moderate intelligence, who were never capable of achieving theoretical virtue, but who nonetheless lived in accordance with the revealed law will experience through God's mercy a relatively easy separation of the soul from the body in the afterlife.[54]

Avicenna's more approving attitude toward the possibility of harmony between philosophical and revealed conceptions of law is exemplified by a famous passage from the *Epistle on the Divisions of the Rational Sciences*. After noting that the three branches of practical philosophy are ethics (governance of the self), economics (governance of the household), and politics (governance of the city) and that both Plato and Aristotle composed treatises on the "laws" (*nomoi*), he writes

> By the law [*namus*], the philosophers do not mean what the common people think, namely that law is deceit and trickery [*hila wa khadi'a*], but rather the law [*namus*] according to them is tradition [*al-sunna*], the fixed and enduring example and the coming down of revelation [*nuzul al-wahi*]. The Arabs too call the angel that comes down with revelation 'law'

[51] See Jon McGinnis, *Avicenna* (Oxford: Oxford University Press, 2010), particularly Ch. 5, "Psychology II" and Ch. 8, "Value Theory."

[52] *Metaphysics*, X.3.5, 369. [53] Ibid., X.3.6, 369. [54] Ibid., IX.7.24, 355.

[*namus*]. This part of practical wisdom makes known the existence of prophecy and the need the human species has of the divine law (*al-shari'a*) for its existence, preservation and life to come. It makes known the wisdom in the universal limits common to all the divine laws [*shara'i'*] and in those particular to one divine law or another, according to one people or another and one time or another. And it makes known the difference between divine prophecy and all of the false claims to it.[55]

Nonetheless, Ibn Sina does preserve the philosophical categories of the elect versus the multitude. He remarks that "*most* of what the populace [*jumhur*] confesses, takes refuge in, and upholds is true,"[56] and observes that a prophet must describe heaven and hell "so that the multitude will hear and obey"[57] but at the same time that such a prophet "must not involve them with anything pertaining to [theology and doctrine] beyond the knowledge that God is One, the Truth, and has nothing similar to Him.... For it is not for everyone that [the acquisition] of divine wisdom is facilitated."[58] Ibn Sina's proof of prophecy takes on a more providential character than Farabi's. He begins with human political needs—humans must live in societies for which they require laws, which can only come from an original lawgiver [*sannin*] and dispenser of justice [*mu'addil*]—and derives from these premises the conclusion that it is not possible "that divine providence should ordain the existence of the benefits [of helpful physical adaptations] and not [a righteous man to legislate and dispense justice]." For Ibn Sina, the necessary precondition of human society and justice is a human lawgiver who must have been endowed with both theoretical and practical virtue. And since we know that the former (human society with laws of justice) exists, then prophecy must also exist.[59]

Like with Farabi, Ibn Sina's prophet is primarily a lawgiver, although the latter's account stresses an active role for God more than the former's. Ibn Sina's prophet–lawgiver lays down laws (*sunan*) "with the permission of God, by His command (*amr*), inspiration (*wahy*) and the descent of the Holy Spirit on him" (from Q. 16:102). Whereas Farabi's first ruler is owed obedience on the basis of his personal charisma, Ibn Sina suggests the more orthodox view that the prophet–lawgiver's claim to obedience is derived from God, quoting the Qur'an that "command must belong to Him who creates" (Q. 7:54)[60] and claiming that "the prophet was commanded by God to impose these acts of worshipping Him."[61] Still, Ibn Sina describes the revelatory and political role of the prophet in ways similar to Farabi. Because humans will disagree and cannot be trusted to set aside personal interest, "law and justice

[55] The Arabic version of *Risala fi aqsam al-ʿulum al-ʿaqliyya* can be found in *Tisʿ rasāʾil fī al-ḥikmah wa-al-ṭabīʿīyāt wa-qiṣṣat Salāmān wa-Absāl* (Beirut: Dār Qābis, 1986). For the English, see the translation by Muhsin Mahdi, "On the Divisions of the Rational Sciences," in Parens and Macfarland, *Medieval Political Philosophy*, 74–76 or the more accurate rendering in Butterworth, "The Political Teaching of Avicenna," 38.

[56] *Metaphysics*, X.1.12, 362. [57] Ibid., X.2.4, 365. [58] Ibid., X.2.5, 365.

[59] Ibid., X.2.3, 365. [60] Ibid., X.2.4, 365. [61] Ibid., X.3.6, 369–370.

necessarily require a lawgiver and a dispenser of justice."[62] He will perform miracles so the people will recognize him as differentiated from them, should keep religious dogma simple so as not to confuse the masses and enable the spread of "views contrary to the city's welfare," and should inform the people of God's majesty through "symbols and similitudes." The prophet should not suggest that he holds hidden knowledge he is not revealing, but is permitted to speak in esoteric or symbolic ways that "call forth those naturally disposed [*musta'idin bi'l-jibilla*] toward theoretical reflection to pursue philosophic investigations."[63]

Where Ibn Sina's treatment of law exceeds that of Farabi is in his philosophical interpretation of certain known precepts and doctrines of Islamic positive law. Chapters 3–5 of Book Ten of the *Metaphysics* contain philosophical commentaries on a number of central aspects of applied law, sometimes in clear reference to Islamic legal terms and sometimes in more abstract language. Thus, the forms of worship legislated by prophets are to guard against collective forgetting of what the Prophet has revealed. Fasting, for example, "so greatly moves one's nature that he who fasts is reminded that what he is engaged in is not a jest. He will thus recall the intention behind this, which is to draw him nearer to God."[64] Ibn Sina mentions *jihad*, the *hajj*, sacrifice, and prayer all in this context, as acts that contribute to the "strengthening and spreading of the law (*sunna*)." He notes that both the common people (*al-'amma*) and the elect (*al-khassa*) will benefit from such acts, although the former benefit more in the afterlife because they would have been less likely to purify their souls in this world had laws and rituals not been legislated.

His account of the necessity for the lawgiver to divide the city into three classes (administrators, artisans, and guardians), with each person occupying his proper place and function,[65] is more Platonic and Farabian than Islamic. But his prescription for a common public treasury includes reference to the *fiqhi* term for war booty (*ghanima; ghana'im*) to be taken from "those who [obstinately] resist the law" (*al-mu'anidin li'l-sunna*), which corresponds to *fiqhi* descriptions of the rationale for fighting unbelievers.[66] Ibn Sina's ideal law for the city also includes provisions for imposing fines not only on perpetrators of crimes but also on their extended family who failed to restrain them, prohibitions on gambling and all professions that benefit only some without any social welfare or utility (such as theft, brigandage, and usury), and the criminalization of sexual acts that undermine the family ("the best foundation on which the city stands").[67]

In fact, Ibn Sina devotes particularly close attention to the institution of marriage, which he says is the first area on which the lawgiver must legislate. The laws on marriage must ensure that it takes place in a public way (to guard against illegitimacy and property disputes), that it endures the inevitable quarrels of conjugal life,

[62] *Metaphysics*, X.2.2, 364–365. [63] Ibid., X.2.7, 366.
[64] Ibid., X.3.2, 367. [65] Ibid., X.4.1, 370. [66] Ibid., X.4.2, 370.
[67] Ibid., X.4.4, 371.

and that it leads to the responsibility for children on the part of both parents. In this discussion, he rationalizes a number of distinctly Islamic family law provisions. Thus, the law must allow for divorce since "some natures cannot adapt themselves to others ... someone might get an unequal partner ... or they may not be able to cooperate in procreation."[68] Yet, the right to divorce is not placed in the hands of the woman "for, in reality, she is of feeble intellect and is quick to follow passion and anger.[69] As in *fiqh*, a woman can sue for divorce on grounds of mistreatment only through a judge, whereas a man is accorded the autonomous decision but with financial obligations attached so that he does not initiate divorce rashly. Similar references are made to the demanding requirements for reconciliation after a triple-*talaq* divorce (the woman must first marry another man, including consummation) as a deterrent to cruel or reckless men, to the veiling and seclusion of women (since their sexual desire is ravenous and acting on it is a cause of social shame), to the basic characteristic of Islamic marriage as a strict sexual contract, and to the permissibility of polygyny on condition of equity.

In his final chapter, Ibn Sina gives a brief sketch of the constitutional law of the just city, recapitulating in essence many of the standard doctrines of Sunni public law (*al-ahkam al-sultaniyya*). The legislator must prescribe obedience to all those who follow him (using the terms derived from *kh-l-f*, as in "caliph"), must ordain the necessary qualifications of a candidate for the supreme office, and must identify a number of methods for choosing or appointing rulers in the future, with direct designation (what would have been established practice by Ibn Sina's time) being the best since it avoids partisanship and unrest. Usurpers, rebels, and pretenders must be fought to the death and this is an obligation of all citizens. However, if one such rebel (*khariji*) wins and claims that his predecessor was defective in intellect and political skill, then he must be obeyed as the rightful Caliph. This treatment of obedience and rebellion mirrors quite faithfully *fiqhi* doctrines.

Some of his rules of war also track *fiqhi* provisions—like sanctioning the taking of women and property as spoil—although the explanation for them has a certain Aristotelian hue: "for, when such property and women are not administered according to the constitution of the virtuous city, they will not bring about the good for which property and women are sought."[70] Likewise belonging more to Aristotle than the Islamic laws of war is his claim that certain peoples (Turks and Africans) are "slaves by nature." More familiarly Islamic are his considerations of the justness of going to war, which include discussions of just wars to bring other cities under the divine law as well as of the permissibility of sparing them on the condition of paying tribute (*jizya*). In addition to listing prescriptions analogous to Islamic legal rulings, he gives a semi-philosophical, semi-prudential rationale for the principle of fighting non-aggressing peoples in the name of the law's universality. He argues

[68] *Metaphysics*, X.4.6, 372–373. [69] Ibid., X.4.6, 372. [70] Ibid., X.5.7, 376.

that even a city with "a good way of life" that nonetheless rejects the universality of Islamic law "must also be punished and war waged on them" because their denial weakens the law and might encourage other cities to reject it as well. However, he adds, "this war must not be pursued with the same severity as against the people utterly in error."[71]

Ibn Sina concludes with a discussion of criminal law and political virtues. As in the preceding discussions, his treatment is a mix of asserting provisions derived from the shari'a and philosophical accounts of the purposes and rationales behind them. For example, the crimes he identifies as public (i.e. as against the social order) include adultery as well as theft and treason. He notes that laws should be moderate and aspire to the mean, and that some matters of criminal and public law must be left to the judgment of future rulers and authority figures, in accordance both with Greek notions of political judgment and Islamic *siyasa shar'iyya* doctrines. Similarly, his claim that the mean in morals is sought in "the breaking of the dominance of the powers [of the passions], for the soul's purification and for enabling it to acquire the power of self-mastery" might encounter no objection either from a Hellenistic Peripatetic or from a Sufi moralist. The three supreme virtues moderating the pursuit of pleasure and comfort—temperance, practical wisdom, and courage—combine to create justice. The man who can combine justice with theoretical wisdom (i.e. philosophy) is the happy man. But Ibn Sina concludes by acknowledging a rank above the Aristotelian peak: the Prophet, who "becomes almost like a human god. Worship of him, after God, becomes almost allowed. He is indeed the world's earthly king and God's deputy on Earth."[72] Unlike Farabi, however, there is no suggestion that such a demigod might reappear in the life of the virtuous city.

IV. Ibn Bajja and Ibn Tufayl

Farabi and Ibn Sina shared an elitist conception of human perfection and natural human inequality, but both also subscribed to the Aristotelian view that humans are naturally sociable and require for their attainment of the good harmonious social existence. The task of politics is to design laws and institutions based on true knowledge and virtue, and to persuade all citizens of the justice and virtue of this order. Most citizens will have to be persuaded through the use of rhetoric and the symbolic imagery found in religious speech, while only a few will be shown the truth

[71] *Metaphysics*, X.5.8, 376. [72] Ibid., X.5.11, 378.

on the basis of philosophical demonstration (*burhan*). But, as long as all citizens acknowledge the justice of the political order and perform the duties appropriate to their station, a virtuous city in which all persons attain their highest possible level of virtue and perfection is possible and potentially stable. Conflict between the aims of philosophy and the ordinary desires and inclinations of the public is always a possibility (indeed, it is the default *presumption* and framing problem of political philosophy), but the perpetual and stable resolution of that conflict is also realizable.

In turning to the great philosophers of the western lands of Islam, we find between Ibn Sina and Ibn Rushd a tradition that portrays the relationship between philosophy and the city in a much more pessimistic light. The primary figures here are Ibn Bajja (Avempace, d. 533/1138) and Ibn Tufayl (d. 580/1185–86). Ibn Bajja is known to political philosophers primarily for his treatise *Tadbir al-mutawahhid* (*Governance of the Solitary*),[73] although he wrote two other treatises—*Risalat al-wadaʿ* and *Risalat ittisal al-ʿaql bi'l-insan*[74]—that are relevant for his views on political science. *Tadbir al-mutawahhid* treats the problem of the philosopher who has the misfortune of living in one of the imperfect cities, and examines how this better kind of human may nonetheless rise to virtue and happiness.[75]

Following Farabi, Ibn Bajja refers to those who hold opinions at odds with the dominant creed or ideology of their city as "Weeds" (*nawabit*), although he is only concerned with the species of weed represented by those who alight upon *true* opinions in a society dominated by corrupt ones. In such corrupt, unhealthy cities, philosophical concerns with good governance are thus limited to these isolated, solitary individuals who live as "strangers" in the world. How are such individuals to pursue and attain happiness and virtue in social and political conditions that either do not help them in this pursuit or actively obstruct and burden it? For Ibn Bajja, man has three true ends: maintenance of his body, perfection of his particular spiritual form, and perfection of his universal spiritual form (his intellect). The philosopher must always prefer the higher to the lower ends. He must not entirely neglect his corporeal form, since this is what allows him to exist as a human, but he

[73] Ibn Bajja, "The Governance of the Solitary," Lawrence Berman, trans., in *Medieval Political Philosophy*, 2nd edn., 97–104 (henceforth: *Solitary*).

[74] Both in *Rasa'il Ibn Bajja al-ilahiyya*, Majid Fakhry, ed. (Beirut: Dar al-Nahar, 1968).

[75] The prime irony of Ibn Bajja's life is that this solitary "weed" was exceptionally active politically. He is believed to have served as minister (*wazir*) to the rulers of Saragossa and Seville and to have been favored at the Almoravid (*al-Murabit*) court in Fez, before dying after eating an eggplant poisoned by one of his political enemies. On Ibn Bajja's biography, see D.M. Dunlop, "Remarks on the Life and Works of Ibn Bājjah (Avempace)," in *Proceedings of the Twenty-Second Congress of Orientalists* (Leiden: Brill, 1957), 188–196. On Ibn Bajja's political philosophy more generally, see Erwin I.J. Rosenthal, "The Place of Politics in the Philosophy of Ibn Bāja," *Bulletin of the School of Oriental and African Studies* 15, no. 2 (1953): 246–278, Lenn E. Goodman, "Ibn Bajjah," in *History of Islamic Philosophy*, ed. Seyyed Hossein Nasr and Oliver Leaman (London: Routledge, 1996), 294–312, and Steven Harvey, "The Place of the Philosopher in the City According to Ibn Bājjah," in *The Political Aspects of Islamic Philosophy*, ed. Butterworth, 199–233.

must never prefer the goods of the body to the cultivation of his virtue, soul, and nobility. However, even these latter particular spiritual acts are only to be put in the service of his intellect. A man who has perfected the latter achieves the highest level of virtue and divinity open to humans. These goods are most easily achieved in the virtuous city where philosophers on the path to union (or connection: *ittisal*) with the divine intellect can benefit from encountering (*liqa'*, or *iltiqa'*) others on the same path and emulating one another in their efforts.[76] However, the perfections sought after by the philosopher are also attainable in unjust cities as long as the would-be virtuous man only associates with others like himself. In this way, even the solitary man may be a part of the virtuous city, even as he spends his life in exile in one of the corrupt cities.

Notably, for Ibn Bajja law is a necessary science and art *only* in the imperfect cities. He writes: "The virtuous city is characterized by the absence of the art of medicine and of the art of adjudication (*sina'at al-qada'*). For friendship binds all the citizens, and they do not quarrel among themselves at all. Therefore, it is only when a part of the city is bereft of friendship and quarrelsomeness breaks out that recourse must be had to the laying down of justice and the need arises for someone, who is the judge, to dispense it."[77] Ibn Bajja's virtuous city is thus perhaps better compared to Augustine's City of God than to the Platonic model Islamized in different ways in Farabi and Ibn Sina. For Ibn Bajja's two Muslim predecessors, lawgiving was not an exceptional activity to be reached for when things go awry in the virtuous city, but one of the core characteristic activities of the ideal ruler and one of the permanent features of life within his city. For Ibn Bajja, law and coercive governance arise to manage problems that might conceivably not emerge in human society—both medicine and adjudication "disappear completely in the virtuous city."

A somewhat more detailed treatment of how life in a city looks to a true philosopher is found in Ibn Tufayl's celebrated philosophical allegory, *Hayy ibn Yaqzan* (*Alive the Son of Awake*). Ibn Tufayl was even more deeply enmeshed in political life than Ibn Bajja had been, serving as secretary to multiple governors and enjoying a long intimate friendship with the third Almohad (*al-Muwahhid*) ruler, the Caliph Abu Ya'qub Yusuf. [78] The conflict between Ibn Tufayl's public life and most celebrated work is sharpened further by the fact that, whereas Ibn Bajja spoke

[76] Ibn Bajja, "Risalat al-wada'," in *Rasa'il Ibn Bajjah al-ilahiyya*, 142. See also Hans Daiber, "Political Philosophy," in *History of Islamic Philosophy*, eds. Nasr and Leaman, 855.

[77] *Solitary*, Ch. 1 §3, 100.

[78] On Ibn Tufayl's biography see B. Carra de Vaux, "Ibn Tufayl," *Encyclopedia of Islam*, second edition; Lawrence I. Conrad, "An Andalusian Physician at the Court of the Muwahhids: Some Notes on the Public Career of Ibn Tufayl," *Al-Qantara: Revista de estudios árabes* 16, no. 1 (1995): 3–14, and the introduction to Lenn E. Goodman, Ibn Tufayl's *Hayy ibn Yaqzan* (Chicago: University of Chicago Press, 2009). On his political philosophy, see also Hillel Fradkin, "The Political Thought of Ibn Ṭufayl," in *The Political Aspects of Islamic Philosophy*, ed. Butterworth, 234–261; Michael S. Kochin, "Weeds: Cultivating the Imagination in Medieval Arabic Political Philosophy," *Journal of the History of Ideas* 60, no. 3 (1999): 399–416; and Murad Idris, "Ibn Ṭufayl's Critique of Politics," *Journal of Islamic Philosophy* 7 (2011): 67–101.

about life in unspecified corrupt cities, *Hayy ibn Yaqzan* presents a portrayal of the inadequacies of a revealed law that look unmistakably like the sacred law so literally and uncompromisingly enforced by the Almohad regime.

Hayy ibn Yaqzan presents the story of a child born autochthonously on a deserted island who, on the basis of his inborn nature (*fitra*), is able to ascend a path of theoretical and spiritual learning to the point where he achieves unmediated knowledge of God and perfect happiness. Not until the age of fifty was Hayy made aware of the existence of another island not far from his, "in which had settled the followers of a certain true religion, based on the teaching of a certain ancient prophet." Like Farabi, Ibn Tufayl characterizes mass religion as representing "all reality in symbols, providing concrete images of things and impressing their outlines on the people's souls, just as orators do when addressing a multitude." In addition to presenting symbolic accounts of metaphysical reality (the realm of opinion or doctrine), the religion of the second island also prescribed "laws and precepts for living."[79]

Although Ibn Tufayl does describe Hayy as living by certain dietary restrictions and other self-designed and enforced laws, the allegory initially describes Hayy's forceful rejection of religious law. "When [Hayy] saw all the provisions of the Law to do with money, such as the regulations regarding the collection and distribution of welfare or those regulating sales and interest, with all their statutory and discretionary penalties, he was dumbfounded. All this seemed superfluous."[80] As in Ibn Bajja's *Tadbir al-mutawahhid*, the presence of law is symptomatic of an imperfect, corrupt, misguided people. A people aware of truth would accumulate no property beyond their most basic needs, there would be no struggle, and no need to adjudicate conflicts through law.

However, the allegory is clearly best read not as a manifesto for superseding law, but for leaving things exactly as they are. Hayy's objection to the regulation of human behavior and mutual dealings through law was due to "his naïve belief that all men had outstanding character, brilliant minds and resolute spirits."[81] Hayy attempts to lead promising representatives of the community to a deeper, more immediate understanding of truth, but is only rewarded for his efforts with resentment and rejection.

He quickly comes to the understanding that "most men are no better than unreasoning animals, and realized that all wisdom and guidance, all that could possibly help them was contained already in the words of the prophets and the religious traditions. None of this could be different. There was nothing to be added.... everyone belongs to the life for which he was created."[82] We see again the common philosophical view that conventional religious beliefs and laws are to be valued insofar

[79] Goodman, *Ibn Tufayl's* Hayy ibn Yaqzan, 156.
[80] Ibid., 161–162. [81] Ibid., 162. [82] Ibid., 164.

as they provide ordinary people with their only means for preserving social stability and acquiring outward virtues. As inadequate as the life of blindly following conventional religious law is, Hayy comes to the realization that this is the closest those raised in society will ever get to the truth and the only thing allowing them to live decent, peaceful lives.

v. Ibn Rushd

One of the most prolific writers in the Arabic philosophical tradition, best known for his extraordinary commentaries on Aristotle and his monumental defense of philosophy against Ghazali (*Incoherence of the Incoherence*), Ibn Rushd (Averroes, d. 595/1198) had relatively little to say about law in his philosophical writings, although probably more than any philosopher since Farabi. (As a jurist of the Maliki school, he was the author of an important manual of comparative Islamic law, *Bidayat al-mujtahid wa niyahat al-muqtasid*.) He composed neither a systematic work of the place of politics in philosophy nor a treatise on the relationship between philosophical and revealed conceptions of law.[83] However, dispersed through his many writings are nonetheless some important discussions of the meaning and status of law.

His philosophically informed reflections on law can be divided into three types: first, his defense of the philosophers' loyalty to the religious law in response to the accusations of the theologians; second, remarks in his juridical writings that suggest possible Aristotelian influences; and third, discussions of politics to be found in his commentaries on Plato's *Republic* (to which he dedicated himself in the absence of an Arabic translation of Aristotle's *Politics*) and Aristotle's *Ethics* and *Rhetoric*.

Ghazali had famously put philosophers on trial in his *Tahafut al-falasifa* (*The Incoherence of the Philosophers*), at times arguing that the philosophers held knowledge to be certain that was rationally doubtful and at times arguing that they

[83] On political and ethical philosophy in Ibn Rushd's writings, see Erwin I.J. Rosenthal, "The Place of Politics in the Philosophy of Ibn Rushd," *Bulletin of the School of Oriental and African Studies* 15, no. 2 (1953): 246–278; George F. Hourani, "Averroes on Good and Evil," *Studia Islamica* (1962): 13–40; Charles E. Butterworth, "Averroës: Politics and Opinion," *American Political Science Review* 66, no. 3 (1972): 894–901; and "The Political Teaching of Averroes," *Arabic Sciences and Philosophy* 2, no. 2 (1992): 187–202; Oliver Leaman, "Ibn Rushd on Happiness and Philosophy," *Studia Islamica* (1980): 167–181; Michael Blaustein, "The Scope and Methods of Rhetoric in Averroes' *Middle Commentary on Aristotle's Rhetoric*," in *The Political Aspects of Islamic Philosophy*, ed. Butterworth, 262–303; and Maroun Aouad, "Does Averroes Have a Philosophy of History?" in *The Greek Strand in Islamic Political Thought*, eds. E. Gannagé et al.

held doctrines (three in particular) that were wholly incompatible with belief in Islam. Ibn Rushd answered Ghazali's philosophical criticisms point-by-point in *Incoherence of the Incoherence*,[84] but also addressed the more *ad hominem* concern about the philosophers' personal fidelity to the religious law of Islam. In the last section of this text (Question 20), ostensibly about the question of bodily resurrection after death, Ibn Rushd gives a stirring but back-handed defense of obedience to revealed law.[85]

The philosophers' denial of bodily resurrection, an event whose possibility was affirmed as certain by the Qur'an, was one of the three doctrines that Ghazali regarded as tantamount to unbelief. Somewhat disingenuously, Ibn Rushd responds that "this is something for which no statement is found among any one of those who have gone before."[86] Rather than provide a philosophical account of bodily resurrection, however, Ibn Rushd focuses exclusively on the philosophers' general support for the religious law(s), indeed that the philosophers are "the people who make the most of them and the most faith in them."[87]

His account of this, however, is strictly practical and, indeed, political. He immediately explains that the intensity of the philosophers' support for the revealed laws is "their being of the opinion that they direct to the governance of people [*tadbir al-nas*] by means of which a human being exists insofar as he is human and obtains the happiness particular to him."[88] Ibn Rushd declines to clarify in any detail why belief in bodily resurrection is necessary for love of and obedience to God, or even why these latter are necessary for moral virtue and practical wisdom. He merely asserts that "with respect to what is said in [the Islamic shari'a] about the hereafter, it urges more to virtuous acts than what is said in the others."[89] What religious imagery describes by way of corporeal existence in the hereafter (*ma'ad*) is described as *better* or *preferable* (*afdal*) than merely spiritual descriptions, and only those "heretics" (*zanadiqa*) "intent upon rejecting the Laws and rejecting virtuous actions [and] who are of the opinion that a human being has no other end than the enjoyment of pleasures."[90]

[84] For a full English translation of the text see Averroës, *Tahafut al-tahafut (The Incoherence of the Incoherence)*, trans. Simon van den Bergh (Oxford: Oxford University Press, 1954) and online at http://www.muslimphilosophy.com/ir/tt/index.html

[85] In the van den Bergh translation, this is found at 359–363. This section of the *Incoherence* is also translated and included as the Appendix, "Averroës' defense of the philosophers as believing in happiness and misery in the hereafter," in Averroës, *Decisive Treatise & Epistle Dedicatory*, trans. Charles E. Butterworth (Provo, UT: Brigham Young University Press, 2002), 43–46. The Butterworth translation appears more accurate (see the critical Arabic edition of *Tahafut al-Tahafut*, ed. Muhammad 'Abid al-Jabiri (Beirut: Markaz al-Dirasat al-Wahda al-'Arabiyya, 1998), 553–559), and so the citations here are to that translation.

[86] Averroës, *Decisive Treatise & Epistle Dedicatory*, 43.

[87] Ibid. [88] Ibid. [89] Ibid., 45. [90] Ibid., 45–46.

Thus, Ibn Rushd's canny response to Ghazali's charge of unbelief is located strictly within a more general discussion about the proper philosophical attitude toward obedience to the revealed law. Again, there is little doubt that Ibn Rushd's account assigns a strictly instrumental role for divine law: "In sum, the [philosophers] are of the opinion that the Laws are the necessary civic arts whose principles are taken from the intellect and Legislation [*al-shara'*], especially those that are common to all the Laws—even if they [the Laws] differ about the lesser and the greater with respect to that."[91]

Here and elsewhere Ibn Rushd advances views quite similar to those of Farabi. Religious laws and doctrines are the best means for the multitude to learn as much of wisdom and virtue as will be possible for them. However, Ibn Rushd does seem more charitable to the religious law than Farabi. He argues both that "the moral virtues are not firmly established but through knowledge of God"[92] and that "we do not find any one of the Laws that has not been attentive to what particularly characterizes the wise, even though it is concerned with what the multitude share in."[93] Moreover, the "elect" only perfects its own conditions and attains happiness through association with the multitude, which relies on law. Thus, the philosophers hold that following the law is obligatory. He appears to take a step even further than this. While philosophy remains self-sufficient and the truest path to knowledge and virtue, religions can also evolve in the direction of truth and virtue and philosophers should adopt the best religion of their day. By his day, Islam had achieved superiority in inciting to virtue through prayer and removing irrational doctrines, and thus all philosophers were under a rational obligation to choose Islam.[94]

Nonetheless, ambiguities in Ibn Rushd's commitment to religious orthodoxy remain. For example, he does not give a philosophical defense of bodily resurrection but instead insists that philosophers must on all accounts refrain from (publicly) objecting to the common religious doctrines of society. In fact, any philosopher who scorns the doctrines of the masses, raises doubts about religious principles, or offers an interpretation that contradicts the prophets does indeed deserve the label—and the punishment—of atheist. However, having said this, Ibn Rushd concludes by asserting that "it should be posited that what comes back are likenesses [*amthal*] of the bodies that existed in this abode, not these very ones, because what has perished does not come back as an individual entity. Existence comes back only to a likeness of what has perished, not to what has perished." And he goes as far as saying that the doctrine of the orthodox theologians, "that the soul is an accident and that the bodies that come back are those that have perished, is not correct."[95] This statement

[91] Ibid., 44. [92] Ibid., 43. [93] Ibid., 44.
[94] Ibid., 45–46. [95] Ibid., 46.

would either seem to contradict much of what he argued in the preceding section about the reticence of the philosophers to contradict the law, or to rest on the assumption that it is the theologians who contradict the statements of revelation.

Although Ibn Rushd appears to call in these sections for certain limits to the public expression of philosophy that would cast doubt on doctrines and practices useful to the community, he elsewhere composed a famous defense of the practice of the philosophy as such. Ibn Rushd's *Fasl al-maqal ma bayna al-shariʿa wa'l-hikma min al-ittisal* (commonly translated as the *Decisive Treatise* (*On the Union of Shariʿa and Philosophy*))[96] is relevant here insofar as it takes the form of an inquiry from within law, that is, an investigation into the legal ruling (*hukm*) on philosophizing, which involves some important reflections on the meaning of the revealed law itself.[97]

Among the claims Ibn Rushd makes in the *Decisive Treatise* to defend philosophy in Islam, two are particularly relevant. First, he asserts that there are three sorts of people and thus three ways that religion calls people to truth. These methods are demonstration (*burhan*), dialectics, and rhetoric. A small elite is capable of assenting to truth through philosophy, while the masses are reached only through the rhetorical language of the Qur'an and prophetic preaching. In between are those who are capable of the dialectical defense of religion not from first principles but on the basis of assumed premises. For Ibn Rushd, it is the beauty of revelation that all three of these methods are called for and validated so that all might achieve happiness regardless of their innate intelligence: "assent was extended to every human being."[98]

Second, Ibn Rushd argues that in practical matters the revealed law provides for the attainment of bodily and spiritual virtue. Revelation aims at nothing other than to teach true science (*ʿilm*; knowledge) and true practice. "True practice is to follow the actions that promote happiness and to avoid the actions that promote misery . . . these are of two kinds. One is the apparent, bodily actions. The science of these is what is called 'jurisprudence.' The second division is actions of the soul—like gratitude, patience and other moral habits [*akhlaq*]—that the Law calls to or bans. And the science of these is what is called 'asceticism' and 'the sciences of the hereafter.'"[99] In this context he offers the classical analogy from Plato's *Laws* that a physician is to the health of the body as the lawgiver is to the health of the soul.[100] As the practices of the law such as fasting and prayer are conducive to the disciplining

[96] Translated by Butterworth in Averroës, *Decisive Treatise & Epistle Dedicatory*, 43.

[97] For a gripping account of the significance of this event, see Daniel Heller-Roazen, "Philosophy before the Law: Averroës's Decisive Treatise," *Critical Inquiry* 32, no. 3 (2006): 412–442.

[98] Averroës, *Decisive Treatise & Epistle Dedicatory Decisive*, 8, citing Q. 16:125: "Call to the path of your Lord by wisdom, fine preaching, and arguing with them by means of what is finest."

[99] Ibid., 23. [100] Ibid., 28–29.

of the self and development of virtue, obeying the strictures of the law is a reliable means to the health of the soul.

Statements like this inevitably invite the question of the extent to which philosophy informed Ibn Rushd's juridical works. Evidence of this is sparse but at times striking. For example, the last paragraphs of his juridical treatise *Bidayat al-mujtahid wa nihayat al-muqtasid*[101] include the following discussion of the overall pattern of Islamic law:

> It is necessary to know that the legal rules (*sunan*) pertaining to conduct have as their purpose the virtues of the believer. Some of them refer to glorification ... and gratitude ... the acts of worship are of this type. Some relate to the virtue known as continence ('iffa) ... to the requirement of justice and abstention from tyranny.... There are also rules pertaining to society, which is a condition for human life and the preservation of its practical and intellectual virtues, which are expressed by the idea of leadership. This is why there must also be rules on the *imamate* and upholding religion. Among the most important rules on society are those on love and hate, and cooperation in preserving these rules, which is called "commanding right and forbidding wrong." This is a form of love and hate, namely a religious kind, which occurs either from the evasion of these rules or the bad intent of the believer in *shari'a*.... [The main books of law] pertain to the four categories which are the [four cardinal] virtues of continence, justice, courage and generosity, and worship, which is the condition for establishing these virtues."[102]

In addition to this statement, which depicts the most general rules of Islamic law as in principle harmonious with the main virtues identified in philosophical ethics, some scholars have noted the influence of Aristotle's idea of equity (from Book V.10 of the *Nicomachean Ethics*), which calls for a correction of what a law posits as a just general rule when the application of it to a particular case would subvert the law's aim. One example comes in a discussion of *jihad* in his commentary on the *Nicomachean Ethics*. Whereas the general rule in Islamic law is to call for *jihad* against non-Muslims, "there are times when peace is more choiceworthy than war."[103] He makes a similar remark as part of his discussion of the virtue of lenience as part of equity in his *Middle Commentary on Aristotle's* Rhetoric when he compares it to the suspension of the punishment for theft "among us."[104]

But Ibn Rushd's debt to Aristotle in his approach to reasoning from equity should not be overstated. Consider his discussion of whether an elderly ill man may remarry to the possible detriment of his heirs: "reluctance to pay attention to welfare

101 English translation: *The Distinguished Jurist's Primer* (2 vol), trans. Imran Ahsan Khan Nyazee (Reading, UK: Garnet, 2000).

102 See *The Distinguished Jurist's Primer*, vol. 2, 572, but I have modified the Nyazee translation based on my understanding of the Arabic.

103 Noah Feldman, "War and Reason in Maimonides & Averroes," *Journal of Islamic Law & Culture* 9 (2004): 83–84. Ibn Rushd's commentary on the *Ethics* is lost in Arabic but has been preserved in Hebrew and Latin.

104 *Commentaire moyen à la Rhétorique d'Aristote/Averroès (Ibn Rušd)*, trans. and ed. Maroun Aouad (Paris: Vrin, 2002), 118.

[*maslaha*] might cause the people to be pushed, because of a lack of precedents in [a particular area], toward injustice. Such interests should be brought to the scholars of the wisdom [*hikma*] of the law … to examine the evidence in the circumstances of the case. [i.e. does the ill man intend betterment or harm?]."[105] It is true that Ibn Rushd states this ordinary legal dilemma in a somewhat more philosophical language than other jurists might, but the basic terms here—public welfare (*maslaha*) and choosing between multiple legal rulings to arrive at an optimal outcome (*istihsan*)—are central to ordinary Islamic legal reasoning and hardly need to be derived from Aristotle. This is most likely a case where Ibn Rushd sees two parallel traditions as naturally converging on a shared procedure. This is not to say that Ibn Rushd thought that the Islamic legal community was univocal on the questions at stake, but rather, that he perceived concepts and methods analogous to equity as fully indigenous to the Islamic legal tradition.[106]

However, in his various philosophical commentaries on Plato and Aristotle, Ibn Rushd's relationship to orthodox Islamic law is more ambiguous. More than with his philosophical predecessors, with Ibn Rushd we see the question of the shari'a's relationship to a universal or natural law treated in fascinating, yet elusive, ways. The lack of an extant Arabic manuscript and the nature of philosophical commentary in general make it difficult for us to discern the relationship of Ibn Rushd's commentary to his personally held views, but we can at least present here some intriguing discussions of law in the Commentary on Plato's *Republic*[107] and Middle Commentary on Aristotle's *Rhetoric* (*Talkhis al-khitaba*).

In his commentary on the *Republic*, Ibn Rushd repeatedly advances a distinction between a human rational law (translated by Lerner as "nomos") and a divinely revealed shari'a (translated by Lerner as Law). At many points, Ibn Rushd treats the "nomoi and Laws" in tandem,[108] but at other points he distinguishes them, and seems to suggest either the superiority of nomos to the shari'a or the shari'a's validation through its similarity to the universal law taught by the philosophers. For example, he writes that good governance requires "knowledge of the end of man since this governance moves in that direction. And it is evident that we can only perceive the end of man through the theoretical sciences."[109]

[105] *The Distinguished Jurist's Primer*, vol. 2, 54.

[106] On these themes, see Frank Griffel, "The Relationship between Averroes and al-Ghazālī," in *Medieval Philosophy and the Classical Tradition: In Islam, Judaism and Christianity*, ed. John Inglis (London: Curzon, 2002), 51–63.

[107] References here are to *Averroes on Plato's* Republic, trans. Ralph Lerner (Ithaca, NY: Cornell University Press, 1974). For an earlier translation with a critical edition of the extant Hebrew manuscript, see *Averroes' Commentary on Plato's* Republic, trans. E.I.J. Rosenthal (Cambridge, UK: Cambridge University Press, 1956).

[108] *Averroes on Plato's* Republic, trans. Lerner, 47–48.

[109] Ibid., 49–50.

This text also contains some important statements of Ibn Rushd's belief in a kind of natural law and a critique of orthodox Islamic divine voluntarism. He writes that the *mutakallimun*'s "legal inquiry led them to the position that what God wills has no definite nature and merely turns on what the will of God lays down for it. According to this, there is nothing beautiful or base other than by fiat. Furthermore, there is no end of man other than by fiat.... [But] this leads them to an opinion close to sophistry, very far from the nature of man, and far from being the content of a Law."[110] It is important to note, however, that Ibn Rushd does not suggest that a superior natural law trumps the Islamic shari'a, but rather, that the proper understanding of the shari'a is harmonious with natural law, at least in the area of action and practical philosophy, if not creed and theoretical wisdom: "our Law's intention ... regarding [action] is identical with the intention of philosophy in genus and purpose. That is why humans assert that these Laws only follow ancient wisdom. It is evident that, in the opinion of all these, the good, the bad, the useful, the harmful, the beautiful, and the base are something existing by nature, not by convention. For whatever leads to the end is good and beautiful, and whatever hinders one from it is bad and base."[111]

Similar notions are presented in the Middle Commentary on the *Rhetoric*. Following Aristotle, Ibn Rushd discusses the distinction between unwritten and written laws, broadly tracking the distinction between universal ideals of justice or equity and particular instantiations of them: "The unwritten law is eternal and unchanging because it is in the nature of people [*ṭabi'at al-nas*] and the written laws are replaceable and changing."[112] As in the Commentary on the *Republic*, it seems that Ibn Rushd accepts the idea of universal justice, or natural law, but sees the Islamic shari'a and its various practices and institutions as almost perfectly harmonious with it.

At the same time, Ibn Rushd recognizes the limited and contingent attributes of the revealed law. He introduces Aristotle's view that "the goal of the skillful legislator is to lay down what holds for the most part ... The more that the legislator struggled so that the law might be beneficial for the longest possible time, for the greatest number of people, the better the law. Since this is the case necessarily, determined [posited] laws are not true permanently ... This is why they need addition and subtraction." But he then notes confidently: "You will see this clearly from the written religions in our time. Adding to or subtracting from them is an improvement if this is associated with praise and honor."[113] Here and elsewhere Ibn Rushd seems to be suggesting that the posited, revealed shari'a is, perhaps, the best that

110 *Averroes on Plato's* Republic, trans. Lerner, 81–82.

111 Ibid., 81.

112 *Commentaire moyen à la Rhétorique d'Aristote*, trans. Aouad, 125.

113 Ibid., 117.

any lawgiver could legislate, but does not exhaust or limit human possibilities in the areas of individual virtue or legal justice.

VI. Conclusion

We must avoid the outdated view that *falsafa* ended with Ghazali's critique of it and that Ibn Rushd represents the last hurrah of Islamic philosophy before passing the torch to the Latins. By ending this survey with Ibn Rushd I do not wish to make any such implication. It is well known that independent philosophical investigation continued long after the thirteenth century (particularly in the eastern Islamic lands) and that Avicennan logic and metaphysics were incorporated into dogmatic theology (*kalam*). But the thinkers surveyed here provide a necessary, if not sufficient, introduction to the main themes, problems, and concepts produced by the encounter between Greek philosophy in Muslim contexts and the mainstream Islamic legal tradition. They are also the thinkers whose thought is most accessible to non-specialists hoping to study Islamic philosophy in translation.

By way of conclusion, I would like to suggest that a promising area for further work in this field is not only the increasing investigation of lesser known periods of philosophy in Muslim lands, but also the study of mainstream Islamic theology and law as articulations of political philosophy. For these discourses did not only contain formal arguments from reason as well as revelation, but also offered rich theoretical reflections on anthropology, the purpose of governance, the best that could be hoped for from political society and the relationship between law and ideals of justice.

References

Alfarabi, *The Political Writings, Volume II: "Political Regime" and "Summary of Plato's Laws,"* trans. Charles Butterworth (Ithaca, NY: Cornell University Press, 2015).

Al-Farabi, *On the Perfect State (Mabadi' ara' al-madina al-fadila)*, Richard Walzer ed. and trans. (Chicago, IL: Kazi Publications, 1988).

Averroës, *Tahafut al-tahafut (The Incoherence of the Incoherence)*, trans. Simon van den Bergh (Oxford: Oxford University Press, 1954).

Averroës, *Bidayat al-mujtahid/The Distinguished Jurist's Primer The Distinguished Jurist's Primer* (2 vol), trans. Imran Ahsan Khan Nyazee (Reading, UK: Garnet, 2000).

Averroës, *Commentaire moyen à la Rhétorique d'Aristote/Averroès (Ibn Rušd)*, trans. and ed. Maroun Aouad (Paris: Vrin, 2002).

Averroës, *Averroes on Plato's Republic*, trans. Ralph Lerner (Ithaca, NY: Cornell University Press, 1974).

Avicenna, *The Metaphysics of The Healing*, trans. Michael E. Marmura (Provo, UT: Brigham Young University Press, 2005).

Avicenna, *Tis' rasā'il fī al-ḥikmah wa-al-ṭabī'īyāt wa-qiṣṣat Salāmān wa-Absāl* (Beirut: Dār Qābis, 1986).

Brague, Rémi, *The Law of God: The Philosophical History of an Idea*, trans. Lydia G. Cochrane (Chicago: University of Chicago Press, 2007).

Butterworth, Charles E., "Philosophy of Law in Medieval Judaism and Islam" in Fred D. Miller Jr. (ed.) *A History of the Philosophy of Law from the Ancient Greeks to the Scholastics vol. 6 of A Treatise of Legal Philosophy and General Jurisprudence* (Dordrecht: Springer, 2007) 219–250.

Carra de Vaux, B., "Ibn Tufayl" in P. Bearman, Th. Bianquis, C.E. Bosworth, E. van Donzel, W.P. Heinrichs (eds.) *Encyclopedia of Islam*, secone edition (Brill Online, 2015) http://referenceworks.brillonline.com/entries/encyclopaedia-of-islam-2/ibn-tufayl-SIM_3394

Daiber, Hans, "Political Philosophy" in Seyyed Hossein Nasr and Oliver Leaman (eds.) *History of Islamic Philosophy*, 841–885 (London: Routledge, 1996).

Feldman, Noah, "War and Reason in Maimonides & Averroes." *Journal of Islamic Law & Culture* 9, 1 (2004): 65–86.

Goodman, Lenn E., "Ibn Bajjah" in Seyyed Hossein Nasr and Oliver Leaman (eds.) *History of Islamic Philosophy*, 294–312 (London: Routledge, 1996).

Goodman, Lenn E., *Ibn Tufayl's Hayy ibn Yaqzan* (Chicago: University of Chicago Press, 2009).

Gutas, Dimitri, *Greek Thought, Arabic Culture: The Graeco-Arabic Translation Movement in Baghdad and Early 'Abbāsid Society (2nd–4th/8th–10th centuries)* (New York: Routledge, 1998).

Gutas, Dimitri, "The Study of Arabic Philosophy in the Twentieth Century: An Essay on the Historiography of Arabic Philosophy." *British Journal of Middle Eastern Studies* 29, no. 1 (2002): 5–25.

Heller-Roazen, Daniel, "Philosophy before the Law: Averroës's Decisive Treatise." *Critical Inquiry* 32, no. 3 (2006): 412–442.

Ibn Bajja, "*Risalat al-wada'*" in Majid Fakhry (ed.) *Rasa'il Ibn Bajja al-ilahiyya* (Beirut: Dar al-Nahar, 1968) 113–144.

Ibn Bajja, "*Risalat ittisal al-'aql bi'l-insan*" in Majid Fakhry (ed.) *Rasa'il Ibn Bajja al-ilahiyya* (Beirut: Dar al-Nahar, 1968) 153–174.

Kraemer, Joel L., "The *Jihād* of the *Falāsifa*." *Jerusalem Studies in Arabic and Islam* 10, (1987): 288–324.

McGinnis, Jon, *Avicenna* (Oxford: Oxford University Press, 2010).

Parens, Joshua, and Joseph C. Macfarland, eds. *Medieval Political Philosophy: A Sourcebook* (Ithaca, NY: Cornell University Press, 2011).

PART II

LEGAL THEORY AND INSTITUTIONS

A

LEGAL THEORY

CHAPTER 7

IJTIHAD

ANVER M. EMON

THE topic of *ijtihad* has occupied researchers of Islamic law for decades if not centuries. Moreover, polemicists and reformists in more popular venues invoke it to question the relevance and ongoing significance of Islamic law in the world today. This chapter will canvass a range of issues pertaining to the historiography of *ijtihad*. It will start by addressing the highly fraught concept of the "gates of *ijtihad*" and the debates about whether the "gates" were ever closed, what "closure" implies about Islamic law, and how calls for its "reopening" seem to reflect less about the study of Islamic law and more about the conditions of modernity that pose new questions to a tradition with a considerable history. Thereafter, the chapter will explore the scholarship on *ijtihad* as a topic of legal theory in the *usul al-fiqh* genre, and the intersection of that discussion with contemporary issues in legal philosophy and interpretation. The chapter will then turn to the discourse of *ijtihad* in the modern period, and its significance as a proxy for underlying concerns about epistemology, legal education, and authority. The chapter will conclude with gestures toward new scholarly directions in research on *ijtihad*.

I. The Politics of "the Gates of *Ijtihad*"

Ijtihad is not a new term of art; indeed it is a term with a long and rich history in the Islamic tradition. It is an Arabic term derived from the trilateral root *j-h-d*, and can mean many different things. It generally refers to exertion or doing one's utmost in a particular task. In the context of law, though, it takes on the special meaning of a jurist "exerting the faculties [of the mind] to the utmost, for the purpose of forming an opinion in a case of law."[1] The antonym of *ijtihad* is *taqlid*, which has been variously defined. Often with polemical tenor, *taqlid* has been defined as blind obedience, namely blind obedience to historical legal doctrines.[2] In more scholarly writings, the term often reflects adherence to precedent, or even rule of law.[3] Throughout the twentieth century and more feverishly in the twenty-first century, many have called for the gates (or alternatively the doors) of *ijtihad* to be reopened, on the assumption that the gates have been closed and that *taqlid* has reigned supreme with rigid inflexibility. For instance, self-styled Muslim reformer Irshad Manji has written that for political reasons, the tenth century witnessed the closing of "the gates of *ijtihad* and therefore the tradition of independent thought … Got a new question? The four existing Sunni schools of thought can address it. They've never dealt with a question as novel as yours? Then they'll imitate past verdicts. No trailblazing tolerated."[4] That the gates were closed is presumed by many polemicists writing about Islam, and contributes to the conception of Islamic law as ancient, antiquated, and rigid, at least when viewed from a presentist perspective. Indeed, that presentist perspective is perhaps what most animates popular debates about *ijtihad* specifically, and explorations of the methods of Islamic legal inquiry generally, suggesting that modern Muslims need to break away from the rigidity of the premodern past and opt, instead, for a more fluid conception of law. For example, after acknowledging some epistemic flexibility in premodern Islamic legal theory, Pakistani Anglican Bishop Michael Nazir-Ali, now living in Britain, notes that, when "[f]aced with present realities, such flexibility may be practically very useful."[5] Useful in what sense, to what end, or for what reason?—Nazir-Ali is not entirely clear. But if these calls for flexibility are recognized as presentist ruminations on Islamic law, then the answers about practicalities and usefulness are presumably understood by all readers. What is important for these authors is to identify that the problem with Islamic law lies in the tradition's own legal history, as opposed to the impact of European colonialism, for instance. Indeed, Manji goes so far as to say that "[t]o this day, Muslims use the white man as a weapon of mass distraction—a distraction from the fact that we've never needed the 'oppressive' West to oppress

[1] E.W. Lane, *Arabic-English Lexicon* (Cambridge: Islamic Texts Society, 1984), 1:473.

[2] Muneer Fareed, "Against Ijtihad," *The Muslim World* 91, no. 3–4 (2001): 355–370.

[3] Mohammad Fadel, "The Social Logic of *Taqlid* and the Rise of the *Mukhtasar*," *Islamic Law and Society* 3, no. 2 (1996): 193–233, 197.

[4] Irshad Manji, *The Trouble with Islam Today* (New York: St Martin's Griffin, 2005), 59.

[5] Michael Nazir-Ali, "Islamic Law, Fundamental Freedoms, and Social Cohesion: Retrospect and Prospect," in *Shari'a in the West*, eds. Rex Ahdar and Nicholas Aroney (Oxford: Oxford University Press, 2010), 71–89, 74.

our own."[6] For her, the trope of "closing the gates of *ijtihad*" serves her larger argument that Muslims have stunted the capacity of their faith tradition to engage, innovate, and remain responsive to changing realities.

II. On the Gates of *Ijtihad*: Closed, Open, Ajar?

In a well-written, balanced, and accessible article published in 1994, Shaista Ali-Karamali and Fiona Dunne surveyed the competing scholarly positions on both the meaning of *ijtihad* and whether the gates of *ijtihad* were closed.[7] Ali-Karamali and Dunne outlined three scholarly trends regarding the gates of *ijtihad*: (1) those that adhered to their closure; (2) those that denied they ever closed; and (3) those that lay somewhere in between, based on a more complex understanding of *ijtihad* and its various uses within the historical Islamic intellectual tradition. Ali-Karamali and Dunne traced each of these arguments back into the nineteenth century, and offered an important historical record of those early views. This chapter will not reproduce that history. Rather, starting with this 1994 entry, the current chapter will extend the analysis into more recent debates on *ijtihad* that take the scholarly interest beyond the narrow, though important, one about the "gates" and their closure.

The first argument about the gates of *ijtihad*, namely that they were closed, is well-represented by North Atlantic scholars such as Joseph Schacht and Noel Coulson. Joseph Schacht, the early twentieth-century scholar of Islamic law, devoted the tenth chapter of his *An Introduction to Islamic Law* to what he called the "Closing of the Gate of Independent Reasoning." He described a whittling away of independent reasoning as jurists in the period of ʿAbbasid rule articulated strict methods of legal reasoning, qualifications for those who would exercise legal reasoning, and different degrees to which differently qualified personnel could reason to legal conclusions. From these restrictive qualifications, Schacht argued that the scope of independent reasoning increasingly diminished. He stated:

> By the beginning of the fourth century of the hijra (about A.D. 900) ... the point had been reached when the scholars of all schools felt that all essential questions had been thoroughly discussed and finally settled, and a consensus gradually established itself to the effect that from that time onwards no one might be deemed to have the necessary qualifications for

[6] Manji, *Trouble with Islam*, 57.

[7] Shaista P. Ali-Karamali and Fiona Dunne, "The Ijtihad Controversy," *Arab Law Quarterly* 9, no. 3 (1994): 238–257.

independent reasoning in law, and that all future activity would have to be confined to the explanation, application, and, at most, interpretation of the doctrine as it has been laid down once and for all.[8]

Inferring normative implications from his historicist approach, Schacht concluded that the historical legacy of Islamic law reflects an 'Abbasid historical reality that grew "more and more out of touch with later developments of state and society."[9]

Noel J. Coulson likewise stipulated that the doors of *ijtihad* were indeed closed. He wrote: "Muslim jurisprudence of the early tenth century formally recognized that its creative force was now spent and exhausted ... The right of *ijtihād* was replaced by the duty of *taqlīd* or 'imitation'. Henceforth every jurist was an 'imitator' (*muqallid*), bound to accept and follow the doctrine established by his predecessors."[10] Coulson briefly alluded to various reasons for this shift, such as the full exploitation of existing materials, and over-indulgent respect for prior scholars. Whatever the historical factors may have been, for Coulson the more interesting point is that the decline of *ijtihad* was given conceptual cover by the rise of *ijma'*, or rule by consensus. Coulson linked the closure of the gates of *ijtihad* to the rise of *ijma'*, by which whole areas of legal dispute were rendered subject to consensus, thus precluding ongoing debate and deliberation. According to Coulson, the increasingly restrictive attitude on independent reasoning was "naturally closely linked to the enervating effect of the spread of *ijmā'*." As a natural sequel to the classical theory it represents the *post facto* rationalization of an existing state of affairs reached with the culmination of the quest to express the law in terms of the will of God."[11] The political implications of such a reading of Islamic legal history, though, is evident only later in Coulson's work, when he addressed the advent of "neo-*ijtihad*" in the nineteenth century. The more contemporary debates about *ijtihad* were, on Coulson's reading, pretext for a more overtly political dispute between conservative and progressive factions within the Muslim world. As he wrote: "Those who saw the established law as the ideal order of things upheld the doctrine of *taqlīd*, while those who sought reform argued for the legitimacy of *ijtihād* as the ultimate and proper means of changing legal rules which rested on the unanimous authority of the mediaeval manuals."[12]

Expositors of this first position recognize, at least historically, that there remained ongoing disputes about the capacity to exert *ijtihad*. If the gates of *ijtihad* were definitively closed, how must we interpret these later arguments in support of *ijtihad*? Schacht acknowledges some opposition to this closure, but discounts them as merely theoretically relevant.[13] Coulson also recognized that the closure argument

[8] Joseph Schacht, *An Introduction to Islamic Law* (reprint, 1993; Oxford: Clarendon Press, 1964), 70–71.

[9] Schacht, *Introduction*, 75.

[10] Noel J. Coulson, *A History of Islamic Law* (reprint, 1997; Edinburgh: Edinburgh University Press, 1964), 80.

[11] Coulson, *History*, 81. For a similar argument, see Falzur Rahman, *Islam*, 2nd edn. (Chicago: University of Chicago Press, 1979), 77.

[12] Coulson, *History*, 203.

[13] Schacht, *Introduction*, 72.

was not without its early premodern detractors, but again suggested that these debates on *ijtihad* were more theoretical than practical, and that in more recent history, the resort to *ijtihad* is theoretical cover for underlying political tensions between those wanting to preserve the status quo and others seeking to subvert it.[14] What they mean by "theoretical," though, is not explicated, and begs important questions about theory, practice, and the conception of law. For instance, if theoretically the door of *ijtihad* remained opened, despite jurists in later periods claiming they were not exerting *ijtihad*, must a historian necessarily infer that the gates of *ijtihad* were in fact closed? Or does their reliance on the metaphor of door or gates as either opened or closed unduly reduce the enterprise of law to a zero-sum game? Might the metaphor of "door" and "gate" actually over-determine what jurists were actually doing when they argued about *ijtihad* and *taqlid*, whether prior to the tenth century or thereafter?

These questions prompt consideration of the second argument about the gates of *ijtihad*, namely that they were never closed. This argument is perhaps best represented by Wael B. Hallaq in a set of articles in the 1980s. His conclusion was quite straightforward, namely that the claims about the gates of *ijtihad* being closed are "entirely baseless and inaccurate" and that the "gate of *ijtihad* was not closed in theory nor in practice."[15] He rested his conclusion upon a series of interlocking arguments, which warrant discussion herein. He began by arguing that premodern Islamic legal theory manuals, *usul al-fiqh*, always addressed the significance of *ijtihad*, whether through express focus on the concept of *ijtihad*, or on the methods that imply the ongoing salience of *ijtihad* to the enterprise of law as an ongoing concern.[16] Relatedly, legal theory manuals outlined the conditions that a jurist must fulfill in order to become a *mujtahid*, or, one who can exercise *ijtihad*. Hallaq noted that those who espouse the closure of the door of *ijtihad* assumed that the prerequisites for exercising *ijtihad* were so demanding as to render *ijtihad* practically impossible.[17] Reviewing various premodern juristic accounts that outlined the disciplinary training required to perform *ijtihad*, Hallaq remarked on how jurists consistently stipulated qualifications that were hardly impossible to reach. Consequently, Hallaq argued that legal theory and the educational requirements for exercising *ijtihad* were not responsible for ushering in the demise of *ijtihad* in Islamic legal history.

This is not to suggest that all premodern Muslims supported the use of *ijtihad*. Indeed, some such as the Zahiris were outright critics of basic modes of legal reasoning, such as *qiyas* (analogical reasoning by precedent). Hallaq argued, however, that this opposition to *ijtihad* does not imply the demise of *ijtihad*, but rather

[14] Coulson, *History*, 202–203.
[15] Wael B. Hallaq, "Was the Gate of *Ijtihad* Closed?" *International Journal of Middle East Studies* 16 (1984): 3–41, 4.
[16] Ibid., 5. [17] Ibid.

reflects a larger contest over what would become Sunni legal practice. Opposition to *ijtihad* cannot be fully appreciated without reflecting on the broader contest within Sunni Islam between adherents of tradition and adherents of opinion (*ahl al-hadith* and *ahl al-ra'y*). That larger contest set the terms by which Sunni Islam would ultimately take shape.[18] For Hallaq, the groups that opposed *ijtihad* "found no place inside the pale of Sunnism."[19]

Indeed, staying within the confines of a Sunni communal identity may also explain why creative Sunnis nonetheless framed their legal argument within the bounds of the four established Sunni schools. Of course, there were some jurists who outright disagreed with the doctrines of established schools, although as Hallaq noted, by the eleventh century, jurists were affiliated with one school or another. The fact that such schools effectively disciplined the scope of legal interpretation does not imply, for Hallaq, that *ijtihad* ceased to exist. Rather, legal creativity simply had to be framed in a particular, disciplined fashion in order to be recognized as legitimate and authoritative: "[C]reative scholars of the fourth/tenth century attributed their own doctrines to a great master. By so doing, they could avoid attacks that were the automatic reaction against fissiparous tendencies and could certainly earn immediate recognition once their opinions were put under the aegis of a great jurist . . ."[20]

A continued commitment to *ijtihad* also animated the political role jurists imagined themselves to play in relation to the ruling authorities. Jurists such as al-Mawardi, al-Juwayni, and al-Ghazali could not repudiate *ijtihad* or suggest it had closed so long as the aspired-for political order was to be Islamically oriented. For some such as al-Mawardi, a key qualification for one to be an imam or political leader was that he be a *mujtahid*. For al-Ghazali, on the other hand, the religious authority of political leaders was no longer taken for granted given the proliferation of multiple caliphates (Andalusian, Fatimid, and 'Abbasid), as well as the erosion of the 'Abbasid caliphate into a symbolic office. Consequently jurists such as al-Ghazali argued that ruling authorities who did not achieve the rank of *mujtahid* could delegate their religious authority to jurists who could exercise that function. Hallaq concludes from this history of Islamic political thought that *ijtihad* remained integral to the jurists as they imagined the conditions for legitimate Islamic rule and the relationship between the ruling class and the juristic one: "The weakening of the Caliphate which found its expression, *inter alia*, in the legal impotency of the Caliph, constituted for the ulama an urgent problem that was seriously treated,

[18] Indeed, see also Jonathan Brown's work on hadith canonization and how the canonization of Bukhari and Muslim was a mechanism for creating a corporate Sunni identity in opposition to a Shi'a corporate identity. Jonathan A.C. Brown, *The Canonization of al-Bukhari and Muslim: The Formation and Function of the Sunni Hadith Canon* (Leiden: Brill Publications, 2011).

[19] Hallaq, "Was the Gate of *Ijtihad* Closed?" 8.

[20] Ibid., 11.

although ineffectively, in a mass of [political] writings. The insistence of jurists on the requirement of *ijtihad*, whether fulfilled by the Caliph himself or by others, furthermore enhances the fact that inasmuch as *ijtihad* was indispensable in legal matters it was equally indispensable in political matters."[21]

Of course, one might object that all of the above arguments are theoretical arguments about *ijtihad*. Certainly they attest to the ongoing significance of *ijtihad* in the imagination of Muslim jurists. But does that necessarily mean that *ijtihad* featured expressly in the way jurists developed the doctrines of a school's tradition? In his seminal article on the issue, Hallaq addresses this point only briefly, where he notes that a diachronic review of *fiqh* sources within a school reveals an ongoing development in the legal discourse, whether in terms of organization and arrangements, robustness of argument, and precision in terminology.[22] Notably, in his later work, Hallaq addresses the role of the scholar-jurist who issues *fatawa* (sing. *fatwa*), i.e. legal responsa. *Fatawa* offer a legal site where doctrine meets the thick narrative context of a legal dispute. Reviewing the *fatawa* of the Maliki judge Ibn Rushd al-Jadd, Hallaq shows how his resolution of disputes later became incorporated in Maliki *fiqh* collections, thus showcasing a particular mechanism to diachronically track legal change, and thus the ongoing significance of *ijtihad* in the development of Islamic law.[23]

But if the gates of *ijtihad* were never closed, why do later jurists in the Islamic legal tradition write about *ijtihad*'s demise? In a second article, Hallaq explains that premodern debates about *ijtihad*'s demise were premised upon a separate and much earlier debate, namely whether or not there could be a period in time when *mujtahids* no longer existed.[24] If *mujtahids* were extinct, then it follows that the era of *ijtihad* was over. But what explains the concern about *mujtahids* and their extinction? Part of the answer lies in the political history of the caliphate and what that history implied about the role of jurists in an Islamically defined polity. According to Hallaq:

By the middle of the fifth/eleventh century it had become quite clear that a revival of the institution of caliphate was out of the question. The caliph was no more than a religious symbol whose authority and dominion over the Muslim subjects could hardly reach the peripheries of Baghdad. Instability of political regime and political and social strife were predominant ... The Muslim community in general and the urban communities in particular lacked any sort of all-inclusive political or economic organization ... In the fourth/tenth and especially in the fifth/eleventh century the ulama emerged as the sole uniting social force in the Muslim community. Their leadership was accepted by virtually all segments of

[21] Ibid., 15.

[22] Ibid., 19.

[23] Wael B. Hallaq, *Authority, Continuity and Change in Islamic Law* (Cambridge: Cambridge University Press, 2001).

[24] Wael B. Hallaq, "On the Origins of the Controversy about the Existence of Mujtahids and the Gate of *Ijtihad*," *Studia Islamica* 63 (1986): 129–141, 133.

society … By the nature of the functions they occupied, they were undoubtedly most instrumental in preserving the social fabric of Islam."[25]

Among the "*ulama*," the *mujtahids* were of particular importance. They were the only ones qualified "to inform the community and its military rulers of what was lawful and what was not, particularly when an unprecedented situation arose."[26] But in the wake of the caliphate's demise, it was not impossible to imagine a world also without *mujtahids*. Indeed, this imagined world was made more pressing, argued Hallaq, by certain apocalyptic doctrines about the end of the world and the Day of Judgment. Prophetic traditions calculate that the world would end after 7000 years from its creation, and that the Prophet came into the world in the final thousand years of the world's life. Consequently, by the fifth/eleventh century, it was believed that the world would come to an end within the next five centuries. Muslim jurists addressed in great detail the various signs that mark the end of the world. As Hallaq noted: "[o]ne of these signs was the disappearance of religious knowledge, *'ilm*. But *'ilm* could disappear only with the demise of the scholars … Thus, the extinction of *mujtahids,* the bearers of *'ilm,* was one of the signs of the Hour."[27] Ahmad Atif Ahmad, on the other hand, characterized this debate less in terms of theology (without denying the theological basis) and more in terms of legal philosophy. For Ahmad, this early debate—which he called "the fatigue of Shari'a" by reference to early *usul al-fiqh* debates about the end of shari'a and the jurists who represent it—concerned determinacy in and authority of the law, and in particular the authority of reason unaided by revelation.[28]

In their analysis of the two extreme positions in the debate on *ijtihad*, Ali-Karamali and Dunne suggest that a third, middle position exists. For them, that third approach to *ijtihad* is more focussed on the way in which the capacity to exercise *ijtihad* was restricted, based on the qualifications of a given individual: "Their writings display an awareness of the different levels of *ijtihad* and who may practice it, an aspect not as prevalent in the writings" of those who argued the door of *ijtihad* had closed.[29] The authors they review seem to regard *ijtihad* as having been restricted, but never closed off entirely. As a key reference point for this third position, the authors reviewed the writings of W. Montgomery Watt, in particular his 1974 article "The Closing of the Door of *Ijtihad*" in which he takes issue with the Schactian argument about the closing of the doors of *ijtihad*: "I have long been uneasy about this view, and more particularly about the fact that the closing is placed in the early tenth century."[30]

[25] Ibid., 135. [26] Ibid. [27] Ibid., 138–139.

[28] Ahmad Atif Ahmad, *The Fatigue of the Shari'a* (New York: Palgrave MacMillan, 2012).

[29] Ali-Karamali and Dunne, "The *Ijtihad* Controversy," 251.

[30] W. Montgomery Watt, "The Closing of the Door of *Iǧtihād*," in *Orientalia Hispanica 1*, ed. J.M. Barral (Leiden: E.J. Brill, 1974), 675–678, 675.

For Ali-Karamali and Dunne, Watt's rather ambiguous, middle position "is probably attributable to the different levels of *ijtihad* ... for example, as well as to confusion regarding who was entitled to exercise *ijtihad* and whether it was exercised in practice, in theory, or both."[31] As much as they situate Watt and others in this middle position, it may be that they represent less a middle position on the door of *ijtihad* issue, and instead the threshold of a different set of questions about the conditions of authority that permit one to undertake *ijtihad*. In other words, one way to see what Ali-Karamali and Dunne describe as a third, middle position on the gates of *ijtihad* is to see that position as not being about the gates of *ijtihad* so much as the epistemic conditions that make *ijtihad* possible. In fact, as shown later in this chapter, a considerable development in the scholarship on *ijtihad* is less interested in whether the gates/doors of it are open or closed, but rather, on different facets of authority that invocations of *ijtihad* call forth.

III. Legal Philosophy, Authority, and *Ijtihad*

As the field of Islamic legal studies grows and develops in an interdisciplinary fashion, it should not be surprising to see legal philosophy offering a lens through which to view debates in different aspects of *usul al-fiqh*, as in the case of *ijtihad*. For some scholars, *ijtihad* debates offer an insight into competing theoretical camps that address the implication of Islamic legal pluralism on legal determinacy. If Islamic law is characteristically pluralistic, with its various legal schools and their affiliated doctrines, how does one ever know what the right answer to a legal question is? Alternatively, is the very idea of a "right answer" problematic? Instead, should we be asking how a range of possible legal answers become authoritative as a matter of law? This set of philosophical questions take their starting point from a question often posed in premodern *usul al-fiqh* texts, namely whether every jurist is correct (*hal kull mujtahid musib*).

For Khaled Abou El Fadl and Anver M. Emon, this premodern issue opens up a series of questions about legal interpretation and legal pluralism, and moreover their implications on the objectivity and authority of a jurist's *ijtihad*. Further, their focus on objectivity and authority are focal points for a range of studies that explore the theological and jurisprudential significance of legal pluralism,

[31] Ali-Karamali and Dunne, "The *Ijtihad* Controversy," 254.

objectivity, and authority. Their approach, though, concentrates on the Sunni tradition, though Normal Calder illustrates that similar issues pervaded Shi'a debates on *ijtihad* as well.[32] Jurisprudential concerns about objectivity and authority will frame the analysis of this section in order to illuminate the stakes underlying a range of important scholarly contributions to the more theoretical study of *ijtihad*.

Abou El Fadl's approach to this topic reflects his broader interest in challenging authoritarian tendencies in modern Islamic thought. Using the image of the text as open, he argued that the "text speaks with a renewed voice to successive generations of readers because its meaning is unfixed and actively evolving."[33] An open text permits an expansion of meaning-possibilities, whereas a closed text is one in which meaning has been determined for all time. Abou El Fadl went on to say: "I am not claiming that closing a text is never justified ... The readers or the interpretive community must be willing to claim that human knowledge and God's knowledge have become one and the same on this particular point, and that the human determination cannot possibly threaten to replace the Divine Word."[34] He concluded, however, that "[i]n all likelihood, this claim will be an act of usurpation of the Divine authority, and will be a constructed authoritarianism."[35]

In this analytic context, Abou El Fadl then turned to debates on *ijtihad*, in particular on the question of whether every *mujtahid* is correct. Acknowledging that most jurists agreed that God only required diligent efforts made in good faith, Abou El Fadl outlined two camps that posed their own distinct answer to the above question. In the first camp, the *mukhatti'a* argued that on any given issue with a range of opinions, only one is correct, and the others are wrong. However, jurists are not required to be right in order to reap God's reward, nor are they liable for being wrong. Indeed, only God knows the right answer. But due to their effort in investigating the law, jurists can claim some limited authority for their positions, even if they cannot claim with certainty that their position is right. At most, their opinions enjoy what premodern jurists called *ghalabat al-zann*, or the preponderance of opinion, which was sufficient for purposes of adjudicating disputes and fixing answers to questions of law.

Emon analyzes the two hadith on which the *mukhatti'a* built their argument. In the first hadith, the prophet Muhammad states:

There are three types of judgments: one leads to heaven, and two lead to hell. The one leading to heaven [involves] one who knows the truth and decides in accordance with it. One who

[32] Norman Calder, "Doubt and Prerogative: The Emergence of an Imami Shi'I Theory of Ijtihad," *Studia Islamica* 70 (1989): 57–78.

[33] Khaled Abou El Fadl, *Speaking in God's Name: Islamic Law, Authority, and Women* (Oxford: Oneworld Publications, 2001), 146.

[34] Ibid., 147. [35] Ibid.

knows the truth but deviates from ruling [according to it] goes to hell, and one who ignorantly adjudicates for the people goes to hell.[36]

As Emon pointed out, this hadith "sets up the importance of epistemic excellence in adjudication."[37] The second hadith from Muhammad reads: "When a judge decides on a legal ruling and gets the right answer, he receives two rewards. If he adjudicates but gets the wrong answer, he gets one reward."[38] Emon noted that the emphasis on expertise in the first hadith glosses the second one on *ijtihad* to emphasize the issue of authority. The second hadith already assumes that those who are rewarded for their *ijtihad*, whether "right" or "wrong," are those with knowledge and expertise whose due diligence contributes to the authority of their legal rulings. For the *mukhatti'a*, the second hadith provides them with the basis for claiming that there is in fact a right answer, regardless of its epistemic accessibility. On this approach, *ijtihad* grants the law determinacy, at least in the mind of God, while rendering authoritative a range of answers to a legal question. For the *mukhatti'a*, correctness "means that the *mujtahid* is to be commended for putting in the effort, but it does not mean that all responses are equally valid."[39]

In contrast to this Sunni reading, Calder remarked that Shi'a theories of *ijtihad* did not so much reward the incorrect *mujtahid*, but rather held the erring *mujtahid* forgiven and unpunished for his error, while requiring adherence to his *ijtihad*ic view.[40] The fact that adherence is still required, however, speaks to the authority of *ijtihad*, whereas the point of forgiveness may have had more to do with distinguishing the Shi'a approach from the Sunni one.

The second Sunni camp, called the *musawwiba*, held that all jurists are indeed correct, although what they meant by "correct" must be carefully examined: "The *musawwiba* argued that there is no specific and correct answer (*hukm mu'ayyan*) that God wants human beings to discover, in part, because if there were a correct answer, God would have made the textual evidence conclusive and clear."[41] In other words, humans are not required to find or discover some preordained, right answer, but rather are "charged with the duty to search and honestly and diligently ascertain what they believe to be true and correct."[42] This particular approach was rejected by various Shi'a jurists, as Calder noted. The phrase in Sunni texts about all *mujtahids* being correct "was a slogan ascribed by the Shi'a to other sects, and taken to be symbolic of their juristic weakness."[43] But as Calder deftly noted, this rejection

[36] Anver M. Emon, "To Most Likely Know the Law: Objectivity, Authority, and Interpretation in Islamic Law," *Hebraic Political Studies* 4, no. 4 (2009): 415–440, 433.

[37] Ibid., 433.

[38] Ibid., 432 (footnote omitted).

[39] Abou El Fadl, *Speaking in God's Name*, 148.

[40] Calder, "Doubt and Prerogative," 71.

[41] Abou El Fadl, *Speaking in God's Name*, 148.

[42] Ibid., 149.

[43] Calder, "Doubt and Prerogative," 63.

was a means of ensuring a distinctive Shi'a approach,[44] one that could not ignore the tension between aspiring to clarity and certainty in the divine law, on one hand, and recognizing the inevitability of interpretive diversity on the other.[45] In other words, despite sectarian reasons for presuming different approaches, there is some consensus across the Islamic sects on the fundamental tensions posed by *ijtihad* concerning objectivity and authority.

For instance, as Abou El Fadl situates these camps in opposition to one another, his focus on authority reveals a greater proximity between both groups: "Importantly, both the *mukhatti'ah* and *musawwibah* do not adopt positions that mandate the closing of the text. The *mukhatti'ah* endorses the theoretical possibility of closing the text upon locating the truth, but as a practical matter, that might not be possible as long as there is juristic disagreement upon the meaning of the text ... However, the *musawwibah* adopts a position that normatively would refuse closing the text."[46] The difference between them, at least in terms of legal authority, is more of degree than of kind.

Emon also addresses both theoretical camps, but he utilizes the analytic lens of "objectivity" as framed in contemporary debates in legal philosophy. Whereas Abou El Fadl's concern was with authoritarianism among Muslims regarding the Islamic legal tradition (with specific focus on Saudi Arabia's council on *fatwa* and research), Emon's concern was with a common North Atlantic image of Islamic law as archaic, rigid, and inflexible. He took as his starting point the words of US Supreme Court Justice Felix Frankfurter when addressing the Supreme Court's power of review: "This is a court of review, not a tribunal unbounded by rules. We do not sit like a *kadi* under a tree dispensing justice according to considerations of individual expediency."[47] For Frankfurter J., Islamic law is a tradition of legal expediency. This particular image was drawn from Max Weber's depiction of Islamic law and the Muslim judge,[48] one that has prompted various scholars to reflect on the relationship between legal doctrine, judicial decision-making, and the nature of discretion. For instance, Lawrence Rosen offers an anthropological account of a modern Muslim judge in Morocco to suggest that the consistency and coherence of judicial decision-making lies in the judge's ability to recognize the negotiative space in the social relationships between litigants. Less interested in legal doctrine, the Muslim judge on Rosen's account, interprets the law less by reference to legal doctrine and more by reference to the social facts that link the litigants together, both inside

[44] Calder, "Doubt and Prerogative," 59–60. [45] Ibid., 61–63.

[46] Abou El Fadl, *Speaking in God's Name*, 150.

[47] Emon, "To Most Likely Know the Law," 415, quoting from *Terminiello v. Chicago*, 337 US 1 at 11; 69 S.Ct 894, 899 (1949).

[48] For an insightful discussion of Weber, his reference to *kadijustiz*, and what it implies about law generally and Islamic law specifically, see Baber Johansen, *Contingency in a Sacred Law: Legal and Ethical Norms in the Muslim Fiqh* (Leiden: Brill, 1999), 48–51.

and outside the courtroom.[49] David Powers, in his impressive study on adjudication in the fourteenth and fifteenth centuries, challenges Rosen's characterization by showing through historical analysis that a judge (*qadi*) was neither slave to doctrine nor an agent of mere expediency. Rather the judge as legal interpreter decided complex conflicts with a legal pragmatism that blended both factual and legal analysis.[50]

In contrast to the Weberian image of the *qadi* as legal interpreter is another that represents Islamic law as "so highly determinate as to prevent effective interpretive engagement with source-texts and the contingencies of particular conflicts."[51] Indeed, this image draws upon the characterization addressed above about *taqlid* as demanding blind obedience to legal doctrine. These two images of Islamic law frame the fundamental questions concerning *ijtihad*, objectivity and authority in the law, which animate the jurisprudential stakes to debates on *ijtihad*.

For instance, as much as Emon responds against competing perceptions of Islamic law, his reference to Ronald Dworkin's interpretive theory of law reveals a slightly different intellectual agenda, namely to situate *ijtihad* debates within the larger framework of legal philosophy, and thereby undercut the exceptionalism that often attends to popular and even scholarly analyses of Islamic law. For example, he wrote:

> [P]remodern Muslim jurists from the ninth through fifteenth centuries developed a jurisprudence of Shari'a that acknowledged the inevitability of interpreting within the law. This should not be surprising if we take into account that legal systems generally require a degree of interpretive agency, whether they are premodern or modern ... I suggest that concerns about determinacy, authority, and reason are significant features of legal systems, whether common law, rabbinic law, or as in this case, Islamic law.[52]

For Emon, the *mukhatti'a* and *musawwiba* approaches to *ijtihad* reflect competing approaches to objectivity in the law, and thereby competing metaphors for the jurist, whether as an archaeologist who must find or discover the law, or as a constructivist who must exercise creative agency in developing the law.[53] These two camps staked out their competing positions in their respective responses to the question of whether every jurist is correct. However, this question begged a further one about scope of interpretation, namely whether there are some questions that are outside the bounds of interpretation. Premodern Muslim jurists from among the

[49] Lawrence Rosen, *The Anthropology of Justice: Law as Culture in Islamic Society* (Cambridge: Cambridge University Press, 1989). For a critique of Rosen's method and analysis, see Khaled Abou El Fadl, "Islamic Law and Ambivalent Scholarship: A Review of Lawrence Rosen, *The Justice of Islam: Comparative Perspectives on Islamic Law and Society* (Oxford: Oxford University Press, 2000)," *Michigan Law Review* 100, no. 6 (May 2002): 1421–1443.

[50] David S. Powers, *Law, Society and Culture in the Maghreb, 1300–1500* (Cambridge: Cambridge University Press, 2002).

[51] Ibid., 416. [52] Ibid., 418.

[53] Ibid., 419; Anver M. Emon, *Religious Pluralism and Islamic Law: Dhimmis and Others in the Empire of Law* (Oxford: Oxford University Press, 2012), 203.

Sunni and Shiʿa generally held core or foundational values (the *usul*) to lie outside the ambit of *ijtihad*: "According to Muslim jurists, the *usul*, or core values, are those that are universal and are subject to neither dispute nor interpretation. In fact, for the thirteenth-century jurist al-Qarafi (d. 1285 CE) and others, the *usul* are so fundamental that one is effectively compelled, whether by nature, reason or otherwise, to believe them."[54] And while this was the predominant position, there were some who disputed whether in fact the *usul* were immune from *ijtihad*. For instance, al-ʾAnbari (d. 785) "held that there can be differences of opinion over the *usul* and that all competing views about core values are correct."[55] As much as al-ʾAnbari's position was critiqued, that did not prevent someone such as al-Jahiz from suggesting that there can be debate on the *usul*. This is not because the *usul* themselves are debatable, but rather because people have different capacities to know the *usul*. In other words, al-Jahiz doubted that all people shared the same epistemic capacities to know the *usul*.[56]

But if the *usul* are not subject to dispute, that does not mean they are necessarily determinate. Indeed, jurists who held the *usul* immune to *ijtihad* nonetheless disagreed on what they were. For some such as al-Juwayni, the *usul* had to do with broad, theological issues such as the nature of God's speech, the eternity of the Qur'an, and so on. Others considered the obligations to pray and give charity among the *usul*.

This indeterminacy in the *usul* prompted Abou El Fadl to examine whether and to what extent one can explore the formulations of these core values. He too noted the indeterminacy among premodern jurists on defining the *usul*. He responded to this indeterminacy with three postulates. First, he argued that "[i]t is one thing to argue that there are matters so clear and obvious in the pertinent Islamic texts that it is sinful to attempt to re-interpret them, and it is quite another to argue that it is appropriate to censor someone who wishes to reinterpret the matters."[57] Second, whether something is an *usul* or precludes reinterpretation is a matter of proof, whose burden may shift depending on the nature of the claim being made. For instance, to claim something as fundamental is indeed a weighty claim. As such, Abou El Fadl argued that the claimant bears a heavy burden of proof. Alternatively, if something has been held to be a core value within the Islamic tradition, and this position has been "consistently and cumulatively accepted as supported by evidence, one can presume that it is a legitimate and sound determination."[58] But it is a rebuttable presumption, where the burden of proof lies on the one who seeks to open the issue to reinterpretation. Third, Abou El Fadl addressed the concern that whether a value is fundamental or not may depend on certain assumptions that are themselves

[54] Emon, "To Most Likely Know the Law," 426. On the Shiʿa view, see Calder, "Doubt and Prerogative," 75.

[55] Emon, "To Most Likely Know the Law," 428.

[56] Ibid., 430.

[57] Abou El Fadl, *Speaking in God's Name*, 151.

[58] Ibid., 152.

contextually limited. It may be that the very idea of a fundamental value is authoritarian. Abou El Fadl remarked that this position turns on the nature of the assumption. He described four types of assumptions that may underlie a foundation value: value-based, methodological, faith-based, and reason-based. For Abou El Fadl, the fact that such assumptions operate within the law is not a problem. The problem is that they may unduly close down inquiry. As he wrote: "There is a difference between assuming a certain starting point for the analysis so that the analysis may proceed further, and the closing of the interpretive process by the adoption of non-negotiable convictions about matters of ultimate truth. It is the closing of the interpretive process and the violation of the conditions of agency that can be described as authoritarian."[59]

If the *usul* are immune from *ijtihad* (whatever the *usul* may be), Emon noted that Muslim jurists held the *furu'*, or particular legal issues, to be matters ripe for *ijtihad*. The debate between the *mukhatti'a* and *musawwiba* was focussed on this particular arena of legal interpretation. For the *mukhatti'a*, the objectivity of the law, at least in the mind of God, contributed to the law's determinacy. But given its inaccessibility, *ijtihad*ic products must be framed as having limited authority. For the *musawwiba*, the lack of objective determinacy in the law did not preclude jurists from having the authority to interpret and adjudicate disputes. The absence of an objective, determinate answer did not preclude the jurist from exercising *ijtihad*.

Both schools ultimately acknowledged the epistemic impossibility of determining the law of God with certitude. At most, the jurist exercises a qualified authority to interpret the law and adjudicate disputes. They expressed that qualified authority by using the same Arabic phrase *ghalabat al-zann*. "Ghalabat al-zann, which can be translated as 'the preponderance of opinion,' reflects the authority of a legal argument that, at the same time, preserves one's epistemic humility before an infinite God, [and] grants epistemic authority" to the *ijtihad*ic ruling.[60]

Moreover, the commonality between both schools also lay in their theo-legal conception of objectivity in the law. For the *mukhatti'a*, there was a law in the mind of God, despite it being epistemically inaccessible. The Arabic phrase they used to denote the "law in the mind of God" was *hukm mu'ayyan*. This determinate conception of God's law is what allowed the *mukhatti'a* to hold fast to commitment to a right answer in Islamic law. This particular conception of God and God's will implied that *ijtihad* was a means of "*finding* or *discovering* God's law … *Ijtihad* for the *mukhatti'a* is about finding God's law, knowing that one may not do so, admitting human imperfection, and being satisfied with *ghalabat al-zann* as a basis for legal authority."[61] As much as the *musawwiba* denied the *mukhatti'a* claim of legal objectivity, they could not avoid offering their own telos to which *ijtihad* must

[59] Abou El Fadl, *Speaking in God's Name*, 158.
[60] Emon, *Religious Pluralism and Islamic Law*, 205.
[61] Emon, "To Most Likely Know the Law," 437–438.

be directed, which they called *al-ashbah*. Emon wrote: "As is often formulaically expressed, the *al-ashbah* rule is what God would have ruled had he legislated on the matter ... For the *musawwiba*, there is only one *al-ashbah;* all others are wrong."[62] On the one hand, their theory of the *al-ashbah* evinces their ongoing concern with objectivity in the law even as they emphasize qualified authority and epistemic excellence as central to debates on *ijtihad*. On the other hand, their ongoing concern with objectivity in the form of *al-ashbah* should not be overstated. Their doctrine of *al-ashbah* is not analogous to the *mukhatti'a* claim of the metaphysical objectivity of the *hukm mu'ayyan*. Rather, the *al-ashbah* is counter-factual: "[i]t is the rule that would have existed had God actually ruled. But he did not."[63] Hence, as much as the *mukhatti'a* and *musawwiba* start from competing positions on the objectivity of law, their competing doctrines culminate in a similar end point, the emphasis on epistemic excellence and due diligence, and their implication for the qualified authority of the *ijtihad*ic product.

IV. *Ijtihad*, Reform, and Contested Conditions of Epistemic Legitimacy: New Directions for Research

The above theoretical discussion on *ijtihad* that links authority to epistemic standards becomes particularly relevant for more recent debates about Islamic law and reform. Specifically, scholarship that addresses *ijtihad* in particular social settings or *ijtihad* as a reform strategy reveals how the underlying issue of authority begs important questions about the requisite curriculum of training that renders one competent to exercise *ijtihad*. Moreover, with contests over the appropriate curriculum of training to enable the legitimate exercise of *ijtihad* comes a contest over the boundaries that delineate who can exercise *ijtihad* and who cannot. Indeed, debates about *ijtihad* and reform therefore call into question how presumptions about education and curriculum feed into corporate identities of competing scholarly communities, and the authority of a particularly trained community of scholars to exercise *ijtihad* at all. Indeed, as will be suggested below, these presumptions demand investigation and inquiry, and thus offer possible avenues for further research and inquiry.

[62] Emon, "To Most Likely Know the Law," 438. [63] Ibid.

The background conditions that animate this contest over the conditions of epistemic legitimacy in recent decades are often described in broad terms. Modernity, colonialism, migration—all contribute to changed background conditions that elicit contested views about authority. Muneer Farid has written extensively on the topic of Islamic reform. In his focus on nineteenth- and twentieth-century reform movements, he has emphasized the role of modernity and European colonialism in galvanizing reform movements to espouse the virtues of *ijtihad*. In an article published in 2000, he explained why this historical period is especially important for thinking about reform and *ijtihad*:

> [T]his is when the cultural hegemony of colonialism was most palpable. Muslim social structures such as the court system of the Muslim *qadi* were rapidly being replaced by European judicial structures. The educational structure was also being replaced, as was the medium of communication. Upwardly mobile Egyptian and Indian civil servants for instance, no longer required Arabic, Persian or Urdu to communicate but rather English, German, and French. Muslim intellectual leaders were understandably alarmed at this deracination of culture, language and law ... Because of their exposure to western society—more so in the case of some than others—[Muslim reformists'] views represent a critique of both traditional Islamic and contemporaneous western perspectives. Each of these thinkers conducted his discourse at the point where classical Islamic and modern Enlightenment thought intertwined and each used traditional symbols such as *ijtihad* and *taqlid* to set in motion what [Fazlur] Rahman calls "a program of reconstruction ... within the basic framework of orthodoxy."[64]

Elsewhere he argued that *ijtihad* offered reformists an Islamic tool or mechanism by which to reverse the effects of colonialism and usher a return of Islam's grandeur in the Muslim world: "To undo the corrosive effects of European colonialism on their civil societies, Muslim reformists turned to their past, to what they believed was the catalyst that spawned early Islam's intellectual efflorescence: for many, *ijtihad* was that impulse, the single element from the sacred heritage with the potential to restore the sacred law to Muslim society."[65] Murteza Bedir, on the other hand, offered a different angle on *ijtihad* and reform in the case of nineteenth- and twentieth-century Turkey.[66] While European legal culture was certainly in many people's minds involved in Ottoman and Turkish legal reform, so too were other considerations such as the role of government and educational institutions; presumptions about curricular and pedagogic design of Islamic studies; notions of the public weal (however defined); and changing attitudes toward the scope of what counts as law in an increasingly centralizing state system.

Whatever the relationship between *ijtihad* and legal reform movements, Muslims did not agree on what *ijtihad* entailed or who could exercise it. In a close and careful

[64] Muneer Fareed, "*Ijtihad and Taqlid*: Classical Metaphors in Modernist Discourse," *Journal for Islamic Studies* 20 (2000): 1–14, 2 (footnote omitted).

[65] Fareed, "Against *Ijtihad*," 356.

[66] Murteza Bedir, "*Fikih* to Law: Secularization through Curriculum," *Islamic Law and Society* 11, no. 3 (2004): 378–401.

analysis of intra-Muslim debates in South Asia on *ijtihad*, Muhammad Qasim Zaman illuminated important differences between modern Muslim intellectuals of distinct and at times competing attitudes on Islam and reform:

> Against the overlapping challenges of the Salafis and the Islamists, modernist Muslims and modernizing Muslim governments, many among the Sunni *'ulama'* of modern times, especially in South Asia, have often expressed grave misgivings about *ijtihad*. Their discomfort has rested, *inter alia*, on the conviction that the scholarly tradition is not only a repertoire of authoritative norms but also of agreed-upon methods for interpreting the foundational texts. Any willingness to set aside these time-honoured methods immediately raises the spectre of wilfully subordinating God's word to ill-informed guesswork which serves only to pave the way towards interpretive anarchy.[67]

Having said that, Zaman also noted that many of these same *ulama* also recognized the importance of *ijtihad* as a means of meeting the changes brought on in contemporary times.[68] Through his analysis, the reader can better appreciate how intellectual exchanges between the Middle East and South Asia shaped debates on *ijtihad*; how the development of institutional sites of *ijtihad* affected attitudes toward *ijtihad*; and how the discourse of *ijtihad* slowly decentered "strict fidelity to the established school of law as a way of articulating claims to religious authority."[69]

Through a comparison between Deoband scholar and jurist Muhammad Anwar Shah Kashmiri (d. 1933) and the well-studied Rashid Rida of the Arab world, Zaman keenly observed a distinction in how the two men understood *ijtihad* and the prerequisites for its exercise. For Rida, the basic conditions for *ijtihad* required an understanding of the Qur'an, the Sunna of the Prophet Muhammad, and the purposes of the law, or what are often called in Arabic the *maqasid al-shari'a*. Kashmiri, though, held a different view on *ijtihad*. He did not deny its importance, but set out different and more extensive conditions for its use. *Ijtihad* implied a methodology of interpretation, a lacuna in the law, and an acceptance of a degree of indeterminacy in ultimate legal outcomes. Zaman quoted Kashmiri, who stated:

> By questions of *ijtihad*, I mean those on which no ruling from the Qur'an exists, nor do any of the most authoritatively transmitted teachings of the Prophet (peace be upon him) (*sunna mutawatirah*). The correct position in such matters can be varied. But if there is a definitive text [from the foundational sources], there is no *ijtihad*. There is a single true position in such cases, which is what accords with the definitive text.[70]

Between Rida's and Kashmiri's approach to *ijtihad*, Zaman noted, lay a difference in scope. That difference was not lost on Rida, who considered the Deobandi scholars far too committed to the doctrines of the Hanafi school. But in proffering competing conceptions of *ijtihad*, Rida and Kashmiri had very different goals. Rida's support of

[67] Muhammad Qasim Zaman, "Evolving Conceptions of *Ijtihad* in Modern South Asia," *Islamic Studies* 49, no. 1 (2010): 5–36.

[68] Zaman, "Evolving Conceptions of *Ijtihad*," 6.

[69] Ibid., 7.

[70] Ibid., 10 (citation omitted).

an *ijtihad* with wide scope reflected, as Zaman noted: "his lifelong concern with the degeneration of the *Madhhab*-bound *ulama* of al-Azhar."[71] Kashmiri, on the other hand, may have had his own reasons for framing the scope of *ijtihad* more narrowly. When Kashmiri described the Deobandi approach on the occasion of Rida's visit in 1912, the former related the importance of the Deoband movement in preserving the true Islam on the peripheries of the Muslim world (i.e. the Arab world). For Kashmiri, these efforts were all the more important, as Zaman noted: "with the onset of colonial rule, which not only brought Christian missionaries to India but had also employed people who were 'Muslim only in name' for the propagation of anti-Islamic ideas."[72]

This difference between Rida and Deobandi scholars such as Kashmiri could be explained in various ways. Of the ones that Zaman presented, the first is of particular interest, in light of what follows below. Specifically, he suggested that the different tendencies and scopes of analyses reflected the status and training of those seeking to exercise *ijtihad*. As Zaman wrote: "in Egypt and elsewhere in the Arab Middle East and North Africa, some of the leading proponents of *ijtihad* were themselves recognized, or recognizable, as *ulama* ... In South Asia, on the other hand, there was a much sharper divide between the Muslim modernists advocating *ijtihad* and the *ulama*, especially the Deobandis, resisting it or at least being highly suspicious of modernist calls for *ijtihad*."[73] So for instance, it is one thing for a Mustafa Maraghi (d. 1945), a *Shaykh al-Azhar*, or today's Yusuf al-Qaradawi, to call for *ijtihad*. They were and are recognized as being trained in a particular curriculum of Islamic legal learning, which provide a context to their calls for *ijtihad*. It's quite another, however, for Muhammad Iqbal (d. 1938) of South Asia, who was trained in the Common Law, and "had a poor view of many among the *ulama*" and whose view of *ijtihad* "was nothing if not radical: he was interested ... in a thoroughgoing rethinking of the entire legal tradition in light of the foundational texts."[74]

Zaman and Fareed presented important background conditions that explain what animates more recent debates in the Muslim world on *ijtihad*. Indeed, their contributions help us appreciate what is at stake when someone invokes *ijtihad* today. *Ijtihad* invokes questions about authority, curriculum, and training. Stepping back from these questions allows us to appreciate how debates about *ijtihad*, especially

[71] Ibid., 13. [72] Ibid., 8. [73] Ibid., 19.

[74] Ibid., 14–15, 19. Zaman's other explanations had to do with the emphasis of Anglo-Mohammad courts on determinacy and predictability in the law (and hence a disincentive for *ijtihad*); the tendency toward traditionalist scholarship in South Asia; and the greater scope in Middle Eastern and North African states to manage religious affairs for their majority Muslim population. Ibid., 19–21. On Anglo-Mohammad courts and their rarifying tendencies, see Anver M. Emon, "Islamic Law and the Canadian Mosaic: Politics, Jurisprudence, and Multicultural Accommodation," *Canadian Bar Review* 87, no. 2 (2009): 391–425, 402–410.

in the Muslim world, are rhetorical sites for broader contests over the appropriate modes of training and curriculum, the authoritative institution(s) of knowledge, the implication of migration from the Muslim world, and the relationship between institutions of the state and the authority to interpret Islamic law, in particular in Muslim majority contexts, though not exclusively so.

A. The Institutional Turn in *Ijtihad*

For example, in a 1999 article, Killian Balz examined the pre-2011 jurisprudence of the Supreme Constitutional Court (SCC) of Egypt in a constitutional challenge against legislation that banned the *niqab* (face veil) in state-run schools, but permitted the *hijab* (headscarf).[75] Article 2 of the then-Egyptian constitution deemed that the principles of Islamic law are the main source of law for the state. The SCC had to determine whether legislation that banned the *niqab* violated Article 2. As Balz outlined, the SCC developed a jurisprudence that distinguished between Islamic legal issues that had clear solutions, and others that were disputed. In the case at hand, the SCC held that however central modesty may be in the Islamic tradition, there were a variety of ways for a woman to achieve modesty. Hence, whether a woman must cover just her hair, or her hair and face, is a matter of dispute in Islamic law, and thus an appropriate topic on which the legislature can act. Though Balz was specifically interested in the relationship between different modalities of law (the Islamic and the secular state law), his analysis revealed an "institutional turn"[76] in the discourse on *ijtihad*. To incorporate Islamic law in the modern state is "not to subordinate state-enacted 'secular' legislation under the 'principles of Islamic law', but rather to 'nationalize' Islamic law by submitting it under the control of the nation-state."[77] In other words, at the intersection of Islam and the state, the discourse of *ijtihad* now includes whether and to what extent state institutions can assume the authority to interpret Islamic law. Indeed, as Zaman explained, "a popularly-elected legislature represents the marriage of an evolving *shari'a* with parliamentary democracy, rendering Islamic law simultaneously an expression of divine *and* popular will."[78]

Inside Muslim majority states, the more conservative "*ulama*" may exercise some suspicion of state-cooptation of *ijtihad*. In some cases, as Zaman noted, these "*ulama*" have created their own institutions for collective *ijtihad* such as the Dar al-Ifta' of Egypt (est. 1895) and the Dar al-Ifta' of India in Deoband, which was

[75] Killian Balz, "The Secular Reconstruction of Islamic Law: Egyptian Supreme Constitutional Court and the 'Battle Over the Veil' in State-Run Schools," in *Legal Pluralism in the Arab World*, eds. Baudouin Dupret et al. (The Hague: Kluwer Law International, 1999), 153–174.

[76] On the "institutional turn" in the study of law and legal theory, see Cass Sunstein and Adrian Vermeule, "Interpretation and Institutions," *Michigan Law Review* 101, no. 4 (2003): 885–951; Scott Shapiro, *Legality* (Cambridge: Belknap Press, 2011).

[77] Balz, "Secular Reconstruction," 237.

[78] Zaman, "Evolving Conceptions of *Ijtihad*," 22.

established two years before the Egyptian one.[79] Outside of Muslim majority states, collective *ijtihad* can take shape as non-governmental organizations (NGOs) that bring together Muslim scholars from different contexts to expound upon issues of contemporary relevance. For instance, the popular cleric Yusuf al-Qaradawi has founded two such institutions: the European Council for Fatwa and Research[80] and the International Union of Muslim Scholars (IUMS).[81] The European institute reflects al-Qaradawi's keen interest in developing a *fiqh* for Muslim minorities, whereas IUMS seeks to support *ijtihad* for all times and places, and in light of changing circumstances and conditions.[82] In both forms of *ijtihad*ic institutionalization, whether as government institution or NGO, the corporate forms within which *ijtihad* takes place beg a series of questions about the underlying conditions of authority that make *ijtihad* possible and meaningful.

B. Curricular Conditions of Authority: The Case of Islamic Feminism

Of particular interest in more recent decades on Islamic law and interpretive authority is the implication of an Islamic feminist critique of Islamic law, whose exponents are often trained in the university setting, as opposed to the more traditional *madrasas*. The historiography on women in traditional settings of training suggests that these venues are not entirely open to Muslim women. Historians of premodern Islamic education have recognized that women were certainly trained in traditional settings, though their numbers were limited.[83] And in the contemporary Muslim world women encounter a ceiling in how far they can advance, whether as students or as authorities of Islam and Islamic law.[84] Moreover, the bounded pedagogic framework potentially limits the scope of intellectual inquiry. As Zareena Grewal has noted, pedagogy in more traditional settings in the Middle East vacillates between transmitting a presumed content, and creating a more open space for creative methods at knowing the divine and one's place within it:

> [I]s the purpose of Islamic higher learning to teach fidelity to a fixed and finished canon and set of methodologies and to simply apply them to new contexts and new questions in order

[79] Zaman, "Evolving Conceptions of *Ijtihad*," 23.

[80] http://e-cfr.org/new/

[81] http://iumsonline.org/portal/en-US/Home/28/

[82] Zaman, "Evolving Conceptions of *Ijtihad*," 25–26.

[83] Jonathan Berkey, *The Transmission of Knowledge in Medieval Cairo: A Social History of Islamic Education* (Princeton: Princeton University Press, 1992); Ruth Roded, *Women in Islamic Biographical Collections: From Ibn Sa'd to Who's Who* (London: Lynne Reinner Publishers, 1994).

[84] Zareena Grewal, *Islam is a Foreign Country: American Muslims and the Global Crisis of Authority* (New York: New York University Press, 2014), 246–252; Julianne Hammer, *American Muslim Women, Religious Authority, and Activism* (Austin: University of Texas Press, 2012), 114–120.

to assimilate them? Or should Islamic education cultivate an ethical sensibility, as a mode of scholarly inquiry focused outward that continuously expands the canon, that embraces a plurality of methods and disciplines in order to engage creation and revelation?[85]

With such limited access and pedagogic possibilities, it is perhaps not surprising that feminism in these contexts is viewed through a postcolonial framework as foreign, western, and imperial.[86] Moreover, it is not surprising that feminist critiques of Islamic law have often self-consciously situated their critique from outside the Islamic tradition, such as in terms of human rights, for instance. This tendency, however, has changed with the development of Islamic feminist movements that seek a gender egalitarian framework from *within* the Islamic tradition, as does the Muslim feminist group *Musawah*. *Musawah*'s signature distinction from many women's equality groups is its engagement with the Islamic tradition. In her exposition of the *Musawah* model, Ziba Mir-Hosseini has argued that in the twentieth century, it was almost commonplace to link religion with the oppression of women (especially Islam). A corollary of that link was to suggest that any feminist or gender equality agenda had to be framed using materials external to the religious tradition of Islam. The problem, she argues, is that this narrow notion of feminism has been repeatedly used in the service of colonial projects, and as such has become discredited in the minds of many in the Muslim world. She makes a similar case for the cause of human rights. Consequently, the *Musawah* model works from *within* the Islamic legal tradition toward a tradition of gender equality. Only in this fashion, she argues, can Muslim women free themselves "from an apparent choice between the devil of those who want to impose patriarchal interpretations of Islam's sacred texts, and the deep blue sea of those who pursue a neo-colonialist hegemonic global project in the name of human rights and feminism."[87]

The feminist scholars who work from within the Islamic tradition toward gender equality tend to share an important characteristic, which bears upon the conditions of authority for purposes of *ijtihad*. Quite often, they are either trained in or teach in university settings (especially North Atlantic ones, though not exclusively so) as opposed to more conservative, traditional seminary-like settings.[88] On the one

[85] Grewal, *Islam is a Foreign Country*, 184. [86] Ibid., 241.

[87] Ziba Mir-Hosseini, "Women in Search of Common Ground: Between Islamic and International Human Rights Law," in *Islamic Law and International Human Rights Law: Searching for Common Ground?*, Anver M. Emon, Mark Ellis, and Benjamin Glahn (eds.) (Oxford: Oxford University Press, 2012), 291–303, 299.

[88] For instance, Ziba Mir-Hosseini did her Ph.D. in anthropology at Cambridge University and has published widely on issues pertaining to gender equality and Islamic law. She is also a leading member of *Musawah*. See her website: http://www.zibamirhosseini.com (accessed November 26, 2013). Kecia Ali, author of *Sexual Ethics and Islam* (Oxford: Oneworld Publications, 2006), completed her Ph.D. in the United States at Duke University and teaches at Boston University: http://www.bu.edu/religion/faculty/bios/kecia-ali/ (accessed November 26, 2013). Laury Silvers, a scholar of Sufism and a well-known activist committed to gender and LGBT equality in Islam, did

hand, this may raise postcolonialist critiques inspired by Edward Said's *Orientalism*. And indeed, historians of Islamic law have illuminated how European scholars of Islamic law represented Islamic law with an implicit aim of supporting their particular country's colonial endeavors in the Muslim world.[89] On the other hand, the dynamics of power and domination in the majority Muslim world cannot discount the way in which patriarchy operates upon a woman's body and mind in ways that may preclude certain modes of critical analysis or methods of inquiry. As such, the development of an Islamic feminism emanating from North Atlantic universities calls out for innovative research not only on the limits of some forms of postcolonial critique, but also, and most pertinently for this chapter, on the implications of curriculum, institution, and even academic freedom on the conditions of interpretive authority and the doctrine of *ijtihad*.

c. Migration and the Racialization of Interpretive Authority: A North American Example

The third and final area that calls out for research concerns the context of Muslims as minorities. Muslim minorities in Europe and North America are topics of increasing scholarly interest. In these contexts, which have historically had few curricular institutions to support Islamic training, questions of authority take on a different hue. Writing about the North American context, Ali Albarghouthi has noted that "the *ijtihad*ic discourse in North America inherits this debate [on authority] and imbues it with the particularities of the continent."[90] Though Albarghouthi elides North America and the United States, he frames the US debate on authority in ways that draw upon the history of the

her doctoral work in the United States and works in Canada. See her website at: http://laurysilvers.com/ (accessed November 26, 2013). Sa'diyya Shaikh, a Sufi and gender specialist, trained in both South Africa and in the United States, completed her Ph.D. at Temple University, and now teaches in South Africa. Ayesha Chaudhry, author of *Domestic Violence and Islamic Law* (Oxford: Oxford University Press, 2013) completed her Ph.D. at New York University and teaches in Canada at the University of British Columbia. http://www.grsj.arts.ubc.ca/faculty2/ayesha-s-chaudhry/ (accessed November 26, 2013). This is not meant to give preference to North Atlantic universities. Indeed, Lila Abu-Lughod remarks that 50 percent of students in Arab universities are women, and some of those women lead important feminist activist organizations, such as the Center for Egyptian Women's Legal Assistance (CEWLA). Lila Abu-Lughod, *Do Muslim Women Need Saving?* (Cambridge, MA: Harvard University Press, 2013), 153.

89 See for instance, David Powers, "Orientalism, Colonialism and Legal History: The Attack on Muslim Family Endowments in Algeria and India," *Comparative Studies in Society and History* 31, no. 3 (July 1989): 535–571.

90 Ali Albarghouthi, "Authority and Representation in North America: The *Ijtihad* Criteria and the Construction of New Religious Authority," *Journal of Islamic Law and Culture* 13 no. 1 (2011): 18–33, 18.

continent. Muslims in the region live as a minority; Muslims have few if any established institutions that "anchor debates over authority"; the Muslim population in the continent is diverse and thus lacks any shared, collective vision or frame of reference to determine questions of authority; and lastly Muslims in this region are embedded in the highly populist notions of religion that have animated American religious life.[91] In the American context, the debate on authority, though often framed in terms of knowledge and expertise, is arguably a pretext for a racialized discourse that maps on to preconceived notions of an Islamic center (the Arab world) and an Islamic periphery. Recent studies on Islamic authority in the United States certainly attest to the racialized character around knowledge and authority.[92] Amina Wadud has written about this quite powerfully:

> Leadership roles, authority, and public representation rest overwhelmingly upon the shoulders of male immigrants ... [T]hose who participate at the grassroots level are marginalized when it comes to the establishment of authority. Immigrant Muslims privilege their own status as authorities on the basis of their centuries-long heritage of Islam.[93]

Wadud describes a tension between African-American Muslims and "immigrant" Muslims in the United States that requires unpacking. The very term "immigrant" is a catch-all that does not adequately reflect on the differences that occur within that category. Nonetheless, she and others writing on authority and American Muslims have tapped into an important theme that calls out for theoretical reflection. Racialized notions of authority are mapped onto a geography of Islam that posits a center (the Arab world) and a periphery (everywhere else) that serve as proxies for authority in contexts where institutions that referee claims to authority do not exist.

To draw upon the work of historian Richard Bulliet, the particularity of the American experience suggests that further theoretical research on *ijtihad* might benefit by viewing the nature of knowledge, expertise, and authority from the edge, all the while interrogating whether there is a center at all.[94]

[91] Albarghouthi, "Authority and Representation," 26.

[92] Grewal, *Islam is a Foreign Country*.

[93] Amina Wadud, "American Muslim Identity: Race and Ethnicity in Progressive Islam," in *Progressive Muslims: On Justice, Gender, and Pluralism*, ed. Omid Safi (Oxford: Oneworld Publications, 2003), 270–285, 271–272. See also, Sherman A. Jackson, *Islam and the Blackamerican: Looking Toward the Third Resurrection* (Oxford: Oxford University Press, 2005).

[94] Richard Bulliet, *Islam: The View from the Edge*, new edn. (New York: Columbia University Press, 1995).

References

Abou El Fadl, Khaled, *Speaking in God's Name: Islamic Law, Authority, and Women* (Oxford: Oneworld Publications, 2001).

Abou El Fadl, Khaled, "Islamic Law and Ambivalent Scholarship: A Review of Lawrence Rosen, *The Justice of Islam: Comparative Perspectives on Islamic Law and Society* (Oxford: Oxford University Press, 2000)." *Michigan Law Review* 100, no. 6 (May 2002): 1421–1443.

Abu-Lughod, Lila, *Do Muslim Women Need Saving?* (Cambridge, MA: Harvard University Press, 2013).

Ahmad, Ahmad Atif, *The Fatigue of the Shari'a* (New York: Palgrave MacMillan, 2012).

Albarghouthi, Ali, "Authority and Representation in North America: The *Ijtihad* Criteria and the Construction of New Religious Authority." *Journal of Islamic Law and Culture* 13 no. 1 (2011): 18–33.

Ali, Kecia, *Sexual Ethics and Islam* (Oxford: Oneworld Publications, 2006).

Ali-Karamali, Shaista P., and Dunne, Fiona, "The Ijtihad Controversy." *Arab Law Quarterly* 9, no. 3 (1994) 238–257.

Balz, Killian, "The Secular Reconstruction of Islamic Law: Egyptian Supreme Constitutional Court and the 'Battle Over the Veil' in State-Run Schools" in Baudouin Dupret et al (eds.) *Legal Pluralism in the Arab World* (The Hague: Kluwer Law International, 1999) 229–243.

Bedir, Murteza, "*Fikih* to Law: Secularization through Curriculum." *Islamic Law and Society* 11, no. 3 (2004): 378–401.

Berkey, Jonathan, *The Transmission of Knowledge in Medieval Cairo: A Social History of Islamic Education* (Princeton: Princeton University Press, 1992).

Brown, Jonathan A.C., *The Canonization of al-Bukhari and Muslim: The Formation and Function of the Sunni Hadith Canon* (Leiden: Brill Publications, 2011).

Bulliet, Richard, *Islam: The View from the Edge* (2nd edn. New York: Columbia University Press, 1995).

Calder, Norman, "Doubt and Prerogative: The Emergence of an Imami Shi'i Theory of Ijtihad." *Studia Islamica* 70 (1989): 57–78.

Chaudhry, Ayesha, *Domestic Violence and Islamic Law* (Oxford: Oxford University Press, 2013).

Coulson, Noel J., *A History of Islamic Law* (reprint, 1997; Edinburgh: Edinburgh University Press, 1964).

Emon, Anver M., "To Most Likely Know the Law: Objectivity, Authority, and Interpretation in Islamic Law." *Hebraic Political Studies* 4, 4 (2009): 415–440.

Emon, Anver M., "Islamic Law and the Canadian Mosaic: Politics, Jurisprudence, and Multicultural Accommodation." *Canadian Bar Review* 87, no. 2 (2009): 391–425.

Emon, Anver M., *Religious Pluralism and Islamic Law: Dhimmis and Others in the Empire of Law* (Oxford: Oxford University Press, 2012).

Fadel, Mohammad, "The Social Logic of *Taqlid* and the Rise of the *Mukhtasar*." *Islamic Law and Society* 3, 2 (1996): 193–233.

Fareed, Muneer, "*Ijtihad* and *Taqlid*: Classical Metaphors in Modernist Discourse." *Journal for Islamic Studies* 20 (2000): 1–14.

Fareed, Muneer, "Against Ijtihad." *The Muslim World* 91, no. 3–4 (2001): 355–370.

Grewal, Zareena, *Islam is a Foreign Country: American Muslims and the Global Crisis of Authority* (New York: New York University Press, 2014).

Hallaq, Wael B., "Was the Gate of *Ijtihad* Closed?" *International Journal of Middle East Studies* 16 (1984): 3–41.
Hallaq, Wael B., "On the Origins of the Controversy about the Existence of Mujtahids and the Gate of *Ijtihad.*" *Studia Islamica* 63 (1986): 129–141.
Hallaq, Wael B., *Authority, Continuity and Change in Islamic Law* (Cambridge: Cambridge University Press, 2001).
Hammer, Julianne, *American Muslim Women, Religious Authority, and Activism* (Austin: University of Texas Press, 2012).
Jackson, Sherman A., *Islam and the Blackamerican: Looking Toward the Third Resurrection* (Oxford: Oxford University Press, 2005).
Johansen, Baber, *Contingency in a Sacred Law: Legal and Ethical Norms in the Muslim Fiqh* (Leiden: Brill, 1999).
Lane, Edward W., *Arabic-English Lexicon* (Cambridge: Islamic Texts Society, 1984).
Manji, Irshad, *The Trouble with Islam Today* (New York: St Martin's Griffin, 2005).
Mir-Hosseini, Ziba, "Women in Search of Common Ground: Between Islamic and International Human Rights Law" in Anver M. Emon, Mark Ellis, and Benjamin Glahn (eds.) *Islamic Law and International Human Rights Law: Searching for Common Ground?* (Oxford: Oxford University Press, 2012) 291–303.
Nazir-Ali, Michael, "Islamic Law, Fundamental Freedoms, and Social Cohesion: Retrospect and Prospect" in Rex Ahdar and Nicholas Aroney (eds.) *Shari'a in the West* (Oxford: Oxford University Press, 2010) 71–89.
Powers, David S., *Law, Society and Culture in the Maghreb, 1300–1500* (Cambridge: Cambridge University Press, 2002).
Roded, Rut, *Women in Islamic Biographical Collections: From Ibn Sa'd to Who's Who* (London: Lynne Reinner Publishers, 1994).
Rosen, Lawrence, *The Anthropology of Justice: Law as Culture in Islamic Society* (Cambridge: Cambridge University Press, 1989).
Schacht, Joseph, *An Introduction to Islamic Law* (reprint, 1993; Oxford: Clarendon Press, 1964).
Shapiro, Scott, *Legality* (Cambridge: Belknap Press, 2011).
Sunstein, Cass and Vermeule, Adrian, "Interpretation and Institutions." *Michigan Law Review* 101, 4 (2003): 885–951.
Wadud, Amina, "American Muslim Identity: Race and Ethnicity in Progressive Islam" in Omid Safi (ed.) *Progressive Muslims: On Justice, Gender, and Pluralism* (Oxford: Oneworld Publications, 2003) 270–285.
Watt, W. Montgomery, "The Closing of the Door of *Iğtihād*" in J.M. Barral (ed.) *Orientalia Hispanica 1* (Leiden: Brill, 1974) 675–678.
Zaman, Muhammad Qasim, "Evolving Conceptions of *Ijtihad* in Modern South Asia." *Islamic Studies* 49, 1 (2010): 5–36.

CHAPTER 8

IMAMI SHIʿI LEGAL THEORY

FROM ITS ORIGINS TO THE EARLY TWENTIETH CENTURY

ROBERT GLEAVE

I. Introduction

The Twelver Shiʿa (sometimes called al-Imamiyya, the Imamis)[1] are the most productive of the Shiʿi intellectual traditions in terms of legal works generally, and works of legal theory (*usul al-fiqh*) in particular. Imami works of *fiqh* and *usul*, the numerous collections of *fatwas* and the many commentaries on the fundamental works in the tradition form an extensive body of literature, easily comparable to the other Muslim traditions of legal theory. To an extent, they form an internally continuous and self-referential system of legal thought. Though Imami writers

[1] I will use the term Imami here to designate Twelver Shiʿism more generally, though I recognize the term is occasionally used to include Ismaʿili thought in the medieval period. Here I mean by Imami that element of the Shiʿa more generally who hold that the leadership of the Muslims was passed down through the Twelve Imams, the last of whom has gone into hiding (*ghayba*).

are aware of (and react to) other intellectual trends (in particular Sunni *usul* and theology, but also philosophical findings), the majority of their explicit references are to other works of Imami legal theory. It is important to note at the outset that the Imami tradition of legal theory (*usul al-fiqh*) continues to be highly influential in the Shiʿi seminary cities (known as the *hawza ʿilmiyya*—the precinct of knowledge) in Iran and Iraq. In Najaf and Karbala, and in Qum and Mashhad, the most important and influential scholars are those who write detailed and advanced works of *usul al-fiqh*. Legal innovations often come first through the development of new and challenging methods of deduction as found in works of *usul*. The most advanced scholars, with the greatest student following, and the best institutional structure become known as sources of emulation (*marjiʿ al-taqlid*) and hold great power in the contemporary Twelver Shiʿi community. *Usul al-fiqh*, then, is one important element of scholarly authority in the modern world, and this has been obvious most vividly in the contemporary era in the Iranian revolution of 1979, the clerical leadership of Imami movements in Lebanon, Bahrain and other Gulf states, and, since 2003, in the leadership of the Imami Shiʿi community in Iraq.

Undoubtedly, the Imami juristic tradition has individual features and distinctive doctrines when compared to other traditions of *usul* scholarship. These include the broadly Muʿtazili theological assumptions concerning the ability of reason to produce knowledge the law (the ramifications of which are worked out in detail in Imami *usul al-fiqh*), and the notion of the Lawgiver (*al-shariʿ*) as including the Imam as an individual present in the world (following the Imami doctrine of the Twelfth Imam, having gone into hiding, but remaining present but not directly available). These two fundamental theological assumptions give rise to numerous distinctive doctrines. On the first, if reason (*ʿaql*) can determine the moral properties of acts independent of revelation, does this mean that apparently harmless acts which are not explicitly mentioned in the texts of revelation are simply licit? That they are licit (a doctrine known as *al-baraʾa al-asliyya*—"fundamental licitness") became a much discussed doctrine in Imami *usul* works (see later in the chapter). The second distinctive theological doctrine (namely the notion that an individual with perfect knowledge of the law—the Imam—is present but unknown) gave rise to distinctive Imami doctrines, such as the justification of *ijmaʿ* (consensus). For Sunnis, *ijmaʿ* is a source of law, generally, justified through revelatory sources (such as the famous Prophetic report, "My community shall never agree upon an error"). Put simply, for the Imamis, *ijmaʿ* is a source because when all agree, the Imam must have been present amongst those forming the consensus. *Ijmaʿ* has no probative force (*hujjiya*)in itself; it is only a useful mechanism for uncovering the opinion of the Imam.

These distinctive features, and a distinctive technical vocabulary which came with it, has mitigated against the incorporation of Imami legal theory into the general study of Islamic legal theory. The tradition remains understudied in the secondary literature: at times it is viewed as a marginal variant of the dominant

Sunni legal tradition;[2] at other times, it is a system with such complicated internal dynamics that it is impenetrable to the outsider.[3] A few scholars, such as Zysow and Reinhart, have managed to integrate the perspectives of Imami writers into their studies of *usul al-fiqh*.[4] Most though have presented their findings as covering "Islamic legal theory" or "Islamic jurisprudence" whilst feeling able to restrict their sources to broadly Sunni accounts. Whilst a monograph on exclusively Sunni legal theory can, it seems, claim to be an account of "Islamic" jurisprudence, every monograph on Imami jurisprudence needs to be explicitly labeled as focussed on that tradition of thought. Having said this, there is a growing body of scholarship in the field. In addition to the more detailed shorter studies referred to below, there are a few academic monographs on aspects of Imami legal theory. The first is probably Harald Loschner's 1991 monograph, *Die dogmatischen Grundlage des Si'itischen Rechts: Eine Untersuchung zur modernen imamitischen Rechtsquellenlehre*[5] which focuses on the contemporary discussions and does not shy away from tackling the more abstruse matters of contemporary *usul* (particularly the *usul'amaliyya*, on which see later in the chapter). The account is a synthetic, and generally ahistorical one, which provides much useful information about the content of contemporary Imami discussions, but little about how it came to be as it is. More historical in its emphasis is Devin Stewart's *Islamic Legal Orthodoxy: Twelver Shiite responses to the Sunni Legal System*. Published in 1998, Stewart gives a detailed account of the development of Islamic jurisprudence and the Imami place within it, and whilst not solely focussed on *usul al-fiqh* (it contains much important information on the transmission of legal texts and teaching practices), it does define the framework within which much subsequent historical scholarship has developed. My own *Inevitable Doubt: Two Shīʿī Theories of Islamic Jurisprudence* is but a comparison of two major late classical Imami thinkers and their legal systems. A study of the legal theory of contemporary Iranian Imami thinkers is Ashk Bahlen's *Islamic Law, Epistemology and Modernity: Legal Philosophy in Contemporary Iran*. The work gives a useful introduction to Imami legal theory, and then explores the reformist ideas of ʿAbd al-Karim Surush. More recently, Ali-Beza Bhojani published his *Moral Rationalism and the Shari'a: Independent rationality in modern Shi'i uṣūl al-fiqh*. This is clear, detailed account of contemporary Imami *usul* thinking, its theological positions

[2] J. Schacht, *Origins of Muhammadan Jurisprudence* (Oxford: Clarendon Press, 1950), 262–8.

[3] Wael Hallaq in his *A History of Islamic Legal Theories* (Cambridge: Cambridge University Press, 1997) viii, writes: "The Shi'ite and other legal theories are appreciably different both in their historical development and, consequently, structure. No doubt they stand on their own, and, like their Sunni counterpart, they demand an independent treatment. Thus no apology is in order for excluding non-Sunni legal theories."

[4] A. Zysow, *The Economy of Certainty: An Introduction to the Typology of Islamic Legal Theory* (Michigan: Lockwood, 2013), formerly his Harvard Ph.D. thesis, completed in 1984; A.K. Reinhart, *Before Revelation: The Boundaries of Muslim Moral Thought* (Albany: SUNY, 1995).

[5] Harald Loschner, *Die dogmatischen Grundlage des Si'itischen Rechts: Eine Untersuchung zur modernen imamitischen Rechtsquellenlehre* [The Religious Basis of Shīʿī Law: An investigation into Imāmī Legal Theory] (Cologne: Heymann, 1971).

(regarding God's justice) and their legal theoretical implications. One outcome of Bhojani's book is to question why the theoretical commitment to independent reason as a legal source has not changed continued practical emphasis on revelatory textual sources in Imami jurisprudence. These, to date, constitute the major book-length treatments of Imami *usul al-fiqh*. They can be supplemented by recent translations of major Imami texts of *usul al-fiqh*. Roy Mottahedeh and Arif Abdol Hussain have each produced translations of Muhammad Baqir al-Sadr's *Durus fī ʿilm al-uṣūl*.[6] As outlined below, al-Sadr is a highly originally thinker in the Imami *usul* tradition. In some ways his work of *usul* is unusual (and innovative), and hence doesn't always act as a useful introduction to the genre. More mainstream, one might say, is the work of al-'Allama al-Hilli, *Mabādiʾ al-wuṣūl ilāʿilm al-uṣūl*, which has recently been translated by Amjad Shah Naqvi.[7] This is not to say that there have not been many important articles and chapters on Imami *usul al-fiqh* in recent scholarship (see in the references at the end of this chapter); however, these represent the principal book-length publications devoted to the field. The aim of this chapter is to outline, in broad terms, the historical development of Imami *usul al-fiqh*, and provide for the reader the major themes within Shi'i *usul* which make it a distinctive system of jurisprudence within the broader history of *usul al-fiqh*, and an introduction to the principal research findings on Imami *usul* found in current Western academic literature.

II. Periodization of Shi'i *Usul*

The presentation of an intellectual tradition's history is often about the future rather than the past. In the Shi'i legal tradition, the various periodizations found within the juristic literature represent different projections of how the tradition should develop next. An example of this is the twentieth-century jurist Muhammad Baqir al-Sadr's (d. 1980) well-known introductory section to his *al-Maʿālim al-Jadīda lil-Uṣūl*. In a section title "The history of the Science of *Usul*" (*tārīkh ʿilm al-uṣūl*) he divides the history of Shi'i *usul* into three periods:

1. The early period (including, it seems, the time of the Imams' presence) until the time of al-Shaykh al-Tusi (d. 460/1067)

[6] *Lessons in Islamic Jurisprudence*, trans. Roy Mottahedeh (Oxford: One World, 2010); *Principles of Islamic Jurisprudence According to Shi'i Lawī*, trans: Arif Abdol Hussein (London: ICAS, 2005).

[7] *Foundations of Jurisprudence—An Introduction to Imāmī Shīʿī Legal Theory*, trans. Amjad Shah Naqvi (Leiden: Brill, 2016).

2. From the time of al-Shaykh al-Tusi to the Usuli movement associated with Muhammad Baqir al-Bihbihani (d. 1205/1791)
3. From al-Bihbihani to the present.[8]

Such a schema inevitably gives al-Tusi and al-Bihbihani pivotal roles in the development of the science. Whilst Muhammad Baqir al-Sadr recognizes sub-sections within each of the time periods, he establishes his own work within the period of the Usuli school's dominance initiated by al-Bihbihani. His periodization can be contrasted with periodization found in the classic work of the anti-Usuli movement (known as Akhbaris), *al-Fawāʾid al-Madaniyya* of Muhammad Amin al-Astarabadi (d. 1036/1626–7). He views the history of Shiʿi legal theory up to this point as essentially split between the periods before and after al-ʿAllama al-Hilli (d. 726/1325). For al-Astarabadi, al-ʿAllama was responsible for the introduction of Sunni methodology into Imami Shiʿi legal thinking, and since then Imami jurists have slavishly followed his lead.[9] The period before al-ʿAllama is portrayed as a time when Shiʿi jurists, notwithstanding their differences, were continuing to work within the way laid down by the Imams themselves. It is al-Astarabadi's aim to revive this earlier method, and thoroughly discredit the "innovations" of al-ʿAllama. By doing so, he hopes to prevent the corruption of the Imami Shiʿi community, and re-establish the way of the Imams. Here, clearly, the ante- and post-Allama framework facilitates al-Astarabadi's broader argument concerning the tradition's deviation.

In the rather limited secondary literature, there are different periodizations of Imami Shiʿi legal theory. Perhaps the most influential can be found in an important article "Rationalism and Traditionalism in Shiʿi Jurisprudence,"[10] by Hossein Modarressi. He itemizes the various works of legal theory giving the impression of a gradual historical development, punctuated by significant works. He begins with formal works of jurisprudence, rather than with theoretical legal thinking, with the most influential works creating commentary traditions in their wake. These can be identified from his account as:

Al-Shaykh al-Tusi (*ʿUddat al-Uṣūl*)
Al-Allama al-Hilli (various works)
Hasan b. Zayn al-Din al-Shahid al-Thani al-ʿAmili (d. 1011/1653-4, *Maʿālim al-Dīn*)
The period of Akhbari dominance
Muhammad Baqir al-Bihbihani (no specific works, but pupils wrote *usul*-extensively)
Al-Shaykh Murtada al-Ansari (d. 1281/1791, *Farāʾid al-uṣūl*) to the present day.[11]

[8] Muḥammad Bāqir al-Ṣadr, *al-Maʿālim al-jadīda lil-uṣūl* (Najaf: n.p., 1975), 46.

[9] Muḥammad Amīn al-Astarābādī, *al-Fawāid al-Madaniyya* (Qum: Muʾassasat al-Nashr al-Islāmī, 2003), 37.

[10] Hossein Modarressi, "Rationalism and Traditionalism in Shiʿi Jurisprudence: A Preliminary Survey," *Studia Islamica* 59(1984), 141–158. The article jumps back and forth across time periods, and hence an overall scheme is difficult to identify, but these appear to be the principal period markers for Modarressi.

[11] Hossein Moddarressi, *Introduction to Shīʿī law* (London: Ithaca, 1984), 23–58.

This schema too serves to illustrate a particular conclusion: namely that the principles of Shi'ite jurisprudence (as given by Modarressi in the introductory section) can be characterized as being generally stable across history, and that the challenges to those rationalist principles (posed in particular by the Akhbaris) did not make a significant dent on the overall trajectory of the rationalist school. That is, the current dominance of the framework of al-Shaykh al-Ansari is a natural outgrowth of the previous centuries of Shi'i legal deliberation.

I cite these examples, from both inside the Shi'i tradition and in the secondary literature, to demonstrate that describing the history of this legal tradition requires an identification of significant works, schools of thought, and time periods, which are hardly neutral and undisputed. Instead, each periodization serves to bolster particular depictions of contemporary trends (as traditionalist, innovative or even deviant), and enable particular arguments to be made about the future direction of the discipline. I am, of course, fully aware that the historical account I am about to present is not immune from these characteristics (and potential criticisms).

III. Legal self-reflection at the time of the Imams

That there were debates amongst early Imami thinkers around issues which later became major discussion in works of *usul al-fiqh* seems quite clear. There are reports outlining how the Imams used principles of exegesis and legal reasoning in the various collections of *akkhbar* (reports) in early Shi'ism. These books of reports, and the authenticity of the material within them, is an area for extensive future research. In lieu of that, one finds *usul*-related material in al-Kulayni's (d. 329/941) *al-Kāfī*, Ibn Babawayh's (d. 381/991) *Man Lā Yaḥduruhu al-Faqīh*, and in al-Shaykh al-Tusi's two famous book *al-Istibṣār* and *al-Tahdhīb*. These four books were particularly prized by later writers as the so-called "four books," which supposedly functioned like the Sunni *hadith* collections as the database for future legal deduction. The origin and provenance of these reports remains to be tested, but that they represent views within the Imami community before the time of al-Kulayni can be safely assumed.

Even if the reports documenting, for example, the discussions of the Imams around issues such as *qiyas* and *ijtihad* cannot be dated to the time of Imams Muhammad al-Baqir (d.c. 114/745) or Ja'far al-Sadiq (d. 148/765), they were undoubtedly being circulated before the minor occultation of the Twelfth Imam in 260/874.[12] The reports are reasonably clear in the condemnation of *qiyas/ijtihad*, and therefore

[12] We find them circulated in reports found in al-Kulayni's collection, taken from collections which predate him by at least a generation and probably more.

can be initially dated to sometime after these terms (and the hermeneutic practices they designate) became established elements of Muslim legal theory. This period is normally associated with the period contemporary with, or possibly following Muhammad b. Idris al-Shafiʿi (d. 204/820). Similarly the exchanges between Jaʿfar al-Sadiq and Abu Hanifa (d. 150/767) in which the Imam condemns Abu Hanifa for employing *qiyas* reflect, at least in their final wording, the point when the school of Abu Hanifa and his students had adopted the terminology and mechanisms of *qiyas*, which may have dated to sometime after the eponym himself.[13] These famous exchanges include the dialogue:

Abu Hanifa dropped in on Abu ʿAbdallah (al-Sadiq); he said to him, "O Abu Hanifa, I hear you practise *qiyas*." He replied positively. He said, "Do not practise *qiyas*. The first to practice *qiyas* was Satan ..."[14]

Other hints at the beginning of legal theoretical discussion can be found in the statements attributed to the Imams. If we take such statements as (perhaps) not reflecting the Imams' own words but the intellectual discussions of Imami scholars at the time of circulation, then we find numerous hermeneutic procedures (later incorporated into the discipline of *usul al-fiqh*) mentioned and either approved, or rejected by the Imam.[15] So, for example:

> It is reported from Zurara and Muḥammad b. Muslim that they said, 'We said to Abu Jaʿfar [Muhammad al-Baqir], "What do you say about the prayer when you are travelling? How is it and how many is it?"[16]
>
> He said, 'God says, *If you go on a journey, there is no blame on you (laysa ʿalaykum junah) for shortening your prayer* (Q. 4.101). So it is obligatory when travelling, just as a complete [prayer] is obligatory when stationary.'
>
> (They continue) So we said, 'God only says *there is no blame on you*. He did not say, "Do it!" So how can this become obligatory, just as a complete [prayer] is obligatory when stationary?
>
> He said, 'Has not God said concerning Safa and Marwa, *He who is making pilgrimage to the House or ʿumra, then there is no blame on him (la junah ʿalayhi) if he goes around them both* (Q. 2.158). Do you not see that going around them both is obligatory-commanded (*wajibmafrud*), because God mentions it in his Book, and his Prophet did it? And in the same way, shortening [prayer] is something that the Prophet did, and God mentions in his book.'[17]

[13] See Schacht, where he considers Abu Hanifa's use of anaological reasoning, without terming it *qiyas*: Schacht, *Origins*, 111–112; R. Gleave, "Imāmī Shīʿī Refutations of *qiyās*," in *Studies in Islamic Legal Theory*, ed. Bernard Weiss, 267–292 (Leiden: Brill, 2002).

[14] Al-Kulayni, *al-Kāfīī* (Qum: D al-Ḥadīth, 2008), v.1, 58.

[15] For more examples, see R. Gleave, "Early Shīʿī Hermeneutics. Some Exegetical Techniques Attributed to the Shiʿi Imams," in *Aims, Methods and Contexts of Qur'anic Exegesis (2nd/8th–9th/15th c.)*, ed. Karen Bauer, 141–72 (Oxford: Oxford University Press, 2013).

[16] "How is it?," that is: "Is it a *rukhṣa* [dispensation] or an *ʿaẓīma* [the law's full requirement]?," and "How many is it?"—i.e. "how many *rakʿāt* [prayer sequences] are there in it?"

[17] Ibn Babawayh, *Man lā yaḥḍuruhu al-faqīh* (Qum: Jamāʿat al-Mudarrisīn, 1984) v.1, 434–5, no. 1265 (extract).

Here the issue is whether an obligation can be established through a linguistic form ("there is no blame on you") in the textual source. It seems for Imam al-Baqir it can, as it does for the later Hanafis and Malikis. This was contrary to the position later proposed by Shafi'is, who appears to view that the phrase indicated a lessening from God (*takhfif*) rather than an obligation to shorten one's prayer. The comparison between this case with Q. 2.158 (on the obligation to perform Safa and Marwa) is regularly found in later *fiqh* and *usul* works as a stock example, and refuted by al-Shafi'i and, interestingly Ibn Hazm (d. 456/1064).[18]

One might expect there to be no need for such hermeneutic procedures and the emergence of juristic theoretical reflection, given the presence of an infallible guide in the form of the Imam himself.[19] But it is clear from this (and other evidence) that the doctrine of the Imam being the repository of perfect knowledge of religion (and the Shari'a in particular) took some time to become unchallenged Imami orthodoxy.[20] Imami discussion of legal hermeneutic principles in these early periods indicate that their discussions were related to discussions in early legal literature more generally. This is an area which should be developed as a major line of future research, though little can be said with any certainty at this point.

A. Early emergence of Shi'i *usul*

Systematic reflection on juristic issues in the Shi'i tradition is normally attributed to two controversial figures, known as "the Two Ancients (*qadimayn*): Ibn Abi 'Aqil al-'Umani (d. early tenth century) and Ibn Junayd al-Iskafi (d. 381/991). Both appear to have ignored the Imams' condemnations of *qiyas* and *ijtihad* (if indeed they knew of them), and composed works of legal theory promoting both techniques, which might give us rise to consider how well circulated these traditions might have been. Ibn Abi 'Aqil appears to have been more "rationalist" as he reportedly rejected reports (*akkhbar*) as legal sources (presumably on epistemological grounds). Ibn Junayd's views, in so far as they can be known, are often portrayed as reducing the Imam's role as similar to that of the *mujtahid* in emergent Sunni theory, who engages in legal deduction based on his own *ijtihad*. This, it might be argued, reduces the Imam's role to nothing more than the position of a school eponym (comparable to Malik b. Anas, d. 179/795, or al-Shafi'i), something which subsequent Shi'i scholars

[18] Al-Shafi'i, *Kitāb al-Umm* (Beirut: Dār al-Marifa, 1973), v.1, 207; Ibn Hazm, *al-Iḥkām fī uṣūl al-aḥkām* (Dār al-Kutub al-'Ilmiyya, n.d.), v.3, 288. The Imami discussion and comparison can be found in Al-Tusi, *al-Khilāf* (Qum: Jamā'at al-Mudarrisīn, 1990), v.1, 569.

[19] Hossein Modarresssi, *Crisis and Consolidation in the Formative Period of Shi'ite Islam* (Princeton: Darwin, 1993).

[20] See the collected works of Etan Kohlberg, *Law and Belief in Imāmī Shi'ism* (Aldershot: Variorum, 1991) and T. Bayhom Daou, *al-Shaykh al-Mufid* (Oxford: Oneworld, 2005).

found theologically problematic. The works of both scholars though are lost, though their opinions appear cited in subsequent works. Their association with *qiyas* and *ijtihad* has either been explained away (e.g. with the argument that what they meant by *qiyas* was not what we understand from mature Sunni theory), or their views were not taken into account in the acceptable views (*khilaf*) of the Shiʿa. What we might be able to reconstruct of their legal theories requires forensic research, and represents another important future area of investigation.

Ibn Junayd's pupil, al-Shaykh al-Mufid (d. 413/1022)is reportedly the first to write a substantive work of legal theory in the Imami Shiʿi tradition. Only a summary of that work has survived, collected in a pupil's (namely al-Karajiki (d. 449/1057–8)) miscellanea work *Kanz al-Fawāʾid*. The title of al-Mufid's work is sometimes recorded as *al-Tadhkira fī uṣūl al-fiqh* (as it is named in the *Kanz*), but this may itself be an abbreviated title. The work itself is extremely brief, almost to the point of being opaque to someone not schooled in the debates of *usul*. It is epistemological, uncompromising—demanding certain knowledge (*ʿilm*) of the law as a requirement of legal derivation. For this reason he rejects central doctrines of Sunni *usul al-fiqh* at his time such as the probative force of the isolated tradition (*hujjiya khabar al-wahid*, discussed later in this section) and the legitimacy of *qiyas* and *ijtihad*. At other points, he adopts certain Sunni positions (such as the issue of *al-hizr wa'l-ibaha* to be discussed below).

Whilst the *Tadhkira* is rather limited in its scope, the works of al-Mufid's two star pupils, al-Shaykh al-Tusi and al-Sayyid al-Murtada (d. 436/1044), can be said to establish the genre within the Imami legal tradition. The order of composition of their works is not obvious. Al-Shaykh al-Tusi is the younger of the two scholars, though his work makes reference to al-Sayyid al-Murtada (who was at one point al-Tusi's teacher), but neglects to mention his work in *usul*. Indeed al-Tusi claims to be the first Imami to engage properly with the discipline of *usul*, indicating that either he didn't think al-Murtada's work was serious, or he did not know of it, or he composed his work first. Whilst the two works are different in approach, there are similarities: the sections on *qiyas* in the two works for example are very similarly worded, and reach similar conclusions (i.e. that *qiyas* has no place in Imami jurisprudence).

The *ʿUddat al-Uṣūl* of al-Shaykh al-Tusi and *al-Dharīʿa ilā uṣūl al-sharīʿa* of al-Sayyid al-Murtada are works which appear to speak to one another, and to have been written contemporaneously, as each author refers to the other's doctrines, as found in their works of *usul*. Al-Murtada's *al-Dharīʿa* is more obviously rationalist (under Muʿtazili influence). For example, the treatment of "prohibition and permission" (*al-hizr wa'l-ibaha*) in the two works indicate al-Murtada's association with (Basran) Muʿtazili doctrine, and al-Tusi's adoption of less "rationalist" positions. This issue in *usul al-fiqh* is intimately linked to the power of reason (*ʿaql*) to discern the moral and legal properties of things in the absence of any order from God and the Prophet (and, in the case of Shiʿism, the Imams also). If there has been no revealed regulation concerning the category into which an action should be placed, then what is the default category of that action? Writers of *usul al-fiqh* had discussed this issue in some detail. In the two works under consideration here, there is a difference of opinion. In his *al-Dharīʿa*, al-Murtada writes:

[Regarding things which have no revelatory assessment;] there are those who argue that they are forbidden; and there are those who argue they are permitted; and there are those who suspend [making an assessment] between the two ... The correct position is that of the one who declares that the aforementioned type of actions are permitted.[21]

Al-Tusi, on the other hand, writes:

Most people say that [the assessment for such things] is suspending [the decision] since either one of the two orders (permission and prohibition] is possible, and one awaits the arrival of a revelatory declaration (al-samʿ) indicating to one of the two [categories]. This was the view that our Shaykh Abu ʿAbdallah [al-Mufid] championed, and it is the strongest position in my view.[22]

For al-Murtada, through reason alone, one can determine that acts unregulated by revelation are permitted. For al-Tusi, one cannot reach such a conclusion, and one must suspend judgment concerning the assessment of such actions. At stake in this dispute is the extent to which reason (an imperfect but necessary translation of Arabic term *ʿaql*) can provide knowledge of legal assessments; al-Murtada, more precisely in line with Muʿtazili thinking, is more optimistic about reason's potential in this area.

It was al-Tusi's views on jurisprudence generally, and *usul* in particular, which proved the more authoritative for subsequent scholars. There is a tendency within the tradition (and in the secondary literature also) to portray the generations of scholars after al-Tusi as simply following his lead in most matters.[23] Certainly, his influence was considerable, and the lines of argument in his *ʿUddat al-uṣūl* appear to have been broadly accepted. Aside from Ibn Zuhra's (d. 585/1189–90) theoretical introductory comments to his *Ghunyat al-nuzūʿ* (see below), no major works of Imami *usul* have survived, indicating perhaps that al-Tusi's work was seen as a sufficient statement of the discipline, at least for the moment.

This is not to say there were no legal theoretical debates. Ibn Zuhra al-Halabi adopted *usul* positions contrary to those put forward by al-Tusi on a number of points; he appears in closer agreement with al-Murtada on most issues. On the issue mentioned above, he adopts the "permission" position, and criticizes those who suspend judgment.[24] Indeed on many areas of legal theory he held views at odds with

[21] Al-Sharif al-Murtada, *al-Dharīʿa ilā uṣū-al-sharīʿa* (Tehran: University of Tehran, 1985) v.2, 808–809.

[22] Al-Shaykh al-Tusi, *ʿUddat al-uṣūl* (Qum: Muʾassasat ahl al-bayt, 1983), v.2, 742.

[23] See Robert Gleave, "Shiʿi Jurisprudence During the Seljuq Period: Rebellion and Public Order in an Illegitimate State," in *The Seljuqs: Politics, Society and Culture*, eds. Christian Lange and Songul Mecit (Edinburgh University Press, 2011), 205–27.

[24] Ibn Zuhra al-Halabi, *Ghunyat al-nuzūʿ fī ʿilmay al-uṣūl wal-furūʿ* (Qum: Muʾassasat al-Imām al-Ṣādiq, 1996) v.2, 416.

al-Shaykh al-Tusi. These included the probative force of the isolated report (*hujjiya khabar al-wahid*) being less than certain, the lack of a specific legal, literal meaning of the imperative and general forms (*sighat al-amr* and *sighat al-ʿumum*) and that the negative imperative form does not imply that the thing forbidden is necessarily morally corrupt (*fasad*). Similarly, Ibn Idris al-Hilli (d.c. 598/1201), though not the author of a dedicated work of *usul al-fiqh*, objected to many of al-Tusi's methodological principles, in particular al-Tusi's adoption of isolated reports as legal proofs. For Ibn Idris, isolated reports fall short of knowledge, and therefore cannot act as legal proofs (in line with the view of al-Murtada and, in some respects, overlapping with Ibn Zuhra's position).

Whilst undoubtedly there were objections to the position put forward by al-Tusi, there emerged no work of *usul* to challenge the primacy of his *al-ʿUdda* until the *Maʿārij al-uṣūl* of al-Muhaqqiq al-Hilli (d. 676/1278), and more systematically, his nephew and student al-ʿAllama al-Hilli. In their works, we have a more structured approach to *usul*; these works appear to follow the styles of argumentation of the (by-now established) Sunni discipline of *usul* more closely than that found in earlier works, such as *al-Dharīʿa* and *al-ʿUdda*. In Muhaqqiq's *Maʿārij*, for example, one has a clear and well-organized section on the issue of *al-hizr wa'l-ibaha*, described above. He identifies the areas of dispute; he examines the arguments for each position; and then he offers his own argument. His view, and that adopted by subsequent Imami writers of *usul* is that there is a general permission to use things in the world if there is no harm caused to anyone else. The examples they use are breathing and sitting in the shade of a wall. In neither case is the owner harmed by one's actions. This general permission in the absence of harm can then be generalized as a presumption of permission in the absence of harm (*darar*) or evil (*mafsada*). This is backed up with citation from the Qur'an (such as "All that is in the world is created for you" Q. 2.29), and by the consensus of the community (where the scholars agree that one can, for example, eat a substance without a specific text permitting one to do so).[25] The presentation is straightforward, and much more orderly (and refined) than the previous discussion.

On epistemological matters, tentatively in al-Muhaqqiq's *Maʿārij*, and then more assertively in the *usul* works of al-ʿAllama (*al-Tahdhīb, Mabadiʾ al-wuṣūl* and the more expansive *Nihāyat al-wuṣūl*), there is an adoption of the principle that legal assessments need not be based on certain evidence (*yaqini*); uncertain but persuasive evidence (*zanni*) can also give rise to legal obligations. As with Sunni theories, the legal opinion should be produced by a properly qualified scholar (a *mujtahid*) who expends his effort to acquire an opinion (*ijtihad*). It was married with the traditional Imami emphasis on certain knowledge (*ʿilm*) in legal matters by positing that during the absence of the twelfth Imam, and whilst awaiting his return, the jurists were confined to work with the available sources of legal knowledge. This included

[25] Al-Muhaqqiq al-Hilli, *Maʿārij al-uṣūl* (Qum: Muʾassasat Ahl al-Bayt, 1983), 202–206.

sources which could not, on rational terms, be considered certainly authentic; the adoption of *zann* was a sort of regrettable force majeure brought about by the prolongation of the Imam's absence.

The debate around the probative force of isolated report (*hujjiya khabar al-wahid*) illustrates well the new epistemological framework espoused particularly eloquently by al-ʿAllama al-Hilli. These are reports which have one (or at least very few) transmission chains; this paucity of transmission chains led to scholars reducing their reliability; they therefore had a reduced potential to act as a legal proof (that is, they had a lower level of *hujjiyya*). Some Imami Shiʿi legal theorists (including al-Shaykh al-Mufid and al-Sayyid al-Murtada) had argued that such traditions did not bring knowledge of the law, and hence could not act as a proof. Al-Shaykh al-Tusi had controversially argued that at least some reports do bring knowledge and do have probative force, even if, in themselves, a *khabar al-wahid* does not bring knowledge. He placed upon them various conditions: "a *khabar al-wahid* [should be] transmitted by way of our colleagues who support the [Imami] notion of Imamate, and it [should be] related from the Prophet or one of the Imams by someone who is not maligned for his reporting, and is secure in his transmission."[26] Such reports may not bring knowledge (that is a moot point in al-Tusi) but they are permitted to act as the basis of correct action. In a sense they bring knowledge of correct action, even if they do not, as a category and in themselves, produce knowledge. This created a compromise: whilst *khabar al-wahid* do not bring *ʿilm*, they do provide a valid basis for action (or perhaps, to put it more accurately, a basis for valid action), this did not damage the overall Imami commitment to certain knowledge and the rejection of juristic opinion (*raʾy*, or more technically *zann*). Despite the widespread adoption of al-Tusi's ideas, he was subjected to a sustained attack for this position from some subsequent jurists. Most notably, Ibn Idris al-Hilli famously rejected al-Tusi's use of *khabar al-wahid* in his *fiqh* work *al-Sarāʾir*.[27] Al-Tusi's position was broadly maintained by al-Muhaqqiq al-Hilli, though he may have differed over the conditions which qualified an isolated report as a basis for action.

Al-ʿAllama's opening statement in his *Mabādiʾ al-uṣūl* though is quite bold in comparison to the careful:

A *khabar al-wahid* is [a report] which provides [us] with *zann*, however many transmitters there may be. It is a proof in the Law, in opposition to al-Murtada and others.[28]

Here one can see that the literal meaning of "*khabar al-wahid*" (the isolated report) has been replaced with an epistemological definition. It does not matter how many transmitters a report has, if it does not produce knowledge it is to be classed as

[26] Al-Tusi, *ʿUddat*, v.1, 67.

[27] For Ibn Idris's comments on al-Tusi's *usul* see the introduction to his *al-Sarāʾir al-Ḥāwī li-taḥrīr al-fatāwī* (Qum: Muʾassasat al-Nashr al-ʿIslāmī, 1989), v.1, 41–55.

[28] Al-ʿAllama al-Hilli, *Mabādiʾ al-wuṣūl ilā ʿilm al-uṣūl* (Najaf: Maṭbaʿat al-Ādāb, 1970), 203.

an "isolated report." In another of his *usul* works, the *Tahdhīb al-wuṣūl ilā ʿilm al-uṣūl*, he writes that the prohibition on following *zann* found in the Qur'an and other revelatory sources "is not general covering *fatwas* and testimony in court, or [when someone informs you of] the direction of prayer and [his] state of ritual purity."[29] In all these cases, al-ʿAllama argues, the person's individual report is accepted as having established a legal duty. "In the juristic principles (*usul*) one might aim at *ʿilm*, but in the legal details (*furuʿ*) one can act on *zann*" [230].The dispute over isolated reports were perhaps the prime battleground for establishing epistemological structures, and here we see al-ʿAllama securing *zann* as having probative force within the process of legal reasoning. It was an innovation, adopted from his reading of Sunni jurisprudence no doubt, which was to remain a central element in Shiʿi legal theory up to the contemporary period.

Al-ʿAllama's development has been remarked upon by a number of scholars in the secondary literature,[30] and was one of the major criticisms of the later Akhbari scholars. If legal indicators which are less than certain can play a role in legal argumentation, then the early Shiʿi rejection of *ijtihad*, mentioned above, on the basis of it providing only *zann*, can be overturned. In all his major *usul* works (*Mabadiʾ al-wuṣūl*, *Tahdhīb al-wuṣūl* and *Nihāyat al-wuṣūl*), al-ʿAllama includes a chapter on *ijtihad*, not to refute or limit it (as in previous works), but to place it in the centre of Imami legal theoretical discussions. Once established, it became a permanent fixture in Imami Shiʿi legal thinking, and served as a crucial ideological element in the enhancement to scholarly authority. The central place given to *ijtihad* though was just one by-product though of al-ʿAllama's epistemological innovation: that is the establishment of a developing hierarchy of knowledge, from certain to presumptive, to doubtful. Whilst not fully exploited in his works, the framework for subsequent legal theory, in which *zann* was a category of knowledge below *ʿilm* and above *shakk* (or "doubt," laid out in the nineteenth century, on which see Section V), his *usul* thinking does represent a turning point in how to conceptualize in theoretical terms the Imami Shiʿi legal project.

In terms of contribution to the development of Shiʿi *usul*, it is worth comparing, for a moment, the achievements of al-Tusi and al-ʿAllama. Shiʿi tradition views al-Tusi's achievements as so mammoth that subsequent scholars (apart from a few renegades) were compelled to merely follow his model. In *usul* (and in jurisprudence generally), I have indicated that this may not be an entirely accurate account. Advances in jurisprudence were made, albeit incrementally,[31] by the generations immediately following al-Tusi; and in legal theory specifically, his positions were not simply adopted wholesale. The differences with Ibn Zuhra's theory (as found in the *Ghunya*) and the almost scandalous attack of Ibn Idris are evidence of this. With regard to al-ʿAllama, his advancements in legal theory (focussed on the construction

[29] al ʿAllama al-Hilli, *Tahdhīb al-wuṣūl ilā ʿilm al-uṣūl* (Qum: Muʾassasat al-Imām ʿAlī, 2001), 230.

[30] N. Calder, "Doubt and Prerogative: The Emergence of an Imāmī Shīʿī Theory of Ijtihād" *Studia Islamica*, 70 (1989), 57–78; Modarressi, "Rationalism and Traditionalism."

[31] Gleave, "Shiʿi Jurisprudence During the Seljuq Period."

of *zann* as an acceptable, legally probative epistemological category), is not generally viewed within the tradition as having the same revolutionary character. Rather, his work is a formalization of a slippage away from total reliance on certain knowledge which had already been accepted by Imami Shi'i legal theorists in the previous generations. As I have indicated here, it is possible to see his achievements as more than this, and whilst he was not simply aping Sunni *usul al-fiqh* (as later Akhbaris would claim), he certainly had a respect and was influenced by the major elements of Sunni legal theory which, by his time, were firmly established in what has been called the "classical" tradition.

Whilst theoretical thinking within the Imami Shi'i jurists clearly did not cease, there was a not, apparently, the need for an independent monograph of *usul al-fiqh* for nearly two hundred years. There were commentaries on al-'Allama's works, notably by his two nephews. Their commentary on the *Tahdhīb al-Wuṣūl* (mentioned above) remain unpublished.[32] Also unpublished is the *Ghāyat al-Bādī fī sharḥ al-Mabādiʾ* (a commentary on al-'Allama's *Mabādiʾ al-wuṣūl*) by Muhammad b. 'Ali al-Jurjani (d. 729/1328–29), a Shi'i scholar, resident in Hilla, studying with 'Allama. However, it was only with the *Maʿālim al-Uṣūl* of Hasan b. Zayn al-Din al-'Amili that a work is composed which could rival, and soon supplant, al-'Allama's works. This work, though, was never conceived of as a separate work of *usul*. Instead it was an introduction to his work of *fiqh*. Like the *usul* section of Ibn Zuhra's *Ghunya* (which formed a postscript to his *fiqh* work), the intention was clearly to demonstrate, by the fact of colocation, how legal theory and positive law (*fiqh*) are closely linked.

The *Maʿālim al-Uṣūl* achieved a position of dominance in the Imami Shi'i curriculum. It was the principal work on which commentaries were made over the centuries subsequent to its composition. Commentaries were usually called *hashiyya* (marginalia) or *sharh* (full commentary), though the difference between them was regularly little more than terminological. Many *hashiyyas* were as expansive as the *sharhs*. The Imami Shi'i biobibliographical tradition records the names (and manuscripts) of over fifty such commentaries up to the early twentieth century, and the text continues to be the subject of commentary in some parts of the Imami Shi'i seminary today. Its success is usually credited to its straightforward language, its "systematic and well-arranged" structure and its ability to condense the Imami Shi'i *usuli* position in a digestible format. On the question of *khabar al-wahid* for example, *Maʿālim*'s discussion is introduced:

> *Khabar al-Wahid* is that which does not reach the level of well-attested, regardless of whether its transmitters are many or few. Its content does not give rise to knowledge in and of itself (*bi-nafsihi*).[33]

[32] To my knowledge: University of Tehran Library, *Fihrist-e Nuskheh-hā-ye khaṭṭī-ye Dānishgāh-e Tihrān* (Tehran: University of Tehran, 1978) v.5, 1731–1727. They were collected together by al-Shahid al-Awwal al-'Amili (d. 786/1384) in an apparently lost work titled *Jāmiʿ al-Bayān*.

[33] Hasan b. Zayn al-Din al-'Amili, *Maʿālim al-uṣūl maʿa taʿlīqa Sulṭān al-ʿūlamāʾ* (Qum: Dār al-fikr, 1995), 187.

As with al-'Allama's text, there is an explicit rejection of the linguistic definition (*khabar al-wahid*—"the report of one"). But here the principal element of the definition is given by reference to another *usul* category (*tawatur*—"well-attested"). The category of *tawatur* refers to reports so widely transmitted that doubt over their accuracy is unthinkable (indeed, irrational). This internal reference to another *usul* category rather than a reference to a broader epistemological category indicates how *usul*, by the time of Hasan b. Zayn al-Din was developing its own internal set of self-referential definitions (*khabar al-wahid* is defined as something which is not *mutawatir*, rather than by some external epistemological definition). He does go on to describe it in epistemological terms ("does not give rise to knowledge...."), but even here the definition is refined from al-'Allama's formulation (where the notion of "in itself" is understood but not immediately articulated). This is just one way in which the *Maʿālim al-uṣūl* displays a refined and condensed expression of Imami Shiʿi legal theory, the result probably of repeated instruction in educational contexts where memorization is the standard mode of learning. These characteristics resulted in an almost immediate commentarial tradition as this introduction to Hasan b. Zayn al-Din's *fiqh* book *Maʿālim al-Dīn* was separated out and given its own title of *Maʿālim al-uṣūl*. The first major commentary, Sultan al Ulama Husayn al-Mazandarani's (d. 1064/1653–4) *Taʿlīqa*, was already considered a central seminar teaching aid within fifty years of Hasan b. Zayn al-Din's death.[34]

Even more condensed, and from the generation after Hasan b. Zayn al-Din, is the *Zubdat al-Uṣūl* of the important polymath of the Safavid era, al-Shaykh al-Baha'i Muhammad al-'Amili (d. 1030/1621). This, though as the title indicates, was a useful summary of the discipline, it could not compete with the dominance of the *Maʿālim*, signalled by the fact that in the modern period, the edition of the *Zubdat al-uṣūl* remained in lithograph form until the early twenty-first century.[35] Its brevity did attract over twenty commentaries (both *hashiyya* and *sharh*) by subsequent authors.[36]

IV. The Akhbaris

The reaction to the dominance of the model of *usul al-fiqh* which was initiated by al-'Allama and summarized by Hasan b. Zayn al-Din appeared very soon. It was

[34] The most common edition of the *Maʿālim* is published with Sultan al-Ulama's comments—see n. 33.

[35] It was eventually published in 2003 (al-Shaykh al-Baha'i, *Zubdat al-uṣūl* (Qum: Dār al-Bashar, 2003).

[36] See Āghā Buzurg al-Tiḥrānī, *Dharīʿa ilā taṣānīf al-Shīʿa* (Najaf: Maṭbaʿat al-Ghārī, 1936–1970), v.6, 102–104 and v.13, 297–301 for a list of the major commentaries on al-Baha'i's *Zubdat al-uṣūl*.

spearheaded by Muhammad Amin al-Astarabadi and his famous work *al-Fawā'id al-Madaniyya*. This is seen as the foundational tract of the Akhbariyya school of thought. The work itself is a rather disorganized collection of short essays (each termed a *fa'ida* – or "useful comment") on aspects of legal theory, in which al-Astarabadi rejects most of the positions so succinctly laid out in the *Maʿālim al-uṣūl*. Hasan b. Zayn al-Din is not always his main target; most of his criticism is aimed at al-ʿAllama, who (he argues) corrupted Imami Shiʿi *usul al-fiqh* by incorporating Sunni elements into its structure. This led him, at times, to reject the whole enterprise of legal speculation, and its literary expression in the *usul* genre. His primary focus is on the practice of *ijtihad*, validated by al-ʿAllama in his *usul* and expanded upon by subsequent jurists. *Ijtihad* is a Sunni invention, he argues, aimed at coping with the fact that their jurists cannot agree on the meaning of revelation or the message of the Sunna of the Prophet. What distinguished the Shiʿa was the fact that they could be certain in their fulfillment of God's law by recourse to a sinless Imam. The Imami authors who are currently arguing for *ijtihad* because the Imam is absent are, in effect, adopting a Sunni argument. Instead, he argued, they should turn to the reports of the Imams. These reports (collectedly termed *akkhbar*, hence the movement's name "the Akhbaris") provide certainty as to the Imam's words and actions, and following them gives the community a clear path to salvation. The categorization of *hadith* (into *khabar al-wahid* and *al-khabar al-mutawatir*, and then further into categories based on the strength of the *isnad* accompanying them) is, for al-Astarabadi and for many subsequent Akhbaris, irrelevant. The *akhbar*, in their current form and as found in the Shiʿi books of *hadith* (the so-called "Four Books" mentioned at the beginning of the chapter) constitute the sole source of religious guidance for the community.

There are, of course, similarities with the Ahl al-Hadith perspective found in Sunni thinking, which side-lined the enterprise of *usul al-fiqh*, or limited it to particular areas. Ahl al-Hadith similarly viewed *isnad* criticism as having restricted utility in the derivation of legal rulings; their acceptance of transmitters was more relaxed than the stricter "rationalist" trends. But there are differences as well. For example, so all-encompassing were the *akhbar* that the direct interpretation of the Qur'an itself became impossible. The contents of the Book were only known through the sayings of the Imams, for Akhbaris. There are also similarities with the earlier collectors of Shiʿi reports, such as al-Kulayni and Ibn Babawayh, and even with al-Shaykh al-Tusi.This, and the Akhbari claim that they were merely reviving the lost (i.e. true) reflection of these earlier scholars, has led some to see the Akhbari school as a continuous feature of the Shiʿi landscape. Madelung and Newman, for example, trace a history of the Akhbari school to the earliest period; Calder (and myself in my own work) argue that there was something new in Akhbarism which one does not find in the straightforward examples of traditionalism in the earlier period.[37] The Akhbari rejection of *ijtihad*, and the promotion of reports as sources

[37] Wilferd Madelung, "Imamism and Mu'tazilite Theology" in *Le Shīʿisme imâmite: colloque de Strasbourg (6–9 mai, 1968)* ed. T. Fahd (Paris: Presses Universitaires de France, 1970), 13–30; A. Newman, "The Development and Political Significance of the Rationalist (Uṣūlī) and Traditionalist (Akhbārī)

of knowledge led, inevitably, to the denial of *zann* as a useful category of knowledge in legal derivation. At its root, then, the Akhbari polemic against the Usulis (as those maintaining Hasan b. Zayn al-Din's position were termed) was epistemological. For the Akhbaris, the opinion of the jurist was not considered authoritative, simply because of the qualifications of the individual.

The central ideas of the Akhbari movement, as sketched out above, was, in a sense, a rejection of *usūl al-fiqh* as a discipline. Legal derivation was, initially at least, not considered complex or demanding, and answers were always present within the sayings of the Imams. Of course, this simplicity of approach faced serious tests (one could draw the comparison with the impracticality of certain Zahiri approaches). The drive to reject *usul al-fiqh* as a discipline in Astarabadi's writings did not last throughout the movement's popularity. Subsequent Akhbari writers composed works of *usul al-fiqh* in which they attempted to outline a more sophisticated Akhbari legal methodology, whilst staying true to the rejection of *zann* and *ijtihad*. Muhammad Taqi al-Majlisi (d. 1070/1659–60), Mulla Muhsin Fayd al-Kashani (d. 1091/1680), al-Hurr al-Amili (d. 1104/1693) and eventually the last great Akhbari writer Yusuf al-Bahrani (d. 1180/1772), all had to make compromises to Astarabadi's critique. In terms of writings in *usul al-fiqh*, the best known Akhbari works are probably Muhsin Fayd's *al-Uṣūl al-Aṣīla* and al-Bahrani's *Muqaddimāt* ("Introductory comments") to *al-Ḥadā'iq al-Nāḍirā*. Whilst not a regular work of legal theory, it is divided into ten sections (each termed an *asl*) dealing with standard Akhbari doctrines.

He does however move away from al-Astarabadi's position. For example, al-Astarabadi had argued:

> If one does not know a ruling of God in an issue, he cannot make his own efforts [i.e. *ijtihad*] in this area. Rather he is forbidden [by the Imams] from doing this. This is the path of the suspension of opinion (*tawaqquf*) and caution (*ihtiyat*), as has been related many times from the Imams for every case in which the ruling of God is not clear.[38]

This appears to be the position of "suspension" in cases of revelatory silence (or lack of clarity), which would appear as a continuation of that advocated by al-Tusi in the question of *al-hizr wa'l-ibaha* outlined earlier. In relation to this issue Muhsin Fayḍ takes a different view:

> The truth in this issue has already been demonstrated, and you already know that it is permitted to act on the basis of the original status [of a thing] being free of assessment (*asalat al-bara'a*); this is what the Imams have permitted, and to what reason testifies.[39]

Schools in Imāmī Shī'ism History from the Third/Ninth to the Tenth/Sixteenth Century" (Unpublished Ph.D. thesis, University of California Los Angeles, 1986); Calder, "Doubt and Prerogative." For an analysis of the debate around the "origins" of Akhbarism, see, Gleave, *Scripturalist Islam: The History and Doctrines of the Akhbārī Shī'ī School* (Leiden: Brill, 2007), 1–31.

[38] Muhammad Amin al-Astarabadi, *al-Fawā'id al-Madaniyya* (Qum: Mu'assasat al-Nashr al-Islāmī, 2003), 122.

[39] Muhsin Fayd al-Kashani, *al-Uṣūl al-Aṣīla* (Tehran: Sazimān-e Chāp-e Dānishgāh, 1971), 143.

Muhsin Fayd's position would appear to be, then, a softening of al-Astarabadi's rejection of the assumption of freedom of assessment in cases of revelatory silence. Fayd argues that the Imams themselves decreed that in the absence of revelatory indicators, all things are to be considered permitted, and this creates knowledge of one's obligations under the law of God. Interestingly, Fayd's argument here is based mainly on the Akhbari notion that one should always take the statements of the Imams as one's principal source of legal knowledge. He appeals to the *akkhbar* in order to demonstrate that he is more Akhbari, as it were, than Astarabadi himself. One finds similar softening of some of Astarabadi's more "extreme" or anti-rationalist positions in the other major work of Akhbari *usul al-fiqh*, the introduction to Yusuf al-Bahrani's *fiqh* work *al-Ḥadāʾiq al-Nādira*.[40]

One interesting work of *usul al-fiqh* of the period of Akhbari dominance is *al-Wāfiyya* of ʿAbdallah al-Tuni (d. 1071/1600). Al-Tuni's work is normally accepted as a mainstream Usuli work; though Akhbaris also claim he was, at heart, an Akhbari. On the question of *al-baraʾa al-asliyya* (that is, the fundamental freedom of things from assessment, also termed *asalat al-baraʾa*), he is quite cautious. He argues that although it is permitted to adopt the presumption of freedom of assessment in cases of revelatory silence, it can only be in issues which are of such common occurrence that, had there been a ruling, the Imams would have expressed. He terms this *ʿumum al-balwa*: a widespread unavoidable, common matter. In a remarkable mixture of Akhbari and *Usuli* themes, he argues that the *akkhbar* of the Imams must contain all the rulings which are required for the believer:

> The expert one, knowledgeable in *hadith* follows the reports transmitted from the Imams in an issue. If there is a ruling which contradicts the assumption [of there being an assessment and therefore a general permission], then it would have been disseminated, on account of *ʿumum al-balwa*. If he finds no report which indicates that [opposing] rule, then he gains an overwhelming opinion (*al-zann al-ghalib*) that there is no rule. This is because a huge number of the *ulama*—4000 alone who were pupils of al-Imam al-Sadiq alone...—were closely associated with the Imams during a period of time over 300 years. Their aim was the same as the Imams themselves: to make clear the religion for us, and to record everything they heard from them.[41]

The argument is basically a historical one, closely linked to notion of "wide-attestation" (*tawatur*). Those who studied with the Imams were so numerous, that if there was a rule which was different from the assumption of permission, then they would have heard it. If the expert knowledgeable in *hadith* (*al-muhaddith al-mahir*) finds no rule, then he gains an overwhelming opinion there is no ruling. In this

[40] I have analyzed al-Bahrani's position extensively in my *Inevitable Doubt*, and though his is a less vehement or dogmatic position than Astarabadi, it certainly held on to the fundamental Akhbari notions of a rejection of *ijtihad* and *zann* and a preservation of the total historical integrity of the reports.

[41] ʿAbdallah al-Tuni, *al-Wāfiyya* (Qum: Majmaʿ al-Fikr al-Islāmī, 1992), 178.

sense *al-baraʾa al-asliyya* is a valid source of law. The Akhbari elements in this argument include the promotion of the "expert in *hadith*" (rather than the *mujtahid* as a pure Usuli might say) and the promotion of the *akkhbar* as the source of all necessary legal knowledge. The Usuli elements include the notion that this *muhaddith mahir* gains an opinion (*zann*) which overwhelms him (rather like a *mujtahid*) that the rule of God is in accordance with *al-baraʾa al-asliyya.*

By the time of Yusuf al-Bahrani, the Akhbari dominance of the Shiʿi seminaries in Iraq and Iran had begun to wane, and he was the last of the great Akhbari scholars. This is not to say there were not Akhbaris after him, but they were not as influential or powerful in the seminary, and Akhbarism never regained its position of dominance. The great reviver of Usulism, Muhammad Baqir al-Bihbihani, a contemporary of Yusuf al-Bahrani, and his intellectual sparring partner on numerous occasions, was to re-establish a revived Usuli school in which the *zann* of the *mujtahid* was to become the central concern of Imami legal theory.

V. Contemporary Usulism

Akhbarism continued to influence the development of Imami Shiʿi legal theory well after the Akhbari School petered out as a viable intellectual force. *Usul* writers continued to write refutations of the Akhbari position well after the school was largely defunct within the principal seminaries of Najaf, Karbala, and Mashhad. In works written well into the twentieth century, one finds detailed critiques of Akhbari positions on various *usul* topics, as well as rejections of the Akhbari approach to *usul* more generally. Akhbarism remained a strictly minority interest, with schools continuing in the Persian Gulf (particularly Bahrain and Ahsa) and in India up to the present day. Some have argued that the Akhbari tendency may have lost its independent status as a school, but it has not disappeared. Rather the impetus has transformed into movements within Usulism, most notably the so-called "School of Separation" (*Maktab-e Tafkik*), Iranian anti-philosophy which emerged in the twentieth century as a rejection of the philosophy of Mulla Sadra al-Shirazi (d. 979/1640–41). The Tafkikis (as they are known) wish to limit the role of reason in matters of religious thought (including *usul al-fiqh*), and are accused by some of being inspired by Akhbarism. Similarly, there were elements of Muhammad Baqir al-Sadr's legal theory (in particular, his promotion of caution—*ihtiyaṭ*—to new areas of legal derivation—see later in this chapter) which revived Akhbari doctrines.

The end of Akhbari dominance saw, in the early decades of the nineteenth century, a revival in *usul al-fiqh* as a genre of writing, and a flurry of important *usul* works were published. Most notable are by the pupils (or the pupils of the pupils of al-Bihbihani):

Qawanin al-usul of Mirza Abu al-Qasim al-Qummi (d. 1231/1816)
Mafatih al-Usul of Muhammad al-Tabataba'i, known as al-Mujahid (d. 1242/1826)
al-Fusul al-Gharwiyya of Muhammad Husayn al-Ha'iri (d. 1250/1834)
Dawabit al-usul of Ibrahim b. Muhammad Baqir al-Qazwini (d. 1262/1846)

Al-Bihbihani's achievements were partly institutional (he followed al-Bahrani in Karbala as the leading scholar, and re-established the dominance of the Usuli school), and also literary (he published many books which influenced the immediate generation of scholars). But his works of *usul al-fiqh* do not become standard seminary texts. They are rather disorganized and inchoate. The systematic presentation of his position was left to his pupils to work out.

Apart from the *usul* monographs listed above, the surviving *usul* production from this early post-Akhbari period is voluminous. Authors, both established and less so, took advantage of the space for *usul* discussions created by the establishment of Usulism. Aside from monographs (always the preserve of the truly dedicated *usuli*), many hundreds of shorter *usul* treatises were composed and have survived, and quite a few important commentaries on past *usul* masterpieces, such as the *Hidāyat al-Mustashidīn* (a lengthy commentary on al-Hasan b. al-Shahid al-Thani's *Maʿālim al-dīn*) by Muhammad Taqi al-Isfahani (d. 1248/1833).

The authors of these works were clearly experimenting with the rediscovered framework of *zann* and *ijtihad*, and this led them to adopt positions which later Shiʿi *usul* would reject or heavily modify. For example, Mirza Qummi credited with holding a series of quite radical *usul* positions by later writers, and his views, whilst respected, have not formed the central doctrines of the mainstream. For example, in his *Qawānīn al-uṣūl* he developed a set of arguments defending the rather radical position that every opinion (*zann*) of the *mujtahid* has the authority or "probative force" (*hujjiyya*) to establish a legally valid ruling. By this he implies that it is not the interpretive process whereby the *mujtahid* reaches his opinion that established the authority of his assessment; rather it is the fact that he is a *mujtahid* which assures his opinion has probative force legally speaking. By arguing in this way, Mirza Qummi locates the probative force in the person of *mujtahid* rather than in the hermeneutic techniques he employs. Such a view, of course, probably enhances the *mujtahid*'s status as an interpreter of the law, giving him almost acharismatic authority. The doctrine was broadly criticized by subsequent writers of *usul al-fiqh*, as the mainstream argued that *zann* in itself has no probative force. It only gains this force when there is a clear and indubitable sanction for the jurist to use a particular mechanism. So, analogical reasoning (*qiyas*) is condemned both because it leads to *zann* and also because there are explicit indicators (in this case statements by the Imams) condemning it. On the other hand, the apparent meaning of the verses in the Qur'an (*hujjiyat al-zawahir*) have probative force because that has been specifically allowed by a certain indicator (*dalil*—from reason or from revelation). This mainstream position formed the basis for much Shiʿi *usuli* thought in writings after Mirza Qummi.[42]

Al-Shaykh Murtada al-Ansari often counted within the tradition, and in the secondary literature, as the founder of the contemporary school of Imami jurisprudence. Certainly in terms of power within the seminary, he was unparalleled, and his collected *usul* thinking in his *Farāʾid al-uṣūl* (also known as "The Treatises" – *al-Rasāʾil*) certainly represents an innovative structuring of *usul al-fiqh*. Al-Ansari divides his work into three sections and on the basis of epistemological categories (certainty, opinion and doubt—*yaqin, zann* and *shakk*). In each section he discusses those indicators of the law which fall into each category. The largest section, inevitably is *zann*. The division of *usul* subject matter into epistemological categories is significant. It represents the foregrounding of a feature of Imami *usul* discussions which was latent in *usul al-fiqh* before al-Ansari, but which he exploited to the full. The emphasis is firmly on the unobtainability of knowledge. That is, acquiring certainty (*yaqin*) of the ruling of much of God's law depend on indicators (*adilla*) which guide us to the law's content. The *adilla* though are uncertain in terms of their provenance (apart from the Qur'an), and uncertain in terms of what they indicate. The individual, standing before the sources, is required to interpret indicators which are, in themselves, of uncertain indication. Any conclusions which he reaches is therefore not going to be the law of God but a personal understanding of the *adilla* which point to the law of God. He will reach an opinion, but it will be an "apparent rule" (*hukm zahiri*) rather than rule itself (*hukm waqiʿi*). Amongst the tools he might use in cases of uncertain indication are the "procedural principles" (*al-usulal-ʿamaliyya*). These are principles of exegesis which a jurist should use in order to reach an opinion about the rule, even if the rule itself will never be known to be the actual rule. Placing the procedural principles at the centre of the Imami juristic project was, perhaps, the most important result of al-Shaykh al-Ansari's *usul al-fiqh*. Hence he writes:

> When [the individual legal subject] is in a position of doubt (*shakk*), the source for him in such circumstances are the legal principles established for situations of doubt. These are called *al-usul al-ʿamaliyya* (procedural principles).[43]

Al-Ansari then divides the doubt of the believer into different types of doubt. For example, he may be in doubt over the ruling itself, or he be certain for the rule, but be in doubt over whether it applies to this particular circumstance. He decreed different principles for the believer in these different circumstances. So if he knows the ruling but is not sure of its application, he should find the most cautious course

[42] Abu al-Qasim al-Qummi, *Qawanīn al-uṣūl* (Qum: Dār al-Iḥyāʾ al-Kutub al-Islāmī, 2008), v.3–4, 341.

[43] Al Shaykh al-Ansari, *Farāʾid al-uṣūl* (Qum: Muʾassasat Dār al-Kitāb, 1999), v.1, 25.

of action and do that (*ihtiyaṭ*). If, on the other hand, he is uncertain of the rule itself (i.e. the revelation is silent or unclear on this issue), then he can operate on the assumption that there is no obligation placed upon him (*al-bara'a al-asliyya*).

The discussion here is clearly an extension of the discussion outlined above, concerning *al-hizr wa'l-ibaha*. However, here the discussion is not about whether the ruling of God is that there is no assessment; rather al-Shaykh al-Ansari is arguing that the individual believer will have fulfilled his obligation to God if he follows this or that procedural principle in this or that situation of doubt. The aim of *usul al-fiqh* is no longer to find out the law of God but to find out how the individual fulfills their obligations to God. Al-Ansari continues the line of argument laid out by previous jurists, that God "cannot ask his believers to do the impossible" (*taklif mala yutaq*), which was for Mu'tazilis (and hence Imamis) demonstrated by reason alone. It would be irrational for God to provide uncertain indicators (as he surely does in the revelatory texts) and then expect the believer to be certain about the law; and it would be unjust of God to punish a believer if he followed these uncertain indicators to the best of his ability, but still transgressed the law. Rather, the aim of legal theory is to construct a framework whereby the individual has fulfilled his legal responsibility, not necessarily a mechanism for discovering legal certainty. This emphasis on how the law appears to the believer rather than what the law actually is led to the introduction of a range of innovative *usul* concepts in contemporary Imami legal theory since al-Ansari. For example, the *bina' al-'uqala'* (and similar locutions), which could be translated as "the findings of rational people," replaces at times the findings of pure reason (*'aql*). There is an implicit recognition that what appears rational to the individual may not be (objectively speaking) rational. Therefore, what rational beings have considered rational over the years (and in the present) is, in a sense, a valid source of legal knowledge. Similarly the "practice of religious people" (*sirat al-mustasharri'a*) over the centuries becomes a potential source of legal knowledge, since it is improbable (rationally speaking) that truly religious people would have been following a dangerously illegal path for all this time without identifying a rule (rational or revelatory) which modifies their behavior. Therefore, their practice becomes a source for religious practice in the absence of clear guidance from other sources (replacing the similar notion of *ijma'*).

Al-Shaykh al-Ansari's general position, which was probably not more than a formalization of previous post-Akhbari *usul al-fiqh*, was taken up and condensed in the central *usul* text of modern times, the *Kifāyat al-uṣūl* of Akhund al-Khurasani (d. 1911).[44] Whilst Khurasani disagrees with al-Ansari on various issues, the

[44] Al-Akhund Kazim al-Khurasani, *Kifāyat al-uṣūl* (Qum: Dār al-Ḥikma, 1992). On contemporary *usul al-fiqh* and its use of tradition see Robert Gleave "Modern Shi'ite Legal Theory and the Classical Tradition," in *Reclaiming Islamic Tradition: Modern Interpretations of the Classical Heritage*, eds. Elisabeth Kendall and Ahmad Khan 12–32 (Edinburgh: Edinburgh University Press, 2016).

compressed expression found in the *Kifāya* made it a perfect candidate for subsequent commentary. In the seminaries, it was this text which became the principal focus for commentary, replacing, to an extent, the *Maʿālim al-uṣūl* of Hasan b. Zayn al-din. In the twentieth century, there have been numerous commentaries on the *Kifāya*; indeed producing a commentary on it was seen as an important step to becoming a senior scholar, even when the scholar disagreed with Akhund's views as laid out in the *Kifāya*. The total number of commentaries is almost impossible to determine, given the popularity of this text as a focus of comment; many commentaries remain unpublished and available only within the Hawza circles. This estimation is yet further exacerbated by the common twentieth century practice of setting down the lecture notes of a teacher, asking him to check them, and then producing a commentary publication of them (known as *taqrirat*). The *Nihāyat al-Dirāya* of the great teacher of *usul al-fiqh* Muhammad Husayn al-Isfahani (d. 1947) is perhaps the most referenced commentary on the *Kifāya*, but the comments of the great Ayatallah Burujirdi (d. 1961), the leader of the Qum *hawza* in the late 1950s, are also extensively used, based on the lecture notes (*taqrir*) of his pupil Baha' al-Din Hujjati. The major scholars of the twentieth century, including Ayatallahs Ruhallah Khumayni (Khomeini, d. 1989) and Abu al-Qasim al-Khu'i (Khoie, d. 1992), and the current "sources of emulations" Ayatallahs 'Ali al-Sistani, Ishaq Fayyad, Bashir Najafi and Sa'd al-Hakim all cut their teeth in *usul* by studying the *Kifāya*, and their independent *usul* works are often evidence of the *Kifaya's* influence upon them. Even the rival text to the *Kifāya*, Muzaffar al-Rida's (d. 1964) widely used teaching text, called simply *Uṣūl al-fiqh*, is considered a more accessible expression of the system, laid out in the *Kifāya*. Muzaffar's work has not become a source of commentary, though it has enabled a wider number of students to grasp the fundamentals of *usul al-fiqh* without having to struggle with the archaic language and compressed expression of the *Kifāya*. This is unsurprising as it came out of his own attempts to link the *hawza* methodology with a more university style "College of Law."

VI. Conclusion

The *Kifāya's* role, both as a text for commentary and as the central teaching text, has only really been challenged in recent times. The most successful *usul* text to challenge the *Kifāya's* dominance are to be found in the writings of the Iraqi seminarian Muḥammad Baqir al-Sadr (d. 1980), specifically his *al-Maʿālim al-Jadīda fī uṣūl al-fiqh* ("the New Ma'alim" which as the name suggests, aims replace the *Maʿālim al-uṣūl* of Hasan b. Zayn al-Din), and his three part text book course in legal theory *Durūs fī ʿilm* al-*uṣūl*. The first "turn" (*al-Ḥalaqa al-Ūla*, as it is often referred to) has been translated into English.[45] For those used to reading Imami classical *usul* works, even a cursory reading of Sadr's writings reveals an attempt to reform Imami *usul*, and his project in *usul* is but one part of his more general project of reforming the *hawza* seminary educational system in Iraq. Whilst still working within the framework established by al-Bihbihani (around the uncertainty of indicators), al-Sadr devises radical *usul* positions. An example of this is his reaction to the doctrine of the general license for unregulated actions (*al-bara'a al-asliyya*) already discussed. For al-Sadr, the presumption that there is no assessment when the indicators do not provide clear rulings runs the danger of contravening a fundamental theological principle (established for him through rational investigation). All agree that the Lawgiver (i.e. God) has the right to expect the obedience of his servants, by virtue of his role as originator and sustainer of creation. This "right of obedience" (*haqq al-ṭa'a*) due to the Lawgiver established a duty placed upon the servants to do all within their power to fulfill his law. This duty extends not only to issues which are clear within the text, but also those which appear to the readers to be unclear. It could be argued that the lack of clarity within the text may be due to the readers' deficiencies rather than the Lawgiver's failure to communicate effectively. This "right of obedience" doctrine has many ramifications for legal derivation, but (in reference to *al-bara'a al-asliyya* discussed above), it amounts to a rejection of the untrammelled application of the doctrine of "fundamental freedom from assessment." God's right to demand obedience from his servants extends to those areas where the servants, due to their own limitations, cannot fully grasp the message. In such cases, Baqir al-Sadr argues, one should exercise caution wherever possible (*ihtiyat*), and this means placing greater emphasis on extending the rules only vaguely known in the sources to new situations which previously were thought to be unregulated. This return to the promotion of the "principle of caution" has led to some characterizing his ideas as a continuation of some major Akhbari themes. It might be more accurate to say that he is re-emphasizing the "cautious" elements of al-Shaykh al-Ansari's *usul*.

Contemporary Imami *usul* then has, since al-Sadr's death, been characterized by debates between these various approaches. There have been attempts, particularly in Iran, to reform (for some to the point of abandoning entirely) the hermeneutic project found in religious texts such as *usul al-fiqh*. There is the reform proposed by the followers of al-Sadr, which is often accompanied by a desire to reform the *hawza* curriculum more generally. These are amongst the challenges to the more conservative approach of maintaining the legacy of al-Shaykh al-Ansari, as encapsulated in Akhund's *Kifāyat al-uṣūl*. All the indications are that the intellectual vibrancy of the debate within Imami *usul al-fiqh* will continue both within and without the *hawza* system for some years to come.

[45] See n. 6.

CHAPTER 9

CUSTOM IN THE ISLAMIC LEGAL TRADITION

AYMAN SHABANA

1. Definition and Scope

The two Arabic terms associated with the concept of custom are *'urf* (pl. *a'raf*) and *'ada* (pl. *'adat*). The word *'urf* shares the root of several derivatives that signify, among other things, what is "known," "famous," or "commendable." The two words *'urf* and *ma'ruf* are used as synonyms and both are mentioned in the Qur'an and Hadith to denote commendable and praiseworthy deeds.[1] The same relationship also exists between the opposites of these two terms, *nukr* and *munkar*, which denote what is unknown or condemnable.[2] The two terms *ma'ruf* and *munkar* are conjoined in the moral exhortation to command good and to forbid evil (*al-amr bi-al-ma'ruf wa-al-nahy 'an al-munkar*), which is considered one of the fundamental principles in the Islamic moral-legal tradition.[3] The word *'urf* refers to well-established conventions and practices in a given society or among a group of people. This would include common linguistic and moral practices such as idiomatic expressions, types of transactions, or definition of proper conduct. The word *'urf* was used by the early jurists in this general sense before the development of new classifications to distinguish different customs in terms of types (e.g. linguistic

[1] Ibn Manzur, *Lisan al-'Arab*, 10:112.

[2] Ibid.; Isfahani, *al-Mufradat fi Gharib al-Qur'an*, 334–335.

[3] Michael Cook, *Commanding Right and Forbidding Wrong*, 9.

and practical), scope (e.g. specific and general), or relationship to shariʿa (approved and disapproved). According to some contemporary jurists, the most common definition for custom in the Islamic legal tradition is traced back to Hafiz al-Din ʿAbd Allah ibn Ahmad al-Nasafi (d. 710/1310),[4] according to which custom is defined as "well-established practices that can be rationally justified and that are not deemed repulsive to good nature."[5] The word *ʿada* shares the root of several derivatives that denote repetition or recurrence. As a noun it refers to a habit, continuous practice, or character trait.[6] While some premodern as well as modern jurists use the two terms *ʿurf* and *ʿada* interchangeably,[7] others distinguish them. The latter disagree over which one of the two terms is broader in scope.[8] The majority of scholars are of the opinion that *ʿada* is broader than *ʿurf*. While *ʿada* covers both personal habits as well as collective customs, *ʿurf* refers only to the latter. Therefore, every *ʿurf* is *ʿada* but not every *ʿada* is *ʿurf*. The most important distinction between *ʿurf* and *ʿada* is made on the basis of their rational justification. While the emergence of an *ʿurf*-based custom involves an element of human volition such as the prevalence of particular types of transactions due to their utility or convenience, an *ʿada*-based custom may also be attributed to natural phenomena that do not involve human volition. The attainment of puberty, for example, is considered an *ʿada*-based rather than *ʿurf*-based custom because not only does it differ from one person to another but it also depends on factors such as the average temperature or other natural factors specific to particular geographical locations. Some definitions of *ʿada*, therefore, emphasize the lack of this rational volitional element in *ʿada*, to distinguish it from *ʿurf*. The distinction between the two terms is based also on factual as well as formal considerations. While *ʿurf* involves a factual element (the actual recurrence of an action) as well as a formal element (the recognition of such recurrence as normative), *ʿada* involves only the former. In other words, while the collective recognition of *ʿurf* is intrinsic, recognition of *ʿada* as normative requires further legal or cultural confirmation and ascertainment.[9] Accordingly, and depending on whether *ʿurf* and *ʿada* are considered synonyms, these factual and formal elements are the criteria by which a common convention or practice is considered normative. References to the concept of normative custom permeates the different sections of Islamic substantive law (*fiqh*), especially in the area of commercial transactions where it is used as a method to determine values, measures, and other information that change over time or across regions.

[4] Ahmad Fahmi Abu Sunnah, *al-ʾUrf wa-al-ʾAdah fi Raʾy al-Fuqahaʾ*, 28.

[5] Nasafi, *al-Mustasfa*, 425.

[6] Ibn Manzur, *Lisan al-ʾArab*, 10:326; Jurjani, *al-Taʿrifat*, 149; Ibn ʿAbidin, "*Nashr al-ʾArf fi Binaʾ baʿd al-Ahkam ʿala al-ʾUrf*," in *Majmuʿat Rasaʾil Ibn ʿAbidin*, 112; Sunnah and Ahmad, *al-ʾUrf wa-al-ʾAda*, 31.

[7] Nasafi, *al-Mustasfa*, 425; Ahmad Fahmi Abu Sunnah, *al-ʿUrf wa-al-ʾAda*, 34.

[8] Ahmad Fahmi Abu Sunnah, *al-ʿUrf wa-al-ʾAda*, 31–34.

[9] Ibid.

II. Custom and Islamic Law in Modern Scholarship

Studies on the role of custom in the Islamic legal tradition have to be placed within the context of the debates that have occupied the field of Islamic studies since the late nineteenth century. These debates centered on two important issues: the origins of Islamic sources; and the dichotomy between theory and practice in the development of Islamic law. These two issues have been of utmost significance for scholarly assessments of the role and function of custom in Islamic legal history. The first issue concerns the development not only of Islamic law but also Islam's foundational sources: the Qur'an and the Sunna of the Prophet. The second issue concerns juristic methods for the construction of Islamic legal rules and the extent to which these rules responded to social reality. In general, as Rudolph Peters notes, western scholarship on the Islamic legal tradition has been dominated by two main assumptions: the closure of the gate of *ijtihad* after the formative period of the tradition; and the highly theoretical nature of Islamic law.[10] Although these assumptions are no longer defensible, they are important to keep in mind while tracing the historiography of custom in the Islamic legal tradition.

A. Custom and the Origins of Islamic Law

The debate on the origins and authenticity of Islam's foundational sources, specifically of the Sunna of the Prophet Muhammad, is important for the historiography of custom in the Islamic legal tradition. The term "sunna" originally stood for "custom," "practice," or "way" broadly construed. Only later did it become a term of art reserved for the normative practice of the Prophet. The earlier, pre-Islamic, use of the term became a key problem in the historiography of the later development of the normative concept of sunna. The main question has been the extent to which the pre-Islamic connotations of the term "sunna" continued after Islam, and the point at which the new normative sense of the term started to take root. Fazlur Rahman and Zafar Ishaq Ansari indicate that although the pre-Islamic connotation of the term "sunna" continued after Islam, and although its normative usage was not exclusively reserved for the Prophet, the normative concept of the Sunna of the Prophet can be traced back to the first century, prior to the composition of the major hadith collections.[11]

[10] Rudolph Peters, "[Book Review]: *The Islamic Law on Land Tax*," 245.

[11] Fazlur Rahman, *Islamic Methodology*, 12; Zafar Ishaq Ansari, "Islamic Juristic Terminology," *Arabica* 19 (1972): 259–282.

Apart from the linguistic and semantic association between sunna and custom in the debate over the historicity of the Sunna of the Prophet, the larger implication of this relationship between sunna and custom has been the role of the latter in the development of the Islamic legal tradition. This is illustrated by the view that the genesis of Islamic law owes more to indigenous, pre-Islamic, customs than to Islam's original sources, which became known as the foreign origins thesis. The role of custom in the development of the Islamic legal tradition has been at the center of a heated debate since the publication of the first edition of Joseph Schacht's *The Origins of Muhammadan Jurisprudence* in 1950 and later his *An Introduction to Islamic Law* in 1964. Schacht argued that it was not the Prophet's original intent to establish a comprehensive legal system but rather to establish a moral system that is geared towards the attainment of salvation in the Hereafter.[12] According to Schacht, the creation of a comprehensive legal system commenced in Iraq, rather than in Medina, long after the death of the Prophet in light of the more developed social and cultural context in Iraq.[13] More particularly, according to Schacht: "The literary period of Islamic law begins about the year 150 of the hijra (AD 767), and from then onwards the development of technical legal thought can be followed step by step from scholar to scholar."[14] Building on the ideas of Christiaan Snouck Hurgronje and Ignaz Goldziher concerning the foreign origins of Islamic law, Schacht notes that: "the first considerable body of legal traditions from the Prophet originated towards the middle of the second century."[15] Schacht's argument on the precedence of juridical opinions to Prophetic reports supporting these opinions is based on examples of contracts and legal maxims, which he traces back to the commercial practice in Iraq.[16] Similar to Schacht, Patricia Crone used the foreign origins thesis but she argued that these origins go back to Ummayad Syria rather than Iraq.[17]

Schacht's work on the origins of the Sunna generated a heated debate not only on the historicity of the Sunna but on the early development of Islamic legal thought. Muslim scholars vehemently criticized Schacht's conclusions because they conflict with the standard view in Muslim sources, according to which authentic Prophetic reports predate systematic legal thought.[18] In western academic study of Islam, Schacht's ideas have been well received, but they have not been immune to

[12] Joseph Schacht, *An Introduction to Islamic Law*, 11.

[13] Ibid., 19, 20, 29. [14] Ibid., 40.

[15] Joseph Schacht, *Origins of Muhammadan Jurisprudence*, 4. For a review of Schacht's work in light of the works of Snouck Hurgronje, Goldziher, and Max Weber, see Baber Johansen, "The Muslim Fiqh as a Sacred Law, Religion, Law and Ethics in a Normative System," in *Contingency in a Sacred Law, Legal and Ethical Norms in the Muslim* Fiqh, 42–72.

[16] Joseph Schacht, "Foreign Elements in Ancient Islamic Law," *Journal of Comparative Legislation and International Law* 32 (1950): 9–17.

[17] Patricia Crone, *Roman, Provincial and Islamic Law*, 8.

[18] Stephen Humphreys, *Islamic History*, 84, Tarif Khalidi, *Arabic Historical Thought in the Classical Period*, 26; Harald Motzki, *The Origins of Islamic Jurisprudence*, 35.

criticism.[19] For example, in response to Schacht's emphasis on the role of the Sunna in the development of the legal tradition, S.D. Goitein argued that the legal import of many verses in the Qur'an suggests that Islamic legal thought began during the Prophet's lifetime.[20] More recently, several studies have rekindled the debate on the origins of Islamic law by questioning the foreign origins thesis and the suggested chronology of Islamic legal thought. For example, Hallaq argues against the foreign origins of Islamic law, which he traces to two main sources: "the Qur'anic legal ethic and the customary laws of Peninsular Arabs—laws that underwent a gradual transformation under the influence of emerging religious values."[21] Obviously, Hallaq's opinion does not question the role of pre-Islamic Arabian customs in the development of Islamic law but rather the extent to which these customs had been Islamized as a result of a creative interaction with Islamic normative values and the mode of such interaction.

Other studies argued against Schacht's estimation of the beginning of legal thought on the basis of textual analysis of early hadith works. For example, Harald Motzki's study of the *Musannaf* of 'Abd al-Razzaq al-San'ani (d. 179/795), which was not available at Schacht's time, challenges Schacht's conclusion that Islamic legal thought did not commence before the middle of the second Islamic century. It also questions the thesis of the foreign origins of Islamic law for lack of concrete evidence.[22] Similarly, Yasin Dutton's study of the Qur'anic elements in the *Muwatta'* of Malik ibn Anas (d. 179/795) sheds more light on both: the relationship between the concept of Medinan *'amal* (lit. practice) and the Sunna of the Prophet; and the role of the Qur'an in the development of Islamic law.[23] Dutton argues that within the framework of the *Muwatta'*, *'amal* is considered more authoritative than a statement attributed to the Prophet (*hadith*) because it is not based on a singular report (one from one) but rather on the practice of the community in which the Prophet lived. It is, therefore, reinforced by collective confirmation (one thousand from one thousand).[24] In this sense *'amal* is seen as coextensive with practical Sunna, before its later development within the Maliki school to include recognized custom within the framework of the legal school. Dutton's study shows also that the early formulation of the concept of *'amal*, as the normative Sunna-based practice of the people of Medina, traces the roots of Islamic legal thought to Medina prior to further developments in Iraq and elsewhere.

19 Motzki, *The Origins of Islamic Jurisprudence*, 28.

20 S.D. Goitein, "The Birth-Hour of Muslim Law?: An Essay in Exegesis," *Muslim World* 50 (1960): 23–29.

21 Wael Hallaq, *Origins and Evolution of Islamic Law*, 4; Wael Hallaq, "Groundwork for the Moral Law: A New Look at the Qur'an and the Genesis of Sharia," *Islamic Law and Society* 16 (2009): 239–279.

22 Motzki, *The Origins of Islamic Jurisprudence*, xv.

23 Yasin Dutton, *The Origins of Islamic Law, the Qur'an, the* Muwatta' *and Madinan* 'Amal, 5, 42.

24 Yasin Dutton, "'*Amal V Hadíth* in Islamic Law, The Case of *Sadl al-Yadayn* (Holding One's Hands By One's Sides) When Doing the Prayer," *Islamic Law and Society* 3 (1996): 13–40, 38–40.

B. Custom and the Dichotomy Between Theory and Practice

In addition to the issue of the origins of both Islam's foundational sources and Islamic law, another related issue that impacted the historiography of custom in modern scholarship has been the role of custom in the construction of Islamic legal rules. What is important to note here is the relationship between the new (western) understanding of the role of custom in the development of Islam's original sources on evaluating the role of custom in the construction of Islamic substantive rules. For example, Noel Coulson pointed out the significance of research on the origins of Islamic law on understanding the role of custom in the development of this law. Referring to Schacht's *Origins* in an article that was published in 1959, he notes: "Recent research, however, has now clearly demonstrated that the actual role of custom in the formation of the law was infinitely more important than hitherto suspected."[25] In this article Coulson compares the findings of western scholarship on the origins of Islamic law with the traditional view of Muslim jurists on the role of custom in the construction of Islamic law, according to which custom is accommodated within the framework of the main four sources: the Qur'an, the Sunna, analogical reasoning, and juristic consensus. Within this traditional view, Coulson observes, *'urf* had only "subsidiary and supplementary value."[26] He gave four examples of how the classical jurists made use of *'urf* within the framework of the four sources in substantive law.

From Coulson's account two different pictures of the role of custom in Islamic legal history emerge: the first, which is unofficial and implicit, describes the role of custom in the development of Sunna in the early formative period. The second, which is official and explicit, describes the role of *'urf* in the development of Islamic law, which remained unable to acquire the status of a "principal source of law."[27] This double image of custom in Islamic legal history is clearly expressed in this paragraph from Schacht's *Introduction:*

> If later Maliki doctrine in the West thus took limited notice of custom and actual practice, it remains, nevertheless, true that Islamic law, including the Maliki school, ignores custom as an official source of law. Custom (*'urf, 'ada*) is recognized as a restrictive element in dispositions and contracts ... and as a principle in interpreting declaration; it also serves occasionally as a basis of *istihsan* ... or *istislah*. Besides, custom and customary law have coexisted with the ideal theory of Islamic law, while remaining outside its system, in the whole of Islamic world. As a point of historical fact, custom contributed a great deal to the formation of Islamic law, but the classical theory of Islamic law was concerned not with its historical development but with the systematic foundation of the law, and the consensus of the scholars denied conscious recognition to custom.[28]

[25] Noel Coulson, "Muslim Custom and Case-Law," *Die Welt des Islams* 6 (1959): 13–24, 14.
[26] Ibid., 15. [27] Ibid., 13.
[28] Schacht, *An Introduction to Islamic Law*, 62.

A careful literature review of the topic should reveal that Schacht's view of custom has greatly influenced surveys of Islamic legal history in modern western scholarship. These surveys often speak about a persistent tension between legal theory and legal practice because Islamic law reached theoretical maturity during the Abbasid period, after which it "has grown more and more out of touch with later developments of state and society."[29] This depiction of Islamic law often emphasizes the gulf between legal theory and social reality, which was bound to increase over time. In the absence of formal recognition of custom as a source of law, any functional legal system must have methods to accommodate custom in order to remain relevant to contemporary concerns. Schacht observes that the jurists were able to accommodate custom and in general mitigate the tension between legal theory and social reality through employment of different types of legal stratagems or notions such as necessity (*darura*).[30]

The best expression of this standard narrative is to be found in Coulson's account of Islamic history in terms of a series of conflicts and tensions between revelation and reason; unity and diversity; authoritarianism and liberalism; idealism and realism; law and morality; and stability and change.[31] Within this narrative, with the exception of the early formative period (often associated with the period prior to al-Shafi'i), when Islamic law enjoyed a considerable degree of flexibility, it gradually lost this flexibility until: "In the tenth century the law was cast in a rigid mould from which it did not really emerge until the twentieth century."[32] The point that Coulson refers to in the tenth century is usually identified with the closure of the gate of *ijtihad* and the ushering of the system of imitation (*taqlid*).

Baber Johansen reports that this was the dominant view of the development of Islamic legal history in western scholarship until the 1980s, when it was challenged by scholars such as Rudolph Peters and Wael Hallaq who argued that there has never been a consensus on the closure of the gate of *ijtihad* in Islamic history.[33] Moreover, along with this revision of the standard view of the development of Islamic law, more studies started to address later periods of Islamic legal history, beyond the main concentration on the early formative period. For the purpose of understanding the role of custom in Islamic legal history, this shift of focus away from the early formative period enables a more nuanced understanding of the longitudinal

[29] Ibid., 75. [30] Ibid., 76–85.

[31] Noel Coulson, *Conflicts and Tensions in Islamic Jurisprudence*; Noel Coulson, "Doctrine and Practice in Islamic Law: One Aspect of the Problem," *Bulletin of the School of Oriental and African Studies* 18 (1956): 211–226.

[32] Noel Coulson, *A History of Islamic Law*, 5.

[33] Baber Johansen, "Legal Literature and the Problem of Change: the Case of Land Rent," in *Contingency in a Sacred Law, Legal and Ethical Norms in the Muslim* Fiqh, 446; Rudolph Peters, "*Idjtihad* and *Taqlid* in 18th and 19th Century Islam," *Die Welt des Islams* 20 (1980): 131–145; Wael Hallaq, "Was the Gate of Ijtihad Closed?" *International Journal of Middle East Studies* 16 (1984): 3–41.

or diachronic development of the role of custom throughout the entire course of Islamic legal history. Below I give some examples of studies that aim to shed more light on the role of custom and examine the extent to which these studies improve our understanding of custom as a legal source and its role in effecting legal change.

c. Custom as a Source of Islamic Law

One of the important questions for the historiography of custom in the Islamic legal tradition has been whether custom is recognized as a source of law, and, if yes, how or where it ranks within the hierarchy of Islamic legal sources. One of the recent studies that explore this question in light of modern western scholarship is undertaken by Gideon Libson in his comparative survey of the status of custom in Jewish and Islamic law.[34] Libson argues that while Jewish law recognizes custom as a formal source of law, Islamic law does not.[35] Despite this lack of formal recognition of custom in Islamic law, Libson notes, it was often used as a material source by means of *de facto* recognition through other legitimate sources of law, particularly *istihsan* (juristic preference in consideration of equity).[36] In addition to this *de facto* recognition, Libson notes that custom was also integrated through identification with Sunna and *ijma'*, or through written stipulation.[37] Libson's view, therefore, accords with the standard double image of custom (its "unrecognized" role in the development of Sunna and its "recognized" role in the development of Islamic law as a subsidiary method) that Schacht articulated, as shown earlier.

The main focus of Libson's study is the Hanafi school from the seventh to eleventh centuries CE, which corresponds with the Geonic period in Iraq, but he also offers a general outline of the development of custom throughout the course of the Islamic legal tradition. Following Chafik Chehata's periodization—dividing the Islamic legal tradition into three main periods: preclassical (until the end of the ninth century), classical (from the tenth to twelfth centuries), and postclassical (from the twelfth century onwards)—Libson identifies five main stages of development that custom underwent. The first, during the preclassical period, marks the incorporation of custom through Sunna and *ijma'*. Libson concentrates on the connection between custom and Sunna, particularly insofar as Sunna itself originates in custom, which conforms to the foreign origins thesis.[38] The second corresponds with early

[34] Gideon Libson, "On the Development of Custom as a Source of Law in Islamic Law," *Islamic Law and Society* 4 (1997): 131–155; Gideon Libson, *Jewish and Islamic Law, a Comparative Study of Custom during the Geonic Period*; see also his entry on *'Urf* in the *Encyclopedia of Islam*, second edition.

[35] Libson, "On the Development of Custom," 136–137.

[36] Ibid., 138. [37] Ibid. [38] Ibid., 139.

unsuccessful attempts to recognize custom as a formal source. The third marks the incorporation of custom as a material source through other sources such as *istihsan*. The fourth, from the eleventh century onwards, marks the infusion of custom with the power of written stipulations. And the fifth, from the sixteenth century onwards, denotes its consolidation as a formal source of law.[39]

Libson's account of the development of custom in the Hanafi school, which he extends to the entire Islamic legal tradition, offers an illustrative example of the current state of scholarship and serves as a working model for further scholarly explorations of the topic. The model shows the gradual and incremental development that custom went through but it leaves several gaps that need to be filled in each stage of this development. Before addressing this developmental framework, it should be noted that the reluctance of Muslim jurists to recognize custom as a primary or formal source may be attributed to a concern to preserve the relationship of legal sources to divine authority, believed to be inherent in the scriptural sources, rather than to a deliberate attempt to conceal the foundational role of custom in the development of legal thought. As Baber Johansen notes: "the normative structure of *fiqh* is based on scriptural authority and the notion that 'undisputable and certain knowledge' (*'ilm yaqin*) can only be found in the texts of revelation."[40] Legal constructions must, therefore, be anchored in or attached to this divine guidance. While the fixed nature of the primary sources can keep this connection intact, the circumstantial and changeable nature of custom cannot.[41]

To return to Libson's framework, his account of the development of custom in the preclassical period does not address the Qura'nic treatment of the concept of custom. As noted earlier, the two terms *'urf* and *ma'ruf* occur in the Qur'an quite frequently to denote not only what is known but also what is good, praiseworthy, and commendable. In fact this connection between what is known/customary and what is commendable at this linguistic level may allude to the prima facie positive connotation of custom in the Islamic tradition. Apart from direct references in the Qur'an and the Sunna to *'urf* and *ma'ruf*, several passages also include indirect references to the concept of *'urf*, and this is where many of the relevant paradigmatic cases of substantive law originate. Those cases often involve exceptions made to general rules in observance of customary practices such as the sale with advance payment (*salam*), in which payment is made for a commodity to be delivered at a future date. This type of sale is an exception to the ban on the sale of goods that are not readily available at the conclusion of the transaction.[42]

According to Libson's account, the early unsuccessful attempts to elevate the status of custom to a formal source of law are traced back to opinions in the early

[39] Libson, "On the Development of Custom," 141–142.

[40] Johansen, "The Muslim *Fiqh*," 25.

[41] Mohammad Hashim Kamali, *Principles of Islamic Jurisprudence*, 381.

[42] For more on this and other examples, see Ayman Shabana, *Custom in Islamic Law*, 45–58.

Hanafi tradition concerning methods of determining the units of measurement for certain items. More particularly, the discussion is traced back to a *hadith* that bans unequal exchange of the six items constituting common types of staple food and which are known in the tradition as *al-asnaf al-ribawiyya*. According to this *hadith* four items are measured by volume (wheat, barley, dates, salt) and two by weight (gold and silver). The question that was debated in the tradition was whether the *hadith* was meant to fix the units of measurement for these items or was rather meant to accommodate the custom that determined these units. According to the first view, these units should remain unchangeable because this is based on a clear text. According to the second view, they can change because these units were determined on the basis of the contemporary common custom, and therefore if the custom changes, so also should the rule. The majority opinion in the Hanafi tradition supported the first view on the grounds that whatever the text stipulates cannot be trumped by a weaker authority (i.e. custom). The minority opinion, which is attributed to Abu Yusuf (d. 182/798), reasoned that accommodation of custom does not amount to conflict with the text because the text in this case is based on custom.

The question raised in the literature is whether Abu Yusuf's opinion was meant to give precedence to custom even if it conflicts with the Sunna in general or if it conflicts with a Sunna that was based on custom. On this point Libson seems to support the former view: "Abu Yusuf's position was rejected in the classical *fiqh* literature in favor of the opposing view: *nass* prevails over custom—and it was this latter view that colored much of the treatment of custom by Hanafi jurists."[43] Similarly Wael Hallaq notes: "Sarakhsi's recognition of custom on a case-by-case basis is but one illustration of the success of the thesis of the divine origins of the law, a thesis that ensured the near decimation of Abu Yusuf's doctrine and its likes."[44] Hallaq highlights the role of custom in the process of legal construction by offering a close analysis of the famous treatise on custom by the Syrian Hanafi jurist Ibn ʿAbidin (d. 1252/1836).[45] On the opinion attributed to Abu Yusuf, Ibn ʿAbidin notes:

> If you say it was reported that Abu Yusuf recognized custom in these [six] textually-indicated items to the extent that he allowed equal exchange of gold by volume and of wheat by weight if this exchange is based on common custom, since this (the implementation of custom) justifies overlooking the text, which means that according to him (Abu Yusuf) it would be permissible to engage in similar transactions even when they involve usury if they (the transactions) are based on common custom, I [Ibn ʿAbidin] respond by saying: God forbid that this would be what Abu Yusuf did indeed mean. What he meant, rather, was to justify the rationale of the text on the basis of custom, meaning that the text specified the measurement of wheat, barley, dates, and salt by volume and the measurement of gold and silver by weight due to the contemporary custom [at the time of the Prophet]. Therefore, the text in

[43] Shabana, *Custom in Islamic Law*, 145; Libson, *Jewish and Islamic Law*, 74.

[44] Wael Hallaq, *Authority, Continuity, and Change*, 219.

[45] On Ibn ʿAbidin's treatment of custom, see also Ahmad Atif Ahmad, *Islam, Modernity, Violence, and Everyday Life*, 83–115.

this case is based on the common custom. If the custom at that time was the measurement of wheat by weight and gold by volume, the text would have indicated so as well. The rule then would be whenever the operative cause of a text in the determination of measurement either by volume or weight is custom, it becomes the main factor in question. Whenever it changes, so also does the rule. In this case, the recognition of the changing custom does not entail violation of the text but implementation thereof. The discussion of the eminent jurist Ibn al-Humam seems to support this interpretation.[46]

Hallaq recognizes that Abu Yusuf's opinion on the authority of custom is interpreted by Ibn 'Abidin as being applicable to a certain type of prophetic Sunna, rather than to the category of prophetic Sunna per se.[47] It is, however, unclear the extent to which there were opinions in the Hanafi tradition that resisted the view attributed to Abu Yusuf in view of its giving precedence to custom over prophetic Sunna in general, not just over a custom-based Sunna, as Ibn 'Abdin observes. The above passage from Ibn 'Abidin's treatise reveals the controversy in the Hanafi tradition surrounding the opinion of Abu Yusuf and also how Ibn 'Abidin interprets it. The question that Libson's and Hallaq's studies raise on the extent to which there were efforts in the Hanafi school, or other legal schools, to elevate custom to the status of a formal source that could trump a text in cases of conflict seems to be worthy of further investigation in future research. In this regard it is important to note that juristic discussions on the negotiation of potential conflicts between a text (*nass*) and any other subsidiary source or evidence deemed to be of lesser weight (or exceptions to general rules due to common custom) is expressed in terms of particularization (*takhsis*), by means of which the scope of a general text is limited in a manner that allows exclusion of certain cases out of the domain of a general principle. Sherman Jackson studied some of the juristic procedures that comparative legal scholars refer to as "legal scaffolding" and how custom is used in the process. This process characterizes the attitude of jurists at a more developed stage of a legal tradition. Through legal scaffolding, Jackson notes: "rather than abandon existing rules in favor of new interpretations of the sources (i.e. *ijtihad* proper), jurists seek needed adjustments through new divisions, exceptions, distinctions, prerequisites, and expanding or restricting the scope of existing laws."[48]

The third stage that Libson marks for the incorporation of custom as a material source through other sources, especially *istihsan*, underscores a process that most of what later became known as secondary or subsidiary sources—*istihsan* itself, *maslaha* (benefit/welfare/utility/interest), custom—underwent: i.e. inductive abstraction of norms out of numerous substantive cases. Again the example of *salam* is instructive because in the early stages of the tradition it is found in Prophetic

[46] Ibn 'Abidin, "*Nashr al-'Arf fi Bina' ba'd al-Ahkam 'ala al-'Urf*," 116.

[47] Hallaq, *Authority, Continuity, and Change*, 225.

[48] Sherman Jackson, "*Taqlid*, Legal Scaffolding and the Scope of Legal Injunctions in post-Formative Theory, *Mutlaq* and *'Amm* in the Jurisprudence of Shihab al-Din al-Qarafi," *Islamic Law and Society* 3 (1996): 165–192, 167; see also Shabana, "*'Urf* and *'Adah*."

reports in which the Prophet allows this type of sale in view of a common custom in Medina.[49] Early Hanafi discussions on *istihsan* are centered on a number of examples which, similar to *salam*, constitute departure from a general rule. *Istihsan* is considered a type of implicit analogical reasoning (*qiyas khafi*), in which a conclusion on the basis of a straightforward *qiyas* is overlooked in favor of another conclusion deemed to be more equitable. The Hanafi jurist al-Bazdawi (d. 482/1089) notes that departure from a straightforward *qiyas* to *istihsan* may be justified on the basis of three considerations: tradition (such as the case of *salam*), *ijma*ʿ (such as the case of the contract of manufacture or *istisna*ʿ), and necessity.[50] Later juristic discussions on custom began to appeal to the logic of *istihsan* with or without reference to *istihsan* itself. This can be seen in the examples that these discussions invoke, which were often traced back to cases such as *salam* and *istisna*ʿ.[51] Both these types of contracts, though involving a departure from the general principle that prohibits the sale of non-existent commodities, were approved on the basis of common custom, which the Prophet explicitly approved in the case of *salam*. This process of inductive abstraction reveals the gradual and incremental development of the concept of custom from scattered references in various substantive cases into a full-fledged legal norm that is used in its own right, even without reference to these substantive cases.[52] Following the debates on the origins of Islamic law, a skeptical attitude toward the historicity of these origins would view paradigmatic cases such as *salam* and *istisna*ʿ as being antecedent to the prophetic reports in the tradition, which were meant to provide textual support for these cases. Therefore, rather than seeing a development from *hadith*-based cases to abstract norms such as *istihsan* or custom, later cases are seen as having been projected backwards as *hadith* to enhance the legal authority of these cases.

The fourth and fifth stages that Libson identifies in the development of custom, from the eleventh century on, mark its steadily increasing significance. It is clear that custom acquired more prominence in the later stages of the tradition and this is clearly reflected in the juristic works of later scholars who tended to modify elements in the legal doctrines of their schools in view of changing customs. Two general observations, which Libson does not address thoroughly, should be made here. The first is the role of non-legal discussions, particularly in theology, in the development of custom as a legal norm. Muslim theologians appealed to the various connotations of custom in several debates on issues such as religious obligation

[49] Ibn Hajar al-ʾAsqalani, *Fath al-Bari*, 4:534 (*hadith* no. 2240); Nawawi, *Sahih Muslim*, 11:220.

[50] ʿAlaʾ al-Din Abd al-Aziz al-Bukhari, *Kashf al-Asrar ʿan Usul Fakhr al-Islam al-Bazdawi*, 4:6–7.

[51] Ibn ʿAbidin, "*Nashr al-ʿArf fi Binaʾ baʿd al-Ahkam ʿala al-ʿUrf*," 114. On this point see Libson, "On the Development of Custom," 147 (fn. 42), for more on *istihsan*, see J. Makdisi, "Legal Logic and Equity in Islamic Law," *The American Journal of Comparative Law* 33 (1985): 63–92.

[52] For a similar explanation of the concept of *ʿamal*, see Umar Faruq Abd-Allah, "Malik's Concept of *ʿAmal* in the light of Maliki Legal Theory." Ph.D. diss., University of Chicago, 1978.

(*taklif*) and causality (*sababiyya*). Echoes of these discussions can be traced in similar debates in legal theory, especially in the works of theologian-jurists such as al-Juwayni (d. 478/1085) and al-Ghazali (d. 505/1111).[53] The second is the role of custom in the development of legal genres such as legal maxims and legal objectives (*maqasid*). In the later periods of the Islamic legal tradition, and with higher levels of the inductive abstraction mentioned earlier concerning the development of notions such as *istihsan*, several legal genres gradually emerged to both explain and inform the process of legal construction. This is clearly illustrated in legal maxims that underscore the importance of a recognized common custom by equating it with a written stipulation.[54]

D. Custom and Legal Change

Apart from the question of whether the gate of *ijtihad* was closed or not, students of Islamic legal history are more interested in the question of legal change and the mechanisms through which such change is effected. Tracing a legal system's response to changing social customs is an important measure of its ability to accommodate change and still maintain its continuity. Shifting the focus from theoretical issues such as the origins of Islamic sources or the scope of *ijtihad* to tracing actual change coincided with scholarly interest in Islamic legal genres as sources from which invaluable information for the reconstruction of social, political, and economic history can be gleaned. This is evident in the work of several scholars who paid close attention to changes in legal doctrines due to changes in social customs.

One illustrative example is Baber Johansen's examination of developments in the later Hanafi legal corpus concerning the question of land tax and rent. Johansen explains changes in Hanafi legal doctrines by pointing out the role and function of legal genres. Different legal genres serve different purposes, so when competing legal opinions are found therein they should not be seen as contradictory. While textbooks maintain older doctrines and are used mainly for teaching purposes, other genres such as commentaries, treatises, and *fatawa* may introduce new solutions for new problems in the process of legal practice.[55] Johansen emphasizes the dual function of Islamic law as a tool for preserving legal and religious doctrines and also as an applied legal system. In this latter capacity Islamic law had to contend with social realities, which often involved changing social customs and emerging needs of particular social, cultural, and economic contexts. He illustrates this point by tracing the change in the Hanafi school doctrine, both in Central Asia during

[53] Shabana, *Custom*, 59–70. [54] Ibid., 111–124.
[55] Johansen, "Legal Literature," 447–448.

the eleventh century and in Ottoman and Mamluk Egypt and Syria, concerning the definition of authorized and unauthorized land use with implications on eligibility for payment of land rent and tax. The examples are meant to assess the extent to which this change was in response to prevalent customs and common social and economic standards.[56]

Johansen also explores the role of custom in legal construction by examining the emergence of casuistic reasoning, which he considers a tool that the jurists used to reconcile the demands of real life with those of legal doctrine.[57] As a legal method, casuistry investigates the applicability of legal concepts to actual incidents and responds to the limits of such applicability to particular cases. An important example that Johansen uses is the contract of *salam* sale. As noted earlier, this type of sale is considered exceptional because, unlike a regular sale contract, the commodity is not exchanged at the time of payment, which necessitates the enumeration of detailed specifications of such commodity to preclude potential disagreement between the buyer and the seller. To a large extent, determination of these specifications is made in light of prevalent customs and standards.[58] Johansen's historical analysis of the examples of land rent and rise of casuistic reasoning in the Hanafi legal tradition offers many insights. In both cases he emphasizes the role of the socio-economic context in the development of legal thought and argues against pure theoretical approaches to the study of Islamic legal issues, which tend to treat Islamic law as a unique or exceptional legal system. He makes analogies to similar developments in European socio-economic history,[59] but these analogies remain in need of further studies to confirm their accuracy and applicability, especially for other contexts and time periods in Islamic history.

Similar to Johansen's work on land rent and casuistic reasoning, Wael Hallaq studied the role of *fatwa* literature in the development of Islamic substantive law. By responding to social needs (and accommodating social customs), the *fatwa* literature was essential for both maintaining the currency of the law while preserving the legal doctrine of legal schools. Hallaq emphasizes the rootedness of the *fatwa* literature in social reality as it responds to actual questions, not hypothetical or fictitious ones.[60] Insofar as the *fatwa* literature is a reflection of social reality, it bears special significance for the evaluation of the role of customary practices in shaping constructed legal rules in particular contexts. As Hallaq notes, the choice

[56] Johansen, "Legal Literature," 450–464; see also Baber Johansen, *The Islamic Law on Land Tax and Rent.*

[57] Baber Johansen, "Casuistry: Between Legal Concept and Social Praxis," *Islamic Law and Society* 2 (1995): 135–156, 149.

[58] Johansen, "Casuistry: Between Legal Concept and Social Praxis," 149–151.

[59] Johansen, "Legal Literature," 461–462; Johansen, "Casuistry: Between Legal Concept and Social Praxis," 140.

[60] Wael Hallaq, "From *Fatwas to Furu'*: Growth and Change in Islamic Substantive Law," *Islamic Law and Society* 1 (1994): 29–65, 32–38, 61.

of particular *fatawa* for inclusion in substantive legal works (*fiqh*) depended largely on "contemporary needs" and cases of "wide occurrence." The process also excluded cases that "ceased to be of relevance to the community and its needs."[61] Hallaq's analysis of the different legal genres and their functions draws upon a classification of the four main roles that the jurists assumed in the tradition: the judge, the juris-consult, the author–jurist, and the professor. Hallaq argues that it was through the efforts of both the juris-consult and the author–jurist that legal doctrines incorporated and reflected legal change.[62] Although judges and professors may also have participated in the process, the major part of the task fell to juris-consults, who performed the necessary hermeneutical tasks required for the adjustment of legal doctrines with changing social conditions, and author–jurists, who integrated new legal opinions within the corpus of legal schools through several juristic and editorial procedures. As biographical dictionaries indicate, many eminent jurists served in more than one capacity and assumed more than one role, but even in those cases these jurists were able to effect legal change more in their roles as juris-consults and author–jurists than as judges and professors.[63]

III. Conclusion and Suggestions for Further Research

This outline of the historiography of custom in the Islamic legal tradition is not meant to serve as an exhaustive survey of the topic but rather as a guide to the important methods used and also to give some examples of representative studies. It shows that custom has been an integral part of discussions of the main questions that have occupied the field of Islamic studies over the past two centuries. This is clearly illustrated in the debate over the origins of Islam and Islamic law and also the debate over the dichotomy between legal theory and social reality. The outline also shows that the final word in these debates has not yet been announced. These debates are periodically rekindled, especially with the discovery and publication of new sources. Therefore, the status, role, and function of custom in the Islamic legal tradition will remain tied to these questions, and current opinions remain subject to reevaluation in light of new evidence.

[61] Hallaq, "From *Fatwas* to *Furu'*: Growth and Change in Islamic Substantive Law," 48–49.
[62] Hallaq, *Authority, Continuity, and Change*, 174.
[63] Ibid., 166–168.

In this outline, the works of Joseph Schacht and Noel Coulson are taken as a starting point because they represent the most authoritative synthesis of the works of earlier authorities in western Islamic studies such as Snouck Hurgronje and Ignaz Goldziher and also because these works have left a lasting impact on the field of Islamic legal studies. In these works, a double image of custom can be clearly identified. The first is custom as a constitutive element in the development of Islam's foundational sources, particularly the Sunna during the formative period of Islam. In this role custom is said to have played a more prominent role than what Muslim sources say explicitly. The second is custom as *'urf*, which Muslim jurists recognized as a source of law, but only in a subsidiary capacity. Another view of the status and role of custom, which accords more with the standard view in the Muslim sources, focuses on the gradual and cumulative nature of the development that custom underwent in Islamic legal history, which begins with references to the *concept* of custom in both the Qur'an and the Sunna.[64]

Available literature suggests that there are at least two possibilities for future research on the topic. The first is to continue the exploration of the historical development of custom itself as a legal tool and, in turn, its role in the development of the entire Islamic legal tradition. Given the current state of scholarship, there is a greater need for more synchronic studies that target specific works, authors, or topics in given social and historical contexts. More accurate diachronic studies will only be possible on the basis of many synchronic studies representing different periods and legal schools in Islamic history. The second is to continue the exploration of the role of custom in the mechanics of the legal process. Here research should not be limited to the usual question as to whether custom is considered a primary source of law. More attention should be devoted to other uses of custom in legal hermeneutics as in the discussions over particularization and justification, or in particular legal genres such as the study of Hallaq on the *fatwa* literature.

More serious research on the role of custom in the Islamic legal tradition is of prime importance mainly because it lies at the interface between abstract legal thought and legal practice. It can improve our understanding of how Islamic law has developed not only in theory but also in real life. Most importantly, custom reveals clearly the balance that legal scholars within the Islamic legal system, or any functional legal system for that matter, seek to achieve between two main objectives: preserving the normative character of the system through commitment to its guiding principles, and responding to the needs of social reality. This balance has proven to be all the more challenging when these guiding principles are believed to be rooted in divine revelation.

[64] Kamali, *Principles of Islamic Jurisprudence*, 381.

References

Abd-Allah, Umar Faruq, "Malik's Concept of *'Amal* in the light of Maliki Legal Theory" (Ph.D. diss., University of Chicago, 1978).

Abu Sunnah, Ahmad Fahmi, *al-'Urf wa-al-'Adah fi Ra'y al-Fuqaha'* (Cairo: Dar al-Basa'ir, 2004).

Ahmad, Ahmad Atif, *Islam, Modernity, Violence, and Everyday Life* (New York: Palgrave, 2009).

Ansari, Zafar Ishaq, "Islamic Juristic Terminology before Safi'i: A Semantic Analysis with Special Reference to Kufa." *Arabica* 19 (1972): 255–300.

Bukhari, 'Ala' al-Din Abd al-Aziz, *Kashf al-Asrar 'an Usul Fakhr al-Islam al-Bazdawi* (Beirut: Dar al-Kutub al-'Ilmiyyah, 1997).

Cook, Michael, *Commanding Right and Forbidding Wrong in Islamic Thought* (Cambridge: Cambridge University Press, 2000).

Coulson, Noel, "Doctrine and Practice in Islamic Law: One Aspect of the Problem." *Bulletin of the School of Oriental and African Studies* 18 (1956): 211–226.

Coulson, Noel, "Muslim Custom and Case-Law." *Die Welt des Islams* 6 (1959): 13–24.

Coulson, Noel, *Conflicts and Tensions in Islamic Jurisprudence* (Chicago: University of Chicago Press, 1969).

Coulson, Noel, *A History of Islamic Law* (Edinburgh: Edinburgh University Press, 1964).

Crone, Patricia, *Roman, Provincial and Islamic Law* (Cambridge: Cambridge University Press, 1987).

Dutton, Yasin, "'*Amal v. Hadith* in Islamic Law, The Case of *Sadl al-Yadayn* (Holding One's Hands By One's Sides) When Doing the Prayer." *Islamic Law and Society* 3 (1996): 13–40.

Dutton, Yasin, *The Origins of Islamic Law, the Qur'an,* the *Muwatta'* and *Madinan 'Amal* (New York: Routledge, 2002).

Goitein, Shelomo Dov, "The Birth-Hour of Muslim Law?: An Essay in Exegesis." *Muslim World* 50 (1960): 23–29.

Hallaq, Wael, "Was the Gate of Ijtihad Closed?" *International Journal of Middle East Studies* 16 (1984): 3–41.

Hallaq, Wael, "From Fatwas to Furu: Growth and Change in Islamic Substantive Law." *Islamic Law and Society* 1 (1994): 29–65.

Hallaq, Wael, *Authority, Continuity, and Change* (Cambridge: Cambridge University Press, 2001).

Hallaq, Wael, *Origins and Evolution of Islamic Law* (Cambridge: Cambridge University Press, 2005).

Hallaq, Wael, "Groundwork for the Moral Law: A New Look at the Qur'an and the Genesis of Sharia." *Islamic Law and Society* 16 (2009): 239–279.

Humphreys, Stephen, *Islamic History, a Framework for Inquiry* (Princeton: Princeton University Press, 1991).

Ibn 'Abidin, Muhammad Amin, "*Nashr al-'Arf fi bina' ba'd al-ahkam 'ala al-'Urf*" in *Majmu'at Rasa'il Ibn 'Abidin* (Beirut: Dar Ihya' Dar al-Turath al-'Arabi, n.d.).

Ibn Hajar al-'Asqalani, *Fath al-Bari bi Sharh Sahih al-Bukhari* (Cairo: Maktabat al-'Ilm, 2000).

Ibn Manzur, *Lisan al-'Arab* (18 vols. Beirut: Dar Sadir, 2008).

Jackson, Sherman, "Taqlid, Legal Scaffolding and the Scope of Legal Injunctions in post-Formative Theory: *Mutlaq* and *'Amm* in the Jurisprudence of Shihab al-Din al-Qarafi." *Islamic Law and Society* 3 (1996): 165–192.

Johansen, Baber, *The Islamic Law on Land Tax and Rent: the Peasants' Loss of Property Rights as Interpreted in the Hanafite Legal Literature of the Mamluk and Ottoman Periods* (London: Croom Helm, 1988).
Johansen, Baber, "Casuistry: Between Legal Concept and Social Praxis." *Islamic Law and Society* 2 (1995): 135–156.
Johansen, Baber, "Legal Literature and the Problem of Change: the Case of Land Rent" in Baber Johansen (ed.) *Contingency in a Sacred Law, Legal and Ethical Norms in the Muslim Fiqh* (Leiden: Brill, 1999) 446–464.
Johansen, Baber, "The Muslim Fiqh as a Sacred Law, Religion, Law and Ethics in a Normative System" in Baber Johansen (ed.) *Contingency in a Sacred Law, Legal and Ethical Norms in the Muslim Fiqh* (Leiden: Brill, 1999) 1–77.
Jurjani, 'Ali b. Muhammad, *al-Ta'rifa* (Beirut: Dar al-Kutub al-'Ilmiyyah, 2009).
Kamali, Mohammad Hashim, *Principles of Islamic Jurisprudence* (Cambridge: The Islamic Texts Society, 2003).
Libson, Gideon, "On the Development of Custom as a Source of Law in Islamic Law." *Islamic Law and Society* 4 (1997): 131–155.
Libson, Gideon, *Jewish and Islamic Law: A Comparative Study of Custom during the Geonic Period* (Cambridge, MA: Harvard University Press, 2003).
Makdisi, J., "Legal Logic and Equity in Islamic Law." *The American Journal of Comparative Law* 33 (1985): 63–92.
Motzki, Harald, *The Origins of Islamic Jurisprudence, Meccan Fiqh before the Classical Schools* (Leiden: Brill, 2002).
Nawawi, *Sahih Muslim bi Sharh al-Nawawi* (Cairo: Dar al-Manar, 2003).
Peters, Rudolph, "Idjtihad and Taqlid in 18th and 19th Century Islam." *Die Welt des Islams* 20 (1980): 131–145.
Peters, Rudolph, "[Book Review]: *The Islamic Law on Land Tax and Rent: the Peasants' Loss of Property Rights as Interpreted in the Hanafite Legal Literature of the Mamluk and Ottoman Periods,* by Baber Johansen," *Die Welt des Islams* 30 (1990): 245–247.
Raghib al-Isfahani, *al-Mufradat fi Gharib al-Qur'an* (Beirut: Dar al-Ma'rifa, 2010).
Rahman, Fazlur, *Islamic Methodology in History* (Karachi: Central Institute of Islamic Research, 1965).
Schacht, Joseph, "Foreign Elements in Ancient Islamic Law." *Journal of Comparative Legislation and International Law* 32 (1950): 9–17.
Schacht, Joseph, *Origins of Muhammadan Jurisprudence* (Oxford: Clarendon Press, 1967).
Schacht, Joseph, *An Introduction to Islamic Law* (Oxford: Clarendon Press, 1982).
Shabana, Ayman, "'*Urf* and '*Adah* within the Framework of Al-Shatibi's Legal Methodology." *UCLA Journal of Islamic and Near Eastern Law* 6 (2006–07): 87–100.
Shabana, Ayman, *Custom in Islamic Law and Legal Theory, the Development of the Concepts of* 'Urf *and* 'Adah *in the Islamic Legal Tradition* (New York: Palgrave, 2010).

CHAPTER 10

THE HISTORIOGRAPHY OF SUNNI USUL AL-FIQH

YOUCEF SOUFI

USUL *al-fiqh* can and has been translated by the cognate terms "Islamic jurisprudence," "legal theory," "source law," and "legal methodology."[1] A historically common definition of the term among Muslim jurists was "the proofs of the law" (*usul al-fiqh adillatuhu*), meaning that *usul al-fiqh* referred to the types of proofs admissible when deriving legal rulings.[2] Thus for these jurists the study or science (*'ilm*) of *usul al-fiqh* was the inquiry into those valid categories of proofs: its purpose was both to explicate these categories as well as to provide arguments for their validity. Importantly, *usul al-fiqh* was different from *furu' al-fiqh* (substantive law): the former literally meant the roots (*usul*) of the law (*fiqh*) and the latter its branches (*furu'*), conveying the tree-like image that from *usul al-fiqh* substantive law developed. By the fourth/tenth century, the production of books dedicated to *usul al-fiqh* historically became common across Sunni schools of law. As some contemporary

[1] Joseph Schacht used the term jurisprudence in *The Origins of Muhammadan Jurisprudence*; Bernard G. Weiss has suggested the more nuanced view that Islamic jurisprudence includes both *usul al-fiqh* and *fiqh* (the elaboration of rules of law), the former being more properly called theoretical jurisprudence, Weiss, *The Spirit of Islamic Law*, xi. This has led him and others like Wael Hallaq to speak of it also as legal theory or methodology. Hallaq, *A History of Islamic Legal Theories*, 1; Hallaq, *Shari'a*, 18. Taha Jabir al-Alwani for his part prefers to use the expression "source methodology," an expression conveying the sense that *usul al-fiqh* acts as the foundation of the law. Al-Alwani, *Source Methodology in Islamic Jurisprudence*.

[2] For an elaboration of this definition within the work of Sayf al-Din al-Amidi (d. 631/1233), see Weiss, *The Search for God's Law*, 23.

scholars of Islamic law have pointed out, these texts form a distinct genre of Islamic legal literature.[3]

This chapter surveys scholarship on the history of Sunni *usul al-fiqh* during the premodern period.[4] In the first part, the chapter examines scholarship on the history of *usul al-fiqh* from the second AH/eighth CE to the middle of the fourth/tenth centuries. It focuses on debates about when and how jurists began to produce texts dedicated to the exposition of *usul al-fiqh*. In doing so it traces scholarly accounts of the gradual shift from early rudimentary discussions on legal methodology to systematic and detailed elaborations in what Joseph Lowry calls mature texts of *usul al-fiqh*.[5] The second part of the chapter examines scholarship on *usul al-fiqh* sources from the late fourth/tenth up until the tenth/sixteenth century. Though *usul al-fiqh* continued to develop in this period, it had become a stable genre in which jurists of all Sunni schools debated over a similar set of methodological questions. The historical studies reviewed in this section therefore turn to understanding the key intellectual debates within this genre and their relevance to legal practice.

I. The Emergence of *Usul al-fiqh*

Scholarship is divided on the question of the origins of *usul al-fiqh*. Scholars debate how the genre emerged, when it gained currency, and which jurist or group of jurists were responsible for its initiation. Muhammad ibn Idris al-Shafi'i (d. 204/820), is often credited by Muslim sources as having founded *usul al-fiqh* with his famed epistle, *al-Risala*.[6] Recently, however, several scholars have questioned this attribution, arguing that the term *usul al-fiqh* should only be reserved for methodology texts written a century or so after Shafi'i. This section makes use of the debate about whether al-Shafi'i can properly be considered the founder of *usul al-fiqh* in order to lay bare the historiography on *usul al-fiqh*'s early development.

[3] See in particular Devin Stewart, "Muhammad b. Da'ud al-Zahiri's Manual of Jurisprudence, al-Wusul ila Ma'rifat al-Usul" in *The Formation of Islamic Law*, ed. Wael B. Hallaq (Burlington: Ashgate, 2004) 277–315. Weiss countered this view, arguing that Muslim jurists themselves would have seen *usul al-fiqh* not as a genre but as a "science" (*'ilm*), "Alta Discussion," 396.

[4] Although the premodern/modern periods can be dated differently, Hallaq identifies the nineteenth century as the turning point in which new legal methodologies were produced to grapple with the challenges of modernity. Hallaq, *A History of Islamic Legal Theories*, 212.

[5] Lowry, *Early Islamic Legal Theory*, 13.

[6] Al-Shafi'i, *The Epistle on Legal Theory* translated by Joseph Lowry.

A. The Argument that al-Shafi'i is the Founder of *Usul al-Fiqh*

Early western scholarship uncritically accepted Muslim accounts that identified al-Shafi'i as the founder of *usul al-fiqh*. Ignác Goldziher in the late nineteenth century wrote of the *Risala*: "This work... is the point of departure of Islamic legal sciences."[7] Joseph Schacht's seminal *Origins of Mohammadan Jurisprudence* further promoted this view such that by the 1960s, Noel Coulson felt fully justified in calling al-Shafi'i the "master architect" of *usul al-fiqh*.[8] Coulson et al. argued that al-Shafi'i was the first Muslim jurist to pen a treatise fully explaining his legal methodology. They saw al-Shafi'i as breaking from the early jurists, who were content to simply catalogue their conclusions in jurisprudence, and considered his *Risala* to have provided the schematic foundation for all later texts of *usul al-fiqh*.

Schacht's *Origins* exposited what became the standard view on the state of *usul al-fiqh* prior to al-Shafi'i. Legal debates were concentrated in Medina and Iraq at the time and Schacht tended to minimize the differences between these early geographical schools of law.[9] He characterized law as being grounded in "the 'living tradition' of the ancient schools," by which he meant the traditional legal practice of a locality.[10] This practice developed over time, originally articulated through gubernatorial decrees, judicial rulings, and jurists' non-textual—and therefore independent—reasoning (*ra'y*). Eventually, these positions were given sanction through traditions (*hadith*) traced back to respected individuals, including but not limited to, the Prophet.[11] The basic outlines of this view have not been significantly challenged, though historians have amended features of it.[12]

According to Schacht, al-Shafi'i wrote the *Risala* because of his dissatisfaction with the living traditions' lack of methodological consistency. For instance, in his polemical work *Ikhtilaf Malik wa al-Shafi'i*, al-Shafi'i attacked the Medinese reliance on the customary practice (*'amal*) of its jurists as involving an arbitrary use of personal reason:

> You claim that the judges give judgment only in accordance with the opinion of the scholars, and you claim that the scholars do not disagree. But it is not so ... Where is the

[7] Goldziher, *Muslim Studies*, 2:86. [8] Coulson, *A History of Islamic Law*, 53.

[9] Schacht, *The Origins of Muhammadan Jurisprudence*, 7.

[10] Ibid., 5. Hallaq disputed the existence of geographical schools, asserting that they were always personal, see Hallaq, "From Regional to Personal Schools of Law?"

[11] Schacht, *The Origins of Muhammadan Jurisprudence*, 99.

[12] Fazlur Rahman for instance agreed that the *ra'y* of a variety of authorities was considered part of the *sunna* in this period, but contended that this *sunna* was still conceived as a continuation of an ideal prophetic *sunna*, Rahman, "Concepts Sunnah, Ijtihad and Ijma' in the Early Period." Yasin Dutton in his study of the concept of *'amal* in the thought of Malik ibn Anas, the chief of the Medinan jurists, agreed that the law was transmitted through practice, but suggested early Muslims conceived of this practice as a non-textual means of linking back to the prophet and his *sunna*, Dutton, *The Origins of Islamic Law: The Qur'an, the Muwatta' and Madinan 'Amal* (Surrey, England: Curzon, 1999), 4.

practice? ... We do not know what you mean by practice, and you do not know either, as far as we can see. We are forced to conclude that you call your own opinions practice and consensus, and speak of practice and consensus when you mean only your own opinions.[13]

Responding to this state of affairs, al-Shafi'i sought to bring methodological coherence to legal reasoning by clearly enumerating the valid sources of law. The result was what many have called the "classical theory" of *usul al-fiqh*, which traces the whole of the legal system to four sources, or, valid proofs: "The Koran, the sunna of the Prophet, that is his ideal behaviour, the consensus of the orthodox community, and the method of analogy."[14]

Schacht and others identified in al-Shafi'i's intervention a remarkable shift in the self-awareness of juristic practice. Goldziher spoke of the "disciplining of reason" by limiting the *ra'y* of previous periods to analogical reasoning based on a source-text, i.e. the Qur'an or prophetic *sunna* (exemplary behavior).[15] More recently, Ahmed El Shamsy has contended that al-Shafi'i's methodology elevated the texts of revelation to independent sources of law. Rather than sifting and interpreting the Qur'an and *hadith* through the experiences of the Muslim community, al-Shafi'i's methodology made these texts the "fount of normativity itself."[16]

Historians point out that al-Shafi'i's theory emerged from his particular socio-historical context, which straddled two dominant movements of his time. On the one hand, Schacht identified al-Shafi'i with the emerging traditionist (*ahl al-hadith*) movement.[17] Schacht considered this group to have emerged in the first half of the second/eighth century in opposition to those exercising independent reasoning, namely the "people of opinion" (*ahl al-ra'y*) The traditionists, in Schacht's account, held that "[F]ormal traditions from the Prophet supersede the 'living tradition' of the early schools."[18] Al-Shafi'i's *usul al-fiqh* aimed at defending and developing a coherent legal methodology for this movement. On the other hand, Schacht noted that many of al-Shafi'i's propositions on *hadith* and analogical reasoning (*qiyas*) had been influenced by his sojourn in Iraq and interactions with the Hanafi authority Muḥammad ibn Ḥasan al-Shaybani. Thus, distinctly recognizable elements of *usul al-fiqh*, such as its terminology and many of its key propositions, predate

13 Schacht, *The Origins of Muhammadan Jurisprudence*, 69.

14 Ibid., 1. See also Coulson, *A History of Islamic Law*, 55.

15 Goldziher, *The Zahiris*, 20–21.

16 El Shamsy, *The Canonization of Islamic Law*, 4. For changes to the concept of *ijma'*, see Rahman, "Concepts *Sunnah, Ijtihad* and *Ijma'* in the Early Period," 20.

17 Schacht, *The Origins of Muhammadan Jurisprudence*, 56–57.

18 Ibid., 253. For the methodology of the traditionists, see Lucas, "Principles of Traditionist Jurisprudence Reconsidered"; Lucas, "Where Are the Legal Hadith?"; Melchert, "Traditionist-Jurisprudents and the Framing of Islamic Law"; Spectorsky, "Ahmad Ibn Hanbal's Fiqh."

al-Shafiʿi.[19] As John Burton put it, al-Shafiʿi did not "invent" "the rules of *usul al-fiqh*, any more than Aristotle 'invented' the rules of logic, but rather … extracted and codified them."[20]

In sum, those who view al-Shafiʿi as the founder of the science of *usul al-fiqh* emphasized the extent to which he shifted Islamic legal methodology's reliance on a communal living tradition based upon independent juristic reasoning to a scriptural and largely prophetic *hadith*-based tradition with a limited role for reason. This scholarship nonetheless recognized that al-Shafiʿi's thought extended, refined, and systematized that of his predecessors, namely the traditionist movement and the Iraqi jurists. These historians acknowledged the inchoate elements of *usul al-fiqh* in legal reasoning prior to al-Shafiʿi, but considered al-Shafiʿi to have formulated its elements together in a way that permanently shifted the history of Islamic legal thought.

B. On the Emergence of *Usul al-Fiqh* as a Post-Shafiʿi Event: Legal Methodology from 820–981 CE

From the preceding section, one discerns two reasons for considering al-Shafiʿi as the founder of *usul al-fiqh:* 1) he was the first jurist to compose a treatise outlining his legal methodology; and 2) he ushered in what became widely known as classical Islamic legal methodology in the form of his four source theory which subsequent texts of Sunni *usul al-fiqh* emulated. Scholarship in the last thirty years has contested both these propositions. Some have offered an alternative view of the emergence of the genre of *usul al-fiqh* and others have simply sought to qualify the importance of al-Shafiʿi to its development. What follows traces these scholarly debates about the development of *usul al-fiqh* during the third/ninth and fourth/tenth centuries.

George Makdisi, in an article entitled "The Juridical Theology of al-Shafiʿi: Origins and Significance of *Usul al-Fiqh*," was the first to present evidence questioning the influence of al-Shafiʿi on subsequent texts of *usul al-fiqh* (proposition 2). Makdisi noted that it took two centuries after al-Shafiʿi wrote the *Risala* (late fourth/tenth–early fifth/eleventh centuries) for the term *usul al-fiqh* to formally designate the science of legal methodology, or, jurisprudence.[21] He also identified in later *usul al-fiqh* texts a thematic departure from the *Risala* in that they incorporated questions and postulates pertaining to another Islamic science, namely rationalistic theology (*kalam*). In spite of his findings, Makdisi maintained that the *Risala* was the first

[19] As Z.I. Ansari demonstrated, the Iraqis' use of terms such as *hadith, ijmaʿ*, and *qiyas* prior to al-Shafiʿi evince a "comparative lack of fixity in the technical connotation of their jurisprudential language." Ansari, "Islamic Juristic Terminology before Safiʿi," 255.

[20] Burton, *The Sources of Islamic Law*, 15.

[21] Makdisi, "The Juridical Theology of Shafiʿi": 8–9.

book of legal methodology and that al-Shafiʿi was therefore the founder of *usul al-fiqh*.

In contrast, Wael Hallaq's article "Was al-Shafiʿi the Master Architect of Islamic Jurisprudence?" denied both that al-Shafiʿi had written a text of legal methodology and that his epistle gave rise to the production of texts of *usul al-fiqh* (propositions 1 and 2). Hallaq not only pointed to the time separating the *Risala* from later texts of *usul al-fiqh*, but also affirmed that the *Risala* was completely ignored for a century after its composition. Beyond causation, Hallaq contended that the *Risala's* structure and purpose distinguished it from later texts of *usul al-fiqh*. On the basis of these later texts, he defined *usul al-fiqh* as "a systematic, comprehensive, and organically structured legal methodology whose purpose in turn is to derive legal rulings from the material sources."[22] The *Risala*, in his view, did not conform to these characteristics. He identified it instead as a treatise concerned with arguing for the privileged use of prophetic *hadith* in legal reasoning.[23]

Hallaq contended that the appearance in the fourth/tenth century of several works of *usul al-fiqh* was therefore a product not of the *Risala*, but of what he calls the synthesis between the *ahl al-raʾy* and the *ahl al-hadith*. Hallaq believed that a rapprochement took place between these two movements during the third/ninth century, making propitious the development of a legal theory that established the primacy of *hadith* as a source of law, while also acknowledging a place for reason through *qiyas*. Rather than al-Shafiʿi, Hallaq considered that the Baghdad leader of the Shafiʿi school, Ibn Surayj (d. 306/918), and his students should be credited with first theorizing the key questions found in classical texts of *usul al-fiqh* and then producing the first treatises dedicated to their full exposition. This generation's scholarly endeavors sparked a new interest in the *Risala*, evidenced by several fourth/tenth century commentaries on it, resulting in a reverse-attribution of the treatise as the founding text of what, in reality, was a newly emerging genre.[24]

Joseph Lowry, who has offered the most sustained engagement with the *Risala* to date, also denied that the *Risala* is a text of *usul al-fiqh*.[25] While arguing that the *Risala* was a treatise of methodology—"perhaps the first work of Islamic legal theory"—Lowry pointed out five differences between the *Risala* and later, more mature texts of *usul al-fiqh*.[26] First, the *Risala* was more immediately concerned with positive or substantive legal questions. Second, the *Risala's* use of examples made it less abstract and theoretical than later works. Third, later texts incorporated questions of theology absent in the *Risala*. Fourth, rules of scriptural hermeneutics were barely addressed in the *Risala*, despite figuring prominently in mature *usul*

[22] Hallaq, "Was al-Shafiʿi the Master Architect of Islamic Jurisprudence?," 588.

[23] Ibid., 592–593. [24] Ibid., 599; see also Reinhart, *Before Revelation*, 15–17.

[25] Lowry saw the *Risala* primarily as a text seeking "to eliminate the apparent conflicts" between the Qur'an and the Sunna. Lowry, *Early Islamic Legal Theory*, 359. It therefore sought to provide not only a defense of prophetic *hadith*, but also to provide a coherent vision of the structure of the law, 23.

[26] Ibid., 359–368.

al-fiqh texts. And last, the function of the *Risala* was neither to help judges adjudicate between claims nor to train jurists, in the manner that mature texts of *usul al-fiqh* sought to do. One might add that Lowry also rejected that al-Shafiʿi posited the classical four source theory of law.[27]

The thesis that Shafiʿi was not the architect of *usul al-fiqh* has prompted several scholarly rejoinders. Most of these critiqued Hallaq's sweeping claim that the *Risala* elicited little interest in the fouth/ninth century. Sherman Jackson, for instance, has gestured toward the numerous Maliki texts with the title *al-Radd ʿala al-Shafiʿi* (The Refutation of al-Shafiʿi) in this period, and Devin Stewart has argued that Ibn Dawud al-Zahiri (d. 270/884), among others, did compose fourth/ninth century treatises belonging to the genre of *usul al-fiqh*.[28] It is however, Murtaza Bedir's "An Early Response to al-Shafiʿi: ʿIsa ibn Aban on the Prophetic Report" that most clearly highlighted the *Risala*'s nearly immediate impact on methodological debates. Bedir gathered the Hanafi jurist Ibn Aban's (d. 221/836) methodological propositions recorded in Abu Bakr al-Jassas's (d. 370/981) later text of *usul al-fiqh*, and demonstrated that Ibn Aban critiqued the status that al-Shafiʿi granted single-narrator (*ahad*) prophetic *hadith* when determining law. Though his article indicated that al-Shafiʿi did influence early discussions on legal methodology, Bedir nonetheless conceded to Hallaq that the *Risala* was primarily concerned with the defense of prophetic *hadith*, rather than with expositing a complete methodological system.[29] This concession indicates his agreement with Hallaq's attack of proposition 1.

Bedir's study also suggested a more modest influence of the *Risala* on the other Sunni schools of law than Schacht and other early historians supposed. Bedir showed through Ibn Aban that Hanafis attempted to formulate their own *usul al-fiqh* based largely upon earlier developments within their own school of law, such as the school's almost exclusive reliance on widely spread *hadith*, known as *hadith al-jamaʿa* or *mashhur*, as opposed to single-narrator (*ahad*) *hadith*.[30] Based on Bedir's findings, al-Shafiʿi would be seen as a key interlocutor during the formation of the different schools' *usul al-fiqh*, and not the founder of a single classical methodology. Umar F. Abd-Allah Wymann-Landgraf recently added weight to this position in his study of the early Medinan concept of *ʿamal*. Wymann-Landgraf contended, *contra* Schacht, that the early schools of law did possess a remarkably consistent methodology and that this methodology largely endured post-Shafiʿi. He pointed toward the acceptability of disconnected (*mursal*) *hadith* and post-prophetic reports in the non-Shafiʿi schools of law, including the Hanbalis, to buttress his argument.[31]

[27] See Lowry, "Does Shafiʿi Have a Theory of 'Four Sources' of Law?"

[28] Jackson, "Setting the Record Straight" 122; Stewart, "Muhammad b. Daʾud al-Zahiri's Manual of Jurisprudence, *al-Wusul ila Maʿrifat al-Usul*"; Stewart, *Islamic Legal Orthodoxy*, 33–36.

[29] Bedir, "An Early Response to Shafiʿi," 309.

[30] Bedir defined *hadith al-jamaʿa* as "communal reports that do not qualify as *al-mutawatir*," that is, as being transmitted by so many that one is certain of its authenticity, ibid, 297.

[31] Wymann-Landraf, *Malik and Medina*, 13.

A final challenge in identifying al-Shafi'i as the founder of *usul al-fiqh* came from Norman Calder, who argued that early canonical texts of Islamic law cannot be ascribed to their purported authors. Calder considered them to be "organic texts" that were composed over generations by multiple authors. He dated the *Risala's* final redaction to approximately the beginning of the fourth/tenth century.[32] It follows that al-Shafi'i could not be the founder of *usul al-fiqh* because he did not write its founding document. However, it is difficult to sustain Calder's thesis today. Jackson, Bedir, El Shamsy, and Lowry have all advanced claims that make the application of the "organic texts" theory to al-Shafi'i highly unlikely.[33]

The debate about al-Shafi'i as the founder of *usul al-fiqh*, as fascinating as it might be, threatens to obscure the fact that *usul al-fiqh* as a genre underwent rapid development from the late second/eighth–early fourth/tenth centuries. It appears that the *Risala* and al-Shafi'i's legal thought ushered in, or was at the very least seminal, to intense methodological debates in the third/ninth century. The authority of prophetic *hadith* and other legal concerns were hotly debated by Malikis such as Ibn al-Labbad, Hanafis such as Ibn Aban, Zahiris such as Ibn Dawud al-Zahiri, and the early Hanbalis of the *ahl al-hadith* movement.[34] Despite retaining some of their original legal methods, these schools followed al-Shafi'i in elevating the status of prophetic *hadith* and in limiting the authority of non-textual sources of law in *usul al-fiqh*.[35] Whether or not treatises like the *Risala* were composed with the sole intent of outlining a legal methodology is a matter of debate, but what is certain is that the study of legal methodology developed at a faster rate than in the preceding century. This development is what enabled historians to discern in the beginning of the fourth/tenth century the existence of an unmistakable preoccupation among Ibn Surayj and his Shafi'i disciples in Baghdad with producing texts that systematically and comprehensively dealt with the subject-matter of *usul al-fiqh*. As Vishanoff has noted, other schools of law were not far behind in following their example of incorporating *usul al-fiqh* within their teaching curriculum and producing texts on the subject.[36]

Extant texts from the late fourth/tenth century, such as al-Jassas's *Al-Fusul fi al-Usul*, not only confirm the existence of a legal literary genre dealing systematically with methodology, but they also shift scholarly concerns toward understanding this genre and its historical legal relevance, which is the subject of the next section.[37]

[32] Calder, *Studies in Early Muslim Jurisprudence*, 224.

[33] Lowry, "The Legal Hermeneutics of al-Shafi'i and Ibn Qutayba," 15; Jackson, "Setting the Record Straight: Ibn Labbad's Refutation of Al-Shafi'i"; El Shamsy, "Al-Shafi'i's Written Corpus"; Bedir, "An Early Response to Shafi'i."

[34] For the Hanbali response, see El Shamsy, "The First Shafi'i: The Traditionalist Legal Thought of Abu Ya'qub al-Buwayti (d. 231/846)," 319.

[35] Jackson, "Setting the Record Straight" 141–146; Dutton, "'Amal v. Hadith in Islamic Law."

[36] Vishanoff, *The Formation of Islamic Hermeneutics*, 196.

[37] Here I omit Abu al-Hasan al-Karkhi's (d. 340/951) and Abu 'Ali al-Shashi's (d. 344/955) earlier texts of usul al-fiqh because of their fragmentary nature. For these texts, see 'Ubaidallah Ibn al-Husain

II. Understanding the Genre of *Usul al-Fiqh*: Late Tenth–Sixteenth Century

This section presents Islamic law scholars' analyses of extant texts of *usul al-fiqh* (late tenth/fourth–tenth/sixteenth century). It focuses upon three areas of historical concern. The first is the classification of texts of *usul al-fiqh*. Historians have attempted to complicate the traditional Muslim classification of two historical *usul al-fiqh* streams (*tariqa*), namely, that of the theologians (*mutakallimun*) and that of the jurists (*fuqaha'*). The second is the relationship between *usul al-fiqh* and the substantive legal rulings (*furu' al-fiqh*). While *usul al-fiqh* texts allegedly provide a method for developing legal rulings, historians have debated whether and how these texts actually impacted the development of Islamic law. The last area covered in this section is an analysis of the major intellectual themes of *usul al-fiqh*. These themes include, among others, the jurists' rich theories of language and hermeneutics, epistemology, and ethics.

A. Classifying Texts of *Usul al-Fiqh*: The Streams of the *Mutakallimun* and the *Fuqaha'*

Although *usul al-fiqh* texts covered similar topics of legal methodology, they often diverged based on their incorporation, or not, of arguments from rationalistic theology (*kalam*).[38] Ibn Khaldun explained this difference by referring to two historical streams (*tariqa*) of *usul al-fiqh*. He attributed one stream to the theologians (*mutakallimun*), gesturing toward its authors' reliance on theological postulates in the course of developing their legal principles, and identified Shafi'i jurists as its representatives. The second stream he termed that of the jurists (*fuqaha'*), because of its authors' inferred principles of *usul al-fiqh* from examples of existing substantive legal doctrine. He attributed this stream to the Hanafi school of law. Ibn Khaldun's dichotomy has persisted in contemporary Muslim scholarship.[39] M.H. Kamali has elaborated upon the distinction, comparing the *mutakallimun* approach to the work of a legal draftsman and the *fuqaha'* approach to that of a

al-Karkhi, *Risalat Abi'al-Hasan al-Karkhi fi al-Usul*; and Abu 'Ali al-Shashi, *Usul al-Shashi*. They are in any case not much prior to the text of al-Jassas.

[38] Makdisi distinguished rationalistic theology (*kalam*) from traditionalist theology (*usul al-din*) by the former's use of reason in determining its theological postulates, see Makdisi, "Ash'ari and the Ash'arites in Islamic Religious History I," 48. See also for a fuller account of the meaning of *kalam*, Wolfson, *The Philosophy of the Kalam*, 1–2.

[39] Abu Zahra, *Usul al-Fiqh*., 18–24.

judge: "The former is mainly concerned with the exposition of principles whereas the latter tends to develop a synthesis between the principle and the requirements of a particular case."[40] Scholars of Islamic legal studies have sought to significantly complicate Ibn Khaldun's simple dichotomy and in the process posit alternative ways to categorize texts of *usul al-fiqh*.

Makdisi was largely responsible for initiating the historical inquiry into the nature of the dichotomy between the theological and juristic approaches to *usul al-fiqh*.[41] Makdisi explained that *kalam* was in ill-repute after the *mihna* (inquisition from 218/833–233/848), as the traditionalist creed championed by Ahmed ibn Hanbal gained ascendancy and rationalism was vilified.[42] *Mutakallimun*, whether Muʿtazili or the Ashʿari, could henceforth make "a bid for legitimacy" only by their "gaining admission into one of the school's of law."[43] *Mutakallimun* working under the aegis of legal schools, like the Shafiʿi Qadi ʿAbd al-Jabbar (d. 415/1025–26) and his student Abu al-Husayn al-Basri (d. 426/1044), included within their texts of *usul al-fiqh* a heavy dose of arguments and topics drawn from the science of *kalam*. This was responsible for the emergence of the theological stream of *usul al-fiqh*.

Makdisi, however, departed from Ibn Khaldun's contention that the division between a *mutakallimun* and a *fuqaha'* stream can be attributed to the Shafiʿi and Hanafi schools respectively. He argued that there existed traditionalist jurists within each and every legal school who rejected *kalam*'s rationalism and deplored its incorporation within *usul al-fiqh*. He focussed his evidence upon the Shafiʿi school which had long been identified as a bastion of Ashʿari theology.[44] Makdisi for instance contended that the famed fifth/eleventh-century Shafiʿi jurist, Abu Ishaq al-Shirazi (d. 476/1083) rejected Ashʿari *kalam* and belonged to the *fuqaha'* stream of *usul al-fiqh*.[45]

Since Makdisi, the question of al-Shirazi's appurtenance to Ashʿarism has been the subject of intense scrutiny, particularly among French scholars. Marie Bernand's publication of al-Shirazi's creed and her and C. Guillot's subsequent analysis of it made it difficult to uphold the view that al-Shirazi was not an Ashʿari.[46] Nonetheless, Eric Chaumont soon thereafter argued for a subtle distinction not previously countenanced: Shirazi was an Ashʿari in theology but not in *usul al-fiqh*.[47] He supported his position by showing how al-Shirazi overwhelmingly rejected and

[40] Kamali, *Principles of Islamic Jurisprudence*, 9. Kamali's monograph is an overview of *usul al-fiqh*, other overviews include Nyazee, *Islamic Jurisprudence*; Hallaq, *A History of Islamic Legal Theories*; Weiss, *The Spirit of Islamic Law*.

[41] Makdisi, *The Rise of Humanism*, 2–14; Makdisi, "The Juridical Theology of Shafiʿi," 12–13.

[42] Makdisi, *The Rise of Humanism*, 2–14.

[43] Ibid., 22.

[44] See Makdisi, "Ashʿari and the Ashʿarites in Islamic Religious History I."

[45] Ibid., 27–28.

[46] Claude Gilliot, "Deux professions de foi"; Marie Bernand, Introductions to *La Profession de foi d'Abu Ishaq al-Sirazi*, by Abu Ishaq al-Sirazi. See for a divergent view, Turki, "ʿAqida al-Shirazi.

[47] Chaumont, "Encore au sujet de l'Ashʿarism d'Abu Ishaq al-Shirazi."

critiqued Ashʿari *usul al-fiqh* positions. His conclusions buttressed Makdisi's contention that not all Shafiʿis belonged to the approach of the *mutakallimun*.[48]

Conversely, Aron Zysow effectively challenged the claim that Hanafis avoided *kalam* in their *usul al-fiqh*. He illustrated that many Central Asian Hanafi jurists, for example, Abu al-Yusr al-Bazdawi (d. 482/1089) and ʿAla al-Din al-Samarqandi (d. 539/1144), utilized the genre of *usul al-fiqh* to discredit the Muʿtazili doctrines of their Iraqi Hanafi predecessors in favour of their Maturidi theology. One example is the debate on juristic infallibility (*taswib*).[49] The Central Asian Hanafis rejected the Iraqis' position that all juristic interpretations were correct, affirming instead that the truth concerning God's law is singular.[50] Zysow highlighted how the Central Asian Hanafis explicitly affirmed their doctrine as belonging to the people of orthodoxy (*ahl al-haqq*) in opposition to the Muʿtazila, thus making evident the wider theological relevance of the debate.

David Vishanoff recently added another twist to the division between theological and juristic streams. Vishanoff contended that the marker of the *fuqaha'* approach to hermeneutics was its paradoxical view of scriptural language as "ambiguous enough to be manipulated into a coherent system of legal rules, yet clear enough that those rules can be regarded as the plain and obvious meaning of the revealed texts."[51] This approach created a pragmatic legal system by maximizing jurists' interpretive power and interpretive flexibility. In contrast, the Muʿtazili and Ashʿari theologians' legal hermeneutics each lacked one of these twin virtues. By the middle of the fifth/eleventh century, the *fuqaha'* approach consequently triumphed over the *mutakillimun* model of hermeneutics such that "even the most theologically inclined thinkers had found ways to reconcile their hermeneutical principles with the law-oriented theorists' interpretative rules."[52] If Vishanoff is correct, the division between theological and juristic streams—at least in the realm of hermeneutics—most properly belongs to the third/ninth and fourth/tenth centuries.

Alternative categorizations of *usul al-fiqh* texts are possible. Hallaq for instance distinguished between features common to all texts of *usul al-fiqh* and those that admit of variation and should therefore be studied diachronically.[53] He included the four sources of the law, i.e. the Qur'an, the Sunna, *ijmaʿ*, and *qiyas* as part of the former. The diachronic variation between texts included not only *kalam* but also subjects like Greek logic, the debate about the continued existence of jurisconsults

[48] This being said, Chaumont has recently identified in al-Shirazi's *usul al-fiqh* an eclectic combination of Muʿtazili and Ashʿari positions, see Chaumont, "La notion de *wajh al-hikmah*."

[49] Zysow, "Muʿtazilism and Maturidism in Ḥanafi Legal Theory," 239. See also, Zysow, *The Economy of Certainty*, about which Zysow stated "I wished to show that Hanafi *usul al-fiqh* is informed by the same theological concerns as the writings of famous Shafiʿi theologians such as al-Ghazali and Fakhr al-Din al-Razi," 2.

[50] Zysow, "Muʿtazilism and Maturidism in Hanafi Legal Theory," 240.

[51] Vishanoff, *The Formation of Islamic Hermeneutics*, 2.

[52] Ibid., 196.

[53] Hallaq, *A History of Islamic Legal Theories*, vii.

(*mujtahidun*), and the examination of grammatical prepositions (*huruf*).[54] Hallaq's categorization suggests that the division between the *mutakallimun* and the *fuqaha'* is but one among many possible classifications of *usul al-fiqh* texts.

In sum, historians have complicated the simple theological/juristic dichotomy in *usul al-fiqh*. Neither should the Shafi'i school be labeled theological in its entirety nor should the Hanafis be deprived of this appellation. This being said, the distinction is useful analytically because *usul al-fiqh* texts reliance upon *kalam*-based arguments do vary. This remains true in the fifth/eleventh century, even if Vishanoff is right that the juristic approach had made significant inroads in influencing the positions of the theological stream. Thus when Bernard Weiss categorized al-Amidi within the theological stream, he effectively informed his reader of al-Amidi's intellectual lineage and debts to his theologically-inclined Shafi'i predecessors such as Imam al-Haramayn al-Juwayni (d. 478/1085) and Abu Hamid al-Ghazali (d. 505/1111).[55]

B. The Relationship Between *Usul al-Fiqh* and *Furu'*

According to Hallaq, Muslim jurists articulated two purposes in writing *usul al-fiqh* texts. The first consisted in developing a methodology to guide the jurist's derivation of new laws. In this sense, *usul al-fiqh* was *prescriptive* of the law. Hallaq explained that "The primary objective of legal theory, therefore, was to lay down a coherent system of principles through which a qualified jurist could extract rulings for novel cases. From the third/ninth century onwards this was universally recognized by jurists to be the sacred purpose of *usul al-fiqh*."[56] The second was to provide a "reasoned defense" of the legal doctrines of a school. Because it presented and supported methodological principles that lent credibility to school doctrine, *usul al-fiqh* could also be said to *justify* the law. While the prescriptive purpose of *usul al-fiqh* made it a forward-looking means to derive new laws, its justificatory purpose involved the ex post facto defense of already existing laws.

Most historians have argued for seeing *usul al-fiqh* as predominantly, if not completely, justificatory. Ahmed, for instance, explained that by the time the genre of *usul al-fiqh* emerged, the substantive legal doctrines of a school "had already achieved a large degree of fixity."[57] The derivation of new laws was therefore not

[54] For more on the variation between texts of *usul al-fiqh*, see also, Hallaq, "Usul al-Fiqh."

[55] Weiss, *The Search for God's Law*, 19–20. Weiss called al-Amidi's text of *usul al-fiqh* a "kind of sea in relation to which the previous literature forms a gigantic tributary. Within the tributary flow not only the works of Amidi's great predecessors within the Ash'ari/Shafi'i camp but also, further upstream, the works of the great Mu'tazili masters, especially 'Abd al-Jabbar and Abu'l-Husayn, through whom Amidi may have acquired much of his information concerning earlier Mu'tazilis." 22.

[56] Hallaq, *A History of Islamic Legal Theories*, ix; see also Hallaq, "Was the Gate of Ijtihad Closed?," 4.

[57] Ahmed, *Narratives of Islamic Legal Theory*, 6.

of primary importance. Ahmed distinguished, however, between apology and justification. While the former merely defends the validity of existing law, the latter makes a case for its proper application in the present.[58] Very different court rulings are possible depending on *how* one justifies a school's legal injunctions. A jurist like the Hanafi Abu Zayd al-Dabusi (d. 430/1039), whose justification of the law posited an understanding of revelation as inextricable from context, would pay far greater attention to the circumstances of a case than a jurist who viewed divine law as a straightforward set of injunctions to be applied with minimal consideration to historical context. Ahmed explained that the justificatory nature of *usul al-fiqh* texts could only be understood if one saw them "as products of religious devotion."[59] Because communal rituals necessitate "an inherited template" delineating their proper execution, jurists across generations largely reasserted the already established school principles. Their variations on how the law should be applied reflected their desire "to create a stronger bond between God and man."[60]

Norman Calder's study of the introduction to the *Majmu'* of the Shafi'i jurist Sharaf Muhyi al-Din al-Nawawi (d. 676/1277) likewise led him to conclude that a jurist used *usul al-fiqh* to "to explain and justify the *madhhab* [i.e. the legal doctrine of a school]."[61] Calder critiqued the idea that *usul al-fiqh* served to determine new legal rules, contending instead that new legal cases "were worked out by interpretation of, or were otherwise drawn out of, the statements and opinions of previous jurists within the school."[62] New legal cases were therefore beholden to and largely derivative of the school's existing body of substantive legal doctrine. Calder's position finds support in Brannon Wheeler, who showed the extent to which each generation of Hanafi jurists had to countenance their predecessors' legal rulings.[63]

Sherman Jackson also viewed *usul al-fiqh* as justificatory, but for different reasons than the authors above. For Jackson, *usul al-fiqh* justified the law by lending authority to legal opinions whose raison d'être lay elsewhere. Jackson argued that while *usul al-fiqh* appeared to determine or predict legal rulings, it was in reality often used to shore up a variety of contrary positions. Jackson referenced the ideas of Legal Realists and Critical Legal Studies to contend that practical and political realities were the main determinants of the law. Even when applied to novel cases, *usul al-fiqh* merely served the rhetorical function of providing the law with recognizable and therefore convincing forms of argumentation. *Usul al-fiqh* for Jackson was about legal authority: it partook in what Jackson calls "legal scaffolding," i.e. the attempt to maintain "conspicuous links" with "authorities of the past" even while producing new law.[64]

58 Ibid., 7. 59 Ibid., 152. 60 Ibid., 153.

61 Calder, "Al-Nawawi's Typology of Muftis," 139. 62 Ibid., 158.

63 Wheeler, *Applying the Canon in Islam*.

64 Jackson, *Islamic Law and the State*, xxxi; idem, "Fiction and Formalism: Towards a Functional Analysis of Usul al-Fiqh," in *Studies in Islamic Legal Theory*, ed. Bernard Weiss, 177–201 (Leiden: Brill, 2002). Vishanoff echoed Jackson's position in his study on hermeneutics. He affirmed that *usul al-fiqh*'s

The most sustained treatment of the relationship between *usul al-fiqh* and *furu'* came from Ahmad Atif Ahmad, who recently argued that *usul al-fiqh* and *furu'* mutually influenced one another throughout their historical development. Ahmad supported his theory by examining six books from among the largely overlooked legal genre called *Takhrij al-furu' 'ala al-usul*. This genre's purported goal was to show the basis in *usul al-fiqh* for the legal rulings of a school. These books' authors revised and changed accepted principles of *usul al-fiqh* and substantive legal doctrine in order to establish consistency between both. Ahmad's analysis led him to conclude that there was a "constant adjustment of both the theoretical and practical aspects of the law."[65] He called this dialectic "the structural interrelations" of *usul al-fiqh* and *furu'*.

Some have sought to move the debate away from the dichotomy between prescription and justification. Mohammad Fadel spoke of the "puzzling" fact that "the vast majority of actual Islamic law" was derived from non-revelatory sources.[66] He illustrated through the example of the Maliki school's law of pledges (*ruhun*) that *usul al-fiqh* was oftentimes unable or only marginally capable of providing an explanation for the law. In the case of pledges, revealed texts (i.e. Qur'anic and *hadith*) were few and seemingly disconnected from the content of the law. Rather than being based on the revelatory sources that *usul al-fiqh* texts since al-Shafi'i focussed upon, the law of pledges appeared to be mainly based on *istihsan*, often translated as the jurist's "personal preference" for one ruling over another, but also denoting his use of "practical reason" on a legal matter.[67]

Fadel's puzzle might be solved if one follows Robert Gleave in seeing the function of *usul al-fiqh* as largely independent from consideration of the existing and developing corpus of substantive law. Building from Calder's assertion that *usul al-fiqh* was a "closed and independent science," Gleave abandoned attempts at making generalizations about the relationship between *usul al-fiqh* and *furu'*.[68] He argued that the impact of *usul al-fiqh* in substantive legal reasoning varied from one jurist to another. Nonetheless, he identified the main purpose of *usul al-fiqh* as pedagogical. Its function was to "hone the intellectual skills of students."[69] This is a point to which Fadel himself has gestured, suggesting that *usul al-fiqh*, while not necessarily determining law, did provide jurists with a set of analytical tools for thinking about the law.[70]

The historical studies reviewed above suggest a modest role for *usul al-fiqh* in the production of *furu'*. The schools' *furu'* was already well developed by the time the

hermeneutical principles posited a theory of language as ambiguous and therefore capable of accommodating a variety of juridical opinions, Vishanoff, *The Formation of Islamic Hermeneutics*, 9.

65 Ahmad, *Structural Interrelations of Theory and Practice in Islamic Law*, 23.

66 Fadel, "Istihsan Is Nine-Tenths of the Law," 164.

67 Weiss, "Alta Discussion," 402.

68 Cited in Gleave, *Inevitable Doubt*, 3 n. 3.

69 Gleave, *Inevitable Doubt*, 3.

70 Weiss, "Alta Discussion," 417.

genre of *usul al-fiqh* emerged, making *usul al-fiqh*'s primary task its ex post facto justification. Although new cases of law arose, they were primarily dealt with as extensions of already existing legal doctrine. Historians have nonetheless disagreed on how to describe the impact of *usul al-fiqh* on the law. *Usul al-fiqh* was for Jackson, primarily rhetorical; for Rumee Ahmed, a claim for the law's proper application; for Ahmad Atif Ahmad, a way to mutually adjust theory and practice; and for Gleave, a means to train new jurists.

c. Intellectual Debates in *Usul al-Fiqh*

A large body of literature on *usul al-fiqh* has bracketed the question of the genre's relationship to substantive law and has focussed instead on the texts' contents. Aron Zysow's now published 1984 dissertation *The Economy of Certainty* is sometimes credited for initiating this approach.[71] Zysow encouraged Islamic legal studies scholars to pay attention to the rich intellectual debates contained in books of *usul al-fiqh*. As A. Kevin Reinhart and Rumee Ahmed have suggested, many of these debates are embedded in texts of *usul al-fiqh*: they are implicit yet pervasive throughout.[72] Since Zysow's dissertation, many historians have grappled with the theories of language, epistemology, and ethics within *usul al-fiqh*. In doing so, they brought to the fore the intricacies of Muslim jurists' legal-theoretical thought. In what follows, I present but a cursory overview of the literature covering some of *usul al-fiqh*'s intellectual debates.

Zysow analyzed *usul al-fiqh* debates on legal epistemology.[73] He contended that the most basic pattern in *usul al-fiqh*, and the one that most distinguished it from other legal systems, was its epistemological categorization of legal proofs.[74] He argued that "certainty and probability were the fundamental categories from which they [jurists] approached every question of law." He showed that the authority of scriptural texts like prophetic *hadith*, communal consensus (*ijma'*), and analogy (*qiyas*) depended on jurists' assessments of their epistemic value in discovering God's law. Zysow's thesis was that Muslim jurists were historically either formalists, belonging to the surviving Sunni schools who accepted the probative value of the law, or materialists, made up of the Zahiris and early Twelver Shi'is who did not accept anything other than complete epistemic certainty in legal rulings. Zysow focussed on the Hanafi school as a representative of the former, giving great attention to the thought of the six/twelfth century jurist 'Ala al-Din al-Samarqandi (d. 539/1144).

[71] Robert Gleave, foreword to *The Economy of Certainty*, xi.

[72] Ahmed, *Narratives of Islamic Legal Theory*, 9; Reinhart, *Before Revelation*, 7–9.

[73] Zysow, *The Economy of Certainty*, 2. [74] Ibid., 1–2.

Reinhart and Anver Emon have provided the most sustained investigation into Islamic legal ethics. Reinhart focussed on *usul al-fiqh* debates pertaining to the legal status of acts "before the advent of revelation" (*qabla wurud al-shar'*). He showed that because "Muslim law assesses all acts against the norms of Revelation, and judges them to be Proscribed, Permitted, or Obligatory," jurists were uncertain of the status of these acts before revelation.[75] Reinhart analyzed the jurists' positions: some argued that prior to revelation all acts were permitted, some that they were all prohibited, and others saying that they could not be assessed and were in suspension until the advent of revelation. At stake were wider questions about the source of morality and the means to apprehend it.[76] When jurists argued over reason's ability to determine the goodness and therefore permissibility of an act prior to revelation, they indirectly argued "about the limitations of human moral-epistemological capacity."[77] Likewise when they argued over the permissibility of all acts before revelation, they indirectly argued over the permissibility of post-revelation acts on which the scripture was silent.

Emon for his part used *usul al-fiqh* to investigate natural law theories in Islam. He demonstrated that Muslim jurists no less than western natural law philosophers grappled with reason's ability to extract normative rules from objective facts about nature.[78] He focussed on juristic discussions on the nature of the good (*husn*) and the bad (*qubh*) as well as on whether and when the perceived good (*maslaha*) constituted a valid source of law.[79] This allowed Emon to discern the existence of two cohorts of Muslim natural law theorists. The first were the hard natural law theorists who built upon the premise that "God only does good and is incapable of evil" to argue "that one could rationally deduce the goodness from nature."[80] Worried about limiting God's omnipotence, the second cohort, the soft natural law theorists, contended that nature did not in itself need to be a source for normative rules, but that God, out of his grace, made it so. Moreover, this second cohort embraced this form of reasoned deliberation only in the absence of normative texts.

A series of studies have examined *usul al-fiqh* theorizations on language. Bernard Weiss's dissertation *Language in Orthodox Muslim Thought* presented the historical development of the jurists' semantic theory of language, commonly called *wad' al-lugha* (the givenness of language). At its simplest, the theory suggested that words have a historically determined and therefore "given" meaning. Early texts of *usul al-fiqh* debated whether the origins of this given language were divine or human.

75 Reinhart, *Before Revelation*, 3. 76 Ibid., 5.

77 Ibid; Reinhart spoke of the interrelated questions of the debate as the "before revelation complex."

78 Emon, *Islamic Natural Law Theories*, 3.

79 Discussions of *husn* and *qubh* are also dealt with in Hourani, *Islamic Rationalism*; and Hourani, *Reason and Tradition in Islamic Ethics*. Hourani's approach is however that of an academic philosopher who explicates and critiques the ideas of his interlocutors rather than historicizing them. For more on Maslaha, see Felicitas Opwis, *Maslaha and the Purpose of the Law*.

80 Emon, *Islamic Natural Law Theories*, 25 and 26.

Weiss would later compare the theory of *wad'* to that of Ferdinand De Saussure's linguistics which sees a speaker as operating "within a context of signifiers and signifieds (*dallat, madlulat*)."[81] When referring to the language of revelation in determining law, jurists were to assume that words carried this given meaning unless contextual evidence pointed toward an alternative intended meaning.[82]

Mohamed Yunus Ali then supplemented this theory of semantics by positing two historical juristic theories of pragmatics, or language use. The first, to which Ali claimed the majority of jurists subscribed, saw communication as the product of four elements: the given meaning of words, the intention of speakers, the context of speech, and the interpretation of the hearer. The second approach, belonging to Ibn Taymiyya (d. 728/1328) and his student Ibn al-Qayyim al-Jawziyya (d. 751/1350), affirmed that a word's meaning did not exist outside of a context: words have "elastic rather than firmly fixed meanings" such that context is the main determinant of meaning.[83]

Finally, Vishanoff focussed on the jurists' legal hermeneutics. He contended that jurists held four different conceptions of how scripture communicates God's law. The first assumed that language is "purely a verbal entity" making legal interpretation dependent on a linguistic analysis of scripture.[84] He associated this model with Ibn Hazm (d. 456/1064) and the Zahiris, among others. The second, held by the Mu'tazila, based interpretation on a speaker's intentions. The Mu'tazila therefore read scripture through the lens of their theological assumption that God benevolently intends to inform humans of what is beneficial and harmful. In contrast, the early Ash'aris posited a third conception in which verbal language is a reflection of a speaker's internal speech. They held that revelation only provided dim clues about God's "eternal inner command."[85] And the fourth and last conception, which Vishanoff believed became dominant by the fifth/eleventh century, considered revelation to be a speech-act. This position saw God's utterances as legal commands only if and when they conformed to the act of "requesting something from an inferior." Through this speech-act, God performatively brought the law into existence.[86]

The above studies show that through texts of *usul al-fiqh*, jurists probed a series of complex philosophical–legal questions. Part of their value is putting Muslim jurists' thought in conversation with other contemporary academic debates. Emon's study makes Islamic law relevant to the natural law theories of John Finnis and others; Ali's to Paul Grice's pragmatics; Vishanoff's to J.L. Austin's theory of speech-acts. Such studies enrich these academic debates, injecting them with new ideas, while simultaneously revealing what is singular and unique about Muslim juristic thought.

[81] Weiss, *The Search for God's Law*, 115.

[82] Weiss, "Language in Orthodox Muslim Thought." See also Weiss, "A Theory of the Parts of Speech in Arabic"; Weiss, "Language and Tradition in Medieval Islam"; Weiss, "'Ilm Al-Wad'."

[83] Ali, *Medieval Islamic Pragmatics*, 8.

[84] Vishanoff, *The Formation of Islamic Hermeneutic*, 248.

[85] Ibid., 247.

[86] Ibid., 13. For an overview of hermeneutic principles, see also Ramic, *Language and the Interpretation of Islamic Law*.

III. Conclusion

The historians of *usul al-fiqh* have countenanced two critical moments in the emergence of the genre. The first is al-Shafiʿi's *Risala.* Early historical studies considered al-Shafiʿi as having systematized his predecessors' legal discussions into the first explicit exposition of methodology. It affirmed that all Sunni schools of law subsequently followed the general outlines of this methodology. The second moment is Ibn Surayj's incorporation of the study of *usul al-fiqh* to the training of Shafiʿi jurists in early fourth/tenth-century Baghdad. The great numbers of treatises of *usul al-fiqh* that Shafiʿis and subsequently other schools' jurists composed in this period mark the beginning of mature *usul al-fiqh.* I have shown that scholarship vacillates between identifying al-Shafiʿi and Ibn Surayj's circle as the founder(s) of *usul al-fiqh.*

Academic scholarship focusing on the late fourth/tenth century onward turned toward a new set of concerns. I have grouped these concerns under three headings in the second part of this chapter. The first is the identification of differences within the genre of *usul al-fiqh.* It focuses upon and complicates the traditional Muslim distinction between the theological and juristic streams of the discipline. The second is *usul al-fiqh*'s relationship to substantive law. It too seeks to complicate the Muslim account of *usul al-fiqh* as determining jurist's legal reasoning. Finally, the third examines the major intellectual debates within *usul al-fiqh.*

It is the period covered in the second part of this chapter that most merits increased scholarly attention. Our picture of the genre remains blurry and research should seek to supplement the current state of our knowledge. It is not clear how the multitude of texts of *usul al-fiqh* should be grouped together or distinguished from each other. We are not destitute in this matter: school and theological affiliations tell us much about the types of arguments one will find in the writings of any given jurist. Yet it is clear from our current scholarship that this is not always sufficient. The problem is largely that scholars have shown the inadequacy of the juristic versus theological typology without offering a new one in its place.

Much can also be gained by continuing to grapple with the key or major debates within the genre. *Usul al-fiqh* texts string together a multitude of topics of investigations—approximately eight thousand according to the eighth/fourteenth-century Shafiʿi Badr al-Din al-Zarkashi[87]—many of these revealing competing understandings about the nature of God, language, knowledge, ethics, natural science, and legal authority. As Zysow puts it, for scholars not to attend to these questions "is not only for them to miss an opportunity to bring an apparently arcane corner of Islamic studies into the wider fold of human learning but equally to impoverish Islamic studies."[88] Scholars who have attended to them (e.g. Emon,

[87] Zysow, *The Economy of Certainty*, 1.

[88] Ibid., xxiv.

Vishanoff, etc.) demonstrate their potential richness for future studies of *usul al-fiqh*. The great number of texts and topics of *usul al-fiqh* suggest that there is much that historians using this approach can still explore.

References

Abu Zahra, Muhammad, *Usul al-Fiqh* (Cairo: Dar al-Fikr al-'Arabi, 1958).

Ahmad, Ahmad Atif, *Structural Interrelations of Theory and Practice in Islamic Law: A Study of Six Works of Medieval Islamic Jurisprudence* (Leiden, Boston: Brill, 2006).

Ahmed, Rumee, *Narratives of Islamic Legal Theory* (Oxford: Oxford University Press, 2012).

Al-Alwani, Taha Jabir, *Source Methodology in Islamic Jurisprudence* (3rd edn. London: The International Institute of Islamic Thought, 2003).

Ali, Mohamed Mohamed Yunis, *Medieval Islamic Pragmatics: Sunni Legal Theorists' Models of Textual Communication* (Richmond: Curzon, 2000).

Al-Shafi'i, Muhammad ibn Idris, *Al-Shafi'i's Risala: Treatise on the Foundations of Islamic Jurisprudence* translated by Majid Khadduri (reissue edn. Cambridge: Islamic Texts Society, 1997).

Al-Shafi'i, Muhammad ibn Idris, *The Epistle on Legal Theory*, translated by Joseph Lowry (New York: New York University Press, 2013).

Al-Shashi, Abu 'Ali, *Usul al-Shashi* (Beirut: Dar al-Kitab al-'Arabi, 1982).

Ansari, Zafar Ishaq, "Islamic Juristic Terminology before Safi'i: A Semantic Analysis with Special Reference to Kufa" *Arabica* 19, 3 (1972): 255–300.

Bedir, Murteza, "An Early Response to Al-Shafi'i: 'Isa b. Aban on the Prophetic Report (Khabar)." *Islamic Law and Society* 9, no. 3 (2002): 285–311.

Bernand, Marie, "Introductions to *La profession de foi d'Abu Ishaq al-Sirazi*, by Abu Ishaq al-Sirazi," 3–16 and 51–61. Marie Bernand (ed.) (Cairo and Paris: IFAO, 1987).

Burton, John, *The Sources of Islamic Law: Islamic Theories of Abrogation* (Edinburgh: Edinburgh University Press, 1990).

Calder, Norman, "Al-Nawawi's Typology of Muftis and its Significance for a General Theory of Islamic Law." *Islamic Law and Society* 3, no. 2 (1996): 137–164.

Calder, Norman, *Studies in Early Muslim Jurisprudence* (Oxford: Clarendon Press, 1993).

Chaumont, Eric, "Encore au sujet de l'Ash'arism d'Abu Ishaq al-Shirazi." *Studia Islamic* 79 (1994): 79–102.

Chaumont, Eric, "La notion de wajh al-hikmah dans les usul al-fiqh d'Abu Ishaq al-Shirazi (m. 476/1083)" in A. Kevin Reinhart, Robert Gleave, and Peter Sluglett (eds.) *Islamic Law in Theory: Studies on Jurisprudence in Honor of Bernard Weiss* (Leiden: Brill, 2014) 39–53.

Coulson, Noel J., *A History of Islamic Law* (Edinburgh: Edinburgh University Press, 1964).

Dutton, Yasin, "'Amal v. Hadith in Islamic Law: The Case of Sadl al-Yadayn (Holding One's Hands by One's Sides) When Doing the Prayer." *Islamic Law and Society* 3, no. 1 (1996): 13–40.

Dutton, Yasin, *The Origins of Islamic Law: The Qur'an, the Muwatta' and Madinan 'Amal* (Surrey, England: Curzon, 1999).

El Shamsy, Ahmed, "The First Shafi'i: The Traditionalist Legal Thought of Abu Ya'qub al-Buwayti (d. 231/846)." *Islamic Law and Society* 14, 3 (2007): 301–341.

El Shamsy, Ahmed, "Al-Shafi'i's Written Corpus: A Source-Critical Study." *The Journal of the American Oriental Society* 132, 2 (2012): 199–220.
El Shamsy, Ahmed, *The Canonization of Islamic Law : A Social and Intellectual History* (New York: Cambridge University Press, 2013).
Emon, Anver M., *Islamic Natural Law Theories* (New York: Oxford University Press, 2010).
Fadel, Mohammad, "'Istihsan is Nine-Tenths of the Law': The Puzzling Relationship of Usul to Furu' in the Maliki Madhhab" in Bernard Weiss (ed.) *Studies in Islamic Legal Theory* (Leiden: Brill, 2002) 161–176.
Gilliot, Claude, "Deux professions de foi du juriste-théologien Abu Ishaq as-Sirazi." *Studia Islamica* 68 (1988): 170–186.
Gleave, Robert, *Inevitable Doubt: Two Theories of Shi'i Jurisprudence* (Leiden; Boston: Brill, 2000).
Gleave, Robert, "Foreword" in *The Economy of Certainty* by Aron Zysow (Atlanta: Lockwood Press, 2013) xi–xix.
Goldziher, Ignác, *Muslim Studies* in S.M. Stern (ed.) translated by C.R. Barber and S.M. Stern. vol. 2 (2 vols. London: Allen & Unwin, 1971).
Goldziher, Ignác, *The Zahiris: Their Doctrine and Their History; A Contribution to the History of Islamic Theology* translated by Wolfgang Behn and Camilla Adang (Leiden: Brill, 1971).
Hallaq, Wael B., "Was the Gate of Ijtihad Closed?" *International Journal of Middle East Studies* 16, 1 (1984): 3–41.
Hallaq, Wael B., "Usul al-Fiqh: Beyond Tradition." *Journal of Islamic Studies* 3, 2 (1992): 172–202.
Hallaq, Wael B., "Was al-Shafi'i the Master Architect of Islamic Jurisprudence?" *International Journal of Middle East Studies* 25, 4 (1993): 587–605.
Hallaq, Wael B., *A History of Islamic Legal Theories: An Introduction to Sunni Usul Al-Fiqh* (New York: Cambridge University Press, 1997).
Hallaq, Wael B., "From Regional to Personal Schools of Law? A Reevaluation." *Islamic Law and Society* 8, 1 (2001): 1–26.
Hallaq, Wael B., *Shari'a : Theory, Practice, Transformations* (Cambridge: Cambridge University Press, 2009).
Hourani, George, *Islamic Rationalism: The Ethics of 'Abd Al-Jabbar* (Oxford: Clarendon Press, 1971).
Hourani, George, *Reason and Tradition in Islamic Ethics* (New York: Cambridge University Press, 1985).
Jackson, Sherman, *Islamic Law and the State: The Constitutional Jurisprudence of Shihab al-Din al-Qarafi* (Leiden; New York: E.J. Brill, 1996).
Jackson, Sherman, "Setting the Record Straight: Ibn Labbad's Refutation of Al-Shafi'i." *Journal of Islamic Studies* 11, 2 (2000): 121–146.
Jackson, Sherman, "Fiction and Formalism: Towards a Functional Analysis of Usul al-Fiqh" in Bernard Weiss (ed.) *Studies in Islamic Legal Theory* (Leiden: Brill, 2002) 177–201.
Kamali, Mohammad Hashim, *Principles of Islamic Jurisprudence* (3rd edn. Cambridge: Islamic Texts Society, 2003).
al-Karkhi, 'Ubaidallah Ibn-al-Husain, "Risalat Abi'al-Hasan al-Karkhi fi al-Usul" in 'Abdallah Ibn 'Umar al-Dabusi (ed.) *Kitab Ta'sis an-nazar* (Cairo: Zakariya 'Ali Yusuf, 1971).
Lowry, Joseph E., "Does Shafi'i Have a Theory of 'Four Sources' of Law?" in Bernard Weiss (ed.) *Studies in Islamic Legal Theory* (Leiden: Brill, 2002) 23–50.
Lowry, Joseph E., "The Legal Hermeneutics of al-Shafi'i and Ibn Qutayba: A Reconsideration" *Islamic Law and Society* 11, 1 (2004): 1–41.

Lowry, Joseph E., *Early Islamic Legal Theory: The Risala of Muḥammad Ibn Idris Al-Shafiʿi* (Leiden: Brill, 2007).
Lucas, Scott, "Where Are the Legal Hadith? A Study of the Musannaf of Ibn Abi Shayba." *Islamic Law and Society* 15, 3 (2008): 283–314.
Lucas, Scott, "Principles of Traditionist Jurisprudence Reconsidered." *The Muslim World* 100, 1 (2010): 145–156.
Makdisi, George, "Ashʿari and the Ashʿarites in Islamic Religious History I." *Studia Islamica* 17 (1962): 37–80.
Makdisi, George, "The Juridical Theology of Shafiʿi: Origins and Significance of Usul al-Fiqh." *Studia Islamica* 59 (1984): 5–47.
Makdisi, George, *The Rise of Humanism in Classical Islam and the Christian West: With Special Reference to Scholasticism* (Edinburgh: Edinburgh University Press, 1990).
Melchert, Christopher, "Traditionist-Jurisprudents and the Framing of Islamic Law." *Islamic Law and Society* 8, 3 (2001): 383–406.
Nyazee, Imran Ahsan Khan, *Islamic Jurisprudence: Usul al-Fiqh* (Islamabad: Islamic Research Institute, 2000).
Opwis, Felicitas, *Maslaha and the Purpose of the Law: Islamic Discourse on Legal Change from the 4th/10th to 8th/14th Century* (Leiden: Brill, 2010).
Rahman, Fazlur, "Concepts Sunnah, Ijtihad and Ijmaʿ in the Early Period." *Islamic Studies* 1, no. 1 (1962): 5–21.
Ramic, Sukrija Husejn, *Language and the Interpretation of Islamic Law* (Cambridge: Islamic Texts Society, 2003).
Reinhart, A. Kevin, *Before Revelation: The Boundaries of Muslim Moral Thought* (Albany: State University of New York Press, 1995).
Schacht, Joseph, *The Origins of Muhammadan Jurisprudence* (Oxford: Clarendon Press, 1959).
Spectorsky, Susan A., "Ahmad ibn Hanbal's Fiqh." *Journal of the American Oriental Society* 102, 3 (1982): 461–465.
Stewart, Devin, *Islamic Legal Orthodoxy: Twelver Shiʿite Responses to the Sunni Legal System* (Salt Lake City: University of Utah Press, 1998).
Stewart, Devin, "Muhammad b. Da'ud al-Zahiri's Manual of Jurisprudence, al-Wusul ila Maʿrifat al-Usul" in Wael B. Hallaq (ed.) *The Formation of Islamic Law* (Burlington: Ashgate, 2004) 277–315.
Turki, A.-M., "Aqida al-Shirazi" in *Sharh al-Lumaʿ* by Abu Ishaq al-Shirazi A.-M. Turki (ed.) (Beirut: Dar al-Gharb al-Islami, 1988) 73–89.
Vishanoff, David, *The Formation of Islamic Hermeneutics How Sunni Legal Theorists Imagined a Revealed Law* (New Haven: American Oriental Society, 2011).
Weiss, Bernard, "Language in Orthodox Muslim Thought: A Study of 'Wad' Al-Lughah' and Its Development." (Ph.D. Dissertation, Princeton University, 1966).
Weiss, Bernard, "A Theory of the Parts of Speech in Arabic (Noun, Verb and Particle): A Study in 'Ilm Al-Wad'." *Arabica* 23, 1 (1976): 23–36.
Weiss, Bernard, "Language and Tradition in Medieval Islam: The Question of Al-Tariq ila Ma'rifat Al-Lugha." *Der Islam: Zeitschrift Fur Geschichte Und Kultur Des Islamischen Orients* 61, 1 (1984): 92–99.
Weiss, Bernard, "ʿIlm Al-Wadʿ: An Introductory Account of a Later Muslim Philological Science." *Arabica* 34, 3 (1987): 339–356.
Weiss, Bernard, "Alta Discussion" in Bernard Weiss (ed.) *Studies in Islamic Legal Theory* (Leiden: Brill, 2002) 385–429.

Weiss, Bernard, *The Spirit of Islamic Law* (2nd edn. Athens: University of Georgia Press, 2006).
Weiss, Bernard, *The Search for God's Law: Islamic Jurisprudence in the Writings of Sayf Al-Din al-Amidi* (revised edn. Salt Lake City: University of Utah Press, 2010).
Wheeler, Brannon M., *Applying the Canon in Islam: The Authorization and Maintenance of Interpretive Reasoning in Ḥanafi Scholarship* (Albany: State University of New York Press, 1996).
Wolfson, Harry Austryn, *The Philosophy of the Kalam* (Cambridge and New York: Harvard University Press, 1976).
Wymann-Landraf, Umar F. Abd-Allah., *Malik and Medina: Islamic Legal Reasoning in the Formative Period* (Leiden: Brill, 2013).
Zysow, Aron, *The Economy of Certainty: An Introduction to the Typology of Islamic Legal Theory* (Atlanta: Lockwood Press, 2013).
Zysow, Aron, "Mu'tazilism and Maturidism in Hanafi Legal Theory" in Bernard Weiss (ed.) *Studies in Islamic Legal Theory* (Leiden: Brill, 2002) 235–265.

CHAPTER 11

IJMAʿ

MAIRAJ U. SYED

THERE are three main approaches in modern scholarship on consensus in Islamic thought: source-critical, phenomenological, and hermeneutical-theological. These approaches are not mutually exclusive and a single scholar often combines elements of each approach. The source-critical approach uses contextual interpretations of the oldest Muslim sources on consensus, such as Qurʾanic verses and ḥadiths, to question a received theological understanding of the texts' relationship to the doctrine of consensus. This approach often attempts to supplant the theologically valanced understanding of the oldest Muslim texts with a conception of consensus that gradually developed over time, mainly as the result of the intellectual interaction of groups competing with each other for influence and adherents. This approach predominates among historians who work the formative period of Islamic thought (roughly first–fourth AH/seventh–tenth CE centuries).

The phenomenological approach takes the description of the main contours of the doctrine and the arguments surrounding it among Muslim religious scholars as its basic aim and dominates the scholarship on consensus in classical Muslim thought. It insists on a close reading of classical Muslim sources (especially legal theory (*usul al-fiqh*)) in order to reconstruct more clearly how classical Muslim thinkers conceived of the doctrine.

The hermeneutical-theological approach, used by Muslim thinkers, and often relying on the results of scholarship of the first and second approaches, attempts to reinterpret the doctrine of consensus to meet contemporary Muslim theological or political needs. This approach sees consensus as a living doctrine—a potentially persuasive authority that has a vital role now in Islamic thought. Because all three approaches regard the *classical* Muslim articulation of the doctrine of consensus as a starting point, I will begin my survey of the historiography on consensus with the scholarship that sought to clarify how classical Muslim scholars substantiated its proof-value and the conditions for its occurrence. I will then proceed to survey important critical and reconstructive theories on how consensus developed in the formative period before it took its classical shape. Given the importance of the doctrine in some modern debates, I will then survey the current scholarship on their shape in postcolonial Islamic thought. Before concluding with my thoughts on the quality of the historiography surveyed, I will analyze some scholarship on how consensus has been used as a legal proof in specific matters, namely the laws of slavery and the marriage of minors.

Three works, in particular, exemplify the phenomenological approach to consensus, all of which focus on its classical articulation: Ahmad Hasan's *The Doctrine of Ijmāʿ in Islam*, Bernard Weiss's *In Search of God's Law*, and Wael Hallaq's *A History of Islamic Legal Theories*. These works largely confine themselves to the conception of consensus as it is articulated in works of legal theory (*usul al-fiqh*). Hasan provides a general survey of medieval Sunni debates on different aspects of the doctrine of consensus. Weiss provides a detailed analysis of the Shafiʿi-Ashʿari Sayf al-Din al-Amidi's (d. 631/1233) writing on legal theory, a substantial portion of which is devoted to an exploration of consensus's authority. Hallaq traces the historical development of the main ideas that form Sunni legal theory, consensus being one of them.

I. Substantiating Consensus as Proof-value

Ideally, consensus in classical Muslim thought refers to a type of legal or theological proof, functioning in a way similar to the citation of scriptural text or rational argument. It occurs when those judged competent to participate in it concur on a legal or theological position. For those who accept its authority, the occurrence of a consensus is an authoritative proof for the validity of the position agreed upon; an indication of the Divine will on the issue at hand.

Classical Muslim scholars faced two conceptual problems regarding consensus. First, they needed to substantiate its proof-value. Second, they needed to define the criteria by which an occurrence of consensus may be ascertained.

According to Hallaq, the first known attempt to substantiate its authority was by one of the founders of Hanafism, Muhammad b. al-Hasan al-Shaybani

(d. 188/804). Shaybani grounded the authority of consensus in the following Prophetic hadith: "whatever the Muslims see as good is good in the eyes of God, and whatever they see as bad is bad in the eyes of God." Hallaq adds that Shaybani's contemporary, Muhammad b. Idris al-Shafiʿi (d. 204/820) disagreed with this reasoning because it too closely resembled a mode of Hanafi legal argument—*istihsan*—which al-Shafiʿi rejected. Shafiʿi himself seems to have been perturbed by how to substantiate consensus's proof-value: later Muslim sources apparently record that when he was asked about how we know consensus to be a source of law, Shafiʿi read through the Qur'an over 300 times—or alternatively consulted it for three days—before happening on the verse (4:105) that would later become one of the cornerstones of Sunni argumentation for consensus's authority.[1] In his own works, he cites and interprets Prophetic hadiths that encourage Muslims to cling fast to the community as establishing the validity of consensus.[2]

Both Schacht and Joseph Lowry, author of a detailed study of Shafiʿi's legal theory, describe Shafiʿi as holding the view that it is not so much that the relevant community's consensus occurs in a scriptural vacuum, such that a law is simply established just by the community's agreement on it. Rather, consensus elevates the epistemic status of a legal position originally based on an interpretation of the Qur'an, hadith, or reasoning by analogy from being conjectural, and thereby susceptible to error, to being infallible, and thereby uncontaminated by the occurrence of human mistakes.[3] For Shafiʿi consensus is a derivative source: it not so much creates law as it reveals the Sunna.[4]

[1] Goldziher cites the former in his Muslim Studies. See Ignaz Goldziher, *The Ẓāhirīs: their Doctrine and their History* (Leiden: Brill, 1971), 85. Weiss cites the latter on Goldziher's authority. See Bernard G. Weiss, *The Search for God's Law: Islamic Jurisprudence in the Writings of Sayf al-Dīn al-Āmidī* (Salt Lake City: University of Utah Press, 1992), 195. Ahmad Hasan and Wael Hallaq are skeptical that Shāfiʿī substantiated consensus through the interpretation of this verse, because his actual writings on consensus do not refer to it. See Ahmad Hasan, *The Doctrine of Ijmāʿ in Islam: a Study of the Juridical Principle of Consensus* (New Delhi: Nusrat Ali Nasri for Kitab Bhawan, 1992), 37 and Wael B. Hallaq, "On the Authoritativeness of Sunni Consensus," *International Journal of Middle East Studies* 18, no. 4 (1986): 432.

[2] See *The Origins of Muhammedan Jurisprudence* (Oxford: Clarendon Press), 91. There is some disagreement on Shāfiʿī's conception of consensus. Schacht held that for Shāfiʿī, the consensus-makers are not just the specialists of law, but the community as a whole. On this point, in the most detailed study of Shāfiʿī's work of legal theory (*al-Risāla*) to date, Joseph Lowry makes a persuasive argument that this is not the case. According to Lowry, only the legal specialists are the valid consensus-makers in Shāfiʿī's theory of consensus. On this, see Joseph E. Lowry, *Early Islamic Legal Theory: the Risāla of Muḥammad ibn Idrīs al-Shāfiʿī* (Leiden: Brill, 2007): 351–357.

[3] *The Origins of Muhammedan Jurisprudence*, 91.

[4] See ibid., 90–91. See Lowry, where he summarizes the function of consensus in Shāfiʿī's legal theory in the following way: "It aids exclusively the interpretation of the Qur'ān and Sunna, and it does not, on its own, furnish rules." "Early Islamic Legal Theory: the Risāla of Muḥammad ibn Idrīs al-Shāfiʿī," 319. See also ibid., 327: "Shāfiʿī suggested that ijmāʿ derived its authority from its proximity to the collectively maintained Sunna."

Given the centrality of Shafiʿi in the historiography of the emergence of Islamic legal theory (*usul al-fiqh*), it is not surprising that his arguments on consensus's authority would attract attention. But how do later classical legal theorists treat the problem of consensus's authority? The most comprehensive description of the arguments for and against consensus is found in Ahmad Hasan's monograph. Later Shafiʿis hold on to Shafiʿi's conception of consensus as the revealer of a Sunna that was simply preserved in a textual source. Other thinkers, for example the fifth/eleventh century Hanafiʿ Ali b. Muhammad al-Bazdawi (d. 480/1088), take very seriously the community's ability to consensually create law. For Bazdawi, the community's collective immunity from error, which is the basis of consensus, is a gift of Divine grace. The purpose of consensus is to ensure God's ongoing guidance of the community even after revelation's termination.[5] Though no historian frames the issue as such, there seem to be two contrasting conceptions of consensus in classical Islam: Is it a mere revealer of what was once a scripturally mandated norm or a creator of a norm in and of itself?

Later classical legal theorists largely tended to reject the idea that consensus's authority can be substantiated through reason.[6] This left only one other avenue: scriptural interpretation. Scriptural substantiations of consensus run into two problems: uncertainty about the authenticity of some scriptural texts or ambiguity over their legal meaning. The main Qur'anic verse adduced by the legal theorists for establishing consensus's proof value was 4:115:

> But as for him who, after guidance has been vouchsafed to him, cuts himself off from the Apostle *and follows a path other than that of the believers*—him shall We leave unto that which he himself has chosen, and shall cause him to endure hell: and how evil a journey's end! (Emphasis added.)

The most important phrase in the verse is "and [whoever] follows a path other than that of the believers ... [We] shall cause him to endure hell: and how evil a journey's

[5] See Hasan, *The Doctrine of Ijmāʿ in Islam: a Study of the Juridical Principle of Consensus*, 64–65 and Marie Bernand, "Idjmāʿ," in *Encyclopedia of Islam, Second Edition*, eds. P. Bearman, et al. (Leiden: Brill, 1980–2004) for a similar point. Bazdawi may have been inspired by a similar argument given by Sarakhsi, who thinks that the conjunction of the premise that the shariʿa is eternal with the premise that prophecy ended with Muḥammad requires that the Muslim community be protected from committing error in its consensus. For this, see Hasan, *The Doctrine of Ijmāʿ in Islam: a Study of the Juridical Principle of Consensus*, 62. For a summary of a later Hanafite, Bukhari's, criticism of Bazdawi's arguments, see ibid., 65–66.

[6] Even the so-called rationalist school of theology, Muʿtazilism, explicitly rejected reason as the source of consensus's authority. The fifth/eleventh century Muʿtazili Qadi ʿAbd al-Jabbar (d. 415/1035) holds, that it is rationally impossible that a group of people will be free from error. See Bernand, "Idjmāʿ." The earlier Hanafi Muʿtazili, Abu Bakr al-Jassas (371/982) held the same view—that reason is incapable of substantiating consensus's authority, "for reason allows that the community can agree on an error, like the Jews, Christians and others." For the description and citation to this view see Hasan, *The Doctrine of Ijmāʿ in Islam: a Study of the Juridical Principle of Consensus*, 50.

end." The legal theorists construed the prohibition of following "a path other than that of the believers" as forbidding the contravention of Muslim consensus.

Attempts at substantiating consensus through interpretation of scripture were not limited to the Qur'an. From the perspective of legal theory, the problem with the Qur'an was not its authenticity but the clarity of passages legal theorists wanted to construe as authorizing consensus. The situation is slightly reversed when it came to hadith. The hadith texts, perhaps especially the one that declares "my community will never agree on error," are relatively clearer in grounding consensus as a source of law, but they lack the Qur'an's unimpeachable authenticity. While most Muslim scholars held that hadith texts of probable authenticity are sufficient as a legal proof for laws on specific issues, the legal theorists preferred certainty to establish consensus as a source.[7] Hallaq notes that the legal theorists overcame this obstacle by noting that while the individual hadiths are not so profligately narrated as to constitute proofs of certain authenticity (*tawatur lafzi*), taken together the general theme that Divine grace makes the community safe from committing error is transmitted on a certain basis (*tawatur maʿnawi*).[8]

While most Sunni scholars held that the consensus of any generation is binding on subsequent ones, a few held that *only* the consensus of the Prophet's companions counts as an unimpeachable legal authority. Goldziher notes that the eleventh-century Spanish scholar, Ibn Ḥazm, is recorded to have held this view.[9] Hasan attributes what amounts to the same view to the founder of Hanbalism, Ahmad b. Hanbal. According to discussions of his views in later sources, Ibn Ḥanbal seems to have practically ruled out consensus as a source of law by requiring almost impossible standards to establish its existence: "one cannot possess the knowledge of

[7] Weiss says that Amidi reports two positions on whether certainty is required to establish consensus as a source of law. One position holds that since practical legal positions are valid even if established on mere probable grounds there is no need for consensus's authority to be certain. Scholars who insisted on certainty said its authority needed to be established decisively because it is a source for law, akin to a core theological position, like God's existence. Weiss notes that Amidi does not come down explicitly on one side or another, but says "Looking at the larger context of Amidi's thinking as a whole, we must consider him as coming down, in the final analysis, on the side of those who regarded the authority of the ijmaʿ as probable in the highest possible degree." See also Weiss, *Search*, 198 for the two positions, and 201 for Weiss's interpretation of where Amidi himself fell. For an overview of al-Amidi's arguments on consensus's basis, see "Al-Āmidī on the Basis of Authority of Consensus," in *Essays on Islamic Civilization Presented to Niyazi Berkes*, ed. Donald P. Little (Leiden: Brill, 1976), 342–356.

[8] Wael Hallaq, *A History of Islamic Legal Theories: an Introduction to Sunnī Uṣūl al-Fiqh* (Cambridge; New York: Cambridge University Press, 1997), 76.

[9] Juwaynī, in his *Sharḥ al-Waraqāt*, attributes this view to all of the Zahiris, who thought that only during the time of the companions was it practically possible for one to document the occurrence of agreement. Later on the learned became geographically dispersed and it became practically impossible to ascertain the occurrence of agreement. See Goldziher, *The Ẓāhirīs: Their Doctrine and their History*, 34. Āmidī also attributes this view to the Zahiris, and engages in a lengthy rebuttal of the view. See Weiss, *Search*, 216–219.

*ijma*ʿ of the scholars unless one meets each and every scholar and witnesses his actions."[10]

While the vast majority of scholarship is devoted to explicating the Sunni concept of consensus, there are a few scholars who describe Twelver-Shiʿi discussions of consensus. The classical Shiʿis also accepted consensus as a valid proof, though their argumentation for it was somewhat different from that of the Sunnis. Hossein Modarressi notes that Shiʿi legal theorists defined it as the agreement of the Shiʿi legal jurists, and did not consider it a truly independent source of the law. Rather, it functioned to reveal the hidden Imam's legal position, on the assumption that the Imam, whose legal positions are inerrant, is one of the consensus-makers.[11] Despite the Shiʿis' distinct conception of consensus, the procedural criteria for identifying whether it exists are remarkably similar to those of their Sunni counterparts, with one exception. Because infallibility of consensus derives only from the presumption that it indicates the hidden Imam's legal opinion, Shiʿi legal theorists also worried about the possibility that he may not have participated in the consensus out of precautionary dissimulation (*taqiyya*).[12] For if the hidden Imam did not voice his view on the law because of his fear of persecution, then a consensus cannot be taken to indicate the Divine will, because the Imam has not in fact articulated the law on the matter.

Overall, there is little disagreement in the scholarship describing the classical doctrine of consensus, and it consist largely of description. What progress there was, was made mostly in analyzing new sources, and providing a more detailed description of how classical theorists conceived of consensus. There are two exceptions to this general trend. The first exception is criticism of the Orientalist Christiaan Snouck Hurgronje's (d. 1355/1936) description of consensus. Hurgronje accused the classical legal theorists of circular reasoning in their justification of consensus as a legal authority. He believed that the Muslim community's consensus on the authority of consensus was taken to prove the validity of consensus as a source of law.[13] Hourani notes that Hurgronje's fundamental flaw was to think that consensus was the sole authority for validating interpretations of scripture and that he overestimated the centrality of consensus in Muslim thought.[14]

[10] See Hasan, *The Doctrine of Ijmāʿ in Islam: a Study of the Juridical Principle of Consensus*, 179. Hasan adds that Ibn Taymiyya construes Ibn Hanbal's position as only accepting the consensus of the companions.

[11] See Hossein Modarressi Tabataba'i, *An Introduction to Shīʿī Law: A Bibliographical Study* (London: Ithaca Press, 1984), 3; Hasan, *The Doctrine of Ijmāʿ in Islam: A Study of the Juridical Principle of Consensus*, 174–175; and Robert Gleave, "Intra-madhhab Ikhtilāf and the Late Classical Imami Shiite Conception of the Madhhab," in *The Islamic School of Law Evolution, Devolution, and Progress*, eds. P. J. Bearman, Rudolph Peters, and Frank E. Vogel (Cambridge, MA: Islamic Legal Studies Program, Harvard Law School, 2005), 136–137.

[12] "Intra-madhhab Ikhtilāf and the Late Classical Imami Shiite Conception of the Madhhab," 137.

[13] See Hourani's presentation in George F. Hourani, "The Basis of Authority of Consensus in Sunnite Islam," *Studia Islamica* 21 (1964): 49–52.

[14] For Hourani's criticism, see ibid., 52–54. Hallaq also notes that there is no circularity in the way that the legal theorists argued for consensus's basis. Hallaq, *A History*, 76.

The second exception is Hourani's attempt to go beyond mere description of debates on the authority of consensus. Hourani puts classical Muslim understanding of consensus's authority in conversation with classical Islamic theological discussions and mid-twentieth-century Western philosophical debates on moral epistemology. Hourani considers, before rejecting, the possibility that the classical understanding of consensus is simply a form of what he labels the social subjectivist or conventionalist theory of moral knowledge. This view holds that judgments of ethical value do not track objective moral features. Rather, they merely manifest the attitudes of the relevant moral community. The Muslim theory of consensus then is "merely a religious way of expressing the social subjectivist definition of value."[15] This construal of consensus is susceptible to criticisms that apply to social subjectivism, generally contradict classical Islamic theological theories of ethical value, and the moral objectivism implicit in the Qur'an and the Prophet's teachings. Hourani criticizes social subjectivism in two ways. It does not properly account for the intentionality of moral beliefs, nor can it account for criticism of or change in moral ideas. From the perspective of Islamic theology, Muʿtazilite moral objectivism and Ashʿarite theistic subjectivism posit value-making features of acts beyond the community's mere agreement, and therefore conflict with a social subjectivist construal of consensus. Lastly, the very fact that the Qur'an criticizes the first Muslim community's preferences, as in the verse that describes its attitude toward fighting—"Prescribed for you is fighting, though it be hateful to you"—seems to undermine the community's authority to make morality.

II. The Classical Legal Theorists on Procedural Conditions for a Consensus

Sunni legal theorists writing on consensus devoted attention to two broad themes: substantiating its proof-value and delineating the features identifying its occurrence. The following types of questions dominated their discussion of the latter theme. Who counts as a consensus-maker? Is tacit consensus valid? Precisely when does a consensus occur? The scholarship on the answers developed by Islamic

[15] Hourani, "The Basis of Authority of Consensus in Sunnite Islam," 46. Hourani notes Shaybani's justification of the consensus through the Prophetic hadith that asserts "Whatever the Muslims see as good is good with God" comes closest to expressing a social subjectivist understanding of moral knowledge, and in this case, consensus.

thought to these questions is mostly descriptive and hence does not give us much insight into historiographical trends in consensus scholarship. But because much of the content of modern Islamic thought is an attempt to reconfigure the doctrine of consensus through its procedural features, it behooves us to gain a working understanding of some of them.

One of the procedural questions that occupied legal theorists was whether individual consensus-makers needed to expressly assent to a rule in order to establish a consensus, or whether their silence or lack of explicit dissent was sufficient. Bernand notes that only the Hanafis seem to have accepted the legitimacy of tacit consensus, and even they confined it to laws dealing with dispensations for extenuating circumstances (*rukhas*), not those that govern a normal state of affairs (*aza'im*).[16] Amidi holds that a tacit agreement of all consensus-makers yields a consensus, but only with probabilistic and not certain proof-value.[17] A related issue was whether the unanimous actions of consensus-makers that presupposed a law was sufficient to establish the consensus-makers' assent to that law and therefore a consensus on it. Those who considered such a consensus valid argued that just as the Prophet's act presupposes his approval of it, the community's act ought to be regarded in the same fashion. The Shafi'is rejected this type of consensus on the grounds that it is impossible to know whether each member of the community has in fact acted in the same fashion.[18]

Another procedural question was whether it is a condition for the validity of a consensus that each individual mujtahid die off before a consensus can be declared. Saying that the death of all the consensus-makers was a condition preserved an individual consensus-maker's prerogative to change his mind, and thereby cause the failure of the consensus to materialize. The Hanafi legal theorist, Abu Bakr al-Sarakhsi (d. 490/1096) and the Shafi'i scholar, Abu Hamid al-Ghazali (d. 505/1111) rejected the condition. Ghazali simply held that the moment a consensus is reached, it is binding. Sarakhsi held that to make it a requirement is in fact to foreclose the possibility of consensus completely.[19]

One of the central procedural issues the legal theorists discussed is who counts as a consensus-maker. The settled classical doctrine holds that only those competent to do *ijtihad*, or derive the law from scripture, count as consensus-makers—a position that excludes the laity. A more refined version of the position holds that on

[16] Bernand, "Idjmā'."

[17] The upshot of classifying a tacit consensus as of only probabilistic proof-value may be that a dissenter from the consensus need not be regarded as committing a sin. See Bernard G. Weiss, *The Spirit of Islamic Law* (Athens, GA: University of Georgia Press, 2006), 226–228 for a discussion of this issue.

[18] Bernand, "Idjmā'."

[19] See ibid.; Hallaq, *A History*, 78–79. Amidi agrees with the majority that a consensus is binding as soon as all the consensus-makers concur. There is no special requirement that they must die off. See Weiss, *Search*, 229–230.

issues of general religious obligations, the laity's judgments count, but on technical points of law, only that of the *mujtahids* count.[20]

Related to the issue of who counts is whether consensus can be generated by the consensus-makers of a single region, most notably Medina. Early Medinan scholars may have thought that the consensus of the scholars of Medina constituted a legal proof. Both Shaybani and Shafiʿi reject this argument and insist that a valid consensus requires consensus-makers from all regions to concur on a law.[21]

Weiss ultimately concludes that while, theoretically, consensus was a legal proof not rooted in a historical moment, insofar as the contemporaneous concurrence of all consensus-makers, regardless of time period, occasions it, the procedural conditions delimiting its occurrence proved too onerous to be practicable. In practice, therefore, claims of consensus were entirely those that occurred in the past, and thus acted much as a scriptural text does in legal argument. Weiss says that Amidi himself must have been aware of this character of consensus, which is the reason why he listed consensus under the broader heading of "matn" or "textual proof."[22]

The equivocality of the main Qur'anic proof text, the lack of certain authenticity of the hadith texts, and the fact that some scholars limited consensus to the generation of the companions would all be cited by thinkers desiring to reconfigure consensus in the modern age or eliminate it entirely.

III. Consensus Before the Classical Doctrine

If one does not accept the interpretations that later Muslim scholars gave to verses of the Qur'an as substantiating consensus, it is far from clear that the Qur'an has anything to say about consensus as a type of authority. Though the hadith texts used by legal theorists seem to be a bit more clear, Western scholars, and even some

[20] See Hallaq, *A History*, 80. Amidi identifies the mujtahids-only view of consensus-makers as the majority opinion among legal theorists, even though he himself is committed to the minority view which holds that the assent of the laity must be included for a valid consensus. For the details of this position and arguments for it, see Weiss, *Search*, 213–214.

[21] See Umar F. Abd-Allah Wymann-Landgraff, *Mālik and Medina: Islamic Legal Reasoning in the Formative Period* (Leiden: Brill, 2013), 200 for a summary of Shaybani and Shafiʿi's criticisms of the Medinan consensus position. For the arguments of later legal theorists, see ibid., 215–216. See also the summary of the debate between Malikis and non-Malikis in Hallaq, *A History*, 80. On Amidi's presentation of this issue, see Weiss, *Spirit*, 220–221.

[22] Weiss, *Search*, 182.

modernist Muslim intellectuals, seem skeptical that they can be dated with any confidence, much less authenticated to the Prophet Muhammad. In the absence of these literary sources, scholars can only mount conjectural theories about what consensus could have meant to the earliest Muslims and how it initially developed into its classical form. Muslim modernists, such as Manzooruddin Ahmed, rely on assumptions about the character of common deliberation on issues facing the community during the time of the Prophet Muhammad and the first four caliphs. Orientalists and more recent Western scholars rely on assumptions about how ideas emerge and develop to help groups retain authority and power in a contentious and competitive environment in the Umayyad and early Abbasid time periods. Both groups reject the accounts that had crystallized in the classical doctrine on the authority of consensus: that the Prophet, through the Qur'an and hadith established consensus as a legal proof.

Most scholars think that evidence of premodern consensus theorists' attempts at substantiation of consensus as a type of legal proof appears at the earliest from the second half of the second/eighth century. This position presumes that the Qur'anic verses and hadiths used by classical legal theorists to substantiate consensus were originally intended to do no such thing. This begs the question of how Muslims regarded consensus before that time. Scholars that pursued this question employed historical-critical methods of analysis, and can be divided into two camps: scholars belonging to the Orientalist tradition and those belonging to the Muslim modernists. The famous nineteenth-century Orientalist, Ignaz Goldziher (d. 1340/1921) sees two conflicts as especially important to the development of consensus in the history of early Islam: the conflict between religious scholars on the content of and basis for legal norms, and the conflict between religious scholars and political elites on what legitimizes caliphal rule. For Goldziher, the emergence of consensus as a type of legal proof is rooted in the conflict between early religious scholars about where the normative Sunna, a source for religious norms, may be found. In his view, traditionalist religious scholars insisted that the Sunna is only found in hadith texts and wanted to reform existing customary social norms according to the information found in them. Other scholars thought that the customary practice of local societies already reflected the normative Sunna, and invoked consensus to argue for the legitimacy of this conception of the Sunna. Goldziher writes:

> The ijmāʿ is thus a counterweight to the attempt of traditionalists to reform existing customs according to their own views and to oppose sharply the customary laws of society. As we have just seen, they had to admit their weakness in the face of such power and they were clever enough to find a form for this admission which made the recognition of ijmāʿ an element of the sunna.[23]

[23] Ignaz Goldziher, *Muslim Studies*, trans. C.R. Barber and S.M. Stern, 2 vols. (London: Geo. Allen & Unwin, 1971), 87.

In addition to being involved in arguments between religious scholars on the sources of norms, consensus developed as a tool for political legitimation. After the Abbasid revolution in the middle of the second/eighth century, consensus became involved in arguments about political legitimacy between religious scholars and caliphs. Against the hereditary argument advocated by the Abbasids, religious scholars insisted that it is the community's consensus that confers legitimacy on a caliph's accession to the office.[24]

Ultimately, Goldziher theory supposes that consensus as a legal proof emerged because of the competition between social groups in early Islam. Schacht similarly links its emergence to conflict, albeit one between the ancient geographical schools and Shafiʿi. Each of the ancient geographical schools accepted the authority of their local consensus as a legal proof in practice, even if in theory they did not. The Medinese accepted the authority of local consensus in both theory and practice, and in fact tended to accept the opinion of the majority of scholars as sufficient to generate a consensus.[25] The Iraqis, although in practice tended to regard the consensus of local scholars as a sufficient legal proof, in theory insisted that it be universal, and not generated in a particular city.[26] According to Schacht, much of the authority of the legal doctrine of the ancient schools was consensus-based. And, insofar as Shafiʿi's life project was devoted to articulating a non-parochial law, he was devoted to dismantling the attractiveness of the ancient schools by enshrining the principle that only properly authenticated Prophetic hadith may serve as decisive legal proofs. This meant undermining the authority of provincial consensus. He did this by insisting that only the universal agreement of all Muslims, lay and scholars alike, generated a valid consensus.[27] Consistent with Schacht's view of Shafiʿi as predominantly responsible for introducing a new paradigm in legal theory, he regards Shafiʿi's interventions as generally successful. On the doctrine of consensus, Shafiʿi won acceptance for the idea that for an agreement to count as a consensus it must be universal, and not provincial. But Shafiʿi lost on the idea that it must consist of the concurrence of all Muslims, scholars and lay alike.[28]

Hallaq adds to aspects of Schacht's understanding of the historical emergence of a technical legal doctrine of consensus. Relying on Bravmann's work on the pre-Islamic values of the Arabs, Hallaq holds that consensus is likely rooted in the authority given by the Arabs to the "conscious formal agreement of the tribe."[29] Before the solidification of consensus as a technical legal doctrine was addressed explicitly and at length in works of classical legal theory, and during the age of the dominance of the geographical schools of law, Hallaq thinks that consensus served as a mechanism that conferred legitimacy on the "average" doctrine of a given locale.[30]

[24] Ibid., 97–99. [25] Schacht, *The Origins of Muhammedan Jurisprudence*, 83–85.
[26] Ibid., 85–88. [27] *An Introduction to Islamic Law* (Oxford: Clarendon Press, 1964), 59.
[28] *The Origins of Muhammedan Jurisprudence*, 59. [29] Hallaq, *A History*, 20. [30] Ibid.

The tradition of Islamic studies in the academic West tended to explain the emergence of consensus as rooted in the competition of different groups for social legitimacy and power. Muslim modernists, largely from Pakistan in the 1960s and '70s, on the other hand locate it in the practices of communal deliberation in early Islamic history. While the former's view is seemingly premised on the assumption that the development of ideas in history can be largely reduced to human nature's universal desire for wealth and power, the latter's view is premised on a view of the first community as one guided by virtues, and yet unsullied by the tragic conflicts associated with subsequent civil wars.

Manzooruddin Ahmed holds that consensus was intimately linked with the deliberative processes that produced law in the time of the Prophet.[31] On issues not directly legislated in the Qur'an or the Sunna, the Muslim community engaged in a process of deliberative consultation (*shura*), part of which was made up of independent legal opinions of individuals (*ijtihad*) in the community. Over time a consensus would emerge on the best policy or law for the community: "This emergent consensus of opinions was, perhaps, the earliest crude form of ijma‘ (consensus)."[32] After the death of the Prophet, this same deliberative process established the institution of the caliphate. In fact, Ahmed conjectures that the legal institutions of the people of loosening and binding (*ahl al-ḥall wa al-ʿaqd*) and oaths of political loyalty (*bay'a*) were originally interchangeable with consensus, and it is the consensus of the community that legitimated the caliphates of Abu Bakr, 'Umar, and 'Uthman.[33] Perhaps inspired by Ibn Khaldun's concept of *'asabiyya* (group solidarity), Ahmed considers social solidarity or group feeling as the animating spirit behind consensus.[34] Subsequent civil wars and conflicts undermined this solidarity, and it became increasingly difficult and well-nigh impossible for deliberative decision-making to take place within the community and therefore, consensus to be reached on issues of public importance. The community ultimately failed to develop institutional mechanisms that sustained political integration, deliberative decision-making, and the resultant opportunities to generate consensuses.[35] The result: "The natural evolution of the Islamic community in the political sphere was arrested and stagnation followed which had continued until the advent of the twentieth century."[36] Ahmed concludes his genealogical recovery of the consensus's original meaning and role in the political life of the early community with a moral

[31] See Manzooruddin Ahmed, "Shūrā, Ijtihād and Ijmāʿ in the Early State," *University Studies (Karachi)* 1, no. 1 (1964): 46. Ahmed Hasan also sees consensus in the Prophet's community, though informal, as stemming from the practice of consultation, which is itself recommended in the Qur'an. On this see, Ahmad Hasan, "The Political Role of Ijmāʿ," *Islamic Studies* 8 (1969): 140.

[32] Ahmed, "Shūrā, Ijtihād and Ijmāʿ in the Early State," 52.

[33] See ibid., 54. Hasan also thinks there is a connection between consensus and the people who loosen and bind, though by consultation. In the time of the pious caliphs, the people who loosened and bound were a specialized group of people that the caliph consulted. See Hasan, "The Political Role of Ijmāʿ," 141 and 144.

[34] Ahmed, "Shūrā, Ijtihād and Ijmāʿ in the Early State," 58. [35] Ibid., 60. [36] Ibid.

demand: "that the Islamic community should once again galvanize its intellectual potentialities in an organized manner with a view to restore the process of Shura, Ijtihad and Ijmaʿ within the framework of modern democratic government."[37]

Despite the contrasting presumptions that informed scholarship on consensus, it is a mistake to distinguish too sharply between Western Islamic studies scholars and those working in Muslim majority countries, for the simple reason that they often read each other's works, and incorporated each other's findings, even if they may have imagined their prospective audiences a bit differently.[38] This is especially the case with Ahmed Hasan. While Manzooruddin Ahmed sees consensus as intimately linked to the processes of political deliberation in the early community, Ahmed Hasan sees its origin as closely connected to other normative ideals operative in early Islamic history, namely Sunna and communal unity (*jamaʿa*). Both of these ideas—Sunna and communal unity—played the same functional role as consensus, and were essentially synonymous during the time of the Prophet and the early caliphs. They all emphasized the value of maintaining the community's unity. Over time, through their invocation in the conflicts of the period, the concepts came to acquire distinct meaning. Originally, invocation of the Sunna, which referred to the Prophet's model practice, accomplished this goal.[39] Importantly, at this stage, the Sunna was a diffuse normative idea that was not strictly gleaned from hadith texts. As hadith came to be systematically collected in the second century, and religious scholars started advocating legal and religious norms that contrasted with existing communal practice through interpretation of hadith texts, the hadith texts came to represent the Sunna. For this reason, Invocations of the Sunna no longer played the role of emphasizing communal unity. It is at this moment in the middle of the second century that explicit appeals to the unity of the community (*jamaʿa*) along with invocations of its consensus as a binding normative ideal emerged. Hasan thinks that the contours of consensus as a technical legal doctrine emerged from the same impulse and started to be articulated in the third century.[40] Only later on, in response to the changing meanings of the Sunna in the second and third centuries, the civil wars of the first century, and the emergence of distinct religious movements in the third century, did consensus come to fulfill Sunna's role, before it ultimately became a highly technical legal doctrine in the fifth/eleventh century. In the later medieval period, consensus was used to restrict *ijtihad* and prevent the emergence of legal traditions outside the four main Sunni ones. Consistent with modernist understandings of Islamic legal history, Hasan interprets this latter development in starkly negative terms, writing: "Any opinion other than that of the four schools of law became a solitary opinion carrying no weight. Conformity provided sustenance to *Ijmaʿ* and a death-blow to creativity."[41]

[37] Ibid.

[38] Though I might add that the traffic has not always been equal in both directions. It is notable that while Hasan is aware of Goldziher and Schacht, his studies are not cited by Western academics who came after him.

[39] Ahmad Hasan, "Ijmāʿ, an Integrating Force in the Muslim Community," *Islamic Studies* 6 (1967): 390.

[40] Ibid., 390–393.

[41] Ibid., 404.

In many ways Hasan's account shares assumptions with Orientalist and modernist descriptions of the historical development of consensus: both regard the concept as having amorphous content in the earliest period, only to acquire ever-increasingly distinct features in response to changing social and political needs. Legal theorists articulate a definitive legal doctrine of consensus in the classical period, and in doing so inaugurate a period of doctrinal stasis in the postclassical period.

IV. Consensus in Modern Postcolonial Islamic Thought

Scholarship on consensus has skipped the postclassical period entirely, and moves almost immediately to a postcolonial modern context. As far as I know, there exist no studies on consensus from the sixteenth and seventeenth centuries. Similar to scholars who examined the classical period, the authors writing about consensus in modern Islamic thought by and large adopt a phenomenological approach, for the simple fact that there exist many literary sources that scholars can analyze, something that poses a problem for those who want to examine consensus in the first two centuries of Islamic history. In addition to the phenomenological approach, some scholarship on consensus in modern thought is also explicitly theological. This strand of scholarship undertakes an analysis of the historical Muslim debates on the authority and use of consensus in order to take an explicit theological position on a live issue in the contemporary Muslim community.

There is one crucial difference between the historical scholarship on the classical and the modern periods. The scholarship on the classical period is largely descriptive and restricts itself to describing the logic of the argumentation amongst legal theorists debating consensus. The texts analyzed are highly technical scholastic works of legal theory, and therefore very difficult to examine as responses to either events or larger social, cultural, and political trends. This is not the case for figures writing about consensus in the modern period. They stem from a much wider stratum of Muslim society; they are not solely composed by religious scholars (*ulama*). Moreover, they write in genres beyond the technical textbooks, and they focus on time periods where a much more extensive body of literary materials documenting the context of the figures exists.

Two works in particular are important for surveying modern Islamic thought on consensus: Ahmad Hasan's article "Modern Trends in Ijmāʿ" and Muhammad Qasim Zaman's "Consensus and Religious Authority in Modern Islam: The Discourses of the ʿUlamāʾ." Hasan divides the contestations over the concept in Islamic thought as being between the liberal reformers and orthodoxy, while Zaman frames the modern discussion as taking place between the modernist intellectuals or those inspired by them and the more traditionalist religious scholars. For Zaman, the debate about the authoritativeness of consensus, its scope, and its procedures reveal how religious scholars incorporated and responded to voices outside of themselves, and how internally differentiated they were. Both authors adopt a genealogical approach in their surveys of modern thought on consensus, and for both, the intellectuals and religious scholars from the Indian sub-continent play a large role in the modern debates over consensus.

Both Hasan and Zaman begin their survey of modern thought on consensus with recounting Shah Waliullah's (d. 1176/1762) thoughts on the matter, elements of which end up being quite influential in modern Islamic thought, especially for Indian Muslims in the early twentieth century. In contrast to the classical legal theorists, Waliullah interprets the hadith "my community does not agree on error" not as directly establishing the authority of consensus, but as recommending the integration of the community, a value that can then in turn justify consensus's authority.[42] Waliullah regards the integration of the community on a common issue as intimately tied to the process of deliberation that precedes the formation of an opinion. He is critical of the classical conception that required the unanimity of consensus-makers, because it was impracticable and impossible, and was never really achieved. Rather, for Waliullah, historically consensus was reached when the caliph decided on a legal position after consultation with the people of knowledge and the community accepted it.[43] When these two conditions are fulfilled: the caliph decides on a given legal opinion as the correct one and the community accepts that decision, you have a law sanctioned with consensus's authority.[44] Historically, this procedure was successfully implemented only during the time of the first three caliphs. Afterwards, the community was too riven by disagreement and conflict to successfully execute the proper consensus procedure.[45] The most relevant feature in Waliullah's conception of consensus for the postcolonial period is his suggestion that some type of political institution plays an integral part in the creation of consensus.

If Waliullah's thoughts on consensus play the role of precursor in modern Islamic thought, the Indian modernist Sayyid Ahmad Khan's (d. 1315/1898) writings on the issue take place firmly in the British colonial period. Khan explicitly rejected the doctrine of consensus as formulated by the classical jurists.[46] He takes his aim at a view, which must have been quite widespread at his time, that consensus does not

[42] See "Modern Trends in Ijmāʿ," *Islamic Studies* 12 (1973): 122 and Muhammad Qasim Zaman, "Consensus and Religious Authority in Modern Islam: The Discourses of the ʿUlamāʾ," in *Speaking for Islam*, eds. Gudrun Krämer and Sabine Schmidtke (Leiden: Brill, 2010), 164.

[43] Hasan, "Modern Trends in Ijmāʿ," 123, 126. The decisions of the second caliph ʿUmar are the paradigmatic examples of this type of consensus.

[44] Ibid., 122. [45] Ibid. [46] Ibid., 127.

simply equate with the dominant customary practices of a Muslim society. Rather, a consensus emerges only after the community agrees to follow a rule that was the result of the active deliberation upon the evidences of the shari'a. Only the latter and not the former is consensus.[47] In one departure from the classical conception, he does not think that a consensus reached by one generation is binding on subsequent generations, if the context that occasioned the consensus-sanctioned law changes. When the context changes, the consensus is no longer valid.[48]

The next thinker, also an Indian, whom Hasan and Zaman identify as a crucial reformer of consensus, is the Deobandi-trained former Sikh 'Ubayd Allah Sindhi (d. 1363/1944). Sindhi identified the emergence of the four sources of Sunni jurisprudence with the historical development of the early Muslim community. While the Qur'an is the basic eternal law of Islam, the Sunna consists of the interpretations of Qur'anic law by the first four Caliphs and the companions generally, and consensus consists of the interpretations of the successors till the end of the Umayyad regime, which for Sindhi constitutes the fundamental bedrock of Islamic positive law (*fiqh*). Sindhi thinks that consensus is not confined to only that period, even if that period is the paradigmatic example of how consensuses are reached and how they relate to the previous two sources. Similar to Khan before him, Sindhi does not consider consensus to be an independent source, nor does he think only unanimous agreement produces it. Rather consensus may be reached by the majority of virtuous and knowledgeable people in their confrontation with new issues after their deliberation on the Qur'an and the Sunna.[49] Unlike Waliullah, Sindhi does not seem to stipulate a special role for rulers or ruling institutions in the formation of consensus.

Zaman's interpretation of Sindhi's conception departs significantly from Hasan's description above. According to Zaman, Sindhi's conception is informed by Shah Waliullah's intellectual output and must be seen as a response to the problems Indian Muslims faced in late colonial British India. Zaman summarizes Sindhi's conception of consensus as composed of two types: local and overlapping. Sindhi's local consensus is genealogically related to the classical doctrine and debates between modernists and conservatives about the concept. Sindhi departs from the classical doctrine in three ways. Whereas the classical theorists limited the consensus-makers to the religious scholars (*ulama*, or more specifically the *mujtahids*), based on an

[47] Ibid. Khan's colleague, Muhsin Mahdi 'Ali Khan (d. 1325/1907) agreed with this aspect of his thought. He considered consensus to be a secondary proof, with no authority independent of scripture. He also rejects the idea that a consensus is indication of a law's inerrancy on the grounds that unanimous agreement on a law as the correct interpretation of scripture does not eliminate the possibility of human error. If a single human may err in interpreting scripture, aggregating humans does nothing to eliminate this possibility, and hence the possibility of error remains. See ibid., 130.

[48] Ibid.

[49] Ibid., 132 and Zaman, "Consensus and Religious Authority In Modern Islam: The Discourses of The 'Ulamā'," 165.

interpretation of Qur'anic verse 9:100, Sindhi extends the consensus-franchise to simply those who follow the first generation of Muslims in doing good.[50] Sindhi does not require unanimity for a binding consensus to take place, a majority is sufficient. At the same time, similar to other modernists, he does not think that consensuses are universally binding. The only timeless universal source is the Qur'an, and Qur'anic law alone is not limited to any particular age.[51] What Zaman labels as Sindhi's doctrine of "overlapping consensus," a choice of terminology that evokes the political philosopher John Rawls's ideas on deliberation in pluralistic societies, has less of a relationship to medieval and modern debates about consensus. Rather it is inspired by the influential Sufi thinker Ibn 'Arabi's (d. 638/1240) ideas. Sindhi envisages the possibility of moral agreement between Muslims and other religious communities on issues facing them in common: "Hindus, Christians, and Muslims can all stand and collaborate on this common ground, but do so in terms of their own scriptural justifications."[52] Sindhi's views of the possibility of moral agreement and collaboration with religious others is underpinned by his philosophical commitment to Akbarian doctrine of the "unity of being (*wahdat al-wujud*)," which he construes as allowing for agreement on moral norms because "adherents of different faiths believe in different manifestations of what is ultimately the same reality."[53] Zaman frames both of Sindhi's notions of consensus as deeply involved in debates amongst Indian Muslims in the first half of twentieth-century British India about the extent to which local culture ought to inform their conception of Islam and the moral possibility of collaborating with non-Muslims on shared goals.

No individual better exemplifies the modernist desire to invest a concrete political institution with the authority to make consensus legitimized law than the revivalist Indian intellectual and poet Muhammad Iqbal (d. 1357/1938). Iqbal wrote his views on consensus at the closing of the First World War, with political developments in Turkey rapidly unfolding. Iqbal wanted to back those figures in the Ottoman Empire that wanted to authorize state institutions with the power and capacity to make Islamic law.[54] He held that one way to invest those institutions with social legitimacy was to root its authority in the doctrine of consensus.[55] Making the argument for this innovative way of conceiving of consensus though required a historical examination of why the classical legal theorists themselves did not vest institutions with the authority to make consensus backed law. For Iqbal, the Umayyad and Abbasid caliphs prevented the formation of an institution which produced consensus-legitimized law because they thought it would become a competing and therefore

[50] The category is based on a phrase in the verse: "And those leading the way (*al-sabiqun*), the first of the Emigrants and the Helpers, and those who followed them in doing good (*wa-lladhina ittaba'uhum bi-ihsan*)—God will be well-pleased with them and they are well-pleased with Him ...."

[51] Zaman, "Consensus and Religious Authority in Modern Islam: The Discourses of The 'Ulamā'," 165.

[52] Ibid., 167. [53] Ibid.

[54] S.M. Yusuf, "A Study of Iqbal's Views on 'Ijma," *Iqbal Review* 3, no. 3 (1962): 17–19.

[55] Zaman, "Consensus and Religious Authority in Modern Islam: The Discourses of the 'Ulamā'," 159.

constraining center of power, something which was against their interests and their absolutist monarchical conception of political authority. But, in the early twentieth century, the political landscape had changed with the spread of republican ideas and institutional forms in the Muslim world. Given a vastly different political situation, Iqbal saw a renewed historical opportunity to vest legislative institutions with the authority to make consensus-legitimized law.[56] But, this would require transferring the competence of engaging in *ijtihad* from scholars who belonged to legal schools to a legislative assembly, inevitably populated by laymen, who, though ignorant of the niceties of the shariʿa, are well-versed in the affairs of the age. This transfer of competence raised its own issues. Given that the legislative assemblies would be peopled by those who were not trained in Islamic law, how are they to avoid mistakes in their interpretation of the Divine sources? Iqbal ultimately suggests that the religious scholars should form a part of the assembly and guide its deliberations with their knowledge of Islamic law.[57]

Similar to other modernists and his contemporary, ʿUbaydallah Sindhi, Iqbal seems to largely reject historical consensuses as binding on subsequent generations. Even in the case of the consensus of the companions, he does not uniformly accept all of them as generating binding laws. Iqbal holds that the companions' consensuses only on points of law, as opposed to points of fact, bind subsequent generations, because the "companions alone possess the knowledge of those questions."[58]

Similar to other modernists, Muhammad ʿAbduh (d. 1323/1905) disagrees fundamentally with the conception of consensus represented in the classical articulation of the doctrine. He thinks that classical interpretations of scripture do not substantiate the doctrine's authority, nor do classical authors get its definition correct, with the end result being a rigid, inflexible, and ultimately unworkable doctrine. Similar to Waliullah and Iqbal, ʿAbduh thinks that political authority has an essential role to play in the creation of consensus. Whereas Waliullah made the executive command of the caliph and its acceptance conditions for the creation of a consensus, and Iqbal located the authority to make it in a formal law-making body, ʿAbduh identifies it as the result of a consultative and deliberative process by those in authority (*ulu 'l-amr*), who possess knowledge of temporal affairs, and are competent to derive the law from scripture.[59] While he considers a consensus reached in this way as infallible, ʿAbduh is at pains to delimit the jurisdiction of issues that those in authority may consider and the sources that they must rely on during their deliberation: "The questions dealt with by them [possessors of political authority] must relate to public interest. They have no say in the questions relating to dogma

[56] Yusuf, "A Study of Iqbal's Views on 'Ijma,'" 19; Hasan, "Modern Trends in Ijmāʿ," 134–135.

[57] Yusuf, "A Study of Iqbal's Views on 'Ijma,'" 20.

[58] Hasan, "Modern Trends in Ijmāʿ," 136.

[59] On this point Rashid Rida, ʿAbduh's influential student, is very similar to his mentor. See Zaman, "Consensus and Religious Authority in Modern Islam: The Discourses of The 'Ulamā'," 157 ʿAbduh

and rituals. These matters will be decided directly on the basis of the Qur'an and the Sunna."[60] If agreement occurs within these parameters, it is indeed infallible, but it is not irrevocable. The consensus of preceding generations does not forever constrain future ones, because the fact that it is binding derives not from its infallibility but from its "utility, advantage and public interest (*maslaha*)."[61] If circumstances change such that complying with a past consensus is against the public interest, there is no reason to continue following it.[62]

While Hasan concluded his survey of consensus in modern Islamic thought with Iqbal, Zaman traces the genealogy of the institutionalist conception of consensus down to Mahmud Shaltut, rector of al-Azhar from 1958–63, who also conceives of the concept largely along the lines developed by ʿAbduh and Rida. For Shaltut, consensus-makers are not only the jurists, nor even all Muslims, but the people of discernment "*ahl al-nazar*," similar to the group identified by ʿAbduh: those people who have knowledge of the community's temporal affairs, and can therefore deliberate on the courses of action facing it based on their consideration of its welfare.[63] Because this body makes its decisions based on welfare and public interest, its determinations, and indeed consensuses are local in character and presumably revocable.[64]

Though Hasan organizes his survey of modern Islamic thought on consensus as taking place within the struggle between modernists and orthodoxy, Zaman notes orientations that do not fall squarely into one camp or another. Take the Egyptian Azhari Islamist religious scholar, Yusuf al-Qaradawi, who neither reproduces the classical doctrine nor quite adopts the modernist view. For Qaradawi, consensus represents the unity of Muslims on "the beliefs, basic principles and understandings, and the fundamental laws on which the community has agreed" (*dawabit*). The function of this type of consensus is to encourage unity amongst Muslims against united non-Muslim enemies who oppose their moral values and material interests.[65] Yet, unlike modernist scholars who restrict consensus in order to advocate change in the law, Qaradawi does not use his reconfigured notion to advocate substantial change in concrete premodern legal inheritance.[66]

and Rida think the "people who loosen and bind," "those in authority," and those consulted in people's affairs are in fact those that are vested with the authority to conclude a consensus. This group is not constituted by the religious scholars alone.

60 Hasan, "Modern Trends in Ijmāʿ," 143.

61 Ibid., 144–145; Zaman, "Consensus and Religious Authority in Modern Islam: The Discourses of the ʿUlamāʾ," 158, Zaman adds that Rida's holds the same position as ʿAbduh.

62 Hasan, "Modern Trends in Ijmāʿ," 145.

63 Zaman, "Consensus and Religious Authority in Modern Islam: The Discourses of the ʿUlamāʾ," 161.

64 Ibid., 162. Zaman describes Shaltut's conception of consensus as amounting to admitting it as having local, as opposed to universal relevance.

65 Ibid., 171–172.

66 Ibid., 174–175.

The mid-twentieth-century modernist intellectual and scholar, Kemal Faruki, adopts many features of Iqbal's institutionalist view of consensus. Similar to other modernists, Faruki assumes a narrative of decline as caused by the prevalence of *taqlid* (deference to inherited law of the madhhabs) in classical times.[67] He says that in the postclassical period consensus was discovered retrospectively because there existed no institutionalized mechanism for creating it.[68] He denies that absolute infallibility is a feature of consensus, because infallibility is something that can only characterize an omniscient being, in essence God.[69] If *ijtihad* is the principle of energy and movement (as Iqbal describes it) in Muslims' attempts to grapple with moral and legal problems as they arise in their societies, consensus is supposed to be a stabilizing principle, but one that ought not to strangle creative engagement with existing problems.[70] Faruki does not think this type of consensus is generated by simply the agreement of Muslims.[71] Not only must consensus-makers be morally trustworthy, but they must also have knowledge of all of the relevant sciences, both religious and secular, to properly evaluate the issue at hand. Faruki does not think that the latter qualification may be found in individuals. But this does not matter because a collective body, institutionally organized, may as a whole fulfill the requirement.[72]

The modernist proposal to institionalize consensus did not go unchallenged. The Pakistani intellectual and scholar S.M. Yusuf is especially critical of Iqbal's proposal to institutionalize consensus. Yusuf highlights the dangers of institutionalizing a consensus-building process that had been organic and diffuse.[73] The historical process of generating consensus allowed individual Muslim scholars whom the community had freely come to recognize as having the authority to offer solutions to its moral and legal problems, to engage in *ijtihad* in a way free from state intervention. Yusuf sees state interference as the real threat to the conscientious and free exercise of *ijtihad* and consensus, something the institutionalized view of consensus and *ijtihad* in fact reinforces. His view merits quotation in full:

> Really *Ijtihad* can be free only in one sense i.e., in the sense of freedom of the conscience of the *Mujtahid* from political pressure and surveillance to temporal authority. Paradoxically enough, this is best achieved in the absence of a rigid mechanism and regularized institution. It is always easier to influence and corrupt a concentrated well-defined body, even though it be an elected one (in the mechanical Western way) than an unlimited body of independent scholars recognised spontaneously by the people at large for their personal qualities and achievements.[74]

He is skeptical that Iqbal's proposal of allowing laymen the competence to engage in *ijtihad* and therefore *ijma'* would not lead grave errors in the interpretation of the Divine will.[75]

[67] Kemal A. Faruki, "Ijma' and Ijtihad for Modern Conditions," *Islamic Order* 1, no. 2 (1979): 78, 80.
[68] Ibid., 79. [69] Ibid. [70] Ibid., 80–81. [71] Ibid., 81. [72] Ibid.
[73] Yusuf, "A Study of Iqbal's Views on 'Ijma,'" 20. [74] Ibid., 24.
[75] Ibid., 23. Part of the reason for this is Yusuf's skepticism that the common man has the requisite moral knowledge to decipher the Divine will. He provides the "offensive examples of alcoholism,

He also disagrees with central components of the modernists' historical narrative of the possibility of change in Islamic law and its relation to the broader social, political, and scientific stagnation of Muslim societies. He is of the view that the reason Muslim societies did not progress in the same way and at the same rate as those of Europe has much to do with Islamic law's inability to change and develop. He also holds that Iqbal had the causation in the wrong direction. It is not the law's stagnation that caused society's stasis, but rather the law's stability was caused by the lack of radical social change that required it.[76] Simply put, for centuries the law was stable because it worked for a myriad of Muslim societies.[77] In Yusuf's view of history, consensuses emerged in traditional Muslim societies very slowly and only after a long period of time, and this is a good thing. It allows for a society's religious authorities to deliberate and debate solutions to problems, and an attendant process of whittling away the weak opinions occurs naturally: "When the individual *mujtahids* have put forward their opinions there sets forth a process of conflict and survival of the fittest comparable to the natural selection in the physical world."[78] In Yusuf's eyes this gradual process of natural selection, has an important political benefit: it protects the rights of those who hold minority opinions on an issue. Presumably, the state's abstention from the consensus-producing process, allows consensus to emerge only when minority opinions disappear in an uncoerced way, which has the political effect of encouraging the toleration of those who hold minority positions.[79]

Similar to Yusuf's criticism of Iqbal's ideas on consensus, Moroccan-educated America-based theologian, Abdullah bin Hamid Ali, offers an explicit theological critique of the classical conception. For Ali, claims of consensus are a discursive practice that can have both good and bad consequences. Its good consequences include generating ideological uniformity, preserving social order, and decreasing the possibility of violent dissent. But its bad consequences consist of undermining an ideological minority's right to legitimate criticism of majoritarian positions within Islam, and also providing regimes cover to oppress ideological minorities.[80] In the classical conception, the consequences of violating a consensus are serious; amounting effectively to accusing someone of violating a universal teaching of Islam. Given these two bad functional consequences of the traditional doctrine, how would one go about reconfiguring it to preserve its social goods?[81]

While Ali does not deny the theoretical authority of unanimous consensus, he holds that most claims of unanimous consensus are in fact invalid.[82] But why are

homosexuality, adultery, racialism, colonialism and imperialism" as evidence of the "ignorant will of the common man." For this see ibid.

76 Ibid., 22. 77 Ibid., 21–22. 78 Ibid., 20. 79 Ibid., 21.

80 Abdullah bin Hamid Ali, "Scholarly Consensus: Ijmāʿ: Between Use and Misuse," *Journal of Islamic Law & Culture* 12, no. 2 (2010): 93.

81 Ibid., 94. 82 Ibid., 94–95.

there so many historical claims of consensus that in fact do not qualify as such, in Ali's view? Because there is no consensus on the criteria for identifying when a consensus occurs.[83] Theoretically, according to the classical doctrine, the consequence of intentionally upholding a consensus that contravenes a law based on a different but explicit and unanimous consensus is to render oneself a disbeliever. Yet, Ali notes that the Spanish scholar Ibn Hazm (d. 456/1064), claims that scholars rarely ever castigate a consensus violator in such a grave way. Ali reasons that scholars in the past resisted this because they inherently sensed the weakness of consensus as a compelling authority, and did not want to accuse a consensus violator of disbelief.[84] However, if we eliminate the classical doctrine of consensus, would we not also eliminate one non-arbitrary way of defining Islam's essence? Based on his reading of Juwayni, who viewed the authority of consensus as substantiated not by scripture, but by the fact that a widely transmitted clear text causes agreement, he argues similarly that the epistemic status of Islam's core principles are ensured by the concept of things "known by immediate necessity ... That is, matters known by immediate necessity result from decisively transmitted (*mutawatir*) and unambiguous scriptural pronouncements (*qat'i al-dalala*)."[85] It is in fact just such a process that itself creates the unanimous consensus.

Ali further adds that even if one were to admit some form of the classical doctrine of consensus as valid, most postclassical historical claims of consensus in fact do not even meet the classical criteria, because they exclude minority objectors, scholars not working within one's legal tradition, or non-Sunnis, all of whom classical legal theorists counted as having the competence to participate in a consensus.[86]

The end result of Ali's argument is to restrict the areas which constitute Islam's essence to a few basic fundamental teachings, which are guaranteed not by unanimous scholarly consensus, but rather by things that are known necessarily because they were widely transmitted from the earliest Muslim community. Moreover, he thinks that the historical claims of consensus ought not to be construed in such a way that violating it amounts to committing an act of apostasy. This opens up the possibility that Muslims may rethink many different detailed legal doctrines, without fear of contravening a consensus. A concrete example of one such law deals with rates of compensation for victims of homicide who were women or non-Muslim. Ali considers the reasoning that led to such conclusions as possibly flawed, and believes that contemporary scholars ought to revisit the issue without fear of contravening a consensus.[87]

[83] Ibid., 95. Ali cites the modern writer of a popular work of legal theory, 'Abd al-Wahhab Khallaf (d. 1956/1375) as holding the opinion that not a single instance of a unanimous scholarly consensus, as defined by the majority of religious scholars, has occurred in Islamic history. For this see ibid., 96.

[84] Ibid., 101. [85] Ibid., 100. [86] Ibid., 102–108. [87] Ibid., 104–105.

Whereas Ali's nuanced understanding of both the functional discursive roles that claims of consensus play in Muslim societies and the internal logic of the classical doctrine informed his normative recommendation of how it ought to be reconfigured, other modern thinkers, such as the Pakistani scholar, Javed Ghamidi, simply deny outright that consensus is an independent source of legislation in Islam, because it has no definitive textual sanction in either the Qur'an or the hadith. Specifically Ghamidi denies that 4:115, a lynchpin proof-text for those that want to substantiate consensus as an independent source, does any such thing. Rather, when read in its narrative context, the verse counsels believers to refrain from joining and supporting the hypocrites. The verse "certainly does not mean that one cannot differ from the interpretations, opinions, and *ijtihads* nor does it mean that if in the light of the Qur'an and Sunna a person criticizes a view on which there is consensus, then he would become worthy of Hell."[88]

V. Consensus in Practice

As we have seen, the vast majority of twentieth-century scholarship on consensus is about its authority as a source for law. There is very little scholarship that investigates actual claims of consensus on specific issues in a systematic way. Carolyn Baugh's "An Exploration of the Juristic Consensus (*ijma*ʿ) on Compulsion in the Marriage of Minors" and Bernard K. Freamon's "Slavery, Freedom, and the Doctrine of Consensus in Islamic Jurisprudence" are two exceptions to this overall trend. Baugh's investigation of the legal debates about the power of fathers to marry off their minors traces the historical role of consensus and its relationship to other types of arguments in early classical Islamic law. Both Baugh and Freamon's inquiries are motivated by practical normative concerns. Freamon is explicit in his, and Baugh's is implicit in her writing. Baugh seeks to weaken the consensus argument for allowing fathers the ability to marry off their minor daughters. Freamon seeks to demonstrate that a consensus-based legal argument can be made for the prohibition of slavery.

In Baugh's analysis, the earliest legal arguments on the issue of the legal capacity of fathers to marry off their minor children were myriad in nature, and seem to reflect the customary practice of different cities. The earliest debates also presuppose that the father's power to marry off his minors applies to both sons and daughters. Two things whittle down this initial heterogeneity of legal argument and undermine

[88] Javed Ahmad Ghamidi, "The Consensus of the Muslims," http://www.javedahmadghamidi.com/books/view/the-consensus-of-muslims.

the assumption that the power to compel marriage covers both genders: the hadith referring to 'A'isha's age at the time of her marriage to the Prophet becomes the main proof-text on the issue, as well as claims of consensus.

The early scholars, al-Marwazi (d. 371/982) and Ibn al-Mundhir (d. 318/930), ground the consensus on the power of the father to marry off his minors on the report recording 'A'isha's marriage contract with the Prophet.[89] Though many classical legal theorists envision the possibility that the simple unanimous agreement of religious scholars could create a law, in practice, Baugh notes: "Further exploration of the consensus on prepubescent marriage throughout the genre of consensus/disagreement writing finds that rather than being a scholarly-wide legal opinion on child marriage, it is little more than a validation of the report of 'A'isha."[90] Baugh demonstrates, at least on one particular issue, that claims of consensus rarely operate in an interpretive vacuum; they are amongst an array of other types of legal arguments on a given issue. Baugh adds that even the scope of the consensus claimed in the early works of comparative law, which explicitly claim the father's power to marry off minors of both genders, is whittled down in works of later law to support explicit discussion of the father's power to compel only prepubescent daughters.[91] In addition to this historical development, Baugh also demonstrates how very little that a consensus on a law actually settles, and in fact raises more issues than it settles. Baugh speculates that this may have been the reason why juristic discussion of compelling boys to marry eventually dropped out of the discussion.[92]

If Baugh emphasizes the limited role that consensus plays in actually settling and developing law, especially as it relates to the morally problematic issue of allowing fathers to compel minors to marry, Freamon makes the argument that Muslims may use the concept of consensus to make a compelling shari'a-based normative argument against the practice of slavery and slave-trading.[93] Freamon contests much of the existing historiography on the abolition of slavery in Muslim lands, which sees movement toward abolishing it as largely inspired by outside European efforts. In Freamon's view, a historical argument can be made for the beginnings of the emergence of specifically Islamic arguments to abolish slavery in the latter half of the nineteenth and early twentieth centuries.[94] Given the passive validation of

[89] Carolyn Baugh, "An Exploration of the Juristic Consensus (ijmāʿ) on Compulsion in the Marriages of Minors," *Comparative Islamic Studies* (2011): 52.

[90] Ibid., 53.

[91] Ibid., 74. In contradistinction to earlier writers, it is not so much that the later authors deny that the father can compel his minor son to marry someone the father chooses as much as they simply do not discuss the issue.

[92] Ibid., 64–65, 88–89.

[93] Bernard K. Freamon, "Slavery, Freedom, and the Doctrine of Consensus in Islamic Jurisprudence," *Harvard Human Rights Journal* 11 (1998): 6–8.

[94] Ibid., 56–63. In particular, Freamon thinks that the discourse of the religious scholars on the issue in this time period have not been examined thoroughly.

the permissibility of slavery in the Qur'an and the Sunna, Freamon thinks that the most effective religious argument for its abolition must come from the creation of a consensus:

In my view, the *ijma'* that would articulate the abolition of slavery is probably an *ijma'* that would take into account the views of the community as a whole and not just the view of the *mujtahidun*. This kind of *ijma'* is one that was contemplated by Imam Shafi'i and recently confirmed as viable in the writing of scholars like Wael Hallaq. All of these views make it clear that the Islamic doctrine of consensus or *ijma'*, in the hands of the modern-day 'ulema', could effectively authorize an Islamic declaration that slavery is now forbidden by the *Shari'a*.[95]

VI. Room for Growth in Consensus Studies

Not surprisingly the advances made and the shortcomings that afflict the scholarship on consensus are ones that beset the historical investigation of Islamic thought generally. The early, classical, and postcolonial modern periods of Islamic thought have received all of the scholarly attention devoted to investigation of the concept of consensus in Islamic thought. I do not think a single investigation of consensus in the postclassical period has been done, despite the existence of a vast number of texts, written often as commentaries on prominent legal text books. The existing scholarship has done a reasonably good job in outlining the contours of the substance of the classical doctrine of consensus, often informed by deep reading of classical texts. Bernard Weiss's periphrastic elucidation of al-Amidi's writings on the topic, and Hourani's reconstruction of the classical arguments for consensus's authority, stand out as exemplary in this respect. The latter goes beyond a simple descriptive presentation of the arguments and counter-arguments and engages in a comparative analysis of the classical consensus discourse.

Much more progress can be made on consensus in early Islam because of the emergence of newer methods of dating individual hadiths, most notably the *isnad-cum-matn* method, and the travelling traditions test.[96] There are a handful of hadiths used by early and classical Islamic scholars as potential proof-texts

[95] Ibid., 63–64.

[96] Behnam Sadeghi, "The Travelling Tradition Test: A Method for Dating Traditions," *Der Islam: Zeitschrift für Geschichte und Kultur des Islamischen Orients* (2010); Harald Motzki, "Dating Muslim Traditions: a Survey," *Arabica* 52, no. 2 (2005).

("My community will not agree on error") for establishing the authority of consensus. Contrary to Schacht, I think it is implausible that the "my community" hadith only became attributed to the Prophet after Shafi'i and was created either by or shortly before the classical collections of hadith. Many of the recent attempts at dating hadith have tended to establish *terminus ante quem* of within the first half of the second century, and I would be surprised if something contrary is the case with the "my community" hadith.[97] A historical study of the chains of transmission (*isnad*) of this and all other texts relating to the Muslim community's authority, using the latest methods of dating them, may provide a much more granular and detailed picture of when, how, where, and in whose hands the idea of the community as a religious authority developed in the formative period. As such, it is a desideratum for consensus studies specifically, and the history of early Islam generally.

Those adopting the source-critical method of investigation tended to concentrate on the formative period of Islamic history. Those that used a phenomenological approach concentrated on the classical period. Much as is the case with Islamic legal studies generally, the phenomenologists of classical legal thought are mainly interested in works of legal theory (*usul al-fiqh*) as opposed to positive law (*fiqh*) or responsa (*fatawa*). What we have gained from this is pretty good knowledge of the structure of arguments for and against consensus as a proof, at least in the classical period. What we do not know much about is how the writers of positive law and the givers of *fatwas* used consensus as an argument on concrete issues. The few small studies that have investigated this in some depth indicate that, in fact, consensus does not seem to have been used as an independent proof. Other authors have noted the claims to consensus made by religious scholars on concrete issues rarely, if ever, meet the criteria stipulated by the legal theorists. These latter authors make these observations often in passing, and not based on any systematic study of the issue. The fact that no systematic study of claims of consensus on concrete issues exists, renders certain foundational assertions about it in current scholarship curious and unsubstantiated. These claims have to do with the so-called centrality of consensus to Islam (particularly Sunnism), or more specifically to Islamic law. Those that restrict their remarks to Islamic law hold that consensus validates or ratifies specific solutions to legal and theological problems as expressive of orthodoxy.[98] But, to my mind, no study exists which actually documents this process of selection and validation, hence the claim that consensus as a legal argument or social procedure that

[97] See, e.g., Mairaj U. Syed, "The Construction of Historical Memory in the Exegesis of Kor 16, 106."

[98] See, e.g., Patricia Crone's representative remarks: "Ijmāʿ is classically described as the third source of law, but it was only a source in the sense that it put doctrinal constructions to the test, eliminating some, endorsing others and thereby adding a new layer of accepted views, on which the next generations could build." Patricia Crone, *God's Rule: Government and Islam* (New York: Columbia University Press), 140.

generates orthodoxy after a time of uncertainty and disagreement at a minimum remains unsubstantiated. I do not think consensus, at least as defined by the legal theorists, has in fact played much of a role in the history of Islamic law, but we need a much more systematic set of studies to tell for sure.

References

Abd-Allah Wymann-Landgraff, Umar F., *Mālik and Medina: Islamic Legal Reasoning in the Formative Period* [in English] (Leiden: Brill, 2013).

Ahmed, Manzooruddin, "Shūrā, Ijtihād and Ijmāʿ in the Early State." *University Studies (Karachi)* 1, no. 1 (1964): 46–60.

Ali, Abdullah bin Hamid, "Scholarly Consensus: Ijmāʿ: between Use and Misuse." *Journal of Islamic Law & Culture* 12, no. 2 (2010): 92–113.

Baugh, Carolyn, "An Exploration of the Juristic Consensus (ijmāʿ) on Compulsion in the Marriages of Minors." *Comparative Islamic Studies* (2011): 33–92.

Bernand, Marie, "Idjmāʿ" in Peri Bearman, Th. Bianquis, Clifford E. Bosworth, Emeri van Donzel, and Wolfhart P. Heinrichs (eds.) *Encyclopedia of Islam*, second edition (Leiden: Brill, 1980–2004).

Crone, Patricia, *God's Rule: Government and Islam* (New York: Columbia University Press, 2003).

Faruki, Kemal A., "Ijmaʿ and Ijtihad for Modern Conditions." *Islamic Order* 1, no. 2 (1979): 76–83.

Freamon, Bernard K., "Slavery, Freedom, and the Doctrine of Consensus in Islamic Jurisprudence." *Harvard Human Rights Journal* 11 (1998): 1–64.

Ghamidi, Javed Ahmad, "The Consensus of the Muslims" http://www.javedahmadghamidi.com/books/view/the consensus of muslims.

Gleave, Robert, "Intra-madhhab Ikhtilāf and the Late Classical Imami Shiite Conception of the Madhhab" in Peri J. Bearman, Rudolph Peters, and Frank E. Vogel (eds.) *The Islamic School of Law Evolution, Devolution, and Progress* (Cambridge, MA: Islamic Legal Studies Program, Harvard Law School, 2005).

Goldziher, Ignaz, *Muslim Studies* (translated by C.R. Barber and Samuel M. Stern. 2 vols. London: Geo. Allen & Unwin, 1971).

Goldziher, Ignaz, *The Ẓāhirīs: their Doctrine and their History* (Leiden: Brill, 1971).

Hallaq, Wael, *A History of Islamic Legal Theories: an Introduction to Sunnī Uṣūl al-Fiqh* (Cambridge; New York: Cambridge University Press, 1997).

Hallaq, Wael B., "On the Authoritativeness of Sunni Consensus." *International Journal of Middle East Studies* 18, no. 4 (1986): 427–454.

Hasan, Ahmad, "Ijmāʿ, an Integrating Force in the Muslim Community." *Islamic Studies* 6 (1967): 389–406.

Hasan, Ahmad, "The Political Role of Ijmāʿ." *Islamic Studies* 8 (1969): 135–150.

Hasan, Ahmad, "Modern Trends in Ijmāʿ." *Islamic Studies* 12 (1973): 121–153.

Hasan, Ahmad, *The Doctrine of Ijmāʿ in Islam: a Study of the Juridical Principle of Consensus* (New Delhi: Nusrat Ali Nasri for Kitab Bhawan, 1992).

Hourani, George F., "The Basis of Authority of Consensus in Sunnite Islam." *Studia Islamica* 21 (1964): 13–60.

Lowry, Joseph E, *Early Islamic Legal Theory: the Risāla of Muḥammad ibn Idrīs al-Shāfiʿī* (Leiden: Brill, 2007).
Modarressi Tabataba'i, Hossein, *An Introduction to Shīʿī Law: A Bibliographical Study* (London: Ithaca Press, 1984).
Motzki, Harald, "Dating Muslim Traditions: A Survey." *Arabica* 52, no. 2 (2005): 204–253.
Sadeghi, Behnam, "The Travelling Tradition Test: a Method for Dating Traditions." *Der Islam: Zeitschrift für Geschichte und Kultur des Islamischen Orients* (2010): 203–242.
Schacht, Joseph, *The Origins of Muhammedan Jurisprudence* (Oxford: Clarendon Press, 1950).
Schacht, Joseph, *An Introduction to Islamic law* (Oxford: Clarendon Press, 1964).
Syed, Mairaj U., "The Construction of Historical Memory in the Exegesis of Kor 16, 106." *Arabica* 62, no. 5–6 (2015): 607–651.
Weiss, Bernard G., "Al-Āmidī on the Basis of Authority of Consensus" in Donald P. Little (ed.) *Essays on Islamic Civilization Presented to Niyazi Berkes* (Leiden: Brill, 1976) 342–356.
Weiss, Bernard G., *The Search for God's Law: Islamic Jurisprudence in the Writings of Sayf al-Dīn al-Āmidī* (Salt Lake City: University of Utah Press, 1992).
Weiss, Bernard G., *The Spirit of Islamic Law* (Athens, GA: University of Georgia Press, 2006).
Yusuf, S.M., "A Study of Iqbal's Views on 'Ijma'." *Iqbal Review* 3, no. 3 (1962): 17–25.
Zaman, Muhammad Qasim, "Consensus and Religious Authority in Modern Islam: The Discourses of the ʿUlamāʾ" in Gudrun Krämer and Sabine Schmidtke (ed.) *Speaking for Islam* (Leiden: Brill, 2010) 153–180.

B

INSTITUTIONS

CHAPTER 12

AL-QADI

MOHAMMAD FADEL

I. Introduction

ISLAM, it is often said, is a religion of law, an observation that derives from the pre-eminent place that the law, the shari'a, occupies in Muslims' self-understanding of what it means to be a Muslim.[1] Muslims' interest in law manifested itself in the area of theoretical jurisprudence (*usul al-fiqh*) as well as substantive law (*furu' al-fiqh*). But what distinguished Islamic law's place in the history of Muslim societies, particularly with regard to Christendom and Judaism, was the fact that its norms, while certainly serving the role of a general moral law, also served as the generally applicable rules of the secular legal system in Muslim societies until the third-quarter of the nineteenth century. Accordingly, Islamic law was deeply embedded in the state institutions of the premodern Islamic world to a much greater extent than occurred in the two other Abrahamic religions. The central, albeit not the exclusive, institution for the application of the norms of Islamic law was the court of the *qadi*, the Islamic law judge. As will be discussed in greater detail below, Muslim jurists paid special attention to the rules governing this office, writing numerous specialized treatises that set out the substantive doctrines regulating its operation as well as routinely dedicating chapters of their general works on substantive law to the subject. This chapter will discuss the history of the office and the methodological questions associated with studying this institution.

[1] Joseph Schacht, *An Introduction to Islamic Law* (London: Oxford University Press, 1964), 1.

As is the case with Islamic history generally, any attempt to understand the institution of the *qadi* must confront the problem of the sources that are available to study the institution. As a general rule, only literary evidence is available for the earliest periods of Islamic history regarding the *qadi*. Any discussion of the office during the Prophet Muhammad's lifetime, that of his first four successors—the so-called "rightly-guided caliphs," and even during the Umayyad period, will raise the controversial question of the reliability of the Arabic literary sources for the first 150 years of Islamic history. This chapter will not attempt to resolve that debate, and will instead touch on issues such as the reliability of historical sources in connection with particular issues that arise in contemporary scholarship surrounding the institution of the *qadi*.

There have generally been two approaches to the study of the *qadi*. The first may be called a doctrinal approach which focuses on the theoretical norms that were articulated in connection with the institution in various times and places. Unsurprisingly, this approach tends to be most commonly used by academically trained lawyers and specialists in Islamic law. The second method is less concerned with the normative framework of the institution and instead attempts to understand how the institution actually operated in particular social and historical contexts using empirical methods. This second approach, however, does not represent a single method, but includes studies that have taken a number of different disciplinary approaches to understanding how the *qadi* functioned: sociology (social history), anthropology, political science, and economics. Empirical investigations into the history of this office, however, are necessarily limited by the availability of the relevant empirical evidence, a fact that has substantially restricted empirical approaches to the modern period and to early modern Muslim polities such as the Ottomans which retained extensive records reflecting the *qadi's* activities.

This chapter will proceed chronologically, beginning with the pre-Islamic Arabian context, and concluding in the modern period. It will then conclude with an assessment of research on the *qadi* and suggestions for future research.

II. Adjudication in the Pre-Islamic Period

Little is known of the details of the legal system that prevailed in pre-Islamic Arabia. Both Joseph Schacht and Noel Coulson give very cursory treatments of the pre-Islamic legal system, and emphasize the absence of any institutionalized means to enforce whatever law existed aside from appeal to arbitrators (*hakam* (s.)/*hukkam* (p.)) and self-help, either in the form of direct action by the aggrieved individual, or if the offender was from another tribe, by the direct action of the victim's tribe.[2] They both concur that most pre-Islamic law was customary Bedouin law, with the exceptions of Makka and Madina; in the former, a kind of commercial law was said to have developed and in the latter a kind of real property law as well as agricultural contracts came into existence.[3] In addition, pre-Islamic Arabian law and institutions, from the perspective of Schacht and Coulson, existed in isolation from the wider legal cultures of their Near Eastern imperial neighbors, the Byzantines and the Sassanians.[4] Wael Hallaq, by contrast, emphasizes the deep connections of the Arabian Peninsula with its neighboring empires, commercially, politically, and legally, and argues that Bedouin and sedentary Arabs, far from operating in distinctive political, legal, and cultural spheres, lived together in a complementary civilizational system in which trade, religion, and politics bound them to the wider Near East. Although he does not discuss the particulars of how pre-Islamic Arabians resolved their legal disputes, Hallaq's analysis inevitably leads to the conclusion that the pre-Islamic Arabs must have had greater institutional sophistication than that suggested by Coulson and Schacht.[5]

III. Adjudication in the Prophetic Period

The Prophetic period did not, according to most accounts, represent a sharp break from pre-existing Arabian dispute resolution mechanisms. Most authorities take the view that the Prophet Muhammad viewed himself primarily as a moral reformer, and not a lawgiver, at least until he was forced to leave Makka and emigrate to Madina.[6] Once there, however, the logic of heading up the new community of Muslims led to the increasingly substantive legal content of Qur'anic revelations, and the political expectation that Muslims would submit all their disputes to the Prophet himself, who was their natural arbitrator, if only to make clear Muslims'

[2] Schacht, *An Introduction to Islamic Law*, 7–8; N.J. Coulson, *A History of Islamic Law* (Edinburgh: Edinburgh University Press, 1964), 9–10.

[3] Schacht, *An Introduction to Islamic Law*, 6; Coulson, *A History of Islamic Law*, 10.

[4] Schacht, *An Introduction to Islamic Law*, 8–9; Coulson, *A History of Islamic Law*, 10.

[5] Wael B. Hallaq, *The Origins and Evolution of Islamic Law* (New York: Columbia University Press, 2005), 8–19, 25.

[6] Schacht, *An Introduction to Islamic Law*, 10; Coulson, *A History of Islamic Law* 11–12; Hallaq, *The Origins and Evolution of Islamic Law*, 19–20.

independence from other laws, whether pagan or religious in the form of Christian or Jewish law.[7] As Schacht pointed out, however, the Qur'an referred to the Prophet's dispute resolution activities using the pre-Islamic term *hakam* and the new, Qur'anic term *qada*, from which the term *qadi* is derived, indicating, in his view, the transition from a purely consensual arbitral form of dispute resolution to a state-based system for the administration of justice.[8]

The only real dissent from the view that law was only a secondary concern of the Prophet Muhammad comes from Hallaq. Although he largely affirmed the opinions of Coulson and Schacht in his 2005 book on the origins of Islamic law, he subsequently repudiated that position and argued that law had been a central concern of the Qur'an from the very beginning of the Prophet's mission in Makka.[9] Hallaq does not, however, depart from the views of Schacht and Coulson with respect to their belief that the Prophet did not establish a new infrastructure for the administration of justice, but instead largely took over the pre-Islamic institution of the arbitrator.[10]

The conviction that the Prophet did not establish a new system for the administration of justice is at odds with the claims of Muslim tradition, however, which portray the Prophet, among other things, as appointing some of his companions, for example, Mu'adh b. Jabal, to serve as judges for various regions of the new state as it gradually expanded to encompass all of the Arabian Peninsula.[11]

IV. Adjudication in the Madinese Caliphate (*al-Khilafa al-Rashida*) and the Umayyad Caliphate

Probably due to the paucity of sources for this period, contemporary scholarship largely follows traditional Muslim accounts of the institution of the *qadi* in this period. According to the prevailing view of contemporary scholars, after the death of the Prophet Muhammad in 632 CE, the Islamic state consolidated its control over the Arabian Peninsula during the reign of the first of four so-called "rightly-guided caliphs," Abu Bakr al-Siddiq. Then, during the reigns of his two immediate successors, 'Umar b. al-Khattab and 'Uthman b. 'Affan, it expanded into the Fertile

[7] Schacht, *An Introduction to Islamic Law*, 11; Coulson, *A History of Islamic Law* 11; Hallaq, *The Origins and Evolution of Islamic Law*, 20–22.

[8] Schacht, *An Introduction to Islamic Law*, 10.

[9] Wael B. Hallaq, "Groundwork of the Moral Law," *Islamic Law & Society* 16, no. 3/4 (2009): 239–279.

[10] Hallaq, *The Origins and Evolution of Islamic Law*, 24.

[11] Ibid., 34.

Crescent into the borders of the Anatolian Peninsula, North Africa, Iran and Central Asia. By the time 'Ali b. Abi Talib, the fourth rightly-guided caliph assumed office, the Islamic state could no longer be effectively ruled from Madina, and he moved his government to the newly established Arab garrison town of Kufa, located in southern 'Iraq.

The rapid expansion of the Islamic state in the immediate aftermath of the Prophet's death created immense political and administrative challenges.[12] As a general rule, the conquering Arab armies chose to found new towns, such as Kufa and Basra in 'Iraq, and Fustat in Egypt, in the vicinity of more established towns rather than settle with the native population. The one major exception to this pattern was Damascus, where the Muslim Arabs, probably because of extensive trading ties to that city dating to the pre-Islamic period, felt comfortable settling in the city itself. During this period, the caliphs in Madina relied on their field commanders to wield both administrative and legal powers, in addition to control over military issues.[13] They typically only exercised jurisdiction over those Muslims settled in the garrison towns, with the non-Muslim inhabitants of the empire and the Bedouin Arabs generally left to follow their own laws.[14] Governors, when adjudicating disputes, would typically rely on legal rulings found in the Qur'an, as well as their individual (and communal) memory of Prophetic precedent, and failing that, use their individual judgment (*ra'y*), often after consulting with the caliph in Madina.[15] Later Umayyad caliphs began a process of centralizing the judiciary by directly appointing judges instead of delegating that function to local governors, as had been the practice in the earlier days of the dynasty.[16]

Traditional Muslim sources, however, indicate that the rightly-guided caliphs designated specific persons to serve as *qadis*,[17] and that the caliphs gave them very specific instructions on how they should conduct themselves while in office. For example, Muslim authorities on the history of judgeship regularly reference 'Umar b. al-Khattab's alleged letter of appointment of Abu Musa al-Ash'ari as *qadi* for the basic parameters of the judge's functions and the ethical norms that govern the office.[18] In any case, it is clear that the process of rationalizing and professionalizing the administration of justice as a function distinctive from political administration began in earnest only with the Umayyad caliphate. With the Umayyads the office of the *qadi* became clearly separated from that of the regional governor, and evidence recently uncovered by Wadad Kadi suggests that Umayyad-era judges were granted regular stipends from the treasury.[19] At the same time, however, Arabic historical

[12] Coulson, *A History of Islamic Law*, 21.

[13] Schacht, *An Introduction to Islamic Law*, 15; Hallaq, *The Origins and Evolution of Islamic Law*, 29–32.

[14] Hallaq, *The Origins and Evolution of Islamic Law*, 36. [15] Ibid., 55–56. [16] Ibid., 57.

[17] Ibid., 34.

[18] R.B. Sergeant, "The Caliph 'Umar's Letters to Abu Musa al-Ash'ari and Mu'awiya," *Journal of Semitic Studies* XXIX, no. 1 (1984): 65–79.

[19] Wadad Kadi, "The Salaries of Judges in Early Islam: The Evidence of the Documentary and Literary *Sources*," *Journal of Near Eastern Studies* 68, no. 1 (2009): 9–30.

sources indicate that judges did not necessarily limit themselves to the administration of justice; they often exercised other administrative powers in addition to the resolution of disputes between private persons, a pattern that would be repeated throughout the Muslim world until modernizing reforms in the late nineteenth century.[20]

During the Umayyad caliphate the outlines of a distinctively Islamic law began to take shape. While legal reasoning was still in its infancy, and certainly primitive relative to what it would reach a mere hundred years later during the 'Abbasid caliphate,[21] evidence suggests that early jurists—including judges—had already begun the process of rationalizing their decision-making, largely by attempting to harmonize different precedents that had been reported as well as the different ad hoc solutions to various legal problems that had been proposed by various authorities through the exercise of *ra'y*. This process of rationalizing judicial decisions, opinions of a nascent group of legal specialists, caliphal decisions, Prophetic practice, and Qur'anic law gradually gave rise to formal doctrines which would eventually crystallize into the various schools of Islamic law a few centuries later.

There is also the controversial question of the role that non-Islamic law or legal systems played in the formation of what would come to be known as Islamic law. Authors such as Schacht and Coulson generally took the view that the Arab Muslims emerged from the Arabian Peninsula virtually *tabula rasa* with respect to questions of law, and as a result, much of what became Islamic law was in fact adopted from the laws of the various non-Muslim peoples who were incorporated into the Islamic state as it had rapidly expanded. Hallaq, by contrast, contends that the Arabs, even prior to Islam, had been more or less integrated into the various legal systems of the Near East, and accordingly, early Muslims did not "borrow" foreign law as much as they simply continued doing what they had always done: apply the law of the Near East, subject to the new Islamic ethos that reformed the historical law of the Near East.

V. The Judiciary in the Early 'Abbasid Caliphate (750–945)

The two trends already established during the Umayyad caliphate, namely rationalization of the law and bureaucratization of the judiciary, were heightened with the rise of the 'Abbasid caliphate. This was partially a result of the rise of a proto-corporate

[20] Hallaq, *The Origins and Evolution of Islamic Law*, 36–37.

[21] Ibid., 34–35.

identity among the jurists which resulted in their self-identification as partisans of specific traditions of jurisprudence, for example, the people of 'Iraq or the people of the Hijaz (or Madina), a trend that eventually produced what would come to be known as the Hanafi school of law and the Maliki school of law, respectively. It was also a result of the attempts of the 'Abbasids to centralize control over the territories of the Islamic caliphate which began in earnest when Abu Ja'far al-Mansur, the second 'Abbasid caliph, built his new capital, Baghdad, in 'Iraq. Harun al-Rashid, the fifth 'Abbasid caliph and al-Mansur's grandson, applied the 'Abbasids' centralizing zeal to the administration of justice, appointing Abu Yusuf, the chief disciple of Abu Hanifa, the eponym of the Hanafi school of law, as chief justice of the caliphate.[22]

This office, although it did not create a hierarchical system of judicial review, authorized the chief justice, in his capacity as the chief administrator of the judiciary, to appoint and dismiss judges throughout the territory subject to the control of the 'Abbasids.[23] The judges appointed by the chief judge were understood to be, in the first instance, his delegates or lieutenants, which gave the chief judge immense power to influence the character of the judiciary. For reasons that are not at all clear, it appears that a tacit alliance emerged between the early 'Abbasid caliphs and the early Hanafis, which resulted in the Hanafis enjoying a virtual monopoly over the office of chief judge. Control over this office allowed the Hanafis to appoint their protégés to judicial positions throughout 'Abbasid territory, a fact that could not have hurt them in their efforts to attract adherents.[24] Tsafrir, however, suggests that Hanafi control over the judiciary in the early 'Abbasid period is exaggerated, and that more often than not, local factors were often decisive in determining judicial appointments.[25]

The Maliki school was the only school of law that successfully resisted Hanafi attempts to monopolize the judiciary in the first 150 years of the 'Abbasid caliphate. While the Maliki school originally emerged in the Hijaz, by the early 'Abbasid period its center of strength had shifted westward to Egypt, Ifriqiyya (present-day Tunisia), and Andalus. The 'Abbasids never gained complete control over the Islamic west, with an Umayyad refugee, 'Abd al-Rahman b. Mu'awiya b. Hisham b. 'Abd al-Malik, successfully establishing an independent Umayyad dynasty in Andalus for almost 300 years. The Umayyad rulers of Andalus, unlike the 'Iraqi-based 'Abbasids, favored Maliki jurists, and chose to give them control over the dynasty's judiciary.[26] Like the 'Abbasids, the Andalusian Umayyads also attempted to centralize the administration of justice in their realm, and so pursued many of the same

[22] Ibid., 79–80. [23] Ibid., 80.

[24] Nurit Tsafrir, *The History of an Islamic School of Law: The Spread of Early Hanafism* (Cambridge, MA: Islamic Legal Studies Program, Harvard Law School, 2004), 20–21.

[25] Ibid., 21.

[26] Maribel Fierro, "Proto-Malikis, Malikis and Reformed Malikis in al-Andalus," in *The Islamic School of Law: Evolution, Devolution and Progress*, eds. Peri Bearman, Rudolph Peters, and Frank E. Vogel (Cambridge, MA: Harvard University Press, 2005), 61–70.

administrative policies introduced by the ʿAbbasids, including the appointment of a head of the judiciary who, like the ʿAbbasid chief justice, exercised supreme administrative power over the judiciary. Although the name of the Umayyad office was the more modest sounding "the judge of the community" (*qadi al-jamaʿa*), it does not appear that his substantive powers differed from those of the ʿAbbasid chief justice. Like his ʿAbbasid counterpart, lesser judges were considered the lieutenants or delegates of the judge of the community, and he too was authorized to appoint and dismiss judges in his discretion. The Umayyads did, however, introduce a uniquely Anadalusian judicial institution, that of the *shura*, or assembly of learned jurists, who assisted the judge in resolving difficult legal questions or in the exercise of judicial discretion in appropriate cases.[27]

The political independence of Umayyad Andalus from the ʿAbbasids therefore permitted the Maliki school's jurists to become important judicial actors in a fashion that was impossible for non-Hanafi jurists in the Islamic east, at least for the earliest decades of the ʿAbbasid caliphate. Likewise, as ʿAbbasid power began to wane over the Islamic west with the rise of quasi-independent local dynasts, such as the Aghlabids in Ifriqiyya (present-day Tunisia) and the Tulunids in Egypt, the Malikis began to make substantial inroads into the judiciaries of these territories. For example, the Aghlabid *amir* of Ifriqiyya appointed Sahnun, the compiler of the *Mudawanna*, the fundamental source of Maliki positive law, the chief judge of Ifriqiyya toward the end of his life. Sahnun used his position to appoint Malikis to the judiciary of this province, and even where he retained Hanafis, Mohammad Fadel reports that he required them to rule based on Maliki doctrines.[28] The Maliki–Aghlabid alliance proved sufficiently durable that it outlasted the fall of the Aghlabids to the Shiʿi Fatimids in the tenth century. Maliki jurists based in Qayrawan, such as Ibn Abi Zayd al-Qayrawani, led Sunni resistance against attempts by the Fatimid rulers to convert the population to Shiʿism. The same pattern is confirmed by Mathieu Tillier in his study of the Egyptian judiciary in the ninth and tenth centuries: as effective ʿAbbasid control over the province waned, the Hanafi monopoly over the judiciary likewise weakened.[29]

Most secondary scholarship ignores the often cooperative relationship between some of the most important figures of what would become the Hanafi and the Maliki schools of law in favor of a view of Islamic law as a practice that arose in *opposition* to the state, rather than in support of it. This may be true of figures such as al-Shafiʿi, who only served for a brief period of time as a judge in the relative backwater of Yemen, or more fundamentally with respect to Ahmad b. Hanbal, the putative

[27] Emile Tyan, *Histoire de L'Organisation Judiciare En Pays D'Islam* 2nd edn. (Leiden: Brill, 1960), 214–217, 232–234; Mohammad Fadel, *Adjudication in the Maliki Madhhab: A Study of Legal Process in Medieval Islamic Law.* Ph.D. diss., University of Chicago, 1995, 100.

[28] Fadel, *Adjudication in the Maliki Madhhab*, 283.

[29] Mathieu Tillier, "The *Qadis* of *Fustat-Misr* Under the *Tulunids* and the *Ikhshidids*: The Judiciary and Egyptian Autonomy," *Journal of the American Oriental Society* 131, no. 2 (2011): 207–222.

founder of the Hanbali law school, or even Malik b. Anas and Abu Hanifa insofar as the Arabic literary sources preserve evidence demonstrating their reluctance to serve the state. For example, historical sources claim that the second 'Abbasid caliph, al-Mansur attempted to appoint Abu Hanifa as a judge, but the latter refused and even went into hiding. So too, the tradition preserves reports that al-Mansur punished Malik b. Anas for his refusal to cease narrating a Prophetic tradition that could be read to imply that coerced pledges of fealty to the caliph were invalid as well as Malik's reluctance to assist al-Mansur in his project of legal centralization by advising him, against al-Mansur's wishes, not to impose Malik's compilation of Madinan law, the *Muwatta'*, throughout the empire.

These reports and others indicating a pious reticence against government service, however, should be viewed in light of the fact that many important 'Abbasid-era Hanafi jurists such as Abu Yusuf and Muhammad b. al-Hasan al-Shaybani willingly served the early 'Abbasids, and that many Andalusian Malikis, including Yahya b. Yahya, the most prominent transmitter of Malik's *Muwatta'*, willingly cooperated with the Spanish Umayyads, to say nothing of Sahnun's cooperation with the Aghlabids in North Africa with the decline of effective 'Abbasid control over those provinces. Whatever else may be said about the development of Islamic law during the early 'Abbasid period, it is clearly an oversimplification to portray Islamic law, as it is often claimed, as having arisen in opposition to the state, or that it was the product purely of intellectual reflection disconnected with the institutional development of the caliphate. To the contrary, it would be hard to explain the relative success of the Hanafi and Maliki schools of law, both in terms of winning adherents and in terms of successfully obtaining appointments to the judiciary, without taking into account their willingness to cooperate with the state-building agendas of Muslim political elites in this period.

The early 'Abbasid period, however, not only introduced greater centralized control over the judiciary and greater formalization of the legal profession with the rise of the law schools; it also introduced a basic template for judicial administration that numerous Muslim dynasties would replicate long after the 'Abbasids themselves lost effective political power. In addition to the office of the chief judge who oversaw the daily work of his lieutenant judges, the 'Abbasids also introduced institutions such as the *mazalim* (the tribunal of complaints) and the *muhtasib* (market regulator) that would become mainstays of the administration of law in subsequent Muslim polities and dynasties. The tribunal of complaints arose primarily as a forum for addressing complaints of official wrongdoing, whether in cases involving a government official and a private citizen, or complaints by government officials that they had wrongly been denied an entitlement, for example, a pension or income from a fief. Its primary function as a means to redress official wrongdoing gave its decision-maker both greater investigatory powers relative to the *qadi*—he did not, for example, need to wait for a complaint before initiating a case—and greater power to consider circumstantial evidence and to adopt as rules of decision norms that went beyond the formal doctrines of the jurists.[30]

The specialized judicial institutions introduced by the ʿAbbasids also proved to be significant for their impact on the rule of law and the different standards of legality that eventually came to govern each institution. The *qadi* essentially administered the laws developed by the jurists of the legal schools, and relied on an adversarial procedure. A passive administrator of the law, the *qadi's* jurisdiction required claimants to present their claims before him. Until he received a complaint, he had no role to play in the administration of the law. When he did receive a complaint, the formalistic rules of evidence and procedure of the various legal schools, as well as their substantive laws, governed proceedings and effectively limited his discretion in the majority of cases. The tribunal of complaints, by contrast, afforded the relevant decision-maker, who could be a *qadi* or other senior public official, greater discretion, both as a matter of substantive and procedural law. Scholarship on this has generally viewed the development of institutions like the *mazalim* and the *muhtasib* as a recognition of the failure of the law developed by Muslim jurists and administered by the *qadis* to meet the needs of an increasingly complex urban-based empire. According to the prevailing narrative, these new offices represented a sharp break with Islamic standards of legitimacy and represented a secular legal system that was, in its fundamental ethos, inconsistent with the shariʿa's ideal of divine law. Demarcating the precise boundaries between the jurisdictions of *qadis* and other judicial officials would become an important issue in later Muslim dynasties.

VI. Adjudication in the Buyid Era Until the Sack of Baghdad

The entrance of the Buyids into Baghdad in 945 is conventionally taken as representing the end of the early ʿAbbasid state and its effective disintegration into a series of statelets governed by various military strongmen whose submission to the ʿAbbasid caliph was merely nominal. The effective fragmentation of the ʿAbbasid state also put a practical end to the ʿAbbasid project of judicial centralization and the privileged position of the Hanafis in the judicial hierarchy. As a practical matter, this meant that the virtual monopoly Hanafis had enjoyed over judicial offices in the early ʿAbbasid period came to an end, and even the office of chief justice was opened to the followers of the other Sunni schools of law. The Buyid policy of expanding

[30] Hallaq, *The Origins and Evolution of Islamic Law*, 99–101.

judicial positions to non-Hanafis expanded dramatically with the rise of the Turkish Seljuks, particularly under the administration of Nizam al-Mulk, who sought to calm the Hanafi-Shafi'i conflicts that plagued the eastern (Persian) cities of the empire by ensuring that appointments were given to the followers of both schools.

It is not clear, however, whether this ecumenical policy was pursued equally in the Seljuks' Arab domains. We know that the Ayyubid successors to the Seljuks in Egypt and greater Syria extensively patronized the Shafi'i school,[31] and for a time there was a virtual Shafi'i monopoly over the office of chief judge in Ayyubid territory[32] in a broader context of Shaf'i domination over the administration of justice. The attempt to create an Ayyubid-Shafi'i state was short-lived, however, and came to an end with the collapse of the Ayyubids and the rise of the Mamluk dynasty.

Neither the rise and the subsequent collapse of the Fatimid Shi'ite state in North Africa and Egypt, nor the collapse of the Umayyad caliphate in Andalus lessened the virtual stranglehold Malikis held over the judiciary in the Maghrib and Andalus. The strength of the Maliki juristic establishment generally, and of judges in Andalus specifically, is evidenced in part by the prominent political role that *qadis* played as political leaders, even rulers, during the period of the petty kingdoms (eleventh century) that came in the wake of the Umayyad collapse, their role as leaders of rebellions in various Andalusian cities during the Murabitun period (twelfth century),[33] and as leaders resisting the Muwahhidun.[34] Even though there is evidence of the spread of non-Maliki ideas in Andalus during the end of the Umayyad period, such as Zahirism[35] and Shafi'ism,[36] they were never strong enough to challenge the Maliki domination of the judiciary, much less produce a system of legal pluralism such as that which was coming into existence in the Arab east.[37] Even the Muwahhidun, despite their quasi messianic ethos, were unable to displace the Maliki judiciary from their hegemonic position in Andalus and North Africa.[38] We are fortunate, however, to have documentary evidence regarding the administration

31 Sherman Jackson, "The Primacy of Domestic Politics: Ibn Bint al-A'azz and the Establishment of Four Chief Judgeships in Mamluk Egypt," *Journal of the American Oriental Society* 115, no. 1 (1995): 53.

32 Ibid., 62.

33 Maribel Fierro, "The Qaḍi as Ruler," in *Saber Religioso Y Poder Politíco En El Islam: Actas del Simposio Internacional (Granada, 15–18 octubre 1991)* eds. Manuela Marín and Mercedes García-Arenal (Madrid: Agencia Española de Cooperación Internacional, 1994), 71–116.

34 Hanna E. Kassis, "Qadi 'Iyad's Rebellion Against the Almohades in Sabtah (A.H. 542–43 /A.D. 1147–48): New Numismatic Evidence," *Journal of the American Oriental Society* 103, no. 3 (1983): 504–514.

35 Camilla Adang, "The Beginnings of the Zahiri Madhhab in al-Andalus," in *The Islamic School of Law: Evolution, Devolution and Progress*, eds. Peri Bearman, Rudolph Peters, and Frank E. Vogel (Cambridge, MA: Harvard University Press, 2005), 117–126.

36 Fierro, "Proto-Malikis, Malikis and Reformed Malikis," 70–71.

37 Fierro, "Proto-Malikis, Malikis and Reformed Malikis."

38 Camilla Adang, "*Ẓahiris of Almohad Times*," in *Biografías Almohades. II*, eds. María Louisa Ávila and Maribel Fierro (Madrid-Granada: Consejo Superior de Investigaciones Científicas, 2000), 413–479.

of the Muwahhid state in the form of various official documents of appointments of provincial officials, including, judges.[39]

VII. Adjudication in the Arab Middle East and North Africa in the Post-Caliphal Era

A. The Judicial System in the Arab Middle East in the Mamluk Period

Unlike previous periods of Islamic history, the Mamluk era is rich with sources that can be used to reconstruct the history of the judiciary in this period, including numerous historical chronicles, biographical works on the leading jurists of the day, and countless normative legal sources, both theoretical and applied. With the exception of Mamluk-era legal documents discovered in the Masjid al-Aqsa, a catalogue of which has been published by Donald Little, there is a dearth of documentary evidence attesting to the practices of the Mamluk-era judiciary. This means that, as a practical matter, legal historians of this period have had to rely almost entirely on various literary sources in an attempt to reconstruct the judicial history of the period. Despite this shortcoming, other than the Ottoman era, the Mamluk-era legal system has perhaps been the subject of more studies than any other premodern Islamic regional legal system. The rich historical legacy of Mamluk-era historians, combined with what appears to have been their natural interest in judicial affairs (many Mamluk-era historians were themselves jurists), have, however, allowed modern historians to write detailed histories of various aspects of the Mamluk judiciary, such as the office of the Mamluk chief judge[40] and the Damascene judiciary in the generation prior to the Ottoman conquest.[41]

The Mamluks are largely remembered for their military prowess in defending Egypt and greater Syria from the simultaneous threats posed by the Crusaders and the Mongols. They also introduced some of the most far reaching institutional innovations in the judicial system of the eastern Arab world since the founding

[39] Pascal Buresi and Hicham El Aallaoui, *Governing the Empire: Provincial Administration in the Almohad Caliphate (1224–1269)* (Boston: Brill, 2013).

[40] Joseph H. Escovitz, *The Office of* Qadi al-Qudat *in Cairo Under the Bahri Mamluks* (Berlin: Klaus Schwarz Verlag, 1984).

[41] Jon Mandaville, *The Muslim Judiciary of Damascus* (Ph.D. diss., Princeton University, 1969).

of the Arab state. The first of these far reaching innovations was introduced by the second Mamluk sultan, al-Zahir Baybars. Reversing the Ayyubid policy of attempting to consolidate the judicial power in the Shafi'i school of law, al-Zahir Baybars instead institutionalized a system of legal pluralism by appointing four chief justices, one from each Sunni school of law.[42] The legal pluralism introduced by the Malikis would characterize the judicial system of the Arab Middle East until the nineteenth century when, under modernizing pressures, the Ottoman Empire attempted to create a unified system of Islamic law.[43]

Scholarship has been divided on the reasons that led Baybars to introduce this daring innovation between some who saw this innovation as recognition on the part of Baybars that pursuing a policy of judicial centralization that gave primacy to one legal school, for example, the Shafi'is, at the expense of the other schools, was futile,[44] and other scholars who viewed the introduction of the system of the four chief judges as a tool to make the legal system more responsive to the needs of the state and the public by allowing both the populace and the government to exploit, systematically, the substantive differences found in the doctrines of the four schools.[45]

The second institutional innovation introduced by the Mamluks began with the introduction of the *Dar al-'Adl*, the Palace of Justice. While it began as a kind of court of complaints along the lines of the 'Abbasid *mazalim* tribunal, its jurisdiction gradually expanded to include some matters of commercial law, including disputes between foreign and local merchants, and even family law cases.[46] The gradual expansion of the jurisdiction of the *Dar al-'Adl*, as well as the jurisdiction of other courts staffed by Mamluk officers, into what had been traditionally the exclusive preserve of the *qadi* courts was the cause of substantial controversy within the Mamluk legal class of the time, and its significance for Mamluk law and society is also the subject of heated controversy among Mamluk historians.

Some historians, such as Albrecht Fuess, have taken the view that this development was not, in itself, abusive, even if in practice it often led to a great deal of abuse of power. Others, however, have taken a much dimmer view of these developments, describing them sometimes as a "usurpation" of judicial authority by the Mamluk rulers at the expense of the ordinary courts,[47] and at other times as producing little more than an extortion racket that undermined the coherence of the Mamluk

[42] Jackson, "Chief Judgeships in Mamlūk Egypt."

[43] Hallaq, "Groundwork of the Moral Law."

[44] Jackson, "Chief Judgeships in Mamlūk Egypt," 54.

[45] Yossef Rapoport, "Royal Justice and Religious Law: Siyasah and Shari'ah Under the Mamluks," *Mamluk Studies Review* XVI (2012): 77–79.

[46] Ibid., 81–92.

[47] Robert Irwin, "The Privatization of 'Justice' Under the Circassian Mamluks," *Mamluk Studies Review* VI (2002): 64.

state.[48] Rapoport, on the other hand, interprets the expanding jurisdiction of the *Dar al-ʿAdl* and other courts headed by Mamluk *amirs* as an important development in the history of the Islamic legal system in the Arab Middle East whereby state authorities began to challenge the monopoly enjoyed by the jurists over the interpretation of the shariʿa. Far from representing a derogation from the shariʿa, Rapoport argues that the Mamluk rulers saw themselves as giving greater effect to the shariʿa by circumventing what they perceived to be the numerous loopholes in the formal legal doctrines of the various legal schools. In contrast to the formalist understanding of the shariʿa advanced by the jurists, the rulers according to Rapoport advanced a more common-sense understanding of the shariʿa that sought to vindicate its substantive ends, even if that at times violated the formalistic rules of the jurists.[49] It is clear that some jurists, including the controversial Ibn Taymiyya, were not unsympathetic to giving the rulers a greater normative role in the administration of Islamic law.[50]

The controversy over how to understand the increasing importance of non-*qadi* courts in the Mamluk state grows out of the question previously considered with regard to the legitimacy of the various tribunals established by the ʿAbbasids—most prominently the *mazalim*—that were not necessarily subject to the control of the jurists. While previous generations of Islamic legal historians such as Schacht and Coulson were quick to take the existence of such tribunals as evidence of an unbridgeable gap between the theory of Islamic law and the practice of Muslim states (the existence of such an unbridgeable gap being taken as evidence of the essential non-adaptivity of Islamic law as a religious, in contrast to a secular, legal system), contemporary scholarship has sought to portray these non-*qadi* tribunals as existing in a complementary relationship with that of the *qadi* court and not in a parallel system that undermined it. Mohammad Fadel, for example, argued that Mamluk-era jurists such as the Maliki Ibn Farhun and the Hanafi al-Tarabulusi, under the rubric of siyasa, explicitly incorporated these non-*qadi* courts into their treatises on the judiciary, treating them and the norms they used—even if different from those that applied in *qadis*' courts—as legitimate parts of their legal system.[51]

Consistent with Fadel's argument that the Mamluk period witnessed the increasing incorporation of *siyasa* into the shariʿa and in the formal institutions, including the courts, Baber Johansen argued that the rise of *siyasa* in the Mamluk era fostered a revolution in the Islamic law of evidence at the hands of the iconoclastic

[48] John L. Meloy, "The Privatization of Protection: Extortion and the State in the Circassian Mamluk Period," *Journal of the Economic and Social History of the Orient* 47, no. 2 (2004): 195–212.

[49] Rapoport, "*Siyasah* and Shariʿah Under the Mamluks."

[50] Baber Johansen, "A Perfect Law in an Imperfect Society: Ibn Taymiyya's Concept of 'Governance in the Name of the Sacred Law'," in *The Law Applied: Contextualizing the Islamic Shariʿa—A Volume in Honor of Frank E. Vogel*, eds. Peri Bearman, Wolfhart Heinrichs, and Bernard G. Weiss (New York: I.B. Tauris, 2008), 259–294.

[51] Fadel, *Adjudication in the Maliki Madhhab*, 82–130.

Syrian Hanbali theologian and jurist, Ibn Taymiyya and his disciple, Ibn Qayyim al-Jawziyya, which gave circumstantial evidence a prominent and legitimate role in the investigation, proof, and punishment of crime, in contrast to the classical approach of the jurists which typically eschewed reliance on circumstantial evidence in favor of eyewitness testimony or confession as the exclusive means to establish criminal conduct.[52] In a similar vein to Fadel and Johansen, Kristen Stilt, in her study of the market inspector (*muhtasib*) in Mamluk Cairo, advanced the thesis that the office of the *muhtasib* incorporated both the formal jurisprudential traditions of the jurists and the political concerns of the Mamluk rulers for effective enforcement of the law.[53]

Jackson, in his study of Shihab al-Din al-Qarafi, an Egyptian jurist who witnessed the end of the Ayyubid state and the rise of the Mamluks, emphasized Qarafi's legal project as one designed to establish a pure system of law that could be used to protect the integrity of the judiciary from manipulation, either by overzealous rulers or jurists themselves. Jackson's study, although it is a skilful reading of Qarafi and represents an excellent rejoinder to older scholars' claims regarding the immutability (and consequent unadaptability) of Islamic law to changing social circumstances, avoids the question of the growing importance of *siyasa* to the Mamluk-era legal system. Jackson's reading of Qarafi suggests that Qarafi, perhaps like the fourteenth-century Mamluk-era Shafi'i jurist Taj al-Din al-Subki, would have been opposed to the expansion of the jurisdiction of the non-*qadi* courts into the purely "legal" domains of the *qadi*.[54]

B. The Judiciary in the Islamic West (Maghrib) and Andalus

The collapse of the Muwahhids in the Maghrib produced three different successor states: the Nasrids in what remained of Muslim Spain, with their capital in Granada; the Marinids in Morocco, based in Fez; and, the Hafsids in Ifriqiyya (present-day Tunisia). Although politically divided, a shared commitment to Maliki *fiqh*, one of whose distinguishing features was a relatively greater concern with the precedential practice of its legal system, which was called *'amal* (practice) and *nawazil* (precedents), gave the Maghreb a distinctive legal culture throughout this period that helped overcome the political divisions that arose with the collapse of the al-Muwahhids.

52 Baber Johansen, "Signs as Evidence: The Doctrine of Ibn Taymiyya (1263–1328) and Ibn Qayyim al-Jawziyya (d. 1351) on Proof," *Islamic Law and Society* 9, no. 2 (2002): 168–193.

53 Kristen Stilt, *Islamic Law in Action: Authority, Discretion and Everyday Experiences in Mamluk Egypt* (New York: Oxford University Press, 2011).

54 Jackson, *Islamic Law and the State.*

Several contemporary scholars have taken advantage of the rich Maliki literature in the genres of 'amal and *nawazil* to explore with greater empirical precision Islamic legal scholars' concern with the question of the relationship of law to practice. David Powers pioneered the use of *fatwas* as a tool to explore both the social and legal history of the post-Muwahhid Maghreb in a series of studies beginning the 1990s. Using *fatwas* from the monumental collection of al-Wansharisi, Powers published a series of articles focusing on particular disputes, often dealing with complex legal and social questions involving the intergenerational transfer of wealth, gender, and the intersecting practices of courts and muftis in the Maghrib. Powers's research represented a broader turn toward the "practical" in studying Islamic law, with less concern about issues regarding the origins of Islamic law, or the authenticity of its early texts, whether religious, for example, Qur'anic or Prophetic, or scholarly, for example, the attribution of early works such as the *Muwatta'* to their traditional authors, and more toward understanding how Islamic law worked in particular social circumstances, both from a normative perspective with respect to the kinds of legal and customary norms that regulated disputes and from an institutional perspective to understand what kinds of institutions mediated legal disputes.[55] Another excellent example of such an approach, although it deals with a case predating the political disintegration of the Maghrib, is Hallaq's *Murder in Cordoba*, in which he analyzes the particularities of a case of murder involving next of kin who are minors, and how Ibn Rushd the Grandfather sought to resolve that case in light of established norms of Maliki doctrine by proposing a novel solution.[56] Other scholars have also used this method to investigate the North African legal system as it existed during the later days of the Murabitun.[57]

Another approach to using *fatwas* as a tool for exploring the tension between law as norm and law as practiced is found in Fadel's article, "Rules, Discretion and the Rule of Law in Nasrid Granada."[58] Using a collection of fourteenth- and fifteenth-century Granadan fatwas, Fadel examined the extent to which the responses recorded in the various *fatwas* were consistent with an obligation to adhere closely to formal legal doctrine, or reflected a willingness to depart from established rules willy-nilly in furtherance of some particularized conception of substantive justice

[55] David Powers, "The Maliki Family Endowment: Legal Norms and Social Practices," *International Journal of Middle East Studies* 25 (August 1993): 379–406; David Powers, "*Kadijustiz* or *Qadi-Justice*: A Paternity Dispute from Fourteenth-Century Morocco," *Islamic Law and Society* 1, no. 3 (1994): 332–366; David Powers, *Law, Society and Culture in the Maghrib, 1300–1500* (New York: Cambridge University Press, 2002).

[56] Wael B. Hallaq, "Murder in Cordoba: *Ijtihad, Ifta'* and the Evolution of Substantive Law in Medieval Islam," *Acta Orientalia* 40 (1994, 1995): 1–29.

[57] Delfina Serrano, "Legal Practice in an Andalusi-Maghribi Source from the 12th Century CE: The *Madhahib al-Hukkam fi Nawazil al-Ahkam*," *Islamic Law and Society* 7, no. 2 (2000): 187–234.

[58] Mohammad Fadel, "Rules, Judicial Discretion, and the Rule of Law in Nasrid Granada," in *Islamic Law: Theory and Practice*, eds., Robert Gleave and Eugenia Kermali (New York: I.B. Tauris, 1997), 49–86.

as exemplified in the Weberian ideal-type of *qadi-justiz*. Whether used for micro-studies or macro-studies, scholars of Islamic law in the post-Muwawhhid Maghrib (and sometimes even in Muwahhid-era Maghrib where sources exist) are making increasing use of the *fatwa* and *nawazil* literature to produce a richer social and legal history of the judiciary during this period and its broader relationship to society. One can reasonably expect that this trend will continue.

VIII. The Judiciary in the Ottoman, Safavid (and its Successors), and Mughal Empires

Our knowledge of the legal history of the Islamic world improves substantially with the rise of what Marshall Hodgson has called the "gunpowder empires," i.e. the Ottomans, Safavids, and the Mughals. This is particularly true in the case of the Ottoman Empire, which kept meticulous records of court proceedings. Social historians of the Middle East in the last forty years have used these judicial records to produce scores of studies exploring many facets of early modern Middle Eastern social history, including history of gender, status of non-Muslim Ottomans, and the economic history of the Ottoman Empire. While these studies have greatly enriched—and in many cases has forced a substantial reconsideration of—our understanding of the social and economic history of the territories comprising the early modern Ottoman Empire, researchers have only begun to make full use of documentary evidence the Ottoman archives have preserved.

Unlike other periods of Islamic history,[59] the existence of these court records has allowed Islamic legal historians access to the operation of the Ottoman court system in a fashion unrivalled for any other period of Islamic history. Ahmed Akgündüz has provided a detailed overview of how the administration of the Ottoman judicial system worked, the different kinds of documents it generated, how those documents were preserved, and how they changed over the lengthy 500-year history of the Ottoman Empire.[60] Records pertaining to the *qadi's* courts were known as *sijillat-i shar'iyya*, and each court kept its own records. According to Akgündüz, these records are massive, with the *qadi* court in Istanbul by itself having over

[59] Wael B. Hallaq, "The Qadi's Diwan (Sijill) Before the Ottomans," *Bulletin of the School of Oriental and African Studies, University of London* 61, no. 3 (1998): 415–436.

[60] Ahmed Akgündüz, "Shari'ah Courts and Shari'ah Records: The Application of Islamic Law in the Ottoman State," *Islamic Law and Society* 16 (2009): 202–230.

20,000 volumes of records.[61] Legal historians have only recently begun to make use of these documents to explore in a detailed fashion how the Ottoman legal system operated. The Ottomans, unlike prior Muslim states in the Mediterranean region, abolished the dualistic jurisdiction of the *qadi* court and the *mazalim* court, assimilating the latter into the former. While the Ottomans were prolific in issuing positive laws, known as *qanun-namehs*, many of which dealt with fiscal and criminal law, they entrusted the enforcement of their positive laws to the Ottoman *qadis*. The Ottomans, paradoxically, were the most prolific of the premodern Muslim states as "secular" law-makers, but also the regime that most successfully enlisted ordinary *qadis* for the implementation of those laws.

Most of the Ottoman records have not been edited and published, and as a result, can only be accessed from archival sources. Some collections of court decisions, however, have been edited and published, including a four-volume collection of judicial documents related to the diasporic community of Maghribis in Egypt (in Arabic), ('Abd al-Rahim); a two-volume collection of judicial documents from the city of Bursa in Anatolia for the years 1670–71 (transliterated Ottoman Turkish, with English summary and occasional Arabic text of judicial decree), (Abaci); and a ten-volume collection of judicial records from seventeenth-century Istanbul organized topically (transliterated Ottoman Turkish with modern Turkish and English summary of judicial decree), (Kuran).

Unfortunately, we lack equivalent archival data for the Safavid legal system. Willem Floor has written a lengthy article on the Safavid legal system which confirms that, from a structural perspective, it differed little from that of the prior Timurid-Sunni states that dominated the Persian-speaking world following the Mongol invasions. The Safavids maintained a dualist judiciary, one called the "customary" or *'orfi* court that dealt largely with criminal matters, including, against the king, and the shari'a courts that dealt largely with personal claims. The main judicial official was known as the *divan-begi*, who acted as the king's representative with respect to all matters of criminal law. Another official, called the *sadr*, oversaw the shari'a courts, but was often consulted by the *divan-begi* on matters pertaining to criminal law.[62] The same author has also published a detailed study on the office of the *sadr* and its role in supervising the judiciary responsible for the administration of the shari'a in the Safavid state.[63]

The situation in Mughal India, although not as well-studied as the Ottoman Empire, is better than Safavid Persia. At least two English-language monographs on the Mughal legal system have been published. One is a general administrative history of the Mughal empire, including, that of its *qadi* courts,[64] and the other is on

[61] Ibid., 205.

[62] Willem Floor, "The Secular Judicial System in Safavid Persia," *Studia Iranica* 29 (2000): 10.

[63] Ibid., 416.

[64] M.L. Bhatia, *Administrative History of Medieval India (A Study of Muslim Jurisprudence Under Aurengzeb)* (New Delhi: Radha Publications, 1992).

criminal law in the Mughal Empire.[65] Both works rely largely on historical chronicles and imperial decrees but lack the judicial records of the sort generated by the Ottoman court system.

IX. Introduction of "Secular" (*Nizami*) Courts and the Rise of State Courts

Beginning in the latter half of the nineteenth century (or earlier if one counts British and Dutch colonial reforms in India and Southeast Asia), Muslim states began a process of judicial reform that eventually led to the displacement of the traditional *qadi* court with "secular" (*nizami*) courts, and the replacement of the uncodified *fiqh* administered by *qadis* with codified law. This process began with a codified version of Hanafi law promulgated by the Ottomans known as the *Majalla* and concluded with the wholesale implementation of legal codes imported from Europe. This effort began in earnest in the Ottoman Empire with the promulgation of the "New Order" through a series of far-reaching legal and administrative reforms known as the *tanzimat* (literally, "the organizational decrees").[66] Although it is often assumed that the new, *nizami* courts introduced in furtherance of the Ottoman reform programs had the practical, if not the intended effect, of circumventing the traditional juristic class, traditional jurists often staffed the *nizami* courts, both at the trial and the appellate levels.[67] The one state that resisted this trend was the Kingdom of Saudi Arabia, which was able to maintain a relatively traditionalist legal system largely because its poverty and relative isolation allowed it to escape direct colonization or incorporation into the world economy until after the discovery of oil in the twentieth century.[68]

An older generation of scholars has essentially taken these developments as representing the displacement of the shari'a with secular law, largely of European civil law provenance.[69] More recent scholarship, however, has attempted to complicate this narrative, challenging the notion that Muslim states abandoned Islamic law in order to distance themselves from Islamic law,[70] or that they passively

[65] Satya Prakesh Sangar, *Crime and Punishment in Moghul India* (New Delhi: Reliance Publishing House, 1998).

[66] Hallaq, "Groundwork of the Moral Law," 401–425.

[67] Ruth A. Miller, "Apostates and Bandits: Religious and Secular Interaction in the Administration of Late Ottoman Criminal Law," *Studia Islamica* 97 (2003): 155–178.

[68] Frank Vogel, *Islamic Law and Legal Systems: Studies of Saudi Arabia* (Boston: Brill, 2000), xiv.

[69] Schacht, *An Introduction to Islamic Law*, 92–93; Coulson, *A History of Islamic Law*, 149–152.

[70] Nathan J. Brown, *The Rule of Law in the Arab World* (New York: Cambridge, 1997), 30.

received European civil law without attempting to "domesticate" it, so to speak, by synthesizing it with historical norms of Islamic law.[71] The debate on the "Islamic" character of the legal systems of contemporary Muslim states has only become more contentious with the rise of populist movements demanding the restoration of the shariʿa as the basis for the legal systems of various Muslim-majority nation states. Even in the extreme case of the Islamic Republic of Iran, however, it would be a mistake to think that restoration of the shariʿa means simply a restoration of the *status quo ante*: modern Islamic legal forms are indelibly stamped with modernity in a way that makes them radically distinct from their premodern ancestors.[72]

There is little doubt that many Muslim-majority states have acted, to one degree or another, to Islamize their legal systems. One prominent example is Egypt whose constitution affirms that the shariʿa is the primary source for the state's legislation. Modern scholarship is bitterly divided on whether these attempts at Islamization have been successful,[73] with some going so far as to assert an irreducible conflict between modern conceptions of the state and its legality and Islamic conceptions of governance and legality.[74] There is little disagreement, however, regarding the effects of the modernization of the judiciary: little trace has been left of the traditional *qadi* court, which has largely been replaced—even if there are pockets of the Muslim world where *qadi* courts continue to exist applying uncodified Islamic law—by courts created by modernizing and centralizing states whose judges are an indelible part of the state's bureaucracy.

Scholars have taken different approaches to the study of the judiciary in modern Muslim states. The literature on the modern period is of course too extensive to discuss in depth in a survey such as this, but it is crucial to point out the broad diversity in approach that has been taken to the study of contemporary Muslim courts. Broadly speaking, one can speak of the rise of social science, particularly, legal anthropology, as a pre-eminent mode for the study of modern Muslim courts.[75] With the opportunity to observe Muslim courts in action, it should not be surprising that scores of works have been written by contemporary scholars from the perspective

[71] Enid Hill, "The Place and Significance of Islamic Law in the Life and Work of ʿAbd al-Razzaq Ahmad al-Sanhuri," *Arab Law Quarterly* 3, no. 1 (1988): 33–64 (Part I); Enid Hill, "Al-Sanhuri and Islamic Law: The Place and Significance of Islamic Law in the Life andWork of ʿAbd al-Razzaq Ahmad al-Sanhuri," *Arab Law Quarterly* 3, no. 2 (1988): 182–218 (Part II); Amr Shalakany, "Between Identity and Distribution: Sanhuri, Genealogy and the Will to Islamise," *Islamic Law and Society* 8, no. 2 (2001): 201–244.

[72] Louise Halper, "'Legal Realism' in Tehran: Gender Law and the Transformative State," in *The Law Applied: Contextualizing the Islamic Shariʿa—A Volume in Honor of Frank E. Vogel*, eds., Peri Bearman, Wolfhart Heinrichs, and Bernard G. Weiss (New York: I.B. Tauris, 2008), 47.

[73] Oussama Arabi, *Studies in Modern Islamic Law and Jurisprudence* (London: Kluwer Law International, 2001).

[74] Wael B. Hallaq, *The Impossible State: Islam, Politics and Modernity's Moral Predicament* (New York: Columbia University Press, 2013).

[75] Lawrence Rosen, *The Anthropology of Justice: Law as Culture in Islamic Society* (New York: Cambridge University Press, 1989).

of legal anthropology, often dealing with the practice of Muslim courts in the so-called "Muslim periphery," for example, Yemen,[76] Southeast Asia,[77] and Zanzibar.[78] Political scientists have also become involved in the study of modern Muslim courts, bringing their own methods to the study of these institutions.[79] Conventional legal analysis of formal doctrine, and how courts understand legal doctrine, however, still occupies an important place in the contemporary scholarship of courts in the Muslim world.[80]

X. Conclusion

Scholarship on the *qadi* and the *qadi's* court has made substantial progress over the last generation, but it still remains haunted by questions first formulated in the nineteenth century at its birth: religion versus secular; theory versus practice; formal rationality versus substantive rationality; stability versus change; and law versus politics. While these binaries are hardly unique to the study of Islamic law, prior generations of Islamic law scholarship approached these problems from an ideological, indeed, Orientalist perspective, in which the answers to the questions were assumed, rather than demonstrated, in accordance with prevailing essentializing assumptions about the Muslim world. Legal scholars of the Muslim world, particularly for those working on materials after the thirteenth century, are now in a position to investigate these traditional questions empirically, based on a much richer set of historical evidence, both literary and sometimes documentary. In the modern period, direct observation is often an additional source available for the researcher. Indeed, one can say with some confidence that we are now on the cusp of achieving, for the first time, a genuine history of the *qadi* and his court.

76 Brinkley Messick, *The Calligraphic State: Textual Domination and History in a Muslim Society* (Berkeley: University of California Press, 1993).

77 Sharifah Zaleha et al., *Managing Marital Disputes in Malaysia: Islamic Mediators and Conflict Resolution in the Syariah Courts* (Richmond, England: Curzon Press, 1997); John R. Bowen, *Islam, Law and Equality in Indonesia: An Anthropology of Public Reasoning* (New York: Cambridge University Press, 2003).

78 Erin Stiles, *An Islamic Court in Context: An Ethnographic Study of Judicial Reasoning* (New York: Palgrave MacMillan, 2009).

79 Brown, *The Rule of Law in the Arab World*; Tamir Moustafa, *The Struggle for Constitutional Power: Law, Politics and Economic Development in Egypt* (New York: Cambridge University Press, 2007).

80 Clark B. Lombardi, *State Law as Islamic Law in Modern Egypt: The Incorporation of the Sharīʿa into Egyptian Constitutional Law* (Boston: Brill, 2006).

References

Abaci, Nurcan, *The Ottoman Judges and Their Registers: The Bursa Court Register B-90/295 (Dated AH 1081/AD 1670–71)* (Cambridge, MA: The Department of Near Eastern Languages and Civilizations, Harvard University, 2007) (2 vols).

ʿAbd al-Rahim, ʿAbd al-Rahim ʿAbd al-Rahman. *Watha'iq al-Maghariba min Sijillat al-Mahakim al-Sharʿiyya Ibban al-ʿAsr al-ʿUthmani.* Zaghwan, Tunisia: Markaz al-Dirasat wa-al-Buhuth al-ʿUthmaniyah wa-al-Muriskiyah wa-al-Tawthiq wa-al-Maʿlumat, 1992–2004 (4 vols).

Adang, Camilla, "*Zahiris of Almohad Times*" in María Louisa Ávila and Maribel Fierro (eds.) *Biografías Almohades. II* (Madrid-Granada: Consejo Superior de Investigaciones Científicas, 2000) 413–479.

Adang, Camilla, "The Beginnings of the Zahiri Madhhab in al-Andalus" in Peri Bearman, Rudolph Peters and Frank E. Vogel (eds.) *The Islamic School of Law: Evolution, Devolution and Progress* (Cambridge, MA: Harvard University Press, 2005) 117–126.

Akgündüz, Ahmed, "Shariʿah Courts and Shariʿah Records: The Application of Islamic Law in the Ottoman State." *Islamic Law and Society* 16 (2009): 202–230.

Arabi, Oussama, *Studies in Modern Islamic Law and Jurisprudence* (London: Kluwer Law International, 2001).

Al-Atrushi, Lawlaf Mustafa Salim, *Al-Qada' fi Misr wa'l-Sham fi'-ʿahd al-Ayyubi* (Baghdad: Dar Dijla, 2007).

Bhatia, M.L, *Administrative History of Medieval India (A Study of Muslim Jurisprudence Under Aurengzeb)* (New Delhi: Radha Publications, 1992).

Bowen, John R, *Islam, Law and Equality in Indonesia: An Anthropology of Public Reasoning* (New York: Cambridge University Press, 2003).

Brown, Nathan J., *The Rule of Law in the Arab World* (New York: Cambridge, 1997).

Buresi, Pascal, and El Aallaoui, Hicham, *Governing the Empire: Provincial Administration in the Almohad Caliphate (1224–1269)* (Boston: Brill, 2013).

Cammack, Mark E., and Feener, R. Michael, "Joint Marital Property in Indonesian Customary, Islamic, and National Law" in Peri Bearman, Wolfhart Heinrichs, and Bernard G. Weiss (eds.) *The Law Applied: Contextualizing the Islamic Shariʿa—A Volume in Honor of Frank E. Vogel* (New York: I.B. Tauris, 2008) 92–115.

Coulson, Noel J, *A History of Islamic Law* (Edinburgh: Edinburgh University Press, 1964).

Escovitz, Joseph H, *The Office of* Qadi al-Qudat *in Cairo Under the Bahri Mamluks* (Berlin: Klaus Schwarz Verlag, 1984).

Fadel, Mohammad, *Adjudication in the Maliki Madhhab: A Study of Legal Process in Medieval Islamic Law* (Ph.D. diss., University of Chicago, 1995).

Fadel, Mohammad, "Rules, Judicial Discretion, and the Rule of Law in Nasrid Granada" in Robert Gleave and Eugenia Kermali (eds.) *Islamic Law: Theory and Practice* (New York: I.B. Tauris, 1997) 49–86.

Fierro, Maribel, "The Qadi as Ruler" in Manuela Marín and Mercedes García-Arenal (eds.) *Saber Religioso Y Poder Politíco En El Islam: Actas del Simposio Internacional (Granada, 15–18 octubre 1991)* (Madrid: Agencia Española de Cooperación Internacional, 1994) 71–116.

Fierro, Maribel, "Proto-Malikis, Malikis and Reformed Malikis in al-Andalus" in Peri Bearman, Rudolph Peters, and Frank E. Vogel (eds.) *The Islamic School of Law: Evolution, Devolution and Progress* (Cambridge, MA: Harvard University Press, 2005) 57–76.

Floor, Willem, "The Secular Judicial System in Safavid Persia." *Studia Iranica* 29 (2000): 9–60.

Floor, Willem, "The *Sadr* or Head of the Safavid Religious Establishment, Judiciary, and Endowments and Other Members of the Religious Institution." *Zeitschrift der Deutschen Morgenländischen Gesellschaft* 150 (2000): 461–500.

Fuess, Albrecht, "*Zulm* by *Mazalim*? The Political Implications of the Use of *Mazalim* Jurisdiction by the Mamluk Sultans." *Mamluk Studies Review* XIII, no. 1 (2009): 121–147.

Hill, Enid, "Al-Sanhuri and Islamic Law: The Place and Significance of Islamic Law in the Life and Work of ʿAbd al-Razzaq Ahmad al-Sanhuri." *Arab Law Quarterly* 3, no. 1 (1988): 33–64 (Part I).

Hill, Enid, "Al-Sanhuri and Islamic Law: The Place and Significance of Islamic Law in the Life andWork of ʿAbd al-Razzaq Ahmad al-Sanhuri." *Arab Law Quarterly* 3, no. 2 (1988): 182–218 (Part II).

Hallaq, Wael B., "Murder in Cordoba: *Ijtihad, Ifta'* and the Evolution of Substantive Law in Medieval Islam." *Acta Orientalia* 40 (1994, 1995): 1–29.

Hallaq, Wael B., "The Qadi's Diwan (Sijill) Before the Ottomans." *Bulletin of the School of Oriental and African Studies, University of London* 61, no. 3 (1998): 415–436.

Hallaq, Wael B., *The Origins and Evolution of Islamic Law* (New York: Cambridge University Press, 2005).

Hallaq, Wael B., "Groundwork of the Moral Law." *Islamic Law & Society* 16, no. 3/4 (2009): 239–279.

Hallaq, Wael B., *Shariʿa: Theory, Practice, Transformations* (New York: Cambridge University Press, 2009).

Hallaq, Wael B., *The Impossible State: Islam, Politics and Modernity's Moral Predicament* (New York: Columbia University Press, 2013).

Halper, Louise, "'Legal Realism' in Tehran: Gender Law and the Transformative State" in Peri Bearman, Wolfhart Heinrichs, and Bernard G. Weiss (eds.) *The Law Applied: Contextualizing the Islamic Shariʿa—A Volume in Honor of Frank E. Vogel* (New York: I.B. Tauris, 2008) 42–56.

Irwin, Robert, "The Privatization of 'Justice' Under the Circassian Mamluks." *Mamluk Studies Review* VI (2002): 63–70.

Jackson, Sherman, "The Primacy of Domestic Politics: Ibn Bint al-Aʿazz and the Establishment of Four Chief Judgeships in Mamluk Egypt." *Journal of the American Oriental Society* 115, no. 1 (1995): 52–65.

Jackson, Sherman, *Islamic Law and the State: The Constitutional Jurisprudence of* Shihab al-Din al-Qarafi (New York: Brill, 1996).

Johansen, Baber, "Signs as Evidence: The Doctrine of Ibn Taymiyya (1263–1328) and Ibn Qayyim al-Jawziyya (d. 1351) on Proof." *Islamic Law and Society* 9, no. 2 (2002): 168–193.

Johansen, Baber, "A Perfect Law in an Imperfect Society: Ibn Taymiyya's Concept of 'Governance in the Name of the Sacred Law'" in Peri Bearman, Wolfhart Heinrichs, and Bernard G. Weiss (eds.) *The Law Applied: Contextualizing the Islamic Shariʿa—A Volume in Honor of Frank E. Vogel* (New York: I.B. Tauris, 2008) 259–294.

Kadi, Wadad, "The Salaries of Judges in Early Islam: The Evidence of the Documentary and Literary Sources." *Journal of Near Eastern Studies* 68, no. 1 (2009): 9–30.

Kassis, Hanna E., "Qadi ʿIyad's Rebellion Against the Almohades in Sabtah (A.H. 542–43 / A.D. 1147–48): New Numismatic Evidence." *Journal of the American Oriental Society* 103, no. 3 (1983): 504–514.

Kuran, Timur, *Social and Economic Life in Seventeenth-Century Istanbul: Glimpses from Court Records* (Istanbul: Türkiye İş Bankası, 2011) (10 vols).

Lindsey, Tim, and Kingsley, Jeremy, "Talking in Code: Legal Islamisation in Indonesia and the MMI Shariʿa Criminal Code" in Peri Bearman, Wolfhart Heinrichs, and Bernard G. Weiss (eds.) *The Law Applied: Contextualizing the Islamic Shariʿa—A Volume in Honor of Frank E. Vogel* (New York: I.B. Tauris, 2008) 295–320.

Little, Donald P., *A Catalogue of the Islamic Documents from al-*Haram al-Sharif *in Jerusalem.* Beirut: In Kommission bei F. Steiner (Verlag, Wiesbaden, 1984).

Lombardi, Clark B., *State Law as Islamic Law in Modern Egypt: The Incorporation of the Shariʿa into Egyptian Constitutional Law* (Boston: Brill, 2006).

Mandaville, Jon, *The Muslim Judiciary of Damascus in the Late Mamluk Period* (Ph.D. diss., Princeton University, 1969).

Meloy, John L., "The Privatization of Protection: Extortion and the State in the Circassian Mamluk Period." *Journal of the Economic and Social History of the Orient* 47, no. 2 (2004): 195–212.

Messick, Brinkley, *The Calligraphic State: Textual Domination and History in a Muslim Society* (Berkeley: University of California Press, 1993).

Messick, Brinkley, "Shariʿa Ethnography" in Peri Bearman, Wolfhart Heinrichs, and Bernard G. Weiss (eds.) *The Law Applied: Contextualizing the Islamic Shariʿa—A Volume in Honor of Frank E. Vogel* (New York: I.B. Tauris, 2008) 173–193.

Miller, Ruth A., "Apostates and Bandits: Religious and Secular Interaction in the Administration of Late Ottoman Criminal Law." *Studia Islamica* 97 (2003): 155–178.

Moustafa, Tamir, *The Struggle for Constitutional Power: Law, Politics and Economic Development in Egypt* (New York: Cambridge University Press, 2007).

Peters, Rudolph, "Sharecropping in the Dakhla Oasis: Shariʿa and Customary Law in Ottoman Egypt" in Peri Bearman, Wolfhart Heinrichs, and Bernard G. Weiss (eds.) *The Law Applied: Contextualizing the Islamic Shariʿa—A Volume in Honor of Frank E. Vogel* (New York: I.B. Tauris, 2008) 79–91.

Powers, David, "The Maliki Family Endowment: Legal Norms and Social Practices." *International Journal of Middle East Studies* 25 (August 1993): 379–406.

Powers, David, "*Kadijustiz* or *Qadi-Justice*: A Paternity Dispute from Fourteenth-Century Morocco." *Islamic Law and Society* 1, no. 3 (1994): 332–366.

Powers, David, *Law, Society and Culture in the Maghrib, 1300–1500* (New York: Cambridge University Press, 2002).

Rapoport, Yossef, "Royal Justice and Religious Law: *Siyasah* and Shariʿah Under the Mamluks." *Mamluk Studies Review* XVI (2012): 71–102.

Rosen, Lawrence, *The Anthropology of Justice: Law as Culture in Islamic Society* (New York: Cambridge University Press, 1989).

Sangar, Satya Prakesh, *Crime and Punishment in Moghul India* (New Delhi: Reliance Publishing House, 1998).

Schacht, Joseph, *An Introduction to Islamic Law* (London: Oxford University Press, 1964).

Sergeant, R.B., "The Caliph ʿUmar's Letters to Abu Musa al-Ashʿari and Muʿawiya." *Journal of Semitic Studies* XXIX, no. 1 (1984): 65–79.

Serrano, Delfina, "Legal Practice in an Andalusi-Maghribi Source From the 12th Century CE: The *Madhahib al-Hukkam fi Nawazil al-Ahkam*." *Islamic Law and Society* 7, no. 2 (2000): 187–234.

Shalakany, Amr, "Between Identity and Distribution: Sanhuri, Genealogy and the Will to Islamise." *Islamic Law and Society* 8, no. 2 (2001): 201–244.

Stiles, Erin, *An Islamic Court in Context: An Ethnographic Study of Judicial Reasoning* (New York: Palgrave MacMillan, 2009).

Stilt, Kristen, "Price Setting and Hoarding in Mamluk Egypt: The Lessons of Legal Realism for Islamic Legal Studies" in Peri Bearman, Wolfhart Heinrichs, and Bernard G. Weiss (eds.) *The Law Applied: Contextualizing the Islamic Shariʿa—A Volume in Honor of Frank E. Vogel* (New York: I.B. Tauris, 2008) 57–78.

Stilt, Kristen, *Islamic Law in Action: Authority, Discretion and Everyday Experiences in Mamluk Egypt* (New York: Oxford University Press, 2011).

Tillier, Mathieu, "The *Qadis* of *Fustat-Misr* Under the *Tulunids* and the *Ikhshidids*: The Judiciary and Egyptian Autonomy." *Journal of the American Oriental Society* 131, no. 2 (2011): 207–222.

Tsafrir, Nurit, *The History of an Islamic School of Law: The Spread of Early Hanafism* (Cambridge, MA: Islamic Legal Studies Program, Harvard Law School, 2004).

Tyan, Emile, *Histoire de L'Organisation Judiciare En Pays D'Islam* (2nd edn. Leiden: Brill, 1960).

Vogel, Frank, *Islamic Law and Legal System: Studies of Saudi Arabia* (Boston: Brill, 2000).

Zaleha, Sharifah, et al., *Managing Marital Disputes in Malaysia: Islamic Mediators and Conflict Resolution in the Syariah Courts* (Richmond, England: Curzon Press, 1997).

CHAPTER 13

HISBA AND MUHTASIB

KRISTEN STILT AND M. SAFA SARAÇOĞLU[1]

I. Definitions of *Hisba* and *Muhtasib* and Their Origins

Hisba is typically defined as encompassing both the duty of Muslim individuals to command right and forbid wrong and the jurisdiction of the person who is officially appointed to carry out that activity, the *muhtasib*.[2] But how these terms came to have these meanings is a matter of speculation and their origins are uncertain. Both are believed to originate in the Qur'anic concept of "commanding right and forbidding wrong," so the question of definitions often begins with this Qur'anic phrase. Several Qur'anic verses contain the language of commanding right and forbidding wrong, as in Q. 3:104: "Let there be one community of you, calling to good, and commanding right and forbidding wrong; those are the prosperers."[3] These verses do not specify who is meant to do the commanding and forbidding (beyond the community generally, or perhaps in two cases, those engaged in warfare), to whom,

1 The authors thank Oxford University Press for permission to borrow, sometimes verbatim, from Kristen Stilt, *Islamic Law in Action* (New York, 2011). The authors thank Alice Di Concetto, Policy Fellow, Animal Law and Policy Program, Harvard Law School, and Roozbeh Jabbarizadeh, SJD candidate, Harvard Law School, for their very helpful research assistance.

2 *EI2*, s.v. "Hisba" (Cahen and Talbi), 3: 485–493.

3 Similar phrasing is found in Q. 3:110, 3:114, 7:157, 9:71, 9:112, 22:41, and 31:17. These verses are discussed in Michael Cook, *Commanding Right and Forbidding Wrong in Islamic Thought* (Cambridge: Cambridge University Press, 2000), 13–14, from where the translation of Q. 3:104 is taken.

for what purposes, or even what behavior is considered right and wrong, and the views of early scholars who examined these verses were not uniform.

Qur'anic exegetes debated the meaning of the terms *right* (*ma'ruf*) and *wrong* (*munkar*) in these verses. Some limited right and wrong to particular acts—al-Tabari (d. 923), in particular, said that commanding right refers to all that God and the Prophet commanded and forbidding wrong likewise refers to all that they forbade.[4] Later jurists who addressed the topic do not seem to have reached a clear view. A basic question is whether *ma'ruf* and *munkar* match any of the five moral classifications that legal scholars developed. *Ma'ruf* seems to have been treated as referring to those acts covered by *wajib* (required) but the treatment of *munkar* is more complicated. According to al-Ghazali (d. 1111), for example, *munkar* contains two categories: forbidden (*haram*) and disapproved or repugnant (*makruh*). In his view, preventing a wrong that is merely *makruh* is commendable but not obligatory.[5]

As for who was supposed to do the commanding and forbidding, Michael Cook concludes that the exegetes determined that the duty was "to be performed by individual believers to each other. The overall effect is to insert the duty into the daily life of the community in a far more concrete way than the Koran, read as naked scripture, would seem to require."[6] Some historical sources describe individual Muslims carrying out this duty, such as the goldsmith who famously confronted the Abbasid leader Abu Muslim, verbally criticized him, and then was executed. The goldsmith was "known as a devotee of commanding right" and clearly did not listen to the learned advice "that this duty (unlike others) was not one that a man could undertake alone."[7] Scholarship that discusses the individual duty, and notably Michael Cook's book, is discussed more fully later.

Importantly, the concept was not understood to be limited to an individual duty. Rulers appointed individuals to carry out the duty on behalf of that authority by way of a position that came to be known as *muhtasib*. Historically, the scholars who elaborated on the duty of individuals to carry out *hisba* typically did not discuss the appointed *muhtasib*.[8] Very little is known therefore about the origins of this appointed official or the terminology used to describe the position, which includes not only *muhtasib* but also two phrases meaning "guardian of the market": *sahib al-suq* and *'amil al-suq*.

The standard account of the *muhtasib*'s origins focuses on market regulation, beginning with the assumption that in pre-Islamic Arabia, markets had their own regulatory and dispute resolution mechanisms.[9] These markets continued in the early Islamic period and others developed that also needed some kind of system

[4] Cook, *Commanding Right and Forbidding Wrong*, 24. [5] Ibid., 442. [6] Ibid., 31.

[7] Ibid., 6–7.

[8] Cook points to one exception among the exegetes in particular: the Qur'anic commentary of Nizam al-Din al-Naysaburi (fl. 14th century), *Ghara'ib al-Qur'an*, which is basically a highly condensed version of al-Mawardi's discussion of the *muhtasib* (discussed later). Ibid., 21 n. 36.

[9] See Ahmad Ghabin, "Some Jahili Origins of the *hisba*," *JSAI* 35 (2008): 59–90. R.P. Buckley asserts, however, that there is no mention of any official in the pre-Islamic period charged with market

of regulation. The Prophet reportedly appointed people to look after the markets in Medina—including a woman—under the title *ʿamil al-suq* or the virtual synonym *ʿamil ʿala al-suq*. The second successor to the Prophet, ʿUmar b. al-Khattab, continued on this path, also appointing at least one woman to oversee Medinan markets. Some sources claim that he was the first to perform *hisba*; others praise ʿAli for engaging in *hisba*.[10] The appointment of market inspectors persisted throughout the Umayyad period (661–750). When some members of the Umayyad family fled westward upon the rise of the Abbasids, they took the concept of the market inspector with them. In the Umayyad-era sources of the Islamic West, the position appears as *sahib al-suq*. The explanation of the position is usually accompanied by the assertion that the Umayyad market inspector focussed exclusively on market affairs and not on a larger concept of commanding right and forbidding wrong.[11]

The standard account of the development of the position called *muhtasib* states that in an effort to "Islamize" the institutions of the former Umayyad rulers, the Abbasids (r. 750–1258) gave what had been a market inspector position wide-ranging powers that went beyond market matters and connected it to the broader Qur'anic notion of commanding right and forbidding wrong. Thus, the link with the Qur'anic concept was a later Abbasid-era development, intended to infuse the position with a broad Islamic component. The position continued in the central and eastern Islamic lands under this name, fully flourishing in the Fatimid (r. 909–1171), Ayyubid (r. 1171–1250), and Mamluk (r. 1250–1517) eras in particular.[12]

This standard account of origins, beginning with the narrow concept of market inspector who became an Islamic *muhtasib* with fuller powers under the Abbasids, is not entirely persuasive. Patricia Crone has suggested that "the term *muhtasib* must be as early as that of *sahib al-suq*: the two terms merely happen to be attested at slightly different times in the extant literature."[13] Also, the claim that market

regulation responsibilities. R.P. Buckley, trans., *The Book of the Islamic Market Inspector*, Journal of Semitic Studies Supplement, vol. 9 (Oxford, 1999), 2; Buckley, "The *Muhtasib*," *Arabica* 39 (1992): 59–117.

[10] Buckley, *Book of the Islamic Market Inspector*, 6.

[11] Buckley, "*Muhtasib*," 60–63; Buckley, *Book of the Islamic Market Inspector*, 5.

[12] Buckley, "*Muhtasib*," 60–67; Buckley, *The Book of the Islamic Market Inspector*, 5. *The Encyclopaedia of Islam*, second edition article on *hisba* states that (3: 487),

> about the time of the caliphate of al-Maʾmun [r. 813–833], the *sahib al-suk* was replaced by the *muhtasib* .... This change in nomenclature evidently took place within the framework of the Islamization of institutions carried out by the ʿAbbasids, particularly during the period of the Muʿtazila; but it is difficult to tell to what extent there really took place a transformation in the spirit and content of the office of *hisba*.... The classical *muhtasib* then was characterized by the integration of his task as controller of the market within the wider duty, basically religious, of maintaining the seemly ordering of social life.

EI2 does not contain a separate article on the *muhtasib*, directing readers to the *hisba* article instead. The first edition did include a short entry on the *muhtasib* (R. Levy), which was mainly a composite summary of al-Mawardi's chapter on the office (see Section III), the *muhtasib* manual of al-Shayzari (see Section III), and al-Ghazzali's discussion of the concept of commanding right and forbidding wrong (see later in this section).

[13] Patricia Crone, *Roman, Provincial and Islamic Law: The Origins of the Islamic Patronate* (Cambridge, 1987), 108.

regulation under the *sahib al-suq* was purely commercial, and not infused with legal and ethical concerns derived from the Qur'an, is misplaced. The writings that make this claim often list the Qur'anic verses that deal with the obligation to give proper weights and measures and the many *hadith* on this topic, and then go on to conclude that market regulation was largely a secular operation. These accounts seem to assume that if an area of regulation is undertaken today by a modern secular authority, then it should also be called secular when performed by an early Muslim official, even when the basis for the Muslim performance derives from the texts of Islamic law.[14]

The origins of the terminology of *hisba* and *muhtasib* are also contested. A prominent view sees *sahib al-suq* as the Arabic translation of the Greek term *agoranomos* (market inspector), an official in cities charged with checking for fraud in the market and watching over temples that were located in the market areas.[15] Under this theory, the Arabs found this position to be a useful one and retained it, although with an Arabic name. Benjamin Foster, however, has traced carefully the use of the term *agoranomos* in pre-Islamic Egypt, Syria, and Palestine to show that its usage in the sense of market inspector had ceased around the end of the third century.[16]

The term *muhtasib* was used in the eleventh century by al-Mawardi (discussed later in Section III) to describe the official appointed to command right and forbid wrong (which he referred to as *hisba*); he called any other Muslim who undertook this duty by another term, *mutatawwiʿ*, indicating that the person was an unappointed volunteer.[17] A half-century later, al-Ghazzali used *hisba* as a general term for commanding right and forbidding wrong, but he did not explain the word choice. For al Ghazzali, everyone who carries out the duty is considered a *muhtasib*. According to Michael Cook, "What Ghazzali fails to explain is just why he chose the word *hisba* as a general term for forbidding wrong, and I am not entirely clear why he did so.... The modern reader tends to assume that Ghazzali is implying an analogy between the duty of the individual to forbid wrong and the obligation of the officially appointed censor (*muhtasib*) to police morals and markets—for all that Ghazzali has nothing to say about the duties of the censor."[18] Cook then speculates about al-Ghazzali's choices of *hisba* and *muhtasib*. The terms (including the cognate verb *ihtsaba*) suggest "doing something for God's sake, without personal or worldly motives of any kind."[19] However, "forbidding wrong is far from

[14] Buckley, "*Muhtasib*," 63–64.

[15] See, for example, Joseph Schacht, *An Introduction to Islamic Law* (Oxford, 1964), 25; *EI2*, s.v. "Hisba" (Cahen and Talbi), 3: 487. Crone summarizes this view, beginning with its original proponent Gaudefroy-Demombynes in 1939. Crone, *Roman, Provincial and Islamic Law*, 107–8.

[16] Benjamin R. Foster, "Agoranomos and Muhtasib," *JESHO* 13 (1970): 128–44, at 135–36.

[17] As al-Mawardi explained, the duties of the volunteer are limited in comparison to those of the official. Al-Mawardi, *al-Ahkam al-sultaniyya wa-l-wilayat al-diniyya* (Beirut, 1985), 299–300.

[18] Cook, *Commanding Right and Forbidding Wrong*, 447–48.

[19] Ibid., 448 and n. 136; see Ibn Manzur, *Lisan al-ʿarab*, ed. ʿAli Shiri, 18 vols. (Beirut, 1988), 3: 164–66 (entry *ḥ-s-b*).

being the only thing that can or should be done for God's sake."[20] Furthermore, it is difficult to say that the *muhtasib*, an appointed official, was carrying out the duty without personal or worldly motives, since he was paid a salary for his work from the treasury.

The translation of "market inspector" for *muhtasib* in Western literature is possibly influenced by the many descriptions of the jurisdiction that involve commerce and commercial transactions or by the related title of *sahib al-suq*, with its clear emphasis on the market. Such a translation is, however, too narrow. The jurisdiction of the *muhtasib* extended to any manifest public action, whether in the fields of devotional practice, commerce, or crime. The position is better expressed as an inspector and regulator of the markets and public behavior generally.

II. Scholarship Dealing with *Hisba* as Applied to Individual Muslims

The most significant scholarship dealing with *hisba* as applied to individuals is Michael Cook's *Commanding Right and Forbidding Wrong in Islamic Thought*, published in 2000. As Cook states in the preface, "my interest here is in the duty of individual believers; this book is only tangentially concerned with the place of rulers in forbidding wrong, or with the officially appointed censor (*muhtasib*) or his administrative role (*hisba*)."[21] This 700-page book offers as extensive a treatment of *hisba* as can be found today—in the Qur'an and Qur'anic exegesis; in the *hadith*; in biographical literature about early Muslims; and in the scholarship of sects and schools, that is, the Hanafis, Shafi'is, Malikis, and Hanbalis, the Mu'tazilis, and the Shi'a. It includes a section on al-Ghazzali, one on "Classical Islam in Retrospect," and, finally, one entitled "Beyond Classical Islam," which includes "Modern Islamic Developments" and "Origins and Comparisons."

Cook's extensive bibliography provides the researcher with a full list of primary sources and secondary works. Because the book's bibliography is so extensive, researchers will find it an invaluable resource for any publication on *hisba* published before 2000. More generally, this book is the necessary point of departure for any subsequent scholarship on commanding right and forbidding wrong as applied to individual Muslims; it remains the state of the field on this topic and no doubt will for quite some time to come.

[20] Cook, *Commanding Right and Forbidding Wrong*, 448. [21] Ibid., xii.

It should be noted that Cook found that "the Imamis provide the richest and most continuous documentation of the doctrine of forbidding wrong of any sect or school," so that he was able to write a "more sustained narrative of the history of the doctrine in Imamism than is possible for any other sect or school."[22] As for the practice of the *muhtasib* under Shiʿi rule, however, as will be discussed, the literature is less developed than in Sunni contexts because the actual position of *muhtasib* appears to have been far less important.

Cook's main goal of the book is to "set out an intelligible account of the duty as it appears in the scholastic literature of Islam."[23] This was not a straightforward task because "there are very many such accounts" and "the doctrine they present is far from uniform."[24] Cook further aims to explain "why Islam came to have such a doctrine, and why this doctrine varied as it did from one milieu to another" as well as "how this intellectual tradition was related to the society in which it flourished, and what difference it made to life on the street."[25] Cook admits that his achievement in these latter two goals "is a much more limited one" due in part to the fact that, out of necessity given the sheer volume of material, he had to limit his reading of any particular work to the chapter on commanding right and forbidding wrong.[26] Further, "'practice' in this book almost invariably means practice as described in Islamic literary sources."[27]

Commanding Right and Forbidding Wrong does not lend itself to general conclusions or overarching arguments, given its encyclopedic nature. The last chapter is a conclusion only to the book's final part, "Beyond Classical Islam," and it mainly compares "Muslim and Western notions of the duty to stop wrongdoing."[28] One such comparison is that "while Islam has definite notions of privacy and gives them strong articulation, there seems to be a difference between Islamic and Western thinking.... In a Western perspective, certain kinds of behavior tend to be thought of as an inherently private matter, whether or not they happen to become public knowledge. In Islamic thought, by contrast, such behavior may be only contingently private. Wrongdoing that does not affect others will tend for that very reason to remain in the private domain; and by and large, it is urged, it should be allowed to remain there. But once it ceases to be private ... more drastic norms may properly come into play."[29] In the final few pages, Cook hints at the issues that arise in modern Muslim societies in which the "Muslim doctrine of forbidding wrong now confronts a theory of minding one's own business significantly different from its own."[30] As will be discussed, a line of contemporary scholarship addresses issues related to *hisba* and *muhtasib* in the modern period, such as in countries that have an official performing the work of the *muhtasib* or that allow arguments based in *hisba* to be made in courts of law.

[22] Ibid., 252–253. [23] Ibid., xii. [24] Ibid., xiii. [25] Ibid. [26] Ibid.
[27] Ibid. [28] Ibid., 590. [29] Ibid., 593–594. [30] Ibid., 594.

III. Scholarship on the *Muhtasib*

Scholars studying the *muhtasib* (who were nearly exclusively male) have focussed on the issues of the official's job description and jurisdiction, especially vis-à-vis certain other officials; his sources of law, including the manuals written to guide him in his work; the biographies of individuals holding the position, and what prosopography reveals about the position itself; and the larger socio-legal question of how he worked in practice and what effects he had on social life in the regulated communities. This section discusses each topic in turn.

A. Job Description and Jurisdiction

Scholars have sought to understand the duties and the jurisdiction of the *muhtasib*, who, like the institution of *mazalim*, does not have an obvious counterpart in the Western legal system. In doing so, virtually all scholarship relies upon the description of the *muhtasib* presented in *al-Ahkam al-sultaniyya wa-l-wilayat al-diniyya* by the Shafi'i jurist al-Mawardi, who was born in Basra and died in 1058 in Baghdad.[31] No other author treated the *muhtasib* as fully as al-Mawardi did in the chapter on this position in his masterful work of Islamic public law, and so it is worth discussing it here in detail. In addition, al-Mawardi's successors copied his language, and the *muhtasib* manuals (discussed later) in particular quoted al-Mawardi extensively, showing that his work was not just of theoretical interest but was used by the authors of manuals in their efforts to guide *muhtasib*s in their work.[32] Further, al-Mawardi was interested in constitutional structure and jurisdictional concerns, and not just in the substance of the *muhtasib*'s duties, although he commented on them in order to provide examples of his larger points. He described the *muhtasib*

[31] This is true dating back to the earliest scholarship on the official. For example, Émile Tyan's discussion of the *muhtasib*'s position is based in large part on al-Mawardi's *al-Ahkam al-sultaniyya wa-l-wilayat al-diniyya*, along with al-Qalqashandi's *Subh al-a'sha* and three *muhtasib* manuals. Émile Tyan, *Histoire de l'organisation judiciaire en pays d'Islam* (Leiden, 1960), 2: 436–62. The perceived connection between al-Mawardi and *hisba* is so strong that his name has been attached to a manuscript of a *hisba* manual that is identical to Ibn al-Ukhuwwa's manual (discussed later in this chapter). Carl Brockelmann, *GAL* (Leiden, 1937–1949), S 1: 668. References within the manual indicate that it could not have been al-Mawardi's and biographical entries for al-Mawardi do not list the manual; Maurice Gaudefroy-Demombynes identified it as pseudo-Mawardi. Gaudefroy-Demombynes, "Sur quelques ouvrages de hisba," *Journal Asiatique* 230 (1938): 456. The manual was published as al-Mawardi, *al-Rutba fi talab al-hisba*, in Cairo in 2002.

[32] This is true for other types of literature on the *muhtasib* as well. For example, the section dealing with the *muhtasib* in al-Nuwayri's encyclopedia is nearly identical to al-Mawardi's chapter on the *muhtasib*. Al-Nuwayri (d. 1333), *Nihayat al-arab fi funun al-adab* (Cairo, 1964–), 6: 291–315.

as having connections to the authority of both the judge and legal doctrine (*fiqh*) on the one hand, and the sultan and policy (*siyasa*) on the other. He also identified the tensions inherent in a position that simultaneously applies *fiqh* rules and makes decisions of strategy and policy.

The Hanbali scholar Ibn Taymiyya (d. 1328) also deserves mention for dealing with the duty generally and with the *muhtasib* in particular in his short work published as *al-Hisba fi-l-Islam*. For Ibn Taymiyya, the *muhtasib*'s jurisdiction was simply the commanding right and forbidding wrong that was not otherwise in the jurisdiction of any other authority, whether judges or other appointed officials. In other words, the *muhtasib* was supposed to fill in the gaps, commanding right and forbidding wrong when it was not done by someone else. Aside from this brief sketch of jurisdiction and constitutional structure, the remainder of Ibn Taymiyya's work describes substantive areas of law that the *muhtasib* should deal with and the rules that he should apply, and some of these views seem particular to Ibn Taymiyya. In terms of the origins of this writing, Michael Cook remarks that *al-Hisba fi-l-Islam* is "something of a biographical puzzle," and he doubts that the work was originally meant to be an independent one.[33]

Returning to al-Mawardi, three aspects of his chapter on the *muhtasib* stand out as particularly significant on their own terms and also in terms of the specific interests that modern scholars have taken in al-Mawardi's writing: the *muhtasib*'s qualifications; the jurisdictional divisions between the *muhtasib* and others who command right and forbid wrong—the volunteer, the judge, and the *mazalim* court; and the substance of the *muhtasib*'s jurisdiction. As a preliminary matter, al-Mawardi defined the concept of *hisba* as "commanding right when it is conspicuously neglected, and forbidding wrong when it is conspicuously done."[34] A first significant question about the *muhtasib* (or anyone carrying out *hisba*) is the meaning of conspicuous and how much investigation is appropriate to identify offenses, such as when suspicious sounds are heard from behind a neighbor's closed door.[35] Al-Mawardi specified that the *muhtasib* may not spy on people, which involves looking beyond what takes place in the public view.[36] This rule implicitly recognizes that forbidden acts will take place in private, but also considers respect for privacy to be more important than catching and punishing those acts. There are exceptions, however—if the situation suggests the occurrence of an imminent crime the damage of which will not be remediable, the *muhtasib* may spy in order to investigate. Al-Mawardi provided the examples of when the *muhtasib* is informed by a reliable source that a man is alone with a woman in order to commit fornication (*zina*) or

[33] Cook, *Commanding Right and Forbidding Wrong*, 151 n. 48.

[34] Al-Mawardi, *al-Ahkam al-sultaniyya*, 299.

[35] This topic is discussed in each chapter of Cook, *Commanding Right and Forbidding Wrong*. See, e.g., 80–82 (defending privacy in biographical literature); 99–100 (the privacy limits according to Ibn Hanbal).

[36] Al-Mawardi, *al-Ahkam al-sultaniyya*, 314.

a man is alone with another man in order to kill him. In these cases, the *muhtasib* is entitled to uncover the act in order to stop it. If the situation does not rise to this level of urgency, he may not so investigate.[37]

In terms of qualifications, for al-Mawardi the *muhtasib* must be a free man, of good character (*'adl*), have sound judgment, and be strong in matters of faith. He must know what actions are obviously wrong, meaning that he must know what acts the jurists agreed are wrongful, but he does not need to be familiar with acts that some consider wrongful but others consider permissible.[38] This leads al-Mawardi into a contested area among the Shafi'i scholars: What if the *muhtasib* is considered a *mujtahid*, able to reach his own opinion through his own *ijtihad* ? May he do so and impose upon people rules about which there is disagreement? The Shafi'i majority opinion, also held by al-Mawardi, is that the *muhtasib* may not impose his opinion and the results of his *ijtihad*, even if he is able and qualified to conduct *ijtihad*, nor may he lead people toward his school. The minority Shafi'i opinion, articulated by al-Istakhri,[39] argued that a *muhtasib* competent in *ijtihad* may impose his opinion resulting from his *ijtihad* on a matter of disagreement.[40]

In terms of jurisdiction, al-Mawardi began his chapter with a discussion of the differences between the *muhtasib*, who was appointed, and the *mutatawwi'*, who volunteers.[41] The remainder of the chapter deals explicitly with the *muhtasib*, and not the volunteer, but one important distinction between them is that the *muhtasib* may inflict a punishment (*ta'zir*) for wrongs committed in the open whereas the volunteer may not physically punish wrongful acts at all. Al-Mawardi specified that in punishing through *ta'zir*, the *muhtasib* may not exceed the *hadd* penalties, which is both a comment on the limits of *ta'zir* in al-Mawardi's view (which is the Shafi'i position) and also implicitly a statement that adjudication of *hadd* crimes is beyond the *muhtasib*'s jurisdiction, a position reinforced in the discussion of the distinction between the *muhtasib* and the judge.[42]

Next, al-Mawardi compared the *muhtasib* to the judge. The *muhtasib* is more powerful than the judge in two ways. First, he has the authority to initiate an investigation of an action taking place in the open without a complaint being brought to him, whereas the judge must wait for a party to initiate a suit. Secondly, the *muhtasib* carries the ruler's power in regard to wrongful acts. This means that the *muhtasib* should instill fear in people in a way that a judge is not permitted to do, and he may even display a lack of restraint and general harshness.[43] However, the *muhtasib* has less power than the judge because the *muhtasib* may only hear complaints about wrongs that are factually manifest and take place out in the open. The *muhtasib*

[37] Ibid. [38] Ibid., 300.

[39] Abu Sa'id al-Istakhri (d. 939) was a Shafi'i jurist who also served as *muhtasib* of Baghdad. Ibn Khallikan, *Wafayat al-a'yan wa-anba' abna' al-zaman* (Beirut, 1398/[1977]), 2: 74–75.

[40] Al-Mawardi, *al-Ahkam al-sultaniyya*, 300. [41] Ibid., 299–300. [42] Ibid., 300.

[43] Ibid., 302.

may use his own knowledge or rely on what he is told, but he may not hold a formal evidentiary hearing or ask anyone to take an oath to deny a claim. Only judges may hear evidence and administer oaths.[44] Finally, a decision of a *muhtasib* is merely that; unlike the judge, the *muhtasib* does not issue a legal judgment (*hukm*).

Al-Mawardi then compared the authority of the *muhtasib* to that of the sultan's tribunal (*mazalim*). The *mazalim* as an institution and the *muhtasib* as an individual are faces of the law that should inspire fear and awe, in contrast to the judge who is supposed to be even-tempered and impartial. Further, what might lead to achieving public interest is an independent criterion that both the *muhtasib* and the sultan in the *mazalim* forum may take into consideration in their deliberation process. Al-Mawardi did not discuss the judge's use of public interest, presumably because he expected judges to use public interest as a factor in the process of *ijtihad* and not as an independent basis. For the *muhtasib* and the sultan in the *mazalim* court, however, public interest is a free-standing basis for decision-making, one that can guide the entire process.[45]

Al-Mawardi's concern with the *muhtasib*'s jurisdiction and with the position's relationship to other officials, and judges and the *mazalim* in particular, have remained areas of focus in studies of the position of *muhtasib*. Modern-day scholars have written extensively about al-Mawardi's work and also have used his framework to assess the jurisdiction and the nomenclature of an official that functioned as *muhtasib* in different historical contexts.

One issue raised by al-Mawardi that has been of particular interest to scholars is the public-private distinction and the limits of the *muhtasib*'s jurisdiction.[46] These questions are also discussed in the *hisba* literature (see above) since the basic issue is the same; the Muslim carrying out *hisba* as an individual duty also has to decide the degree to which he or she will intrude into someone's private space in pursuit of a wrongdoing. The divisions between public and private were the focus of an article by Roy Mottahedeh and Kristen Stilt,[47] and they conclude that "the line between public and private was not rigidly fixed but, rather, shifted according to the relations among the people involved in any particular situation." For example, "what is considered outside the jurisdiction of the *muhtasib* ... may not be considered private in relation to another official, such as the police (*shurta*) or judge."[48]

In the same volume, Frank Vogel compares the distinction between public and private as articulated by al-Mawardi, as discussed above, with the rules governing the office of the contemporary *muhtasib* in Saudi Arabia, which is known colloquially as the *mutawwa*ʿ, "the religious police."[49] The term *mutawwa*ʿ is itself a curious choice,

44 Ibid., 301–302. 45 Ibid., 302.

46 Among scholars who have written on this topic is Yaron Klein, "Between Public and Private: An Examination of *hisba* Literature," *Harvard Middle Eastern and Islamic Review* 7 (2006): 41–62.

47 Roy P. Mottahedeh and Kristen Stilt, "Public and Private as Viewed through the Work of the *Muhtasib*," *Social Research* 70.3 (2003): 735–748.

48 Ibid., 736.

49 Frank E. Vogel, "The Public and Private in Saudi Arabia: Restrictions on the Powers of Committees for Ordering the Good and Forbidding Evil," *Social Research* 70.3 (2003): 749–68.

and Vogel speculates that "one cannot help but think that the term has its origins in the term *mutatawwiʿ*, literally 'volunteer,' used to refer to the private individual" in al-Mawardi's terminology, in contrast to the officially appointed *muhtasib*.[50] Vogel describes al-Mawardi as "working consciously and carefully to circumscribe the power of the state to invade the private sphere to correct or punish immorality."[51] In contrast, the *mutawwaʿ* "are granted much greater and more intrusive authority than Mawardi's *muhtasib*—and this is true as a matter of doctrine, without considering the vast augmentation in surveillance and enforcement powers now available to governments and their agents as compared with their medieval ancestors."[52]

B. Sources: *Fiqh* and Manuals

Scholars have been very interested in the question of what sources of law guide the *muhtasib*s in their work. As noted, the fundamental task of the *muhtasib* was to command right and forbid wrong, which the jurists commented and elaborated upon in their works of *fiqh*. But since the *muhtasib* was supposed to apply only agreed-upon rules, the position did not inherently require knowledge of complex discussions of proof texts and disagreements on views within or across schools. Aside from the appointment document (discussed later) and occasional orders from the sultan, how did a *muhtasib*, who might have had little in the way of legal education (see heading B. in this section for the discussion of biographies), know how to carry out the demands of his position? Manuals written for the express purpose of guiding *muhtasib*s in their work provided the official with detailed and practical legal guidance. These may have been written by jurists, but often the authors were fairly unknown men who must have had enough education to provide short summaries of *fiqh* rules and enough experience in the market to describe the daily challenges the appointed official faces.

Critical editions of many of the extant *muhtasib* manuals have been produced, and lists of manuals are available in several publications with varying amounts of accompanying information. Pedro Chalmeta provides a list, beginning with the earliest extant manual of Yahya b. ʿUmar (d. 901) (discussed later).[53] Mu'il ʿIzz al-Din also provides a list of manuals in his critical edition of ʿUmar b. Muhammad al-Sunami's *Kitab Nisab al-ihtisab*, published as *The Theory and the Practice of Market Law in Medieval Islam*.[54] Maya Shatzmiller also lists *muhtasib* manuals in her *Labour in the Medieval Islamic World*.[55] These manuals form what should be considered a distinct genre of "rules for the *muhtasib*" (*adab al-muhtasib*).[56]

[50] Ibid., 758 n. 14. [51] Ibid., 757. [52] Ibid., 759.

[53] Pedro Chalmeta, *El zoco medieval: Contribución al estudio de la historia del mercado* (Alméria, 2010), 35–50.

[54] Mu'il ʿIzz al-Din, *The Theory and Practice of Market Law in Medieval Islam: A Study of Kitab Nisab al-ihtisab of ʿUmar b. Muhammad al-Sunami* (Cambridge, 1997).

[55] Maya Shatzmiller, *Labour in the Medieval Islamic World* (Leiden, 1994), 71–76.

[56] See Stilt, *Islamic Law in Action*, 55 n. 63.

The manuals typically list the qualifications for the person serving as *muhtasib*, describe the *muhtasib's* areas of duties, caution against specific types of fraud and how to detect them, and suggest means of punishment. For example, according to doctrinal rules, a transaction should be based on accurate information in order to ensure that it does not subject the buyer or seller to excessive risk (*gharar*), such as in the object of the sale itself or the sale's terms and conditions. But how would a *muhtasib* know how to enforce this general rule in the face of a creative merchant trying to cheat his customer in devious ways, perhaps by mixing oak bark into a bag of musk so that the customer cannot even see that what she is buying is not pure? The manual tells the *muhtasib* the typical tricks engaged in by each type of merchant and how to detect them, and provides simplified versions of rules of doctrine.

Scholars sometimes treat these manuals as quasi-chronicles, assuming that they depict historical events. Without corroborating evidence from chronicles or other descriptive sources, relying on the manuals for evidence of social practice in a particular time and place is problematic.[57] The manuals as a genre contain clauses that appear to have been copied from one manual to the next, and few authors seem to have written their manuals without an awareness of and consultation with previous ones. Each manual contains elements of the prescriptive and descriptive and so each paragraph or rule in a manual needs to be considered individually to determine its significance. Did the author encounter the problem when serving as *muhtasib*? Does the rule respond to a particular incident or pervasive problem? Or did the author include the rule in the manual, perhaps copying it from an earlier manual or a book of *fiqh*, without anyone ever having encountered the issue or having heard that it was a problem in his place and time?

The manual that has received the most scholarly attention, and is discussed here as an example, is *Maʿalim al-qurba fi ahkam al-hisba*, attributed to Diyaʾ al-Din Muhammad b. Muhammad b. Ahmad al-Qurashi al-Shafiʿi, who was known as Ibn al-Ukhuwwa (d. 1329). Ibn al-Ukhuwwa's manual was edited and partially translated in 1938 by Reuben Levy, and since then it has been widely cited by scholars.[58] Despite the popularity of the text, little is known about the author other than his death date and that he was a Shafiʿi and likely an Egyptian.[59] Ibn al-Ukhuwwa's text is composed of seventy chapters and builds on the manual written by al-Shayzari, who died in 1193 and likely lived in Syria.[60] A substantial number of sections or parts of sections are identical to those in al-Shayzari, and the ordering of the chapters is the same to some extent.

Despite these similarities, Ibn al-Ukhuwwa's text is different in fundamental ways, and these differences highlight some of the most interesting aspects of these

[57] As an example of this, *muhtasib* manuals formed the basis for the discussion on the *muhtasib* in Subhi Y. Labib, *Handelsgeschichte Ägyptens im Spätmittelalter (1171–1517)* (Wiesbaden, 1965), 179–83.

[58] Ibn al-Ukhuwwa, *Maʿalim al-qurba fi ahkam al-hisba*, ed. Reuben Levy (Cambridge, 1938). For a discussion of the manuscripts Levy relied upon and subsequent published editions of this manual, see Stilt, *Islamic Law in Action*, 59–60. Citations herein are to Levy's edition.

[59] Ibn al-Ukhuwwa, *Maʿalim al-qurba*, xvii (editor's introduction).

[60] See Stilt, *Islamic Law in Action*, 57.

manuals in general. Al-Shayzari tended to give specific, pragmatic, and direct instructions whereas Ibn al-Ukhuwwa offered the *muhtasib* long discussions of doctrinal rules. For example, he presented the *muhtasib*'s qualifications and jurisdiction succinctly as in al-Shayzari, but then added a long elaboration, including a discussion that comes straight from al-Mawardi, on whether a *mujtahid muhtasib* may impose his own views on the people he regulates.[61]

While organized under topic headings that look like a *muhtasib* manual, Ibn al-Ukhuwwa's manual reads like a *fiqh* text at times. He offers differing opinions in some cases, giving and naming not only the Shafiʿi view, but also that of the Hanafis and Malikis (though never the Hanbali view). Ibn al-Ukhuwwa's manual also cites proof texts with much higher frequency than al-Shayzari's. Like al-Shayzari, Ibn al-Ukhuwwa gave the *muhtasib* doctrinal rules to follow, but he did so in a much longer and more complex way. For Ibn al-Ukhuwwa's text to be used as a practical manual, the *muhtasib* would have to make his own decision as to which rule he would follow, or at least determine how to apply Ibn al-Ukhuwwa's preferred legal rule to factual scenarios. The manual's presentation of a diversity of views also raises the question of whether Ibn al-Ukhuwwa intended a *muhtasib* to pick one view and impose it on those he regulated, in contrast to the general view that the *muhtasib* is supposed to limit himself to agreed-upon rights and wrongs. Alternatively, perhaps Ibn al-Ukhuwwa merely wanted the *muhtasib* to be aware of the range of opinions, while confining himself to those agreed upon.

The manuals are a particular kind of legal text, one that presents simplified rules of doctrine embellished with examples from the market. The familiarity of any particular *muhtasib* with the rules, however, either independently or as expressed in the manuals, depended on that individual's personal abilities and talents. A *muhtasib* who studied doctrine and was considered highly learned would know the details above and beyond what was presented in the manuals, but a *muhtasib* pulled from the ranks of the soldiers—as did happen at the end of the Mamluk period, as discussed below— might have had only basic Arabic literacy, in which case the manuals would have been difficult reading. The less learned *muhtasib* probably relied more heavily on common understandings of the position's jurisdiction and responsibilities and the sultan's instructions, which are discussed next.

c. Sources: Appointment Documents

Scholars have also taken an interest in the documents appointing the *muhtasib*s to their positions, although to a far lesser degree than the manuals just discussed. Appointment decrees are valuable evidence of the job description as produced by the ruler, or at least as written by his scribes. The appointment document that has

[61] Ibn al-Ukhuwwa, *Maʿalim al-qurba*, 7–8.

probably received the most attention is from the Mamluk period; it is translated and discussed at length in Stilt, *Islamic Law in Action*.[62] The Mamluk sultan appointed the *muhtasibs* of Cairo and of Fustat, who served at his pleasure and were expected to follow his periodic instructions. An extensive appointment document (*wasiya*) from the Mamluk period was recorded by al-ʿUmari (d. 1349) in his *al-Taʿrif bi-l-mustalah al-sharif*, and al-Qalqashandi (d. 1418) after him included the same decree (along with several others) in his massive book on secretaryship, *Subh al-aʿsha fi sinaʿat al-inshaʾ*.[63] Al-Qalqashandi was a secretary for the Mamluk sultans and knowledgeable in Islamic law, and in particular the Shafiʿi school. His book on secretaryship contains both its theoretical bases and the specific skills needed by a secretary dealing with official correspondence. Such a secretary should know the appointment decrees used for officials such as the judge and *muhtasib*. The actual process of appointing the *muhtasib* might have involved the reading aloud of such an appointment decree. The appointment document that was recorded by al-ʿUmari and copied by al-Qalqashandi shows vibrant detail about the position's tasks from the perspective of the ruler or other individual making the appointment.

D. Prosopography

Scholars have been interested in the identities of the individuals who have served as *muhtasib*. The question of identity is driven in part by an effort to understand the position of *muhtasib* since, as discussed, it fits somewhere between the position of judge and the institution of *mazalim* but its precise contours are fluid. The question of the nature of the position has often been posed as either a "political" or a "religious" one; in *Islamic Law in Action*, Stilt has suggested that a more productive way to view the position is to see it as one influenced by both the authority of law, represented by *fiqh*, and by the authority of order, represented by the authority of the ruler and his policy decisions, *siyasa*.

In a chapter on *hisba* in an edited volume on the Seljuk period (1040–1194), Lange discusses the biographies of some of the individuals who held the position then and asks "whether *hisba* under the Seljuks was predominately occupied by those connected to the (Sunni) religious elite or by people without affiliation to religious

[62] This appointment document is also translated and discussed briefly in Christian Lange, "Hisba and the Problem of Overlapping Jurisdictions: An Introduction to, and Translation of, Hisba Diplomas in Qalqashandi's Subh al-aʿsha," *Harvard Middle Eastern and Islamic Review* 7 (2006): 85–107. Lange's article discusses briefly all of the appointment documents for the *muhtasib* in al-Qalqashandi's work, regardless of time period. For a discussion of an appointment document for the *muhtasib* in the Seljuq period in particular, see Richard Wittman, "The Muhtasib in Seljuq Times: Insights from Four Chancery Manuals," *Harvard Middle Eastern and Islamic Review* 7 (2006): 108–28.

[63] Al-ʿUmari, *al-Taʿrif bi-l-mustalah al-sharif* (Karak, Jordan, 1992), 178–80; al-Qalqashandi, *Subh al-aʿsha* (Cairo, 1964), 11: 214–15. Unfortunately, neither author provided specific dates for when the document was in use, but evidence points convincingly to the Mamluk period.

learning."[64] With access to only limited biographical information, he concludes that "while a certain number of *muhtasib*s under the Seljuqs, and especially in Baghdad under the Abbasid caliphs, appear to have been close to *ulama* circles, it would be hasty to infer from this that the office was (re-)islamised."[65] Lange concludes that appointments to the office of *hisba* continued to be granted to individuals without Islamic legal training and credentials into the second half of the Seljuk period.[66]

Jonathan Berkey has examined the transformation in the office of the *muhtasib* in Cairo during the Mamluk period.[67] He divides the period into six parts that reflect, in his view, changes in the "*muhtasib*'s character and responsibilities."[68] These changes include the type of person who held the office, beginning with the early period in which members of the *ulama* held the position, to the later period, in which members of the military held the office.[69] Also studying the Mamluk period, Stilt examines the *muhtasib*s of both Cairo and adjacent Fustat, since the two cities, and the positions of *muhtasib*s, were linked in several ways. Stilt divides the types of men who held the position into four groups: recognized jurists, or individuals with at least a strong educational background in the legal sciences; individuals with an administrative background; associates of the sultan or the amirs, who had neither strong scholarly nor administrative backgrounds; and soldiers or even the sultan himself. Finding a similar trend to Berkey, Stilt concludes that over the course of the Mamluk period, the presence of the jurist-*muhtasib* tapers off and then disappears, while at the same time, well-connected individuals and amirs begin to dominate the position, with even the sultan serving toward the end of the period briefly. These trends suggest a change over time in the expectations by the sultan and perhaps society at large for the qualifications of the office.[70]

E. The Practice in Historical Context

Going beyond the identity of the individuals who held the position, scholars have also looked at the practice of the *muhtasib* in particular historical contexts, examining how the position changed according to differing governance structures and rulers. Within specific historical contexts, some scholars have also asked socio-legal questions about the practice of the *muhtasib* and the effects on the regulated population. Some of the most interesting scholarship has developed from this line

[64] Christian Lange, "Changes in the Office of *Hisba* Under the Seljuqs," in *The Seljuks: Politics, Society and Culture*, eds., Lange and Songül Mecit (Edinburgh, 2012), 160.

[65] Ibid., 162. [66] Ibid., 161.

[67] Jonathan Berkey, "The Muhtasibs of Cairo under the Mamluks: Toward an Understanding of an Islamic Institution," in *The Mamluks in Egyptian and Syrian Politics and Society*, eds., Michael Winter and Amalia Levanoni (Leiden, 2004), 245–276.

[68] Ibid., 253. [69] Ibid., 253–257. [70] Stilt, *Islamic Law in Action*, 63.

of thought, and there is still a need and an opportunity for additional work in this area. The challenge is the existence of sources of social history, since the questions asked in this line of scholarship depend on sources that provide evidence of social life and the ways that the *muhtasib* affected and responded to the behavior of individuals on a daily basis.

For the Seljuk period, Lange argues that "while the Seljuqs adopted and continued features of Abbasid, Buyid and Ghaznavid state organization, the office of *hisba* underwent developments which gave it a new and distinctly Seljuq profile."[71] In particular, the *muhtasibs* gained additional powers to punish, encompassing both *hadd* and *ta'zir* penalties.[72] They also "became more interventionist, in the sense that the Seljuq *muhtasibs* acquired greater authority to transgress into the private sphere of Muslim households," which seems to go along with the "Seljuq preoccupation with a comprehensive system of surveillance" more generally.[73]

For Mamluk Egypt, Kristen Stilt's monograph, *Islamic Law in Action*, is the most extensive examination of the practice of the *muhtasibs* of Cairo and Fustat.[74] The book is structured around the substantive areas of the law in which the *muhtasibs* of these adjacent cities took action, and takes up two main and related issues: the dynamics of law and society at the hands of the *muhtasib* and the sources of legal authority that influenced the official. In terms of the first, the books seeks to discover for what, when, and why the *muhtasib* punished people or required that they conform their behavior to his orders, and when and why he chose to pass over wrongful acts.

Regarding sources of authority, *Islamic Law in Action* shows how policy concerns and doctrine interacted, cooperated, and competed. Other studies have justifiably concluded that jurists and rulers recognized the mutual need for the other—their relationship was symbiotic. But this does not mean that they had clear jurisdictions that were well recognized—quite the contrary, they each sought to extend the reach of their own notion of law, even at the expense of the other when they disagreed. The *muhtasib* was influenced by both sources, sometimes in very immediate and tangible ways. *Islamic Law in Action* shows the dynamics of these jurisdictional struggles and in particular the extent to which both jurists and rulers took an interest in the full spectrum of social regulation. As a result, the inhabitants of Cairo and Fustat were governed by both sources of authority, as expressed through the *muhtasib*, in all aspects of public life.

The areas of the *muhtasib*'s actions discussed in *Islamic Law in Action* are Muslim devotional and pious practices; serious crimes and minor offenses; the regulation of Christians and Jews; market regulation and consumer protection, with a particular

71 Lange, "Changes," 157. 72 Ibid., 163–65. 73 Ibid., 166.

74 Berkey also briefly discusses actions of the *muhtasib* under the headings of "activities of a religious or ethical nature"; "prices and food supplies"; "revenue collection"; and "political and administrative duties." Berkey, "Muhtasibs of Cairo," 261–74.

focus on the markets for essential bread; currency and taxes; and keeping the peace. Each of these areas constitutes a separate chapter, and each chapter includes numerous case studies involving the *muhtasib*, such as "prayer lessons for merchants," "wine, women, and hashish," "public dress and the Pact of ʿUmar," "rotten birds," "underselling by the merchants," "counterfeit copper coins," and "the mysterious talking wall."[75] The goal with each particular case study is to piece together a full sense of the dynamics involved in the *muhtasib*'s actions, including the reactions of those affected and the doctrinal and policy interests that were implicated.

For Muslim Spain, Pedro Chalmeta has focussed significant attention on the *muhtasib* in many articles and two substantial monographs: *El ʿseñor del zoco' en España* (1973) and *El zoco medieval* (2010), the latter actually an expanded and updated version of the former publication. *El zoco medieval* has an encyclopedic quality, with a tremendous amount of material from primary and secondary sources.[76] The first part is an overview of pre-Islamic and Islamic markets. The more significant contribution comes in the second part, which treats al-Andalus and then, at the end of the book, Christian Iberia. The last few pages list, cursorily, modern contexts in which an official, whether called the *muhtasib* or something else, have appeared.

In the Shiʿi context, commanding right and forbidding wrong was considered a mandate by Shiʿi jurists, as it was in the Sunni realm, but the lack of a political system through which to apply it throughout most of the medieval period meant that Shiʿi scholars did not elaborate on its institutional mechanisms by way of a *muhtasib*, or another appellation, and focussed on the duty as applied to individual Muslims (see the earlier discussion). Modern-day scholars Willem Floor and Rasul Jaʿfariyan have noted that the position of *muhtasib* underwent, from the Seljuk period on (1040–1194), a structural adjustment insofar as an office of chief *muhtasib*, or *muhtasib al-mamalik*, was created.[77] Most scholarly attention to the official of the *muhtasib* in a Shiʿi institutional structure begins for the Safavid period (1501–1722), in which, according to Jaʿfariyan, the authority of the *muhtasib*'s role was weaker than under the Seljuks and there was less clarity about its precise duties, due to the many and often overlapping offices that dealt with the application of the law.[78]

Both of these scholars took an interest in the kind of duties that the official performed, with Floor focusing on the strictly market-related aspects of the duties. According to Jaʿfariyan, the duties traditionally associated with the *muhtasib* were divided among several new categories of officials, including the Sadr (the head

[75] Carl Petry has also written about the case of the wall, in "The Hoax of the Miraculous Speaking Wall: Criminal Investigation in Mamluk Cairo," in *Mamluks and Ottomans: Studies in Honor of Michael Winter*, eds., David J. Wasserstein and Ami Ayalon (London, 2006), 86–95.

[76] For a concise description of the contents, see the review by Justin Stearns, in *Islamic Law and Society* 20 (2013): 141–55.

[77] Rasul Jaʿfariyan, *Safaviyyah dar ʿarsah- ʿi din, farhang va siyasat*, 3 vols. (Qum, 1379/[2000–1]), 1: 301.

[78] Ibid., 1: 300–301.

of religious institutions), the Shaykh al-Islam (the leading *fiqh* scholar), and the *Darugha* (the city police chief).[79] In the immediate aftermath of the Safavid period, the *muhtasib*'s importance declined under Nadir Shah and under the Zands (1751–1794), attributed to the "unruliness and often anarchy which prevailed in Iran during a great part of this period."[80]

At the beginning of the Qajar period (1779–1925), the position of *muhtasib* was still weak and its functions were limited to strictly those of the market. Even in that limited capacity, the official was subordinate to the *Darugha* in some cities at least, and throughout the nineteenth century the position seems to have slowly disappeared in many Iranian cities.[81] In Tehran, the office of *muhtasib* evolved into the Department of Ihtisab and was responsible for city cleaning and maintenance, a very narrow and limited role in comparison with the full range of duties outlined in the *muhtasib* manuals previously discussed.[82] As a result of the Constitutional Revolution (1905–1911), modern agencies took over all of the tasks that had been performed historically by the *muhtasib*.[83]

Soon after the 1979 Islamic Revolution, Ayatollah Khomeini announced his intention to establish a Ministry for Commanding Right and Forbidding Wrong, but it never developed.[84] The idea was ultimately deemed inefficient, unmanageable, and unnecessary, since the whole state came under the supervision of *mujtahid*s, and the Supreme Leader in particular, and was in its entirety considered to be carrying out the broad mandate of commanding right and forbidding wrong through the entire state system. Agencies that developed to have particular duties regarding commanding and forbidding included the Attorney General Office, Police, Municipalities, the Ministry of Culture and Islamic Guidance, the Ministry of Intelligence, the State Broadcasting, as well as specialized entities like the Prayer Promotion Staff.[85] One very specific example of a state agency carrying out *hisba* was the Police for the Fighting of Wrongs (*munkarat*) in the early years after the Revolution (subsequently, the Social Security Promotion Patrol). Its primary mission was to watch for compliance of the hijab code and the ban on relationships between opposite sexes in public places, by giving notice to or arresting the offenders.

Given the size and duration of the Ottoman Empire, there is a significant amount of scholarship on this topic, for which the related term *ihtisab* alongside the terms *muhtasib* and *hisba* is used; moreover, its focus shifts from the previous historical periods. The literature has concentrated on the office and functions of the *muhtasib* as an appointed official and the concept of *narkh* (setting price ceilings for essential

[79] Rasul Ja'fariyan, *Din va siyasat dar dawrah-'i Safavi* (Tehran: Ansariyan, 1991), 78–118.

[80] Willem Floor, "The Office of Muhtasib in Iran," *Iranian Studies* 18 (1985): 66.

[81] Ibid., 67–68. [82] Ibid., 67.

[83] Ghulam 'Ali Haddad 'Adil et al., eds., *Danishnamah-'i jahan-i Islam*, 21 vols. (Tehran, 1386/[1996]) 13: 6116.

[84] 'Abd al-Husayn Riza-yi Rad, *Amr-i bih ma'ruf dar tarazu-yi tarikh: Gami navin dar fiqh-i siyasi-i Islam* (Qum, 1384/[2005]), 15.

[85] Ibid., 153; Husayn 'Ali Muntaziri, *Mabani-i fiqhi-i hukumat-i Islami* (Tehran, 1367/[1988]), 462.

goods) as a market control mechanism. Scholars have paid limited attention to the social control functions historically associated with the *muhtasib* or to the larger economic transformations in the Ottoman Empire.

Osman Nuri Ergin produced one of the most comprehensive discussions of *ihtisab* in the Ottoman Empire as part of his five-volume set on municipal governance, *Mecelle-i umur-ı belediyye* (published between 1914 and 1922).[86] Ergin worked at the Istanbul prefecture (*şehremaneti*) for forty-six years before retiring in 1947, and was responsible, among other things, for the establishment of the municipal archives.[87] Committed to the modernization of urban governance, Ergin set the tone for an anachronistic association of *ihtisab* with municipal governance rather than "commanding right and forbidding wrong." Following Ergin's focus on modernization, other scholars, such as Ziya Kazıcı[88] and Ahmed Akgündüz,[89] discussed *ihtisab* as an early example of modern municipal governance that developed in the Ottoman Empire based on Islamic principles.

Scholars following the modernization framework focussed on the state-appointed *muhtasib*'s functions in urban governance, examined this office's place within the larger Ottoman administrative hierarchy, and explained its transformation. Until the mid-nineteenth century, *muhtasib*s were organized under the office of *ihtisab ağalığı*, which was established for the security of Istanbul. The functions of the state-appointed *muhtasib*s under this office included tasks associated with commanding right and forbidding wrong to individuals (such as warning those missing their prayers, exposing and punishing people if they skipped fasting during Ramadan, and preventing cattle from walking over graves), as well as protecting the broader public interest (such as ensuring that those selling food used clean utensils and that streets and public areas remained clean).

A great majority of the *muhtasib*'s responsibilities focussed on inspecting the marketplaces and fairs for various irregularities in commercial activity, including faulty scales, tainted goods, and sale of commodities at prices exceeding the established *narkh*.[90] *Muhtasib*s had the authority to tax market activity through fees

[86] For the modern Turkish rendition, see Osman Nuri Ergin, *Mecelle-i umur-ı belediyye*, 9 vols. (Istanbul, 1995).

[87] Müslüm Yılmaz, "Osman Nuri Ergin: Hayatı, şahsiyeti ve eserleri (1883–1961)," *Türkiyat mecmuası* 23 (Spring 2013): 141–88.

[88] Ziya Kazıcı, *Osmanlı'da ihtisab müessesesi: Yerel yönetim* (Istanbul, 2006). This is the only publication devoted entirely to *ihtisab*; it is a slightly revised version of an earlier printing (1987).

[89] Ahmed Akgündüz, *Osmanlı devleti'nde belediye teşkilatı ve belediye kanunları* (Istanbul, 2005). Akgündüz provides a brief analysis of the institution and lists all the laws relevant to *ihtisab* and *narkh* from the fifteenth to the twentieth centuries.

[90] For a detailed list of these tasks, see ibid., 63–120; Kazıcı, *Osmanlı'da ihtisab müessesesi*, 71–245; Charles Wilkins, *Forging Urban Solidarities* (Leiden, 2010), 165 and Amnon Cohen, *Economic Life in Ottoman Jerusalem* (New York, 1989), 16–17, 99; note that the involvement of the *muhtasib* with economic activities resulted in merchants, artisans, and soldiers serving as *muhtasib*s. *Muhtasib*s also had control over the fairs within the empire: Ömer Şen, *Osmanlı panayırları (18.–19. yüzyıl)* (Istanbul, 1996).

they collected from shops and other marketplaces and to impose fines on and punish those whom they caught committing wrong.[91] This meant that their office generated revenue and employed staff to enforce their authority over the commercial activity.[92] Scholars of the modernization framework agree that the combination of these factors made the *muhtasib*'s office a candidate for corruption—a social problem that the imperial administration sought to eliminate through its nineteenth-century reforms.

Within the administrative hierarchy, the *muhtasib*s functioned under a *qadi*'s supervision with staff assisting in the various tasks.[93] They had a close and problematic relationship with the Janissaries due to the latter's increased involvement with guilds and artisanal production after the seventeenth century.[94] Mehmet Sunar notes how the staff inspectors (sing. *koloğlanı*) working for Istanbul's chief *muhtasib* were all from the 56th Ağa Bölük Regiment that controlled the entry of vegetables and fruit into the city.[95] Such cooperation under the *ihtisab ağalığı* system seems to have limited the ability of the *muhtasib* to enforce his will fully. Following the abolishment of the Janissary forces in 1826, the *ihtisab ağalığı* was changed into a ministry, called *ihtisab nezareti*, and soon after that, in 1855, to the modern municipal office of the prefecture (*şehremaneti*) in Istanbul. Ali Akyıldız argues that the Istanbul prefecture was established in an ad hoc manner to address the urban governance issues that emerged due to the Crimean war (1853–56).[96] After 1864, the system was expanded to the whole empire as part of the general transformation of urban governance. The office of the *muhtasib* was gradually eliminated in the nineteenth century and the movement away from the principles of *ihtisab* happened in conjunction with the general transformation of the judicial-administrative institutions of Ottoman governance.[97] Not only did the *muhtasib*s gradually disappear and the practice of *narkh* abandoned, but the Janissaries as well were eliminated and the functions

[91] These taxes and fees were similar to the *octroi*: Ergin, *Mecelle-i umur-ı belediyye*, 1: 349. Both Ergin and Kazıcı refer to a story (from Aşıkpaşazade's *History*) on how the empire's eponymous founder Osman came to establish a market participation fee. Ibid., 1: 352–55; Kazıcı, *Osmanlı'da ihtisab müessesesi*, 188–90. See also Wilkins, *Forging Urban Solidarities*, 165, and Cohen, *Economic Life*, 90.

[92] Ziya Kazıcı (in *İslam ansiklopedisi*, s.v. "Hisbe, Osmanlı Devleti") points out that in 1831 the *muhtasib* of Sofia was tasked with arresting those using faulty scales, putting them in the "*ihtisab* prison," and exiling those who committed an indictable offense if the *qadi* found them guilty.

[93] For a list of the *muhtasib*'s staff (*hüddam-ı ihtisab*), see Kazıcı, *Osmanlı'da ihtisab müessesesi*, 46–56; Akgündüz, *Osmanlı devleti'nde belediye*, 55–62.

[94] Nalan Turna, "Yeniçeri – esnaf ilişkisi: Bir analiz," in *Osmanlı'dan cumhuriyet'e esnaf ve ticaret*, ed. Fatmagül Demirel (Istanbul, 2012), 21–42; Baki Tezcan, *The Second Ottoman Empire: Political and Social Transformation in the Early Modern World* (New York, 2012), 175–213.

[95] Mehmet Mert Sunar, "Cauldron of Dissent: A Study of the Janissary Corps, 1807–1826" (Ph.D. diss., State Univ. of New York, Binghamton, 2006), 80.

[96] *Islam ansiklopedisi*, s.v. "Şehremini" (A. Akyıldız).

[97] M. Safa Saraçoğlu, "Economic Interventionism, Islamic Law and Provincial Government in the Ottoman Empire," *Journal of the Ottoman and Turkish Studies Association* 2 (2015): 59–84.

of the *qadi*s changed drastically. The relationship among all four of these closely connected changes are yet to be explored in the field.

A second line of inquiry into *ihtisab* in Ottoman studies has focussed on the price control mechanism, *narkh*. There are no monographs on the topic, but a few notable studies have explored the Ottoman practice. The earliest significant discussion is a three-part article by Ömer Lütfi Barkan who, in 1942, transliterated early sixteenth-century *ihtisab* regulations for Istanbul, Bursa, and Edirne, which included information on how *narkh* was used at that time.[98] Cemal Kafadar also has examined *narkh* policies.[99] In addition to these, Ahmet Uzun's study on meat provisioning in Istanbul and Seven Ağır's dissertation on grain trade policies discuss the topic in some detail.[100]

Monitoring prices was an essential function of the *muhtasib*, who also played a role in enforcing the *narkh*, which the *qadi* established in consultation with the artisans and the *muhtasib*.[101] Following the rules of *fiqh*, the *muhtasib*'s manuals stated that price setting was generally wrongful, with an exception adopted by the Malikis. Although Hanafi scholars considered price setting in a properly functioning market as repugnant and others considered it forbidden, in the sixteenth-century Ottoman Empire, "systematic government intervention in price rates" was the norm.[102] Ottoman jurists in the sixteenth century did not question the validity of the practice.[103] In fact, Kafadar notes that in condoning price controls, the Ottomans not only sidestepped the "liberal tendency of the classical jurists" to leave the market in God's hands, but also "went further than other [Islamic states as they] systematized and codified [such controls] through secular legislation" in the aftermath of the conquest of Constantinople to establish a "strict control over the bazaar among other realms of economic activity."[104]

[98] Ömer Lütfi Barkan, "XV. Asrın sonunda bazı büyük şehirlerde eşya ve yiyecek fiyatlarının tesbit ve teftişi hususlarını tanzim eden kanunlar I." *Tarih vesikaları dergisi* 1:5 (1942): 326–40; Part II, ibid., 2:7 (1942): 15–40; Part III, ibid., 3:9 (1942): 168–77.

[99] Cemal Kafadar, "When Coins Turned into Drops of Dew and Bankers Became Robbers of Shadows: The Boundaries of Ottoman Economic Imagination at the End of the Sixteenth Century" (Ph.D. diss., McGill Univ., 1986).

[100] Ahmet Uzun, *İstanbul'un iaşesinde devletin rolü: Ondalık ağnam uygulaması, 1783–1857* (Ankara, 2006); Seven Ağır, "From Welfare to Wealth: Ottoman and Castilian Grain Trade Policies in a Time of Change" (Ph.D. diss., Princeton Univ., 2009).

[101] *EI2*, s.v. "Narkh" (M. Kütükoğlu); Akgündüz, *Osmanlı devleti'nde belediye*, 56. Mübahat Kütükoğlu (*İslam ansiklopedisi*, s.v. "Narh, Osmanlı'larda") notes that the author of a seventeenth-century anonymous text, *Kitabü mesalihi 'l-Müslimin ve menafii'l-mü'minin*, suggested that the *muhtasib* should determine the *narkh* because of his close connections with the artisans. Cohen, *Economic Life*, 38–44, explains in detail how the meat prices were fixed in Jerusalem during the sixteenth century and adds (ibid. 53) that "pricing was an administrative prerogative of both the kadi and the *muhtasib*."

[102] *İslam ansiklopedisi*, s.v. "Narh" (C. Kallek).

[103] Saraçoğlu, "Economic Interventionism, Islamic Law and Provincial Government in the Ottoman Empire," 64.

[104] Kafadar, "When Coins Turned into Drops of Dew," 114–16.

The Ottoman use of *narkh*, however, had some backing in *fiqh*. As already mentioned, predominantly Malikis, and post-fourteenth-century Hanbali and Hanafi scholars, commonly tolerated price ceilings, particularly in times of scarcity, "in the public interest."[105] Ottoman administrators and jurists, like the Mamluk sultans, seem to have adopted the Maliki position that justified widespread use of price ceilings because the ruler's *siyasa* powers would allow that. The use of *narkh* from the middle of the fifteenth through the eighteenth centuries made Ottoman intervention into markets a consistent administrative reality. The markets served as one of the important public places where the Ottoman rulers did "command right and forbid wrong" and intervened with the relations between different socio-economic institutions, such as guilds and *waqf*s.[106]

IV. Hisba and Muhtasib in the Modern World

The position of *muhtasib* was replaced with modern bureaucracies virtually everywhere that it existed, although at different points in time. With the rise of political Islam and efforts by some countries to Islamize their legal systems, the position of *muhtasib* has been reinstituted, or recreated, in some parts of the world; in others, notably Egypt, the concept of *hisba* has been used in the modern period even in the absence of a *muhtasib*. There has been some scholarly attention to these developments, although most of the writings in this area have come from human rights organizations and other institutions and NGOs that are concerned about the ways in which modern-day *muhtasib*s violate privacy rights and operate without clearly defined jurisdictions or limitations on the power to punish.

This final section briefly discusses Saudi Arabia and Egypt as the countries that have received the most scholarly focus in this area. The position of *muhtasib* and the concept of *hisba* also exist or have existed in recent years in several other jurisdictions, including Malaysia, Pakistan, and the states of northern Nigeria. One clear conclusion emerges from a study of the modern context: the office of *muhtasib* and the concept of *hisba* function differently in each jurisdiction, and more work

[105] Adam Sabra, "'Prices Are in God's Hands': The Theory and Practice of Price Control in the Medieval Islamic World," in *Poverty and Charity in Middle Eastern Contexts*, ed. Michael David Bonner et al. (Albany, 2003), 76–83.

[106] Kafadar, "When Coins Turned into Drops of Dew," 122; Saraçoğlu, "Economic Interventionism, Islamic Law and Provincial Government in the Ottoman Empire," 65.

is needed to understand the particularities in each context. As has been seen, there was, of course, diversity in the practice of the *muhtasib* and the understanding of the concept throughout the premodern period, but the emergence of the modern state has created an even far broader range of practices.

Saudi Arabia is the country best known for the existence of a modern-era *muhtasib*. According to its own literature, its name in English is the General Presidency of the Promotion of Virtue and the Prevention of Vices, and, as discussed above, the individual members are colloquially known as *mutawwaʿ*. There is a significant amount of literature from Saudi Arabia praising the functioning of the *mutawwaʿ*, a significant amount of materials published by human rights organizations criticizing the practice, and very little academic scholarship on the institution. Frank Vogel's 2003 article in *Social Research*, as has been discussed, is vital for understanding the legal rules governing the *mutawwaʿ* and the divergences from the historical rules regarding the *muhtasib*'s jurisdiction, as explained by al-Mawardi, that the *mutawwaʿ* engage in.[107]

More recently, Nabil Mouline addressed the topic of the General Presidency.[108] His overall argument is that both the political powers and the religious authorities of Saudi Arabia relied on the practice of *hisba* to impose the "cognitive, normative, and symbolic principles" of the "Hanbali-Wahhabi tradition" on the population.[109] Mouline provides a short history of the General Presidency, and argues that "the expansion and renaissance of the Saudi Emirate that began in 1902 went hand in hand with the establishment of hisba as a tool for homogenizing and dominating a public sphere . . . ."[110]

Both Mouline and Vogel discuss the activities of the General Presidency. As Vogel explains, "the activities of the committees—policing attendance at prayers, enforcing closure of shops at prayer times, assuring that women are properly veiled, preventing undue mixing of men and women, suppressing licentious acts like drinking or dancing, and banning public services of religions other than Islam—have attracted notoriety and criticism among Saudis and visitors to the kingdom for many years."[111] Mouline examined the General Presidency's cases across the country for the period 1991–2008. His empirical work is very valuable for showing the range of areas of operation, with matters of ritual—"failure to attend group prayers, working during prayer time, eating in public during Ramadan"—accounting for 75 percent of the cases while public morality accounts for 22 percent.[112] The category of moral behavior in public places includes enforcement of the dress code for men and women and preventing "mixed-gender groups," or *ikhtilat*.[113]

[107] Vogel, "Public and Private in Saudi Arabia."

[108] Nabile Mouline, *The Clerics of Islam: Religious Authority and Political Power in Saudi Arabia*, trans. Ethan S. Rundell (New Haven, 2013; French orig. 2011).

[109] Ibid., 203. [110] Ibid., 206. [111] Vogel, "Public and Private in Saudi Arabia," 758.

[112] Mouline, *Clerics of Islam*, 226–227. [113] Ibid., 228–229.

One event that attracted world attention occurred in 2002, when *mutawwaʿ* allegedly prevented girls from escaping from a fire in their school because they were not properly veiled, causing the deaths of dozens of children.[114]

Criticisms of the *mutawwaʿ* appear frequently in human rights reports and in YouTube videos, in which Saudis are increasingly capturing the excesses of the *mutawwaʿ* and broadcasting them. In response to mounting criticism, the Kingdom announced in April 2016 that it was modifying the operating manual for the *mutawwaʿ*.[115] Under the new rules, "they can no longer detain, pursue or question suspects, and have been told to act 'kindly and gently' and report suspicious activity to law enforcement officers."[116] Studying the contemporary *mutawwaʿ* in order to update the work of Vogel and Mouline and examine these new apparent developments in particular would involve not only legal research but, more importantly, ethnographic research, which may not be possible as a practical matter.

Saudi Arabia has the most active formulation of a modern-day *muhtasib*, but the most scholarly writing in the contemporary period has been on one particular case in Egypt. It did not involve a *muhtasib*—which does not exist as a position in the country—but rather the concept of *hisba*. *Hisba* was not formally part of the Egyptian legal system, but its use in the famous case of Nasr Abu Zayd generated a flurry of scholarship criticizing the decision. Nasr Abu Zayd was an associate professor of Islamic studies and literature at Cairo University in 1992, when he was denied a promotion to full professor. His key opponent was ʿAbd al-Sabur Shahin, who was known to object to Abu Zayd's approach to interpreting the Qur'an. Abu Zayd turned to the Egyptian media with his tenure denial story, and Shahin responded by declaring Abu Zayd an apostate.[117]

A group of plaintiffs, all with ties to the opposition to Abu Zayd led by Shahin, then filed suit against Abu Zayd and his wife in the family court. Their complaint alleged that Abu Zayd's publications were the evidence that he was an apostate and further stated that a Muslim woman cannot marry a non-Muslim man, according to most Islamic legal views. Thus, they asked the court to declare a divorce between Abu Zayd and his wife, Ibtihal Younes, who had no desire to be divorced. The plaintiffs had no relationship to the case, no standing in the conventional sense, but they brought the case on the grounds of *hisba*, claiming that they each had the duty to forbid wrong committed by any other Muslim; this is the doctrine of *hisba* as applied to individuals covered by Michael Cook, as discussed in the beginning

114 Vogel, "Public and Private in Saudi Arabia," 758.

115 Simeon Kerr, "Saudi Arabia Clips the Wings of Feared Religious Police," *Financial Times*, April 14, 2016.

116 Ibid.

117 Kristen Stilt, "Islamic Law and the Making and Remaking of the Iraqi Legal System," *George Washington International Law Review* 36 (2004): 735.

of this chapter. *Hisba* was not a standing doctrine in Egypt at that time according to Egyptian law, but there was a provision in the personal status law providing that Shari'a, and the *fiqh* of the Hanafi school in particular, was the appropriate source of law when Egyptian codified law did not address an issue before the court. The plaintiffs claimed that since *hisba* did not exist in Egyptian codified law, then the judge could rightly look to Islamic law generally, and that of the Hanafi school in particular, which recognized a claim of *hisba*.[118]

The court of first instance rejected the standing argument on the grounds that the residual role of the Shari'a was only for the substantive law of personal status; for procedure, the Civil and Commercial Procedural Law is the only relevant law. The Procedural Law requires plaintiffs to have a direct and personal interest in the claim that is recognized by law. The Court of Appeals reversed, and was in turn affirmed by the Court of Cassation, the highest relevant court. The Court of Cassation concluded that "all capable Muslims had the duty of commanding good and forbidding wrong vis-à-vis all other Muslims."[119] At this point, the Mubarak regime became very concerned about the possibility of a flood of *hisba* cases brought by Islamists as a result of the decision, and it made rapid efforts, from the mid-1990s on, to preclude future *hisba* claims. As a result, the legislature adopted Law No. 3 in 1996, giving the public prosecutor the sole authority to bring claims of *hisba*.[120]

The case of Nasr Abu Zayd generated significant scholarly interest, as well as interest from human rights practitioners around the world. A thorough treatment of the case is found in Jörn Thielmann's *Nasr Hamid Abu Zaid und die wiedererfundene Hisba*.[121] Thielmann provides historical context for what he calls the "rediscovered *hisba*" and he also examines Abu Zayd's literary work that formed the basis of the case and the cast of characters involved in the legal attack. He argues that the use of *hisba* in this case was invented and did not have historical precedent. The persuasiveness of this argument depends on how far back in time one wants to look for precedent and whether one takes a broad or a narrow view of the concept of *hisba* (and the practice of the *muhtasib*), which are questions relevant to any modern jurisdiction that seeks to invoke historical precedent to justify the contemporary use of the concepts discussed in this chapter.

118 Ibid., 734–36. 119 Ibid., 737. 120 Ibid., 738.

121 Jörn Thielmann, *Nasr Hamid Abu Zaid und die wiedererfundene Hisba* (Würzburg, 2003). On the case of Nasr Abu Zayd, see also Nathalie Bernard-Maugiron, "Can Hisba be 'Modernised'? The Individual and the Protection of the General Interest before Egyptian Courts," in *Standing Trial: Law and Person in the Modern Middle East*, ed. Baudouin Dupret (London, 2004), 318–344; Declan O'Sullivan, "Hisba Law and Freedom of Expression in Islam: Two Case Studies of Prosecutions in Contemporary Egypt," *Journal of Mediterranean Studies* 14: 1, 2 (2004): 213–235; Fauzi M. Najjar, "Islamic Fundamentalism and the Intellectuals: The Case of Nadr Hamid Abu Zayd," *British Journal of Middle Eastern Studies* 27:2 (2000): 177–200.

V. Conclusions

From the earliest exegetes, who were the focus of Michael Cook's *Commanding Right and Forbidding Wrong in Islamic Thought*, to the case of Nasr Abu Zayd in contemporary Egypt, the concept of *hisba*, and the related position of *muhtasib*, have been discussed at great length and in great detail throughout many centuries and many genres of literature. But there is certainly room, and a need, for more scholarly attention to these crucial concepts. In terms of future work, Cook's book will stand as the definitive study on *hisba* for quite some time. And while there is no comparable tome for the practice of the *muhtasib*, there have been important and detailed works regarding specific times and places. The most exciting areas of new scholarship have examined particular jurisdictions and have taken a socio-legal approach, seeking to understand how the *muhtasib* operated, the source of his authority, and the significance of such an official for the population in his jurisdiction. While some time periods have been more thoroughly studied than others, there is certainly still room for new scholarship that follows in this line.

The modern period offers many new questions for researchers to pursue, and to date there has been comparatively little scholarship that examines how modern states, or individuals within them, use *hisba* or the position of *muhtasib*. The case of Saudi Arabia, where the *mutawwa*ʿ have played such a significant role in both the public and private lives of the country's inhabitants, is particularly important. The modern-day *muhtasib* in Saudi Arabia is far better known than its counterparts in other jurisdictions, and there is also a tremendous need for analysis of those other jurisdictions as well. Going beyond written sources, there is great potential for ethnographic work on the practice of *hisba* and the *muhtasib* in the modern world that promises to provide valuable insight into the lived experiences in the regulated societies.

Abbreviations

EI2	*Encyclopaedia of Islam*, New Edition, ed. P. J. Bearman et al. Leiden: Brill, 1960–2004
GAL	Carl Brockelmann. *Geschichte der arabischen Litteratur*. 2 vols. and Supplement, 3 vols. (Leiden: E.J. Brill, 1937–1949)
İslam ansiklopedisi	(Istanbul: Türkiye Diyanet Vakfı, 1988–2013)
JESHO	*Journal of the Economic and Social History of the Orient*
JSAI	*Jerusalem Studies in Arabic and Islam*

References

ʿAdil, Ghulam ʿAli Haddad et al., eds., *Danishnamah-ʿi jahan-i Islam*. 21 vols. Tehran: Bunyad-i Daʾirat al-Maʿarif-i Islami, 1386/[1996].

Ağır, Seven, "From Welfare to Wealth: Ottoman and Castilian Grain Trade Policies in a Time of Change." Ph.D. diss., Princeton Univ., 2009.

Akgündüz, Ahmed, *Osmanlı devleti'nde belediye teşkilatı ve belediye kanunları* (Istanbul: Osmanlı Araştırmaları Vakfı, 2005).

Barkan, Ömer Lütfi, "XV. asrın sonunda bazı büyük şehirlerde eşya ve yiyecek fiyatlarının tesbit ve teftişi hususlarını tanzim eden kanunlar I." *Tarih vesikaları dergisi* 1.5 (1942): 326–340.

Barkan, Ömer Lütfi, "XV. asrın sonunda bazı büyük şehirlerde eşya ve yiyecek fiyatlarının tesbit ve teftişi hususlarını tanzim eden kanunlar II." *Tarih vesikaları dergisi* 2.7 (1942): 15–40.

Barkan, Ömer Lütfi, "XV. asrın sonunda bazı büyük şehirlerde eşya ve yiyecek fiyatlarının tesbit ve teftişi hususlarını tanzim eden kanunlar III." *Tarih vesikaları dergisi* 3.9 (1942): 168–77.

Berkey, Jonathan, "The Muhtasibs of Cairo Under the Mamluks: Toward an Understanding of an Islamic Institution" In Michael Winter and Amalia Levanoni (eds.) *The Mamluks in Egyptian and Syrian Politics and Society* (Leiden: Brill, 2004) 245–276.

Bernard-Maugiron, Nathalie, "Can *Hisba* be 'Modernised'? The Individual and the Protection of the General Interest before Egyptian Courts" in Baudouin Dupret (ed.) *Standing Trial: Law and Person in the Modern Middle East* (London: I.B. Tauris, 2004) 318–344.

Buckley, R. P., "The *Muhtasib*." *Arabica* 39 (1992): 59–117.

Buckley, R. P., trans., *The Book of the Islamic Market Inspector*. Journal of Semitic Studies Supplement, vol. 9 (Oxford: Oxford University Press, 1999).

Chalmeta, Pedro, *El zoco medieval: Contribución al estudio de la historia del mercado* (Alméria: Fundación Ibn Tufayl de Estudios Árabes, 2010).

Cohen, Amnon, *Economic Life in Ottoman Jerusalem* (New York: Cambridge Univversity Press, 1989).

Cook, Michael, *Commanding Right and Forbidding Wrong in Islamic Thought* (Cambridge: Cambridge University Press, 2000).

Crone, Patricia, *Roman, Provincial and Islamic Law: The Origins of the Islamic Patronate* (Cambridge: Cambridge University Press, 1987).

EI2. Arts. "Hisba" (Cahen and Talbi); "Narkh" (Kütükoğlu).

Ergin, Osman Nuri, *Mecelle-i umur-ı belediyye*. 9 vols. (Istanbul: İstanbul Büyükşehir Belediyesi Kültür İşleri Daire Başkanlığı, 1995).

Floor, Willem, "The Office of Muhtasib in Iran," *Iranian Studies* 18 (1985): 53–74.

Foster, Benjamin R., "Agoranomos and Muhtasib." *JESHO* 13 (1970): 128–44.

Gaudefroy-Demombynes, Maurice, "Sur quelques ouvrages de hisba." *Journal Asiatique* 230 (1938): 449–57.

Ghabin, Ahmad, "Some Jahili Origins of the *hisba*." *JSAI* 35 (2008): 59–90.

Ibn Khallikan, Ahmad, *Wafayat al-aʿyan wa-anbaʾ abnaʾ al-zaman*. Beirut: Dar Sadir, 1398/[1977].

Ibn Manzur, Muhammad, *Lisan al-ʿarab*, ed. ʿAli Shiri. 18 vols. Beirut: Dar Ihyaʾ al-Turath al-ʿArabi, 1988.

Ibn al-Ukhuwwa, Muhammad, *Maʿalim al-qurba fi ahkam al-hisba*. Reuben Levy (ed.) (Cambridge: E.J.W. Gibb Memorial Series, 1938).

İslam ansiklopedisi, Arts. "Şehremini" (A. Akyıldız); "Hisbe, Osmanlı Devleti" (Z. Kazıcı); "Narh" (C. Kallek); "Narh, Osmanlı'larda" (M. Kütükoğlu).

ʿIzz al-Din, Mu'il Yusuf, *The Theory and Practice of Market Law in Medieval Islam: A Study of Kitab Nisab al-ihtisab of ʿUmar b. Muhammad al-Sunami* (Cambridge: E.J.W. Gibb Memorial Trust, 1977).

Jaʿfariyan, Rasul, *Din va siyasat dar dawrah-ʿi Safavi* (Tehran: Ansariyan, 1991).

Jaʿfariyan, Rasul, *Safaviyyah dar ʿarsah-i din, farhang va siyasat*. 3 vols. (Qum: Pizhuhishkadah-yi Hawzah va Danishgah, 1379/[2000–1]).

Kafadar, Cemal, "When Coins Turned into Drops of Dew and Bankers Became Robbers of Shadows: The Boundaries of Ottoman Economic Imagination at the End of the Sixteenth Century." Ph.D. diss., McGill Univ., 1986.

Kazıcı, Ziya, *Osmanlı'da ihtisab müessesesi: Yerel yönetim* (Istanbul: Bilge, 2006).

Kerr, Simeon, "Saudi Arabia Clips the Wings of Feared Religious Police." *Financial Times*, April 14, 2016.

Klein, Yaron, "Between Public and Private: An Examination of *hisba* Literature." *Harvard Middle Eastern and Islamic Review* 7 (2006): 41–62.

Labib, Subhi Y., *Handelsgeschichte Ägyptens im Spätmittelalter (1171–1517)* (Wiesbaden: Franz Steiner, 1965).

Lange, Christian, "Hisba and the Problem of Overlapping Jurisdictions: An Introduction to, and Translation of, Hisba Diplomas in Qalqashandi's Subh al-aʿsha." *Harvard Middle Eastern and Islamic Review* 7 (2006): 85–107.

Lange, Christian. "Changes in the Office of Hisba Under the Seljuqs" in Christian Lange and Songül Mecit (eds.) *The Seljuks: Politics, Society and Culture* (Edinburgh: Edinburgh University Press, 2012) 157–181.

al-Mawardi, Abu al-Hasan, *Al-Ahkam al-sultaniyya wa-l-wilayat al-diniyya* (Beirut: Dar al-Kutub al-ʿIlmiyya, 1985).

Mottahedeh, Roy P., and Kristen Stilt, "Public and Private as Viewed through the Work of the *Muhtasib*." *Social Research* 70.3 (2003): 735–48.

Mouline, Nabile, *The Clerics of Islam: Religious Authority and Political Power in Saudi Arabia*, trans. Ethan S. Rundell (New Haven: Yale Univ. Press, 2013; French orig. 2011).

Muntaziri, Husayn ʿAli, *Mabani-i fiqhi-i hukumat-i Islami* (Tehran: Kayhan, 1367/[1988]).

Najjar, Fauzi M., "Islamic Fundamentalism and the Intellectuals: The Case of Nadr Hamid Abu Zayd." *British Journal of Middle Eastern Studies* 27:2 (2000): 177–200.

al-Nuwayri, Ahmad, *Nihayat al-arab fi funun al-adab*. 33 vols. (Cairo: al-Mu'assasa al-Misriyya al-ʿAmma li-l-Ta'lif wa-l-Tarjama wa-l-Tibaʿa wa-l-Nashr, 1964–).

O'Sullivan, Declan, "Hisba Law and Freedom of Expression in Islam: Two Case Studies of Prosecutions in Contemporary Egypt." *Journal of Mediterranean Studies* 14: 1,2 (2004): 213–235

Petry, Carl, "The Hoax of the Miraculous Speaking Wall: Criminal Investigation in Mamluk Cairo" in David J. Wasserstein and Ami Ayalon (eds.) *Mamluks and Ottomans: Studies in Honor of Michael Winter* (London: Routledge, 2006) 86–95.

al-Qalqashandi, Ahmad, *Subh al-aʿsha fi sinaʿat al-insha'*. 14 vols. (Cairo: al-Mu'assasa al-Misriyya al-ʿAmma li-l-Ta'lif wa-l-Tarjama wa-l-Tibaʿa wa-l-Nashr, 1964).

Riza-yi Rad, ʿAbd al-Husayn, *Amr-i bih maʿruf dar tarazu-yi tarikh: Gami navin dar fiqh-i siyasi-i Islam* (Qum: Bustan-i Kitab, 1384/[2005]).

Sabra, Adam, "'Prices Are in God's Hands': The Theory and Practice of Price Control in the Medieval Islamic World" in Michael David Bonner, Mine Ener, and Amy Singer (eds.) *Poverty and Charity in Middle Eastern Contexts* (Albany: State Univ. of New York Press, 2003) 76–83.
Saraçoğlu, M. Safa, "Economic Interventionism, Islamic Law and Provincial Government in the Ottoman Empire." *Journal of the Ottoman and Turkish Studies Association* 2 (2015): 59–84.
Schacht, Joseph, *An Introduction to Islamic Law* (Oxford: Clarendon Press, 1964).
Şen, Ömer, *Osmanlı panayırları (18.–19. yüzyıl)* (Istanbul: Eren, 1996).
Shatzmiller, Maya, *Labour in the Medieval Islamic World* (Leiden: E.J. Brill, 1994).
Stearns, Justin, "Review of Chalmeta, *El zoco medieval*." *Islamic Law and Society* 20 (2013): 141–155.
Stilt, Kristen, "Islamic Law and the Making and Remaking of the Iraqi Legal System." *George Washington International Law Review* 36 (2004): 695–756.
Stilt, Kristen, *Islamic Law in Action: Authority, Discretion, and Everyday Experiences in Mamluk Egypt* (New York: Oxford University Press, 2011).
Sunar, Mehmet Mert, "Cauldron of Dissent: A Study of the Janissary Corps, 1807–1826." Ph.D. diss., State Univ. of New York, Binghamton, 2006.
Tezcan, Baki, *The Second Ottoman Empire: Political and Social Transformation in the Early Modern World* (New York: Cambridge University Press, 2012).
Thielmann, Jörn, *Nasr Hamid Abu Zaid und die wiedererfundene Hisba* (Würzburg: Ergon, 2003).
Turna, Nalan, "Yeniçeri – esnaf ilişkisi: Bir analiz" in Fatmagül Demirel (ed.) *Osmanlı'dan cumhuriyet'e esnaf ve ticaret* (Istanbul: Tarih Vakfı Yurt Yayınları, 2012) 21–42.
Tyan, Émile, *Histoire de l'organisation judiciaire en pays d'Islam*. 2 vols 2nd edn. (Leiden: E.J. Brill, 1960).
al-ʿUmari, Ahmad, *al-Taʿrif bi-l-mustalah al-sharif*. (Karak, Jordan: Mu'ta Univ., 1992).
Uzun, Ahmet, *İstanbul'un iaşesinde devletin rolü: Ondalık ağnam uygulaması, 1783–1857* (Ankara: Türk Tarih Kurumu, 2006).
Vogel, Frank E., "The Public and Private in Saudi Arabia: Restrictions on the Powers of Committees for Ordering the Good and Forbidding Evil." *Social Research* 70.3 (2003): 749–768.
Wilkins, Charles, *Forging Urban Solidarities: Ottoman Aleppo, 1640–1700* (Leiden: Brill, 2010).
Wittman, Richard, "The Muhtasib in Seljuq Times: Insights from Four Chancery Manuals." *Harvard Middle Eastern and Islamic Review* 7 (2006): 108–128.
Yılmaz, Müslüm, "Osman Nuri Ergin: Hayatı, şahsiyeti ve eserleri (1883–1961)." *Türkiyat mecmuası* 23 (Spring 2013): 141–188.

CHAPTER 14

THE MAZALIM IN HISTORIOGRAPHY

MATHIEU TILLIER

THE word *mazalim* is the plural form of *mazlima*, meaning "exaction" or a "thing wrongfully taken," and derives from *zulm*, a "wrongdoing" or an "injustice."[1] In a terminological sense, it refers to a specific institution, also called *wilayat al-mazalim* or *al-nazar fi al-mazalim*, which was expected to adjudicate complaints regarding "injustices." The *mazalim* are usually regarded as the expression of the sovereign's direct justice in Medieval Islam.

Mazalim first attracted the attention of scholars in the early twentieth century, with the publication of legal and historiographical texts such as *al-Ahkam al-sultaniyya* by al-Mawardi (d. 450/1058) and the *Book of the Governors and the Judges* by al-Kindi. Following A.F. Amedroz, who published in 1910 an analytical commentary of al-Mawardi's chapter on *mazalim*, a significant number of scholars tried to understand this institution and its historical development. The most important step was taken by Émile Tyan, who devoted a 150-page chapter to *mazalim* in the second volume of his *Histoire de l'organisation judiciaire en pays d'Islam*, during the 1940s. As Amedroz, Tyan only relied on literary sources (*fiqh*, chronicles, biographical dictionaries, and *adab*). Samuel Stern's studies of petitions in the 1960s marked a turning point in the approach of the institution by way of providing documentary evidence of the historical functioning of the *mazalim*. It was not until the 1980s,

[1] W.E. Lane, *Arabic-English Lexicon* (London: Willams & Norgate 1863), 1921, 1923. See also Émile Tyan, *Histoire de l'organisation judiciaire en pays d'Islam* (Paris: Sirey, 1938–43), II, 145.

however, that this approach began to be systematically combined with literary data, as in Jørgen Nielsen's monograph on the *mazalim* under the Mamluks. Since the mid-1990s, and especially in the late 2000s, a number of studies have renewed the historical understanding of the institution, either by relying on documentary evidence (Marina Rustow, Maaike van Berkel) or by shedding new light on the information provided by literary sources (Nasser Rabbat, Albrecht Fuess, Fumihiko Hasebe, Mathieu Tillier, Christian Müller).

One major problem in understanding the *mazalim* institution is that its concept does not fall into any modern legal category, and does not have any equivalent in Occidental languages. In more than a century of research, the first challenge was therefore to define the institution, to understand its origins, and to determine its nature according to modern classifications. The second issue raised by several generations of scholars relates to the historical functioning of the institution, to its articulation with other institutions, and to its symbolic and political uses.

I. What are the *Mazalim*?

A. Problems of Terminology and Definition

The term *mazalim* is attested in Islamic literary sources from the late ninth century at the latest, and designates a kind of court or legal institution. As Émile Tyan noted, however, no Arab author ever provides a satisfactory definition of this word.[2] The first—and most detailed—definition of the institution occurs in al-Mawardi's *al-Ahkam al-sultaniyya* in the middle of the eleventh century CE, which was relied on by the first historians who studied this institution. In his seminal study, Amedroz took over al-Mawardi's text and defined the *mazalim* as "compelling those who would do each other wrong—*mutazalimun*—to mutual justice, and restraining litigants from repudiating claims by inspiring fear and awe in them."[3] However, this vague definition does not describe an institution as such, but rather, its missions. Later historians tried to reach a clearer characterization. As a rule, Tyan saw the *mazalim* as a superior justice, whose scope of practice was not limited by any fixed rule: it was the retained justice of the sovereign, who delegated his judicial powers to secondary authorities—such as the *qadi*s—and could withdraw this delegation at will. As such, *mazalim* corresponded to a kind

[2] Tyan, *Histoire de l'organisation judiciaire*, II, 145.

[3] A.F. Amedroz, "The Mazalim Jurisdiction in the Ahkam Sultaniyya of Mawardi," *Journal of the Royal Asiatic Society of Great Britain and Ireland* (July 1911): 635.

of extraordinary justice, not delegated to anyone on a permanent basis.[4] This theoretical definition is contradicted, however, by Tyan's own analysis of the organization of the institution. Tyan observed that from early on, caliphs appointed permanent judges to the *mazalim* courts, which means that in practice the sovereign did not exercise his retained judicial powers any longer. Practically, Tyan came to characterize the *mazalim* by their organization and functioning. On the basis of al-Mawardi, he defined them as a collegial institution intervening when ordinary justice dispensed by *qadi*s was inefficient, mainly because of the power and social position of the defendant.[5] Tyan's internal contradictions illustrate the difficulty in providing any general overview of the institution. The term *mazalim* is attested early on, but the content, functioning, and purpose of the institution(s) bearing this name changed over time and can only be studied in specific historical contexts.

Another terminological problem is that of the relationship between *mazalim* and *siyasa*. Tyan noticed that classical authors of the Muslim world did not usually distinguish between the two concepts and used them to describe the same institution until the Mamluks, when the term *siyasa* almost replaced that of *mazalim*.[6] Despite this interchangeability, Tyan believed that *mazalim* and *siyasa* are different: dispensing *siyasa* justice, he argued, was possible even when an ordinary *qadi* could have settled the case himself. The powerlessness of normal judges was not a precondition for the administration of *siyasa*, as it was for that of *mazalim* according to Tyan's definition.[7] Following his interpretation, *siyasa* was simply a rival jurisdiction to the *qadi*'s court—notwithstanding the fact that Tyan also regarded the *mazalim* as rival to the *qadi*'s court, which contradicts his restrictive definition of the institution[8]: *siyasa* is exemplified by the kind of justice dispensed by the *hajib* (chamberlain) in the Mamluk period. It is not, therefore, similar to the supreme judicial power exercised by the sovereign.[9] Later authors do not try to establish such distinction between the two concepts: Nielsen noticed a close similarity between *mazalim* and *siyasa*, which was already implicit in al-Mawardi's work.[10] Tyan was probably too keen to distinguish two closely related concepts, and became a prisoner of his own definition of the *mazalim*, which he could only conceive as a superior jurisdiction dedicated to overcome the weakness of ordinary *qadis* in front of powerful litigants. One can still ruminate, however, to what extent the two terms were completely synonymous. Whereas *mazalim* designated an institution, it is likely that *siyasa* referred at first to the methods and procedures implemented in *mazalim* courts, which enjoyed larger

4 Tyan, *Histoire de l'organisation judiciaire*, II, 141, 143.
5 Ibid., 143, 238. 6 Ibid., 161, 164.
7 Ibid., 164. 8 Ibid., 194. 9 Ibid., 166.
10 Jørgen Nielsen, *Secular Justice in an Islamic State: Maẓālim under the Baḥrī Mamluks, 662/1264–789/1387* (Leiden: Nederlands Historisch-Archaeologisch Instituut te Istanbul, 1985), 31–32.

means of investigation and punishment, and by metonymy came to designate the institution itself.

Faced with the difficulty of giving a positive definition of the *mazalim*, Nielsen decided to proceed by exclusion. Any judicial case that is not decided by the *qadi*, the *muhtasib* (market inspector), the *qadi al-ʻaskar* (military judge) or the non-Muslim courts, but is placed under the direct authority of the political ruler, must be regarded as a *mazalim* case. According to the same author, moreover, theoretical prescriptions not corroborated by other sources should not be taken into account for the study of *mazalim*.[11] This empirical approach, which relies on historical practices and compares them to the legal theory only in the second stage, seems to be most fruitful.

B. Origins of the Institution

Islamic tradition regards the *mazalim* as rooted in a pre-Islamic background. The concern of redressing wrongs appeared with the *hilf al-fudul*, an alliance of Qurashi clans in pre-Islamic Mekka. According to this view, repeated in the most sanguine modern historiography, prophet Muhammad's judicial practice is the second source for the development of *mazalim*, which developed as an institution during the Umayyad period.[12]

This vision has long been criticized by more skeptical scholars. Commenting on al-Mawardi's text, in which caliph ʻUmar II appears as one of the earliest upholders of the *mazalim*, Amedroz emphasized the idealized character of reports concerning this caliph, and seemed to doubt the historical existence of the *mazalim* under the Umayyads.[13] Tyan was the first who criticized openly the vision of Islamic sources. Following al-Mawardi's description of the *mazalim*, and considering that their existence was only motivated by injustices committed by powerful people or members of the administration against whom *qadis* were powerless, he refused to categorize pre-Umayyad and Umayyad caliphs' legal decisions as *mazalim* cases.[14] According to Tyan, the *mazalim* institution only developed in the Abbasid period once an Islamic state was fully constituted. The Abbasids did not rely upon any Arabic models, pre-Islamic or prophetic, but were rather inspired by a similar Sassanid institution.[15] Joseph Schacht followed this

[11] Nielsen, *Secular Justice*, 35.

[12] See, e.g., Hamdi ʻAbd al-Munʻim, *Dīwān al-maẓālim. Nashʼatuhu wa-taṭawwuruhu wa-ikhtiṣāṣātuhu muqāranan bi-l-naẓm al-qaḍāʼī al-ḥadīth* (Beirut: Dār al-Shurūq, 1983), 36–38; Mohammad Hashim Kamali, "Appellate Review and Judicial Independence in Islamic Law," in *Islam and Public Law. Classical and Contemporary Studies*, ed. Chibli Mallat (London, Dordrecht, Boston: Graham & Trotman, 1993), 226.

[13] Amedroz, "The Mazalim Jurisdiction," 656.

[14] Tyan, *Histoire de l'organisation judiciaire*, II, 277.

[15] Ibid., 278.

interpretation a few years later.[16] Nielsen has suggested, however, that Islamic *mazalim* are anchored in wider historical phenomenon. Although the Sassanid model is prevalent in Islamic mirrors for princes, other pre-Islamic civilizations developed similar institutions of royal justice: in Byzantine Egypt, for instance, there was a system of appeal to the provincial governor (*dux*).[17]

Tyan's hypothesis is partly justified by the evidence of wider oriental influence on the early Abbasid caliphate. Later research has shown, however, that oriental and Sassanid influences were already perceptible during the late Umayyad period.[18] Furthermore, his main argument—namely that the same terminology is used in Arabic to describe Sassanid royal justice and Islamic *mazalim*—is inconclusive, for Arab authors could only describe Sassanid institutions through their own terminology, and Pahlavi sources are too scarce on this topic to authorize any detailed comparison. Lastly, Tyan's restrictive interpretation of the *mazalim* as a collegial institution obscures the historical existence of other types of royal justice, which should also be part of the category of *mazalim*. According to Tyan, the province of al-Andalus could not have known any *mazalim* institution during the period of the Umayyad emirate, for Persian influence was negligible in the Islamic west at that time.[19] However, although a special administration dedicated to *mazalim* was only created in the tenth century CE, Christian Müller recently argued that justice dispensed by Andalusi *amir*s in earlier periods were already part of a *mazalim* system dedicated to redressing wrongs.[20] In my personal work on the Umayyad period, I have also concluded that the Marwanid caliphs were actively involved in legal administration and were themselves dispensing royal justice that could be assimilated into the *mazalim*.[21]

C. A Judicial Institution?

The first modern scholars who dealt with *mazalim* took for granted that this institution was a judicial court. Amedroz considered it as a purely legal institution.[22]

[16] Joseph Schacht, *An Introduction to Islamic Law* (Oxford: Clarendon Press, 1982; 1st edn. 1964), 51. See also Beatrice Gruendler, "*Tawqīʿ* (Apostille): Royal Brevity in Pre-modern Islamic Appeals Court," in *The Weaving of Words. Approaches to Classical Arabic Prose*, eds. Lale Behzadi and Vahid Behmardi (Beirut: Orient-Institut, 2009), 102–103.

[17] Nielsen, *Secular Justice*, 1–2.

[18] See, e.g., Oleg Grabar, "Notes sur les cérémonies umayyades," in *Studies in Memory of Gaston Wiet*, ed. M. Rosen-Ayalon (Jerusalem: The Hebrew University of Jerusalem, 1977), 59.

[19] Tyan, *Histoire de l'organisation judiciaire*, II, 282–285.

[20] Christian Müller, "Redressing Injustice. Maẓālim Jurisdictions at the Umayyad court of Córdoba (Eighth-Eleventh Centuries CE)," in *Court and Cultures in the Muslim World. Seventh to Nineteenth Centuries*, eds. Albrecht Fuess and Jan-Peter Hartung (London, New York: Routledge, 2011), 95.

[21] Mathieu Tillier, "Califes, émirs et cadis: le droit califal et l'articulation de l'autorité judiciaire à l'époque umayyade," *Bulletin d'Études Orientales* 63 (2014): 154.

[22] Amedroz, "The Mazalim Jurisdiction."

Although Tyan noticed that in principle, Islam did not know any strict separation between the administrative and legal jurisdictions,[23] his long chapter on *mazalim* treats them exclusively as a court. He argued that the principal goal of *dar al-ʿadl* ("house of justice"), under the Mamluks, was to accommodate *mazalim* sessions based on arbitrary procedures (i.e. not limited by *fiqh* regulations), and that other ceremonies held in the same place were only secondary.[24] He also noted that non-judicial cases such as financial demands were presented to *mazalim* sessions, but concluded that this was a marginal phenomenon, resulting from the fact that the ruler received the people during *mazalim* audiences.[25] In the early 1970s, Husam al-Samarra'i described the organization of *mazalim* as exposed by Qudama b. Jaʿfar for tenth-century Baghad as a judicial process.[26] More recently, Wael Hallaq still interpreted *mazalim* as a predominantly judicial institution.[27]

This understanding of the *mazalim* began to change in the 1960s, with the first studies on Fatimid, Ayyubid, and Mamluk petitions by Samuel Stern. Documents found in the Geniza revealed the administrative side of the institution, which had been neglected until then. Stern insisted on the process of petitioning and the bureaucratic treatment of complaints leading to the emission of decrees, which according to him developed especially in the twelfth century CE.[28] Since then, scholars have continued to edit and study petitions and decrees issued in reply. They include Geoffrey Khan, Stefan Heideman, Christian Müller, Yusuf Raġib—and more recently—Marina Rustow.[29] Nielsen, who relied extensively on Mamluk petitions and decrees available to him in the early 1980s, proposed a vision of the *mazalim* quite different from that of Tyan. As Tyan, Nielsen argued that the judicial and administrative aspects of the institution could not be separated. However, he insisted on the primary importance of its bureaucratic process. In his view, the real work of the *mazalim* was the reception and processing of these petitions by different

[23] Tyan, *Histoire de l'organisation judiciaire*, II, 143, 172.

[24] Ibid., 266. On the procedures, see Tyan, 150–157.

[25] Ibid., 144, 202.

[26] Ḥusām Q. al-Sāmarrā'ī, *al-Mu'assasāt al-idāriyya fī al-dawlat al-ʿabbāsiyya khilāl al-fatra 247–334 H./861–945 M.* (Damascus: Maktabat dār al-fatḥ, 1971), 264–267.

[27] Wael B. Hallaq, *The Origins and Evolution of Islamic Law* (Cambridge: Cambridge University Press, 2005), 99–100.

[28] Samuel M. Stern, "Three Petitions of the Fāṭimid Period," *Oriens* 15 (1962): 172–209; Samuel M. Stern, *Fatimid Decrees: Original Documents from the Fāṭimid Chancery* (London: Faber and Faber, 1964). See also Nielsen, *Secular Justice*, 10.

[29] Geoffrey Khan, "A Petition to the Fāṭimid Caliph al-'Āmir," *Journal of the Royal Asiatic Society* 1 (1990): 44–54; Geoffrey Khan, "A Copy of a Decree from the Archives of the Fāṭimid Chancery in Egypt," *Bulletin of the School of Oriental and African Studies* 49 (1986), 439–463; Stefan Heideman, Christian Müller, and Yūsuf Rāġib, "Un décret d'al-Malik al-ʿĀdil en 571/1176 relatif aux moines du Mont Sinaï," *Annales Islamologiques* 31 (1997): 81–107; Marina Rustow, "The Legal Status of ḏimmī-s in the Fatimid East: A View from the Palace in Cairo," in *The Legal Status of ḏimmī-s in the Islamic East (second/eighth-ninth/fifteenth centuries)*, eds. M. Fierro and J.V. Tolan (Turnhout: Brepols, 2013), 307–332.

levels of administrative staff who usually decided cases without referring them to the sultan. Public hearings of litigants were above all a symbolic setting of the ruler's justice.[30] Nielsen concluded that the middle of the thirteenth century represented a turning point in the history of the *mazalim*: before the Mamluks, the institution was still predominantly a judicial one, whereas under the Bahri Mamluks it became an administrative process in which legal complaints only represented a small proportion of cases.[31]

Recent studies point in the direction followed by Nielsen, but qualify his conclusions about the late development of *mazalim* as an administrative process. Maaike van Berkel showed that as early as the tenth century CE, *mazalim* "courts" did not only deal with judicial cases, but likewise processed mere demands of assistance or financial help.[32] Furthermore, she stressed that the essential aspect of the administrative treatment of petitions was already in place in tenth-century Baghdad. A special bureau called *diwan al-mazalim* received petitions (called *qissa*-s or *ruq'a*-s) and sent back replies or decisions called *tawqi'*-s. The vizier, who was officially in charge of the *mazalim* at that time, was assisted by a team of secretaries and only intervened personally when a case could not be resolved without his intervention. Most of the time, petitioners did not appear during hearings; secretaries prepared decisions alone, on the basis of their verifications and enquiries in the archives of various bureaus. Petitions and decisions were themselves registered in the *diwan al-mazalim*'s archives.[33]

Nielsen's model, as reviewed by more recent studies, is certainly more accurate than Tyan's, who was misled both by his training as a jurist and by the absence of available documents at the time. Historians should be careful, however, not to exaggerate Nielsen's conclusions, for his stress on the administrative process was also a way to counterbalance Tyan's insistence on the judicial side of the institution. Recent studies tend to underestimate the judicial functions of the *mazalim* and to see them first and foremost as a governing council.[34] The distinction between administrative and judicial processes—now in favor of the administrative side—is, however, once again artificial. Even when a majority of non-"judicial" cases were examined by the institution, the *mazalim* process remained structurally a judicial process, in a non-restrictive sense. Someone submitted a problem (it did not necessarily have to be a wrong deed committed by a defendant, but could also be unjust fate or need of any kind), and his demand/complaint was examined. In other words, he appealed to the ruler's justice: not his justice in the legal sense, but rather in the

[30] Nielsen, *Secular Justice*, esp. 63–78, 134. [31] Ibid., 135.

[32] Maaike van Berkel, "Embezzlement and Reimbursement. Disciplining Officials in 'Abbāsid Baghdad (8th–10th centuries A.D.)," *Journal of Public Administration* 34 (2011): 714.

[33] Maaike van Berkel, "'Abbāsid Maẓālim between Theory and Practice," *Bulletin d'Études Orientales* 63 (2014): 240.

[34] See, e.g., Mathieu Eychenne, *Liens personnels, clientélisme et réseaux de pouvoir dans le sultanat mamelouk (milieu xiiie–fin xive siècle)* (Beirut: Presses de l'Ifpo, 2013), 206.

broader sense of the equilibrium that a just ruler was supposed to warrant by providing a solution to troubles encountered by his subjects.

D. An Appellate Jurisdiction?

To what extent can the *mazalim*, when regarded as a judicial institution, be compared to an appellate court? This controversial issue leads to another question: the extent to which the *mazalim* courts can be held as the apex of a hierarchical legal system. Although al-Mawardi's theory does not explicitly state that the *mazalim* served for appeal against a *qadi*'s legal decision, their general role as recourse against official abuse suggests that they could function as a court of appeal.[35] Several scholars have interpreted the institution as such, like Joseph Schacht (to a certain extent) and Mohammad Hashim Kamali.[36] Nielsen noticed that in the Mamluk period, *mazalim* could occasionally serve as appellate jurisdiction against a *qadi*'s decision; however, examples of such uses are rare in the sources.[37] The strongest advocate for the appellate role of the *mazalim* is perhaps David Powers, who argued against Tyan and Schacht that a *qadi*'s decision was legally revocable in certain circumstances. His analysis of Marinid cases led him to conclude that the judiciary was indeed structured around a rudimentary hierarchical system, and that the *mazalim* courts may have played the role of an appellate jurisdiction.[38]

Other historians are more reluctant to consider the *mazalim* as an appellate institution. Tyan remarked that complaints against *qadi*s included all kinds of misdeeds or misbehaviors—and were not just directed against their decisions—and concluded that they cannot be considered as proper "appeals." *Mazalim* were rather an expression of the ruler's (or his direct representative's) right to control the general administration of justice.[39] Nielsen's analysis leads to the same conclusion. During the first two centuries of Islam, caliphs and governors progressively delegated their full judicial competences to their *qadi*s. Therefore, they usually preferred dismissing a bad *qadi* instead of modifying his judgment against which a litigant had appealed.[40] Delfina Serrano gave furthermore the example of an *amir* of the Almoravid period to whom a litigant appealed against a *qadi*'s judgment, and who asked another *qadi* to review the decision. She argued that the process of appeal was then controlled by *qadi*s, and not by the *mazalim* institution.[41]

[35] Amedroz, "The Mazalim Jurisdiction," 663.
[36] Schacht, *An Introduction*, 189; Kamali, "Appeal Review," 226.
[37] Nielsen, *Secular Justice*, 121.
[38] David S. Powers, "On Judicial Review in Islamic Law," *Law & Society Review* 26 (1992): 336–337.
[39] Tyan, *Histoire de l'organisation judiciaire*, 188–189.
[40] Nielsen, *Secular Justice*, 3.
[41] Delfina Serrano, "Legal Practice in an Andalusī-Maghribī Source from the Twelfth Century CE: The *Madhāhib al-ḥukkām fī nawāzil al-aḥkām*," *Islamic Law and Society* 7 (2000): 215, 231.

One solution to the problem is perhaps to distinguish situations in which the *mazalim* institution was headed by *qadi*s from those in which they were in the hands of political rulers. In theory, the sovereign was the highest judicial authority. Therefore, whenever litigants appealed to him directly, he could dispense justice himself and his word could have replaced that of the judges he appointed. However, in practice, very few examples have survived of Muslim rulers who reversed decisions previously rendered by a *qadi*. They usually resorted to other means: some asked for a *fatwa* to condemn an unjust ruling,[42] others insisted that the unjust judge reverse his judgment himself,[43] or punished him.[44] From the Abbasid period onwards, if not earlier, caliphs and other Muslim rulers did not usually venture to annul a *qadi*'s judgment, possibly out of fear that such an act would harm their image as sovereigns respectful of Islamic legality. We may conclude, therefore, that the *mazalim* could indeed be used for appeal against a contested legal decision. However, the review was not processed within the *mazalim* themselves when the ruler was directly in charge of this institution, but rather delegated to other judges: the appeal process was therefore distinct from the review process. There are, on the other hand, situations in which *qadi*s were appointed as head of the *mazalim* court.[45] It was probably easier for such *qadi*s to review other *qadis*' judgments, and the *mazalim* may in this situation have functioned as modern appeal courts.

E. A Secular Justice?

Mazalim courts are most of the time interpreted as an expression of "secular" justice as opposed to "religious" institutions like the *qadi*'s court. Defending the "lay" character of this jurisdiction, Tyan argued that the mosque was never considered the normal place of *mazalim* hearings.[46] Joseph Schacht and Nimrod Hurvitz followed him on this issue.[47] From the title of his book on *mazalim*, Nielsen also took for

[42] See the example of al-Ḥārith b. Miskīn in Mathieu Tillier (trans.), *Vies des cadis de Miṣr (257/851–366/976). Extrait du Rafʿ al-iṣr ʿan quḍāt Miṣr d'Ibn Ḥağar al-ʿAsqalānī* (Cairo: Institut français d'archéologie orientale, 2002), 50–51.

[43] See the example of ʿUbayd Allāh b. al-Ḥasan al-ʿAnbarī in Mathieu Tillier, "Judicial Authority and *Qāḍīs'* Autonomy under the Abbasids," *al-Masāq* 26 (2014), 7.

[44] See the example of Bishr b. al-Walīd al-Kindī in Mathieu Tillier, *Les cadis d'Iraq et l'État abbasside (132/750–334/945)* (Damascus: Presses de l'Ifpo, 2009), 600–601.

[45] Mathieu Tillier, "*Qāḍīs* and the Political Use of the *Maẓālim* Jurisdiction under the ʿAbbāsids," in *Public Violence in Islamic Societies: Power, Discipline, and the Construction of the Public Sphere, 7th—18th Centuries CE*, eds. Christian Lange and Maribel Fierro (Edinburgh: Edinburgh University Press, 2009), 43–46.

[46] Tyan, *Histoire de l'organisation judiciaire*, II, 264.

[47] Schacht, *An Introduction*, 54; Nimrod Hurvitz, "The Contribution of Early Islamic Rulers to Adjudication and Legislation: The Case of the Mazalim Tribunals," in *Law and Empire. Ideas, Practices, Actors*, eds. Jeroen Duindam, Jill Harries, Caroline Humfress, and Nimrod Hurvitz (Leiden: Brill, 2013), 155.

granted that this institution was a secular one.[48] He questioned, however, the nature of the law that was applied in *mazalim* courts under the Mamluks. According to al-Maqrizi, Mamluks applied the Mongol *yasa*, i.e. a secular Mongol code based on customary law. Al-Maqrizi's statement is polemical, Nielsen argued (following David Ayalon against Poliak), and there is no evidence that the *yasa* was ever codified in writing.[49] Mongol laws, customs, and governmental practices may have had some influence on the Mamluk regime, but not on a systematic basis, and al-Maqrizi's isolated statement cannot be taken as evidence.[50] More recently, Marina Rustow noticed that the petitions addressed to the Fatimids never appealed to the shariʿa nor to the interpretations of the *fuqaha'*, and concluded that the *mazalim* courts were independent of the legal system represented by the *qadi*s and jurists,[51] reinforcing the view yet again that they belonged to the secular sphere.

In al-Andalus, the understanding of the nature of the *mazalim* depends on that of their hierarchical position. According to Tyan, who saw major differences between Oriental and Andalusi *mazalim*, the *sahib al-mazalim* was clearly a subordinate to the *qadi* from the tenth century onwards.[52] Müller remarked however that the political ruler appointed him, and he refutes the conclusion that the *sahib al-mazali* was inferior to the *qadi*. The *sahib al-mazalim* belonged to a different sphere of justice: the political sphere rather than the shariʿa system.[53]

On the other hand, Nedjmeddine Hentati recently argued that such a distinction between religious and secular justice is artificial, and does not match historical realities. He stressed that the *qadi*s did not only rely on shariʿa law, but also took customary rules into consideration. Furthermore, political and secular authorities heard many cases that fell under Islamic law. Lastly, many of the "secular" magistrates were hired among religious scholars—a fact that Tyan and Müller already noted for al-Andalus.[54]

The identification of religious versus secular institution is not straightforward, for the sources do not use these categories, but rather those of shariʿa versus *siyasa*. According to al-Maqrizi, the bad *siyasa* relies on an extra-Islamic code; but there is also a good *siyasa* which is not opposed to the shariʿa, but rather forms part of it.[55] Although al-Maqrizi's description is polemical, it suggests that shariʿa and *siyasa* were not as antithetical as our "religious" and "secular" concepts. If we understand "secular" as qualifying a phenomenon that is connected with neither religious nor spiritual matters, the term is obviously misleading. Islamic rulers—caliphs or sultans—were regarded as religious leaders, whose legitimacy was defined according

[48] Nielsen, *Secular Justice*. [49] Ibid., 33, 105.

[50] Ibid., 109. [51] Rustow, "The Legal Status," 311.

[52] Tyan, *Histoire de l'organisation judiciaire*, II, 287. [53] Müller, "Redressing Injustice," 98.

[54] Nedjmeddine Hentati, "Le pluralisme judiciaire en Occident musulman médiéval et la place du cadi dans l'organisation judiciaire," *Bulletin d'Études Orientales* 63 (2014): 74–75. Cf. Tyan, *Histoire de l'organisation judiciaire*, II, 288; Müller, "Redressing Injustice," 98.

[55] Nielsen, *Secular Justice*, 104.

religious criteria (e.g. sacred genealogy, divine will, ability to defend Islam against its internal and external enemies). According to Abu Yusuf (d. 182/798), the first jurist who mentioned the *mazalim* institution, dispensing justice in person during *mazalim* hearings was an act by which the ruler could please God.[56] Although not limited by shari'a rules, his justice was part of a religious mission. Furthermore, as noticed by Nielsen, rulers used to dispense justice assisted by legal scholars (*fuqaha'*) and *qadis*; the function of *mufti* of the *dar al-'adl* became permanent from the mid-fourteenth century onwards.[57] Nielsen also remarked that administrative and religious functions could hardly be distinguished in the Mamluk period. Chancery scribes who were part of the *mazalim* process had also been trained in religious sciences, and some of them exerted alternatively "civilian" and "religious" functions.[58] Lastly, Tyan's view of *mazalim* as a lay institution—given that the mosque was never regarded as the normal place for their hearings—can easily be refuted. Under the Ayyubids and the early Mamluks, *mazalim* were often organized in madrasas, another kind of "religious" buildings.[59]

Mazalim courts appear as polemical institutions in Mamluk sources not because they were non-religious in nature, but rather because they escaped the strict rules defined by the *fiqh* law, and thus could become arbitrary and unjust. Some modern historians have followed the same logic and wondered whether *mazalim* judges were impartial. Nielsen argued that the litigants' social position had a major impact on the judge's decision. No Mamluk sultan is reported to have lost his trial, and civilians almost never won against soldiers. The institution reflected the balance of powers.[60] Albrecht Fuess confirmed that *mazalim* justice depended on arbitrary powers of the sultan. He concluded that the system was not structurally unjust, but that its equity was limited by personal and political interests of the sultan.[61]

F. *Mazalim* in Theory and Practice

The way historians conceive the origins and the nature of the *mazalim* system depends on their understanding of this concept. For historians like Tyan, who conceived it as a formal and codified institution, no *mazalim* could have existed before the Abbasid period. It is worth noting, however, that the theory of *mazalim* developed only in the eleventh century CE, in the works of al-Mawardi and Ibn al-Farra' (d. 458/1066). What about earlier periods? Tyan remarked that the earliest

56 Tyan, *Histoire de l'organisation judiciaire*, II, 210.
57 Nielsen, *Secular Justice*, 91.
58 Ibid., 88–89.
59 Tyan, *Histoire de l'organisation judiciaire*, II, 266; Nielsen, *Secular Justice*, 13, 50–51.
60 Ibid., 126–131.
61 Albrecht Fuess, "*Ẓulm by Maẓālim*? The Political Implications of the Use of Maẓālim Jurisdiction by the Mamluk Sultans," *Mamluk Studies Review* 13 (2009): 132–133.

traces of *mazalim* in theoretical treatises occur in Abu Yusuf's *Kitab al-Kharaj*, in which the chief *qadi* advises caliph Harun al-Rashid to preside over *mazalim* sessions every two months at least.[62] Tyan concluded implicitly that *mazalim* in the late eighth century were the same institution as that described by al-Mawardi in his treaty of government, which authorizes him to reject as non-*mazalim* any kind of justice that does not fit al-Mawardi's model. This begs the question: were the *mazalim* conceived as a specific institution before al-Mawardi? Was a form of royal justice emerging as soon as the Umayyad period systematically referred to as *mazalim*?

Maaike van Berkel observed that one of the first theoretical developments on the *mazalim* can be found in al-Bukhari's *Sahih* in late ninth century CE. His chapter on this notion remains, however, very abstract. It provides only examples of wrongs and abuses, and never deals with procedures or court organization. *Mazalim* appears thus more as an abstraction than an institution. Van Berkel noticed also the variable terminology used before the eleventh century to refer to what al-Mawardi calls *mazalim*. This could mean, according to her hypothesis, that the concept of *mazalim* could span across several administrative procedures that were not regarded as single mode of justice.[63]

This dissociation between *mazalim* as an abstract concept and the practice of royal justice can also be illustrated by the example of the Umayyad caliph ʿUmar II b. ʿAbd al-ʿAziz (r. 99–101/717–720). This "just" caliph is taken as an early example of *mazalim* practice by Muslim theorists. However, in his early biographies, or in the correspondence attributed to him by Ibn ʿAbd al-Hakam (d. 214/829), the term *mazalim* never appears in an institutional sense. The caliph "gave back properties wrongly acquired" by the Umayyad family (*radda al-mazalim*), or canceled some of his family's privilege; here "*mazalim*" designates exactions, not the institution that is mandated to repress them.[64] It is only subsequently that this word gained terminological meaning, and that ʿUmar II's practice was regarded as an early institutional example of *mazalim*. ʿUmar II's wider involvement in judicial administration suggests that he also presided over judicial sessions, but these were probably not identified by contemporaries as "*mazalim*" audiences. One can therefore hypothesize that "*mazalim*" referred retrospectively a royal judicial practice that existed since the Umayyad period, and developed into structured institution during the Abbasid period.

Although previous administrators like Qudama b. Jaʿfar, in the tenth century CE, offered partial descriptions of the *mazalim* process, al-Mawardi was the first author to provide a complete theory of *mazalim*.[65] Following H.A.R. Gibb, Nielsen

[62] Tyan, *Histoire de l'organisation judiciaire*, II, 209.

[63] Maaike van Berkel, "ʿ*Abbāsid Maẓālim* between Theory and Practice," *Bulletin d'Études Orientales* 63 (2014): 233.

[64] Tillier, "Califes, émirs et cadis," 154.

[65] Van Berkel, "ʿAbbāsid *Maẓālim*," 232, 234.

argued that this theory should not be read as a description of the actual missions and procedures of the institution, but rather as part of a religious and political program aimed at defending the caliphate and enhancing its power in the context of the decline of the Buyid dynasty and the creation of the Seljukid sultanate.[66] This is why this theory insists on the public role played by rulers—under the authority of the Imam/caliph—in dispensing justice, while ignoring administrative procedures that represented the hidden part of the iceberg and the bulk of the institution.[67]

It remains to be understood why no theory of the *mazalim* as an institution developed before al-Mawardi—and why it eventually emerged with that author in particular, with subsequent thinkers merely parroting his theory. According to Nimrod Hurvitz, Muslim jurists long avoided theorizing public law in order to preserve their position of being the principal (if not exclusive) interpreters of sacred texts. For their part, rulers benefited from the absence of any theorization of *mazalim*, for they could escape the constraints of the law as defined by Muslim jurists. Hurvitz thus interpreted this absence of theorization as a division of legislative authority, which did not result from tensions between rulers and jurists, but rather from common interests. Rulers could keep *mazalim* procedures under control and therefore ensure their efficiency.[68]

Yet, Hurvitz's interpretation remains unsatisfactory. There was no clear separation between *fiqh* and state law; *fiqh* itself did not rely exclusively on sacred texts, but depended to a large extent on personal opinions or interpretations by previous jurists, precedents, etc. Furthermore, contrary to Hurvitz's statement, Muslim jurists did not leave public law in the hands of the state. From early on, they authored long chapters detailing rules and procedures of the judiciary—part of the state organization—and of fiscal administration and criminal law, which were all part of public law. Another explanation must therefore be found in the absence of early theorization of *mazalim*. Other state institutions were excluded from *fiqh* books, such as the police (*shurta*). Considering that *mazalim* were regularly used against the ordinary judiciary, and that their judges were often regarded as illegitimate rivals to *qadi*s, it is possible that Muslim jurists long refused to provide a legal background to an institution they were reluctant to acknowledge.[69] In theory, *qadi*s should have been able to render justice to anyone, whatever the respective social position of the litigants, on the sole basis of *fiqh* law. In practice, the system sometimes failed because *qadi*s had no coercive power against high-ranking officers or because the strict application of *fiqh* court procedures was insufficient to ascertain facts. The intervention of the ruler was necessary, but jurists could not admit it easily, and royal justice remained confined to mirrors for princes. If this hypothesis is true, why did al-Mawardi and Ibn al-Farra' suddenly decide to provide a theory of

[66] Nielsen, *Secular Justice*, 17–27. [67] Ibid., 134.
[68] Hurvitz, "The Contribution of Early Islamic Rulers," 155.
[69] Cf. Tyan, *Histoire de l'organisation judiciaire*, II, 160.

mazalim in books that pertained to *fiqh*—even in an unconventional manner? Here again, answers can be found in the political context. Including the *mazalim* in an original legal theory of the government, and defending caliphal prerogatives—even those criticized by previous jurists—may have been a way to insist on the necessity for new military rulers to submit to Islamic law and judicial institutions.

II. The Historical Functioning of *Mazalim*

A. *Mazalim* Staff

There is little disagreement about the historical composition of *mazalim* staff. Tyan was followed by Sourdel and Nielsen in his analysis of the early development of the institution. Abbasid caliphs presided over hearings until al-Ma'mun (r. 198–218/813–833), and al-Muhtadi (r. 255–256/869–870) was the last one who did so. Viziers already played an important role in the *mazalim* process under al-Rashid (r. 170–193/786–809). During the *mihna*—an inquisition demanding *qadi*s, witnesses, and scholars to adhere to the doctrine of the created Qur'an (c. 218–234/833–848)—the chief *qadi* took over the supervision of *mazalim*. He was replaced by the vizier, who retained this function until the beginning of the Buyid period (334–447/945–1055), and reprised this role under the Fatimids (especially when the vizier belonged to the military) and the Seljuks. The vizier was succeeded by the *na'ib* under the Ayyubids and the early Mamluks. The Buyids entrusted this task to the *naqib al-ashraf*, head of the 'Alid family. Under the Mamluks, the sultan often presided over *mazalim* sessions, but this ceased in periods of troubles or political weakness.[70]

The actual role played by the sovereign, though, has been questioned. Although the *mazalim* were supposed to represent his direct justice, the sovereign (the caliph, later the sultan) ceased presiding over hearings during long periods, across dynasties. Paying only attention to the external organization of the institution, Tyan claimed that no Fatimid caliph played any active role in the *mazalim*.[71] On the basis of documentary evidence, however, Stern argued that Fatimid caliphs were still dealing with petitions when solicited during their administrative treatment, even though they did not preside over hearings.[72] Nielsen suggested, on the contrary, that

[70] Tyan, *Histoire de l'organisation judiciaire*, II, 208–215; Dominique Sourdel, *Le Vizirat 'abbāside de 749 à 936* (Damascus: IFEAD, 1959–60), 641–644; Nielsen, *Secular Justice*, 4–7.

[71] Tyan, *Histoire de l'organisation judiciaire*, II, 213.

[72] Stern, "Three Petitions," 194.

during the Mamluk period, the sultan's appearance at *mazalim* sessions concealed a very limited involvement in the actual process: his role was mostly confined to the signature of decrees.[73]

Historians also agree that *mazalim* were soon delegated to lower officials. Tyan noted that the title of *sahib al-mazalim*, which designated an auxiliary of the *mazalim* judge during the early Abbasid period, became that of a delegate judge in the tenth century.[74] Under the Fatimids, a *sahib al-bab* was in charge of *mazalim* when the vizier did not belong to the military.[75] The title of *na'ib dar al-'adl*, which developed under the Ayyubids and the Mamluks in relationship with the institution of *dar al-'adl* (house of justice), came to designate the main delegate of the sultan, and could be entrusted to scholars (*'ulama'*).[76] The main debate regards the actual functions of the *hajib* (chamberlain) during the Mamluk period. Tyan noted that the title of *sahib al-mazalim* disappeared definitively under the Mamluks, and relied on al-Maqrizi to suggest that his functions passed into the hands of the *hajib*.[77] However, Nielsen challenged al-Maqrizi's statements about the *hajib* and proposes that the latter did not play an important role in the *mazalim* process. According to his interpretation, the *hajib* was a military judge who only dealt with disputes between soldiers and had no part in *mazalim* sessions.[78]

Focussed as he was on the apparent judicial process of the *mazalim*, Tyan passed quickly over the lower staff of the *mazalim*, whom he considered of secondary importance.[79] Because Nielsen is more interested in highlighting the administrative process of the institution, he rather insists on the crucial role of scribes and other officials of the *diwan*s during the Mamluk period. He showed how different agents intervened in the processing of petitions, from their reception to the decision sent back to the petitioners, and describes the respective roles of the *sahib diwan al-insha'*, the *katib al-daraj*, the *katib al-dast*, the *dawadar*, and other chancery secretaries.[80] I have myself tried to suggest that the *mazalim* organization in provincial cities could be different from that of the capital during the Abbasid period, and argued that *qadi*s were irregularly entrusted with this institution, on a temporary basis, in order to solve a particular crisis. In Baghdad, from the early Abbasid period onwards, *qadi*s often joined *mazalim* sessions held by rulers in order to provide decisions (sometimes political ones) with an aura of legitimacy.[81]

[73] Nielsen, *Secular Justice*, 80.
[74] Tyan, *Histoire de l'organisation judiciaire*, II, 221–222.
[75] Ibid., 233; Nielsen, *Secular Justice*, 10; Stern, "Three Petitions," 197.
[76] See Nielsen, *Secular Justice*, 14.
[77] Tyan, *Histoire de l'organisation judiciaire*, II, 234.
[78] Nielsen, *Secular Justice*, 83–85.
[79] Tyan, *Histoire de l'organisation judiciaire*, II, 234.
[80] Nielsen, *Secular Justice*, 85–92.
[81] Tillier, "Qāḍīs and the Political Use," 46–47, 52–53.

B. The Locus of the *Mazalim* Sessions

There are few controversies about the place of *mazalim* hearings during the first centuries of Islam. Tyan noted that they were held in the caliph's palace or in the official residence of the viziers, governors, or other officials in charge of the institution.[82] The basic principle was that royal justice needed to be public and accessible to any subject.[83] Tyan also stressed the importance of the official cortege (*mawkib*), in which the sovereign showed himself to the people, with a *mazalim* session at times coming at the end of the procession.[84]

The most important change in the locus of the *mazalim* was the adoption of a designated place, called *dar al-ʿadl* (house of justice), attributed to Nur al-Din Zanki (r. 541–569/1146–74) by Islamic tradition.[85] Nielsen adopted the same chronology and considered that the first *dar al-ʿadl* was invented shortly after 549/1154, whereas Nasser Rabbat mentioned a date around 1163.[86] Tyan had however questioned this tradition. He noted that Islamic history had punctually adopted specialized places for *mazalim* before Nur al-Din. Caliph al-Hadi (r. 169–170/785–786) may have had a *Dar al-mazalim* in Baghdad. In Samarra, caliph al-Muhtadi (r. 255–6/869–870) had built a *Qubbat al-mazalim* (dome of the *mazalim*) opened on each side, in which he dispensed justice.[87] Such sporadic attempts prefigured the adoption of the *dar al-ʿadl*, which became the permanent center of *mazalim* justice only in late twelfth century CE.

Tyan was puzzled by complex changes in the *dar al-ʿadl* implantation and architecture, especially during the Mamluk period. He misunderstood certain evolutions in the spatial organization of audiences. He thought, for instance, that the *dikka*, which appeared in the late Mamluk period, designated an actual courtroom, whereas later scholars such as Albrecht Fuess interpreted it more accurately as a wooden platform covered by a large tent.[88] Likewise, Tyan failed to conceive that the *istabl* in which *mazalim* sessions were organized in the late fourteenth century was in fact an actual "stable," and apparently thought the term was just the name of a hall.[89] More recent research suggests that sessions were actually held in the royal stables.[90] Drawing on Tyan and Nielsen, the latter having provided a detailed

[82] Tyan, *Histoire de l'organisation judiciaire*, II, 264.

[83] Ibid., 259–260. [84] Ibid., 261. [85] Ibid., 265–266.

[86] Nielsen, *Secular Justice*, 13, 49; Nasser O. Rabbat, "The Ideological Significance of the *Dār al-ʿAdl* in the Medieval Islamic Orient," *International Journal of Middle East Studies* 27 (1995): 3.

[87] Tyan, *Histoire de l'organisation judiciaire*, II, 265. See also Alastair Northedge, *The Historical Topography of Samarra* (London: British School of Archaeology in Iraq-Fondation Max van Berchem, 2005), 134, 137, 139, 140.

[88] Tyan, *Histoire de l'organisation judiciaire*, II, 267; Fuess, "*Ẓulm* by *Maẓālim*," 126.

[89] Tyan, *Histoire de l'organisation judiciaire*, II, 252.

[90] Fumihiko Hasebe, "Sultan Barqūq and his Complaining Subjects in the Royal Stables," *Al-Masāq* 21 (2009), 315–330.

account of successive locations of the *dar*-s *al-'adl* under the Mamluks,[91] Fuess proposed that these periodic changes allowed each sultan to reinvent the way he represented himself, and to leave his mark upon the administration.[92]

C. Social and Political Use of *Mazalim*

1. *Relationships between* qada' *and* mazalim

The relationship between the *mazalim* and ordinary justice dispensed by the *qadi*s is difficult to define. Were the *mazalim* a superior form of justice (see Section I, D. about the question of appeal)? Were they competing jurisdictions? Were the two complementary institutions? Tyan hesitated: as an expression of the sovereign's justice, it must have been superior. In his view, the two systems could also be regarded as complementary, for *mazalim* judges used to transfer common cases to *qadis*.[93] (However this last generalization only relies upon an isolated example dating from the reign of sultan Barquq.) Tyan remarked that the *mazalim* were delegated to appointed officials on a permanent basis from the tenth century onwards. *Mazalim* judges and *qadi*s stood therefore on an equal footing, and certain competition opposed the two jurisdictions. As a result, the frontier between *mazalim* justice and ordinary justice became blurred.[94] They sometimes became so close that a *mazalim* judge could replace a *qadi* temporarily.[95] Tyan noted that *qadi*s could also be appointed as *mazalim* judges.[96] On al-Andalus, he even regarded the *mazalim* institution that developed in Cordova in the early tenth century as subordinated to the *qadi*'s court.[97] The picture drawn by Tyan is far from clear and conclusive, and some of his generalizations are contradicted by other examples.

Nielsen also observed different kinds of relationships between the two institutions. Before the Fatimids, he noted that some Egyptian *qadi*s were dismissed and replaced by *mazalim* judges, and concluded that the two institutions were close to one another. He explained this proximity by the existence of an Egyptian administration simpler than the central one in Iraq.[98] Nielsen noted that under the Mamluks, the *mazalim* integrated *qadi*s in the judicial process, especially when confronted with cases covered by shari'a law. He concluded that the religious establishment understood how to benefit from the *mazalim* system.[99] In general, Nielsen

[91] Tyan, *Histoire de l'organisation judiciaire*, II, 266–267; Nielsen, *Secular Justice*, 50–53.
[92] Fuess, "*Ẓulm* by *Maẓālim*," 128. [93] Tyan, *Histoire de l'organisation judiciaire*, II, 197.
[94] Ibid., 224–226. [95] Ibid., 229. [96] Ibid., 234.
[97] Ibid., 286. This analysis has since been refuted by Müller. See Müller, "Redressing Injustice," 98.
[98] Nielsen, *Secular Justice*, 8. [99] Ibid., 114, 117.

considered the two institutions as complementary rather than competing ones. So has Wael Hallaq on the basis of a few Egyptian examples from the ninth century CE, about which he argued that *mazalim* only replaced ordinary justice when no qualified *qadi* was to be found.[100] In his study on Barquq's reign, Hasebe followed Nielsen and remarked that the sultan, who acted himself as a judge, did not want to infringe upon other courts, and only accepted to examine cases that had unsuccessfully been presented to a *hajib* or a *qadi*.[101] He showed, however, that Barquq's justice was criticized by Muslim scholars like Ibn Hajar, who denounced the sultan's political use of *mazalim*.[102]

In my own work on the Abbasid period (eighth to tenth century CE), I have argued that the *mazalim* institution can be seen as a political tool in the hands of rulers. This court was used to regain control over a judicial system that rulers delegated to Muslim jurists on a permanent basis. I disagree with Nielsen's analysis of the pre-Fatimid period. The alternation between *qadi*s and *mazalim* judges in Fustat should not be explained by the proximity between the two institutions, but rather by their competition. I have shown that a ruler usually dismissed his *qadi* and appointed a *mazalim* judge in his place when he needed to assert his judicial authority during or after a political crisis.[103] Moreover, in ninth- and tenth-century Egypt, appointing a *mazalim* judge was a way newly autonomous governors (Tulunids and Ikhshidids) could assert their local judicial authority against caliphs who still claimed to be the only source of *qadis*' appointments.[104]

We should be careful not to overvalue the instances highlighted by Tyan in which *qadi*s were also in charge of *mazalim* without taking the historical context into consideration. Yahya b. Aktham and Ahmad b. Abi Du'ad, whom Tyan gave as examples,[105] were also chief *qadi*s and as such were not judges in ordinary courts. Therefore they were not really holding multiple positions. As chief *qadi*s, they were the caliph's legal advisers and, at the time (middle of the ninth century), the most powerful men of the empire after the caliph himself.[106] Their holding of the *mazalim* at the caliph's court expressed their hierarchical superiority in the whole judicial system. In the Orient, although distinctions between titles and functions were occasionally blurred, *mazalim* and *qada'* never merged. They represented two different judicial tools that the rulers could use, play against one another, and reshape according to their needs. In this game, *mazalim* remained the favorite expression of the ruler's direct justice.

[100] Hallaq, *The Origins*, 101.
[101] Hasebe, "Sultan Barqūq," 318.
[102] Ibid., 322.
[103] Tillier, "*Qāḍīs* and the Political Use," 47–49.
[104] Ibid., 49–51.
[105] Tyan, *Histoire de l'organisation judiciaire*, II, 235.
[106] See Tillier, *Les cadis d'Iraq*, 443–454.

2. *The symbolic and political use of* mazalim

The ruler's direct justice appeared indeed as a major expression of his legitimacy. Émile Tyan had already noted that the exercise of the *mazalim* was one of the most characteristic and the most striking attributes of supreme power in Islam.[107] Therefore, the first autonomous rulers, like Ibn Tulun and Kafur, demonstrated a special attachment to this institution.[108] Under the Mamluks, official justice dispensed during ceremonies in *dar al-ʿadl* expressed publicly the sovereign power of the ruler.[109]

Drawing on Tyan's first investigations, Nielsen highlighted that as a building, the *dar al-ʿadl* became an essential symbol of power that helped legitimize the sultan's regime from the Ayyubids onwards.[110] Under the Mamluks, it hosted coronation rites as well as official public ceremonies twice a week, called *khidma* (homage), during which the sultan paraded in his cortege and demonstrated the military legitimacy of the state.[111] Protocols of hearing at the *dar al-ʿadl*, and selection of different categories of officials to participate in the ceremony, as well as their respective place vis-à-vis the sultan, were all significant. Any adjustment reflected an evolution in the relationships between the ruler and his agents. The organization of the *dar al-ʿadl* provides therefore a changing picture of the Mamluk religious and legal politics. In Nielsen's view, although the *dar al-ʿadl* was originally conceived to host *mazalim* sessions, this legal function soon became secondary and the term of *dar al-ʿadl* came to designate the *khidma* in general.[112]

Nielsen suggested that the location of the *dar al-ʿadl* itself was significant of the symbolic use of *mazalim* by rulers, and conveyed a message to the people. Nur al-Din built the first one in Damascus outside the Citadel, in order to highlight its accessibility to his civil subjects. In Mamluk Cairo, however, the *dar al-ʿadl* was transferred into the Citadel, which expressed a strong connection between the army and *mazalim* justice.[113] According to Nasser Rabbat's later analysis of all the *dar al-ʿadl* known from the sources (in Damascus, Alep, and Cairo), the position of such buildings reflected the way rulers defined their relationship with the city.[114]

Mazalim audiences came to feature the legitimacy of a sultan anxious to solve his subjects' concerns. The study of their theatrical setting was pursued by Nasser Rabbat, who showed how the great *iwan* of the Citadel, under Sultan al-Nasir Muhammad (r. with two interruptions 693–741/1293–1341), adopted an open plan layout (unlike the previous hearings rooms) that expressed the litigants' accessibility to the sultan.[115] Rabbat also argued that the significance of the *dar al-ʿadl* went beyond the mere

107 Tyan, *Histoire de l'organisation judiciaire*, II, 151.
108 Ibid., 207.
109 Ibid., 205, 248 *et seq.*
110 Nielsen, *Secular Justice*, 14.
111 Ibid., 53–54.
112 Ibid., 56–58.
113 Ibid., 60–61.
114 Rabbat, "The Ideological Significance," 10.
115 Ibid., 17.

development of the *mazalim* system: the appearance of this type of building, he said, is related to the context of war against the Crusaders and the Mongols, and to the ideological revival that accompanied it. The *dar al-ʿadl* visually represented justice and provided the ruler with a forum in which he publicly proclaimed his adherence to Islamic codes. From this point of view, the *dar al-ʿadl* appears as a propaganda tool used to legitimize the actions of the sultans.[116] Rabbat's theory has thereafter been partly refuted by Fuess, who argued that the construction of *dar al-ʿadl* was not limited to the context of the counter crusade.[117] Fuess nevertheless accepted that this type of building helped to establish the legitimacy of the Mamluks.[118]

Fumihiko Hasebe, for his part, investigated the transfer of the *dar al-ʿadl* to the Royal Stables of the Citadel under sultan Barquq (r. 784–791/1382–89), and interpreted this reform in the context of the contemporary economic crisis in Egypt. The sultan magnanimously encouraged the population, including those living in rural areas, to complain about the abuses of his emirs, whom he then punished. Installing the *mazalim* in the Royal Stables carried therefore a socio-political meaning: justice descended into the lower enclosure of the Citadel, where subjects gained easier access to the sultan's audience.[119] Using a similar anthropological interpretation, Albrecht Fuess noted that sultan al-Nasir Muhammad used to sit next to an empty *minbar*-looking throne during his *mazalim* audiences, which could give the impression that he was almost equal to the rest of the society.[120]

III. Concluding Remarks

Defining the *mazalim* remains a challenge for modern historians. The term itself appeared early on, but mostly in an abstract or general sense. It designated various kinds of judicial practices, whether dispensed by the ruler himself or by his appointed representatives. The only precise definition of the *mazalim* as an institution is provided by al-Mawardi, who idealized some judicial practices at work in the tenth and eleventh centuries CE. His definition must therefore be taken with a grain of salt. Émile Tyan's seminal analysis of the institution is marked by a concern for systematization that corresponds primarily to a legal approach. Some of his generalizations rely only upon one or two examples that may not be representative of the whole medieval period, and do not give consideration to the high terminological fluidity of classical Arabic. His view of the *mazalim* should thus be taken with caution.

116 Rabbat, "The Ideological Significance," 19–20. 117 Fuess, "*Ẓulm* by *Maẓālim*," 125.
118 Ibid., 122. 119 Hasebe, "Sultan Barqūq," 320–325.
120 Fuess, "*Ẓulm* by *Maẓālim*," 125.

Modern historians willing to study the *mazalim* must therefore choose between either sticking with what is referred to as such in historical sources, or speculating about what Muslims may have considered as *mazalim* without using this term on a systematic basis. As sticking with what is explicitly called *mazalim* in historical sources would dramatically reduce the number of usable examples, most historians choose an empirical approach and extend the appellation to other cases not described as such in the sources, including assemblies gathered for political trials.[121]

None of these methodological choices is entirely satisfactory, for they require either that certain historically identifiable phenomena be ignored—such as early existence of royal direct justice—or force the interpretation by imposing terminological frameworks that are likely to be inadequate. This choice is highly dependant on the systematization of al-Mawardi and Ibn al-Farra', who defined *mazalim* as an institution. However, if we attempt to disregard the rigid vision proposed by the two Sunni authors, it appears that the term *mazalim* conveyed at least two meanings: a general principle, and an institutional manifestation of this principle.

As a general principle, *radd al-mazalim* can broadly be understood as the ruler's duty to ensure the achievement of equity and to remedy injustices, whether caused by individuals or by state agents. In this sense, *mazalim* existed from the Umayyad period onwards, at the very least, although at that time no institution bore that name. This duty was not legal by nature: it was both political—the ruler appearing as a warrant of the world's order—and ethical. It had also a social equivalent: the great notables' duty to respond when solicited by lower people seeking support or a service—or what Arabic sources describe as *haja*. Whenever someone could not satisfy a need by himself, he could ask some richer or more powerful man and present him with an oral or written request. This practice appeared as a pillar of the social game, allowing those enjoying a dominant position (politically, socially, or economically) to create a clientele network and thereby strengthen their power. At the summit of the social pyramid, the ruler had to act as the warrant of equity and help those whose needs could compromise the stability of the system. In this sense, *radd al-mazalim* did not need a special institution with a specific name. It only needed access to the ruler, and the privileged way of securing such access was by petitioning. Therefore, all procedures using petitions to the ruler—whatever the subject of the request—could be regarded as a *mazalim* process in the broader sense, whereby the ruler was solicited as warrant of social equilibrium.

This governing principle, which had concrete expression in the ruler's willingness to answer petitions, periodically took on other institutional manifestations.

[121] See, e.g., Louis Massignon, *La Passion de Husayn Ibn Mansûr Hallâj* (Paris: Gallimard, 1975; 1st edn. 1922), I, 436, 542.

On the legal level, it could take the form of special courts, either held by the ruler himself or his representative, or by assemblies of scholars and/or state servants. It could also assume administrative form by the development of a bureau (*diwan*) supervising the handling of petitions. The existence of the underlying principle of *radd al-mazalim* and its nature explain some of the characteristics of its legal expression, notably the fact that the *mazalim* courts were partly (but only partly) detached from the shari'a system: when the legal *fiqh* system was unable to help establishing equity, the ruler had to solicit other legal references, or even the reason of the state.

The institutionalization of the *radd al-mazalim* principle was reinforced by the creation and the development of the *dar al-'adl* in the Zengid period. The adoption by the Mamluks of this kind of building, originally conceived as a place for dispensing justice, as the center of court ceremonies and general sultanian hearings, sanctioned the complete assimilation of the governing principle by state institutions. One should not be surprised, therefore, that *mazalim* sessions were rarely legal in nature, nor consider this fact as a major break from previous practices. Ensuring equity and redressing injustices appeared as the main governing principle by which the sultan could keep the society's equilibrium, and thereby prove his legitimacy. The hearing of legal cases and complaints against state agents were only representative of the sultan's wider concern for the well-being of his subjects. "*Mazalim*" became therefore a metonymical appellation for the public part of the government's activity.

Further research is needed to understand better the articulation between legal and governmental institutions, in which *mazalim* played a major role. Renewal of historical research will probably come from the study of documentary sources, especially petitions and decrees. While narrative sources convey a normative view of the *mazalim*,[122] documents allow a more precise analysis of the social use of petitioning, of representations filtering through formulae employed by petitioners and administrative staff, and of the process of governmental decision-making. Maaike van Berkel and Marina Rustow's recent investigations along this approach are already promising. In order to overcome the barriers represented by a conservative terminology, it will also be necessary to multiply studies of *mazalim* processes in relation to their precise historical contexts. Only such contextualization may enable us to move the analysis beyond the conventional image provided by literary sources, and to understand the various uses of institutions placed under the aegis of the general principle of redressing injustices.

122 Van Berkel, "'Abbāsid *Maẓālim*," 234.

References

'Abd al-Mun'im, Ḥamdi, *Diwan al-mazalim* (Beirut: Dar al-Shuruq, 1983).

Amedroz, Henry Frederick, "The Mazalim Jurisdiction in the Ahkam Sultaniyya of Mawardi." *Journal of the Royal Asiatic Society of Great Britain and Ireland* 2 (July 1911): 635–674.

Berkel, Maaike van, "Embezzlement and Reimbursement. Disciplining Officials in 'Abbasid Baghdad (8th–10th centuries A.D.)." *Journal of Public Administration* 34 (2011): 712–719.

Berkel, Maaike van, "'Abbāsid *Maẓālim* between Theory and Practice." *Bulletin d'Études Orientales* 63 (2014): 229–242.

Eychenne, Mathieu, *Liens personnels, clientélisme et réseaux de pouvoir dans le sultanat mamelouk (milieu xiiie-fin xive siècle)* (Beirut: Presses de l'Ifpo, 2013).

Fuess, Albrecht, "*Ẓulm by Maẓālim*? The Political Implications of the Use of *Maẓālim* Jurisdiction by the Mamluk Sultans." *Mamluk Studies Review* 13 (2009): 121–146.

Grabar, Oleg, "Notes sur les cérémonies umayyades" in M. Rosen-Ayalon (ed.) *Studies in Memory of Gaston Wiet* (Jerusalem: The Hebrew University of Jerusalem, 1977) 51–60.

Gruendler, Beatrice, "*Tawqī'* (Apostille): Royal Brevity in Pre-modern Islamic Appeals Court" in Lale Behzadi and Vahid Behmardi (eds.) *The Weaving of Words. Approaches to Classical Arabic Prose* (Beirut: Orient-Institut, 2009) 101–129.

Hallaq, Wael B., *The Origins and Evolution of Islamic Law* (Cambridge: Cambridge University Press, 2005).

Hasebe, Fumihiko, "Sultan Barqūq and his Complaining Subjects in the Royal Stables." *Al-Masāq* 21 (2009): 315–330.

Heideman, Stefan, Müller, Christian, and Rāġib, Yūsuf, "Un décret d'al-Malik al-'Ādil en 571/1176 relatif aux moines du Mont Sinaï." *Annales Islamologiques* 31 (1997): 81–107.

Hentati, Nedjmeddine, "Le pluralisme judiciaire en Occident musulman médiéval et la place du cadi dans l'organisation judiciaire." *Bulletin d'Études Orientales* 63 (2014): 57–78.

Hurvitz, Nimrod, "The Contribution of Early Islamic Rulers to Adjudication and Legislation: The Case of the Mazalim Tribunals" in Jeroen Duindam, Jill Harries, Caroline Humfress, and Nimrod Hurvitz (eds.) *Law and Empire. Ideas, Practices, Actors* (Leiden: Brill, 2013) 135–156.

Kamali, Mohammad Hashim, "Appellate Review and Judicial Independence in Islamic Law" in Chibli Mallat (ed.) *Islam and Public Law. Classical and Contemporary Studies* (London, Dordrecht, Boston: Graham & Trotman, 1993) 49–83.

Khan, Geoffrey, "A Copy of a Decree from the Archives of the Fāṭimid Chancery in Egypt." *Bulletin of the School of Oriental and African Studies* 49 (1986): 439–463.

Khan, Geoffrey, "A Petition to the Fāṭimid Caliph al-'Āmir." *Journal of the Royal Asiatic Society* 1 (1990): 44–54.

Massignon, Louis, *La Passion de Husayn Ibn Mansûr Hallâj*. 4 vols (Paris: Gallimard, 1975; 1st edn. 1922).

Müller, Christian, "Redressing Injustice. *Maẓālim* Jurisdictions at the Umayyad court of Córdoba (Eighth-Eleventh Centuries CE)" in Albrecht Fuess and Jan-Peter Hartung (eds.) *Court and Cultures in the Muslim World. Seventh to Nineteenth Centuries* (London, New York: Routledge, 2011) 94–104.

Nielsen, Jørgen, *Secular Justice in an Islamic State: Maẓālim under the Baḥrī Mamlūks, 662/1264–789/1387* (Leiden: Nederlands Historisch-Archaeologisch Instituut te Istanbul, 1985).

Northedge, Alastair, *The Historical Topography of Samarra* (London: British School of Archaeology in Iraq-Fondation Max van Berchem, 2005).
Powers, David S., "On Judicial Review in Islamic Law." *Law & Society Review* 26 (1992): 315–342.
Rabbat, Nasser O., "The Ideological Significance of the *Dār al-ʿAdl* in the Medieval Islamic Orient." *International Journal of Middle East Studies* 27 (1995): 3–28.
Rustow, Marina, "A Petition to a Woman at the Fatimid Court (413–414 A.H./1022–23 C.E.)." *Bulletin of the School of Oriental and African Studies* 73 (2010): 1–27.
Rustow, Marina, "The Legal Status of *ḏimmī*-s in the Fatimid East: A view from the Palace in Cairo" in M. Fierro and J.V. Tolan (eds.) *The Legal Status of ḏimmī-s in the Islamic East (second/ eighth- ninth/ fifteenth centuries)* (Turnhout: Brepols, 2013) 307–332.
Al-Samarra'i, Husam Q, *Al-Mu'assasat al-idariyya fī al-dawlat al-ʿabbasiyya khilal al-fatra 247–334 H./861–945 M* (Damascus: Maktabat dar al-fath, 1971).
Schacht, Joseph, *An Introduction to Islamic Law* (Oxford: Clarendon Press, 1982; 1st edn. 1964).
Serrano, Delfina, "Legal Practice in an Andalusī-Maghribī Source from the Twelfth Century CE: The *Madhāhib al-ḥukkām fī nawāzil al-aḥkām*." *Islamic Law and Society* 7 (2000): 187–234.
Sourdel, Dominique, *Le Vizirat ʿabbāside de 749 à 936* (Damascus: IFEAD, 1959–60).
Stern, Samuel M., "Three Petitions of the Fāṭimid Period." *Oriens* 15 (1962): 172–209.
Stern, Samuel M., "Petitions from the Ayyūbid Period." *Bulletin of the School of Oriental and African Studies* 27 (1964): 1–32.
Stern, Samuel M., *Fatimid Decrees: Original Documents from the Fāṭimid Chancery* (London: Faber and Faber, 1964).
Stern, Samuel M., "Petitions from the Mamlūk Period (Notes on the Mamlūk Documents from Sinai)." *Bulletin of the School of Oriental and African Studies* 29 (1966): 233–276.
Tillier, Mathieu, *Les cadis d'Iraq et l'État abbasside (132/750–334/945)* (Damascus: Presses de l'Ifpo, 2009).
Tillier, Mathieu, "*Qāḍīs* and the Political Use of the *Maẓālim* Jurisdiction under the ʿAbb āsids" in Christian Lange and Maribel Fierro (eds.) *Public Violence in Islamic Societies: Power, Discipline, and the Construction of the Public Sphere, 7th—18th Centuries CE* (Edinburgh: Edinburgh University Press, 2009) 42–66.
Tillier, Mathieu, "Judicial Authority and *Qāḍīs*' Autonomy under the Abbasids." *al-Masāq* 26 (2014): 1–13.
Tillier, Mathieu, "Califes, émirs et cadis: le droit califal et l'articulation de l'autorité judiciaire à l'époque umayyade." *Bulletin d'Études Orientales* 63 (2014): 147–190.
Tillier, Mathieu, (trans.) *Vies des cadis de Misr (257/851-366/976). Extrait du Rafʿ al-isr ʿan quḍāt Misr d'Ibn Ḥağar al-ʿAsqalānī* (Cairo: Institut français d'archéologie orientale, 2002).
Tyan, Émile, *Histoire de l'organisation judiciaire en pays d'Islam* (Paris: Sirey, 1938–1943).

PART III

ORIGINS, EMPIRES, AND STATES

A

HISTORICAL STUDIES

CHAPTER 15

ORIGINS OF AND INFLUENCES ON ISLAMIC LAW

BENJAMIN JOKISCH

I. Introduction

ISLAMIC law as it became manifest in a literary form at the end of the eighth century displays a considerably high degree of evolution both in content and structure. About 150 years after the formation of the Muslim community it proves to be on a par with other legal systems at the time such as Byzantine–Roman law, Jewish law, or Zoroastrian law which look back at a history of many centuries or even millennia. It is the rapidity of development on the one hand and the complexity of the system on the other that raised the interest of Islamicists, historians, and jurists since the mid-nineteenth century and gave rise to a number of studies on the "mystery" of its origins.

The almost total lack of early foundational texts presents scholars with serious problems. Apart from the revelation text itself, a handful of reports concerning legal aspects of pre-Islamic Arab society, and a few very small legal works or legally relevant sources dating to the second half of the eighth century, there is no first hand evidence giving insight into the early development of Islamic law. In fact, historical research is restricted to legal and related prosopographical texts emerging after the formative period and, last but not least, to a bulk of legal traditions purported to go back to the Prophet Muhammad or early Muslim authorities.[1] According to the heuristic value attributed to that latter category of sources, scholars draw quite different pictures of the early development of Islamic law. One camp, largely represented by Muslim scholars,[2] but also by some western Islamicists,[3] regards most of the legal traditions as trustworthy and therefore emphasizes the continuous and autopoietic character of the early Islamic evolution. The other camp, prevalent within the western academic discourse,[4] qualifies most or even all of these traditions as later fabrications, concluding that there must have been room for external influences from outside Islam.[5]

Apart from the general controversy on sources, which is still going on and sometimes has a doctrinal impetus,[6] we find a spectrum of approaches and theories focussed on single aspects of the topic. As a first step, this chapter provides a survey of the major issues of Islamic law discussed by the sharīʿa experts. These central aspects refer to the general conception of Islamic law, the role of pre-Islamic tribal law, Islamic substantive law and the question of interaction with non-Islamic legal systems, and, last but not least, the early development of Islamic legal institutions such as judgeship, market inspection, law schools, and colleges. Since all of these aspects prove to be controversial, we are faced with quite different historical outlines, the most representative of which will be presented in a separate chapter.

[1] Harald Motzki, "Quo vadis, Ḥadīt-Forschung? Eine kritische Untersuchung von G. H. A. Juynboll: 'Nāfiʿ the mawlā of Ibn ʿUmar, and his position in Muslim Ḥadīt literature,'" *Der Islam* 73 (1996): 41.

[2] Birgit Krawietz, *Hierarchie der Rechtsquellen im tradierten sunnitischen Islam* (Berlin: Duncker & Humblot, 2002), 12–70.

[3] Harald Motzki, "Die Entstehung des Rechts," in *Der islamische Orient—Grundzüge seiner Geschichte*, eds. A. Noth et al. (Würzburg: Ergon-Verlag, 1998), 151–172; Asaf Fyzee, *Outlines of Muḥammadan Law* (Oxford: Oxford University Press, 1964); Yasin Dutton, *The Origins of Islamic Law. The Qurʾān, the Muwaṭṭaʾ and Madinan ʿAmal* (Surrey: Curzon, 1999).

[4] Gavin Picken, "General Introduction," in *Islamic Law: Critical Concepts in Islamic Studies, Vol. 1: Origins and Sources*, ed. Gavin Picken (London: Routledge, 2011), 13.

[5] For further surveys of the different approaches see Harald Motzki, *Die Anfänge der islamischen Jurisprudenz. Ihre Entwicklung in Mekka bis zur Mitte des 2./8. Jahrhunderts* (Stuttgart: K.F. Steiner, 1991), 8–49; Mohyddin Yahia, *Šāfiʿī et les deux sources de la loi islamique* (Turnhout: Brepols Publishers, 2009), 11–78; Patricia Crone, *Roman, Provincial and Islamic Law. The Origins of the Islamic Patronate* (Cambridge: Cambridge University Press, 1987), 1–17; Ulrike Mitter, *Das frühislamische Patronat. Eine Untersuchung zur Rolle von fremden Einflüssen bei der Entwicklung des islamischen Rechts* (Nijmwegen, 1999), 9–18; Cilardo, Agostino *Teorie sulle origine del diritto islamico* (Rome: Istituto per l'Oriente 1990); Maribel Fierro, "Nuevas perpectivas sobre la formaciòn del derecho islàmico," *al-Qanṭara* 21 (2000): 511–523; see also Christopher Melchert, "The Early History of Islamic Law," in *Method and Theory in the Study of Islamic Origins*, ed. H. Berg (Leiden: Brill, 2003), 293–324; Kurt Rasim Güner, "The Origins of Islamic Legal Theory: The Traditionalist and Western perspectives," *Utah Historical Review* 4 (2014): 205–226.

[6] John Hursh, "The Role of Culture in the Creation of Islamic Law," *Indiana Law Journal* 84, no. 4 (2009): 1423.

A. Conception of Law

One fundamental question revolves around the early conception of law: was there any idea of law when the Prophet Muhammad received the divine revelation, or did it develop only later, and if so, which factors contributed to its evolution? With regard to the legal content of the Qur'an, which contains between eighty to six hundred rulings in the narrow sense, it is postulated that there emerged a particularly Islamic conception of law already in Muhammad's time.[7] According to this perspective an Islamic conception of law is inherent in the revelation text on the basis of which it was systematically developed by pious scholars. Other scholars point to the ambiguity and change in meaning that central legal terms such as *fiqh*,[8] *ra'y*,[9] or *shari'a*[10] underwent in the early centuries of Islam. The fact that western scholars tended to apply western terms and their specific connotations to the Islamic system of normativity—the term "Islamic law" (or, *droit islamique, diritto islamico, islamisches Recht*, etc.) is in fact an invention by European scholars,[11] but will be used in this context in the more general sense of Islamic normativity—confused rather than elucidated the discussion on that issue.

The discourse on the early conception of Islamic law is largely focussed on the role that the four-sources scheme, the core of Islamic legal theory, played in the elaboration of substantive law. In its classical form, the scheme determines the hierarchy of sources: Qur'an as the basic revelation text represents the primary source, followed by Sunna as the secondary source. In case these material sources leave room for speculation, the consensus of the scholars (*ijma'*) becomes binding. Only if there is no explicit ruling in Qur'an and Sunna and no *ijma* can be reached, analogy (*qiyas*) is allowed. While being fully established in the tenth or eleventh century at the latest, the question remains to what extent the four-sources scheme was developed and applied by the Prophet and his successors.

Closely related to the question of legal conception, but no less disputed, is the relationship between state and law. Most scholars, both traditionalists and skeptics, take the view that Islamic law from the beginning—that is after the Prophet's death—was a jurists' law, evolving more or less independently of the state.[12] According to

[7] George-Henri Bousquet, "Le mystère de la formation et des origins du fiqh," in *Revue Algérienne, Tunisienne et Marocaine de Législation et de Jurisprudence* 63 (1947): 66–81; Wael Hallaq, *The Origins and Evolution of Islamic Law* (Cambridge: Cambridge University Press, 2005), 4, 31–32, 195; Wael Hallaq, *A History of Islamic Legal Theories* (Cambridge: Cambridge University Press, 1997).

[8] Joseph Schacht, "Art. Fiḳh," *Encyclopaedia of Islam*, II, 886; see also Tilman Nagel, *Das islamische Recht. Eine Einführung* (Westhofen: WVA Skulima, 2001), 171, 184.

[9] Jeanette Wakin and Aaron Zysow, "Art. Ra'y," *Encyclopaedia of Islam*, Supplement (Leiden: Brill 2004), 687.

[10] Norman Calder, "Art. Sharīʿa," *Encyclopaedia of Islam*, IX, 321.

[11] Baudouin Dupret and Leon Buskens, "L'invention du droit musulman. Genèse et diffusion du positivisme juridique dans le contexte normatif islamique," in *Après l'orientalisme: l'orient crée par l'orient*, ed. François Pouillon (Paris: Karthala, 2011), 71–92.

[12] Hallaq, *Origins*, 204.

another perspective, however, the state, in particular the Umayyad[13] and/or early Abbasid[14] caliphate had a considerable impact on legal development, introducing a great number of rulings not contained in Qur'an and Sunna. Only later, when caliphal power diminished, did the domain of law become exclusively reserved for independent scholars (*ulama*).

B. Pre-Islamic Tribal Law

Muslims make a clear distinction between the Islamic and pre-Islamic eras, the latter also called *jahiliyya* (era of ignorance). Islamic law is regarded as a new legal system that in principle has no foundation in the time of ignorance. Nevertheless some elements of Islamic law are supposed to go back to Arab tribal law. In a few cases the Prophet himself is reported to have accepted some customs practiced by pre-Islamic Arab tribes. However, due to the scarcity of sources, scholars disagree about the extent of that transfer, some of them assuming that tribal law formed part of a broader legal culture in the Near East. This would mean that elements of foreign legal systems could well have entered Islamic law by way of tribal law. By any means, there seems to be unanimity as to tribal law representing a significant potential foundation of early Islamic law and therefore deserving to be studied in detail.[15]

C. Islamic Substantive Law

Many studies deal with the origins and early development of particular institutions of Islamic substantive law such as property,[16] ritual,[17] endowment,[18] inheritence,[19] debt bondage,[20] and patronage,[21] each covering only a small part of the vast and

[13] Patricia Crone, *God's Caliph. Religious Authority in the First Centuries of Islam* (Cambridge: Cambridge University Press, 1986), 45–46.

[14] Benjamin Jokisch, *Islamic Imperial Law. Hārūn al-Rashīd's Codification Project* (Berlin/New York: De Gruyter, 2007), 261ff.

[15] Carlo Nallino, "Considerazioni sui rapporti fra diritto romano e diritto musulmano," *Raccolta di scritti editi e inediti*, Rome 4 (1942): 85–94; G. Bergsträsser, "Anfänge und Charakter des juristischen Denkens im Islam. Vorläufige Betrachtungen," *Der Islam* 14 (1925): 80.

[16] Hiroyuki Yanagihashi, *A History of the Early Islamic Law of Property. Reconstructing the Legal Development, 7th–9th Centuries* (Leiden: Brill, 2004).

[17] Arent Wensinck, "Die Entstehung der islamischen Reinheitsgesetzgebung," *Der Islam* 5 (1914): 62–80.

[18] Carl H. Becker, "Zur Entstehung der Waqfinstitution," *Der Islam* 2 (1911): 404–405.

[19] David Powers, *Studies in Qur'ān and Ḥadīth: The Formation of the Islamic Law of Inheritance* (Berkeley: University of California Press, 1986).

[20] Irene Schneider, *Kinderverkauf und Schuldknechtschaft. Untersuchungen zur frühen Phase des islamischen Rechts* (Stuttgart: K.F. Steiner, 1999).

[21] Crone, *Roman, Provincial and Islamic Law.*

highly heterogeneous field. Depending on the degree of authenticity accorded to legal traditions, the reconstruction of the institutions is based either on the *hadith* material, which we will call a "traditionalist" approach, or on comparative analysis, the latter starting from the premise that Islamic institutions that bear similarity to foreign legal systems must have been borrowed sometime in the formative period. The comparative approach, by its nature, tends to undermine the legitimacy of Islamic law, and up to the present provokes criticism by the opposite camp. One of the arguments put forward against the comparative approach—most recently by Wael Hallaq[22]—is inspired by a growing criticism of Orientalism, emphasizing the biases of most western Orientalists. But this provoked reactions from comparativists, as may be seen in a counterstatement by David Powers,[23] who tries to defend the scientific and non-ideological character of western studies in the field. Apart from the ideological argument, the traditionalists usually point to the indigenous character of Islamic law, which they regard as completely different both in content and in structure from neighboring legal systems. Similarities may be explained by convergent developments independent of foreign influences. Furthermore, it is the lack of textual evidence—both with regard to the borrowed material and the circumstances of borrowing—that puts comparative analysis in question. In response, adherents of the comparative hypothesis point to the interaction and entanglement of cultures in early Islam, which necessarily implies a transfer of knowledge. Many comparative studies have unveiled a bulk of similarities which, in the comparativists' opinion, indicate reception.[24] As a result the origins of most of the institutions of substantive law remain controversial, being essentially Islamic for one camp and non-Islamic for the other.

D. Institutions of Learning and Judiciary

While it is generally accepted that legal institutions such as judgeship, market inspection, etc. witnessed a considerable maturation in the formative period as integral parts of the emerging Islamic state,[25] the details of this development as well as the provenance of the institutions remain controversial. Apart from its formal aspects, the institution of an Islamic judiciary highlights the practical aspects of law, because jurists, by deciding on concrete cases, demonstrate a penchant for

[22] Hallaq, *Origins*.

[23] David Powers, "Wael B. Hallaq on the Origins of Islamic Law: A Review Essay," *Islamic Law and Society* 17 (2010): 126–157.

[24] For a survey of comparative studies see Crone, *Roman, Provincial and Islamic Law*, preface. More recent studies are: Irene Schneider, *Kinderverkauf und Schuldknechtschaft. Untersuchungen zur frühen Phase des islamischen Rechts* (Stuttgart: K.F. Steiner, 1999); Jokisch, *Islamic Imperial Law*.

[25] Émile Tyan, *Histoire de l'organisation judiciaire en pays d'Islam* (Leiden: Brill, 1960).

modifying law and adapting it to real life. But since we do not have court records and other legal documents from the formative period it is difficult to get deeper insight into the field of legal practice, which presumably would have shed light on the early development of Islamic normativity.

Another significant phenomenon contributing to the institutionalization of Islamic law is the law school (*madhhab*). This institution gave rise to a number of specialized studies[26] describing its evolution from loose circles of pious scholars in the eighth century via personal schools to highly professionalized doctrinal schools organized in colleges (*madaris*) in the tenth century. As to the regional character of the earliest schools and their transformation into personal schools, there is a fierce debate, notably between Wael Hallaq[27] and Christopher Melchert,[28] the former emphasizing a transfer from non-regional schools oriented around individual juristic doctrines to schools oriented around the doctrines of like-minded scholars. While the details of this development, which goes far beyond the formative period in the narrow sense, as well as the interdependence of the different law schools—including Shiʿi institutions of learning—still need to be investigated, scholars agree upon the tremendous impact that these academic platforms had on the elaboration of Islamic law.

II. Traditionalists Versus Skeptics

In the following, the origins and evolution of Islamic law will be outlined according to the approaches of the traditionalists and skeptics respectively, admitting that many of the approaches have to be placed somewhere between the two poles. While the former group tends to accept the sources as more or less authentic, the latter shows a more critical attitude towards many early sources. Interestingly, the fronts are not so much between Muslim insiders and non-Muslim outsiders, but rather between revisionists and anti-revisionists within the western camp. In fact, the debate is fueled by a dialectical process of developing and refining *hadith*-critical

[26] George Makdisi, *The Rise of Colleges. Institutions of Learning in Islam and the West* (Edinburgh: Edinburgh University Press, 1981); Miklos Muranyi, *Beiträge zur Geschichte der Ḥadīt- und Rechtsgelehrsamkeit der Mālikiyya in Nordafrika bis zum 5. Jh. D.H.* (Wiesbaden: Reichert, 1997); Christopher Melchert, *The Formation of the Sunnī Schools of Law, 9th—10th Centuries C.E.* (Leiden: Brill, 1997).

[27] Wael Hallaq, "From Regional to Personal Schools of Law? A Reevaluation," *Islamic Law and Society* 8 (2001): 3. See also Nimrod Hurvitz, "Schools of Law and Historical Context. Re-examining the Formation of the Ḥanbalī *Madhhab*," *Islamic Law and Society* 7 (2001): 42–46.

[28] Melchert, *The Formation of the Sunnī Schools of Law*, 32–47.

methods encouraged by the increase of available sources since the second half of the nineteenth century. In the following, the focus is on the extreme positions, although members of each camp nuance and modify these positions in creative and substantive ways.

A. Traditionalists

The early history of Islamic law as exposited by many Muslim scholars[29] as well as by western Islamicists[30] such as E. Sachau, A. v. Kremer, A. Sprenger, or D. Margoliouth essentially follows the pattern given by the four sources of law: Qur'an, Sunna, *ijma'*, and *qiyas*. Starting from the premise that there existed from the beginning a specifically Islamic idea of law, scholars of the traditionalist wing take the four-sources scheme as reflective of a more or less authentic description of early legal development.[31] After coming down step-by-step to the Prophet Muhammad, the legal content of the Qur'an was very soon put into practice. Since the number of explicit Qur'anic rulings was limited, the Prophet, through his words and actions, established new precedents, interpreted and complemented the revelation text, accepting, whenever compatible, the validity of pre-Islamic customs. The great bulk of prophetic sayings, deeds, and acknowledgements (*sunna*), which in quantity by far surpass the Qur'anic rulings, represent the second material source of Islamic law. This means that both sources, closely connected in authority and supporting each other, and already established in the lifetime of the Prophet, formed the essential basis for a more detailed elaboration of law after Muhammad's death.

The main task of the succeeding generation, known as "the Companions," was to preserve the prophetic heritage, and transmit it to later generations. Along with their immediate successors, the *tabi'un*, they represent the link between the Prophet at the beginning of the seventh century and the founders of the first law schools emerging in the second half of the eighth century. While they themselves didn't leave any contemporary texts disclosing the quantity of transmissions and quality of the transmitters, their closeness to the Prophet (*suhba*) is taken to prove their reliability. At the same time, they are credited with a particular knowledge of early Islamic law that helped them to exercise the highest degree of *ijtihad* (use of

29 Muḥammad Khuḍarī al-, *Tārīkh al-tashrīʿ al-islāmī* (Beirut: Dar al-Kutub al-ʿIlmiyya, 1985).

30 Eduard Sachau, "Zur ältesten Geschichte des muhammedanischen Rechts," in *Sitzungsberichte der Kaiserlichen Akademie der Wissenschaften in Wien, Phil.-Historische Klasse*, vol. 65, 699–723; Alois v. Kremer, *Culturgeschichte des Orients unter den Chalifen* (Wien: W. Braumüller, 1875), vol. 1, 470–504; Alois Sprenger, "Eine Skizze der Entwicklungsgeschichte des muslimischen Gesetzes," in *Zeitschrift für vergleichende Rechtswissenschaft* 10 (1892): 1–31; David Margoliouth, *The Early Development of Mohammedanism* (London: C. Scribner's Sons, 1914).

31 M. Bakar, "The Origins of Islamic Legal Theory (uṣūl al-fiqh)," *Intellectual Discourse* 5 (1997): 121–144.

individual reasoning) and to find adequate legal solutions to new cases. This latter procedure, in the time of the Companions, implies the observation of the four sources in a strictly hierarchical order: the revelation text comes first, and, if there is no ruling in the Qur'an, the prophetic Sunna has to be examined. Only then, if this hierarchical search proves unsuccessful, the Companion may turn to *ra'y* (personal opinion), which may potentially form the basis for *ijma'* (consensus). For proving the historicity of this procedure, scholars usually point to a famous, but highly controversial, tradition in which the Companion Mu'adh b. Jabal (d. 640) is told by the Prophet to proceed in this way.[32]

In spite of the methodological frame given by the four-sources scheme, the Companions often disagreed on particular cases, so that *ikhtilaf* (disagreement) became a characteristic element of early Islamic law. This is essentially due to the fact that the Companions split in two groups, one remaining in Medina and the other migrating to the provinces of the new caliphate. While the Medinese (later called *ahl al-hadith*/people of *hadith*) were theoretically closer to the practice of the Prophet, the other Companions, most of them Iraqis (later called *ahl al-ra'y*/ people of personal opinion) and living under conditions quite different from the Medinese, tended to derive law more freely. All of them, however—and this is true also for all succeeding generations—elaborated early Islamic law more or less independently of any political encroachment, establishing the evolving legal system as a jurists' law.[33]

What followed in the eighth and ninth centuries—the final stage of the formative period—is the collecting, systematizing and, to a certain degree, writing down of legal knowledge consisting of traditions and rulings derived from the material sources. This process, called the era of *talab al-'ilm* (search for knowledge), eventually resulted in the emergence of law schools, which in many respects—both in

[32] Jokisch, *Islamic Imperial Law*, 243, 526 (however, the element of consensus does not occur in this tradition).

[33] The characterization of Islamic law as a jurists' law is common to both the traditionalist and the skeptic view: Crone, *God's Caliph*, 87; Baber Johansen, *Islam und Staat* (Berlin: Argument, 1982), 9; Tamara Sonn, "The State and the Sacred in Classical Islamic Thought," in *Religion and the Political Order. Politics in Classical and Contemporary Christianity, Islam, and Judaism*, ed. J. Neusner (Atlanta: Scholars Press, 1996), 216; H. Motzki, "Die Entstehung des Rechts," in *Der islamische Orient—Grundzüge seiner Geschichte*, ed. A. Noth et al. (Würzburg: Ergon-Verlag, 1998), 167, 171; J. Schacht, *An Introduction to Islamic Law* (Oxford: Clarendon Press, 1984), 28, 209–210; Ira Lapidus, "The Separation of State and Religion in the Development of Early Islamic Society," *International Journal of Middle East Studies* 6 (1975), 369; N. Coulson, *A History of Islamic Law* (Edinburgh: Edinburgh University Press, 1964), 52; Dominque Sourdel, "Gouvernement et administration dans l'orient Islamique jusqu'au milieu du XIe siècle," in *Handbuch der Orientalistik* Abteilung 1: Der Nahe und Mittlere Osten/Vol. 6: Geschichte der islamischen Länder/Abschnitt 5: Regierung und Verwaltung des Vorderen Orients in islamischer Zeit/Part 2, 34; N. Calder, *Studies in Early Muslim Jurisprudence* (Oxford: Oxford University Press, 1993), 220; Aharon Layish, "The Transformation of the Sharī'a from Jurists' Law to Statutory Law in the Contemporary Muslim World," *Welt des Islam* 44 (2004): 86; Sami Zubaida, *Law and Power in the Islamic World* (London: I.B. Tauris, 2003), 82.

substantive law and legal theory—differ from each other, but nevertheless share the foundation set by the Prophet and the Companions.

B. Skeptics

One of the first scholars to criticize the traditionalist picture of the early legal evolution in Islam just described is I. Goldziher.[34] By doubting the authenticity of legal traditions he sketched a legal development that, instead of following the *usul*-pattern mentioned above, was strongly exposed to external factors such as *ra'y* and, no less important, the influence of foreign legal systems, particularly Roman law. The development of Islamic law, in his opinion, did not start until the mid-eighth century while the first Islamic century remains in obscurity. *Ra'y*, defined as independent legal reasoning of the Companions and their successors, did not evolve from the divine sources but preceded them, with the consequence that the majority of legal traditions must be qualified as fabrications.

Somewhat later, after the Second World War, a more elaborate version of Goldziher's approach was presented by J. Schacht.[35] Starting from the radical premise that all legal traditions have to be considered spurious until the contrary is proved, he turned upside down the traditionalist picture of early Islamic law. He developed a complex *hadith*-critical method for proving the continuous growth of *isnads* (chains of transmitters), concluding that the traditions, in fact, were produced ex post facto. Just like Goldziher he regarded Islamic jurisprudence as non-existent before the first quarter of the eighth century. It was the ancient schools of law centered in Kufa, Basra, Mecca, Medina, and Damascus and represented by scholars such as Hammad b. Abi Sulayman (d. 738), al-Zuhri (d. 742), and Malik b. Anas (d. 795) that showed the first attempt to develop a legal system inspired by general Islamic ethics. However, the role of Qur'an and Sunna was limited and gained in importance only step by step. The pious scholars largely relied on their personal opinion, taking recourse to the legal practice of conquered peoples, and the decrees and decisions of the caliphs. It is in that time that elements of foreign legal systems such as Roman (provincial) law, Jewish law, Canon law, and even Babylonian law entered the Islamic legal system—most probably by way of converts who had some knowledge of rhetoric. What the ancient schools produced is the so-called "living tradition," which in the second half of the eighth century became the object of

[34] Ignaz Goldziher, "Fiḳh," in *Enzyclopaedie des Islam*, 1st edn., vol. 2 (Leiden/Leipzig: Brill, 1924), 106–111.

[35] Joseph Schacht, *The Origins of Muhammadan Jurisprudence* (Oxford: Clarendon Press, 1959); Schacht, *An Introduction to Islamic Law*; Joseph Schacht, "Pre-Islamic Background and Early Development of Jurisprudence," in *Law in the Middle East, vol. 1: Origin and Development of Islamic Law*, ed. M. Khadduri et al. (Washington: The Middle East Institute, 1955), 28–56.

harsh criticism advanced by a growing movement of traditionalists. The process that followed may be described, according to Schacht, as a conflict between the ancient schools of law on one side and the traditionalists on the other, all of them competing for religious authority. Challenged by the traditionalists who brought into circulation formal traditions opposed to the living tradition, the ancient schools of law in turn projected their decisions back to early Muslim authorities—first to the successors, then to the Companions, and finally to the Prophet. In the second half of the ninth century, the overriding importance of prophetic tradition was explicitly formulated in the *Risala* of al-Shafi'i (d. 820), the first extant work on Islamic legal theory.[36] It is in this way that Companions such as Ibn Mas'ud, Hasan al-Basri, and the "seven lawyers of Medina" were made out to be the earliest specialists of Islamic law. At the same time the ancient schools of law—originally anonymous in character—turned into personal schools associated with eponyms, such as Abu Hanifa (d. 767) for the 'Iraqis, and Malik b. Anas for the Medinese. According to Schacht, these eponyms also mark the beginning of the literary period of Islamic law. To justify his view of the early legal development, and particularly his critical approach to the sources, Schacht presented a number of arguments that may be summarized as follows:

The early sources used by Schacht seem to point to the priority of traditions traced back to successors, followed by those attributed to Companions. Prophetic traditions came to play a role only later after the beginning of the literary period of Islamic law. The criterion used by Schacht for determining the priority of specific traditions is quantity: the more traditions going back to successors found in the texts, the more importance must be credited to this category of traditions. Since the quantity of successor traditions supersedes that of Companion traditions, Schacht concludes that successor traditions must have been regarded as most important at the beginning of the conflict between traditionalists and the ancient schools of law, followed later by the Companion traditions and prophetic traditions respectively.

By investigating the earliest legal discourses on specific topics, Schacht argued that the relevant prophetic traditions contained in later *hadith* collections were not used by the early scholars. According to the *argumentum e silentio*, Schacht concluded that the relevant prophetic traditions did not yet exist at the time that their legal injunctions were being practiced. In a second step, he generalized the results of his investigation by declaring all traditions to be spurious, assigning the burden of proof to those who claim prophetic traditions to be authentic.

It was only after the first quarter of the eighth century that traditions were formalized by introducing *isnad*s (chains of transmitters). This conclusion is primarily based on two traditions which, according to Schacht's interpretation, seem to point to a regular use of *isnad*s only after the second Islamic century.

[36] While Schacht presupposes al-Shafi'i's Risala to be authentic, later Orientalists raise some doubt as to the originality and import of this work (Calder *Studies*, 67; W. Hallaq, "Was al-Shāfiʿī the Master Architect of Islamic Jurisprudence?," *International Journal of Middle East Studies* 25 (1993): 587–605.

By analyzing *isnads*, Schacht—and after him in some more detail, G.H.A. Juynboll[37]—detected that most of the traditions prove to be single-stranded in the first three or four generations; that is, in the first generations after the Prophet, the scholars seemingly used to transmit traditions to no more than one person. Only then did the transmitters—called *common links*—begin to hand down the traditions to several persons. This phenomenon is interpreted by Schacht as pointing to the period (lifetime of the *common link*) in which the traditions were brought into circulation. Accordingly, the great bulk of traditions were deemed to have come into being in the second half of the eighth century or later.

III. Assessment

Both approaches, traditionalist as well as skeptic, gave rise to criticism, which in fact contributed to bringing the contrary positions closer to each other. In the same way as the mechanical projection of the four-sources scheme to the early period of Islamic law, as described by the traditionalists, in many respects proves untenable, the wholesale rejection of traditions, as postulated by Schacht and other skeptics, provoked more cautious and more sophisticated approaches to the *hadith* material. The most important objections to each of the approaches may be summarized as follows.

A. Critical Aspects of the Skeptic View

Schacht restricted himself to a small selection of legal works, which he accepted as authentic sources. Apart from the fact that, in the last few decades, more early works—particularly in the field of Maliki law[38]—have been discovered and edited, Schacht's selection and interpretation of sources seems arbitrary. For instance, he regards the reports attributed to Abu Hanifa as authentic although this latter scholar himself didn't leave any legal work. In the same way Schacht relies upon a tradition of Ibn Sirin (d. 729) concerning the first use of *isnads*. In this special case he accepts the tradition, because it seems to confirm his conviction that *isnads* came into being only in the second quarter of the eighth century.

37 G.H.A. Juynboll, *Muslim Tradition* (Cambridge: Cambridge University Press, 1983).

38 Miklos Muranyi, *Ein altes Fragment medinensischer Jurisprudenz aus Qairawān. Aus dem K. al-ḥağğ des ʿAbd al-ʿAzīz b. ʿAbd Allāh b. Abī Salama al-Māğišūn* (Stuttgart: Harrassowitz, 1985).

According to Schacht there was no specifically Islamic conception of law before the beginning of the eighth century. He strictly ignores the indications in the traditions, but also in the relevation text, pointing to the legal reforms introduced by the Prophet. The same applies to central terms such as *fiqh*, *sunna*, or *ra'y*, which well may be interpreted as having a specifically Islamic connotations.[39]

The *e silentio* argument, adduced by Schacht, does not necessarily prove the non-existence of a tradition at a certain time. According to Azami[40] there are many reasons (simple ignorance, loss of works in which the report is mentioned, etc.), why a report was not mentioned in a legal discourse, or why it may not be found.

Schacht's *hadith*-critical method is almost exclusively focussed on the *isnad*, ignoring the *matn* (text of tradition). But formal defects do not necessarily imply defects in content. As H. Motzki's *isnad-cum-matn* analysis shows,[41] there is good reason to analyze traditions both in form and in content. By comparing the different strands of a tradition—including those with considerable textual variants—he found out that the text of the tradition shows specific features within each strand and sub-strand. Since it is unimaginable that all the transmitters agreed on using specific textual features in each strand, he concludes that this tradition must be authentic. It is on the basis of this *hadith*-critical method that Motzki is able to disprove Schacht's conviction that all traditions *a priori* have to be regarded as spurious. On the other hand the use of this method is limited because most of the traditions are single stranded in the first generations and even common links may be exposed as only seemingly common links.[42]

B. Critical Aspects of the Traditionalist View

Anti-revisionist reactions to the hypotheses of Schacht and his followers did not lead, however, to the unreserved acceptance of the traditionalist view. Though it may be possible that legal development in Muhammad's lifetime and afterwards had a more or less Islamic foundation, the question remains, to what extent did other factors contribute to the early formation of Islamic law? Many traditions in fact do not meet Muslim *hadith* criticism standards as laid down in works on *'ilm al-hadith* (science of hadith),[43] and there is even a specific literary genre in classical Islam

[39] M. Bravmann, *The Spiritual Background of Early Islam* (Leiden: Brill, 1972).

[40] Muhammad Mustafa Azami al-, *On Schacht's Origins of Muhammadan Jurisprudence* (Lahore: Suhail Academy, 2004), 118–119.

[41] Mitter, *Das frühislamische Patronat*, 11–12.

[42] Stephen Shoemaker, "In search of 'Urwa's *sīra*: Some methodological issues in the quest for 'authenticity' in the life of Muḥammad," *Der Islam* 85 (2008): 266. Melchert, "The Early History of Islamic Law," 303: see also Gautier H. Juynboll, *Encyclopedia of Canonical Hadith* (Leiden: Brill, 2007), preface.

[43] Benjamin Jokisch, *Islamisches Recht in Theorie und Praxis. Analyse einiger kaufrechtlicher Fatwas von Taqī'd-Dīn Aḥmad b. Taymiyya* (Berlin: Klaus Schwartz, 1996), 256–257.

for collecting forged traditions (*kutub al-mawdu'at*) or weak transmitters (*kutub al-du'afa'*). Furthermore, Shi'is and Sunnis—and even the different sub-groups within the two confessions—in a number of fields (inheritance law, family law) rely upon mutually exclusive traditions. Consequently, it is generally accepted that at least parts of the *hadith* material have to be treated with caution.[44] The same applies to legal theory, the details of which didn't become manifest until the tenth or eleventh century. The fact that there was a considerable disagreement amongst early jurists in deciding single cases—and this is clearly confirmed in the *Risala*[45] of Ibn al-Muqaffa' (d. 758), one of the few works of the pre-literary period generally accepted as authentic—seems to point to a vast spectrum of conflicting sources and methods used by these jurists. We may suppose the heterogeneous character of early Islamic law allowed tremendous leeway in formulating new precedents.[46]

It is particularly in this context of accommodating and adjusting law to new circumstances that the legal systems of conquered peoples come into play. To what extent, we may ask, was it regarded as "non-Islamic" in that time to take recourse to elements of "foreign" law? Apart from the fact that customary law, when compatible with Islamic ethics, was approved by some early jurists, the clear predominance of non-Islamic laws within the early caliphate, the growing number of converts, and, last but not least, the general openness to foreign cultures, seem to be strong arguments for potential legal transfer—a phenomenon that may be observed in many other cultures as well.[47] But this does not necessarily mean that the bulk of similarities presented by the proponents of legal interaction[48] may be taken as indicative of foreign influence. With regard to the complexity of the legal systems involved, the diversity of sources (Greek, Pahlavi, Syriac, Aramaic, Hebrew, etc.) and the lack of appropriate methods for proving legal transfers, it is difficult to reconstruct the entanglement of laws in the early Islamic period. The fact that proponents of foreign influence often trace back one and the same institution to different roots—so, for instance, that the four-sources scheme or parts of it are taken from Roman[49] and

[44] Schneider, *Kinderverkauf und Schuldknechtschaft*, 65.

[45] C. Pellat, *"Ibn al-Muqaffa' conseilleur" du calife* (Paris: Maisonneuve et Larose, 1976), 41.

[46] So the outstanding Hanafi jurist Muhammad al-Shaybani (d. 805) is reported to have derived about 27,000 rulings by way of analogy (Jokisch, *Islamic Imperial Law*, 32, 78).

[47] Allan Watson, *Legal Transplants. An Approach to Comparative Law* (Charlottesville: University Press of Virginia, 1974); Watson, *The Evolution of Law* (Baltimore: Johns Hopkins University Press, 1985).

[48] Joseph Schacht, "Vom babylonischen zum islamischen Recht," *Orientalistische Literaturzeitung* 30 (1927): 664–669; Joseph Schacht, "Foreign Elements in Ancient Islamic Law," *Memoires de l'Academie International de Droit Comparé* 3 (1955): 127–141; for a summary of parallels see Mitter, *Das frühislamische Patronat*, 19–84; Crone, *Roman, Provincial and Islamic Law*, 103–108; Antonio D'Emilia, "Il diritto musulmano comparato con il bizantino dal punto di vista della tipologia del diritto," *Studia Islamica* 4 (1955): 57–76; Antonio D'Emilia, "Roman Law and Muslim Law. A Comparative Outline," *East and West* 4 (1953): 73–80.

[49] Schacht, *Introduction*, 20.

Jewish law[50]—raises suspicion,[51] and requires more conclusive methods of comparison.[52]

Starting from the premise that legal transfer may have taken place not only accidently and unconsciously (*en voie diffuse*), but also on the basis of texts (*en voie érudite*), it is necessary to compare in detail potentially interlinked texts with regard to cases, terms, formulations, arguments, and structures. Unlike general similarities, the congruency of a bundle of highly specific features may be taken to indicate legal interaction. As a consequence, before conducting comparative studies on a broad, systematic, and interdisciplinary basis it would be rash to reject out of hand the possibility of legal transfer.

IV. Future Research

About 150 years after the emergence of the first studies on the origins of Islamic law the topic still represents a highly fascinating, but also controversial, object of research. As is apparent in the most recent research, the central problem of sources and their authenticity remains unsolved. At the same time, we observe an increasing number of studies taking a middle position between the camps. In fact the seemingly contrary positions need not necessarily be interpreted as incompatible, since the major part of substantive law, manifest in the first extant legal works, is not covered by the *hadith* material anyway or, no less important, forms the object of *ikhtilaf* (disagreement). Islamic law, when defined in a broader sense as a continuous process of interaction between the divine sources on one side and eager human beings on the other—and not as a corpus of fixed precepts—leaves much room for formulating, changing, and refining concrete rulings, and this is what most probably also happened in the formative period.

[50] Judith Wegner, "Islamic and Talmudic Jurisprudence: The Four Roots of Islamic Law and their Talmudic Counterparts," *American Journal of Legal History* 26 (1982): 25–71.

[51] Wael Hallaq, "The Use and Abuse of Evidence," *Journal of the American Oriental Society* 110 (1990): 79–91; Mitter, *Das frühislamische Patronat*, 86, 89; Ze'ev Maghen, "First blood. Purity, Edibility, and the Independence of Islamic Jurisprudence," *Der Islam* 81 (2004): 49–95; Gamal Moursi Badr, "Islamic Law: Its Relation to Other Legal Systems," *The American Journal of Comparative Law* 26 (1978): 187–198.

[52] Some first criteria for analyzing legal transfer are mentioned in Gustave v. Grunebaum, "The Problem of Cultural Influence," in *Islam and Medieval Hellenism: Social and Cultural Perspectives*, ed. D. Wilson (London: Variorum, 1976), VIII, 86–99; Jokisch, *Islamic Imperial Law*, 11–50; Fritz Pringsheim, "Reception," *Revue International des Droits de l'Antiquité* 8 (1961): 243–255; Max Rheinstein, "Types of Reception," *Annales de la Faculté de Droit d'Istanbul* 6 (1956): 31–40; Alan Watson, "Aspects of Reception of Law," *American Journal of Comparative Law* 44 (1996): 335–351.

The complexity of the subject has shown that there is a growing need for interdisciplinary work, particularly in the field of legal transfer. Not only Islamicists, historians, and shariʿa experts—Muslims as well as non-Muslims—but also specialists in other religious legal systems are requested to collaborate in common research platforms, starting from the premise that Islamic legal culture developed in a multicultural context. This approach, which closely correlates with most recent theories on cultural transfer,[53] is not intended to be opposed to, but rather complementary to, specialization tendencies in *hadith* research, which deserves the same attention in the near future.

References

Azami al-, Muhammad, *On Schacht's Origins of Muḥammadan Jurisprudence* (Lahore: Suhail Academy, 2004).

Badr, Gamal Moursi. "Islamic law: Its Relation to Other Legal Systems." *The American Journal of Comparative Law* 26 (1978): 187–198.

Bakar, M., "The Origins of Islamic Legal Theory (uṣūl al-fiqh)." *Intellectual Discourse* 5 (1997): 121–144.

Becker, Carl H., "Zur Entstehung der Waqfinstitution." *Der Islam* 2 (1911): 404–405.

Bergsträsser, Gotthelf, "Anfänge und Charakter des juristischen Denkens im Islam. Vorläufige Betrachtungen." *Der Islam* 14 (1925): 76–81.

Bousquet, George-Henri, "Le mystère de la formation et des origins du fiqh." *Revue Algérienne, Tunisienne et Marocaine de Législation et de Jurisprudence* 63 (1947): 66–81.

Bravmann, M., *The Spiritual Background of Early Islam* (Leiden: Brill, 1972).

Calder, Norman, *Studies in Early Muslim Jurisprudence* (Oxford: Oxford University Press, 1993).

Cilardo, Agostino, *Teorie sulle origine del diritto islamico* (Rome: Istituto per l'Oriente, 1990).

Coulson, Noel, *A History of Islamic Law* (Edinburgh: Edinburgh University Press, 1964).

Crone, Patricia, *God's Caliph. Religious Authority in the First Centuries of Islam* (Cambridge: Cambridge University Press, 1986).

Crone, Patricia, *Roman, Provincial and Islamic law. The Origins of the Islamic Patronate* (Cambridge: Cambridge University Press, 1987).

D'Emilia, Antonio, "Roman Law and Muslim Law. A Comparative Outline." *East and West* 4 (1953): 73–80.

D'Emilia, Antonio, "Il diritto musulmano comparato con il bizantino dal punto di vista della tipologia del diritto." *Studia Islamica* 4 (1955): 57–76.

Dupret, Baudouin and Buskens, Leon, "L'invention du droit musulman. Genèse et diffusion du positivisme juridique dans le contexte normatif islamique" in François Pouillon (ed.) *Après l'orientalisme: l'orient crée par l'orient.* (Paris: Karthala, 2011) 71–92.

[53] Jörg Feuchter, ed. *Cultural Transfers in Dispute: Representations in Asia, Europe and the Arab World Since the Middle Ages* (Frankfurt: Campus, 2011).

Dutton, Yasin, *The Origins of Islamic Law. The Qur'ān, the Muwaṭṭa' and Madinan 'Amal* (Surrey: Curzon, 1999).
Feuchter, Jörg, ed. *Cultural Transfers in Dispute: Representations in Asia, Europe and the Arab World Since the Middle Ages* (Frankfurt: Campus, 2011).
Fierro, Maribel, "Nuevas perpectivas sobre la formaciòn del derecho islàmico." *al-Qanṭara* 21 (2000): 511–523.
Fyzee, Asaf, *Outlines of Muḥammadan Law* (Oxford: Oxford University Press, 1964).
Goldziher, Ignaz, *Muhammedanische Studien*. vol. 2. Leipzig, 1890.
Goldziher, Ignaz Fiḳh, *Enzyclopaedie des Islam*. 1st edn., vol. 2 (Leiden/Leipzig: Brill, 1924) 106–111.
v. Grunebaum, Gustave, "The Problem of Cultural Influence" in D. Wilson (ed.) *Islam and Medieval Hellenism: Social and Cultural Perspectives*, VIII (London: Variourum, 1976) 86–99.
Güner, Kurt Rasim, "The Origins of Islamic Legal Theory: The Traditionalist and Western Perspectives." *Utah Historical Review* 4 (2014): 205–226.
Hallaq, Wael, "The Use and Abuse of Evidence." *Journal of the American Oriental Society* 110 (1990): 79–91.
Hallaq, Wael, *A History of Islamic Legal Theories* (Cambridge: Cambridge University Press, 1997).
Hallaq, Wael, "From Regional to Personal Schools of Law? A Reevaluation." *Islamic Law and Society* 8 (2001): 1–16.
Hallaq, Wael, *The Origins and Evolution of Islamic Law* (Cambridge: Cambridge University Press, 2005).
Hallaq, Wael, "Was al-Shāfiʿī the Master Architect of Islamic Jurisprudence?" *International Journal of Middle East Studies* 25 (1993): 587–605.
Khuḍarī al-, Muḥammad, *Tārīkh al-tashrīʿ al-islāmī*. (Beirut: Dar al-Kutub al-'Ilmiyya, 1985).
Hursh, John, "The Role of Culture in the Creation of Islamic Law." *Indiana Law Journal* 84, no. 4 (2009): 1401–1423.
Hurvitz, Nimrod, "Schools of Law and Historical Context. Re-examining the Formation of the Ḥanbalī *Madhhab*." *Islamic Law and Society* 7 (2001): 37–64.
Johansen, B., *Islam und Staat* (Berlin: Argument, 1982).
Jokisch, Benjamin, *Islamisches Recht in Theorie und Praxis. Analyse einiger kaufrechtlicher Fatwas von Taqī'd-Dīn Aḥmad b. Taymiyya* (Berlin: Klaus Schwartz, 1996).
Jokisch, Benjamin, *Islamic Imperial Law. Hārūn al-Rashīd's Codification Project* (Berlin/New York: De Gruyter, 2007).
Juynboll, G.H.A. *Muslim Tradition* (Cambridge: Cambridge University Press, 1983).
Juynboll, Gautier H., *Encyclopedia of Canonical Hadith* (Leiden: Brill, 2007).
Krawietz, Birgit, *Hierarchie der Rechtsquellen im tradierten sunnitischen Islam* (Berlin: Duncker & Humblot, 2002.
v. Kremer, *Alois Culturgeschichte des Orients unter den Chalifen* vol. 1, 470–504 (Wien: W. Braumüller, 1875).
Lapidus, Ira, "The Separation of State and Religion in the Development of Early Islamic Society." *International Journal od Middle East Studies* 6 (1975): 38–85.
Layish, Aharon, "The Transformation of the Sharīʿa from Jurists' Law to Statutory Law in the Contemporary Muslim World." *Welt des Islam* 44 (2004): 85–113.

Maghen, Z., "First Blood. Purity, Edibility, and the Independence of Islamic Jurisprudence." *Der Islam* 81 (2004): 49–95.
Makdisi, George, *The Rise of Colleges. Institutions of Learning in Islam and the West* (Edinburgh: Edinburgh University Press, 1981).
Margoliouth, David, *The Early Development of Mohammedanism* (London: C. Scribner's Sons, 1914).
Melchert, Christopher, *The Formation of the Sunnī Schools of Law, 9th–10th Centuries C.E* (Leiden: Brill, 1997).
Melchert, Christopher, "The Early History of Islamic Law" in H. Berg (ed.) *Method and Theory in the Study of Islamic Origins* (Leiden: Brill, 2003) 293–324.
Mitter, U., *Das frühislamische Patronat. Eine Untersuchung zur Rolle von fremden Einflüssen bei der Entwicklung des islamischen Rechts*. Nijmwegen, 1999.
Motzki, Harald, *Die Anfänge der islamischen Jurisprudenz. Ihre Entwicklung in Mekka bis zur Mitte des 2./8. Jahrhunderts* (Stuttgart: K.F. Steiner, 1991).
Motzki, Harald, "Quo vadis, Ḥadīt-Forschung? Eine kritische Untersuchung von G.H.A. Juynboll: 'Nāfi' the mawlā of Ibn 'Umar, and his Position in Muslim Ḥadīt literature.'" *Der Islam* 73 (1996): 40–80.
Motzki, Harald, "Die Entstehung des Rechts" in A. Noth et al. (eds.) *Der islamische Orient—Grundzüge seiner Geschichte* (Würzburg: Ergon-Verlag, 1998) 151–172.
Muranyi, Miklos, *Ein altes Fragment medinensischer Jurisprudenz aus Qairawān. Aus dem K. al-ḥağğ des 'Abd al-'Azīz b. 'Abd Allāh b. Abī Salama al-Māğišūn* (Stuttgart: Harrassow itz, 1985).
Muranyi, Miklos, *Beiträge zur Geschichte der Ḥadīt- und Rechtsgelehrsamkeit der Mālikiyya in Nordafrika bis zum 5. Jh. D.H* (Wiesbaden: Harrassowitz, 1997).
Nagel, Tilman, *Das islamische Recht. Eine Einführung* (Westhofen: WVA Skulima, 2001).
Nallino, Carlo, "Considerazioni sui rapporti fra diritto romano e diritto musulmano." *Raccolta di scritti editi e inediti* Rome 4 (1942): 85–94.
Pellat, C., *Ibn al-Muqaffa' "conseilleur" du calife* (Paris: Maisonneuve et Larose, 1976).
Picken, Gavin, "General Introduction" in Gavin Picken (ed.) *Islamic Law: Critical Concepts in Islamic Studies, Vol. 1: Origins and Sources* (London: Routledge, 2011) 1–29.
Powers, David, *Studies in Qur'ān and Ḥadīth: The Formation of the Islamic Law of Inheritance* (Berkeley: University of California Press, 1986).
Powers, David, "Wael B. Hallaq on the Origins of Islamic law: A Review Essay." *Islamic Law and Society* 17 (2010): 126–157.
Pringsheim, Fritz, "Reception." *Revue International des Droits de l'Antiquité* 8 (1961): 243–255.
Rheinstein, Max, "Types of Reception." *Annales de la Faculté de Droit d'Istanbul* 6 (1956): 31–40.
Sachau, Eduard, "Zur ältesten Geschichte des muhammedanischen Rechts." In *Sitzungsberichte der Kaiserlichen Akademie der Wissenschaften in Wien, Phil.-Historische Klasse*, vol. 65 (Wein: Akademie der Wissenschaften), 699–723.
Schacht, Joseph, "Vom babylonischen zum islamischen Recht." *Orientalistische Literaturzeitung* 30 (1927): 664–669.
Schacht, Joseph, "Foreign Elements in Ancient Islamic Law." *Memoires de l'Academie International de Droit Comparé* 3 (1955): 127–141.
Schacht, Joseph, "Pre-Islamic Background and Early Development of Jurisprudence" in M. Khadduri et al. (eds.) *Law in the Middle East, vol. 1: Origin and Development of Islamic Law* (Washington: The Middle East Institute, 1955) 28–56.

Schacht, Joseph, *The Origins of Muhammadan Jurisprudence* (Oxford: Clarendon Press, 1959).

Schacht, Joseph, *An Introduction to Islamic Law* (Oxford: Clarendon Press, 1984).

Schneider, Irene, *Kinderverkauf und Schuldknechtschaft. Untersuchungen zur frühen Phase des islamischen Rechts* (Stuttgart: K.F. Steiner, 1999).

Shoemaker, Stephen, "In Search of 'Urwa's *sīra:* Some Methodological Issues in the Quest for 'Authenticity' in the Life of Muḥammad." *Der Islam* 85 (2008): 257–344.

Sonn, Tamara, "The State and the Sacred in Classical Islamic Thought" in J. Neusner (ed.) *Religion and the Political Order. Politics in Classical and Contemporary Christianity, Islam, and Judaism* (Atlanta: Scholars Press, 1996) 209–230.

Sourdel, Dominique, "Gouvernement et administration dans l'orient Islamique jusqu'au milieu du XIe siècle" in *Handbuch der Orientalistik* Abteilung 1: Der Nahe und Mittlere Osten/Vol. 6: Geschichte der islamischen Länder/Abschnitt 5: Regierung und Verwaltung des Vorderen Orients in islamischer Zeit/Part 2 (Leiden: Brill, 1997).

Sprenger, Alois, "Eine Skizze der Entwicklungsgeschichte des muslimischen Gesetzes." *Zeitschrift für vergleichende Rechtswissenschaft* 10 (1892): 1–31.

Tyan, Émile, *Histoire de l'organisation judiciaire en pays d'Islam* (Leiden: Brill, 1960).

Wakin, Jeanette and Zysow, Aaron, "Art. Ra'y," *Encyclopaedia of Islam*, Supplement, 687–690 (Leiden: Brill, 2004).

Watson, Alan, *Legal Transplants. An Approach to Comparative Law* (Charlottesville: University Press of Virginia, 1974).

Watson, Alan, *The Evolution of Law* (Baltimore: Johns Hopkins University Press, 1985).

Watson, Alan, "Aspects of Reception of Law." *American Journal of Comparative Law* 44 (1996): 335–351.

Wegner, J., "Islamic and Talmudic Jurisprudence: The Four Roots of Islamic Law and their Talmudic Counterparts." *American Journal of Legal History* 26 (1982): 25–71.

Wensinck, A., "Die Entstehung der islamischen Reinheitsgesetzgebung." *Der Islam* 5 (1914): 62–80.

Yahia, Mohyddin, *Šāfiʿī et les deux sources de la loi islamique* (Turnhout: Brepols Publishers, 2009).

Yanagihashi, Hiroyuki, *A History of the Early Islamic Law of Property. Reconstructing the Legal Development, 7th–9th Centuries* (Leiden: Brill, 2004).

Zubaida, Sami, *Law and Power in the Islamic World* (London: I.B. Tauris, 2003).

CHAPTER 16

THE CLASSICAL PERIOD

SCRIPTURE, ORIGINS, AND EARLY DEVELOPMENT

MARIAM SHEIBANI, AMIR TOFT, AND AHMED EL SHAMSY

MUCH of the historiography of Islamic law in the period between the seventh and eleventh centuries is rooted in positions taken on one central question: is the traditional Muslim account of the genesis of Islamic law reliable? This traditional account, in a nutshell, says that Islamic law originated in the rules and instructions propounded by Muhammad, and that after the exodus to Medina and the establishment of a Muslim polity these rules grew into an extensive body of laws rooted in the Qur'an. After Muhammad's death, his successors continued to implement the Qur'anic laws as well as others based on the Prophet's precedent. In addition, they solved issues that were not explicitly covered by the former two sources by employing individual reasoning (*ra'y*). Some of Muhammad's companions who were recognized for their legal acumen settled in the newly founded garrison towns, establishing regional traditions of legal learning in these locations. Between the second quarter of the second Islamic century and the middle of the third (roughly 740–860 CE), a handful of prominent jurists systematized earlier legal thought and laid the foundations for enduring legal schools with their own legal literatures. Within this traditional narrative, the aspects that have prompted extensive debate concern the following questions: whether the Qur'an actually served as a source for the early jurists; whether Hadith reports contain authentic information regarding Muhammad's sayings and actions (and if they do not, when and how they became attributed to him); whether and how the regional legal traditions were transformed into legal schools centered around particular individuals; and how the nature of legal reasoning changed within this period.

This chapter is divided into six sections. The first two address debates regarding the role of the Qur'an and Hadith, respectively, in the formulation of Islamic law. The remaining four sections engage with scholarship on the phases of Islamic law's development, beginning with the emergence of geographically defined legal traditions and culminating in the formation of the legal schools and their distinctive theoretical principles and substantive doctrines.

I. Law in the Qur'an

Classical works of Sunni legal theory (*usul al-fiqh*) take as axiomatic that the Qur'an is the foundation of Islamic law, complemented by the precedent, or Sunna, of the prophet Muhammad. Western scholars writing in the second half of the nineteenth and beginning of the twentieth centuries drew heavily on the narrative provided by these works for their understanding of legal developments in the first two centuries AH (roughly the seventh and eighth centuries CE).[1] But shortly into the twentieth century, and in earnest after about 1950, scholars started questioning whether this narrative reliably represented the historical reality of the first two centuries of Islamic law.

Building on his nineteenth-century predecessors, Ignaz Goldziher (1850–1921) put forward a highly influential challenge to the classical narrative, and his critical engagement with the earliest legal sources set a benchmark for succeeding scholarship. His most cutting critique, elaborated in the next section, was of the authenticity of Hadith, the body of reports of the statements and deeds of the Prophet, his Companions, and other early figures whom later jurists regarded as legal authorities. Goldziher asserted that the Qur'an and Hadith (which over time came to serve as the textual substance of the prophetic Sunna) were accorded legal authority only at a secondary stage of Islamic legal formation.[2] Since Goldziher, scholars who have

[1] See e.g. Sachau, "Zur ältesten Geschichte"; von Kremer, *Culturgeschichte*, 1:470–504; Hurgronje, "Nieuwe bijdragen"; Sprenger, "Skizze der Entwicklungsgeschichte"; MacDonald, *Development of Muslim Theology*, 65–117.

[2] Goldziher, *Muslim Studies*.

cast doubt on the Qur'an's legal content have approached the matter from two broad but complementary angles.

The first, and by far the more influential, is a historiographical approach that focuses, as Goldziher did, on the appearance of early scriptural texts and their reception by the first generations of Muslims. It asks whether those early generations took the Qur'an's black-letter imperatives as a basis for legislation and, if so, when they began to do this. The most prominent proponent of this approach is Joseph Schacht (1902–1969). It is scarcely possible to overstate the influence of Schacht's work on the modern study of Islamic law. Since the publication of his *Origins of Muhammadan Jurisprudence* (1950), Schacht has without question become the most frequently cited authority in western studies in the fields of legal origins and Islamic law, and his work has elicited paeans of acclaim as well as sweeping rebuttals. Despite its waning influence under the force of increasingly successful critiques, to a large extent Schacht's conclusions still frame the debate for both his admirers and his detractors.

Did Schacht view the Qur'an as a source of early Islamic law? With respect to its content, Schacht saw the Qur'an as providing a moral take on legal matters.[3] This perspective, likely influenced by Goldziher, is rooted in a vision of Near Eastern cultural continuity that informed Arabian custom both before and during Muhammad's prophetic mission and is reflected in the language of the Qur'an. Where the Qur'an speaks of the Prophet's judicial functions, therefore, it speaks of his role in settling disputes (*hukm*)—which Schacht saw as a continuation of the pre-Islamic Arabian custom of the wise arbiter (*hakam*)—and augments it with a new rudimentary notion of administering justice (*qada'*).[4] For Schacht, the Prophet was only marginally elevated to the status of "lawgiver" by virtue of his political and military leadership at Medina. His primary role was to rectify society's fallen standards, and the Qur'an implicitly registers this mission through its prescriptions and prohibitions regarding commercial dealings, family relations, and public conduct. The Qur'an's verses in favor of women and orphans and against usury, blood feuds, and lax sexual mores were therefore declarations of right and wrong, not instances of legislation.

Schacht argued that the Qur'an's incorporation into Islamic law proper was a much later development. He complemented his impressions about the Qur'an's language with a critical analysis of early Hadith collections and legal works, dating the beginning of a truly "Islamic" articulation of law about twenty years into the second/

[3] Schacht, *Introduction*, 10–14; cf. Coulson, *Conflicts and Tensions*, 81–82.

Schacht, *Introduction*, 80. Though published about fifteen years after *Origins*, Schacht's introductory book is a good entry into his scholarship. It provides a synopsis of major elements and themes in Islamic law (e.g. origins, theory and practice, modern iterations) and summaries of the substantive content areas of law (e.g. property, family, penal, procedural). It is informed by the same premises guiding Schacht's more ambitious work.

[4] Schacht cites Q. 4:65.

eighth century. Preceding it was what he called the customary (e.g. marriage and divorce) and administrative (e.g. fiscal and military) law of the Umayyad Caliphate (41–132/661–750). These doctrines he regarded as the starting point for what later developed into Islamic law: later jurists either affirmed doctrines they deemed theologically and rationally acceptable and clothed them in legitimizing scriptural authority or, alternatively, discarded unacceptable ones in favor of other doctrines which they equally clothed in the same scriptural authority.[5] To Schacht, this scriptural clothing was woven of Hadith reports, which he, like Goldziher before him, considered almost entirely fabricated (for Schacht's Hadith critique, see the next two sections). With regard to the Qur'an, what is important to note is that Schacht viewed Islamic law-making as essentially the invention of early Hadith masters who systematically islamized existing legal doctrines by fabricating reports that linked them to the authority of the Prophet and the early Muslim community. According to this narrative, Qur'anic injunctions became important only after the process of islamization began and were used to pad the new religious law at a decidedly secondary stage. Schacht thus dispatched the Qur'anic "element" of Islamic law in a precious few pages toward the end of his study, further emphasizing his view of the Qur'an's marginal role in the formation of a functional legal system.[6]

Schacht sharpened Goldziher's skeptical view of the classical narrative by grounding it in a more thoroughgoing analysis of a broader range of Arabic primary texts, some of which had not been available to scholars before him. But not all were convinced by Schacht's demotion of the Qur'an. An alternative but complementary approach is exemplified by the work of Noel Coulson (1928–1986). Coulson too characterized the Qur'an as essentially moral, but it was precisely because of its moral imperative that he argued that it must have provided the ethical seeds for later Islamic legal doctrine. On this view, Islamic law developed alongside Umayyad regulatory law.[7] Still, Coulson seemed to view Islamic law—though not islamized law—as emerging when jurists "cloth[ed Qur'anic] norms of behavior with legal consequences."[8]

Shortly after Coulson, S.D. Goitein (1900–1985), best known for his magisterial studies on the Cairo geniza,[9] disputed the notion that the Qur'an is bereft of legal material.[10] He was unconvinced by the quantitative argument—namely, that because the Qur'an has no more than 500 verses of legal import (out of over 6,000), it cannot be considered to have significant legal weight.[11] Goitein pointed out that verses with legal import are often long and detailed, and that in any case quantity does not outweigh substance and thus can tell us nothing of how the early community viewed the role of scripture in their lives. Paralleling the old Israelite

[5] Schacht, *Origins*, 190 ff. [6] Ibid., 224–227. [7] Coulson, *History*, 34.
[8] Coulson, *Conflicts and Tensions*, 81–82. [9] Goitein, *Mediterranean Society*.
[10] Ibid., "Birth-Hour."
[11] Coulson, too, observed that this quantity is "not great by any standards"; see Coulson, *History*, 12.

conception and in keeping with Near Eastern tradition, Muhammad's followers, Goitein argued, viewed law not as a contingent human institution but as an eternal and ontologically independent expression of truth accessible only through divinely conferred wisdom or revelation. Like Schacht, Goitein affirmed the Prophet's status as wise arbiter (*hakam*), but unlike Schacht, he took this broadened scope of the Prophet's office—from preacher to arbiter—as evidence that religious law existed as an instrument of social governance during the Prophet's lifetime. Goitein identified a particular Qur'anic passage (5:42–51) as anointing the Prophet as arbiter and, using the chronology of the Qur'anic text proposed by earlier scholars, he pinpointed the "birth-hour" of Islamic law at around the year 5 AH (637 CE).[12] But Goitein seemed unprepared to take on Schacht in so short an article, sidestepping the latter's main contention that law lay outside of religion in the first century. Instead, he drew a distinction between (sacred) law and (formal) jurisprudence, which somewhat diluted his argument into a variation on Schacht's thesis.

After a period of dormancy, studies on the origins of Islam and its law acquired fresh vigor beginning around 1980, and the doubts Schacht raised about the early sources were taken to new heights. Patricia Crone (1945–2015) stands out as promoting the most sweepingly skeptical position. Crone viewed the Qur'an as a confounding hodgepodge of statements whose disorganization and amorphous origins severely compromised its usefulness as a source of historical information. Later exegetical works, which she contended were heavily infiltrated by the tales of nameless storytellers, offer no help; and early jurists, she argued, chronically misunderstood the true import of legal verses.[13] What she identified as severe discontinuities between the real meanings of the Qur'an and the provisions of Islamic law bolstered her conclusion, prevalent in much of her work, that the Qur'an coalesced into its canonical form at a period substantially later than that claimed in the traditional Muslim narrative.[14] An authoritative Qur'anic canon was either non-existent in the Hejaz at an early period or, if it existed, was considered irrelevant for the purpose of deriving law.[15] In a separate study on the foreign borrowings in Islamic law, Crone took the

[12] Goitein, "Birth-Hour," 26–28.

[13] On Qur'anic exegesis and history, see Crone, *Meccan Trade*. On the Qur'an in law, see Crone, "Two Legal Problems."

[14] Dating the Qur'anic text was never one of Schacht's main concerns. Crone was part of a wave of skeptical scholarship in Qur'anic studies that included John Wansbrough, who argued in *Quranic Studies* (1977) and *Sectarian Milieu* (1978) that the Qur'an came to its final form in Syria (not the Hejaz) around 800 CE and therefore had nothing originally to do with the Prophet Muhammad. Crone expressed ambivalence about dating the Qur'an quite this late and disagreed with Wansbrough's claim that it originated outside of Arabia. See Crone, "Two Legal Problems," 16–19. On the skeptical school, see Donner, *Narratives*, 20–25 (overview), 35–40 (dating the Qur'anic text). Following the groundbreaking work of Behnam Sadeghi and Uwe Bergmann on dating early Qur'an manuscripts (see Sadeghi and Bergmann, "Codex"), Crone eventually came to affirm the view that the Qur'anic text does indeed originate in the seventh century (see Crone, *Qur'anic Pagans*, xiii).

[15] Crone, "Two Legal Problems," 19–21.

Qur'an's irrelevance for granted, and the Qur'an's complete absence in this work stands out even more than the passing treatment it receives in Schacht's *Origins*.[16] Crone earned considerable praise from some scholars for her daring, while others attacked her for what they described as a polemical, high-handed tone and an inadequate, even arbitrary handling of the Qur'an and exegetical sources.[17]

Since then, several studies that focus on specific areas of the legal corpus have in great measure disproved the sweeping claim that the Qur'an was absent in early Islamic law. David S. Powers's 1986 study on inheritance law, while partially in agreement with Schacht, was reserved about marginalizing the Qur'an's early importance, which would leave an unaccountable space of about a century before the Hadith masters got to work.[18] Not long after, Harald Motzki and Yasin Dutton, each studying an early Hadith collection, noted that figures from the first/seventh century are observed routinely employing both direct and indirect references to the Qur'an as evidence for legal doctrine.[19] Finally, in her study on Islamic purity law, Marion Holmes Katz made the sensible observation that the basic rules governing ritual washing for daily acts of worship are all articulated in the Qur'an, which makes it implausible that the Qur'an had no legal relevance for early Muslims whatsoever.[20]

A more resounding recent critique, however, belongs to Wael B. Hallaq. Hallaq's views on the subject appear to have undergone a slight evolution, or else perhaps a shift in emphasis. His 2005 synoptic study of legal origins described a view of the Qur'an as eminently concerned with carving out a unique Muslim moral identity that absorbed acceptable pre-Islamic customs while rejecting immoral pagan practices as well as correcting the errant ways of previous monotheistic communities (i.e. Jews and Christians).[21] This "Islamic legal ethic," his narrative suggested, grew organically after the Prophet's death. But in a 2009 article, he re-centered the debate explicitly on the philosophical question of morality and the law.[22] Drawing on the writings of modern moral and legal philosophers, Hallaq upbraided scholars for what he deemed their misguided habit of exporting a modern European dichotomy between the moral and legal spheres across time and space into seventh-century Arabia. To him, the Qur'an's juxtaposition of "faith" (*iman*) and "practice" (*'amal*) comports with the premodern conviction that the "moral" and the "legal" were identical concepts. Therefore, the Qur'an, by virtue of being a moral text, cannot but have been seen by its first recipients as an expression of law as well.

Other studies have sought to combine the respective historical values of the Qur'an and Hadith to see whether a coherent and continuous historical picture

16 Crone, *Roman, Provincial and Islamic Law*, ch. 2.

17 In praise of Crone's *Meccan Trade*, see reviews by Wansbrough and by Paxton. For a thoroughgoing and particularly acid assessment of the same book, see review article by Serjeant, as well as Crone's long and equally acid response.

18 Powers, *Studies*.

19 Motzki, *Origins*, 108–117, 152–157; Dutton, *Origins*, 61–77, 157–161.

20 Katz, *Body of Text*, 33.

21 Hallaq, *Origins and Evolution*, 19–25.

22 Hallaq, "Groundwork."

emerges.[23] These studies use the Qur'anic reception as a springboard to explain what happened in the first century after the Prophet's death. But because so much of this story is bound up in the reliability of Hadith reports, they tend to focus considerably on this source, to which we, too, now turn.

II. Law in the Hadith

As we have seen, historians reconstructing Islamic legal history in the first two Islamic centuries are faced with the challenge of doing so on the basis of limited and incomplete sources. The majority of legal material available to historians is contained in the vast corpus of Hadith reports (also referred to by many as "traditions"). Each Hadith report is composed of a narrated text (*matn*), which recounts an event from the prophetic age, appended to a chain of transmitters (*isnad*), which traces the text back to its putative source. Given that the earliest extant Hadith collection was compiled around the middle of the second/eighth century, historians of early Islam have applied the critical tools of modern historical inquiry, particularly source criticism, to evaluate the historicity of Hadith reports and to accurately date when specific reports first appeared and to which authorities they may be correctly ascribed.

Nineteenth-century scholars such as D.S. Margoliouth (1858–1940) drew heavily on the classical narrative for their understanding of the Hadith (just as they did for their understanding of the Qur'an), taking the canonical works[24] as more or less reliable.[25] On this account, during the first/seventh century, the Companions of the Prophet and their Successors derived Islamic law on the basis of (in hierarchical order) the Qur'an, the Sunna, and the consensus of the Companions. The second/eighth century saw the emergence of *ra'y*, the exercise of a jurist's individual reasoning to resolve legal questions, which was later systematized as legal analogy (*qiyas*) and constituted the fourth source of law.[26] Despite the relative emphasis placed on Hadith in Medina and *ra'y* in Iraq, by the middle of the second/eighth

[23] See e.g. Maghen, *Virtues*; Lowry, "Reading the Qur'an"; Stodolsky, "New Model."

[24] In particular the two *Sahih* collections of al-Bukhari (d. 256/870) and Muslim (d. 261/875). For the history and status of these and other "canonical" Hadith collections, see Brown, *Canonization*.

[25] See n. 1. D.S. Margoliouth also largely followed in the line of scholarship before Goldziher, but he asserted that initially the term *sunna* denoted the normative practice of the general community and only later acquired the restricted sense of prophetic precedent; see Margoliouth, *Development*, 65–98. Schacht cites Margoliouth and incorporates similar findings into his thesis; see Schacht, *Origins*, 58–81.

[26] These comprise the four "sources" (which is the literal translation of *usul*) commonly referred to in classical jurisprudence.

century the foundations of a coherent legal system were discernible and served as the basis for the later schools of law.

Goldziher's source-critical approach and his rejection of this classical account, as already noted, altered the course of all subsequent research on the formation and early development of Islamic law. First in his study of the Zahiri school and later in his *Muslim Studies*, Goldziher posited the reverse trajectory: in the first/seventh century, Islamic legal doctrine was developed primarily from *ra'y*, and only later were Hadith reports fabricated to justify existing *ra'y*-based jurisprudence.[27] Goldziher characterized the jurisprudence of the first/seventh century as underdeveloped and attributed the evolution of legal doctrine in the following century to the religious policies of the early Abbasids, who sought to ground religious and social life in prophetic precedents, which in turn gave rise to the mass forgery of Hadith reports. Goldziher adduced as evidence the fact that legal works preceded Hadith collections; the latter, he argued, did not appear until the third/ninth century. This claim turns on Goldziher's own classification of second/eighth-century works—such as Ibn Jurayj's (d. 150/767) collection and Malik b. Anas's (d. 179/796) *Muwatta'*—as legal manuals. He also categorized older collections (*suhuf* and *kutub*) as mere *scripta*, or rough notes of individual sayings intended for private use.[28]

Schacht furthered Goldziher's ideas by developing methods for dating Hadith reports, or at least establishing a *terminus post quem* for various categories of reports, and integrating his findings into a comprehensive master narrative of the development of Islamic law. In his *Origins*, Schacht maintained that legal traditions from the first/seventh century—those ascribed to the Prophet and the Companions—should be assumed fictitious unless proven otherwise, and that the reports of Successors are likewise largely inauthentic. Schacht proposed several methods for dating reports. One was based on an argument *e silentio*. He assumed that a legal report would have been adduced as evidence immediately after it came into circulation, and from there he concluded that reports that were not mentioned in a legal discussion to which they would have pertained did not yet exist at that historic moment.[29] Schacht further proposed that a report's initial circulation could be dated based on when it first appeared in legal or Hadith literature, or when the earliest common transmitter in the *isnad*—whom Schacht termed a "common link"—appeared in a chain.[30]

Schacht related his dating of Hadith to his broader interest in the origins of Islamic law. In his studies of the earliest extant legal works, Schacht observed a generational frequency in the Hadith reports adduced by early Iraqi jurists. They ascribed more reports to Successors than to Companions and cited the former more frequently

27 Goldziher, *Zahiris*; Goldziher, *Muslim Studies*, 2:73.
28 Goldziher, *Muslim Studies*, 2:182, 211.
29 Schacht, *Origins*, 140–151.
30 Ibid., 171–175.

than the latter, and these in turn more frequently than reports that extended all the way back to the Prophet. Schacht also noted that the quantity of Hadith reports in circulation grew considerably between 150/767 and 250/864, and that the quantity of prophetic reports in particular expanded during the first half of the third/ninth century, which coincided with the period after the death of al-Shafiʿi (d. 204/820). These observations led Schacht to posit the "backward growth of *isnads*": legal doctrines were first ascribed to the Successors, then later to the Companions, and finally to the Prophet. In this schema, *isnad*s were gradually improved through the steady projection of teachings back to earlier and higher authorities, culminating in the unbroken *isnad*s found in the Hadith collections of the third/ninth centuries. For Schacht, the most complete *isnad*s were forged most recently, and therefore, "the more perfect the *isnad*, the later the tradition."[31]

Schacht's contemporaries generally received his work with approbation,[32] and its significance has been so enduring in the field of Hadith studies that it has provided the starting point and the dominant paradigm for virtually every subsequent study in the field. While several scholars, such as Johann Fück (1894–1974), Fuat Sezgin, and Muhammad Mustafa Azami,[33] have disputed Schacht's methods and conclusions, among western scholars the most significant challenge to Schacht's legacy has been posed by the so-called *isnad-cum-matn* method, most extensively developed by Harald Motzki.

Motzki criticized Schacht's conclusions as circular, overly generalized, and arbitrary. He proposed an alternative and, in his view, more rigorous and robust way of judging the historicity of Hadith reports, one that accounts for both the *isnad* and the *matn*. First, all available narrations are compiled, diagrammed, and compared to identify any variant transmissions in both the *isnad* and the *matn*. Then, groups of *matn* variants and groups of *isnad* variants are compared to identify any correlations.[34] By applying this method to Hadith collections from the first two centuries, including previously unexamined ones such as the *Musannaf* of ʿAbd al-Razzaq (d. 211/827), Motzki challenged Schacht's categorical conclusions of fabrication and back projection. Against Goldziher's and Schacht's findings, Motzki argued that the growth of reports does not necessarily entail forgery and that common links should not be assumed to be forgers. Further, he asserted that the age and provenance of early Hadith reports *can* be determined through careful study and comparison of chains of transmission with the earliest collections available to us. His own study of the *Musannaf* led him to conclude that Islamic law began at the end of the first/seventh century and was the result

[31] Schacht, "Revaluation," 147.

[32] See e.g. separate reviews by Watt, Gibb, and Anderson.

[33] For a critical assessment, see review by Fück. For more extended criticism, see review by Sezgin; see also Sezgin, *Bukhari'nin kaynaklari*. And for a more direct rebuttal, see Azami, *Studies*; Azami, *Schacht's Origins*.

[34] Motzki, "Dating Traditions."

of systematic collecting, not merely forging, of Hadith reports.[35] Motzki's results also called into question Schacht's argument from silence. The complexity of the process of gathering and evaluating Hadith reports means that the absence of a particular report from the legal discussion of one scholar cannot be taken as evidence that it was not known to other scholars at the time.

Motzki's novel research agenda has inaugurated a new era in the study of early Islam, and his method is now being employed by a new generation of scholars.[36] While Motzki's work has been misinterpreted as incorporating an *a priori* assumption of authenticity for Hadith reports,[37] he has emphatically repudiated this claim, maintaining that he has intended only to judiciously retrace the transmission history of individual texts—which may very well contain forgeries—with a view to dating individual reports or groups of reports.[38]

III. The Debate on Origins, First/Seventh Century

Having evaluated how scholars have engaged with the historical sources of Islamic law, we now turn to contending visions of its early development. The first century of Islam played a formative role in determining the course of the subsequent development of Islamic law. Already in the first three generations after the Prophet, foundational legal institutions were established and the characteristic features of Islamic law became discernible. Regrettably, the paucity of contemporaneous sources from this period also makes it the one about which the least is known with certainty. We have already described the traditional narrative of development elaborated in classical Sunni sources from the fourth/tenth century onward, to which many early European historians generally adhered. Some nineteenth-century scholars, however, postulated unacknowledged borrowings from other legal systems in the Near East. Abraham Geiger (1810–1874) wrote an influential study that argued for a strong Jewish influence on Islamic thought, particularly in the area of law.[39] Alfred von Kremer (1828–1889) was one of the first to consider the influence of Roman law

[35] Motzki, *Origins*, 295–297.

[36] Motzki, Boekhoff-van der Voort, and Anthony, *Analysing Muslim Traditions*.

[37] Berg, "Competing Paradigms," 260. For Motzki's response to Berg, see Motzki, "Question of Authenticity."

[38] Motzki et al., *Analysing Muslim Traditions*, 234–235.

[39] Geiger, *Was hat Mohammed aufgenommen?*

on the formation of Islamic legal doctrines and to hypothesize an indirect transfer through the medium of Jewish law.[40] Goldziher not only saw Islamic law as primarily derived from the practical *ra'y* accommodations of first-century jurists but also considered it deeply indebted to Roman law.[41]

As on so many other questions in Islamic legal history, Schacht furthered Goldziher's theories concerning Islamic legal origins. According to Schacht, "during the greater part of the first century Islamic law, in the technical meaning of the term, did not yet exist."[42] Instead, he argued, apart perhaps from the narrow scope of worship and ritual law, early Muslims were generally indifferent to legal matters and largely retained the practice and institutions of the territories they conquered. During the first/seventh century, legal maxims and customs originating from Roman law, canon law of the Eastern Churches, Jewish law, and Sassanian law infiltrated Umayyad popular and administrative practices and appeared later in legal doctrines of the second/eight century. Schacht identified cultured non-Arab converts, whose education in Hellenistic rhetoric had comprised the study of Roman law at a rudimentary level, as the chief conduit of this transfer.[43] On Schacht's account, these borrowings, alongside the *ra'y*-based judgments of Umayyad judges and the remnants of pre-Islamic customary law, combined to form the "living tradition" of the ancient schools, which was subsequently islamized and buttressed with fabricated post-prophetic and then prophetic reports starting in the early second/eighth century.

In her study on foreign elements in Islamic law, Crone held to the basic outlines of Schacht's paradigm, but she described his findings (as well as Goldziher's) on extra-Islamic legal sources as far-fetched.[44] She disputed his work on two specific fronts. First, she argued that since the early Islamic community took shape in the Roman Fertile Crescent, borrowings must have taken place through this geographical area, not through Iraq as Schacht had supposed.[45] While she accepted borrowings from Jewish law as self-evident,[46] Crone maintained that the principal source of classical and Umayyad institutions was neither Arab custom nor ancient Roman law but "Roman provincial law," that is, Roman law that incorporated foreign elements and was applied in the provinces of the Roman Empire, especially in the east.[47] Second, Crone argued that the list of supposed borrowings given by Goldziher and Schacht was unconvincing, going so far as to state that "not a single item of Goldziher's and Schacht's list of Roman elements in Islamic law has been proved, and several are demonstrably wrong."[48]

[40] Von Kremer, *Culturgeschichte*, 1:532–1:547.

[41] Goldziher, *Muslim Studies*, vol. 2, appendix 2. For a survey of the scholarship on this topic, see Crone, *Roman, Provincial and Islamic Law*, ch. 1.

[42] Schacht, *Introduction*, 19.

[43] Ibid., 21.

[44] Crone, *Roman, Provincial and Islamic Law*, 3, 9.

[45] Ibid., 7–8.

[46] Ibid., 2–3; Crone and Cook, *Hagarism*.

[47] Crone, *Roman, Provincial and Islamic Law*, 1.

[48] Ibid., 11.

Paralleling her critique of earlier studies of foreign influences on Islamic law, Crone's own findings have attracted both substantive and methodological criticism. Kevin Reinhart argued that Crone's evidence in fact contradicts her conclusions. He contended that the eastern Mediterranean world of the first/seventh century, in which Islam emerged, was not a cultural vacuum, but a heterogeneous region with shared cultural institutions. It should, therefore, be no surprise if Muslims inherited some of these institutions.[49] Accordingly, Reinhart interpreted Crone's evidence as a carefully documented history of the "creativity of an Islamic culture that felt free to borrow but also to discard and that both integrated itself into and distinguished itself from its predecessors."[50]

Hallaq criticized Crone for misreading legal texts; for leaving unanswered important questions, such as what exactly the sources of provincial law were and who was applying it; for not taking into account important findings in the fields of Roman and Byzantine studies; and, above all, for a deprecating assumption of Arabian cultural inferiority which, he argued, colored her interpretation of the evidence[51] and prompted her to search for the true origins of legal norms, which she believed could not possibly have been an indigenous Arab development.[52] In his own study on legal origins, Hallaq emphasized that the genuine sources of Islamic law are to be found in the Hejaz, not in cultural borrowings from the Fertile Crescent or elsewhere in the wake of the Muslim conquests. Much like Reinhart, Hallaq held that Islam emerged within an indigenous Arabian legal tradition, and to the extent that pre-Islamic Arabs absorbed Greco-Roman and Semitic laws and Near Eastern legal institutions, these could be unproblematically incorporated into Islamic law.[53]

Motzki's studies on early legal developments in Mecca, which used the method of Hadith analysis outlined earlier, concluded that Schacht's date for the beginnings of a properly "Islamic" law was at least half to three-quarters of a century too late.[54] Motzki identified reliable and precise examples of legal reasoning that drew on the Qur'an and prophetic Hadith reports as early as the second half of the first/seventh century.[55] He also argued that during the Umayyad period, the rulings of judges and governors played "a very marginal role in the formation of the opinions of the early [jurists]," at least in the issues of private law (e.g. marriage and divorce) with which Motzki's study was concerned. El Shamsy has likewise argued for an early inauguration of a properly Islamic law, noting that the founding document of the Islamic polity in Medina shows that the early Muslims saw their community as religiously constituted, and that the laws of this community could therefore be legitimately

49 Reinhart, review of *Roman, Provincial and Islamic Law*. 50 Ibid., 216.

51 Hallaq, "Use and Abuse." Hallaq also presented a broader critique of Crone's work in "Origins or Doctrine."

52 Hallaq, "Use and Abuse," 80. 53 Hallaq, *Origins and Evolution*, 18–19, 24–28, 197–198.

54 Motzki, *Origins*, 297. 55 Ibid., 131.

considered Islamic.[56] Consequently, Muslim jurists in the formative period did not enjoy the luxury of a tabula rasa in their law-making: they had to operate within the framework of an existing Islamic legal tradition that must have possessed considerable authority.

One possible way of shedding light on the transition from early, preliterary Islamic legal thought to the law as articulated in second/eighth-century legal literature is offered by the systematic study of the opinions of the earliest jurists, which were transmitted orally or in note form. Such a study was undertaken on a limited scale by Motzki,[57] but a comprehensive survey has yet to be attempted, even though extensive lists of the early jurists are available in the works of Ibn Hazm (d. 456/1064) and Ibn al-Qayyim (d. 751/1350).[58] Muhammad Rawas Qalʿaji has compiled the legal opinions of many of these early jurists into individual volumes, ordering all of their known legal views alphabetically and carefully referencing the various Hadith collections in which their transmissions appear. Qalʿaji's more than a dozen volumes draw together the legal reports attributed to Companions such as ʿUmar b. al-Khattab, ʿAbdullah b. ʿUmar, ʿAli b. Abi Talib, Ibn ʿAbbas, and ʿAʾisha, as well as Successors such as Ibrahim al-Nakhaʿi and al-Layth b. Saʿd. These volumes could serve as a propitious beginning for a historical and analytical study on this topic.

IV. Master Jurists and the Emergence of a Legal Literature, Second/Eighth Century

Many scholars mark the middle of the second/eighth century as the beginning of a formal Islamic law. The first surviving books on Islamic law proper—that is, works that were deliberately composed and disseminated—originate from around the middle of the second Islamic century. The emergence of a written discourse at this time is not limited to Islamic law. Owing primarily to the adoption of paper and the advantages this medium offered over parchment and papyrus, the same shift can be observed across the landscape of Islamic learning.[59] These surviving works do not appear to have been preceded by similar ones that were later lost; they seem in fact

[56] El Shamsy, *Canonization*, 21. To what extent these laws match those in the legal literature of the second/eighth century onward is a separate question.

[57] Motzki, *Origins*.

[58] Ibn Hazm, *al-Ihkam*, 5:89–5:105; Ibn al-Qayyim, *Iʿlam*, 2:17–2:49.

[59] The importance of writing as a tool of knowledge transmission cannot be overstated. For a review of its growth and interaction with oral transmission, see Schoeler, *Genesis*, 1–15.

to have been the first. Schacht accordingly called the stretch of time roughly from 150 to 250 AH the "literary period."[60] Still, the works of this period represent a legal system that was still taking shape, and scholars studying these works have reached varying conclusions about the nature of early law and its sources of authority.

The new urban centers in the vast Islamic Empire were far enough apart to develop separate characters but close enough to maintain strong commercial and cultural exchange, which included religious knowledge. The main regions of learning in the second century were the Hejaz, represented by Medina, less so by Mecca; Iraq,[61] represented by Kufa, the southern port city of Basra, and the emerging metropolis of Baghdad; and Syria, represented by Damascus. After the Abbasid revolution in 132/750, Damascus ceased to be the capital of the caliphate, and Syria's importance faded. By contrast, over the course of the second/eighth century and in the beginning of the third/ninth, Egypt, with its center at Fustat (Old Cairo), grew in importance, and its influence eventually extended across the Muslim domains in North Africa and Iberia.

An important scholarly discussion on this period concerns the space in which early legal thinking took place. At what point did early jurists begin to view themselves as part of an increasingly defined juristic community, and what was the nature of juristic thought before that point? Schacht regarded the first half of the second/third century as the period of the "ancient" schools of Medina and Iraq.[62] These schools, he suggested, were not homogeneous, but they were characterized by common patterns of legal thinking expressed in regional terms. The scholars of Medina determined normativity through reliance on the communal practice (*'amal*) of the city's leading jurists, while Iraqi scholarship was known for its rigorous application of *ra'y* as a way of generating legal decisions out of a set of well-attested normative principles. Toward the end of the second century, these regional styles of legal thinking were reworked into "personal" schools named after the influential masters who were thought to represent them best. Abu Hanifa (d. 150/767), whose disciples were the Hanafis, represented the Iraqi school; Malik (d. 179/796) and his disciples, the Malikis, represented the Medinan. Hallaq, however, vehemently contested this geographical partitioning of the early intellectual landscape, arguing that known legal disputes among jurists within each region clearly indicate that there was no such thing as uniform schools delimited by regional boundaries.[63] Some scholars have supported Hallaq's stance against Schacht's notion of regional schools, while others have pointed out that Hallaq may have misread Schacht's intended meaning

[60] Schacht, *Origins*, 140–151.

[61] "Iraq" here denotes the historical region of Iraq, which roughly coincides with but does not extend as far north as the modern state of Iraq.

[62] Schacht, *Origins*, 2–10 and passim.

[63] Hallaq, "Regional to Personal." See also Hallaq, *Origins and Evolution*, 153–167.

for "regional" and "personal."[64] This disagreement extends to views on the schools' subsequent development in the third/ninth century, discussed in the next section.

Another central debate on the second/eighth century relates to the question of who had the authority to formulate and apply the law. It has become something of a commonplace in legal scholarship, particularly on Sunnism,[65] to describe Islamic law as a "jurist's law"[66]—that is, a law whose binding authority derives not from judicial rulings or government legislation but from the collective efforts of private jurists who issued opinions on legal questions. Because of the generally private nature of their occupation—in the sense that the government did not actively regulate it—early Muslim jurists possessed significant independent social and religious authority. This was based on their claim to represent the heirs and guardians of the normative practice of the sacred past, from the Prophet and his Companions down to their own time. This autonomous status, coupled with such regional variation as may have existed, created a legal diversity that could prove disruptive to the new Abbasid dynasty's efforts to bring unity and centralized control to the sprawling empire.

That the new administration saw both decentralization and diversity in the law as a problem is brought out in Joseph Lowry's study of a well-known letter written by the courtier Ibn al-Muqaffaʿ (d. c. 139/756) to the caliph al-Mansur (r. 136–58/754–75). In this letter, Ibn al-Muqaffaʿ advises the caliph to assume final discretion in selecting and promulgating legal doctrine out of what he saw as a hash of conflicting opinions from regional judges and jurists. Beyond its pragmatic plea to mitigate legal indeterminacy, Lowry argued, the letter contains an early typology of the religious law that prefigured later legal theory, which divided the law into spheres of interpretation: a non-interpretable sphere, which covered such fundamental obligations as prayer, and an interpretable one, which included nearly everything else.[67] Ibn al-Muqaffaʿ suggests placing legal interpretation within the caliphal domain, thereby linking obedience to sacred law with obedience to the caliph.

Examining the thought of this one courtier largely in the abstract, Lowry made no clear historical judgment about the political relationship of jurists and rulers. This was done much earlier in an influential but highly controversial book by Patricia Crone and Martin Hinds (1941–1988).[68] Crone and Hinds argued that religious authority was initially invested in the caliph, who was seen as "God's representative on earth" rather than as a temporal and non-inspired successor of Muhammad. This

[64] In support of Hallaq's critique, see e.g. Powers, "Schools of Law"; Wymann-Landgraf, *Malik and Medina*, 21. Against Hallaq, see El Shamsy, *Canonization*, 42; Christopher Melchert, "Basra and Kufa," 174.

[65] Because of the role of the infallible imam, legal authority was, at least in theory, less ambiguous for most branches of Shiʿism. For an overview of the bases of Shiʿi law, see Modarressi, *Introduction*, 2–6.

[66] For the foundational statement of this view, see Schacht, *Introduction*, 5, 209.

[67] Lowry, "First Islamic Legal Theory," 25–40. Lowry was careful to point out that later legal theory is likely not genetically related to the courtier's typology despite their similarities.

[68] Crone and Hinds, *God's Caliph*.

framework pitted the caliphate from the outset against the increasingly influential class of scholars (*ulama*), which included jurists and theologians. The conflict swelled into the Abbasid period and culminated in the Qur'anic Inquisition (218–34/833–49), or *Mihna*, wherein the caliphs attempted to determine official theology against the scholars' protestations. The scholars triumphed, successfully wresting legal and theological authority from the caliphs, and, in Crone and Hinds's account, they proceeded to erase the past by systematically linking normative religion to the prophetic age. Unlike Schacht, Crone and Hinds held that caliphal law was seen ipso facto as religious law; like him, they argued that the victorious scholars rewrote history.

Crone and Hinds's thesis is emblematic of a trend in Islamic legal historiography that depicts early tensions as a fierce, sometimes violent dialectic between two irreconcilable enemies, with one winner who proceeds to obliterate the legacy of the loser. Such zero-sum terms often exaggerate the conflict's intensity and obscure the exchange of ideas between scholars and rulers. In rebuttal to Crone and Hinds, Muhammad Qasim Zaman has argued that the caliphs, particularly the Abbasids, sought to legitimize their rule not by sidelining religious scholars but by enlisting them in their centralizing project through patronage and other means.[69] Whether this strategy is better called inclusion or cooptation, according to Zaman, is a trifling point. Similarly, El Shamsy has proposed that the major shift in the late Umayyad and early Abbasid period was from a communitarian vision of Islamic law, one based on regional practice that amalgamated caliphal and judicial decisions and scholarly opinions, to a regularized system of legal interpretation. This system produced an influential class of jurists to which rulers increasingly turned for legal opinions and on which, in turn, they exercised significant influence through judicial appointments and patronage of scholars.[70]

What unifies all of the studies we have surveyed, despite their often radically different emphases and conclusions, is a quest to determine how legal thought evolved and spread, a process that took on new dimensions in the following century.

V. The Early Schools, Third/Ninth Century

In the third/ninth century, as well as in the decades leading up to it, we see the emergence and establishment of the four *madhhabs*, the classical schools of Sunni

[69] Zaman, *Religion and Politics*. For a short version of one of his central arguments, see Zaman, "The Caliphs, the 'Ulama', and the Law."

[70] El Shamsy, *Canonization*, 84–87.

Islamic law.[71] Until the modern period, these four schools constituted the preeminent formal institution through which Sunni legal doctrine in Muslim lands was interpreted and debated and legal cases involving Muslims adjudicated.[72] And even though the secular nation-state has now long been the operative political order in most of the historical Muslim lands, the *madhhab* continues to guide many Muslims in ritual and civil matters (and increasingly commercial ones) and to serve as the framework for teaching Islamic law in many traditional colleges and schools.[73] The label "classical" here denotes that in this period each school's discursive repertoire (e.g. a legal vocabulary) and general institutional contours (e.g. a distinct body of legal opinion and methodology) more or less assumed the forms that would carry legal thought for the following millennium.[74]

The traditional Muslim account of the emergence of the legal schools can be summarized as follows. In the first two centuries, the development of Islamic law was to a large extent driven by practical needs and expressed in legal responsa (*fatawa*, sg. *fatwa*) from jurists and judicial rulings (*ahkam*, sg. *hukm*) from judges and rulers.[75] These legal authorities—many of them either students of the Companions or students of these students—drew first and foremost on the recent memory of the Prophet's community in issuing their opinions and rulings. Jurists in the generations thereafter cultivated these opinions and rulings into a body of substantive doctrine, applying a set of largely implicit principles of legal interpretation (*ijtihad*) to address emergent issues. These jurists' legal acumen and social standing attracted followings of disciples, creating master–disciple associations that were often numerous and not necessarily exclusive, with students typically attending the learning circles of more than one master. But these associations gradually contracted and formalized over the course of the third/ninth century (and to some extent the following century as well), until Sunni law came to be dominated by the four institutionalized schools, each named after its principal founder: Hanafi, Maliki, Shafiʿi, and Hanbali.[76] Of the early Sunni schools that did

[71] "School," like most translations, is not a perfect one, and scholars have rightly taken the time to explore the semantic shades of *madhhab*; see e.g. Hallaq, *Origins and Evolution*, 150–153.

[72] The following section discusses the emergence of a distinctly Shiʿi law, whose history and theoretical underpinnings distinguish it qualitatively from Sunni law.

[73] See Hefner and Zaman, *Schooling Islam*, for a rich set of essays by leading experts on the various regions of the Muslim world.

[74] Both the endurance and the elasticity of the legal school as an institution is brought out in the essay collection by Bearman, Peters, and Vogel, *The Islamic School of Law*.

[75] Many jurists (*fuqaha'*, s. *faqih*) were called upon to issue opinions in response to inquiries put to them either by private individuals or, in more formal settings, by judges. The responsum was known as a *fatwa*, the issuer a *mufti* (often translated as a jurisconsult for the role he historically played as an authority to a judge). Note, then, that the jurist did not necessarily serve formally as a *mufti*, nor did the functions of *fatwa* and *mufti* remain the same over time. For an excellent overview of the *mufti*'s developing roles, see Masud, Messick, and Powers, "Muftis, Fatwas, and Islamic Legal Interpretation."

[76] For general information on these four figures, see their entries in the *The Encyclopaedia of Islam*, second edition, "Abu Hanifa al-Nuʿman" (J. Schacht); "al-Shafiʿi" (E. Chaumont); "Malik b. Anas"

not survive, the most notable is the Zahiri school, named after the literalist scholar Dawud al-Zahiri (d. 270/884).

By the end of the third/ninth century, the Hanafi, Maliki, and Shafiʿi schools were firmly established, with the Hanbali school soon to follow. Each had a body of law and a legal methodology, as well as an extensive literature produced by a robust community of dedicated students. In order to guarantee the (relative) predictability of judicial rulings, the ruling authorities patronized the legal schools and began to appoint judges on the explicit condition that they adhere to a specific school in their judgments. But how and when the schools changed from loose associations to formal institutions remain among the more vexing questions for historians of Islamic law today. Apart from the dearth of sources already mentioned, two aspects of the early schools make their history hard to pin down. First, religious law was not decreed by sovereign power, which precludes finding a reliable narrative in the historical chronicles alone. Second, the early networks of jurists were diffused across place and time, which means that a robust narrative must account for considerably more than fifty or a hundred years. Because school formation was fluid and gradual, scholars have attempted to impose order by highlighting a particular conceptual category of historical agents that they believe propelled the process. For the sake of simplicity, one could characterize the various approaches as focussed on individuals, institutions, or ideas.[77]

The first approach focuses on prominent figures and is represented by Schacht, who, as seen earlier, propounded a two-stage narrative. In the first stage, the early, "ancient" schools, expressed in terms of regional normative traditions, emerged in Iraq, Medina, Syria, and later on in Egypt. In the second stage, before and after the turn of the third/ninth century, these transitioned into "personal" schools defined by exclusive adherence to the doctrine of an eponymous imam.[78] Schacht's thesis gave prominent credit to al-Shafiʿi, whose distinct synthesis of textual and rational interpretation enabled legal doctrine to be packaged, transported, and systematically applied without reliance on local tradition.[79] Schacht's narrative is largely based on al-Shafiʿi's writings and ends with his death in 204/820, but the implication is that he set the schools on their new trajectory. The novel legal theory formulated by al-Shafiʿi became the new way of articulating law, but it was al-Shafiʿi's personal authority, and that of the other eponymous imams, that served as the new organizing principle for the legal schools.

The second approach emphasizes the importance of social and political institutions for the development and spread of the classical schools. George Makdisi

(J. Schacht); "Ahmad b. Hanbal" (H. Laoust). For short but more informative biographies on al-Shafiʿi and Ibn Hanbal, see Ali, *Imam Shafiʿi*; Melchert, *Ahmad ibn Hanbal*.

[77] These are, of course, not rigidly defined categories, but notional centers of gravity for the respective scholars' analysis.

[78] Schacht, *Origins*, 6–10.

[79] Subsequent debates regarding al-Shafiʿi's importance and impact are discussed in Section VI.

(1920–2002), and after him his student Christopher Melchert, took up Schacht's early periodization and extended the narrative into the third/ninth century (and beyond). Makdisi saw in this period the evolution of the personal schools into de facto guilds that featured a hierarchical structure of leadership and were dedicated to the education of students and the reproduction of knowledge, a mission that eventually came to be performed within the space of the law college (*madrasa*).[80] Melchert considered the regularization of legal education to be *the* defining moment for a school's birth. He proposed precise dates of formation—either in the late third/ninth century or in the early fourth/tenth—for each school based on the lives of particular teachers who established regular systems for transmitting legal doctrines.[81]

Both Makdisi and Melchert accorded tremendous (in Melchert's case, nearly exclusive) weight to biographical works in the construction of their narratives.[82] This source preference generated a certain historiographical bias in favor of scholarly activity in Iraq in general and of Hadith scholarship in Baghdad in particular.[83] Makdisi's emphasis on Baghdad seems in great measure a function of his interest in the city's Hadith-minded jurists and theologians (whom he termed "traditionalists" in opposition to the "rationalists") and in the emergence of Hanbalism. He saw the Qur'anic Inquisition in Baghdad as the decisive showdown between the rationalists and the traditionalists[84] in a conflict that had been put into motion by al-Shafi'i and was brought to a conclusion by Ahmad b. Hanbal, whose unyielding stance on the textual primacy of the Qur'an and Hadith carried the day for the traditionalists.[85] This is another example of the tendency, mentioned earlier, to depict intellectual conflicts in overtly martial terms. In the end, the victorious Hanbalis forced the hand of the rationalist jurists, who by the fourth/tenth century had largely begun to reframe their legal thought to square with the compulsions of Hadith reports. In more certain terms, Melchert saw this rapprochement between traditionalists and rationalists as the decisive moment in which the law acquired its classical framework.[86]

Other scholars have linked the schools' growth and spread to the relative levels of state patronage they enjoyed. Using later biographical dictionaries, Nurit Tsafrir constructed chronological charts of judicial tenure in the various regions in the second/eighth and third/ninth centuries and correlated the spread of the Hanafi school with the increasing number of Hanafi jurists taking up posts in

[80] Makdisi, *Rise of Colleges*. [81] Melchert, *Formation of the Sunni Schools*, xxvii.

[82] Makdisi, "*Tabaqat*-Biography"; Melchert, *Formation of the Sunni Schools*, xxvii–xxviii. For an overview of the genre of Muslim intellectual biography, see Kadi, "Biographical Dictionaries."

[83] The bias may have been directly or indirectly influenced by a subtle but similar bias in Schacht's work. According to Schacht, Medina shared Iraq's ancient doctrine, but where cross-influences existed, they nearly always moved from Iraq to Medina. See Schacht, *Origins*, 220.

[84] He thus viewed it differently from Crone and Hinds, who, as seen earlier, interpreted the inquisition as a political struggle for religious authority.

[85] Makdisi, *Rise of Colleges*, 6–9. [86] Melchert, "Traditionist-Jurisprudents."

the empire's expanding judiciary.[87] Her work supported the general thesis that the Hanafi school flourished chiefly thanks to the backing of the Abbasid center. She conceded, however, that in so early a period school identities were still ill defined, and she coined the term "semi-Hanafi" to describe jurists of ambiguous affiliation.

The third approach to school formation shifts the emphasis from the personages of the imams and the formal institutions of learning and patronage to the idea of doctrinal authority. It has been articulated most extensively by Hallaq, who, as described earlier, contested Schacht's progression from regional to personal schools. Rejecting the notion of regional schools altogether, Hallaq argued that the first schools of the second/eighth century were personal, marked by the dominance of individual master jurists and consisting of their positive legal opinions. In the third/ninth century these schools then acquired a "doctrinal" framework that defined the classical schools from then on. The doctrinal schools, Hallaq maintained, were composite systems, comprising the cumulative legal rulings of successive generations of jurists (e.g. Abu Hanifa and his two leading students, Abu Yusuf and al-Shaybani) as well as a clear methodology for addressing legal problems. Each of the schools was also defined by the loyalty of its adherents, who abandoned its doctrines on pain of rejection from the school. The eponymous imams, by this view, were not founders of their schools but were accorded this status fictitiously by later jurists in order to provide the schools with an axis of authority.[88] This authority was preserved by the widely accepted principle of legal conformism (*taqlid*), discussed further in the next section.

More recent studies, wary of the pitfalls of singling out historical causes, forgo the impulse to date and attempt instead to unpack the socio-political contexts and gradual intellectual processes that underpinned the formation of the classical schools. This scholarship revises the preceding theses by combining and complicating their categories. For example, Umar Faruq Abd-Allah studied the life and works of Malik, parsing his legal terminology and contending that his rulings embody an interpretive process that was far more systematic and sophisticated than the nebulous "living tradition" that Schacht and others had made it out to be. Though not concerned with the school's formalization and spread beyond the second/eighth century, Abd-Allah maintained that a richer understanding of Malik's thought could change how we understand the formation of the schools.[89] El Shamsy returned to Schacht's historical scheme of regional schools followed by personal ones but further theorized personal schools as communities of jurists centered on a discursive "paradigm" founded by the eponym. This paradigm allowed successive jurists, through the development of a secondary literature, to extend and

[87] Tsafrir, *History of an Islamic School of Law*.
[88] Hallaq, *Origins and Evolution*, 155–167; Hallaq, *Authority, Continuity, and Change*.
[89] Abd-Allah, *Malik and Medina*; cf. Dutton, *Origins of Islamic Law*.

even disagree with the founder's opinions while remaining faithful to his methods of interpretation.[90] Saud Al-Sarhan pursued a similar approach in an article-length study of the Hanbali school. By reviewing the legal responsa collected by eight of Ibn Hanbal's students, Al-Sarhan offered examples of how these students tried to extract the imam's legal-theoretical principles from his rulings.[91]

Put together, the findings of these recent studies suggest that an integrated examination of the ideas expressed in early legal texts alongside the narratives in historical and biographical works produces more fruitful results than impressionistic interpretations of a limited and often arbitrary selection of sources. Such a holistic approach allows for a clearer understanding of how legal thought developed over the course of the third/ninth century, which facilitates a better understanding of the trajectory it took in the two centuries that followed.

VI. Legal Developments in the Fourth/Tenth and Fifth/Eleventh Centuries

This section addresses three of the most significant developments in the evolution of Islamic law in the fourth/tenth and fifth/eleventh centuries. The first is the putative closing of the gate of *ijtihad*; the second, the development of legal theory following al-Shafi'i; and the third, the emergence of a distinctive Shi'i jurisprudence.

A. Closing the Gate of *Ijtihad*

When Snouck Hurgronje first put forward the idea—adopted from indigenous Muslim historiography[92]—that the exercise of *ijtihad*, or independent legal reasoning, had ceased around the turn of the third/ninth century, he could not have anticipated the controversy that would ensue.[93] Indeed, few controversies in the field of Islamic legal history have gained as much traction as the debate concerning the "closing of the gate of *ijtihad*." Schacht, who studied under Snouck Hurgronje,

[90] El Shamsy, *Canonization*, ch. 7.

[91] Al-Sarhan, "Responsa of Ahmad Ibn Hanbal."

[92] See e.g. El Shamsy, "*Hashiya* in Islamic Law."

[93] Hurgronje, review of *Muhammedanisches Recht* by Sachau. The idea acquired particular salience in the context of the Orientalist view of the Islamic world's historical decline.

popularized his teacher's view, and his authority lent the topic weight. In his clearest statement on the subject, Schacht wrote:

> [B]y the beginning of the fourth/tenth century ... the point had been reached when the scholars of all schools felt that all essential questions had been thoroughly discussed and finally settled, and a consensus gradually established itself to the effect that from that time onwards no one could be deemed to have the necessary qualifications for independent reasoning in religious law, and that all future activity would have to be confined to the explanation, application, and, at the most, interpretation of the doctrine as it had been laid down once and for all. This "closing of the gate of *ijtihad*," as it was called, amounted to the demand for *taklid* ... which now came to mean the unquestioning acceptance of the doctrines of established schools and authorities.[94]

This thesis fit within Schacht's broader account of the decline of intellectual sophistication in the later tradition. While Schacht acknowledged that the work of later jurists was "no less creative ... than that of their predecessors" and noted the ongoing dispute regarding *ijtihad* among them, the fact that he never elaborated on the character of their innovative contribution led his successors to view as conclusive his emphatic remarks about the stagnation of the later tradition.[95]

The thesis of the closure of the gate of *ijtihad* remained largely unchallenged for several decades, and its influence is evident in every major work written on Islamic law in the twentieth century.[96] Hallaq reignited the debate and advanced the most sustained challenge to Schacht's work in a series of articles written in the 1980s and 1990s. His essay "Was the Gate of Ijtihad Closed?" in many ways reset the course of inquiry on the topic. In it, he argued that the gates of *ijtihad* were never closed in either theory or practice. As evidence, Hallaq characterized the requirements for reaching the rank of *mujtahid* as relatively easy; typified *ijtihad* as indispensable for the derivation of rulings through legal theory; documented the exclusion from Sunnism of groups who opposed *ijtihad*; listed jurists who lived after the fourth/tenth century and were labeled *mujtahid*s or practiced *ijtihad*; and traced the persistence of the controversy regarding *ijtihad* in classical works.[97] In a follow-up article, Hallaq addressed the question of why the controversy concerning the existence of *mujtahid*s existed when *ijtihad* never ceased. He located the answer beyond the confines of the law, in "the theological doctrine of the end of religion and the coming of the Day of Judgment."[98]

Hallaq's studies generated renewed interest in the question. Norman Calder steered a middle course between Schacht and Hallaq. He followed Schacht by upholding the Islamic legal tradition's distinction between *ijtihad* as direct

[94] Schacht, *Introduction*, 70–71.
[95] Schacht, *Introduction*, 73; Schacht, "Taklid."
[96] See e.g. Coulson, *History of Islamic Law*, 80; Gibb, *Whither Islam?*, 67.
[97] Hallaq, "Was the Gate of Ijtihad Closed?"
[98] Hallaq, "On the Origins of the Controversy," 134.

confrontation with revelation, which generally ceased after al-Shafiʿi, and *ijtihad* as innovative responses to new cases and creative legal thinking within the constraints of *taqlid*, which was ongoing. He conceded Hallaq's central thesis: that creative legal reasoning did not cease or even necessarily decline after the third/ninth century. Beyond this point, however, Calder thoroughly critiqued Hallaq's study, particularly for failing to make systematic distinctions between various types of *ijtihad* and for not qualifying the depiction of *ijtihad* as a sustained phenomenon.[99] Importantly, Calder differed on the role of legal theory. He saw this discipline only as an ex post facto justification of law, while Hallaq conceived of the process of *ijtihad* as it is described in works of legal theory, namely, as a "coherent system of principles through which a qualified jurist could extract rulings for novel cases."[100]

Despite their sharply divergent accounts, Schacht's and Hallaq's theses share one major premise: they both typify *ijtihad* as creative legal thought while associating *taqlid* with blind imitation, lack of originality, and a qualitative decline in legal scholarship. Several scholars have challenged this negative depiction of *taqlid* and the concomitant depiction of *ijtihad* as the natural *telos* of Islamic law. They have argued that *taqlid* is in fact a more advanced stage of legal development with its own social logic as the mainstay of a mature legal system. Sherman Jackson maintained that *taqlid* was not motivated by "any real or perceived inability on the part of post-formative jurists to come up with novel interpretations."[101] Rather, he characterized post-formative *taqlid* as a dynamic institution whose primary function was to appropriate the established authority of the earlier tradition and thereby to legitimize the interpretations of later jurists by virtue of their affiliation to the *mujtahid* imams.[102] In a similar vein, Mohammad Fadel drew on the sociology of law and an analysis of legal process to highlight the crucial social logic of *taqlid*: not only was it essential for guaranteeing a stable and determinate legal system that ensured uniform rules, but it also limited the discretionary power of legal officials, especially those at the bottom of the legal hierarchy.[103] Beyond the *taqlid–ijtihad* dichotomy, El Shamsy identified a discourse that theorized precedent as a "distinct locus of normativity" in discussions of the *qibla* (direction of prayer) in Shafiʿi legal works.[104] This justification of precedent enabled later jurists to bypass al-Shafiʿi's explicit prohibition of *taqlid* and to assign his legal views a privileged status as binding interpretations that were distinct from but consistently bolstered by revelatory evidence.

[99] Calder, "Al-Nawawi's Typology."

[100] Ibid., 158; Hallaq, "Was the Gate of Ijtihad Closed?," 5. Sadeghi largely agreed with Calder on this issue in *The Logic of Law Making in Islam*.

[101] Jackson, "*Taqlid*, Legal Scaffolding and the Scope of Legal Injunctions," 172.

[102] Ibid., 169, 172.

[103] Fadel, "Social Logic of *Taqlid*."

[104] El Shamsy, "Rethinking *Taqlid*."

B. Legal Theory After al-Shafiʿi

Conventional accounts of the history of legal theory see al-Shafiʿi's *Risala* as the work that gave birth to the discipline and formed the basis of subsequent contributions. However, the development of legal theory in the century and a half that followed al-Shafiʿi's death has been difficult to reconstruct. The second extant treatise dedicated to legal theory is *al-Fusul fi al-usul* by al-Jassas (d. 370/981). This work was closely followed by a proliferation of writings on legal theory in all four Sunni schools, as well as among the Muʿtazila and the Zahiris in North Africa, by such illustrious scholars as al-Baqillani (d. 403/1013), al-Dabbusi (d. 430/1039), Abu Yaʿla b. al-Farraʾ (d. 458/1065), al-Juwayni (d. 478/1085), Abu al-Husayn al-Basri (d. 436/1044), and Ibn Hazm (d. 456/1064).

The apparent gap in the extant record between al-Shafiʿi and al-Jassas led Hallaq to argue, against Schacht, that al-Shafiʿi's centrality in the inauguration of legal theory has been greatly overstated and that his allegedly foundational work in fact had little resonance until Ibn Surayj (d. 306/918) and his students popularized it in the fourth/tenth century.[105] By contrast, other scholars have argued that the formative influence of al-Shafiʿi on subsequent legal theory is evident in the significant body of fragmentary and indirect evidence available from the third/ninth and fourth/tenth centuries. In the past few decades, several studies have successfully demonstrated how intellectual history can be reconstructed in the absence of contemporaneous sources. They have shown that the period after al-Shafiʿi was a dynamic one: al-Shafiʿi's ideas were continuously discussed and reworked in the form of abridgments, commentaries, and refutations, and a technical vocabulary was developed, debated, and refined.[106] For example, Murteza Bedir has used al-Jassas's work to establish the views and significance of ʿIsa b. Aban (d. 221/836), a much earlier jurist, and to trace his engagement with al-Shafiʿi's ideas.[107] Using a similar methodology, Devin Stewart has reconstructed a lost treatise on legal theory by Dawud al-Zahiri (d. 271/884) from the copious quotations of it in al-Qadi Nuʿman's (d. 363/974) *Ikhtilaf usul al-madhahib*.[108] And El Shamsy has found al-Shafiʿi's theoretical discussions reproduced and expanded by Ibn Surayj in the late third/ninth century and by Abu Bakr al-Khaffaf in the early fourth/tenth century.[109]

When compared with al-Shafiʿi's *Risala*, works of legal theory written after the second half of the fourth/tenth century exhibit certain literary features that reveal the discipline's course of development in the intervening century and a half. First and foremost, mature legal theory demonstrates how thoroughly the Shafiʿi paradigm won out

[105] Hallaq, "Was al-Shafiʿi the Master Architect?"

[106] In addition to the references in the following notes, see El Shamsy and Zysow, "Al-Buwayti's Abridgment"; El Shamsy, "Wisdom of God's Law"; Stewart, "Al-Tabari's *al-Bayan*"; Temel, "Missing Link."

[107] Bedir, "Early Response to Shafiʿi."

[108] Stewart, "Muhammad b. Dawud al-Zahiri's Manual of Jurisprudence."

[109] El Shamsy, "Bridging the Gap."

over contending approaches. There is considerable evidence that as early as the first half of the third/ninth century, scholars from other schools had already assimilated the central feature of the Shafiʿi paradigm—namely, the prioritization of textual evidence rooted in the canonized revelatory sources, especially the Hadith—and that they adopted some of al-Shafiʿi's conceptual tools and hermeneutic techniques.[110] David Vishanoff has carefully documented the debates surrounding legal hermeneutics in the period after al-Shafiʿi, showing that while Sunni theorists were initially torn between four different hermeneutical visions representing distinctive conceptual models of how language reveals the law (the literalist Zahiri, the Basran Muʿtazili, the Ashʿari theological, and the law-oriented paradigms), in the fifth/eleventh century the law-oriented paradigm championed by Abu Yaʿla b. al-Farraʾ triumphed, assisted by the resurgence of traditionalism and the rise of the legal schools.[111]

A second feature of developed legal theory is its incorporation of the theological concerns of rationalist theology and the sharply deductive theoretical and dialectical methods it employed. This feature was first noted by Makdisi, who placed the development in its historical context and highlighted its departure from the legal theory articulated by al-Shafiʿi, which contained a pronounced antirationalist dimension.[112] In his study of legal theory after al-Shafiʿi, El Shamsy showed that Shafiʿis in the early fourth/tenth century were undeterred by their master's condemnation of rationalist theology. They embedded legal theory both substantively and methodologically within a rationalist ethical framework: reason and revelation were assigned complementary roles; the securing of human interest (*maslaha*) was posited as the structuring principle of the law; and the formalistic method of dialectics (*jadal*) formed the basis of analogical reasoning. With the advent of Ashʿarism, however, law was extracted from the realm of theology, while a "detheologized" variety of *maslaha* was integrated into a firmly legal methodology of reasoning.[113] The most detailed examination of a theological controversy developed in legal theory is Reinhart's comprehensive study of legality in the absence of revelation, a controversial problem that was debated vigorously in classical works of legal theory. Reinhart analyzed the underlying epistemological and moral issues that this debate indexes, including the limits of human intellect, the significance of revelation, and moral categorization and its relation to ontology.[114]

c. Emergence of a Distinct Shiʿi Law

Early Shiʿi legal history remains an understudied field, as Shiʿism in general and early Shiʿism in particular have been seen primarily as subjects of theological and

[110] See e.g. Dutton, "ʿAmal v Hadith"; Jackson, "Setting the Record Straight"; El Shamsy, *Canonization*, ch. 8.
[111] Vishanoff, *Formation of Islamic Hermeneutics*.
[112] Makdisi, "Juridical Theology of Shafiʿi."
[113] El Shamsy, "Wisdom of God's Law."
[114] Reinhart, *Before Revelation*.

political, not legal, interest.[115] Consequently, most accounts of early Twelver Shiʿi (or Imami) law have adopted a theological periodization. This framework describes the period before the occultation (*ghayba*) of the twelfth imam in 260/874 as one in which Shiʿi law remained relatively underdeveloped, owing to the accessibility of the imam, who presided over the community as the exclusive source of infallible judgment. The sudden absence of the imam then necessitated the development of a more systematic approach to law. In the most comprehensive work to date on Shiʿi (in particular, Imami) legal history written in a European language, Hossein Modarressi disputed this picture as overly simplistic, arguing that the earliest sources depict a dynamic and heterogeneous circle of followers, who were encouraged by the imams to exercise their individual reason and who expressed a variety of legal opinions even in the presence of the imams.[116]

After the twelfth imam's occultation, the fourth/tenth and fifth/eleventh centuries represented a period of crucial intellectual ferment and doctrinal crystallization for the nascent Imami Shiʿi community. The first Imami Hadith collections were compiled in the last decades of the third/ninth century and in the early fourth/tenth, and the first works of legal theory were written in the century that followed.[117] Sunni Hadith collections and jurisprudence thus predate their Shiʿi counterparts by more than a century, and the former exercised a significant formative influence on the latter, both in terms of structure and substantively in the incorporation of select elements of legal theory and positive law. This fact has shaped an important debate in the field of Shiʿi legal studies, namely, how to characterize the historical interaction between the Sunni and Shiʿi legal systems. In his terse treatment of Shiʿi legal history, Schacht maintained that in the first three centuries, Shiʿi law was closely identified with Sunni law, and that modifications introduced to "orthodox" legal doctrines were only "superficial" concessions necessitated by political exigencies or essential Shiʿi doctrines.[118] It was only after the occultation, Schacht argues, that Shiʿi legal doctrine gradually distinguished itself as a separate legal system.[119]

Several scholars after Schacht have likewise supported the thesis of extensive Shiʿi borrowing of legal thought from the Sunni schools.[120] Devin Stewart's study has been the most comprehensive to date. He examined structural features adopted by Shiʿi jurists from Sunni law, especially consensus, which he argued became the hallmark of orthodoxy in the fourth/tenth and fifth/eleventh centuries.[121] Stewart created a typology of three responses to Sunni orthodoxy among Shiʿi jurists: first, outward

115 Haider, "Prayer, Mosque, and Pilgrimage," 152.

116 Modarressi, *Introduction*, 24–25.

117 However, Shiʿi thinkers were clearly engaging with questions of legal theory already; see Gleave, "Early Shiite Hermeneutics."

118 Schacht, "Fikh"; Schacht, *Introduction*, 16.

119 Schacht, *Origins*, 54, 99, 262.

120 Muzaffar, *Usul al-fiqh*, 3:97; Cole, "Imami Jurisprudence," 35; Modarressi, *Introduction*, 44, 48; Madelung, "Authority in Twelver Shiism," 168; Moussavi, *Religious Authority in Shiʿite Islam*, 26, 30, 85, 164 n. 47, 170.

121 Stewart, *Islamic Legal Orthodoxy*.

conformity with the Sunni consensus and adherence to the Shafiʿi school among the four Sunni schools; second, adoption of a modified version of consensus and a parallel legal school for Twelver Shiʿis; and third, outright rejection of the Sunni legal system on the grounds that it violates fundamental Shiʿi principles. Stewart posited a trajectory that was diametrically opposed to that outlined by Schacht. On the level of legal theory, he contended, early Shiʿi law was originally quite different from Sunni law and only gradually came to conform to the more dominant Sunni legal system.[122] Furthermore, although the dominant view continues to be that the institution of the Shiʿi *madhhab* and the development of Shiʿi legal theory were engendered by the urgent need to fill the vacuum in religious authority after the disappearance of the imam,[123] Stewart has argued that a more decisive factor was the formation of the Sunni schools, which created a desire among Shiʿi legal scholars to be included within the wider community of jurists.[124]

VII. Conclusion: Directions for Future Research

We conclude this survey of modern debates regarding the origins and early development of Islamic law by pointing to a few of the many promising avenues for further inquiry in this field.

There is still much room to improve our understanding of the origins of Islamic law by comparing the emerging Islamic norms with preexisting legal systems. However, such studies ought to be carried out holistically. Narrow and formalistic comparisons between legal systems are of limited use, since parallels between individual laws are often coincidental and cannot provide concrete evidence of a genetic relationship.[125] A good example of a holistic study is Motzki's examination of how pre-Islamic Arabian norms on the treatment of defaulting debtors were transformed into classical Islamic rules.[126] Motzki's legal-historical analysis is preceded and supported by painstaking authentication of the relevant source material, which brings us to a second area of fruitful future concern.

122 Ibid., 17.

123 In the case of Ismaʿilism, however, these developments took place in the presence of the imam; see al-Qadi al-Nuʿman, *Disagreements of the Jurists*; Qutbuddin, "Fatimid Legal Exegesis of the Qur'an."

124 Stewart, *Islamic Legal Orthodoxy*.

125 A study that illustrates the perils of the latter approach is Jokisch, *Islamic Imperial Law*; see esp. 627–650.

126 Motzki et al., *Analysing Muslim Traditions*, ch. 3, esp. 194–204.

While the revisionist trend succeeded in pressing home the need for a more rigorous approach to the sources for early Islamic history, it impoverished the study of early Islamic law by dismissing the bulk of the available material on the subject—namely, Hadith and reports on the early generations of Muslims. The *isnad-cum-matn* analysis represents a methodological offensive to reclaim these sources and to use them critically for the study of early Islam, including Islamic law. But it is neither the only nor the most obvious way to bring out new sources. Another is to examine the enormous body of surviving early Islamic papyri, which remain largely unmined for insights into early Islamic law.[127] As historical artifacts, papyri are not subject to the authenticity questions that afflict other types of sources. There are also important manuscripts from the early literary period of Islamic law that have not been edited or studied, including manuscripts held in well-known and accessible libraries.[128] Moreover, even many key works that have been published remain curiously understudied. Such works include the foundational opus of the Hanafi school, al-Shaybani's *Kitab al-Asl*, which was fully edited and published only in 2012.[129] The problem of understudied sources is closely related to our final point, namely, how to study them to begin with.

The big questions that animate the field of early Islamic legal history have been debated since the nineteenth century, but this interest has not, by and large, been accompanied by the kind of foundational research that is necessary to provide a reliable basis for answering these larger questions. Until the end of the twentieth century, the dearth of such research could be traced to the small number of scholars working on Islamic law. The expansion of the field since then has created new opportunities, but the present academic ecosystem in the humanities does not reward the unglamorous and laborious spadework of reading manuscripts and compiling documents. Collaborative projects, such as the European Research Council project "Islamic Law Materialized," led by Christian Müller, should be commended for the service they render to the field.[130] The corpus of early Arabic legal documents assembled by this project is an important contribution toward the vertical integration of sources, from documents such as wills and contracts up through the most abstract discussions of theory. Such integration of sources can reveal the connections between private ritual observance, everyday contracts between individuals, adversarial encounters in court, debates among jurists on fine points of law, and theories of the relationship of law to reason and revelation. It is thus a precondition for writing a truly comprehensive history of Islamic law in the classical period.

[127] Sijpesteijn, "*Hadith* Fragment on Papyrus," is a relatively rare exception; but see also El Shamsy, "Debates on Prayer."

[128] As but one example, a manuscript copy of Abu Ishaq al-Marwazi's (d. 340/951) important work *al-Tawassut bayn al-Shafi'i wa-l-Muzani* languishes unstudied in Yale's Beinecke Library, misattributed to Ibn al-Qass in the catalog.

[129] A partial edition by Abu al-Wafa' al-Afghani was published in 1966–1973.

[130] See the project's database at http://cald.irht.cnrs.fr/php/ilm.php.

References

Abd-Allah Wymann-Landgraf, Umar F, *Malik and Medina: Islamic Legal Reasoning in the Formative Period* (Leiden: Brill, 2013).

Ali, Kecia, *Imam Shafiʿi: Scholar and Saint* (Oxford: Oneworld, 2011).

Al-Sarhan, Saud, "The Responsa of Ahmad Ibn Hanbal and the Formation of Hanbalism." *Islamic Law and Society* 22 (2015): 1–44.

Anderson, James Norman Dalrymple, Review of *Origins of Muhammadan Jurisprudence*, by Joseph Schacht. *Die Welt des Islams* 2, no. 2 (1952): 136.

Azami, Muhammad Mustafa, *Studies in Early Hadith Literature* (Beirut: al-Maktab al-Islami, 1968).

Azami, Muhammad Mustafa, *On Schacht's Origins of Muhammadan Jurisprudence* (Riyadh: King Saud University, 1985).

Bearman, Peri, Peters, Rudolph, and Vogel, Frank E., eds. *The Islamic School of Law: Evolution, Devolution, and Progress* (Cambridge, MA: Harvard University Press, 2005).

Bedir, Murteza, "An Early Response to Shafiʿi: ʿIsa b. Aban on the Prophetic Report (*Khabar*)." *Islamic Law and Society* 9, no. 3 (2002): 285–311.

Berg, Herbert, "Competing Paradigms in Islamic Origins: Qur'an 15:89–91" in Herbert Berg (ed.) *Method and Theory in the Study of Islamic Origins*. (Leiden: Brill, 2003) 259–290.

Brown, Jonathan A. C., *The Canonization of al-Bukhari and Muslim: The Formation and Function of the Sunni Hadith Canon* (Leiden: Brill, 2007).

Calder, Norman, "Al-Nawawi's Typology of Muftis and Its Significance for a General Theory of Islamic Law." *Islamic Law and Society* 3, no. 2 (1996): 137–164.

Chaumont, E., *The Encyclopaedia of Islam*, second edition s.v. "Al-Shafiʿi."

Cole, Juan R., "Imami Jurisprudence and the Role of the Ulama" in Nikki R. Keddie (ed.) *Religion and Politics in Iran: Shiʿism from Quietism to Revolution* (New Haven, CT: Yale University Press, 1983) 33–46.

Coulson, Noel J., *A History of Islamic Law* (Edinburgh: Edinburgh University Press, 1964).

Coulson, Noel J., *Conflicts and Tensions in Islamic Jurisprudence* (Chicago: University of Chicago Press, 1969).

Crone, Patricia, *Meccan Trade and the Rise of Islam* (Princeton, NJ: Princeton University Press, 1987).

Crone, Patricia, *Roman, Provincial and Islamic Law: The Origins of the Islamic Patronate* (Cambridge: Cambridge University Press, 1987).

Crone, Patricia, "Serjeant and *Meccan Trade*." *Arabica* 39, no. 2 (1992): 216–240.

Crone, Patricia, "Two Legal Problems Bearing on the Early History of the Qur'an." *Jerusalem Studies in Arabic and Islam* 18 (1994): 1–37.

Crone, Patricia, *The Qur'anic Pagans and Related Matters. Vol. 1 of Collected Studies in Three Volumes* Hanna Siurua (ed.) 3 vols (Leiden: Brill, 2016).

Crone, Patricia, and Cook, Michael A., *Hagarism: The Making of the Islamic World* (Cambridge: Cambridge University Press, 1977).

Crone, Patricia, and Hinds, Martin, *God's Caliph: Religious Authority in the First Centuries of Islam* (Cambridge: Cambridge University Press, 1986).

Donner, Fred M., *Narratives of Islamic Origins: The Beginnings of Islamic Historical Writing* (Princeton, NJ: Darwin Press, 1998).

Dutton, Yasin, "ʿAmal v Hadith in Islamic Law: The Case of *Sadl al-Yadayn* (Holding One's Hands by One's Sides) When Doing the Prayer." *Islamic Law and Society* 3, no. 1 (1996): 13–40.

Dutton, Yasin, *The Origins of Islamic Law: The Quran, the Muwatta', and Madinan 'Amal* (London: Curzon, 1999).

El Shamsy, Ahmed, "Rethinking *Taqlid* in the Early Shafi'i School." *Journal of the American Oriental Society* 128, no. 1 (2008): 1–23.

El Shamsy, Ahmed, *The Canonization of Islamic Law: A Social and Intellectual History* (Cambridge: Cambridge University Press, 2013).

El Shamsy, Ahmed, "The *Hashiya* in Islamic Law: A Sketch of the Shafi'i Literature." *Oriens* 41, no. 3/4 (2013): 289–315.

El Shamsy, Ahmed, "The Wisdom of God's Law: Two Theories" in Robert Gleave and A. Kevin Reinhart (eds.) *Islamic Law in Theory: Studies on Jurisprudence in Honor of Bernard Weiss* (Leiden: Brill, 2014) 19–37.

El Shamsy, Ahmed, "Debates on Prayer in Second/Eighth-Century Islam: Some Remarks on Sijpesteijn's Papyrus." *Journal of Near Eastern Studies* 75, no. 2 (2016): 335–337.

El Shamsy, Ahmed, "Bridging the Gap: Two Early Texts on Islamic Legal Theory." *Journal of the American Oriental Society* 137, no. 3 (2017): 505–536.

El Shamsy, Ahmed, and Aron Zysow, "Al-Buwayti's Abridgment of al-Shafi'i's *Risala:* Edition and Translation." *Islamic Law and Society* 19, no. 4 (2012): 327–355.

Fadel, Mohammad, "The Social Logic of *Taqlid* and the Rise of the *Mukhtasar*." *Islamic Law and Society* 3, no. 2 (1996): 193–233.

Fück, Johann, "Review of *Origins of Muhammadan Jurisprudence*, by Joseph Schacht." *Bibliotheca Orientalis* 10 (1953): 196–199.

Geiger, Abraham, *Was hat Mohammed aus dem Judenthume aufgenommen?* (Bonn: F. Baaden, 1833).

Gibb, Hamilton A. R., Review of *Origins of Muhammadan Jurisprudence*, by Joseph Schacht. *Journal of Comparative Legislation and International Law*, 3rd ser., 33, no. 3/4 (1951): 113–114.

Gibb, Hamilton A. R., *Whither Islam? A Survey of Modern Muslim Movements in the Moslem World* (London: V. Gollancz, 1932).

Gleave, Robert, "Early Shiite Hermeneutics and the Dating of *Kitab Sulaym ibn Qays*." *Bulletin of the School of Oriental and African Studies* 78, no. 1 (2015): 83–103.

Goitein, Shelomo Dov, "The Birth-Hour of Muslim Law? An Essay in Exegesis." *Muslim World* 50, no. 1 (1960): 23–29.

Goitein, Shelomo Dov, *A Mediterranean Society: The Jewish Communities of the Arab World as Portrayed in the Documents of the Cairo Geniza*. Berkeley: University of California Press, 1967–. Edited into one volume by Jacob Lassner as *A Mediterranean Society: An Abridgment in One Volume* (Berkeley: University of California Press, 1999).

Goldziher, Ignaz, *Muslim Studies*. Edited by S. M. Stern. Translated by C. R. Barber and S. M. Stern. 2 vols (Chicago: Aldine, 1971). Page references are to the pagination of the German edition, which appears bracketed in the translation's margins.

Goldziher, Ignaz, *The Zahiris: Their Doctrine and Their History*. Translated by Wolfgang Behn (Leiden: Brill, 1972).

Haider, Najam, "Prayer, Mosque, and Pilgrimage: Mapping Shi'i Sectarian Identity in 2nd/8th Century Kufa." *Islamic Law and Society* 16, no. 2 (2009): 151–174.

Hallaq, Wael B., "Was the Gate of Ijtihad Closed?" *International Journal of Middle East Studies* 16, no. 1 (1984): 3–41.

Hallaq, Wael B., "On the Origins of the Controversy about the Existence of Mujtahids and the Gate of Ijtihad." *Studia Islamica*, no. 63 (1986): 129–141.

Hallaq, Wael B., "The Use and Abuse of Evidence: The Question of Provincial and Roman Influences on Early Islamic Law." *Journal of the American Oriental Society* 110, no. 1 (1990): 79–91.

Hallaq, Wael B., "Was al-Shafi'i the Master Architect of Islamic Jurisprudence?" *International Journal of Middle East Studies* 25, no. 4 (1993): 587–605.

Hallaq, Wael B., *Authority, Continuity, and Change in Islamic Law* (Cambridge: Cambridge University Press, 2001).

Hallaq, Wael B., "From Regional to Personal Schools of Law? A Reevaluation." *Islamic Law and Society* 8, no. 1 (2001): 1–26.

Hallaq, Wael B., "The Quest for Origins or Doctrine? Islamic Legal Studies as Colonialist Discourse." *UCLA Journal of Islamic and Near Eastern Law* 2, no. 1 (2002–3): 1–31.

Hallaq, Wael B., *The Origins and Evolution of Islamic Law* (Cambridge: Cambridge University Press, 2005).

Hallaq, Wael B., "Groundwork of the Moral Law: A New Look at the Qur'an and the Genesis of the Shari'a." *Islamic Law and Society* 16 (2009): 239–279.

Hefner, Robert W., and Zaman, Muhammad Qasim, eds. *Schooling Islam: The Culture and Politics of Modern Muslim Education* (Princeton, NJ: Princeton University Press, 2007).

Hurgronje, Christian Snouck, "Nieuwe bijdragen tot de kennis van de Islam." In *Bijdragen tot de Taal-, Land- en Volkenkunde van Nederlandsch-Indië*, 4th ser., vol. 6 (1882). Reprinted in Hurgronje, *Verspreide Geschriften*, vol. 2 (Bonn: Kurt Schroeder, 1923).

Hurgronje, Christian Snouck, Review of *Muhammedanisches Recht nach schafiitischer Lehre*, by Eduard Sachau. *Zeitschrift der Deutschen Morgenländischen Gesellschaft* 53 (1899): 141–142.

Ibn Hazm, *Al-Ihkam fi usul al-ahkam*. 8 vols (Beirut: Dar al-Afaq al-Jadida, 2008).

Ibn al-Qayyim, *I'lam al-muwaqqi'in 'an rabb al-'alamin*. 7 vols (Dammam: Dar Ibn al-Jawzi, 1423 [2002]).

Jackson, Sherman A., "*Taqlid*, Legal Scaffolding and the Scope of Legal Injunctions in Post-Formative Theory: *Mutlaq* and *'Amm* in the Jurisprudence of Shihab al-Din al-Qarafi." *Islamic Law and Society* 3, no. 2 (1996): 165–192.

Jackson, Sherman A., "Setting the Record Straight: Ibn al-Labbad's Refutation of al-Shafi'i." *Journal of Islamic Studies* 11, no. 2 (2000): 121–146.

Jokisch, Benjamin, *Islamic Imperial Law: Harun-Al-Rashid's Codification Project* (Berlin: Walter de Gruyter, 2007).

Kadi, Wadad, "Biographical Dictionaries: Inner Structure and Cultural Significance" in George N. Atiyeh (ed.) *The Book in the Islamic World* (Albany: State University of New York Press, 1995) 93–122.

Katz, Marion Holmes, *Body of Text: The Emergence of the Sunni Law of Ritual Purity* (Albany: State University of New York Press, 2002).

Kremer, Alfred von, *Culturgeschichte des Orients under den Chalifen*. 2 vols (Vienna: W. Braumüller, 1875–1877).

Laoust, H., "Ahmad b. Hanbal." In *Encyclopaedia of Islam*, second edition.

Lowry, Joseph E., "The First Islamic Legal Theory: Ibn al-Muqaffa' on Interpretation, Authority, and the Structure of the Law." *Journal of the American Oriental Society* 128, no. 1 (2008): 25–40.

Lowry, Joseph E., "Reading the Qur'an as a Law Book." Yale Law School Occasional Papers, 13 (New Haven, CT: Yale Law School, 2015).

MacDonald, Duncan B., *The Development of Muslim Theology, Jurisprudence and Constitutional Theory* (New York: Scribner's Sons, 1903).
Madelung, Wilferd, "Authority in Twelver Shiism in the Absence of the Imam" in George Makdisi et al. (eds.) *La notion d'autorité au Moyen Age: Islam, Byzance, Occident* (Paris: Presses Universitaires de France, 1982) 163–173.
Maghen, Ze'ev, *Virtues of the Flesh: Passion and Purity in Early Islamic Jurisprudence* (Leiden: Brill, 2005).
Makdisi, George, *The Rise of Colleges: Institutions of Learning in Islam and the West* (Edinburgh: Edinburgh University Press, 1981).
Makdisi, George, "The Juridical Theology of Shafi'i: Origins and Significance of *Usul al-Fiqh*." *Studia Islamica*, no. 59 (1984): 5–47.
Makdisi, George, "*Tabaqat*-Biography: Law and Orthodoxy in Classical Islam." *Islamic Studies* 32, no. 4 (1993): 371–396.
Margoliouth, D.S., *The Early Development of Mohammedanism* (London: Williams and Norgate, 1914).
[al-Marwazi, Abu Ishaq], *Al-Tawassut bayn al-Shafi'i wa-l-Muzani*. Manuscript. Landberg 314, Beinecke Library, Yale University.
Masud, Muhammad Khalid, Messick, Brinkley, and Powers, David S., "Muftis, Fatwas, and Islamic Legal Interpretation" in Muhammad Khalid Masud, Brinkley Messick, and David S. Powers (eds.) *Islamic Legal Interpretation: Muftis and Their Fatwas* (Cambridge, MA: Harvard University Press, 1996) 3–32.
Melchert, Christopher, *The Formation of the Sunni Schools of Law, 9th–10th Centuries C.E* (Leiden: Brill, 1997).
Melchert, Christopher, *Ahmad ibn Hanbal* (Oxford: Oneworld, 2006).
Melchert, Christopher, "Traditionist-Jurisprudents and the Framing of Islamic Law." *Islamic Law and Society* 8, no. 3 (2001): 383–406.
Melchert, Christopher, "Basra and Kufa as the Earliest Centers of Legal Controversy" in Behnam Sadeghi, Asad Q. Ahmed, Adam J. Silverstein, and Robert G. Hoyland (eds.) *Islamic Cultures, Islamic Contexts: Essays in Honor of Professor Patricia Crone* (Leiden: Brill, 2015) 173–194.
Modarressi, Hossein, *An Introduction to Shi'i Law: A Bibliographical Study* (London: Ithaca Press, 1984).
Motzki, Harald, *The Origins of Islamic Jurisprudence: Meccan Fiqh before the Classical Schools*. Translated by Marion H. Katz (Leiden: Brill, 2002).
Motzki, Harald, "The Question of the Authenticity of Muslim Traditions Reconsidered: A Review Article" in Herbert Berg (ed.) *Method and Theory in the Study of Islamic Origins* (Leiden: Brill, 2003) 211–258.
Motzki, Harald, "Dating Muslim Traditions: A Survey," *Arabica* 52, no. 2 (2005): 204–253.
Motzki, Harald, Nicolet Boekhoff-van der Voort, and Sean W. Anthony, *Analysing Muslim Traditions: Studies in Legal, Exegetical and Maghazi Hadith* (Leiden: Brill, 2010).
Moussavi, Ahmad Kazemi, *Religious Authority in Shi'ite Islam: From the Office of Mufti to the Institution of Marja'* (Kuala Lumpur: International Institute of Islamic Thought and Civilization, 1996).
Muzaffar, Muhammad Rida, *Usul al-fiqh*. 4 vols. in 2 (Najaf: Dar al-Nu'man, 1966–1967).
Paxton, Frederick S., Review of *Meccan Trade and the Rise of Islam*, by Patricia Crone. *Journal of Asian Studies* 48, no. 3 (1989): 574–575.
Powers, David S., *Studies in Qur'an and Hadith: The Formation of the Islamic Law of Inheritance* (Berkeley: University of California Press, 1986).

Powers, Paul, "The Schools of Law" in Rudolph Peters and Peri Bearman (eds.) *The Ashgate Research Companion to Islamic Law* (Surrey: Ashgate, 2014) 42–47.

al-Qadi al-Nuʿman, *Disagreements of the Jurists: A Manual of Islamic Legal Theory*. Translated by Devin J. Stewart (New York: New York University Press, 2015).

Qutbuddin, Husain K.B., "Fatimid Legal Exegesis of the Qur'an: The Interpretive Strategies Used by al-Qadi al-Nuʿman (d. 363/974) in His *Daʿa'im al-Islam*." *Journal of Qur'anic Studies* 12 (2010): 109–146.

Reinhart, A. Kevin, Review of *Roman, Provincial, and Islamic Law*, by Patricia Crone. *American Historical Review* 95, no. 1 (1990): 215–216.

Reinhart, A. Kevin, *Before Revelation: The Boundaries of Muslim Moral Thought* (Albany: State University of New York Press, 1995).

Sachau, Eduard, "Zur ältesten Geschichte des muhammedanischen Rechts." In *Sitzungsberichte der Philosophisch-historischen Classe der Kaiserlichen Akademie der Wissenschaften*, vol. 65 (Vienna: K. K. Hof- und Staatsdruckerei, 1870).

Sadeghi, Behnam, *The Logic of Law Making in Islam* (Cambridge: Cambridge University Press, 2012).

Sadeghi, Behnam, and Uwe Bergmann, "The Codex of a Companion of the Prophet and the Qur'an of the Prophet." *Arabica* 57 (2010): 343–436.

Schacht, Joseph, "A Revaluation of Islamic Tradition." *Journal of the Royal Asiatic Society*, no. 2 (1949): 143–154.

Schacht, Joseph, *Origins of Muhammadan Jurisprudence* (Oxford: Clarendon Press, 1950).

Schacht, Joseph, *An Introduction to Islamic Law* (Oxford: Clarendon Press, 1964).

Schacht, Joseph, *Encyclopedia of Islam* s.v. "Taklid."

Schacht, Joseph, "Abu Hanifa al-Nuʿman." In *Encyclopaedia of Islam*, 2nd edn.

Schacht, Joseph, *Encyclopedia of Islam*, second edition, s.v. "Fikh."

Schacht, Joseph, *Encyclopedia of Islam*, second edition, s.v. "Malik b. Anas."

Schoeler, Gregor, *The Genesis of Literature in Islam: From the Aural to the Read*. Translated by Shawkat Toorawa (Edinburgh: Edinburgh University Press, 2009).

Serjeant, R.B., Review article on *Meccan Trade*, by Patricia Crone. *Journal of the American Oriental Society* 110, no. 3 (1990): 472–486.

Sezgin, Fuat, *Bukhari'nin kaynaklari hakkinda araştirmalar* (Istanbul: Ibrahim Horoz Basimevi, 1956).

Sijpesteijn, Petra M., "A *Hadith* Fragment on Papyrus." *Der Islam* 92, no. 2 (2015): 321–331.

Sprenger, Alois, "Skizze der Entwicklungsgeschichte des muslimischen Gesetzes." *Zeitschrift für vergleichende Rechtswissenschaft* 10 (1892): 1–31.

Stewart, Devin J., *Islamic Legal Orthodoxy: Twelver Shiite Responses to the Sunni Legal System* (Salt Lake City: University of Utah Press, 2007).

Stewart, Devin J., "Muhammad b. Dawud al-Zahiri's Manual of Jurisprudence: *Al-Wusul ila Maʿrifat al-Usul*" in Bernard G. Weiss (ed.) *Studies in Islamic Legal Theory* (Leiden: Brill, 2002) 99–137.

Stewart, Devin J., "Muhammad b. Jarir al-Tabari's *al-Bayan ʿan Usul al-Ahkam* and the Genre of *Usul al-Fiqh* in Ninth-Century Baghdad" in James Montgomery (ed.) *Abbasid Studies: Occasional Papers of the School of Abbasid Studies* (Leuven: Peeters, 2004) 321–349.

Stodolsky, Volkan, "A New Historical Model and Periodization for the Perception of the Sunnah of the Prophet and His Companions." Ph.D. diss., University of Chicago, 2012.

Temel, Ahmet, "The Missing Link in the History of Islamic Legal Theory: The Development of *Usul al-Fiqh* between al-Shafiʿi and al-Jassas during the 3rd/9th and Early 4th/10th Centuries." Ph.D. diss., University of California at Santa Barbara, 2014.

Tsafrir, Nurit, *The History of an Islamic School of Law: The Early Spread of Hanafism* (Cambridge, MA: Harvard University Press, 2004).
Vishanoff, David, *The Formation of Islamic Hermeneutics How Sunni Legal Theorists Imagined a Revealed Law* (New Haven, CT: American Oriental Society, 2011).
Wansbrough, John, *The Sectarian Milieu: Content and Composition of Islamic Salvation History* (Oxford: Oxford University Press, 1978).
Wansbrough, John, Review of *Meccan Trade and the Rise of Islam*, by Patricia Crone. *Bulletin of the School of Oriental and African Studies* 52, no. 2 (1989): 339–340.
Wansbrough, John, *Quranic Studies: Sources and Methods of Scriptural Interpretation* (Oxford: Oxford University Press, 1997).
Watt, W. Montgomery, Review of *Origins of Muhammadan Jurisprudence*, by Joseph Schacht. *Journal of the Royal Asiatic Society*, no. 1/2 (1952): 91.
Zaman, Muhammad Qasim, "The Caliphs, the 'Ulama', and the Law: Defining the Role and Function of the Caliph in the Early 'Abbasid Period." *Islamic Law and Society* 4, no. 1 (1997): 1–36.
Zaman, Muhammad Qasim, *Religion and Politics under the Early 'Abbasids: The Emergence of the Proto-Sunni Elite* (Leiden: Brill, 1997).

CHAPTER 17

THE AGE OF DEVELOPMENT AND CONTINUITY, 12TH–15TH CENTURIES CE

MARION KATZ

UNTIL fairly recently, it was widely believed in the western academy that the period from the eleventh through fifteenth centuries CE (the fifth through eighth century AH) was one of stasis, rigidity, and decline in the history of Islamic law. The leading European authority on Islamic law in the mid-twentieth century, Joseph Schacht, declared in a phenomenally influential survey that,

> [b]y the beginning of the fourth century of the hijra (about A.D. 900) ... the point had been reached when the scholars of all schools felt that all essential questions had been thoroughly discussed and finally settled, and a consensus gradually established itself to the effect that from that time onwards no one might be deemed to have the necessary qualifications for independent reasoning in law, and that all future activity would have to be confined to the explanation, application, and, at the most, interpretation of the doctrine as it had been laid down once and for all.[1]

[1] Joseph Schacht, *An Introduction to Islamic Law* (Oxford: Oxford University Press, 1964), 70–71.

In another widely cited survey published in the same year (1964), N.J. Coulson concurred that beginning in the fourth/tenth century, "[t]he spring of juristic speculation, which had supplied the rapidly moving stream of Islamic jurisprudence in its early stages, gradually ceased to flow; the current slowed, until eventually and inevitably, it reached the point of stagnation."[2] In Islamic legal terminology, the stage of *ijtihad* (intellectual "exertion" to produce new rulings) was irrevocably succeeded by the age of *taqlid* (the following of authoritative precedent). In this view, not only did Islamic legal thinking after the tenth century lack the vitality and originality to merit serious intellectual interest; its supposed inflexibility rendered it unresponsive to the changing needs of society, so that it was gradually supplanted by customary or dynastic law in most areas of practical import. For instance, Schacht argues that shariʿa-based contract law was largely displaced by "practice and custom" because "the ideal theory, being essentially retrospective, was ... unable to keep pace with the ever-changing demands of society and commerce."[3]

More recently, it has become clear that this understanding of the development of Islamic law is untenable both in chronology and in substance. It certainly places the crystallization (let alone the fossilization) of legal doctrine too early; legal thought had scarcely reached full maturity—let alone senescence—by the tenth century. According to this view, creativity would have ceased in the Hanafi school before the time of al-Sarakhsi, in the Maliki before the elder Ibn Rushd, and the Hanbali before Ibn Qudama (who produced their spectacularly creative and influential works in the eleventh, twelfth, and thirteenth centuries, respectively). More fundamentally, it is now recognized to be a fallacy that legal doctrine definitively stagnated at any particular point in history, whatever the prevalence of internal laments of dependency or decline in comparison with the early masters. This recognition was initially stimulated by a 1984 article by Wael Hallaq, who demonstrated that there was never any consensus either on the "closure of the gate of *ijtihad*" or on the non-existence of *mujtahid*s. Even those scholars who asserted either the impermissibility of *ijtihad* or the extinction of *mujtahid*s were generally referring to the absolute and unlimited degree of *ijtihad* that would have enabled a scholar to found a new school analogous to those associated with Abu Hanifa, Malik, al-Shafiʿi, and Ibn Hanbal, rather than simply to the generation of new rulings based on the methodologies of existing schools.[4] As the thirteenth-century Shafiʿi jurist Ibn ʿAbd al-Salam al-Sulami (d. 660/1262) put it, on this level the issue of the "closure of the gate of *ijtihad*" was in any case moot "because if a new case comes up and no solution is found in the scripture, or when the case is a subject of *khilaf* [dispute] among our forefathers, *ijtihad* is needed (to determine the ruling of the case)."[5]

[2] N.J. Coulson, *A History of Islamic Law* (Edinburgh: Edinburgh University Press, 1964), 73.

[3] Schacht, *Introduction*, 77.

[4] Wael Hallaq, "Was the Gate of Ijtihad Closed?" *International Journal of Middle East Studies* 16 (1984).

[5] Hallaq, "Was the Gate," 26.

This chapter will survey the current state of the field of the study of Islamic law in the twelfth through fifteenth centuries in three basic areas: the progressive stabilization and institutionalization of the four classical Sunni *madhhabs* (schools of law) and the corresponding developments in Imami Shiʿism; developments in legal theory (*usul al-fiqh*); and the practical administration of the law.

I. Fiqh, the Madhhab, and Interpretation

Although our period did not see the final crystallization of the law, a significant shift in attitudes did occur starting around its beginning. There is no doubt that in the twelfth to fifteenth centuries CE Islamic legal doctrine (*fiqh*) was more stable and institutionalized than ever before. In particular, this period immediately follows the closure of the long process by which the exuberant diversity of early legal opinion was gradually reduced to the recognition of four "classical" Sunni schools of law (*madhahib*, sing. *madhhab*), a stage Sherman Jackson has defined as the "post-formative" period.[6] Hallaq notes that "all [Sunni] jurists from the fifth/eleventh century onwards officially follow one school or another,"[7] and in the following centuries authorities including Ibn al-Salah (d. 643/1245) and Ibn Rajab al-Hanbali (d. 795/1393) overtly asserted that only the eponymous founders of the four schools were legitimate objects of legal emulation (*taqlid*).[8] Hallaq observes that the debate over the extinction of *mujtahid*s seems to have begun at the end of the eleventh century or the beginning of the twelfth.[9] Scholars in this period also often held that even a routine level of *ijtihad* (that is, the ability to derive rulings in response to practical needs, rather than to found a new methodology or school) was increasingly rare. Hallaq demonstrates in another article that while all of the eleventh-century jurists whose works he consulted affirmed that only *mujtahid*s were qualified to

[6] Sherman Jackson, "*Taqlid*, Legal Scaffolding, and the Scope of Legal Injunctions in Post-Formative Theory: *Mutlaq* and *ʿAmm* in the Jurisprudence of Shihab al-Din al-Qarafi," *Islamic Law and Society* 3 (1996): 165–192, 168.

[7] Hallaq, "Was the Gate," 11.

[8] See Ibn Rajab al-Hanbali, *Majmuʿ rasaʾil al-hafiz Ibn Rajab al-Hanbali*, ed. Abu Musʿab Talʿat ibn Fuʾad al-Hulwani, 5 vols. (N.p.: Al-Faruq al-Hadithiya liʾl-Tibaʿa waʾl-Nashr, 1423/2002), 2:619–638; al-Hattab al-Ruʿayni, ed. *Mawahib al-jalil li-sharh Mukhtasar Khalil*, ed. Zakariya ʿUmayrat, 8 vols. (Beirut: Dar al-Kutub al-ʿIlmiya, 1416/1995), 1:42.

[9] Hallaq, "Was the Gate," 23.

give *fatwas*,[10] "[b]y the middle of the thirteenth century, the concession allowing muqallids to occupy the office of ifta' seems to have become commonplace."[11] In this context as well, the perceived waning of *ijtihad* was merely a relative phenomenon; jurists continued to recognize a range of competencies in the field of legal reasoning, with only the highest levels of *ijtihad* increasingly asserted to be unavailable.

Even if it did not effectively foreclose the possibility of fresh legal reasoning, the stabilization of the four *madhahib*, and the increasing assertion among Sunnis that they cumulatively exhausted the legitimate range of legal diversity, had concrete implications for the administration of the law. Thinkers such as Ibn al-Salah and Ibn 'Abd al-Salam al-Sulami affirmed a *qadi*'s obligation to rule according to the received doctrine of his *madhhab*.[12] The Mamluk dynasty (1250–1517) obligated judges to rule according to the established doctrines of their schools of law; judges (and even *muftis*) could be disciplined for diverging from the accepted rulings of their *madhhabs*, and deviant verdicts could be overturned.[13] In the realm of legal education as well, the role of the *madhhab* was structurally entrenched; the institution of the *madrasa*, vitally important in the Islamic East throughout this period, offered salaried and prestigious teaching posts to scholars based on their *madhhab* identity.

In some ways, the trajectory of Shi'i legal thought in the period under consideration tended in the opposite direction. Norman Calder has demonstrated that, while Buyid-era (eleventh-century) authorities such as al-Sharif al-Murtada and al-Tusi firmly rejected *ijtihad* (on the grounds that it introduced inadmissible elements of subjectivity and doubt into the law), in our period Ibn Idris al-Hilli (d. 598/1201) and al-'Allama al-Hilli (d. 726/1325) denounced *taqlid* and promoted *ijtihad*.[14] This emphasis on *ijtihad* would prove dominant until the temporary reassertion of the textualist (Akhbari) trend in the seventeenth century, and ultimately achieved a dominance that has lasted until the present. Nevertheless, in many respects Imami law stabilized in ways quite reminiscent of the Sunni schools, with the works of the most influential scholars functioning as base texts that enjoyed authority and attracted commentaries for centuries thereafter; for instance, al-Muhaqqiq al-Hilli's (d. 676/1277) *Shara'i' al-islam* "has remained to this day one of the foremost works

[10] Wael Hallaq, "*Ifta'* and *Ijtihad* in Sunni Legal Theory: A Developmental Account," in *Islamic Legal Interpretation: Muftis and Their Fatwas*, eds. Muhammad Khalid Masud, Brinkley Messick, and David S. Powers (Cambridge, MA: Harvard University Press, 1996), 34.

[11] Hallaq, "*Ifta'* and *Ijtihad*," 37.

[12] Yossef Rapoport, "Legal Diversity in the Age of Taqlid: The Four Chief Qadis under the Mamluks," *Islamic Law and Society* 10 (2003): 210–228, 214.

[13] Rapoport, "Legal Diversity," 216–217; Leonor Fernandes, "Between Qadis and Muftis: To Whom Does the Mamluk Sultan Listen?" *Mamluk Studies Review* 6 (2002): 95–108, 98, 104. The stipulation that a *qadi* judge exclusively according to the doctrine of a specific school was theoretically problematic outside of the Hanafi school (see *al-Mawsu'a al-fiqhya* [Kuwait: Wizarat al-Awqaf wa'l-Shu'un al-Islamiya, 1416/1995], s.v. *qada'*, §29 (33:300–301).

[14] Norman Calder, "Doubt and Prerogative: The Emergence of an Imami Shi'i Theory of *Ijtihad*." *Studia Islamica* 70 (1990): 57–78, 65, 67; see also *Encyclopaedia Iranica*, art. "Ejtehad" (by Aron Zysow).

in Shi'i jurisprudence."[15] As Devin Stewart has argued, to some extent Imamis framed their own legal works and doctrines so as to position themselves effectively as a *madhhab* parallel to the Sunni schools.[16] For instance, towards the beginning of our period the Abbasid Caliph al-Qadir (r. 381-422/991–1031) "commissioned four leading jurists to write four epitomes of law representing the four legal schools"; the prominent Imami scholar al-Sharif al-Murtada appears to have responded by producing his legal manual *al-Intisar*, which focuses on opinions distinctive to the Imamis.[17] Robert Gleave has shown that by the end of this period, Imami authors (much like their peers in Sunni *madhhabs*) routinely cited the works of a canon of earlier jurists, rather than resorting directly to the texts of Qur'an and hadith; they legitimized their interpretations in part by placing them within a range of established *ikhtilaf* (acceptable difference of opinion), again much like members of a Sunni legal school.[18]

Since the 1990s, a large and growing body of research has demonstrated the continuing creativity and dynamism of Islamic legal thinking in the post-formative period, as well as probed the lively dialectic between legal rulings and social practice. While it is no longer possible to assert that "the door of *ijtihad* was closed" after the tenth (or, indeed, any other) century, however, there is still lively debate over the extent of legal change and the mechanisms by which it occurred. Furthermore, unreflective celebration of the values of progress and originality has given way to more serious examination of the ways in which *fiqh* was institutionalized and made socially effective.

In an analysis of the genre of the *mukhtasar* (a succinct "summary" of authoritative legal doctrine) in the Maliki school beginning in the thirteenth century, Mohammad Fadel argues that "taqlid resulted from the desire to have uniform rules rather than ... [from] intellectual stagnation."[19] *Mukhtasars*, which state school doctrine in condensed form and often become the object of centuries' worth of commentaries and super-commentaries, epitomize the kind of literature that scholars like Schacht and Coulson deemed unworthy of serious analysis. Their mono-vocal enunciation of doctrine, their lack of intellectually interesting argumentation, and their accretion of layer upon layer of commentarial literature were

[15] Moojan Momen, *An Introduction to Shi'i Islam* (New Haven: Yale University Press, 1985), 95; see also Hossein Modarressi Tabataba'i, *An Introduction to Shi'i Law* (London: Ithaca Press, 1984), 48.

[16] Devin Stewart, *Islamic Legal Orthodoxy: Twelver Shiite Responses to the Sunni Legal System* (Salt Lake City: The University of Utah Press, 1998), 111–173.

[17] Devin Stewart, "al-Sharīf al-Murtaḍā," in *Islamic Legal Thought: A Compendium of Muslim Jurists*, eds. Oussama Arabi, David S. Powers, and Susan A. Spectorsky (Leiden: Brill, 2013), 177–179.

[18] Robert Gleave, "Intra-Madhhab *Ikhtilaf* and the Late Classical Imami Shiite Concept of the Madhhab," in *The Islamic School of Law: Evolution, Devolution, and Progress*, eds. Peri Bearman, Rudolph Peters, and Frank E. Vogel (Cambridge, Massachusetts: Islamic Legal Studies Program, Harvard Law School, 2005), 126–146.

[19] Mohammad Fadel, "The Social Logic of *Taqlid* and the Rise of the *Mukhtasar*," *Islamic Law and Society* 3 (1996): 193–233, 193.

long assumed to reflect the sterility of Islamic legal thought in this period, as well as later generations' mindless subservience to the authorities of the past. However, as Fadel's analysis makes clear, the very qualities that make them unattractive as intellectual documents make them useful as statements of the law. Muslims seeking to know what provisions could validly be included in a marriage contract or which party bore liability in a commercial transaction presumably craved not creativity, but predictability.

Furthermore, it is the uniformity of legal judgments that lends them legitimacy and protects them from suspicions of arbitrariness or bias. Writing of Mamluk-era Egypt and Syria, Leonor Fernandes observes that *fatwas* diverging from the received doctrines of the schools of law could indeed bring about lasting legal change—but that far from being viewed by contemporaries as evidence of intellectual vitality, such instances were often perceived as evidence of the subversion of the law in the service of those in power. She notes,

> Muftis like al-Bulqini and al-Subki were known to have defied the traditional views of their school of law without hesitation, despite the disapproval of their peers, because their legal opinions were supported by the ruler and the military elite. Al-Suyuti ... provided an apologetic explanation for their behavior, saying that even though they had opened the door for illegal practices, they were responding to the needs of their time.[20]

Legal "flexibility" is thus a double-edged sword; it may amount to manipulability (often, although certainly not always, on behalf of the powerful) as well as responsiveness to implicitly neutral or shared "social needs." As Sherman Jackson has observed in a study of a legal work of a slightly later period, "the tendency to associate such categories as 'liberal' or 'progressive' with ijtihad and 'conservative' or even 'patriarchal' with taqlid is not only unwarranted but dangerously misleading."[21]

Scholars concerned with the mechanisms of legal creativity and change in this period have also examined the various forms of *ijtihad* and *taqlid* that could generate new legal rulings. Having defined *ijtihad* as the application of "the tools of *usul al-fiqh*" directly to the revealed texts of Qur'an and hadith, Sherman Jackson has directed interest to "the highly intricate and spirited institution of *taqlid*."[22] He argues that under a "regime of *taqlid*" demanding formal deference to the doctrine of a school, scholars resort to what he calls (following Alan Watson) "legal scaffolding": "rather than abandon existing rules in favor of new interpretations of the sources ..., jurists seek needed adjustments through new divisions, exceptions, distinctions, prerequisites and expanding or restricting the scope of existing law."[23] Far from being limited to the mechanical reproduction of received doctrine, he

[20] Fernandes, "Between Qadis and Muftis," 101.

[21] Sherman Jackson, "Kramer versus Kramer in a Tenth/Sixteenth Century Egyptian Court: Post-Formative Jurisprudence between Exigency and Law," *Islamic Law and Society* 8 (2001): 27–51, 50.

[22] Jackson, "*Taqlid*, Legal Scaffolding," 165, 167, n. 5.

[23] Ibid., 167.

argues that *taqlid* amounted to "an attempt to gain authority for one's interpretation by associating it with the name or doctrine of an already established authority-figure."[24] Given that multiple competing opinions were transmitted within individual schools in almost all areas of the law, the construction of a case that a given opinion constituted valid school doctrine could itself be a highly creative and sophisticated enterprise—and allow significant responsiveness to perceived social needs.

Even short of the (formal or informal) recognition of code-like works like the *Mukhtasars* of Ibn al-Hajib (646/1249) and Khalil b. Ishaq al-Jundi (776/1374), analyzed by Fadel, there were systematic efforts in this period to identify authoritative doctrines among the welter of competing opinions that were transmitted in the long-accumulating bodies of legal literature of the various schools. While the multi-vocality of legal texts could provide a wealth of alternatives to scholars or judges seeking viable precedents within a school, legal practice could not tolerate an infinite degree of indeterminacy; means were required to identify the most widespread or authoritative opinion on any given point. To this end, jurists developed sophisticated techniques of *tarjih* and *tashih* (both terms that designated the process of evaluating an opinion's relative strength as compared to other candidates transmitted within the school). It was in the period under consideration here that scholars began to produce works that "attempt to develop a systematic set of technical terms whose purpose was to classify the legal status of the different opinions within the ... school."[25] Such works include the *Minhaj* of al-Nawawi (d. 672/1273) in the Shafi'i school and the *Kashf al-niqab* of Ibn Farhun (d. 799/1397) in the Maliki school. Rudolph Peters has similarly noted that "during the late twelfth century jurists began to argue that there was a hierarchy of authority among the founders of the Hanafi *madhhab* and to formulate rules to determine whose opinion was most authoritative if there was a difference of opinion on a specific issue"; as a result, "Hanafi opinion by the sixteenth century had become standardized, unequivocal, and easy to apply."[26]

Perhaps the most vital example of the "operative terminology" (in Hallaq's phrase) that served to designate the degrees of validity associated with different opinions, particularly in the Maliki and Shafi'i schools, was the term *mashhur* (literally, "well-known"). This label designated the doctrine deemed most widespread or authoritative within a *madhhab*; some scholars considered it obligatory for lower-ranking (i.e. non-mujtahid) jurists to apply the *mashhur* of the *madhhab*. Fadel observes that, among Malikis starting in the thirteenth century, the *mashhur* was increasingly defined as the final doctrine of Malik as transmitted from Ibn al-Qasim

[24] Ibid., 169. [25] Fadel, "Social Logic," 215.

[26] Rudolph Peters, "What Does It Mean to Be an Official Madhhab? Hanafism and the Ottoman Empire," in *The Islamic School of Law: Evolution, Devolution, and Progress*, eds. Peri Bearman, Rudolph Peters, and Frank E. Vogel (Cambridge, MA: Islamic Legal Studies Program, Harvard Law School, 2005), 150.

in the *Mudawwana*, and further identified with the content of the *Mukhtasar* of Khalil. Thus, the concept of the *mashhur* produced—with respect to that majority of jurists unqualified to engage in fresh legal reasoning—a univocal and consistent law. Hallaq, in contrast, emphasizes that "a salient feature of operative terminology, which evolved as a response to the indeterminacy of legal rules, is its own indeterminacy"[27] and argues that even Ibn Farhun's work demonstrates "fundamental uncertainty in the Malikite school as to what exactly the mashhur was"—most importantly, whether it designated the quantitative prevalence of the opinion or the strength of the evidence supporting it.[28] Thus, in Hallaq's view the actual identity of the *mashhur* doctrine could remain highly negotiable. Indeed, in a study of an Egyptian Maliki legal work from a somewhat later period, Jackson demonstrates that it was possible for a member of this school to advance a novel interpretation precisely by generating ambiguity about the identity of the *mashhur* opinion (here understood as the quantitatively preponderant view).[29] Thus, it would seem that the definition of the *mashhur* remained somewhat fluid long after the thirteenth century.

It is worth noting that, unlike Sunni jurists, Imami thinkers do not appear to have developed elaborate frameworks or terminology for the comparative evaluation of different opinions within the body of Imami teaching or the designation of uniquely valid doctrines. This may have been related to their requirement that a non-qualified person follow a living *mujtahid*, which would have militated against the definitive designation of authoritative individuals or texts from the past. The limitation of *ikhtilaf* continued to depend in large part on the *ijtihad* of the individual jurist.[30]

II. Legal Theory (*Usul al-Fiqh*)

The period under consideration here also saw the composition of some of the most lastingly influential works in the field of legal theory (*usul al-fiqh*), including the *Mukhtasar* of the Maliki Ibn al-Hajib, which was the subject of many centuries of commentaries by scholars of various legal schools, including Imami Shi'is.[31] There is a vast body of texts in this field, often easily accessible (although rarely in critical

[27] Wael Hallaq, *Authority, Continuity and Change in Islamic Law* (Cambridge: Cambridge University Press, 2001), 165.

[28] Hallaq, *Authority, Continuity and Change*, 151.

[29] Jackson, "Kramer vs. Kramer," 39–45.

[30] Gleave, "Intra-Madhhab *Ikhtilaf*," 135–136.

[31] See Stewart, *Islamic Legal Orthodoxy*, 98.

editions). The challenge facing the researcher is thus not a paucity of evidence, but the need for orienting principles to guide her through a sea of voluminous and often formidably technical writings. The discipline of *usul al-fiqh* can be approached in two different ways that, although not mutually exclusive, are fundamentally distinct. One approach posits that *usul al-fiqh* is basically a set of procedures for the generation of concrete legal rules (*furu'*); in Hallaq's words, "[t]he primary objective of legal theory ... was to lay down a coherent system of principles through which a qualified jurist could extract rulings for novel cases."[32] From this point of view, the flourishing of the discipline of *usul al-fiqh* in this period can be understood to reflect the ongoing need for tools of creative legal reasoning. The second approach emphasizes the discipline's nature as an autonomous and sophisticated form of Islamic thought whose significance is by no means exhausted by its pragmatic usefulness in generating legal rules.

The first approach is overtly espoused by Bernard Weiss, whose monumental study of the legal theories of Sayf al-Din al-Amidi (d. 631/1233) seeks to address the western legal community[33] and expressly aims "to focus the attention of the reader upon that aspect or component of the shari'a that has a bearing upon the process whereby an Islamic state, through its appointed judges and enforcement agencies, regulates the conduct of its members toward each other and thus achieves social order and peace."[34] (In practice, it is notable that the content of Weiss's analysis sometimes appears to reflect a deep interest on Amidi's part—and indeed on Weiss's—with theoretical issues far transcending the practical administration of justice.) The second approach is exemplified by the work of Aron Zysow who, while acknowledging "the importance of *usul al-fiqh* for the practicing jurist,"[35] strongly asserts that "[f]or the historian of Islamic intellectual history, the study of these systems of legal theory is an end in itself. Their identification and elucidation is as legitimate as the analogous activity undertaken in the study of Islamic philosophy, theology, or mysticism."[36] His work focuses on epistemology as a central focus of legal theorizing, demonstrating how different presuppositions regarding the possibility and necessity of certain knowledge create fundamental divisions between different schools of legal thought.

Even among those who emphasize the speculative nature of much *usul* thinking in this period, there may be a tacit assumption (based in part on testimony from within the tradition) that this trend represents a failure or perversion of the proper function of *usul*. For instance, Kevin Jaques cites Ibn Khaldun's (d. 784/1382)

[32] Hallaq, "Was the Gate," 5.

[33] Bernard G. Weiss, *The Search for God's Law: Islamic Jurisprudence in the Writings of Sayf al-Din al-Amidi* (Salt Lake City: University of Utah Press, 1992), 8.

[34] Weiss, *Search for God's Law*, 7.

[35] Aron Zysow, *The Economy of Certainty: An Introduction to the Typology of Islamic Legal Theory* (Atlanta, GA: Lockwood Press, 2013), 4, 5.

[36] Zysow, *The Economy of Certainty*, 5.

critique of a "theological" current in post-formative *usul* that ultimately became an academic discipline pursued as an end in itself.[37] Basing himself on the work of the fifteenth-century Shafi'i scholar Ibn Qadi Shuhba, Jaques argues that while *usul al-fiqh* had by then long since become an entrenched part of the legal curriculum of the madrasas, it was no longer the primary means to the generation of new legal rulings, which were instead produced by extrapolation based on the *ikhtilaf* (diversity of opinion) transmitted within the *madhhab*.[38] To the extent that the promotion of substantively new legal opinions in the post-formative period involved "legal scaffolding" or the re-evaluation of existing options transmitted within the school, the interpretive tools involved are not centrally reflected in works of *usul al-fiqh*. For instance, Hallaq notes that the definitions of "operative terminology" and the process of *tarjih* have no place in conventional *usul* works.[39] He further argues that many of the rules presented in manuals of substantive law (*furu'*, "branches," contrasting with *usul*, "roots") in fact function to exemplify abstract principles that can be extrapolated in a sophisticated form of *taqlid* (rather than merely being mechanically applied to individual instances precisely matching the subject matter of the rule).[40]

Scholars examining the *de facto* correlation between the rules of *usul al-fiqh* and the substance of *furu'* in a given *madhhab* (or the arguments of a given thinker) have generally found the nexus between the two to be notably loose.[41] One manifestation of the tenuous nature of this connection is that scholars of different *madhhabs* (who held differing opinions in the realm of *furu'*, and thus generally did not write commentaries on works of other schools in that area) routinely borrowed from and commented on the same works of *usul* regardless of school identity. Thus, Ibn al-Hajib's *Mukhtasar* on *usul al-fiqh* was copiously commented on by members of various schools, and even became a widely studied and commented authority among Imami Shi'a. Although *usul* principles had always crossed school boundaries to some extent, this phenomenon was particularly notable in our historical period; Ayman Shabana notes that after the fifth/eleventh century, "juristic discussions in the *usul al-fiqh* literature developed into a shared, interschool theoretical framework."[42]

The genre of legal maxims (*qawa'id*) reflected a mature stage of legal development where scholars identified the broad regularities and principles discernible in

[37] R. Kevin Jaques, *Authority, Conflict, and the Transmission of Diversity in Medieval Islamic Law* (Leiden: Brill, 2006), 201–202.

[38] Jaques, *Authority, Conflict, and the Transmission of Diversity*, 198, 200–201.

[39] Hallaq, *Authority, Continuity and Change*, 133.

[40] Ibid., 88–101.

[41] Mohammad Fadel, "*Istihsan* is Nine-Tenths of the Law: The Puzzling Relationship of Usul to *Furu'* in the Maliki Madhhab," in *Studies in Islamic Legal Theory*, ed. Bernard G. Weiss (Leiden: Brill, 2002), 163, n. 6; see also Sherman Jackson, "Fiction and Formalism: Toward a Functional Analysis of Usul al-fiqh," in Weiss, 179.

[42] Ayman Shabana, *Custom in Islamic Law and Legal Theory* (New York: Palgrave Macmillan, 2010), 96.

the law as developed in earlier centuries. While such maxims often reproduced or at least paraphrased statements from the Qur'an or hadith, they fundamentally reflected scholars' inductive inferences about the overall logic of the law. While Hanafi examples of this genre go back to the fourth/tenth century, it flourished particularly in the eighth/fourteenth century with works by scholars such as Taj al-Din al-Subki (d. 771/1370) and Ibn Rajab al-Hanbali. A related genre, *furuq* ("distinctions") analyzed the factors differentiating superficially similar cases; the *Kitab al-Furuq* of Shihab al-Din al-Qarafi (d. 682/1281) comprises both maxims and distinctions. Like *usul al-fiqh*, the genre of maxims crossed school boundaries, with most major maxims common to the Sunni *madhahib*; *qawa'id* works were also composed by Imami Shi'is such as 'Allama Ibn Mutahhar al-Hilli (d. 771/1369) and al-Shahid al-Awwal (d. 782/1389).[43]

III. The Fatwa as Interpretive Site

Beyond the question of the interpretive tools that were used to generate fresh legal judgments, scholars have sought to understand the textual forms and real-world interactions within which such judgments were sought and expressed. Perhaps the most important genre of legal writing in this respect is the *fatwa*, which consists of a legal opinion issued in response to an inquiry (*istifta'*). The pairing of a concrete question with a specific response offers insight into the process by which legal reasoning was elicited in real situations. Although *fatwas* from this period only occasionally survive as original documents, they are available in vast numbers in collections that may reflect the output of a single scholar or those of a number of authorities from the same school or locality. One of the greatest *fatwa* collections of this period is al-Wansharisi's (d. 914/1508) *al-Mi'yar al-mu'rib*, which presents more than 6,000 fatwas originating with hundreds of jurists of North Africa and Spain; it has been studied in great depth by David Powers, who demonstrates the wealth of information it yields on both legal practice and social history.[44] However, not all preserved *fatwas* are formally equivalent to each other or offer comparable data about the specific situation that gave rise to the original legal inquiry. As Hallaq has set forth in detail, raw "primary fatwas" (like many of those in al-Wansharisi's

[43] See Mohammad Hashim Kamali, "Legal Maxims and Other Genres of Literature in Islamic Jurisprudence," *Arab Law Quarterly* 20 (2006): 77–108; Wolfhart Heinrichs, "*Qawa'id* as a Genre of Legal Literature," in *Studies in Islamic Legal Theory*, ed. Bernard G. Weiss (Leiden: Brill, 2002), 365–384.

[44] D.S. Powers, *Law, Society and Culture in the Maghrib, 1300–1500* (Cambridge: Cambridge University Press, 2002).

compilation) may offer a wealth of specific information about the parties to the conflict that gave rise to the inquiry and the context (familial, economic, geographic) in which it occurred. Even at this stage, the question may be drafted with the help of trained legal personnel to frame the problem in terms appropriate for legal analysis; it does not necessarily represent an unmediated reflection of the ways in which the situation would have been understood by laypeople. Subsequently, in a process of abstraction (*tajrid*), a *fatwa* of some legal significance (due to its originality or usefulness) might be stripped of superfluous details and identifying particulars to produce a more universal expression of the legal issue and its solution. Finally, an abbreviated and abstracted form of the *fatwa* could be included in a work of positive law (*furuʿ*) in one of the *madhhabs*, thus enshrining an opinion originally elicited in the context of concrete social events as new school doctrine.[45]

While the existence and importance of the process described by Hallaq seems undeniable, this direct (if multi-staged) path from social exigency to legal doctrine does not necessarily represent the full spectrum of situations and modes in which *fatwas* were produced. Hallaq repeatedly emphasizes that the majority of *fatwas* were generated in the context of litigation, an idea that he adduces in support of the argument that they responded to genuine (rather than hypothetical) conflicts and problems.[46] By situating the production of *fatwas* primarily within the setting of court practice, he underlines the real-world relevance (and genuinely "legal" quality) of the production of juristic opinions; *fatwas* become somewhat similar to case law, generating new precedents that may become authoritative for later jurists. Without denying the importance of this aspect of the *fatwa* literature, however, it is important to remember that vast numbers of *fatwas* produced by scholars and preserved for posterity address issues (such as ritual law) that would rarely, if ever, be subject to litigation.

A very different approach to the *fatwa* literature is provided in a posthumously published work by Norman Calder, who emphasizes that the "basic" (and most common) *fatwa* is the one requested by a layperson rather than a judge, and observes that "the process of asking questions and getting the answers of the learned went considerably beyond a concern with the merely practical." Furthermore, "[q]adis, students and fellow jurists used the device of the formal question in search of education, instruction, advice, recreation, amusement and play."[47] Focusing on the *Fatawa* of Taqi al-Din al-Subki (d. 756/1355), he argues that al-Subki often used questions addressed to him to initiate scholarly debate (*munazara*), which then contributed to the content of *fatwas* that went far beyond a pragmatic response to the original questions; "[c]onversely, it is clear ... that questions that started as debate were

45 Hallaq, *Authority, Continuity and Change*, 174–194.

46 Ibid., 173, 177, 178, 180.

47 Norman Calder, *Islamic Jurisprudence in the Classical Era*, ed. Colin Imber (Cambridge: Cambridge University Press, 2010), 169–170.

written up in the literary form of the fatwa."[48] It is worth noting that Hallaq names al-Subki as a "mufti who engages in discourse that transcends the limits of the fatwa strictly defined."[49] To a certain extent, the issue here is simply definitional; Calder himself observes that when al-Subki incorporated accounts of scholarly disputation in his opinions, "the end product was no longer a basic fatwa of the type that was described in the manuals."[50] Nevertheless, there is more at stake; while Hallaq valorizes legal discourses by emphasizing their pragmatic realism, their responsiveness to social needs, and their more strictly "legal" qualities (in the sense of generating judicially enforceable norms), Calder insists on the central value of the literary and intellectual dimensions of *ifta'*.

Even to the extent that *fatwas* provide insight into practical social issues that arose in specific times and places, however, they have some limitations as sources for a history of legal practice. As non-binding advisory opinions, *fatwas* do not inherently tell us anything about the ultimate disposition of the cases they address. Indeed, even those produced in the context of litigation need not have been applied or enforced; more than one competing *fatwa* may have been solicited by a judge or presented by parties to the case, so we can rarely be confident that the opinion at hand was the one that dictated the resolution of the problem. In some cases, supplementary information can be derived from works of other genres (for instance, if an important case is mentioned in a chronicle) or another *fatwa* clearly addresses a subsequent stage of the same dispute. In most cases, such corroborating material is not forthcoming. *Fatwa* collections, although often voluminous, also suffer from selection bias. For obvious reasons, *fatwas* reflecting routine responses to undisputed points of law were unlikely to be anthologized; an opinion that was sufficiently notable to warrant preservation is also likely to be, from a historian's point of view, somewhat unrepresentative of the daily run of legal practice.[51]

IV. Courts and Jurisdiction

The question of the application and enforcement of legal rulings brings us to the issue of courts and jurisdictions. To the extent that scholars once believed *fiqh* to have become fossilized by the beginning of our period—or to have evolved from its origins as an idealistic counter-discourse to political and social reality—they

[48] Calder, *Islamic Jurisprudence*, 171.
[49] Hallaq, *Authority, Continuity and Change*, 170.
[50] Calder, *Islamic Jurisprudence*, 171.
[51] See Mohammad Fadel, *Adjudication in the Maliki* Madhhab: *A Study of Legal Process in Medieval Islamic Law* (Ph.D. dissertation, University of Chicago, 1995), 2:297.

have tended to posit that the pragmatic regulation of society largely eluded its grasp. Particularly with respect to issues of criminal law and social order, they have emphasized the importance of the concept of *siyasa* (roughly translatable as "statecraft," and used to designate the discretionary powers exercised by the ruler) and the institution of *mazalim* ("grievance") courts. Drawing in part on sources of this period, Bernard Lewis draws a sharp dichotomy between *siyasa* and shari'a. He notes that the fifteenth-century Egyptian historian al-Maqrizi not only contrasts the two, but (wrongly) traces the etymology of the term *siyasa* to the Turko-Mongol legal code attributed to Genghis Khan, thus labeling it as a system fundamentally alien to the Islamic dispensation.[52] This contention, even if historically ill-founded, illustrates in Lewis's view that "the Muslim authors were aware of [a] distinction between Shari'a justice and another kind of jurisdiction which, according to strict Shari'a concepts, should not have been admitted at all."[53] In this view, Ibn Taymiyya's initiative to subsume the ruler's discretionary penal and administrative rulings under the aegis of the shari'a was an effort to assimilate a fundamentally alien element into the framework of religious law.

Somewhat similarly, the institution of *mazalim* tribunals—where the ruler or his deputies responded to petitions alleging abuses by government officials or other grievances unresolved in the *qadi* courts—has been seen as a pragmatic response to the impractical procedural limitations imposed by the shari'a, particularly in the area of penal law. In a widely cited study, Jorgen S. Nielsen characterized the *mazalim* under the Mamluks as "Secular Justice in an Islamic State," and emphasized that the participation of *qadis*, although frequently noted in the sources, was marginal to the institution. He depicted the *mazalim* as fora for summary justice by the ruler, lacking any formalized procedure or established legal rules.[54] In his view, this situation arose because "whatever criminal, fiscal, and commercial provisions there existed" in the shari'a "were largely ignored," because it had long been "left behind by practical developments."[55]

In contrast, Muhammad Khalid Masud has argued based on a study of the definition and use of the term *siyasa* over the centuries that "the duality of siyasa and shari'a as a tension between theory and practice is over exaggerated"; after the early period Muslim scholars did not, overall, perceive an irreducible incompatibility between the two, but saw a role for *siyasa* within the context of the legitimate operation

[52] Bernard Lewis, *Political Words and Ideas in Islam* (Princeton: Markus Wiener Publishers, 2008), 43.

[53] Bernard Lewis, "Siyasa," in *In Quest of an Islamic Humanism: Arabic and Islamic Studies in Memory of Mohamed al-Nowaihi*, ed. A.H. Green (Cairo: The American University in Cairo Press, 1986), 10.

[54] See Jorgen S. Nielsen, *Secular Justice in an Islamic State: Mazalim under the Bahri Mamluks*, 662/1264–789/1387 (Leiden: Nederlands Historisch-Archaeologisch Instituut te Istanbul, 1985), esp. 10–11, 26, 33.

[55] Nielsen, *Secular Justice in an Islamic State*, 95.

of shariʿa.[56] Similarly, Yossef Rapoport notes that over the course of the expansion of the jurisdiction of the Mamluk *mazalim* tribunals in the fourteenth and fifteenth centuries, "some religious scholars ... come to accept them as beneficial and indeed integral elements in the application of Islamic law."[57] He also emphasizes that *mazalim* panels routinely included *qadis*, and "the Islamic legal tradition delineates the legal procedure to be followed in *mazalim* sessions"; "the eventual result was based on shariʿa reasoning, even if the jurists were not present."[58] Overall, Rapoport questions the tacitly ideological and moralizing assumption that shariʿa was fundamentally idealistic and non-political, and that any state involvement in its content or administration thus inherently reflected corruption or interference.[59]

The actual workings of *qadi* courts (and the legal transactions over which they presided) are indirectly accessible to us through two primary forms of evidence. One, the formulary literature comprising model documents and guidance on notarial practice, is literary in nature but offers insights into an aspect of legal practice far closer to the ground-level transactions that would have punctuated the lives of ordinary people. This genre (known in Arabic as *shurut* or *watha'iq*) consists of fill-in-the-blank documents for a vast range of purposes, ranging from marriage and bequests to commercial partnerships; perhaps the most notable example in our period is the ninth/fifteenth century Egyptian al-Asyuti's *Jawahir al-ʿuqud*. Amalia Zomeño notes that such works "give extensive recommendations on how to meet the demands of the parties involved while at the same time respecting the law"; in addition to providing practical tools, each document "is explained with reference to Islamic legal doctrine (fiqh), so that the notaries know why one formula should be used instead of another."[60] Hallaq has emphasized that notarial practice is merely one aspect of the discipline of *fiqh*; "we have no evidence to indicate that the shurutis [notaries] came from other than the 'ulama's ranks." [61] In this view, there is no basis for the widespread assumption that works of positive law (*furuʿ*) are "theoretical" while formularies reflect actual practice; indeed, "model shurut works structurally and organically constitute an integral part of the *furuʿ* and *adab al-qadi* manuals which have been decried as abstract and theoretical by modern scholarship."[62] Not all scholars have seen the professional conventions of the notaries as quite so seamlessly

[56] Muhammad Khalid Masud, "The Doctrine of Siyasa in Islamic Law," *Recht van de Islam* 18 (2001): 1–29, 23.

[57] Yossef Rapoport, "Royal Justice and Religious Law: *Siyasah* and Shariʿah under the Mamluks," *Mamluk Studies Review* 16 (2012): 71–102, 76.

[58] Rapoport, "Royal Justice and Religious Law," 80–81.

[59] Ibid., 72.

[60] Amalia Zomeño, "The Islamic Marriage Contract in al-Andalus (10th–16th Centuries)," in *The Islamic Marriage Contract: Case Studies in Islamic Family Law*, eds. Asifa Quraishi and Frank E. Vogel (Cambridge, MA: Islamic Legal Studies Program, Harvard Law School, 2008), 138.

[61] Wael Hallaq, "Model Shurut Works and the Dialectic of Doctrine and Practice," *Islamic Law and Society* 2 (1995): 109–134, 115.

[62] Ibid., 112.

integrated into the discipline of *fiqh*; in a study of Islamic marriage contracts in al-Andalus in the tenth to sixteenth centuries, Zomeño notes that "the muftis at the time were critical of the notaries and their methods of drafting marriage contracts, since many of the legal problems about which the muftis were consulted had their origins in the contracts' imprecise phrasing and, sometimes, shaky legality."[63] However, she also notes that according to Lisan al-Din Ibn al-Khatib (d. 776/1375)—who was otherwise quite critical of the notaries—"they were highly specialized jurists trained to write down the transactions according to the principles and rules of Islamic law."[64]

Even closer to lived practice, of course, are actual surviving documents. In this area, we are limited by the widely lamented dearth of surviving pre-Ottoman archives. One notable source of original documents—although only for the early part of our period—has been the Cairo Geniza, containing centuries' worth of discarded documents emanating from the local Jewish community. Following the overall approach of S.D. Goitein, which emphasized the embeddedness of the community represented in the Geniza within the broader Muslim society, Abraham Udovitch noted in 1970 that: "One observes a striking similarity between the outlines of commercial institutions as we find them in early Hanafi texts and the actual documented business practice of the 11th to 13th century merchants whose business records have been preserved in the Cairo Geniza."[65] He concludes that, rather than assuming the direct influence of Hanafi doctrine on commercial practice (particularly among non-Muslim traders), we should infer that Hanafi law "was, with minor qualification, a reflection of actual practice, and that this practice, while containing components of varying provenance, was international and interdenominational."[66] More recently, Phillip Ackerman-Lieberman has argued for the distinctively Jewish character of the contractual conventions reflected in the Geniza documents and cautioned against their use to reconstruct the practice of Islamic commercial law.[67] Studies comparing archival legal and commercial documents (in this case, of Muslim origin) with normative Islamic legal sources have also been produced by Werner Diem, who focuses in part on Egyptian papyri.[68]

[63] Zomeño, "Islamic Marriage Contract," 139.

[64] Amalia Zomeño, "Notaries and Their Formulas: The Legacies from the University Library of Granada," in *From al-Andalus to Khurasan: Documents from the Medieval Muslim World*, eds. Petra M. Sijpesteijn, Lennart Sundelin, Sofía Torallas Tovar, and Amalia Zomeño (Leiden and Boston: Brill, 2007), 60.

[65] Abraham L. Udovitch, "Theory and Practice of Islamic Law: Some Evidence from the Geniza," *Studia Islamica* 32 (1987): 289–303, 290.

[66] Udovitch, "Theory and Practice of Islamic Law, 291; see also Mark R. Cohen, "Geniza for Islamicists, Islamic Geniza, and the New Cairo Geniza," *Harvard Middle Eastern and Islamic Review* 7 (2006): 129–145.

[67] Phillip I. Ackerman-Lieberman, *The Business of Identity: Jews, Muslims, and Economic Life in Medieval Egypt* (Stanford: Stanford University Press, 2014).

[68] See, for instance, Werner Diem, *Arabischer Terminkauf: Ein Beitrag zur Rechts- und Wirtschaftsgeschichte Ägyptiens im 8. Bis 14. Jahrhundert* (Wiesbaden: Harrassowitz Verlag, 2006);

Another important trove of documentary sources for our period is the Haram Documents, a collection of more than 900 documents discovered within the precincts of al-Haram al-Sharif in Jerusalem in the 1970s. The vast majority of these are in Arabic, originate from within Syria, and date from the Mamluk period; of these, a large number are concentrated between the years 793 and 797 AH (the end of the fourteenth century of the Common Era). The documents include estate inventories, contracts, legal depositions, contracts, and court records. The collection is of vital significance, not least in that it provides "specimens of several types of documents [that] were not known to exist except in chancery and notarial manuals."[69] However, part of the significance of the collection depends on our hypothesis about how and why it was assembled. A notable proportion of the documents were drawn up under the auspices of (or otherwise mention) a single individual, a Shafiʿi *qadi* of Jerusalem thus raising the question of whether the documents "constituted a typical *qadi*'s archive or might have been gathered for purposes other than archival conservation."[70] As Christian Müller has observed, some of the documents bear filing notations that suggest that they were formally archived, and some have holes that would have allowed them to be tied together in groups.[71] However, the disparate nature of the markings, formats, and holes suggest that the documents "were not created by a single administration with the intention of long-term archival use."[72] Rather, he suggests that this portion of the collection may have been generated in the context of an (ultimately aborted) investigation into accusations of corruption against the judge. All of this is not to deny, as Müller emphasizes (and has been argued in detail by Hallaq) that pre-Ottoman courts generated and preserved sophisticated documentation.[73] However, if the Haram documents are understood to be the product of a specific investigation rather than of routine record-keeping, then we can no longer assume them to have the representative qualities that would otherwise be associated with a court archive.

Another significant documentary source that preserves direct evidence of a central legal and economic institution of the Mamluk period are the *waqf* deeds that established pious foundations benefitting charitable causes and/or the family of the founder. More than a thousand of these are preserved in various collections; they not only set forth the original provisions of the foundation, but often "continued to be working documents, providing successive details of manipulation and change

Werner Diem, *Ein arabisches Rechtsgutachten zum Eherecht asu dem 11.-12. Jahrhundert aus der Heidelberger Papyrussammlung* (Wiesbaden: Harrassowitz Verlag, 2007).

69 Ibid., 15.

70 Christian Müller, "The Haram al-Sharif Collection of Arabic Legal Documents in Jerusalem: A Mamluk Court Archive?" *al-Qantara* 32 (2011): 435–459, 438.

71 Ibid., 444, 445.

72 Ibid., 446.

73 See Wael Hallaq, "Qadi's *diwan (sijill)* Before the Ottomans," *Bulletin of the School of Oriental and African Studies* 61 (1998): 415–436.

for the ongoing life and transformation of a perpetual trust."[74] Other troves of original documentation continue to be recognized and analyzed; for instance, in a 2007 monograph Maya Schatzmiller examines a body of fifteenth-century Granadan court documents recording the private transactions of Muslims, which were preserved by the Christian administration following the Reconquista.[75] Yet another intriguing non-literary source for legal practice is suggested by Ruba Kana'an, whose study of a richly embellished twelfth-century Khurasanian vessel demonstrates how the various roles and transactions associated with the commissioning and production of metalwork in contemporary Hanafi legal discussions are reflected in its inscriptions.[76]

It is tempting to regard preserved original documents as direct evidence of the concrete reality of legal transactions. However, to some extent they share the conventional and ideological dimensions of our normative sources. Zomeño observes that "the documents do not always reflect actual practice"; for instance, in the Andalusian context she studied "although the custom of the notaries was to record the receipt of a certain marriage gift, this gift was never exchanged by the parties at that time ... "[77] Rapoport has similarly noted fictive features in marriage contracts from Mamluk Egypt and Syria, which often enhanced the status of the families involved by doubling the value of the marriage gifts or by denominating them prestigiously in gold coins, even when the parties "had never had the chance to hold a gold piece in their hand."[78]

It might be assumed that with respect to discursive traditions like *fiqh* and *usul al-fiqh*, as opposed to social practices such as adjudication, our voluminous textual sources would suffice to provide near-comprehensive insight. After all, in such cases the text is not merely evidence of the practice, but in some sense constitutive of it. However, this is not completely the case (even allowing for the fact that not all texts were equally likely to survive); rather, written texts reflect merely a fraction of a wider array of discursive practices including oral debate and face-to-face teaching. Although his study analyzes a vast body of literary work, Weiss notes that in Amidi's time "the energies of the learned were always focused ... on live debate, that it was principally in the arena of ongoing disputation that they proved their intellectual worth to their contemporaries, and that the literature was geared largely to equipping them to perform effectively in live debate."[79] Whether we are

[74] Hallaq, "Qadi's *diwan*, 53.

[75] Maya Shatzmiller, *Her Day in Court: Women's Property Rights in Fifteenth-Century Granada* (Cambridge, MA: Islamic Legal Studies Program, Harvard Law School, 2007), 1.

[76] Ruba Kana'an, "The *de Jure* 'Artist' of the Bobrinksi Bucket: Production and Patronage of Metalwork in pre-Mongol Khurasan and Transoxiana," *Islamic Law and Society* 16 (2009): 175–201.

[77] Zomeño, "Islamic Marriage Contract," 139; see also 142.

[78] Yossef Rapoport, *Marriage, Money and Divorce in Medieval Islamic Society* (Cambridge: Cambridge University Press, 2005), 54.

[79] Weiss, *Search*, 23.

seeking to understand the legal expectations, transactions, and rulings that shaped people's everyday lives or the religious and intellectual worlds of the scholars, our data reflect only a fraction of a multi-faceted reality. Only by careful coordination of different genres of sources can we reconstruct any aspect of legal thought or practice in this period.

V. Conclusion

Scholarship has by now succeeded in refuting many of the polemical distortions (as well as the simple errors of fact) disseminated by pioneering scholars such as Schacht and Coulson, not to mention their predecessors of earlier generations. However, discussion of the historical development and social and intellectual functioning of Islamic law often remains driven by the issues they raised. Conscious critique of the tacit assumptions and ideological overtones of debates over the "rigidity," "creativity," or "practicality" of legal discourses has helped to dispel the lingering traces of an outmoded paradigm. However, this legacy lives on in the polarization of many interpretations—*fiqh* is *either* a pragmatic discourse whose proper center of gravity is in the courtroom, *or* a form of intellectual play best understood in purely literary terms; we focus *either* on documents as supposedly direct reflections of actual social transactions, *or* on literary texts as manifestations of disembodied ideas. As scholarship moves away from holistic arguments about the fundamental nature of *fiqh* to address the content and texture of different facets of the law, however, we come closer to appreciating the many insights into intellectual, social, and political history afforded by the full variety of the preserved sources. Serious exploration of many individual areas of the law in this period, particularly on the level of substantive doctrine (*furuʿ*), remains in its infancy.

References

Ackerman-Lieberman, Phillip I., *The Business of Identity: Jews, Muslims, and Economic Life in Medieval Egypt* (Stanford: Stanford University Press, 2014).

Calder, Norman, *Islamic Jurisprudence in the Classical Era* in Colin Imber (ed.) (Cambridge: Cambridge University Press, 2010).

Cohen, Mark R, "Geniza for Islamicists, Islamic Geniza, and the "New Cairo Geniza." *Harvard Middle Eastern and Islamic Review* 7 (2006): 129–145.

Coulson, N.J., *A History of Islamic Law* (Edinburgh: Edinburgh University Press, 1964).

Fadel, Mohammad, *Adjudication in the Maliki Madhhab: A Study of Legal Process in Medieval Islamic Law*. Ph.D. dissertation, University of Chicago, 1995.
Fadel, Mohammad, "'*Istihsan* is Nine-Tenths of the Law': The Puzzling Relationship of Usul to *Furu'* in the Maliki Madhhab" in Bernard G. Weiss (ed.) *Studies in Islamic Legal Theory*, 161–176 (Leiden: Brill, 2002).
Fernandes, Leonor, "Between Qadis and Muftis: To Whom Does the Mamluk Sultan Listen?" *Mamluk Studies Review* 6 (2002): 95–108.
Gleave, Robert, "Intra-Madhhab *Ikhtilaf* and the Late Classical Imami Shiite Concept of the Madhhab" in Peri Bearman, Rudolph Peters, and Frank E. Vogel (eds.) *The Islamic School of Law: Evolution, Devolution, and Progress* (Cambridge, MA: Islamic Legal Studies Program, Harvard Law School, 2005) 126–146.
Hallaq, Wael, *Authority, Continuity and Change in Islamic Law* (Cambridge: Cambridge University Press, 2001).
al-Hattab al-Ru'ayni, *Mawahib al-jalil li-sharh Mukhtasar Khalil*, Zakariya 'Umayrat (ed.) 8 vols (Beirut: Dar al-Kutub al-'Ilmiya, 1416/1995).
Heinrichs, Wolfhart, "*Qawa'id* as a Genre of Legal Literature" in Bernard G. Weiss (ed.) *Studies in Islamic Legal Theory* (Leiden: Brill, 2002) 365–384.
Ibn Rajab al-Hanbali, 'Abd al-Rahman ibn Ahmad, *Majmu' rasa'il al-hafiz Ibn Rajab al-Hanbali*. Edited by Abu Mus'ab Tal'at ibn Fu'ad al-Hulwani. 5 vols (N.p.: Al-Faruq al-Hadithiya li'l-Tiba'a wa'l-Nashr, 1423/2002).
Jackson, Sherman, "*Taqlid*, Legal Scaffolding, and the Scope of Legal Injunctions in Post-Formative Theory: *Mutlaq* and *'Amm* in the Jurisprudence of Shihab al-Din al-Qarafi." *Islamic Law and Society* 3 (1996): 165–192.
Jackson, Sherman, "Kramer versus Kramer in a Tenth/Sixteenth Century Egyptian Court: Post-Formative Jurisprudence between Exigency and Law." *Islamic Law and Society* 8 (2001): 27–51.
Jackson, Sherman, "Fiction and Formalism: Toward a Functional Analysis of Usul al-fiqh" in Bernard G. Weiss (ed.) *Studies in Islamic Legal Theory* (Leiden: Brill, 2002) 177–201.
Jaques, R. Kevin, *Authority, Conflict, and the Transmission of Diversity in Medieval Islamic Law* (Leiden: Brill, 2006).
Kamali, Mohammad Hashim, "Legal Maxims and Other Genres of Literature in Islamic Jurisprudence." *Arab Law Quarterly* 20 (2006): 77–108.
Kana'an, Ruba, "The *de Jure* 'Artist' of the Bobrinksi Bucket: Production and Patronage of Metalwork in pre-Mongol Khurasan and Transoxiana." *Islamic Law and Society* 16 (2009): 175–201.
Lewis, Bernard, "Siyasa" in A.H. Green (ed.) *In Quest of an Islamic Humanism: Arabic and Islamic Studies in Memory of Mohamed al-Nowaihi* (Cairo: The American University in Cairo Press, 1986) 3–14.
Lewis, Bernard, *Political Words and Ideas in Islam* (Princeton: Markus Wiener Publishers, 2008).
Masud, Muhammad Khalid, "The Doctrine of *Siyasa* in Islamic Law." *Recht van de Islam* 18 (2001): 1–29.
al-Mawsu'a al-fiqhya, 45 vols. (Kuwait: Wizarat al-Awqaf wa'l-Shu'un al-Islamiya, 1404/1983–1427/2006).
Modarressi Tabataba'i, Hossein, *An Introduction to Shi'i Law* (London: Ithaca Press, 1984).
Momen, Moojan, *An Introduction to Shi'i Islam* (New Haven: Yale University Press, 1985).
Müller, Christian, "The Haram al-Sharif Collection of Arabic Legal Documents in Jerusalem: A Mamluk Court Archive?" *al-Qantara* 32 (2011): 435–459.

Nielsen, Jorgen S., *Secular Justice in an Islamic State: Mazalim under the Bahri Mamluks, 662/1264–789/1387* (Leiden: Nederlands Historisch-Archaeologisch Instituut te Istanbul, 1985).

Peters, Rudolph, "What Does It Mean to Be an Official Madhhab? Hanafism and the Ottoman Empire" in Peri Bearman, Rudolph Peters, and Frank E. Vogel (eds.) *The Islamic School of Law: Evolution, Devolution, and Progress* (Cambridge, MA: Islamic Legal Studies Program, Harvard Law School, 2005) 147–158.

Powers, David S., *Law, Society and Culture in the Maghrib, 1300–1500* (Cambridge: Cambridge University Press, 2002).

Rapoport, Yossef, "Legal Diversity in the Age of Taqlid: The Four Chief Qadis under the Mamluks." *Islamic Law and Society* 10 (2003): 210–228.

Rapoport, Yossef, *Marriage, Money and Divorce in Medieval Islamic Society* (Cambridge: Cambridge University Press, 2005).

Rapoport, Yossef, "Royal Justice and Religious Law: *Siyasah* and Shariʿah under the Mamluks." *Mamluk Studies Review* 16 (2012): 71–102.

Schacht, Joseph, *An Introduction to Islamic Law* (Oxford: Oxford University Press, 1964).

Shabana, Ayman, *Custom in Islamic Law and Legal Theory* (New York: Palgrave Macmillan, 2010).

Shatzmiller, Maya, *Her Day in Court: Women's Property Rights in Fifteenth-Century Granada* (Cambridge, Massachusetts: Islamic Legal Studies Program, Harvard Law School, 2007).

Stewart, Devin, *Islamic Legal Orthodoxy: Twelver Shiite Responses to the Sunni Legal System* (Salt Lake City: The University of Utah Press, 1998).

Stewart, Devin, "al-Sharīf al-Murtaḍā" in Oussama Arabi, David S. Powers, and Susan A. Spectorsky (eds.) *Islamic Legal Thought: A Compendium of Muslim Jurists* (Leiden: Brill, 2013) 167–210.

Udovitch, Abraham L., "Theory and Practice of Islamic Law: Some Evidence from the Geniza." *Studia Islamica* 32 (1987): 289–303.

Weiss, Bernard G., *The Search for God's Law: Islamic Jurisprudence in the Writings of Sayf al-Din al-Amidi* (Salt Lake City: University of Utah Press, 1992).

Zomeño, Amalia, "Notaries and Their Formulas: The Legacies from the University Library of Granada" in Petra M. Sijpesteijn, Lennart Sundelin, Sofía Torallas Tovar, and Amalia Zomeño (eds.) *From al-Andalus to Khurasan: Documents from the Medieval Muslim World* (Leiden and Boston: Brill, 2007) 58–77.

Zomeño, Amalia, "The Islamic Marriage Contract in al-Andalus (10th–16th Centuries)" in Asifa Quraishi and Frank E. Vogel (eds.) *The Islamic Marriage Contract: Case Studies in Islamic Family Law* (Cambridge, MA: Islamic Legal Studies Program, Harvard Law School, 2008) 136–155.

Zysow, Aron, *The Economy of Certainty: An Introduction to the Typology of Islamic Legal Theory* (Atlanta, Georgia: Lockwood Press, 2013).

CHAPTER 18

THE HISTORIOGRAPHY OF ISLAMIC LAW DURING THE MAMLUK SULTANATE

MATTHEW B. INGALLS

The Mamluk sultanate lasted from 1250 until the Ottoman conquest of Egypt in 1517. With its capital in Cairo, the sultanate exercised direct political control over the Levant, the Hijaz, Egypt into Cyrenaica (eastern Libya) in the west, and Nubia and Massawa (Eritrea) in the south. The Mamluks (literally, "one who is owned") were Turkic slave soldiers who constituted a political elite that would rule over predominantly Arabic-speaking indigenous populations under the leadership of a manumitted sultan. As a political dynasty, the Mamluks are traditionally divided into two ethnic lines of sultans: the Bahri line, which lasted from 1250 until 1390 and was comprised mainly of Kipchak Turks from the southwestern Eurasian Steppe; and the Burji line, which lasted from 1382 until 1517 and was comprised mainly of Circassians from the northern Caucasus.

Taking pride in their origins as slave legionaries, the Mamluks viewed themselves as defenders of Islamdom, and their military defeat of the Mongols in 1260 at 'Ayn Jalut would help in cementing this reputation in the minds of the civilian population over which they ruled. Moreover, their general disdain for hereditary rule—notwithstanding several noteworthy attempts at it—was unique to the Mamluks' model of political succession in medieval times. Although it would be a source of political instability especially in the waning years of the sultanate, it would also serve as an indirect impetus for many of the legal institutions that the present chapter analyzes.

Because the Mamluk sultanate represents a *political* dynasty with a fixed temporal and geographic scope, we must frame our examination of the historiography of Islamic law within the boundaries of this dynasty by asking: What is specifically "Mamluk" about Islamic law and legal scholarship during the Mamluk sultanate? Is there any benefit in viewing legal scholarship and the application of law through the lens of this particular political dynasty?

As current scholarship on the Mamluks will attest, the answer is both yes and no. If we consider the institutions that (1) fostered legal scholarship and (2) applied the law during Mamluk times then, yes, there is benefit for historians in delineating a distinctly Mamluk interpretation of Islamic law. However, if we consider the structure and content of *fiqh* and *usul* texts that emerged from scholars living in Mamluk lands, then no. That is, with the possible exception of certain *fatawa* (sing. *fatwa*) that are specific to Mamluk socio-political considerations, the Mamluk period appears too parochial in space and time to serve as a useful signpost in charting the development of legal literature. Rather, in order to account for such a development we must think in broader terms, although this should certainly not be read as an endorsement of the formative/classical/postclassical framework that informed twentieth-century scholarship on Islamic intellectual history.

I have divided the remainder of this chapter according to the two answers to the framing question above. The first section thus addresses current scholarship on the institutions that might allow for an understanding of Islamic law that is clearly Mamluk in its essence. As it relates to the historiography of Islamic law, I have arranged this section to flow hierarchically downwards from the Mamluk executive, to the judiciary, to, finally, law enforcement. A second section next analyzes the historiography of Mamluk educational institutions, which fall in a gray area between institutions that are distinctly Mamluk and those that are not, as is explained. A third section then references the most current scholarship on three larger intellectual trends that would shape the development of medieval Islamic law but which are not readily confined to the Mamluk period alone. Finally, I conclude the chapter with a brief assessment of the state of the field and some questions for future researchers to consider.

1. The Historiography of Mamluk Legal Institutions

If we begin our historiographical survey at the top—that is, with the Mamluk executive—we immediately confront a number of daunting challenges. For one, the shariʿa would function as the equivalent of a constitution throughout Islamic legal history, and this would certainly remain the case in Mamluk times. However, Patricia Crone has cautioned that the shariʿa comprises "a set of rules which organize, but do not restrain, the exercise of power. In order for the rules to yield constitutional government, they have to include restraints, normally identified as a bill of rights and institutional devices for securing their observance."[1] Thus, although the Mamluks were unique in their embrace of election (*pace* hereditary succession) in deciding who among their ranks would accede to the sultanate, they lacked a constitutional foundation to formalize the process of election, delineate a clear electoral body, and, most importantly, establish a legal recourse with which to appeal infractions that might occur during the electoral process.

But it would be anachronistic to expect such institutions from a political dynasty that emerged in the thirteenth century, and, in fact, scholarly concepts like *siyasa sharʿiyya* (discussed later) would provide a theoretical alternative to many of the ideas found in modern constitutional government. We also find a variety of rituals and traditions amongst the Mamluks which would buttress the process of succession and ameliorate the violence that inevitably followed the transfer of power and legitimacy amongst a cadre of highly seasoned warriors. Here we can turn to P.M. Holt's 1975 article "The Position and Power of the Mamluk Sultan" to understand the nature of these rituals and traditions and grasp their symbolic relationship to the sultan and his function in the eyes of his constituents. Specifically, Holt examines practices such as the state procession, accession-banquet, oath of allegiance, and enthronement to show how these rituals legitimized the Mamluk sultans as lawful successors to the dynasty of Ayyubid sultans who preceded them.[2] Holt's article, moreover, uses the Mamluk sultanate as a case study to illustrate larger themes in Islamic constitutional law, which are accepted as axiomatic today. For example, the author explains that the Mamluk sultan "was as much bound by the Holy Law of Islam as any of his Muslim subjects, although the absence of means to compel his submission to the *shariʿa* deprived this concept of effective sanctions."[3] However, even without a means to compel the sultan's submission to the shariʿa, the theory in itself meant that the sultan "was left formally with no scope in legislation."[4] As was the case in many Islamic dynasties of premodern times, this theoretical arrangement would reaffirm the prerogative of the *ulama* in legislating through their interpretations of the shariʿa in their *fatwas* and *fiqh* texts.

To be sure, the sultan alone embodied the Mamluk executive, but we should mention that the Mamluk sultan al-Zahir Baybars (r. 1260–77) re-established the ʿAbbasid Caliphate in Cairo in 1261 by appointing two successive caliphs. Once again P.M. Holt

[1] Patricia Crone, *God's Rule: Government and Islam* (New York: Columbia University Press, 2004), 281.

[2] Peter M. Holt, "The Position and Power of the Mamluk Sultan," *Bulletin of the School of Oriental and African Studies* 38, no. 2 (1975): 237–249, 241–245.

[3] Ibid., 247. [4] Ibid.

provides us with an authoritative, albeit terse, study into this development with his 1984 article "Some Observations on the 'Abbasid Caliphate of Cairo." Although the 'Abbasid Caliph would always be a puppet in the hands of the Mamluk sultan, Holt identifies several essential functions that the caliphate performed for the Mamluks. The first, which Holt establishes as the impetus behind Baybars' abrupt recognition of the first of two caliphs whom he himself would appoint, was "a desire to legitimate his power," as Baybars "was not only personally a usurper, having obtained the throne by the killing of his predecessor Qutuz but the Mamluk sultanate itself had supplanted the Ayyubids."[5] The second caliph appointed by Baybars additionally served a diplomatic function. As a descendent of the Prophet and symbol of pious governance, he "could usefully serve as a mouthpiece in communicating with the convert to Islam" Berke Khan, who led the Golden Horde against the Mamluks' chief rival Hülegü, leader of the Il Khanids.[6] This latter caliph's direct descendants would constitute the dynasty of shadow-caliphs who reigned until the end of the Mamluk sultanate; their ceremonial importance in legitimizing the ascendance of a new sultan would grow after the thirteenth century.[7]

Holt's articles start with the historical data contained in Mamluk chronicles, necrologies, and biographical dictionaries and then work backwards to piece together a theoretical picture of the Mamluk executive and its relationship to offices like that of the caliphate. But would it not be simpler, if not more illuminating, to start with political treatises written by the *ulama* and then attempt to reconcile them with the historical data? Unfortunately we do not have that luxury, as the relative paucity of such treatises in Mamluk times is another challenge to historians of the Mamluk sultanate. In his influential 1988 article "Rather the Injustice of the Turks than the Righteousness of the Arabs," Ulrich Haarmann uses the biography and writings of a late-Mamluk scholar named Abu Hamid al-Qudsi (d. 1483) to account for the "petrified conservatism" of political scholarship in Mamluk Egypt and Syria by the fifteenth century.[8] Although his analysis is vague at times and perhaps relies too heavily on psychological speculation, Haarmann ultimately concludes that the despotism and foreignness of the Mamluk political elite would alienate the scholarly class and foster a despondency among them that undercut any hopes for political reform.[9] Their political reticence, we must assume, is the reason why Mamluk-era scholars have left us with relatively few political writings, in contrast to the prodigiousness of contemporaneous scholarship from Iran and central Asia.

[5] Peter M. Holt, "Some Observations on the 'Abbasid Caliphate of Cairo," *Bulletin of the School of Oriental and African Studies* 47, no. 3 (1984): 501–507, 501–502.

[6] Ibid., 503. [7] Ibid., 504ff.

[8] Ulrich Haarmann, "Rather the Injustice of the Turks than the Righteousness of the Arabs: Changing *'Ulamā'* Attitudes Towards Mamluk Rule in the Late Fifteenth Century," *Studia Islamica* 68 (1988): 61–77, 62.

[9] Ibid., 74ff.

This dearth of political texts from the Mamluk period suggests that Mamluk constitutional law represents relatively unfertile soil for the scholar of Islamic legal history. We are fortunate that the same cannot be said about the Mamluk judicial system, which is one of the most popular objects of study in the subfield of Mamluk legal history today. However, the popularity of the Mamluk judiciary amongst scholars makes a concise historiographical survey of it nearly impossible, and so let us return to our original framing question to make the secondary literature more manageable: What is specifically "Mamluk" about the Mamluk judiciary? In answering this question we find two institutions—namely, the office of chief justice and *siyasa* courts—that take on a decidedly "Mamluk" flavor during the Mamluk sultanate. I thus focus the rest of my discussion of the Mamluk judiciary on these.

Although the office of chief justice (*qadi 'l-qudat*) existed already under the Ayyubid dynasty that preceded them, the Mamluks were the first to appoint a chief justice for each of the four Sunni schools of law (*madhhabs*) beginning in 1265. Joseph Escovitz meticulously analyzed the office of chief justice in his 1984 study *The Office of Qāḍī al-Quḍāt in Cairo under the Baḥrī Mamlūks*; it stands as a pioneering treatment of the subject if we exclude Jon Mandaville's unpublished dissertation on the Mamluk judiciary of Damascus.[10] According to Escovitz, although the Shafi'i chief justice retained a degree of pre-eminence over the other three chief justices, this paled in comparison to Shafi'i pre-eminence under the Ayyubids or, for example, the institutionalized pre-eminence of the Hanafi *madhhab* under the Ottomans.[11] At the same time, the new Mamluk system was perhaps "more evolutionary than revolutionary," according to the author, as the four-justice system emerged in the wake of earlier educational reforms in which major *madrasas* like the Salihiyya would establish professorships for each of the four *madhhabs*.[12] In his 2003 article "Legal Diversity in the Age of *Taqlīd*," Yossef Rapoport criticizes Escovitz, among others, for failing to account for the essential motives behind, and the judicial implications of, this reform of the judiciary. Specifically, Rapoport argues that the four-justice system would ultimately be adopted in urban centers throughout the Mamluk realm in order to achieve "the double purpose of uniformity and flexibility" in the application of the law.[13] The new system achieved uniformity and predictability, as appointment decrees

[10] Jon E. Mandaville, "The Muslim Judiciary of Damascus in the Late Mamluk Period" Ph.D. diss., Princeton University, 1969; see also Émile Tyan, *Histoire de l'organisation judiciaire en pays d'Islam*, 2nd edn. (Leiden: E.J. Brill, 1960), 138–142.

[11] Joseph H. Escovitz, *The Office of Qāḍī al-Quḍāt in Cairo Under the Baḥrī Mamlūks* (Berlin: Klaus Schwarz Verlag, 1984), 20–28, 74, 258, and passim; cf. Mandaville, "The Muslim Judiciary of Damascus in the Late Mamluk Period," 7–8, 67–68, 85.

[12] Escovitz, *The Office of Qāḍī al-Quḍāt in Cairo Under the Baḥrī Mamlūks*, 22, 27.

[13] Yossef Rapoport, "Legal Diversity in the Age of *Taqlīd*: The Four Chief *Qāḍīs* under the Mamluks," *Islamic Law and Society* 10, no. 2 (2003): 210–228, 226.

required a judge to adjudicate according to the most authoritative doctrines of his *madhhab*, while it simultaneously achieved flexibility, as particular legal matters would be referred to the judge whose *madhhab* espoused those idiosyncratic positions that promoted the greatest social good.

In piecing together his description of the chief judgeship under the Bahri Mamluks, Escovitz relies primarily on Mamluk chronicles and biographical dictionaries, while he uses the court cases described in such sources to compile his chapter on "Judicial Activities." It is here, in passing, that the author notes a significant methodological hurdle that we face whenever we attempt to understand the Mamluk judiciary and its day-to-day activities. Since we possess no systematic docket of Mamluk court proceedings (with the exception of a court archive from fourteenth-century Jerusalem),[14] how representative should we assume the cases in Mamluk historical sources to be? As Escovitz explains, "The very fact that these cases were recorded might indicate that they were in some way out of the ordinary."[15] Indeed, it might not be farfetched to analogize the court cases recorded in Mamluk chronicles and biographical dictionaries to the headlines of 24-hour news outlets today: sex, violence, and otherwise sensational events seem to dominate both media and displace the quotidian affairs of everyday people. The contemporary historian of the Mamluk judiciary is left with perhaps no better corrective to this problem than awareness of its existence.

We can supplement the findings of Escovitz with those of Leonor Fernandes as contained in the latter's 2002 article "Between Qadis and Muftis: To Whom Does the Mamluk Sultan Listen?." According to Fernandes, a Mamluk *mufti* (a scholar who issues *fatawa*) would attain his office through the license (*ijaza*) of a previously recognized *mufti*; the position implied an advanced knowledge of one or more *madhhabs* but, unlike the office of *qadi* (shariʿa court judge), it was not dependent on a political appointment. Nevertheless, issuing legal opinions traditionally secured the qualified *mufti* a fixed salary, which Fernandes suggests exposed the office to bribery and political pressures of many sorts. Though some capable *qadis* might be qualified to employ independent legal reasoning (*ijtihad*) in their rulings, more often than not they were compelled to consult a *mufti*. The latter possessed a broader knowledge of legal evidences than most *qadis*, which "often allowed the mufti to propose opinions and solutions to problems which sometimes clashed with the narrower interpretations of the qadis."[16] For this reason, Fernandes explains, the Mamluk political elite was wont to consult with flexible *muftis* to garner legitimacy

[14] For a catalogue of the 900 documents that comprise this archive, see Donald P. Little, *A Catalogue of the Islamic Documents from al-Ḥaram aš-Šarīf in Jerusalem* (Beirut: Orient-Institut der Deutschen Morgenländischen Gesellschaft, 1984).

[15] Escovitz, *The Office of Qāḍī al-Quḍāt in Cairo Under the Baḥrī Mamlūks*, 134.

[16] Leonor Fernandes, "Between Qadis and Muftis: To Whom Does the Mamluk Sultan Listen?," *Mamlūk Studies Review* 6 (2002): 95–108, 99.

for any of their acts (e.g. confiscating property) that had the potential to stir controversy among the scholarly establishment.[17]

Both Escovitz and Fernandes highlight the potential for corruption in Mamluk shariʿa courts and in this way are representative of much scholarship on the Mamluk judiciary. We walk away from their writings with a picture of a Mamluk state that is dominated by corrupt judges and *muftis* who cower before a political elite that acts, more or less, with impunity. But a 2012 article by Rapoport has questioned this picture and provides us with the final word on the subject, for now. In his "Royal Justice and Religious Law: *Siyāsah* and Shariʿah under the Mamluks," Rapoport identifies two grounds on which to criticize the "moralizing, caricature-like accounts of the Mamluk legal system" that predominate in contemporary scholarship.[18] First, such accounts are premised in the assumptions of Joseph Schacht, who famously argued that Islamic law would become ossified by the later Abbasid period and would progressively lose more and more of its practical utility. Citing important scholarship in Islamic law from the past thirty years, Rapoport reminds us that Schacht's position is no longer tenable, as more recent studies of *fatawa*, legal commentaries, and court documents reveal that the gulf between legal theory and positive law in premodern times was nowhere near as large as Schacht describes it.[19] Second, Rapoport criticizes the tendency of many modern scholars to position the Mamluk state in a binary relationship with a "pure, perfect sphere of Islamic law," whereby the state might appear to exist as a supra-legal entity. Rather, the remainder of Rapoport's article makes a compelling case for viewing the Mamluk legal system as one "in which the state takes an active role in adapting the sacred law, the shariʿah, to social practice."[20] The Mamluk legal system, in fact, shares much in common with the more bureaucratized system of the Ottoman state, particularly as regards the theoretical importance that both systems would ascribe to the ruler's *siyasa sharʿiyya*, or governance according to the broader guidelines of Islamic law and, here, notions of equity.[21]

Rapoport's important article charts the jurisdictional expansion of Mamluk *siyasa* courts over the course of the Mamluk sultanate. By showing how this expansion was viewed as necessary to upholding broader conceptions of equity in response to the formalism of the shariʿa courts, his framework supplants earlier, overly simplistic narratives that posit a dual system of justice in which *siyasa* courts held jurisdiction over the affairs of the Mamluk elite while commoners settled their affairs in shariʿa courts. According to Rapoport, no such jurisdictional line existed, and in fact Mamluk chamberlains (*hujjab*) and other military officers would adjudicate the cases of common citizens in *siyasa* courts starting in the mid-fourteenth century.

[17] Ibid., 99–101.

[18] Yossef Rapoport, "Royal Justice and Religious Law: *Siyāsah* and Shariʿah under the Mamluks," *Mamlūk Studies Review* 16 (2012): 71–102, 72.

[19] Ibid., 72–74. [20] Ibid., 75. [21] Ibid., 74–75.

In the end, the encroachment of *siyasa* jurisdiction upon that of the Shariʿa courts functioned—at least in the popular perception—to provide the people with "justice, not just the law."[22] And, inasmuch as this justice reflected the ethical imperatives and timeless objectives of sacred law, then Rapoport is justified in his claim that "the expansion of the *siyāsah* jurisdiction set out to bolster the shariʿa rather than defeat it."[23]

Rapoport's broader definition of shariʿa here intersects nicely with Kristin Stilt's 2011 study into the office of the Mamluk *muhtasib*, or "market inspector," which will epitomize Mamluk law enforcement for the purposes of the present chapter.[24] Although earlier scholars like Émile Tyan have examined the institution of *hisba* through the prescriptive lens of *hisba* manuals written by Muslim scholars,[25] Stilt's *Islamic Law in Action* stands as the first monograph study of the Mamluk office of *muhtasib* written in a European language and, more importantly, is unafraid to bring its discussion into the descriptive realm of social history. To do so, Stilt mines Mamluk chronicles for details into the actual conduct of Mamluk *muhtasibs* and then compares these details with the prescriptive ideals of *hisba* manuals, *fiqh* texts, and the directives of Mamluk sultans. The picture that we gather from this comparison reveals an office with one foot in the *fiqh* concerns of Muslim jurists and one foot in the *siyasa* (here, public order) considerations of the Mamluk state. But in light of Rapoport's broader framework already outlined, we would be mistaken to take only the *fiqh* texts of the jurists as synonymous with the shariʿa, as the sultan's *siyasa* policies were grounded in the ethical objectives of this same law. The *muhtasib* thus emerges—at least in theory—as perhaps the perfect embodiment of shariʿa-oriented law enforcement.

II. A Gray Area: Mamluk Institutions of Learning

Any study of medieval Islamic law would be remiss if it failed to mention the role of *madrasas* (Islamic educational institutions) in the production of legal scholarship. The Mamluks, of course, did not invent the *madrasa*, but their largess through *waqf* endowments, as motivated by both piety and political expediency, took *madrasa*

[22] Ibid., 86–92; quotation at p. 89. [23] Ibid., 101.

[24] Kristen Stilt, *Islamic Law in Action: Authority, Discretion, and Everyday Experiences in Mamluk Egypt* (Oxford: Oxford University Press, 2011).

[25] Tyan, *Histoire de l'organisation judiciare en pays de l'Islam*, 436–462.

building to the next level of complexity. The Mamluks constituted one of the earliest Muslim political dynasties to exist long enough to require a symbolic means of relating their power to the local population and thereby garner for themselves the legitimacy needed for long-term rule.[26] Moreover, they relied on slaves to provide whatever military manpower they needed, and by not conscripting the local population into military service, a "cultural, linguistic and ethnic wedge" persisted between the Mamluk political elites and the people over whom they ruled.[27] Although the Mamluks would establish a strong bureaucratic apparatus, it was not their primary means of projecting themselves into the public sphere. Rather, they performed their authority symbolically through their patronage of educational institutions, thereby "creating some of the largest *madrasas* and entrenching their control of the population deeper and with more lasting effect than any dynasty had done hitherto."[28] The massive *madrasas* that they built and which still stand today also served to foster an environment of relative collegiality between the four Sunni *madhhabs*. But it was the policies of the Ayyubids who preceded the Mamluks that set the stage for such an environment of inter-*madhhab* collegiality,[29] and here we see the rationale for placing Mamluk educational institutions in an intermediate space between things that were unique to Islamic law during Mamluk times and things that were not. Mamluk patronage of *madrasas* and legal scholarship, in other words, was novel in degree but not in kind.

The Mamluk *madrasa* nevertheless represents a unique object of study for social historians of the medieval Middle East because of the existence of *waqf* endowment deeds, which, on the whole and unlike Mamluk court records, have reached us today. A good example of what can be gleaned from such endowment deeds appears in Jonathan Berkey's 1992 study *The Transmission of Knowledge in Medieval Cairo: A Social History of Islamic Education*. Berkey draws his most valuable data from twenty-nine *waqf* deeds for major educational institutions in Mamluk Cairo, and his study offers groundbreaking insights into, among other things: ancillary institutions of learning, such as *khanqahs* (Sufi hospices, which are discussed again in this chapter) and mausoleums, the relationship of Mamluk sultans to such institutions, and the role of women in the larger educational system. Berkey concludes his book with an attempt to situate these institutions of learning within the larger urban environment of Mamluk Cairo.

Beyond Berkey's foundational study, the methodology behind any investigation into Mamluk educational institutions would benefit immensely from Michael Chamberlain's 1994 monograph *Knowledge and Social Practice in Medieval*

[26] Wael B. Hallaq, *Sharīʿa: Theory, Practice, Transformations* (Cambridge; New York: Cambridge University Press, 2009), 148, 152.

[27] Ibid., 197. [28] Ibid., 152.

[29] Ira M. Lapidus, "Ayyubid Religious Policy and the Development of Schools of Law in Cairo," in *Colloque international sur l'histoire du Caire*, ed. André Raymond (Cairo: Wizārat al-Thaqāfa, 1969), 285 and passim.

Damascus, 1190–1350. Chamberlain views the transmission of knowledge in medieval Damascus as a function of power struggles and competition over *mansibs* (stipendiary positions); the competitive ethic that prevailed in the political and social spheres he terms "positive *fitna*" (struggle).[30] Furthermore, the author proposes a radical rethinking of the traditional European approach to the medieval Middle East, as Continental assumptions and theoretical lenses too often taint our interpretations of Middle Eastern social history. In the end, Chamberlain views the production and transmission of knowledge as largely a cultural performance of competition between the intellectual elites for which the *madrasa* itself serves as the central stage. Whether his conclusions are ultimately specific to Damascus or not, Chamberlain furnishes social historians with a compelling methodological starting point from which to analyze the social dynamics of Mamluk cities, particularly as they relate to patronage and the production of knowledge.

A final note on the *khanqah* and its role in Mamluk education is worth mentioning here. An essential study on this subject is Leonor Fernandes' 1988 monograph *The Evolution of a Sufi Institution in Mamluk Egypt: The Khanqah*, while Th. Emil Homerin's 1999 article "Saving Muslim Souls: The *Khānqāh* and the Sufi Duty in Mamluk Lands" helps to update Fernandes' research and situate it within a larger historical framework. For his part, Homerin admits that the difference between the *madrasa*, the *khanqah*, and the comparable Sufi institution of the *zawiya* "resulted largely from differences in size and focus, not their underlying Sunni mission."[31] Nevertheless, the *khanqah* could be viewed as a median point between the other two institutions, as most *khanqah* endowment deeds would stipulate that recipients of their stipends be initiated Sufis, as was the case with most *zawiyas*, while also providing an educational curriculum that included many of the traditional Islamic disciplines. Although both Fernandes and Homerin rely on similar methodologies and sources to reach their conclusions, they filter their data through conflicting worldviews and thus generate divergent narratives. Leaning toward the cynical side of the spectrum, Fernandes explains the *khanqah* as a means by which the Mamluk ruling elite would monitor and control the religious practices of the local population through the establishment of an "orthodox" vision of Sufism. Homerin, on the other hand, adopts a more sanguine stance and points to the relative autonomy that these institutions enjoyed once they were consecrated as *waqf* endowments. We are thus left with two conflicting accounts that likely cannot be reconciled without recourse to undue speculation; the reader must interpret the results in light of their own understandings of the world.

[30] Michael Chamberlain, *Knowledge and Social Practice in Medieval Damascus* (Cambridge; New York: Cambridge University Press, 1994), 7–8, 47–51, 125.

[31] Th. Emil Homerin, "Saving Muslim Souls: The *Khānqāh* and the Sufi Duty in Mamluk Lands," *Mamlūk Studies Review* 3 (1999): 59–83, 76.

III. Larger Intellectual Trends in the Study and Practice of Islamic Law

The legal institutions outlined above each possess some trait that defines them as quintessentially Mamluk, albeit some more subtly so than others. Other intellectual trends that predominated during Mamluk times would shape the study and practice of Islamic law to an equal, if not greater, extent. However, they cannot be as easily confined to the temporal and geographic boundaries of the Mamluk sultanate. They are nevertheless worth mentioning, as their influence would characterize the Mamluk legal texts that have reached us today. I list three of them here briefly and in descending order of significance to the study of Islamic law, while also providing references to some of the most recent scholarship on them.

A. The Proliferation of Commentary Works

The advent of the Mamluk sultanate in the thirteenth century coincides with the beginning of what many Muslim reformers and twentieth-century scholars have dismissed as "the era of commentaries and supercommentaries."[32] This designation reflects the distaste that many such reformers and scholars held toward the outward form and rhetorical tone of commentary works, which would appear in the thousands and within all of the Islamic scholarly disciplines from the thirteenth century onwards. Taking their cues from Romantic ideas of the creative genius, the overwhelming majority of twentieth-century scholars accepted at face value the (often tacit) claim of Muslim commentators to do nothing more than explicate, through their commentaries, what is otherwise implicit in a base-text. Once one accepts this claim, the base-text then assumes all agency in setting the creative agenda of a given discipline, while the commentarial form comes to symbolize intellectual and creative stagnancy.

But to uncritically accept the rhetoric of commentary disregards both commentary's function as an important locus for knowledge brokerage and specialization, and its propensity to subvert the received tradition, notwithstanding its rhetorical claims to the contrary. Contemporary scholars of Islamic law have begun to examine the creative merits of legal commentaries as an object of study in themselves,[33] as is being done with a variety of other Islamic disciplines that witnessed a proliferation

[32] For an example of this sentiment, see, inter alia, Muhammad Qīṭāz, "Al-Shaykh ʿAlwān ʿAlī b. ʿAṭiyya al-Hītī," *Al-Turāth al-ʿArabī* 10 (1983): 135–154, 138–139.

[33] e.g. see Matthew B. Ingalls, "*Šarḥ, Iḫtiṣār*, and Late-Medieval Legal Change," *Annemarie Schimmel Kolleg Working Paper* 17 (2014): 1–20.

of commentary works in medieval times.[34] Notwithstanding these positive trends in twenty-first century scholarship, assumptions from the study of western history still beset the field and inform the research agendas of many. In this light, Thomas Bauer's critique of the study of Mamluk literature, namely that "what is described as 'stagnation' is therefore not the lack of development per se, but the lack of developments that mimicked and confirmed Western models," might also be leveled at the study of Mamluk legal commentaries to date.[35]

B. The Institution of the *Ijaza* (License; Certification)

How did Mamluk legal scholars garner legitimacy for themselves and transmit their authority to the next generation of scholars? This question has proven surprisingly difficult to answer and has polarized contemporary scholars into two camps. In one camp, scholars like Berkey and Chamberlain have highlighted the organic and informal nature of the Mamluk educational system, which rested its foundation upon the skill and charisma of individual scholars, while they simultaneously downplay the role of institutions like the *madrasa* and the *ijaza*. The latter term denotes a complex and dynamic institution that served, in the majority of contexts, as a merely symbolic mechanism to link a new generation to an existing chain of transmission back to a *hadith* text or book, but in other contexts its usage suggests a formal, written certificate that functioned almost like an academic degree today. Berkey and Chamberlain categorically deny this second understanding of the *ijaza*.[36] Opposed to them is the camp of George Makdisi, whose famous 1981 study *The Rise of Colleges* emphasizes the central role of formal institutions like *madrasas* and written, degree-like *ijazas* in certifying the next generation of Muslim scholars.[37]

In his 2004 article "The Doctorate of Islamic Law in Mamluk Egypt and Syria," Devin Stewart traces the source of this debate back to two historiographical problems that confront scholars of the Mamluk educational system. The first, which has already been discussed in this chapter, is the dearth of Mamluk documentary sources that have survived until today that might otherwise provide us with direct examples of *ijaza* certificates functioning like academic degrees. Without direct access to such certificates, however, we are left with only recensions of them as they have reached us in literary sources like al-Qalqashandi's famous secretarial manual

[34] See, e.g., the twelve articles that comprise volume 41:3–4 (2013) of the journal *Oriens*.

[35] Thomas Bauer, "Mamlūk Literature: Misunderstandings and New Approaches," *Mamlūk Studies Review* 9, no. 2 (2005): 105–132, 116.

[36] Jonathan P. Berkey, *The Transmission of Knowledge in Medieval Cairo* (Princeton: Princeton University Press, 1992), 16, 22, 43; Chamberlain, *Knowledge and Social Practice in Medieval Damascus*, 87–90.

[37] George Makdisi, *The Rise of Colleges: Institutions of Learning in Islam and the West* (Edinburgh: Edinburgh University Press, 1981), 148–152, 172–175, 270–276.

Subh al-a'sha. Stewart, in fact, relies heavily on this latter source in his examination of Mamluk *ijaza* practices, and his resulting analysis places him closer to the camp of Makdisi, his former teacher. A second and more general historiographical problem that Stewart identifies is the difficult nature of interpreting medieval Muslim biographical dictionaries. Muslim biographers would employ a highly idiosyncratic technical vocabulary when documenting the scholarly practices of their subjects, and their terms of art are not only subtle in themselves, but it is not always clear when they intend the conventional register of a term that might ostensibly appear technical and vice versa.[38]

Stewart's article demonstrates a profound appreciation for the subtleties of the *ijaza*, and his results are persuasive. Nevertheless, the debate remains far from settled. To date, the most sophisticated treatment of the *ijaza* as an evolving institution throughout Islamic intellectual history appears in Garrett Davidson's 2014 dissertation "Carrying on the Tradition: An Intellectual and Social History of Post-Canonical Hadith Transmission."[39] A published version of this dissertation promises to shed much needed light on an institution that was at the heart of the medieval Muslim discourse on authority.

c. Encyclopaedism in Mamluk Literature

In his 2012 dissertation "Encyclopaedism in the Mamluk Period," Elias Muhanna examines the "aggregative ethos" that would define Mamluk scholarship and would lead to the sudden proliferation of compilatory texts after the thirteenth century. In response to earlier historians who have linked the encyclopaedic push of the times to the trauma of the Mongol conquests, Muhanna explains this trend instead as a function of Mamluk imperial and administrative expansion, which generated a broader, universal understanding of the Islamic intellectual heritage amongst scholars. With this new understanding came "the feeling of an *overcrowding* of authoritative sources," and Muslim writers in a variety of disciplines would respond with compendia and compilations in an attempt to systematize these sources and structure their relationship to them.[40]

[38] Devin J. Stewart, "The Doctorate of Islamic Law in Mamluk Egypt and Syria," in *Law and Education in Medieval Islam: Studies in Memory of Professor George Makdisi*, eds. Joseph Lowry, Devin Stewart, and Shawkat Toorawa (Cambridge: The E.J.W. Gibb Memorial Trust, 2004), 45–90, 48–53 and passim.

[39] For an important discussion of the confusion in the secondary literature on the differing types of *ijazas*, see Garrett Davidson, "Carrying on the Tradition: An Intellectual and Social History of Post-Canonical Hadith Transmission," Ph.D. diss., University of Chicago, 2014, 130–133.

[40] Elias I. Muhanna, "Encyclopaedism in the Mamluk Period: The Composition of Shihāb al-Dīn al-Nuwayrī's (d. 1333) *Nihāyat al-arab fī funūn al-adab*." Ph.D. diss., Harvard University, 2012, chapter two (quoted material at p. 97).

Although not a focus of Muhanna's study, Muslim legal scholarship would also reflect such encyclopaedism, and it behooves the contemporary scholar of Islamic law to consider the causes for it and the effects that it would have on the textual tradition. Of course, much has been written on the practical dynamics of legal compendia as they relate to questions of authority and legal change, but Muhanna's research offers us new methodological avenues for linking these questions to larger forces in Muslim social and political history.

IV. A Brief Assessment of the Historiography and Questions for Future Research

Mamluk Studies is a subfield that, by defining itself according to a fixed temporal and geographic range, manages to bring together political, economic, social, and intellectual historians who research within that range, thereby fostering synergy and creativity between them. In fact, the formative/classical/postclassical framework that informed twentieth-century scholarship in Muslim intellectual history is now seen as far too broad to be of use. Examining legal thought through the lens of a more circumscribed political dynasty, like that of the Mamluk sultanate, might provide us with a more fruitful means of refining the contours of change in Islamic legal thought and practice.

Nevertheless, Muslim intellectual history does not lend itself to fixed borders, and the historiography of the larger intellectual trends discussed in Section III above is only beginning to garner the scholarly attention that it deserves. In light of the framing question that has structured this chapter—namely, what is specifically "Mamluk" about Islamic law and legal scholarship during the Mamluk sultanate?—future researchers might benefit from asking some of the following questions as they approach their primary sources: Is there a particularly Mamluk tone or rhetorical style that we can identify in the legal commentaries that emerged in Mamluk times? Similarly, how do educational and judicial institutions that *are* particular to the Mamluk sultanate affect the intellectual content of the law that they produced and applied in the process of adjudication? How does the *mukhtasar* (abridgement) style of writing—here taken in its generic sense—relate to the Mamluk *madrasa* and the explosion of commentary works that defined the medieval tradition? Can we link the emergence of legal compendia to larger social, administrative, and political developments that are specific to the Mamluk period? Additionally, how might we uncover more historical data on the *formal* aspects of the Mamluk educational system and its processes of certification? For a lead in answering this last question, scholars might wish to consider Stewart's passing remark that *waqf* documents have been "underutilized for the examination of educational, social, and economic history."[41]

Though far from exhaustive, this list of research questions for future historians reveals some of the gaps in our knowledge—gaps that form especially in those places where social and intellectual history intersect. On the other hand, previous scholarship has laid a solid foundation for our understanding of the Mamluk legal institutions discussed in Sections I and II, and future scholars must now continue to expand upon the details of these institutions. Finally, if Rapoport's study into Mamluk *siyasa* courts is any indication, much of a scholar's methodology rests upon his or her theoretical conceptions of Islamic law and the institutions and personalities that he or she chooses to prioritize when defining it. As Rapoport demonstrates convincingly, it is sometimes the broadest conceptions of shariʿa—those that can accommodate the theoretical elaborations of the "*ulama*," the applied practices of the *qadis* and *muhtasibs*, and the political exigencies of the sultans—that best reveal the integration of Islamic law into all segments of Mamluk society.

References

Bauer, Thomas, "Mamlūk Literature: Misunderstandings and New Approaches." *Mamlūk Studies Review* 9, no. 2 (2005): 105–132.

Berkey, Jonathan P., *The Transmission of Knowledge in Medieval Cairo: A Social History of Islamic Education* (Princeton: Princeton University Press, 1992).

Chamberlain, Michael, *Knowledge and Social Practice in Medieval Damascus, 1190–1350* (Cambridge; New York: Cambridge University Press, 1994).

Crone, Patricia, *God's Rule: Government and Islam* (New York: Columbia University Press, 2004).

Davidson, Garrett, "Carrying on the Tradition: An Intellectual and Social History of Post-Canonical Hadith Transmission." Ph.D. diss., University of Chicago, 2014.

Escovitz, Joseph H., *The Office of Qāḍī al-Quḍāt in Cairo Under the Baḥrī Mamlūks* (Berlin: Klaus Schwarz Verlag, 1984).

Fernandes, Leonor, *The Evolution of a Sufi Institution in Mamluk Egypt: The Khanqah* (Berlin: Klaus Schwarz Verlag, 1988).

Fernandes, Leonor, "Between Qadis and Muftis: To Whom does the Mamluk Sultan Listen?" *Mamlūk Studies Review* 6 (2002): 95–108.

Haarmann, Ulrich, "Rather the Injustice of the Turks than the Righteousness of the Arabs: Changing *ʿUlamāʾ* Attitudes Towards Mamluk Rule in the Late Fifteenth Century." *Studia Islamica* 68 (1988): 61–77.

41 Stewart, "The Doctorate of Islamic Law in Mamluk Egypt and Syria," 48 (n. 12).

Hallaq, Wael B., *Sharīʿa: Theory, Practice, Transformations* (Cambridge; New York: Cambridge University Press, 2009).

Holt, Peter M., "The Position and Power of the Mamlūk Sultan." *Bulletin of the School of Oriental and African Studies* 38, no. 2 (1975): 237–249.

Holt, Peter M., "Some Observations on the ʿAbbāsid Caliphate of Cairo." *Bulletin of the School of Oriental and African Studies* 47, no. 3 (1984): 501–507.

Homerin, Th. Emil, "Saving Muslim Souls: The *Khānqāh* and the Sufi Duty in Mamluk Lands." *Mamlūk Studies Review* 3 (1999): 59–83.

Ingalls, Matthew B., "*Šarḥ, Iḫtiṣār*, and Late-Medieval Legal Change." *Annemarie Schimmel Kolleg Working Paper* 17 (2014): 1–20.

Lapidus, Ira M., "Ayyubid Religious Policy and the Development of Schools of Law in Cairo" in André Raymond (ed.) *Colloque international sur l'histoire du Caire* (Cairo: Wizārat al-Thaqāfa, 1969) 279–286.

Little, Donald P., *A Catalogue of the Islamic Documents from al-Ḥaram aš-Šarīf in Jerusalem* (Beirut: Orient-Institut der Deutschen Morgenländischen Gesellschaft, 1984).

Makdisi, George, *The Rise of Colleges: Institutions of Learning in Islam and the West* (Edinburgh: Edinburgh University Press, 1981).

Mandaville, Jon E., "The Muslim Judiciary of Damascus in the Late Mamluk Period." Ph.D. diss., Princeton University, 1969.

Muhanna, Elias I., "Encyclopaedism in the Mamluk Period: The Composition of Shihāb al-Dīn al-Nuwayrī's (d. 1333) *Nihāyat al-arab fī funūn al-adab*." Ph.D. diss., Harvard University, 2012.

Qīṭāẓ, Muḥammad ʿAdnān, "Al-Shaykh ʿAlwān ʿAlī b. ʿAṭiyya al-Hītī." *Al-Turāth al-ʿArabī* 10 (1983): 135–154.

Rapoport, Yossef, "Legal Diversity in the Age of *Taqlīd*: The Four Chief *Qāḍīs* under the Mamluks." *Islamic Law and Society* 10, no. 2 (2003): 210–228.

Rapoport, Yossef, "Royal Justice and Religious Law: *Siyāsah* and Shariʿah under the Mamluks." *Mamlūk Studies Review* 16 (2012): 71–102.

Stewart, Devin J., "The Doctorate of Islamic Law in Mamluk Egypt and Syria" in Joseph Lowry, Devin Stewart, and Shawkat Toorawa (eds.) *Law and Education in Medieval Islam: Studies in Memory of Professor George Makdisi* (Cambridge: The E.J.W. Gibb Memorial Trust, 2004) 45–90.

Stilt, Kristen, *Islamic Law in Action: Authority, Discretion, and Everyday Experiences in Mamluk Egypt* (Oxford: Oxford University Press, 2011).

Tyan, Émile, *Histoire de l'organisation judiciare en pays de l'Islam* (2nd edn. Leiden: E.J. Brill, 1960).

CHAPTER 19

LAW IN THE OTTOMAN EMPIRE

HAIM GERBER

THOUGH it is difficult to tell this from general histories of Islamic law, Ottoman law occupies a special place in the history of Islamic law. While no doubt still part and parcel of classical Islamic culture, this law was characterized by several new features. The most basic one seems to be a matter of coincidence, but one that turns out to be the most important—this is the fact that while for classical Islam we practically have no court registers, for the Ottoman period we possess thousands of such registers (*sicill*). As a consequence, while many (most?) studies on classical Islamic law are about legal philosophy (the development of the doctrine), origins of the doctrine, etc., the study of Ottoman law permits an emphasis on law in practice, as it actually functioned in Muslim courts of law. This must be of some importance: we shall see for example that most of the Qur'anic punishments, the *hudud*, were not implemented in their literal sense, thus forcing a relaxation of the former harsh opinion of the traditional Islamic shari'a. In the same context of the relations between Ottoman law and classical Islamic law, it has been claimed recently that we can assume that what the Ottoman *sicills* tell us about the law is more or less what took place in the classical Islamic shari'a courts.[1] This statement needs much more research to be considered convincing.

[1] Wael B. Hallaq, *Shari'a: Theory, Practice, Transformations* (Cambridge: Cambridge University Press, 2009).

The fact that we possess for the Ottoman period an incredible abundance of court records, should not blind us to the fact that there is another crucially important source shedding light on this law—the *fetva* (Arabic, *fatwa*) collections. *Fetva* as it developed in the classical law was a legal opinion supplied by an expert, *mufti*, to a person, usually, though not exclusively, a party to a lawsuit before the *kadi*. The item of knowledge supplied by the *mufti* is expressly legal–theoretical, but it usually relates to a practical and worldly issue, what makes the *mufti* a bridge between Islamic law and real life. Needless to say, in the future, legal historians will have to come back to the *fetva* collections to look more carefully into the relations between *fetvas* and *kadi* rulings. But in the last three decades or so the surge of *sicill* studies has been such as to push aside almost any interest in areas that are not part of hard core legal practice. Space limitations will necessarily limit my own approach in this historiographic essay to the law in action, that is, *kadi* court records.

Space limitations will also prevent me from delving in any detail into the thorny question of the methodological problems besetting the *kadi* court records as a historical source. I will mention just a few points. The main issue has to do with the fact that the record is not a verbatim transcription of what went on in the court, but only a skeletal summary, leaving out the interrogations, hesitant retractions, expressions of personal feeling, and the like. Also, there is no information on the judges and their approaches to various issues, as we can see in the materials surrounding the debates on American legal realism, where the objectivity of the judge was declared a myth, hence the identity of judges became important in understanding their rulings.[2] No such sensitivity or problem ever arose in Ottoman or Islamic law in general (I devote some more space to Islamic-law related insights that can be distilled from legal realism later in this chapter). But what bridges many of these faults is that we basically get what the claims of the parties were, and we have the decisions of the *kadis*. Despite claims to the contrary, these factors nonetheless make this source all-important for Ottoman-Islamic legal history for generations, especially if we bear in mind that no other source is problem-free.

In looking for one succinct question that would contain as much of the research on Ottoman law as possible, the research agenda of Max Weber seemed to me to be the most appropriate. Weber's findings may not be considered fully valid today; but his theoretical model is still ingenious, and his influence still enormous. Even his substantive findings have in recent years been resuscitated to a certain extent. Weber used Islamic law (for which he dubbed the famous, or infamous, term *kadi* justice) as a term of art to describe legal systems that are far removed from the ordeal type of law, in which there is no weighing of the evidence of the litigants. The *kadi*'s system of thought was substantively rational, but not formally rational: the *kadi* weighed the validity of litigants' arguments without the direction of a law code, but rather on the

[2] On American legal realism see Jerome Frank, *Law and the Modern Mind* (New York: Anchor Books, 1963).

basis of ethical considerations, expediency, whims, corruption, or at the prodding (or under the pressure) of political authorities.[3] Weber knew full well about the oceanic volume of law literature in Islam, known under the term of shari'a or *fiqh*. But he lived under the assumption, universal until the 1970s, that after the closure of the gates of *ijtihad* somewhere in the high Middle Ages, Islamic law ceased to develop, and with the passage of time became increasingly removed and detached from real life, leaving the *kadi* no option but to resort to his own common sense and other intellectual resources in deciding legal cases. The shari'a itself remained sacred on paper, but ossified, and in real life no one heeded it after the tenth or eleventh century, CE. And since the shari'a was a sacred law, no one could devise a new code, or even a way of resuscitating the old one.[4] The attribution to the *kadi* of heavy involvement in corruption and susceptibility to bend rules under the pressure of the political authorities tinged the concept of *kadi* justice and made of it an arbitrary, primitive, and barbaric legal system, eternalized in analyses of famous western judges, and top playwrights like Bertold Brecht. Judging by the Ottoman case all this was extremely exaggerated.

That something was amiss with Weber's theory should have been obvious with the appearance of the first studies of Ottoman law based on actual *kadi* court records, an honor that goes indisputably to Ronald Jennings in the late 1970s.[5] But just a few years later, under the influence of American legal realism and (I would say) post-modernism in general, a new development started that gave Weber a new lease of life. This was the idea that Ottoman, Islamic, or any other law, should not be seen as the document(s) containing the theoretical law, but the actual process of bargaining between the judge and the litigants, bargaining that was often free-floating and unrelated to the contents of the law books. The judge was now seen as a negotiator between litigants, seeking to smooth over differences and keep the social harmony of the society, rather than a judge enforcing a law code. This new theory—a central feature of what is fashionably called "law and society"—is a reincarnation of course, mainly of Weber's main argument, viz., that the *kadi*'s deliberations were not so much formal statements of law, but rather reflected the dynamic and contingent context in which judgment was made, although it has to be borne in mind that for Weber this was not a sign of the strength or health of Islamic law but the opposite, a clear sign of its decline and socio-political obsolescence and irrelevance.

Weber's questions can be phrased thus:

- To what extent was formal Islamic law (the shari'a) also the law in practice? What other sources of law were there?

[3] Max Weber, *Economy and Society*, 2 vols. (New York: Bedminster Press, 1968), 795, 845, 976, 978, 1395.

[4] Weber, *Economy and Society*, 818–822.

[5] Ronald C. Jennings, "Kadi, Court and Legal Procedure in 17th Century Ottoman Kayseri," *Studia Islamica* 48 (1978): 133–172; Ronald C. Jennings, "Limitations on the Judicial Powers of the Kadi in 17th Century Ottoman Kayseri," *Studia Islamica* 50 (1979): 151–184.

- What was the place and role of the *kadi*? Did the *kadi* share law enforcement with other state office-holders (like the provincial governor)?
- Was the *kadi*'s mode of working based on arbitrariness, as suggested by Weber? And more generally, was decision-making by the *kadi* more or less structured or simply based on free-floating bargaining and mediation between litigants, with little or no reference to any law code?

I. Islamic Law in Practice—The Shari'a and Other Sources of Law

My own study of the legal system of seventeenth-century Bursa and the Ottoman Empire in general was the first to deal head on with this specific problem.[6] For some reason, most other studies on Ottoman law are not really interested in the shari'a, but are in effect social histories based on *kadi* court records. My own interest in this topic probably harks back to my early interest in Weber in general and Weber and Islam in particular. For anyone whose starting point is Weber, interest in the shari'a is unavoidable.

Maybe because of the distinguished place of Bursa as the focal point of Ottoman Islam and Ottoman culture in general, the study of its seventeenth-century *kadi* court records showed surprising and unexpected affinity between the law as practiced and the formal shari'a. It was by no means a one to one correspondence, but nevertheless an impressive similarity, far reaching enough to undermine Weber's claim that the shari'a became decadent and obsolete after 1258. But even in areas of the law where divergence between the shari'a and the law in practice existed, the law was more or less stable over time, and hence *pace* Weber, there was a great deal of predictability. Resort to formal shari'a and predictability went hand in hand.

If we take as an example the all-important case of the penal code of the shari'a, many (though not all) of the laws in this field in seventeenth-century Bursa were the shar'i laws. The entire area of law connected with homicide was fully governed by the shari'a. According to shari'a manuals, if a murderer was brought to trial and his guilt proven, the next of kin of the slain person could demand retaliation, that is, the death penalty, or blood money (*diyet*) instead. A large number of documents from several places show that this law was fully operative in the seventeenth and eighteenth centuries. Formal shari'a doctrines were decisive also in the extremely

[6] Haim Gerber, *State, Society and Law in Islam: Ottoman Law in Comparative Perspective* (Albany: State University of New York Press, 1994).

common case of the discovery of a corpse, where the killer was not known. Islamic law solved the issue by using the oath of *kassama*, or oath of compurgation: fifty oaths were required from people living in the vicinity that they were not the perpetrators and did not know who was. And then they had to pay the blood money of the dead person. Sometimes that person was severely wounded before dying, and occasionally he was willing to attest before a *na'ib* (deputy judge, usually the person sent to investigate the whereabouts of found bodies) that in case he died, none of the citizens of the neighborhood was responsible for his death, thus removing the burden on them altogether. All this legal material could be cited from Hanafi legal manuals; but in the Ottoman context it was operative in real court documents, showing again the vibrancy of the formal shari'a four to six centuries after the end of the medieval period, when the shari'a was supposed to have ossified and gone into practical oblivion, according to Weber.

A no less interesting issue is that of *hudud*, or Qur'anic punishments, also called *huquq Allah* (rights of God), the offences considered most severe in the Islamic law book, (an additional topic considered in my book on Bursa and some additional places). These offences were wine drinking; theft; illicit sexual relations (*zina*), punishable by one hundred lashes for an offender who has not been married and death by stoning for someone who has; *kazf* (Arabic, *qadhf*), or false accusation of *zina* (including casual curses insinuating involvement in *zina*); and highway robbery (entailing the death penalty if involving killing). The problem was that the onus of proof demanded in some of the cases was almost impossible to attain: illicit sex required four eye witnesses attesting to seeing the actual act of coitus, while stealing required two eyewitnesses. It is common among historians to deduce from this that the *hudud* were enacted just as deterrence or warning, not to be actually implemented. Whether this was actually the intention of the forefathers of Islamic law is hard to say, but it is true that in the Ottoman Empire most of the *hudud* were only implemented in a mild form. Besides one famous case from eighteenth-century Istanbul[7] no case of stoning is known to have taken place. Lighter punishments were imposed (mainly being forced to serve as oarsmen in the Ottoman navy for a number of years). But on the other hand circumstantial evidence was admitted: known prostitutes were captured by the Bursa police with unrelated men in one house. In no case was full-fledged *zina* proven (or even carefully looked for), but it was assumed that illicit sex had taken place, and a discretionary punishment (*ta'zir*) was imposed in all these cases, conveying the idea that the infraction was a lesser offense than *zina*. Circumstantial evidence was also accepted in the case of theft, though again with the resulting reduced punishment of time served in the Ottoman navy. Most importantly, the crime of highway robbery became a focal point of legal development and innovation in the Ottoman period. Highway robbery by permanent

[7] Madeline Zilfi, *The Ottoman Ulema* (Chicago: Bibliotheca Islamica, 1988), 202f.

gangs of hardened criminals was a common feature of country life in the Ottoman Empire in the seventeenth century, targeting not only merchants and travelers, but also government officials transporting tax money to Istanbul. The frequency of its occurrence called for extraordinary measures, which reflected innovations and developments in the law of highway robbery. These developments do not appear in formal shari'a manuals. What took place on the ground was that a special legal category of criminals was defined—*sai bil-fesad*, or *sai be fesad el-arz*, "a fomentor of evil in the world," who was in effect a repeat robber. The evidentiary requirements for this new offense were limited, thus making prosecution more successful. The only requirement was the attestation of the community leaders of a certain village or quarter, bypassing the sacred shari'a requirement of individual proof according to shar'i evidentiary laws. And on top of all this, this offense entailed the death penalty, even if no killing was involved. Thus, the most important *hadd* punishment was considerably augmented in relation to the Hanafi legal manuals, and may be said to have been applied on a wide scale. The law was no doubt closely related to shar'i conceptions of justice and proper behavior on the roads, but in itself it was an innovation. It was also unrelated to the *kanun* (state law enacted by the ruler in areas where the shari'a was judged insufficient). Was it enacted by the central government in some order that has not yet been discovered? My own feeling is that this was not the case; it was probably a customary law developed on the ground by people facing dire necessities.

Some mistake my critique of Weber, in the book of mine that is being surveyed here, as betraying a stand against legal realism. This is far from being the case: if Salmond defines legal realism as seeing "law" as the practice of the courts, then my approach is exactly that.[8] Although I did not analyze individual cases in detail, none of the rules and laws that I have already spoken about were read by any *kadi* (or by myself) from a law book or a *kanun*. They are based entirely on Ottoman court records, and are nothing more than distillations of the meaning extracted from the substantial number of cases appearing in them. It is simply a fact that the laws and verdicts that transpired from this sea of documentation do not convey the idea of meaningless chaos, but rather, a coherent set of rules that show some correspondence with formal shari'a, *kanun*, and customary law, with shari'a and customary law dominant.

The main criticism that I have of this (my own) book is that not enough attention was devoted to a minute analysis of individual cases, which would have allowed a more detailed reconstruction of the modes of working of the court, checking and possibly proving the points made in the last paragraph.

Another study that is of great importance for the topic at hand (the sources of law in Ottoman Islamic courts—shari'a, customary law, or state legislation) is Elyse

[8] See J. Salmond and P.J. Fitzgerald, *Salmond on Jurisprudence* 12th edn. (London: Sweet & Maxwell, 1966), 25–43.

Semerdjian's study of illicit sexual relations in Ottoman Aleppo, published in 2005.[9] Illicit sex, or *zina* in the parlance of Islamic law, is a major penal offence and a Qur'anic *hadd*, or punishment, and Semerdjian's book is a good example of how this offence was treated in practice—was the full force of the shari'a applied, or was a milder interpretation used instead? The main source of information is the *kadi* court records Aleppo, which—despite a barrage of denigration—prove yet again that they are indispensable for reconstructing the life the common people in the past. (This study, by the way, proves that it was not just the middle class who appeared in the *sicills*, as is often claimed, but also the lowest strata of society). So basically the book deals with the *zina* offence as applied in Aleppo. However, there are no cases among the materials surveyed of adultery among married couples, and the main topic discussed is prostitution.

Prostitution was rife in Ottoman Aleppo. Prostitutes were often brought to court by the people of their quarter and put on trial for being "immoral." For the most part they were immigrants from the rural areas around the city and from rural areas in Southern Anatolia. Their numbers swelled in time of economic crisis. These are all signs that prostitutes came from the lowest strata of society.

One of the interesting aspects of prostitution is again the legal side of it. No physical punishments were imposed on the prostitutes who were prosecuted and found guilty in Aleppo's courts. The usual punishment was simply banishment from the quarter. It is reported that when this happened prostitutes simply took their pimps and moved calmly to another quarter—it was not considered a serious punishment at all, lighter in fact than in Istanbul where prostitutes were banished to another area of the state, and were thus cut off from family and acquaintances.

It may be asked why the Ottoman government was so lenient on the crime of *zina*, which carries such a grievous punishment in the formal shari'a? Judging the severity of the punishments brings to mind *shirk* (heresy), highway robbery, and the like. But possibly *zina* was singled out for a more lenient treatment. Why? Semerdjian suggests a likely explanation was that prostitution was simply unavoidable because Aleppo was a place where a large body of troops was stationed, and, like it or not, troops needed prostitutes. Displacing prostitutes from the city could probably be done, but it would surely lead to major security issues in the city in general, and for the elite in particular.

Another major contribution relevant to the topic at hand (namely, the sources of Ottoman law—shari'a, customary law, and *kanun*) is Fariba Zarinebaf's 2010 book on crime and the application of penal laws in eighteenth-century Istanbul.[10] This study relies on Ottoman court records like most other legal studies in the Ottoman

[9] Elyse Semerdjian, *Off the Straight Path: Law and Community in Ottoman Aleppo* (Syracuse: Syracuse University Press, 2005).

[10] Fariba Zarinebaf, *Crime and Punishment in Istanbul, 1700–1800* (Berkeley and Los Angeles: University of California Press, 2010).

Empire, but in addition deploys two new sources, both archival in nature: one is police records and the other is registers of convicted criminals sent to serve as oarsmen on the ships of the Ottoman navy. We shall devote some attention to these methodological questions later on; our first interest here is to consider the relation between the treatment of the criminals in Istanbul's courts and the formal shari'a.

Most of the documents found by Zarinebaf in relation to criminal behavior concerned theft and robbery.[11] These were common problems in eighteenth-century Istanbul. Thieves targeted mainly rooms in *hans* (inns) and *odalar* (bachelors' residences, rented out by religious endowments), and stole anything they could find. But rather than being punished by the supposedly standard *hadd* punishment of amputation of the hand, they were sentenced instead to serve as oarsmen in the Ottoman navy for a certain period of time (usually a number of months, as apparently most oarsmen were released after that time due to petitions presented to the sultan calling for mercy). Even a short period was considered a harsh punishment, and mortality rates among rowing convicts was extremely high.

Another important topic addressed by Zarinebaf is prostitution. This provides another good opportunity to observe how the shari'a was handled in practice in an Ottoman city. The issue of prostitution was a serious worry for the authorities in Istanbul, because it was extremely widespread, and because it was connected to wine-drinking, which was, in turn, often associated with more serious crimes, like assault and murder, which threatened to undermine public order and thus the legitimacy of the regime. So prostitution was not just a matter of enforcing the law, or the shari'a, but also a question of law and order in the city. But of course (as was the case in Aleppo) trying to eradicate prostitution altogether was unthinkable, because such an outcome could result in more danger from soldiers, or even unruly bachelors who resided in rented rooms, as noted earlier. Thus, the government had to tread very carefully and this it certainly did: prostitution was effectively permitted in the traditional entertainment quarters of the city, in Galata and Pera, and was tolerated as long as prostitutes kept low profiles. But often prostitutes spilled over to "respectable" residential areas, which often aroused the ire of the residents, who complained to the authorities, which were then forced to take action. This is a hazy topic in Islamic law, with some jurists, notably Ibrahim al-Halabi failing even to mention the issue in his foundational treatise on Islamic jurisprudence, *Multaqa al-Abhur*. Formally, prostitutes should have been subjected to the law of *zina*. But the jurists were undecided because some claimed that by paying for the services rendered, the client assumed temporary quasi-ownership of the prostitute, making the relationship akin to concubinage. Despite this logic, most jurists pronounced prostitution to be illegal, though one treated it as full-fledged *zina*. Again, Ottoman *fetva* collections from the seventeenth and eighteenth centuries do not deal directly

[11] Zarinebaf, *Crime and Punishment in Istanbul*, chapter 4.

with prostitution, but anyone calling another person by names related to prostitution was liable to the *hadd* punishment of *kazf*, false accusation of *zina*. Hence, it remained in the area of *ta'zir*, discretionary punishment. I do not think that the reason was that they simply learnt to live with prostitution as an inevitable fact of life: this much could be said also of the law of *zina* itself, that it could hardly be enforced due to the impossible evidential requirements, yet it was consistently upheld as the sole valid law in a large number of Ottoman *muftis' fetvas* throughout the seventeenth and eighteenth centuries. Part of the reason probably was the aforementioned legal similarity between prostitution and concubinage in the formal shari'a.

An important topic related to *zina* and prostitution is that of punishment. Islamic law imposes the punishment of stoning for illicit sex committed by someone who is or has been married and one hundred lashes for someone who has not been married. Zarinebaf did not find evidence that these punishments were applied in Istanbul. In Zarinebaf's materials no real case of *zina* (adultery, that is) surfaced, but only prostitution, a subordinate form of *zina* at best. The punishments meted out were a far cry from that appropriate for *zina*—punishments invariably involving banishment from the city, often to Bursa, sometimes to various islands in the Aegean Sea. It was not really the case that the shari'a's *hudud* were disregarded or put aside—in no case of this sort was *zina* in the full case provable. Consequently, just as in seventeenth-century Bursa, the issue was relegated to the somewhat gray area of *ta'zir*—discretionary punishment by the *kadi*, though formally still within the *hudud*.

Zarinebaf also speaks about killing (chapter 6), and this topic deserves attention here, since it is important to consider whether the actual law applied was the formal shari'a or not. Zarinebaf claims that violent murder was on the rise in Istanbul in the eighteenth century, though she admits herself that this is an impressionistic conclusion, and that we lack hard evidence to sustain this. In any event, much violence in the city is certainly cited, much of it directed against lone women in their houses, in the streets, or in bathhouses. Many of these violence cases resulted in rape (often also involving boys and girls). Much violence and killing in Istanbul was carried out by gangs of soldiers who came from the Kasim Pasha quarter.

To conclude our discussion of Zarinebaf, the writer is to be commended for using sources other than the shari'a records, as we certainly need diversification of sources, but nevertheless, I feel that some more effort should be spent on the documents of the *kadi*, that do not yet appear to have been used extensively enough.

Looking into the future, there is place for additional studies of *sicills*, both for socio-legal studies and for analytical studies devised to advance the understanding of the law. In fact, most of the *sicill* studies undertaken so far are social histories, mostly of women, with few references to the implications of the *sicills* for an understanding of the law. There is considerable room for legal historians to enter the field. The many faults of the *sicill* as a source should not dissuade us. There is no point trying to investigate the behind the scenes structure of any individual *sicill*, not because it is unimportant, but because there is no material making this possible. We should resign ourselves to the study of the *sicill* as it is, and bear in mind that it is the best possible source for this period of Islamic legal history.

II. The Status and Role of the *Kadi*

We learn from Weber that part of the so-called process of decline of the shari'a resulted from the decadence of the role of the *kadi* (with less importance being assigned to him by the public and the government), the *kadi*'s diminished control over the judicial process, and the rise of other forces, like civil and military authorities, as authorities within the law. In any case, the status and role of the *kadi* within the legal framework provide historiographically important focal points from which to explore the nature of adjudication and professionalization of the judiciary.

It is clear that the *kadi*'s court was not the only forum where conflict resolution could take place. The *kadi* records of Bursa and other places show the existence of many instances where cases were resolved by mediation of *muslihun*, or Muslim mediators from outside of the judicial process. The *kadi* always accepted the compromise, though he seems to have never effected it himself. But if we concentrate on the work of the *kadi* himself, the first thing that we observe here is that in earlier historical periods, the *kadi* had competition from several competing bodies, such as the *mazalim* court, which dealt with criminal and other issues; and the *muhtasib*, which had wide authority in market affairs. None of these bodies existed in the Ottoman Empire (the *muhtasib* did in fact exist at least in some places, certainly with much reduced authorities). This means that the role of the *kadi* was formidable in the Ottoman Empire in comparison to earlier periods. Ronald Jennings has a great deal to say here, and he was the first to say it, in the late 1970s. He described the *kadi* as the real legal pillar of the city, eclipsing entirely the *muhtasib*, whereas the *mazalim* court did not exist at all, and the imperial *divan* was barely noticeable. The *kadi* enjoyed full and unrestricted legal authority, apparently enjoying the complete trust of the population and the imperial center.[12] This general picture was fully replicated in the case of seventeenth-century Bursa.

The main competition to the *kadi*, in terms of judicial function, was the provincial governors (*sancak beys*), who were responsible for law and order, but who, most of the time, fought against highway robbers. For instance, though it is not entirely clear what the *sancak bey* of Kayseri did in this respect, it is doubtful

[12] Jennings, "Kadi, Court and Legal Procedure"; Jennings, "Limitations."

that he was really involved with court work. His subordinate officials, mainly the *sabasi* (chief of police), were in charge of investigating criminal cases and arresting suspects; but they were to bring such cases to the *kadi*'s court immediately, and Jennings shows that in a number of cases that is in fact what they did. Officials of the *sancak bey* were present in some criminal cases dealt with by the *kadi*, but what they did there is not at all clear. Furthermore, in several cases citizens sued the *sancak bey* himself (for example, demanding debts due), and the *kadi* dealt with such cases unexceptionally.

Important information on the relations between the provincial governor and the *kadi* in the context of adjudication is supplied by Leslie Peirce's book on sixteenth-century Ayntab, to be surveyed more extensively later. As noted, the book deals with among other things the relations between the provincial governor and the *kadi*, and reaches the conclusion that Sultan Suleyman I (1520–66) was seeking to introduce a reform that would drastically reduce the role of the governor and augment the role of the *kadi*. The policy was in fact to render adjudication by the governor as illegal altogether. This policy seems to have borne fruit. There seems to be a direct line between this study and between the finding of Jennings and Gerber, cited earlier, which indicated that a change of this nature did indeed take place when we move from the sixteenth century to the seventeenth and eighteenth centuries. But a divergent view was put forward by Michael Ursinus, who utilized a small collection of complaints sent to the provincial governor of Rumeli (Ottoman Balkans) toward the end of the eighteenth century.[13] One of Ursinus' conclusions is that though the *kadi* was supreme in the matter of adjudication, many cases were judged by *kadi*s in provincial offices, in the presence of the governor, as opposed to a separate courthouse, which constituted something less than full-fledged autonomous proceedings, in as much as the governor could exert pressure on the *kadi*. But this conclusion seems to be contradicted by the views of other researchers. Had the governor contributed anything substantial to the process, then Ursinus' point would be convincing. But as long as the trial itself was procedurally in line with regular Hanafism, some objections may be raised. It is true that Peirce claimed Suleyman I ordained that a shari'a trial is illegal if not carried out in a formal building designated as a court, but Michael Winter has shown that the court of Damascus in Ottoman times was not in a fixed location, and the court in Ottoman Jerusalem is well-known to have always resided in a madrasa.

An exceptional case is Zarinebaf's study on eighteenth-century Istanbul. She claims that in Istanbul the *kadi* had little authority to judge criminal cases, and his role was limited mainly to investigating the case and suggesting punishments to the central government. Punishment for theft, for example, was mainly imposed by police officers. It may be thought that in Istanbul the government wished to deal

[13] Michael Ursinus, *Grievance Administration (sikayet) in an Ottoman Province* (London: Routledge Curzon, 2005).

with crime more resolutely than in other places, because in Istanbul street crime might escalate to become an issue jeopardizing the security of the entire government. In any event, and to revert to the role of police officers in law enforcement, the process was probably not a proper trial, since it seems that most theft cases came to be decided on as perpetrators were apprehended in the act, and immediately admitted their guilt to avoid the harsher punishments they might suffer if they did not plead guilty. But this case is not yet entirely clear: throughout the book there are quite a few *kadi* court trials reported. So the *kadi* did have some authority to judge, possibly with some limitations, the nature of which is not yet entirely clear. In any event, it is suggested that alternative adjudication was carried out by the Imperial Ottoman Council, a theoretical claim, since no supporting evidence is supplied on this. To my mind, the last word on the *kadi*'s authority in Istanbul is yet to be decided.

Jennings devotes a great deal of attention to professional witnesses (*'udul*—those witnesses who did not actually participate in the legal process, but signed their names at the bottom of the *kadi*'s protocol, as if to approve its legality). The issue is relevant to our discussion, in as much as the professional witnesses also detracted somewhat from the authority of the *kadi*. Jennings was the first to draw attention to this topic. He shows that the role of the *'udul* in the Ottoman court was considerably different from the situation in medieval Islam. The latter were usually part of a formal list of witnesses, well-known to the *kadi*, who likely knew all of them personally, because he would serve in the locality for a long period of time. Witnesses in medieval Islam fulfilled all sorts of functions, notably as notaries, that is, people who knew how to phrase petitions to be presented to the court, or those whom the *kadi* would send to verify the whereabouts of bodies found in deserted places in suspicious circumstances. But also, they were the most trustworthy source of information when the *kadi* needed socio-legal information on individuals, such as whether a person was trustworthy enough for purposes of giving acceptable testimony.

In the Ottoman period, witnesses in places like Kayseri (and this was again, exactly the same in Bursa) were more like ordinary citizens with reasonable reputations who happened to be in the courthouse on that particular day, and were asked to serve as professional witnesses (called in the Ottoman documents *shuhud el-hal*, never *'udul*). The number of these witnesses in both Bursa and Kayseri was very large, and there is no evidence that many of them carried out this role repeatedly. There is also no evidence that they fulfilled other legal functions for the court. At least part of the reason for this is quite clear—the Ottoman *kadi* served in any one place for no more than one or two years, and was not in fact expected to develop "friendly" relations with the local elite—a clear temptation for corruption.

However, Hulya Canbakal's recent study of professional witnesses in the town of Ayntab in the eighteenth century shows that the professional witnesses in that town were not part of a random group, but members of the elite families of Ayntab, an elite that controlled Ayntab economically and politically.[14] Professional witnesses in Ayntab appeared in court many times, and were thus something else altogether than the diverse group of citizens that we have seen in Kayseri and Bursa. What might have been the reason for the difference? Notably, eighteenth-century Ayntab was geographically on the Ottoman periphery, enjoyed considerable local autonomy, and was controlled by an entrenched local elite. Maybe the difference between the two patterns had to do with distance from Istanbul and from major trade arteries, and similar factors.

III. Free-floating Bargaining or Structured Law Enforcement

As noted earlier, Weber claimed that the Muslim judge was not truly directed by any code of law in his decisions, but was either acting from expediency, or, at best, from some sort of cultural intuition. I claimed in my book that this really reduced the *kadi* to a mere mediator between kinship groups to avoid major conflagration. Surprisingly, this Weberian approach has received a new lease of life in recent years, the prime example in this field being Leslie Peirce's book on sixteenth-century Ayntab. Peirce seems to be an enthusiast of the law-and-society approach to Ottoman law; I myself am much less enthusiastic about the applicability of this approach to Ottoman law and Islamic law generally, both because Islamic law, being considered as coming down from the revelation, seems to me less amenable to free-ranging manipulations of the law than expressly secular laws, and because the Ottomans had a clear-cut approach to move *kadi*s around their state every year or two specifically in order to prevent their being able to create connections with local groups, thereby serving their interests rather than those of the state. Thus, we have here two divergent opinions about an important aspect of Ottoman law, which only future research will elucidate further.

Peirce's book revolves around the topic of women and the law, but within this, there is an emphasis on women and the penal law, and thus a focus on the *kadi*, which makes it pertinent to the present survey. Peirce is interested mainly in the lives of lower class women, trying to demonstrate that despite their patriarchal law and society, nevertheless they were able to marshal their personal resources to

[14] Hulya Canbakal, *Society and Politics in an Ottoman Town* (Leiden: Brill, 2007).

withstand societal pressure and protect their own interests. The core of the study is the story of three women who prevailed amidst considerable impediment. More within the legal domain, Peirce claims that the Ottoman court of Ayntab did not work the way former Ottoman legal historians claimed it did. According to Peirce, the Ottoman *kadi* did not in fact enforce a body of laws known as Ottoman law, since such a body of law did not really exist. By emphasizing the specific (and variable) outcomes of litigation, Peirce claims that Ottoman law was rather the product of negotiation and deliberations between *kadi*s and litigants: "Legal codes ... were of course critical in shaping the legal life of communities like Aintab [sic], but it was only in local interpretation that formal rules acquired vitality and meaning. The chapters that follow argue that it was the people of Aintab who, negotiating with and through the court, were responsible for that interpretation."[15] Space limitations prevent me from surveying the book in detail here, thus analyzing the section on killing and murder will have to do, particularly since Peirce claims explicitly that the thesis of her book is particularly salient for this area. Talking about the five murder cases, she says that they are the most complicated in the book, "and perhaps the record's most vivid demonstration that the study of legal culture needs to be grounded in the dialectic between action and prescription."[16] Careful analysis of these murder cases seems to indicate Peirce's view that every kind of bargaining that takes place in the process of trial leads to an outcome which is unique to that particular trial, hence an outcome of a unique process of interpretation and an interplay between action and prescription. In the first case a man was attacked while sleeping on his roof and killed. The heirs of the deceased were awarded compensation (*diyet*) of 46,000 *akce*, after some bargaining between the parties.[17] Intense negotiation is also evident in the other murder cases, and obviously, this negotiation is relevant to the outcome. In that sense Peirce is clearly right in concluding all these cases by saying that "Each of these cases is remarkable in demonstrating a complex mobilization of legal resources that is not entirely predictable from prescriptive legal text described earlier."[18] The point Peirce is making here is that those litigants with more resources are likely to secure a better outcome, like a better paid lawyer hired by a rich litigant in our own times. But Peirce's approach is less convincing when it comes to the law itself, which in all the cases she cites remains unaffected, while every important case in nineteenth-century America changed the law in such a way that no lawyer could come to court without citing the new emendation. In Ottoman and Islamic law this never happened. The law remained exactly as it had been before. At the same time, the bargaining that obviously took place between the parties did not necessarily involve the *kadi*; in no document

[15] Leslie Peirce, *Morality Tales: Law and Gender in the Ottoman Court of Aintab* (Berkeley: University of California Press, 2003), 1.

[16] Ibid., 336. [17] Ibid. [18] Ibid., 337.

cited by Peirce (or seen by this writer elsewhere) is there any sign that the *kadi* was himself involved in the bargaining that took place either in and around the case, or in and around the court. Also, there is no sign that *kadi*s were deciding cases without reference to the law, as is claimed.

Thus, Peirce has done an important job of showing how a minute analysis of *kadi* court records can yield fruitful results by showing that people with greater access to legal resources can sway the court's decision in their favor, thereby affecting the law at least in an ad hoc manner. But judging by the studies written so far, this approach may be limited by the fact that the core of the Ottoman–Islamic legal system may have been more resilient and less malleable than Peirce's approach suggests.

IV. Summary and Conclusion

Following the lead of Max Weber, I have dealt with Ottoman law under three headings: in the first section I was interested in gauging the extent to which the formal shariʿa was actually practiced in the Ottoman Empire, a society that certainly prided itself for being a shariʿa enforcing society. I pursued this question mainly via a discussion of two legal monographs that were published in recent years: namely, Semerdjian's study of women in Ottoman Aleppo and Zarinebaf's study of women in eighteenth-century Istanbul. Zarinebaf surveys the scene of crime and punishment in eighteenth-century Istanbul. Crime is said to have been widespread, and included theft, mainly of items from rooms in inns and the like; rape, particularly involving women living alone; prostitution; unlawful killing, often as a consequence of brawls, etc. What is interesting from the point of view of this study is that while many of these cases were liable to the *hudud* punishments, these were in fact never inflicted and the punishments used were much lighter. Prostitution in particular was treated lightly, mainly by banishment from the city, when it could have entailed the death penalty if treated in the harsh manner required by the theoretical law. Other crimes were punishable by the requirement to work as an oarsman in the Ottoman navy for a number of years, often shortened to a number of months. A similar phenomenon is evident in Semerdjian's study on Aleppo: prostitutes were not at all harshly treated by the courts, and were simply banished to another quarter of town. Thus the *hudud* were applied only leniently, and one is left wondering why? Vogel's article on *siyasa sharʾiyya* seems to provide a good explanation—the doctrine became widespread at the end of classical Islam that a shariʿa enforcing Islamic government, enjoying a good reputation as such, could in fact implement the shari'a selectively and still keep its reputation—if that was in the interest of its government.[19]

The second section of this chapter dealt with the role and status of the *kadi*. The main finding here was that although the *kadi* suffered from competition from many directions, notably provincial governors, the *kadi* nevertheless kept a near monopoly on adjudication. This was a direct outcome of government policy, because the central Ottoman government was well aware of, and in fact obsessed by, the powers of high-level bureaucrats and the dangers fraught in their authority over the peasantry and their ability to extract illegal taxes from them. Thus, the Ottoman *kadi* by no means lost power and control as Weber suggested. Nor did the *kadi* become marginal or obsolete as was formerly suggested. On the contrary, his position grew in importance, without any connection to religion or religiosity, and he now fulfilled many "civil" and administrative functions, in addition to enjoying near monopoly of adjudication.

The third section of this chapter dealt with a question subject to an ongoing debate, and on which no definitive conclusion can yet be reached. It is the question of whether the adjudication process that took place in the *kadi*'s court was based on and tied to law codes and fundamental rules directing everything that went on there, or whether the process was free-floating, subject to debates and bargaining between the parties and the judges. Weber believed that at the beginning of Islamic history the name of the game was structured order, but that as the gates of *ijtihad* were closed, there was nothing to guide judges in new cases, and then intuition came to rule the process. Two lines of research are observable within this area of research. Leslie Peirce's study from 2003 devoted particular attention to showing how different pools of legal resources (taking the term "legal resources" in the widest possible sense) have helped litigants to reach outcomes better for themselves than might have been the situation with less legal resources. In this sense they were able to mold the law to work better for them than might have been the case otherwise. It makes sense to claim that in such cases the law was interpreted in a unique way. But in my 1994 book on Ottoman law I looked at two other aspects of the same general topic: I was interested to find out whether the *kadi* himself might engage with the litigants in ways that are contrary to formal shari'a (did he, for example, choose arbitrarily who would be charged with giving the oath that would allow him to win the case?). I was also interested to find out whether the *kadi* handed down legal decisions that were simply an outcome of bargaining, unrelated to the formal shari'a. To the best of my understanding and knowledge, in these two important areas Ottoman law was much less prone to amorphous mode of action than in the areas discussed by Peirce. But either way, this is a major question that awaits the attention of future researchers.

19 Frank Vogel, "Siyāsa," in *Encyclopaedia of Islam*, eds. P. Bearman, Th. Bianquis, C.E. Bosworth, E. van Donzel, W.P. Heinrichs 2nd edn. (Brill Online, 2014).

References

Canbakal, Hulya, *Society and Politics in an Ottoman Town* (Leiden: Brill, 2007).

Frank, Jerome, *Law and the Modern Mind* (New York: Anchor Books, 1963).

Gerber, Haim, *State, Society and Law in Islam: Ottoman Law in Comparative Perspective* (Albany: State University of New York Press, 1994).

Hallaq, Wael B., *Shari'a: Theory, Practice, Transformations* (Cambridge: Cambridge University Press, 2009).

Jennings, Ronald C., "Kadi, Court and Legal Procedure in 17th Century Ottoman Kayseri." *Studia Islamica* 48 (1978): 133–172.

Jennings, Ronald C., "Limitations on the Judicial Powers of the Kadi in 17th Century Ottoman Kayseri." *Studia Islamica* 50 (1979): 151–184.

Peirce, Leslie, *Morality Tales: Law and Gender in the Ottoman Court of Aintab* (Berkeley: University of California Press, 2003).

Salmond, J. and Fitzgerald, P.J., *Salmond on Jurisprudence* (12th edn. London: Sweet & Maxwell, 1966).

Semerdjian, Elyse, *Off the Straight Path: Law and Community in Ottoman Aleppo* (Syracuse: Syracuse University Press, 2005).

Ursinus, Michael, *Grievance Administration (sikayet) in an Ottoman Province* (London: Routledge Curzon, 2005).

Vogel, Frank, "Siyāsa" in P. Bearman, Th. Bianquis, C.E. Bosworth, E. van Donzel, W.P. Heinrichs (eds.) *Encyclopaedia of Islam* (2nd edn. Brill Online, 2014).

Weber, Max, *Economy and Society*. 2 vols (New York: Bedminster Press, 1968).

Zarinebaf, Fariba, *Crime and Punishment in Istanbul, 1700–1800* (Berkeley; Los Angeles: University of California Press, 2010).

Zilfi, Madeline, *The Ottoman Ulema* (Chicago: Bibliotheca Islamica, 1988).

CHAPTER 20

A HISTORIOGRAPHY OF ISLAMIC LAW IN THE MUGHAL EMPIRE

M. REZA PIRBHAI

THE Mughal Sultanate (1526–1858) dominated the political landscape of South Asia during the early modern period with considerable influence extending into the present. Putting aside histories produced in the period of Mughal rule, the state's importance to both South Asian and Islamic Studies has produced over a century and a half of scholarship on dynastic, administrative, fiscal, military, diplomatic, and cultural history. The study of Islamic law as theorized and practiced under the state's auspices, however, is less clearly outlined and remains a fertile and necessary area for research. Journal articles and book chapters devoted to the subject are few in number and of varying quality, while no comprehensive book-length work, monograph or anthology, dedicated to the subject has been published in the postcolonial era. The most pressing question for a historiography of Islamic law in the Mughal context, therefore, is how to account for this dearth?

It is argued here that two factors are primarily responsible. First and most obvious is the qualitative and quantitative paucity of extant documentation relative to such contemporaries as the Ottoman Sultanate. This is particularly so in the case of works related to legal practice. The type of court documents (*mahadir* and *sijills*) upon which the scholarly understanding of legal practice has been constructed in Ottoman and other domains are conspicuously rare in the case of the Mughals. Such deficiencies can be primarily accounted for by the lack of Mughal state archives, and additionally as a result of the fact that contemporary collections of documents originated with British colonialism late in the Mughal period. A second, but no less significant contributor to the thin study of Islamic law under the Mughals, is the approach to Islam and Muslims too often taken by historians of South Asia. In essence, early writings make little to no distinction between treatises reflexive of legal theory (treatises on *usul al-fiqh* and *fatawa* collections) and the actual practice of the Mughal judiciary. On the other hand, many influential late works compensate for early errors by considering theory entirely divorced from practice, thus placing all emphasis on Indic, Indo-Persian and/or Turko-Mongol institutes at the expense of an Islamic framework. This later trend reflects the presumed irrelevance of Islamic law apparent in the works of many contemporary South Asianists, and dissuades others from pursuing the line of inquiry. For the study of Islamic law under the Mughals to progress, therefore, the hurdles on the scholar's path are both practical and theoretical.

To begin to come to grips with the legal history of the Mughal Sultanate as it is currently understood, it is useful to briefly outline the state's rise and fall.[1] When Sultan Zahir al-Din Muhammad Babur (r. 1526–30) dethroned the Lodi Sultan Ibrahim of Delhi in 1526, his venture into South Asia had been driven by no more than political expediency. His memoir, titled *Babur Nama*, soundly establishes the fact that the gaze of this descendant of Amir Timur (a.k.a. Tamerlane, d. 1405) and Genghis Khan (d. 1227) remained focussed on his ancestors' homelands in Central Asia, from which he had been driven by Uzbek rivals. His descendants, however, would not only consider Delhi their primary capital, but eventually extend their sovereignty over virtually all of South Asia, establishing the region's most prominent and long-lived Muslim regime. It is most significant to the state's legal institutes, however, that this lengthy history falls into two distinct phases: the era of the "Great Mughals" (1526–1707) and that of the "Lesser Mughals" (1707–1858). The first phase begins with Sultan Babur's establishment of Mughal authority over the former territories of the Lodi Sultans, extending from Kabul in the west to the borders of Bengal in the east. In the reign of his son and successor, Sultan Humayun (r. 1530–56), the state was contested by local rivals, but eventually placed on firmer footing. Thus, it was not until the reign of Humayun's son and successor, Sultan Jalal al-Din Muhammad Akbar (r. 1556–1605), that the state's territorial possessions were expanded west to Qandahar and Baluchistan, north to Kashmir, east into Bengal, and south to Gujarat. It was also in this period that the bureaucratic and ideological features for

[1] For a sample of contemporary monographs together covering the state's rise and fall as summarized here, see, C.A. Bayly, *Indian Society and the Making of the British Empire* (Cambridge: Cambridge University Press, 1988); D.E. Streusand, *The Formation of the Mughal Empire* (Delhi: Oxford University Press, 1989); J.F. Richards, *The Mughal Empire* (Cambridge: Cambridge University Press, 1996); A. Hintze, *The Mughal Empire and its Decline* (Aldershot: Ashgate, 1997).

which the state is known were instituted. The borders and the institutions established under Akbar passed onto his successors: his son Nur al-Din Muhammad Salim Jahangir (r. 1605–27) and grandson Shahab al-Din Muhammad Shah Jahan (r. 1625–58). A further period of expansion began in the late years of Shah Jahan's reign and continued throughout the extensive rule of his son and successor, Muhyi al-Din Muhammad Aurangzeb (r. 1658–1707); the loss of Qandahar in the northwest being more than made up for by the annexation of almost the entire southern peninsula of the region, known as the Deccan.

The death of Aurangzeb in 1707 marks the end of the era of Great Mughals and the advent of the Lesser Mughals. Between 1707 and 1719, no less than seven sultans rose to the throne, mostly maneuvered on and off by powerful *wazirs*, until the last of them, Sultan Muhammad Shah (r. 1719–48), re-established some semblance of sovereignty. By his reign, however, the writ of the sultan over his viceroys (*nizams*) and governors (*subahdars*/*nawabs*) beyond the environs of Delhi had been eroded to the point that most established themselves as independent rulers in all but name, leaving Delhi itself open to the predations of the Iranian Afsharid ruler, Nadir Shah (r. 1736–47), followed by the Afghan Abdali ruler, Ahmad Shah Durrani (r. 1747–72). The first sacked Delhi in 1739, after annexing all of the Indus Valley provinces, while the second invaded, sacked, and annexed Mughal territory five times between 1747 and 1761. Six more sultans would sit on the throne of Delhi after Muhammad Shah, but as no more than pawns of their *wazirs*, local potentates like Ahmad Shah Durrani or the Maratha Peshwas, and after 1765, as pensioners of the English East India Company. The last mentioned force occupied Delhi in 1803 on the way to colonizing all of South Asia, dethroning the last sultan and abolishing the Mughal state in 1858, promulgating in its place the direct rule of the British government on the heels of the Mughal-backed 1857 Uprising (a.k.a. "The Great Indian Mutiny"). Nevertheless, it must be noted that many of these successor states, including the British Indian Empire, inherited a variety of the institutions established in the heyday of the Mughal Sultanate. As for the precipitous fall of the Mughal regime during the eighteenth century, most contemporary scholars offer the well-documented argument that the state was a victim of its own success. The law, order, and economic development instituted by the Great Mughals gave rise to various capital-holding classes (petty landlords, tribal heads, merchants, bankers, entrepreneurs, etc.) outside the state's fiscal ambit; classes that ultimately allied together on more local levels and with European trading companies to undermine central authority and form multiple, sub-regional successor states before the rise of British authority.

Given this long and more lately torturous history, Mughal primary sources are scattered in archives and libraries across South Asia and Europe. Two of the largest repositories of Mughal manuscripts and documents are the National Archives of India and the British Library. In both cases, the vast majority date from the period of Lesser Mughals, only stray records of the Great era surviving. Important legal works from the earlier period, however, are included in the Oriental Records and Manuscripts division at the National Archives of India. For example, the Inayat Jung Collection dates back to the period of the last Great Mughal, Aurangzeb, and represents the day-to-day administrative records of the state's southern provinces. A number of smaller collections also gather documents related to revenue, endowments, grants, and other administrative records from a patchwork of locales in Arabic, Persian, Urdu, and more local vernaculars. As well, the Fort William College Collection contains works that span the tenth to the twentieth century, including histories and (auto)biographies, jurisprudential works (*usul* and *fatawa*), and records (e.g. *madad-i ma'ash, akhbarat, hukum, parwana, dastur, insha', taqsim, fatawa*, and *farman*). The vast majority of this collection's documents, however, were eventually transferred to the British Library. Along with the types of administrative records available at the National Archives of India, therefore, the latter archive also holds a number of Arabic, Persian, and Urdu works of relevance to legal study, as well as treatises on theology (*kalam*), mysticism (*tasawwuf*), and jurisprudence (*fiqh*). What treasures may be held in other archives, university libraries, and private collections scattered across South Asia and elsewhere is naturally difficult to summarize, but there can be no doubt that valuable supplementary sources can be extracted. A case in point is the M. Iqbal Mujaddidi Collection at the Punjab University Library in Pakistan, which includes a variety of manuscripts relevant to the legal theory and practice of Lahore and environs under the Great Mughals. Various collections in more local Indian libraries similarly shed light on the legal practices of their localities.

Although a considerable body of primary literature is extant, and some of it has even been translated and published, in comparison with the type of sources available in other contexts, particularly concerning the day-to-day practice of courts beyond the imperial center, scholars of Mughal law are at a disadvantage. Records (*mahadir/sijills*) of specific cases tried in the state-sponsored courts and by independent jurists of even the capital, let alone in provincial towns and districts, are few and far between in the major collections, or have yet to be sifted from the mass of documents in more local collections. This can primarily be attributed to the fact that the Mughals did not establish centralized archives, as was the case in Ottoman realms, apparently leaving individual judges to retain their own records. The value of such documents, however, is proven beyond a doubt by the legal and social history produced on the Ottoman setting, and their effective absence in the Mughal is undeniably a factor in explaining the relative lack of writing on Mughal legal theory and practice.

The deficiency of Mughal archiving also explains why the brunt of sources available to scholars of Mughal history date from the mid-eighteenth century on, and not before. In fact, the major collections mentioned are at their core the work of British Orientalists in the employ of the English East India Company. Their interest in collecting works was largely driven by the administrative need to come to grips with the region's institutes for the purpose of increasingly governing it. This plays an additional part in explaining the difficulties faced by contemporary scholars of Islamic law in the Mughal context, for the coincidence of scholarly knowledge and imperial power, of course, implies that the works they collected and the approach to Mughal history they applied remains a potent example of Orientalism as discourse. Regarding legal history in particular, beginning in the 1780s, Company rule limited the exercise of Islamic law to the personal realm (i.e. marriage, divorce, inheritance, etc.), reserving all other legal domains (civil and criminal) for British jurisprudence administered by British judges.[2] Furthermore, few works were collected even to ascertain Islamic personal law and those accessed were read from the perspective of British jurisprudential norms of the day, eschewing case law and allowances for custom ("'urf" *ada*), equity (*istislah*), and juristic preference (*istihsan*) in favor of codification based on literal readings of primary sources (i.e. Qur'an and Hadith).[3] For example, *Al-Hidaya* of Burhan al-Din 'Ali al-Marghinani (d. 1196)—a Central Asian work—was judged most authoritative and first translated in the mid-nineteenth century for official use, while works such the South Asian *Fatawa-i Ghiyathiyya* (c. 1200s), *Fatawa-i Qarakhani* (c. 1200s), *Fatawa-i Tatar Khani* (c. 1300s), as well as four collections from the era of Great Mughals themselves, including the *Fatawa-i Barahaniyya* (c. 1500s) from the time of Akbar and *Fatawa-i 'Alamgiri* (a.k.a. *Fatawa al-Hindiyya*; c. 1600s) compiled under the patronage of Aurangzeb, were largely ignored.[4] The writing of Anglo-Muhammadan Law, rather than an understanding of Islamic legal theory and practice in the Mughal context, therefore, underwrites the legal sources initially gathered for consideration in the major collections mentioned above. Thus, the works on Islamic law produced by British authors were, in R.S. Humphrey's appraisal, "culturally naïve, conceptually inadequate, and full of errors."[5]

While British jurists were codifying Islamic personal law according to their own interpretations of limited sources, the same and other officers of the British Empire began writing Mughal history, paying as little heed to the complexities of Mughal administrative norms. As represented by the works of H.M. Elliot, G.B.

[2] See, e.g., A. Hamid, *A Chronicle of British Indian Legal History* (Jaipur: RBSA Publishers, 1991).

[3] S.A. Kugle, "Framed Blamed and Renamed: The Recasting of Islamic Jurisprudence in Colonial South Asia," *Modern Asian Studies* 35, no. 2 (2001): 257–313.

[4] For the mid-nineteenth century translations of segments of *Al-Hidaya* and *Fatawa-i 'Alamgiri*, see Charles Hamilton, trans., *The Hedaya or Guide: A Commentary of the Mussulman Laws* (Lahore: Premier Book House, [reprint] 1963); N.B.E. Baillie, trans., *The Moohummudan Law of Sale according to the Huneefeea Code: from the Futawa Alumgeeree, a Digest of the Whole Law. Prepared by Command of the Emperor Aurungzebe Alumgeer* (Delhi: Delhi Law House, [reprint], n.d.); and N.B.E. Baillie, trans., *A Digest of Moohummudan Law Compiled and Translated from Authorities in the Original Arabic with an Introduction and Explanatory Notes Containing the Doctrines of the Hunifeea Code of Jurisprudence* (Lahore: Premier Book House, n.d.).

[5] R.S. Humphrey, *Islamic History: A Framework for Inquiry* (Princeton: Princeton University Press, 1991), 210.

Malleson, W.W. Hunter, V.A Smith, S. Lane-Poole, and others, these historians also reflected the inadequacies of their legist colleagues. Both sets of scholars rested on the assumption of their subject's resolutely despotic nature.[6] The only saving grace they found, in fact, was the perceived persecution of Islam begun by Akbar under the influence of Hindu thought, which they argued led to his forming a new religion of his own, while the collapse of the Empire was ultimately attributed to his great-grandson Aurangzeb's revival of Islamic jurisprudence. Such ideas also carried into the writings of South Asians contributing to Mughal history by the turn of the twentieth century, and in some ways continue to maintain influence into the present. This point is well-illustrated by the works and influence of J.N. Sarkar. His *Mughal Administration*, first delivered as a series of lectures in 1920, then published as a book in 1925, is groundbreaking insofar as it seeks to take scholarship beyond the Orientalist's dynastic history to consider Mughal institutions.[7] However, like the Orientalists whom he acknowledges with admiration, Sarkar begins by pointing out that the Mughal state, as an "Islamic" regime, is essentially an example of "centralized despotism," or "military rule" by "one man." The raison d'etre of the state, according to Sarkar, was to extract revenue, expending nothing on social structures such as schools and courts of justice. It is therefore somewhat ironic that Sarkar initiates the historical discussion of Mughal legal institutions. He points out that the "only law recognized" was "Quranic law" (which he considers "incapable of growth"), but "Hindu caste courts" and "Brahmanic courts [were] sanctioned" for the non-Muslim population. The sultan himself acted as the "highest court of appeal," advised by various *qadi*s (judges) and *mufti*s (jurisconsults) particularly of the Hanafi *madhhab*, but below him ranged a formal institutional structure headed by a *Qadi al-Qudat* and a *Sadr al-Sudur*—the former presiding over the *qadi*s of the realm trying cases, the latter administering the judiciary and grants/endowments for schools (*maktab*s, *madrasa*s, *khanqah*s, and non-Muslim institutions) and individual scholars. *Muhtasib*s were also under the purview of the *Sadr*. Sarkar notes that the same institutions and functions were replicated in every provincial capital, but concludes that beyond those cities, community-based, custom-bound bodies (e.g. *panchayat*) prevailed in the villages, while in the cities where *qadi*-courts were present, pragmatism or corruption ameliorated the exercise of Islamic legal theory and the dispensation of justice.[8]

[6] These authors' works were first gathered in two major book series published in the late-nineteenth and early-twentieth centuries: W.W. Hunter, ed., *Rulers of India*, 28 vols. (Oxford: Clarendon Press, 1893–95); A.V.W. Jackson, ed., *History of India*, 9 vols. (London: Grolier, 1906–07). For a late review of such works, see S.C. Mittal, *India Distorted: A Study of British Historians on India* (New Delhi: M.D. Publications, 1996).

[7] See J.N. Sarkar, *Mughal Administration, Six Lectures* (Patna: Government Print Office, 1920); and J.N. Sarkar, *Mughal Administration* (Patna: Patna University Press, 1925).

[8] Sarkar, *Mughal Administration, Six Lectures*, 3–14.

Sarkar apparently did not recognize it, but what he began revealing was a state dependent on a vast network of Islamic legal thought and institutions rather than the capricious whims of "one man." Later scholarship in the colonial era added to the scale of legal institutions, the sense of an Islamic character comparable to such contemporaries as the Ottomans, as well as change over time, though none more so than W. Husain's *Administration of Justice during the Muslim Rule in India* (1934), Ibn Hasan's *The Central Structure of the Mughal Empire* (1936), and M.B. Ahmad's *The Administration of Justice in Medieval India* (1941).[9] These works reconfirmed the basic institutional structure outlined by Sarkar, but challenged some of the shallowness and venality of legal institutions he had portrayed under the influence of Orientalist assumptions. Most significantly, they showed that *qadi*-courts, administered by an array of qualified jurists and administrators beside the *qadi* (e.g. *mir* 'adls), extended to the district (*pargana*) level, and *naib-i qadi*s (deputy judges) were present further below. *Panchayat*s were indeed frequently resorted to by villagers, but only for minor issues, while serious cases (civil and criminal) came under the purview of *qadi*s. As well, under Aurangzeb, various clarifications of the appeals process, requirements for recording judgments through particular documents (*mahadir*/*mahzar nama*s) and advocates (*wakil*s) were added to the judicial process, while the theoretical domain was vastly expounded upon in the compilation of the *Fatawa-i* 'Alamgiri.

Although a number of books adding to the scholarly understanding of Mughal law have appeared in the postcolonial era, few have ventured further than those mentioned above in providing deeper analysis of theory or practice, viewing the subject of law within the context of administrative history. Early examples are S.R. Sharma's *Mughal Government and Administration* (1951), and U.N. Day's *The Mughal Government, 1556–1707* (1970).[10] These works are, however, complemented by a far richer consideration of economic history, most thoroughly examined by I. Habib, beginning with his seminal *The Agrarian System of Mughal India, 1556–1707* (1963).[11] Occasionally translated and published collections of documents in the field are also important, such as B.N. Goswamy and J.S. Grewal's focus on *madad-i ma'ash* grants in *The Mughals and the Jogis of Jakhbar* (1967), and S.P. Gupta and S.H. Khan's review of taxation papers in *Mughal Documents: Taqsim, 1649–1800* (1996).[12] It is also

[9] See W. Husain, *Administration of Justice during the Muslim Rule in India* (Calcutta: University of Calcutta, 1934); Ibn Hasan, *The Central Structure of the Mughal Empire* (London: Oxford University Press, 1936); M.B. Ahmad's *The Administration of Justice in Medieval India* (Allahabad: Aligarh Historical Research Institute, 1941).

[10] See S.R. Sharma, *Mughal Government and Administration* (Bombay: Hind Kitabs, 1951); U.N. Day, *The Mughal Government, 1556–1707* (New Delhi: Munshiram Manoharlal, 1970).

[11] I. Habib, *The Agrarian System of Mughal India, 1556–1707* (Delhi: Oxford University Press, [reprint] 1999).

[12] B.N. Goswamy and J.S. Grewal, *The Mughals and the Jogis of Jakhbar* (Simla: Indian Institute of Advanced Study, 1967); and S.P. Gupta and S.H. Khan, *Mughal Documents: Taqsim, 1649–1800* (Jaipur: Publications Scheme, 1996).

in this field that women most directly enter the discussion of Mughal history, as in R.M. Bilgrami's "Women Grantees in the Mughal Empire."[13] Although these and other works on fiscal policy, land tenure (including *awqaf*), contracts, and trade shed much light on *hisba* under the Mughals, they are generally less concerned with viewing evidence in relation to Islamic doctrine than outlining Mughal institutes in isolation and evaluating their ramifications in terms of local institutions and subjects.

A few books have also ventured to pick legal institutions out of the general administrative structure of the state, including M.J. Akbar's *The Administration of Justice by the Mughals* (1948), S.P. Sangar's *Crime and Punishment in Mughal India* (1967), and B.S. Jain's *Administration of Justice in Seventeenth Century India* (1970). However, Orientalism continues to color interpretation.[14] Thus, for example, Jain's book begins with the statement that Mughal rulers were "absolute despots." Nevertheless, Jain must be credited for appeals to various sources representing not just theory, but the judicial practice of the sultans. He draws some enlightening conclusions, therefore, including the fact that cases of judicial despotism among the sultans are "exceptions and not the rule." As well, reflecting a growing body of scholarship aware of the ideal nature of Islamic legal theory relative to practice, he argues that the Mughals followed earlier sultanic practice of putting into effect whatever was "judged to be for the better government of the country ... [whether it] ... was or was not authorized by the law."[15] Later works, such as Z. Islam's *Socio-Economic Dimensions of Fiqh Literature in Medieval India* (1990), and M.L. Bhatia's *Administrative History of Medieval India: A Study of Muslim Jurisprudence Under Aurangzeb* (1992) and *The Ulama, Islamic Ethics and Courts Under the Mughals: Aurangzeb Revisited* (2006), have further developed both these themes, though no monographs or anthologies on the subject of Mughal law specifically have followed Bhatia.[16]

Although spanning nearly a century of scholarship, the books mentioned reveal the slim number devoted to a subject as vast and important as Islamic law in the Mughal context. Of course, they have been supplemented by journal articles and book chapters by such celebrated scholars as A. Ahmad and J. Schacht, but

[13] R.M. Bilgrami, "Women Grantees in the Mughal Empire," *Journal of the Pakistan Historical Society* 36, no. 3 (1988): 207–214.

[14] See M.J. Akbar, *The Administration of Justice by the Mughals* (Lahore: M. Ashraf Publishers, 1948); S.P. Sangar, *Crime and Punishment in Mughal India* (New Delhi: Reliance Publishing, [reprint] 1998); B.S. Jain, *Administration of Justice in Seventeenth Century India* (Delhi: Metropolitan Book Company, 1970).

[15] Jain, *Administration of Justice*, 2, 12.

[16] See Z. Islam, *Socio-Economic Dimensions of Fiqh Literature in Medieval India* (Lahore: Dyal Singh Trust, 1990); M.L. Bhatia's *Administrative History of Medieval India: A Study of Muslim Jurisprudence Under Aurangzeb* (1992), and Z. Islam, *The Ulama, Islamic Ethics and Courts Under the Mughals: Aurangzeb Revisited* (New Delhi: India Manak Publications, 2006).

the tally of in-depth study remains meagre.[17] Nevertheless, those works mentioned have been very influential in the late writing of Mughal history, whether related to the law or not, and for better or worse. On the positive side, thanks in part to the complex legal structures outlined by everyone from Sarkar to Bhatia, as well as late critiques of Orientalist approaches, the Mughal state is no longer broadly understood as despotic, but rightly as a vast, bureaucratic regime, inclusive of non-Muslims with various centers of power. The Orientalist's eternally fixed dichotomies of Islam/Muslim versus Hindu/Indic have been largely forfeited for more subtle readings of Mughal sources, taking into account the distance between theory held in Islamic texts and the practice of Muslims interpreting them in light of pragmatic realities. Other sources of Islamic doctrine, such as mysticism and philosophy, have supplemented the Orientalist's elevation of law as the only truly Islamic creed, and Indic, Indo-Persian, and Turko-Mongol fonts of inspiration for the state's institutional and ideological initiatives have also been explored. Such trends are wellrepresented in some monographs and by the articles included in a number of anthologies at least partially concerned with the law. These works include: R.M. Bilgrami's *Religious and Quasi-Religious Departments of the Mughal Period* (1984); B.D. Metcalf's *Moral Conduct and Authority: The Place of Adab in South Asian Islam* (1984); E.P. Ewing's *Shari'at and Ambiguity in South Asian Islam* (1988); M. Alam and S. Subrahmanyam's *The Mughal State, 1526–1750* (1998); D. Gilmartin and B.B. Lawrence's *Beyond Turk and Hindu: Rethinking Religious Identity in Islamicate South Asia* (2000); and, R.M. Eaton's *India's Islamic Traditions, 711–1750* (2003).[18]

On the more negative side, many of the former authors' representations of the Islamic legal system as a long-ago ossified, foreign code describable as Qur'anic law, has not been entirely jettisoned. That is to say, the works of specialists in the discipline of Islamic Studies that not only reveal Islamic law to be a rich, jurisprudential process, but reconcile theory and practice as in G. El-Nahal's recognition that the shari'a represents an "ideal doctrine for a very real society"—are not uniformly reflected in the works of South Asianists.[19] Rather, evidence of the Mughal assimilation of Indic, Indo-Persian, or Turko-Mongol norms, whether intellectual, institutional, or cultural, as well as the influence of other expressions

[17] See A. Ahmad, "The Role of the Ulema in Indo-Muslim History," *Studia Islamica* 31 (1970): 1–13; J. Schacht, "On the Title of the *Fatawa- al-'Alamgiriyya*," in *Iran and Islam: In Memory of the Late Vladimir Minorsky*, ed. C.E. Bosworth (Edinburgh: Edinburgh University Press, 1971), 475–478.

[18] See R.M. Bilgrami's *Religious and Quasi-Religious Departments of the Mughal Period* (New Delhi: Munshiram Manoharlal Publishers, 1984); B.D. Metcalf, ed., *Moral Conduct and Authority: The Place of Adab in South Asian Islam* (Berkeley: University of California Press, 1984); E.P. Ewing, ed., *Shari'at and Ambiguity in South Asian Islam* (Berkeley: University of California Press, 1988); M. Alam and S. Subrahmanyam, eds., *The Mughal State, 1526–1750* (Oxford: Oxford University Press, 1998); D. Gilmartin and B.B. Lawrence, eds., *Beyond Turk and Hindu: Rethinking Religious Identity in Islamicate South Asia* (Gainesville, FL: University of Florida Press, 2000); R.M. Eaton, ed., *India's Islamic Traditions, 711–1750* (New Delhi: Oxford University Press, 2003).

[19] Cited in Humphreys, *Islamic History*, 210.

of Islamic thought and institutions, have been read as the transgression of ideal Islam, which often remains equated with an inflexible conception of the shari'a. This is easily identifiable in the legal connotations of contemporary South Asian history, including some of those articles concerned with the Mughal Sultanate in the aforementioned anthologies. In Eaton's *India's Islamic Traditions*, for example, I.A. Khan's "The Nobility Under Akbar and the Development of His Religious Policy, 1560–80," argues that Akbar's initiatives (such as the ideological adoption of the Sufi concept of *sulh-i kull* [peace with all]) represent an "attempt to distance himself from a pro-Islamic policy."[20] S. Chandra's "Jizya and the State in India during the Seventeenth Century," sees the abolition of this poll tax as the reflection of a "concept of state [that] was strikingly modern and secularist."[21] And looking beyond the state, the identical approach to Islamic law is evident in various works concerned with society at large. For example, in Y. Friedmann's contribution to precisely the subject of "Islamic Thought in Relation to the [Mughal] Indian Context," Islamic law is presented as "[d]iametrically opposed" to "the attempt to find a common denominator" with local cultural traditions. Thus, only in the life and work of the legalistic Naqshbandi Sufi, Shaykh Ahmad Sirhindi (d. 1624)—a vocal critic of the Mughal legal regime—does Friedmann find that "Islam preserved its pristine purity and refused to make concessions to the pagan environment," while other Islamic philosophers, mystics, theologians, and jurists accommodating the local environment within Islamic frameworks are judged "deviant" and placed "beyond the pale of medieval Indian Islam."[22]

Given such approaches to Islam by the experts in the field of South Asian Studies, there can be no doubt the same understanding of Islamic legal theory and its implications in practice are also represented in more general histories of the Mughals. H. Mukhia, at a loss to explain how Islamic law is related to Mughal practice in his *The Mughals of India* (2004), reverts to Orientalist ideas by pinning Akbar's enterprises on the ideological construction of the Mughal ruler himself as "divinity," thus empowering him to make his own religious law.[23] Aurangzeb's reimposition of *jizya*, on the other hand, is roundly considered an attempt to re-emboss an "Islamic

[20] I.A. Khan, "The Nobility Under Akbar and the Development of His Religious Policy, 1560–80," in *India's Islamic Traditions*, 120–132. Also by the same author, see "Tracing Sources of Principles of Mughal Governance: A Critique of Recent Historiography," *Social Scientist* 37, nos. 5/6 (2009): 45–54.

[21] S. Chandra's "Jizya and the State in India during the Seventeenth Century," in *India's Islamic Traditions*, 133–149. It should be noted that the same idea of transgression is carried through at least into the reign of Sultan Jahangir, as typically represented in S. Alvi's assertion that this son of Akbar was not interested in legal "Islam," so was "liberal" and "just" in his rule. See S. Alvi, "Religion and State during the Reign of Mughal Emperor Jahangir (1605): Nonjuristical Perspectives," *Studia Islamica* 69 (1989): 95–119.

[22] Y. Friedmann, "Islamic Thought in Relation to the [Mughal] Indian Context," in *India's Islamic Traditions*, 50–63.

[23] H. Mukhia, *The Mughals of India* (Oxford: Blackwell, 2004), 49.

character onto the political culture," as in J.F. Richard's *The Mughal Empire* (1996).[24] What an Islamic character means to such scholars as well as those drawing from their insights to write the Mughals into broader South Asian history is described most plainly in B. Stein's *A History of India* (1998), as "religious bigotry," eschewing "practical political rationale" to "place most ... subjects under continuous pressure to convert."[25] The entire thesis is repeated most succinctly in S. Bose and A. Jalal's *Modern South Asia* (1999), considering Akbar's purported distance from doctrinal Islam as a sign of "a pragmatic streak and determination to adapt to the Indian environment," while Aurangzeb's legalism, alone considered Islamic, is argued to be representative of a "reversal of the politics of alliance building and religious flexibility."[26]

The historiography of the Mughals, therefore, renders it most evident that the late scholarly understanding of Islamic legal theory as more than the Qur'anic code assumed by Orientalists is not uniformly returned in the writing of Mughal history. Not only is an informed understanding of the relationship between the ideal and practical absent, the implications of other related fields of Islamic doctrine, including political philosophy, let alone more esoteric disciplines, are also often absent. For example, the latitude allowed Muslim rulers to appeal to customary law in state legislation (*dawabit*) is evidently not considered in the above mentioned evaluations of Akbar's institutes, and the variety of modes by which custom, equity, and juristic preference is accommodated by Hanafi jurisprudence in particular does not figure in appraisals of Aurangzeb's legal reforms. Indeed, even in works such as Friedmann's on Islamic thought itself, the fact that "custom had become a virtually independent source" of Hanafi jurisprudence by the sixteenth century, as pointed out by G. Libson more than a decade ago and others even earlier, plays no role in judging what is pristine and what is deviant.[27] Rather, in the study of legal theory and its influence on practice by the Mughal state and those living under its watch, Orientalism's assumptions and essentialisms live on. The result is that the Mughals, once erroneously characterized as uniformly Islamic by Orientalists, are now often shorn from their Muslim contemporaries outside South Asia, to be branded as Indic, Indo-Persian, and/or Turko-Mongol, at the expense of broadly common Islamic identifiers. Given that the aforementioned assumptions about Islam and its legal tradition are implicit in even late evaluations of the Mughal regime, it must be said that they have undoubtedly contributed to the dearth of study in the field of Islamic legal theory and practice in the Mughal context, diverting attention to other categorizations of thought and institutions.

[24] Richards, *The Mughal Empire*, 164.

[25] B. Stein, *A History of India* (Oxford: Blackwell, 1998), 171–173.

[26] S. Bose and A. Jalal, *Modern South Asia: History, Culture, Politics, Economy* (London: Routledge, 1999), 40–41.

[27] G. Libson, *Jewish and Islamic Law: A Comparative Study of Custom during the Geonic Period* (Cambridge, MA: Harvard University Press, 2003), 69–71. For custom more generally, see M.Z. Othman, "The Status of "Urf in Islamic Law," *IIUM Law Journal* 3, no. 2 (1993): 40–51; and "Ada," *Encyclopedia of Islam* (Leiden: Brill, CD ROM Edition).

There are, as always, exceptions to the rule, particularly in articles appearing most lately. Regarding legal theory, A.M. Guenther's "Hanafi Fiqh in Mughal India: The *Fatawa-i* 'Alamgiri," redeems the representation of Mughal legal pursuits in Eaton's anthology by placing this monumental work in the context of previous legal compendiums, illustrating development over time while outlining the ideal relationship between jurists and the state sought by its compilers in the seventeenth century.[28] Also focussed on this source, M. Khalfoui's "Together But Separate: How Muslim Scholars Conceived of Religious Plurality in South Asia in the Seventeenth Century," further reveals the development of Hanafi *fiqh* in the region over time, making the important observation that the *Fatawa-i* 'Alamgiri not only legitimated the accommodation of South Asia's non-Muslim majority within an Islamic legal framework, but did so by placing emphasis on eighth to tenth century 'Iraqi works, rather than more recent Central Asian contributions like *Al-Hidaya*.[29] And finally, M.R. Pirbhai's "British Legal Reform and Pre-Colonial Trends in Islamic Jurisprudence," builds on a large body of scholarship begun by the likes of F. Rahman, A. Ahmad, J.M.S. Baljon, and B. Metcalf to use the *Fatawa-i* 'Alamgiri as the launching pad for a discussion of non-state legal trends in the eighteenth century that sought to remove the accommodation of customary law in Hanafi *fiqh* known in the period of the Great Mughals, thus recalibrating the ideal relationship between Muslims and non-Muslims in the era of the Lesser, with significant implications for the rise of late Muslim movements and colonial legal codes.[30]

Turning to legal practice, a number of works have lately illustrated the functioning of Islamic law, rather than its transgression, in South Asia's majority non-Muslim environs with anything but the one-sided bigotry assumed by earlier scholars and carried forth in more general histories. R.A. Khan's "The Practice of Escheat and the Mughal Nobility" illustrates the widespread use of this Islamic legal principle by the state, with its broad acceptance among the nobility, to confiscate property upon the holder's death in the case of Muslims of all ethnicities, but not Hindus.[31] As well, G.C. Koslowski's "Imperial Authority, Benefactions and Endowments (Awqaf) in Mughal India" provides an overview of the state's extensive use of grants and endowments with specifically Islamic theoretical roots issued to Muslim and

[28] A.M. Guenther, "Hanafi Fiqh in Mughal India: The *Fatawa-i 'Alamgiri*," in *India's Islamic Traditions*, 209–233.

[29] M. Khalfoui, "Together But Separate: How Muslim Scholars Conceived of Religious Plurality in South Asia in the Seventeenth Century," *Bulletin of SOAS* 74, no. 1 (2011): 87–96.

[30] M.R. Pirbhai, "British Legal Reform and Pre-Colonial Trends in Islamic Jurisprudence," *Journal of Asian History* 42, no. 1 (2008): 36–63. Also see F. Rahman, *Islam* (Chicago: University of Chicago Press, 1979); J.M.S. Baljon, *Religion and Thought of Shah Wali Allah Dihlawi* (Leiden: E.J. Brill, 1986); A. Ahmad, *Studies in Islamic Culture in the Indian Environment* (New York: Oxford University Press, 1964); B.D. Metcalf, *Islamic Revival in British India: Deoband, 1860–1900* (Princeton: Princeton University Press, 1982).

[31] R.A. Khan, "The Practice of Escheat and the Mughal Nobility," *Historicity Research Journal* 1, no. 2 (2014): 1–3.

non-Muslim religious figures and institutions, though in the interests of pragmatic rather than pious state interests throughout the period of Great Mughals.[32] S. Moosvi's consideration of marriage contracts (*nikah nama*) in Gujarat reveals the strict imposition of Islamic norms on the groom, such as the condition of monogamy, restrictions on violence, and compensation for desertion and the wife's right to divorce/annulment if any of these conditions are violated.[33] Regarding the role of the *qadi* and his court, N. Chatterjee's "Hindu City and Just Empire: Banaras and India in Ali Ibrahim Khan's Legal Imagination" shows how well into the period of Lesser Mughals, custom, locality, and colonial exigencies continued to shape and be influenced by Islamic legal principles and procedures.[34] On the other hand, S. Sen's "Retribution in the Subaltern Mirror: Popular Reckonings of Justice, and the Figure of the Qazi in Medieval and Precolonial Bengal" considers how the judge was perceived by subaltern non-Muslims, both as an exponent of Islam and that of elite authority.[35]

The critique of historians that interpret or assume Islamic legal theory to be rigid, exclusionary, and divorced from practice—scholars who therefore consider the inclusiveness of the Mughal regime a sign of its un-Islamic character—also extends beyond works dealing exclusively with *fiqh*. M. Alam is one of a few historians who have long drawn from works written by Islamic mystics and philosophers to illustrate the vibrant debates among Muslims regarding legalism and their impact on Mughal ideology and legal praxis, most lately in the article: "The Debate Within: A Sufi Critique of Religious Law, Tasawwuf and Politics in Mughal India."[36] That is to say, *fiqh* is not the only Islamic discipline to be considered when evaluating the Mughal legal regime and the state's legitimation as Islamic. Mysticism and philosophy espouse alternative approaches to the definition of shari'a. Thus, in stark opposition to Friedmann's general thesis, noted above, Alam writes, "Sirhindi's condemnation of Akbar was not shared by all Muslims, nor even by the other Sufi shaikhs [sic] ... The Sunni Muslim view of religion and politics is thus not solely represented by Shaikh Ahmad Sirhindi ... Rather ... this view must be complicated

[32] G.C. Koslowski, "Imperial Authority, Benefactions and Endowments (Awqaf) in Mughal India," *Journal of the Economic and Social History of the Orient* 38, no. 3 (1995): 355–370.

[33] See S. Moosvi, *People, Taxation and Trade in Mughal India* (Delhi: Oxford University Press, 2009).

[34] N. Chatterjee's "Hindu City and Just Empire: Banaras and India in Ali Ibrahim Khan's Legal Imagination," *Journal of Colonialism and Colonial History* 15, no. 1 (2014): e-journal accessed April 1, 2015.

[35] S. Sen, "Retribution in the Subaltern Mirror: Popular Reckonings of Justice, and the Figure of the Qazi in Medieval and Precolonial Bengal," *Postcolonial Studies* 8, no. 4 (2005): 439–458.

[36] M. Alam, "The Debate Within: A Sufi Critique of Religious Law, Tasawwuf and Politics in Mughal India," *South Asian History and Culture* 2, no. 2 (2011): 138–159. Among other works by the same author, see "Shari'a and Governance in the Indo-Islamic Context," in *Beyond Turk and Hindu*, 229–233. A scholar and work of great influence on Alam is S.A.A. Rizvi, *Religious and Intellectual History of Akbar's Reign* (Delhi: Munshiram Manoharlal, 1975), and both Alam and Rizvi's influence can be read in, M.R. Pirbhai, *Reconsidering Islam in a South Asian Context* (Leiden: E.J. Brill, 2009).

if we are to understand the full range of Muslim political and religious positions in Mughal India."[37]

Although not an exhaustive survey, such late works force the conclusion that knowledge of the administrative structure of Islamic law in the Mughal Sultanate has steadily grown for well over a century, but a similarly developed appreciation of the theory and practice of Islamic law under Mughal aegis begs further consideration. The approaches these late scholars take and the conclusions they draw most starkly reveal that for the study of Islamic law to proceed, the advantages of expunging the remnants of Orientalism's perspective on Islam in general and its legal disciplines in particular bears much fruit. This not only references the equation of legal theory with an unchanging, exclusionary form of Qur'anic code, but encompasses the revisionist implication based on this assumption that Islamic legal theory has little to no bearing on the practice of the Mughal state or its subjects. That is not to say that Indic, Indo-Persian, or Turko-Mongol institutes and customs are inconsequential, or that political pragmatism does not come into play. It is a question of appreciating how these influences and exigencies are accommodated by and wrapped in an Islamic legal framework, rather than assuming that their acknowledgement is a natural signifier of Islamic doctrine's transgression. Yet, it must be added that the scholar's theoretical approach is not the only obstacle in the way of further study. The shallow reading of legal practice beyond courts presided over by the sultan himself is, no doubt, additionally a consequence of the absence of court registers and other such records in the largest collections of Mughal documents. Although this can be partially explained by the fact that the foundations of contemporary archival collections were laid by Britons in the late-eighteenth century—thus reflecting the wants and ideological perspectives of colonialists—the more direct explanation is the lack of Mughal state archives. Lesser Mughal or successor state legal documents, therefore, dominate extant materials. Hopefully, the records of individual judicial officers and the cases over which they presided in the foundational era of the Great Mughals will be located in more minor library and private collections. Perhaps, the scholarly approaches applied to such primary sources and those already read will be carefully reconsidered. Much progress has been made on both fronts over the last century, but acknowledging the importance of the legal theory and practice of any political regime, it is apparent that a concerted effort to leap the hurdles still standing between historians and the law is a necessary condition for the Mughal Sultanate's place in South Asian and Islamic history to be fully realized.

[37] Alam, "The Debate Within," 152.

References

Ahmad, A., "The Role of the Ulema in Indo-Muslim History." *Studia Islamica* 31 (1970): 1–13.

Ahmad, A., *Studies in Islamic Culture in the Indian Environment* (New York: Oxford University Press, 1964).

Ahmad, M.B., *The Administration of Justice in Medieval India* (Allahabad: Aligarh Historical Research Institute, 1941).

Akbar, M.J., *The Administration of Justice by the Mughals* (Lahore: M. Ashraf Publishers, 1948).

Alam, M., "The Debate Within: A Sufi Critique of Religious Law, Tasawwuf and Politics in Mughal India." *South Asian History and Culture* 2, no. 2 (2011): 138–159.

Alam, M., and Subrahmanyam, S., eds. *The Mughal State, 1526–1750* (Oxford: Oxford University Press, 1998).

Alvi, S., "Religion and State during the Reign of Mughal Emperor Jahangir (1605): Nonjuristical Perspectives." *Studia Islamica* 69 (1989): 95–119.

Baillie, N.B.E., trans. *The Moohummudan Law of Sale according to the Huneefeea Code: from the Futawa Alumgeeree, a Digest of the Whole Law. Prepared by Command of the Emperor Aurungzebe Alumgeer* (Delhi: Delhi Law House, [reprint], n.d.)

Baillie, N.B.E., *A Digest of Moohummudan Law Compiled and Translated from Authorities in the Original Arabic with an Introduction and Explanatory Notes Containing the Doctrines of the Hunifeea Code of Jurisprudence* (Lahore: Premier Book House, n.d.)

Baljon, J.M.S., *Religion and Thought of Shah Wali Allah Dihlawi* (Leiden: E.J. Brill, 1986).

Bayly, C.A., *Indian Society and the Making of the British Empire* (Cambridge: Cambridge University Press, 1988).

Bhatia, M.L., *Administrative History of Medieval India: A Study of Muslim Jurisprudence Under Aurangzeb* (Delhi: Radha Publications, 1992).

Bhatia, M.L., *The Ulama, Islamic Ethics and Courts Under the Mughals: Aurangzeb Revisited* (New Delhi: India Manak Publications, 2006).

Bilgrami, R.M., "Women Grantees in the Mughal Empire," *Journal of the Pakistan Historical Society* 36, no. 3 (1988): 207–214.

Bilgrami, R.M., *Religious and Quasi-Religious Departments of the Mughal Period* (New Delhi: Munshiram Manoharlal Publishers, 1984).

Bose, S., and Jalal, A., *Modern South Asia: History, Culture, Politics, Economy* (London: Routledge, 1999).

Chatterjee, N., "Hindu City and Just Empire: Banaras and India in Ali Ibrahim Khan's Legal Imagination." *Journal of Colonialism and Colonial History* 15, no. 1 (2014): e-journal accessed September 2, 2015.

Day, U.N., *The Mughal Government, 1556–1707* (New Delhi: Munshiram Manoharlal, 1970).

Eaton, R.M., ed. *India's Islamic Traditions, 711–1750* (New Delhi: Oxford University Press, 2003).

Ewing, E.P., ed. *Shari'at and Ambiguity in South Asian Islam* (Berkeley: University of California Press, 1988).

Gilmartin, D., and Lawrence, B.B., eds. *Beyond Turk and Hindu: Rethinking Religious Identity in Islamicate South Asia* (Gainesville, FL: University of Florida Press, 2000).

Goswamy, B.N., and Grewal, J.S., *The Mughals and the Jogis of Jakhbar* (Simla: Indian Institute of Advanced Study, 1967).
Gupta, S.P., and Khan, S.H., *Mughal Documents: Taqsim, 1649–1800* (Jaipur: Publications Scheme, 1996).
Habib, I., *The Agrarian System of Mughal India, 1556–1707* (Delhi: Oxford University Press, [reprint] 1999).
Hamid, A., *A Chronicle of British Indian Legal History* (Jaipur: RBSA Publishers, 1991).
Hamilton, C., trans. *The Hedaya or Guide: A Commentary of the Mussulman Laws* (Lahore: Premier Book House, [reprint] 1963).
Hintze, A., *The Mughal Empire and its Decline* (Aldershot: Ashgate, 1997).
Humphreys, R.S., *Islamic History: A Framework for Inquiry* (Princeton: Princeton University Press, 1991).
Hunter, W.W., ed. *Rulers of India*, 28 Vols (Oxford: Clarendon Press, 1893–95).
Husain, W, *Administration of Justice during the Muslim Rule in India* (Calcutta: University of Calcutta, 1934).
Ibn Hasan, *The Central Structure of the Mughal Empire* (London: Oxford University Press, 1936).
Islam, Z., *Socio-Economic Dimensions of Fiqh Literature in Medieval India* (Lahore: Dyal Singh Trust, 1990).
Jackson, A.V.W., ed. *History of India*, 9 Vols (London: Grolier, 1906–07).
Jain, B.S, *Administration of Justice in Seventeenth Century India* (Delhi: Metropolitan Book Company, 1970).
Khalfoui, M., "Together But Separate: How Muslim Scholars Conceived of Religious Plurality in South Asia in the Seventeenth Century." *Bulletin of SOAS* 74, no. 1 (2011): 87–96.
Khan, I.A., "Tracing Sources of Principles of Mughal Governance: A Critique of Recent Historiography," *Social Scientist* 37, nos. 5/6 (2009): 45–54.
Khan, R.A., "The Practice of Escheat and the Mughal Nobility." *Historicity Research Journal* 1, no. 2 (2014): 1–3.
Koslowski, G.C., "Imperial Authority, Benefactions and Endowments (Awqaf) in Mughal India." *Journal of the Economic and Social History of the Orient* 38, no. 3 (1995): 355–370.
Kugle, S.A., "Framed Blamed and Renamed: The Recasting of Islamic Jurisprudence in Colonial South Asia." *Modern Asian Studies* 35, no. 2 (2001): 257–313.
Metcalf, B.D., ed. *Moral Conduct and Authority: The Place of Adab in South Asian Islam* (Berkeley: University of California Press, 1984).
Metcalf, B.D., *Islamic Revival in British India: Deoband, 1860–1900* (Princeton: Princeton University Press, 1982).
Mittal, S.C., *India Distorted: A Study of British Historians on India* (New Delhi: M.D. Publications, 1996).
Moosvi, S., *People, Taxation and Trade in Mughal India* (Delhi: Oxford University Press, 2009).
Mukhia, H., *The Mughals of India* (Oxford: Blackwell, 2004).
Pirbhai, M.R., "British Legal Reform and Pre-Colonial Trends in Islamic Jurisprudence." *Journal of Asian History* 42, no. 1 (2008): 36–63.
Pirbhai, M.R., *Reconsidering Islam in a South Asian Context* (Leiden: E.J. Brill, 2009).
Rahman, F., *Islam* (Chicago: University of Chicago Press, 1979).
Richards, J.F., *The Mughal Empire* (Cambridge: Cambridge University Press, 1996).

Rizvi, S.A.A., *Religious and Intellectual History of Akbar's Reign* (Delhi: Munshiram Manoharlal, 1975).
Sangar, S.P., *Crime and Punishment in Mughal India* (New Delhi: Reliance Publishing, [reprint] 1998).
Sarkar, J.N., *Mughal Administration, Six Lectures* (Patna: Government Print Office, 1920).
Sarkar, J.N., *Mughal Administration* (Patna: Patna University Press, 1925).
Schacht, J., "On the Title of the *Fatawa- al-'Alamgiriyya*" in C.E. Bosworth (ed.) Iran and Islam: In Memory of the Late Vladimir Minorsky (Edinburgh: Edinburgh University Press, 1971) 475–478.
Sen, S., "Retribution in the Subaltern Mirror: Popular Reckonings of Justice, and the Figure of the Qazi in Medieval and Precolonial Bengal." *Postcolonial Studies* 8, no. 4 (2005): 439–458.
Sharma, S.R., *Mughal Government and Administration* (Bombay: Hind Kitabs, 1951).
Stein, B., *A History of India* (Oxford: Blackwell, 1998).
Streusand, D.E., *The Formation of the Mughal Empire* (Delhi: Oxford University Press, 1989).

CHAPTER 21

DELIVERING JUSTICE

THE MONARCH'S ʿURFI COURTS AND THE SHARIʿA IN SAFAVID IRAN

RULA JURDI ABISAAB

MODERN scholarship is dominated by the view that the Safavid legal system was dualistic, sharply divided between dysfunctional shariʿa courts and effective ʿurfi (monarchical/sultanic) courts.[1] Advocates of this view argue that the ʿurfi courts eventually eclipsed the shariʿa courts during the seventeenth century as a remedy for the chaos of the latter, or/and the suffocation of judgeship (*qada'*, *qazavat*) at the hands of the mujtahids' (jurists who use rational legal inference (*ijtihad*) to derive the law in addition to the Qur'an, hadith, and consensus (*ijmaʿ*). This view is substantiated through a reliance on European travelogues, which offer various narratives about the ʿurfi courts, described as "secular." Without a close assessment of the meaning of the term "secular" in its European context at the time, and a deconstruction of the travelogues, it is difficult to arrive at an accurate picture of the activities of the shariʿa experts as well as the so-called "secular" judge, that is, the

[1] See Mohammad Hoseini and Ahmad Rezvanimofrad, "The Structure of Safavid Judicial System," *Law Quarterly-Journal of Faculty of Law and Political Science*, Vol. 41, no. 3 (2011): 155–169; S.H. Amīn, *Tārīkh-i Ḥuqūq-i Īrān* (Tehran: Intishārāt-i Dā'irat al-Maʿārif-i Irānshināsī, 2003), 281, 333; Aḥmad Pakatchī, "Ḥuqūq," Vol.10, *Dā'irat al-Maʿārif-i Buzurg-i Islāmī*, ed. Kāẓim Mūsavī Bojnūrdī (Tehran, 2002); Willem Floor, "Mazalem," *Encyclopedia Iranica*, September 15, 2009 ed. Ehsan Yarshater (1996 web based version); "The Secular Judicial System in Safavid Persia," *Studia Iranica*, vol. 29, no. 1 (2000): 9–60.

divan-begi (the imperial chief of justice) who handles claims at the ʿurfi courts on behalf of the Safavid monarch.

In this chapter, I argue that the alleged split between a sacred and a secular basis for justice in Safavid Iran is largely unfounded, and that the interconnections between the ʿurfi and the shariʿa courts abound.[2] I shed light on the judicial and executive procedures linking the judges (*qazis*) to the *divan-begis*, particularly, in connection to capital offenses and crimes. I also assess the *sadr*'s unique abilities to join together the decisions of the shariʿa experts and the executive authority of the *divan-begis*. Many *sadrs* (heads of religious–legal administration and endowments) exhibited an eclectic scholarly training in the religious and rational sciences, and came from families that included judges. Evidently, the ʿurfi courts enforced many decisions, even on cases of murder, issued by the provincial judges and *shuyukh al-Islam* (chief judges, highest clerical authority). These legal decisions found their way to the *divan-begi*'s council, in the royal palace, in the form of petitions (*ʿarzehs*) sent by the judges themselves. In other words, what went on in a ʿurfi court was informed by recommendations and developments, which either took place earlier in a shariʿa court or adjudicated upon by shariʿa experts and chief judges, attesting to the interconnection between the two court systems.

I. Conceptual Framework and Sources

It goes without saying that many legal agreements and settlements occurred outside the shariʿa court, relying on interpersonal relations, community pressure, and family intervention. But these legal activities, much like the ones carried out within the courts, hardly found their way into court chronicles, which focussed on the sovereign, the imperial court, and the administrative and military elites. Notwithstanding, some of the legal prerogatives of the *qazis*, *qazi ʿaskar* (or *muʿaskar*), and *shuyukh al-Islam*, can be gleaned from an array of chronicles,[3] which depict more frequently

[2] In the last two decades several scholars have offered diverse models for the interaction between the *ʿurfi* and shariʿa courts in the Mamluk and Ottoman contexts, and ways of rethinking *ʿurfi law*. Two works, which speak to some aspects of my study are: Kristen A. Stilt, *Islamic Law in Action: Authority, Discretion, and Everyday Experiences in Mamluk Egypt* (New York: Oxford University Press, 2011), 26. Stilt rejected the use of the term "secular" to describe *ʿurfi* laws in Mamluk Egypt and suggested instead the term "*siyasa*." Başak Tuğ also questioned the perception of the *kanun* in the Ottoman context as secular law. See Tuğ, *Politics of Honor in Ottoman Anatolia: Sexual Violence and Socio-Legal Surveillance in the Eighteenth Century* (Leiden: Brill, 2017), 47–48, 70.

[3] Among these court chronicles are: Amīr Maḥmūd b. Khwāndamīr, *Iran dar Rūzgār-i Shāh Ismāʿīl va-Shāh Tāhmāsb Safavī*, ed. Ghulāmrezā Ṭabāṭabāʾī (Tehran: Bunyād-i Mawqūfāt-i Duktūr Maḥmūd Afshār Yazdī, 1991); Ḥasan Beg Rumlū, *A Chronicle of the Early Safawis (Ahsanu't-Tawarikh)*,

the tribunals (*mazalim* courts) set up by the Shah and his Grand Vizier, and the *'urfi* courts held by the *divan-i 'adalat* (royal council of justice). Unlike the shari'a courts, the *'urfi* ones, which reflected imperial judicial supervision, coercion, and punishment, came more readily to the attention of court historians (*majlis-nevis*), whether they were *munshis* (scribes), astrologers (*munajjims*), or even *qazis*.[4] There is no reason for court historians to be concerned with the ubiquitous, lay-focussed, widely dispersed legal activities taking place at shari'a courts in various Iranian cities and towns. Despite the lack of official court records, one can draw upon other critical sources, including manuals of state,[5] such as *Tadhkirat al-Muluk* and *Dastur al-Moluk*, which delineate normative legal enactments at the highest state levels. A richly textured provincial chronicle titled, *Tadhkirah-yi Safaviyya-yi Kirman*,[6] and a few royal decrees (*farmans*) discussed by Rasul Ja'fariyan, also shed light on the functions of *qazis* and *shuyukh al-Islam* during the second half of the seventeenth century.

A group of European travelogues, written by Raphael du Mans (1664–96), Nicolas Sanson (1683–91), Adam Olearius (August 1637–end of 1638), John Baptista Tavernier (made six trips in and through Iran between 1632 and 1668), Jean Chardin (during the 1660s and the 1670s), and Engelbert Kaempfer (1684–85), provide the greatest number of narratives on the 'urfi courts.[7] Modern scholars have used these

trans. C.N. Seddon, (Baroda: Oriental Institute, 1934); Iskandar Beg Munshī, *'Ālam-ārā-yi 'Abbāsī*, 3 volumes, ed. Muḥammad Ismā'īl Rezvānī (Tehran: Dunyā-yi Kitāb, 1377/1998); Mulla Jalāl al-Dīn Munajjim Yazdī, *Tārīkh-i 'Abbāsī or Rūznāmah-yi Jalāl*, ed. Sayfullah Vaḥīd-Niyā (n.p.: Intishārāt-i Waḥīd, 1366); Mīrzā Muḥammad Ṭāhir Vahīd Qazvīnī, *Tārīkh-i Jahān-ārā-yi 'Abbāsī ('Abbāsnāmah)*, ed. I. Dihgān (Arak: Kitābfurūshī-yi Dāvūdī, 1951); 'Abdī Beg Shīrāzī, *Takmilat al-Akhbār*, ed. 'Abd al-Ḥusayn Navā'ī (Tehran: Nashr-ī Nay, 1369/1990); Qāḍī Aḥmad Qummī, *Khulāṣat al-Tavārīkh*, ed. Iḥsān Ishrāqī, Vol.1 (Tehran: Intishārāt-i Dānishgāh-i Tehran, 1359–63sh/1980–84); Muḥammad Yūsuf Vālih Qazvīnī Iṣfahānī, *Irān dar Zamān-i Shāh Ṣafī va-Shāh 'Abbās Duvvum (1038–1071) or Khuld-i Barīn*, ed. Muḥammad Rezā Nāṣirī (Tehran: Anjuman-i Āthār va-Mafākhir-i Farhangī, 1382/1962–63).

[4] See Sholeh Quinn and Charles Melville, "Safavid Historiography," in *A History of Persian Literature: Persian Historiography*, Vol.10, ed. C. Melville (London: I.B. Tauris, 2012), 209–257.

[5] Mirza Samī'ā's manual of state was edited and translated by Vladimir Minorsky under the title, *Tadhkirat al-mulūk: A Manual of Safavid Administration* (circa 1137/1725). E.J.W. Gibb Memorial Series (Cambridge, 1980); Mīrzā Rafī'ā or Muḥammad Rafī' al-Dīn Anṣārī, *Dastur al-Moluk: A Safavid State Manual*, trans. Willem Floor and Mohammad H. Faghfoory, with commentary by Willem Floor (Costa Mesa: Mazda Publishers, 2007). See also Ali Naqi Nasiri, *Titles and Emoluments in Safavid Iran: A Third Manual of Safavid Administration*, trans. and annotated by Willem Floor (MD: Mage Publishers, 2008).

[6] Mīr Muḥammad Sa'īd Mushīzī (Bardsīrī), *Tadhkirah-yi Ṣafaviyya-i Kirmān* ed. M. Ibrāhīm Bāstānī Pārīzī (Tehran: Ḥaydarī, 1369).

[7] Michele Membré, *Mission to the Lord Sophy of Persia (1539–1542)*, trans. A.H. Morton, London, (Cambridge: Gibb Memorial Trust, 1993); Nicolas Sanson, (1600–67), *The Present State of Persia with a Faithful Account of the Manners, Religion and Government of that People* (London: Printed for M. Gillyflower, J. Tonson, and H. Bonwick, 1695), 137–154; Adam Olearius (1603–71), *The Voyages and Travels of the Ambassadors sent by Frederick Duke of Holstein, to the Great Duke of Muscovy, and the King of Persia* (London: Printed for Thomas Dring and John Starkey, 1662), 356, 367, 370; John Baptista Tavernier, (1605–89), *The Six Voyages of John Baptista Tavernier, Baron of Aubonne, through Turky, into Persia and the East Indies, for the Space of Forty Years* (London: Printed by William Godbid for Robert Littlebury and Moses Pitt, 1677), Book V, 232–234; Sir John Chardin (1643–1713), *The Travels*

travelogues largely in a positivist manner as sources of data. Their authors had diverse backgrounds and included a proselytizing Capuchin like du Mans, a Protestant jeweller like Chardin, a Hugenot gem merchant like Tavernier,[8] a French cartographer like Sanson, and a German naturalist like Kaempfer. They wrote self-consciously to certain European audiences, tweaked and rearranged their "observations" to fit European perceptions, and modeled themselves after earlier travellers. They also integrated sections from other travelogues, which had particular utility for their discourse about the Orientals, a broad and heterogenous category, which included during the sixteenth and seventeenth centuries, Russians and Poles.[9]

An awareness of the travelogues' contexts, dynamics of alterity, intended audiences, and utility helps one understand how a narrative about a dysfunctional shari'a court was authorized in the secondary literature, and how "religious" law came to be contrasted with an efficient "secular" legal system. Willem Floor argued that the *sadr* and *shaykh al-Islam* "influenced" the performance of the *qazi*s, who failed to resolve the laity's legal disputes. Floor concluded that the secular courts monopolized justice not merely with respect to cases dealing with state officials but civilians as well.[10]

The travellers did not use the term "secular" to imply an absence or negation of the "religious" and the non-sacramental. In late medieval Europe it was used by Christian theologians to refer to a transition from monastic life (*regularis*) to the life of canons (*saecularis*) and worldliness.[11] After that period, "secular" referred more specifically to the Reformation (1517–1648) and the "transfer of ecclesiastical real property to laypersons," as private property.[12] The Reformation nurtured a strong faith in a sovereign transcendental God and rejected the agency of saints and angels.[13] Secular affairs in the domains of politics and enconomics were as such "liberated" from the Church. Chardin used the term "secular" in this capacity, and not in the way it was reassembelled by the Enlightenment to refer to an attitude or practice that exhibits an adversarial relationship with religion.[14] Still, it is absurd to think that a transition

of Sir John Chardin into Persia, and the East-Indies; The Coronation of Solyman III (London: Printed for Christopher Bateman, 1691), 59–60, 87–90, 127–128; Engelbert Kaempfer (1651–1716), *Am Hofe des persischen Grosskönig, 1684–85; das erste Buch der Amœnitatum exoticae* (Leipzig: K.F. Koehler, 1940); Cornelis de Bruyn, *Travels into Muscovy, Persia, and Part of the East-Indies*, Vol. 1 of 2. Translated from French (London: MDCCXXXVII, 1737), 202, 207–208, 231.

[8] Both Chardin and Tavernier experienced religious discrimination in France.

[9] Larry Wolff, *Inventing Eastern Europe: The Map of Civilization on the Mind of the Enlightenment* (Stanford: Stanford University Press, 1994), 4–5. Rudi Matthee acknowledged the Orientalist approaches of western travelogues but argued that they offered invaluable sources of information. See Matthee, "The Safavids under Western Eyes: Seventeenth-Century European Travelers to Iran," *Journal of Early Modern History*, no. 13 (2009): 137–171.

[10] Floor, "Mazalem"; "The Secular Judicial," 9–60.

[11] Talal Asad, *Formations of the Secular: Christianity, Islam, Modernity* (Stanford: Stanford University Press, 2003), 192–193.

[12] Ibid., 194.

[13] Charles Taylor, *A Secular Age* (Cambridge, MA: Harvard University Press, 2007), 77–78.

[14] Talal Asad, *Formations*, 194.

from Christian monastic life to worldly endeavors, which fits with the Reformation, has any relevance to Iranian clerics. The legal cases, which Chardin and Sanson referred to appear to be divided between the unworldly sphere of the "Ancients of the Law,"[15] that is, the religious scholars, who execute the "Law of Imam Dgafar,"[16] and the secular worldly sphere of the *divan-begi*, described as the "Chief of the Civil Justice,"[17] who deals with the affairs of civilians, seen as falling outside the ulema's control.

In addition to the conceptual problems posed by using travelogues as repositories of rare "proofs" for the alleged triumph of the 'urfi courts, the nature of these "proofs" themselves is paradoxical. The travellers' perceptions of what they saw or what was explained to them in connection to legal cases of loan disputes, theft, or murder carry gaps, inconsistencies, and unlikely endings. To this, one must add the sketchy references to the shari'a courts, and ignorance of Islamic law. Navigating the travelogues necessitates filling gaps and resolving contradictions. This intervention appears to be necessary in order to clarify what the justice system in Safavid Iran *was not*. To more accurately describe the Safavid legal system, I have tried to decenter European projects embedded in the travelogues, including themes of Asiatic despotism, Persian depravity, as well as Islam's legal failures.[18] This leads me to privilege diverse Safavid sources over travelogues not due to the former's objectivity, but rather due to the absence of an external "gaze," and the sense of an excited otherness. Safavid authors were naturally situated within the system they wrote about, with subjectivities related to their professions, personal loyalties, genre of writing, local politics, social class, and proximity to those in power, all within a Safavid context. Attending to what the Safavid authors themselves had to say about various legal actors and issues, offers us a far superior view of the Safavid legal system as a whole.

II. Administering Justice: the Shah, the *Sadr*, the *Qazis*, the *Shaykh al-Islam*, and the *Divan-Begi*

A. The Shah

Delivering justice was integral to the imperial authority of the Shah who was presented by his chroniclers as the *sahib-i qiran* (master of the auspicious

[15] Chardin, *The Travels of Sir John Chardin: The Coronation of Solyman III*, 43–44, 59.

[16] Sanson, *The Present State of Persia*, 144. [17] Ibid., 137.

[18] On Asiatic despotism see Stefan Brakensiek, "Political Judgement between Empirical Experience and Scholarly Tradition: Engelbert Kaempfer's Report on Persia," *The Medieval History Journal* 5, no. 2 (2002): 223–246.

conjunction), divinely blessed,[19] and the *zill-i ilahi* (God's shadow on earth). Celestial conjunctions and astrological predictions confirmed his suitability for kingship and stressed its sacred elements. He must act swiftly and intelligently to prevent disorder, insecurity, and hunger among his subjects. As a dispenser of justice, he is also empowered by his public devotion to the Twelve Imams and the building of shrines dedicated to them and to Safavid Sufi ancestors.[20]

The Shahs' concern for the well-being of the elderly and the weak is a prevalent theme in court chronicles. For one, Shah Tahmasb (r. 930/1524–984/1576) asked the supervisor (*sarkar*) of the royal household, Khwaja Habibullah, to inform him about the conditions of the poor in Herat and to distribute meat to them.[21] He also waived the craft tax for the Tabrizis, and absolved them from *divan* dues.[22] Shah 'Abbas (r. 996/1588– 1038/1629), more than any earlier sovereign, was presented as siding with the weak to the extent of eliminating injustice in his empire.[23] The calamities he endured, his historians liked to say, made him even more sympathetic to those who experienced injustice.[24] He listened to the complaints of the people of Natanz in central Iran and ordered an investigation into the injustices committed by the local governor and the abuses of tax collectors (*tahsildaran*).[25] His Grand Vizier, and the provincial governors held tribunals on his behalf to address the grievances of commoners. The Shah's justice (*'adalat*) was to be manifest through social stability, the security of his subjects, and their goods and money. He was expected to curb excess and the arbitrary actions of state officials.[26] Like Shah Tahmasb, Shah 'Abbas's moral authority and control was enhanced through these assuaging measures such as the remission of taxes for his subjects, tax exemptions for travellers (*tamgha-yi shavari'*) and merchants, and the waiving of taxes on herds and crafts.[27]

These and later Shahs made a concerted effort to attend the court of justice or delegate the task to the Grand Vizier.[28] The medieval Shafi'i jurist and political philosopher, al-Mawardi (d. 450/1058), described this practice, which linked *siyasa shar'iyya* (governance according to shari'a norms) and *qada'* (judgeship), by stating that, through the *mazalim* (tribunal) courts, "the political might of the ruler is joined together with half of judgeship *qada*'."[29] This depiction is key to understanding the

[19] Roger M. Savory, trans., *History of Shah 'Abbas the Great (Tārīkh-e 'Ālamārā-ye 'Abbāsī)*, Vol. 1 (Boulder: Westview Press, 1978), 520–521.

[20] Kishwar Rizvi, *The Safavid Dynastic Shrine: Architecture, Religion and Power in Early Modern Iran* (London: I.B.Tauris, 2011), 76–79.

[21] Rumlū, *A Chronicle of the Early Safawis*, 86, 91; Minorsky, *Tadhkirat al-mulūk*, 105.

[22] Savory, *History of Shah 'Abbas*, Vol. 1, 441, 203–205, 291; vol.2, 752–753, 785, 1227, 1304.

[23] Ibid., 523, 517. See also Mullā Jalāl, *Rūznāmah-yi*, 371, 421, 429.

[24] Savory, *History of Shah 'Abbas*, Vol. 1, 520–521.

[25] Natanzī, *Naqāvat al-Āthār*, 462.

[26] Savory, *History of Shah 'Abbas*, vol. 1, 523.

[27] Ibid., 204, 523, 624, 773–774, 1032; Maḥmūd b. Hidāyatullah Āfūshtah Natanzī, *Naqāvat al-Āthār fī dhikr al-Ākhyār*, ed. Iḥsān Ishrāqī, (Tehran: Intishārāt-i 'Ilmī Farhangī, 1364), 223–224.

[28] Vaḥīd Qazvīnī, *'Abbāsnāmah*, 174–175, 183, 190.

[29] Al-Māwardī, *Al-Aḥkām al-Sulṭāniyya* (Beirut: Dār al-Kutub al-'Ilmiyya, n.d.), 98.

links between ʿurfi and shariʿa courts as well as the tensions. From the viewpoint of the Safavid state, the tribunals and the ʿurfi courts served more than one purpose. They deflected blame and discontent from the Shah to governors, tax collectors, merchants, and viziers among others. The tribunals permitted occasional outlets of class discontent and anger.[30] Like the ʿurfi courts, they offered commoners direct access to the highest executive authority. The sovereign strengthened his imperial authority by keeping such channels open for the laity's grievances and by being seen as capable of regulating the behavior of his state officials and curtailing crime. At the same time, the prerogatives of state officials, governors, and *shuyukh al-Islam* were redrawn and reconfirmed every time the Shah's justice council acted upon their petitions and recommendations.

B. The *Ṣadr*

In early Safavid times, more than one person held the post of *sadr*.[31] At the time of Shah Ṭahmasb, a territorial and administrative division in this post took place, whereby the *sadr-i ʿamma* presided over state lands, and the *sadr–i khassa* over crown lands. The latter also administered the religious endowments (*awqaf*), appointed clerics, and regulated their affairs.[32] In a later period, both posts were combined, and the *sadr* was in charge of appointing the *shuyukh al-Islam*, *qazi*s, teachers, orators, prayer leaders, and superintendents.[33]

Olearius, Sanson, and Le Bruyn associated the *sadr* solely with the religious sphere, yet referred inadvertently, to a mix of "ecclesiastical" and "secular" tasks and roles taken up by him.[34] Sanson's confusion about the nature of the *sadr*'s post is reflected in the title he gave him, namely, the "Sovereign Judge of the Tribunal of Religion."[35] In reality, the *sadr* linked together through his functions, private and public spheres of justice, and balanced imperial jurisdiction with court rulings based on the shariʿa.[36] He presided over the affairs of the royal council of justice including the adjudication and executive tasks of the *divan-begi*, accompanied by the

[30] Munshī, *ʿĀlam-ārā-yi ʿAbbāsī*, Vol. 2, 1401.

[31] Willem Floor, "ṢADR," *Encyclopedia Iranica*.

[32] Muḥammad Shafiʿ Tehrānī (Vārid), *Mir'āt-i Vāridāt: Tārikh-i Suqūṭ-i Ṣafaviyyān, Piyāyād-hā-yi ān va-Farmānravā'ī-yi Malik Maḥmūd Sistānī*, ed. Manṣūr Ṣefatgol (Tehran: Mirāth-i Maktūb, 1383/1964), 227.

[33] Mīrzā Rafīʿā, *Dastur*, 2.

[34] Sanson, *The Present State*, 142–143, 153; Olearius, *The Voyages*, 367; Le Bruyn, *Travels into Muscovy*, 208.

[35] Sanson, *The Present State*, 143, 153.

[36] See Munshī, *ʿĀlam-ārā-yi ʿAbbāsī*, Vol. 1, 225, 243–244, 246, 332, 342; Vol. 2, 877, 993–996,1401, 1464; Vol. 3, 1562–1563, 1732, 1765, 1813–1814. Rasūl Jaʿfariyān noted that *ḥukūmat-i sharʿiyyat* was in the hands of *shaykh al-Islām* but the *ṣadr* can be seen as a supreme legal judge. See Rasūl Jaʿfariyān, *Siyāsat va-Farhang-i Rūzgār-i Ṣafavī*, Vol. 1 (Tehran: Nashr-i ʿIlm, 1388/2009), 319.

shaykh al-Islam.[37] In this respect, he was the legal linchpin of the entire 'urfī-shari'a system.

The *sadr*s exhibited an eclectic intellectual–administrative profile, which placed them in an ideal position to bring together monarchical and shari'a-based law. They cultivated knowledge in the legal and rational sciences and were involved in some aspects of judgeship. It suffices to mention a few examples. Mir Jamal al-Din Muḥammad Astarabadi (d. 931/1524–25), a well-known scholar of jurisprudence and *kalam* (rational theology), was appointed *sadr* by Shah Isma'il (r. 907/1501–930/1524) after the battle of Chaldiran in 920/1514.[38] Another *sadr*, Mir Ni'matullah al-Hilli studied with jurists in Najaf, including al-Muhaqqiq al-Karaki (d. 940/1534), the prominent *shaykh al-Islam*. A similar training was attained by Mir Mu'izz al-Din Muḥammad Isfahani who served as *sadr* for six years starting in 938/1531–32, and Mir Asadullah Mar'ashi Shushtari who succeeded him in 963/1555–56.[39]

A number of *sadr*s also practiced *qazavat* (judgeship) and many others had senior family members who occupied judgeship posts.[40] At the time of Shah 'Abbas, Qazi Khan was practicing judgeship in Qazvin as many of his family members had done earlier. He occupied the post of *qazi 'askar* (army judge) and twelve years afterwards he was appointed *sadr*.[41] The father of yet another *sadr*, known as Mir Muḥammad Yusuf, was the *qazi* of Herat. Mir 'Ala' al-Mulk, a seyyed from Mar'ash, was also *qazi-yi mu'askar* in Qazvin at the time of Shah 'Abbas and was appointed *sadr* in Gilan.[42] As with other professions, many ulema cultivated expertise in fields known to their fathers, grandfathers, or siblings, who acted as *qāzīs, muḥtasibs* (market supervisor and inspector), and *shuyūkh al-Islām*.[43]

c. The *Qazi* and the *Shaykh al-Islām*

The extent to which the shari'a furnished the basis for the regulation of civil life is reflected in court records and documents,[44] as well as treatises and *responsa* to

[37] Mīrzā Rafī'ā, *Dastur*, 3; Minorsky, *Tadhkirat al-mulūk*, 42.

[38] Rula Jurdi Abisaab, "Peasant Uprisings in Astarabad: the *Siyāh Pūshān* (Wearers of Black), the Sayyids, and the Safavid State," *Iranian Studies*, vol. 49, no. 3 (April 2016): 477–481.

[39] Mulla Jalāl, *Rūznāmah-yi*, 428; Iskandar Beg Munshi, *'Ālam-ārā-yi 'Abbāsī*, Vol. 1, 230; Qāḍī Aḥmad Qummī, *Khulāṣat al-Tavārīkh*, Vol. 2, 1050; Qāḍī Aḥmad Ghaffārī Qazvīnī, *Tārīkh-i Jahān-ārā*, ed., 'Allāma Qazvīnī (Tehran: Kitābfurūshī-yi Ḥāfiz, 1363/1964), 291, 308.

[40] See Qāḍī Aḥmad Qummī, *Khulāṣat*, Vol. 1, 565; Rula Jurdi Abisaab, *Converting Persia: Religion and Power in the Safavid Empire, 1501–1736* (London: I.B. Tauris, 2004), 154–155. On references to judgeship and *ṣadārat*, which ran in families, and connections between the two, See Munshī, *'Ālam-ārā-yi 'Abbāsi*, Vol. 1, 246–247, 237, 320, 340; Vol. 2, 1400–1401; Vol. 3, 1813–1814.

[41] Savory, *History of Shah 'Abbās*, Vol. 2, 1188.

[42] Munshī, *'Ālam-ārā-yi 'Abbāsī*, Vol. 1, 232.

[43] Bardsīrī, *Tadhkirah-yi*, 34–36, 262, 349.

[44] Manṣūr Ṣifatgul, "Safavid Administration of Avqaf: Structure, Changes, and Function, 1077–1135/1666–1722," in *Society and Cultures in the Early Modern Middle East: Studies on Iran in the Safavid*

provincial governors, community members, and other ulema.[45] Shah Tahmasb was the first monarch to extend critical financial and socio-political support for the ulema. Aside from giving al-Karaki[46] exceptional powers in standardizing Shiʿa law, he assigned a *qazi-yi ahdath* (judge of the night watch), to protect Tabriz's artisans and merchants from the excesses of the chief of police.[47] The latter had to conduct his activities in the presence of the *qazi-yi ahdath*. Those found guilty of undermining peace and order were subject only to "the penalties prescribed by religious law and cannot be fined."[48] Clearly, the Shah was giving precedence to the judges' decisions over coercive pressure from the chief of police.

The majority of civil cases went through the shariʿa courts. The *shaykh al-Islam* and the *qazis* received peoples' claims (*daʿawa*) and solved legal disputes all weekdays except for Friday.[49] The judge's decisions were executed by the state's *maqamat*, that is, the highest law-enforcement officers. The chief of police was expected to maintain public order based on the general moral edicts of the shariʿa, and hence worked closely with the judges. Other officials were responsible for maintaining public order, and supplied important information about violations and offenders to the judge. The mayor (*kalantar*),[50] the leader of city quarters, senior heads of guilds, town wardens (*kadkhuda*), and night-watches, and the chief of merchants (*malik-al-tujjar*) were expected to uphold the judge's decisions. The manuals of state clearly note that the *shaykh al-Islam* and the *qazi*s attended the ʿurfi courts, and that the *sadr* had to ensure that their "religious–legal judgments" were executed by the *divan-begi*.[51] The *qazi*s appear to have adjudicated on legal offenses and crimes committed by malcontents in their towns and city quarters, but they did not handle those committed by rebels, state officials, governors, army officers, and the like.[52]

Two royal decrees (*farmans*) issued by Shah Suleiman (r. 1077/1666–1105/1694) in 1081 Dhu al-Hijja 1081/May 1671 and 1093 Muḥarram/January 1682, give us a good idea of the tasks which devolved to the *shaykh al-Islam* in the cities of Urdubad

Period, Vol. 46, no. 1 (2003): 397–409. See also R.D. McChesney, *Waqf in Central Asia: Four Hundred Years in the History of a Muslim Shrine, 1480–1889* (Princeton, 1991). See also *Dībācheh-yi Qubāleh Qāzī Shukrullah va-Dībācheh-yi Ṣarīḥ al-Mulk*, MS 3850, Vol. 7, Kitābkhānah-yi Millī Malik, Tehran; *Majmūʿa* MS 1: r 52- p, Vol. 16, Kitābkhānah-yi Markazī-yi Dānishgāh-i Tehran.

45 On legal treatises, *responsas*, and *fatawa* see Hossein Modarressi Tabatabaʾi, *An Introduction to Shīʿi Law: A Bibliographical Essay* (London: Ithaca Press, 1984), 95, 106–108, 182, 200, 203, 204–206; Rula Jurdi Abisaab, *Converting Persia*, Appendix III, 156–165. A good example of these *responsas* are found in al-Karakī, *Rasāʾil al-Muḥaqqiq al-Karakī*, 3 vols., ed. Muḥammad al-Ḥassūn (Qum: Maṭbaʿat al-Khayyām, 1409/1989).

46 Rula Jurdi Abisaab, "Karaki," *Encyclopedia Iranica*, Vol. XV, Fasc. 5, 544–547.

47 Muḥammad Yūsuf Vālih Qazvīnī Iṣfahānī, *Khuld-i Barīn*, ed. Mīr Hāshim Muḥaddith (Tehran: Majmūʿah-yi Intishārāt-i Adabī va-Tārīkhī, 1372/1993), 734.

48 Munshī, *ʿĀlam-ārā-yi ʿAbbāsī*, Vol. 1, 240; Savory, *History of Shah ʿAbbas*, Vol. 1, 441.

49 Mīrzā Rafīʿā, *Dastur*, 9.

50 Tehrānī, *Mirʾāt-i Vāridāt*, 119.

51 Mīrzā Rafīʿā, *Dastur*, 3–4, 30; Minorsky, *Tadhkirat al-Mulūk*, 42.

52 Munshī, *ʿĀlam-ārā-yi ʿAbbāsī*, Vol. 1, 342; Mirzā Rafīʿā, *Dastur*, 3.

and Tabriz respectively.[53] These decrees were highlighted by Rasul Jaʿfariyan. The judge registered deeds, validated contracts, attested transactions, and arbitrated in legal conflicts. He divided inheritance, collected the "fifth" (*khums*) and almsgiving (*zakat*) taxes, and decided how they should be distributed. He managed real and movable property of the orphans and the mentally handicapped. He was expected to "enjoin good and forbid wrongdoing," and prevent *fisq* (immorality), *fujur* (fornication), and wine drinking. He was also in charge of appointing and removing the *nuqaba' al-ashraf*, or, those dignitaries who attended to the affairs of seyyeds, the heads of tribes, the callers for prayer, and ritual washers of the dead. These decrees challenge Floor's view that the *naqib al-ashraf* administered justice for the seyyeds independently from the *qazi* and the *shaykh al-Islam*.[54] Local leaders, headmen, and landholders were commanded by the Shah "not to sever their ties" with the clerics. The local governors (*beglerbegis*) and military commanders were also asked to support the *shaykh al-Islam*. More importantly, the royal decree cautioned against the interference of the *sadr* in the *shaykh al-Islam*'s decision to appoint or remove any of the low-ranking clerics and scribes.[55] In other words, these appointments were no longer in the hands of the *sadr*.

The royal decrees of Shah Suleiman extended similar duties and powers to the *qazi*s of Tabriz.[56] The seyyeds, large landholders, dignitaries, policemen, and the ulema were advised to apply the *shaykh al-Islam*'s legal commands. Even though the decrees do not address theft, murder, or rape specifically, the judge and the *shaykh al-Islam* would have to adjudicate on such cases as they become entangled with "prevention of immorality." The judges also took part in legal decisions tied to public welfare and security, which were then communicated directly to the *divanbegi* or through the *sadr*.[57] Judges petitioned the Shah on behalf of civilians caught in military and political conflicts to guarantee safety for them and their children, and to preserve their possessions.[58] One judge appears to have been entrusted with the civil administration of Lar and was directly in charge of preventing theft and attacks on merchants.[59] Judges also acted in unison with provincial governors, viziers, and chiefs of police to execute death punishments for murder committed by disorderly mobs, the riff-raff (*awbash*), and the unruly (*ajlaf*).[60] European travellers offered distinct narratives about the Safavid judges' corruption. Olearius referred to a "corrupt" *qazi* who was found guilty of accepting bribery from both the claimant and the defendant.[61] He did not, however, offer any details. Tavernier contended

[53] Jaʿfariyān, "Shaykh al-Islām-ī dowreh-yi Safavī," accessed online September 2016, http://www.iranicaonline.org/articles/judicial-and-legal-systems-iv-judicial-system-from-the-advent-of-islam-through-the-19th-century. See also Jaʿfariyān's *Dīn va-Siyāsat dar dowreh-yi Safavī*, 398–399; *Siyāsat va-farhang-i*, Vol. 1, 322.

[54] See Mīrzā Rafīʿā, *Dastur*, 113. [55] Jaʿfariyān, "Shaykh al-Islām-ī." [56] Ibid.

[57] Mīrzā Rafīʿā, *Dastur*, 9–10, 30.

[58] Mulla Jalāl, *Rūznāmah-yi*, 249–250. [59] Munshī, *History of Shah ʿAbbas*, Vol. 2, 807.

[60] Bardsīrī, *Tadhkirah-yi*, 391. [61] Olearius, *The Voyages*, 356.

that the "Officers of Justice" were easily corrupted were it not for the imminent fear or threat of punishment from the Shah.[62] He also emphasized the supremacy of the "secular" 'urfi courts over the shari'a ones in handling "civil" legal cases. Yet, in at least two murder cases, which he cared to highlight, he failed to substantiate his views. Moreover, the judge, not the *divan-begi*, appears to have been the first figure approached by the *mudda'i* (claimant).[63]

Tavernier's own accounts undermine his claim of entrenched corruption, as when he wrote that a baker in Isfahan complained to a judge that he was losing profit due to how low the *muhtasib* had fixed the prices for bread. The judge was unsympathetic and replied that he had no say in the matter. The baker, however, offered the judge a gift of fifty *tomans* to have him raise the price of bread. The judge, Tavernier added, was insulted for being considered "a seller of Justice" and directly commanded the police to carry the baker to the piazza where he received a *bastinado*. The baker was also forced to pay another fifty *tomans*, which the judge distributed to the poor.[64]

Some of the elisions and lacunae in another account provided by Tavernier further undermine his discourse about the judges' corruption and their marginal role in resolving civil legal conflicts. His narrative goes as such: a judge in Shiraz had close ties with an influential man accused of committing a murder. His ties to the murderer undermined his administration of justice, and necessitated the intervention of the Royal Council of Justice in Isfahan. After the mother and widow of the slain man made a legal claim against his alleged murderer, the judge tried to offer the claimants money to persuade them to drop their charges against the defendant.[65] They refused to accept the money and "threatened" to take their case to the Shah. At this point, the judge asked the chief of police to take the defendant to Isfahan. He also sent a letter to the Shah petitioning him through the 'urfi court to execute the punishment for his crime. The Shah ordered that the alleged murderer be put to death.

Some the missing details of this legal case can be readily supplied through standard knowledge of legal procedure in a shari'a court, and information from manuals of state about the way the judges' petitions were handled by the *divan-begi*. When the judge decided to send the defendant handcuffed to Isfahan along with a petition to the justice council, it meant that he had already found the defendant guilty of the crime and that he had him incarcerated. This was due to either the defendant's confession or his non-denial of the claimants' accusations, or through a proof (*bayyina*) based on the testimony of trustworthy witnesses.

What Tavernier failed to understand is that even though the death penalty is prescribed for murder, the charges can be dropped through recompense, that is, the

62 Tavernier, *The Six Voyages*, 232.
63 Ibid., 233–234.
64 Ibid., 234.
65 Ibid., 232.

payment of blood money (*diyya*) to the mother and widow of the slain man. The crime could also be simply forgiven by the victim's family giving the defendant forgiveness (*'afu*). When the judge asked the widow and mother openly if they would accept blood money, which Tavernier had mistaken for "bribery," it meant that the judge had established that the defendant was guilty of murder. When the family refused blood money, the judge had no other option but to recommend the death sentence. As such, whether the judge had close ties with the defendant or not, he followed regular judicial procedure. There is nothing in Tavernier's story that proves that the judge's alleged personal ties undermined his administration of justice.

Lord Stanley, another traveller, attributed the judges' corruption, to the groundless view that they did "not receive pay," and thus were "forced to take bribes."[66] During the late seventeenth century the *qazis* and the *shuyukh al-Islam* each received 200 Tabrizi *tomans* per year, while the *divan-begi* received 500 *tomans*.[67] Sanson found the *divan-begi* corrupt as well. He claimed that the *divan-begi* was unable or unwilling at one point to investigate civilian complaints against injustices committed by a close friend, but Sanson did not provide any further details.[68] To be sure, there were judges who accepted bribery, but the narrative about rampant bribery has no basis in any of the Safavid sources.

Kaempfer, a European traveller who stayed in Isfahan from 1684 to 1685, divided the Safavid justice system into "customary" and "spiritual" law, using church-related terminology to describe the array of posts tied to them. The specificity of this terminology reveals the problems with using a secular–religious dichotomy to describe the Safavid legal system as many modern scholars have done.[69] Kaempfer wrote that "spiritual law" was observed by the *qazi*s and the "pontiff," by which he meant, the *sadr*. He equated the latter, erroneously, with the Grand Mufti of the Ottoman Empire and mixed up some of his tasks with those of the Safavid *shaykh al-Islam*. This confusion is indicative of the problem with sharply dividing the *shari'a-'urfi* justice system, as Kaempfer cannot neatly associate the *sadr*, who combined "worldly and spiritual authorities"[70] with either. Kaempfer noted that civil disputes had to go in front of the *qazi*s who adjudicated all types of violations except capital offences, such as *qatl* (murder), *tajawuz* (transgression), *hatk-i namus* (violating chastity and honor), *irad-i jarh* (intentional injuring), and *sariqat* (theft). The Shah's authority, in his view, was complemented by the clerics, and the "provosts of the mosques," that is, the "spiritual" guides who adjudicated civil matters while the Shah saw to capital offences.[71] In doing so, Kaempfer was superimposing upon the Safavid justice system a particular division between *regularis* and *saecularis*, evident in Europe

[66] Lord Stanley, ed., *Travels to Tana and Persia by Josafa Barbaro and Ambrogio Contarini*, trans. William Thomas (London: Hakluyt Society, 1873), 216. See also Floor, "The Secular Judicial System," 12–13.

[67] Mīrzā Rafī`ā, *Dastur*, 31.

[68] Sanson, *The Present State of Persia*, 112.

[69] Kaempfer, *Am Hofe*, 80–81.

[70] Ibid., 97.

[71] Ibid.

at the time, as an opposition between worldliness and non-worldliness, rather than as an opposition between the Church and state that would develop later in the Enlightenment period. In another place, he notes that, "not only in the capital but also in the country towns the observation of the law lies in the hands of a spiritual judge."[72] This statement does not cohere with Kaempfer's depiction of the clerics as non-worldly, but the terminology he used maintains his artificial division.

With respect to the *qazis*' amenability to corruption, which Kaempfer read about in earlier travelogues, he responded with a narrative about the gullibility of the common believer. He was doubtful that "cunning or corruption" could be the cause for the Shah's or layperson's reverence toward the mujtahid who possessed "unrivalled scholarship" and "apparent holiness." Rather, the "simple-minded credo"[73] of the laity allowed the mujtahid to have such power, for the laity believe that he has the "correct interpretation of the Qur'an and the oral traditions of the Prophet and the holy twelve Imams."[74]

Kaempfer's attention to the laity alerts us to the fact that the "corruption" thesis, in general, rests on the presumption that the Shah held absolute power and reigned supreme, and that monetary reward and fear of the Shah alone guaranteed the delivery of justice. The Shah's authority, however, should be properly placed within a framework of patrimonial politics. As such, at least part of his authority is negotiated. Moreover, as Islamic dynasties rose and fell, judges and chief judges carried out their legal tasks, which were also moral obligations, unhindered. Some judges were amenable to bribery, and found ways to bend the law in self-interest, but this did not prevent the shari'a court system as a whole from functioning effectively and dispensing justice to civilians from all walks of life.[75]

In *Tadhkirah-yi Ṣafaviyya-yi Kirmān*, Bardsiri (alive in 1105) offers rare accounts of a powerful *shaykh al-Islam*, Shah 'Abd al-'Ali, who challenged the authority of Hatam Beg, the vizier of Kirman, and carried out physical threats against others.[76] Bardsiri, was an influential scribe and accountant (*mustawfi*) at the court of Hatam Beg, and shared the latter's animosity toward Shah 'Abd al-'Ali.[77] He paints, however, a complex picture of alliances and competitions, noting that the mayor was also the archenemy of the *shaykh al-Islam* while the chief of police was his ally.[78] He also notes that one *qazi*, Salmanshah, was closely tied to the vizier and Mirza Abu Salih, the *sadr*, and stood up against the succeeding *shaykh al-Islam*, namely, Mirza Muzaffar Husayn.

Bardsiri's loyalties come through when he uses the words, "*mazbur neveshtehjat*" to refer to *qazi* Salmanshah's attempt to buy off certain officials, and calls the same

[72] Ibid., 100. [73] Ibid. [74] Ibid.

[75] For references to upright *qazis* see Iṣfahānī, *Khuld-i Barīn*, ed. Muḥaddith, 123, 199, 319–320, 427, 430, 484; Mulla Jalāl, *Rūznāmah-yi*, 250; ʿAbd al-Ḥusayn Khwātūnābādī, *Vaqāyiʿu Sinīn va'l-Aʿvām*, (Tehran: Intishārāt-i Vahīd, 1352/1973), 542.

[76] Bardsīrī, *Tadhkirah-yi*, 218–219, 311, 473. [77] Ibid., 142–149. [78] Ibid., 261.

act by the *shaykh al-Islam* a "*reshvat*" or bribery.[79] Meanwhile, Bardsiri includes a precarious account tied to Mirza Muzaffar Husayn, and accuses him of forging the signature of the *sadr* Mirza Abu Salih on a letter directing insults at the Shah.[80] The modern Iranian historian, Muhammad Ibrahim Bastani Parizi, correctly argued that the story of the forged signature does not seem to be reliable, a detail that Bardsiri failed to mention.[81] Parizi also added that Kaempfer reproduced a version of this precarious account in his travelogue.[82]

Overall, Bardsiri's chronicle shows that the *shaykh al-Islam* did not have a free hand. He was incapable of undermining the *qazi*'s functions. The multiple spheres of influence at the provincial and central levels, as well as intra-elite competition guaranteed that no one was able to dictate systematically the outcome of a conflict.[83] Judges and *shuyukh al-Islam* were drawn from powerful propertied seyyed families but equally from modest backgrounds.[84] When it came to capital offenses, the *shaykh al-Islam* acted in unison with the *sadr*, the vizier, the mayor, and the chief of police. When a murder was committed by one of the *ashrar* (evildoers) against another, the *shaykh al-Islam* issued a death sentence and all parties signed a petition upholding his ruling, which was then sent to the *divan-begi* in Isfahān.[85] The *divan-begi* acted upon the petition relying only on the legal decision stated therein, for he had no recourse to other proofs in Isfahan. The *shaykh al-Islam* in Kirman appears to have regularly directed official requests to the *divan-i ʿadalat* to execute decisions tied to such crimes.[86]

There are important considerations when trying to understand why the *divan-begi* and not the shariʿa judge executed the death sentence. Shiʿa law like all schools of Islamic law acknowledged three types of shariʿa-based punishments. The first, the *hudud* (pl. of *hadd*) are fixed punishments for offenses against God's right such as adultery, false accusation of adultery, theft, consumption of alcohol, and highway robbery. The second, the *qisas* are punishments in the form of retaliation in kind against transgressions such as injury and homicide, which are considered offenses committed against other humans.[87] *Taʿzir* is discretionary punishment for an array of wrongful acts, decided by the judge.[88]

[79] Ibid., 472–476. [80] Ibid., 349–353. [81] Ibid., 475–476, footnote 2.

[82] Kaempfer, *Am Hofe*, 99. [83] Bardsīrī, *Tadhkirah-yi*, 612–614, 622–624, 643–644.

[84] Ibid., 35, 39, 219, 485–486; Mīrzā ʿAbdullah Afandī, *Riyāḍ al-ʿUlamāʾ wa-Ḥiyāḍ al-Fuḍalāʾ*, Vol. 2, ed. Aḥmad al-Ḥusaynī (Qum: Manshūrāt Maktabat Āyatullah Marʿashī, 1403/1980), 261–266; Vol. 5, 180–182.

[85] Bardsīrī, *Tadhkirah-yi*, 391. [86] Ibid., 391, 456.

[87] There are a few differences between Shiʿa law and the various Sunni schools of law with respect to these areas of punishment. To give but one example, under Shiʿa law, a blind person who kills another is liable to blood money only and not to *hadd*. See al-Ḥurr al-ʿĀmilī, *Wasāʾil al-Shīʿa*, Vol. 29 (Qum: Mehr, 1414/1993), 399.

[88] On punishments see al-ʿAllāma al-Ḥillī, *Taḥrīr al-Aḥkām*, Vol. 5, ed. Ibrāhīm al-Bahādirī (Qum: Iʿtimād, 1422/2001), 301–647. Al-Shahid al-Awwal delineated ten differences between the legal categories of *hadd* and *taʿzir*. See *Al-Qawāʿid wa-al-Fawāʾid*, Vol. 2, ed. ʿAbd al-Hādī al-Ḥakīm (Qum: Manshūrāt Maktabat al-Mufīd, n.d.), 142–143.

A number of Twelver Shiʿa jurists and *shuyukh al-Islam* were reluctant to apply the *hudud* in the absence of the Imām.[89] We do not know the extent to which this view was reflected in judgeship during the Safavid period. What we do know, however, is that judges who issued verdicts in the domains of criminal and penal law needed guarantees that their lives would be protected if the police executed these verdicts. Otherwise, they would suffer retaliation from the defendants' family members or cohort, be they commoners, influential dignitaries, or rebel groups. To give one example, the head of the Bayat tribe in Erevan was displeased by the legal verdict of the *shaykh al-Islam* and killed him.[90]

Even the legal handling of civilians' monies required protection. In Lar, in 1012 Muharram/July 1603 *qazi* ʿAbd al-Ḥayy was robbed and killed by thieves while he was sorting out some accounts (*muhasabat*).[91] The judge's death was blamed on the shortcomings of the chief of police, and his inadequate defense against the attackers. The judges depended, as such, on those who held direct policing and military power. This gave them a good reason to turn to the highest exective authority in the empire, the Shah, to execute their decisions.[92] Yet, the Shah and the *divan-begi* had a free hand in the type of punishment carried out. They were not bound by the stipulations of Shiʿa law.

D. The *Divan-begi*

The *divan-begi*'s post grew in importance and scope due to the policing needs of the state during the late sixteenth century.[93] The *divan-begis* were drawn predominantly from among the Qizilbash households.[94] They watched over politically unstable Iranian regions and frontiers, reporting acts of revolt to the Shah, and subduing them while working closely with the provincial governors and emirs.[95] In time, the *divan-begi*

[89] From the time of al-ʿAllama onward, the Twelver Shiʿa jurists supported the permissibility of applying *qisas* and *hudud* during the absence of the Imam. See al-ʿAllāma, *Taḥrīr al-Aḥkām*, 321. Al-Muhaqqiq al-Karaki, however, hesitated about endorsing its permissibility even though he considered himself a mujtahid who fulfilled all the conditions of *wilaya ʿamma* (general deputyship of the Imam) entrusted with such an authority. See al-Karaki, *Rasāʾil al-Muḥaqqiq*, Vol. 1, 142–143. Al-Muqaddas al-Ardabili, in contrast, and despite his refusal to associate with the Shah, legitimized the application of these punishments in *Majmaʿ al-Fāʾida wa-al-Burhān*, Vol. 12 (Qum: Muʾassassat al-Nashr al-Islāmī, 1414/1994), 18.

[90] Iṣfahānī, *Khuld-i Barīn*, parts 6 and 7, section 8, 303.

[91] Mullā Jalāl, *Rūznāmah-yi*, 242.

[92] Minorsky, *Tadhkirat al-mulūk*, 72, 74.

[93] Naṣīrī Urdūbādī, *Alqāb va-Mavājib-i Dowreh-yi Salāṭīn-i Ṣafaviyya*, ed. Yūsuf Raḥīm-Lū (Mashhad: Dānishgāh-i Firdowsī-yi Mashhadī, 1372/1953), 22–23. See Minorsky, *Tadhkirat al-mulūk*, 44; Munshi, *ʿĀlam-ārā-yi*, Vol. 3, 1765. See also Qādī Aḥmad Qummī, *Khulāṣat*, Vol. 1, 83, 384, 394, 487.

[94] Iṣfahānī, *Khuld-i Barīn*, ed. Muḥaddith, 657; Vahīd Qazvīnī, *ʿAbbāsnāmah*, 187.

[95] Iskandar Beg, *ʿĀlam-ārā-yi ʿAbbāsi*, Vol. 2, 1464; Vol. 3, 1765; Vālih Iṣfahānī, *Irān dar Zamān*, 62–66, 214.

evolved into the chief of the *majlis-i dadresi*, the council of justice, and was charged with executing the Shah's verdicts, and hence, articulate the Safavids' *siyasa shar'iyya*.[96] One account has it that Shah 'Abbas ordered the vizier and the *divan-begi*, known as Kalb-i 'Ali Shamlu, and the chief of police, to summon one of the slaves (*ghulams*) of the royal household to investigate a murder.[97] The *divan-begi*, without waiting for a formal command from the vizier, went to arrest the *ghulam* after which he and his brothers confessed to having committed the murder.

The *divan-begi* relied on the directions of the *sadr-i khassa* primarily or the *vizier* before carrying out his tasks. The *sadr-i khassa* sat jointly with the *divan-begi* in the guardhouse (*keshik-khanah*), at the main gate of the royal palace, the 'Ali Qapu, every Saturday and Sunday to examine petitions and peoples' claims.[98] For two other days during the week, the *divan-begi* addressed "civil cases" brought by commoners at his residence.[99] On Saturdays and Sundays in the guardhouse, however, the *divan-begi* would investigate petitions that fell in four major areas considered capital offences: murder, transgression, violating chastity, and theft.[100] Mirza Rafi'a, however, described the four capital offences (*ahdath-i arba'a*) as murder, rape of virgins (*izalah-yi bakarat*), breaking of teeth, and blinding.[101]

It is only with respect to executing these four capital offences that the *divan-begi* was presented as acting, at least theoretically, independently of the *sadr-i khassa*, the *shaykh al-Islam*, and the *qazis*.[102] Mirza Rafi'a himself and the Safavid chronicles suggest, however, that in practice, this was not always the case.[103] A number of capital offense punishments were executed at the 'urfi court, and appear to have been judicially handled by the *qazis*.[104] The *sadr-i khassa* made sure that the shari'a courts' decisions were executed by the *divan-begi*, and that punishments for religious transgressions were "in accordance with" the verdict of the *qazis*.[105] This would include punishments against intoxication, adultery, and apostasy. The crime of rape, too, was not outside the purview of a *qazi*'s jurisdiction as the implementer of the shari'a. In Tabriz, a *qazi* by the name of Muhammad appears to have adjudicated on a case of rape while the governor, Haydar Beg, executed the punishment, cutting off the ears and noses of those found guilty of committing the rape.[106] Clearly, such a punishment exceeded the stipulations of Shi'a law.

[96] On the various features of this post, see Mulla Jalāl, *Rūznāmah-yi*, 227; Qaḍī Aḥmad Qummī, *Khulāṣat*, Vol. 1, 681, 763.

[97] Iskandar Beg, *ʿĀlam-ārā-yi*, Vol. 2, 1562–1563; Savory, *History of Shah ʿAbbas*, Vol. 2, 1166.

[98] Mīrzā Rafīʿā, *Dastur*, 3; Minorsky, *Tadhkirat al-mulūk*, 42.

[99] Mīrzā Rafīʿā, *Dastur*, 31.

[100] Minorsky, *Tadhkirat al-mulūk*, 12.

[101] Mīrzā Rafīʿā, *Dastur*, 2.

[102] Ibid., 3.

[103] Ibid., 4, 9–10.

[104] Sayyid b. Murtaḍā Ḥusaynī Astarabādī, *Az Shaykh Ṣafī tā Shāh Ṣafī*, ed. Iḥsān Ishrāqī (Tehran, 1364/1985), 250; Jalāl al-Dīn Muḥammad b. Asʿad Dawānī, "Dīvān-i Maẓālim," ed. Hossein Modarressi Tabatabai, *Farhang-i Īrān Zamīn* 27 (1987): 107; Qaḍī Aḥmad Qummī *Khulāṣat*, Vol. 1, 389.

[105] Mīrzā Rafīʿa, *Dastur al-Moluk*, 4, 30.

[106] Qaḍī Aḥmad Qummī, *Khulāṣat*, Vol. 1, 389.

The interconnection between the ʿurfi and the shariʿa systems as such appears to be enhanced through the efforts of the *sadrs*. The latter *sadrs* made sure that the shariʿa court decisions were executed by fusing the sovereign's "political might" with "half of judgeship," to use al-Mawardi's words. Jalal al-Din Dawani (d. 908/1501) elucidated what that means in his *Divan-i Mazalim*.[107] He noted that the awe and retribution of the head of the *mazalim* (tribunal) chancery "prevented people from hiding the truth by using tricks and resorting to falsification."[108] The head of the *mazalim* court is referred to as a "judge" and in our case he would be the equivalent to the *divan-begi*. Certain legal disputes, which may take several years to be resolved in the shariʿa court, were swiftly concluded "in one single *mazalim* court session."[109] This was possible because the *mazalim* judge relied on procedures and proofs that might not be admissibile in a shariʿa court.[110] The *mazalim* judge could admit testimonies, for example, made by absent persons whose trustworthiness is not established. The judge can also add or cancel as many witnesses as he pleases, and may very well start the trial by hearing these witnesses first. But in a shariʿa court, the *qazi* has to ask the claimant to provide a *bayyina* (proof) first for his claim.[111] Witness examiners (*shuhud, ashab al-masa'il*) were asked to attest to the truthfulness of claims and occurrences, and the character of these witnesses was also systematically examined. The judges in a shariʿa court needed to employ permanent inspectors from among the local population. These inspectors became tied to the courts and collaborated with security officers and the police, to learn how, where, and when a person was murdered.

How did the *divan-begi* perform his tasks? In cases of murder, we are told that he relied on a number of local assistants to investigate the matter and report back to him.[112] When he received complaints issued by persons from outside Isfahan, he was, however, unable to rely on these local experts and turned the cases to the Shah. Otherwise, he asked his paid assistants, called *Ajrulu*, to gather specific information about the nature of the crime committed.[113] The *Ajrulu* were located in the neighborhoods of Isfahan or in adjacent towns, which were 10–12 *farsakh* (about 60–70 km) or less away from the court of the *divan-begi*. The *Ajrulu* were permanent employees, paid regular wages based on a declaration of an *iltizam*, that is, an obligation by the plaintiff to pay a fee of five *tomans* to the court to process her/his petition.[114] When the complaint issued from a location quite close to the *divan-begi*, he usually commanded one of his subordinates, through a written requisition called *taʿliqah-yi bayazi*, to summon the two sides and start an investigation

107 Dawānī, "Dīvān-i maẓālim," 107–118. 108 Ibid., 107. 109 Ibid.
110 Al-Māwardī, *Al-Aḥkām*, 105. 111 Ibid. 112 Mīrzā Rafīʿā, *Dastur al-Moluk*, 31.
113 Ibid., 30.
114 Ibid., 3, 30–31. I gave a different translation of the term *iltizam* than the one offered by Floor and Faghfoory. They described the *ilitzam* as "caution-money."

(*ghowr-rasi*). The *ta'liqah* (a written requisition) also carried instructions for the chief of the corpse washers (*ghassal-bashi*) to start a preliminary investigation into cases of murder to specify how a victim had been killed. Clearly, then, the *divan-begi*'s court was not devoid of procedures and the task of providing proofs. It also relied as much as possible on the *qazis*' petitions.

A number of travelogues gave the impression that judges were irrelevant to the 'urfi court, and that no adjudication of any kind took place. Themes about arbitrary and despotic rule appear to be intertwined with a narrative of judicial failure.[115] Sanson wrote that there were "neither Messengers, Councellors, or Attorneys."[116] Everyone "pleads for himself, and defends his own Right," and he who "Speaks loudest has commonly the better of the Day."[117] Tavernier surmised too that the administration of justice is "exact and speedy," without any reliance on "Advocates or Proctors."[118] Yet, he contradicts himself when he stresses in another place the significance of the legal labor of the *qazis* who "do Justice in their Provinces" and who represent the Shah himself.

The ties, which the *divan-begi*'s court maintained with the *sadr*, the judges, and the *shaykh al-Islam*, and the notion of justice, which the Shah projected, reveal the inadequacy of describing the 'urfi courts as "secular." There is no actual separation or hard line between the 'urfi and the shari'a courts. The term also fails to depict the complex connections between various socio-legal actors, activities, and institutions. It does not fit with the way renaissance humanists understood it. Nor does it cohere with the way later Enlightenment thinkers articulated it, namely, as an anti-religious mode of thought. As I noted earlier, the separation between clerics who retreat from public life, and those who handle clerical day-to-day affairs, which took place in Europe, is irrelevant to Islamic society.

Chardin hailed the "secular" courts for protecting non-Muslims.[119] Membré also depicted a secular judicial process at play.[120] Olearius, attempting to fit Safavid legal roles into a European Christian framework, disclosed nonetheless, a form of interdependence between the shari'a and the 'urfi courts. He wrote that the *divan-begi*'s main function was presiding,

> at the judgement of Criminal causes, jointly with the Seder [Sadr] and the Kadi, and the other Ecclesiastical and Secular Judges, whom they call Schehra and OËf, under the Portal of the King's Palace, at the place named Diwan-Chané; and to be personally present at the executions of Malefactors.[121]

That an 'urfi court would have so many shari'a experts, did not change the insistence by modern scholars on a binary legal system. Olearius mentioned the

[115] Sanson, *The Present State of Persia*, 137. [116] Ibid. [117] Ibid., 137–138.
[118] Tavernier, *The Six Voyages*, 232.
[119] Chardin, *The Travels of Sir John Chardin; The Coronation of Solayman III*, 87.
[120] Michele Membré, *Mission to the Lord Sophy of Persia (1539–1542)*, trans. A. H. Morton, London, 1993.35.
[121] Olearius, *The Voyages*, 367.

adjudication process that takes place at the *'urfi* court. After hearing both sides of a civil dispute, he wrote, the *divan-begi* turned to the judges present at the council.[122] The judges gave their decision about the case, which was then mediated to the Shah, who decided what action to take. Yet, in another place, confusion creeps back into Olearius's narrative. He writes that, "Civil causes are commonly try'd before Secular Judges whom they call Oef"[123] and described the "Secular Judges" as "Kind of Lawyers" whose chief is the *divan-begi*, who "ought to be well vers'd in the Law of Mahomet."[124] This confusion about the *divan-begi*'s alleged expertise in the shari'a goes to show that the interconnection between various legal actors is profound and difficult to explain in European terms.

Tavernier too organized his narrative around two spheres of justice, which modern scholars treated as separate from each other. He wrote that Iran's provincial governors tried hard to compensate merchants and travellers for stolen goods, lest they complain to the Shah. On the road from Lar to Shiraz, he was robbed of two bales of goods with the value of 1,400 *piasters*.[125] When he complained to the governor of Shiraz, the latter asked him to take an oath on his own sacred book, in order to confirm the truthfulness of what he said. Tavernier took the oath and the governor paid him all his loss in gold.

It was the case that whenever governors received such complaints, they would only rely on this oath. This extralegal act rests on a shared belief that God would punish a person who evokes His name in a lie. If the provincial governor asked for such an oath, it does not empty it of sacredness. It does not make it secular. Wael Hallaq noted that the oath, "carried with it a major transcendental liability."[126] The Shah's justice too is not simply secular. It is intertwined with a notion of a divinely endowed kingship, which defends the "shari'a *gharra*" (revered shari'a), and famous sayings of the Twelve Imams.

III. Superiority of the 'Urfi Court Revisited

Floor argued that the 'urfi "secular" court was efficient, just, and superior to its "religious" counterpart.[127] His views resonated with those of S.H. Amin, who

[122] Ibid., 370. [123] Ibid. [124] Ibid.
[125] Tavernier, *The Six Voyages*, 233. [126] Hallaq, *Sharī'a*, 173.
[127] Floor, "Mazalem,"; "The Secular Judicial System in Safavid Persia," 9–60.

noted that customary and governmental laws were given "precedence over Islamic law."[128] Ahmad Pakatchi argued in turn that the Shahs' and viziers' execution of punishments was a remedy to the chaos in the religious judicial system.[129] Floor also stated that the mujtahids exercised "considerable influence over the religious courts."[130] The notion of "influence" remains vague, but if it means that they forced the outcome of legal cases handled by the *qazis*, then this is unfounded, for neither the sources nor the travelogues warrant such a conclusion. In fact, there was an organic link between the mujtahid and the judge: the former derives the body of substantive laws which the judge must rely upon to arrive at a legal decision. The mujtahid did not normally sit in the judge's court but the judge consulted with him at times on knotty legal cases.

As for civilians' attitudes toward the courts, Floor stated that the "lower classes were apprehensive" and worried about approaching the 'urfi court officials because "justice was swift and immediate."[131] Yet, in another place he contradicts himself by concluding that civilians favored the "secular court" because decisions were taken within a "reasonable" time framework.[132] In fact, the execution itself was quick but in many cases the decisions were issued earlier and included in the petitions received by the *divan-begi*.[133] If the claimants already knew that the judge's decision was in their favor, then surely they would hail the swiftness by which the *divan-begi* would execute it. Otherwise, swiftness was considered dangerous and risky.

The travellers oscillated between two contradictory views with respect to the 'urfi courts. One view emphasized the cruelty and arbitrariness of the punishments. Another view presented such cruelty and terror as necessary in maintaining security and public order. Sanson regretted that only the *qazis*, the chief of police, and the Shah himself could issue or carry out the death sentence.[134] He and others made numerous references to the "mutation of organs," the cutting off of noses, ears, and sometimes feet and hands for minor offenses.[135] Tavernier commented on the severity of punishments tied to the policing of prices of bread, meat, grains, and

[128] Amīn, *Tārīkh-i ḥuqūq-i Īrān*, 333. [129] Pakatchī, "Ḥuqūq," 626.

[130] Floor, "Mazalem." [131] Floor, "The Secular Judicial System," 30, 31.

[132] Whether Shi'a or Sunnite, Islamic judgeship permitted claimants to seek the opinion of more than one *qazi* and to try and maximize their chances in arriving at a favorable decision. Strangely, however, Floor blamed the delay in resolving disputes to the pluralistic nature of Shi'a legal consultation. He appears to think that the Sunnite juristic principle of "*kull mujtahid musib*," (every grand jurist's legal opinion is authoritative) goes against such pluralism. Yet, this is not the case and the Shi'a also have a cognate principle, namely, "*li-al-mujtahid al-mukhti' ajr wa-li-al-musib ajran*," which denotes that the jurist may err in deriving the law, but he receives one reward for trying and two rewards for arriving at the accurate opinion. See Al-'Allāma, *Mabādi' al-Wuṣūl ilā 'Ilm al-Uṣūl*, ed. 'A. Baqqāl (Tehran: al-Maṭba'a al-'Ilmiyya, 1984), 240; al-Fāḍil al-Tūnī, *Al-Wāfiya fī Uṣūl al-Fiqh*, ed. M. Ḥusayn al-Raḍawī al-Kashmīrī (Qum: Majma' al-Fikr al-Islāmī, 1411/1991), 301–304.

[133] Mīrzā Rafī'ā, *Dastur al-Moluk*, 30. [134] Sanson, *The Present State of Persia*, 137.

[135] Chardin, *The Travels of Sir John Chardin; The Coronation of Solyman III*, 88–89; Olearius, *The Voyages*, 370; Sanson, *The Present State of Persia*, 137–138; Tavernier, *The Six Voyages*, 232–233.

provisions of belly-timber.[136] A person accused of usury in Ardabil had his teeth knocked out. Tavernier mentioned milder punishments for the same violations, and hence, inconsistency. Merchants who were arrested for using "false weights" were led in the streets with a "bonnet like a Bee-hive" placed on their heads and a bell around their necks to expose them to public ridicule.[137] Afterwards they were fined and received a *bastinado*.

Sanson wrote at length in support of the superiority of the 'urfi courts in delivering justice, taking as proof a legal dispute over the payment of debts. His unfamiliarity with the basic features of Islamic law leaves us with an impressionistic view of what actually happened. He noted that it was impossible for a "Plaintiff to prove his Debt" to the judge.[138] The shari'a court, he noted, "always" gave the defendant who confessed a debt, "a reasonable time for payment."[139] The defendant, he added, might deny the debt even against a judge's own testimony, escaping all responsibility despite having affirmed such a debt with his own handwriting.[140] Sanson proceeded to argue that it is unjust on the part of the judge to ask a creditor to provide him with a proof of a loan, which he claimed to have given to a debtor. Sanson's narrative is undermined further by sarcasm and fabrications,

> According to their [Islamic] laws, they must produce Seventy Two witnesses, who must all very near equal the Imams in Integrity, if not wholly. The experts Words of the Law are these, That to be believ'd, the witnesses must be either Imams, or Naib Imams, that is, Saints, or Deputies of Saints. There are not wanting in Persia People that can equal these pretended Saints in Adultery, Knavery, and Murther [Murder].[141]

Sanson's ignorance about the criteria used to establish a witness's qualifications allows him to embellish his discourse about deceitful and adulterous Persians.[142] He is unaware that even a visitor has the right to testify, as well as a slave, unless he is testifying in a case involving his owner. As for loans, it is permissible under Shi'a law to perform a verbal contract for a loan, but it is strongly recommended that a written one be made to avoid problems of verification.[143] If the debt is disputed, the lender can prove it through the testimony of two men, one man and two women, or one man and an oath.[144] Testifying to be a witness to a testimony is also

136 Tavernier, *The Six Voyages*, 234.
137 Ibid., 233–234.
138 Sanson, *The Present State of Persia*, 138, 140.
139 Ibid., 138.
140 Ibid., 139.
141 Ibid., 139–140.
142 On witnesses see al-Muḥaqqiq al-Ḥillī, *Sharā'i' al-Islām fī Masā'il al-Ḥalāl wa-al-Ḥarām*, Vol. 4, ed. Sayyid Ṣādiq al-Shīrāzī (Qum: Dār al-Imān, 1409/1988–89), 910–920.
143 Al-Muḥaqqiq al-Ḥillī, *Sharā'i' al-Islām*, Vol. 2, 324–325; Muḥammad b. al-Ḥasan al-Ḥurr al-'Āmilī (d. 1104), *Wasā'il al-Shī'a ilā Taḥṣīl Masā'il al-Sharī'a*, Vol. 18, 331–334, 338–341, 347–350, 369. Also when performing an oral transaction, the two parties are urged to have two male witnesses, or two female and a male witness, present. See *The Holy Qur'an*, trans. Abdullah Yusuf 'Ali, Sūrat al-Baqara, Āya 282, http://www.muslimaccess.com/quraan/translations/yusufali/002.htm.
144 Al-'Allāma, *Qawā'id al-Aḥkām*, Vol. 3 (Qum: Mu'assassat al-Nashr al-Islāmī, 1419/1998), 499; Al-Shahīd al-Thānī, *Masālik al-Afhām*, Vol. 14 (Qum: Mu'assasat al-Ma'ārif al-Islāmiyya: 1419/1998), 255. Al-Fāḍil al-Hindī, *Kashf al-Lithām*, Vol. 10 (Qum: Mu'assassat al-Nashr al-Islāmī, 1416/1995), 329.

accepted.[145] When the period for paying back the debt is provisional, the borrower can pay back the debt anytime. But when the lender demands her/his property at the expiration of the specified period in which she/he has the right to seek this property, it is obligatory upon the borrower to promptly pay her/his debt immediately.[146] To deliberately delay on repayment of a loan is a transgression. However, if the debtor does not own anything except the house in which she/he lives and money for basic daily needs, it is obligatory upon the lender to grant her/him time to pay. The lender is not permitted to force the debtor to sell her/his house or other bare necessities of life. At the same time, it is obligatory that the debtor strive to pay the loan through some additional earnings or by offering her/his labor to repay the debt. It is recommended but not obligatory for the debtor to return the same property to the lender for she/he can return its value in different ways.[147]

If someone denies a debt, the *qazi* calls witnesses to appear in person to his court and have them deliver their testimonies orally in front of him. The burden of proof (*bayyina*) falls on the claimant, and the oath of denial is allowed to the defendant in case the claimant fails to provide evidence in support of her/his allegations or simply when the *qazi* deems it necessary to do so. The witnesses' testimonies may shed light on the character of the defendant or the claimant or the status of the loan. After studying the testimonies and the details of the case the *qazi* arrives at a decision. Those chosen to be witnesses and allowed to sign papers need a collective social endorsement that they are pious, upright, and trustworthy. Some of them are also expected to be knowledgeable about people and events in their communities.

Practical knowledge, experience, and resourcefulness of the *qazi* within each local setting was critical in gathering proof. In this respect, one must define judgeship (*qazavat*) broadly, and recognize provincial differences and variations as well as change over time.[148] Judgeship also relied on a network of informal ties and negotiations that unfolded outside the walls of a shariʿa court.[149] The transparency, procedures of calling witnesses, gathering proofs, listening to confessions, and issuing legal decisions in a shariʿa court, were, in the eyes of Safavid jurists, superior to the methods evident at the ʿurfi court. In a shariʿa court it was inconceivable that the *qazi* would execute rule purely based on his own discretion. As Hossein Modarressi noted, the judge was not permitted to use any sort of intimidation, coercion, or torture during the investigation.[150] On the other hand, beating and torture were used in many cases to get a confession at the ʿurfi courts. Penalties

145 Al-Shahīd al-Thānī, *Masālik*, Vol. 14, 269.

146 See al-Karakī, *Rasāʾil al-Muḥaqqiq al-Karakī*, Vol. 2, 190; Al-Shaykh al-Ṭūsī, *Tahdhīb al-Aḥkām*, Vol. 7 (Tehran: Khūrshīd, 1365sh/1986–87), 22.

147 al-Karakī, *Rasāʾil al-Muḥaqqiq al-Karakī*, Vol. 2, 310; Vol. 3, 129.

148 Mīrzā Vahīd, *Tārīkh-i Jahān-ārā-yi ʿAbbāsī*, 307.

149 Wael Hallaq, *Sharīʿa: Theory, Practice, Transformation* (Cambridge: Cambridge University Press, 2009), 173–174.

150 Hossein Modarressi Tabatabai, "Dīvān-i maẓālim," *Farhang-i Īrān zamīn*, no. 27 (1366/1987): 98–118. See p. 105.

and punishments exceeded many a time those prescribed by the shariʿa. It is possible that the *mullabashi*,[151] the highest religious authority in the late Safavid period, attempted to check abuses at the ʿurfi courts. He was expected to help the poor, lift injustice, and intercede on behalf of sinners.[152] In other words, he was allowed to intervene in the execution of verdicts and ask for a lesser punishment or forgiveness.

IV. Conclusion

Legal roles and processes in the Safavid justice system unfolded within a religious framework, reflecting the interface between ideal stipulations and practical ends, and between public shariʿa-derived law and private monarchical law. The shariʿa and ʿurfi courts were as such interdependent and provided overlays of jurisdiction. The *sadr* had legal–administrative expertise, and held, through his post, the threads that tied the authority of the shariʿa to the monarch's might. He navigated various public and private domains of the law, consulting regularly with the *shaykh al-Islam* and the *qazis*. He expected the Shah to intervene, coerce, and punish in his capacity as monarch.

The *qazi*s in the provinces appear to have accommodated the discrepancy between the Shah's punishments and the shariʿa-prescribed ones because they did not enjoy full protection against the retaliation of a defendant or his family, cohort, or tribe. The relationship between the shariʿa and ʿurfi courts was not purely cooperative, for the *sadr*s and later the *mullabashi*s, along with other state and community agents, tried to exploit tensions in this relationship. Hallaq referred to "judicial relativism" to describe the medieval *qadi*s' accommodation of an existing power structure or state of affairs.[153] Safavid *qazi*s too were forced to balance competing interests while trying to curb the abuses of the powerful.

Like the ʿurfi courts, the tribunals were explained as acts of benevolence emanating from the practice of justice by a monarch whose rule was seen as blessed and preordained. To this we must add the monarch's support for the ulema in perpetuating Twelver Shiʿism. Meanwhile, holding tribunals and issuing ʿurfi verdicts deflected anger and social discontent away from the Shahs and onto their subordinates and officials. They also provided mechanisms of relief for the poor against oppressive taxes and abuses of government officials. Finally, they allowed the Shahs to offest the interests of the administrative and military officials in the capital city and the provinces.

[151] Said Amir Arjomand, "The Office of Mulla-Bashi in Shiʿite Iran," *Studia Islamica*, no. 57 (1983): 138–140.

[152] Mīrzā Rafīʿā, *Dastur*, 1–2.

[153] Hallaq, *Sharīʿa*, 165.

References

Abisaab, Rula Jurdi, "Peasant Uprisings in Astarabad: the *Siyāh Pūshān* (wearers of black), the Sayyids, and the Safavid State." *Iranian Studies* 49, no. 3 (April 2016): 477–481.

Abisaab, Rula Jurdi, "Karaki," in *Encyclopedia Iranica*, Vol. XV, Fasc. 5, 544–547.

Al-ʿAllāma al-Ḥillī, *Taḥrīr al-Aḥkām*, Vol. 5, ed. Ibrāhīm al-Bahādirī (Qum: Iʿtimād, 1422/ 2001).

Al-ʿAllāma al-Ḥillī, *Qawāʿid al-Aḥkām*, Vol. 3, (Qum: Muʾassasat al-Nashr al-Islāmī, 1419/ 1998).

Al-ʿĀmilī, ʿAlī b. ʿAbd al-ʿĀlī al-Karakī, *Rasāʾil al-Muḥaqqiq al-Karakī*, 3 vols., ed. Muḥammad al-Ḥassūn (Qum: Maṭbaʿat al-Khayyām, 1409/1989).

Al-ʿĀmilī, Muḥammad al-Ḥurr, *Wasāʾil al-Shīʿa*, Vol. 29 (Qum: Mehr, 1414/1993).

Al-Fāḍil al-Hindī, *Kashf al-Lithām*, Vol. 10, (Qum: Muʾassasat al-Nashr al-Islāmī, 1416/1995).

Al-Māwardī, *Al-Aḥkām al-Sulṭāniyya* (Beirut: Dār al-Kutub al-ʿIlmiyya, n.d.)

Al-Muḥaqqiq al-Ḥillī, *Sharāʾiʿ al-Islām fī Masāʾil al-Ḥalāl wa-al-Ḥarām*, Vol. 4, ed. Sayyid Ṣādiq al-Shīrāzī (Qum: Dār al-Imān, 1409/1988–89).

Al-Muqaddas al-Ardabīlī, *Majmaʿ al-Fāʾida wa-al-Burhān*, Vol. 12. (Qum: Muʾassasat al-Nashr al-Islāmī, 1414/1994).

Al-Shahīd al-Awwal, *Al-Qawāʿid wa-al-Fawāʾid*, Vol. 2, ed. ʿAbd al-Hādī al-Ḥakīm (Qum: Manshūrāt Maktabat al-Mufīd, n.d.)

Al-Shahīd al-Thānī, *Masālik al-Afhām*, Vol. 14, (Qum: Muʾassasat al-Maʿārif al-Islāmiyya: 1419/1998).

Al-Shaykh al-Ṭūsī, *Tahdhīb al-Aḥkām*, Vol. 7, (Tehran: Khūrshīd, 1365sh/1986–87).

Amīn, S.H., *Tārīkh-i Ḥuqūq-i Īrān* (Tehran: Intishārāt-i Dāʾirat al-Maʿārif-i Irānshināsī, 2003).

Amīr Maḥmūd b. Khwāndamīr, *Iran dar Rūzgār-i Shāh Ismāʿīl va-Shāh Tāhmāsb Safavī*, ed. Ghulāmrezā Ṭabāṭabāʾī (Tehran: Bunyād-i Mawqūfāt-i Duktūr Maḥmūd Afshār Yazdī, 1991).

Arjomand, Said Amir, "The Office of Mulla-Bashi in Shiʿite Iran." *Studia Islamica*, no. 57 (1983): 138–140.

Asad, Talal, *Formations of the Secular: Christianity, Islam, Modernity* (Stanford: Stanford University Press, 2003).

Astarabādī, Sayyid b. Murtaḍā Ḥusaynī, *Az Shaykh Ṣafī tā Shāh Ṣafī*, ed. Iḥsān Ishrāqī. (Tehran, 1364/1985).

Brakensiek, Stefan, "Political Judgement between Empirical Experience and Scholarly Tradition: Engelbert Kaempfer's Report on Persia." *The Medieval History Journal* 5, no. 2 (2002): 223–246.

Chardin, Sir John (1643–1713), *The Travels of Sir John Chardin into Persia, and the East-Indies; The Coronation of Solyman III* (London: Printed for Christopher Bateman, 1691).

Dawānī, Jalāl al-Dīn Muḥammad b. Asʿad, "Dīvān-i Maẓālim," ed. Hossein Modarressi Tabatabai, *Farhang-i Īrān Zamīn*, no. 27 (1987): 98–118.

De Bruyn, Cornelis, *Travels into Muscovy, Persia, and part of the East-Indies*, Vol. 1 of 2. Translated from French. (London: MDCCXXXVII, 1737).

Hallaq, Wael, *Sharīʿa: Theory, Practice, Transformation* (Cambridge: Cambridge University Press, 2009).

Hoseini, Mohammad and Rezvanimofrad, Ahmad, "The Structure of Safavid Judicial System." *Law Quarterly-Journal of Faculty of Law and Political Science* 41, no. 3 (2011): 155–169.

Floor, Willem, "Mazalem." In *Encyclopedia Iranica*, September 15, 2009.

Floor, Willem, "The Secular Judicial System in Safavid Persia." *Studia Iranica* 29, no. 1 (2000): 9–60.

Floor, Willem, "ṢADR." In *Encyclopedia Iranica*.

Jaʿfariyān, Rasūl, *Siyāsat va-Farhang-i Rūzgār-i Ṣafavī*, Vol. 1, (Tehran: Nashr-i ʿIlm, 1388/ 2009).

Jaʿfariyān, Rasūl, "Shaykh al-Islām-ī dowreh-yi Safavī," http://www.iranicaonline.org/articles/judicial-and-legal-systems-iv-judicial-system-from-the-advent-of-islam-through-the-19th-century

Kaempfer, Engelbert (1651–1716), *Am Hofe des persischen Grosskönig, 1684–85; das erste Buch der Amœnitatum exoticae* (Leipzig: K.F. Koehler, 1940).

Khwātūnabādī, ʿAbd al-Ḥusayn, *Vaqāyiʿu Sinīn va'l-Aʿvām* (Tehran: Intishārāt-i Vahīd, 1352/1973).

Lord Stanley, ed. *Travels to Tana and Persia by Josafa Barbaro and Ambrogio Contarini*, trans. William Thomas (London: Hakluyt Society, 1873).

Matthee, Rudi, "The Safavids under Western Eyes: Seventeenth-Century European Travelers to Iran." *Journal of Early Modern History*, no. 13 (2009): 137–171.

Membré, Michele, *Mission to the Lord Sophy of Persia (1539–1542)*, trans. A.H. Morton, London, 1993.

McChesney, Robert D., *Waqf in Central Asia: Four Hundred Years in the History of a Muslim Shrine, 1480–1889* (Princeton: Princeton University Press, 1991).

Mīrzā ʿAbdullah Afandī, *Riyāḍ al-ʿUlamāʾ wa-Ḥiyāḍ al-Fuḍalāʾ*, Vol. 2, ed. Aḥmad al-Ḥusaynī (Qum: Manshūrāt Maktabat Āyatullah Marʿashī, 1403/1983).

Mirza Rafiʿa or Muḥammad Rafīʿ al-Dīn Anṣārī, *Dastur al-Moluk: A Safavid State Manual*, trans. Willem Floor and Mohammad H. Faghfoory, with commentary by Willem Floor (Costa Mesa: Mazda Publishers, 2007).

Mirza Samiʿa, *Tadhkirat al-mulūk: A Manual of Safavid Administration* (circa 1137/1725). E.J. W. Gibb Memorial Series. (Cambridge Gibb Memorial Trust, 1980).

Munajjim Yazdī, Mulla Jalāl al-Dīn, *Tārīkh-i ʿAbbāsī or Rūznāmah-yi Jalāl*, ed. Sayfullah Vaḥīd-Niyā (n.p.: Intishārāt-i Waḥīd, 1366).

Munshī, Iskandar Beg, *ʿĀlam-ārā-yi ʿAbbāsī*, 3 volumes, Muḥammad Ismāʿīl Rezvānī (Tehran: Dunyā-yi Kitāb, 1377/1998).

Mushīzī (Bardsīrī), Mīr Muḥammad Saʿīd, *Tadhkirah-yi Ṣafaviyya-i Kirmān* in M. Ibrāhīm Bāstānī Pārīzī (ed.) (Tehran: Ḥaydarī, 1369).

Nasiri, Ali Naqi, *Titles and Emoluments in Safavid Iran: A Third Manual of Safavid Administration*, trans. and annotated by Willem Floor (MD: Mage Publishers, 2008).

Natanzī, Maḥmūd b. Hidāyatullah Āfūshtah, *Naqāvat al-Āthār fī dhikr al-Ākhyār*, ed. Iḥsān Ishrāqī (Tehran: Intishārāt-i ʿIlmī Farhangī, 1364).

Olearius, Adam (1603–71), *The Voyages and Travels of the Ambassadors sent by Frederick Duke of Holstein, to the Great Duke of Muscovy, and the King of Persia* (London: Printed for Thomas Dring and John Starkey, 1662).

Patakchī, Aḥmad, "Ḥuqūq," Vol. 10, *Dāʾirat al-Maʿārif-i Buzurg-i Islāmī*, Kāẓim Mūsavī (ed.) Bojnūrdī (Tehran: Center for the Great Islamic Encyclopedia, 2002).

Qazvīnī, Mīrzā Muḥammad Ṭāhir Vahīd, *Tārīkh-i Jahān-ārā-yi ʿAbbāsī (ʿAbbāsnāmah)*, I. Dihgān (ed.) (Arak: Kitābfurūshī-yi Dāvūdī, 1951).

Qazvīnī Iṣfahānī, Muḥammad Yūsuf Vālih, *Irān dar Zamān-i Shāh Ṣafī va-Shāh ʿAbbās Duvvum (1038–1071) or Khuld-i Barīn*, ed. Muḥammad Rezā Nāṣirī (Tehran: Anjuman-i Āthār va-Mafākhir-i Farhangī, 1382/1962–63).

Qazvīnī Iṣfahānī, Muḥammad Yūsuf Vālih. *Khuld-i Barīn*, Mīr Hāshim Muḥaddith (ed.) (Tehran: Majmūʿah-yi Intishārāt-i Adabī va-Tārīkhī, 1372/1993).

Qazvīnī, Qāḍī Aḥmad Ghaffārī, *Tārīkh-i Jahān-ārā*, ʿAllāma Qazvīnī (ed.) (Tehran: Kitābfurūshī-yi Ḥāfiz, 1363/1964).

Quinn, Sholeh and Melville, Charles, "Safavid Historiography" in C. Melville (ed.) *A History of Persian Literature: Persian Historiography*, Vol. 10 (London: I.B. Tauris, 2012).

Qummī, Qāḍī Aḥmad, *Khulāṣat al-Tavārīkh*, ed. Iḥsān Ishrāqī, Vol. 1, (Tehran: Intishārāt-i Dānishgāh-i Tehran, 1359–63sh/1980–84).

Rizvi, Kishwar, *The Safavid Dynastic Shrine: Architecture, Religion and Power in Early Modern Iran* (London: I.B. Tauris, 2011).

Rumlū, Ḥasan Beg, *A Chronicle of the Early Safawis (Ahsanu't-Tawarikh)*, trans. C.N. Seddon (Baroda: Oriental Institute, 1934).

Sanson, Nicolas (1600–67), *The Present State of Persia with a Faithful Account of the Manners, Religion and Government of that People* (London: Printed for M. Gillyflower, J. Tonson, and H. Bonwick, 1695).

Savory, Roger M., trans., *History of Shah ʿAbbas the Great (Tārīkh-e ʿĀlamārā-ye ʿAbbāsī)*, Vol. 1 (Boulder: Westview Press, 1978).

Shīrāzī, ʿAbdī Beg, *Takmilat al-Akhbār*, ʿAbd al-Ḥusayn Navāʾī (ed.) (Tehran: Nhshr-i Nay, 1369/1990).

Ṣifatgul, Manṣūr, "Safavid Administration of Avqaf: Structure, Changes, and Function, 1077–1135/1666–1722." *Society and Cultures in the Early Modern Middle East: Studies on Iran in the Safavid Period* 46, no. 1 (2003): 397–409.

Stilt, Kristen A., *Islamic Law in Action: Authority, Discretion, and Everyday Experiences in Mamluk Egypt* (New York: Oxford University Press, 2011).

Tabatabai, Hossein Modarressi, *An Introduction to Shiʿi Law: A Bibliographical Essay* (London: Ithaca Press, 1984).

Tabatabai, Hossein Modarressi. "Dīvān-i maẓālim." *Farhang-i Īrān zamīn*, no. 27 (1366/1987): 98–118.

Tavernier, John Baptista (1605–89), *The Six Voyages of John Baptista Tavernier, Baron of Aubonne, through Turky, into Persia and the East Indies, for the Space of Forty Years* (London: Printed by William Godbid for Robert Littlebury and Moses Pitt, 1677, Book V).

Taylor, Charles, *A Secular Age* (Cambridge, MA: Harvard University Press, 2007).

Tehrānī (Vārid), Muḥammad Shafīʿ, *Mirʾāt-i Vāridāt: Tārikh-i Suqūṭ-i Ṣafaviyyān, Piyāyād-hā-yi ān va-Farmānravāʾī-yi Malik Maḥmūd Sistānī*, Manṣūr Ṣifatgol (ed.) (Tehran: Mirāth-i Maktūb, 1383/1964).

The Holy Qurʾan, trans. Abdullah Yusuf ʿAli, Sūrat al-Baqara, Āya 282, http://www.muslimaccess.com/quraan/translations/yusufali/002.htm

Tuğ, Başak, *Politics of Honor in Ottoman Anatolia: Sexual Violence and Socio-Legal Surveillance in the Eighteenth Century* (Leiden: Brill, 2017).

Urdūbādī, Naṣīrī, *Alqāb va-Mavājib-i Dowreh-yi Salāṭīn-i Ṣafaviyya*, Yūsuf Raḥīm-Lū (ed.) (Mashhad: Dānishgāh-i Firdowsī-yi Mashhadī, 1372/1953).

Wolff, Larry, *Inventing Eastern Europe: The Map of Civilization on the Mind of the Enlightenment* (Stanford: Stanford University Press, 1994).

CHAPTER 22

ANGLO-MUHAMMADAN LAW

SYED ADNAN HUSSAIN

I. Introduction: What's in a Name?

Anglo–Muhammadan law was a hybrid legal system that combined English common law and principles of equity with a distilled version of Islamic jurisprudence.[1] This was both a combination of law in practice and jurisprudence resulting in a unique blend in India that was then exported to other colonial holdings in Malaysia, Zanzibar, Sudan, and Nigeria. Its origins lie in exigencies of an expanding British Empire, which by the eighteenth century included millions of Muslim subjects in India. The standard narrative is that the British needed to develop a strategy of rule that would avoid the need for constant military intervention. This need was coupled with an initial recognition that India had a sophisticated civilization and that it would be prudent to work, at least initially, within the established power structures. With growing power came growing responsibilities of rule, which came to include the administration of justice. In matters designated as "religious," this was performed with the assistance of local religious scholars. In time this system of consultation was supplanted by a further spread

[1] Researchers in this area would do well to familiarize themselves with the many terms used for referring to Muslims, many of which are derived from French, German, English, and Hindustani terms including: Mahomedan, Muhammadan, Muhammudan, Mohammadan, Moohummudan, Moslem, Mooselman, Mussalman, and Musleman. For my present purpose I have opted for Muhammadan.

of the Common Law (piecemeal, not *en toto*), through translations and codes, and with the work of native professional lawyers who replaced religious consultants. Moreover, in the absence of statute, religious personal law, custom, or case law, judges were to decide cases on English notions of "justice, equity and good conscience."[2] Anglo-Muhammadan law was unpopular amongst many Muslims, particularly the displaced religious elites, but was used extensively to resolve disputes between those with the sufficient means to pay its costs. The system would eventually become incorporated into the postcolonial legal structures although it has since undergone extensive revision.

There is exciting research being done in the field owing to the massive digitization of much of the archive, which has both preserved many texts and made them broadly accessible. What follows in this chapter is a more detailed explanation of its historical origins, sources, and subject-matter jurisdiction. One broad idea to keep in mind is that Anglo-Muhammadan law was being developed at the same time as colonial dispensations of modernity which included the idea of the modern state with all its administrative, legal, and territorial complexity. Similarly, the modern state would need to create, through education and legislation, the modern subject with layers of religious, racial, political, and sexual complexity. Though Anglo-Mohammadan law is something of a relic of the transition period, it nonetheless transformed the legal trajectories of much of the Islamicate world. The term itself was a neologism that would eventually be replaced by "Muhammadan law." In the words of colonial jurist Kenyvet Wilson, the prefix's usage reveals many of its underlying complexities:

> [I]t seems better to distinguish by the prefix "Anglo" that small fragment of each system which an alien Government, making no pretence of sympathy with the general spirit of the whole, has thought suitable for enforcement by its own tribunals. British statesmanship determines from time to time how much of Oriental precept is to be treated as Law in the English sense, how much is left to the consciences of those who acknowledge it as religiously binding, how much forcibly supressed as noxious and immoral; and when this has been determined, European scholarship sifts and classifies the Oriental authorities, the mental habits of English and Scotch lawyers influence the methods of interpretation, and Procedure Codes of modern European manufacture regulate the ascertainment of facts and the ultimate enforcement of the rule.[3]

[2] According to Duncan Derrett, whose article still remains the most cited on this issue, the formula "justice, equity and good conscience" operated as something of a catchall. It would be used to consult other legal systems to reach conclusions in cases where the matter was not considered in English positive or case law, these could include looking at American, civil law sources, or even to natural law. Derrett laments that "the effects of the formula in India have been to smooth out discrepancies between systems of law, and to introduce conceptions which strongly resemble the general character of English law" but he insists that the intent of the formula "was a way to escape English law, not to call it in." For a complete treatment see Duncan M. Derrett, "Justice, Equity and Good Conscience," in *Changing Law in Developing Countries*, ed. J.N.D. Anderson (New York: Frederick A. Praeger, 1963), 150–151.

[3] Roland Knyvet Wilson, *An Introduction to the Study of Anglo-Muhammadan Law* (London: W. Thacker and Co., 1894), 1–2.

The result is hybrid to the core, but with the Anglo unquestionably dominant. If we are obliged to rule, Wilson opines, let it at least be with an eye to civilizing and systematizing with the best parts of our own tradition.

II. Short History: Origins of Anglo-Muhammadan Law

Colonial histories often operate in parallel. The histories of the colony will be intimately tied up with the political and philosophical concerns in the English public sphere. They act on each other. Hence, the rise of classical liberalism in England would eventually challenge the capriciousness of Company rule in India. Once Indians could articulate their opposition to colonialism in the language of liberal Englishmen, they would succeed in pushing for freedom.[4] The logic of rule transformed from economic exploitation to administrative management, and eventually a civilizational mission to bring English liberty to India. This moral justification for colonialism was advanced by English education and the reshaping of subjects whose relationship with the law, and state expanded exponentially.

Part of the colonizing mission was a deployment of the idea of a "rule of law" which was proposed as a progressive strategy to counter "Oriental despotism." Early on, the rule of law meant making the Company a functionary in the Mughal legal system. They were given the grant of the *Diwani* of Bengal, Bihar, and Orissa (1765) and would expand the Company mandate to include the administration of justice on behalf of local figureheads. This phase was marked by a period of "Oriental learning" as facilitated through organizations such as the Asiatic Society (1784) and officially sponsored translations financed by the first Governor General, Warren Hastings (d. 1818). In section 15 of Bengal Regulation IV of 1793, the administration specified that:

> In suits regarding inheritance, marriage, caste and other religious usages and institutions, the Mahomedan laws with respect to the Mahomedans, and the Hindu laws with respect to the Hindus, are to be considered as the general rules by which the Judges are to form their decisions. In the respective cases, the Mahomedan and the Hindu law officers of the Court [Elswhere specified as "Maulvis or Brahmins"] are to Attend to expound the Law[5]

This allowed the Company to extend the indigenous legal system by allowing colonial administrators—often with little legal training—to act in personae *Qadi*.

[4] Britain's empire in India ultimately ended legally. A highly recommended text on the ways in which Indians eroded the necessary "difference" of empire and ultimately mounted their demands as the apotheosis of the British "rule of law" is Thomas R. Metcalf, *Ideologies of the Raj*, The New Cambridge History of India (Cambridge; New York: Cambridge University Press, 1994).

[5] Bengal Regulation IV of 1793, section 15.

Courts were and have remained an expensive option, and much of local justice was meted out by *panchayats* or village and caste councils. Local authorities, such as local *ulema* also retained some residual judicial power. The British set up a Supreme Court at Fort William, as well as maritime, military, arbitral, and equity courts. The most substantial shifts came after the revolt in 1857, which resulted in a massive restructuring of the legal system. In 1864 Hindu and Muslim jurisconsults were dispensed with, as were any residual Persian legal titles (e.g. *qazi*). Most important in the shift was a systemization of law under legal codes, deeply informed by utilitarian philosophy, such as the Indian Penal Code (1862), the Code of Criminal Procedure including the Evidence Act (1872), and the Contracts Act (1872). District courts or local courts dealt with daily suits that were overseen by magistrates. Appeals would involve a finding of fact, which was then sent up the appeals chain. To that end, High Courts were developed in Bombay, Calcutta, Madras, and Allahabad, whose justices were appointed by authority of the Crown. Chief Courts were set up in Lahore and Nagpur, whose justices were appointed by the Viceroy-Governor General. Appeals were sent to the Judicial Committee of the Privy Council in London and were heard by a group of Law Lords, which did not include Indians until Syed Ameer Ali (d. 1928) was appointed in 1909.

III. The Subject Matter of Anglo-Muhammadan Law and Syed Ameer Ali

Roland Kenyvet Wilson's 1895 *A Digest of Anglo-Muhammadan Law: setting forth in the form of a code, with full references to modern and ancient authorities, the special rules now applicable to Muhammadans as such by the civil courts of British India*[6] is one of the most ponderously titled and impressive codes developed during the British colonial period. Wilson made no pretensions to knowing any Islamicate language and had, at the time of the first edition, only visited India once. He had been a reader in Indian Law at the University of Cambridge for fourteen years when he composed the work which was intended to be a work of utility, as opposed to more theoretical works like those of Syed Ameer Ali. The work went through a number of editions, updating for changes in law. After the death of its progenitor, addenda were contributed by Abdullah Yusuf Ali (d. 1953), a Dawoodi Bohra Muslim famous for his extremely popular 1934 translation of the Qur'an. The first edition of the digest provides an excellent overview of the subject matter of the new legal system.

[6] Roland Knyvet Wilson, *A Digest of Anglo-Muhammadan Law* (London: W. Thacker & Co. 1895).

Topics include marriage, divorce, parentage, care of family members, succession, alienation, and choice of law between legal schools. Nearly every successive text on Anglo–Muhammadan law would follow a similar pattern, which in general, rendered Muslim personal law through the lens of private property rights.

One of the most contentious areas of the law was the nature of trust law, or *awqaf* (sing. *waqf*), derived from the Arabic root verb *waqafa* meaning "to stop" or "to hold." Although there is no Qur'anic basis for a *waqf*, each of the legal schools including the Shi'a have ways of transferring ownership of a property to God, in perpetuity, with the primary purpose of benefitting some person or class of persons. The property in question becomes, through this process, inalienable. The property is overseen by an administrator, who may or may not be one of the beneficiaries, and who administers the property according to the wishes of the founder (*waqif*). The activities of the administrator may be overseen by a governmental body; and in the case of the colonial administration, that body assumed the responsibility of oversight invoked through lawsuits. For those familiar with trust law, the *waqf* has some familial similarity, but there are some contentious points. First, the *waqf* at its core is an instrument designed for perpetuity and may therefore run afoul of the rule against perpetuities, which was already a part of the common law following the *Duke of Norfolk's Case* of 1682. Secondly, the colonial administration interpreted *awqaf* narrowly to distinguish between ones designed to benefit the public and those merely designed as a way of securing wealth for a person's heirs. Distinguishing between mere trusts, governed by the common law, and *awqaf* in Muhammadan law was fraught with difficulties. The touchstone text for this peculiarity of the colonial encounter is still Gregory C. Kozlowski's work on Muslim endowments,[7] but for a full account of the complexities of *awqaf*, Syed Ameer Ali's work and legacy is indispensable.

Ameer Ali proves an extraordinary example of the ways in which the local elite became absorbed into the new legal system, and how they assisted in structuring subject matter as well as deciding cases under the rubric of Anglo–Muhammadan law. Ameer Ali was Shi'a-born, but would later refer to himself a "Mutazala"[8] and spent much of his professional career in Bengal. He would graduate from the Inner Temple in 1873 and become a Judge in the Calcutta High Court in 1890. After retirement from the High Court, Ameer Ali moved to England and was appointed to the Judicial Committee of the Privy Council in 1909, where he served till his death in 1928. He authored a number of books on Islam and Anglo–Muhammadan law, and gained some renown as both a modernist scholar of Islam and a loyal servant of Empire. Though his reputation was towering amongst the Anglo–educated elite, he was often maligned by the *maulvis* or local religious elite. His work is magisterial in its scope and relied on both untranslated texts from major Islamic legal schools, and the work of Orientalist scholars, such as

[7] Gregory C. Kozlowski, *Muslim Endowments and Society in British India* (Cambridge: Cambridge University Press, 1985).

[8] Syed Ameer Ali, *The Personal Law of the Mahommedans* (London: W.H. Allen & Co. 1880), xi.

Ignatius Mouradgea d'Ohsson (d. 1807), the Swedish-Armenian scholar whose *Tableau Général de l'Empire Othoman* (seven volumes, 1788–1824) was an excellent text on Maliki law.[9] d'Ohsson, like the English, constructed his understanding of Islam primarily textually as a strategy for wresting Islam from the control of the *maulvis*, who were perceived to be backward-looking traditionalists. Ameer Ali's 1891 *Spirit of Islam*[10] remains an important modernist text that reinterprets Muhammad as a moral exemplar who encouraged rationalism and progress.

One of Ameer Ali's most important contributions to Anglo–Muhammadan law was developed during his year as the Tagore Law Professor at Calcutta University. He lectured on Muhammadan Law and the course he taught was eventually tuned into a text titled, *The Law relating to Gifts, Trusts, and Testamentary Dispositions among the Mahommedans*.[11] He would argue, both in his writings and in the cases in which he was a council and judge, that the British had interpreted *awqaf* too narrowly and that *awqaf* operate in three equally valid but distinct modes. The first is public, or those properties designed for public works or charitable purposes such as the establishment of a mosque. The second is what Ameer Ali calls a *quasi*-public *waqf*, one that has the public as a beneficiary but also provides for the benefit of particular individuals or classes of individuals. The third type is the private *waqf*, or one designated for the settlor's family or relations.[12] The last two types were most hotly debated. In *Abdul Fata v. Russomoy Dhur Chowdhury*[13] the courts refused to allow for a *waqf* that did not substantially benefit the poor, after which Ameer Ali began his agitations which would eventually result in the Wakf Validating Act of 1913 which allowed for private beneficiaries, and beneficiaries of mere shares. Muslim law was being negotiated politically and in statute as well as in courts and textbooks; the sources of the law had expanded considerably.

IV. Sources of Anglo–Muhammadan Law

A. Translations and Textbooks

The most accessible sources on Muslim jurisprudence in English rapidly became textbooks and English translations of primary texts. The codification efforts of the

[9] Ignatius Mouradgea D'Ohsson, *Tableau Général de l'Empire Othoman*, Vol. 1. (Paris: De L'Imprimerie de Mousieur [Firmin Didot], 1788). Other volumes are listed in the bibliography.

[10] Syed Ameer Ali, *The Life and Teachings of Mohammed or The Spirit of Islam* (London: W.H. Allen & Co., 1891).

[11] Syed Ameer Ali, *The Law relating to Gifts, Trusts, and Testamentary Dispositions among the Mahommedans* (Calcutta: Thacker, Spink and Co., 1885).

[12] Ibid., 178. [13] *Abdul Fata v. Russomoy Dhur Chowdhury* (1894) 22 I. A. 76.

Utilitarians in England led to the Penal Code of 1860, which upended any remainder of Muslim criminal jurisdiction, and narrowed the subject matter of Muslim law to personal law. Hornbooks, codes, and digests became the most referenced "sources" of law and effectively functioned as a code of the new legal hybrid system. The broader scope of actionable shariʿa was narrowed to the law that the British were willing to enforce in their courts, as modified by the common law, particularly cases and precedent. Textbooks were designed for both students as study aids and for judges as a restatement of the law. They were written by both European legal scholars, as well as by Muslim and non-Muslim native law officers. They worked with translations as well as with primary sources, and are remarkable documents of heroic effort regardless of their shortcomings.

The first phase of British scholarship was the development of translations of "authoritative," primarily Hanafi texts that would facilitate the work of company judges. The earliest of note was Hamilton's 1791 and Gady's 1870 translation and restatement of the *Hedaya*.[14] Owing to certain "shortcomings" of the *Hedaya*, William Jones translated and edited *Al-Sirajiyah*,[15] a thirteenth-century text on inheritance. Although it was widely recognized that the *Fatawa-e-Alamgiri*, commissioned by Emperor Aurangzeb (d. 1707), was one of the most important Hanafi collections in India, it proved profoundly difficult to translate. Containing broad subject matter and numerous illustrations, the text only appeared piecemeal to satisfy administrative interests in three books translated by Neil B.E. Baillie's (d. 1883) *The Moohummudan Law of Sale*,[16] *The Land Tax of India*,[17] and *Digest of Muhammadan Law*.[18] To add further to this corpus, W.H. Macnaghten distilled and translated a number of judicial opinions of *maulvis* on inheritance from court cases at the Courts of Judicature, subordinate to Fort William. This collection, entitled *Principles and Precedents of Moohummudan Law*,[19] was designed to supplement the *Hedaya* and Jones' texts and is presented both as a code and as a series of questions and answers with local experts. These precedents abstracted the *fatwa*, which was designed to be applied to a single case, into something broader as an expert statement on the law to be applied across cases.

[14] Charles Hamilton, *The Hedaya or Guide a Commentary on the Mussulman Laws*, Vols I and II (London: T. Ben & Ley, 1791); Standish Grove Grady, *The Hedaya or Guide: A Commentary on the Mussulman Laws*, 2nd edn, trans. Charles Hamilton (London: William H. Allen & Co, 1870).

[15] William Jones, *Al Sirajiyyah or the Mohammedan Law of Inheritance* (Calcutta: Joseph Cooper, 1792).

[16] Neil B.E. Baillie, *The Moohummudan Law of Sale, according to the Huneefeea Code: from the Futawa Alumgeeree, a Digest of the Whole Law* (London: Smith, Elder, & Co., 1850).

[17] Neil B.E. Baillie, *The Land Tax of India, according to the Moohummudan Law: Translated from the Futawa Alumgeeree, with Explanatory Notes* (1853, reprint, London: Smith, Elder, & Co. 1973).

[18] Neil B.E. Baillie, *A Digest of Moohummudan Law on the Subjects to which it is usually Applied by British Courts of Justice in India* (London: Smith, Elder & Co. 1865).

[19] W.H. MacNaghten, *Principles and Precedents of Moohummudan Law* (Calcutta: Samuel Smith, Elder, & Co., 1825).

Beyond the textbooks already mentioned, there were a few others of note, which would be frequently cited by colonial judges and administrators. In order of date of appearance these were: Shama Churun Sircar's Tagore Lectures;[20] Dinshah Fardunji Mulla's *Principles of Mahomedan Law*[21], originally published in 1905 and now in its fifteenth edition; Faiz Badruddin Tyabji's *Principles of Muhammadan Law*,[22] originally published in 1913, and republished in numerous editions. Perhaps of greatest renown in the post-independence period is the work of Asaf A.A. Fyzee (d. 1981). Fyzee's *Outlines of Muhammadan Law*[23]—originally published in 1949, now in its fifth edition)—is still a basic text required in many South Asian law programs. Many of these programs were founded on the British model of common law legal education, and their graduates have been key to the expansion of common law in South Asia. Lawsuits became the favored method of dispute resolution for the monied classes, and what follows is an example of an important case from 1922.

B. Case Law and Sample Case: *Narantakh v. Parakkal* (1922)

To gain a sense of how Anglo–Muhammadan law operated in case law, the 1922 case of *Narantakath v. Parakkal*[24] is exemplary. It was decided by an appellate court of two judges: an Englishman, Justice Oldenfeld, and a native non-Muslim, Justice Krishnan. The case at hand was filed in regards to an alleged violation of the Indian Penal Code regulation on bigamy. A woman's husband joined the "new sect of Ahmediyans" which she took, after due consultation with local scholars, to be an act of apostasy, or renunciation of faith,[25] which would result in her marriage being annulled. She thereafter married another man, at which point her first husband accused her of bigamy. To determine whether the wife was guilty of bigamy, the court had first to determine whether becoming an Ahmadi, ipso facto, constituted apostasy. All parties agreed that apostasy severed the marriage. Whereas the lower court ruled that becoming an Ahmadi does constitute apostasy, the appeals court reversed that decision, finding that Ahmadi converts are not apostates, and therefore that the wife was indeed guilty of bigamy. The courts

[20] Shama Churun Sircar, *The Muhammadan Law: Digest of the Law Applicable Especially to the Sunnis of India* (London: Thacker, Spink and Co., 1873).

[21] Dinshah Fardunji Mulla, *Principles of Mahomedan Law* (Bombay: Thacker & Co. 1905).

[22] Faiz Badruddin Tyabji, *Principles of Muhammadan Law* (Bombay: D.B. Taraporevala Sons. 1913).

[23] Asaf A.A. Fyzee, *Outlines of Muhammadan Law*, 2nd edn. (London: Oxford University Press 1960).

[24] *Narantakath v. Parakkal* (1922) 71 Ind Cas 65 (43 MLJ 663).

[25] The council for the defendant was none other than the soon-to-be-famous Muhammad Zafarullah Khan, the brilliant Ahmedi jurist and politician whose removal was demanded by the anti-Ahmedi riots in Pakistan.

ultimately narrowed Islam and adherence to an "essential doctrine" test, which they enunciated as the following:

The essential doctrine of the Muhammadan religion is that God is only one and that Muhammad is His Prophet; hence Ahmediyans who also hold that belief are only a sect of Muhammadans, notwithstanding the fact that they differ from other Muhammadans in some other matters of religious belief. Hence on a Muhammadan becoming an Ahmediyan he does not become an apostate and his wife is guilty of bigamy if she marries another during his lifetime.[26]

The court admitted that there were compelling public policy grounds for the decision that would have risked rendering a large number of Ahmedi Muslims apostates, and possibly dissolving their marriages. This reasoning would also be in line with the legislative directive expressed in the Caste Disabilities Removal Act (XXI of 1850), which removed apostasy as grounds for loss of civil rights or property.

The judges were asked in the first instance to weigh the claims that the Ahmadi converts were apostates. They based their test on an assessment from Abdur Rahim's textbook from 1911,[27] which itself relies on a Hanafi scholar, Muhammad Amin Ibn Abidin (d. 1836), and claims that "the correct law is that when heretical doctrines are opposed to clear and indisputable texts they would amount to unbelief but not otherwise."[28] They combined this text with the following from Ameer Ali: "[a]ny person who professes the religion of Islam ... accepts the unity of God and the prophetic character of Muhammad is a Moslem ... [s]o long as the individual pronounces the *Kalma* of *Tawhid*, the *Credo* of Islam, it is not necessary for him or her to observe any of the rites and ceremonies or to believe in particular doctrines which imply Imam [*sic.*] or belief."[29] This two-tiered essential doctrine test was combined with one further "ripeness test" by the court. Both justices argued that insufficient time had passed since the new sect appeared, and that any hastiness to condemn the sect would be inappropriate until they could be sufficiently vetted by the community. They argued that thirty-three years was insufficient time to develop a consensus (*ijma'*) about the status of Ahmadis, which would have been cold comfort in the present case of the wife who relied on a broadly shared opinion, but was nevertheless charged with bigamy.

Case history from the colonial period at the appellate and higher levels is extensive. The author of a law report by the Civil Justice Committee in 1925 would remark that Punjabis were "greatly addicted to litigation."[30] Land disputes would

26 *Narantakath v. Parakkal*, at 986–987.

27 Abdur Rahim, *The Principles of Muhammadan Jurisprudence* (London: Luzack & Co. 1911).

28 Ibid., 250.

29 *Narantakath v. Parakkal*, at 1001, quoting Ameer Ali, *Mahommedan Law*, 36.

30 India Civil Justice Committee, *Civil Justice Committee, 1924–1925 Report* (Calcutta: Government of India Central Publication Branch, 1925), 590.

make Punjab a hotbed of litigation, but more generally the introduction of a new mode of negotiating power relations and property through the law made it a powerful tool for the wealthy and a prestigious career for the aspiring.

c. Legislation and Custom

John Austin's (d. 1859) legal theories in England would come to form the basis for the philosophy of legal positivism, which included the framing idea that the law was not about moral precepts but rather the law of the lawmaker, or law as a command. Statutes in the fashion of nineteenth-century Europeans were distinct from any extant system of edicts. The *Code Civil des Français* (Napoleonic Code) expurgated some of the capriciousness of the royal system by removing its inconsistencies and restructuring the law to be accessible to the common person. These trends were less popular in England owing to the strength of hereditary power holders, but the agenda was pushed by Utilitarian reformers including Jeremy Bentham (d. 1832), a close friend of Austin. Law as command in this fashion was new to India and it was of particular importance to Muslim communities as much of it was designed, despite the philosophy of legal positivism, to restructure things considered "noxious and immoral" to English sensibilities.

Slavery was abolished in 1843 (Act V of 1843) and the Caste Disabilities Removal Act (XXI of 1850) removed apostasy as grounds for loss of property, but the nature of custom would take many more years to resolve. Custom, for example those of Muslims living in Punjab, could trump the general presumption to apply Muhammadan law. Islamic law was familiar with custom of a fashion, and the Maliki legal school drew heavily from the customary practices of the community in Medina during the Prophet's tenure as a statesman. Lord Symonds, in *Asrar Ahmed v. Durgah Committee, Ajmer* (1943),[31] once quipped that the bar for proving custom lay much lower in India than in England. The courts used the following three-part test: First, the burden to prove the applicability of custom laid with the claimant, who had to prove that they were a member of the communities to which customary law applied, for example, Khojas, Bohoras, or syncretic Hindu–Muslim (or Muslim–Hindu?) communities such as the Satpanthis or Pirpanthis. The custom appealed to must be "ancient and notorious," or well-established in history and widely known, and to prove its existence parties were to rely on previous judgments as well as testimony (the parties had to essentially agree to be bound). Fyzee in his discussion states that the "Court must scrutinize the custom set up jealously and must be careful not to be misled by an unfamiliarity with social conditions."[32] Many Muslim

[31] *Asrar Ahmed v. Durgah Committee, Ajmer* (1943) 49 BOMLR 235.

[32] Fyzee, *Outlines of Muhammad Law*, 54.

reformers at the close of the nineteenth century and in the early twentieth century became involved in promoting Muslim law as better for women than customary laws. Eventually communal agitation culminated in the passage of the Muslim Personal Laws (Shariat) Act of 1937 (Act XXVI of 1937). That law effectively ended the application of custom in marriages and property assignment (with important exceptions for *awqaf* and agricultural land). In 1939 the Dissolution of Muslim Marriages Act (Act VIII of 1939) would allow Muslim women to end marriages for a number of statutory reasons, such as neglect or abandonment. These two laws were some of the last major pieces of legislation in the history of Anglo-Muhammadan law. They used English legislative power to apply a formal version of Islamic law to override customary practices, which was seen at the time as a progressive victory for women's rights—a complicated history indeed.

V. After Independence

Of the many changes in the immediate period after independence and partition, the law proved particularly resistant to being overhauled. Many of the leaders of the independence movement were themselves lawyers and retained a certain reticence toward their largely uneducated countrymen. It cannot be overstated that the law seemed to them to be part of the reason that they achieved independence without revolution, and hence was conceived of by many of the western educated as one of the sweeter fruits of colonialism. Although in each of the colonies some of the terms of Anglo-Muhammadan law would be revised, the system would retain nearly all of its colonial facets, so much so that the textbooks for its study remained the same. The "Anglo" was dropped and terms like "Muhammadan law" or "Islamic Law" or "Shariat" took its place. *Waqf* in India remained the most contentious area of the law through the 1970s. Pakistan's trajectory is slightly more complicated owing to the attempts by Zulfikar Ali Bhutto and later his executioner-successor, General Zia ul Haq, to Islamicize the law. These changes were primarily surface level, and although crimes such as adultery were now reframed as *zina* in the infamous *hudood* ordinances, they were structured in code-like fashion, alien to precolonial Islamic fashion. English remains the language of the appellate system and the leading lawyers and thinkers in the system frequently train in other Commonwealth countries owing to a politics of prestige.

The Anglo-Muhammadan law tends to receive less regard than warranted primarily because many are unfamiliar with the complex and ambivalent relationships it created. It is undeniable that this "jural colonization," Wael Hallaq's term, greatly changed the trajectories of Islamic law, and it remains to be seen the ways that it will continue to evolve in former colonies. It may also be interesting to see the trajectories of Anglo-Muhammadan law as former colonial subjects arrive in Europe and North America and begin agitating to have the law that was created on the periphery returning to the metropole.

Texts cited and others relevant to the Study of Anglo Muhammadan Law

Ali, Syed Ameer, *Mahommedan Law: The Law relating to Succession and Status* (Thacker, Spink and Co., 1917).

Ali, Syed Ameer, *The Law relating to Gifts, Trusts, and Testamentary Dispositions among the Mahommedans* (Calcutta: Thacker, Spink and Co., 1885).

Ali, Syed Ameer, *The Life and Teachings of Mohammed or the Spirit of Islam* (London: W.H. Allen & Co., 1891).

Ali, Syed Ameer, *The Personal Law of the Mahommedans* (London: W.H. Allen & Co., 1880).

Baillie, Neil B.E., *A Digest of Moohummudan Law on the Subjects to which it is Usually Applied by British Courts of Justice in India* (London: Smith, Elder & Co., 1865).

Baillie, Neil B.E., *The Land Tax of India, according to the Moohummudan Law: Translated from the Futawa Alumgeeree, with Explanatory Notes.* 1853; Reprint, (London: Smith, Elder & Co., 1973).

Baillie, Neil B.E., *The Moohummudan Law of Sale, according to the Huneefeea Code: from the Futawa Alumgeeree, a Digest of the Whole Law* (London: Smith, Elder & Co., 1850).

D'Ohsson, Ignatius Mouradgea, *Tableau Général de l'Empire Othoman,* Vol. 1 (Paris: De L'Imprimerie de Mousieur [Firmin Didot], 1788).

D'Ohsson, Ignatius Mouradgea, *Tableau Général de l'Empire Othoman,* Vol. 2 (Paris: De L'Imprimerie de Mousieur [Firmin Didot], 1788).

D'Ohsson, Ignatius Mouradgea, *Tableau Général de l'Empire Othoman,* Vol. 3 (Paris: De L'Imprimerie de Mousieur [Firmin Didot], 1790).

D'Ohsson, Ignatius Mouradgea, *Tableau Général de l'Empire Othoman,* Vol. 4 (Paris: De L'Imprimerie de Mousieur [Firmin Didot], 1791).

D'Ohsson, Ignatius Mouradgea, *Tableau Général de l'Empire Othoman,* Vol. 5 (Paris: Firmin Didot Père et Fils, 1824).

D'Ohsson, Ignatius Mouradgea, *Tableau Général de l'Empire Othoman,* Vol. 6 (Paris: Firmin Didot Père et Fils, 1824).

D'Ohsson, Ignatius Mouradgea, *Tableau Général de l'Empire Othoman,* Vol. 7 (Paris: Firmin Didot Père et Fils, 1824).

Fyzee, Asaf A.A., *An Introduction to the Study of Mahomedan Law* (London: Oxford University Press, 1931).

Fyzee, Asaf A.A., *Cases in the Muhammadan Law of India and Pakistan* (London: Oxford University Press, 1965).

Fyzee, Asaf A.A., *Outlines of Muhammadan Law,* 2nd edn (London: Oxford University Press, 1960).

Grady, Standish Grove, *The Hedaya or Guide: A Commentary on the Mussulman Laws*, 2nd edn., trans. Charles Hamilton (London: W.H. Allen & Co., 1870).

Hamilton, Charles, *The Hedaya or Guide a Commentary on the Mussulman Laws*, Vols I and II (London: T. Ben & Ley, 1791).

India Civil Justice Committee, *Civil Justice Committee, 1924–1925 Report* (Calcutta: Government of India Central Publication Branch, 1925).

Jones, William, *Al Sirajiyyah or the Mohammedan Law of Inheritance* (Calcutta: Joseph Cooper, 1792).

MacNaghten, W.H., *Principles and Precedents of Moohummudan Law* (Calcutta: Samuel Smith, Elder, & Co., 1825).

Morley, William H., *The Administration of Justice in British India* (London: Williams and Norgate, 1858).

Mulla, Dinshah Fardunji, *Principles of Mahomedan Law* (Bombay: Thacker & Co., 1905).

Rahim, Abdur, *The Principles of Muhammadan Jurisprudence* (London: Luzack & Co., 1911).

Sircar, Shama Churun, *The Muhammadan Law: Digest of the Law Applicable Especially to the Sunnis of India* (London: Thacker, Spink and Co., 1873).

Stokes, Whitley, *The Anglo-Indian Codes*, Vols I and II (Oxford, Clarendon Press, 1887).

Tayabji, Faiz Badruddin, *Principles of Muhammadan Law* (Bombay: D.B. Taraporevala Sons, 1913).

Wilson, Roland Knyvet, *A Digest of Anglo-Muhammadan Law* (London: W. Thacker & Co., 1895).

Wilson, Roland Knyvet, *An Introduction to the Study of Anglo-Muhammadan Law* (London: W. Thacker and Co., 1894).

Cases Cited

Abdul Fata v. Russomoy Dhur Chowdhury (1894) 22 I. A. 76
Asrar Ahmed v. Durgah Committee, Ajmer (1943) 49 BOMLR 235
Narantakath v. Parakkal (1922) 71 Ind Cas 65 (43 MLJ 663)

Statutes

Caste Disabilities Removal Act (Act XXI of 1850)
Criminal Procedure Code of 1861
Dissolution of Muslim Marriages Act of 1939 (Act VIII of 1939)
Indian Penal Code of 1860
Indian Slavery Act, 1843 (Act V of 1843)
Indian Evidence Act of 1872
Muslim Personal Laws (Shariat) Act of 1937 (Act XXVI of 1937)
Mussalman Wakf Validating Act, 1913 (Act VI of 1913)
Bengal Regulation IV of 1793

Relevant scholarly literature

Anderson, J.N.D., "The Anglo Muhammadan Law" in *Contributions to the Study of Indian Law and Society: The South Asian Seminar 1966–1967* (Philadelphia: South Asia Regional Studies, University of Pennsylvania 1967) 165–185.

Anderson, Michael R., "Islamic Law and the Colonial Encounter in British India" in David Arnold and Peter Robb (eds.) *Institutions and Ideologies: A SOAS South Asia Reader* (Richmond, UK: Curzon Press, 1993).

Cohn, Bernard S., *Colonialism and Its Forms of Knowledge: The British in India* (Princeton: Princeton University Press 1996).

Derrett, J. Duncan M., "Justice Equality and Good Conscience" in J.N.D. Anderson (ed.) *Changing Law in Developing Countries* (London: George Allen & Unwin Ltd., 1963) 114–153.

De, Rohit, "The Two Husbands of Vera Tiscenko: Apostasy, Conversion, and Divorce in Late Colonial India." *Law and History Review* vol. 28, no. 4 (2010): 1011–1041.

Galanter, Marc, *Law and Soceity in Modern India* Rajeef Dhavan (ed.) (Delhi: Oxford University Press, 1989).

Hallaq, Wael B., *Shari'a: Theory, Practice, Transformations* (Cambridge: Cambridge University Press, 2009).

Kozlowski, Gregory C., *Muslim Endowments and Society in British India* (Cambridge: Cambridge University Press, 1985).

Kugle, Scott Alan, "Framed, Blamed and Renamed: The Recasting of Islamic Jurisprudence in Colonial South Asia." *Modern Asian Studies* vol. 35, no. 2 (2001): 257–313.

Sharafi, Mitra, "The Semi-Autonomous Judge in Colonial India: Chivalric Imperialism meets Anglo-Islamic Dower and Divorce Law." *Indian Social and Economic History Review* vol. 46, no. 1 (2009): 57–81.

Works cited

Derrett, Duncan M., "Justice, Equity and Good Conscience" in J.N.D. Anderson (ed.) *Changing Law in Developing Countries* (New York: Frederick A. Praeger, 1963) 114–153.

Metcalf, Thomas R., *Ideologies of the Raj* (The New Cambridge History of India. Cambridge; New York: Cambridge University Press, 1994).

CHAPTER 23

LEGISLATION AS AN INSTRUMENT OF ISLAMIC LAW

LEONARD WOOD

ALTHOUGH rarely defined by scholars in the fields of Islamic and area studies, the term "legislation" is almost universally used to denote the process by which a government sets forth a law in written form and the resulting written law.[1] Legislation has been a popular medium of power worldwide since the nineteenth century, and ample literature surveys and bibliographies have in turn outlined the legislative projects of different Muslim countries and their contributions to legal categories such as family law, women's law, and criminal punishment.[2] Scholars who address

[1] See the first two definitions in *Black's Law Dictionary*, 9th edn., (2009) s.v. "legislation."

[2] See generally Joseph E. Lowry, "Law," in *Cambridge Companion to Modern Arab Culture*, ed. Dwight F. Reynolds (Cambridge: Cambridge University Press, 2015), 75–95; Norman Calder et al., "Law," in *The Oxford Encyclopedia of the Islamic World*, ed. John L. Esposito (New York: Oxford University Press, 2009), 381–389; Andrew F. March, *Shari'a (Islamic Law): Oxford Bibliographies Online Research Guide* (Oxford: Oxford University Press, 2011), 27–36; Jan Michiel Otto, ed., *Sharia Incorporated: A Comparative Overview of the Legal Systems of Twelve Muslim Countries in Past and Present* (Leiden: Leiden University Press, 2010); Enid Hill, "Comparative and Historical Study of Modern Middle Eastern Law," *American Journal of Comparative Law* 26 (1978): 279–297; Herbert J. Liebesny, *The Law of the Near and Middle East* (Albany: State University of New York Press, 1975); Martin Lau, "The Re-Islamization of Legal Systems," in *The Ashgate Research Companion to Islamic Law*, ed. Rudolph Peters and Peri Bearman (Farnham, Surrey: Ashgate, 2014), 235–248. On topical areas, see e.g. Lynn Welchman, *Women and Muslim Family Laws in Arab States: A Comparative*

legislation of the Muslim world typically do so within larger studies that discuss national legal systems or substantive legal topics, but do not take the varied techniques, practices, and forms of legislation as the primary objects of inquiry.[3]

Few words in the Islamic legal lexicon are so frequently applied and yet so unsettling to Islamic legal sensibilities as legislation. The sources of discomfort are that in widespread understandings of pre-nineteenth-century Islamic history, legislation played a marginal role and that legislation was not, and still is not, as well defined and analyzed as other topics in Islamic legal theory (*usul al-fiqh*).

This article addresses the topic of legislation as an instrument of Islamic law in the history of the Islamic world and in Islamic legal theory, with particular regard to the scholarly analysis of whether Islamic law can be legislated at all, and if so, how. It begins by reviewing the scholarship on legislation in the Islamic world before the mid-nineteenth-century Ottoman reforms (*tanzimat*)—henceforth, the "premodern" centuries. The second section looks at legislation after the mid-nineteenth century—henceforth, the "modern" centuries—elaborating on scholars' preoccupations with the apparent novelty of modern legislation and its debatable Islamicity. The final two sections discuss empirical dilemmas underlying these preoccupations and competing scholarly approaches to theorizing and studying the proper relationship between legislation and Islam. The chapter points to open questions in the literature and suggests opportunities for future research and analysis.

I. Early Islamic Period until the Mid-nineteenth Century

There is no rigorous treatment of legislation as an instrument, technique, or source of Islamic law in canonical works of Islamic history (*ta'rikh*) or legal theory of the premodern centuries. Legislation is given such short shrift by fundamental premodern sources of authority that a newcomer to the field of premodern Islamic

Overview of Textual Development and Advocacy (Leiden: Amsterdam University Press, 2007); Susan E. Rayner, *The Theory of Contracts in Islamic Law: A Comparative Analysis with Particular Reference to the Modern Legislation in Kuwait, Bahrain, and the United Arab Emirates* (London: Graham & Trotman, 1991); Farhat J. Ziadeh, "Criminal Law," in *The Oxford Encyclopedia of the Islamic World*, ed. John L. Esposito (New York: Oxford University Press, 2009), 4–9.

[3] See e.g. R. Michael Feener, *Shari'a and Social Engineering* (Oxford: Oxford University Press, 2013), esp. 129–130; Otto, *Sharia Incorporated*, 21, 34; Wael B. Hallaq, *Shari'a: Theory, Practice, Transformations* (Cambridge: Cambridge University Press, 2009), esp. 443–499; Nathan J. Brown, *The Rule of Law in the Arab World: Courts in Egypt and the Gulf* (Cambridge: Cambridge University Press, 1997), esp. 32–33.

history and Islamic law will encounter relatively scarce treatment in primary and secondary sources. Scholars widely accept the notion that the elaboration of shari'a in the premodern centuries was the work of jurists who conducted their elaborations through jurisprudential writing (*fiqh*) and, as judges, applied Islamic law outside of direct and routine governmental control. According to this view, it is a matter of historical truth that jurists elaborated shari'a with this kind of independence, and of rightly-guided Islamic practice that they did so.

The history of legislation in Islamic history, however, has been documented going as far back as the eighth century, found in the legal instrument type known as *qanun*.[4] The Arabic term is said to have derived from the Byzantine Greek word *κανών*, which most likely entered Arabic vocabulary as a result of the Muslim conquests of Egypt and Syria in the seventh century.[5] Like its Greek precursor, *qanun* in the early Islamic centuries most commonly consisted of the governmental authorities' imposition of taxes, tariffs, and other administrative and regulatory policies. In the Islamic legal context, *qanun* was most commonly a response to those areas of public law where the rules of shari'a were not evident. Already by the eleventh century, the chief *qadi* of Baghdad, Abu al-Hasan al-Mawardi, used the term *qanun* in his writings in the sense of "legal prescriptions independent of the shari'a laid down by the sultan by virtue of his authority as ruler."[6] The term expanded to include the discretionary (*ta'zir*) punishments, such as imprisonment or fines, meted out by executive authorities for crimes against the public order. Some leading scholarship on *qanun* in the premodern centuries includes studies of the fiscal and criminal laws from the fifteenth-century reign of Ottoman Sultan Mehmed II;[7] legislation under the subsequent sultan Beyazit II;[8] and for the eighteenth and nineteenth centuries, the issuance in Egypt of *qanun* regulating agriculture, conscription, local governance, personal injury, crimes, and political corruption.[9] The past twenty years have

[4] See generally Khaled Abou El-Fadl, "Qanun," in *Encyclopedia of Islam and the Muslim World*, ed. Richard C. Martin et al. (New York: Macmillan Reference USA, 2004), 560–61; Halil İnalcık, "Kanun, 3. Financial and Public Administration," in *The Encyclopaedia of Islam*, 2nd edn., vol. 4. ed. C.E. Bosworth, E. van Donzel, W.P. Heinrichs and Ch. Pellat, 556–562. (Leiden: Brill, 1960–2004).

[5] Frede Løkkegaard, *Islamic Taxation in the Classic Period* (Copenhagen: Branner og Korch, 1950), esp. 118–120.

[6] İnalcık, "Kanun." For evidence of *qanun* governing taxation in twelfth-century Mamluk Egypt, see Richard S. Cooper, "The Assessment and Collection of Kharaj Tax in Medieval Egypt," *Journal of the American Oriental Society* 96, no. 3 (1976): 365–382.

[7] Rudolph Peters, *Crime and Punishment in Islamic Law: Theory and Practice from the Sixteenth to the Twenty-First Century* (Cambridge: Cambridge University Press, 2006), 73–74; Uriel Heyd, "Kanun and Sharia in Old Ottoman Criminal Justice," *Proceedings of the Israel Academy of Sciences and Humanities* 3, no. 1 (1967): 1–18; Uriel Heyd, *Studies in Old Ottoman Criminal Law* (Oxford: Clarendon Press, 1973).

[8] Avi Rubin, "Ottoman Modernity: The Nizamiyye Courts in the Late Nineteenth Century," Ph.D. diss., Harvard University, 2006, 46; Colin Imber, *Ebu's-Su'ud: The Islamic Legal Tradition* (Stanford, CA: Stanford University Press, 1997), 46–47.

[9] Gabriel Baer, *Studies in the Social History of Modern Egypt* (Chicago: University of Chicago Press, 1969), esp. 109–113.

additionally seen a flourishing of writing by revisionist historians investigating the life of pre-European-colonial *qanun* and courts in the Ottoman Empire of the eighteenth and nineteenth centuries. Among the contributions of this revisionist history of the later Ottoman centuries is that it downplays European influence in the narrative of modern legal change and shows how innovations in legislation and adjudication in the Middle East were attributable to autochthonous Arab, Turco-Circassian, and Ottoman design.[10]

The most defining characteristic of premodern *qanun* for historians is not its substance, form, or sources (i.e. other texts, or the rational faculties of the legislators), but rather its maker: the state, that is, the governing authorities.[11] As already noted, the prevailing understanding of historians has long been that that shari'a was elaborated by jurists independent of the state, and therefore the general trend in scholarship has focussed above all on the claim that *qanun* was "state-enacted law" and not jurists' law.[12] According to this line of argument, premodern jurists elaborated shari'a through *fiqh*, but the state's *qanun*, issued by political rulers, was not an instantiation of shari'a. One origin of this understanding is a thesis argued by Joseph Schacht that Muslim jurists of the ninth century wrested from political leaders the monopoly to elaborate the rules of shari'a.[13] Thus, as Martin Hinds contended, beginning in the ninth century, "It was now unquestionably the *ulama* (the jurists), rather than the caliphs, who were 'the legatees of the prophets'; and henceforward it would be they who, armed with this spiritual authority, and at a distance from those who held temporal power, elaborated classical Islam."[14] Shelomo Goitein concurred,

[10] See e.g. Reem Meshal, *Sharia and the Making of the Modern Egyptian: Islamic Law and Custom in the Courts of Ottoman Cairo* (Cairo: American University in Cairo Press, 2014); Khaled Fahmy, "The Anatomy of Justice: Forensic Medicine and Criminal Law in Nineteenth-Century Egypt," *Islamic Law and Society* 6, no. 2 (1999): 224–271; Rudolph Peters, "Islamic and Secular Criminal Law in Nineteenth Century Egypt: The Role and Function of the Qadi," *Islamic Law and Society* 4, no. 1 (1997): 70–90; Rudolph Peters, "State, Law and Society in Nineteenth Century Egypt," *Die Welt des Islams* 39 (1999): 267–272; Avi Rubin, *Ottoman Nizamiye Courts: Law and Modernity* (New York: Palgrave Macmillan, 2011); Omar Cheta, "Rule of Merchants: The Practice of Commerce and Law in Late Ottoman Egypt, 1841–1876," Ph.D. diss., New York University, 2014.

[11] Nazih N. Ayubi, Nader Hashemi, and Emran Qureshi, "Islamic State," in *Oxford Encyclopedia of the Islamic World*, ed. John L. Esposito (New York: Oxford University Press, 2009), 165–75; Shahrough Akhavi, "Dawlah," in *Oxford Encyclopedia of the Islamic World*, (New York: Oxford University Press, 2009), 43–47; Antony Black, *The History of Islamic Political Thought: From the Prophet to the Present* (New York: Routledge, 2001).

[12] Peters, *Crime and Punishment*, 71–72. See also René David and John E.C. Brierley, *Major Legal Systems in the World Today: An Introduction to the Comparative Study of Law* 3rd edn. (London: Sweet & Maxwell, 1985), 470.

[13] Joseph Schacht, *An Introduction to Islamic Law* (Paperback reprint, Oxford: Oxford University Press, 1982), 49–56; and this volume's chapter "*On Reading Fiqh*."

[14] Martin Hinds, "Mihna," in *The Encyclopaedia of Islam*, 2nd edn., vol. 7, ed. C.E. Bosworth, E. van Donzel, W.P. Heinrichs, and Ch. Pellat, 2–6. (Leiden: Brill, 1960–2004). See also Bernard G. Weiss, "Interpretation in Islamic Law: The Theory of Ijtihad," *The American Journal of Comparative Law* 26, vol. 2 (1978): 201.

claiming that "with the exception of some local statutes promulgated and abrogated from time to time, the states as such did not possess any law."[15]

The thesis of a simultaneous existence of both a religious and an apparently secular-oriented law of the state therefore holds that a practical and theoretical dichotomy existed in premodern Islamic institutional history and legal theory, separating the law-making powers of the state from those of the jurists. A recent book by Wael Hallaq freshly insists that the dichotomy was largely firm in history, although he problematizes the dichotomy in other ways.[16] In an extreme version of this thesis, the two bodies of law and their respective makers never met—politics did not interfere in *fiqh*, jurists were not influenced or co-opted by politics, and the subject matter of *qanun* and *fiqh* did not co-mingle. On this basis, for Jan Michiel Otto, writing an introduction to a formidable survey of legal systems of the modern Muslim world, the Middle East before 1500 was a place where "a dual system of state law and religious law operated."[17]

To some observers of modern legislation, the limited range of the subject-matter jurisdiction of premodern *qanun* is an important supposition because it helps to distinguish the past from the present.[18] Whereas the rules of *fiqh* elaborated by jurists historically and ostensibly regulated most aspects of private dealings between people—for example, in contracts, marriages, succession, and certain crimes and torts—it has often been said that *qanun* filled the gaps where shariʿa was silent.[19] By contrast, in the modern Islamic world, legislation regulates every area of law, not only the premodern *qanun* areas of taxation, administration, conscription, and criminal punishment. A question that has gained momentum, meanwhile, is whether a separation between temporal law and the jurisdiction of shariʿa was as clear in premodern centuries as scholars once thought.

A counter narrative to the dichotomy thesis exists, including one put forward by Joseph Schacht himself, who referred to the distinction between the law of jurists and law of the state as a "fiction."[20] Noel Coulson similarly argued that there was a co-mingling of authority between the state and the jurists (although some scholars think Coulson claimed the opposite).[21] More recently, Kristen Stilt's study

[15] Shelomo D. Goitein, *A Mediterranean Society: The Jewish Communities of the Arab World as Portrayed in the Documents of the Cairo Geniza, vol. 1: Economic Foundations* (Berkeley: University of California Press, 1967), 66. See also Emile Tyan, "Judicial Organization," in *Law in the Middle East: Origin and Development of Islamic Law*, ed. Majid Khadduri and Herbert J. Liebesny (Washington, DC: Middle East Institute, 1955; reprint, 2010), 236–278.

[16] Wael B. Hallaq, *The Impossible State: Islam, Politics, and Modernity's Moral Predicament* (New York: Columbia University Press, 2012), 56, 59.

[17] Otto, *Sharia Incorporated*, 43.

[18] See e.g. Anver Emon, Mark Ellis, and Benjamin Glahn, eds., *Islamic Law and International Human Rights Law* (Oxford: Oxford University Press, 2012), 6.

[19] See e.g. Peters, *Crime and Punishment*, 72; İnalcık, "Kanun."

[20] Schacht, *An Introduction to Islamic Law*, 54.

[21] Compare Noel J. Coulson, *A History of Islamic Law* (Edinburgh: Edinburgh University Press, 1964; reprint, 2006), 120–134 and Noel J. Coulson, *Conflicts and Tensions in Islamic Jurisprudence*

of market regulators in Mamluk Cairo (1250–1517) argues that the holders of this office embodied and combined the law and authority of jurists on the one hand and law and authority of the state on the other hand.[22] Mohammad Fadel and Yossef Rapoport have each produced evidence of premodern courts of the state integrating rules of shariʿa, and have shown that early political leaders intervened in jurists' administration and elaboration of shariʿa.[23] David Powers' examination of legal responsa (sg. *fatwa*) from the fourteenth and fifteenth centuries also illustrates the overlapping jurisdictions of *mufti*, *qadi*, and *sultan*.[24]

Contemporary legal theorists working outside of Islamic and area studies have helped establish analytical groundwork for problematizing the jurist/state dichotomy. Janet Halley and Kerry Rittich, for example, have suggested that areas typically considered to have been the least penetrable bastion of premodern jurists' authority—"family law" and rules governing the home[25]—cannot, as a practical matter, ever be wholly separated from rules in areas such as taxation, market regulation, administration, and conscription.[26] It is conceivable that the very notion of such categorical divisions is a fiction, or at least an exaggeration, of a category-obsessed, nineteenth-century continental European legal ideology that Europeans foisted on legal systems of Muslim countries and simultaneously back-projected onto understandings of Islamic legal history.[27]

Recognizing that early religious authorities vested in the caliph the qualities of a jurist in order to protect public order and the shariʿa,[28] scholars have researched the premodern doctrine of *siyasa sharʿiyya*. The term may be translated as

(Chicago: University of Chicago Press, 1969), 59–70 with Amr A. Shalakany, "Islamic Legal Histories," *Berkeley Journal of Middle Eastern and Islamic Law* 1 (2008): 21–22. See also Gustave E. von Grunebaum, *Medieval Islam* (Chicago: University of Chicago Press, 1946), 167–168.

22 Kristen Stilt, *Islamic Law in Action: Authority, Discretion, and Everyday Experiences in Mamluk Egypt* (New York: Oxford University Press, 2011). See also Marshall G. S. Hodgson, *The Venture of Islam: Conscience and History in a World Civilization, vol. 3: The Gunpowder Empires and Modern Times* (Chicago: University of Chicago Press, 1974), 346–347.

23 Yossef Rapoport, "Royal Justice and Religious Law: Siyasah and Shariʿah under the Mamluks," *Mamluk Studies Review* 16 (2012): 71–102; Mohammad Fadel, "Adjudication," 61–75, 79–105, 185–198, as cited in Fadel, "State and Sharia," in *The Ashgate Research Companion to Islamic Law*, ed. Rudolph Peters and Peri Bearman (Farnham, Surrey: Ashgate, 2014), 100.

24 David S. Powers, *Law, Society, and Culture in the Maghrib, 1300–1500* (Cambridge: Cambridge University Press, 2002).

25 Liebesny, *Law of the Near and Middle East*, 16.

26 Janet Halley and Kerry Rittich, "Critical Directions in Comparative Family Law: Genealogies and Contemporary Studies of Family Law Exceptionalism," *American Journal of Comparative Law* 58, no. 4 (2010): 753–776.

27 On legal categories, see John Henry Merryman and Rogel Pérez-Perdomo, *The Civil Law Tradition: An Introduction to the Legal Systems of Europe and Latin America*, 3rd edn. (Stanford, CA: Stanford University Press, 2007), 91–94.

28 Schacht, *An Introduction to Islamic Law*, 53–54; Weiss, "Interpretation," 201.

"Shari'a-compliant policy."[29] This doctrine held that man-made law promulgated by the political ruler, and created for political expedience but compliant with fundamental principles of shari'a, should be considered part of shari'a insofar as it served necessary and beneficial ends for the people. Frank Vogel has published an elaborate study of the interplay between classical *fiqh* and *siyasa shar'iyya*, based on Saudi Arabia as a case-study.[30] Related to *siyasa shar'iyya* doctrine, studies of Ottoman jurists show how they expanded the doctrine of custom (*'urf*)—a well-established source of Islamic law in canonical theoretical literature—to legitimize state-made law as an instantiation and part of the overall shari'a-compliant legal order.[31]

Although all recognize the existence of *siyasa shar'iyya* doctrine in historical legal theory, scholars are divided over whether the doctrine emphasized a distinction between law of the jurists and law of the state, or whether the doctrine's intent and effect was to lessen or deny such distinction. Likewise, they differ on whether state-produced *qanun* and shari'a coexisted in conflict or harmony. Halil İnalcık maintains that in the earlier centuries of Islam, the appearance of *qanun* "did not shock even the strictest of the [jurists], because in administrative matters there was no conflict between the *qanun* and the shari'a, the latter generally being silent on such matters."[32] But he claims that in later times the difference between *qanun* and *fiqh* was a source of tension between jurists and the *sultan*.[33] Likewise, Colin Imber has argued that although theoretical justifications of *qanun* existed in Islamic legal thought, those justifications arose out of and coexisted with an ongoing conflict between *qanun* and shari'a. "The *qanun*," he says, "was a systematization of specifically Ottoman feudal practice which ... ran directly counter to the doctrines of the jurists."[34]

Others argue that a higher degree of harmony existed.[35] Michael Winter asserts that *qanun* in Mamluk Egypt empowered and extended the law of the shari'a courts, but did not seek to compromise the jurisdiction of those courts.[36] Ahmet Akgündüz

[29] Frank E. Vogel, "Siyasa 3. In the Sense of siyasa shar'iyya," in *The Encyclopaedia of Islam*, 2nd edn., vol. 9. ed. C.E. Bosworth, E. van Donzel, W.P. Heinrichs and Ch. Pellat, 694–96. (Leiden: Brill, 1960–2004). See also Fadel, "Adjudication," 61–75, 79–105, 185–198.

[30] Frank E. Vogel, *Islamic Law and Legal System: Studies of Saudi Arabia* (Leiden: Brill, 2000).

[31] See e.g. Meshal, *Sharia*, 49–50; Leslie P. Peirce, *Morality Tales: Law and Gender in the Ottoman Court of Aintab* (Berkeley, CA: University of California Press, 2003), 117–120; G. Libson and F. H. Stewart, "'Urf," in *The Encyclopaedia of Islam*, 2nd edn., vol. 10. ed. C.E. Bosworth, E. van Donzel, W.P. Heinrichs and Ch. Pellat, 887–892. (Leiden: Brill, 1960–2004).

[32] İnalcık, "Kanun." [33] İnalcık, "Kanun."

[34] Imber, *Ebu's-Su'ud*, 24, 40, 50–51. See also von Grunebaum, *Medieval Islam*, 167–169.

[35] See e.g. Peters, *Crime and Punishment*, 74; Seyyed Hussein Nasr, *The Heart of Islam: Enduring Values for Humanity* (San Francisco: HarperCollins, 2002), 122; Karen Meerschaut and Serge Gutwirth, "Continuities and Ruptures in the Governance of Islam in Malaysia," in *Colonial and Post-Colonial Governance of Islam: Continuities and Ruptures*, ed. Marcel Maussen, Veit Bader, and Annelies Moors (Amsterdam: Amsterdam University Press, 2011), 177; Muzaffar Alam, *The Languages of Political Islam: India 1200–1800* (Chicago: University of Chicago Press, 2004).

[36] Michael Winter, "The Ottoman Occupation," in *The Cambridge History of Egypt, vol. 1: Islamic Egypt, 640–1517*, ed. Carl F. Petry (Cambridge: Cambridge University Press, 1998), 516.

argues that Ottoman *qanun* reflected attempts by the state to apply *fiqh* and claims that Islamic jurists influenced the production of *fiqh*.[37] He emphasizes that legislators used canonical sources and *fiqh* methods to produce legislation, including custom and juristic preference (*istihsan*). Douglas Howard states that "by the middle of the fifteenth century" Ottoman legal theory had accomplished "the equation of justice with the application of the *qanun*."[38] The idea that state-made *qanun* coexisted in relative harmony with the jurisdiction of the jurists corresponds with findings of research into other aspects of premodern Islamic legal practice.[39]

Historiography of premodern Islamic societies therefore presents competing claims about the presence of state-legislated *qanun* and about its relationship with shariʿa. Although legislation was once thought to have been relatively scarce in premodern Muslim societies, scholars have been finding greater evidence of it and positing that it was prevalent. There is still debate as to whether the separation of jurisdiction and authority between the state and jurists in legal practice was as strict as once thought, and as to the degree to which premodern Muslims accepted *qanun*, in legal theory, as being evocative of shariʿa. Either the two areas of law were in theoretical conflict, or Islamic legal theory genuinely accepted the coexistence and co-mingling of the jurisdictions, to the extent that the jurisdictions were separated.

II. Mid-nineteenth Century until the Present Day

Like *fiqh*, legislation is an instrument and a genre, and also a technique and a practice. There are many conceivable methods for determining what legislation's content should be and how to write and use legislation. But unlike *fiqh*, no canonical Islamic discourse explains how to style the genre, how to interpret and apply it, and how to fill its infinite gaps through adjudication. The discourse about how to legislate consists only of the modern-era volleying and polemics of intellectuals and jurists,

[37] Akgündüz, *Osmanlı kanunnameleri ve hukuki tahlileri* as cited in Boğaç A. Ergene, "*Qanun* and Shariʿa," in *The Ashgate Research Companion to Islamic Law*, ed. Rudolph Peters and Peri Bearman (Farnham, Surrey: Ashgate, 2014), 115.

[38] Douglas A. Howard, "Ottoman Historiography and the Literature of 'Decline' of the Sixteenth and Seventeenth Centuries," *Journal of Asian History* 22, no. 1 (1988): 52–77. But see Hallaq, *The Impossible State*, 69.

[39] See e.g. Baber Johansen, "Legal Literature and the Problem of Change: The Case of Land Rent," in *Islam and Public Law: Classical and Contemporary Studies*, ed. Chibli Mallat (London: Graham & Trotman, 1993), 29–47. Reprinted in Baber Johansen, *Contingency in a Sacred Law: Legal and Ethical Norms in the Muslim Fiqh* (Leiden: Brill, 1999), 446–64.

none of whom carry the authoritative weight or renown of a premodern Muslim jurist writing from within *fiqh* literature. Whoever wants to know how to legislate in a shariʿa-compliant matter must either innovate or follow earlier historical examples.

An oft-cited historical example of Islamic legislation is the Ottoman civil code, the Mecelle, on account of the way its drafters—jurists—combined formal aspects of the Napoleonic Civil Code of 1804 with legal substance and methodology from *fiqh*.[40] But neither the Mecelle nor the methodology of its drafters achieved canonical status in the Islamic world. Modern-day legislation in the Islamic world appears through parliamentary process, importation of foreign law, fiat, and the work of legislators commissioned by states, with only varying levels of input from traditionally educated jurists and the teachings of *fiqh* literature.

Scholars typically make three preliminary decisions when discussing legislation of recent centuries. One, they call the period from approximately the mid-nineteenth century onward "modern" even though this terminology risks nurturing a teleological presumption that phenomena of recent centuries must somehow be significantly different from correlating phenomena of eras past.[41] Two, they assume that the analysis of legislation and the modern nation-state, including the colonial state,[42] go hand-in-hand.[43] As a practical matter, this has meant that scholars attribute features they find in modern legislation to the modern state, and they attribute features they find in the modern state to legislation.[44] And, three, scholars often take as a premise one particular concept of what "Islamic law" is and should be in a legislative context.[45]

Against this background, the most common preoccupations in scholarly analyses of modern legislation have focussed on its apparent newness from a broader historical perspective and its contestable Islamicity from the theoretical perspective. A common ambition of scholars is, in other words, to address how modern legislation has integrated, contravened, modified, or sidelined the true or authentic shariʿa. Combined with these preoccupations is an epistemological disjuncture of perspective between scholars who write from different disciplines, principally specialists in Islamic and area studies on one hand, and lawyers and full-time specialists of western legal theory on the other hand. These preoccupations and epistemological

40 Şerif Arif Mardin, "Some Explanatory Notes on the Origins of the Mecelle," *Muslim World* 51, nos. 3–4 (1961): 189–196, 274–279. But see Frederic Maurice Goadby, *Introduction to the Study of Law: A Handbook for the Use of Law Students in Egypt and Palestine*, 3rd edn. (London: Butterworth, 1921), 165.

41 Compare Otto, *Sharia Incorporated*, 41 with Meshal, *Sharia*, 3–4.

42 Otto, *Sharia Incorporated*, 41; Nathan J. Brown, "Law and Imperialism: Egypt in Comparative Perspective," *Law and Society Review* 29, no. 1 (1995): 103–126; Marcel Maussen and Veit Bader, "Introduction," in *Colonial and Post-Colonial Governance of Islam: Continuities and Ruptures*, ed. Marcel Maussen, Veit Bader, and Annelies Moors (Amsterdam: Amsterdam University Press, 2011), 12.

43 Hallaq, *Shariʿa*, 357–360; Hallaq, *The Impossible State*, 19–36.

44 See e.g. Sami Zubaida, *Law and Power in the Islamic World* (London: I.B. Tauris, 2003), esp. 121–157, 183–219.

45 See Shalakany, *Islamic Legal Histories*, 10.

disjunctures pervade the arena of analysis but pose striking dilemmas, which will be discussed in the following sections.

A. Preoccupations with Newness from a Broader Historical Perspective

The treatment of post-Ottoman and other modern, non-Ottoman legislation as new phenomena in Muslim historical experience is based on facts that are hard to dispute. For example, the Iranian civil code of 1928 was indisputably new for Iran as both a matter of form—its style was modeled on continental European precedents—and of substance—it incorporated some rules from the continental European codes.[46] Likewise, the legislative process that the Malaysian state of Kelantan implemented in 1993 for adopting criminal statutes was representative of a relatively new process for the elaborating of shari'a (despite the fact that Malaysian criminal law is federal and that Kelantan's new law had no chance of surviving within the framework of the federal system).[47] However, the inclination to treat modern legislation as new persists also because some still endorse the thesis of a premodern jurist/state dichotomy.[48] Hallaq, for example, accepts that *qanun* existed in premodern times, but he finds modern legislation so qualitatively different on account of the state's degree of penetration in society and in law-making itself that he considers modern Islamic legislation to be, overall, a radically new phenomenon.[49]

Scholars have commonly traced the newness and difference of modern legislation to four attributes of modern political and legal practice:

1. Hegemony. Scholars assert that the modern, post-Ottoman state has proved hegemonic in historically unprecedented ways, centralizing power and invading the legal sphere with a measure of top-down definitiveness and decisiveness unknown to most Islamic history and unjustified in Islamic legal theory.[50] This

[46] Yeganeh, "Civil Code." Cf. Hadi Enayat, *Law, State, and Society in Modern Iran: Constitutionalism, Autocracy, and Legal Reform, 1906–1941* (New York: Palgrave Macmillan, 2013), 134–139; Herbert J. Liebesny, "Stability and Change in Islamic Law," *Middle East Journal* 21, no. 1 (1967): 30.

[47] Kamaruzzaman Bustamam-Ahmad, *Islamic Law in Southeast Asia: A Study of Its Application in Kelantan and Aceh* (Bangkok: Asian Muslim Action Network, 2009), 19–27.

[48] See e.g. Roel Meijer, "The Problem of the Political in Islamist Movements," in *Whatever Happened to the Islamists? Salafis, Heavy Metal Muslims and the Lure of Consumerist Islam*, eds. Amel Boubekeur and Olivier Roy (London: Hurst, 2012), 27–28.

[49] See generally Hallaq, *The Impossible State*, esp. 72.

[50] Hallaq, *Shari'a*, 361; Maurits S. Berger, "Sharia and Nation State," in *The Ashgate Research Companion to Islamic Law*, eds. Rudolph Peters and Peri Bearman (Farnham, Surrey: Ashgate, 2014), 224; Sherman A. Jackson, "Jihad and the Modern World," *Journal of Islamic Law and Culture* 7, no. 1 (2002): 4–5; Enayat, *Law, State, and Society*, 142.

assertion sets up legislation as not merely a legal instrument but also as an unprecedented manifestation of top-down political and law-making power.

2. Usurpation. Scholars emphasize that the modern nation-state usurped law-making power from the Islamic jurists in ways that were uncommon in Islamic legal history and impermissible in Islamic legal theory.[51] This follows the view that the isolation of jurists from the state was enshrined in Islamic legal theory and also prevailed in history as a matter of practice, and distinguishes legislation from other instruments for articulating Islamic law in its being state-made.
3. Uniformity. Scholars argue that modern legislation provides one answer to every legal question, whereas classical Islamic law generally accepted the existence of multiple, competing answers (*ikhtilaf*) to each legal question both in theory and practice, without threatening the integrity of the shariʿa-compliant normative order.[52]
4. Secularity. Scholars claim that the secular, modern nation-state newly marginalized Islamic law by relegating its subject-matter jurisdiction to a historically unprecedented, narrow range of matters, such as family law and inheritance. Similarly, scholars depict modern states as having disingenuously incorporated rules from *fiqh* by manipulating them to achieve secular policy, all in a way broadly unknown to Islamic legal history and unapproved in Islamic legal theory.[53]

Although there must be degrees of truth in these listed claims about the newness and difference of legislation in the Islamic world, the harder questions arise when one seeks to ascertain the degrees more precisely. Not all of the arguments of newness and difference between legislation and Islamic law are rigorously reconciled with developments in premodern Islamic historiography or in modern legal science.

[51] Hallaq, *Shariʿa*, 364; Berger, "Sharia and Nation State," 225, 255; Emon, Ellis, and Glahn, *Islamic Law*, 6; Enayat, *Law, State, and Society*, 139; Asghar Schirazi, *The Constitution of Iran: Politics and the State in the Islamic Republic* (London: I.B. Tauris, 1997), 243.

[52] Marc Galanter, "The Modernization of Law," in *Modernization: The Dynamics of Growth*, ed. Myron Weiner (New York: Basic Books, 1996), 154; Jackson, "Jihad and the Modern World," 4–5; Enayat, *Law, State, and Society*, 139.

[53] Hallaq, *Shariʿa*, 412; Wael B. Hallaq, "Can the Shariʿa Be Restored?" in *Islamic Law and the Challenges of Modernity*, ed. Yvonne Yazbeck Haddad and Barbara Freyer Stowasser (Walnut Creek, CA: AltaMira, 2004), 25; Zubaida, *Law and Power*, 125, 140–142, 160–165; Knut S. Vikør, *Between God and the Sultan: A History of Islamic Law* (New York: Oxford University Press, 2006), 241; Talal Asad, *Formations of the Secular: Christianity, Islam, Modernity* (Stanford, CA: Stanford University Press, 2003), 4–17, 218–227; Hussein Ali Agrama, *Questioning Secularism: Islam, Sovereignty, and the Rule of Law in Modern Egypt* (Chicago: University of Chicago Press, 2012), 23–36; Butti Sultan Butti Ali Al-Muhairi, "The Development of the UAE Legal System and Unification with the Judicial System," *Arab Law Quarterly* 11, no. 2 (1996): 116, 129–130, 135–138; Mehdi Pirhaji et al., "Investigation of Defects of Article 264 of Iranian Civil Code," *Asian Social Science* 10, no. 7 (2014): 40; Enayat, *Law, State, and Society*, 138.

The newness of the factor of nation-state hegemony is a false premise when premodern governmental institutions of the Islamic world are shown to have hegemonic aspects. Ample instances of governmental hegemony and centralization can be found in the history of politics of the medieval Muslim world.[54] Historians such as Stilt, Rapoport, and Powers have demonstrated the co-mingling of states' and jurists' powers in the premodern eras. Also, credence in the idea that Islamic legal theory is averse to state-made law and considers state-made law as apart from the shariʿa is undermined where scholars have shown that Islamic legal theories, including popular ones such as *siyasa sharʿiyya*, accepted the coexistence and co-mingling of state-made and jurist-made law.

B. The Dilemma of Islamicity

The combined conclusion of scholars about newness and difference in modern legislation of shariʿa opens the door to concerns about Islamicity. This door is particularly inviting to very many scholars who assume that what Muslims did in the premodern periods that was viewed by anyone in those times as compliant with Islam can confidently be called Islamic, while anything that Muslims do in the modern period that some may view today as non-Islamic—or insufficiently Islamic—may be plausibly entertained as such.[55] This prevalent assumption, once exposed, is problematic. It is understandable from an Islamic worldview that venerates precedent and finds anything "new" in the legal practice of Muslims potentially suspect (*taqlid*), but not from an alternative Islamic worldview that holds that new developments in the legal practice of Muslims may be readily considered a service to Islam (*tajdid*), especially where such developments do not contravene the norms or aims (e.g. *maqasid*) of Islam.

Asifa Quraishi-Landes among other scholars has indicated that the presumption that legislation must be or could ever be compliant with shariʿa stems from western intellectual innovation or was imposed by Westerners on Islamic legal consciousness through colonialism.[56] One extension of this thesis is a view that colonial conquerors, who sought to codify shariʿa laws as part of their colonial projects, imposed on Muslims a transformative, western-driven, positivist conception of Islamic law that holds that Islamic law can, hypothetically, be reduced to monolithic,

[54] Hodgson, *Venture of Islam*, 345–348; Meshal, *Sharia*, 89–93; Efraim Karsh, *Islamic Imperialism: A History* (New Haven: Yale University Press, 2006), 31–42; Coulson, *Conflicts and Tensions in Islamic Jurisprudence*, 67–76; von Grunebaum, *Medieval Islam*, 167; Schacht, *An Introduction to Islamic Law*, 53–54.

[55] See e.g. Hallaq, *The Impossible State*, 2–3.

[56] See Asifa Quraishi-Landes, "The Sharia Problem with Sharia Legislation," *Ohio Northern University Law Review* 41, no. 3 (2015): 546 fn. 2, 552.

state-produced codes. In this view, the imposition of secular rule in some countries also inspired Islamicity concerns of Muslims by newly supplanting the jurisdiction of shari'a with secular or foreign law. Wael Hallaq, famously but not alone, has taken the position that this transformative influence produced an "impossible" expectation, for premodern Islamic law was effectively a jurists' common law elaborated in isolation from political forces. Thus Islamic law cannot be legislated by the modern state and still be Islamic law.[57]

A second viewpoint, as Leonard Wood has proposed, is that indigenous Muslims of the Islamic world in recent centuries exercised equal or greater agency in putting the Islamicity preoccupation to the fore. Faced with importation of western-style legislation through colonialism, they themselves played an equal or greater role than westerners in transforming the conception of shari'a—i.e. from non-legislatable to legislatable—to the extent that such a conceptual transformation happened at all.[58]

A third view is that the alleged transformation in conceptions of shari'a never took place, or has at least been overstated. Therefore it is in the ordinary course of Islamic legal theory and historical practice that Muslims should both seek to legislate in shari'a-compliant ways and debate the extent to which they have succeeded.[59]

Assessing whether legislation is Islamic is, to begin with, a bedeviling ambition of the first order because it is challenging, if not impossible, to uncontroversially specify the criteria for determining Islamicity. Despite this, an industry of writing has been dealing with the topic since the British occupation of India and more concertedly since the French occupation of Algeria. A paradigmatic example is J.N.D. Anderson's article "Shari'a and Civil Law" (1954), which examined the Egyptian and Syrian civil codes provision-by-provision, identifying Islamic and non-Islamic parts.[60] The pertinent question, however—which can be asked of all such works—is whether Anderson selected the correct criteria for assessing the Islamicity of the rules he studied.

Some modern legislative examples illustrate, if only very generally, the depth of the *a priori* dilemma of evaluating legislation's Islamicity. The first example comes from legislation enacted in Iran before and after the Islamic Revolution of 1979. The government of post-revolutionary Iran, which fashions itself as Islamic, has long championed the imperative to produce only Islamic legislation and to Islamize all

[57] Hallaq, *The Impossible State*. See also H.A.R. Gibb, "Constitutional Organization," in *Law in the Middle East: Origin and Development of Islamic Law*, ed. Majid Khadduri and Herbert J. Liebesny (Washington, DC: Middle East Institute, 1955; reprint, 2010), 3.

[58] Leonard Wood, "Shari'ah Revivalist Thought in the First Years of the Shari'ah Lawyers' Bar Association Journal," *Maghreb Review* 32, no. 2 (2007): 196–217.

[59] See Shalakany, "Islamic Legal Histories."

[60] J.N.D. Anderson, "The Shari'a and Civil Law: The Debt Owed by the New Civil Codes of Egypt and Syria to the Shari'a," *Islamic Quarterly* 1 (1954): 29–46. See also Yvon Linant de Bellefonds, "Le droit

pre-revolutionary non-Islamic legislation.[61] Yet the government has kept in place and effectively endorsed pre-revolutionary commercial, administrative, and procedural legislation, all without evident connections to Islamic legal sources, as a means to provide order, address necessities, and support social objectives.[62] One criterion of Islamicity, then, is that it can be claimed for laws that *serve a legitimate public purpose*.[63] A second criterion of Islamicity is that a self-declared Islamic state may confer Islamicity on laws by *fiat*.[64] A third criterion is located in the *political and cultural origins* of legislation—steadfast critics deride the above laws for their origins in non-Islamic polities, whether pre-revolutionary Iran or western countries.[65]

The second example comes from the conclusions of a rural shariʿa court judge in Egypt in the 1870s who was commissioned to compare each article of the Napoleonic Code to rules of *fiqh*; he concluded that much of the Napoleonic law substantively complied with *fiqh* and was thus evocative of shariʿa.[66] A fourth criterion of Islamicity in legislation is thus the *substantive correspondence of norms* with rules found in classical books of *fiqh*. However, it was commonplace in Egypt for jurists of that era to dismiss the Napoleonic code—significant portions of which were adopted in Egypt's civil code of 1883—as generally non-compliant with shariʿa because it was not authored by Muslim jurists.[67] A fifth criterion of Islamicity is thus that the legislated rule should be directly *extracted from books of fiqh*. On this basis, in 1983, the Sudanese government produced a new Islamic criminal code and claimed it was Islamic because it was derived from principles articulated in *fiqh* literature. The Sudanese legal scholar Abdullahi An-Naʿim questions its Islamic credentials, however, observing that it was not produced by a more democratic or consultative procedure where each person can consider "the valid concerns of the other."[68] A sixth criterion for Islamicity may therefore emphasize that a *democratic or consultative process* is necessary to make legislation sufficiently Islamic.

musulman et le nouveau code civil égyptien," *Revue algérienne, tunisienne et marocaine de législation et de jurisprudence* 72 (1956): 211–222.

61 Schirazi, *Constitution of Iran*, 161–162.

62 Ibid., 165–175, 194, 200, 202.

63 Cf. Quraishi-Landes, "The Sharia Problem," 556.

64 Schirazi, *Constitution of Iran*, 171–172. 65 Ibid., 163.

66 Makhluf ibn Muhammad al-Badawi al-Minyawi, *Al-Muqaranat al-tashriʿiyya: Tatbiq al-qanun al-madani wa-l-jinʿi ʿala madhhab al-imam Malik*, ed. Muhammad Ahmad Siraj and ʿAli Jumʿa Muhammad (Cairo: Dar al-Salam, 1999), 1–13.

67 Leonard Wood, "Reception of European Law, Origins of Islamic Legal Revivalism, and Foundations of Transformations in Islamic Legal Thought in Egypt, 1875–1960." Ph.D. diss., Harvard University, 2011, 119.

68 Abdullahi Ahmed An-Naʾim, *Toward an Islamic Reformation: Civil Liberties, Human Rights, and International Law* (Syracuse, NY: Syracuse University Press, 1990), 82–83, 104, 131, 134. See also Sayyid Abu'l-Aʿla Mawdudi, "The Islamic Law," in *Princeton Readings in Islamist Thought: Texts*

The *a priori* obstacles to determining the Islamicity of legislation stem, then, from a deficit of consensus over whether legislation can ever be a legitimate instrument of shari'a; which political procedures are legitimate for legislating shari'a; which methods for determining the right rules are correct; and which methods should be used for testing a given rule's compliance with shari'a, assuming the foregoing criteria are already answered and satisfied. Additionally, there is no agreement on how statutes in an Islamic legal order should be interpreted, applied, and reconciled, or how its gaps should be filled through adjudication. Baudoin Dupret has shown that in Egypt, where many judges infuse Islamic norms into their statutory interpretation, the theories and methods used by judges are extremely divergent.[69]

Scholars who generalize on the types of legislation in the modern Muslim world typically group legislation, explicitly or implicitly, into categories of Islamic, non-Islamic, and hybridic, following how given bodies of legislation have been publicly advertised or otherwise commonly perceived in the Muslim world.[70] But this categorizing can be misleading if one's primary concern is to analyze the relationship of legislation to Islam. Such a classification demands and implicitly assumes an answer to what Islamic legislation is. Legislation cannot definitively claim anything about itself. No person or institution can definitively claim that legislation is Islamic or non-Islamic, including the drafters. For most legislation in the world that one would claim is Islamic, someone can and likely has alleged insufficient Islamicity, and the inverse applies for many pieces of legislation that some people claim are non-Islamic. Consider, for example, An-Na'im's claim that legislation is more evocative of Islamic norms when it is made through a consultative process,[71] or 'Abd al-Razzaq al-Sanhuri's proposition that legislation can be considered Islamic when made out of economic necessity.[72] These types of theories dramatically expand the possibilities for creating shari'a-compliant legislation. The result of this situation is that most legislation existing in the Islamic world can be subjected to an earnest Islamicity inquiry, even when the legislation is facially secular, imported from the West, or widely recognized as having been derived from sources other than *fiqh*.

and Contexts from al-Banna to Bin Laden, ed. Roxanne L. Euben and Muhammad Qasim Zaman (Princeton: Princeton University Press, 2009), 105.

[69] Baudouin Dupret, "A Return to the Shariah? Egyptian Judges and Referring to Islam," in *Modernizing Islam: Religion in the Public Sphere in the Middle East and Europe*, ed. John L. Esposito and François Burgat (New Brunswick, NJ: Rutgers University Press, 2003), 125–143.

[70] See e.g. Lau, "Re-Islamization of Legal Systems," 235; David and Brierley, *Major Legal Systems*, 473; Emon, Ellis, and Glahn, *Islamic Law*, 6.

[71] An-Na'im, *Toward an Islamic Reformation*, 82–83, 104, 131, 134.

[72] Chibli Mallat, "The Debate on Riba," in *Islamic Law and Finance*, ed. Chibli Mallat (London: Graham & Trotman, 1988), 76–85.

III. Epistemological Differences and New Directions in Scholarship

In order to examine supposed differences between law in the premodern and modern Islamic world, it is helpful to have a sophisticated understanding of what modern legislation is as a technique and an instrument of legal practice across cultures and countries. Yet while scholars of Islamic and area studies habitually caution against the dangers of reducing Islamic law to a construct, they habitually rely on reductive constructs of western-style legislation, which are partially Weberian[73] and partially precepts of continental European, nineteenth-century, civil law ideology.[74] In this view, legislation is monolithic; internally consistent;[75] predictable; comprehensive; clear;[76] rationalizing;[77] shaped from the top down;[78] typically applied without reference to uncodified canons of interpretation and construction; typically applied without reference to uncodified doctrines of application, such as doctrines of equity and judicial aversion to negative practical consequences of legal formalism; a reliable primary source for understanding how the law is lived; special as compared to other forms of law because it is written down; and special as compared to other forms of law because it is controlled by agents of a political power as opposed to jurists and judges who are politically independent and policy-neutral.

One finds a persistent dominance in Islamic and area studies of such constitutive elements of a reductive construct of western legislation, even though those precepts have been qualified and discarded for over a century in other disciplines. Since the late nineteenth century, legal scholars working far from Islamic and area studies—especially lawyers writing from within law faculties about western law and legal theory—have labored to show that legislation is not monolithic but exists concurrently with other formal and informal sources of law; not internally consistent but internally inconsistent; not predictable but unpredictable; not comprehensive but riddled with gaps; not clear but subject to manifold interpretations; not shaped from

[73] Max Weber, *From Max Weber: Essays in Sociology*. Translated and edited by Hans H. Gerth and C. Wright Mills (New York: Oxford University Press, 1958), 78; Max Weber, *Economy and Society: An Outline of Interpretive Sociology*, ed. Guenther Roth and Claus Wittich (Berkeley: University of California Press, 1978), 34; Galanter, "Modernization of Law," 153–163, 154.

[74] See Ann Elizabeth Mayer, "Universal Versus Islamic Human Rights: A Clash of Cultures or a Clash with a Construct?" *Michigan Journal of International Law* 15 (1994): 307–404; Andrew F. March, "What Can the Islamic Past Teach Us about Secular Modernity?" *Political Theory* 43 (December 2015): 838–49.

[75] See e.g. Hallaq, *Sharīʿa*, 368; Enayat, *Law, State, and Society*, 138.

[76] See e.g. Hallaq, *Sharīʿa*, 367, 369.

[77] Ibid., 417; Enayat, *Law, State, and Society*, 138.

[78] Ibid., 142. But see Leopold J. Pospisil, *Anthropology of Law: A Comparative Theory* (New Haven, CT: HRAF Press, 1974), 104; Max Weber, *Wirtschaft und Gesellschaft* (Tübingen: J.C.B. Mohr, 1922), 373.

the top down but shaped from the bottom up; typically applied by means of reference to competing, uncodified canons of interpretation and construction; typically applied by means of reference to uncodified doctrines of application, like doctrines of equity and judicial aversion to negative practical consequences of formalism; not a reliable primary source for understanding how the law is lived; written down but containing rules that existed for centuries in an uncodified form; and controlled by both agents of political power as well as judges and jurists who claim to be independent and policy-neutral, but are, in fact, neither.[79]

Greater attention by scholars in Islamic and area studies to western legal history and theory could create new opportunities to achieve greater precision when discussing legislation's newness and its effects within any Islamic context. An example is found in the use of the term "codification," which scholars of Islamic and area studies habitually link with "legislation," as if to mean that the terms always have the same meaning.[80] In contrast, Guy Bechor has discussed in depth how codification in the nineteenth century was a species of legislation and not a synonym of legislation.[81] Codification in this era was an exacting science with arguably no precedent in the Islamic world. Codes were meant to set out a comprehensive set of rules for specific fields of law that were taken to be wholly distinct, and codifiers intended that their codes should be interpreted according to precise methods that they specified in separate technical treatises.[82] With the passing of decades, predominating theories for writing and interpreting codes shifted in perceptible waves. Some legislation in the Islamic world has resulted from these movements, and other legislation has not. A few scholars have acknowledged the distinction and apprehended this aspect of the history of European codification and legal education when looking at legislation of the Islamic world.[83] Yet in the colonial era,

[79] See e.g. William Lucy, "Adjudication," in *The Oxford Handbook of Jurisprudence and Philosophy of Law*, eds. Jules Coleman and Scott J. Shapiro (Oxford: Oxford University Press, 2004), 206–267 and Martin Stone, "Formalism," in *The Oxford Handbook of Jurisprudence and Philosophy of Law*, eds. Jules Coleman and Scott J. Shapiro (Oxford: Oxford University Press, 2004), 166–205; Dennis Patterson, ed., *A Companion to Philosophy of Law and Legal Theory* (Malden, MA: Blackwell, 1996), 223–396; Roberto Unger, "The CLS Movement," *Harvard Law Review* 96 (1983): 561–573, 665–675; Gary Minda, *Postmodern Legal Movements: Law and Jurisprudence at Century's End* (New York: New York University Press, 1995).

[80] See Brown, *Rule of Law*, 32–33; Hallaq, *Shari'a*, 368; Zubaida, *Law and Power*, 134.

[81] Guy Bechor, *The Sanhuri Code, and the Emergence of Modern Arab Civil Law (1932 to 1949)* (Leiden: Brill, 2007), 50–57.

[82] See generally Katarzina Sójka-Zielińska, "Codification," in *Dictionnaire encyclopédique de théorie et de sociologie du droit*, eds. André Jean Arnaud and Jean-Guy Belley (Paris: Libraire générale de droit et de jurisprudence, 1993), 69–72. See also André Jean Arnaud, *Les origines doctrinales du code civil français* (Paris: Libraire générale de droit et de jurisprudence, 1969); Taylor Arthur von Mehren and James Gordley, *The Civil Law System: An Introduction to the Comparative Study of Law* (Boston: Little, Brown, 1977), 54–55.

[83] Amr A. Shalakany, "Between Identity and Redistribution: Sanhuri, Genealogy and the Will to Islamise," *Islamic Law and Society* 8, no. 2 (2001): 201–244.

when Muslim lawyers studied in colonial law schools and then erected the pillars of modern legislation in their countries, this knowledge was considered fundamental.[84]

Existing scholarship on legislation as an instrument of Islamic law has therefore produced powerful arguments, yet it struggles with dilemmas and contradictions. The scholarship of arm's length researchers is characterized by a stalemate in the question of what constitutes proper Islamic legislation because invested proponents of Islamic legislation, i.e. stakeholders, are themselves locked in conflict over how to produce Islamic legislation and the question of whether such a project should be pursued at all. But it cannot suffice to leave the discussion on that conclusion. If for no other reason, the need for breaking the current stalemate is urgent because a pressing need is still felt in parts of the Islamic world to reconcile desires for Islamic normativity with the ubiquity of legislation as a contemporary phenomenon.[85] This desire has been voiced by leaders of the Arab Spring, as well as in the advocacy of Islamists in Asia, India, Africa, and the Americas.

In a 2008 article, Amr Shalakany sought to bridge disjunctures between the fields of Islamic history, revisionist legal history of the Ottoman Empire, and western legal scholarship on legislation. In the two following subsections, his law-in-action approach to understanding legislation is compared with its "opposite," the scripturalist approach.

A. The Law-in-Action Concept

Shalakany begins by observing that the notion of "Islamicity" is methodologically problematic because it involves essentializing the complex shari'a and making selective decisions about what counts as shari'a and what does not.[86] In his view, writers consciously and unconsciously make selective decisions about what "Islamic law" is in form and substance before putting pen to paper, and these decisions in turn affect, and skew, their evaluations of Islamicity in legislation.

He calls one end of the spectrum of approaches for defining Islamic law the "scripturalist" (or "positivist") approach.[87] This approach, typified by Anderson, holds that Islamic law is a legal practice based entirely on the methodological and substantive doctrines of predominant juristic writers (*fuqaha'*) of the past and as recorded in their *fiqh* books.[88] The approach focuses on what falls within the pages

[84] See e.g. Goadby, *Introduction to the Study of Law*, 150–173; Bechor, *Sanhuri Code*, 59–61, 94–97; 'Abd al-Razzaq al-Sanhuri, "Wujub tanqih al-qanun al-madani al-misri," *Majallat al-qanun wa-l-iqtisad* 6, no. 1 (1936): 3–144.

[85] See March, "What Can the Islamic Past Teach Us?"

[86] Shalakany, "Islamic Legal Histories," 10.

[87] Ibid., 5. See also Baudouin Dupret, "Modern Law and Arab Societies in Recent French-Speaking Literature," *Journal of Law and Religion* 15, nos. 1–2 (2000–01): 289.

[88] See Majid Khadduri, *War and Peace in the Law of Islam* (Baltimore: Johns Hopkins Press, 1955), 22–29, 41.

of *fiqh* books and excludes examination of state law and other sources of law such as custom. Writers of scripturalist accounts often begin their accounts by questioning the legitimacy of legislating Islamic law—since they do not find it within traditional *fiqh*—but subsequently take legislation for granted as they proceed with their critique, notwithstanding their reservations.[89] In this vein, one looks to the rules in *fiqh* books, usually premodern books, to determine whether legislation faithfully integrates, contravenes, modifies, or ignores Islamic law.

At the other end of the spectrum is the "law-in-action" approach,[90] which Shalakany calls "new history" and "archival history"[91] and which might also include "interpretivist" methods.[92] This approach holds that Islamic law is not merely what past writers of *fiqh* claim it is, in substance and method. It could include other law that Muslim societies applied in the past and considered legitimate, regardless of what the writers of *fiqh* said on the topic in the mainstream of their doctrinal writings.[93] Practitioners of this approach have shown a commitment to sociology, anthropology, political science, and economics, or else they have been trained in advanced theories of legal studies.[94] These disciplines provide research methods for discerning what law historically was apart from what it merely seems to have been when one limits the study of law to written law and *fiqh* alone. These scholars of law and legal practice have studied sources beyond legislation and *fiqh* such as court records, commercial documents, and families' archives, to learn about how law was lived in the premodern past or at least the precolonial past. In this regard the contemporary revisionist historians of Ottoman-era law and legal culture provide models for advanced research and sources of information for law-in-action scholars who are not specialists in the Islamic world, Arabic, or Ottoman Turkish. Law-in-actionists consider both legislation and custom as historically having been part of the general shariʿa-compliant legal order of past Muslim societies.

A law-in-action understanding of Islamic law expands the possibilities for what Islamic legislation is, could be, or need not be, because indications from

[89] See e.g. Norman Solomon, "Codification of Law," *Maghreb Review* 13, nos. 1–2 (1988): 109–115; David S. Powers, "Orientalism, Colonialism, and Legal History: The Attack on Muslim Family Endowments in Algeria and India," *Comparative Studies in Society and History* 31, no. 3 (1989): 535–571; Wood, "Reception of European Law," 172–249.

[90] See Roscoe Pound, "Law in Books and Law in Action," *American Law Review* 44 (1910): 12–36.

[91] Shalakany, "Islamic Legal Histories," 60–82.

[92] Tina Hunter, "Interpretive Theories: Dworkin, Sunstein, and Ely," *Bond Law Review* 17, no. 2 (2005): 78–101.

[93] See Bernard Botiveau, "Culture juridique islamique," in *Dictionnaire encyclopédique de théorie et de sociologie du droit*, ed. André Jean Arnaud and J.-G. Belley (Paris: Libraire générale de droit et de jurisprudence, 1993), 154–159; Lama Abu-Odeh, "Commentary on John Makdisi's 'Survey of AALS Law Schools Teaching Islamic Law,'" *Journal of Legal Education* 55 (2005): 589; Pound, "Law in Books"; Stewart Macaulay, Lawrence Meir Friedman, and Elizabeth Mertz, *Law in Action: A Socio-Legal Reader* (New York: Foundation Press, 2007).

[94] See Dupret, "Modern Law and Arab Societies"; Macaulay, Friedman, and Mertz, *Law in Action*. See also references to revisionist Ottoman historiography in Section I of this chapter.

legal-historical sources beyond *fiqh* literature and even historical legislation itself suggest that legal practice of Muslim societies was broader and more flexible methodologically and substantively than what most written *fiqh*, especially in the Sunni tradition, would suggest. Since law-in-actionists consider legislation a viable and legitimate source of law for shariʿa-compliant societies, they readily dispense with the notion that legislation is a non-Islamic practice from the start; they see legislation as justified by theory and realities of historical practice. They also emphasize that premodern Islamic legal practice tolerated custom and concepts of general welfare as sources for legitimizing certain norms as shariʿa-compliant, even when such were not typically endorsed by *fiqh* manuals.

The value of Shalakany's contribution is on multiple levels. He maps out competing approaches to assessing Islamicity in law; he undermines scripted constructs of the Islamic past and challenges skeptical perspectives about legislation by reference to revisionist Ottoman legal history and western legal theory;[95] and, by challenging scripturalism, he sets up the law-in-action understanding of Islamic law as a basis for supporting certain rights agendas that do not have equivalents in premodern *fiqh* and which, at least in his view, could be instantiated in modern, shariʿa-compliant legislation. This advocacy of law-in-action supports the concept that modern law-making need not be made only through processes known to premodern *fiqh*.

B. Contending with Deeply Rooted Scripturalism

Although law-in-action methods are attractive to scholars who wish to advance the state of thinking about substantive Islamic law, legislation, and Islamicity, Shalakany's contribution also highlights some dangers posed by adopting a holistic dismissal of scripturalism. These dangers relate to understandings of both historiography and history. On the historiographical front, Shalakany blames Orientalists for making scripturalism a popular analytic in scholarship, and he takes aim at Joseph Schacht and Noel Coulson in particular.[96] Since he sees scripturalism as a force that distorts shariʿa by enforcing atavism and close-mindedness,[97] Shalakany's critique effectively blames Orientalists for contemporary distortions in popular understanding of Islamic law worldwide. From this standpoint, for example, one can blame Orientalists, as Shalakany does, for the common understanding of Muslims that a shariʿa-compliant legal order must impose severe *hadd* punishments for

[95] March, "What Can the Islamic Past Teach Us?"

[96] Cf. Hill, "Orientalism and Liberal-Legalism"; Johansen, "Legal Literature," (1976): 29–47; Dupret, "Modern Law and Arab Societies," 289.

[97] Shalakany, "Islamic Legal Histories," 4–14, 78–80. Cf. Lama Abu-Odeh, "The Politics of (Mis) recognition: Islamic Law Pedagogy in American Academia," *American Journal of Comparative Law* 52 (2004): 789–824; Johansen, "Legal Literature."

homosexual intercourse.[98] A scripturalist reading of Islamic law dictates this result, but a law-in-action reading may suggest a more favorable outcome for the accused. The problem here, however, is that Schacht, Coulson, and many Orientalists in fact addressed what Schacht himself called the "relation between theory and practice, especially the detection of practice via the distorting lens of theory."[99] For the sake of maintaining a precise understanding of historiography, it may be necessary to revisit the extent to which Orientalists can be blamed for scripturalism in evaluations of Islamic law and legislation.

A historical reality that law-in-actionists should not ignore is that scripturalism (and the accompanying atavism and close-mindedness that Shalakany critiques) has long been a dominant approach among Muslim jurists who have evaluated the relationship between sharīʿa and legislation. This has been true for at least a century in the Arab and Turkish world, and possibly centuries more if one looks to the history of southeast Asia and India where the legacy of European colonial penetration started earlier. Even if it was true that westerners are to blame for the prevalence of scripturalism in the Islamic world, this would not, and does not, change the reality that scripturalism has been and continues to be deeply entrenched among Muslim thinkers.

When western lawyers traveled to the famed mosque-university of al-Azhar in Egypt in the later nineteenth century, they found jurists there advancing a scripturalist version of Islamic law, even though al-Azhar's jurists had negligible experience with western law.[100] In that same era, Muhammad ʿAbduh became a celebrated character in western scholarship on Islamic law because he was an unpopular critic of scripturalism at al-Azhar.[101] Ottoman legal reformers of Istanbul in the

[98] Shalakany, "Islamic Legal Histories," 15.

[99] Joseph Schacht, *Esquisse d'une histoire du droit musulman*. Translated by Jeanne and Félix Arin (Paris: Librairie orientale et américaine, 1953), 7. See also, inter alia, Jeanette A. Wakin, *Remembering Joseph Schacht (1902–1969)*. Occasional Publications of the Islamic Legal Studies Program, 4 (Cambridge, MA: Islamic Legal Studies Program, Harvard Law School, 2003); Noel J. Coulson, "Doctrine and Practice in Islamic Law: One Aspect of the Problem," *Bulletin of the School of Oriental and African Studies* 18, no. 2 (1956): 224; Coulson, *A History of Islamic Law*, 3–5, 20, 137; Noel J. Coulson, "The Concept of Progress and Islamic Law," *Quest* 40, no. 10 (1964): 17; J.N.D. Anderson, "Law as a Social Force in Islamic Culture and History," *Bulletin of the School of Oriental and African Studies* 20 (1957): 13–40; J.N.D. Anderson, "Modern Trends in Islam in Islam: Legal Reform and Modernisation in the Middle East," *International and Comparative Law Quarterly* 20, no. 1 (1971): 2; Abraham Udovitch, "Theory and Practice of Islamic Law: Some Evidence from the Geniza," *Studia Islamica* 32 (1970): 289; Farhat J. Ziadeh, "Permanence and Change in Arab Legal Systems," *Arab Studies Quarterly* 9, no. 1 (1987): 21–23; R. Stephen Humphreys, *Islamic History: A Framework for Inquiry* (Minneapolis, MN: Bibliotheca Islamica, 1988), 209–210.

[100] Adolf Heidborn, "A Muslim University," *Imperial and Asiatic Quarterly Review* 16, nos. 31–32 (1903): 300–326; Pierre Arminjon, *L'enseignement, la doctrine et la vie dans les universités musulmanes d'Égypte* (Paris: Felix Alcan, 1907), 254–273.

[101] Charles C. Adams, *Islam and Modernism in Egypt: A Study of the Modern Reform Movement Inaugurated by Muhammad Abduh* (London: Oxford University Press, 1933); Heidborn, "A Muslim University," 311.

1870s were scripturalist reformers, as were the Ottoman legal reformers of the 1910s, drawing legislation entirely from classical *fiqh* manuals.[102] The Wahhabi jurists in early twentieth-century Saudi Arabia were famously self-proclaimed scripturalists.[103] They cut from their Hanbali school curricula the works of Ibn Taymiyya and Ibn Qayyim al-Jawziyya, two celebrated Hanbali jurists who had crystallized the doctrine of *siyasa shar'iyya*.[104] In the 1930s Saudi Arabia's jurists celebrated the publication of a scripturalist codification of Hanbali *fiqh*, and they again celebrated its new edition in the 1980s.[105] Islamic legal revivalists in Morocco, Yemen, and Libya were similarly preoccupied with reforming *fiqh* by adhering to scripture and using well-established methodologies from the canonical *fiqh*.[106] When 'Abd al-Razzaq al-Sanhuri wrote a new Egyptian civil code in the 1930s and 1940s, in order to make Egyptian civil law more compliant with the shari'a, he was not an adherent of the scripturalist version of Islamic law,[107] but voluminous "preparatory drafts" (*travaux préparatoires*) show that he employed a scripturalist analytic at various points in his drafting.[108] Lawyers and parliamentarians later critiqued the code for insufficient Islamicity, from a scripturalist approach.[109]

In the second half of the twentieth century, across the Middle East multiple academic and legislative projects with a view to codifying shari'a also adopted the scripturalist premise. In Egypt alone, there were acclaimed academic codifications[110] and Islamic legislation drafts by the legislature in the 1970s.[111] As late as 1994, the politician Sufi Abu Taleb, who directed the legislative effort in Egypt in the 1970s, still conceived of the Islamization and legislation-of-shari'a project in Egypt in largely scripturalist terms.[112] Similar interests can be found in the scripturalist legislation of

[102] Mardin, "Some Explanatory Notes."

[103] Motleb Abdullah Nafisa, "Law and Social Change in Muslim Countries: The Concept of Islamic Law Held by the Hanbali School and the Saudi Arabian Legal System," SJD. diss., Harvard University, 1975, 193; Vogel, "Islamic Law and Legal System," 1993, 203, 296, 576–581.

[104] Nafisa, "Law and Social Change," 124, 185; George N. Sfeir, "The Saudi Approach to Law Reform," *American Journal of Comparative Law* 36, no. 4 (1988): 732.

[105] Ahmad ibn 'Abd Allah al-Qari et al. *Majallat al-ahkam al-shar'iyya* (Jedda: Matbu'at Tihama, 1981).

[106] Gilbert Delanoue, *Moralistes et politiques musulmans dans l'Égypte du XIXe siècle (1798–1882)* (Cairo: Institut français d'archéologie orientale du Caire, 1982), 128.

[107] Leonard Wood, "Sanhuri, 'Abd al-Razzaq Ahmad al-," in *Dictionary of African Biography*, ed. Emmanuel K. Akyeampong and Henry Louis Gates Jr., vol. 5 (New York: Oxford University Press, 2012), 266–268.

[108] Wizarat al-'Adl, *Al-Qanun al-madani: Majmu'at al-a'mal al-tahdiriyya* (Cairo: Matba'at Dar al-Kitab al-'Arabi, 1950).

[109] Bechor, *Sanhuri Code*, 87.

[110] See e.g. Majma' al-Buhuth al-Islamiyya et al., *Mashru' taqnin al-shari' a al-islamiyya 'ala madhhab al-imam al-a'zam Abi Hanifa*. (Cairo: Majma' al-Buhuth al-Islamiyya, 1972); Majma' al-Buhuth al-Islamiyya et al., *Mashru' taqnin al-shari'a al-islamiyya 'ala madhhab al-imam Malik* (Cairo: Majma' al-Buhuth al-Islamiyya, 1972).

[111] M. Martin and R.M. Mas'ad, "Return to Islamic Legislation in Egypt," in *Islamic Law and Change in Arab Society*, ed. Université Saint-Joseph (Beirut: Dar El-Mashreq Publishers, 1978), 47–78.

[112] See Sufi Abu Taleb, "La shari'a islamique et le droit positif dans les pays arabes: Histoire et prospective," in *Politiques législatives: Égypte, Tunisie, Algérie, Maroc* (Cairo: CEDEJ, 1994), 145–149.

Islamic law in Libya,[113] Tunisia,[114] Sudan,[115] Iran,[116] and Pakistan.[117] In sum, a challenge for scholars who advocate for law-in-action approaches to understanding *qanun* is to deal with the fact that law-in-action is popular among western-trained scholars but far less highly regarded among wholly indigenously trained scholars.

IV. Legislation and Constitutional Order

Much of the scholarly literature has approached legislation and the topic of Islamicity with the questionable premise that the perceived Islamicity of the government is only an ancillary issue to the Islamicity of legislation. Maurits Berger observes that "discussions on shari'a and on the nature of the Islamic state were—and still are—not about legal structures, but about legal content. When it [comes] to the role of the shari'a in the legal modernization projects, the question [is] therefore reduced to that of codification: what fields of national law will be governed by shari'a and, when it comes to the codification of that field, what elements of shari'a will be selected to make up the law?"[118] This statement accurately summarizes the state of debates and scholarly literature, but it also points to a contradiction. The contradiction is that it may not be possible—or Islamic—to divorce analysis of the content of legislation from an analysis of the institutional structure that produces legislation.

For scholars who take premodern practice as the standard for judging the Islamicity of modern practice, the apparently new hegemony of the modern state

[113] See Ann Elizabeth Mayer, "Le droit musulman en Libye, à l'âge du 'Livre vert'," *Maghreb, Machrek* 93 (1981): 5–22.

[114] See Muhammad ibn Ibrahim Buzughayba, *Harakat taqnin al-fiqh al-islami bi-l-bilad al-tunisiyya, 1857–1965* (Tunis: Markaz al-Nashr al-Jami'i, 2003).

[115] See Carolyn Fluehr-Lobban, *Shari'a and Islamism in Sudan: Conflict, Law and Social Transformation* (London: I.B. Tauris, 2012); Aharon Layish and Gabriel R. Warburg, *The Reinstatement of Islamic Law in Sudan under Numayri: An Evaluation of a Legal Experiment in the Light of Its Historical Context, Methodology, and Repercussions* (Leiden: Brill, 2002).

[116] See Bahman Baktiari, "Iran: Shari'a Politics and the Transformation of Islamic Law," in *Shari'a Politics: Islamic Law and Society in the Modern World*, ed. Robert W. Hefner (Bloomington, IN: Indiana University Press, 2011), 121–145; Ziba Mir-Hosseini, "Sharia and National Law in Iran," in *Sharia and National Law: Comparing the Legal Systems of Twelve Islamic Countries*, ed. Jan Michiel Otto (Leiden: Leiden University Press, 2010), 319–372.

[117] Martin Lau, *The Role of Islam in the Legal System of Pakistan* (Leiden: M. Nijhoff, 2006); S.M. Yusuf, "The Supremacy of Shari'at Law in Islamic Society," *Islamic Quarterly* 20–22, nos. 1–2 (1978): 15–23.

[118] Berger, "Sharia and Nation State," 224.

presents a serious problem. If legitimate shari'a can only be produced by independent jurists as opposed to the state—some would add, produced thereby from the bottom up as opposed to from the top down—then it is conceivable that true Islamic legislation can never be produced by the modern state in its current form. As pointed out earlier, for Hallaq this means that Islamic legislation in a modern state is an "impossible" expectation.[119] A challenging question for this and similar approaches, however, is whether the separation between jurists and state was indeed so clear in premodern centuries. Another challenging question is whether modern Muslims must be bound to practices and theories of the past, particularly when present-day understandings of the past are in flux.

Several studies have focussed on the "secular" state as a problematic force in contemporary legislation, even as a defeater to true Islamic legislation. In the context of Islamic legal studies, however, "secularism" does not have much currency because few states officially pursue this objective. In place of understanding the term to signify a separation between religion and state, Talal Asad and Husain Ali Agrama have articulated a now widely recognized understanding of secularism for Muslim countries.[120] They suggest that for the purpose of studying Islamic societies secularism refers not to a situation where the state and religion are wholly separated, but to a situation where the state, as opposed to the jurists, controls the articulation of shari'a. The state does this by relegating shari'a to more limited jurisdictions than was known in the past, and by subsuming shari'a into the field of state law and thereby subjecting shari'a to substantive manipulation. Noteworthy about this approach is that its premise is the jurist/state dichotomy hypothesis—the view that jurists and the state did not, do not, and should not co-mingle. If one rejects that thesis as historically inaccurate or theoretically erroneous, or if one believes that states have always been and may always be involved with the elaboration of shari'a, then the anti-state critique of modern Islamic legislation—implied and sustained by the Asadian perspective on secularism—falls apart.

When Egyptians were developing and reforming their civil code in the twentieth century, even the Islamist-inclined among them found ways to accept and to justify the co-mingling of state power and jurists' authority. For Egypt's leading legislator, 'Abd al-Razzaq al-Sanhuri, Islam was a "religion and a state." However, he added to this aphorism his view that where the state's law serves the ends of Islam, the state's law is therefore compliant with and part of the shari'a order.[121] This is a perspective on the role of the state in articulating and influencing shari'a that embodies the Asadian concept of secularism in action. But, whereas for Asad and others this

[119] Hallaq, *The Impossible State*.

[120] See Asad, *Formations of the Secular*, 205–227; Agrama, *Questioning Secularism*, 23–36. See also Bernard Botiveau, *Loi islamique et droit dans les sociétés arabes* (Paris: Iremam, 1993), 144; Enayat, *Law, State, and Society*, 138.

[121] 'Abd al-Razzaq al-Sanhuri, "Al-Din wa-l-dawla fi l-islam," *Al-Muhama al-shar'iyya* 1, no. 1 (1929): 8–14.

behavior by the state reveals the state's betrayal of true Islam, for al-Sanhuri this behavior by the state facilitated pious Islamic ordering. The most important point, however, is that concerns for shari'a-legitimacy in legislation are assuaged if one is convinced that a given government has become a legitimate authority for making pronouncements about the shari'a.

Several scholars have pointed to the concept that discussions of Islamic legislation cannot be separated from discussions about constitutional order. Noah Feldman's *The Fall and Rise of the Islamic State* (2008) suggests that a legitimate state is indispensable to producing a law that is broadly considered by the population to be Islamic.[122] Abdullahi An-Na'im's argument that only a democratic or consultative process can produce shari'a-compliant legislation has been noted earlier,[123] while Intisar Rabb has suggested that the key to legitimate law-making is involving jurists in the legislative process.[124]

People who desire an Islamic normativity expressed through legislation will probably not be satisfied with legislation until they are at least moderately satisfied with the institutions that make it. The choice of institutions falls on a spectrum. At one end is legislation through popular democracy; at the other end is legislation by authoritarian cliques of politicians, monarchs, generals, warlords, or jurists. Various options lie between the poles. If a given Muslim polity could settle on a choice about which institutions are legitimate, that settlement could ease conflicts and tensions over the legitimacy of legislation. But Muslims are presently just as divided over the question of what kind of legislative procedure is legitimate as they are over the question of which criteria should be employed to evaluate the substantive Islamicity of legislation itself. While scholars and intellectuals debate these questions, the people with the greatest influence are currently those who wield such influence by force, for better or worse.

V. Conclusion

The foregoing discussion suggests at least four paths forward in the analysis of legislation as an instrument of Islamic law. One, scholars may want to think more

[122] Noah Feldman, *The Fall and Rise of the Islamic State* (Princeton: Princeton University Press, 2008).

[123] An-Na'im, *Toward an Islamic Reformation*, 134–135. See also Quraishi-Landes, "The Sharia Problem," 560 fns. 38–39.

[124] Initsar A. Rabb, "'We the Jurists': Islamic Constitutionalism in Iraq," *University of Pennsylvania Journal of Constitutional Law* 10 (2008): 527, 577–579; compare with Baber Johansen, "A Perfect Law in an Imperfect Society: Ibn Taymiyya's Concept of 'Governance in the Name of the Sacred Law'," in *The Law Applied: Contextualizing the Islamic Shari'a*, ed. Peri Bearman, Wolfhart Heinrichs, and Bernard G. Weiss (London: I.B. Tauris, 2008), 275.

about how reductive constructs of the past limit investigations of contemporary legislation. So long as our understandings of premodern legal history are in flux, discussions about newness and difference in legislation of the modern period should be undertaken cautiously. New waves of Ottoman historiography are suggesting that changes between the modern and premodern periods are not as stark as they once appeared, and that modernizing trends in law and legislation had pre-European, autochthonous antecedents. Two, scholars of the legal history of Islamic countries may want to take more seriously the insights of over a century of legal scholarship that is focussed not on Islam or on area studies, but on legislation itself in its technical, theoretical, and comparative aspects. Adopting more critical, rigorous, and nuanced understandings and expectations of legislation could facilitate more sophisticated and critical assessments of the relationship between legislation and Islam. Three, scholars interested in legislation must also be interested in political theory and constitutional law, because legislation is an effect of the former. And, finally, scholars may want to consider moving beyond concerns for newness, difference, and Islamicity. It will always be useful to investigate and debate the ways in which modern legislation differs from law of ages past. There will probably never be agreement as to whether given statutes or codes are sufficiently Islamic. Despite this, legislation has played and still plays an important role in the functioning and welfare of society. The most practical and helpful investigations into the creation and application of legislation are probably those that draw on practical experience of actual human legal systems, that have a robust appreciation for comparative studies of legislation, and that are realistic and practical-minded in evaluating the potential as well as the inevitable pitfalls of legislation. For this reason, the methods of law-in-action, archival history, and interpretivist legal studies will most likely inform the next wave of leading scholarship on legislation in the Islamic world. This is already happening to an exemplary degree in revisionist historiography of the later Ottoman centuries.

References

Abou El-Fadl, Khaled, "Qanun" in Richard C. Martin et al. (eds.) *Encyclopedia of Islam and the Muslim World* (New York: Macmillan Reference USA, 2004) 560–561.

Abu Taleb, Sufi, "La shariʿa islamique et le droit positif dans les pays arabes: Histoire et prospective" in Nabil ʿAbd al-Fattah (ed.) *Politiques législatives: Égypte, Tunisie, Algérie, Maroc* (Cairo: CEDEJ, 1994) 137–156.

Abu-Odeh, Lama, "The Politics of (Mis)recognition: Islamic Law Pedagogy in American Academia." *American Journal of Comparative Law* 52 (2004): 789–824.

Abu-Odeh, Lama, "Commentary on John Makdisi's 'Survey of AALS Law Schools Teaching Islamic Law.'" *Journal of Legal Education* 55 (2005): 589–591.

Adams, Charles C., *Islam and Modernism in Egypt: A Study of the Modern Reform Movement Inaugurated by Muhammad Abduh* (London: Oxford University Press, 1933).
Agrama, Hussein Ali, *Questioning Secularism: Islam, Sovereignty, and the Rule of Law in Modern Egypt* (Chicago: University of Chicago Press, 2012).
Akhavi, Shahrough, "Dawlah" in John L. Esposito (ed.) *Oxford Encyclopedia of the Islamic World* (New York: Oxford University Press, 2009) 43–47.
Al-Muhairi, Butti Sultan Butti Ali, "The Development of the UAE Legal System and Unification with the Judicial System." *Arab Law Quarterly* 11, no. 2 (1996): 116–160.
Alam, Muzaffar, *The Languages of Political Islam: India 1200–1800* (Chicago: University of Chicago Press, 2004).
An-Na'im, Abdullahi Ahmed, *Toward an Islamic Reformation: Civil Liberties, Human Rights, and International Law* (Syracuse, NY: Syracuse University Press, 1990).
Anderson, J.N.D., "The Shari'a and Civil Law: The Debt Owed by the New Civil Codes of Egypt and Syria to the Shari'a." *Islamic Quarterly* 1 (1954): 29–46.
Anderson, J.N.D., "Law as a Social Force in Islamic Culture and History." *Bulletin of the School of Oriental and African Studies* 20 (1957): 13–40.
Anderson, J.N.D., "Modern Trends in Islam: Legal Reform and Modernisation in the Middle East." *International and Comparative Law Quarterly* 20, no. 1 (1971): 1–21.
Arminjon, Pierre, *L'enseignement, la doctrine et la vie dans les universités musulmanes d'Égypte* (Paris: Felix Alcan, 1907).
Arnaud, André Jean, *Les origines doctrinales du code civil français* (Paris: Libraire générale de droit et de jurisprudence, 1969).
Arnaud, André Jean, and Belley, J.-G. eds., *Dictionnaire encyclopédique de théorie et de sociologie du droit* (Paris: Libraire générale de droit et de jurisprudence, 1993).
Asad, Talal, *Formations of the Secular: Christianity, Islam, Modernity* (Stanford, CA: Stanford University Press, 2003).
Ayubi, Nazih N., Hashemi, Nader, and Qureshi, Emran, "Islamic State" John L. Esposito (ed.) *Oxford Encyclopedia of the Islamic World* (New York: Oxford University Press, 2009) 165–175.
Baer, Gabriel, *Studies in the Social History of Modern Egypt* (Chicago: University of Chicago Press, 1969).
Baktiari, Bahman, "Iran: Shari'a Politics and the Transformation of Islamic Law" in Robert W. Hefner, (ed.) *Shari'a Politics: Islamic Law and Society in the Modern World* (Bloomington, IN: Indiana University Press, 2011) 121–145.
Bechor, Guy, *The Sanhuri Code, and the Emergence of Modern Arab Civil Law (1932 to 1949)* (Leiden: Brill, 2007).
Berger, Maurits S., "Sharia and Nation State" in Rudolph Peters and Peri Bearman (eds.) *The Ashgate Research Companion to Islamic Law* (Farnham, Surrey: Ashgate, 2014) 223–234.
Black's Law Dictionary, (9th edn. St. Paul, MN: West, 2009).
Black, Antony, *The History of Islamic Political Thought: From the Prophet to the Present* (New York: Routledge, 2001).
Botiveau, Bernard, "Culture juridique islamique" in André Jean Arnaud and J.-G. Belley (eds.) *Dictionnaire encyclopédique de théorie et de sociologie du droit* (Paris: Libraire générale de droit et de jurisprudence, 1993) 154–159.
Botiveau, Bernard, *Loi islamique et droit dans les sociétés arabes* (Paris: Iremam, 1993).
Brown, Nathan J., "Law and Imperialism: Egypt in Comparative Perspective." *Law and Society Review* 29, no. 1 (1995): 103–126.

Brown, Nathan J., *The Rule of Law in the Arab World: Courts in Egypt and the Gulf* (Cambridge: Cambridge University Press, 1997).

Bustamam-Ahmad, Kamaruzzaman, *Islamic Law in Southeast Asia: A Study of Its Application in Kelantan and Aceh* (Bangkok: Asian Muslim Action Network, 2009).

Buzughayba, Muhammad ibn Ibrahim, *Harakat taqnin al-fiqh al-islami bi-l-bilad al-tunisiyya, 1857–1965* (Tunis: Markaz al-Nashr al-Jami'i, 2003).

Calder, Norman, Kéchichian, Joseph A., Ziadeh, Farhat J., Sachedina, Abdulaziz, Hendrickson, Jocelyn, Mayer, Ann Elizabeth, and Rabb, Intisar A., "Law" in John L. Esposito (ed.) *The Oxford Encyclopedia of the Islamic World* (New York: Oxford University Press, 2009) 381–389.

Cheta, Omar, "Rule of Merchants: The Practice of Commerce and Law in Late Ottoman Egypt, 1841–1876." Ph.D. diss., New York University, 2014.

Cooper, Richard S., "The Assessment and Collection of Kharaj Tax in Medieval Egypt." *Journal of the American Oriental Society* 96, no. 3 (1976): 365–382.

Coulson, Noel J., "Doctrine and Practice in Islamic Law: One Aspect of the Problem." *Bulletin of the School of Oriental and African Studies* 18, no. 2 (1956): 211–226.

Coulson, Noel J., "The Concept of Progress and Islamic Law." *Quest 40*, no. 10 (1964): 16–25.

Coulson, Noel J., *Conflicts and Tensions in Islamic Jurisprudence* (Chicago: University of Chicago Press, 1969).

Coulson, Noel J., *A History of Islamic Law* (Edinburgh: Edinburgh University Press, 1964; reprint, 2006).

David, René and Brierley, John E.C., *Major Legal Systems in the World Today: An Introduction to the Comparative Study of Law*, (3rd edn. London: Sweet & Maxwell, 1985).

Delanoue, Gilbert, *Moralistes et politiques musulmans dans l'Égypte du XIXe siècle (1798–1882)* (Cairo: Institut français d'archéologie orientale du Caire, 1982).

Dupret, Baudouin, "A Return to the Shariah? Egyptian Judges and Referring to Islam" in John L. Esposito and François Burgat (eds.) *Modernizing Islam: Religion in the Public Sphere in the Middle East and Europe* (New Brunswick, NJ: Rutgers University Press, 2003) 125–143.

Dupret, Baudouin, "Modern Law and Arab Societies in Recent French-Speaking Literature." *Journal of Law and Religion* 15, nos. 1–2 (2000–01): 289–301.

Emon, Anver M., Ellis, Mark, and Glahn, Benjamin, eds., *Islamic Law and International Human Rights Law* (Oxford: Oxford University Press, 2012).

Enayat, Hadi, *Law, State, and Society in Modern Iran: Constitutionalism, Autocracy, and Legal Reform, 1906–1941* (New York: Palgrave Macmillan, 2013).

Ergene, Boğaç A., "Qanun and Shariʿa" in Rudolph Peters and Peri Bearman (eds.) *The Ashgate Research Companion to Islamic Law* (Farnham, Surrey: Ashgate, 2014) 109–122.

Fadel, Mohammad, "State and Sharia" in Rudolph Peters and Peri Bearman (eds.) *The Ashgate Research Companion to Islamic Law* (Farnham, Surrey: Ashgate, 2014) 93–107.

Fahmy, Khaled, "The Anatomy of Justice: Forensic Medicine and Criminal Law in Nineteenth-Century Egypt." *Islamic Law and Society* 6, no. 2 (1999): 224–271.

Feener, R. Michael, *Shari'a and Social Engineering* (Oxford: Oxford University Press, 2013).

Feldman, Noah, *The Fall and Rise of the Islamic State* (Princeton: Princeton University Press, 2008).

Fluehr-Lobban, Carolyn, *Shariʿa and Islamism in Sudan: Conflict, Law and Social Transformation* (London: I.B. Tauris, 2012).

Galanter, Marc, "The Modernization of Law" in Myron Weiner (ed.) Modernization: *The Dynamics of Growth* (New York: Basic Books, 1996) 153–163.

Gibb, Hamilton Alexander Rosskeen, "Constitutional OrganizationOrganization" in Majid Khadduri and Herbert J. Liebesny (eds.) *Law in the Middle East: Origin and Development of Islamic Law* (Washington, DC: Middle East Institute, 1955; reprint, 2010) 3–27.

Goadby, Frederic Maurice, *Introduction to the Study of Law: A Handbook for the Use of Law Students in Egypt and Palestine*, (3rd edn. London: Butterworth, 1921).

Goitein, Shelomo D., *A Mediterranean Society: The Jewish Communities of the Arab World as Portrayed in the Documents of the Cairo Geniza, vol. 1: Economic Foundations* (Berkeley: University of California Press, 1967).

von Grunebaum, Gustave E., *Medieval Islam* (Chicago: University of Chicago Press, 1946).

Hallaq, Wael B., "Can the Shari'a Be Restored?" in Yvonne Yazbeck Haddad and Barbara Freyer Stowasser (eds.) *Islamic Law and the Challenges of Modernity* (Walnut Creek, CA: AltaMira, 2004) 21–54.

Hallaq, Wael B., *The Impossible State: Islam, Politics, and Modernity's Moral Predicament* (New York: Columbia University Press, 2012).

Hallaq, Wael B., *Shari'a: Theory, Practice, Transformations* (Cambridge: Cambridge University Press, 2009).

Halley, Janet and Rittich, Kerry, "Critical Directions in Comparative Family Law: Genealogies and Contemporary Studies of Family Law Exceptionalism." *American Journal of Comparative Law* 58, no. 4 (2010): 753–776.

Heidborn, Adolf, "A Muslim University." *Imperial and Asiatic Quarterly Review* 16, nos. 31–32 (1903): 300–326.

Heyd, Uriel, "Kanun and Shari'a in Old Ottoman Criminal Justice." *Proceedings of the Israel Academy of Sciences and Humanities* 3, no. 1 (1967): 1–18.

Heyd, Uriel, *Studies in Old Ottoman Criminal Law* (Oxford: Clarendon Press, 1973).

Hill, Enid, "Orientalism and Liberal-Legalism." *Review of Middle East Studies* 2 (1976): 57–70.

Hill, Enid, "Comparative and Historical Study of Modern Middle Eastern Law." *American Journal of Comparative Law* 26 (1978): 279–297.

Hinds, Martin, "Miḥna" in C. E. Bosworth, E. van Donzel, W. P. Heinrichs and Ch. Pellat (eds.) *The Encyclopaedia of Islam*, 2nd edn., vol. 7 (Leiden: Brill, 1960–2004) 2–6.

Hodgson, Marshall G. S., *The Venture of Islam: Conscience and History in a World Civilization, vol. 3: The Gunpowder Empires and Modern Times* (Chicago: University of Chicago Press, 1974).

Howard, Douglas A., "Ottoman Historiography and the Literature of 'Decline' of the Sixteenth and Seventeenth Centuries." *Journal of Asian History* 22, no. 1 (1988): 52–77.

Humphreys, R., Stephen, *Islamic History: A Framework for Inquiry* (Minneapolis, MN: Bibliotheca Islamica, 1988).

Hunter, Tina, "Interpretive Theories: Dworkin, Sunstein, and Ely." *Bond Law Review* 17, no. 2 (2005): 78–101.

Imber, Colin, *Ebu's-Su'ud: The Islamic Legal Tradition* (Stanford, CA: Stanford University Press, 1997).

İnalcık, Halil, "Kanun, 3. Financial and Public Administration" in C. E. Bosworth, E. van Donzel, W. P. Heinrichs and Ch. Pellat (eds.) *The Encyclopaedia of Islam*, 2nd edn., vol 4 (Leiden: Brill, 1960–2004) 556–562.

Jackson, Sherman A., "Jihad and the Modern World." *Journal of Islamic Law and Culture* 7, no. 1 (2002): 1–26.

Johansen, Baber, "A Perfect Law in an Imperfect Society: Ibn Taymiyya's Concept of 'Governance in the Name of the Sacred Law'" in Peri Bearman, Wolfhart Heinrichs, and Bernard G. Weiss (eds.) *The Law Applied: Contextualizing the Islamic Shari'a* (London: I.B. Tauris, 2008) 259–294.

Johansen, Baber, "Legal Literature and the Problem of Change: The Case of Land Rent." in Chibli Mallat (ed.) *Islam and Public Law: Classical and Contemporary Studies.* (London: Graham & Trotman, 1993) 29–47. Reprinted in Baber Johansen, Contingency in a Sacred Law: Legal and Ethical Norms in the Muslim Fiqh (Leiden: Brill, 1999) 446–464.

Karsh, Efraim, *Islamic Imperialism: A History* (New Haven: Yale University Press, 2006).

Khadduri, Majid, *War and Peace in the Law of Islam* (Baltimore: Johns Hopkins Press, 1955).

Khadduri, Majid and Liebesny, Herbert J., eds., *Law in the Middle East: Origin and Development of Islamic Law* (Washington, DC: Middle East Institute, 1955; reprint, 2010).

Lau, Martin, "The Re-Islamization of Legal Systems" in Rudolph Peters and Peri Bearman (eds.) *The Ashgate Research Companion to Islamic Law* (Farnham, Surrey: Ashgate, 2014) 235–248.

Lau, Martin, *The Role of Islam in the Legal System of Pakistan* (Leiden: M. Nijhoff, 2006).

Layish, Aharon and Warburg, Gabriel R., *The Reinstatement of Islamic Law in Sudan under Numayri: An Evaluation of a Legal Experiment in the Light of Its Historical Context, Methodology, and Repercussions* (Leiden: Brill, 2002).

Libson, Gideon, and Stewart, F.H., "'Urf" in C.E. Bosworth, E. van Donzel, W.P. Heinrichs and Ch. Pellat (eds.) *The Encyclopaedia of Islam*, 2nd edn., vol. 10 (Leiden: Brill, 1960–2004) 887–892.

Liebesny, Herbert J., "Stability and Change in Islamic Law." *Middle East Journal* 21, no. 1 (1967): 16–34.

Liebesny, Herbert J., *The Law of the Near and Middle East: Readings, Cases, and Materials* (Albany: State University of New York Press, 1975).

Linant de Bellefonds, Yvon, "Le droit musulman et le nouveau code civil égyptien." *Revue algérienne, tunisienne et marocaine de législation et de jurisprudence* 72 (1956): 211–222.

Løkkegaard, Frede, *Islamic Taxation in the Classic Period* (Copenhagen: Branner og Korch, 1950).

Lowry, Joseph E., "Law" in Dwight F. Reynolds *Cambridge Companion to Modern Arab Culture* (Cambridge: Cambridge University Press, 2015) 75–95.

Lucy, William, "Adjudication" in Jules Coleman and Scott J. Shapiro (eds.) *The Oxford Handbook of Jurisprudence and Philosophy of Law* (Oxford: Oxford University Press, 2004) 206–267.

Macaulay, Stewart, Friedman, Lawrence Meir, and Mertz, Elizabeth, *Law in Action: A Socio-Legal Reader* (New York: Foundation Press, 2007).

Majma'al-Buhuth al-Islamiyya et al., *Mashru'taqnin al-shari'a al-islamiyya 'ala madhhab al-imam al-a'zam Abi Hanifa* (Cairo: Majma' al-Buhuth al-Islamiyya, 1972).

Majma' al-Buhuth al-Islamiyya et al., *Mashru' taqnin al-shari'a al-islamiyya 'ala madhhab al-imam Malik* (Cairo: Majma' al-Buhuth al-Islamiyya, 1972).

Mallat, Chibli, "The Debate on Riba" in Chibli Mallat (ed.) *Islamic Law and Finance.* (London: Graham & Trotman, 1988) 69–88.

March, Andrew F., "What Can the Islamic Past Teach Us about Secular Modernity?" *Political Theory* 43 (December 2015): 838–49.

March, Andrew F., *Shari'a (Islamic Law): Oxford Bibliographies Online Research Guide* (Oxford: Oxford University Press, 2011).

Mardin, Şerif Arif, "Some Explanatory Notes on the Origins of the Mecelle." *Muslim World* 51, nos. 3–4 (1961): 189–196, 274–279.

Martin, M. and Mas'ad, R.M., "Return to Islamic Legislation in Egypt" in Université Saint-Joseph (ed.) *Islamic Law and Change in Arab Society* (Beirut: Dar El-Mashreq Publishers, 1978) 47–78.

Maussen, Marcel, and Veit Bader, "Introduction" in Marcel Maussen, Veit Bader, and Annelies Moors (eds.) *Colonial and Post-Colonial Governance of Islam: Continuities and Ruptures* (Amsterdam: Amsterdam University Press, 2011) 1–26.

Maussen, Marcel, Bader, Viet, and Moors, Annelies, eds., *Colonial and Post-Colonial Governance of Islam: Continuities and Ruptures* (Amsterdam: Amsterdam University Press, 2011).

Mawdudi, Sayyid Abu'l-A'la, "The Islamic Law" in Roxanne L. Euben and Muhammad Qasim Zaman (eds.) *Princeton Readings in Islamist Thought: Texts and Contexts from al-Banna to Bin Laden* (Princeton: Princeton University Press, 2009) 86–106.

Mayer, Ann Elizabeth, "Le droit musulman en Libye, à l'âge du 'Livre vert'." *Maghreb, Machrek* 93 (1981): 5–22.

Mayer, Ann Elizabeth, "Universal Versus Islamic Human Rights: A Clash of Cultures or a Clash with a Construct?" *Michigan Journal of International Law* 15 (1994): 307–404.

Meerschaut, Karen and Gutwirth, Serge, "Continuities and Ruptures in the Governance of Islam in Malaysia" in Marcel Maussen, Veit Bader, and Annelies Moors (eds.) *Colonial and Post-Colonial Governance of Islam: Continuities and Ruptures* (Amsterdam: Amsterdam University Press, 2011) 175–198.

von Mehren, Taylor Arthur, and Gordley, James, *The Civil Law System: An Introduction to the Comparative Study of Law* (Boston: Little, Brown, 1977).

Meijer, Roel, "The Problem of the Political in Islamist Movements" in Amel Boubekeur and Olivier Roy (eds.) *Whatever Happened to the Islamists? Salafis, Heavy Metal Muslims and the Lure of Consumerist Islam* (London: Hurst, 2012) 27–60.

Merryman, John Henry and Pérez-Perdomo, Rogelo, *The Civil Law Tradition: An Introduction to the Legal Systems of Europe and Latin America*, (3rd edn. Stanford, CA: Stanford University Press, 2007).

Meshal, Reem, *Sharia and the Making of the Modern Egyptian: Islamic Law and Custom in the Courts of Ottoman Cairo* (Cairo: American University in Cairo Press, 2014).

Minda, Gary, *Postmodern Legal Movements: Law and Jurisprudence at Century's End* (New York: New York University Press, 1995).

al-Minyawi, Makhluf ibn Muhammad al-Badawi, *Al-Muqaranat al-tashri'iyya: Tatbiq al-qanun al-madani wa-l-jina'i 'ala madhhab al-imam Malik*. Muhammad Ahmad Siraj and 'Ali Jum'a Muhammad (eds.) (Cairo: Dar al-Salam, 1999).

Mir-Hosseini, Ziba, "Sharia and National Law in Iran" in Jan Michiel Otto (ed.) *Sharia and National Law: Comparing the Legal Systems of Twelve Islamic Countries* (Leiden: Leiden University Press, 2010) 319–372.

Nafisa, Motleb Abdullah, "*Law and Social Change in Muslim Countries: The Concept of Islamic Law Held by the Hanbali School and the Saudi Arabian Legal System.*" SJD. diss., Harvard University, 1975.

Nasr, Seyyed Hossein, *The Heart of Islam: Enduring Values for Humanity* (San Francisco: HarperCollins, 2002).

Otto, Jan Michiel, ed., *Sharia Incorporated: A Comparative Overview of the Legal Systems of Twelve Muslim Countries in Past and Present* (Leiden: Leiden University Press, 2010).

Patterson, Dennis, ed., *A Companion to Philosophy of Law and Legal Theory* (Malden, MA: Blackwell, 1996).

Peirce, Leslie P., *Morality Tales: Law and Gender in the Ottoman Court of Aintab* (Berkeley, CA: University of California Press, 2003).

Peters, Rudolph, "Islamic and Secular Criminal Law in Nineteenth Century Egypt: The Role and Function of the Qadi." *Islamic Law and Society* 4, no. 1 (1997): 70–90.

Peters, Rudolph, "State, Law and Society in Nineteenth Century Egypt." *Die Welt des Islams* 39 (1999): 267–272.

Peters, Rudolph, *Crime and Punishment in Islamic Law: Theory and Practice from the Sixteenth to the Twenty-First Century* (Cambridge: Cambridge University Press, 2006).

Peters, Rudolph and Bearman, Peri, eds., *The Ashgate Research Companion to Islamic Law* (Farnham, Surrey: Ashgate, 2014).

Pirhaji, Mehdi, Yusoff, Sakina Shaik Ahmad, Isa, Suzanna Mohamed, and Jalali, Mahmoud. "Investigation of Defects of Article 264 of Iranian Civil Code." *Asian Social Science* 10, no. 7 (2014): 38–47.

Pospisil, Leopold J., *Anthropology of Law: A Comparative Theory* (New Haven, CT: HRAF Press, 1974).

Pound, Roscoe, "Law in Books and Law in Action." *American Law Review* 44 (1910): 12–36.

Powers, David S., "Orientalism, Colonialism, and Legal History: The Attack on Muslim Family Endowments in Algeria and India." *Comparative Studies in Society and History* 31, no. 3 (1989): 535–571.

Powers, David S., *Law, Society, and Culture in the Maghrib, 1300–1500* (Cambridge: Cambridge University Press, 2002).

al-Qari, Ahmad ibn 'Abd Allah et al., *Majallat al-ahkam al-shar'iyya* (Jedda: Matbu'at Tihama, 1981).

Quraishi-Landes, Asifa, "The Sharia Problem with Sharia Legislation." *Ohio Northern University Law Review* 41, no. 3 (2015): 545–566.

Rabb, Intisar A., "'We the Jurists': Islamic Constitutionalism in Iraq." *University of Pennsylvania Journal of Constitutional Law* 10 (2008): 527–579.

Rapoport, Yossef, "Royal Justice and Religious Law: Siyasah and Shari'ah under the Mamluks." *Mamluk Studies Review* 16 (2012): 71–102.

Rayner, Susan E., *The Theory of Contracts in Islamic Law: A Comparative Analysis with Particular Reference to the Modern Legislation in Kuwait, Bahrain, and the United Arab Emirates* (London: Graham & Trotman, 1991).

Rubin, Avi, "*Ottoman Modernity: The Nizamiyye Courts in the Late Nineteenth Century.*" Ph.D. diss., Harvard University, 2006.

Rubin, Avi, *Ottoman Nizamiye Courts: Law and Modernity* (New York: Palgrave Macmillan, 2011).

al-Sanhuri, 'Abd al-Razzaq. "Al-Din wa-l-dawla fi l-islam." *Al-Muhama al-shar'iyya* 1, no. 1 (1929): 8–14.

al-Sanhuri, 'Abd al-Razzaq, "Wujub tanqih al-qanun al-madani al-misri." *Majallat al-qanun wa-l-iqtisad* 6, no. 1 (1936): 3–144.

Schacht, Joseph, *Esquisse d'une histoire du droit musulman*. Translated by Jeanne and Félix Arin, (Paris: Librairie orientale et américaine, 1953).

Schacht, Joseph, *An Introduction to Islamic Law* (Paperback reprint, Oxford: Oxford University Press, 1982).

Schirazi, Asghar, *The Constitution of Iran: Politics and the State in the Islamic Republic* (London: I.B. Tauris, 1997).

Sfeir, George N., "The Saudi Approach to Law Reform," *American Journal of Comparative Law* 36, no. 4 (1988): 729–757.
Shalakany, Amr A., "Between Identity and Redistribution: Sanhuri, Genealogy and the Will to Islamise." *Islamic Law and Society* 8, no. 2 (2001): 201–244.
Shalakany, Amr A., "Islamic Legal Histories." *Berkeley Journal of Middle Eastern and Islamic Law* 1 (2008): 1–82.
Sójka-Zielińska, Katarzyna, "Codification" in André Jean Arnaud and J.-G. Belley (eds.) *Dictionnaire encyclopédique de théorie et de sociologie du droit.* (Paris: Libraire générale de droit et de jurisprudence, 1993) 69–72.
Solomon, Norman, "Codification of Law." *Maghreb Review* 13, nos. 1–2 (1988): 109–115.
Stilt, Kristen, *Islamic Law in Action: Authority, Discretion, and Everyday Experiences in Mamluk Egypt* (New York: Oxford University Press, 2011).
Stone, Martin, "Formalism" in Jules Coleman and Scott J. Shapiro (eds.) *The Oxford Handbook of Jurisprudence and Philosophy of Law* (Oxford: Oxford University Press, 2004) 166–205.
Tyan, Emile, "Judicial Organization" in Majid Khadduri and Herbert J. Liebesny (eds.) *Law in the Middle East: Origin and Development of Islamic Law* (Washington, DC: Middle East Institute, 1955; reprint, 2010) 236–278.
Udovitch, Abraham, "Theory and Practice of Islamic Law: Some Evidence from the Geniza." *Studia Islamica* 32 (1970): 289–303.
Unger, Roberto, "The CLS Movement." *Harvard Law Review* 96 (1983): 561–573, 665–675.
Vikør, Knut S., *Between God and the Sultan: A History of Islamic Law* (New York: Oxford University Press, 2006).
Vogel, Frank E., "*Islamic Law and Legal System: Studies of Saudi Arabia.*" Ph.D. diss., Harvard University, 1993.
Vogel, Frank E., *Islamic Law and Legal System: Studies of Saudi Arabia* (Leiden: Brill, 2000).
Vogel, Frank E., "Siyasa. 3. In the Sense of siyasa shar'iyya" in C.E. Bosworth, E. van Donzel, W.P. Heinrichs and Ch. Pellat (eds.) *The Encyclopaedia of Islam*, 2nd edn., vol. 9. (Leiden: Brill, 1960–2004) 694–696.
Wakin, Jeanette A., *Remembering Joseph Schacht (1902–1969).* Occasional Publications of the Islamic Legal Studies Program, 4 (Cambridge, MA: Islamic Legal Studies Program, Harvard Law School, 2003).
Weber, Max, *From Max Weber: Essays in Sociology.* Translated and edited by Hans H. Gerth and C. Wright Mills (New York: Oxford University Press, 1958).
Weber, Max, *Economy and Society: An Outline of Interpretive Sociology* in Guenther Roth and Claus Wittich (eds.) (Berkeley: University of California Press, 1978).
Weber, Max, *Wirtschaft und Gesellschaft* (Tübingen: J.C.B. Mohr, 1922).
Weiss, Bernard G., "Interpretation in Islamic Law: The Theory of Ijtihad." *The American Journal of Comparative Law* 26, vol. 2 (1978): 199–212.
Welchman, Lynn, *Women and Muslim Family Laws in Arab States: A Comparative Overview of Textual Development and Advocacy* (Leiden: Amsterdam University Press, 2007).
Winter, Michael, "The Ottoman Occupation" in Carl F. Petry (ed.) *The Cambridge History of Egypt, vol. 1: Islamic Egypt, 640–1517* (Cambridge: Cambridge University Press, 1998) 490–516.
Wizarat al-'Adl, *Al-Qanun al-madani: Majmu'at al-a'mal al-tahdiriyya* (Cairo: Matba'at Dar al-Kitab al-'Arabi, 1950).
Wood, Leonard. "Shari'ah Revivalist Thought in the First Years of the Shari'ah Lawyers' Bar Association Journal." *Maghreb Review* 32, no. 2 (2007): 196–217.

Wood, Leonard, "Reception of European Law, Origins of Islamic Legal Revivalism, and Foundations of Transformations in Islamic Legal Thought in Egypt, 1875–1960." Ph.D. diss., Harvard University, 2011.

Wood, Leonard, "Sanhuri, 'Abd al-Razzaq Ahmad al-" in Emmanuel K. Akyeampong and Henry Louis Gates Jr., (eds.) *Dictionary of African Biography* vol. 5 (New York: Oxford University Press, 2012) 266–268.

Yeganeh, Naser, "Civil Code" in *Encyclopaedia Iranica*, http://www.iranicaonline.org/articles/civil-code.

Yusuf, S. M., "The Supremacy of Shari'at Law in Islamic Society." *Islamic Quarterly* 20–22, nos. 1–2 (1978): 15–23.

Ziadeh, Farhat J., "Criminal Law" in John L. Esposito (ed.) *The Oxford Encyclopedia of the Islamic World* (New York: Oxford University Press, 2009) 4–9.

Ziadeh, Farhat J., "Permanence and Change in Arab Legal Systems." *Arab Studies Quarterly* 9, no. 1 (1987): 20–34.

Zubaida, Sami, *Law and Power in the Islamic World* (London: I.B. Tauris, 2003).

PART IV

REGIONAL VARIATIONS

A

MUSLIM-MAJORITY STATES

CHAPTER 24

ISLAMIC LAW AND SOCIETY IN SOUTHEAST ASIA

MELISSA CROUCH[1]

Of more than 1.57 billion Muslims around the world today, over 60 percent live in Asia.[2] The region of Southeast Asia is particularly important to the Muslim world because it is home to the largest Muslim majority country, Indonesia. Yet the study of Islamic law is often associated with the study of the Middle East. Scholars of Islamic law in Southeast Asia, however, have long advocated for the importance of Southeast Asia and its pluralist legal history to the field of Islamic law.

Like the majority of the Islamic world, most Muslims in Southeast Asia are Sunni Muslims, although there are small Shiʿa communities.[3] Despite the large number of Muslims in Southeast Asia, the only country in the region that

[1] Dr Melissa Crouch is a Lecturer at the Law Faculty, University of New South Wales, Sydney. She would like to thank Matthew Erie, Andrew Harding, and the editors, for their comments on an earlier version of this article.

[2] Pew Research Center's Forum on Religion & Public Life, *Mapping the Global Muslim Population: A Report on the Size and Distribution of the World's Muslim Population*, (2009) http://www.pewforum.org.

[3] Chiara Formici and Michael Feener, eds., *Shi'ism in South East Asia: Alid Piety and Sectarian Constructions* (London: I.B. Tauris, 2014).

unambiguously recognizes Islam as the religion of the state is Brunei. The relationship between Islam and the state, and the extent to which Islamic law is reflected in state structures and authorities in the region has been a central issue of scholarly inquiry.

It has long been recognized that the legal traditions of Southeast Asia are inherently plural and that Islamic law coexists with state law and customary law, in some places formally recognized by the state, but in others not. In terms of the state legal systems, Myanmar, Singapore, Malaysia, and Brunei share a similar common law heritage due to the British colonial legacy. The influence of the civil law in other countries has been more diverse—Indonesia's legal system was inherited from Dutch colonial authorities; the Philippines' system was influenced by the Spanish but also has traces of American common law; and Thailand[4] was never colonized, strictly speaking. Across the common law–civil law divide, the state legal systems of all of these countries recognize some aspects of customary law, and this at times overlaps with Islamic law.

This article seeks to provide an introduction to the ways Islam is recognized by the state in Southeast Asia, and the particular scholarly debates that have arisen in response to these Islam-state configurations. It begins by highlighting the work of a pioneer of the field of comparative law in Southeast Asia, Professor M.B. Hooker. His work demonstrates the preoccupation of early scholarship with documenting the sophisticated systems of Islamic law, and therefore pushing scholars to look beyond the state, as well as confronting the false assumption that western law was more developed than Islamic law. It then turns to examine how scholars have addressed the regulation and institutionalization of Islam in Malaysia, Indonesia, Brunei, and Singapore.[5] This is contrasted with the focus on explaining conflict and violence in Muslim minority contexts, particularly in the Southern Philippines and Southern Thailand, while Muslim minorities of Myanmar (Burma) have largely been overlooked by scholars.[6] This review demonstrates the rich body of empirical literature in this area, its potential for comparative legal inquiries, and the emerging scholarship analyzing the establishment, role, and function of Islamic institutions and authorities. It concludes with the ongoing challenge of advocating for the importance of the study and contribution of Islamic law in Southeast Asia to the broader field of Islamic legal studies.

[4] Formerly known as Siam.

[5] In Singapore, Malay Muslims constitute a significant minority.

[6] In this article, I do not cover Cambodia, Laos, Vietnam, and Timor-Leste, as these jurisdictions have very small Muslim populations and little has been written on the practice of Islamic law there. A brief overview of Islam in Cambodia and Vietnam can be found in Jacob Ramsay, "Cambodia and Vietnam," in *Voices of Islam in Southeast Asia: A Sourcebook*, eds. Greg Fealy and Sally White (Singapore: ISEAS, 2006), 31–37.

I. Pioneers of the Study of Islamic Law in Southeast Asia

The academic field of Islamic law in Southeast Asia is indebted to the pioneering work and historiography of Professor M.B. Hooker.[7] Hooker has not only published broad ranging volumes on the legal traditions of Southeast Asia that include analysis of Islamic law,[8] but he has specifically examined the origins, sources, and development of Islamic law in Southeast Asia.[9] His early work sheds light on the gradual adoption and development of Islamic law in Southeast Asia. His research pays tribute to the inherent diversity in Islamic legal practice in the region, while also searching for comparable features. In his work he identifies three particular characteristics of Islamic law in the region: the way in which local traditions have accommodated shari'a; the inevitable reconstruction of shari'a by colonizers in building the colonial state; and the "Islamization" of state policies and institutions in post-independent states, particularly since the 1970s.[10]

Hooker developed particular expertise in the legal traditions of Malaysia and Indonesia, and published extensively on issues of *adat* (customary law) and its interaction with Islamic law, as well as on *fatawa* (Islamic legal opinions). The range and depth of his compilations and commentary on Islamic case law in the region are impressive, given that for the most part he was writing in an era without the internet, and most of the legal texts he relied upon were only available in hardcopy (although this is still the case to some extent today). Throughout his work, he has emphasized the reality of legal pluralism in the region, and was one of the foundational contributors to this broader theoretical field.[11]

An early, comprehensive survey of Islamic legal history in the region is contained in Hooker's work *Islamic Law in South-East Asia*.[12] This volume builds upon his previous concise legal history of the region,[13] his historiography of Islamic law in particular,[14] and his pioneering work on legal pluralism that included a brief section

[7] See Gary Bell, "Pluralism in the Life and Work of M. B. Hooker," *Journal of Legal Pluralism* (forthcoming). See also Gary Bell and Mike Dowdle, eds., *Pluralism, Transnationalism and Culture in Asian Law: In Honour of MB Hooker* (Singapore: ISEAS, forthcoming).

[8] M.B. Hooker, *The Laws of Southeast Asia. Vol 1* (Singapore: Butterworths, 1988).

[9] M.B. Hooker, *Islamic Law in Southeast Asia* (New York: Oxford University Press, 1984).

[10] Hooker, *Islamic Law in Southeast Asia*, v.

[11] M.B. Hooker, *Legal Pluralism: An Introduction to Colonial and Neo-colonial Laws* (Oxford: Clarendon Press, 1975).

[12] M.B. Hooker, *Islamic Law in Southeast Asia* (New York: Oxford University Press, 1984).

[13] M.B. Hooker, "The Islamic Legal World: The Law Texts of Island Southeast Asia," in *A Concise Legal History of Southeast Asia*, ed. M.B. Hooker (Oxford: Clarendon Press, 1978).

[14] M.B. Hooker, "The Law Texts of Muslim South-East Asia," in *The Laws of Southeast Asia. Vol 1*, ed. M. B. Hooker (Singapore: Butterworths, 1986).

on Islam and the law in Indonesia during the colonial period.[15] He demonstrates the ways Islamic law was reformulated by European colonizers, and then traces the gradual Islamization of state law across Southeast Asia as states became independent from colonial powers. Overall, his work has primarily been that of a comparative lawyer, with a focus on conflicts of law and plural legal systems.

Heavily influenced by, and explicitly drawing upon Hooker's work, Tim Lindsey and Kerstin Steiner have published a major series on *Islam, Law and the State in Southeast Asia*, which includes volumes on Indonesia and Singapore, and a combined volume on Malaysia and Brunei.[16] These volumes provide an extensive overview and insight into modern state institutions in the region, including on Islamic education, Islamic finance, Islamic courts, Islamic personal law, Islamic philanthropy, and contemporary debates arising from the state regulation of Islam. Lindsey and Steiner focus on modern states in Southeast Asia and demonstrate the ways in which states have selected from among Islamic legal traditions in order to achieve public policy objectives in shifting political environments.

The work of scholars such as Hooker, Lindsey, and Steiner has contributed to the task of documenting Islamic practice and its manifestation in state structures over time in the region, and in doing so has advocated for the serious study of law and Islam in Southeast Asia. I turn now to consider the scholarship on Islamic law and the state in Muslim majority countries of Southeast Asia.

II. Islamic Law and the State in Muslim Majority Southeast Asia

Countries where Muslims form a majority of the population in Southeast Asia have experienced similar tensions in terms of Islam and the state, and scholarly research has centered on a set of common themes. First, scholars have considered how modern governments in Southeast Asia regulate religious affairs and the impact of such regulations on Muslims and non-Muslims. They have found that, while constitutional recognition of Islam plays a role, it has often been government policies

[15] M.B. Hooker, *Legal Pluralism: An Introduction to Colonial and Neo-colonial Laws* (Oxford: Clarendon Press, 1975), 265–286.

[16] Tim Lindsey, *Islam, Law and the State in Southeast Asia. Vol I: Indonesia* (New York: I.B. Tauris, 2012); Tim Lindsey and Kerstin Steiner, *Islam, Law and the State in Southeast Asia. Vol III: Malaysia and Brunei* (New York: I.B. Tauris, 2012); Tim Lindsey and Kerstin Steiner, *Islam, Law and the State in Southeast Asia. Vol II: Singapore* (New York: I.B. Tauris, 2012). In the interests of disclosure, from 2007–10, I was one (of many) research assistants on this project.

and regulations that have had the greatest impact on Islamic affairs. Further, concerning the compatibility of Islam, constitutionalism, and democracy, scholars have affirmed the coexistence of Islamic legal norms and democratic principles.

Second, scholars have examined the increasing regulation of the family through Islamic personal law on matters of marriage, divorce, child custody, and inheritance. The codification of Islamic law raises several puzzles that have occupied scholars, such as whether Islamic courts or the general civil courts are most suited to adjudicate these cases; whether a system of Islamic courts should be supervised by the general courts through a system of appeals; which legal texts should be used to determine Islamic personal law cases and whether Islamic texts should be codified, and if so, how; and the procedures for training, selecting, and appointing of Islamic court staff, not least the judges and lawyers.

A third theme for scholars is the sources of Islamic law and religious authority. Some Islamic authorities are recognized as part of the state structure in Southeast Asia. The institutionalization of Islam has had a significant impact on the form and shape of Islamic legal traditions and determines who gets to speak for Islam. I turn now to consider how scholars have sought to understand the regulation and bureaucratization of Islam in Indonesia, Malaysia, Brunei, and Singapore.

A. Indonesia: Nationalizing Islamic Law

In response to the increasing regulation of Islamic affairs by the state, a major subject of scholarly debate unique to Southeast Asia has been the emergence of a national *madhhab* (Islamic school of law). This possibility has been raised by scholars of Indonesia such as Professor Hazarin, former president of the State Islamic University of Indonesia (1960–75). His call for a new *ijtihad* (independent reasoning) was developed later by western scholars such as Professor Dan S. Lev[17] and Hooker. This line of reasoning has never intended to suggest that Islamic law in Indonesia does not derive from one of the recognized four schools of Islamic law, but rather reflects the aspects of Islamic legal doctrine that have developed in a unique way across the Indonesian archipelago.

The institutionalization and regulation of religion in Indonesia is embodied in studies of the Ministry of Religion, which recognizes six religions—Buddhism, Confucianism, Hinduism, Protestantism, Catholicism, and Islam. From the beginning, however, its main focus and efforts have been on Islamic affairs, and Islamic education in particular. The creation of the Ministry of Religion was a crucial part of the bureaucratization of Islam.[18] Hooker has observed that the Ministry plays

[17] Dan Lev, *Islamic Courts in Indonesia: A Study of the Political Bases of Legal Institutions* (Berkeley: University of California Press, 1972), 219.

[18] Lev, *Islamic Courts in Indonesia*, 58–59.

an influential—and lucrative—role in the administration and commodification of matters such as the *hajj* (pilgrimage to Mecca).[19] This phenomenon forms part of Hooker's broader thesis on the concept of an Indonesian *madhhab*, in which he argues that the shape of shari'a in Indonesia has taken on an "indigenous originality."[20] The concept of an Indonesian *madhhab* was later affirmed by Lindsey as a framework through which to analyze Islamic institutions in Indonesia.[21]

Despite its status as the world's largest Muslim majority country, Indonesia is not an Islamic state and its constitution does not recognize Islamic law as a source of law. The constitution does, however, recognize the state ideology of the Pancasila, and one of its tenets is the "Belief in One God." Scholars have demonstrated that, although there has been vigorous debate over whether to include an obligation in the constitution for Muslims to follow shari'a, proponents of this view have never enjoyed majority support.[22] The more pressing issue in contemporary Indonesia is the way religions are managed and regulated through government policies at the national level, because the national government retains the power to make laws on matters of religion. Since 2003, applications for judicial review of national laws can be heard by the Indonesian Constitutional Court. In reviewing cases on religious issues, such as the legitimacy of polygamy, the authority of the Religious Courts,[23] and the legality of the criminal offense of blasphemy,[24] the Constitutional Court has generally upheld state policies on the regulation of religion.

The only province in Indonesia that has the right to legislate on matters of Islamic law is Aceh, according to the terms of special autonomy it was given in 1999. While Aceh has been the subject of a number of significant studies,[25] Feener has recently published the most advanced thesis that analyzes the development of Islamic law in Aceh as a form of social engineering.[26] Based on his extensive field research in Aceh since the tsunami in 2004, Feener captures not only the rapid pace of development since this time, but the underlying tensions that have accompanied the expansion of Islamic law in public institutions and policies, and its tangible social consequences. He identifies the way in which Islamic reform has gone hand-in-hand with the

[19] M.B. Hooker, *Indonesian Syariah: Defining a National School of Islamic Law* (Singapore: ISEAS, 2008), 205–234.

[20] Hooker, *Indonesian Syariah*, xi.

[21] Lindsey, *Islam, Law and the State in Southeast Asia. Vol I: Indonesia.*

[22] Nadirsyah Hosen, *Sharia and Constitutional Reform in Indonesia* (Singapore: ISEAS, 2007).

[23] Simon Butt, "Islam, the State and the Constitutional Court in Indonesia," *Pacific Rim Law and Policy Review* 19, no. 2 (2010): 279.

[24] Melissa Crouch, "Law and Religion in Indonesia: The Constitutional Court and the Blasphemy Law," *Asian Journal of Comparative Law* 7, no. 1 (2012): 1–46.

[25] For an excellent legal anthropology of public reasoning and the concept of equality in the context of Aceh, see John Bowen, *Islam, Law and Equality in Indonesia: An Anthropology of Public Reasoning* (Cambridge: Cambridge University Press, 2003).

[26] R. Michael Feener, *Shari'a and Social Engineering: The Implementation of Islamic Law in Contemporary Aceh* (Oxford: Oxford University Press, 2013).

expansion of Indonesian nationalism and efforts of economic developmentalism. His book considers the key actors and institutions that comprise the Islamic legal system in Aceh and the way these institutions are both public manifestations of religiosity, but also a means for the Indonesian state to exert control over the province of Aceh.

The study of the local regulation of religion has at times overlapped with the study of *adat* (custom).[27] For example, the province of West Sumatra, the home of the Minangkabau, has presented a particular paradox for scholars who have struggled to reconcile its matrilineal social structure with its adherence to Islam.[28] Franz and Keebet von Benda Beckmann provided the most sustained legal anthropology of the Minangkabau.[29] An impressive study that spans the 1970s to 2010s, a period of over forty years, the von Benda Beckmanns examine the impact of state policies on local village governance and the shifting dynamics of *adat* and Islam in West Sumatra. Their study finds that, according to the Minangkabau, property is equated with inheritance and so when state law affects property rights, it also affects Islamic law and *adat* law, a reality that has been overlooked by scholars.[30]

There has been consistent scholarly emphasis on the Religious Courts (*Pengadilan Agama*) as institutions that mediate the scope and content of legal pluralism in Indonesia. Indonesia's Religious Courts exist under the authority of the general court system. That is, while Islamic courts may hear cases at first instance, the final level of appeal lies with the general court system. On the one hand, changes in Indonesia's political context have led to reform in the Religious Courts, yet at the same time these courts are restricted by positive state law.[31] Writing before the introduction of a national law on the Religious Courts (which occurred in 1989) and the introduction of the Compilation of Islamic Law (introduced in 1993 as a guide for the courts), Lev demonstrates that one of the key roles of the courts at this time was to respond to the demands of women, particularly in matters of divorce and inheritance.[32] This finding has been strengthened through recent empirical research that confirms the Religious Courts in Indonesia are widely respected and provide an avenue of divorce for women.[33] There has also been an increase in the regulation

[27] M.B. Hooker, *Adat Law in Modern Indonesia* (Oxford: Oxford University Press, 1978), 91–111.

[28] Franz von Benda-Beckmann, *Property in Social Continuity: Continuity and Change in the Maintenance of Property Relationships through Time in Minangkabau, West Sumatra* (The Hague: M Nijhoff, 1979); Franz and Keebet von Benda-Beckmann, "Adat and Religion in Minangkabau and Ambon," in *Time Past, Time Present and Time Future*, eds. Henri J.M. Claessen and David S. Moywer (Dordrecht: Foris, 1998).

[29] Franz and Keebet von Benda-Beckmann, *Political and Legal Transformations of an Indonesian Polity: The Nagari from Colonisation to Decentralisation* (Cambridge: Cambridge University Press, 2013).

[30] Benda-Beckmann, *Political and Legal Transformations*, 27.

[31] Dan S. Lev, *Islamic Courts in Indonesia: A Study of the Political Bases of Legal Institutions* (Berkeley: University of California Press, 1972).

[32] Lev, *Islamic Courts in Indonesia*, 182.

[33] Cate Sumner and Tim Lindsey, *Courting Reform: Indonesia's Islamic Courts and Justice for the Poor* (Lowy Institute Paper No 31, 2012) Lowy Institute for International Policy, New South Wales.

of the Islamic judiciary in Indonesia since it was formalized at the national level in 1989, and Nurlaelawati has demonstrated how this has strengthened the professionalism of and respect for the judiciary.[34]

B. Malaysia: The Islamization of the State

Scholarship on Islam and the state in Malaysia has struggled to understand the interaction between common law and Islam; the position of women under Islamic law; the power of state governments to pass laws on Islam; and the jurisdiction of the Syariah Courts in relation to the civil court system. To begin with, Malaysia's constitution has been the source of significant debate because Article 3(1) states that Islam is the religion of the state. At independence this was generally understood to be confined to the recognition of Islamic personal law for Muslims. The constitution also blurs Islamic identity with Malay identity (Article 160(2)), so that being Malay is often thought to be synonymous with being Malay Muslim. In 2001, the debate over whether Malaysia is an Islamic or secular state peaked when Prime Minister Mahathir Mohamed, of the ruling United Malays National Organization (UMNO), declared Malaysia to be an Islamic state. This and subsequent incidents spurred a large body of scholarship that has sought to unpack the tensions and trajectory of secularism, liberal conceptions of rights, and Islam in Malaysia.[35] The general consensus, as described by Harding, is that the state is more "secular" than Islamic, despite fierce political rhetoric to the contrary.[36]

Aside from the constitutional position of Islam, a distinction between the Indonesian and Malaysian governments is that the power to regulate religion is held by regional states in Malaysia (rather than the central government in Indonesia). This is partly a legacy of the localized history of Islam in the region, and the subsequent fragmentation of British colonial rule, which saw present day Malaysia, Singapore, and Brunei ruled in several distinct ways: the Straits Settlement, the Federated Malay States, the Unfederated Malay States, and British Borneo.[37] This

[34] Euis Nurlaelawati and Abdurrahman Rahim, "The Training, Appointment and Supervision of Islamic Judges in Indonesia," *Pacific Rim Law and Policy Journal* 21, no. 1 (2012): 43.

[35] Tamir Moustafa, "Judging in God's Name: State Power, Secularism, and the Politics of Islamic Law in Malaysia," *Oxford Journal of Law and Religion* 3, no. 1 (2014): 152–167; Tamir Moustafa, "Liberal Rights v Islamic Law? The Construction of a Binary in Malaysian Politics," *Law and Society Review* 47, no. 4 (2013): 771; Amanda Whiting, "Secularism, the Islamic State and the Malaysian Legal Profession," *Asian Journal of Comparative Law* 5 (2010): 1–34.

[36] Andrew Harding, "The Keris, the Crescent and the Blind Goddess: The State, Islam and the Constitution in Malaysia," *Singapore Journal of International and Comparative Law* 6 (2002): 154–180; see e.g. Hooker, *Islamic Law*, 130–170.

[37] See Hooker, *Islamic Law*, for a more detailed history of Islamic law and legal texts in this region, including the Straits Settlement and Singapore (84–129); the Malay States and Peninsula Malaysia (130–160); and Sarawak and Sabah (of former British Borneo, 189–220).

has affected the way scholars approach the regulation of Islam, and there has been greater focus at the state level. For example, scholars have considered the impact and implementation of the Administration of Muslim Law Acts that were passed by nearly all of the states in Malaysia between the 1950s and 1970s.[38] This was followed in the 1980s and 1990s by a strategic national push to establish greater uniformity in the approach and application of Islamic law across Malaysia under the cover of "upgrading" state laws and institutions across the country.[39]

Another reason for a focus at the state level is that the Shariʿa Courts are regulated by each state in Malaysia through respective Administration of Islamic Law state statutes, and the Administration of Islamic Law Act for the Federal Territories. The structure and composition of the Shariʿa Courts was revised in the 1980s,[40] and since 1988, the Shariʿa Courts are the final level of appeal. This means that the Shariʿa Courts, rather than the general courts, have the final say on any case that is first heard by the Shariʿa Courts, but it also means that the choice of jurisdiction is even more important. In terms of the composition of these courts, unlike in Indonesia, women do not have a history of serving as judges in the Shariʿa Courts in Malaysia and it was only in 2010 that the first female judges were appointed.[41] Whiting has shown that in other sectors such as practising lawyers, the gender representation is more balanced; for example, in the Federal Territories women make up 50 percent of *peguam syarie* (shariʿa lawyers).[42]

Since then, there has been growing concern from scholars that the civil courts have given up matters concerning Islam to the Shariʿa Courts at the expense of individual rights, particularly on matters of conversion, burial, and child custody. The role and position of women in Islam has been debated by scholars seeking to understand the tensions between liberal Islam and more conservative perspectives,[43]

[38] Horowitz, "The Qur'an and the Common Law," 267. See generally Mohammad Hashim Kamali, *Punishment in Islamic Law: An Enquiry into the Hudud Bill of Kelantan* (Petaling Jaya: Ilmiah Publishers, 1995); Mohammad Hashim Kamali, *Islamic Law in Malaysia: Issues and Developments* (KL: Ilmiah Publishers, 2000).

[39] Horowitz, "The Qur'an and the Common Law," 233.

[40] See generally Michael G. Peletz, *Islamic Modern: Religious Courts and Cultural Politics in Malaysia* (Princeton NJ: Princeton University Press, 2002); Farid Sufian Shuaib, *Powers and Jurisdiction of Syariah Courts in Malaysia* 2nd edn. (Petaling Jaya: Lexisnexis, 2008).

[41] Najibah M. Zin, "The Training, Appointment and Supervision of Islamic Judges in Malaysia," *Pacific Rim Law and Policy Journal* 21, no. 1 (2008): 115.

[42] Amanda Whiting, "The Training, Appointment and Supervision of Islamic Lawyers in the Federal Territories of Malaysia," *Pacific Rim Law and Policy Journal* 21 (2012): 151.

[43] Tamir Moustafa, "Islamic Law, Women's Rights, and Popular Legal Consciousness in Malaysia," *Law and Social Inquiry* (2013): 1–21; Jaclyn Ling-Chien Neo, "Anti-God, anti-Islam and anti-Quran: Expanding the Range of Participants and Parameters in Discourse over Women's Rights and Islam in Malaysia," *UCLA Pacific Basin Law Journal* 21 (2004): 29; Li-Ann Thio, "Recent Constitutional Developments: Of Shadows and Whips, Race, Rifts and Rights, Terror and Tudungs, Women and Wrongs," *Singapore Journal of Legal Studies* 1 (2002): 414.

as has the prohibition on conversion in some states of Malaysia, which is in contrast to its neighbor Indonesia, which does not explicitly ban apostasy.[44]

The Malaysian context has also raised discussions about the interaction between Islam and the common law.[45] Horowitz argues that the influence of the common law is stronger than that of Islam on most legal matters in Malaysia; moreover, on matters that Islamic law does not cover, "the model is invariably English law."[46] This has led scholars such as Hooker to describe the form of Islamic law that has developed in modern Malaysia as an "Anglo-Malay *madhhab*."[47] In some states of Malaysia, such as Negri Sembilan, Hooker has also highlighted the way in which *adat* interacts and overlaps with Islamic law in relation to property and land disputes.[48]

Scholarship on Islam and the state in Singapore is more recent, because Singapore only became independent from Malaysia in the 1960s. Singapore also has a system of Shari'a Courts for Muslims (who are overwhelmingly Malay), although unlike Malaysia, appeals from the Shari'a Courts can still be brought to the general courts. In 1966 the Administration of Muslim Law Act was passed to regulate all aspects of Islamic personal law in Singapore.[49] As Lindsey and Steiner note, the regulation of Islamic practice in Singapore aligns with the broader nature and philosophy of the Singapore state, which seeks to control and contain any potential or perceived sources of social conflict.[50]

c. Brunei: Islam and the Sultan

The other Muslim majority state in Southeast Asia, Brunei, has a population of just over 400,000, of whom 60 percent are Malay Muslims. Brunei's constitution explicitly recognizes that Islam is the religion of the state and that the Sultan of Brunei is the leader of Islam.[51] Scholars have demonstrated the way that Islam is heavily regulated and centrally controlled by the Sultan of Brunei, and the state bureaucracy has been subject to a process of increasing Islamization.[52] In May 2014, the

[44] Although there is no legal ban on apostasy in Indonesia, the Blasphemy Law has at times been used to the same effect as an apostasy law: see Melissa Crouch, *Law and Religion in Indonesia: Conflict and the Courts in West Java* (New York: Routledge, 2014).

[45] Horowitz, "The Qur'an and the Common Law."

[46] Ibid., 272, 292.

[47] Steiner and Lindsey, *Islam, Law and the State in Southeast Asia: Malaysia and Brunei*, 7.

[48] M.B. Hooker, *Adat Laws in Modern Malaya: Land Tenure, Traditional Government and Religion* (New York: Oxford University Press, 1972), 209–250.

[49] Hooker, *Islamic Law*, 102–122; Lindsey and Steiner, *Islam, Law and the State in Southeast Asia: Singapore*.

[50] Lindsey and Steiner, *Islam, Law and the State in Southeast Asia: Singapore*.

[51] Constitution of Brunei, Art. 3(1) and (20).

[52] See Hooker, *Islamic Law*, 177–188; Lindsey and Steiner, *Islam, Law and the State in Southeast Asia. Vol III: Malaysia and Brunei*; Ann Black, "Ideology and Law: The Impact of the MIB Ideology on Law

oil-rich Sultanate made world headlines when the Sultan introduced the first of three stages of a new Penal Code based on Islamic law.[53] This is just one indication of the shifting nature of Islamic law in Southeast Asia, and such developments need to be considered and analyzed by scholars in the future.

There are a wide range of issues regulated by the state, that this section lacks the space to examine, that are the subject of more recent scholarly research, such as the role of the state in the collection of *zakat* (alms), the implementation of Islamic criminal law, and the regulation of Islamic banking and finance. One of the gaps in past research is a focus on Islamic legal professionals, and the importance of studying judges and lawyers in Islamic courts across Southeast Asia has only recently begun to receive attention.[54]

III. Islamic Law and the State in Muslim Minority Southeast Asia

There has been less scholarly attention on Islamic law in Muslim minority Southeast Asia, partly because scholarship has tended to focus on conflict, violence, and the need to resolve demands for separatism or special autonomy.[55] There is nevertheless a small body of scholarship that provides a basis from which we can further develop our understanding of Islamic law in Southern Thailand, the Southern Philippines, and Myanmar. Thailand and the Philippines scholarship are discussed together, as these countries raise similar issues. While Myanmar has often been lumped in together with these two countries,[56] it is argued that a distinctive set of issues set Myanmar apart, and needs to be reflected in future scholarship.

and Dispute Resolution in the Sultanate of Brunei Darussalam," *Asian Journal of Comparative Law* 3, no. 1 (2008); A. V. M. Horton, "Brunei in 2004: Window-Dressing an Islamizing Sultanate," *Asian Survey* 45, no. 1 (2005): 180–185.

[53] BBC, "Brunei introduces tough Islamic penal code," 30 April 2014, http://www.bbc.com/news/world-asia-27216798.

[54] Clark B. Lombardi and R. Michael Feener, "Why Study Islamic Legal Professionals?" *Pacific Rim Law and Policy Journal* 21, no. 1 (2012): 1.

[55] See e.g. Michelle Miller, ed. *Autonomy and Armed Separatism in South and Southeast Asia* (Singapore: ISEAS, 2012).

[56] See e.g. Moshe Yegar, *Between Integration and Secession: The Muslim Communities of the Southern Philippines, Southern Thailand and Western Burma/Myanmar* (New York: Lexington Books, 2002).

A. Thailand and the Philippines: Conflict Against the State and State Recognition of Islam

Scholarship on Thailand and the Philippines inevitably focuses on understanding the tensions and armed conflict between Muslim minorities and the state. A critical part of this focus has also been the codification of Islamic personal law within the nation-state, and the paradox that this potentially brings to the practice of Islam under greater state control.

Thailand is a Buddhist majority country but its largest minority religious group is Muslims, who make up 4.9 percent of the population. These Muslims are ethnically Malay and the majority live in one of four provinces—Yala, Songkhla, Pattani, and Narathiwat—in Southern Thailand, bordering Malaysia. The most significant monograph that has addressed the historical role of the state in relation to its Muslim minority is by Tamara Loos.[57] Loos seeks to dispel the common assumption that Siam was something of an exception given that it was never formally colonized by a foreign power. Instead, she highlights the way that the state of Siam played the role of both colonizer and colonized, and demonstrates the central role of law in relation to the colonization of the Muslim minority areas, and the construction of family law in particular.

The most recent attempt by the state to regulate Islam is the Royal Act Concerning the Administration of Islamic Law 1997, which only applies to Southern Thailand.[58] This allows for the application of Islamic personal law, including family law and inheritance, in the four provincial courts. While there have been demands in the past for a separate Islamic Court at the national level, these demands have not yet been realized. There have been few detailed analyses of the actual practice of Islamic law, formal or informal, in Southern Thailand,[59] although there have been recent studies on particular issues such as Islamic education,[60] and of Islamic philanthropy in Thailand.[61]

Aside from the codification of Islamic personal law, most scholarship has focussed on the violent conflict between the Thai government and its Muslim minorities who desire some form of independence from the Thai state. Various legal options have been considered, yet the inadequacy of a purely legal response is also

[57] Tamara Loos, *Subject Siam: Family, Law, and Colonial Modernity in Thailand* (Ithaca, NY: Cornell University Press, 2006).

[58] Ramizah Wan Muhammad, "The Dato' Yuthitham and the Administration of Islamic Law in Southern Thailand" (*ARC Federation Fellowship Policy Paper*, 2011) http://www.law.unimelb.edu.au/files/dmfile/Ramizah_web1.pdf.

[59] See Hooker, *Islamic Law*, 164.

[60] Joseph Chinyong Liow, *Islam, Education and Reform in Southern Thailand* (Singapore: ISEAS, 2009).

[61] Rajeswary Ampalavanar Brown, *Islam in Modern Thailand: Faith, Philanthropy and Politics* (New York: Routledge, 2013).

acknowledged.[62] Since the conflict escalated in the mid-2000s, several scholars have demonstrated both the complexity of the conflict and the competing demands that have been made, but also the complicity of the Thai (Buddhist) state and Buddhist monks.[63] This scholarship, and the work of Michael Jerryson in particular, has helped to dispel the myth that Buddhism is a peaceful religion and Islam in contrast is violent, by leveling the field and demonstrating that violence may originate from adherents across the religious divide. This also demonstrates the importance of studying Islamic communities in their local context, rather than in isolation from other religious communities.

Scholarship on Islamic law and the Muslim community in the Philippines has taken a similar tone, with a particular focus on understanding the history of conflict against the (non-Muslim) state.[64] The Philippines is a Catholic majority country, but has a Muslim population of between 5 and 10 percent. Known as the "Moro," these Muslims trace their background to the former Malay Sultanate established in the fourteenth century. Hooker's work remains the most complete discussion on Moro Islamic texts and state responses to demands from the Muslim community.[65]

Scholars have been drawn to study the impact of changes in governance in the Muslim south. In the past, the Muslim south had been governed separately during the period of Spanish rule, and then when the United States took control of the Philippines in 1898, the southernmost major island of Mindanao remained separate from the rest of the country. While resistance to the state had a long history,[66] attacks by Muslims increased in response to the declaration of martial law in 1972. Scholars have highlighted the intersection of ethnic identity with religious identity, similar to other parts of Southeast Asia, and Federspiel has demonstrated how a heightened sense of connection with the broader Islamic world has developed as a way of defining Moro Muslim identity as distinct from the state.[67]

[62] Peter Leyland, "Thailand's Troubled South: Examining the Case for Devolution from a Comparative Perspective," *Australian Journal of Asian Law* 11, no. 1 (2009): 1–28; John Funston, "Malaysia and Thailand's Southern Conflict: Reconciling Security and Ethnicity," *Contemporary Southeast Asia* 32, no. 2 (2010): 234.

[63] See e.g. Michael Jerryson, *Buddhist Fury: Religion and Violence in Southern Thailand* (Oxford: Oxford University Press, 2011); Duncan McCargo, *Rethinking Thailand's Southern Violence* (Singapore: NUS, 2007); Duncan McCargo, *Mapping National Anxieties: Thailand's Southern Conflict* (Copenhagen: NIAS Press, 2012).

[64] The only major anthropology is Thomas M. Kiefer, *The Tausug: Violence and Law in a Philippine Moslem Society* (New York: Holt Rinehart and Winston, 1972).

[65] Hooker, *Islamic Law*, 221–244.

[66] On the politics of daily resistance, see Thomas M. McKenna, *Muslim Rulers and Rebels: Everyday Politics and Armed Separatism in the Southern Philippines* (Berkeley: University of California Press, 1998.).

[67] Howard M. Federspiel, "Islam and Muslims in the Southern Territories of the Philippine Islands During the American Colonial Period (1898 to 1946)," *Journal of Southeast Asian Studies* 29, no. 2 (1998): 340 356.

The perceived need to formalize Islamic law, as Emon has shown, has been part of efforts to define the position of Muslims in the past, present, and future.[68] In 1977, the state accommodated Islamic personal law through the adoption of the Code of Muslim Personal Laws of the Philippines.[69] Mastura, as a participant in the process, captured the challenges of this drafting process through the lens of legal pluralism.[70] The introduction of the Code of Muslim Personal Laws has been depicted as both an expression of Islamic consciousness, and as a mechanism for the state to institutionalize and therefore limit the expression of Islam.[71] Chiarella has highlighted that real practical issues of implementation remain, such as the insufficient number of judges and qualified Islamic legal professionals, as well as unresolved issues arising from the multiple and at times competing sources of Islamic authority.[72] Despite the introduction of a codified form of Islamic personal law, the violent struggle against the state has continued. In 2012, a peace agreement was signed between the government and the Moro Islamic Liberation Front.[73] The ongoing challenge to the system of Islamic personal law, and the fragile agreement with the state, are developments that require further research in both comparative and historical contexts.

B. The Muslim Minorities of Myanmar

While Muslim communities of Myanmar have often been studied simultaneously as part of comparative scholarship on Thailand and the Philippines, this has obscured the differences in the identity and experiences of the Muslim communities in Myanmar. Figures on the Muslim population range from the government's conservative estimate of 4 percent to up to 15 percent. Muslim communities are characterized by a high degree of diversity, and include Burmese Muslims, Indian Muslims, Shan Muslims, Chinese Muslims, Rohingya, Kaman, and others. There is an urgent need for in-depth historical studies on Muslim communities in Myanmar. Keck has begun this task, and his work explains why Muslims were an "invisible minority" during the British colonial period, rarely receiving a mention in the records

[68] Anver Emon, "Techniques and Limits of Legal Reasoning in Shar'ia Today," *Berkeley Journal of Middle Eastern and Islamic Law* 2, no. 1 (2009): 101–124.

[69] Hooker, *Islamic Law in Southeast Asia*, 231–245; Matthew Stephens, *Islamic Law in the Philippines: Between Appeasement and Neglect* (ARC Federation Fellowship Policy Paper, Melbourne University, 2011) http://www.law.unimelb.edu.au/files/dmfile/Stephens_web2.pdf.

[70] Michael O. Mastura, "Legal Pluralism in the Philippines," *Law & Society Review* 28, no 3 (1994): 461–475.

[71] G. Carter Bentley, "Islamic Law in Christian Southeast Asia: The Politics of Establishing Shari-a Courts in the Philippines," *Philippine Studies* 29, no. 1 (1981): 45–65.

[72] Gregory M. Chiarella, "Sources of Law, Sources of Authority: The Failure of the Philippines' Code of Muslim Personal Law," *Pacific Rim Law and Policy Journal* 21, no. 1 (2012): 223.

[73] Human Rights Resource Centre, *Keeping the Faith: A Study of Freedom of Thought, Conscience and Religion in ASEAN* (Jakarta: University of Indonesia, 2015), 363–409.

of British colonial authorities, because they were perceived to be "transitory" and "alien" to Burma.[74] It was assumed that Muslims did not really "belong" to Burma and that Muslims were "non-Burmese," despite the fact that Islam in Burma long preceded the arrival of the British. While there were several prominent Burmese Muslims and Islamic organizations in the independence movement,[75] the declining political situation in the late 1950s followed by the military coup and introduction of socialism in the 1960s led to a particularly hostile period for Muslims. This has led Berlie to argue that Muslims have been subject to a conscious attempt at "Burmanisation,"[76] although this claim is not unique to Muslims, as it has been made to describe the policies of the military government towards other non-Buddhist, non-Burman groups.

Islamic personal law was recognized in Myanmar during the period of British colonialism based on the Anglo-Muhammadan law of British India, and this persisted after independence. Yet unlike the rest of Southeast Asia, Myanmar is the only country where cases concerning Islamic personal law are heard and determined by the general courts. The jurisprudence developed by the courts is based on early Anglo-Muhammadan textbooks in English,[77] although we know little about the case law since the 1960s.[78] While the Department of Religion is solely focussed on the propagation of Buddhism, there are several Islamic organizations recognized by the state and some of these do issue *fatawa*, such as the Islamic Religious Affairs Council. There is an informal system of Islamic education in Myanmar, but this also remains unregulated by the state.[79] The practice of Islam in Myanmar is therefore among the least regulated by the state in Southeast Asia.

Of particular concern to both scholars and human rights advocacy groups has been the precarious situation of the Muslim group that primarily resides in Rakhine State, often referred to as the Rohingya,[80] and where they form a majority near the border of Bangladesh. Concerns have been raised regarding human rights violations, and even allegations of genocide, as well as challenges concerning their

[74] Stephen L. Keck, "The Making of an Invisible Minority: Muslims in Colonial Burma," in *Living on the Margins: Minorities and Borderlines in Cambodia and Southeast Asia* (Center for Khmer Studies, Cambodia, 2008).

[75] Moshe Yegar, *The Muslims of Burma* (Germany: Otto Harrassowitz, 1972).

[76] Jean Berlie, *The Burmanisation of Myanmar Muslims* (Bangkok: White Lotus, 2008).

[77] See Hooker, *Islamic Law*, 44–82. Hooker provides a basic description of Anglo-Muhammedan law as adopted in Burmese case law up to the 1950s, but it should be noted that his claim that Islamic personal law ceased to exist from the 1960s is factually incorrect.

[78] But see Melissa Crouch, "Islamic Personal Law in Myanmar," in *Islam and the State in Myanmar: Muslim-Buddhist Relations and the Politics of Belonging*, ed. M. Crouch (India: Oxford University Press, 2015).

[79] Mohammed Mohiyuddin Mohammed Sulaiman, "Islamic Education in Myanmar: A Case Study," in *Dictatorship, Disorder and Decline in Myanmar*, eds. Monique Skidmore and Trevor Wilson (Acton, Australia: ANU Press, 2008).

[80] Moshe Yegar, *Between Integration and Secession: The Muslim Communities of the Southern Philippines, Southern Thailand and Western Burma/Myanmar* (New York: Lexington Books, 2002).

citizenship, irregular migration, and the risk of terrorism. Yet, as Selth[81] points out, while there were terrorist connections with Rohingya groups in the 1970s, these groups were very small and were never a real threat to the government, and there is no evidence of such radicalism today. While severe human rights concerns remain, there is the potential for academia to provide a more informed analysis, given the often polemic nature of human rights reports.

Overall, while Muslim minorities of the Southern Philippines, Southern Thailand, and Myanmar present a challenging environment for scholars conducting field research, there is a need for ethnographic scholarship that can illuminate how communities in these fragile contexts maintain practices of Islam both within and beyond the view of the state, and this can provide an informed response to critical policy debates.

IV. Conclusion

This review began with the work of M.B. Hooker because his research has laid a foundation for the comparative study of Islamic texts and state recognition of Islamic law in Southeast Asia. Hooker devoted a great amount of energy in rebutting the presumption that western law was superior to Islamic law, arguing that evolutionary theories of legal change were flawed, and in demonstrating the way western and colonial law sought to contain and control Islamic law through the state. In particular, Hooker focussed on unmasking the myth that Islamic law in countries such as Indonesia is a "corruption" of its classical Middle Eastern origins and texts.

Many of the original questions Hooker explored in the context of Southeast Asia remain relevant. These includes questions such as "what counts as Islamic law?"; "who is a Muslim for the purpose of applying Islamic law?"; "to what extent is Islamic law reflected in state law?"; "which institutions have the power to interpret Islamic law?"; "where does the source or authority for Islamic law come from?"; "which authorities have the power and legitimacy to determine the scope of Islamic law?"; and "how are conflicts of laws between Islamic law and state or customary law resolved?" These questions have begun to be explored from new perspectives, beyond a doctrinal comparative law approach, and within a broader theoretical framework of the modern, secular state and religion–state relations.

[81] Andrew Selth, "Burma's Muslims and the War on Terror," *Studies in Conflict & Terrorism* 27, no. 2 (2004): 107–126.

The strengths of this scholarly field are that it is inherently socio-legal, it has embraced the plurality of legal traditions in the region, and has pioneered empirically based understandings of Islamic law in the region. In Muslim majority contexts such as Indonesia and Malaysia, there has been a focus on Islamic institutions and religious authorities, while the development of Islamic legal professionals remains an ongoing area for research. In Muslim minority contexts such as Thailand, the Philippines, and Myanmar, scholarly research has often focussed on the demand for legal solutions to conflicts between Muslim communities and the state; yet the everyday practices of Islamic law also deserver greater attention.

Another reason why scholarship on Islamic law and society in Southeast Asia is valuable is because it challenges us to re-examine many of the assumptions that are taken for granted in scholarship on Islamic legal studies more generally. In particular it forces us to confront the interaction between local customs and traditions, and the practice of Islamic law. It also highlights the fluid and dynamic nature of the interaction between Islamic authorities and institutions, and state actors and organizations, as well as between contested concepts of constitutionalism, democracy, and Islamic law.

To conclude, Anderson's classic book on *Imagined Communities*, which draws on his extensive knowledge of Southeast Asia, aimed to "de-Europeanise the theoretical study of nationalism."[82] In the same way, the review of scholarship in this chapter reminds us of the work that still needs to be done to "de-Arabicize" or "de-Middle Easternize" Islamic legal studies. Contemporary Southeast Asian expressions and practices of Islamic law should not be treated as peripheral to Islamic legal studies, but should rather be considered as a dynamic and exciting vantage point from which to explore core questions at the heart of the study of Islamic law and society.

References

Anderson, Benedict, *Imagined Communities* (New York: Verso, First published 1983, 2006).

Bell, Gary. "Pluralism in the Life and Work of MB Hooker." *Journal on Legal Pluralism* (forthcoming).

Bell, Gary and Mike Dowdle, eds. *Pluralism, Transnationalism and Culture in Asian Law: In Honour of MB Hooker* (Singapore: ISEAS, forthcoming).

Berlie, Jean, *The Burmanisation of Myanmar Muslims* (Bangkok: White Lotus, 2008).

Benda-Beckmann, Franz von, *Property in Social Continuity: Continuity and Change in the Maintenance of Property Relationships through Time in Minangkabau, West Sumatra* (The Hague: M Nijhoff, 1979).

82 Benedict Anderson, *Imagined Communities* (New York: Verso, first published 1983, 2006), 209.

Benda-Beckmann, Franz von, and Benda-Beckmann, Keebet von, "Adat and Religion in Minangkabau and Ambon" in Henri J. M. Claessen and David S. Moywer (eds.) *Time Past, Time Present and Time Future* (Dordrecht: Foris, 1998) 195–212.

Benda-Beckmann, Franz von, and Benda-Beckmann, Keebet von, *The Minangkabau of West Sumatra* (Cambridge: Cambridge University Press, 2013).

Bowen, John, *Islam, Law and Equality in Indonesia: An Anthropology of Public Reasoning* (Cambridge: Cambridge University Press, 2003).

Black, Ann, "Ideology and Law: The Impact of the MIB Ideology on Law and Dispute Resolution in the Sultanate of Brunei Darussalam." *Asian Journal of Comparative Law* 3, no. 1 (2008): art 5.

Butt, Simon, "Islam the State and the Constitutional Court in Indonesia." *Pacific Rim Law and Policy Review* 19, no. 2 (2010): 279.

Chiarella, Gregory M., "Sources of Law, Sources of Authority: The Failure of the Philippines' Code of Muslim Personal Law." *Pacific Rim Law and Policy Journal* 21, no. 1 (2012): 223.

Crouch, Melissa, "Law and Religion in Indonesia: The Constitutional Court and the Blasphemy Law." *Asian Journal of Comparative Law* 7, no. 1 (2012): 1–46.

Crouch, Melissa, *Law and Religion in Indonesia: Conflict and the Courts in West Java* (New York: Routledge, 2014).

Crouch, Melissa, "Personal Law and Colonial Legacy: State-Religion Relations and Islamic Law in Myanmar" in M. Crouch (ed.) *Islam and the State in Myanmar: Muslim-Buddhist Relations and the Politics of Belonging* (India: Oxford University Press, 2016).

Emon, Anver, "Techniques and Limits of Legal Reasoning in Shar'ia Today." *Berkeley Journal of Middle Eastern and Islamic Law* 2, no. 1 (2009): 101–124.

Federspiel, Howard M., "Islam and Muslims in the Southern Territories of the Philippine Islands During the American Colonial Period (1898 to 1946)." *Journal of Southeast Asian Studies* 29, no. 2 (1998): 340–356.

Formici, Chiara, and Feener, Michael, eds. *Shi'ism in South East Asia: 'Alid Piety and Sectarian Constructions* (London: I.B. Tauris, 2014).

Funston, John, "Malaysia and Thailand's Southern Conflict: Reconciling Security and Ethnicity." *Contemporary Southeast Asia* 32, no. 2 (2010): 234.

Harding, Andrew, "The Keris, the Crescent and the Blind Goddess: The State, Islam and the Constitution in Malaysia." *Singapore Journal of International and Comparative Law* 6 (2002): 154–180.

Hooker, M.B., *Adat Laws in Modern Malaya: Land Tenure, Traditional Government and Religion* (New York: Oxford University Press, 1972).

Hooker, M.B., *Legal Pluralism: An Introduction to Colonial and Neo-colonial Laws* (Oxford: Clarendon Press, 1975).

Hooker, M.B., *Adat Law in Modern Indonesia* (Oxford: Oxford University Press, 1978).

Hooker, M.B., *A Concise Legal History of Southeast Asia* (Oxford: Clarendon Press, 1978).

Hooker, M.B., *Islamic Law in Southeast Asia* (New York: Oxford University Press, 1984).

Hooker, M.B., "The Law Texts of Muslim South-East Asia" in M. B. Hooker (ed.) (Singapore: Butterworths, 1986) 347–434.

Hooker, M.B., *Indonesian Islam: Social Change through Contemporary Fatwa* (Honolulu: University of Hawaii Press, 2003).

Hooker, M.B., *Indonesian Syariah: Defining a National School of Islamic Law* (Singapore: ISEAS, 2008).

Horowitz, Donald L., "The Qur'an and the Common Law: Islamic Law Reform and the Theory of Legal Change." *American Journal of Comparative Law* 42 (1994): 233.

Horton, A. V. M., "Brunei in 2004: Window-Dressing an Islamizing Sultanate." *Asian Survey* 45, no. 1 (2005): 180–185.

Hosen, Nadirsyah, *Sharia and Constitutional Reform in Indonesia* (Singapore: ISEAS, 2007).

Human Rights Resource Centre, *Keeping the Faith: A Study of Freedom of Thought, Conscience and Religion in ASEAN* (Jakarta: University of Indonesia. 2015).

Jerryson, Michael, *Buddhist Fury: Religion and Violence in Southern Thailand* (Oxford University Press, 2011).

Kamali, Mohammad Hashim, *Punishment in Islamic Law: An Enquiry into the Hudud Bill of Kelantan* (Petaling Jaya: Ilmiah Publishers, 1995).

Kamali, Mohammad Hashim, *Islamic Law in Malaysia: Issues and Developments* (KL: Ilmiah Publishers, 2000).

Keck, Stephen L., "The Making of an Invisible Minority: Muslims in Colonial Burma" in *Living on the Margins: Minorities and Borderlines in Cambodia and Southeast Asia*, 221–234 (Center for Khmer Studies, Cambodia, 2008).

Lev, Dan, *Islamic Courts in Indonesia: A Study of the Political Bases of Legal Institutions* (Berkeley: University of California Press, 1972).

Lindsey, Tim, *Islam, Law and the State in Southeast Asia. Vol I: Indonesia* (New York: I.B. Tauris, 2012).

Lindsey, Tim, and Steiner, Kerstin, *Islam, Law and the State in Southeast Asia. Vol II: Singapore* (New York: I.B. Tauris, 2012).

Lindsey, Tim, and Steiner, Kerstin, *Islam, Law and the State in Southeast Asia. Vol III: Malaysia and Brunei* (New York: I.B. Tauris, 2012).

Leyland, Peter, "Thailand's Troubled South: Examining the Case for Devolution from a Comparative Perspective." *Australian Journal of Asian Law* 11, no. 1 (2009): 1–28.

Liow, Joseph Chinyong, *Islam, Education and Reform in Southern Thailand* (Singapore: ISEAS, 2009).

Lombardi, Clark B., and Feener, R. Michael Feener, "Why Study Islamic Legal Professionals?" *Pacific Rim Law and Policy Journal* 21, no. 1 (2012) 1.

Loos, Tamara, *Subject Siam: Family, Law, and Colonial Modernity in Thailand* (Ithaca, NY: Cornell University Press, 2006).

Mastura, Michael O., "Legal Pluralism in the Philippines." *Law and Society Review* 28, no. 3 (1994): 461.

McCargo, Duncan, *Mapping National Anxieties: Thailand's Southern Conflict* (NIAS Press, 2012).

McCargo, Duncan, *Rethinking Thailand's Southern Violence* (Singapore, NUS, 2007).

McKenna, Thomas M., *Muslim Rulers and Rebels: Everyday Politics and Armed Separatism in the Southern Philippines* (Berkeley: University of California Press, 1998).

Miller, Michelle, ed., *Autonomy and Armed Separatism in South and Southeast Asia* (Singapore: ISEAS, 2012).

Moustafa, Tamir, "Judging in God's Name: State Power, Secularism, and the Politics of Islamic Law in Malaysia." *Oxford Journal of Law and Religion* 3, no. 1 (2014): 152–167.

Moustafa, Tamir, "Islamic Law, Women's Rights, and Popular Legal Consciousness in Malaysia." *Law and Social Inquiry* 38 (2013) 168–188.

Moustafa, Tamir, "Liberal Rights v Islamic Law? The Construction of a Binary in Malaysian Politics." *Law and Society Review* 47, no. 4 (2013): 771.

Muhammad, Ramizah Wan, *The Dato' Yuthitham and the Administration of Islamic Law in Southern Thailand*. ARC Federation Fellowship Policy Paper, 2011 http://www.law.unimelb.edu.au/files/dmfile/Ramizah_web1.pdf.

Neo, Jaclyn Ling-Chien, "Anti-God, Anti-Islam and Anti-Quran": Expanding the Range of Participants and Parameters in Discourse over Women's Rights and Islam in Malaysia." *UCLA Pacific Basin Law Journal* 21 (2004): 29.

Nurlaelawati, Euis and Rahim, Abdurrahman, "The Training, Appointment and Supervision of Islamic Judges in Indonesia." *Pacific Rim Law and Policy Journal* 21, no. 1 (2012): 43.

Pew Research Center's Forum on Religion & Public Life. Mapping the Global Muslim Population: A Report on the Size and Distribution of the World's Muslim Population (2009) http://www.pewforum.org.

Rajeswary Ampalavanar Brown, *Islam in Modern Thailand: Faith, Philanthropy and Politics* (New York: Routledge, 2013).

Ramsay, Jacob, "Cambodia and Vietnam" in Greg Fealy and Sally White (eds.) *Voices of Islam in Southeast Asia: A Sourcebook* (Singapore: ISEAS, 2006) 31–37.

Selth, Andrew, "Burma's Muslims and the War on Terror." *Studies in Conflict & Terrorism* 27, no. 2 (2004): 107–126.

Stephens, Matthew, Islamic Law in the Philippines: Between Appeasement and Neglect, ARC Federation Fellowship Policy Paper, Melbourne University, 2011, http://www.law.unimelb.edu.au/files/dmfile/Stephens_web2.pdf.

Sulaiman, Mohammed Mohiyuddin Mohammed, "Islamic Education in Myanmar: A Case Study" in Monique Skidmore and Trevor Wilson (eds.) *Dictatorship, Disorder and Decline in Myanmar* (ANU E-Press, 2008) 177–192.

Whiting, Amanda, "Secularism, the Islamic State and the Malaysian Legal Profession." *Asian Journal of Comparative Law* 5 (2010) 1–34.

Whiting, Amanda, "The Training, Appointment, and Supervision of Islamic Lawyers in the Federal Territories of Malaysia." *Pacific Rim Law & Policy Journal* 21, no. 1 (2012): 133–161.

Yegar, Moshe, *The Muslims of Burma* (Germany: Otto Harrassowitz, 1972).

Yegar, Moshe, *Between Integration and Secession: The Muslim Communities of the Southern Philippines, Southern Thailand and Western Burma/Myanmar* (New York: Lexington Books, 2002).

CHAPTER 25

ISLAMIC LAW IN POST-REVOLUTIONARY IRAN

ANTONIA FRASER FUJINAGA

THIS chapter aims to present a "bird's-eye view" of scholarship available to a foreign audience concerning Islamic law in post-revolutionary[1] Iran. Crucially, there are areas of Iranian law, such as maritime law or some aspects of commercial or criminal law,[2] which have been diligently studied but were not significantly Islamized after the revolution or are outside the purview of scripture. Likewise there are manifestations of Islam in Iran (such as women's theological meetings) which, though subjected to painstaking investigation, are outside the realm of law. Here we must limit ourselves to areas where the two coincide.

Outside Iranian academic institutions, some areas of Islamic law in Iran have received more detailed academic attention abroad than others. For instance, family law (marriage, divorce, child custody, and so on) in theory and practice has been analyzed in depth, often from a feminist perspective. Another popular

[1] For an analysis of the Iranian revolution in 1979 and events leading to it, see Abrahamian 1982, Keddie 2003, McDaniel 1991, Dabashi 1993, Kamali 1998, Arjomand 1988c, Irfani 1983, and Fajri 1992. For an introduction to Shiʿism, see Momen 1985. For the basics of Islamic law, see Schacht 1982.

[2] Examples: Maleki 2009; McDonald; Iwasaki 2011; Smythe 2006; Rahmdel 2002; Aliverdinia and Pridemore 2007; Farajiha 2006; Rezapour et al. 2007; Wiswall 1991; Samii 2005; Sanei 2001; Shahshahani 2007; Yazdani 2000; Zahedi 2007.

area of study is constitutional law. This encompasses *velayat-e faqih*, the arguably innovative juristic argument justifying the very existence of the Islamic Republic, as well as the tension between "Islam" (conformity to Shiʿi scripture and jurisprudence) and "Republic" (popular input and considerations of the common good) within the constitution and hence the law and the functioning of the state. Notably, there have not been comparably detailed studies of criminal law and its practical application, probably in part because of the political sensitivity of the subject and consequent restrictions on the availability of materials to foreign researchers.

Space limitations and the number of topics to be discussed preclude a detailed exposition of each legal area and a differentiated analysis of the scholarship involved, but it is hoped that this presentation will facilitate a general understanding of which major areas of Iranian Islamic law have been investigated outside Iran or for a foreign audience, and which sources exist on each topic.

I. Legal Overviews

For those interested in a general picture of Islamic law in post-revolutionary Iran, there are studies that offer an overview of the subject or trace the history of various stages of Iran's adoption of Islamized laws.[3] Ansari-Pour's "Iran" entries in the *Yearbook of Islamic and Middle-Eastern Law* (starting in 1994) are useful sources on legal developments in Iran in any given year. Ansari-Pour, a former judge and professor, would have had access to primary sources not necessarily easily available to "outsiders," and would have been well-placed to follow developments in the law and courts. Tellingly, however, even he mentions imperfect access to sources. Another detailed source on the Islamization of laws and the establishment of the post-revolutionary legal system is Schirazi's *The Constitution of Iran*.[4] There are also many descriptions, whether brief and introductory or highly analytical, of the structures and general functioning of the Iranian governmental and judicial systems; these may be free-standing or may form part of studies of specific related issues.[5] There are

[3] Examples: Niknam, 1999a,b; Rezaei 2002; Rahami 2005; Mavani 2001; Akhavi 1996; Behrooz 1996; Roy 1999; Abrahamian 1993; Bakhash 1989; Arjomand 1993, 2007; Mayer 1993, 1987; Owsia 1991; Shaaban 1999–2000; Zubaida 1997, 2010; Tabarestani 1993; Tabari 1983; Lawyers' Committee; Keddie and Monian 1993; Menashri 1980; Martin 1993; Amanat 2007; Sachedina 2001; Mir-Hosseini 2007, 2010c; Schirazi 1997; Valibeigi 1993; Moroni 1993 [1995]; Entessar 2002.

[4] Ansari-Pour 1996, "Iran" entries in *YIMEL* (from vol. 1, 1994/5); Schirazi 1997.

[5] e.g. Shambayati 2004, 2008; Sahimi 2010; *Economist* 2003; Wright 2010; BIA 2007; Durham University 2006; Entessar 2002.

large numbers of studies, including very detailed ones, of post-revolutionary Iranian political and social issues[6]; these may unavoidably touch on aspects of law, without necessarily having law as their main focus.

II. Constitutional Law and Islamic Reformism

When the Iranian revolution of 1978–79 culminated in the formation of an "Islamic Republic" purporting to be rooted in Shi'i law ("Islamic") while also upholding popular representation ("Republic"), there was a proliferation of scholarly studies aiming to understand this new system and how it was being justified on the basis of extant Shi'i jurisprudence. Hence there have been, and continue to be, many intellectual histories of the following:

government in Twelver Shi'ism;
the evolution of Khomeini's thought and his arguably innovative or even radical elaboration of *velayat-e faqih*;
the manner in which the Iranian constitution was drafted and has subsequently attempted to combine Islamic with democratic elements, and the continuing tension between these two elements in Iranian politics.[7]

A useful overview of the nature and history of the post-revolutionary Iranian constitution, and of the Islamization of laws, is Schirazi's monograph mentioned earlier.

A prevalent and frequently noted element of Shi'i *fiqh* (jurisprudence) is continuous *ijtihad*.[8] This contrasts with the pre-eminence given by the constitution to the *vali-e faqih* (Guardian Jurist: head of state according to *velayat-e faqih*, also called

[6] Examples: Keddie 2003; Bakhash 1984; Martin 2000; Boroujerdi 2001; Kamalipour 2010; Kamrava 2008; Arjomand 1988c; Ashraf and Banuazizi 2001; Diamond et al. 2003; Rezaei 2004; Mirbagheri 2007; Sreberny and Khiabany 2007; Rajaee 1999; Zeydabadi-Nejad 2007; Wells 1999; Behnia 1997.

[7] Examples: Mavani 2001; Hairi 1977; Rose 1983; Sachedina 1998, 2001; Akhavi 1996; Calder 1982; Arjomand 1988a, 1988b, 2000a, 2000b; Enayat 1983; Amanat 1988; Fukuyama 2009; Cole 1983; Kelidar 1981; Tamadonfar 2001; Eslami Somea 2001; Arminjon 2010; Bahar 2010; Bakhash 1989; Entessar 2002; Schirazi 1997; Chehabi and Schirazi 2012; Chehabi 2012; Malekahmadi 1999; Martin 1996; Mayer 2008; Strong 1997–98; Usman 2002; Brown 2008; Lamloum 2006/4; Ramazani 1980; Saffari 1993.

[8] Arjomand 2000b, 1980, 156, 1988c, 13–14, 163, 167, 184, 1988a, 5–9, 16–17; Mohammadi, 1996/7, 345–351, 355; Halm, 1991, 67–71, 101–105; Tabataba'i, 2004, 122; Khomeini/Curzu, 1982 183, point 1; Niknam 1999b, "The Islamization," 18; Martin 1993, 43–45; Kamrava, 169; Bakhash 1989, 73; Gleave, 1997, 24–28; Menashri, 1980, 121, 123; Newman, 1982, 573; Mir-Hosseini 1993/2000, 7; Cole 2001, 83–84; Dahlén, 70–76, 87–90; Amanat 2007, 124–125; Walbridge, 2001, 4–5; Picheca, 40, 45; Keddie, 19–20, 310; Khatami, 1998, 145; Matsunaga 2011, 365; Constitution, article 2.

rahbar: "Leader"), whose rulings are incorporated by the Iranian authorities into the "Islam" component of the "Islam-Republic" dyad.[9] Indeed a governmentally endorsed concept is that adherence to "Islam" implies acceptance of *velayat-e faqih*,[10] the "guardianship of the jurist," meaning rule by Shi'i jurists (or the most learned among them) during the Twelfth Imam's Occultation. Since previous conceptions of government during Occultation generally stopped short of positing Shi'i jurists as out-and-out rulers, some current jurists reject *velayat-e faqih* as insufficiently supported by scripture. However, without it an "Islamic Republic" ruled by Shi'i jurists would be impossible; hence it is a major element of the post-revolutionary constitution (for discussion of this see sources in note 7).

Many studies of the Iranian constitution and governmental structure note the evolution of post-revolutionary Iranian governmental ideology to the point where it condoned the subordination of Shi'i law to state power through Khomeini's doctrine, promulgated in 1988, of the "absolute rule of the jurist" (*velayat-e motlaqeh-ye faqih*), permitted by the historically mostly Sunni mechanism of *maslahat* (best interests). This concept has itself undergone much evolution and interpretation; more cautious jurists permit it as a source of law only where scripture is silent.[11] At the other end of the spectrum is Khomeini's interpretation which led in 1988 to the formation of the "Council for Assessing the Benefits of the State" (*Majma'-e Tashkhis-e Maslahat-e Nezam*, often translated as "Expediency Council"). According to this doctrine, so crucial is the existence of the Islamic state to the continued survival of Islam itself that if the functioning of that state requires contravention of Islamic norms, this is permitted, even necessitated, paradoxically on Islamic grounds. In practical terms, laws rejected as un-Islamic by the Guardian Council (GC)—which screens every law for compliance with "Islam"—can be passed by the Expediency Council (EC) notwithstanding that veto. Indeed, it was the repeated showdowns over proposed laws between the parliament and the GC which precipitated the EC's creation, with Khomeini favoring raison d'état over Islamic orthodoxy.

Scholars have perceived one or both of the almost diametrically opposed implications of *maslahat*. On the one hand, it gives potentially limitless discretion to unelected authoritative interpreters of Islam (Leader, GC, EC), and as such is yet another tool strengthening these unelected, hence non-democratic, institutions. On the other, it provides an instant "workaround" for inconvenient scriptural commandments, which means that if the people demand reforms which are deemed un-Islamic, the government has the power to accommodate them,

[9] Arjomand 2000b, e.g. 292–294 and note 1; Bahar, 161; Chehabi and Schirazi 2012. Instead, codified laws, e.g. some criminal laws, were often lifted wholesale from Khomeini's 2007/8 legal treatise *Tahrir al-Vasileh*.

[10] IRNA 2011; Arjomand 2000b, note 1; Schirazi, 74–81.

[11] Schirazi, 63–81, 206–253; Opwis 2007.

instead of throwing its hands up and rejecting these demands on Islamic grounds. In other words it allows the unelected institutions to comply with popular input *should they choose to do so*. The missing link here is a coercive nexus between popular input and *maslahat*: if elected institutions could force legal reforms on the basis of *maslahat*, it could be a formidable tool in the service of adaptability to popular needs. Popular demands have sometimes eventually caused legal reform through the EC. Inconveniently for democracy, however, this council is unelected and populated with conservatives by the Leader (though it occasionally favors popular opinion or the parliament (*Majles*)).[12] The procedural regulations for membership of the council could be reformulated to introduce a conduit (however indirect) between popular input and legal flexibility, as some scholars have noted.[13] A more common view among scholars outside Iran, however, appears to be that *maslahat* is a pro-Leader force, and hence democratically deficient.[14] Also, since any given Leader is not necessarily bound by previous Leaders' choices, a new Leader could potentially undo developments wrought through *maslahat* by his predecessor(s),[15] again suggesting that lasting and less easily reversible change would require greater popular access to *maslahat*.

Substantial scholarly and media attention has been received by Iranian Islamic reformism and its thinkers, such as Montazeri, Kadivar, Soroush, Qabel, Yousefi Eshkevari, Mojtahed Shabestari, and Sa'idzadeh. They have tried to conceptualize Islam in such a way as to accommodate, *inter alia*, popular representation and adaptability to changing social and cultural preferences, and have often been persecuted as a result.[16]

The Constitution seeks to embody two sometimes contradictory elements: Shi'i law (and/or its governmentally endorsed interpretations) and the exigencies of a modern state. The latter includes responsiveness to popular and parliamentary demands for legal reform, which could contradict the concept of God as legislator. The dance between these two poles characterizes not only the constitution, but also the codification, interpretation, and (attempted) reform of the other laws of which it is the "fountainhead."

[12] e.g. Arjomand 2000b, note 4.

[13] Bahar, 163; Malekahmadi, 127–134; Valibeigi, 799–800; Schirazi, 236.

[14] Rezaei and Aghababaei, 109–110; Schirazi, 63–65, 95–96; Bahar, 154; Chehabi and Schirazi, 196–197; Strong, 216; Rejali, 127–129; Arjomand 2000a; Cohen, 262–263; Rasekh, 2005–06, 73; Gheissari and Nasr, 2004, 98–105; Freedom House 2012; Mir-Hosseini and Tapper, 29–36, 174–181.

[15] Strong, 216.

[16] Künkler 2009; Dahlén 2003; Usman 2002; Fathi 2001; Eslami Somea 2001; Foody 2009; Gheytanchi 2001; Arjomand 2000b; Entessar 2002, 30–5; Hajatpour 2011; Schirazi, 277–288; Mayer 1987, 172–178; Lamloum 2006/4; Matsunaga 2007; Radio Farda 2012; Sadri 2002; Matin-asgari 1997, 103–106, 113–115; Zubaida 2010; Mir-Hosseini and Tapper 2006; Esfandiari 2011; Kurzman 2001; Mir-Hosseini, 2010c, 336–337, 2008, 224–228, 2010d, 2001; Sa'idzadeh 2001; Keddie, 260, 274–275, 283, 309–310; Press TV 2010; Abdo 2000; CSM 2010; Payvand 2010.

III. Family Law

Resources available outside Iran about Iranian family law range from brief descriptions of relevant codified law to detailed studies of the law, its Shi'i underpinnings, and the practical applications of both. Criminal and family law are two branches of Iranian law that are sometimes discussed by foreign media and human rights organizations.[17]

Two well-known, relatively early works concerning post-revolutionary Iranian family law are Mir-Hosseini's *Marriage on Trial* (1993) and Shahla Haeri's *Law of Desire* (1989). The first analyzes Iranian and Moroccan divorce law and cases, with a detailed exposition of relevant laws, their roots in Shi'i *fiqh*, and their interpretation in divorce trials, often intersecting with socio-economic forces and extra-legal belief systems. The second focuses on temporary marriage (*ezdevaj-e movaqqat, sigheh*, or *mut'a*) in Iran shortly before and shortly after the revolution. Since *mut'a* is only vaguely defined in codified law, the study concentrates chiefly on the relevant *fiqh*, informants' accounts of their own experiences with, and/or conceptions of, temporary marriage, the socio-economic ramifications of these experiences, and the ways in which the institution is used creatively, such as the facilitation of co-educational travel or work, or the creation of fictive kinship bonds circumventing the necessity to veil in front of unrelated men. Osanloo and Yassari have also conducted fieldwork in Iranian family courts.

The history, nature, and implementation of family law in Iran before and after the revolution have been well documented, particularly regarding marriage, divorce, and child custody. Briefly, the Pahlavi regime preceding the 1979 revolution had introduced the Family Protection Law (FPL) in 1967 and amended it in 1975. These laws raised marriage ages for girls and boys respectively to eighteen and twenty, and gave wives and mothers rights approaching those of men in marriage, divorce, and child custody. Men could no longer contract polygynous marriages without any existing wives' consent, and had to secure a court order (and therefore submit to court arbitration) before obtaining a divorce, despite prevailing conceptions of Shi'i family law permitting men to divorce their wives unilaterally and extra-legally without providing reasons (arbitration of divorcing parties, however, is also enjoined in Qur'an 4:35). Wives were given grounds for initiating divorce, and conditions inserted into marriage contracts allowed wives to divorce themselves if certain circumstances arose, for instance a husband's unauthorized re-marriage. The previous situation, whereby a man could divorce his wife extra-judicially without stated grounds and

[17] e.g. Fathi 2001; Sherman 2009; *Asia News Monitor* 2009; Terman 2007; Terman and Fijabi 2010; Amnesty International 2007, FIDH, and Human Rights Watch 2013 documents.

automatically obtain custody of daughters over the age of seven and sons over the age of two, was modified in women's favor.

Almost immediately after the Pahlavi regime fell, Khomeini declared the FPL un-Islamic and therefore suspended, announcing that divorces granted under it were null and void and that "shari'a" marriage norms would be reinstated. The curbs on men's prerogatives of unilateral divorce, unauthorized polygyny, and automatic child custody were seemingly abandoned. Wives had to secure their husbands' permission to travel and, theoretically, to work or even leave their homes. Women who had spent their lives in the role of wife and mother could find themselves repudiated, unemployable, bereft of their children, and without any recourse, despite the post-revolutionary regime's incessant rhetoric exalting mothers. Widows lost custody of their children to their husbands' relatives. Judges in divorce cases were torn between the duty to implement the law and their frequent perception of that law's unfairness.

Over the years, public opinion and awareness of the social ills resulting from inequitable family laws stimulated legal amendments introducing safeguards recalling those provided by the FPL. For instance, the plight of war widows—who were both numerous and institutionally praised for their sacrifice during the Iran–Iraq war (1980–88)—losing custody of their children; the problem of unemployable long-term housewives and mothers being repudiated; and the harm that could result from children invariably being assigned to their fathers were the catalysts for legal change. Conditions (which must be validated by the husband's signature) were reinserted into standard marriage contracts; wives divorced on their husbands' initiative through no fault of their own could receive "up to" half of the wealth accumulated during the marriage; girls' minimum marriage age was raised from nine (*bulugh*, the age of legal majority in Shi'i *fiqh*) to thirteen; wives were given the theoretical (though often ineffectual) ability to request a divorce on grounds of "harm" (a concept drawn from *fiqh*); the age when boys' custody reverted to their fathers, previously two, was raised to seven on a par with girls; and mothers could obtain custody of children whose fathers were demonstrably unsuitable (following a public outcry after a little girl, Arian Golshani, died at the hands of her abusive divorced father despite her mother's repeated warnings and attempts to retrieve her, thwarted by custody laws which then unequivocally favored fathers). The EC often provided the final push for the passage of such laws. Increasingly open public debate, though punctuated by persecutions of those advocating reform (such as the *mujtahid* Mohsen Sa'idzadeh), has focussed *inter alia* not only on examining and reinterpreting the minutiae of scripture concerning family law and male–female relations, but also on elaborating a new conception of how "Islamic law" relates to changing social needs—the status of women being one of the areas of Islamic law that have provided an impetus for reformist thought.

All of this—the details of pre- and post-revolutionary family law, the timelines of legal reform, the dynamics of marriage and divorce negotiations—is documented by a large number of studies in far greater detail than space allows here.[18]

Areas of family law which have received less frequent attention have included inheritance and the issue of "illegitimate" children. Both are similar to marriage, divorce, and custody law in that they have been the subject of reforms to accommodate practical necessity. For example, a legal reform used reinterpretations of scripture to expand the categories of property from which a widow can inherit from her husband's estate, thereby helping to alleviate the problem of impoverished widows.[19] As for "illegitimate" children, current Iranian law mirrors prevailing Shi'i *fiqh* in identifying filiation and its concurrent obligations—custody, maintenance, inheritance, family name, and such parental duties as obtaining children's identity documents—only through marriage. Court cases regarding unmarried fathers' obligations have produced varying results. Some exonerated the fathers of any obligation. Others invoked such legal mechanisms as *tasbib*—"causation," whereby the father, being responsible for the child's existence, cannot avoid all responsibility—as well as Khomeini's *fatwas* acknowledging that an "illegitimate" parent is nevertheless a parent, to conclude that the only difference in treatment between "legitimate" and "illegitimate" children is that the second are excluded from inheritance. All other parental responsibilities remain in force regardless of children's "birth status." This position was consolidated in 1997 by a "judicial uniformity" (*vahdat-e ravieh*) ruling of the General Council of the Supreme Court, which consists of three-quarters of presiding judges and their assistants and issues binding rulings when detecting inconsistency between court judgments. This ruling, while displaying the potential adaptability of *fiqh* despite prima facie inflexibility, also illustrates the limits of that adaptability, since as a result of scriptural commandments deemed inviolable, these blameless children are still "punished" for their parents' behavior by being excluded from inheritance.[20]

[18] Mir-Hosseini 1993/2000, 1999, 2002, 1996a, 1996b, 2008; Yassari 2002–03; Haeri 1989, 1990, 1994; Hoodfar 1996; Osanloo 2006a,b, 2002, 2008; Gheytanchi 2001; Strong, 163–170, Yeganeh 1993, Aghajanian 1986; Ardehali (esp. 83–87); Mohaqeq Damad 2004; Safa'i 2004; Hamidian 2004; Kian 1997; Bahramitash and Kazemipour 2006; Entessar 2002, 30; Fatemi 2006; Bernardi 1986–87; Ebrahimi 2005; Habibi 1997; Schirazi 1997, 215–220; Malekahmadi, 218; Esfandiari 1994; Moghadam 1994; Sa'idzadeh 2001; Ansari-Pour 2001–02; Kar and Hoodfar 1996; Pakzad 1994; Higgins 1985; Mokhtari 2005; Lamloum 2006/4; Williams 2009; Niknam 1999b, "The Islamization," 20–21.

[19] Yassari 2009; Mehrpour 2004.

[20] Ansari-Pour 1999–2000; Syed 2008. Though the stigma of "illegitimacy" appears anachronistic and barbaric, it remains legally entrenched even in secular and supposedly "civilized" countries, such as Britain, which still forbids nationality through unmarried fathers (British Nationality Act 1981, sections 2, 3(6)c).

IV. The Status of Women

There are many studies that, rather than concentrating on one topic within Iranian law, note women's inferior status in multiple areas of law. For example, inheritance mandates male–female inequality by generally assigning female heirs half the share of analogous male heirs. Female testimony, where accepted, is most frequently given half the weight of male testimony, so that a male witness may be substituted by two female witnesses (and there are instances where female testimony is rejected altogether, or at least one male witness is required). The *diyeh* or "blood money"—compensation for murder or injuries—for a murdered female is half that of a murdered male, so a murdered woman's heirs must compensate her male murderer's heirs for his execution by paying them half his blood money. Women are buried deeper in the ground than men when being stoned for adultery, making escape (which cancels the conviction if it was based on confession) more difficult. Women must veil, and cannot convey Iranian citizenship to their children or fill the position of judge or head of state (though there are female "assistant investigative magistrates"). Such legal inequalities are enumerated as examples of the female condition in post-revolutionary Iran, often alongside others, such as the fluctuating policies regarding limits on female students in certain university courses, which are not strictly speaking "Islamic," and others which are not necessarily within the domain of law, such as interpersonal relations, family dynamics, or the political ramifications of the "woman question." Given the high visibility of the issues "women in Islam" and "women in Iran," it is not surprising that this is a frequent starting point for academic study as well as less specialized investigations such as newspaper reporting. Therefore, while some areas of law such as marriage, divorce, and child custody have been thoroughly studied, others (e.g. testimony and inheritance) have attracted less painstaking investigation, figuring instead as examples in studies of women's status in Iran or Islam. There are occasional mentions of women's comparatively better status (in some fields) in Iran than in most Muslim countries (e.g. Mir-Hosseini).[21]

[21] Higgins 1985; Esfandiari 2001; Ardehali 1986; Yeganeh 1993; Bahramitash and Kazemipour 2006; Nashat 1983; Afkhami and Friedl 1994; Namayandeh 2010; Tremayne 2006; Zahedi 2007; Sepehrrad 2010; Williams 2009; Mir-Hosseini 1996b, 1993; Hoodfar 2000; Abbasi-Shavazi et al., 2008c "Family"; Betteridge 1983; Kian 1997; Fazaeli 2007; Ulrey 2011; Halper 2007.

v. Criminal Law

The most common conception of Islamic criminal law, which is mirrored in codified Iranian law, is that crimes fall into four categories: *hudud, qesas, diyeh*, and *ta'zirat*.

Hudud (singular: *hadd*; literally, "boundaries" or "limits"), also known as "Islamic fixed penalties," are described in scripture (notably, stoning is not in the Qur'an) for certain crimes including fornication, rape, adultery (fornication while married), sodomy, alcohol consumption, and theft. *Hudud* are inalterable (they cannot be commuted or "bargained down") and mostly consist of a specified number of lashes (maximum 100), with some exceptions including the penalties for theft (amputation of four fingers of the right hand), adultery (stoning), and rape or sodomy (death). *Qesas* is retaliation for murder (through execution) or injuries (through infliction of equivalent injuries on the perpetrator). *Diyeh* is "blood money" payable in lieu of *qesas* to the victim or the deceased victim's heirs. *Ta'zirat* are discretionary (literally: "disciplinary") penalties, covering crimes outside the other categories. In Iranian codified law they generally involve combinations of incarceration, flogging, or fines, each crime legally having a maximum and minimum sentence. The prevalent view before the revolution, however, was that their discretionary nature was incompatible with predetermined maximum and minimum sentences, and their codification was one of the struggles between the GC and the parliament which triggered the creation of the EC, explained earlier. Despite the EC's potentially sweeping powers, reform attempts in areas of criminal law covered by scripture, particularly *hudud*, have been slow or ineffectual, showing that the GC and the criterion of "Islamicity" (or "being seen to be Islamic") still have considerable weight. For example, stoning generated substantial public debate and came close to abrogation several times (e.g. in 2002 with a frequently ignored moratorium from the head of the judiciary, and in 2008 and 2012 with proposed laws), ultimately to no avail. However, there is talk of emphasizing rehabilitation over punishment for some narcotics and other offenders and HIV-positive individuals; similar arguments have been made regarding prostitutes.[22]

Post-revolutionary codification of Shi'i criminal law began in 1982 with the introduction of the *Hudud* and *Qesas* Law. In 1983, parliament attempted to codify *ta'zirat*, as described earlier.[23] The *Hudud, Qesas*, and *Ta'zirat* law remained in force until a new penal code, named "Law of Islamic Penalties" (*Qanun-e Mojazat-e Eslami*), was introduced in similar stages: its *hudud* and *qesas* portions in 1991, and its *ta'zirat* portion in 1996. It was given "experimental" validity for five years, renewed

[22] Farajiha 2006; Aliverdinia and Pridemore 2007; Mayer 1987, 171–174; Rejali 126–129; Nobahar, 1996, 204–206, 216–217; Samgiss, 2005, 68–73; Navai, 2005, 83–87; Kusha, 223–229; Abu-Raddad et al. 2010, 119–126, 202; Keddie, 289; Majdi et al. 2011.

[23] e.g. Schirazi, 223–231; Niknam 1999a,b, "L'Islamisation," 48–62, "The Islamization."

several times, most recently until mid-March 2012. A replacement bill (which made stoning commutable) was approved by parliament in 2008, but rejected by the GC; it never became law. A significantly different (and harsher) version was approved by parliament and by the GC in 2012, which subsequently withdrew its approval.[24] That version notably omitted any explicit mention of stoning for adultery, but left a loophole encouraging judges to refer to *fiqh* where the law was silent, effectively allowing stoning through the back door. With some changes including the explicit reintroduction of stoning for adultery (commutable by the head of the judiciary) in article 225, this penal code was approved by parliament on April 21, 2013 for an "experimental" five-year period, confirmed by the GC on May 1, and signed by Ahmadinezhad shortly thereafter, becoming fully fledged law.[25] The new law differs from the old one in the details of *ta'ziri* penalties, but seems to bring no advantages to those accused of *qesas* or *hadd* crimes, notwithstanding superficial claims of leniency to those aged under eighteen (e.g. article 91); indeed, the *hudud* section omits elements formerly favorable to defendants.

The coverage of criminal law, like that of family law, available outside Iran has ranged from mentions in the media[26] to academic studies, though to a lesser extent than with family law. One notable difference is that while family law has been the subject of investigations combining breadth with depth—such as Mir-Hosseini's *Marriage on Trial* which combines an overview of Iranian marriage and divorce law with a detailed account of its practical implementation and interpretation, aided by case studies—works on post-revolutionary Iranian criminal law tend to be either very focussed on one issue, or very general but without much detailed analysis of legal theory and practice.

Focussed studies come from scholars both within and outside Iran. Their topics include legal principles (e.g. double jeopardy or the legality principle), drug-related convictions, the sociological ramifications of murder, women's treatment by judicial authorities, and the law of political opposition.[27]

Very general overviews often come from Iranian scholars addressing a foreign audience, assuming no prior knowledge. These may paraphrase parts of the penal code or, less frequently, other codes relevant to criminal law; delineate the

[24] Fararu 2012; Tabnak 2012; Golduzian, 2003/4, 26; Alborz 2010; UN General Assembly, GA/SHC/3925; Paygah-e Ettela'-resani-e Basij-e Huquqdanan 2010; ISNA 2013; Bultan 2013; Tasnim 2013; ICANA 2013.

[25] Aminizadeh 2013; Safa'i 2013; *Mehr News* 2013; ICARC 2013.

[26] e.g. Sherman 2009; *Asia News Monitor* 2009.

[27] Rahmdel 2004; Kusha 2002; Rezaei and Aghababaei 2005–06; Tamadonfar 2001; Habibzadeh 2005; Tabari 2003; Jalali-Karveh 2006; Ghodsi 2003, 2004; Brajer and Rahmatian 2005; Schneider 2012; Keshavarz 2006–07 [2009]; Ghassemi 2009; Mahmoudi 2006a, 2006b; Gholami 2006; Shams Nateri 2006; Haddad and Moghadam 2011; Mousavi et al. 2012; Nayyeri 2012; Mokhtari 2004; Attari et al. 2006. The work of Rabb (2009) and Fierro (2007), though not focussed on post-revolutionary Iran, is useful for understanding the principle "avert *hudud* through doubt" (*qa'edeye darr'*), used with great frequency in Iranian *hadd* trials.

structure of the criminal justice system; describe the categories of Islamic penal law and how they relate to those in the Iranian penal code; or describe the history of the Islamization of criminal law. They occasionally refer to one or more court judgments or *fiqh* principles.[28] Some focussed studies, or studies of related subjects, also include general overviews of this nature.

Human rights organizations such as Amnesty International, Human Rights Watch, Fédération Internationale des Droits de l'Homme (FIDH), and Women Living Under Muslim Laws monitor human rights abuses in various countries, including Iran, and produce or commission reports on these and relevant laws, such as Iran's penal code. Their legal information mostly consists of paraphrased or translated portions of the penal code. However, these texts (especially FIDH) provide some understanding of legal developments relevant to human rights, and sometimes contain one or more case studies.[29] Studies without a specific affiliation to human rights organizations, which address the subject of human rights in Iran, sometimes contain legal analysis or *fiqh* perspectives.[30]

Comparatively few studies set out to perform a detailed investigation of Iranian criminal law, or a branch thereof, in its own right; and those which do, as noted earlier, generally analyze very specific points of law. Forays into Iranian criminal law are frequently ancillary to studies of some other aspect of Iran, most often its human rights record, its treatment of women, or its political repression. Hence the emphasis of many texts is not on understanding the law's minutiae, but on displaying its incompatibility with international law or standards of human rights, which may be accorded more attention than Iranian law. Portions (usually brief) of Iranian law are displayed chiefly to illustrate points pertaining to the greater aim of the studies.

The resultant conception of Iranian law is often colored by the main raison d'être of the texts. A notable example of this is the frequent filtering of *hudud* through the issue (whose importance it is not my intention to diminish) of "women in Iran." Stoning, for instance, is often presented as a women's issue. Though females are apparently convicted of adultery far more often than males, many if not most people known to have perished by stoning since the 2002 stoning moratorium have been men. A more nuanced view could acknowledge the gender biases in the law and its application while noting the relevance of *hudud* not exclusively to "women's rights" but to "human rights" generally. Conceptualizing "Islamic penalties" as "women's

[28] Examples: Asli 2006; Gontowska 2005; Entessar 1988, 2002; Rezaei 2002; Picheca 1982; Rahami 2005, 2006; Lawyers' Committee; Sadeghi and Kendall 2001; Mir-Hosseini 2010b, 2010a; Shambayati 2008; Kusha 2002; Rejali 1994; Schirazi, 223–231, 244, note 61; Malekahmadi 1999.

[29] Examples: Amnesty International 2007, 2008, 2009a, 2009b and yearly reports on Iran; FIDH 2009, 2010, 2013; IHRDC 2013a, 2013b; Terman 2007; Terman and Fijabi 2010; Iran-e Azad 2011; ICAS 2010, 2011; Mir-Hosseini, 2010a, 2010b; Eghtedari 1997.

[30] Karadsheh 1996; Organization for Islamic Culture and Communications 2003; Afshari 1996; Taheri 1983; Mayer 1996, 2006, 2007, 2008; Mokhtari 2008; Mokhtari 2004; Price 2006; Bielefeldt 2006; Morgan-Foster 2008; Kar 2007; Matsunaga 2011; Sepehrrad 9, 65–67.

issues" may partially account for the relative rarity of investigations of other *hudud*, such as hand amputation, compared to stoning. I have tried to aid the study of *hudud* in Iran through my research on Iranian *hadd* law, its relationship with Shi'i law, and its practical implementation in courts as observed through original documents pertaining to Iranian *hadd* trials.[31]

VI. Minorities

Iran is ethno-linguistically diverse, with a Persophone majority living alongside such minorities as Kurds, Baluchis, Arabs, and Turkic-speaking groups including Azaris and Turkmen, *inter alia*. However, relations with ethno-linguistic minorities are not the domain of Islamic law, which instead plays a role in the treatment of non-Muslims living in Muslim lands, irrespective of ethnic or linguistic differences from the rulers. The standard Muslim tolerance for "people of the book" is well-known. "People of the book" are generally conceptualized as worshippers of the same God as Muslims, and followers of earlier divine revelations whose imperfect retention over time necessitated the new dispensation represented by the Qur'an. Followers of pre-Islamic Abrahamic religions (Jews, Christians, and Sabians) are Qur'anically recognized as belonging in this category, to which have historically been added other groups depending on practical necessity and the resultant juristic adaptations—for example, Hindus in Mughal India and Zoroastrians in Iran. Post-Islamic Abrahamic religions are most emphatically excluded from the category because they reject the finality of Muhammad's prophetic role, positing prophets after him: hence the persecution of Baha'is in post-revolutionary Iran. These recognized religious minorities, or *dhimmis*, can retain their religion and their religious laws (where these do not interfere with the functioning of the state) subject to a tax called *jizya*, and, though tolerated, are not on an equal footing with Muslims, are excluded from important posts (notably head of state), and are subject to some discrimination within the criminal law.[32] Constitutionally (articles 13–14), the only religious minorities recognized by the Islamic Republic of Iran are Jews, Christians, and Zoroastrians, who have the full protection of the law and remain subject to their own religious laws regarding personal affairs and religious education within the (unspecified) limits of the law; parliamentary seats are reserved for Armenians,

[31] Fraser Fujinaga 2013, *Life and Limb*.

[32] Hemmasi and Prorok, 63–66; Higgins 1984, 53–55; Samii 2000; Bernardi 1986–87; Cohen 2008; Valavioun 2004; Tsadik, 2003, 380–405; Mayer, 1987, 147–149, 182–183; Eslami Somea, 158–161; Berween 2008; Rehman 2008; FIDH 2010, 2009, 32–34.

Jews, Assyrians, and Zoroastrians.[33] Other schools of Islam (the constitution explicitly mentions Sunnis and Zaydis) also retain some religious autonomy (article 12) though, notwithstanding some calls for harmony, in practice they have been discriminated against, for instance through the struggle over permission to build Sunni mosques, the fact that the Sunni call to prayer is not broadcast, and the absence of parliamentary seats reserved for Sunnis. The few available sources on the Ismailis, who are not explicitly mentioned in the constitution, suggest that they are considered somewhat heretical, because their conception of the finality of Muhammad's prophecy is interpreted as different from that of Twelvers or Sunnis. Some sources suggest little official discrimination but some individual instances of discrimination.[34] Despite theoretical constitutional protections of ethnic minorities and their languages (articles 15, 19, etc.) and some gestures toward minorities such as a small amount of state broadcasting in minority languages,[35] there have been and continue to be controversies over minority languages and bitter ethnic struggles, for example, those involving the Kurds, Turkmen, and Baluchis who are, however, mostly Sunni.[36] The non-Persian but mostly Shiʿi Azaris tend to be more integrated,[37] though they too have not been immune from strife.[38] Generally, the Islamic emphasis in the constitution and the post-revolutionary law makes it such that religious, rather than ethnic, minority status can be expected to create the greater hindrance to integration into the dominant system: Higgins notes that "individuals of non-Persian Shiʿi background should find integration into the Islamic Republican state easier than should Persian-speaking non-Shiʿi,"[39] emphasizing the minority status of non-Shiʿis and non-Muslims by pointing out the large proportion of non-Persophones (less than 50 percent) but small proportion of non-Shiʿis (less than 10 percent) in the Iranian population.[40] Ethno-linguistic minority status does intersect with the deployment of Islamic law in unexpected ways: for instance, my research on Iranian *hadd* cases repeatedly displayed the disadvantage borne by members of linguistic minorities who could not understand interrogators and legal proceedings, because the law requiring interpreters for non-Persian speakers was ignored.

A detailed account of the formation and implementation of post-revolutionary policy regarding religious minorities is provided by Eliz Sanasarian in *Religious Minorities in Iran*. It uses published minutes of meetings during which the new constitution was elaborated in the summer and autumn of 1979 to recount how minority policy was decided, emphasizing the crucial role of the four minority

[33] Samii 2000, 130, 133.

[34] Human Rights Watch 2013; Buchta 2000 (Ismailis: 346); Samii 2000, 130, 133; FIDH 2010, 22–23; IRBC 2000; MRGI 2009.

[35] Samii 2000, 131, 133.

[36] Higgins 1984, 55–59; KHRP 2009; FIDH 2010; Samii 2000; Vercellin 1980; Sanati 2008; Brown, 70.

[37] Higgins 1984, 59–62. [38] Samii 2000, 133–134. [39] Higgins 1985, 1984, 47.

[40] Higgins 1984, 47; Samii 2000; Hemmasi and Prorok 2002.

representatives (Zoroastrian, Armenian, Jewish, and Chaldaean/Assyrian) whose "impact in proportion to their numbers was remarkable"[41] (the Assembly of Experts had seventy-three members) in securing at least some rights for the minorities. While they did not obtain everything they wanted, and minorities remain resolutely discriminated against in their exclusion from some important posts, the requirement that they outwardly comply with certain standards of "Islamic" behavior, and their inferior position in parts of the criminal law (e.g. the reduced "blood money" for their murder and the automatic death penalty for non-Muslim males fornicating with Muslim females), they retained autonomy in some other areas of life such as marriage, divorce, child custody, inheritance, and private worship and religious instruction. The Shi'i and Persophone authorities did make incursions into the educational prerogatives of religious and linguistic minorities, and the resulting struggle played out differently in different locations. The author points out the variance in the situation of different minority groups, with Armenians and Zoroastrians generally managing to achieve social upward mobility and retain some self-determination,[42] Assyrians and Chaldaeans not faring as well, and Jews and especially Baha'is contending with the constant possibility of assault (including the threat of Jews being charged as Israeli or Zionist spies, which occasionally still happens).[43] Zoroastrians have benefited from being characterized as inalienably Iranian and free of perceived affiliations with foreign enemies (e.g. Israel for Jews and America and other formerly proselytizing western powers for Christians).[44]

Despite some legal protections and social integration as described by Sanasarian, Cohen emphasizes "the dark side of the coin," pointing out that despite the regime's vaunted religious tolerance,[45] first the status of religious minorities does resolutely remain one of subordination rather than equal citizenship with all its corollaries, and secondly that status is limited to Jews, Christians, and Zoroastrians, including some and leaving others vulnerable to veritable persecution. She concludes that religious tolerance compatible with international law is impossible in Iran without a radical overhaul of the way in which laws must comply with literal interpretations of scripture.[46]

Studies of religious minorities, usually by scholars outside Iran, are often performed not only with a focus on Islamic law but within an investigation of their sociology or history, or of ethno-linguistic minorities. Besides Sanasarian, good sources for the post-revolutionary history and/or sociology of religious minorities include Vivier-Muresan, Hemmasi and Prorok, Higgins (1984), and Samii (2000); Helfgott 1980 provides pre-revolutionary background, and Tsadik describes relevant scripture and *fiqh*.

[41] Sanasarian, 2000, 71.
[42] Also noted in Hemmasi and Prorok, 76.
[43] Hemmasi and Prorok, 78.
[44] Hemmasi and Prorok, 76.
[45] e.g. Noori and Amin, 1987, 73.
[46] Cohen, 262–266.

VII. Medicine

There has been much analysis of Shi'i *fiqh*'s relationship with various fields of medicine within Iran, for readily comprehensible reasons of practical necessity; and this field has also received some scholarly attention from abroad. Areas that face prima facie obstacles from *fiqh*, and which have therefore been studied meticulously, include certain fertility treatments, organ transplant, and abortion. Works on medical ethics in post-revolutionary Iran often emphasize the flexibility of Shi'i *fiqh* due to its dynamic use of *ijtihad*. Jurists have been hard at work accommodating the law to medical advances, and clinics generally keep collections of medical rulings and precepts (*ahkam-e pezeshki*) in their offices, including relevant portions of Khomeini's and Khamenei's legal treatises and the most recent *fatwas* on cutting-edge issues, to assuage any misgivings about the possible illicitness of their services.[47]

Gamete and embryo donation are problematic because of the *fiqhi* emphasis on biological parentage to establish filiation. Additionally, carrying a child created by the seed of someone other than one's spouse may suggest the possibility of adultery (*zena*). One way of circumventing the adulterous implications of donor gametes has been to divorce one's infertile husband before accepting donor gametes and subsequently remarry him, or, for men, to contract a temporary marriage (*sigheh*) with the egg donor for the duration of the pregnancy. Stratagems have also been discovered for permitting embryo donation. The prohibition of donor gametes in many Sunni nations has led to "IVF tourism" in Iran. Various IVF techniques have been permitted through the introduction of new laws.[48]

Such creative use of *fiqh* suggests other potential areas of investigation. For instance, the law criminalizes gay couples but permits gender reassignment surgery[49]—another example of adaptive *fiqh*. It would be interesting to investigate whether couples with one "reassigned" partner could qualify for IVF treatments (which could require surrogacy).

Fiqh has been used creatively in other areas of medicine.[50] For instance, the *fiqh* prohibition of mutilating oneself or others, including cadavers, interferes with organ donation. Live donations have been encouraged by a governmental program of infrastructure development and monetary compensation for donors. Physicians, noting the shortage of cadavers for organ donation due to objections to mutilating cadavers, have called for the permissibility of cadaveric donation to be publicized. The resulting juristic and publicity efforts have increased popular awareness,

[47] Larijani et al. 2005; Abbasi-Shavazi et al., 2008b "ART;" Tober 2007.

[48] Larijani et al. 2005; Abbasi-Shavazi et al., 2008b "ART."

[49] Omani Samani et al. 2007; Papan-Matin, 2009, 128.

[50] Akrami et al. 2004; Larijani et al., 2004, 2005; Einollahi 2004; Zali et al. 2002; Hessini 2007; Afshar, 1996, 136; Akrami and Osati 2007; Abbasi-Shavazi et al. 2008a, "Modernization."

encouraging more people to compile organ donor cards. Legal reforms and juristic debate on relevant *fiqh* have promoted not only live and cadaveric donation but a host of other practices including stem cell research, "therapeutic cloning," genetic research, and abortion in certain medically necessary cases, while scholars have sought to discourage consanguineous marriage (which increases the risk of genetic defects) by arguing that Islam does not necessarily recommend it.

Family planning is another area where Shiʿi law and medicine have intertwined.[51] Iranian population policy in the latter twentieth century was characterized by two about-faces. In 1967 the Pahlavi regime launched a population control program, whose aggressive promotion caused several Shiʿi jurists to denounce contraception even though mostly it has historically been considered permissible in Islam. Although after the revolution jurists did concede that contraception was not Islamically forbidden, supplies became unreliable and prices correspondingly inflated, while pre-revolutionary family planning infrastructures were dismantled; indeed, the new rulers reportedly considered the previous regime's family planning programs to be tools of western imperialism to keep Muslim populations under control.[52] Several concepts promoted by the new government, such as the importance of the Muslim family (including the Muslim wife and mother, newly emancipated from her objectified western role), the function of early marriage (as permitted and even encouraged by *fiqhi* sources) in satisfying bodily urges and preventing uncontrolled promiscuity, and, with the advent of war, the need for a supply of soldiers to defend the motherland, combined to form an amalgam of policies which were decidedly pronatalist, and a rapid population explosion followed. A crucial theme characterizing the struggle against the Shah's regime had been to rectify the injustices that it had wrought—including economic ones. The post-revolutionary regime emphasized social justice and the provision of basic necessities, education, and health care to all.[53] This, however, backfired when combined with its pro-natalist policies, because the rapid population growth created too many claimants for the promised services, with demand rapidly outstripping supply. Hence, in a second about-face with initial stirrings in 1985, the authorities once again reversed course. They first encouraged publications and broadcasts about the ills of overpopulation to increase awareness and stimulate public debate, and then solicited the involvement of jurists to add the necessary ingredient of Islamic approval. Eventually they instituted a national conference on family planning policy whose result was an intensive family planning program, ratified by Khomeini in 1989 shortly before his death.

The program included heavily promoted slogans ("fewer children, better life" etc.), highly efficient family planning clinics, community health workers going

[51] Hoodfar and Assadpour 2000; Hoodfar 2008; Tober et al. 2006; Tober 2007; Afshar, 1996, 135–137; Hessini 2007; Abbasi-Shavazi et al., "Family"; Fathi. For pre-revolutionary background, see Mosavvar-Rahmani 1983.

[52] Hoodfar and Assadpour, 20.

[53] Messkoub, 202–218.

from door to door, and easy access to contraception; later developments included collaboration with the Ministry of Education to introduce relevant instruction in schools, and a reduction in child benefits for state employees after the fourth child. The program was remarkably successful. (On a related note, Underwood notes that overall child health improved after the revolution, possibly in part because of the state ideology's egalitarian elements and emphasis on development.)[54] There were debates about whether various forms of contraception were Islamically permissible. For instance, tubal ligation and vasectomy were controversial because they may be categorized as irreversible mutilation, so more funds were allocated to training doctors in reversing these procedures. Though abortion was considered by many jurists to be permissible until "ensoulment" (before the second trimester) if medically necessary, it remained controversial and was placed outside the family planning program, being categorized instead as a health issue, to avoid tarnishing the family planning program with this potentially destructive controversy. Research into premodern *fiqh* on contraception was encouraged, with family planning being cast not as a western import but as a tool to alleviate poverty and other ills (with which many Iranians were familiar) which had been discussed by Muslim scholars long before its examination in the west. In such a manner, negotiation with Islamic authorities allowed gradual expansion and wider acceptance of the family planning program, as did the involvement of local clerics whose familiarity with both Islamic norms and their communities made them a useful additional vehicle for promoting family planning services, especially in rural or low-income areas.

VIII. Islamic Banking

The field of Islamic banking in Iran has received copious amounts of attention,[55] whether in its own right, as part of a comparison with Islamic banking in other countries, or as an aid to understanding economic or investment conditions in Iran.

[54] Underwood, e.g. iii, 33–46, 106–112, 123–137, 270–271.

[55] Nomani 2003; Ansari-Pour 1994, 1995, 1996; Khan and Mirakhor, 1987, 1990; Anwar 1992; Haron 1998; Kuran 1995, 1997; Behdad 1994, 1995; Valibeigi 1993; Iqbal and Molyneux 2005 (basic ideas); Chong and Liu 2009; Makiyan 2001; Aggarwal and Yousef 2000; de Belder and Hassan 1993; Khan 1986; Zenganeh 1989; Bader et al. 2008; Atai 2005–06 [2008]; Kordvani 2009; Dusuki and Abozaid 2007 (basic ideas); Yazdani 2000; Karbassian 2000; Yousefi et al. 1997; Mazarei 1996; Zaher and Hassan 2001; Ariff 1988; Solé 2008; Imam and Kpodar 2010; Mirakhor 1987; Guru et al. 2003; Raqibuz zaman and Movassaghi 2001, 2002; Ghasimi 1992; Iqbal and Llewellyn 2002; Iqbal 1997; Van Schaik (basic ideas); Mayer 1987, 166–169; Owsia, 65; Shaaban, 29–32; Schirazi, 239.

The consensus among most Muslim jurists is that Islam prohibits *riba* ("excess or increase") and *gharar* ("hazard"), but there is less agreement about what these really mean, with some equating *riba* with any interest on loans or transactions, and others only defining it as usury, meaning *excessive* interest. Similarly *gharar* is often viewed as speculation, but its interpretations vary. In any case, Iran, Pakistan, and Sudan claim to have rendered their entire banking systems compatible with Islam. However, the Iranian banking system, which characterizes *riba* as any interest but provides workarounds, has been characterized by pragmatism and flexibility, such that some observers, noting the "tricks" with which it circumvents Islamic prohibitions, have deemed it neither Islamic nor economically efficient, with much discussion of the consequent problems.

The revolutionary movement focussed on ousting the Shah and elaborated few details on a future economic system other than self-sufficiency, autarchy, and an end to the Shah's usurpation of wealth. *Riba* is mentioned in articles 43 and 49 of the post-revolutionary constitution, the passing of which occurred with little controversy. Unlike the pre-revolutionary criminal code, civil and contract laws were deemed sufficiently Islamic not to require great changes. All banks were nationalized in 1979, mainly because their owners had either fled or become insolvent. Parliament approved the Law of *Riba*-free Banking in August 1983; it came into force on March 21, 1984, and was pragmatic, allowing many workarounds for obstacles found in Shi'i *fiqh*. The Islamization of banking was reportedly gradual and unaccompanied by fierce debate. From 1981 various types of interest were replaced by service charges, "minimum profit" rates, "prizes," or "bonuses" (whose magnitude should not be predetermined and could be in kind or in cash) on deposits or loans, the sharing of profit and loss on loans used for productive enterprises, price markups conceptualized as repurchase for an increased price, and pecuniary penalties for delayed payment of loans. (These and similar mechanisms have technical names, such as *mudaraba, musharaka, murabaha*, and *jo'ala*, which are familiar to specialists in Islamic banking, on which primers are readily available.) "Islamic" sanction often postdated actual practice: for instance, in 1988 the GC approved interest for dealings with non-Muslims by invoking *fiqh* interpretations. However, Iranian banks and authorities had already been giving and receiving interest on international transactions, even though the GC had also, on other occasions (e.g. 1985), declared any interest illicit. Despite the prohibition on transactions involving chance and selling what one does not possess (e.g. futures), which may be considered obstacles to a stock market, the Iranian system manages to permit a stock market explicitly.

Other concepts advanced by Iranian jurists have been that the Qur'an's prohibition of *riba* refers to private loans but not to a national banking system such as did not exist in the Prophet's time, and that because of inflation, a lender who receives the same amount originally lent will be losing money, in effect become the victim of *riba*, so the amount returned should be increased to compensate for inflation, though any more than that would constitute *riba*. Inflation-replacing rates became lower than inflation rates, causing various problems including a widespread preference for informal, unregulated, and sometimes risky lending. This has elicited pressure from Iranian economists to adopt a parallel banking system, as exists in Malaysia and some Iranian free economic zones in the Persian Gulf, with Islamic and "conventional" banks operating alongside each other. Increasing acknowledgement of such problems has led to the permission of private banking, with the first private bank and insurance company opening in 2002.

The Iranian banking system is integrated into governmental development policies in various ways (a role emphasized by a *fatwa* from Khomeini).[56] Through the medium of parliamentary budget bills, banks have been encouraged to invest in such projects as low-income housing and profit-sharing cooperatives rather than luxuries and non-essential goods, and are required to keep a portion of their resources for *qarz al-hasan* (interest-free loans, literally "correct/benevolent loan"). These are intended for such personal needs as dowries (*mehrieh*, payable to wives by husbands), medical and educational costs, and house repairs, as well as financial assistance for small farmers and craftsmen or production and service cooperatives.

IX. Other Areas of Law

Islamic and Iranian law intersect in other areas which have been the subject of some scholarly inquiry. For example, the history of music in post-revolutionary Iran involved juristic developments from the government's initial stance against all music, through Khomeini's permission of purchasing musical instruments provided they were also usable for "licit" music, to the expanding of permitted musical categories and the partial reinstatement of female vocalists (only in groups, or only for female audiences). Similar developments occurred with cinema.[57] The struggle over post-revolutionary land reform and redistribution saw Khomeini claimed both by landowners—as a paladin of Islamic protections of private property—and by the would-be land occupiers—as a proponent of Islamic egalitarianism—both of which he propounded at different times. Labor law was another area where *fiqh* posed problems, and one of the catalysts for the articulation of *maslahat* as a promoter of raison d'état. Any restrictions on wages, working hours, and so on were deemed incompatible with Islamic laws regarding freedom of contract, yet the

[56] Khan and Mirakhor 1990, 359.

[57] Zahir 2008; Schirazi, 67–68, 240–244; Zeydabadi-Nejad 2007; Motlagh, 2012, 132–136.

Labor Minister's appeal to Khomeini yielded the response that such laws could be overridden in the public interest.[58] The topic of post-revolutionary Iran and international relations (the Iranian hostage crisis, the nuclear program, etc.) has been much discussed, mostly from the perspective of international law and politics. However, some studies have investigated Islamic perspectives on international relations with Iran.[59] A study of Iranian driving habits and regulations,[60] though its subject is not strictly Islamic, sheds light on people's attitudes about the authorities' cynically selective use of Islamic law which could be relevant to the study of some or all branches of Islamic law in Iran. Some issues which are tangential to, but potentially influential upon, the evolution and application of Islamic law in Iran have received attention; examples include police forces, prisons, torture, political parties, repression, laws and events related to journalism, and health policy which, though not always contingent upon the minutiae of *fiqh*, are shaped by the Islamic-inflected state ideology.[61]

X. Conclusion

Unsurprisingly, interest in post-revolutionary Iran frequently originates in a desire to understand various highly visible aspects of it: its politics, its repression of dissent, its treatment of women, its human rights record, its economic resources, its militarily strategic importance, its professed enmity towards "the west," and so on. A focus on its law is often, though not exclusively, secondary to these interests. Hence, referring to studies conducted outside Iran or addressing a foreign audience, we see a proliferation of texts with a tangential, and not always very detailed, legal "arm": enumerations of Iran's human rights abuses or forms of female subordination; descriptions of diplomatic difficulties; analyses of Iran's economy or suitability as a potential target for investment; histories of the Islamic Republic's formation; highly detailed accounts of Iranian politics; and so on, with varying amounts of

[58] Bakhash 1989; Behdad 1994, 803–813; Valibeigi 1993; Kuran 1995, 1997; Underwood, 33–6; Schirazi, 175–192, 206–215; Malekahmadi, 121–134.

[59] Bahar 1992; Cherif Bassiouni 2008; Elahi 1987–88; Scott 2000; Algar 1993; Bsoul 2003 (Islamic international relations).

[60] Banakar and Nasrolahi Fard 2012.

[61] Zamani and Jordan 1989; Samii 2005; Shahidi, 2008, 746 onwards; Dinmore 2001; Eslami Somea 2001; Hooglund 1989; Underwood 1993; Matin-Asgari 2006; Mokhtari 2004; Abrahamian 1999; Kamalipour 2010; Osborne 2009; Parvaz 2003; Messkoub 2006; Alfoneh 2008; Diamond et al. 2003; Osanloo 2010; Redaelli 2007; Rejali 1994.

legal information illustrating various arguments. These appear to be more common than studies where the law is the starting point.

Where the law is the main focus, this apparently occurs most often with constitutional law, family law, and to some extent Islamic banking. Studies of Iranian medical law most often come from scholars writing within Iran for a foreign audience, though some scholars outside Iran have investigated it. The study of minorities is mostly conducted by a relatively small number of scholars outside Iran. This contrast may be partly due to the political sensitivity of the religious minority issue (addressing the treatment of non-Muslims may quickly imply that Islam is incompatible with "international standards of equality"), the comparatively lower political sensitivity of many medical topics, and the desire to optimize health services and promote Iran as a center for certain medical procedures. A similar dynamism seems to characterize discussions of Iran's banking practices, whose goal of being both Islamic and viable has, however, occasioned charges from Islamic jurists and economists of being neither.

Constitutional, criminal, and family law are often addressed in studies of politics or, especially for the latter two, human rights or female subordination. Constitutional analyses may have a mainly political focus, or instead may come from scholars of Islamic law seeking to establish a pedigree, or lack thereof, for *velayat-e faqih* and other Iranian governmental doctrines in pre-revolutionary Shiʿi *fiqh*; both frequently identify the role of practical necessity or Khomeini's increasing political awareness in forming what were subsequently termed "Islamic" doctrines.

While criminal and family law have both been addressed by human rights organizations and the foreign media, a notable difference between them is that family law has also received painstaking academic attention outside Iran; this is less true for criminal law, whose academic treatment for a non-Iranian audience has mostly consisted of either greatly focussed studies of individual issues (from outside or inside Iran), or very general presentations, often coming from within Iran and avoiding controversial analysis. There are also sub-divisions within these two fields. For example, stoning has received much attention, mostly from the media or human rights organizations, whose texts occasionally contain some deeper analysis. However, other Iranian *hadd* or other Islamically influenced penal laws have received far less detailed analysis, and that mostly from a human rights perspective with less specialized information about relevant *fiqh*. Likewise, intensive academic studies of marriage, divorce, and child custody abound, while inheritance and filiation are examples of less likely subjects of study. Overall, family law is the focus of dedicated studies presenting codified laws, their relationship with Shiʿi law, and their practical application, while criminal law has less frequently received comparable attention.

The general impression, therefore, is that some areas of Islamic law in Iran have been studied in their own right in great detail, while analysis of other areas remains mostly tangential to various non-legal topics and is often partial in its presentation of codified law, *fiqh*, practical application, or any combination thereof. It is consequently desirable for these areas to become the focus of dedicated scholarly studies.

References

Abbasi-Shavazi, McDonald, Peter, and Hosseini-Chavoshi, Meimanat, "Modernization or Cultural Maintenance: The Practice of Consanguineous Marriage in Iran." *Journal of Biosocial Science* 40 (2008a): 911–933.

Abbasi-Shavazi, Inhorn, Marcia C., Razeghi-Nasrabad, Hajiieh Bibi, and Toloo, Ghasem, "The 'Iranian ART Revolution': Infertility, Assisted Reproductive Technology, and Third-Party Donation in the Islamic Republic of Iran." *Journal of Middle East Women's Studies* 4, no. 2 (Spring 2008b): 1–28.

Abbasi-Shavazi, Jalal, Mohammad, McDonald, Peter, and Hossein-Chavoshi, Meimanat, "The Family and Social Change in Post-revolutionary Iran" in Kathryn M. Yount and Hoda Rashad (eds.) *Family in the Middle East: Ideational Change in Egypt, Iran, and Tunisia* (Abingdon: Routledge, 2008c) 217–235.

Abdo, Genevieve, "Re-thinking the Islamic Republic: A 'Conversation' with Ayatollah Hossein 'Ali Montazeri." *The Middle East Journal* 55 (Winter 2000): 9–24.

Abrahamian, Ervand, *Iran Between Two Revolutions* (Princeton: Princeton University Press, 1982).

Abrahamian, Ervand, *Khomeinism: Essays on the Islamic Republic* (London: I.B. Tauris, 1993).

Abrahamian, Ervand, *Tortured Confessions: Prisons and Public Recantations in Modern Iran* (Berkeley: University of California Press, 1999).

Abu-Raddad, Laith J., Ayodeji Akala, Francisca, Semini, Iris, Riedner, Gabriele, Wilson, David, and Tawil, Ousama, *Characterizing the HIV/AIDS Epidemic in the Middle East and North Africa: Time for Strategic Action* (Washington: The World Bank, 2010).

Afkhami, Mahnaz and Friedl, Erika, eds., *In the Eye of the Storm: Women in Post-revolutionary Iran* (Syracuse: I.B. Tauris, 1994).

Afshar, Haleh, "Women and Political Fundamentalism in Iran" in Haleh Afshar (ed.) *Women and Politics in the Third World* (London: Routledge, 1996) 121–141.

Afshari, Reza, "An Essay on Scholarship, Human Rights, and State Legitimacy: The Case of the Islamic Republic of Iran." In *Human Rights Quarterly* 18, no. 3 (August 1996): 544–593.

Aggarwal, Rajesh K. and Yousef, Tarik, "Islamic Banks and Investment Financing." *Journal of Money, Credit and Banking* 32, no. 1 (February 2000): 93–120.

Aghajanian, Akbar, "Some Notes on Divorce in Iran." *Journal of Marriage and Family* 48, no. 4 (November 1986): 749–755.

Akhavi, Shahrough, "Contending Discourses in Shi'i law on the Doctrine of *Wilayat al-Faqih*." *Iranian Studies* 29, no. 3–4 (Summer/Fall 1996): 229–268.

Akrami, S. M., Osati, Z., Zahedi, F., and Raza, M. "Brain Death: Recent Ethical and Religious Considerations in Iran." *Transplantation Proceedings* 36 (2004): 2883–2887.

Akrami, Mohammad and Osati, Zahra, "Is Consanguineous Marriage Religiously Encouraged? Islamic and Iranian Considerations." *Journal of Biosocial Science* 39 (2007): 313–316.

Alborz, "Tamdid-e ejraye Qanun-e Mojazat-e Eslami." December 19, 2010. http://www.alborznews.co/view/8785.aspx Opened 20/8/11. Archived at http://www.webcitation.org/616KkhrLj.

Alfoneh, Ali, "The Revolutionary Guards' Role in Iranian Politics." September 1, 2008. http://www.aei.org/article/foreign-and-defense-policy/regional/middleeast-and-north-africa/the-revolutionary-guards-role-in-iranian-politics/ Archived at http://www.webcitation.org/6EvgSyvGE.

Algar, Hamid, "The Problem of Retaliation in Modern Warfare from the Point of View of Fiqh" in Farhang Rajaee (ed.) *The Iran–Iraq War: The Politics of Aggression* (Gainesville: University Press of Florida, 1993) 191–197.

Aliverdinia, Akbar and Pridemore, William Alex, "A First Glimpse at Narcotics Offenders in an Islamic Republic: A Test of an Integrated Model of Drug Involvement Among a Sample of Men Incarcerated for Drug Offenses in Iran." *International Criminal Justice Review* 17 (2007): 27.

Amanat, Abbas, "In Between the Madrasa and the Marketplace: The Designation of Clerical Leadership in Modern Shi'ism" in Saïd Amir Arjomand (ed.) *Authority and Political Culture in Shi'ism* (Albany: State University of New York Press, 1988) 98–132.

Amanat, Abbas, "From *Ijtihad* to *Wilayat-i faqih*: The Evolution of the Shiite Legal Authority to Political Power" in Abbas Amanat and Frank Griffel (eds.) *Shari'a: Islamic Law in the Contemporary Context* (Stanford: Stanford University Press, 2007) 120–136.

Aminizadeh, Mohammad, "Eblagh-e qanun-e jadid-e mojazat-e Eslami" (Announcement of the new penal code). May 28, 2013. http://aminizadeh.blogfa.com/post/40. Archived at http://www.webcitation.org/6N2onveZI.

Amnesty International, "Iran, The Last Executioner of Children." June 27, 2007. Index number: MDE 13/059/2007. http://www.amnesty.org/en/library/info/MDE13/059/2007 Accessed August 20, 2011. Archived at http://www.webcitation.org/616KkhrQe.

Amnesty International, "Iran: End Executions by Stoning." January 13, 2008. http://www.amnesty.org/en/library/asset/MDE13/001/2008/en/2b087fb2-c2d2-11dc-ac4a-8d7763206e82/mde130012008eng.pdf. Accessed December 13, 2011. Archived at http://www.webcitation.org/63upQkeUa.

Amnesty International, "Death Penalty/Stoning." AI Index: MDE 13/015/2009. February 24, 2009a. http://www.amnesty.org/fr/library/asset/MDE13/015/2009/fr/2a4eac90-d433-493e-be49-27399b73e21d/mde130152009en.pdf. Accessed August 20, 2011. Archived at http://www.webcitation.org/616KkhrQM.

Amnesty International, "Iran: Demand Judiciary Halts Stoning: Sakineh Mohammadi." August 7, 2009b. AI Index number: MDE 13/082/2009.307 http://www.amnesty.org/en/library/asset/MDE13/082/2009/en/7fdb4e30-712a-4fca-b807-1365834fcd17/mde130822009en.html Accessed August 20, 2011. Archived at http://www.webcitation.org/616KkhrQV.

Ansari-Pour, M.A., "Interest in International Transactions Under Shiite Jurisprudence." *Arab Law Quarterly* 9, no. 158 (1994): 158–170.

Ansari-Pour, M.A., "Iran" entries in *Yearbook of Islamic and Middle Eastern Law* (from vol. 1, 1994/5).

Ansari-Pour, M.A., "Prohibition of Interest Under the Iranian Legal System Since the Revolution" in Hilary Lewis Ruttley and Chibli Mallat (eds.) *Commercial law in the Middle East* (London: Kluwer Law International, 1995) 167–191.

Ansari-Pour, M.A., "The Illegality of Taking Interest from Muslim Countries." *Arab Law Quarterly* 11, no. 3 (January–December 1996): 281–284.

Ansari-Pour, M.A., "The Legal Relationship of a Father with his Illegitimate Child under Islamic and Iranian Law." *Yearbook of Islamic and Middle Eastern Law* 6 (1999–2000): 140–155.

Ansari-Pour, M.A., "Remuneration for Work Done by a Wife under Islamic and Iranian Law." *Yearbook of Islamic and Middle Eastern Law* 8 (2001–02): 108–121.

Anwar, Muhammad, "Islamic Banking in Iran and Pakistan: A Comparative Study." *The Pakistan Development Review* 31, no. 4 part II (Winter 1992): 1089–1097.

Ardehali, Paula-Elizabeth, *Arranging Marriages in Iran*. Unpublished Ph.D. thesis, Rutgers University, 1986.

Ariff, Mohamed, "Islamic Banking." *Asian-Pacific Economic Literature* 2, no. 2 (September 1988): 48–64.

Arjomand, Saïd Amir, "The State and Khomeini's Islamic Order." In *Iranian Studies* vol. XIII, no. 1–4 (1980): 147–164.

Arjomand, Saïd Amir, "Introduction: Shiʿism, Authority, and Political Culture" in Saïd Amir Arjomand (ed.) *Authority and Political Culture in Shi'ism* (Albany: State University of New York Press, 1988a) 1–22.

Arjomand, Saïd Amir, "Ideological Revolution in Shi'ism" in Saïd Amir Arjomand (ed.) *Authority and Political Culture in Shi'ism* (Albany: State University of New York Press, 1988b) 178–212.

Arjomand, Saïd Amir, *The Turban for the Crown: The Islamic Revolution in Iran* (New York: Oxford University Press, 1988c).

Arjomand, Saïd Amir, "Shi'ite Jurisprudence and Constitution Making in the Islamic Republic of Iran" in Martin E. Marty and R. Scott Appleby (eds.) *Fundamentalisms and the State* (Chicago: University of Chicago Press, 1993) 88–109.

Arjomand, Saïd Amir, "Authority in Shiism and Constitutional Developments in the Islamic Republic of Iran" in Rainer Brunner and Werner Ende (eds.) *The Twelver Shia in Modern Times: Religious Culture and Political History* (Leiden: Brill, 2000a) 301–332.

Arjomand, Saïd Amir, "Civil Society and the Rule of Law in the Constitutional Politics of Iran under Khatami." *Social Research* 67, no. 2 (Summer 2000b): 283–301.

Arjomand, Saïd Amir, "Shariʿa and Constitution in Iran: A Historical Perspective" in Abbas Amanat and Frank Griffel (eds.) *Shariʿa: Islamic Law in the Contemporary Context* (Stanford: Stanford University Press, 2007) 156–164.

Arminjon, Constance, "L'instauration de la 'guidance du juriste' en Iran: Les paradoxes de la modernité chiite." *Archives de sciences sociales des religions* 149 (January–March 2010): 211–228.

Ashraf, Ahmad and Banuazizi, Ali, "Iran's Tortuous Path Towards 'Islamic Liberalism.'" *International Journal of Politics, Culture and Society* 15, no. 2 (Winter 2001): 237–256.

Asia News Monitor, "Iran: Stoning in the Islamic law of Iran." 5 February 2009.

Asli, Mehrdad Rayejian, "Iranian Criminal Justice System in Light of International Standards Relating to Victims." *European Journal of Crime, Criminal Law and Criminal Justice* 14, no. 2 (2006): 185–207.

Atai, Ardeshir, "Comparative Analysis of the Iranian Foreign Investment Law and the World Bank Guidelines on Treatment of Foreign Direct Investment." *Yearbook of Islamic and Middle Eastern Law* 12 (2005–06 [2008]): 111–128.

Attari, A., Dashty, S., and Mahmoodi, M., "Post-traumatic Stress Disorder in Children Witnessing a Public Hanging in the Islamic Republic of Iran." *Eastern Mediterranean Health Journal* 12, no. 1/2 (2006): 72–80.

Bader, Mohammed Khaled I., Mohamad, Shamsher, Ariff, Mohamed, and Hassan, Taufiq, "Cost, Revenue, and Profit Efficiency of Islamic versus Conventional Banks: International Evidence Using Data Envelopment Analysis." *Islamic Economic Studies* 15, no. 2 (January 2008): 23–76.

Bahar, Sarvenaz, "Khomeinism, the Islamic Republic of Iran, and International Law: The Relevance of Islamic Political Ideology." *Harvard International Law Journal* 33 (1992): 145–190.

Bahramitash, Roksana and Kazemipour, Shahla, "Myths and Realities of the Impact of Islam on Women: Changing Marital Status in Iran." *Critique: Critical Middle Eastern Studies* 15, no. 2 (Summer 2006): 111–128.

Bakhash, Shaul, "The Politics of Land, Law, and Social Justice in Iran." *The Middle East Journal* 43, no. 2 (Spring 1989): 186–201.

Bakhash, Shaul, *The Reign of the Ayatollahs: Iran and the Islamic Revolution* (New York: Basic Books, 1984).

Banakar, Reza and Fard, Shahrad Nasrolahi, "Driving Dangerously: Law, Culture and Driving Habits in Iran." *British Journal of Middle Eastern Studies* 39, no. 2 (August 2012): 241–257.

Behdad, Sohrab, "A Disputed Utopia: Islamic Economics in Revolutionary Iran." *Comparative Studies in Society and History* 36 (October 1994): 775–813.

Behdad, Sohrab, "Islamization of Economics in Iranian Universities." *International Journal of Middle East Studies* 27 (1995): 193–217.

Behnia, Behnam, *Political Repression, Socialization, and Frame of Interpretation: A Comparative Study of the Establishment of a Constitutional Regime (1906) and an Islamic Regime (1979) in Iran*. Unpublished Ph.D. thesis, Carleton University (Ottawa), 1997.

Behrooz, Maziar, "The Islamic State and the Crisis of Marja'iyat in Iran." *Comparative Studies of South Asia, Africa and the Middle East* XVI, no. 2 (1996): 93–100.

Bernardi, Albert, "Iran: Family Law After the Islamic Revolution." *Journal of Family Law* 25 (1986–87): 151–154.

Berween, Mohamed, "Non-Muslims in the Islamic State: Major Rule and Minority Rights" in Mashood A. Baderin (ed.) *International Law and Islamic Law* (Aldershot: Ashgate, 2008) 599–610.

Betteridge, Anne H., "To Veil or Not to Veil: A Matter of Protest or Policy" in Guity Nashat (ed.) *Women and Revolution in Iran* (Boulder: Westview Press, 1983) 107–128.

BIA (Islamic Republic of Iran, Bureau of International Affairs of the Judiciary), *An Introduction to the Legal System of the Islamic Republic of Iran*. Tehran: Nashr-e Tose'eye Iran, 1386 AP (2007).

Bielefeldt, Heiner, "Muslim Voices in the Human Rights Debate" in Shahram Akbarzadeh (ed.) *Islam and Globalization: Critical Concepts in Islamic Studies* (vol. 4) (London: Routledge, 2006) 226–254.

Boroujerdi, Mehrzad, "The Paradoxes of Politics in Postrevolutionary Iran" in John L. Esposito and R. K. Ramazani (eds.) *Iran at the Crossroads* (New York: Palgrave, 2001) 13–27.

Brajer, Victor and Rahmatian, Morteza, "From Diye to Value of Statistical Life: A Case Study for the Islamic Republic of Iran." Paper presented at the Economic Valuation of Caspian Environment (Caspian EVE) Training Program, November 13–18, 2005,

Ashgabat, Turkmenistan. http://www.caspianenvironment.org/newsite/DocCenter/Traning/Caspian%20EVE/Supporting%20Papers/Session%2010%20B%20Paper%20%28English%29.pdf. Accessed August 20, 2011. Archived at http://www.webcitation.org/61EFxZkrk.

Brown, Nathan J., "Bargaining and Imposing Constitutions: Private and Public Interests in the Iranian, Afghani and Iraqi Constitutional Experiments" in Saïd Amir Arjomand (ed.) *Constitutional Politics in the Middle East, With Special Reference to Turkey, Iraq, Iran and Afghanistan* (Oxford: Hart Publishing, 2008) 63–76.

Bsoul, Labeeb Ahmed, *International Treaties (Mu'ahadat) in Islam: Theory and Practice in the Light of Siyar (Islamic International Law)*. Unpublished Ph.D. thesis, McGill University, 2003.

Buchta, Wilfried, "Tehran's Ecumenical Society (*Majma' al-Taqrib*): A Veritable Ecumenical Revival or a Trojan Horse of Iran?" in Rainer Brunner and Werner Ende (eds.) *The Twelver Shia in Modern Times: Religious Culture and Political History* (Leiden: Brill, 2000) 333–353.

Bultan News, "Mojazat-e sangsar as qanun-e jadid-e Eslami hazf shod." February 16, 2013. Archived at http://www.webcitation.org/6EgifepEA.

Calder, Norman, "Accommodation and Revolution in Imami Shi'i Jurisprudence: Khumayni and the Classical Tradition." *Middle Eastern Studies* 18, no 1 (1982): 3–20.

Chehabi, H.E., "Islam and Constitutionalism in the Persianate World." *Journal of Persianate Studies* 5 (2012): 93–94.

Chehabi, H.E. and Asghar Schirazi, "The Islamic Republic of Iran." *Journal of Persianate Studies* 5 (2012): 175–204.

Cherif Bassiouni, Mahmoud, "Protection of Diplomats Under Islamic Law" in Mashood A. Baderin (ed.) *International Law and Islamic Law* (Aldershot: Ashgate, 2008) 243–267.

Chong, Beng Soon and Ming-Hua Liu, "Islamic Banking: Interest-Free or Interest- Based?" *Pacific-Basin Finance Journal* 17 (2009): 125–144.

Cohen, Jennifer F., "Islamic Law in Iran: Can It Protect the International Legal Right of Freedom of Religion and Belief?" *Chicago Journal of International Law* 9, no. 1 (Summer 2008): 247–274.

Cole, Juan R., "Imami Jurisprudence and the Role of the Ulama: Mortaza Ansari on Emulating the Supreme Exemplar" in Keddie, Nikki (ed.) *Religion and Politics in Iran: Shi'ism from Quietism to Revolution* (New Haven: Yale University Press, 1983) 33–46.

Cole, Juan R. I., "Shaykh Ahmad al-Ahsa'i on the Sources of Religious Authority" in Linda S. Walbridge (ed.) *The Most Learned of the Shi'a: The Institution of the Marja' Taqlid* (New York: Oxford University Press, 2001) 82–93.

CSM (Christian Science Monitor), "Iran Move to Defrock Dissident Ayatollah Opens Rifts in Theocracy." January 6, 2010. http://www.csmonitor.com/World/Middle-East/2010/0106/Iran-move-todefrock-dissident-ayatollah-opens-rifts-in-theocracy (Part 1, archived at http://www.webcitation.org/6Evi4qgwk); http://www.csmonitor.com/World/Middle-East/2010/0106/Iran-move-todefrock-dissident-ayatollah-opens-rifts-in-theocracy/%28page%29/2 (Part 2, archived at http://www.webcitation.org/6EviBpMmS).

Dabashi, Hamid, *Theology of Discontent* (New York: New York University Press, 1993).

Dahlén, Ashk, *Islamic Law, Epistemology and Modernity: Legal Philosophy in Contemporary Iran* (New York: Routledge, 2003).

de Belder, Richard T. and Hassan, Mansoor, "The Changing Face of Islamic Banking." *International Financial Law Review* 12, no. 11 (1993): 23–26.

Diamond, Larry, Plattner, Marc F., and Brumberg, Daniel, eds. *Islam and Democracy in the Middle East* (Baltimore: Johns Hopkins University Press, 2003).

Dinmore, Guy, "Reform Tide Helps Wash Rule of Law into Iran." *Financial Times*, May 31, 2001: 12.

Durham University, Centre for Iranian Studies, "Understanding Iran's Assembly of Experts." November 2006. http://www.dur.ac.uk/resources/iranian.studies/Policy%20Brief%201.pdf Archived at http://www.webcitation.org/6EviXkH4c.

Dusuki, Asyraf Wajdi and Abozaid, Abdulazeem, "A Critical Appraisal on the Challenges of Realizing Maqasid al-shari'ah in Islamic Banking and Finance." *IIUM Journal of Economics and Management* 15, no. 2 (2007): 143–165.

Ebrahimi, S.N., "Child Custody (*Hizanat*) under Iranian Law: An Analytical Discussion." *Family Law Quarterly* 39, no. 2 (Summer 2005): 459–476.

The Economist, "Iran: Constitution and Institutions." February 21, 2003.

Eghtedari, Goudarz, "Islamic Republic of Iran and Execution for Adultery and Homosexuality." Paper presented at the Center for Iranian Research Analysis (CIRA) Conference, Atlanta, 1997. http://web.archive.org/web/20010615192731/www.ihrwg.org/CP/cirapaper.pdf Accessed August 20, 2011. Archived at http://www.webcitation.org/61DQoLBQA.

Einollahi, Behzad, "Iranian Experience with Non-related Renal Transplantation." *Saudi Journal of Kidney Diseases and Transplantation* 15, no. 4 (2004): 421–428.

Elahi, Maryam, "The Rights of the Child Under Islamic Law: Prohibition of the Child Soldier." *Columbia Human Rights Law Review* 19 (1987–88): 259–280.

Enayat, Hamid, "Iran: Khumayni's Concept of the 'Guardianship of the Jurisconsult'" in James P. Piscatori (ed.) *Islam in the Political Process* (Cambridge: Cambridge University Press, 1983) 160–180.

Entessar, Nader, "Criminal Law and the Legal System in Revolutionary Iran." *Boston College Third World Law Journal* 8 (1988): 91–102.

Entessar, Nader, "Limits of Change: Legal Constraints to Political Reform in Iran." *Journal of Third World Studies XIX*, no. 1 (2002): 25–36.

Esfandiari, Golnaz, "Exiled Iran Religious Scholar Calls for Debate on Nuclear Safety." *Radio Free Europe*, March 31, 2011. http://www.rferl.org/content/interview_exiled_iran_religious_scholar_debate_nuc lear_safety/3542999.html Archived at http://www.webcitation.org/6EviwkEga.

Esfandiari, Haleh, "The Majles and Women's Issues in the Islamic Republic of Iran" in Mahnaz Afkhami and Erika Friedl (eds.) *In the Eye of the Storm: Women in Post-revolutionary Iran* (Syracuse: I.B. Tauris, 1994) 61–79.

Esfandiari, Haleh, "The Politics of the 'Women's Question' in the Islamic Republic, 1979–1999" in John L. Esposito and R. K. Ramazani (eds.) *Iran at the Crossroads* (New York: Palgrave, 2001) 75–92.

Eslami Somea, Reza, *Human Rights in Shari'a and Iran's Constitutional and Legal System: The Case of Freedom of Expression*. Unpublished LLD thesis, Montréal University, 2001.

Fajri, Nurul, *The Role of Religious Symbols in the Iranian Revolution of 1979*. Unpublished MA thesis, McGill University, 1992.

Farajiha, Mohammad, "Community Involvement in Administration of Criminal Justice in Iran." *International Journal of Humanities* 13, no. 1 (2006): 93–106.

Fararu News, "Qanun-e jadid-e Mojazat-e Eslami bargasht khurd." August 31, 2012. Accessed 16 January 2013. Archived at http://www.webcitation.org/6DYkRuAvJ.

Fatemi, Mohammad Ghari S., "Autonomy and Equal Right to Divorce with Specific Reference to Shi'i *fiqh* and the Iranian Legal System." *Islam and Christian-Muslim Relations* 17, no. 3 (2006): 281–294.

Fathi, Nazila, "Ayatollah, Reviewing Islamic Law, Tugs at Ties Constricting Iran's Women." *New York Times*, July 29, 2001.

Fazaeli, Roja, "Contemporary Iranian Feminism: Identity, Rights and Interpretations." *Muslim World Journal of Human Rights* 4, no. 1 (2007): article 8.

FIDH (International Federation for Human Rights), "Death Penalty—A State Terror Policy." April 28, 2009. http://www.fidh.org/IMG/pdf/Rapport_Iran_final.pdf Accessed February 9, 2014.

FIDH, "The Hidden Side of Iran: Discrimination Against Ethnic and Religious Minorities." October 21, 2010. http://www.fidh.org/IMG/pdf/IrandiscrimLDDHI545a.pdf Accessed February 9, 2014.

FIDH, "Death Penalty—A State Terror Policy: Special Update for 11th World Day against the Death Penalty." October 11, 2013. http://www.fidh.org/en/asia/iran/death-penalty-in-iran-a-state-terror-policy-14075 Accessed February 9, 2014.

Fierro, Maribel, "*Idra'ū al-ḥudūd bi-l-shubuhāt*: When Lawful Violence Meets Doubt." *Hawwa* 5, no. 2–3 (2007): 208–238.

Foody, Kathleen, *Contesting the Jurists' Authority: Muslim Critique and CounterTraditions in the Islamic Republic of Iran*. Unpublished MA thesis, UNC Chapel Hill, 2009.

Fraser Fujinaga, Antonia, *Life and Limb: Irreversible Hadd Penalties in Iranian Criminal Courts and Opportunities to Avoid Them*. Unpublished Ph.D. thesis, Edinburgh University, 2013.

Freedom House, "Freedom in the world 2012: Iran." http://www.freedomhouse.org/report/freedom-world/2012/iran Archived at http://www.webcitation.org/6Evja2QSI.

Fukuyama, Francis, "Iran, Islam and the Rule of Law." *Wall Street Journal*, July 28, 2009.

Ghasimi, M.R., "The Iranian Economy After the Revolution: An Economic Appraisal of the Five-year Plan." *International Journal of Middle East Studies* 24 (1992): 599–614.

Ghassemi, Ghassem, "Criminal Punishment in Islamic Societies: Empirical Study of Attitudes to Criminal Sentencing in Iran." *European Journal of Criminal Policy and Research* 15 (2009): 159–180.

Gheissari, Ali and Nasr, Vali, "Iran's Democracy Debate." *Middle East Policy* 11, no. 2 (Summer 2004): 94–106.

Gheytanchi, Elham, "Civil Society in Iran: Politics of Motherhood and the Public Sphere." *International Sociology* 16, no. 4 (2001): 557–576.

Ghodsi, Ebrahim, "Legitimate Defence in the Criminal Law of Iran and Islam." *Journal of Criminal Law* 67 (2003): 349–358.

Ghodsi, Ebrahim. "Murder in the Criminal Law of Iran and Islam." *Journal of Criminal Law* 68 (2004): 160–169.

Gholami, Hussein, "Restorative Traditions in Violent Conflicts in Iran" in Hans-Jörg Albrecht, Jan-Michael Simon, Hassan Rezaei, Holger-C. Rohne, and Ernesto Kiza (eds.) *Conflicts and Conflict Resolution in Middle Eastern Societies—Between Tradition and Modernity* (Berlin: Duncker & Humblot, 2006) 457–470.

Gleave, Robert, "Akhbari Shi'i *usul al-fiqh* and the Juristic Theory of Yusuf b. Ahmad al-Bahrani" in Robert Gleave and Eugenia Kermeli (eds.) *Islamic Law: Theory and Practice* (London: I.B. Tauris, 1997) 24–45.

Golduzian, Iraj, *Huquq-e Jaza'i-e Ekhtesasi*. Tehran: Entesharat-e Daneshgah-e Tehran, 1382 AP (2003/4).

Gontowska, Maria, "Human Rights Violations under the Sharia'a [*sic*]: A Comparative Study of the Kingdom of Saudi Arabia and the Islamic Republic of Iran." Unpublished honors dissertation, Pace University, 2005. http://digitalcommons.pace.edu/cgi/viewcontent.cgi?article=1010&context=honor scollege_theses&seiredir=1#search=%22gontowska%20 human%20rights%20viol ations%22. Accessed August 21, 2011. Archived at http://www.webcitation.org/61EGPFBlp.

Guru, Balachandher Krishnan, Shanmugam, Bala, Alam, Nafis, and Perera, Corrine J., "An Evaluation of Internet Banking Sites in Islamic Countries." *Journal of Internet Banking and Commerce* 8, no. 2 (November 2003): 1–11.

Habibi, Nader, "An Economic Analysis of the Prenuptial Agreement (*Mahrieh*) in Contemporary Iran." *Economic Development and Cultural Change* 45, no. 2 (1997): 281–293.

Habibzadeh, Jafar, "The Legality Principle of Crimes and Punishments in the Iranian Legal System." *Global Jurist Topics* 5, no. 1 (2005): article 1.

Haddad, Gholamreza Keshavarz and Moghadam, Hamed Markazi, "The Socioeconomic and Demographic Determinants of Crime in Iran (a Regional Panel Study)." *European Journal of Law and Economics* 32 (2011): 99–114.

Haeri, Shahla, "Divorce in Contemporary Iran: A Male Prerogative in Self-will" in Chibli Mallat and Jane Connors (eds.) *Islamic Family Law* (London: Graham and Trotman, 1990) 55–69.

Haeri, Shahla, *Law of Desire: Temporary Marriage in Shi'i Iran* (Syracuse, NY: Syracuse University Press, 1989).

Haeri, Shahla, "Temporary Marriage: An Islamic Discourse on Female Sexuality in Iran" in Mahnaz Afkhami and Erika Friedl (eds.) *In the Eye of the Storm: Women in Post-revolutionary Iran* (Syracuse: I.B. Tauris, 1994) 98–114.

Hairi, Abdul-Hadi, *Shi'ism and Constitutionalism in Iran* (Leiden: E.J. Brill, 1977).

Hajatpour, Reza, "Reflections and Legal Analysis of the Relationship between 'Religious Government and Human Rights' from the Perspective of Grand Ayatullāh Muntaẓirī." *Die Welt des Islams* 51 (2011): 382–408.

Halm, Heinz, *Shiism* (Edinburgh: Edinburgh University Press, 1991).

Halper, Louise, "Disputed Societies, Transformative States: Politics of Law and Gender in Republican Turkey and Iran." *Hawwa* 5, no. 1 (2007): 90–110.

Hamidian, Hassan, "Jurisdiction of Family Courts in Iran" in Jürgen Badow and Nadjma Yassari (eds.) *Iranian Family and Succession Laws and their Application to German Courts* (Tübingen: Mohr Siebeck, 2004) 81–95.

Haron, Sudin, "A Comparative Study of Islamic Banking Practices." *J.KAU: Islamic Economics* 10 (1998): 23–50.

Helfgott, Leonard M., "The Structural Foundations of the National Minority Problem in Revolutionary Iran." *Iranian Studies* 13, no. 1/4, *Iranian Revolution in Perspective* (1980): 195–214.

Hemmasi, Mohammad and Prorok, Carolyn V., "Demographic Changes in Iran's Recognized Religious Minority Population After the Islamic Revolution." *African and Asian Studies* 1, no. 2 (2002): 63–86.

Hessini, Leila, "Abortion and Islam: Policies and Practice in the Middle East and North Africa." *Reproductive Health Matters* 15, no. 29 (2007): 75–84.

Higgins, Patricia J., "Minority-State Relations in Contemporary Iran." *Iranian Studies* 17, no. 1 (Winter 1984): 37–71.

Higgins, Patricia J., "Women in the Islamic Republic of Iran: Legal, Social, and Ideological Changes." *Signs* 10, no. 3 (Spring 1985): 477–494.

Hoodfar, Homa, "Family Law and Family Planning Policy in Pre- and Post-revolutionary Iran" in Kathryn M. Yount and Hoda Rashad (eds.) *Family in the Middle East: Ideational Change in Egypt, Iran, and Tunisia* (Abingdon: Routledge, 2008) 80–110.

Hoodfar, Homa, "Women and Personal Status Law in Iran: An Interview with Mehranguiz Kar." *Middle East Report* 26, no. 198 (1996): 36–38.

Hoodfar, Homa, "Iranian Women at the Intersection of Citizenship and the Family Code: The Perils of 'Islamic Criteria'" in Suad Joseph (ed.) *Gender and Citizenship in the Middle East* (Syracuse, NY: Syracuse University Press, 2000) 287–313.

Hoodfar, Homa and Assadpour, Samad, "The Politics of Population Policy in the Islamic Republic of Iran." *Studies in Family Planning* 31, no. 1 (2000): 19–34.

Hooglund, Eric, "The Fear Can Drive You Crazy: A Prisoner's Testimony." *Middle East Report* no. 156 (January–February 1989): 25–28.

Human Rights Watch, "Iran: Lift Restrictions on Sunni Worship." November 9, 2013. http://www.hrw.org/news/2013/11/09/iran-lift-restrictions-sunni-worship Archived here: http://www.webcitation.org/6N1hnTwvH.

ICANA (Islamic Consultative Assembly News Agency), "Neshast-e barresi-e 'Akherin tahavvolat-e Qanun-e Mojazat-e Eslami' bar gozar mishavad." March 5, 2013. http://vista.ir/news/7416237 Archived at http://www.webcitation.org/6Eu60Rdzn.

ICARC (Islamic Consultative Assembly Research Centre), "Qanun-e Mojazat-e Eslami baraye ejra\' eblagh shod—va matn-e kamel." May 29, 2013. http://rc.majlis.ir/fa/news/show/845002 Archived at http://www.webcitation.org/6N21x5XAr (contains full text of 2013 penal code).

ICAS (International Committee Against Stoning), "Islamic Judiciary Apparatus Prepares to Stone a Man and a Woman in Orumiya." December 23, 2010. http://stopstonningnow.com/wpress/4311. Accessed August 20, 2011. Archived at http://www.webcitation.org/61DQoLBSh.

ICAS (International Committee Against Stoning), "The Islamic Regime of Iran is to Execute Two Young Men for Homosexuality by Stoning." January 16, 2011. http://stopstonningnow.com/wpress/4323. Accessed August 20, 2011. Archived at http://www.webcitation.org/61DQoLBSz.

IHRDC (Iran Human Rights Documentation Centre), "Islamic Penal Code of the Islamic Republic of Iran: Book One & Book Two." April 4, 2013a. http://www.iranhrdc.org/english/human-rights-documents/iranian-codes/3200-islamic-penal-code-of-the-islamic-republic-of-iran-book-one-and-book-two.html#. UvdIjfuDItM Accessed February 9, 2014.

IHRDC (Iran Human Rights Documentation Centre), "Islamic Penal Code of the Islamic Republic of Iran: Book Five." July 18, 2013b. http://www.iranhrdc.org/english/human-rights-documents/iranian-codes/1000000351-islamic-penal-code-of-the-islamic-republic-of-iran-book-five.html#. UvdH-PuDItM Accessed February 9, 2014.

Imam, Patrick and Kpodar, Kangni, "Islamic Banking: How Has it Spread?" International Monetary Fund, March 2010.

Iqbal, Munawar and Llewellyn, David T., eds. *Islamic Banking and Finance: New Perspectives on Profit-sharing and Risk* (Cheltenham and Northampton (MA): Edward Elgar Publishing, 2002).

Iqbal, Munawar and Molyneux, Philip, *Thirty Years of Islamic Banking: History, Performance and Prospects* (London: Palgrave Macmillan, March 2005).

Iqbal, Zamir, "Islamic Financial Systems." *Finance and Development*, June 1997: 42–45.

Iran-e Azad, "Stoning to Death in Iran: A Crime Against Humanity Carried Out by the Mullahs' Regime." http://www.iran-e-azad.org/stoning/women.html Accessed August 20, 2011. Archived at http://www.webcitation.org/61DQoLBUg.

IRBC (Immigration and Refugee Board of Canada), "Iran: Treatment of Ismailis by the Iranian Authorities." November 29, 2000. http://www.refworld.org/docid/3df4be448.html Accessed March 7, 2014.

Irfani, Suroosh, *Revolutionary Islam in Iran: Popular Liberation or Religious Dictatorship?* (London: Zed Books, 1983).

IRNA (Islamic Republic News Agency), "Asas va payeye estevar-e din bar mehvar-e velayat-e faqih ast." November 12, 2011. Archived at http://www.webcitation.org/6ELGozsbB.

ISNA (Iranian Students' News Agency), "Ra'is-e koll-e dadgostari-e Khuzestan: Qanun- e jadid-e Mojazat-e Eslami mored-e niaz-e kollieye maraje'-ye qaza'i ast." February 14, 2013. Archived at http://www.webcitation.org/6EgifepEA.

Iwasaki, Yoko, "*Sar-qofli* in the Customs and Laws of Modern Iran: The Emergence of *Haqq-e Kasb o Pishe o Tejarat* and the Evolution of the Shop-lease Contract System." *Iranian Studies* 44, no. 2 (March 2011): 147–174.

Jalali-Karveh, Mahmoud, "Theory and Practice of Arbitration as a Peaceful Means of Dispute Settlement in the Iranian Legal System" in Hans-Jörg Albrecht, Jan-Michael Simon, Hassan Rezaei, Holger-C. Rohne, and Ernesto Kiza (eds.) *Conflicts and Conflict Resolution in Middle Eastern Societies—Between Tradition and Modernity* (Berlin: Duncker & Humblot, 2006) 429–446.

Kamali, Masoud, *Revolutionary Iran: Civil Society and State in the Modernization Process* (Aldershot: Ashgate, 1998).

Kamalipour, Yahya R., ed. *Media, Power, and Politics in the Digital Age: The 2009 Presidential Election Uprising in Iran* (Plymouth: Rowman and Littlefield, 2010).

Kamrava, Mehran, *Iran's Intellectual Revolution* (Cambridge: Cambridge University Press, 2008).

Kar, Mehrangiz, "Iranian Law and Women's Rights." *Muslim World Journal of Human Rights* 4, no. 1 (2007): article 9.

Kar, Mehranguiz and Hoodfar, Homa, "La loi sur le statut personnel telle que définie par la République Islamique d'Iran: une évaluation" in Mehranguiz Kar and Homa Hoodfar (eds.) *Les frontières mouvantes du mariage et du divorce dans les communautés musulmanes* (Grabels: Women Living Under Muslim Laws, 1996) 11–36.

Karadsheh, Rose Marie, "Creating an International Criminal Court: Confronting the Conflicting Criminal Procedures of Iran and the United States." *Dickinson Journal of International Law* 14, no. 243 (Winter 1996): 243–289.

Karbassian, Akbar, "Islamic Revolution and the Management of the Iranian Economy." *Social Research* 67, no. 2, *Iran: Since the Revolution* (Summer 2000): 621–640.

Keddie, Nikki R., *Modern Iran: Roots and Results of Revolution* (London: Yale University Press, 2003).

Keddie, Nikki R. and Monian, Farah, "Militancy and Religion in Contemporary Iran" in Martin E. Marty and R. Scott Appleby (eds.) *Fundamentalisms and the State* (Chicago: The University of Chicago Press, 1993) 511–538.

Kelidar, Abbas, "Ayatollah Khomeini's Concept of Islamic Government" in Alexander S. Cudsi and Ali E. Hillal Dessouki (eds.) *Islam and Power* (London: Croom Helm, 1981) 72–92.

Keshavarz, Sharbanoo Baharak, "Honor Killing in Iran, a Legal Point of View." *Yearbook of Islamic and Middle Eastern Law* 13 (2006–07 [2009]): 87–96.

Khan, Mohsin S., "Islamic Interest-Free Banking: A Theoretical Analysis." *Staff Papers—International Monetary Fund* 33, no. 1 (March 1986): 1–27.

Khan, Mohsin S. and Mirakhor, Abbas, eds. *Theoretical Studies in Islamic Banking and Finance* (Houston: Institute for Research and Islamic Studies, 1987).

Khan, Mohsin S. and Mirakhor Abbas, "Islamic Banking: Experiences in the Islamic Republic of Iran and in Pakistan." *Economic Development and Cultural Change* 38, no. 2 (January 1990): 353–375.

Khatami, Mohammad, *Islam, Liberty and Development* (Binghamton: Institute of Cultural Studies, 1998).

Khomeini, Ruhollah, "Due Decreti" (Two Decrees). Translated by Silvia Curzu. *Oriente Moderno* 62, New Series no. 1 (1982): 183–188.

Khomeini, Ruhollah Mousavi, *Tahrir al-Vasileh* (volume 4). Persian translation by Hojjatoleslam Mousavi Hamedani (Qom: Dar al-'Ulum, 1386 AP (2007/8)).

KHRP (Kurdish Human Rights Project), "Human Rights and the Kurds in Iran." KHRP briefing paper, 26 August 2009. Available at http://www.khrp.org/khrp-news/human-rights-documents/cat_view/40-briefing-papers-and-speeches.html (accessed February 8, 2014).

Kian, Azadeh, "Women and Politics in Post-Islamist Iran: the Gender Conscious Drive to Change." *British Journal of Middle Eastern Studies* 24, no. 1 (1997): 75–96.

Kordvani, Amir, "A Legal Analysis of the Islamic Bonds (*Sukuk*) in Iran." *International Journal of Islamic and Middle Eastern Finance and Management* 2, no. 4 (2009): 323–337.

Künkler, Mirjam, "The Special Court of the Clergy (dadgah-e vizheh-ye ruhaniyat) and the Repression of Dissident Clergy in Iran." May 13, 2009. Available at http://papers.ssrn.com/sol3/papers.cfm?abstract-id=1505542.

Kuran, Timur, "Islamic Economics and the Islamic Subeconomy." *The Journal of Economic Perspectives* 9, no. 4 (Autumn 1995): 155–173.

Kuran, Timur, "The Genesis of Islamic Economics: A Chapter in the Politics of Muslim Identity." *Social Research* 64, no. 2 (Summer 1997): 301–338.

Kurzman, Charles, "Critics Within: Islamic Scholars' Protests Against the Islamic State in Iran." *International Journal of Politics, Culture and Society* 15, no. 2 (Winter 2001): 341–359.

Kusha, Hamid R., *The Sacred Law of Islam: A Case Study of Women's Treatment in the Islamic Republic of Iran's Criminal Justice System* (Aldershot: Ashgate, 2002).

Lamloum, Olfa, "Femmes, Islamisme et féminisme in Iran" (interview with Fariba Adelkhah). *Confluences Méditerranée* 59 (2006/4): 163–171.

Larijani, B., Zahedi, F., and Taheri, E., "Ethical and Legal Aspects of Organ Transplantation in Iran." *Transplantation Proceedings* 36 (2004): 1241–1244.

Larijani, B., Zahedi, F., and Malek-Afzali, H., "Medical Ethics in the Islamic Republic of Iran." *Eastern Mediterranean Health Journal* 11, nos. 5/6 (2005): 1061–1072.

Mahmoudi, Firouz, "Alternative Sanctions in Iranian Penal Law" in Hans-Jörg Albrecht, Jan-Michael Simon, Hassan Rezaei, Holger-C. Rohne, and Ernesto Kiza (eds.) *Conflicts and Conflict Resolution in Middle Eastern Societies—Between Tradition and Modernity* (Berlin: Duncker & Humblot, 2006a) 447–455.

Mahmoudi, Firouz, "The Informal Justice System in Iranian Law" in Hans-Jörg Albrecht, Jan-Michael Simon, Hassan Rezaei, Holger-C. Rohne, and Ernesto Kiza (eds.) *Conflicts and Conflict Resolution in Middle Eastern Societies—Between Tradition and Modernity* (Berlin: Duncker & Humblot, 2006b) 411–428.

Majdi, M.R., Khani, H., Azadmarzabadi, E., Montazeri, A., Hallajian, E., Babamahmodi, F. and Kariminasab, M.H., "Knowledge, Attitudes and Practices Towards HIV/AIDS Among Iranian Prisoners in Mazandaran Province in the South-coast Area of the Caspian Sea." *Eastern Mediterranean Health Journal* 17, no. 12 (2011): 904–910.

Makiyan, Nezameddin, "The Role of Rate of Return on Loans in the Islamic Banking System of Iran." *International Journal of Islamic Financial Services* 3, no. 3 (2001).

Malekahmadi, Farshad, *The Sociological Intersection of Religion, Law, Politics in Iran: Judicial Review and Political Control in the Islamic Republic.* Unpublished Ph.D. thesis, SUNY Stonybrook, 1999.

Maleki, Abbas, "Oil Economies and Social Welfare: Iran." CeSPI / Institute of Caspian Studies, March 2009. http://www.caspianstudies.com/article/maleki/Iran%20Oil%20Economies%20and%20Social%20Welfare%20CeSPI.pdf. Accessed November 16, 2011. Archived at http://www.webcitation.org/63Fq3BpIA.

Martin, Vanessa, "Religion and State in Khumaini's *Kashf al-Asrar*." *Bulletin of the SOAS*, 56i (1993).

Martin, Vanessa, "A Comparison Between Khumaini's Government of the Jurist and the Commentary on Plato's Republic of Ibn Rushd." *Journal of Islamic Studies* 7, no. 1 (1996): 16–31.

Martin, Vanessa, *Creating an Islamic State: Khomeini and the Making of a New Iran* (London: I.B. Tauris, 2000).

Matin-Asgari, Afshin, "'Abdolkarim Sorush and the Secularization of Islamic Thought in Iran." *Iranian Studies* 30, no. 1V2 (Winter/Spring 1997): 95–115.

Matin-Asgari, Afshin, "Twentieth Century Iran's Political Prisoners." *Middle Eastern Studies* 42, no. 5 (2006): 689–707.

Matsunaga, Yasuyuki, "Mohsen Kadivar, an Advocate of Postrevivalist Islam in Iran." *British Journal of Middle Eastern Studies* 34, no. 3 (December 2007): 317–329.

Matsunaga, Yasuyuki, "Human Rights and New Jurisprudence in Mohsen Kadivar's Advocacy of 'New-Thinker' Islam." *Die Welt des Islams* 51 (2011): 358–381.

Mavani, Hamid, "Analysis of Khomeini's Proofs for *al-Wilaya al-Mutalqa* (Comprehensive Authority) of the Jurist" in Linda S. Walbridge (ed.) *The Most Learned of the Shi'a: The Institution of the Marja' Taqlid* (New York: Oxford University Press, 2001) 183–201.

Mayer, Ann Elizabeth, "Law and Religion in the Muslim Middle East." *The American Journal of Comparative Law* 35, no. 1 (Winter 1987): 127–184.

Mayer, Ann Elizabeth, "The Fundamentalist Impact on Law, Politics, and Constitutions in Iran, Pakistan, and the Sudan" in Martin E. Marty and R. Scott Appleby (eds.) *Fundamentalisms and the State* (Chicago: University of Chicago Press, 1993) 110–151.

Mayer, Ann Elizabeth, "Islamic Rights or Human Rights: An Iranian Dilemma." *Iranian Studies* 29, no. 3–4 (Summer/Fall 1996): 269–296.

Mayer, Ann Elizabeth, "The Universality of Human Rights: Lessons from the Islamic Republic" in Shahram Akbarzadeh (ed.) *Islam and Globalization: Critical Concepts in Islamic Studies* (vol. 4) (London: Routledge, 2006) 307–320.

Mayer, Ann Elizabeth, "The Islam and Human Rights Nexus: Shifting Dimensions." *Muslim World Journal of Human Rights* 4, no. 1 (2007): article 4.

Mayer, Ann Elizabeth, "The Respective Roles of Human Rights and Islam: An Unresolved Conundrum for Middle Eastern Constitutions" in Saïd Amir Arjomand (ed.) *Constitutional Politics in the Middle East with Special Reference to Turkey, Iraq, Iran and Afghanistan* (Oxford: Hart, 2008) 77–97.

Mazarei, Adnan, "The Iranian Economy under the Islamic Republic: Institutional Change and Macroeconomic Performance (1979–1990)." *Cambridge Journal of Economics* 20 (1996): 289–314.

McDaniel, Tim, *Autocracy, Modernization and Revolution in Russia and Iran* (Princeton: Princeton University Press, 1991).

Mehr News, "Ejraye qanun-e jadid-e mojazat-e Eslami dar mahakem-e qaza'i: tafavothaye qanun-e jadid." June 19, 2013. http://www.mehrnews.com/detail/News/2079662 Archived at http://www.webcitation.org/6N21Tozde.

Mehrpour, Hossein, "An Overview of Inheritance in the Legal System of Iran" in Jürgen Badow and Nadjma Yassari (eds.) *Iranian Family and Succession Laws and their Application to German Courts* (Tübingen: Mohr Siebeck, 2004) 103–109.

Menashri, David, "Shi'ite Leadership: In the Shadow of Conflicting Ideologies." *Iranian Studies* XIII, no. 1–4 (1980): 119–145.

Messkoub, Mahmood, "Constitutionalism, Modernisation and Islamisation: The Political Economy of Social Policy in Iran" in Massoud Karshenas and Valentine M. Moghadam (eds.) *Social Policy in the Middle East: Economic, Political and Gender Dynamics* (New York: Palgrave Macmillan / UNRISD, 2006) 190–220.

Mirakhor, Abbas, "Analysis of Short-Term Asset Concentration in Islamic Banking." Washington: International Monetary Fund, October 8, 1987.

Mirbagheri, Farid, "Narrowing the Gap or Camouflaging the Divide: An Analysis of Mohammad Khatami's 'Dialogue of Civilisations.'" *British Journal of Middle Eastern Studies* 34, no. 3 (December 2007): 305–316.

Mir-Hosseini, Ziba, "Women, Marriage and the Law in Post-revolutionary Iran" in Haleh Afshar (ed.) *Women in the Middle East: Perceptions, Realities and Struggles for Liberation* (New York: St. Martin's Press, 1993) 59–84.

Mir-Hosseini, Ziba, *Marriage on Trial: A Study of Islamic Family Law* (London: I.B. Tauris, 1993/2000).

Mir-Hosseini, Ziba, "Stretching the Limits: A Feminist Reading of the *Shari'a* in Post-Khomeini Iran" in Mai Yamani (ed.) *Feminism and Islam: Legal and Literary Perspectives* (Reading: Ithaca Press, 1996a) 285–319.

Mir-Hosseini, Ziba, "Women and Politics in Post-Khomeini Iran: Divorce, Veiling and Emerging Feminist Voices" in Haleh Afshar (ed.) *Women and Politics in the Third World* (London: Routledge, 1996b) 142–170.

Mir-Hosseini, Ziba, "Family Law," section iii: "In Modern Persia." *Encyclopaedia Iranica*, volume 9 (1999): 192–196.

Mir-Hosseini, Ziba, "Hojjat al-Eslam Sa'idzadeh—Iran." In WLUML (Women Living Under Muslim Laws) Dossier 21 (2001): 56–59.

Mir-Hosseini, Ziba, "The Politics of Divorce Laws in Iran: Ideology Versus Practice" in Rubya Mehdi, Werner Menski, and Jørgen S. Nielsen (eds.) *Interpreting Divorce Laws in Islam* (Copenhagen: DJØF Publishing, 2002) 65–83.

Mir-Hosseini, Ziba, "When a Woman's Hurt Becomes an Injury: 'Hardship' as Grounds for Divorce in Iran." *Hawwa* 5, no. 1 (2007): 111–126.

Mir-Hosseini, Ziba, "A Woman's Right to Terminate the Marriage Contract: The Case of Iran" in Asifa Quraishi and Frank E. Vogel (eds.) *The Islamic Marriage Contract: Case Studies in Islamic Family Law* (Cambridge, MA: Harvard University Press, 2008) 215–230.

Mir-Hosseini, Ziba, "Criminalising Sexuality—Zina Laws as Violence Against Women in Muslim Contexts" in Ziba Mir-Hosseini and Vanja Hamzić (eds.) *Control and Sexuality: The Revival of Zina Laws in Muslim Contexts* (London: Women Living Under Muslim Laws, 2010a) 19–48.

Mir-Hosseini, Ziba, "Iran" in Ziba Mir-Hosseini and Vanja Hamzić (eds.) *Control and Sexuality: The Revival of Zina Laws in Muslim Contexts* (Women Living Under Muslim Laws, 2010b) 81–115.

Mir-Hosseini, Ziba, "Sharia and National Law in Iran" in Jan Michiel Otto (ed.) *Sharia Incorporated: A Comparative Overview of the Legal Systems of Twelve Muslim Countries in Past and Present* (Leiden: Leiden University Press, 2010c) 319–371.

Mir-Hosseini, Ziba, "The Secularization of Shari'a in Iran" in Marie-Claire Foblets and Jean-Yves Carlier (eds.) *Islam and Europe: Crises Are Challenges* (Leuven: Leuven University Press, 2010d) 109–115.

Mir-Hosseini, Ziba and Tapper, Richard, *Islam and Democracy in Iran: Eshkevari and the Quest for Reform* (London and New York: I.B. Tauris, 2006).

Moghadam, Fatemeh, "Commoditization of Sexuality and Female Labor Participation in Islam: Implications for Iran, 1960–90" in Mahnaz Afkhami and Erika Friedl (eds.) *In the Eye of the Storm: Women in Post-revolutionary Iran* (Syracuse: I.B. Tauris, 1994) 80–97.

Mohammadi, Abolhassan, *Mabani-e Estenbat: Huquq-e Eslami ya Osul-e Feqh* (Tehran: Entesharat-e Daneshgah-e Tehran, 1375 AP (1996/7)).

Mohaqeq Damad, Mostafa, "Legal and Civil Aspects of Marriage in Islam According to the Shi'i Tradition" in Jürgen Badow and Nadjma Yassari (eds.) *Iranian Family and Succession Laws and their Application to German Courts* (Tübingen: Mohr Siebeck, 2004) 57–68.

Mokhtari, Ali, *Torture and other Cruel, Inhuman or Degrading Treatment or Punishment: A Comparative Study between International law, Islamic Jurisprudence and the Iranian Legal System*. Unpublished LLM thesis, McGill University, 2004.

Mokhtari, Shadi, *A Constructivist Analysis of the Impact of International Human Rights Norms: The Case of Women's Rights under Islamic law in Iran*. Unpublished LLM thesis, York University (Toronto), 2005.

Mokhtari, Shadi, "The Search for Human Rights Within an Islamic Framework in Iran" in Mashood A. Baderin (ed.) *International Law and Islamic Law* (Aldershot: Ashgate, 2008) 613–623.

Momen, Moojan, *An Introduction to Shi'i Islam* (New Haven: Yale University Press, 1985).

Morgan-Foster, Jason, "A New Perspective on the Universality Debate: Reverse Moderate Relativism in the Islamic Context." In Mashood A. Baderin, 365–397. *International and Islamic Law* (Aldershot: Ashgate, 2008).

Moroni, Ferminia, "*Kashf-e Asrar*, o la fenomenologia di uno spirito inquieto." *Oriente Moderno*, New Series 12, no. 73 vii-xiii (1993 [1995]): 229–239.

Mosavvar-Rahmani, Yasmin L., "Family Planning in Post-revolutionary Iran" in Guity Nashat (ed.) *Women and Revolution in Iran* (Boulder: Westview Press, 1983) 253–262.

Motlagh, Amy, *Burying the Beloved: Marriage, Realism, and Reform in Modern Iran* (Stanford: Stanford University Press, 2012).

Mousavi, Shohreh, Shapiee, Rohimi, and Nordin, Rohaida, "Child Offenders in Iran: Legal Analysis on the Age of Criminal Responsibility and Sentencing." *International Journal of West Asian Studies* 4, no. 1 (2012): 31–48.

MRGI (Minority Rights Group International), "Iran Overview." April 2009. http://www.minorityrights.org/?lid=5092 Accessed March 7, 2014.

Namayandeh, Hajar, Yaacob, Siti Nor, and Juhari, Rumaya, "The Effect of Gender Role Orientation on Work Interference with Family (WIF) and Family Interference with Work (FIW) among Married Female Nurses in Shiraz-Iran." *Asian Culture and History* 2, no. 2 (July 2010): 165–171.

Nashat, Guity, ed. *Women and Revolution in Iran* (Boulder: Westview Press, 1983).

Navai, Ramita, "Le vie della droga." *Limes: rivista italiana di geopolitica, n.5: L'Iran tra maschera e volto* (2005): 79–87.

Nayyeri, Mohammad Hossein, "New Islamic Penal Code of the Islamic Republic of Iran: An Overview." University of Essex, Human Rights in Iran Unit, 2012.

Newman, Graeme, "Khomeini and Criminal Justice: Notes on Crime and Culture." *The Journal of Criminal Law and Criminology* 73, no. 2 (1982): 561–581.

Niknam, Azadeh, "L'islamisation du droit pénal à l'épreuve des réalités en Iran." (The Islamization of Penal Law as a Test of Realities in Iran) *Revue des Mondes Musulmans et de la Mediterranee* 85/86 (1999a): 47–62.

Niknam, Azadeh, "The Islamization of Law in Iran: A Time of Disenchantment." *Middle East Report* 29, part III/212 (1999b): 17–21.

Nobahar, Rahim, "Qachaq-e zanan baraye ruspigari az manzar-e amuzeshhaye Eslami ba negah be moqarrarat-e beinolmellali va huquq-e Iran." *Modarres* Series 10, no. 3 (Autumn 1375 AP / 1996): 187–220.

Nomani, Farhad, "The Problem of Interest and Islamic Banking in a Comparative Perspective: The Case of Egypt, Iran and Pakistan." *Review of Middle East Economics and Finance* 1, no. 1 (2003): article 4: 37–70.

Noori, Yahya and Amin, Hassan, *Legal and Political Structure of an Islamic State: The Implications for Iran and Pakistan* (Glasgow: Royston, 1987).

Omani Samani, Reza, Dizaj, Ahmad Vosough Taghi, Moalem, Mohammad Reza Rezania, Merghati, Taha, and Alizadeh, Leila, "Access to Fertility Treatments for Homosexual and Unmarried Persons, through Iranian Law and Islamic Perspective." *Iranian Journal of Fertility and Sterility* 1, no. 3 (November–December 2007): 127–130.

Opwis, Felicitas, "Islamic Law and Legal Change: The Concept of *Maslaha* in Classical and Contemporary Islamic Legal Theory" in Abbas Amanat and Frank Griffel (eds.) *Shari'a: Islamic Law in the Contemporary Context* (Stanford: Stanford University Press, 2007) 62–82.

Organization for Islamic Culture and Communications, Directorate of Research and Education, Centre for Cultural-International Studies. *Islamic Views on Human Rights: Viewpoints of Iranian Scholars* (New Delhi: Kanishka, 2003).

Osanloo, Arzoo, *At the Juncture of Islam and Republic: Socio-legal Constructions of Women's Rights in Iran*. Unpublished Ph.D. thesis, Stanford, 2002.

Osanloo, Arzoo, "Islamico-civil 'Rights Talk': Women, Subjectivity, and Law in Iranian Family Court." *American Ethnologist* 33, no. 2 (May 2006a): 191–209.

Osanloo, Arzoo, "The Measure of Mercy: Islamic Justice, Sovereign Power, and Human Rights in Iran." *Cultural Anthropology* 21, no. 4 (2006b): 570–602.

Osanloo, Arzoo, "Whence the Law: the Politics of Women's Rights, Regime Change, and the Vestiges of Reform in the Islamic Republic of Iran." *Radical History Review* 101 (Spring 2008): 42–58.

Osanloo, Arzoo, "Refusing Mercy: Challenges to the State's Monopoly on Violence in Iran" in Laleh Khalili and Jillian Schwedler (eds.) *Policing and Prisons in the Middle East: Formations of Coercion* (New York: Columbia University Press, 2010) 263–277.

Osborne, Bethany J., *The Learning of Embattled Bodies: Women Political Prisoners of Iran*. Unpublished MA thesis, University of Toronto, 2009.

Owsia, Parviz, "Sources of Law under English, French, Islamic and Iranian Law: A Comparative Review of Legal Techniques." *Arab Law Quarterly* 6, no. 1 (1991): 33–67.

Pakzad, Sima, "The Legal Status of Women in the Family in Iran" in Mahnaz Afkhami and Erika Friedl (eds.) *In the Eye of the Storm: Women in Post-revolutionary Iran* (Syracuse: I.B. Tauris, 1994) 169–179.

Papan-Matin, Firoozeh, "The Case of Mohammad Khordadian, an Iranian Male Dancer." *Iranian Studies* 42, no. 1 (February 2009): 127–138.

Parvaz, Nasrin, "Beneath the Narcissus: A Woman's Experience of Iranian Prisons and Beyond." *Feminist Review* 73 (2003): 71–85.

Paygah-e Ettela'-resani-e Basij-e Huquqdanan, "Layeheye Qanun-e Mojazat-e Eslami be Majles baz migardad." September 5, 2010. http://basijuristics.ir/NSite/Fullstory/?Id=54. Opened 20/8/11. Archived at http://www.webcitation.org/616KkhrOO.

Payvand, "Iranian Reformist Cleric, Ayatollah Sanei, Disowned by Hardliners." January 2, 2010. http://www.payvand.com/news/10/jan/1008.html Archived at http://www.webcitation.org/6EvnBogEA.

Picheca, Giulio, "Analisi della situazione giudiziaria in Iran attraverso la casistica emersa nella prassi rivoluzionaria." *Oriente Moderno*, 62 new series 1 (1982): 37–59.

Press TV, "Ayatollah Sanei No Longer Qualified: Clerical Body." January 2, 2010. http://edition.presstv.ir/detail/115179.html Retrieved 17/1/13. Archived at http://www.webcitation.org/6Dl2rX6dm.

Price, Daniel, "Islam and Human Rights: A Case of Deceptive First Appearances" in Shahram Akbarzadeh (ed.) *Islam and Globalization: Critical Concepts in Islamic Studies* (vol. 4) (London: Routledge, 2006) 278–293.

Rabb, Intisar A., Doubt's Benefit: Legal Maxims in Islamic Law, 7th–16th Centuries. Unpublished Ph.D. thesis, Princeton, 2009.

Radio Farda, "Prominent Iranian Dissident Cleric Ahmad Ghabel Dies." Radio Free Europe, October 23, 2012. http://www.rferl.org/content/iran-ahmad-ghabeldead/24748342.html Archived at http://www.webcitation.org/6Evo3CeLr.

Rahami, Mohsen, "Development of Criminal Punishment in the Iranian Post Revolutionary [*sic*] Penal Code." *European Journal of Crime, Criminal Law and Criminal Justice* 13, no. 4 (2005): 585–602.

Rahami, Mohsen, "The Constitution as Means of Conflict Prevention in the Middle East with a View to the Iranian Experience" in Hans-Jörg Albrecht, Jan-Michael Simon, Hassan Rezaei, Holger-C. Rohne, and Ernesto Kiza (eds.) *Conflicts and Conflict Resolution in Middle Eastern Societies—Between Tradition and Modernity* (Berlin: Duncker & Humblot, 2006) 471–491.

Rahmdel, Mansour, "Money Laundering in Iranian Law: Present and Future." *Journal of Money Laundering Control* 6, no. 2 (Autumn 2002): 182–190.

Rahmdel, Mansour, "The *Ne Bis in Idem* Rule in Iranian Criminal Law." *Journal of Financial Crime* 11, no. 3 (February 2004): 277–281.

Rajaee, Farhang, "A Thermidor of 'Islamic Yuppies'? Conflict and Compromise in Iran's Politics." *Middle East Journal* 53, no. 2 (Spring 1999): 217–231.

Ramazani, Rouhollah K., "Constitution of the Islamic Republic of Iran." *Middle East Journal* 34, no. 2 (Spring 1980): 181–204.

Raquibuz Zaman, M. and Movassaghi, Hormoz, "Islamic Banking: A Performance Analysis." *The Journal of Global Business* 12, no. 22 (Spring 2001): 31–38.

Raquibuz Zaman, M. and Movassaghi, Hormoz, "Interest-free Islamic Banking: Ideals and Reality." *The International Journal of Finance* 14, no. 4 (2002): 2428–2443.

Rasekh, Mohammad, "The Iranian Constitutional System in Context." *Yearbook of Islamic & Middle Eastern Law* 12 (2005–06): 69–96.

Redaelli, Riccardo, "Constitutional Complexity and Political Paradoxes of the Islamic Republic of Iran." *Oriente Moderno* New series, Year 87, no. 2, *Islams and Democracies* (2007): 483–496.

Rehman, Javaid, "Accommodating Religious Identities in an Islamic State: International Law, Freedom of Religion and the Rights of Religious Minorities" in Mashood A. Baderin (ed.) *International Law and Islamic Law* (Aldershot: Ashgate, 2008) 571–597.

Rejali, Darius, *Torture and Modernity: Self, Society, and State in Modern Iran* (Boulder: Westview Press, 1994).

Rezaei, Hassan, "Islamic Sharia and Cyberspace: Reflections on the Interactions of Sharia and Iranian Society in Cyberspace" in Sylvia Tellenbach (ed.) *Beiträge zum Islamischen Recht IV* (Frankfurt: Peter Lang, 2004) 105–124.

Rezaei, Hassan, "The Iranian Criminal Justice under the Islamization Project." *European Journal of Crime, Criminal Law & Criminal Justice* 10, no. 1 (2002): 54–69.

Rezaei, Hassan and Aghababaei, Hussein, "Iranian Criminal Law on Political Opposition." *Yearbook of Islamic and Middle Eastern Law* 12 (2005–06): 97–110.

Rezapour, Morteza, Rashtchi, Kamran Bagheri Maryam, and Bakhtiari, Mohammad Reza, "The Iranian Patenting System: An Introduction." *World Patent Information* 29 (2007): 250–254.

Rose, Gregory, "*Velayat-e Faqih* and the Recovery of Islamic Identity in the Thought of Ayatollah Khomeini" in Nikki Keddie (ed.) *Religion and Politics in Iran: Shi'ism from Quietism to Revolution* (New Haven: Yale University Press, 1983) 166–188.

Roy, Olivier, "The Crisis of Religious Legitimacy in Iran." *Middle East Journal* 53, no. 2 (Spring 1999): 201–216.

Sachedina, Abdulaziz Abdulhussein, *The Just Ruler in Shi'ite Islam* (Oxford: Oxford University Press, 1998).

Sachedina, Abdulaziz, "The Rule of the Religious Jurist in Iran" in John L. Esposito and R. K. Ramazani (eds.) *Iran at the Crossroads* (New York: Palgrave, 2001) 123–147.

Sadeghi-Fassaei, Soheila and Kendall, Kathleen, "Iranian Women's Pathways to Imprisonment." *Women's Studies International Forum* 24, no. 6 (2001): 701–710.

Sadri, Mahmoud, "Attack from Within: Dissident Political Theology in Contemporary Iran." February 13, 2002. http://web.archive.org/web/20030226124152/ http://kadivar.com/Htm/English/Reviews/reform.htm Archived at http://www.webcitation.org/6EvoZ7hGA.

Safa'i, Hamed, "Ba emzaye Rais-e Jomhur, Qanun-e Mojazat-e Eslami eblagh shod." May 26, 2013. Archived at http://www.webcitation.org/6N219V7UK.

Safa'i, Hossein, "Le mariage et le divorce en droit iranien" in Jürgen Badow and Nadjma Yassari (eds.) *Iranian Family and Succession Laws and their Application to German Courts* (Tübingen: Mohr Siebeck, 2004) 69–80.

Saffari, Said, "The Legitimation of the Clergy's Right to Rule in the Iranian Constitution of 1979." *British Journal of Middle Eastern Studies* 20, no. 1 (1993): 64–82.

Sahimi, Muhammad, "Tehran Bureau: Who's in Charge?" June 29, 2010. http://www.irannewsnow.com/2010/07/tehran-bureau-whos-in-charge/ Archived at http://www.webcitation.org/6EvohNW78.

Sa'idzadeh, Mohsen, "Foundations of the Equality Perspective in Modern *Fiqh*: The Case of Divorce." In *WLUML (Women Living Under Muslim Laws) Dossier* 21 (2001): 60–63.

Samgiss, Banafsheh, "Poveri giovani." *Limes: rivista italiana di geopolitica*, 5: *L'Iran tra maschera e volto* (2005): 67–73.

Samii, A. William, "The Nation and Its Minorities: Ethnicity, Unity, and State Policy in Iran." *Comparative Studies of South Asia, Africa and the Middle East* 20, nos. 1&2 (2000): 128–137.

Samii, Abbas William, "The Changing Landscape of Party Politics in Iran: A Case Study." *Vaseteh: The Journal of the European Society for Iranian Studies* 1, no. 1 (Winter 2005): 53–62.

Sanasarian, Eliz, *Religious Minorities in Iran* (Cambridge: Cambridge University Press, 2000).

Sanati, Kimia, "Intolerance Marks Sunni Student's Death Sentence." *IPS News*, February 9, 2008. http://ipsnews.net/news.asp?idnews=41247. Accessed August 21, 2011. Archived at http://www.webcitation.org/61DQoLBZR.

Sanei, Faraz, "The Caspian Sea Legal Regime, Pipeline Diplomacy, and the Prospects for Iran's Isolation from the Oil and Gas Frenzy: Reconciling Tehran's Legal Options with its Geopolitical Realities." *Vanderbilt Journal of Transnational Law* 34 (2001): 681–846.

Schacht, Joseph, *An Introduction to Islamic Law* (Oxford University Press, 1982).

Schirazi, Asghar, *The Constitution of Iran: Politics and the State in the Islamic Republic*. Translated by John O'Kane (London: I.B. Tauris, 1997).

Schneider, Irene, "The Concept of Honor and its Reflection in the Iranian Penal Code." *Journal of Persianate Studies* 5 (2012): 43–57.

Scott, Catherine V., "Bound for Glory: The Hostage Crisis as Captivity Narrative in Iran." *International Studies Quarterly* 44, no. 1 (March 2000): 177–188.

Sepehrrad, Ramesh, *Gender Conflict in Iran: A Critique of Human Rights and Conflict Resolution*. Unpublished Ph.D. thesis, George Mason University, 2010.

Shaaban, H.S., "Commercial Transactions in the Middle East: What Law Governs?" *Law & Policy in International Business* 31 (1999–2000): 157–172.

Shahidi, Hossein, "Iranian Journalism and the Law in the Twentieth Century." *Iranian Studies* 41, no. 5 (December 2008): 739–754.

Shahshahani, Sepehr, "Politics under the Cover of Law: Can International Law Help Resolve the Iran Nuclear Crisis?" *Boston University International Law Journal* 25 (2007): 369–426.

Shambayati, Hootan, "A Tale of Two Mayors: Courts and Politics in Iran and Turkey." *International Journal of Middle East Studies* 36 (2004): 253–275.

Shambayati, Hootan, "Courts in Semi-democratic/Authoritarian Regimes: The Judicialization of Turkish (and Iranian) Politics" in Tom Ginsburg and Tamir Moustafa (eds.) *Rule by Law: The Politics of Courts in Authoritarian Regimes* (New York: Cambridge University Press, 2008) 283–303.

Shams Nateri and Ebrahim, Mohammad, "Formal and Informal Means of Conflict Resolution in Murder Cases in Iran" in Hans-Jörg Albrecht, Jan-Michael Simon, Hassan Rezaei, Holger-C. Rohne, and Ernesto Kiza (eds.) *Conflicts and Conflict Resolution in Middle Eastern Societies—Between Tradition and Modernity* (Berlin: Duncker & Humblot, 2006) 401–410.

Sherman, Bill, "Pastor Fighting Faith Killings: A Law Proposed in Iran Calls for Executing Men Who Leave the Muslim Faith." *McClatchy—Tribune Business News*, January 2, 2009.

Smythe, Chloë Keshree, Keeping Iran's Nuclear Programme Civil: The Legality of Using Force Against Iran in Respect of Its Nuclear Activities. Unpublished LLM thesis: University of Toronto, 2006.

Solé, Juan, "Introducing Islamic Banks into Conventional Banking Systems." *Journal of Islamic Economics, Banking and Finance* 4, no. 2 (2008): 9–34.

Sreberny, Annabelle and Khiabany, Gholam, "Becoming Intellectual: The Blogestan and the Public Political Space in the Islamic Republic." *British Journal of Middle Eastern Studies* 34, no. 3 (December 2007): 267–286.

Strong, Stacie I., "Law and Religion in Israel and Iran: How the Integration of Secular and Spiritual Laws Affects Human Rights and the Potential for Violence." *Michigan Journal of International Law* 19 (1997–98): 109–217.

Syed, Safir, "The Impact of Islamic Law on the Implementation of the Convention on the Rights of the Child: The Plight of Non-marital Children under Shari'a" in Mashood A. Baderin (ed.) *International Law and Islamic Law* (Aldershot: Ashgate, 2008) 499–533.

Tabarestani, Cirus, "Fundamental Contradictions of the Islamic Republic of Iran: An Iranian View." *Capital and Class* 49 (1993): 19–35.

Tabari, Azar, "The Role of the Clergy in Modern Iranian Politics" in Nikki Keddie (ed.) *Religion and Politics in Iran: Shi'ism from Quietism to Revolution* (New Haven: Yale University Press, 1983) 47–72.

Tabari, Keyvan, "The Rule of Law and the Politics of Reform in Post-revolutionary Iran." *International Sociology* 19, no. 1 (March 2003): 96–113.

Tabataba'i, 'Allamah Sayyid Muhammad Husayn, *Shi'ah*. Translated by Sayyid Husayn Nasr (Qum: Ansariyan, 2004).

Tabnak, "Hazf-e sangsar az Qanun-e jadid-e Mojazat-e Eslami." October 11, 2012. Accessed January 16 2013. Archived at http://www.webcitation.org/6DjBOCZIR.

Taheri, Amir, "Divine Law and Human Rights." *Index on Censorship* 12 (1983): 19–21.

Tamadonfar, Mehran, "Islam, Law, and Political Control in Contemporary Iran." *Journal for the Scientific Study of Religion* 40, no. 2 (June 2001): 205–219.

Tasnim News. "Shuraye Negahban be hazf-e 'rajm' as Qanun-e Mojazat-e Eslami irad nagereft." March 1, 2013. Archived at http://www.webcitation.org/6EsWPDocB.

Terman, Rochelle, "The Stop Stoning Forever Campaign: A Report." Women Living Under Muslim Laws, November 2007. http://www.meydaan.net/UserFiles/File/Terman_stoning-2.pdf Accessed August 21 2011. Archived at http://www.webcitation.org/61DQoLBb1.

Terman, Rochelle and Fijabi, Mufuliat, "Stoning is Not Our Culture: A Comparative Analysis of Human Rights and Religious Discourses in Iran and Nigeria." The Global Campaign to Stop Stoning and Killing Women, March 2010. http://www.stop-stoning.org/files/Terman_Fijabi.pdf Opened 21/8/11. Archived at http://www.webcitation.org/61DQoLBb9.

Tober, Diane M., "Kidneys and Controversies in the Islamic Republic of Iran: The Case of Organ Sale." *Body and Society* 13, no. 3 (2007): 151–170.

Tober, Diane M., Taghdisi, Mohammad-Hossein, and Jalali, Mohammad, "'Fewer Children, Better Life' or 'As Many as God Wants'?: Family Planning Among Low-income Iranian and Afghan Refugee Families in Isfahan, Iran." *Medical Anthropology Quarterly* 20, no. 1 (March 2006): 50–71.

Tremayne, Soraya, "Modernity and Early Marriage in Iran: A View from Within." *Journal of Middle East Women's Studies* 2, no. 1 (Winter 2006): 65–145.

Tsadik, Daniel, "The Legal Status of Religious Minorities: Imami Shi'i Law and Iran's Constitutional Revolution." *Islamic Law and Society* 10, no. 3 (2003): 376–408.

Ulrey, LeAnne, *The Women Who Stayed.* Unpublished MA thesis, Southern Illinois University (Carbondale), 2011.
Underwood, Carol Ruth, *Child Health Under Revolutionary Regimes: The Case of the Islamic Republic of Iran.* Unpublished Ph.D. thesis, Johns Hopkins University, 1993.
Usman, Jeffrey, "The Evolution of Iranian Islamism from the Revolution Through the Contemporary Reformers." *Vanderbilt Journal of Transnational Law* 35 (2002): 1679–1730.
Valavioun, Reza, "Succession Laws of Religious Minorities" in Jürgen Badow and Nadjma Yassari (eds.) *Iranian Family and Succession Laws and their Application to German Courts* (Tübingen: Mohr Siebeck, 2004) 111–122.
Valibeigi, Mehrdad, "Islamic Economics and Economic Policy Formation in Post-Revolutionary Iran: A Critique." *Journal of Economic Issues* 27, no. 3 (September 1993): 793–812.
Vercellin, Giorgio, "La minoranza turkmena d'Iran secondo una recente pubblicazione locale." *Oriente Moderno Year 60, no. 1/6, Studi in memoria di Paolo Minganti* (January–June 1980): 357–372.
Walbridge, Linda S., "Introduction: Shi'ism and authority" in Linda S. Walbridge (ed.) *The Most Learned of the Shi'a: The Institution of the Marja' Taqlid* (New York: Oxford University Press, 2001) 3–13.
Wells, Matthew C., "Thermidor in the Islamic Republic of Iran: The Rise of Muhammad Khatami." *British Journal of Middle Eastern Studies* 26, no. 1 (May 1999): 27–39.
Williams, Juliet A., "Unholy Matrimony? Feminism, Orientalism, and the Possibility of Double Critique." *Signs: Journal of Women in Culture and Society* 34, no. 3 (2009): 612–632.
Wiswall, F. L. Jr., "Neutrality, the Rights of Shipping and the Use of Force in the Persian Gulf." *Virginia Journal of International Law* 31 (1991): 619–629.
Wright, Robin, ed. *The Iran Primer: Power, Politics and U.S. Policy* (Washington, DC: United States Institute of Peace, 2010).
Yassari, Nadjma, "Iranian Family Law in Theory and Practice." *Yearbook of Islamic & Middle Eastern Law* 9 (2002–03): 43–64.
Yassari, Nadjma, "The Reform of the Spousal Share under Iranian Succession Law—An Example of the Transformability of Islamic Law." *Rabels Zeitschrift fuer auslaendisches und internationales Privatrecht* 73, no. 4 (October 2009): 985–1004.
Yazdani, Majid, The Place of International Sale of Goods Under Iranian Law: Theory and Practice. Unpublished JD thesis, York University (Toronto), 2000.
Yeganeh, Nahid, "Women, Nationalism and Islam in Contemporary Political Discourse in Iran." *Feminist Review* 44, *Nationalisms and National Identities* (Summer 1993): 3–18.
Yousefi, Mahmood, Abizadeh, Sohrab, and McCormisk, Ken, "Monetary Stability and Interest-free Banking: The Case of Iran." *Applied Economics* 29, no. 7 (1997): 869–876.
Zahedi, Ashraf, "Transnational Marriages, Gendered Citizenship, and the Dilemma of Iranian Women Married to Afghan Men." *Iranian Studies* 40, no. 2 (April 2007): 225–239.
Zaher, Tarek S. and Hassan, M. Kabir, "A Comparative Literature Survey of Islamic Finance and Banking." *Financial Markets, Institutions & Instruments* 10, no. 4 (November 2001): 155–199.
Zahir, Sanam, The Music of the Children of Revolution: The State of Music and Emergence of the Underground Music in the Islamic Republic of Iran with an Analysis of Its Lyrical Content. Unpublished MA thesis, University of Arizona, 2008.

Zali, Mohammad Reza, Shahraz, Saeed, and Borzabadi, Shokoufeh, "Bioethics in Iran: Legislation as the Main Problem." *Archives of Iranian Medicine* 5, no. 3 (2002): 136–140.

Zamani, Amir and Jordan, Casey, "Law Enforcement in the Islamic Republic of Iran and the Socialist Peoples' Libyan Arab Jamahiriya." *Police Studies* 12, no. 2 (Summer 1989): 39–50.

Zenganeh, Hamid, "Islamic Banking: Theory and Practice in Iran." *Comparative Economic Studies (Association for Comparative Economic Studies)* 31, no. 3 (Fall 1989): 67–84.

Zeydabadi-Nejad, Saeed, "Iranian Intellectuals and Contact with the West: The Case of Iranian Cinema." *British Journal of Middle Eastern Studies* 34, no. 3 (December 2007): 375–398.

Zubaida, Sami, "Is Iran an Islamic State?" in Joel Beinin and Joe Stork (eds.) *Political Islam* (London: I.B. Tauris, 1997) 103–119.

Zubaida, Sami, "Contemporary Trends in Muslim Legal Thought and Ideology" in Robert W. Hefner (ed.) *The New Cambridge History of Islam. Volume 6: Muslims and Modernity, Culture and Society Since 1800* (Cambridge: Cambridge University Press, 2010) 270–295.

CHAPTER 26

THE TURKISH REPUBLIC

RUTH A. MILLER

I. Introduction

TURKEY's constitution defines the Turkish Republic as a secular state and thus as a state that is formally disconnected from Islamic law. The importance of eradicating Islamic law does not appear explicitly in the text of the constitution, but that goal is more than suggested by its caution against "sacred religious feelings" that might become political or legal, and thus a threat to Turkish secularism.[1] Turkey's Constitutional Court has been more vocal about the need to cleanse the secular Republic of religious law, and its rulings have rarely shied away from describing Islamic law as a menace to the state.[2] Similarly, in 2001, when the European Court of Human Rights upheld Turkey's right to ban the *Refah* (Welfare) Party from politics, it did so because *Refah* seemed likely to "establish Islamic law."[3] Not only has Turkey abolished Islamic law, therefore; both national and regional juridical bodies have defined Islamic law as one of the most pernicious threats to Turkish sovereignty.

[1] *Constitution of the Republic of Turkey* (Ankara: Türkiye Büyük Millet Meclisi, 1995), 2.

[2] Aslı Ü. Balı, "The Perils of Judicial Independence: Constitutional Transition and the Turkish Example," *Virginia Journal of International Law* 53 (2012): 250–251 and Güneş Murat Tezcür, "Constitutionalism, Judiciary, and Democracy in Islamic Societies," *Polity* 39, no. 4 (October, 2007): 490. See also Güneş Murat Tezcür, *Muslim Reformers in Iran and Turkey* (Austin: University of Texas Press, 2010), 103.

[3] Tezcür, "Constitutionalism," 492. Note that there were two decisions: the first in 2001 by a chamber of the Court, and the second in 2003 by the Grand Chamber of the Court. The second decision affirmed the first decision.

So what is Turkey doing in a handbook on Islamic law? If Turkey's secularism, reiterated since 1924 in every one of the Republic's amended constitutions, entails the radical rejection of religious law, what is there to say about its presence in twentieth- and twenty-first-century Turkish history? Turkey's Republicanism is a secular Republicanism, and secularism in Turkey has been defined at least in part as the vigilant shoring up of Turkish jurisdictional boundaries against the menace of *şeriat* (shariʿa). One would expect an essay on the historiography of Islamic law in the Turkish Republic to be very short indeed.

And yet, since the middle of the twentieth century, historians have remained intrigued by the problem of Islamic law in the Turkish Republic. In particular, they have wondered what role Islamic law might play in a majority Muslim state whose parliament and judiciary have persistently rejected or repudiated it. Taking the Turkish constitution at its word, these commentators have asked not only how *official* Republican law has developed since 1923, but what a legal system predicated on the revolutionary removal of a pre-existing religious law might demand of its citizens and its jurists. They have asked, in short, whether the radical rejection of Islamic law has perhaps enshrined *şeriat* not only as a rhetorical trope in Turkish political discourse, but also as an unofficial and unacknowledged source of Turkish legal doctrine and practice.

Responses to these questions about the role that Islamic law has played in Republican Turkey have, however, ranged widely. Some have meditated on the problem of legal absence or legal borrowing, while others have analyzed Islamic law as a fundamental, if spectral, constitutional problem in the Republic. More recent work has gone further, questioning the Republican progress-narrative of legal transformation—in which a supposedly backward and irrational system of religious law gave way to a rational, coherent non-religious law—and looking for specific, concrete traces of an Ottoman–Islamic legacy in Turkey. Other scholars, similarly suspicious of the idea that Islamic law exists only in its much-discussed absence, have suggested that *new* interpretations of Islamic law have arisen in the Republic. These studies see contemporary Turkish *şeriat* less as an Ottoman holdover and more as an idiosyncratic product of Republican secularism itself.

Given these multifaceted trends in scholarship on Islamic law in the Turkish Republic, commentators today are in an excellent position to reconceive the problem, if any, that Islamic law poses in Turkey. Students, indeed, can begin now to address Turkish *şeriat* without the ideological anxiety that underpinned so much of the earliest work on the topic. They can address Turkish Islamic law in the same way that their contemporaries have addressed other legal systems, structures, or theories. To provide one example, scholars might now finally be able to move away from Islamic law in Turkey as a symptom of failed secularism or of resurgent religious feeling, and consider it instead as an alternative mode of expressing what it means to be a Turkish legal subject or what it means to delimit Turkish legal space or territory. The groundwork, in other words, has been set for a series of exciting new scholarly conversations about the dynamism or fluidity of Republican law writ large.

II. Islamic Law as a Constitutional Problem

Much of the early to mid-twentieth-century scholarship on Turkish legal doctrine and practice accepted that Islamic law had been abolished upon the establishment of the Republic. As of 1924, Turkey was a secular state, and as of 1927, it had replaced its pre-existing Ottoman–Islamic codes with a Swiss Civil Code, an Italian Criminal Code, a German Code of Criminal Procedure, and a largely German and Swiss Commercial Code.[4] Judges and advocates were educated or re-educated in European procedure, and if a memory of Islamic legal doctrine or practice survived in what were usually described as "local" or "rural" areas, this memory soon dissipated. Something called *şeriat* may have remained an obstacle to Republican social engineering, but this *şeriat* had little to do with state law. *Şeriat* was instead a catch-all term for reactionary opposition to Republican progress, and commentators were optimistic that it would soon fade away in the face of universal education. Scholarship on law in Republican Turkey, therefore, whether it praised the ostensible modernity of eradicating *şeriat*[5] or questioned this move for its authoritarianism,[6] took for granted that religious law had indeed ceased to operate.

As Islamic law—or simply the rhetorical trope, *şeriat*—endured in Turkish public discourse, however, historians of Turkish law began to reconsider their assumptions about its passing. Islamic law seemed, if anything, more *rhetorically* persistent in its absence than it had ever been when it was the basis of Ottoman legal theory and practice.[7] Or, put differently, the European civil law that Turkey had adopted seemed to occupy the Turkish legal imagination far less than the Islamic law that Turkey had repudiated. Moving away, therefore, from the problem of "legal borrowing"—of whether the law of culture A (say, Switzerland) could be grafted onto the society of culture B (say, Turkey), with "culture" defined as a monolithic, unquestioned object

[4] Tuğrul Ansay and Don Wallace Jr., *Introduction to Turkish Law* (The Hague: Kluwer Law International, 2005), 9.

[5] Bernard Lewis, *The Emergence of Modern Turkey* (New York: Oxford University Press, 2002 [1961]), 265.

[6] Feroz Ahmad, *The Making of Modern Turkey* (London: Routledge, 1993), 80.

[7] M. Hakan Yavuz, *Islamic Political Identity in Turkey* (Oxford: Oxford University Press, 2003), 220.

of inquiry[8]—historians instead began to consider the problem of legal *revolution*, of the total destruction of a legal system of the sort undertaken in Turkey. Their concern focussed less on grafting and more on eradication, on whether abolishing a legal system in its entirety was even possible.

By the time scholars began to reconsider this history of the elimination of Islamic law in Turkey, however, it seemed that if *şeriat* did exist, it was only as a constitutional problem. No one questioned that criminal law, civil law, commercial law, and legal procedure in Turkey had become "European," and thus not religious—and observers could see that Turkish courts, along with those who staffed them, facilitated Turkey's secular ideology. Historians saw no need to discuss, say, Islamic commercial law or Islamic building codes because these laws were derived from non-Islamic sources. There was little analysis of a Turkish–Islamic legal doctrine or practice in this earlier work—rather, historians asked how Islamic law as a rhetorical trope had or had not influenced Turkish constitutionalism.[9]

But this purely constitutional problem that Islamic law seemed to pose was by no means minor. Historians exploring the issue discussed both the menace to Turkish sovereignty that Islamic law was supposed to represent and the confusion that Islamic law seemed capable of introducing into Republican theories of jurisdiction or Republican interpretations of the rights and duties of citizens.[10] In general, these earliest scholars focussed primarily on how Turkish jurisprudence addressed Islamic law as a rhetorical, rather than legal, threat to sovereignty. As these histories of Islamic law in Turkey developed, however, the possibility that *şeriat* might also pose a properly legal threat to jurisdiction and to theories of citizenship began to occupy their attention. By the 1990s, scholars of the Turkish Constitutional Court especially had begun to discuss how Turkish jurists were dealing with *şeriat* as an apparently pervasive hazard, both ideological and functional, to Republican constitutionalism.[11]

Turkey's Constitutional Court has traditionally concerned itself with sovereignty writ large rather than with jurisdiction or citizenship when it rules on Islamic law. According to the Constitutional Court, Islamic law unravels Turkey's self-definition, and it does so for ideological, rather than doctrinal or practical, reasons.[12] If secularism is a key characteristic of the Turkish state, the Court has suggested, and if secularism in Turkey is defined as the state's total control over public religious expression, then the existence of religious *law*, in particular, upsets this secular hierarchy. Law is explicitly immune from such political control in a rule-of-law

[8] Lewis, *The Emergence of Modern Turkey*, 64.

[9] June Starr, *Law as Metaphor: From Islamic Courts to the Palace of Justice* (Albany: State University of New York Press, 1992), xxxviii.

[10] Şerif Mardin, "Center-Periphery Relations: A Key to Turkish Politics?" *Daedalus* 102, no. 1 (Winter 1973): 185.

[11] Ahmad, *The Making of Modern Turkey*, 158.

[12] Balı, "The Perils of Judicial Independence," 306.

Republic like Turkey, and so if law becomes religious, religion will elude proper political regulation and potentially invert the regulatory relationship on which Turkish statehood rests. Islamic law is a threat to Turkish secular self-definition, in other words, less because it is Islamic than because it is law.

When the Constitutional Court bans political parties because these parties seem, potentially, interested in advocating *şeriat*, however, it is not making a commentary on the inappropriateness of introducing a competing or replacement legal system into the Republic. Rather, as this first generation of historians emphasized, the Constitutional Court dwelt on Islamic law's ideological qualities. Even as Islamic law posed, as law, a constitutional threat, it was rarely evaluated—by jurists or by scholars—as a legal system per se. Instead, Islamic law was, according to the Constitutional Court, ideologically inappropriate, and according to scholars, therefore an ideological issue. As Jacob Landau influentially wrote in the 1970s, the Constitutional Court was brought into being specifically to counteract this ideological rather than legal threat.[13]

Scholars in fact emphasized repeatedly that the politicians, voters, and intellectuals who advocated—or who were accused and convicted of advocating—Islamic law were uninterested in Islamic legal theory, doctrine, or practice. Rather, writers such as Ruşen Çakır suggested that praising (or for that matter condemning) something called "Islamic law" had become a way to express dissatisfaction with a political elite that had left other avenues of communication closed.[14] While they acknowledged the persistence of Islamic law as a trope in Turkish political discourse, these scholars for the most part did not acknowledge its legal qualities. Its mobilization was shorthand for economic, populist, or socially conservative political agendas. The Turkish people were still "secular" in this writing—with, again, "secularism" described in large part as opposed to Islamic law. But these people were also unhappy with twentieth-century Republican politics, and speaking positively of *şeriat* was a way to express this unhappiness. Or, as Hakan Yavuz has repeatedly stressed, Islamic identity in Turkey is "ethical" or communicative, never legal.[15]

This trend in the early scholarship on Islamic law in Turkey without question reinforced Republican progress narratives of national unity, strength, and secularism. Even if Islamic law endured as a trope, it by no means constituted a failure of secularist social engineering. The population, throughout the country, and regardless of background or identity, remained convinced of the validity of the Republican project. The persistence of *şeriat* may have raised questions about the uniformly positive popular *attitude* toward Republican revolution; it did not, however, in any way threaten the *efficacy* of this revolution.

[13] Jacob M. Landau, *Radical Politics in Modern Turkey* (Leiden: Brill, 1974), 11.

[14] Ruşen Çakır, *Ne Şeriat Ne Demokrasi: Refah Partisini Anlamak* (Istanbul: Metis, 1994), 21.

[15] Yavuz, *Islamic Political Identity*, 115; M. Hakan Yavuz, "Ethical Not Shari'a Islam: Islamic Debates in Turkey," *Review of Faith and International Affairs* 10, no. 4 (2012): 30–31.

But this scholarship also, if inadvertently, placed Turkey's Constitutional Court in a difficult position. If Islamic law was a threat to Turkish sovereignty not only because it was religious but also, importantly, because it was law, then its advocates could reasonably be convicted only if they promoted its legal application. If, contrarily, and as scholarship increasingly suggested, those who spoke positively of Islamic law did so for non-legal reasons,[16] then the Court's activities were not as legitimate as they appeared to be. Already on shaky ground because it traditionally convicted politicians for their *potential* to do harm rather than for any harm done—or for *hinting* at a positive attitude toward Islamic law rather than for any explicit statement in favor of instituting this law[17]—the Constitutional Court was now faced with an additional criticism in that it seemed to promote the policing of pure rhetoric.

In the mid- to late 1990s, therefore, scholars such as Ayşe Saktanber and Jenny White, and media outlets such as *Hürriyet* and *Milliyet* began, albeit from quite different perspectives, once more to reconsider the constitutional problems that Islamic law raised in Turkey. As the Constitutional Court's untenable framework for addressing *şeriat* became ever more fragile, commentators both inside and outside of Turkey, both supportive and critical of the Court's work, began to wonder whether Islamic law might still resonate legally, as well as politically or ideologically, in the Turkish Republic. And, as a result, scholarship on Islamic law in Turkey began to shift focus away from Turkish sovereignty writ large and toward, first, the jurisdictional hazards that Islamic law might represent, and second, the damage to Republican theories of citizenship rights and duties that it might do. Gradually, in other words, Islamic law became a problem for legal scholarship as well as for scholarship on politics or political rhetoric. As researchers began to look at how Turkish citizens interpreted or interacted with Islamic law, and away from the broad statements that Parliament or the Constitutional Court had prepared on the threat of *şeriat*, *şeriat* took on legal salience.

This turn to the everyday life of Turkish–Islamic law, however, did not mean that commentators significantly re-evaluated *şeriat* as a constitutional *challenge*. Indeed, the popular media in Turkey in many ways pre-empted scholarly work in this direction, especially as it related to jurisdiction—and mainstream Turkish journalism is rarely sympathetic to Islamic legal doctrine or practice. A major pillar of the media's case against the *Refah* Party, for example, was that the *Refah* Prime Minister, Necmettin Erbakan was prone not only to praising *şeriat* but to convening temporary Islamic law courts.[18] Erbakan, that is to say, not only destabilized the abstract

[16] Yavuz, *Islamic Political Identity*, 220; Richard Tapper, *Islam in Modern Turkey: Religion, Politics, and Literature in a Secular State* (London: I.B. Tauris, 1991), 55.

[17] A position reflected by the rulings of the European Court of Human Rights. Tezcür, "Constitutionalism," 492.

[18] e.g., among many, Oya Armutçu, "Erbakan, 'Şeriat Mahkemesi' Kurdurmuş," *Hürriyet*, February 13, 1999: 1.

secular hierarchies that supported Turkish sovereignty; more perniciously, he undercut the concrete, daily work of Turkish courts, and thus the rule of law. Islamic law in this way became a constitutional threat because it was blurring Turkish *jurisdictional* boundaries rather than because it was inverting ideological hierarchies. Islamic law was transformed in writing about Turkey from pure ideology to something resembling law.

Scholarship on the persistence of the Islamic law courts in Turkey was usually more nuanced than media reports, but for the most part it explored similar themes. Anthropologists, especially, began to work on the apparent continuity of the Islamic law court in both urban and rural neighborhoods. Coinciding with the popularity of identity theory in the late 1990s, this scholarship asked how the discourse surrounding these courts produced or fractured Turkish or Muslim subjectivity.[19] As a corollary, it also explored the jurisdictional and constitutional issues that unofficial Islamic law courts raised. The question animating this more legal take on the issue was what might happen if Turkish citizens imagined their rights and duties with reference to an Islamic law rather than, or in addition to, official law.

The answer, in this earliest literature, was emphatically *not* that a pluralistic legal compromise might be reached. Rather, as scholars such as Saktanber made clear, the rhetoric surrounding Islamic legal or political identity inevitably produced sets of impossible choices—fracturing either the Turkish citizen or Turkish sovereignty into a series of dialectical oppositions at best or a chaotic mess at worst. As Saktanber wrote in *Living Islam: Women, Religion, and the Politicization of Culture in Turkey*, women who defined themselves with reference to an unofficial Islamic political order inevitably identified themselves as "Muslim women," against and apart from "Turkish women."[20] Unofficial legal institutions such as the persistent Islamic law court, in other words, both ruptured Turkey's sovereign space by blurring jurisdictional borders *and* transformed formerly Turkish citizens into foreigners (i.e. they self-identified as Muslim, *not* Turkish). The unofficial Islamic law court thus became in this scholarship a constitutional threat in every sense of the word.

Whereas the earliest work on Islamic law as a Turkish constitutional problem explored the problem of absence, later scholarship gradually began to question, first, the rhetorical eradication of *şeriat* from the Republican landscape and, second, its legal suppression. Initially, this scholarship continued to adhere to Republican progress narratives. Islamic law may have possessed rhetorical or ideological force, but its legal relevance was negligible. Neither the population nor the politicians, neither the intellectuals nor the jurists in Turkey had any interest in its actual interpretation or application. Soon, though, even that qualification disappeared, and

[19] Jenny B. White, *Islamist Mobilization in Turkey: A Study in Vernacular Politics* (Seattle: University of Washington Press, 2002), 134.

[20] Ayşe Saktanber, *Living Islam: Women, Religion, and the Politicization of Culture in Turkey* (New York: Palgrave Macmillan, 2002), 28–29.

commentators on Turkish law addressed *şeriat* as, specifically, a legal system with its own theory, doctrine, and practice. In general, scholars explored the *constitutional* implications of the redefinition—and usually the threatening constitutional implications—of Islamic law. But once granted the status of law, *şeriat* in Turkey began to interest scholars in a variety of other fields as well.

III. Traces of an Ottoman Islamic Past

Historians and legal scholars such as İhsan Yılmaz, İbrahim Yılmaz, and Ali Aslan Topçuoğlu, for example, responded to the notion that an Islamic law might operate *as law* in Turkey by looking for the antecedents to this situation. In particular, these commentators began to consider the possibility that *şeriat* might be, and might historically have been, as relevant to Turkish criminal, commercial, and civil law—in their official manifestations—as it had been as a sort of underground threat or a challenge to constitutional law. These scholars wondered, in other words, whether the ongoing presence of Islamic law in the Republic might be more formal than it initially appeared to be, and whether this formality might be traced to an enduring Ottoman legacy in Turkey.

This emergent trend in the history of Islamic law in Turkey was thus very much in line with a more general late twentieth-century shift in Turkish historiography. Increasingly, by the late 1980s, scholars had begun questioning the story of a complete break between the Ottoman Empire and the Turkish Republic. Narratives of the purely self-generating quality of Republican law, society, and politics, in other words, were being greeted with a mounting skepticism by historians at precisely the same time that work on the persistence of Islamic legal theory and practice in Turkey was growing. Ordinarily, however, the more mainstream histories of Turkey's Ottoman past argued that the Republican *rejection* of Islamic law was the continuation of an Ottoman project. They made the case, in other words, that the Ottoman Empire was more Republican than an earlier generation had thought it to be, rather than that the Republic was more Ottoman that it seemed to be.[21]

Historians of Islamic law, as noted at the beginning of this section, took a different approach. Unlike their contemporaries, they were less interested in projecting Republican ideals back in time to the Ottoman period than they were in excavating Ottoman norms and practices later on in the Republic. Rather than making the

[21] Kemal Karpat, ed., *Ottoman Past and Today's Turkey* (Leiden: Brill, 2000), viii.

case for an Ottoman-era rejection of religious law, these scholars instead posited a Republican-era embrace of it. They argued that the persistence of Islamic law in the Republic was an Ottoman inheritance—and thus that the *Republic* was more *Ottoman* that it might initially have appeared to be. This new trend in scholarship in this way reimagined both late Ottoman *and* Turkish Republican attitudes to law. It sought evidence of a dynamic, late Ottoman variation on Islamic legal theory and practice in official, rather than underground, Republican codes and institutions.

In doing so, this scholarship relied primarily on two complementary methodologies. The first of these methodologies involved a shift away from the anthropological interest in law at work on the ground, and back toward close readings of Ottoman and Turkish legal texts. Once again, a major premise of this work was that Turkish *doctrine* was as much influenced by Ottoman–Islamic law as unofficial practice or protest might have been. Instead of describing an underground, idiosyncratic, or local Islamic law working against an officially recognized system—rather than, say, seeking out "*şeriat* courts" or describing the deleterious constitutional effects of making Islamic law an ideological enemy—this writing returned to official pronouncements, rulings, and legislation. It sought concrete traces of specific elements of Islamic legal norms in the text of Turkey's European codes.

Although this work by no means proved that a coherent Islamic legal system remained at work in the Turkish Republic, therefore, it did excavate a sufficient number of impressionistic examples of Ottoman norms embedded in Republican doctrine to demonstrate a continuing Ottoman–Islamic legacy in Turkey. Some scholars showed, for example, that the family law adopted from Switzerland was interspersed with late Ottoman legal norms, most of which were derived from three of the four major schools of Sunni law. The more notoriously gender-biased sections of Turkey's family law were direct translations of their Swiss model. But early Republican jurists had reduced the impact of these chapters by replacing other parts of the Swiss text with the more flexible approaches to divorce, marital property, paternity, legitimacy, domicile, and employment characteristic of late Ottoman–Islamic law.[22]

Other scholars engaged in detailed discussions of doctrinal problems that Republican jurists had taken over from their Ottoman predecessors. Ali Aslan Topçuoğlu, for example, has demonstrated in fascinating detail that the legal confusion that continues to surround the inheritance of property following the declared death of a missing person is the same in the Republic as it was in the Ottoman period. What differences appear to exist, he argues, have to do more with changing technology than with changing law. According to Topçuoğlu's research, both the doctrine and its *interpretation* are a legacy of late Ottoman interpretations of, in

[22] Ruth A. Miller, "The Ottoman and Islamic Substratum of Turkey's Swiss Civil Code," *Journal of Islamic Studies* 11, no. 3 (September 2000): 342–344, 350–353.

particular, Hanafi practice.[23] Republican law in its most mainstream, day-to-day, and acceptable manifestations draws, according to his writing, on a dynamic, functional, Ottoman–Islamic past.

Still others working with this first set of methodological tools have noted how the built environment of the Turkish Republic reflects a distinctly Islamic legal mindset—echoing, they suggest, Ottoman–Islamic attitudes toward construction, residence, and zoning. The residences that make up the shantytowns that surround many of Turkey's cities, for example—called *gecekondus*, or literally, "settled at night"—have received much scholarly attention over the past decades from sociologists, anthropologists, and historians. Legal scholars too have found the *gecekondu* a topic of interest because the legality of the domicile built overnight is tied directly back to Ottoman theory and practice. Ottoman–Islamic doctrine held that any residence built between sunset and sunrise could not be removed by state actors, and Ottoman legal practice respected this rule. Turkish Republican practice also respects it, and thus the *gecekondu* settlements remain for the most part protected. Whereas earlier scholarship referred to the legal "loophole" that made *gecekondus* possible[24]—suggesting that Republican law had somehow not efficiently eradicated this outdated element of Ottoman–Islamic legal practice—more recent writing has been less dismissive. Increasingly, scholars are making the case that the *gecekondu* is one more, now *physical*, example of a quite official Ottoman–Islamic law at work in the Republic.[25]

Once scholars had begun to accept the possibility that even the Turkish landscape might reflect an Ottoman legal legacy, writing on the topic became more confident. The earliest work on the persistence of Ottoman–Islamic law in Turkey, remember, had simply sought examples of Ottoman doctrine lurking in Turkish law. Later, however, historians began to suggest that Republican Turkish jurisprudence did not just accidentally inherit, but actively worked to accommodate, earlier Ottoman–Islamic theory, doctrine, and practice. This new approach, in turn, produced a new set of methodological tools.

In addition to engaging in close readings of legal texts, for example, scholars seeking evidence of an ongoing, dynamic Ottoman law are now also attempting more holistic descriptions of this active, multifaceted legal system. Taking as a given that Republican law is to some extent a product of its Ottoman–Islamic predecessor, these scholars have been asking how, then, these legal systems have worked together,

[23] Asi Aslan Topçuoğlu, "İslâm Hukuku ve Türk Medenî Kanunu Bağlaminda Gâibin/Mefkûdun Hükmen Ölü Sayilmasi Sonucunda Mallarinin Hukukî Durumu," *Ekev Akademi Dergisi* 8, no. 10 (Spring 2004): 159, 176.

[24] Andreas Philippopoulis-Mihalopoulos, *Law and the City* (London: Routledge, 2007), 60 (citing a well-established narrative).

[25] Umut Duyar-Kienast, *The Formation of Gecekondu Settlements in Turkey: The Case of Ankara* (New Brunswick: Transaction Publishers, 2005), 78.

how they have become syncretic, and how they have accommodated one another. The narrative has become a narrative of legal pluralism rather than of opposition, destruction, or danger. Islamic law is not the thing that erases Turkish sovereignty, jurisdiction, or citizenship; it is in this most recent scholarship a pillar of Turkish legal theory and practice.

Yılmaz, for example, has shown not only that Ottoman–Islamic doctrine has influenced Republican Turkish doctrine on marriage and divorce, but that Islamic jurisprudence can add legal value to civil marriage and divorce proceedings. Noting that jurists working within the Islamic tradition have already accepted the validity of civil marriage provided it follows Islamic norms, Yılmaz continues that a conversation is currently developing among these jurists as to whether civil divorce is equally valid under Islamic law. Yılmaz, in other words, is inverting the traditional question of whether Republican law can or cannot accept or incorporate Islamic law into its framework. Islamic law is, in his work, already part of the framework. And indeed, he suggests that what is of interest now is the *exchange* or *dialogue* among the systems—in this case whether Republican norms are valid in an *Islamic* context.[26] It has become possible, that is to say, for scholars to discuss Islamic law in Turkey not only as a threat to an existing legal regime, not only as an unacknowledged secret within legal doctrine, but as an integral element of Turkish legal discourse.

İhsan Yılmaz approaches the syncretic, rather than dysfunctional, quality of Turkey's Ottoman–Islamic legal inheritance from a different direction. Developing a fascinating theory of "dynamic legal pluralism,"[27] Yılmaz explains how the Turkish legal system as a *whole* has accommodated aspects of Islamic law that it inherited from the Ottoman Empire. Yılmaz begins, it is true, by noting that Islamic legal practices remain, according to mainstream political rhetoric, both unofficial and idiosyncratic. The widely accepted assumption among Turkish jurists, he emphasizes, is that Islamic law operates impressionistically and in competition with the official, uniform Republican law that was adopted by Turkey's founders.[28]

After making this point, however, Yılmaz demonstrates that these practices, though local or idiosyncratic, are also pervasive—not just part of a frequently discounted "rural" backwater, but widespread in middle class urban communities, and common to all branches of law.[29] Moreover, and more importantly, Yılmaz shows

[26] İbrahim Yılmaz, "Türk Medeni Kanunu'na (TMK) Göre Gerçekleşen Boşanmaların İslâm Hukuku Açısından Değerlendirilmesi," *Islam Hukuku Araştırmaları Dergisi* 14 (2009): 268, 288.

[27] İhsan Yılmaz, *Muslim Laws, Politics, and Society in Modern Nation States: Dynamic Legal Pluralisms in England, Turkey, and Pakistan* (Aldershot: Ashgate, 2005), 26.

[28] İhsan Yılmaz, "Non-recognition of Post-modern Turkish Socio-legal Reality and the Predicament of Women," *British Journal of Middle East Studies* 30, no. 1 (2003): 28.

[29] Yılmaz, "Non-recognition," 29, 33.

how these unofficial practices *become* formal, not necessarily through legislative change, but through constitutional and sometimes executive accommodation. He describes, in other words, a system that is flexible enough to maintain *both* a Republican ideology of secularism *and* a functional combination of Republican, Ottoman, and Islamic legal theory, doctrine, and practice.

One of the most striking examples that Yılmaz presents of this dynamic legal pluralism at work in Turkey, for instance, appears in his discussion of how Turkish courts and Turkish parliament deal on a daily basis with the outcome of unofficial polygamous marriages. Although not common—the proportion remains the same 2 to 3 percent across the population that it was in the late Ottoman period[30]—polygamous marriages continue to exist in Turkey, where a first wife is contracted under civil law and a second wife under religious law. Although polygamous marriages are both criminal and unrecognized, Yılmaz notes that Turkish judges, if approached, more often than not grant inheritances to second wives as if these wives had been formally married.[31] Similarly, Yılmaz writes, Turkish parliament periodically passes amnesty laws that allow, first, the registration of "consensual marriage," and second, the legitimization of children born to these marriages.[32] Rather than seeking "to improve the legal status of the illegitimate child," Yılmaz concludes, "in Turkey, the legislator has provided for the legitimization not only of the child, but also of the extra-marital union from which the child has been born."[33]

In this way, although polygamy remains officially illegal in Turkey—and indeed, a flashpoint in the modern, imperial civilizational rhetoric that the Republican adoption of European codes sought to rebut—the legal system as a whole accommodates it and other Islamic legal practices. Law in Turkey, according to narratives such as Yılmaz's, is functional *because* it is multifaceted. It works *because* it has never been a bulwark against inroads etched out by something called *şeriat*. Or, as those who have traced the legacy of Ottoman–Islamic legal *doctrine* in Turkey have suggested, there has never been a purely Republican civil law that could be undermined by an alien Islamic interloper. Republican Turkish practice, theory, *and* doctrine, in this account, have always incorporated Islamic norms and ideals. And, as İbrahim Yılmaz notes, Turkish legal discourse also seems increasingly attuned to the interplay, rather than collision, of Islamic law and Republican law. Scholarship on the Republic's inheritance of Ottoman–Islamic law, in short, has helped to frame new conversations about legal functionality in a twenty-first-century Turkish nation-state.

[30] Ibid., 31.
[31] Ibid., 33, 36.
[32] Ibid., 34.
[33] Ibid.

IV. Distinctive Republican Interpretations of Islamic Law

Not all scholars of Turkish–Islamic law, however, have been convinced that this syncretic or plural system is in fact indebted to Ottoman theory and practice. Indeed, many have made the case that Republican jurists *did* successfully rid themselves of Ottoman legal norms—only, however, to cultivate a new, now distinctively *Republican* variation on *şeriat*. In general, this work falls into two categories. The first describes Islamic law in Turkey as a specifically Turkish product—the direct, if paradoxical, result of Republican secular ideology. The second links Islamic law, and especially Islamic legal theory, in Turkey to transnational trends, and especially to either modernist or postmodernist *salafi* interpretation or continental law-derived critiques of *salafiyya*. This second theme in the scholarship, whether critical or supportive, locates contemporary Turkish theories of Islamic law within ongoing debates concerning the validity of *salafi* as opposed to *mezhep* (*madhhab*)-based legal interpretation.

In his recent book, *Ottoman Ulema, Turkish Republic: Agents of Change and Guardians of Tradition*, for example, Amit Bein challenges earlier narratives of a moribund, and then eventually nonexistent, ulema corps in the late Ottoman Empire and Turkish Republic. Demonstrating the active, versatile, and complex role of nineteenth-, twentieth-, and twenty-first-century Ottoman and Turkish religious scholars, Bein makes clear that secularism in the Turkish Republic is more problematic than much historical and political writing on Turkey has till now suggested. In this sense, his research falls comfortably into the category of scholarship seeking out Ottoman antecedents to ongoing issues in Turkish law, society, and politics.

Bein's analysis of the role of Islamic *law* in the Republican period, however, departs from this earlier scholarly trend. He makes a cogent case that neither Islamic legal interpretation nor the discourse surrounding Islamic law in Turkey is solely an Ottoman inheritance, but rather that each is a Republican invention—or at the very least a Republican *re*invention of a problem of Ottoman law. Unlike their Ottoman predecessors, Bein writes, Republican Turks who have advocated the establishment or re-establishment of Islamic law have drawn heavily on, first, a Republican vocabulary of secularism, and second, Republican categories of comparative civilizational analysis.

Far from rejecting Republican ideologies altogether, for example, he states that religious legal scholars have historically made the case that a proper *secularism* lends itself to an accommodation with, rather than rejection of, *şeriat*. Moreover, invoking the same European model as their anti-*şeriat* opponents, Turkish advocates of Islamic law have argued that from the earliest days of the Republic "legislation in Turkey could and should rely on Sharia law just as there are many articles of law based on Christian jurisprudence and customs in all the civil law codes of the secular West."[34] Bein demonstrates, in other words, that the interpretive battle over the proper place of Islamic law in Turkey concerned not the nature of *şeriat* but the nature of Republican ideology. Republican Turkish advocates of Islamic law mobilized a uniquely Republican Turkish vocabulary. Or, as he concludes, the conversation surrounding the proper place of Islamic law in the Turkish Republic "hybridized ideals and idioms from late Ottoman times with new Republican vocabulary. Demands for 'genuine' secularism and democracy went along with insistence on favorable positions for Sunni Islam and Islamic legal injunctions."[35]

Bein thus finds antecedents in the rhetoric of early Republican jurists and religious scholars to what has become a powerful theme in contemporary religious politics in Turkey. The notion that accommodating Islamic law is more democratic, more liberal, more European, and indeed more *secular* than rejecting or criminalizing it has been a key platform of many of the political parties that have been banned over the past decades in Turkey. More than this, though, Bein also demonstrates that to the extent Islamic law does operate in the Republic, this law is assumed by many observers to be very much local or unique to the Turkish context. It is local and unique because it is fluid, existing to meet the needs of specific, small communities, and—perhaps more importantly—because it is *Republican*. The Islamic law, or the discourse surrounding Islamic law, that Bein sees operating since the establishment of the Republic is not a transnational, imperial, or delocalized mode of interpretation or practice. On the contrary, it is emphatically territorial, and emphatically embedded in Turkish Republican ideology.

The second theme in the literature that describes a new, rather than inherited, Islamic law at work in the Republic, however, comes to different conclusions about its characteristics. Rather than emphasizing the local or territorial qualities of Turkish *şeriat*, this writing instead links it to transnational trends in Islamic jurisprudence. Murteza Bedir, for example, draws on the writing of local, Turkish jurists and scholars in order to make the case that *fıkıh* (*fiqh*) has lost meaning across the Muslim world as it has been increasingly expressed in a vocabulary of continental European law. Bedir argues, in contrast to Bein, that Republican revolutionaries did successfully eradicate *şeriat* from the Turkish political and legal landscape, and that Islamic law in Turkey today has little to do with either Ottoman legacies or religiously inflected reinterpretations of Republican ideology. It was only after the 1950s, Bedir writes, that Islamic law once again became a topic of study, much less practice, in Turkey—and by that time, any lingering local, Ottoman, *or* Turkish variation on *şeriat* had disappeared. Students of Islamic law in Turkey thus preferred

[34] Amit Bein, *Ottoman Ulema, Turkish Republic: Agents of Change and Guardians of Tradition* (Stanford: Stanford University Press, 2011), 142.

[35] Ibid., 143.

to look to "the post-independence ideology of Islamism of the wider Islamic and Arabic world."[36]

Bedir is unsympathetic, however, to recent modes of legal interpretation that have arisen, in Turkey or elsewhere, in response to these Islamist political goals. Both the work critical of Islamism that appears in "the legal profession and law schools [that] have adopted the European style of writing," and the work of "Islamists" themselves, who "have tended to be anti-*mezheb* and *selefi* [*salafi*]," are as misguided, to Bedir, in Turkey as they are in other contexts.[37] Bedir indeed makes a strong case that both styles of interpretation misunderstand, misinterpret, and unintentionally undervalue *fıkıh* as a mode of jurisprudence that eludes modernist categorization.[38] Significantly, though, he also links these two, related trends in transnational Islamic jurisprudence to an ongoing Republican conversation about the nature of *fıkıh* as well as *şeriat*.

Bedir takes nearly all of his examples of the jurists who join in these conversations—whether, in his view, they do so appropriately or not—from Turkish legal studies. Indeed, although he posits a break between Ottoman and Republican legal interpretation, Bedir concludes his discussion with a reference to what he argues is a very well-established tradition in Turkey—a tradition that started with the first Ottoman justice minister and compiler of the 1876 Ottoman Mecelle, Ahmet Cevdet Paşa, and that had not concluded by the time the Republican Turkish scholar of Islamic law, Hayrettin Karaman, wrote in the 1970s and 1980s—of improperly redefining *fıkıh* as modernist law. Bedir describes Turkey, in other words, as an important battleground for arguments about the validity of classical interpretation, interpretation in line with continental law, and *salafi* interpretation. For Bedir, it is precisely *because* of Turkey's unique Republican history that these ongoing conversations concerning appropriate interpretation have salience there. Turkey is particularly well-suited to debates on Islamic jurisprudence *because* of its territoriality and ideology.

This last trend in writing on Islamic law in Turkey, then, both departs from and develops themes that appeared in earlier writing on *şeriat*. Islamic law is by no means described as a threat in this scholarship, and it certainly has legal value—if not the specific, concrete, and doctrinal legal value that it had in the second trend in the literature. But the Islamic law that writing such as Bein's and Bedir's presents to readers also lends itself less easily to legal pluralism than the law that some have assumed simply carried over from Ottoman times. In both Bein's and Bedir's analyses, Turkish Islamic law is as young as the Republic, and as such, it demands a critical distance or skepticism that a familiar or well-worn post-Ottoman Islamic law might not.

[36] Murteza Bedir, "*Fıkıh* To Law: Secularization Through Curriculum," *Islamic Law and Society* 11, no. 3 (2004): 393.

[37] Ibid., 394. [38] Ibid., 400.

This new variation on Islamic law in Turkey, indeed, could be either demonized as a manipulation of Republican rhetoric, or accommodated—if it is possible to reinterpret Republican ideology in these directions—as a vibrant manifestation of this rhetoric. Likewise, it could be rejected as an anti-territorial and Islamist or as an imperial and European import—that either way damages appropriate modes of Islamic jurisprudence along with Turkish sovereignty—or it could be embraced as a prime example of what Turkish Republican practice has always sought to do, situating Turkey at the center of Asian and European political and legal discourse. This final trend in scholarship on Turkish Islamic law, therefore, leaves open a series of fascinating questions as to the implications of a simultaneously local and outward looking, a simultaneously territorial and transnational, and a simultaneously classical, continental, and *salafi*, interpretation of a relentlessly relevant Turkish *şeriat*.

V. Conclusion: Turkish Islamic Law or Just Islamic Law?

Let us return to the point at which we started: the Turkish Republic is a secular Republic, and there is no official Islamic law in Turkey. Yet, as the past three to four decades of writing on Turkish history, Turkish law, and more pointedly, Turkish Islamic law have made clear, *şeriat* has a dynamic life in the Turkish Republic that the earliest Republican ideologues would likely not have conceded. Indeed, we can see a clear move in the historiography away from ignoring its presence and toward describing it as a plural and multidimensional set of theories and practices.

In the earliest days, scholars accepted Republican progress narratives and assumed the total absence of *şeriat* in Turkey's political and legal landscape. From there, some began to question whether eradicating an embedded legal culture is even possible. Having taken these steps, commentators, first, granted Islamic law a rhetorical and ideological—but not legal—presence in Turkey; second, recognized the theoretical but not doctrinal force of *şeriat*; and finally, third, began to excavate what appeared to be Ottoman norms and practices that lingered both in informal discourse or practice and formal doctrine and judgment. Now, scholars have begun to consider the possibility that Islamic law in Turkey has actually been the product of a specifically Republican environment rather than existing as a historical vestige that simply could not be removed. Turkish *şeriat*, in other words, has now come into its own. It is not only very much present in Republican Turkey, but it is a Republican Turkish invention.

Alongside these shifts in the historiography of Islamic law in Turkey has been a likewise increasingly sophisticated analysis of *şeriat*'s moral value. The earliest writing—even as it abandoned the Republican myth of total absence—reinforced Republican narratives of Islamic law as a threat to the state, and in particular as a threat to sovereignty, citizenship, and the rule of law. To the extent Islamic law became naturalized, accepted as part of a shared Ottoman and Turkish history, however, this fear of *şeriat* began to give way. A second, and continuing, theme in scholarship on Islamic law in Turkey, in fact, is that this law displays the *functionality* of Turkish legal culture—the pluralistic rather than authoritarian quality of law and politics in the Republic. The shift in historiography, in other words, set the groundwork for a shift in politics—away from fear and toward affirmation.

Moreover, although the third major theme in scholarship on Islamic law has been less optimistic about the political force of *şeriat* as a specifically Republican product, it has certainly not returned to the idea that Islamic law is a menace to the state. Rather, taking the religious quality of this law as something of a given, this scholarship has begun to reconsider Turkish law as one part of an Islamic jurisprudence that is increasingly transnational and even de-territorialized. This scholarship has placed Turkey at the center of an ongoing, global conversation about proper interpretations and applications of a rapidly changing Islamic legal discourse.

A possible new development in research on *şeriat* in Turkey, in fact, might concern this alternative spatial perspective on Turkish law—it might consider *şeriat*'s non-territorial, rather than its non-secular, character. Scholars of Turkish law and politics, that is to say, might now begin to examine Islamic law as something that *is* Turkish, but not necessarily *in* Turkey. And in turn, such a trend in the research might revisit and recontextualize some of the conclusions that earlier scholars of *şeriat* in the Republic have drawn. For example, this writing might ask whether the threat that Islamic law poses to Turkish sovereignty—if it *does* pose a threat—might always have been the result of its de-territorializing potential rather than its de-secularizing potential. This research might begin to question, in other words, whether religion and secularism are really the proper focus of conversations concerning Islamic law as Turkey's constitutional demon.

Similarly, a new generation of scholars might ask whether the legal legacy that Turkey inherited from its Ottoman predecessor had less to do with a particular style of religious expression than it had to do with an affinity to permeable borders and boundaries. Perhaps the *Ottoman*-Islamic law that, some have argued, continues to operate in Turkey has never been bounded in the radical way that the law of modern nation-states is supposed to be bounded. Perhaps it will never lend itself to complete territorialization.

Finally, scholars might begin to ask whether Turkish law broadly defined has truly been the result of the relentless, failed comparisons with European models that an earlier generation of scholars claimed it to be. Perhaps, indeed, this law—in its dynamic and functional manifestations—has derived as much or more from repeated, productive intersections among classical, continental, and even *salafi* interpretation of *şeriat*. As research on Islamic law in Turkey develops, in other words, it might become possible to paint the Republic as the traditional "crossroads" that revolutionary rhetoric has always claimed it to be—even the character of this crossroads is quite different from what so many modernist, territory-obsessed revolutionaries dreamed it might be.

References

Ahmad, Feroz, *The Making of Modern Turkey* (London: Routledge, 1993).

Ansay, Tuğrul and Don Wallace Jr., *Introduction to Turkish Law* (The Hague: Kluwer Law International, 2005).

Armutçu, Oya, "Erbakan, 'Şeriat Mahkemesi' Kurdurmuş." *Hürriyet*, February 13, 1999.

Balı, Aslı Ü., "The Perils of Judicial Independence: Constitutional Transition and the Turkish Example." *Virginia Journal of International Law* 53 (2012): 235–320.

Bedir, Murteza, "*Fıkıh* To Law: Secularization Through Curriculum." *Islamic Law and Society* 11, no. 3 (2004): 378–401.

Bein, Amit, *Ottoman Ulema, Turkish Republic: Agents of Change and Guardians of Tradition* (Stanford: Stanford University Press, 2011).

Çakır, Ruşen, *Ne Şeriat Ne Demokrasi: Refah Partisini Anlamak* (Istanbul: Metis, 1994).

Constitution of the Republic of Turkey. Ankara: Türkiye Büyük Millet Meclisi, 1995, http://global.tbmm.gov.tr/docs/constitution_en.pdf.

Duyar-Kienast, Umut, *The Formation of Gecekondu Settlements in Turkey: The Case of Ankara* (New Brunswick: Transaction Publishers, 2005).

Karpat, Kemal, ed., *Ottoman Past and Today's Turkey* (Leiden: Brill, 2000).

Landau, Jacob M., *Radical Politics in Modern Turkey* (Leiden: Brill, 1974).

Lewis, Bernard, *The Emergence of Modern Turkey* (New York: Oxford University Press, 2002 [1961]).

Mardin, Şerif, "Center-Periphery Relations: A Key to Turkish Politics?" *Daedalus* 102, no. 1 (Winter 1973): 169–190.

Miller, Ruth A., "The Ottoman and Islamic Substratum of Turkey's Swiss Civil Code." *Journal of Islamic Studies* 11, no. 3 (September 2000): 335–361.

Philippopoulis-Mihalopoulos, Andreas, *Law and the City* (London: Routledge, 2007).

Saktanber, Ayşe, *Living Islam: Women, Religion, and the Politicization of Culture in Turkey* (New York: Palgrave Macmillan, 2002).

Starr, June, *Law as Metaphor: From Islamic Courts to the Palace of Justice* (Albany: State University of New York Press, 1992).

Tapper, Richard, *Islam in Modern Turkey: Religion, Politics, and Literature in a Secular State* (London: I.B. Tauris, 1991).

Tezcür, Güneş Murat, "Constitutionalism, Judiciary, and Democracy in Islamic Societies." *Polity* 39, no. 4 (October, 2007): 479–501.

Tezcür, Güneş Murat, *Muslim Reformers in Iran and Turkey* (Austin: University of Texas Press, 2010).

Topçuoğlu, Ali Aslan, "İslâm Hukuku ve Türk Medenî Kanunu Bağlaminda Gâibin/Mefkûdun Hükmen Ölü Sayilmasi Sonucunda Mallarinin Hukukî Durumu." *Ekev Akademi Dergisi* 8, no. 10 (Spring 2004): 157–176.
White, Jenny B., *Islamist Mobilization in Turkey: A Study in Vernacular Politics* (Seattle: University of Washington Press, 2002).
Yavuz, M. Hakan, *Islamic Political Identity in Turkey* (Oxford: Oxford University Press, 2003).
Yavuz, M. Hakan, "Ethical Not Shari'a Islam: Islamic Debates in Turkey." *Review of Faith and International Affairs* 10, no. 4 (2012): 28–34.
Yılmaz, İbrahim, "Türk Medeni Kanunu'na (TMK) Göre Gerçekleşen Boşanmaların İslâm Hukuku Açısından Değerlendirilmesi." *Islam Hukuku Araştırmaları Dergisi* 14 (2009): 267–290.
Yılmaz, İhsan, "Non-recognition of Post-modern Turkish Socio-legal Reality and the Predicament of Women." *British Journal of Middle East Studies* 30, no. 1 (2003): 25–41.
Yılmaz, İhsan, *Muslim Laws, Politics, and Society in Modern Nation States: Dynamic Legal Pluralisms in England, Turkey, and Pakistan* (Aldershot: Ashgate, 2005).

CHAPTER 27

ISLAMIC LAW IN SOUTH ASIA

A TESTAMENT TO DIVERSITY

JEFF REDDING

ISLAMIC law in South Asia is a testament to the wide diversity of both Muslims and non-Muslims alike in South Asia. This is not surprising, given that South Asian Muslims live in a wide variety of national and sub-national contexts, and also have historically come to be Muslim in South Asia in a number of different ways, namely migration, heritage, and conversion (often from Hinduism).[1]

This article explores and explains this historical and contemporary diversity, and its several influences on the development of Islamic law in South Asia. It will do so through an examination of a number of different South Asian Islamic trajectories, resulting in distinct but overlapping understandings and practices of Islamic law in the contemporary nations of Pakistan, Bangladesh, and India. Together, these three South Asian countries represent approximately five hundred million Muslims, or

[1] See generally Gauri Viswanathan, *Outside the Fold: Conversion, Modernity and Belief* (New Jersey: Princeton University Press, 1998), 153–176 for an account of historical, colonial-era discussions of the Hindu origins of many adherents of Islam in South Asia. See also Peter Hardy, "Modern European and Muslim Explanations of Conversion to Islam in South Asia: A Preliminary Survey of the Literature," in *Conversion to Islam*, ed. Nehemia Levtzion (New York: Holmes & Meier, 1979).

almost one-third of the entire global Muslim population.[2] The practice of Islamic law in South Asia then is of significance for Muslims around the globe, whether living in contexts where Muslims comprise an overwhelming majority of a nation's population (like in Pakistan), or where they live along aside a sizeable non-Muslim minority (such as in Bangladesh),[3] or where they themselves form a significant minority population (the situation in India).

To speak of South Asian Islamic law per se, or South Asian Muslims, in any aggregate sense simultaneously highlights and elides important distinctions and diversities. To be sure, the practice of Islamic law in South Asia draws heavily on discussions and dilemmas concerning Islamic law elsewhere, in both a geographical and historical sense. Indeed, some Muslims in South Asia, part of a larger Indian Ocean Muslim network extending to Yemen, still look to Arab lands for contemporary spiritual and community leadership and guidance.[4] However, that being the case, South Asian Islamic law can and should be considered distinct, seeing that the social, cultural, and political milieus in which it is presently situated are quite

[2] According to the Pew Forum on Religion and Public Life, there were approximately 1.6 billion Muslims living all over the globe in 2010. Pakistan had approximately 178 million Muslims (96.4 percent of Pakistan's population; 11 percent of the global Muslim population), India had approximately 177 million Muslims (14.6 percent of India's population; 11 percent of the global Muslim population), and Bangladesh had approximately 149 million Muslims (90.4 percent of Bangladesh's population; 9.2 percent of the global Muslim population). See generally Pew Research Center (Forum on Religion & Public Life), The Future of the Global Muslim Population: Projections for 2010–2030 (2011), available at http://www.pewforum.org/uploadedFiles/Topics/Religious_Affiliation/Muslim/FutureGlobalMuslimPopulation-WebPDF-Feb10.pdf.

[3] Specifically, I am referring here to Bangladesh's Hindu minority. Bangladesh's Hindu population is significant, but the precise percentage of Bangladesh's population which identifies as Hindu is contested. Most people concur that this percentage has shrunk dramatically since Partition in 1947, when huge numbers of Hindus fled (from what was then East Pakistan) to India. Nonetheless, in 1951, Bangladesh was still reported to be more than 20 percent Hindu; today, however, the figures are estimated at about half of that earlier percentage (or, roughly 10 percent). See Rema Nagarajan, "Door out of Dhaka," *The Times of India*, May 22, 2010, available at http://articles.timesofindia.indiatimes.com/2010-05-22/south-asia/28280481_1_hindus-bangladesh-minorities-census.

[4] For example, at the end of the sixteenth century, the Gujarat-centered community of Indian Muslim Bohras (part of the larger community of Tayyibi Shi'a Ismailis) split into two groups, Dawoodi Bohras and Sulaimani Bohras, in a dispute over the proper inheritance of the community's spiritual leadership. Sulaimani Bohras decided to follow a claimant to this position of leadership who was based in Yemen, while Dawoodi Bohras continued to adhere to the authority of the Indian-based claimant. The spiritual leader of the Sulaimani Bohra community is presently based in the south of the Arabian peninsula. See generally Farhad Daftary, *A Short History of the Ismailis* (Edinburgh: Edinburgh University Press, 1998), 188–189, 192–193. More historically too, the well-known Islamic legal scholar, al-Shawkani, was influential during the late eighteenth and early nineteenth centuries in both India and his native Yemen. See generally Daniel W. Brown, *Rethinking Tradition in Modern Islamic Thought* (Cambridge: Cambridge University Press, 1996), 25–27; Brinkley Messick, *The Calligraphic State: Textual Domination and History in a Muslim Society* (Berkeley: University of California Press, 1993), 42–45.

different from dominant contemporary Arab and Persian contexts.[5] Furthermore, South Asian Islamic law has been deeply influenced by the rather profound ruptures with classical Islamic legal traditions that this South Asian law has experienced as a result of South Asia's centuries-long interactions with British colonialism,[6] and now postcolonial nationalisms.

While South Asian Islamic law can and should be differentiated from other Islamic legal traditions—at least to the extent necessary to mitigate against the historical hegemony of Arab and Persian traditions within the Islamic legal canon[7]—to speak of "South Asian Islamic law" writ large is itself to ignore distinct Islamic legal traditions *within* South Asia. These distinct Islamic legal traditions come about as a result of different national, sub-national, and sectarian experiences with and understandings of Islamic law. This chapter will explore these different Islamic legal contexts, first starting with major sectarian differences in the understanding and practice of Islamic law in modern South Asia—differences occasionally so intense that a central question for South Asian Islamic legal practice has been "Who exactly is a Muslim?"—and then moving on to national divisions in these understandings and practices. The chapter will conclude with a discussion of where research and theoretical work about Islamic law in South Asia is particularly needed at this point in time; research on sub-national contexts, and the ways these contexts complicate an already complicated picture of South Asian Islamic law, will be the focus of the concluding section.

[5] That being the case, the discussion and study of Islamic law still suffers from a problem of focus that Asaf Fyzee, a renowned South Asian scholar and explicator of Islamic law, noted almost fifty years ago: "European studies [of Islam] suffer from exclusive preoccupation with the Arabic-speaking countries and with the problems of the cradle of Islam." Asaf A.A. Fyzee, *Cases in the Muhammadan Law of India and Pakistan* (Oxford: Clarendon Press, 1965), ix.

[6] See generally Scott Alan Kugle, "Framed, Blamed and Renamed: The Recasting of Islamic Jurisprudence in Colonial South Asia," *Modern Asian Studies* 35 (2001): 304, in which Kugle argues that British interference in the administration of Islamic law in colonial India "created a lens of texts, terms and experiences which continue to distort the view of shari'ah today." While Kugle's efforts to show how discussions of Islamic law in South Asia changed via the colonial experience are important and helpful, they leave one wondering how any contemporary discussions of the shari'a anywhere could escape being affected—or "distorted"—by non-shari'a actors, including the state.

[7] Justin Jones makes a similar methodological move in his recent manuscript on Shi'ism in colonial India when he notes how his study "seeks to move away from the ... assumption that modern religious developments in Shi'ism can only be discussed with primary reference to globalization and the enhancement of times to the Iraq-Persian heartland" and how his manuscript seeks to "chart ... the emergence of self-consciously 'Hindustani' or 'Indian' forms of Shi'ism, territorially grounded in the Indian subcontinent, with their own religious leadership and inventories of practice." Justin Jones, *Shi'a Islam in Colonial India: Religion, Community and Sectarianism* (Cambridge: Cambridge University Press, 2012), 20.

1. Sectarian Diversity

With respect to sectarian diversity, South Asian Muslims maintain a particularly rich sectarian tapestry, perhaps unmatched anywhere else in the Muslim world. Looking at this diversity in a relatively crude way, one can immediately observe that, with respect to Sunnis and Shi'as, South Asia has a relatively (compared to other regional contexts) diverse Muslim population, with approximately 87 percent of Pakistani and Indian Muslims being Sunni, and 13 percent being Shi'a.[8] Bangladeshi Muslims, however, are reported to be less than 1 percent Shi'a.[9]

However, as elsewhere in the world, there are many sub-divisions within both of these composite groups, with South Asian Sunnis being further divisible largely into Hanafis and Shafiites,[10] and South Asian Shi'as being divisible into Ithna Asharis (Twelvers) and Ismailis. However, even these groupings are often not the salient ones in South Asia, with Hanafis, for example, often further dividing themselves into Deobandis[11] and Barelvis,[12] and Ismailis usually being known more

[8] Again, according to the Pew Forum on Religion and Public Life, in an older 2009 report on global Muslim population statistics, both Pakistan's and India's Muslim populations are estimated to be approximately 87 percent Sunni (13 percent Shi'a), while Bangladesh's Muslims population is estimated to be more than 99 percent Sunni (<1 percent Shi'a). See generally Pew Research Center (Forum on Religion & Public Life), Mapping the Global Muslim Population: A Report on the Size and Distribution of the World's Muslim Population (2009), 39–41.

While giving these statistics here, it is important to emphasize that these statistics—indeed, these *kinds* of statistics—are widely contested because of the syncretic nature of many South Asian Muslims' identities and practices. For example, while nineteenth-century colonial census records indicated that only 3 percent of Muslims were Shi'a in the United Provinces—as the colonial Indian province of which Lucknow (itself approximately 25 percent Shi'a at the time) was the capital city was then known—Justin Jones notes that "the historical links between Shi'ism and state power meant that Shi'ism maintained a profound influence on *sharif* Muslim life and society in general." Jones, *Shi'a Islam in Colonial India*, 13. As a result, "[t]he very different concept of the Shi'a as a separate, clearly defined religious minority community makes sense only against the background of colonial knowledge and the 'politics of enumeration', by which the colonial administration attempted ... to definitively classify India's population on the basis of homogenous religious categories." Jones, 13.

[9] See generally Pew Research Center (Forum on Religion & Public Life), Mapping the Global Muslim Population: A Report on the Size and Distribution of the World's Muslim Population (2009), 39–41.

[10] See generally Barbara D. Metcalf, "A Historical Overview of Islam in South Asia," in *Islam in South Asia in Practice*, ed. Barbara D. Metcalf (New Jersey: Princeton University Press, 2009), 1–2 for a discussion of early (perhaps, in fact, while the Prophet Muhammad was still alive) contact between Arab traders and southwestern and southeastern coastal India (and also Sri Lanka). This early contact left a community of Muslims who follow Shafii jurisprudence, rather than the more predominant Hanafi jurisprudential communities who were established with the later (starting from the eleventh century) Central Asian conquest of the northern parts of South Asia. See generally Metcalf, "A Historical Overview of Islam in South Asia," 3–17.

[11] See generally Barbara D. Metcalf, *Islamic Revival in British India: Deoband, 1860–1900* (New York: Oxford University Press, 1982).

[12] See generally Usha Sanyal, *Devotional Islam and Politics in British India: Ahmed Riza Khan Barelwi and His Movement, 1870–1920* (Oxford: Oxford University Press, 1996). Sanyal notes that the "Barelvi"

particularly as either Khoja Ismailis or Bohras. As well, there are other significant groupings from a religio-legal perspective, including the Ahl-e-Hadees community, which distinguishes itself from other South Asian Muslim communities as a result of Islamic jurisprudential methodologies—resembling those of Middle Eastern Wahhabis—which this community utilizes.[13] While all of these groupings and subdivisions are ones recognized in South Asian Muslim circles, one has to be cautious in overemphasizing them considering that many South Asian Muslims' religious and *madhhabi*[14] identities and practices are fluid and syncretic[15]—so much so that even the boundaries between Islam and Hinduism are often difficult to decipher in South Asia.[16]

South Asian Muslim divisions are both longstanding—for example, the eleventh-century[17] split in the Shiʿa Ismaili community that ultimately led to the present-day Indian Muslim categories of "Khoja Ismaili" and "Bohra"—and also more recent—for example, the nineteenth-century split between Deobandis and Barelvis. Even more contemporarily, late nineteenth- and twentieth-century political and theoretical movements introduced further Islamic legal diversities, distinctions, and groupings, with some Muslims primarily aligning themselves with modernist[18] or progressive/feminist practices of Islamic law[19] (whether Sunni or Shiʿa in origin) and others aligning themselves with conservative/patriarchal practices, of whatever sectarian origin.

appellation is not one that members of this Sunni community themselves prefer, but rather 'Ahl-e Sunnat wa Jamaʿat. See Sanyal, *Devotional Islam and Politics in British India*, 8–9.

13 See generally Brown, *Rethinking Tradition in Modern Islamic Thought*, 27–32. Brown notes that "the two movements were sufficiently similar in general character to encourage the identification of both as Wahhābī. In fact they grew up quite independently of each other." Brown, *Rethinking Tradition in Modern Islamic Thought*, 27.

14 *Madhhab* is commonly translated as "school of law," and my use of it here is intended to denote the different schools of Islamic legal thought with which different Muslims ally themselves. However, *madhhabs* themselves contain much internal diversity, as my mention of the internal diversity of the Hanafi *madhhab* within South Asia, see the text accompanying nn. 11–12, suggests. See generally Peri Bearman et al., eds., *The Islamic School of Law: Evolution, Devolution, and Progress* (Cambridge, MA: Harvard University Press, 2005).

15 See n. 8.

16 See, e.g., Jonah Blank, *Mullahs on the Mainframe: Islam and Modernity among the Daudi Bohras* (Chicago: University of Chicago Press, 2001), 116 for a discussion of how Dawoodi Bohras, until relatively recently, had followed Hindu inheritance practices rather than Islamic legal ones. Similarly, until relatively recently, Bohras had not followed Islamic legal prohibitions against *riba* (or "interest") on loans. See Blank, *Mullahs on the Mainframe*, 197.

17 See generally Daftary, *A Short History of the Ismailis*, 106–107.

18 See generally Charles Kurzman, ed., *Modernist Islam (1840–1940): A Sourcebook* (New York: Oxford University Press 2002); Charles Kurzman, ed., *Liberal Islam: A Sourcebook* (New York: Oxford University Press 1998).

19 See, e.g., Justin Jones, "'Signs of Churning': Muslim Personal Law and Public Contestation in Twenty-first Century India," *Modern Asian Studies* 44 (2009): 175 (discussing the 2004–05 split of the All India Muslim Personal Law Board into rival boards, including a new All India Muslim Women's Personal Law Board).

Indeed, so varied are South Asian Muslim identities and practices, that a central question for Islamic jurisprudence in South Asia has been the question "Who is a Muslim?" This question is relevant for Muslim individuals and communities in light of the prevalence of endogamous marital and family patterns in South Asia, and also the state. Indeed, this very question provides the title of one of the first chapters in an influential mid-twentieth-century textbook on Islamic law (as applied by different South Asian states) compiled by renowned South Asian scholar and explicator of Islamic law, Asaf A.A. Fyzee.[20] This question was perhaps of intense interest to Fyzee himself, since he belonged to a very small sect of Ismaili Shiʿism which is known as the Sulaimani Bohra sect.[21] While Sulaimani Bohras see themselves as belonging to the larger Ismaili Shiʿa grouping, Sulaimani Bohras are distinguished from the more well-known Dawoodi Bohras[22] (as well as Khoja Ismailis), as each Bohra sect follows a different religious/community leader.[23]

Complicating the South Asian Islamic tapestry as well—with many particularly serious implications for both law and social peace—has been a relatively small[24] group of people who follow the teachings of a charismatic nineteenth-century Indian religious leader, Mirza Ghulam Ahmad; individuals belonging to this community are commonly known as "Ahmadis."[25] Ahmadis themselves claim to be Muslim, but given that their community's founder is widely perceived by others to have claimed for himself the status of a post-Muhammad, Muslim prophet,[26] a significant number of Muslims (whether in South Asia or elsewhere)[27] consider this group profoundly heretical.

[20] See Asaf A.A. Fyzee, *Cases in the Muhammadan Law of India, Pakistan and Bangladesh*, 2nd edn., ed. and rev. Tahir Mahmood (New York: Oxford University Press 2005). The first edition of this book was published in 1965.

[21] See Fyzee, *Cases in the Muhammadan Law of India, Pakistan and Bangladesh*, vii.

[22] See Blank, *Mullahs on the Mainframe*, for an ethnography of the Dawoodi Bohra community.

[23] See generally Daftary, *A Short History of the Ismailis*, 188–189 (explaining the sixteenth-century schism between Tayyibi Ismailis—already distinguished by the late eleventh century from Nizari Ismailis, who would later be known in India as Khoja Ismailis, and whose spiritual leader is the present-day Aga Khan—over the legitimate leadership of the community, into the Sulaimani and Dawoodi Bohra groupings). See also n. 4.

[24] The number of Ahmadis living in South Asia (and the world) is a notoriously politicized figure, as well as one very difficult to reliably measure given the widespread hostility that Ahmadis have experienced in South Asia. See text accompanying nn. 36–38.

[25] It is common to find members of this group referred to as "Qadianis" or "Quadianis" as well. See, e.g., n. 36 for the Constitution of Pakistan's use of the term "Qadiani." However, this appellation is widely considered derogatory by Ahmadis themselves.

[26] There are other interpretations of Mirza Ghulam Ahmad's "prophecy" available, and various subgroupings of Ahmadis who believe different things about his status as a prophet (or not). See generally Charles Kennedy, *Islamization of Laws and Economy: Case Studies on Pakistan* (Islamabad: Institute of Policy Studies, 1996), 143–173 (discussing theological nuances of different claims made by Mirza Ghulam Ahmad).

[27] See, e.g., Human Rights Watch, *In Religion's Name* (New York: Human Rights Watch, 2013) (discussing recent violence committed against religious minorities, including Ahmadis, in Indonesia), available at http://www.hrw.org/reports/2013/02/28/religion-s-name.

This majoritarian Muslim hostility against Ahmadis is longstanding. For example, one of the colonial-era Indian cases discussed in Fyzee's chapter on "Who is a Muslim?" concerns the prosecution of a Muslim woman for bigamy under section 494 of the Indian Penal Code. The first husband of the Muslim woman in question professed Islam but also had, at some point, decided to "adhere ... to Ahmediyan tenets."[28] Following this "adherence" by her first husband, the Muslim woman re-married, apparently thinking that her husband's change in beliefs (or "apostasy") had terminated her first marriage. Her first husband, however, had a different interpretation of the meaning and implications of his Ahmadi adherence and, as a result, pressed section 494 bigamy charges against her. Under colonial rule in South Asia, and the system of "personal law" enforced by the British, one's marital status—at least in the eyes of the state—was roughly determined by one's religion; for example, the colonial state applied (a version of)[29] Islamic family law to Muslims, and also ostensibly applied Hindu family law to Hindus, and so on and so forth for the other major Indian religious communities. Under many interpretations of Islamic law, both classical and as enforced by the colonial state at that time, a Muslim husband's apostasy automatically served to terminate a marriage with another Muslim.[30]

The question presented then by this 1922 Madras High Court case, *Narantakath v. Parakkal*,[31] was whether the accused woman's first husband's newfound affinity to Ahmadi teachings amounted to him becoming an apostate (or, *murtad*)[32] such that his and his wife's Muslim marriage was dissolved and the wife was free to re-marry—as she did—or whether there was no apostasy/dissolution and, as a result, the wife's re-marriage amounted to illegal bigamy. The colonial-era Madras High Court refused to find either that Ghulam Ahmad or Ahmadis had strayed from "the fundamental tenets of Islam,"[33] namely a monotheistic belief in Allah, and also a belief that Muhammad is his prophet, and also a belief in "the supreme authority of the Qur'an."[34] As a result, Muslim women like this wife became susceptible to bigamy convictions, even though in this particular case the High Court exercised mercy and refused to sustain a conviction against the wife in question.[35]

More recently, however, South Asian Ahmadis have had a much more difficult time claiming their Muslim bonafides than they did in 1922 in front of a British

[28] Fyzee, *Cases in the Muhammadan Law of India, Pakistan and Bangladesh*, 43.

[29] See n. 6 for a discussion of the Islamic qualifications of this body of law.

[30] See Muhammad Qasim Zaman, *The Ulama in Contemporary Islam: Custodians of Change* (New Jersey: Princeton University Press 2002), 29 for a discussion of how apostasy—of either the husband or wife—was understood to affect a Muslim marital union in colonial India, as well as under dominant traditions in the classical Hanafi school of Islamic legal thought.

[31] *Narantakath v. Parakkal*, (1922) 45 Mad. 986.

[32] See Fyzee, *Cases in the Muhammadan Law of India, Pakistan and Bangladesh*, 47 for the Madras High Court's use of the Urdu term "*murtad*."

[33] Ibid., 47. [34] Ibid., 49. [35] Ibid.

colonial Indian state court. Pakistan, in particular, stands out for its efforts to classify Ahmadis as outside of the Islamic fold, going so far as to declare, in its constitution, that Ahmadis are "non-Muslims."[36] Pakistan's constitutional treatment of Ahmadis has resulted from actions by both Islamic and secular[37] actors and has contributed to many other forms of Ahmadi censure, including social discrimination, physical violence, and even mass murder committed by different (state and non-state) actors against Ahmadis.[38]

Ahmadis clearly present many wrinkles for South Asian Islamic legal practice, whether by the state or by local, non-state religious leaders and communities.[39] Their status and treatment provide a particularly vivid example of the challenges facing both state and non-state legal actors in South Asia given the very diverse tapestry of South Asian Islam, and the uncertain and contested boundaries of that Islam.[40]

While more will be said about sub-national Islamic legal diversities in Section III of this chapter, it is worth mentioning here that some of the variations on Islam discussed in this section might be considered examples of sub-national diversities in South Asian Muslim populations and practices of Islamic law. For example, Shafiite Muslims in India are primarily found in the southern coastal areas of India, where historical trade with and migration from the Arabian peninsula (historically predominately Shafiite) were concentrated.[41] Similarly, many Twelver Shi'as in India

[36] Article 260(3) of the present Constitution of Pakistan defines a "non-Muslim" as follows: "[A] person who is not a Muslim and includes a person belonging to the Christian, Hindu, Sikh, Buddhist or Parsi community, a person of the Quadiani Group or the Lahori Group (who call themselves 'Ahmadis' or by any other name), or a Bahai, and a person belonging to any of the Scheduled Castes." A version of Article 260(3) was first added to the Constitution of Pakistan in 1974, as the Second Amendment to the 1973 Constitution; both this 1973 constitution and the Second Amendment were heavily shaped by then-Prime Minister Zulfiqar Ali Bhutto. The Second Amendment's definition of a Muslim was then reshaped by the Third Amendment in 1985, during General Zia-ul-Haq's military dictatorship; Zia-ul-Haq took power from Zulfiqar Ali Bhutto in a 1977 coup.

[37] It should be recalled that Pakistan's 1973 constitution was first amended to define "Muslim" in an exclusory way under Prime Minister Zulfiqar Bhutto's leadership. Bhutto's Pakistan Peoples Party was then widely characterized as a left-leaning, secular-oriented Pakistani political party. See also Asad A. Ahmed, "The Paradoxes of Ahmadiyya Identity: The Legal Appropriation of Muslim-ness and the Construction of Ahmadiyya Difference," in *Beyond Crisis: Reevaluating Pakistan*, ed. Naveeda Khan (India: Routledge, 2010), 275.

[38] See, e.g., Rizwan Mohammed and Karin Brulliard, "Militants Attack Two Ahmadi Mosques in Pakistan; 80 Killed," *The Washington Post*, May 29, 2010, available at http://www.washingtonpost.com/wp-dyn/content/article/2010/05/28/AR2010052800686.html.

[39] See, e.g., Naveeda Khan, "Mosque Construction or the Violence of the Ordinary," in *Beyond Crisis: Reevaluating Pakistan*, ed. Naveeda Khan (India: Routledge, 2010) for a discussion of how sectarian differences play into civil legal disputes concerning the (sectarian) control of particular mosques.

[40] For discussion of the ways in which one prominent South Asian theologian has drawn the boundaries between legitimate versus illegitimate pluralism in Muslim thought and identity, see Naveeda Khan, "Maulana Yusuf Ludhianvi on the Limits of Legitimate Religious Difference," in *Islam in South Asia in Practice*, ed. Barbara D. Metcalf (New Jersey: Princeton University Press, 2009).

[41] See generally Metcalf, *A Historical Overview of Islam in South Asia.*

live in northern India, in and around the state of Uttar Pradesh, where the city of Lucknow functioned as the seat of the eighteenth- and nineteenth-century Shi'a kingdom of Awadh (or Oudh). These general trends being noted, it is also worth emphasizing that all kinds of Sunnis, Shi'as, progressive Muslims, conservative Muslims, and Ahmadis live throughout South Asia, and no South Asian country or region has a total monopoly on any of these groupings.

II. National Diversity: Pakistan, Bangladesh, and India

Contemporary South Asian national divisions have introduced some of the most profound differences in day-to-day understandings and enforcements of Islamic law in South Asia. This section will explore these differences, but also suggest that there are as many continuities across the dominant, contemporary South Asian national jurisdictions as there are differences. Given that the focus in this section is on contemporary South Asian nations and their different (but overlapping) understandings and enforcements of Islamic law, the emphasis here is on the contemporary South Asian *states* that (in many ways) define the parameters of the nations discussed here, as well as these *states*' pronouncements on Islamic law. Any contemporary state's authority to pronounce upon Islamic law—and whether to consider such state pronouncements part of any properly Islamic legal canon in the first place—is deeply controversial within Muslim communities, including those in South Asia.[42] As a result, such controversies will be discussed briefly in what follows, especially as they have broken out in contemporary South Asia. However, a fuller discussion of the theological and legal issues implicit in such controversies is not the focus of this section.

With respect to South Asian national differences and looking at contemporary national diversity through the top-down lens of constitutionalism, one notices immediately perhaps that, unlike any of the other countries of South Asia discussed here, Pakistan has come to self-consciously define itself constitutionally through the lens of faith, calling itself an "Islamic Republic" in its most recent constitution (often known as the 1973 Constitution).[43] In doing so, Pakistan has fulfilled something of

[42] See generally Kugle, "Framed, Blamed and Renamed"; Matthew J. Nelson, "Islamic Law in an Islamic Republic: What Role for Parliament," in *Constitution-Writing, Religion, and Democracy*, eds. Asli Bali and Hanna Lerner (Cambridge: Cambridge University Press, 2017).

[43] Pakistan Constitution, art. 1.

the desire of one of its most vocal proponents and advocates during the closing days of British colonial rule, namely the theologian Maulana Abul Ala Maududi and his vision for a new Islamic legal category and phenomenon—that of *hukumat-e-ilahiya*, or "divine government."[44] Yet, simultaneously, contemporary Pakistan has also fallen far short of Maududi's vision of an Islamically divine state in light of the quite substantial amount of agency and power exercised by *humans* in running it. Conversely, Maududi "contended that *Allah* must ... be the 'Ruler, Dictator (amir), and Legislator' of the political domain."[45] While Maududi did theorize a role for ordinary Muslims in the administration of government, he simultaneously advocated sharp limitations on human agency vis-à-vis law-making.[46] As a result, contemporary Pakistan would likely be a disappointment for Maududi.

Bangladesh was initially part of Pakistan[47] after the British colonial government's exit from South Asia in 1947, but later parted ways with (West) Pakistan in 1971 after a bloody civil war that deeply called into question the importance and relevance of Pakistan's predominant Islamic religious identity—versus its internal lingual (Bengali vs. Urdu) and ethnic (chiefly Bengali vs. Punjabi) differences—for the purposes of constituting a republic.

Unsurprisingly then, Bangladesh at first rejected the idea of an "Islamic Republic." However, it did later introduce its own form of Islamic constitutionalism. The present-day Preamble to the Constitution of Bangladesh opens with the standard Islamic invocation "bismillah-ar-rahman-ar-rahim"[48] and then goes on to declare in part:

We, the people of Bangladesh, having proclaimed our independence on the 26th day of March, 1971 and, through a historic struggle for national liberation, established the independent, sovereign People's Republic of Bangladesh; Pledging that the high ideals of

44 See Irfan Ahmad, *Islamism and Democracy in India: The Transformation of Jamaat-e-Islami* (New Jersey: Princeton University Press, 2009) for more discussion of Maududi's vision for Pakistan, as well as Ahmad's translation of this expression as either an "Islamic state" (at 61), or, alternatively, "Allah's kingdom" (at 3). I prefer "divine government" as a translation of this expression given the otherworldly/non-human sources of power suggested by the word "divine," and also because Maududi's vision for Pakistan was decidedly modernist and not best captured by the medieval-sounding "kingdom."

45 Ahmad, *Islamism and Democracy in India*, 65 (emphasis added). See also Nelson, "Islamic Law in an Islamic Republic."

46 For example, Maududi wrote that "[e]very Muslim who is capable and qualified to give a sound opinion on matters of Islamic law, is entitled to interpret the law of God when such interpretation becomes necessary. But [my system of governance] is a theocracy in the sense that where an explicit command of God or His Prophet already exists, no Muslim leader or legislature ... can form an independent judgment." S. Abul Al'a Maududi, *Political Theory of Islam*, 5th edn, ed. and trans. Khurshid Ahmad (Lahore: Islamic Publications, 1976), 25.

47 Specifically, East Pakistan.

48 This (transliterated) Arabic invocation is followed by a common English translation of this invocation, namely "In the name of Allah, the Beneficent, the Merciful." Moreover, after the passage of the 2011 Fifteenth Amendment to the Constitution of Bangladesh, an additional English translation—perhaps one less Islamically imbued—was also inserted here, reading "In the name of the Creator, the Merciful." See http://bdlaws.minlaw.gov.bd/pdf_part.php?id=367.

nationalism, socialism, democracy and *secularism* [emphasis added], which inspired our heroic people to dedicate themselves to, and our brave martyrs to sacrifice their lives in, the national liberation struggle, shall be the fundamental principles of the Constitution.[49]

Article 2A of the Constitution of Bangladesh, most recently amended in 2011, declares that "[t]he state religion of the Republic is Islam," while also going on to declare that "the State shall ensure equal status and equal right in the practice of the Hindu, Buddhist, Christian and other religions."[50]

Unlike the constitutions of both Pakistan and Bangladesh, India's constitution contains no profession of a state religion. Simultaneously, it pronounces India a "Sovereign Socialist Secular Democratic Republic."[51] While India is officially and self-consciously secular, India's secularism is one that is widely commented upon, since it offers a different vision of the relationship between religion and state than many other prominent examples of secularism. For example, Indian secularism is not one predicated in American conceptions of *separation of church and state.* Indian secularism is also unlike French (and other European) articulations of *laicité* that often adopt an outright *hostile and domineering* stance toward religion. Instead, India's secularism is one in which the state engages in a delicate balancing act and "dance" with all of India's religious faiths. Most remarkably, this has come to mean that Indian (secular) state courts administer religious law in certain kinds of disputes. For example, India's state courts—populated by judges of all religious faiths—administer Islamic law (or, at least, a form of it often known as "Anglo-Muhammadan Law") for family law disputes involving Muslims. Again, this kind of administration of law is often known as a "personal law system."[52]

India, as a secular republic which officially enforces Islamic law for its very substantial Muslim population, demonstrates something of the surprising incongruities and complicated nature of contemporary national divisions and

[49] Bangladesh Constitution, Preamble (emphasis added). The 2011 Fifteenth Amendment to the Constitution of Bangladesh restored "secularism" as a "high ideal" here after this ideal was put under substantial pressure by a post-independence military regime in Bangladesh during the late 1970s. As a result of this regime, "secularism" was replaced as a constitutional priority with "absolute trust and faith in the Almighty Allah" in different parts of the constitution. See S. Mahmud, S. Ali, *Understanding Bangladesh* (New York: Columbia University Press, 2010), 141; Ali Riaz, "The Politics of Islamization in Bangladesh," in *Religion and Politics in South Asia*, ed. Ali Riaz (New York: Routledge, 2010), 48.

[50] Bangladesh Constitution, art. 2A. The Eighth Amendment to the Constitution of Bangladesh, legislated in 1988 during the military dictatorship of General Husayn Muhammad Irshad, articulated a state religion (Islam) for Bangladesh for the first time. See Rainer Grote, "Westminster Democracy in an Islamic Context: Pakistan, Bangladesh, Malaysia," in *Constitutionalism in Islamic Countries: Between Upheaval and Continuity*, eds. Rainer Grote and Tilmann J. Röder (New York: Oxford University Press, 2012), 454–455. The present Article 2A is the result of the 2011 Fifteenth Amendment to the Constitution of Bangladesh. See http://bdlaws.minlaw.gov.bd/sections_detail.php?id=367&sections_id=24549.

[51] India Constitution, Preamble.

[52] See generally Jeffrey A. Redding, "Slicing the American Pie: Federalism and Personal Law," *New York University Journal of International Law and Politics* 40 (2008): 957–961 (discussing what a "personal law system" is).

their relation to South Asian Muslims and Islamic law. As another example of this complexity, it should be noted that many Indian Muslim theologians rejected the call for the creation of an independent, sovereign Pakistani state in the first half of the twentieth century—including those affiliated with the globally influential Darul Uloom located in Deoband, India—and, in the process, developed an important Islamic legal neologism centered around the idea of *qaum* (or what has been described as "composite nationality").[53] Some of these theologians' primary ideological opponents included the aforementioned Maududi (who subsequently moved to Pakistan, post-Partition)[54] and also a prominent Shi'a Ismaili politician by the name of Mohammad Ali Jinnah, leader of the influential, colonial-era, All-India Muslim League political party and widely considered the "founding father" (in Urdu, the *baba-e-qaum*) of Pakistan. The Shi'a origins of modern-day, Sunni-dominated Pakistan[55] are yet another testament to the surprising incongruities and complicated nature of South Asian Muslims' contemporary national (and sectarian) divisions.

As much as the practice of Islamic law in South Asia is distinguished from other regions and historical periods by its *internal heterogeneity* then, there are also remarkable *transnational synchronicities* which emerge from an examination of the major contemporary South Asian Islamic legal traditions. These synchronicities manifest themselves in at least a couple of different ways. For one, despite the different ways that Pakistan, Bangladesh, and India have understood and implemented (or, in the case of India, have *not* implemented) Islamic constitutionalism, there are profound similarities in the ways that each contemporary state operates, whether in rights-oriented or authoritarian ways. Ayesha Jalal and Anil Kalhan have brought

[53] Among these religious thinkers was Maulana Husain Ahmad Madani, the principal of the Deoband Darul Uloom. Concerning Islam's tolerance of members of other religious faiths, and the ability of Muslims and non-Muslims to join together in the larger enterprise of *qaum* (nation), Madani famously wrote:

> Islam comprises the principles that underlie the rectitude of doctrinal, practical, and moral matters.... We must now consider whether Islam ... allows, on the basis of shared residence, race, color, and language, a shared nationalism with non-Muslims.... To the extent that I can understand its laws, [Islam] can live together with non-Muslims in the same country; it can be at peace with them; it can enter into treaties with them.... [Muslims] can interact with [non-Muslims], participate in matters of joy and grief, and dine with them.... There are countless laws and principles governing social order in Islam that reveal its consideration for and tolerance of others and that are not found in other religions.

See Zaman, *The Ulama in Contemporary Islam*, 34 (translating and quoting Husain Ahmad Madani, *Muttahida Qawmiyyat aur Islam* (1938)).

[54] See Ahmad, *Islamism and Democracy in India*, 63. Maududi apparently went so far as to refer to post-Partition India as "*dar al-kufr*," and also insisted that Pakistani Muslims, coming from a newly constituted "*dar al-Islam*," should not marry Muslims from the ostensibly infidel land of independent India. Ahmad, 78.

[55] Francis Robinson suggests that "the emergence of Pakistan was the last striking expression of Perso-Islamic values in India." Francis Robinson, *The Ulama of Farangi Mahall and Islamic Culture in South Asia* (London: Hurst Publishers Ltd., 2002), 40.

out some of the shared authoritarian tendencies of the Pakistani and Indian states in their work.[56]

Focusing on other synchronicities, some scholars have noted the ways in which (Islamic) family law is similarly operationalized in Pakistan, Bangladesh, and India alike, focusing in particular on how all three nations have inherited a great deal of modern-day legislation pertaining to Islamic (family) law and legal administration from their common British colonial overseer. For example, the 1937 Application of Shariat Act (declaring that "Shariat" would apply to Muslims in most areas of legal life) and, even more importantly, the 1939 Dissolution of Muslim Marriages Act, were legislated in British colonial India and remain in force (with some later additions and amendments) in present-day Pakistan, Bangladesh, and India.

The 1939 Dissolution of Muslim Marriages Act empowered state judges to issue fault-based (e.g. for reasons of abandonment, impotence, or cruelty) divorces for Muslim women married to Muslim men or, in other words, *faskh* divorces. While this 1939 Act is important with respect to its main object—namely, providing an avenue for Muslim women to divorce husbands who are either unable or unwilling to release these women from marriage—this Act is also noteworthy for what it represents about a South Asian Islamic legal jurisprudence that is not tied to *madhhabi* (or geographical) puritanism. Indeed, the 1939 Act has been the subject of much academic interest and commentary because of this Act's genesis in an influential Muslim theologian's openness to *takhayyur*,[57] thereby allowing Maliki *madhhabi* jurisprudence to heavily shape the 1939 Act despite colonial South Asia having a (Sunni) Muslim population which was predominantly Hanafi.

More broadly, Pakistan, Bangladesh, and India also share a British colonial legal infrastructure, whereby state judges administer Islamic law to Muslims in certain areas of legal life. This system of legal administration is known as a "personal law system," and it administers a form of Islamic law—often known as "Anglo-Muhammadan law"—for Muslims with respect to basic questions of family law and also *waqf* administration.

While debated in all three contemporary nations,[58] whether or not Anglo-Muhammadan law is "Islamic law proper" has been a particularly contentious issue

[56] See, e.g., Ayesha Jalal, *Democracy and Authoritarianism in South Asia: A Comparative and Historical Perspective* (Cambridge: Cambridge University Press, 1995); Anil Kalhan, "Constitution and 'Extraconstitution': Colonial Emergency Regimes in Postcolonial Pakistan and India," in *Emergency Powers in Asia: Exploring the Limits of Legality*, eds. Victor V. Ramraj and Arun K. Thiruvengadam (Cambridge: Cambridge University Press, 2010).

[57] See generally Muhammad Khalid Masud, "Apostasy and Judicial Separation in British India," in *Islamic Legal Interpretation: Muftis and their Fatwas*, eds. Muhammad Khalid Masud et al. (Cambridge, MA: Harvard University Press, 1996).

[58] For a discussion of this debate in Pakistan, see Matthew J. Nelson, "Islamic Law in an Islamic Republic: What Role for Parliament," in *Constitution-Writing, Religion, and Democracy*, eds. Asli Bali and Hanna Lerner (Cambridge: Cambridge University Press, 2017). Nelson identifies three major groupings in postcolonial Pakistan with respect to the proper locus of legitimate Islamic legality. The first group is represented by what Nelson terms "traditionalist" *muftis*, who generally share a "commitment to the

in India, where the vast majority of state judges (and other state officials) have been non-Muslim. In India, "the Shah Bano affair" in the late 1980s launched a particularly fevered debate concerning the propriety of non-Muslims deciding Islamic legal questions for Muslims. In this public controversy over a landmark, still widely discussed case,[59] the Supreme Court of India had to decide whether the Indian Code of Criminal Procedure's requirement that a man indefinitely financially maintain his ex-wife after a divorce if she is "unable to maintain herself"[60] was applicable to Muslim men, who supposedly have more limited responsibilities toward their ex-wives under classical Islamic family law. Ultimately, an overwhelming Hindu bench of the Supreme Court determined that 1) the secular Code of Criminal Procedure's requirements superseded any contradictory Muslim personal law rules and requirements and 2) nothing in Muslim personal law forbade indefinite maintenance to a divorced wife "who is unable to maintain herself."

Given that the first holding about the power of the state's own law was sufficient to have settled the case, many observers felt it was gratuitous and provocative for the Supreme Court to have interpreted Muslim personal law, especially given that other portions of the Court's Hindu-authored opinion took a patronizing tone with regard to the content of such personal law.[61] And indeed, this opinion ignited major protests by conservative Muslims across India[62]—protests which, in turn, set off a series of events which many observers believe ultimately (and ironically) led to the political and social empowerment of Hindu nationalism. Indian Muslims in general, and practitioners of Indian Islamic law in particular, have faced continuous scrutiny from this empowered Hindu nationalism for the past twenty-five years.[63]

autonomy of their fatwas [or, in other words] *a common commitment to the autonomy of the fatwa vis-à-vis the 'corrupting' influence of the state*." Nelson (emphasis in original). The second group Nelson terms "nationalists" who "combine … an appreciation for the unifying work of the state with an appreciation for the dynamic quality of the shari'ah"—a group who believes that non-state Islamic legal actors have a voice in debates about Islamic law but ultimately believe in the "*unfettered legislative power*" of the state, whether voiced through a monopolistic executive or more democratic parliament." Nelson (emphasis in original). Finally, the third group, which Nelson terms "Islamists," are best represented (at least in the Pakistani context) as adherents of Maududi's view of the Islamic state, namely one in which "state officials do not 'define' [or legislate] shari'ah; they merely seek to 'enforce' it." Nelson.

[59] The specific Supreme Court decision which ignited this public controversy is that of *Mohd. Ahmed Khan v. Shah Bano Begum* (1985) 3 S.C.R. 844.

[60] India Code of Criminal Procedure § 125(1)(a).

[61] See, e.g., *Mohd. Ahmed Khan v. Shah Bano Begum* (1985) 3 S.C.R. 844, at 849–850, where the majority opinion noted that "it is alleged that the 'fatal point in Islam is the 'degradation of woman.' To the Prophet is ascribed the statement, hopefully wrongly, that 'Woman was made from a crooked rib, and if you try to bend it straight, it will break; therefore treat your wives kindly.'"

[62] See Kirti Singh, "The Constitution and Muslim Personal Law," in *Forging Identities: Gender, Communities and the State*, ed. Zoya Hasan (Boulder: Westview Press, 1994), 101–103.

[63] See, e.g., Jeffrey A. Redding, "Secularism, The Rule of Law, and 'Shari'a Courts': An Ethnographic Examination of a Constitutional Controversy," *Saint Louis University Law Journal* 57 (2013): 339 (discussing a recent Hindu nationalist effort to convince the Supreme Court of India to shut down the Indian Muslim *dar ul qaza* system).

Partly as a result of the contemporary Muslim belief that Hindu nationalism is now deeply embedded within the Indian state, Muslim discomfort with Islamic law being pronounced by non-Muslims, and more recent problems relating to the extreme backlog in Indian courts,[64] Muslim non-governmental organizations around India have recently begun to accelerate the formation of non-state adjudicatory bodies for Muslims. The most widespread network of such non-state adjudicatory bodies is operated by the All India Muslim Personal Law Board (headquartered in Delhi), in conjunction with the Imarat-e-Shariah (based just outside of Patna, the capital of the eastern state of Bihar),[65] and is known as the *dar ul qaza* system. However, other Muslim organizations and individuals also operate similar bodies, with varying levels of organization and formality. Some of these bodies are coordinated by Muslim women's groups, and adopt interpretations and enforcements of Islamic law favorable to women's interests.[66] Whoever the coordinator, the vast majority of "cases" handled by these non-state Muslim dispute resolution bodies concern women's divorce claims.

Any "need" for non-state Islamic legal bodies is less of an issue in Pakistan and Bangladesh, where the vast majority of state judges (and other state officials) are Muslim. In Pakistan, a Council of Islamic Ideology, the Federal Shariat Court, and the Shariat Appellate Bench of the Supreme Court have been constitutionally established within the state, and each has various powers to review, suggest amendments to, and/or annul laws which run afoul of basic Islamic legal principles. Nonetheless, in Pakistan and Bangladesh alike, fierce disputes (including violent insurgency) have broken out as various Muslim groups in each of these countries have contested the Islamic legitimacy of the state. Indeed, the fact that the Islamic bonafides of state pronouncements on Islamic law have erupted in India, Pakistan, and Bangladesh suggests that controversies about South Asian states pronouncing on Islam are less about whether state law can be "Islamic law" than they are about different visions of what "Islamic law" is in the first place.

In this respect, in Muslim majority Bangladesh, the state system of law and courts recently felt it necessary to render ineffective and illegitimate the issuance of *fatawa* (sing. *fatwa*) and other legal opinions by non-state legal personalities. In the 2001

[64] See generally Jeffrey A. Redding, "Institutional v. Liberal Contexts for Contemporary Non-State, Muslim Civil Dispute Resolution Systems," *Journal Islamic State Practices International Law* 6 (2010): 1 (discussing how issues pertaining to the Indian state's judiciary's systemic problems have spurred the creation and expansion of the non-state *dar ul qaza* system).

[65] See generally Papiya Ghosh, "*Muttahidah qaumiyat in aqalliat Bihar*: The Imarat i Shariah, 1921–1947," *Indian Economic & Social History Review* 34 (1997): 1 (describing the historical roots of the *dar ul qaza* system in pre-Partition efforts, by a prominent (Muslim) Indian nationalist organization, to establish a separate system of Muslim governance within a united, independent India).

[66] See, e.g., Mengia Hong Tschalaer, "Competing Model-*Nikahnamas*: Muslim Women's Spaces within the Legal Landscape in Lucknow," *Journal of Law and Social Research* 3 (2012): 72 (discussing the appointment of a female *qazi* in the city of Lucknow by the All India Muslim Women's Personal Law Board).

High Court Division of the Supreme Court case of *Editor, The Banglabazar Patrika v. District Magistrate and Deputy Commissioner, Naogaon*, the High Court acted to control what it saw as the undermining of the Muslim Family Laws Ordinance (MFLO) of 1961—a law promulgated by General Ayub Khan when West Pakistan (now simply Pakistan) and East Pakistan (now Bangladesh) were still united, and a law which Bangladesh inherited and retained after its independence in 1971—by non-state Islamic legal personalities.[67] Under the MFLO, *talaq* divorces are regulated by the state, and can no longer be unilaterally pronounced by the male partner to a marriage without detrimental state legal consequences. Instead, male-initiated (*talaq*) divorces must be first filed by the husband with a state official who must try to effect a reconciliation between the husband and his wife. Notice must also be given to the affected wife, and a ninety-day waiting period must be observed before the divorce takes effect (assuming no reconciliation between the spouses is possible). The MFLO has been controversial for some time now in conservative Islamic circles in both Pakistan and Bangladesh, and the (successful) Bangladesh High Court Division suit was instituted to counteract the practice of conservative Bangladeshi *muftis* issuing *fatawa* declaring the MFLO un-Islamic, and also issuing *fatawa* giving Islamic religio-legal legitimacy to *talaq* divorces undertaken in contravention of the MFLO's requirements.

As this section has suggested, there are differences in Islamic law as operationalized in different South Asian national contexts, but also a number of profound similarities. Indeed, sometimes it is hard to know whether to categorize a given Islamic legal phenomenon—say, Islamic constitutionalism—as a marker of difference or similarity between the different contemporary national contexts, especially given the profound ways that Pakistan, Bangladesh, and India have been shaped by the experience of British colonialism. Indeed, not only constitutionalism, but the rule of law more generally, often seems to be more shaped by these three nations' shared experience of colonialism rather than any particular Islamic/secular performance engaged in.

This being the case, one particularly noteworthy difference vis-à-vis the enforcement of Islamic law that Pakistan exhibits is the Pakistani state's enforcement of (ostensibly) Islamic criminal law. In 1979, General Zia, Pakistan's longest-serving military dictator (1977–88) promulgated the "Hudood Ordinances." These state ordinances attempted to single out for punishment a number of criminal offenses which the Qur'an specifically designates as important to punish in specific ways.[68] While much attention and criticism was leveled at the Hudood Ordinances for

[67] See Alamgir Muhammad Serajuddin, *Muslim Family Law, Secular Courts and Muslim Women of South Asia: A Study of Judicial Activism* (Karachi: Oxford University Press Pakistan 2011), 210–212 for more discussion of and commentary on this case.

[68] For more discussion of the Hudood Ordinances and their impact on Pakistani women, see Shahnaz Khan, *Zina, Transnational Feminism and the Moral Regulation of Pakistan Women* (Vancouver: University of British Columbia Press, 2006).

their criminalization of heterosexual intercourse outside of marriage (whether pre-marital fornication or post-marital adultery), the Hudood Ordinances also singled out other offenses—such as falsely alleging someone's sexual impropriety (or *qazf*), drug and alcohol use, and theft—for "Islamic" *hadd* punishments. These punishments consisted of different variations on whipping, stoning, and dismemberment, depending on the particular offense and other particularities.

However, even here, it must be mentioned that, irrespective of the Hudood Ordinances, the Pakistani state has followed the example of many other states, including other South Asian states, in having already criminalized the offenses to which the Hudood Ordinances brought renewed attention. In other words, while the Pakistani state implemented new methods of "Islamic punishment" with the Hudood Ordinances, it did not necessarily develop new criminal offenses altogether with these laws. Pakistan, like other South Asian states, has inherited some version of the nineteenth-century, colonial-era Indian Penal Code which itself already criminalizes adultery, outraging the modesty of women, and theft.[69] Moreover, Pakistan, like other South Asian states, practiced (and continues to practice) the ultimate form of criminal punishment—namely, the death penalty—irrespective of the Hudood Ordinances.

Finally—and this will be returned to in the closing section—the boundaries between criminal and civil law are hazy ones in any jurisdiction, and perhaps especially so in South Asia.[70] As a result, it is possible to say that, in India, as in Pakistan, there is Islamic criminal law at work in the contemporary period. This is a result both of the "Islamic exception" to the Indian Code of Criminal Procedure that arose in the aftermath of the Shah Bano crisis, and also the complex interaction of non-state and state legal actors.[71]

[69] See India Penal Code § 497 (punishing anyone who "has sexual intercourse with a person who is and whom he knows or has reason to believe to be the wife of another man, without the consent or connivance of that man"); § 354 (punishing anyone who "assaults or uses criminal force to any woman, intending to outrage or knowing it to be likely that he will thereby outrage her modesty"); § 378 (punishing theft).

[70] This is certainly the case in criminal blasphemy/religious offense cases where important criminal legal questions turn on the religious identities and practices of the involved parties. See, e.g., § 296 of the Indian Penal Code which criminally penalizes anyone who "voluntarily causes disturbance to any assembly lawfully engaged in the performance of religious worship, or religious ceremonies." India Penal Code § 296. This criminal law provision was at issue in a well-known colonial-era Allahabad High Court case, that of *Queen Empress v. Ramzan*, concerning a sectarian dispute over legitimate Islamic religious expression in a mosque. In a recent work, Alan Guenther discusses and lays out an influential minority opinion filed in this case by Judge Syed Mahmood, son of the well-known nineteenth-century Islamic modernist Sir Syed Ahmad Khan, in which Mahmood notes how "the application of some of the sections of the Indian Penal Code depends almost entirely upon the correct interpretation of the rules of civil law." See Alan M. Guenther, "A Colonial Court Defines a Muslim," in *Islam in South Asia in Practice*, ed. Barbara D. Metcalf (New Jersey: Princeton University Press, 2009), 299.

[71] Gopika Solanki discusses this interaction of criminal and civil (family) law. See Gopika Solanki, *Adjudication in Religious Family Laws: Cultural Accommodation, Legal Pluralism, and Gender Equality in India* (Cambridge: Cambridge University Press, 2011), 221–223, 254–259, 270.

III. Sub-national Diversity and a Future Research Agenda

Pakistan and Bangladesh separated in 1971 in a bloody civil war, which is one testament to the extreme forms of Muslim diversity (and disagreement) which can and do exist within any one South Asian nation. One result of the 1971 civil war was the establishment of a "secular republic" in Bangladesh[72] and an "Islamic republic" in Pakistan, yet the internal diversity of each country's politics and populations belies such simplistic labels and typologies.

For example, in Pakistan, there are influential regional voices and political parties which have resisted the call for an "Islamic Pakistan" (narrowly conceived), both historically and contemporarily. For example, in the northwest of the country, the secular Awami National Party (ANP) is a small yet influential party based largely in Khyber Pakhtunkhwa province (formerly known as Northwest Frontier Province). In the south of Pakistan, in Sindh province, the Muttahida Qaumi Movement (MQM) political party (formerly known as the Mohajir Qaumi Movement party) has somewhat transformed itself from a narrow, Karachi-focussed political party primarily dedicated to the advancement (often violently) of Urdu-speaking, Partition-era migrants from India (popularly known as *mohajirs*) to a national political party with a commitment to a more federal, yet united (or *muttahida*), and liberal Pakistan.

Yet even here there are subtleties, with certain groups in the northwestern parts of Pakistan recently posing a deep threat to the hegemony of the Pakistani state. In particular, in 2009, militants operating in areas around Swat District in northwest Pakistan seized control of strategic territory and government buildings, and advanced to territory within an hour's drive of Islamabad, Pakistan's capital. While there were many reasons for this outbreak of violence—some recent and related to the Pakistani state's cooperation with the post-2001 United States-led "global war on terror," and others more rooted in this area's historical independence and uneasy absorption into the post-1947 Pakistani state[73]—one of the key demands of militants was for the establishment of an Islamic system of courts enforcing a particular brand of Islamic law.[74] This demand obviously sits in tension with the more secular politics of other regional forces like the ANP.

[72] See text accompanying nn. 48–50 for discussion of the complexity underlying this characterization of Bangladesh.

[73] See generally Sultan-i-Rome, "Swat: A Critical Analysis," Institute of Peace & Conflict Studies Research Papers (2009), available at http://ipcs.org/pdf_file/issue/1542140255RP18-Rome-Swat.pdf.

[74] See Osama Siddique, *The Other Pakistan: Special Laws, Diminished Citizenship and the Gathering Storm* (forthcoming) (on file with author).

If Pakistan and Bangladesh have been witness to intense sub-national differences in the implementation and experience of Islamic law, the same is true in India, with its continuing challenges in Kashmir. Indian-held Kashmir (formally known as the State of Jammu & Kashmir), situated in India's far north, is presently India's only Muslim majority state.[75] To this day, it holds a unique juridical status within India with, for example, many laws otherwise in effect in India not in force in Kashmir.[76] As a result, "Anglo-Muhammadan" law holds less sway here than in the rest of India, while "classical" Islamic law holds more sway.

This concluding section focuses on sub-national diversities in South Asian Islamic law as these sub-national differences are not only underexplored in the literature on South Asian Islamic law, but they also provide some of the richest areas for future work in the study, understanding, and theorizing of Islamic law in South Asia. Furthermore, by focusing on these sub-national diversities, one can hope that a certain nationalist hold (and limitation) on the study of Islamic law in South Asia can be lessened, thereby opening the door to another area in the study of South Asian Islamic law that needs further development, namely the comparative (or transnational) study of Islamic law. While where there is some comparative Islamic legal work which traverses the boundaries of Pakistan and India, there is far less comparative work concerning Bangladesh and India, or even Pakistan and Bangladesh (united from 1947–71).[77] As a result, much more transnational, comparative work could be done concerning South Asian Islamic law—in every aspect of this large area of law, and concerning every articulation of it (e.g. those by progressive feminists, those within the transnational Dawoodi Bohra community, and those concerning Ahmadis).

In addition, a discussion of sub-national diversities and comparative inquiry could fruitfully come together in a more concerted exploration of the continuing importance of non-state Islamic legal actors in South Asia. Non-state pronouncers of Islamic law have come under serious attack by the state not only in Bangladesh as mentioned earlier,[78] but also in India,[79] yet little attention has been directed to the possible connections (whether discursive, ideological, and/

[75] For helpful historical background on this dispute, see Mridu Rai, *Hindu Rulers, Muslim Subjects: Islam, Rights, and the History of Kashmir* (New Jersey: Princeton University Press, 2004).

[76] For example, the Indian Penal Code does not apply to the State of Jammu & Kashmir, see India Penal Code § 1, available at http://indiacode.nic.in, and neither does the 1939 Dissolution of Muslim Marriages Act. See The Dissolution of Muslim Marriages Act, No. 8 of 1939, § 1, available at http://indiacode.nic.in.

[77] For a couple of recent examples of this exceedingly scarce comparative literature, see Sunil Khilnani et al., eds., *Comparative Constitutionalism in South Asia* (New Delhi: Oxford University Press, 2013) (providing some comparative discussion of India and Pakistan); Serajuddin, *Muslim Family Law, Secular Courts and Muslim Women of South Asia* (discussing India, Pakistan, and Bangladesh).

[78] See discussion accompanying n. 67.

[79] See discussion accompanying nn. 64–66. See also Redding, "Secularism, The Rule of Law, and 'Shari'a Courts.'"

or historical) between these relatively simultaneous state actions against the non-state, and also possible transnational connections between "non-state (Islamic) law movements."

For example, in Pakistan, one of the main demands of militants in Swat District during the 2009 insurgency was for the establishment there of an Islamic system of courts; this demand was partially met by the government of Pakistan, and some of the judges and courts in that general area of Pakistan were reorganized under a nomenclature relating to *qazis*[80] and *dar ul qazas*.[81] As discussed earlier, a network of *dar ul qazas* also exists in India, and this network of non-state Islamic legal institutions has been operating more or less in its present manner for the past ninety years. Certainly, the Pakistani context for a system of state-sponsored *dar ul qazas* is different than the situation in India—with its non-state *dar ul qazas*—or the situation in Bangladesh—where the basic nomenclature of non-state Islamic legal institutions is itself different. Nonetheless, in all three national contexts, there is a need felt by some either to engage with a long history of non-state Islamic legal institutions in South Asia, or to build them anew. In all three national contexts as well, the postcolonial state has resisted empowering non-state actors—even if that sometimes takes the form of the state co-opting them through the deployment of certain Islamically informed legal nomenclatures—thereby following (somewhat) the mid-nineteenth-century British decision to sideline Muslim *qazis* and Hindu *pandits* both in the articulation and (official) enforcement of religious personal law.

This shared colonial history may provide the link to explain each contemporary nation-state's hostility to non-state Islamic legal actors, yet this is only a hypothesis. Further scholarly work exploring either this or other potential linkages is needed, as is much more scholarly work on non-state systems and pronouncers of Islamic law and their possible transnational connections. Non-state Islamic legal actors, whether *mullahs, muftis*, or *qazis* continue to provide the vast majority of South Asian Muslims' access to Islamic legal advice and knowledge in the contemporary period (as such non-state actors did in the past), yet there is not enough scholarly analysis of the contemporary South Asian practices of *ifta'* and *qaza*.[82] Moreover, state resistance to non-state Islamic legal actors seems to be largely based on such a lack of information (including stereotypes) about the agendas, priorities, and values

[80] A common English translation of *qazi* would be "Islamic judge." See n. 82.

[81] See generally Siddique, *The Other Pakistan*.

[82] A common English translation of *ifta* is "jurisconsultation," with the person giving such consultation and advice being referred to as a *mufti*, and the actual legal advice referred to as a *fatwa*. See generally Wael B. Hallaq, *A History of Islamic Legal Theories: An Introduction to Sunni Usul Al-Fiqh* (Cambridge: Cambridge University Press, 1997), 123, 145–146, 149, 153–154, 208–209. *Ifta* is generally distinguished from *qaza*, or actual adjudication of disputes resulting in a binding decision—rather than "merely" a legal opinion. As a result, *qazis* (practitioners of *qaza*) are typically referred to in English translation as "Islamic judges." See, e.g., Lawrence Rosen, *The Anthropology of Justice: Law as Culture in Islamic Society* (Cambridge: Cambridge University Press, 1989), 3, 6–11.

of non-state Islamic legal actors. As a result, our lack of scholarly production in these areas has had detrimental effects which more sustained and robust research efforts might mitigate.

References

Ahmed, Asad A., "The Paradoxes of Ahmadiyya Identity: The Legal Appropriation of Muslim-ness and the Construction of Ahmadiyya Difference" in Naveeda Khan (ed.) *Beyond Crisis: Reevaluating Pakistan* (India: Routledge, 2010) 273–314.

Ahmad, Irfan, *Islamism and Democracy in India, The Transformation of Jamaat-e-Islami* (Princeton, NJ: Princeton University Press, 2009).

Ali, S. Mahmud, *Understanding Bangladesh* (New York: Columbia University Press, 2010).

Bearman, Peri et al., eds., *The Islamic School of Law: Evolution, Devolution, and Progress* (Cambridge, MA: Harvard University Press, 2005).

Blank, Jonah, *Mullahs on the Mainframe: Islam and Modernity among the Daudi Bohras* (Chicago: University of Chicago Press, 2001).

Brown, Daniel, *Rethinking Tradition in Modern Islamic Thought* (Cambridge: Cambridge University Press, 1996).

Daftary, Farhad, *A Short History of the Ismailis* (Edinburgh: Edinburgh University Press, 1998).

The Dissolution of Muslim Marriages Act, No. 8 of 1939. http://indiacode.nic.in.

"The Future of the Global Muslim Population: Projections for 2010–2030." *Pew Research Center*, January 27, 2011. http://www.pewforum.org/uploadedFiles/Topics/Religious_Affiliation/Muslim/FutureGlobalMuslimPopulation-WebPDF-Feb10.pdf.

Fyzee, Asaf A.A., *Cases in the Muhammadan Law of India and Pakistan* (Oxford: Clarendon Press, 1965).

Fyzee, Asaf A.A., *Cases in the Muhammadan Law of India, Pakistan and Bangladesh* in Tahir Mahmood (ed.) (2nd edn. New York: Oxford University Press, 2005).

Ghosh, Papiya, "*Muttahidah qaumiyat in aqalliat* Bihar: The Imarat i Shariah 1921–1947." *Indian Economic & Social History Review* 34 (1997): 1–20.

Grote, Rainer, "Westminster Democracy in an Islamic Context: Pakistan, Bangladesh, Malaysia" in Rainer Grote and Tilmann J. Röder (eds.) *Constitutionalism in Islamic Countries: Between Upheaval and Continuity* (New York: Oxford University Press, 2012) 447–460.

Guenther, Alan M., "A Colonial Court Defines a Muslim" in Barbara D. Metcalf (ed.) *Islam in South Asia in Practice* (Princeton, NJ: Princeton University Press, 2009) 293–304.

Hallaq, Wael B., *Islamic Legal Theories: An Introduction to Sunni Usul Al-Fiqh* (Cambridge: Cambridge University Press, 1997).

Hardy, Peter, "Modern European and Muslim Explanations of Conversion to Islam in South Asia: A Preliminary Survey of the Literature" in Nehemia Levtzion (ed.) *Conversion to Islam* (New Jersey: Holmes & Meier, 1979) 68–99.

INDIA CONSTITUTION

India Code of Criminal Procedure §125 (1)(a).

Indian Penal Code. http://indiacode.nic.in.

"In Religion's Name." *Human Rights Watch*. February 28, 2013. http://www.hrw.org/reports/2013/02/28/religion-s-name.

Jalal, Ayesha, *Democracy and Authoritarianism in South Asia: A Comparative Historical Perspective* (Cambridge: Cambridge University Press, 1995).

Jones, Justin, *Shi'a Islam in Colonial India: Religion, Community and Sectarianism* (Cambridge: Cambridge University Press, 2012).

Jones, Justin, "'Signs of Churning': Muslim Personal Law and Public Contestation in Twenty-First Century India." *Modern Asian Studies* 44 (2009): 175–200.

Kalhan, Anil, "Constitution and 'Extraconstitution': Colonial and Emergency Regimes in Postcolonial Pakistan and India" in Victor V. Ramraj and Arun K. Thiruvengadam (eds.) *Emergency Powers in Asia: Exploring the Limits of Legality* (Cambridge: Cambridge University Press, 2010) 89–120.

Kennedy, Charles, *Islamization of Laws and Economy: Case Studies on Pakistan* (Washington: Institute for Policy Studies, 1996).

Khan, Naveeda, "Maulana Yusuf Ludhianvi on the Limits of Legitimate Religious Difference" in Barbara D. Metcalf (ed.) *Islam in South Asia in Practice* (Princeton, NJ: Princeton University Press, 2009) 438–446.

Khan, Naveeda, "Mosque Construction or the Violence of the Ordinary" in Naveeda Khan (ed.) *Beyond Crisis: Reevaluating Pakistan* (India: Routledge, 2010) 482–518.

Khan, Shahnaz, *Zina, Transnational Feminism and the Moral Regulation of Pakistan Women* (Vancouver: University of British Columbia Press, 2006).

Khilnani, Sunil et al., eds., *Comparative Constitutionalism in South Asia* (New Delhi: Oxford University Press, 2013).

Kugle, Scott Alan, "Framed, Blamed and Renamed: The Recasting of Islamic Jurisprudence in Colonial South Asia." *Modern Asian Studies* 35 (2001): 257–313.

Kurzman, Charles, ed., *Liberal Islam: A Sourcebook* (New York: Oxford University Press, 1998).

Kurzman, Charles, ed., *Modernist Islam (1840–1940): A Sourcebook* (New York: Oxford University Press, 2002).

"Mapping the Global Muslim Population: A Report of the Size and Distribution of the World's Muslim Population." *Pew Research Center*, October 7, 2009. http://www.pewforum.org/files/2009/10/Muslimpopulation.pdf.

Masud, Muhammad Khalid, "Apostasy and Judicial Separation in British India" in Muhammad Khalid Masud et al., (eds.) *Islamic Legal Interpretation: Muftis and their Fatwas* (Cambridge, MA: Harvard University Press, 1996) 193–203.

Maududi, S. Abul A'la Maududi, *Political Theory of Islam* in Khurshid Ahmad (ed. and trans.) (5th edn. Lahore: Islamic Publications, 1976).

Messick, Brinkley, *The Calligraphic State: Textual Domination and History in a Muslim Society* (Berkeley: University of California Press, 1993).

Metcalf, Barbara D., "A Historical Overview of Islam in South Asia" in Barbara D. Metcalf (ed.) *Islam in South Asia in Practice* (Princeton, NJ: Princeton University Press, 2009) 1–39.

Metcalf, Barbara D., *Islamic Revival in British India: Deoband, 1860–1900* (New York: Oxford University Press, 1982).
Mohammed, Rizwan and Brulliard, Karin, "Militants attack two Ahmadi mosques in Pakistan; 80 killed." *The Washington Post.* May 9, 2010. http://www.washingtonpost.com/wp-dyn/content/article/2010/05/28/AR2010052800686.html.
Mohd. Ahmed Khan v. Shah Bano Begum, 3 S.C.R. 844 (1985).
Nagarajan, Rema, "Door out of Dhaka." *The Times of India*, 2010. http://articles.timesofindia.indiatimes.com/2010-05-22/south-asia/28280481_1_hindus-bangladesh-minorities-census.
Narantakath v. Parakkal, 45 Mad. 986 (1922).
Nelson, Matthew J., "Islamic Law in an Islamic Republic: What Role for Parliament" in Asli Bali and Hanna Lerner (eds.) *Constitution-Writing, Religion, and Democracy* (Cambridge: Cambridge University Press, 2017).

Pakistan Constitution

Rai, Mridu, *Hindu Rules, Muslim Subjects: Islam, Rights, and the History of Kashmir* (Princeton, NJ: Princeton University Press, 2004).
Redding, Jeffrey A., "Institutional v. Liberal Contexts for Contemporary Non-State Muslim Civil Dispute Resolution Systems." *Journal Islamic State Practices International Law* 6 (2010): 1–25.
Redding, Jeffrey A., "Secularism, The Rule of Law, and 'Shari'a Courts': An Ethnographic Examination of a Constitutional Controversy." *Saint Louis University Law Journal* 57 (2013): 339–376.
Redding, Jeffrey A., "Slicing the American Pie: Federalism and Personal Law." *New York University Journal of International Law and Politics* 40 (2008): 941–1018.
Riaz, Ali, "The Politics of Islamization in Bangladesh" in Ali Riaz (ed.) *Religion and Politics in South Asia* (New York: Routledge, 2010) 45–70.
Robinson, Francis, *The Ulama of Farangi Mahall and Islamic Culture in South Asia* (London: Hurst Publishers Ltd., 2002).
Rosen, Lawrence, *The Anthropology of Justice: Law as Culture in Islamic Society* (Cambridge: Cambridge University Press, 1989).
Sanyal, Usha, *Devotional Islam and Politics in British India: Ahmed Riza Khan Barelwi and His Movement, 1870–1920* (Oxford: Oxford University Press, 1996).
Serajuddin, Alamgir Muhammad, *Muslim Family Law, Secular Courts and Muslim Women of South Asia: A Study of Judicial Activism* (Karachi: Oxford University Press Pakistan, 2011).
Siddique, Osama, *The Other Pakistan: Special Laws, Diminished Citizenship and the Gathering Storm* (forthcoming).
Singh, Kirti, "The Constitution and Muslim Personal Law" in Zoya Hasan (ed.) *Forging Identities: Gender Communities and the State* (Boulder: Westview Press, 1994) 96–107.
Solanki, Gopika, *Adjudication in Religious Family Laws: Cultural Accommodation, Legal Pluralism, and Gender Equality in India* (Cambridge: Cambridge University Press, 2011).

Sultan-i-Rome, "Swat: A Critical Analysis." *Institute of Peace & Conflict Studies*. (Research Paper. January, 2009). http://ipcs.org/pdf_file/issue/1542140255RP18-Rome-Swat.pdf.
Tschalaer, Mengia Hong, "Competing Model-Nikahnamas: Muslim Women's Spaces within the Legal Landscape in Lucknow." *Journal of Law and Social Research* 3 (2012): 65–80.
Viswanathan, Gauri, *Outside the Fold: Conversion, Modernity and Belief* (Princeton, NJ: Princeton University Press, 1998).
Zaman, Muhammad Qasim, *The Ulama in Contemporary Islam: Custodians of Change* (Princeton, NJ: Princeton University Press, 2002).

B

MUSLIM MINORITIES

CHAPTER 28

THE INCORPORATION OF SHARI'A IN NORTH AMERICA

ENFORCING THE MAHR TO COMBAT WOMEN'S POVERTY POST-RELATIONSHIP DISSOLUTION

NATASHA BAKHT

The past decade has been a tumultuous time in Canada and the United States for Muslims. There has been a groundswell of anti-Muslim sentiment and activity stemming acutely perhaps from the September 11, 2001 attacks. Muslims have been regularly targeted as terrorists, Islam has been attacked as a global political/military threat to western civilization and Muslim women have been portrayed as oppressed and in need of protection from the misogyny of Muslim men.[1]

[1] Given the essential (and sometimes intentional) misunderstandings of Islam by its detractors, one can argue that the "debate" has nothing to do with Islam: "[b]eing in contact with another tradition is itself an interesting notion. To recognize another tradition there are threshold requirements of

This rather overwhelming and incessant degradation of Muslims and their religion has also manifested in many commentators, both scholarly and otherwise, suggesting that the tolerance of Canadian and American jurisprudence ought to be tempered. It has been argued that the increasing demographic diversity in North America, which has been the home of policies of inclusiveness such as multiculturalism, has been a failure and that the lenience of "our" ways has permitted a slow but sure danger to recognized—indeed civilized—ways of being.

The first section of this chapter will trace select events in Canadian and American politics to demonstrate the adverse implications of the above trend on Muslims and Islamic law, despite entrenched North American jurisprudential traditions of accommodating minority religious practices. It will examine the false assumptions and myths about shari'a law and its interaction with state law and policy prevalent in two recent controversies: the religious arbitration debate in Ontario and the shari'a bans enacted by several US states.

The second section will examine actual ways in which American and Canadian courts have recognized the diverse desires of their Muslim citizenry. Several recurring themes arise in North America specific to Muslims including requests for accommodating certain religious practices,[2] shari'a-based rules about business transactions,[3] and family law matters. The majority of cases that have grappled with how to treat shari'a law are contract disputes between divorcing Muslim couples who are seeking enforcement of their rights under Islamic marriage agreements. Because conjugal relationships play a pivotal role in how people identify the human experience, the focus of this chapter will be on how Muslims have reconstructed their conjugal identity through North American courts. In particular, the chapter will examine a key element of an Islamic marriage agreement, the *mahr* or bridal gift, through the courts. The enforcement of the *mahr* in North America is important as it is potentially another tool with which to ensure that post-relationship dissolution women are not left poverty-stricken.

knowledge and understanding, so it appears that there is no contact between traditions which does not involve exchange of information"—H. Patrick Glenn, *Legal Traditions of the World: Sustainable Diversity in Law*, 4th edn. (Toronto: Oxford University Press, 2010), 34.

[2] In Canada see, *R. v. N.S.*, 2012 SCC 72, which involved a niqab-wearing Muslim sexual assault complainant's desire to wear her full-face veil while testifying in court in accordance with her right to equality and religious freedom under the Charter. In the United States see *Shaheed Allah v. Adella Jordan-Luster*, No. 04-1083, 2007 WL 2582199 (C.D. Ill. Aug 3, 2007) and *Taylor v. Cook County*, No. 11 C 7427, 2013 WL 2285806, 4 (N.D. Ill. May 23, 2013), both of which involved a Muslim inmate's claim that a prison violated his religious exercise rights by failing to ensure that all meat served to him was prepared in accordance with his Islamic religious beliefs (neither inmate was successful).

[3] See, e.g., *Abd Alla v. Mourssi*, 680 N.W.2d 569, 574 (Minn. Ct. App. 2004).

1. Banning Shariʿa for the Sake of Women

Most pronouncements that shariʿa must be banned in either Canada or the United States stem from the belief that Islam is a threat to western culture and that Muslim men are dangerously sexist against women. Shariʿa in particular evokes extreme images of stoning and other harsh criminal laws, leaving no room in the western imagination to understand shariʿa as having any positive impact on the lives of Muslims. Contrary to the belief that Muslims in the west seek inclusion of shariʿa in the constitutions of their resident countries, most Muslims in North America are in fact quite satisfied with the religious freedom offered by their democracies. "Muslims in the United States are decidedly uninterested in sharia criminal law ... [they] show no interest in having American law criminalize actions such as extramarital sex or alcohol consumption."[4] Yet this disinterest on the part of Muslims does not preclude ongoing tensions regarding the accommodation of religious freedom in certain aspects of daily life.

Legislative and judicial protection in North America of Muslims' shariʿa-based practices is an extension of the long-standing practice in which religious freedom is protected in these highly diverse societies. As the Supreme Court of Canada recently held, "[t]he need to accommodate and balance sincerely held religious beliefs against other interests is deeply entrenched in Canadian law. For over half a century this tradition has served us well."[5] Similarly, the United States Supreme Court held "We have no cause to pretend that the task assigned by Congress to the courts under RFRA [Religious Freedom Restoration Act] is an easy one ... But Congress has determined that courts should strike sensible balances, pursuant to a compelling interest test that requires the Government to address the particular practice at issue."[6] Sadly, despite traditions of being open-minded to minority religious practices, particularly where there is no countervailing reason to limit them, certain political episodes have revealed deep distrust of Muslims and Islam.[7] This suspicion and animosity have resulted in perhaps the most vitriolic of political moments in recent

[4] Asifa Quraishi-Landes, "What is Sharia and is it Creepy?" *The Islamic Monthly* (June 18, 2012), http://www.theislamicmonthly.com/what-is-sharia-and-is-it-creepy/.

[5] *R. v. N.S.*, para. 54.

[6] *Gonzales v. O Centro Espirita Beneficente Uniao do Vegetal*, 546 U.S. 419, 439 (2006).

[7] One example of this disturbing discourse was an interview given by conservative Herman Cain to Fox News on July 17, 2011, against the building of a mosque in Murfreesboro, Tennessee, in which Cain suggested the First Amendment could be used to stop the mosque. He was subsequently lampooned by comedian/commentator Jon Stewart on *The Daily Show*: "You think 'our' first amendment protects 'us' from 'their' mosque, when in reality, 'the' First Amendment protects 'their' mosque from 'us.'"

Canadian and American history in which stereotypes about Islam and Muslims have played prominently.

A. Shariʿa Family Arbitration in Ontario, Canada

In late 2003, the Islamic Institute of Civil Justice in Toronto announced that it would offer family arbitration services using shariʿa. Ontario's Arbitration Act[8] allowed parties to voluntarily agree to have their disputes resolved by an arbitrator using a choice of law provision. Indeed other religious groups including Jewish communities had created arbitration tribunals to resolve civil matters for several years.[9]

The uproar that was created by this announcement was unprecedented, including an onslaught of fear-mongering articles and commentaries that confirmed the view that Islamic fundamentalism was an imminent threat. Protests were led worldwide against "sharia courts" in Canada.[10] The Ontario Liberal Party Women's Caucus led a call for a ban on shariʿa-based arbitration for fear that women's equality would be compromised. That the debates were characterized by hysteria and irrationality was demonstrated by the fact that Quebec politician Fatima Houda-Peppin led a unanimous motion opposing Islamic tribunals in the Quebec National Assembly even though the province's Civil Code specifies that arbitration cannot be used to resolve family law disputes.[11] At its lowest point,

> the debate portrayed the issue as one in which Canadian Muslims, guided by international Islamic fundamentalists, sought to create a parallel legal justice system, which, opponents feared, would weaken the rights of Muslim women and the functioning of the liberal democratic state.[12]

That some Muslims, including Muslim women, may have wanted to resolve their family law disputes using shariʿa was never taken seriously.[13] The absence of any data surrounding the use of private dispute resolution by Muslims at the time of

[8] Arbitration Act 1991, S.O. 1991, c 17.

[9] Natasha Bakht, "Family Arbitration Using Sharia Law: Examining Ontario's Arbitration Act and its Impact on Women," *Muslim World Journal of Human Rights* 1 (2004): 1.

[10] Natasha Bakht, "Were Muslim Barbarians Really Knocking on the Gates of Ontario?: The Religious Arbitration Controversy—Another Perspective," *Ottawa Law Review* 40th Anniversary(2005): 70.

[11] Bakht, "Family Arbitration Using Sharia," 24 and fn. 129.

[12] Jennifer A. Selby and Anna C. Korteweg, "Introduction: Situating the Sharia Debate in Ontario" in *Debating Sharia: Islam, Gender Politics, and Family Law Arbitration*, eds. Anna C. Korteweg and Jennifer A. Selby (Toronto: University of Toronto Press, 2012), 12.

[13] Lori Beaman explores regulation of choice through discourses of agency and harm: "a bad use of judgment can be sufficient to trigger an assessment of incapacity ... " See Lori G. Beaman, *Defining Harm: Religious Freedom and the Limits of the Law* (Toronto: University of British Columbia Press, 2008), 100.

the debate exacerbated the problem.[14] However, mobilization on the issue of shariʿa arbitration pursued a strategy that pushed religion out of the public sphere and insisted on an expansive definition of secularism, which was puzzling given the Canadian commitment to both gender equality and religious freedom.[15]

Opponents of shariʿa arbitration often relied on the slogan "one law for all." But such a characterization was disingenuous since most family law jurisdictions permit parties to opt out of the default statutory regimes.[16] Parties can and do, through negotiation, mediation, and arbitration, agree to almost any resolution of their marital affairs.[17] This suggests that the concern for women's equality in family law ought to extend beyond merely examining Islamic practices.[18]

Eventually, the premier of Ontario announced that shariʿa arbitration in family law matters would be banned from the province. No doubt invoking the dramatic events of 9/11, he made the announcement on September 11, 2005. The premier's announcement was deliberately misleading. The amendment to the Arbitration Act did not specifically target shariʿa the way the public debates did. Instead the Family Statute Law Amendment Act[19] requires that any family arbitration conducted in Ontario be done according to a family law jurisdiction in Canada. Religious arbitrations thus continue to be possible so long as they conform to the regulations regarding arbitrator training and record-keeping and the final text of the rulings use the language of Canadian law, a requirement that is not onerous given the flexibility of family law regimes in Canada.[20] Nonetheless, the myth that shariʿa arbitration has been banned from the province remains ubiquitous even among scholars.[21]

There is now wide consensus that the public debate regarding shariʿa arbitration largely failed to generate a productive or nuanced discussion about the privatization of family law generally, Muslim women's equality in particular, or the development

[14] It has now been demonstrated that though the Muslim community in Ontario never used arbitration, informal mediation with imams was common. See Julie Macfarlane, "Practising an 'Islamic Imagination': Islamic Divorce in North America" in Korteweg and Selby, *Debating Sharia*, 35 and Christopher Cutting, "Faith-Based Arbitration or Religious Divorce: What Was the Issue?" in Korteweg and Selby, *Debating Sharia*, 66. See also, generally, Korteweg and Selby, *Debating Sharia*, and Mohamed M. Keshavjee, *Islam, Shariʿa and Alternative Dispute Resolution: Mechanisms for Legal Redress in the Muslim Community* (London: I.B. Tauris, 2013) for the collection of data on Islamic dispute resolution.

[15] Bakht, "Were Muslim Barbarians Really Knocking?" 71.

[16] See Bakht, "Were Muslim Barbarians Really Knocking?" 79. See also Audrey Macklin, "Multiculturalism Meets Privatization: The Case of Faith-Based Arbitration" and Faisal Kutty, "'Sharia' Courts in Canada: A Delayed Opportunity for the Indigenization of Islamic Legal Rulings," both in Korteweg and Selby, *Debating Sharia*.

[17] Custody of children is the one area in which there are more restrictions on parties' ability to arbitrate. See Bakht, "Family Arbitration Using Sharia Law," 5.

[18] See Bakht, "Were Muslim Barbarians Really Knocking?" 79 and Korteweg and Selby, *Debating Sharia*, 14.

[19] Family Statute Law Amendment Act, 2006, S.O. 2006, c. 1.

[20] Bakht, "Were Muslim Barbarians Really Knocking?" 81.

[21] See, e.g., Nathan B. Oman, "How to Judge *Shariʿa* Contracts: A Guide to Islamic Marriage Agreements in American Courts," *Utah Law Review* 2011, no. 1 (2011): 288.

of Islamic jurisprudence in family law.[22] Unfortunately, the popular understanding of the debate and its aftermath has left the inaccurate impression that because shari'a is incompatible with gender equality, it was banned from the province.

B. Shari'a Bans in the United States

Since 2010 the United States has seen a number of state legislators propose laws to limit the ability of courts to adjudicate lawsuits using shari'a law. Some of the proposed measures expressly single out shari'a for damaging treatment while others do not make explicit reference to shari'a or Islam, but proponents freely admit that their intent is to target Muslims.[23] The effect of these laws would be to place sweeping limitations on the ability of state courts to consider international or foreign law in rendering decisions. The incorporation of rules of contract derived from Islamic jurisprudence is of course very different from the imposition of "foreign law." Yet the proponents of the anti-shari'a legislation conflated the two regularly. As Quraishi-Landes notes: "American accommodation of religious law, within the limits of public policy, has always been part of [legal diversity]."[24]

Bans on shari'a law have been introduced for legislative approval in at least thirty-two states at the time of writing.[25] The most striking of these has been the voter-approved ban on shari'a law in Oklahoma. Although judicially declared invalid,[26] over 70 percent of voters voted for the ban. In Tennessee, the original text of the Shari'a Ban Bill contained the passage "sharia requires the abrogation, destruction, or violation of the United States and Tennessee Constitutions and the imposition of sharia through violence and criminal activity."[27] The Bill was eventually amended to remove all references to Islam and Shari'a and essentially became standard anti-terrorist legislation.

[22] Korteweg and Selby, *Debating Sharia*, 13.

[23] Abed Awad, "The True Story of Sharia in American Courts," *The Nation* (July 2, 2012), http://www.thenation.com/article/168378/true-story-sharia-american-courts#

[24] Asifa Quraishi-Landes, "Rumors of the Sharia Threat Are Greatly Exaggerated: What American Judges Really Do with Islamic Law in Family Courtrooms," *New York Law School Law Review* 57, no. 2 (2012–13): 256–257.

[25] Abdulaziz A. Al-Alami, "32 States Introduce Ban of Sharia Law with Misleading Semantics," *Arab American Institute* (May 21, 2013), http://www.aaiusa.org/blog/entry/anti-shariah-bills/. For more information on a state-by-state basis, see Pew Research, Religion & Public Life Project, "State Legislation Restricting Use of Foreign or Religious Law," http://features.pewforum.org/sharia-law-map/.

[26] The January 10, 2012 US 10th Circuit Court of Appeals decision in *Awad v. Ziriax et al.*, 670 F.3d 1111 (10th Circuit 2012) (Docket 10-6273) upheld a permanent injunction in certifying the result (effectively blocking the amendment).

[27] H.R. 1353, 107th Leg. (Tenn. 2011), http://www.capitol.tn.gov/Bills/107/Bill/HB1353.pdf. See also: http://wapp.capitol.tn.gov/apps/BillInfo/Default.aspx?BillNumber=%20HB1353&GA=107.

Scholars have roundly argued that the wave of anti-shariʿa legislation is steeped in bigotry and discrimination against Muslims that harnesses the moral threat Islam represents in the west,[28] to render Muslims suspect and their faith threatening. Anver Emon has stated: "the current insecurity of the nation—its existential threat—is identified as a tradition that is made to stand for everything America is not, namely Islamic law."[29]

The proponents of the anti-shariʿa laws rely upon a New Jersey case as proof that Islamic law is seeping into and threatening the American court system. In *S.D. v. M.J.R.*,[30] a wife sought a restraining order against her husband who allegedly beat and sexually assaulted her. The court denied the order finding that the husband did not have the requisite mental intent necessary to commit the crime since he held a genuine religious belief that he was entitled to sexual relations on demand from his wife. The ruling was overturned by the New Jersey Appellate Court[31] and whether it was correct according to contemporary versions of shariʿa is debatable. Nonetheless, the reliance on this case as a rallying cry by anti-shariʿa proponents is interesting because it suggests a false conviction that violence against women is tolerated in Islam, but would never be in the United States. It also depicts Muslim women as being in need of protection from Muslim men, even if that means banning their religion to do it.

In Kansas, the ban of foreign law became effective July 1, 2012.[32] One representative called it "a vote to protect women"[33] yet in its application in *Soleimani v. Soleimani*,[34] it specifically prevented a physically and sexually abused wife from claiming a *mahr* of $677,000 from her estranged husband where relief under Kansas' marital property division would be minimal.[35] The court held that the enforcement of the *mahr* agreement would violate the ban on shariʿa in Kansas.

The anti-shariʿa measures proposed and invoked in the United States have been justified in part on the trope of Muslim women's oppression. One of the bases for seeing Islam as a threat to the nation is its perpetual association with gender inequality. For Mrs. Soleimani, her tragic situation could have been corrected by enforcing a contract based in Islamic jurisprudence. Bans on shariʿa that claim to protect women are often driven by hysteria and are highly disingenuous in that any

[28] Sherene Razack, *Casting Out: The Eviction of Muslims from Western Law and Politics* (Toronto: University of Toronto Press, 2008).

[29] Anver Emon, "Banning Shariʿa" *The Immanent Frame* (September 6, 2011), http://blogs.ssrc.org/tif/2011/09/06/banning-shari%e2%80%98a/.

[30] Superior Court of New Jersey, Chancery Division, Family Part, Hudson County, Docket No. FV-09-1792-09 (2009).

[31] 415 N.J. Super. 417 (N.J. Super. App. Div. 2010); 2010 NJ Super LEXIS 143.

[32] H.R. 79, House Substitute for Senate Bill 79, 2011–2012 Legislative Session (Ks, 2012), http://kslegislature.org/li_2012/b2011_12/measures/SB79/.

[33] Associated Press, "Kansas Senate Passes Law Banning Sharia, Other Foreign Laws from State Courts" (May 11, 2012), http://www.nydailynews.com/news/politics/kansas-senate-passes-law-banning-sharia-foreign-laws-state-courts-article-1.1076862.

[34] Johnson County District Ct, Kansas, Docket 11CV4468 (August 28, 2012).

[35] See Rafia Zakaria, "Sharia Law Ban and Muslim Wives," *Al Jazeera* (February 16, 2013), http://www.aljazeera.com/indepth/opinion/2013/02/201321174724878286.html.

concern regarding abuses associated with shari'a can be prevented by established constitutional principles.[36]

II. Enforcing the *Mahr* for the Sake of Women

This chapter turns now to the ways in which North American courts have accommodated the needs of their Muslim citizens. An area in which many North American Muslims seek to live according to their religious views is family law. A qualitative research study in southern Ontario and three American cities, Dearborn, Los Angeles, and Omaha, concluded that "the number of Muslim North Americans who marry using a *nikah* [Islamic marriage contract] is far higher than those who regularly attend prayers or even consider themselves to be observant."[37] Thus, many Muslims, regardless of their level of religious observance, engage with religion at the time of marriage. Because divorce is increasingly common among younger Muslims,[38] the reality is that the required provision for a *mahr* or the gift to be given by the husband to the wife upon a Muslim marriage is often relevant in determining the division of property upon divorce. Indeed the *mahr* is perhaps the most litigated issue amongst Muslims in North America.

Before turning to the specific issue of the *mahr*, some general context related to the dissolution of conjugal relationships in North America should be kept in mind. Regardless of religious affiliation, there are known negative economic consequences of divorce for women and children:

> For most women and children, divorce means precipitous downward mobility—both economically and socially. The reduction in income brings residential moves and inferior

[36] Sarah M. Fallon, "Justice for All: American Muslims, Sharia Law, and Maintaining Comity Within American Jurisprudence," *Boston College International and Comparative Law Review* 36, no. 1 (2013): 153, 176–177. See also Jeremy Grunert, "How Do You Solve a Problem Like Sharia? *Awad v. Ziriax* and the Question of Sharia Law in America," *Pepperdine Law Review* 40, no. 3 (2013): 695, 725.

[37] Julie Macfarlane, *Sustaining the Islamic Imagination: Islamic Marriage and Divorce in North America* (Oxford: Oxford University Press, 2012), 11. Research in Australia and the United Kingdom show similar engagements with Muslims and Islamic law. Samia Bano, "Islamic Family Arbitration, Justice and Human Rights in Britain," *Law, Social Justice & Global Development Journal* 10, no. 1 (2007); Ghena Krayem, "To Recognized or Not to Recognize, That is NOT the Question: Family Law and the Muslim Community in Australia" (Ph.D. diss., unpublished, University of Sydney, 2011); Asifa Quraishi and Najeeba Syeed-Miller, "No Altars: A Survey of Islamic Family Law in the United States," http://papers.ssrn.com/sol3/papers.cfm?abstract_id=1524246.

[38] Macfarlane, *Sustaining Islamic Imagination*, 35.

housing, drastically diminished or nonexistent funds for recreation and leisure, and intense pressures due to inadequate time and money. Financial hardships in turn cause social dislocation and a loss of familiar networks for emotional support and social services, and intensify the psychological stress for women and children alike. On a societal level, divorce increases female and child poverty and creates an ever-widening gap between the economic well-being of divorced men, on the one hand, and their children and former wives on the other.[39]

In Canada, in the first year of separation, women's family income dropped by one-half and men's by one-quarter.[40] Using calculations of income to needs ratios, studies concluded that there was a small rise in men's economic well-being, while women experienced a 40 percent drop in theirs.[41] In the United States, women's standard of living dropped by 27 percent and men experienced a rise in their standard of living by 10 percent.[42] The Supreme Court of Canada has characterized widespread economic effects of divorce on women as a social phenomenon called the "feminization of poverty."[43]

There is no reason to assume that the impact of divorce on Muslim women in North America is much different. Spousal relationships continue to be marked by gender inequality where women have primary responsibility for children and domestic labor. As a result, women who assume stereotypically gendered roles in the home entirely or even in part are economically disadvantaged on the breakdown of spousal relationships. To combat this intractable social problem, women need as many tools as possible at their disposal. Family law statutes in North America are generally aimed at redressing the economic and other injustices created by gendered roles in spousal relationships. Women are reliant upon either these statutory regimes for the economic adjustment packages that they offer or contracts they enter into with their former spouses.

Because many Muslims in North America marry according to shariʿa, litigation around the enforcement of the *mahr* is highly relevant to this population. The *mahr* is a sum of money or some other economically valuable asset that a husband must give to a wife in consideration of the marriage. Upon marriage, which in Islam is understood as a contract between a man and woman, the wife is entitled to the *mahr*. Typically though, the *mahr* is divided into two parts: a nominal payment made at the time of marriage, and the deferred *mahr* due upon divorce or the husband's death. The *mahr* is supposed to provide wives with some measure of

[39] L.J. Weitzman, *The Divorce Revolution: The Unexpected Social and Economic Consequences for Women and Children in America* (New York: Free Press, 1985), 323.

[40] Ross Finnie, "Women, Men, and the Economic Consequences of Divorce: Evidence from the Canadian Longitudinal Data," *Canadian Review of Sociology and Anthropology* 30, no. 2 (1993): 205.

[41] Finnie, "Women, Men, and the Economic Consequences of Divorce," 205.

[42] Weitzman, *The Divorce Revolution*, 326.

[43] *Moge v. Moge* [1992] 3 S.C.R. 813: para. 55.

financial independence, ensuring that they have some pool of property that is uniquely their own.[44]

Though the wife's *mahr* vests upon marriage, shari'a rules dictate that depending on how a divorce is initiated, she may forfeit the deferred amount of the *mahr*.[45] There are three ways in which a marriage can be dissolved in Islamic law: A *faskh* or *tafriq* is a judicial proceeding initiated by the wife in which she petitions an Islamic judge to dissolve the marriage for cause such as abuse or a husband's failure to financially support her. In practice, obtaining a *faskh/tafriq* is very difficult. Where however, one is granted, the wife is entitled to the deferred *mahr*.[46]

The second kind of divorce, also granted by a court, is a *khul'* where the wife again initiates the divorce, but the husband consents to it. "The law requires that the wife provide consideration known as *'iwad*, equal to the amount of *mahr*."[47] Typically, the wife forgoes her claim to the *mahr* in order to pay *'iwad*, although it can also be paid through other means such as providing childcare for minor children of the marriage post divorce. "In Islamic law, by caring for the children, the wife provides the husband with a service for which she may demand compensation."[48] A *khul'* divorce has thus been described as an exchange of the *mahr* for the wife's freedom.[49]

Finally, a *talaq* allows a husband to unilaterally divorce his wife without cause, judicial proceeding, or her consent. This power of exercising *talaq* is sometimes given to a wife in a marriage contract, in effect giving her the same unilateral right.[50] With a *talaq*, the woman is entitled to the deferred portion of her *mahr*. The delayed payment of *mahr* is meant to act as a check upon the husband's otherwise unfettered power of *talaq*, a type of fine to be paid to the wife upon divorce.[51]

Most Muslims who divorce in North America will do so civilly, sometimes in addition to a religious divorce.[52] The effect of a civil divorce in North America, where the system of law essentially provides a no-fault, unilateral divorce, would be that either party has the right to initiate divorce, regardless of consent, but upon the meeting of certain procedural criteria. Where couples seek a religious divorce, outside the civil context, the issue of the *mahr* is sometimes resolved with the advice of an imam. Where that is not possible, Muslims will turn to the courts.

44 Oman, "How to Judge *Shari'a* Contracts," 303.
45 Ibid., 306. 46 Ibid., 303–304.
47 Ibid., 304. 48 Ibid.
49 Pascale Fournier, "In the (Canadian) Shadow of Islamic Law: Translating *Mahr* as a Bargaining Endowment," in *Law and Religious Pluralism in Canada*, ed. Richard Moon (Toronto: UBC Press, 2008), 149.
50 Oman, "How to Judge *Shari'a* Contracts," 305–306. Some Muslim feminists have argued that such provisions should be a standard part of marriage contracts on equality grounds.
51 Ibid., 306.
52 Cutting, "Faith Based Arbitrations and Religious Divorce," discusses so-called limping marriages, where Muslim women are civilly divorced, but not considered religiously divorced.

It is not always clear from the language of *mahr* agreements whether parties intend these agreements as either prenuptial agreements that exclusively divide the marital assets, or contracts that supplement the state's property division schemes.[53] In the absence of the parties' written intentions, courts are split as to how to enforce these agreements. Some courts have enforced the *mahr* as akin to a secular prenuptial agreement, while others have relied on ordinary contract law to enforce the agreement. Other courts have refused to enforce these agreements entirely on a variety of grounds.

A. *Mahr* Enforced as Prenuptial Agreements

Most husbands in the United States have argued that the *mahr* provisions in their marriage contracts constitute prenuptial agreements governing the distribution of marital property upon divorce. They thus claim that their wives have no right to the marital property beyond the sum specified as the *mahr*. Such an argument is particularly likely where the amount of *mahr* is insignificant or at least less than that which would be required under the law of the land. Upholding such an argument by a husband can have harsh results for the wife.

In *Chaudry v. Chaudry*,[54] the Superior Court of New Jersey accepted just such an argument by the husband when it concluded that the wife was not entitled to equitable distribution by reason of the antenuptial agreement. The court rested its finding on conflicts analysis. It was not satisfied that an adequate nexus had been proven between the marriage and the state to justify alimony or equitable distribution of the property. The wife and children had resided in the state for only two years. The court held that there was no public policy reason to refuse to interpret and enforce the agreement in accordance with the law of Pakistan where the agreement was freely negotiated and the marriage took place. Nathan B. Oman has argued that the problem with the court's analysis is that while under Pakistani law the wife's claim on the husband's assets would be limited to the *mahr* provision, this result arose not from the agreement of the parties but from Pakistani property law. In other words,

> [T]he limitation on the wife's rights arose not because she bargained those rights away, but from the fact that there was no marital property under Pakistani law upon which she might have a claim. Hence, in Chaudry, rather than interpreting the scope of the contract in light of Pakistani law, the court in effect adopted Pakistani property law as a whole under the guise of interpreting a contract and applied it to marital property in New Jersey.[55]

[53] Chelsea A. Sizemore, "Enforcing Islamic Mahr Agreements: The American Judge's Interpretational Dilemma," *George Mason Law Review* 18, no. 4 (2010–11): 1094.

[54] *Chaudry v. Chaudry*, 159 N.J. Super. 566; 388 A.2d 1000; 1978 N.J. Super. Lexis 952.

[55] Oman, "How to Judge *Shariʿa* Contracts," 314.

By contrast, other American courts have refused to enforce *mahr* agreements as premarital contracts that waive a wife's claim on marital property. For example, in *Aleem v. Aleem*, the Maryland Court of Appeals stated: "the Pakistani marriage contract in the instant matter is not to be equated with a premarital or post-marital agreement that validly relinquished, under Maryland law, rights in marital property."[56]

Some wives have also sought recognition that the *mahr* provision constitutes a prenuptial agreement that governs property distribution of the marital assets. Assuming that people act in self-interested ways, this tends to occur most often when the marriage is short, and equitable distribution of marital property laws will garner less for the wife and/or where the *mahr* amount is a significant sum of money. For example, in *Akileh v. Elchahal*,[57] the couple's marriage was less than two years in duration. However, they had entered into a *mahr* agreement in which the husband agreed to give the wife an immediate payment of $1, followed by a deferred payment of $50,000 upon divorce. The court concluded that the *mahr* was a valid and enforceable contract. In *Ahmed v. Ahmed*,[58] the Texas Court of Appeal rejected that wife's claim that the *mahr*, worth $50,000, ought to be enforced as a prenuptial agreement because the parties made the agreement after being married. It did however remand the case to the trial court in order to determine if the *mahr* could be enforceable on other grounds.

Canadian courts have mostly enforced *mahr* agreements as valid marriage contracts.[59] The province of British Columbia has been the site of several such agreements that have been recognized as binding marriage contracts as contemplated by the Family Relations Act (FRA).[60] In *Nathoo v. Nathoo*,[61] the husband proposed a *mahr* of $10,000, while the wife requested $40,000. They eventually agreed upon the amount of $20,000. The contract stated that Karim Nathoo accepted Fahrah Mawani as his wife and:

> I hereby agree and undertake to pay an agreed sum of money by way of "Maher" to my said wife. I hereby agree ... that my undertaking to pay the agreed sum of money by way of Maher to my wife shall be in addition, and without prejudice to, and not in substitution of all my obligations provided for by the laws of the land.[62]

According to section 51 of the FRA, the court may vary terms of a marriage agreement if they are found to be unfair considering certain factors. In *Nathoo*, the court

[56] *Aleem v. Aleem*, 404 Md. 404; 947 A.2d 489; 2008 MD Lexis 246 at 1134.

[57] 666. So. 2d 246 (Fla. Dist. Ct. App. 1996) [*Akileh*].

[58] 261 S.W. 3d 190, 2008 Tex. App. Lexis 4660 (2008) [*Ahmed*].

[59] A marriage contract in Canada is generally an agreement entered into by two people before or during their marriage to manage their property and other rights and obligations on the dissolution of their relationship. See, e.g., Family Law Act, R.S.O. 1990, c. F3, [FLA], s. 52(1).

[60] Family Relations Act, R.S.B.C. 1996, c. 128 [FRA].

[61] *Nathoo v. Nathoo*, [1996] B.C.J. no. 2720 [BCSC].

[62] *Nathoo v. Nathoo*, para. 8.

found that there was nothing unfair about enforcing the agreement. Similarly, in *Amlani v. Hirani*,[63] the agreement itself specified that the *mahr* amount of $51,000 was to be paid in addition to and without prejudice, or in substitution of any other obligations provided for by the law of the land. The court again found that the marriage contract met the requirements of the FRA and thus constituted an enforceable marriage agreement. In *N.M.M. v. N.M.*,[64] in terms identical to *Amlani*, the British Columbia Supreme Court held, despite the husband's assertion that he had not read the document and signed it believing it was merely symbolic, that the *mahr* was a fair marriage agreement as defined by the FRA.

Other Canadian provinces have also recognized *mahr* agreements as marriage contracts. In *Nasin v. Nasin*,[65] the Alberta Court of Queen's Bench found that though the *mahr* was a prenuptial contract, it was unenforceable because it did not meet certain formalities per the Matrimonial Property Act.[66] Specifically, the contract was not in writing and no acknowledgement was made before a lawyer that the parties "entered into the marriage of their own free will, knowing that they have property rights but willingly giving up those rights."[67]

In Ontario, the *mahr* was initially unenforceable on public policy grounds,[68] but more recently, has been enforced as a valid marriage contract in two cases. In *Khanis v. Noormohamed*,[69] the Ontario Superior Court of Justice held, and the Ontario Court of Appeal affirmed,[70] that the *mahr* agreement was a valid domestic contract that met the formalities of the Family Law Act.[71] The contract was made in writing, the parties signed it, and it was witnessed. In *Ghaznavi v. Kashif-Ul-Haque*,[72] the Ontario Superior Court of Justice also upheld the Islamic marriage contract, which provided for a *mahr* of $25,000. The court found the contractual obligation binding and enforceable as a civil obligation in Ontario courts.[73]

Nathan B. Oman has convincingly argued that courts ought not to find that *mahr* agreements are akin to prenuptial contracts in the United States. According to the Uniform Premarital Agreement Act, which twenty-seven American jurisdictions have adopted, a prenuptial agreement is "made in contemplation of marriage and effective upon marriage."[74] Theoretically then, the *mahr* fits awkwardly into such a

[63] *Amlani v. Hirani*, 2000 BCSC 1653 [*Amlani*].

[64] *N.M.M. v. N.S.M.*, 2004 BCSC 346.

[65] *Nasin v. Nasin*, 2008 ABQB 219. See also a similar decision, citing *Nasin*, under New Brunswick family law: *M.A.K. v. E.I.B.*, 2008 NBQB 249, additional reasons at (2008), 73 R.F.L. (6th) 372 (NB QB) (refusing to enforce *mahr* based on matrimonial contract provisions).

[66] Matrimonial Property Act, R.S.A. 2000, c. M-8.

[67] Matrimonial Property Act, para. 21.

[68] See *Kaddoura v. Hammoud* [1998] OJ no. 5054 (SC)(QL).

[69] *Khanis v. Noormohamed* [2009] OJ no. 2245 [*Khanis*].

[70] *Khanis v. Noormohamed* 2011 ONCA 127.

[71] Family Law Act, R.S.O. 1990, c. F3.

[72] *Ghaznavi v. Kashif-Ul-Haque*, 2011 ONSC 4062.

[73] *Ghaznavi v. Kashif-Ul-Haque*, para. 30.

[74] Unif. Premarital Agreement Act, 9C U.L.A. 43 (1983), s. 1(1). Available at: http://www.uniformlaws.org/shared/docs/premarital%20agreement/upaa_final_83.pdf.

definition, as under Islamic law, the *mahr* is part of the contract that causes the parties to be married, and no further ceremony is required subsequent to the contract.[75]

A marriage contract, in the Canadian context, can be made either before or during the marriage to manage a couple's property and other marital issues upon the dissolution of the relationship. A *mahr* agreement could technically fit more easily under such a definition of a marriage contract. However, when one examines the function of prenuptial/marriage contracts with *mahr* agreements, it becomes evident that they have differing purposes. A prenuptial/marriage contract typically protects the assets of a wealthier spouse against the future claims of a poorer spouse.[76] These contracts are gender neutral and are typically seen in second marriages when one or both parties have children from a previous relationship for whom they would like to protect their assets. These contracts allow parties to opt out of the default statutory regimes, which generally provide for equal sharing of the couple's property upon divorce.

A *mahr* by contrast, is a formal requirement of all Islamic marriages, is given by the husband to the wife in consideration of marriage, and its purpose is to provide the wife with something of monetary value either upon the marriage itself or when it dissolves. The deferred *mahr* is not a wife's claim on the property of the husband as under Islamic law there is no such thing as marital or community property. Any property brought to the marriage by either the wife or husband or acquired during the marriage remains his/her respective property. The *mahr* is simply a debt owed by the husband to the wife based on a promise to pay a sum of money upon divorce.

Given this analysis, it makes sense for courts to treat *mahr* agreements like ordinary contracts, as opposed to marriage contracts. The heightened requirements in most jurisdictions for prenuptial/marriage contracts such as disclosure obligations and independent legal advice ought not to be applied to *mahr* agreements as parties are not waiving rights under a legislative scheme or "bargaining away claims to property of uncertain value."[77] Instead the couple will have contracted to a specified monetary amount or object of economic value to be given by the husband to the wife.

B. *Mahr* Enforced as General Contracts

Wives have tried to enforce the husband's obligation to pay the *mahr* using the principles of ordinary contract law. This reasoning is alert to the highly contractual

[75] Oman, "How to Judge *Shari'a* Contracts," 323.

[76] See Mary Jane Mossman, *Families and the Law: Cases and Commentary*, 1st edn. (Concord: Captus Press, 2012).

[77] Oman, "How to Judge *Shari'a* Contracts," 332.

nature of Islamic marriage[78] wherein parties negotiate, sign, and have witnesses attest to their *mahr* agreements. Indeed it also correlates with the secular freedom to contract recognized by American and Canadian law, that is, to give effect to the meeting of the minds of contracting parties, so long as its application is not contrary to public policy.

In such instances, the argument is that the *mahr* does not replace the state's property rules upon divorce, but is simply a debt owed by the husband to his wife. In *Aziz v. Aziz*,[79] the Supreme Court of New York held that the *mahr*, which called for the payment of $5000 from the husband to the wife, was enforceable as a contractual obligation, notwithstanding the fact that it was entered into as part of a religious ceremony. This outcome is beneficial to women who are in marriages with few or no marital assets as it allows wives to obtain some financial support from their ex-husbands even where they would not be entitled to any property upon divorce.

In some cases it has also resulted in wives being able to claim the *mahr and* any equitable distribution in the divorce proceeding.[80] In *Odatalla v. Odatalla*,[81] for example, the New Jersey Superior Court asked "Why should a contract for the promise to pay money be less of a contract just because it was entered into at the time of an Islamic marriage ceremony?"[82] In this case, the court utilized neutral principles of law to enforce the *mahr* agreement worth $10,000. The court also awarded alimony and equitable distribution.

Relying on general principles of contract law, the Court of Appeals for Washington did not enforce the *mahr* in *In the Matter of the Marriage of Husna Obaidi*.[83] The husband, who was a US citizen and had lived in the United States since he was three, did not speak, write, or read Farsi, the language in which the negotiations proceeded and the agreement had been made. The court held that a valid contract requires a meeting of the minds on the essential terms. In this case, there was no such meeting of the minds given the language barrier. The Appeal Court seemed to emphasize in particular that the husband was not told that he would be required to participate in a ceremony that would include the signing of the *mahr* until fifteen minutes before he signed the agreement. This information would be relevant if the *mahr* was akin to a prenuptial agreement as several jurisdictions have heightened obligations regarding disclosure and independent legal advice in order to protect spouses entering into domestic contracts where they waive certain rights under the relevant legislative scheme. If however, the *mahr* agreement is treated using general principles of contract law, then the *mahr* ought simply to be viewed as a debt owed by the husband to the wife, requiring

[78] Mona Rafeeq, "Rethinking Islamic Law Arbitration Tribunals: Are They Compatible with Traditional American Notions of Justice?" *Wisconsin International Law Journal 28* (2010–11): 134.

[79] 488 N.Y.S. 2d 123 (1985).

[80] Oman, "How to Judge *Shariʿa* Contracts," 316.

[81] 344 N.J. Super. 305 (N.J. 2002) [*Odatalla*].

[82] *Odatalla*, 310.

[83] *In the Matter of the Marriage of Husna Obaidi and Khalid Qayoum*, 154 Wn. App. 609 (2010).

merely "mutual asset, offer, acceptance and consideration"[84] with little regard to the timing of the agreement.

The general contract approach to enforcing *mahr* agreements is particularly useful for those Muslim women who may only marry religiously or according to Islamic law, but not civilly or in accordance with the law of the land. The Ontario Superior Court of Justice enforced a *mahr* using ordinary contract law where the couple was not civilly married. In *Rashid v. Shaher*,[85] because the couple went through a religious and not civil marriage ceremony, their family law claims could not be addressed using the Divorce Act.[86] The couple had also not lived long enough to be considered common law spouses by virtue of the Family Law Act.[87] However, the couple had signed two contracts—the Islamic marriage contract which stated that the husband had paid an initial *mahr* of $20,000 to the wife and owed her a postponed amount of $40,000, and a second contract signed one year later which affirmed the terms of the original marriage contract. The court held that "there does not seem to be any public policy reason not to honour the agreement that the parties reached."[88] In such situations, the *mahr* would be the only way a woman would be entitled to any monetary relief from the husband.

For Muslim women living in Quebec who are in *de facto* relationships because they only marry according to Islamic law, enforcement of the *mahr* under ordinary contract law is particularly significant since in Quebec there is no legislative entitlement to spousal support or property division if one is unmarried or not part of a registered civil union.[89] Thus, a woman who has been with her spouse for fifteen years, was the primary caregiver of the children and sacrificed career and earning potential while supporting the husband's career, would be left at the end of the relationship without any spousal support or division of property. Although unlikely to be adequate to support a separate household, a Muslim woman could at the very least still have access to her *mahr* where courts do not hold the *mahr* agreement to the stricter requirements of prenuptial agreements.

The benefit of such an approach to *mahr* agreements is that no special legal innovation is required to enforce them. The common law of contracts is perfectly

[84] *In the Matter of the Marriage of Husna Obaidi and Khalid Qayoum*, para. 20.

[85] 2010 ONSC 4351.

[86] Divorce Act, R.S.C. 1985, c. 3 (2nd Supp).

[87] Ontario's FLA defines spouse for the purposes of support as: "either of two persons who are not married to each other and have cohabited, (a) continuously for a period of not less than three years or (b) in a relationship of some permanence, if they are the natural or adoptive parents of a child." FLA, s. 29.

[88] *Rashid*, para. 134. Interestingly, citing *Rashid*, the case of *Booth v. Howser*, 2012 ONSC 4104, noted that "the issue of 'donative intent', which, if present, would prevent a constructive trust remedy in favour of the claimant ... if the claimant intended a gift in favour of the Respondent, there is a juristic reason for the transfer of the asset, in which case there is no unjust enrichment or constructive trust remedy available to the claimant." This reasoning could presumably reinforce a contractual "gift" of *mahr*.

[89] *Quebec (Attorney General) v. A.*, 2013 SCC 5.

capable of dealing with *mahr* agreements like it would any other ordinary contract. This approach is also preferable as it does not impose additional criteria on parties such as onerous disclosure requirements or independent legal advice, as would be required of those signing prenuptial/marriage contracts. For women, who generally face negative economic consequences post divorce, the hope is that enforcement of the *mahr* using contract law principles will provide an easy-to-use additional tool with which to combat poverty.

c. *Mahr* Unenforceable on Public Policy Grounds

In the United States, *mahr* provisions have been attacked on public policy grounds. In an early case, *In re Marriage of Dajani*,[90] the California Court of Appeal refused to enforce the *mahr* on the theory that it violated the state's public policy against contracts that encouraged divorce. The court was of the view that the *mahr* created an incentive for wives to divorce their husbands as they could "profit by a divorce."[91] This case was later overruled in *In re Marriage of Bellio*[92] when the court noted "we believe that Dajani was wrongly decided. A dowry worth only $1,700, payable upon dissolution, is insufficient to seriously jeopardize a viable marriage."[93]

It has also been argued, typically by husbands, that enforcement of the *mahr* would run contrary to the First Amendment's prohibition on the establishment of religion.[94] For the most part, such arguments have not been successful. In *Jones v. Wolf*,[95] the US Supreme Court held that religious contracts can be enforced using neutral principles of law. Thus in *Odatalla* for example, it was held that the *mahr* agreement is not void simply because it was entered into during an Islamic marriage ceremony. "[E]nforcement of the secular parts of a written agreement is consistent with the constitutional mandate for a 'free exercise' of religious beliefs, no matter how diverse they may be."[96] The neutral principles of law approach appears to be a common way in which *mahr* agreements are enforced in the United States.

In a case this is now primarily of historic significance, a Canadian court held that the *mahr* of $30,000 was an unenforceable obligation pursuant to Ontario law. Although the contract between husband and wife conformed to section 52(1) of Ontario's Family Law Act in that the provision was not vague nor was the agreement signed under duress, the court refused to require payment of the *mahr* because the contract had a religious purpose. The court held:

> ... I cannot help but think that the obligation of the Mahr is as unsuitable for adjudication in the civil courts as is an obligation in a Christian religious marriage, such as to love, honour

[90] 204 Cal. App. 3d 1387 (1988).
[91] 204 Cal. App. 3d 1390 (1988).
[92] 129 Cal. Rptr. 2d 556 (2003).
[93] 129 Cal. Rptr. 2d 559 (2003).
[94] See *Odatalla, Aziz*, and *Akileh*.
[95] 443 U.S. 595 (1979).
[96] *Odatalla*, 312.

and cherish . . . Many such promises go well beyond the basic legal commitment to marriage required by our civil law, and are essentially matters of chosen religion and morality . . . not necessarily as a matter of enforceable civil law.[97]

Pascale Fournier makes the apt point that in erroneously importing a Christian, majoritarian comparison with the *mahr*, the judge overlooks that whereas vows constitute moral obligations that are indefinite insofar as they only bind the conscience, the *mahr* is a clear financial obligation.[98] However, the anxiety associated with entering the " 'religious thicket', a place that the courts cannot safely and should not go,"[99] has since been revised by the Supreme Court of Canada.

In *Bruker v. Marcovitz*, a Jewish couple signed a settlement agreement resolving their marital affairs at the end of their relationship. The agreement included a clause, which stipulated that upon the granting of a civil divorce, the spouses would appear before the rabbinical authorities "for the purpose of obtaining the traditional religious Get."[100] In Judaism, for a couple to be religiously divorced the husband must provide a *get*, or a Jewish bill of divorce, to his wife. A woman may be civilly divorced, but under Jewish law, if her husband does not provide her with a *get*, she remains married in the eyes of her religion. The majority of the Supreme Court endorsed the position that in deciding cases involving religion, "the courts cannot ignore religion."[101]

In her majority judgment, Justice Abella held that the agreement between Marcovitz and Bruker, which had a religious element to it, did not immunize it from judicial scrutiny:

I do not see the religious aspect of the obligation . . . as a barrier to its civil validity. [T]here is nothing in the *Civil Code* preventing someone from transforming his or her moral obligations into legally valid and binding ones.[102]

Justice Abella also stated that while some agreements with a religious aspect could potentially be against public order, an agreement to provide the *get* was not. In fact, enforcing a promise by a husband to provide a *get* harmonized with Canada's approach to religious freedom, to equality and to divorce and remarriage generally.[103] *Bruker v Marcovitz* has already been cited in decisions about Islamic marriages holding that the religious aspect of the *mahr* does not preclude a finding of contractual validity.[104]

Sometimes, courts have refused to enforce the *mahr* on the ground of fairness. In *Delvarani v. Delvarani*,[105] the British Columbia Supreme Court did not enforce

97 *Kaddoura*, para. 25.

98 Pascale Fournier, "The Erasure of Islamic Difference in Canadian and American Family Law Adjudication," *Journal of Law & Policy* 10, no.1 (2001): 61.

99 *Kaddoura*, para. 28.

100 *Marcovitz v. Bruker*, 2005 QCCA 835, para. 13.

101 *Marcovitz v. Bruker*, para. 18.

102 *Marcovitz v. Bruker*, para. 51.

103 *Marcovitz v. Bruker*, paras. 62–63.

104 See *Nasin*, paras. 12–14 and *Khanis*, para. 67.

105 2012 BCSC 162, additional reasons at 2012 BCSC 718.

the *mahr* of 3000 Bahar Azadi coins, valued at approximately CAD $750,000 because the court did not accept that the husband would have agreed to such a large amount of money in addition to any other obligations he might have under the laws of British Columbia. The court noted "[e]ven if this is a valid marriage agreement under the *FRA*, it is clearly unfair" given the short duration of the marriage, the need of the wife and the ability of the husband to pay.[106] In *Abdulqasim v. Mahmoud*,[107] despite a shariʿa marriage contracted in Sudan, the case proceeded purely on marital division law.

D. *Mahr* Unenforceable as Terms Too Vague

The Canadian courts have refused to enforce *mahr* agreements where the terms were too vague. In *Aziz v. Al-Masri*,[108] the British Columbia Supreme Court held that the *mahr* was not enforceable as the contract did not clearly state that the wife was the intended recipient of the funds. The express wording of the contract suggested that the wife's uncle was the intended recipient of the *mahr* funds and there was "no suggestion that the uncle received it [the advanced dowry] on behalf of the wife, or gave it to her."[109]

In *In re Marriage of Shaban*,[110] the husband argued that the Islamic marriage contract, which was signed in Egypt where the couple married, excluded any law but Islamic law from governing. In this case, the husband was seeking enforcement of a deferred *mahr* agreement valued at $30, when under state law, the wife was entitled to half of the $3 million marital property. The California Court of Appeal held that the "desire to be governed by the rules of the Islamic religion bore too attenuated a relationship to any actual terms of a prenuptial agreement to satisfy the statute of frauds."[111] Oman has stated that the husband was seeking more than a choice-of-law provision. He was in effect claiming that the parties had agreed, as a matter of contract, to be subject to the whole of Islamic family law.[112] Because the whole of Islamic law was not specified in the contract and would have to be established by parol evidence, the California Court of Appeal concluded that it could not satisfy the Statute of Frauds' requirement that essential terms of agreements made in consideration of marriage be in writing. The *mahr* was thus unenforceable because its terms were too vague.

In Islamic marriage contracts, the rules governing the initiation of divorce and potential forfeiture of the *mahr* are not always written into the contract. They remain

106 2012 BCSC 162, para. 209.

107 (District of Columbia Ct. of Appeals, 08-FM-228, August 9, 2012), affirming District of Columbia Superior Court, DRB-1527-05).

108 2011 BCSC 985.

109 2011 BCSC 985, para. 13.

110 88 Cal. App. 4th 398 (2001).

111 88 Cal. App. 4th 407–408 (2001).

112 Oman, "How to Judge *Shariʿa* Contracts," 312.

in the background, known to Islamic scholars or imams and perhaps to some litigants, but certainly not obvious to western courts or even necessarily to parties to the marriage. Thus, the question becomes whether and to what extent the type of Islamic divorce ought to govern the enforceability of the *mahr* in North America. For the most part, who initiates the divorce has had little impact on whether the *mahr* is deemed enforceable because courts have followed the ordinary meaning of the words of the contract.

Chelsea Sizemore has argued that courts should avoid guessing at the terms of *mahr* agreements and not enforce those that are vague. In practice, *mahr* agreements can be quite skeletal standard form contracts given to parties by an imam or religious leader. The parties will often fill in the blanks for the amount of the prompt and deferred *mahr*. Typically, the boilerplate terms of *mahr* agreements contain no reference to the different forms of Islamic divorce or when the wife may forfeit her *mahr*. Thus, Sizemore worries that it can obscure the operative details of the contract such as the parties' intentions and definitions, such that the court's reliance on neutral principles or an ordinary reading of the contract will enforce *mahr* agreements no matter the type of divorce.[113]

In *Akileh* for example, the court disregarded the husband's interpretation that the wife forfeited the *mahr* because she initiated the divorce.[114]

> Under the guise of using purely neutral principles of contract law, the Florida court ended up selecting one interpretation of Islam over another, which plainly over-stepped the court's constitutional role. Even if the court was completely unaware that its decision supported one school of Islamic doctrine over another, unintentional state action still may violate the Establishment Clause.[115]

Sizemore argues that because parties bargain for agreements within the greater context of Islamic law, courts are forced to rely on Islamic law to illuminate the *mahr* agreement's complete meaning.[116] On the other hand, Nathan Oman argues that parties to a *mahr* agreement do not bargain for the background rules of Islamic law that limit a wife's claim to the *mahr* in certain situations:

> To hold that it was part of the contract would be an innovation in contract interpretation. For example, if two parties enter into a contract in North Carolina they may have expectations about property rights based on North Carolina law. However, it would be extremely odd for a court to hold that merely making a contract in North Carolina means that the whole of North Carolina property laws is an implicitly bargained for term of the contract. Likewise, even if courts use Islamic law to understand the intentions of the parties ... they should still confine themselves to construing the bargained for terms of the contract.[117]

[113] Sizemore, "Enforcing Islamic Mahr Agreements," 1101. [114] *Akileh*, 248.

[115] Sizemore, "Enforcing Islamic Marriage Agreements," 1099–1100, citing *Akileh*.

[116] Sizemore, "Enforcing Islamic Mahr Agreements," 1100.

[117] Oman, "How to Judge *Shari'a* Contracts," 324.

Sizemore encourages Muslim parties to be precise about the terms of their written agreements and argues that judges should only enforce those *mahr* agreements that are specific in such regard. She suggests that parties (1) define the circumstances in which the "deferred" portion of the *mahr* is due, (2) declare what school of Islamic thought will apply, and (3) identify whether the *mahr* sum is the exclusive division of property upon divorce.[118]

Encouraging Muslim parties to be precise about the terms of their written agreements is certainly laudable.[119] It is more likely to ensure predictable judicial outcomes. However, the immense variety of territorial jurisdictions, linguistic and cultural distinctions, levels of religious piety, and gender and class divisions in which these agreements are formed may not always make such certainties possible. To complicate matters, one cannot assume that Muslims themselves fully comprehend the complex doctrinal differences when negotiating the *mahr* or that particular Muslims are bound to particular schools of Islamic thought. Macfarlane found in her research of North American Muslims that the differing schools of Islamic thought, even for imams, had little impact on the actual outcome because of a focus on adapting legal rules to the particular problem at hand.[120] Indeed as is common in many contractual disputes, parties tend to offer self-interested testimony with a view to gaining the most economically. Fournier has demonstrated that interpretations of the *mahr* have differed depending upon what each party sought to gain from the courts.[121]

III. Conclusion

In our increasingly diverse societies, it is crucial for courts to recognize and respond to the changing needs of the community. An outright denial of the *mahr* as contrary to vague notions of public policy is not only unjust, but contrary to longstanding American and Canadian traditions of promoting diversity and accommodation. As the New Jersey Superior Court noted in *Odatalla*, "the challenge faced by our courts today is in keeping abreast of the evolution of our community

[118] Sizemore, "Enforcing Islamic Mahr Agreements," 1112.

[119] Ibid., suggests that parties should draft their *mahr* contracts so that American courts understand the parties' *ex ante* intentions without relying on their *ex post* declarations of intent.

[120] Julie Macfarlane, "Practising an 'Islamic Imagination'" and Christopher Cutting "Faith-Based Arbitration or Religious Divorce," 37.

[121] Pascale Fournier, "Flirting with God in Western Secular Courts: Mahr in the West," *International Journal of Law, Policy and Family* 24 (2010): 78–84.

from a mostly homogenous group of religiously and ethnically similar members to today's diverse community."[122] In enforcing the *mahr*, the British Columbia courts have commented that attempting to accommodate the traditions of other countries and cultures is appropriate.[123]

Some see judicial recognition of the *mahr* as a manifestation of identity. There is something to be said for courts not summarily dismissing the claims of entire populations of people simply because they have a basis in a religion. Such an approach caters to the reductive and offensive reasoning sadly perpetrated in Ontario's shari'a debate and several US states' anti-shari'a measures. North American courts routinely consider cases that touch on religion and Muslims should not be denied the right to utilize the courts in resolving their contractual disputes.

Whether the enforcement of the *mahr* is necessarily about recognition of a minority right in each specific case is perhaps less obvious. Undoubtedly, parties to a divorce will make arguments that are self-serving. Thus, their interests are often opposed when it comes to the recognition and enforcement that the *mahr* deserves. It has been suggested that the enforcement of the *mahr* is not merely an expression of religious recognition by the judiciary, but carries distributive power. The distributional impact of the *mahr* is far from homogenous or predictable from case to case; it can amount to a bonus or penalty depending on the context[124] and perspective.

The preferable approach to the enforcement of the *mahr* is one that interprets such agreements as ordinary contracts. As noted, the *mahr* is not technically a prenuptial agreement as it is part of the Islamic contract that marries the couple. Moreover the differing purposes of *mahr* agreements (that provide a gift from husbands to wives in consideration of marriage to ensure some financial independence of the woman) versus prenuptial/marriage contracts (that are gender neutral and protect the assets of the wealthier spouse from legislative property sharing) suggest that they should not be treated the same. A general contract approach to *mahr* agreements would not impose additional and onerous formal criteria on the parties' agreements and in most cases would be a sum of money owed by the husband to the wife separate from that given by the marital property regime of the state. Importantly, this would mean that women, who generally face negative economic consequences post divorce, would have an additional and accessible legal device available to counter financial hardship.

Both the shari'a debate in Ontario and the anti-shari'a legislation in several US states relied on the oppression of Muslim women as a reason for prohibiting the incorporation or use of shari'a in the North American legal system. Muslim women, like many other women, face perhaps the greatest adversity both economically and

122 *Odatalla*, 311.

123 See *Delvarani*, para. 204, *Aziz v. Al-Masri*, para. 3, and *Nathoo*, paras. 24–25.

124 Fournier, "Flirting with God," 2.

socially when their conjugal relationships come to an end. One way in which to assist Muslim women and their children is to promote the enforcement of *mahr* agreements, particularly where the terms are clear and fair.

References

Cases

Abd Alla v. Mourssi, 680 N.W.2d 569, 574 (Minn. Ct. App. 2004).
Abdulqasim v. Mahmoud, (District of Columbia Ct. of Appeals, 08-FM-228, August 9, 2012), affirming District of Columbia Superior Court, DRB-1527-05).
Ahmed v. Ahmed, 261 S.W. 3d 190, 2008 Tex. App. *Lexis* 4660 (2008).
Akileh v. Elchahal, 666. So. 2d 246 (Fla. Dist. Ct. App. 1996).
Al-Alami, Abdulaziz A. "32 States Introduce Ban of Sharia Law with Misleading Semantics," *Arab American Institute* (May 21, 2013), http://www.aaiusa.org/blog/entry/anti-shariah-bills/
Aleem v. Aleem, 404 Md. 404; 947 A.2d 489; 2008 MD Lexis 246.
Amlani v. Hirani, 2000 BCSC 1653.
Awad v. Ziriax et al., 670 F.3d 1111 (10th Circuit 2012) (Docket 10-6273).
Aziz v. Al-Masri, 2011 BCSC 985.
Aziz v. Aziz, 488 NYS 2d 123 (1985).
Booth v. Howser, 2012 ONSC 4104.
Chaudry v. Chaudry, 159 N.J. Super. 566; 388 A.2d 1000; 1978 N.J. Super. Lexis 952.
Delvarani v. Delvarani, 2012 BCSC 162, additional reasons at 2012 BCSC 718.
Ghaznavi v. Kashif-Ul-Haque, 2011 ONSC 4062.
Gonzales v O Centro Espirita Beneficente Uniao do Vegetal, 546 US 419 (2006).
In re Marriage of Bellio, 129 Cal. Rptr. 2d 556 (2003).
In re Marriage of Dajani, 204 Cal. App. 3d 1387 (1988).
In re Marriage of Shaban, 88 Cal. App. 4th 398 (2001).
In the Matter of the Marriage of Husna Obaidi and Khalid Qayoum, 154 Wn App 609 (2010).
Kaddoura v. Hammoud, [1998] O.J. no. 5054 (S.C.).
Khanis v. Noormohamed, [2009] O.J. no. 2245.
Khanis v. Noormohamed, 2011 ONCA 127.
M.A.K. v. E.I.B., 2008 NBQB 249, additional reasons at (2008), 73 R.F.L. (6th) 372 (N.B. Q.B.).Marcovitz v. Bruker, 2005 QCCA 835.
Moge v. Moge, [1992] 3 S.C.R. 813.
Nasin v. Nasin, 2008 ABQB 219.
Nathoo v. Nathoo, [1996] B.C.J. no. 2720 [BCSC].
N.M.M. v. N.S.M., 2004 BCSC 346.
Odatalla v. Odatalla, 344 N.J. Super. 305 (N.J. 2002).
Quebec (Attorney General) v. A., 2013 SCC 5.
Rashid v. Shaher, 2010 ONSC 4351.
R. v. N.S., 2012 SCC 72.*S.D. v. M.J.R.*, Superior Court of New Jersey, Chancery Division, Family Part, Hudson County, Docket No. FV-09-1792-09.
S.D. v. M.J.R., 415 N.J. Super. 417 (N.J. Super. App. Div. 2010); 2010 NJ Super LEXIS 143.

Shaheed Allah v. Adella Jordan-Luster, No. 04-1083, 2007 WL 2582199 (C.D. Ill. Aug 3, 2007).
Soleimani v. Soleimani, Johnson County District Ct, Kansas, Docket 11CV4468 (August 28, 2012).
Taylor v. Cook County, No. 11 C 7427, 2013 WL 2285806, 4 (N.D. Ill. May 23, 2013).

Legislation

Arbitration Act 1991, SO 1991, c 17.
Divorce Act, R.S.C. 1985, c. 3 (2nd Supp).
Family Law Act, R.S.O. 1990, c. F3.
Family Relations Act, R.S.B.C. 1996, c. 128.
Family Statute Law Amendment Act, 2006, S.O. 2006, c. 1.
H.R. 79, House Substitute for Senate Bill 79, 2011–2012 Legislative Session (Ks, 2012), http://kslegislature.org/li_2012/b2011_12/measures/SB79/.
H.R. 1353, 107th Leg. (Tenn. 2011), http://www.capitol.tn.gov/Bills/107/Bill/HB1353.pdf.
Matrimonial Property Act, R.S.A. 2000, c. M-8.
Uniform Premarital Agreement Act, 9C U.L.A. 43 (1983).
Tennessee House of Representatives. "Bill Information for H.R. 1353." http://wapp.capitol.tn.gov/apps/BillInfo/Default.aspx?BillNumber=%20HB1353&GA=107.

References

Associated Press, "Kansas Senate Passes Law Banning Sharia, Other Foreign Laws from State Courts" May 11, 2012, http://www.nydailynews.com/news/politics/kansas-senate-passes-law-banning-sharia-foreign-laws-state-courts-article-1.1076862.
Awad, Abed, "The True Story of Sharia in American Courts." *The Nation* July 2, 2012, http://www.thenation.com/article/168378/true-story-shariashari'a-american-courts#.
Bakht, Natasha, "Family Arbitration Using Sharia Law: Examining Ontario's Arbitration Act and its Impact on Women." *Muslim World Journal of Human Rights* 1 (2004): 1.
Bakht, Natasha, "Were Muslim Barbarians Really Knocking on the Gates of Ontario?: The Religious Arbitration Controversy—Another Perspective." *Ottawa Law Review* 40th Anniversary (2005): 70.
Bano, Samia, "Islamic Family Arbitration, Justice and Human Rights in Britain." *Law, Social Justice & Global Development Journal* 1 (2007).
Beaman, Lori, *Defining Harm: Religious Freedom and the Limits of the Law* (Toronto: University of British Columbia Press, 2008).
Cutting, Christopher, "Faith-Based Arbitration or Religious Divorce: What Was the Issue?" in Anna C. Korteweg and Jennifer A. Selby (eds.) *Debating Sharia: Islam, Gender Politics, and Family Law Arbitration* (Toronto: University of Toronto Press, 2012) 66.
Emon, Anver, "Banning Shari'a" September 6, 2011 *The Immanent Frame*, http://blogs.ssrc.org/tif/2011/09/06/banning-shari%e2%80%98a/.
Fallon, Sarah M., "Justice for All: American Muslims, Sharia Law, and Maintaining Comity Within American Jurisprudence." *Boston College International and Comparative Law Review* 36 (2013): 153.
Finnie, Ross, "Women, Men, and the Economic Consequences of Divorce: Evidence from the Canadian Longitudinal Data." *Canadian Review of Sociology and Anthropology* 30, no. 2 (1993): 205.
Fournier, Pascale, "The Erasure of Islamic Difference in Canadian and American Family Law Adjudication." *Journal of Law & Policy* 10 (2001): 51.

Fournier, Pascale, "In the (Canadian) Shadow of Islamic Law: Translating *Mahr* as a Bargaining Endowment" in Richard Moon (ed.) *Law and Religious Pluralism in Canada* (Toronto: University of British Columbia Press, 2008) 140.

Fournier, Pascale, "Flirting with God in Western Secular Courts: Mahr in the West." *International Journal of Law, Policy and Family* 24 (2010): 67.

Glenn, H. Patrick, *Legal Traditions of the World: Sustainable Diversity in Law* (4th edn. Toronto: Oxford University Press, 2010).

Grunert, Jeremy, "How Do You Solve a Problem Like Sharia? *Awad v. Ziriax* and the Question of Sharia Law in America." *Pepperdine Law Review* 40 (2013): 695.

Keshavjee, Mohamed M., *Islam, Shariʿa and Alternative Dispute Resolution: Mechanisms for Legal Redress in the Muslim Community* (London: I.B. Tauris, 2013).

Korteweg, Anna C. and Jennifer A. Selby, eds., *Debating Sharia: Islam, Gender Politics, and Family Law Arbitration* (Toronto: University of Toronto Press, 2012).

Krayem, Ghena, "To Recognized or Not to Recognize, That is NOT the Question: Family Law and the Muslim Community in Australia" (Ph.D. dissertation, unpublished, University of Sydney, 2011).

Kutty, Faisal, "'Shariʿa Courts in Canada: A Delayed Opportunity for the Indigenization of Islamic Legal Rulings" in Anna C. Korteweg and Jennifer A. Selby (eds.) *Debating Sharia: Islam, Gender Politics, and Family Law Arbitration* (Toronto: University of Toronto Press, 2012) 123–151.

MacFarlane, Julie, "Practising an 'Islamic Imagination': Islamic Divorce in North America" in Anna C. Korteweg and Jennifer A. Selby (eds.) *Debating Sharia: Islam, Gender Politics, and Family Law Arbitration* (Toronto: University of Toronto Press, 2012) 35.

MacFarlane, Julie, *Sustaining the Islamic Imagination: Islamic Marriage and Divorce in North America* (Oxford: Oxford University Press, 2012).

Macklin, Audrey, "Multiculturalism Meets Privatization: The Case of Faith-Based Arbitration" in Anna C. Korteweg and Jennifer A. Selby (eds.) *Debating Sharia: Islam, Gender Politics, and Family Law Arbitration* (Toronto: University of Toronto Mossman) 91–122.

Mary Jane, *Families and the Law: Cases and Commentary* (1st edn. Concord: Captus Press, 2012).

Oman, Nathan B., "How to Judge *Shariʿa* Contracts: A Guide to Islamic Marriage Agreements in American Courts." *Utah Law Review 2011*, no. 1 (2011): 287.

Pew Research, Religion & Public Life Project, "State Legislation Restricting Use of Foreign or Religious Law," http://features.pewforum.org/shariʿa-law-map/.

Quraishi, Asifa and Najeeba Syeed-Miller, "No Altars: A Survey of Islamic Family Law in the United States," http://papers.ssrn.com/sol3/papers.cfm?abstract_id=1524246.

Quraishi-Landes, Asifa, "Rumors of the Sharia Threat Are Greatly Exaggerated: What American Judges Really Do with Islamic Law in Family Courtrooms." *New York Law School Law Review* 57, no. 2 (2012–13): 245.

Quraishi-Landes, Asifa, "What is Sharia and is it Creepy?" *The Islamic Monthly* June 18, 2012, http://www.theislamicmonthly.com/what-is-sharia-and-is-it-creepy/.

Rafeeq, Mona, "Rethinking Islamic Law Arbitration Tribunals: Are They Compatible with Traditional American Notions of Justice?" *Wisconsin International Law Journal* 28 (2010–11): 108.

Razack, Sherene, *Casting Out: The Eviction of Muslims from Western Law and Politics* (Toronto: University of Toronto Press, 2008).

Selby, Jennifer A. and Anna C. Korteweg, "Introduction: Situating the Sharia Debate in Ontario" in Anna C. Korteweg and Jennifer A. Selby (eds.) *Debating Sharia: Islam, Gender Politics, and Family Law Arbitration* (Toronto: University of Toronto Press, 2012) 12.

Sizemore, Chelsea A., "Enforcing Islamic Mahr Agreements: The American Judge's Interpretational Dilemma." *George Mason Law Review* 18, no. 4 (2010–11): 1085.

Weitzman, L.J., *The Divorce Revolution: The Unexpected Social and Economic Consequences for Women and Children in America* (New York: Free Press, 1985).

Zakaria, Rafia, "Sharia Law Ban and Muslim Wives." *Al Jazeera* February 16, 2013, http://www.aljazeera.com/indepth/opinion/2013/02/201321174724878286.html.

CHAPTER 29

ISLAMIC LAW IN WESTERN EUROPE

MATHIAS ROHE

1. The History of Islamic Law in Western Europe

Islamic law has been applied in Muslim realms in Southern Europe, namely in Spain and Southern Italy, until the end of the Middle Ages.[1] In an exceptional case, the German Staufian emperor Frederic II introduced legislation (constitutions of Melfi, 1231), which allowed the non-Christian part of the population (Muslims, Jews) to live under their respective personal laws within his realm.[2] Besides that, the application of foreign laws was usually regulated by bilateral or international treaties. The first prominent example is the treaty between the Ottoman Empire and the Kingdom of France from 1535, which served as an example for numerous later treaties.[3]

[1] The geographical area covered by this chapter includes central, northern, and the western part of Southern Europe. According to the terminology which emerged after the Second World War, this follows the distinction between West and East until the end of the Cold War. For basic information about Islam and Muslims in contemporary Europe cf. Jocelyne Cesari, ed., *The Oxford Handbook on European Islam* (Oxford: Oxford University Press, 2015).

[2] Cf. (Klaus Heinisch, *Kaiser Friedrich II* (Darmstadt: Wissenschaftliche Buchgesellschaft, 1970), 225ff.; Eberhard Horst, *Der Sultan von Lucera: Freidrich II. und der Islam* (Freiburg im Breisgau: Herder, 1997), 132.

[3] Cf. Mathias Rohe, *Islamic Law in Past and Present* (Leiden and Boston: Brill, 2015), 202.

Given the fact that after the Reconquista (reconquest of former Muslim territories) the Muslim population came under heavy pressure leading to expulsion, emigration, or forced conversion, Islamic law was only applied in few exceptional cases concerning diplomats or other persons protected by treaty regulations. In consequence, academic publications dealing with Islamic law, which emerged since the nineteenth century from a number of European universities, usually only dealt with the history of Islamic law or with the application of it within territories under European colonial control.

Since the late nineteenth century, courts had to decide cases under legal rules inspired by Islamic law in transnational cases (see later in the chapter). Thus, it was mainly courts and legal practitioners who dealt with Islamic law in Western Europe in times when relatively few Muslims were permanently living in the region.

The situation altered significantly after movements of mass immigration to Western Europe particularly since the 1960s for various reasons, for example, labor migration or migration to the United Kingdom by Commonwealth members before severe immigration restrictions were introduced there. Since then, the application of Islamic legal rules became daily practice in Western European courtrooms and administrations due to the laws of these states which enabled or even demanded such application in transborder cases. From the very beginning it was clear that the implementation of Islamic legal norms into the existing legal systems or the introduction of a system of personal laws on the basis of religious or ethnic affiliation was not an option for European states. Historically, since the early Middle Ages, European legal systems tended to replace personal law systems by territorial ones.[4] Legal pluralism in the sense of total equality of different legal norms within one state has no historical precedent and would fundamentally contradict the existing constitutional orders in Europe. Instead, the continuing necessity to balance legal unity as a basis of social cohesion and diversity as an equally important aspect for granting individual freedom and self-determination is met by creating a frame of compulsory norms applicable to everyone and opening broad space within this frame for individual choice. The latter includes the application or acceptance of Islamic legal norms or legal relations under the law of the land which are inspired by Islamic legal thinking (e.g. Islamic investment).[5]

The chapter goes on to discuss the different levels for the application of Islamic law and the respective scope and limits.

[4] Cf. Hans Hattenhauer, *Europäische Rechtsgeschichte* 3rd edn. (Heidelberg: C.F. Müller, 1998), n. 881ff.; Mathias Rohe, "Family and the Law in Europe: Bringing Together Secular Legal Orders and Religious Norms and Needs," in *Family, Religion and Law: Cultural Encounters in Europe*, eds. Prakash Shah, Marie-Claire Foblets, and Mathias Rohe (Farnham: Ashgate, 2014), 51ff.

[5] For details cf. Rohe, "Family and the Law in Europe," 49, 50ff.

II. The Application of Islamic Law in Western Europe since the 1960s

A. Introduction

Regarding the application of foreign law—including foreign state law based on shari'a rules—we have to distinguish between different fields of law. Public law, which regulates the legal relations between the state and its citizens/inhabitants, and penal law in particular are strictly territorial nowadays worldwide. Consequently, no foreign legal rules can apply in these fields, with few exceptions regarding freedom of religion.[6] In contrast, in matters of private law (mainly concerning legal relations between private parties) the situation is different. In this field, Western European legal systems open space for the application of foreign legal norms when they are considered to be the most appropriate rules to decide the case at stake (see more detail on this later). The same is true with respect to the "private" aspects of social security law, i.e. regarding claims concerning contributions paid by private persons to social security systems (e.g. widows' pensions).

Islamic legal rules in Western Europe first made an appearance in courts and administrations, when state law required their application in cross-border cases (e.g. concerning foreign nationals). Thus, it was mainly case law which dealt with such provisions, first in a more tentative way, being more and more replaced by systematic handling of an increasing number of cases. While an abundance of sociological works on Muslims in Europe was published since the 1970s, academic publications[7] dealing with legal issues related to Muslims in Europe in some depth only appeared since the mid-1990s.[8] The first comprehensive volumes on the handling of Islamic legal rules in European legal orders appeared only since the late 1990s.[9] Since 2001,

[6] This is the case of male circumcision on religious grounds among Muslims and Jews alike. Under European laws it is only permitted on the condition that it will be performed according to specific standards For details cf. Mathias Rohe, "Shari'a in Europe," in *The Oxford Handbook of European Islam*, ed. Jocelyne Cesari (Oxford: Oxford University Press, 2015), 458f.

[7] The most comprehensive collection in European libraries is available at the law library of the University of Erlangen-Nürnberg.

[8] Michael King, ed., *God's Law versus State Law: The Construction of an Islamic Identity in Western Europe* (London: Grey Seal, 1995); Jørgen Nielsen, *Muslims in Western Europe* (Edinburgh: Edinburgh University Press, 1995); Wasif Shadid and Pieter Van Koningsveld, eds., *Religious Freedom and the Neutrality of the State: The Position of Islam in the European Union* (Leuven: Peeters, 2002); Stefano Allievi and Felice Dassetto, *Facettes de l'Islam belge* (Louvain-la-Neuve: Bruylant, 1997).

[9] David Pearl and Werner Menski, *Muslim Family Law* (Lahore: Brite Books, 1998); Sebastian Poulter, *Ethnicity, Law and Human Rights* (Oxford: Clarendon Press, 1998); Aldeeb and Bonomi, *Le droit musulman de la famille et des successions à l'épreuve des ordres juridiques occidentaux* (Zürich: Schulthess, 1999); Christian von Bar, ed., *Islamic Family Law and its Reception by the Courts in the West* (Köln: Heymann 1999); Lionel Panafit, *Quand le droit écrit l'islam* (Bruxelles: Bruylant, 1999); Silvio Ferrari and Anthony Bradney, eds., *Islam and European Legal Systems* (Aldershot: Ashgate, 2010).

the number of specialized book publications has considerably increased.[10] In addition, a long-term project (*Yearbook of Muslims in Europe*, edited by Nielsen et al. since 2009, containing country reports) has been published.

In view of the short period of time since the late 1990s, it may be considered to be still too early to write a comprehensive history of shari'a in Europe. Broader scientific research has only started in this millenium, and the public debate is still by and large lacking sound information and often serves merely as a political forum for islamophobic and Muslim extremist voices. The heated and poorly informed debate on the speech of the Archbishop of Canterbury Rowan Williams in 2008 on the treatment of some aspects of shari'a in the UK is a striking example.[11] In addition, the profound differences between European states regarding their historical

[10] Jean-Paul Charnay, *La Charia et l'Occident* (Paris: L'Herne, 2001); Philippe Kahn, ed., *L'étranger et le droit de la famille: pluralité ethnique, pluralisme juridique* (Paris: La Documentation française, 2001); S.N. Shah-Kazemi, *Untying the Knot: Muslim Women, Divorce and the Shari'ah* (London: Nuffield Foundation, 2001); Agostino Cilardo, *Il diritto islamico e il sistema giuridico italiano* (Napoli: Edizioni Scientifice Italiane, 2002); René Pahud de Mortanges and Erwin Tanner, eds., *Muslime und schweizerische Rechtsordnung: Les musulmans et l'ordre juridique suisse* (Freiburg: Universitätsverlag, 2002); Roberta Aluffi Beck-Peccoz and Giovanna Zincone, eds., *Legal Treatment of Islamic Minorities in Europe* (Leuven: Peeters, 2004); Richard Potz and Wolfgang Wieshaider, *Islam and the European Union* (Leuven: Peeters, 2004); Rohe, "Shari'a in Europe"; Marie-Claire Foblets and Jean-Yves Carlier, *Le code marocain de la famille: Incidences au regard du droit international privé en Europe* (Bruxelles: Bruylant, 2005); J. Meeusen, M. Pertegas, G. Straetmans, and Fr. Swennen, eds., *International Family Law for the European Union* (Antwerp and Oxford: Intersentia, 2007); Prakash Shah and Werner Menski, eds., *Migration, Diasporas and Legal Systems in Europe* (London: Routledge Cavendish, 2007); Conseil de la communauté marocaine à l'étranger, *Le statut juridique de l'Islam en Europe* Acte du colloque international organize par le Conseil de la communauté marocaine à l'étranger Fès, 14 et 15 Mars 2009 (Rabat: Marsam, 2010); Rex Ahdar and Nicholas Aroney, eds., *Shari'a in the West* (Oxford: Oxford University Press, 2010); Nathalie Bernard-Maugiron and Baudoin Dupret, eds., *Ordre public et droit musulman de la famille en Europe et en Afrique du Nord* (Bruxelles: Bruylant, 2010); Marie-Claire Foblets, François Gaudreault-Desbiens, and Alison Rentel, eds., *Cultural Diversity and the Law* (Bruxelles: Bruylant, 2010); Pascale Fournier, *Muslim Marriage in Western Courts: Lost in Transition* (Farnham: Ashgate, 2010); Jørgen Nielsen and Lisbeth Christoffersen, eds., *Shari'a as Discourse: Legal Traditions and the Encounter with Europe* (Farnham: Ashgate, 2010); Andrea Büchler, *Islamic Law in Europe? Legal Pluralism and its Limits in European Family Laws* (Farnham and Burlington: Ashgate, 2011); Rubya Mehdi and Jørgen S. Nielsen, *Embedding Mahr (Islamic Mahr) in the European Legal System* (Copenhagen: DJ Ø F Publishing, 2011); Samia Bano, *An Exploratory Study of Shari'ah councils in England with Respect to Family Law* (Reading: University of Reading, 2012); Maleiha Malik, *Minority Legal Orders in the UK* (London: British Academy Policy Centre, 2012); Joel A. Nichols, ed., *Marriage and Divorce in a Multicultural Context* (Cambridge: Cambridge University Press, 2012); Maurits Berger, ed., *Applying Shari'a in the West* (Leiden: Leiden University Press, 2013); Prakash Shah, Marie-Claire Foblets, and Mathias Rohe, eds., *Family, Religion and Law Cultural Encounters in Europe* (Farnham: Ashgate, 2014).

[11] Rowan Williams, "Civil and Religious Law in England: A Religious Perspective." Lecture, Royal Courts of Justice, 2008; John Milbank, "The Archbishop of Canterbury: The Man and the Theology Behind the Shari'a Lecture," in *Shari'a in the West*, ed. Rex Ahdar and Nicholas Aroney (New York: Cambridge University Press, 2010), 43–57; Jean-François Gaudreault-Desbiens, "Religious Court's Recognition Claims: Two Qualitatively Distinct Narratives," in *Shari'a in the West*, ed. Rex Ahdar and Nicholas Aroney (Oxford: Oxford University Press, 2010), 59–69.

experiences and developments of the relations between state and religion lead to a highly differentiated legal scene. While some common legal ground is created by the protection of freedom of religion provided by the European Convention on Human Rights (ECHR), the application of foreign legal rules—including those inspired by shari'a norms—mainly lies in the competence of the nation-states. Thus, for the time being we should restrict ourselves to discerning the fields in which Islamic law is applied and the main reasons for differing approaches in various European states, and to describing major trends regarding Muslim self-understanding in this regard.

Given the significant differences in the legal-sociological backgrounds of Muslims originating from North Africa, East Africa, the Near East, the Balkans and Turkey, Iran, Central Asia, and South and Southeast Asia, it is correct that the needs and creeds as well as publications and case law mirror this plurality on all legal and societal levels. In addition, the readiness to accept forms of legal pluralism under the law of the land differs in Western European states: British communitarianism often leads to results different from French unitarian thinking (*unité de la Republique*).

In general, the application of Islamic law in the form of modern state law may cause considerable tensions in some fields, for example, regarding family and succession law rules which are not gender neutral or which treat adherents of different religions unequally.[12] It is necessary here to distinguish between legal norms enforceable by official state measures on the one hand, and all sorts of norms and acts operating in civil society without validation by the official legal system of enforcement on the other. In the latter field, normative pluralism is indeed widespread. But in case of conflict, compulsory state rules will prevail over social or religiously inspired ones according to the principles of secular legal orders. However, within this framework, the legal system has the flexibility to accommodate pluralism to a considerable extent.[13]

For centuries, personal law systems implementing a kind of legal pluralism have been replaced in Europe by territorially unified laws granting *internal* pluralism, but reserving the final decision to state law in case of conflicting norms.[14] This is true despite the fact of normative pluralism within western societies.[15] Within this scope, legal shari'a norms might be applied to a certain extent under the respective state law. This legal framework is of prime importance for the development of Muslim normativity in Europe: As far as state law leads to or enables such application,

[12] Cf. Wael Hallaq, *An Introduction to Islamic Law* (New York: Cambridge University Press, 2009), 271ff.; Rohe, *Islamic Law in Past and Present*, 100ff., 263ff.

[13] Cf. John Witte, "The Future of Muslim Family Law in Western Democracies," in *Shari'a in the West*, ed. Rex Ahdar and Nicholas Aroney (Oxford: Oxford University Press, 2010), 279ff.

[14] For the problems of legal transplants concerning personal law systems into western legal orders cf. only Gaudreault-Desbiens, "Religious Court's Recognition Claims."

[15] Cf. the most informative volume edited by Nielsen and Christoffersen, *Shari'a As Discourse*, specifically the chapter on situation written by Prakash Shah, 117ff., and the models developed by Zucca, *Law and Religion*, 194–196 in particular.

Muslims who appreciate this application would be satisfied with the existing system. On the other hand, the readiness of state laws to apply shari'a-based norms leads to criticism among other Muslims and many non-Muslims. Given these controversial attitudes, the existing legal systems, including courts and administrations, have to clarify the scope and limits for the application of Islamic legal norms.

B. Fields of Application

1. *Private international law*

In cross-border cases, for example, where foreign citizens are involved, the parties often rely on legal relations created under foreign law.[16] Long-term relations like marriage and the legal aspects of family life in particular require legal stability and reliability. Should the legal framework governing their relations necessarily change in cases of changing citizenship or residence? The legal order can accept pluralistic arrangements to a certain extent under the principle of private autonomy, but has to grant the amount of unity which is necessary to preserve peace in society. Thus, legal differences can be accepted only to a certain degree.

Private international law (PIL) (which regulates conflicting laws pertaining to civil matters) is the most prominent level on which Islamic legal rules can be directly applied. In primarily private matters of an international dimension it is desirable to apply the substantive law having the most significant relationship to the case to be decided. The revolutionary idea underlying this concept is the principal equality of all legal orders; this is why foreign law can be applied.

Nevertheless, is it obvious that sensitive areas of the law, such as family and inheritance law, are highly dependent on social convictions and developments. Hence, substantially different regulations are in existence all over the world. In such cases, the legal community in a particular country may decide that in certain matters the same substantive law should be applicable to every resident there. This would be the case particularly in matters touching the roots of legal and societal common basic convictions like those regulated by family law. When foreign legal norms are applied, the result must comply with the law of the land and public order (*ordre public*). This is the necessary limit drawn by every legal system in order to preserve peace in society by maintaining the most important common standards, human rights standards in particular.

[16] This part of the chapter is based in part on research in the context of RELIGARE (see http://www.religareproject.eu), a three-year project funded under the Socio-economic Sciences & Humanities program of DG Research of the European Commission's Seventh Framework Research Program.

It would certainly be of some interest to know more about the historical development of these fields. However, this would require a full-length monograph based on in-depth research at Ph.D. level to do it justice.

Islamic law contains many provisions that do not contradict western laws (in the area of contract law, for example) and therefore may be easily applied. In the United Kingdom, contracts including a choice of law provision ("principles of the Glorious Shari'a") have been dealt with in courts.[17] The main conflicts between Islamic and European laws concern family matters and inheritance. They arise over constitutional (and human) rights concerns on gender equality and freedom of religion, including the right not to believe, and the protection of minors; provisions reflecting classical Islamic law preserve strict separation between the sexes with respect to their social roles in patriarchal social structures. Far-reaching segregation of religions under the supremacy of Islam is still prevalent, forcing non-believers into the application of religiously based family and inheritance laws, prohibiting inter-religious inheritance even among spouses or leading to forced separation of spouses in cases of alleged or real "apostasy" by one of them.[18] In addition, child marriage has been abolished in some Islamic countries, but is still practised in others. In addition, conflicts arise, for example, with respect to marriage and inheritance doctrines involving religious difference, polygamy, divorce, and gender-biased rules on guardianship and custody for children.

European legal history is familiar with such religion-orientated and gender-based patriarchal legal structures, but has replaced them by secular and gender-neutral regulations during the twentieth century. From there, fundamental conflicts between Islamic law in its traditional form and current European legal orders arise and have to be tackled in daily legal practice. Again, there is no uniform European approach to this task. The different ways of reasoning within European legal orders shall be demonstrated using the most oft-adjudicated issue of divorce (*talaq*).[19]

According to traditional Islamic law, which is still in force in many Islamic countries despite a number of internal reforms in favor of women,[20] only the husband

[17] Cf. Killian Bälz, "A Murabaha Transaction in an English Court," *Islamic Law and Society* 11 (2004): 117–134.

[18] Cf. Rohe, *Islamic Law in Past and Present*, 263ff., 292ff., 324ff.

[19] Cf. Marie-Claire Foblets, Brigitte Marechal, and Jørgen Nielsen, *Convergences musulmanes: Aspects contemporains de l'islam dans l'Europe élargie* (Louvain la-Neuve: Bruylant, 2001); Marie-Claire Foblets, Brigitte Marechal, and Jørgen Nielsen, "The Admissibility of Repudiation: Recent Developments in Dutch, French and Belgian Private International Law," *Hawwa* 5 (2007): 10–32; Verena Gärtner, *Die Privatscheidung im deutschen und gemeinschaftsrechtlichen Internationalen Privat- und Verfahr ensrecht: außergerichtliche Ehescheidung im Spannungsfeld von kultureller Diversität und Integration* (Tübingen: Mohr Siebeck, 2008); Büchler, Islamic Law in Europe?; Rohe, *Islamic Law in Past and Present*, 468ff.; Julia Koch, *Die Anwendung islamischen Scheidungs—und Scheidungsfolgenrechts im Internationalen Privatrecht der EU-Mitgliedstaaten* (Frankfurt: Lang, 2012).

[20] For new developments cf. Ziba Mir-Hosseini, "Islamic Family Law and Social Practice: Anthropological Reflections on the Terms of the Debate," in *Family, Law and Religion. Debates in the Muslim World and their Implications for Co-operation and Dialogue*, ed. Siegfried Hass (Vienna: Austrian Association for the Middle East Hammer-Purgstall, 2009), 37–48 with numerous references; Rohe, *Islamic Law in Past and Present*, 263ff.; Maaike Voorhoeve, ed., *Family Law in Islam: Divorce, Marriage and Women in the Muslim World* (London: I.B. Tauris, 2012).

is entitled to terminate the marriage by a unilateral declaration of repudiation without any reason to be given (*talaq*). This has to be repeated three times, and attempts at reconciliation have to be made; only when reconciliation fails, is the marriage dissolved. Such procedure clearly contradicts the European legal principle of equality of sexes—since wives have only very limited rights to divorce[21]—as well as the principle of life-long marriage which does not allow the dissolution of the marriage by such easy procedures. Thus, according to regulations in European legal orders, a *talaq* is invalid on European soil[22] (as opposed to the so-called *khul'* or other forms of divorce for discord).[23] But how to deal with a *talaq* which has become valid abroad? Would European "public order" prevent its recognition in any case or only in those cases where the wife was not able to defend her rights and did not agree to the divorce?

The traditional PIL approach concerning the application of the civil law concept of public order (*ordre public*) considers the outcome of the application of the respective foreign law, not at the foreign norm as such. The underlying idea is to concentrate on the individual interests of persons who have to navigate between competing legal orders, not to scrutinize foreign legal orders regarding their compatibility with the law of the land in abstract. In recent years, this pragmatic approach has been increasingly challenged by an abstract "human rights approach," which leads to the rejection of foreign norms as such, rather than first to evaluate their outcome.[24] German[25], Italian,[26] and Spanish[27] courts follow the traditional approach broadly. Thus, the recognition of *talaq* would contradict public order in cases where the wife was not able to claim her legitimate interests or was not even informed about the divorce. In other cases, where the prerequisites for divorce according to the law of the land would be fulfilled in a comparable way or if the wife agrees, the legality

[21] Cf. Rohe, *Islamic Law in Past and Present*, 275ff. Courts usually differentiate between these forms of divorce: Foreign decisions are then recognized if the cases meet the prerequisites of an "equal rights" divorce, cf. only the French Court of Cassation, February 23, 2011, no. 10-14.760.

[22] Cf. e.g. Civil Court Brussels, May 26, 1978; House of Lords, *R. v. Secretary of State for the Home Department ex p. Fatima Ghulam*, [1986] A.C. 527 (H.L.).

[23] Cf. French Court of Cassation, 23.02.2011, no. 10-14.760, regarding a French–Moroccan case where the spouses had lived separately for three years and the divorce was not qualified as a unilateral divorce by the Moroccan court; Court of Appeals Versailles, 25.03.2010 no. 08/08808; Dutch Supreme Court, July 13, 2001, rechtspraak.nl LJN AB2623 (WPNR 2001 (6470)); Cour d'appel Antwerpen 30. June 1982, J.D.I. 1982, 740 s.

[24] Cf. Katajoun Alidadi, "The Western Judicial Answer to Islamic Talaq," *UCLA Journal of Islamic & Near Eastern Law* 5 (2005): 1–80; Marie-Claire Foblets, "Recent Developments in Dutch, French and Belgian Private International Law," *Hawwa* 5 (2007): 10–32.

[25] Cf. e.g. Court of Appeals Düsseldorf, FamRZ 1998,1113; Court of Appeals Köln, FamRZ 2000, 895; Court of Appeals Zweibrücken, NJW-RR 2002, 581; Court of Appeals Hamm 7.3.2006, BeckRS 2007, 00423; Court of Appeals Frankfurt a.M. 11.5.2009, 5 WF 66/09; Mathias Rohe, "Islamic Law in German Courts," *Hawwa* 1 (2003): 46, 50.

[26] Cf. Court of Appeals Cagliari, May 16, 2008, no. 198.

[27] Cf. Supreme Court, ATS 21.04.1998, RJ 3563.

of such a divorce according to Islamic tenets would be accepted by the controlling legal authority.

Belgium shared this approach until 2005, when the courts started to handle recognition more strictly after the enactment of the new law on PIL.[28] Similar developments can be seen in court decisions from France since 2004,[29] whereas in the past these nations adopted the method used by German courts.[30] In Austria, the Supreme Court[31] from the beginning refused to accept any kind of *talaq* whatsoever. Thus, there is an emerging trend in PIL to follow a policy of legal symbolism, which means to abstractly defend principles as such instead of deciding concrete cases according to their particular facts only. Whereas the abstract "human rights approach" leads to clear results—the rejection of *talaq* in any case—the concrete approach lacks such clarity. This might be one of the main reasons for the increasing popularity of the abstract approach in several European legal orders. In addition, it can be used as a political instrument to demonstrate western "cultural self-defence" against shari'a-based law.

On the other hand, it may be that only the concrete approach can help the divorced wife, for example, in cases when she herself wants to re-marry and therefore needs the recognition of the previous *talaq*.[32] In case of nonrecognition she would be forced to apply for divorce in European courts, which would often turn out to be equally time-consuming and expensive, in particular if the husband is living in a country which is not easily accessible for judicial correspondence, or if his address is unknown. The abstract "human rights approach" would then turn against the person it intends to protect[33]; the wife is then punished twice. Inclusive even-handedness, instead of mere political symbolism to the disadvantage of already disadvantaged parties, would thus require following the traditional approach.[34]

[28] Court of Cassation April 29, 2002; after 2005 cf. Court of Appeals Mons, December 20, 2007; Civil court Liège, June 26, 2009; Labor court Brussels, May 27, 2010; but also Labor court Brussels, January 12, 2011. Cf. Foblets, "Recent Developments in Dutch, French and Belgian Private International Law," 10–32; Koch, *Die Anwendung islamischen Scheidungs—und Scheidungsfolgenrechts*, 175–178.

[29] Older decisions by the Court of Cassation from 2001 and 2002 have now been overruled since a change of approach in the same court in 2004 (February 17, 2004, no. 01-11.549, and no. 02-11.618; Court of Cassation, January 3, 2006, no. 04-15.231; Court of Cassation November 4, 2009, No. 08-20.574). The decisions of 2004 were implicitly approved by the ECHR in the decision of November 8, 2005 (Affaire D.D. c France, no. 3/02, available in French at the court's website http://hudoc.echr.coe.int), noting the relevant new French decisions.

[30] The last decisions based on this approach were Court of Cassation July 3, 2001 (Rev. crit. int. privé 2002, 704 note Gannagé).

[31] OGH decision of 31.08.2006 (6Ob189/06), Zeitschrift für Rechtsvergleichung 2007, 35; OGH decision of 28.06.2007 (3Ob130/07z); both decisions available at http://ris.bka.gv.at

[32] This was the case in the decisions of the German Supreme Court from 2004 (BGH FamRZ 2004, 1952) and from 2007 (NJW-RR 2007, 145, 148ff.).

[33] Cf. in this context the Spanish Supreme Court, ATS 21.04.1998, RJ 3563; Koch, *Die Anwendung islamischen Scheidungs—und Scheidungsfolgenrechts*, 181.

[34] This part largely corresponds to Rohe, "Shari'a in Europe," 677ff.

2. *Domestic substantive law*

More and more, former "international" cases have turned into "internal" ones, due to the fact that an increasing number of Muslims have obtained citizenship of their country of residence, or were simply born there. Usually it is the law of the land which governs their private transactions and family status and relations. In addition, modern private international law rules in Western Europe now tend to favor the law of residence of the parties over citizenship; thus, foreign nationals living permanently in Europe are governed equally according to the substantive law of the land.[35] Hence, Islamic rules can only be applied under dispositive substantive law—the part of the private law which is not governed by mandatory rules (protective rules which cannot be negotiated by the parties involved, as opposed to dispositive rules).

Regarding economic contracts, there are various methods of investment that do not violate the Islamic prohibition against usury (*riba*, which according to traditional interpretations means not accepting or paying interest).[36] In addition, traditional forms of complex sales contracts (e.g. *murabaha*) are used for the express purpose of circumventing usurious transactions. This form of contract contains at least two sales contracts for one single item, where the margin of profit for the buyer/re-seller (usually a bank) is determined in the second contract. With respect to business financing, Islamic law permits the formation of types of companies (e.g. *mudaraba*).[37] In such companies, gain and loss are shared among the partners according to the success or failure of the company. No usury is present in such cases. None of these transactions would contradict European contract laws.[38] Similarly, Islamic investments prohibiting engagement in alcohol and pork production, pornography etc. are offered now in many Western European countries by Islamic or other banks. This is taken to be a kind of ethical economics which usually does not cause legal problems in principle. Thus, in many European countries such Islam-based contracts are negotiated and can be enforced under domestic law.

In the field of matrimonial law, the introduction of Islamic norms into marriage contracts has also been addressed within several European legal systems, particularly contractual conditions regulating the payment of dower (*mahr* or *sadaq*) in Muslim marriages.[39] It is important to keep in mind that such payments are due

[35] Cf. Rohe, "Shari'a in Europe," 683f.

[36] Cf. Kilian Bälz, "Scharia Jet Set: Islamic Banking," *INAMO Berichte und Analysen* 57 (Spring 2009): 14–17 with rich factual background; Luqman Zakariyah, "Legal Maxims and Islamic Financial Transactions: A Case Study of Mortgage Contracts and the Dilemma for Muslims in Britain," *Arab Law Quarterly* 26 (2012): 255–285.

[37] Cf. Reinhard Klarmann, *Islamic Project Finance* (Zuerich, Bâle, and Genève: Schulthess, 2003); Bälz, "A Murabaha Transaction," 117ff.

[38] Cf. Michael Gassner and Philipp Wackerbeck, *Islamic Finance* 2nd edn. (Köln: Bank-Verlag, 2010).

[39] Cf. Fournier, *Muslim Marriage in Western Courts*, 35–100 in particular.

to the bride under Islamic law,[40] not to her father/family as is customarily the case in countries such as Yemen, Afghanistan, or Pakistan, the latter not recognizable under European laws.[41] Such payments would indeed be considered as a sales price for the bride, which would challenge her human dignity as well as her free will to freely decide whether to marry or not. In contrast, *mahr* paid to the bride would only improve the bride's financial situation and could be used as a "bargaining" tool in case of divorce under Islamic law,[42] and thus cannot be considered to violate her rights.[43] Thus, "false conflicts" in cases where legal institutions are not contradictory in fact, but wrongly mixed up with certain customary practices, have to be avoided, and the scope of private autonomy in contract law has to be interpreted in an even-handed way irrespective of the origin of the regulation at stake.[44]

Consequently, in Britain, according to a court decision in 2010[45] *mahr* was accepted as a legal norm in marriage contracts. Dutch,[46] French,[47] and German[48] courts have accepted it as well in principle. This could indicate an emerging trend toward the "contractualization" of former "foreign" Islamic legal institutions by simply examining them under domestic dispositive contract law.

3. *Implementation of Islamic law/ Islamic legal thinking*

A few Western European states have introduced Islamic legal provisions concerning family matters that can be applied in Muslim communities on a voluntary basis. As to the celebration of marriages, in Britain Muslim institutions may apply to become entitled to register marriages under the Marriage Act 1949 (section 46) with civil effects. The British Adoption and Children Act of 2002 amended the Children Act of 1989 by provisions introducing "special guardianship" to enable parental relationships by legal means other than adoption, which is forbidden by Islamic law.[49] This option

[40] This was stressed by the French Court of Cassation, November 22, 2005, no. 03-14.961: Therefore, the *mahr* cannot be qualified as a "prix de vente."

[41] Cf. e.g. Court of Appeals Hamm, 13.01.2011 (I-18 U 88/10).

[42] For details cf. Rohe, "Shari'a in Europe," 684ff.; Nadjma Yassari, *Die Brautgabe im Vermögensrecht* (Tübingen: Mohr Siebeck, 2014), 34ff.

[43] The *mahr* was misinterpreted in this sense by regional court Köln IPRspr. 1980 no. 83; Court of Appeals Lyon, December 2, 2002, reversed by Court of Cassation (1ère civ) November 22, 2005, no. 03-14.961.

[44] Cf. Rohe, *Islamic Law in Past and Present*, 488ff.

[45] *Radmacher v. Granatino*, [2010] UKSC 42. The prior decision approving *mahr* (*Uddin v. Choudhury*, [2009] EWCA Civ 1205) concerned a case of informal marriage. Dower agreements seem to be taken as contractual in earlier decisions under previous legal rules (cf. *Shahnaz v. Rizwan*, [1964] 2 All ER 993; *Qureshi v. Qureshi*, [1971] 1 All ER 325).

[46] Rb Alkmaar 16-10-2008; Rb Rotterdam 22-02-2010.

[47] Court of Cassation, 02-12-1997, n. 95-20.026 and 22-11-2005, n. 03-14.961.

[48] Federal Supreme Court, NJW 1999, 574; OLG Celle FamRZ 1998, 374ff.; OLG Saarbruecken NJW-RR 2005, 1306ff. Cf. Yassari, *Die Brautgabe im Vermögensrecht*, 333ff.

[49] Cf. Qur'an surah 33, 4. s; art. "tabanni" in: wizārat al-awqāf, al-mawsūʿat al-fiqhīya vol. 10, Kuwait 1987.

resembles the Islamic legal institution of *kafala*, which endeavors to create a stable legal relationship between the child and the persons caring for him/ her, while maintaining legal bonds with the biological parents in cases where these are known.[50] Of course, the British Act is not formulated on the basis of religion and is thus open to all, irrespective of religion. In "internal" *kafala* cases, once the child has obtained residence in a Member State, there are indications from Dutch legal–anthropological research[51] that courts and administrations are prepared to integrate *kafala* by analogy: It is classified as a form of caring for children comparable to foster-parenthood, and thus integrated into the existing legal rules on child benefit payments. Jurisprudence in other states, namely in Italy, reveals that in immigration cases *kafala* is usually rejected as a basis for a residence permit for the child, which leads to highly unsatisfactory "limping" legal situations, where a state of affairs is recognized in one legal order but not others.

In Spain, Islamic legal norms regulating marriage contracts have been applied to Muslims since 1992.[52] However, the Spanish legislator has also amended its international law of divorce (Article 107 of the Civil Code) to enable women living in Spain to get divorced even if matrimonial law in their country of origin or the country in which they married prevents them from doing so. The legislature has stated expressly that this amendment was intended to provide domestic legal remedies for Muslim women in particular.[53] In sum, the formal incorporation of Islamic law is an exceptional case relating to merely formal legal provisions like the procedural aspects of marriage contracts (though not the substantive ones).

In other European countries, such legislation has not been proposed. Most Muslims of Turkish and Bosnian origin would vehemently oppose the introduction of shariʿa legal norms, since shariʿa-based regulations were abolished in Turkey and in the Balkans decades ago and they do not adhere to a personal law system based on religious affiliation any more.[54] Until now, only in the UK has a broader discussion emerged amongst Muslims, mostly originating from the Indian subcontinent, on the (optional) introduction of a Muslim law of personal status and inheritance comparable to the legal situation in their countries of origin.[55] Given the present status of legal developments and evidence from Islamic shariʿa councils in Britain,

[50] There is an obvious lack of information about the different forms of *kafala* in cases where the parents are known or unknown/dead; a Ph.D. thesis by Rabah Mouzaoui supervised by the present author is in its final stage.

[51] Cf. André Hoekema, "Does the Dutch Judiciary Pluralize Domestic Law?" in *Legal Practice and Cultural Diversity*, ed. Ralph Grillo, Roger Ballard, Alessandro Ferrari, André Hoekema, Marcel Maussen, and Prakash Shah (Aldershot: Ashgate, 2009), 177–198.

[52] Cf. Joaquín Mantecón-Sancho, *L'Islam en Espagne. In Islam and the European Union*, eds. R. Potz and W. Wieshaider (Leuven: Peeters, 2004), 130ff.

[53] BOE 30-09-2003, Ley Orgánica 11/2003, de 29 de septiembre, 4.

[54] Cf. Rohe, *Islamic Law in Past and Present*, 259ff. regarding polls on the issue in Turkey.

[55] Cf. Pearl and Menski, *Muslim Family Law*, 51ff.; for further details cf. Rohe, "Shariʿa in Europe," 691ff.

this would lead to forms of legal inequality of sexes and religions.[56] Thus, this would be neither a realistic nor a desirable option for European states.

4. *Alternative dispute resolution*

All over Western Europe mechanisms of conflict resolution outside state courts, namely alternative dispute resolution (ADR), are operating in the field of economic disputes. They are working either on an informal basis, or the parties agree on engaging arbitration boards or institutions for deciding matters in a legally enforceable way.[57]

Muslim institutions involved in ADR ("Islamic Shariʿa Councils") started to emerge in the UK in the 1980s. Besides economic disputes, they are mainly engaged in family affairs, divorce issues in particular. In most cases, Muslim wives seek either an "Islamic" divorce in addition to a British state court's divorce decree or termination of an unofficial "Islamic" marriage, petitioning these councils to convince the husband to agree on an Islamic termination of the marriage by *talaq* or *khul'*. Besides that, British Muslim Arbitration Tribunals (MAT) have been established since 2007 in London, Birmingham, Bradford, Manchester, and Nuneaton under the Arbitration Act (1996).[58] Contrary to the informally working Islamic Shariʿa Councils, the MAT are entitled to issue formal awards under this act, for example, related to commercial disputes including economic issues arising from family disputes. In family status issues (most notably divorce and custody of children) they have no jurisdiction,[59] but aim at providing informal aid, for example, in cases of social need for an Islamic divorce[60] akin to other shariʿa courts. Samia Bano[61] has stated that the twenty-two Shariʿa Councils in the UK she contacted seek to avoid any conflict with civil law, for example, by requiring the civil divorce of a registered marriage before issuing an Islamic divorce.

Thus, the work of such councils and tribunals seems to serve persons seeking religious support, but also for those living a considerable distance from British legal institutions, who seek socially acceptable conflict resolutions within their community. This is equally true for cases when divorces under British law are not fully accepted by the parties or in the community unless an Islamic divorce has also

[56] Cf. Shah-Kazemi, *Untying the Knot*; Bano, *An Exploratory Study of Shari'ah councils in England* and Samia Bano, *Muslim Women and Shari'ah Councils: Transcending the Boundaries of Community and Law* (Basingstoke: Palgrave Macmillan, 2012); Malik, *Minority Legal Orders in the UK*.

[57] For the fields and reasons of religiously driven arbitration among Muslims in Europe cf. Mathias Rohe, "Alternative Dispute Resolution in Europe in Europe under the Auspices of Religious Norms," *RELIGARE working paper*.

[58] A broader report on religious laws and legal institutions in England and Wales including Islamic rules has been published by Douglas et al., *Social Cohesion and Civil Law: Marriage, Divorce and Religious Courts* (Cardiff: Cardiff University, June 1, 2011).

[59] Cf. Douglas et al., *Social Cohesion and Civil Law*, 17, 22f.

[60] Cf. the MAT website, available at http://www.matribunal.com/cases_faimly.html (last accessed 8 February 2013).

[61] Cf. Bano, *Muslim Women and Shari'ah Councils*, 24.

taken place. Nevertheless, the price to be paid then is a considerable lack of rights as compared to the standards of the law of the land.[62] It should be mentioned that there are some efforts by small numbers of extremist Islamist groups and the Salafi movement aimed at the construction of an exclusive Muslim normative order opposing the governing rules of the land, based on the concept of *al-wala' wa l-bara'*, which restricts Muslim loyalty to Muslims.[63] According to research done in the German state of Bavaria in 2012,[64] there are indeed some cases of culturally or—shari'a—inspired "parallel justice" in family matters, where undue pressure was exercised on women to refrain from exercising their rights under German law. More research is necessary in this field and this has been undertaken by the present author and his team in the state of Berlin and other German cities in 2014 and 2015.[65]

III. Islamic Religious Norms in Western Europe

A. Legally Formal Application of Religious Norms

In applying Islamic norms in the West, the state legal systems fundamentally differentiate between religious and legal issues. In Western Europe, religious issues are regulated by the European and national constitutional provisions including Article 9 ECHR, which grants freedom of religion and state neutrality toward religions. Thus, from a legal (certainly not a socio-cultural) point of view there are no "foreign" religious norms as opposed to "domestic" ones.

Regarding religious norms, freedom of religion is not limited to private worship, but also grants an adequate (but not an unlimited) protection of religious needs in various aspects of public life regulated by public law—from building mosques to social security issues.[66] Western European countries vary in their applications of

[62] For details cf. Shah-Kazemi, *Untying the Knot*; Malik, *Minority Legal Orders in the UK*; Bano, *An Exploratory Study of Shari'ah councils in England*; Bano, *Muslim Women and Shari'ah Councils*.

[63] Cf. Uriya Shavit, "Wasaṭī and Salafi Approaches to the Religious Law of Muslim Minorities," *Islamic Law and Society* 19 (2012): 416–457.

[64] The Bavarian Ministry of Justice implemented a research group of legal practitioners and social organizations working on preventive and repressive measures, the former led by the present author. The results are as yet unpublished.

[65] The results will be published in 2016 or 2017.

[66] Cf. Ferrari and Bradney, *Islam and European Legal Systems*; Aluffi and Zincone, eds., *Legal Treatment of Islamic Minorities in Europe*; Potz and Wieshaider, *Islam and the European Union*; Mathias Rohe and Sebastian Elster, "Zur öffentlich-rechtlichen Situation von Muslimen in ausgewählten europäischen Ländern," in *Perspektiven und Herausforderungen in der Integration muslimischer*

these provisions due to differing interpretations regarding the desirable degree of distance between the state and religion. Thus, the debates and demands regarding visible Muslim religiosity (e.g. with respect to religious garments worn in schools or by state officers) largely differ—whereas in France even students are not allowed to wear the hijab,[67] in the UK teachers or police officers may do so. Obviously most Muslims try to live their religion and define their needs within their respective framework. Thus, Muslim life is rather diverse in different western countries due to such different framing conditions.

Another level where religious norms may have an impact are social relations governed by civil law, specifically (but not exclusively) employment law. In this field, possible conflicting interests of employers and employees have to be weighed with respect to the employee's religious needs on one hand and the employer's needs on the other (cf. Hoevels 2003).[68] Often Muslims do not face specific legal problems concerning their employment. For those who need to pray during work hours, acceptable solutions can be found in most cases. Many either pray during regular breaks or concentrate their prayers in the morning and evening. In Britain, a bus driver claiming the right to interrupt his work five times a day for prayer lost his case for obvious reasons.[69] On Fridays employers often allow breaks for Muslim employees to participate in communal prayer at mosques or allow employees to finish working earlier in the day. Muslim workers are also generally allowed to use vacation days during the feasts of Eid ul-Fitr at the end of Ramadan and the Eid al-Adha (Festival of Sacrifice) in the month of pilgrimage. Nevertheless, in many cases women wearing headscarves or other religious garments are discriminated against in western labour markets. This might pose problems in weighing up the necessity of an income from work and the fulfilment of personal religious needs.[70]

MitbürgerInnen in Österreich, ed. Bundesministerium des Inneren Wien & Sicherheitsakademie (Vienna, 2006); European Parliament, Directorate General for Internal Policies of the Union, *Islam in the European Union: What's at Stake in the Future?* (May 2007); Marie-Claire Foblets, François Gaudreault-Desbiens, and Alison Rentel, eds., *Cultural Diversity and the Law* (Bruxelles: Bruylant, 2010); Silvio Ferrari and Sabrina Pastorelli, eds. *Religion in Public Spaces: A European Perspective* (Farnham and Burlington: Ashgate, 2012).

67 Cf. e.g. John R. Bowen, *Can Islam be French? Pluralism and Pragmatism in a Secularist State* (Princeton: Princeton University Press, 2009); John R. Bowen, *Blaming Islam* (Cambridge, MA: Boston Review, 2012).

68 Cf. Rohe, *Islamic Law in Past and Present*, 461ff.; Alidadi, "The Western Judicial Answer to Islamic Talaq."

69 Reported in Shadid and Van Koningsveld, *Religious Freedom*, 102.

70 Cf. only Deutsche Islam Konferenz, *Bessere Integration von Musliminnen und Muslimen in den Arbeitsmarkt* (2nd edn. Nürnberg, 2012), 16f.; for a broader European perspective regarding religion in the workplace cf. Katajoun Alidadi, Marie-Claire Foblets, and Jogchum Vrielink, *A Test of Faith? Religious Diversity and Accommodation in the European Workplace* (Farnham: Ashgate, 2012).

B. Informal Application of Religious Norms

Islamic religious norms can be "applied" at an informal level by simple practice. It is mainly in the sphere of religious rules—concerning the relations between God and human beings (*'ibadat*) and the non-legal aspects of relations between human beings (*mu'amalat*)—where a "European Shari'a" is possibly developing.[71] In such cases, the opinions contained in religious expert opinions (*fatawa*) and books would not address the existing law of the land, but categorize Muslim behavior and transactions only according to religious standards, without any worldly legal sanction. While some publications by Muslim scholars on Islamic education in the West date back to the 1980s,[72] works dealing specifically with normative issues within the European legal context were not published before the 1990s.

Probably the first collection of *fatawa* by a Europe-based scholar mainly aimed at a British Muslim public was published in 1997.[73] On an institutional level, the Dublin-based European Council for Fatwa and Research[74] and the London-based Islamic Shari'a Council[75] are giving *fatawa* particularly pertaining to Muslim life in a secular environment among a non-Muslim majority. They make use of the traditional Islamic distinction between legal and religious categories used for the evaluation of human behavior.[76] Instead of declaring a certain behavior to be "legally invalid" (*batil*) in this world, they merely consider it to be sinful and forbidden (*haram*), thus restricting the consequences to judgment in the hereafter.

The topics they deal with often concentrate on women's and family issues (e.g. How to deal with inter-religious marriages? How to preserve "Muslim family life"?), but also range from labor and education issues to legal and political issues

[71] Cf. Shadid and van Koningsveld, *Religious Freedom*, 149; Jacques Waardenburg, *Muslims and Others: Relations in Context* (Berlin: de Gruyter, 2003), 241, 308 and 336; Mathias Rohe, "The Formation of a European Sharī'a," in *Muslims in Europe: From the Margin to the Centre*, ed. Jamal Malik (Münster: LIT, 2004), 161ff.

[72] One of the first publications was the booklet by the British scholar Syed Mutawalli ad-Darsh, *Muslims in Europe* (London: Ta-Ha Publishers, 1980).

[73] Cf. ad-Darsh, *Questions & Answers About Islam* (London: Ta-Ha Publishers, 1997). A fatwa on the service of Muslims in the British army (p. 155) reveals the intended readership.

[74] The website is available at http://e-cfr.org/new/, also Rohe, "The Formation of a European Sharī'a" in *Muslims in Europe: From the Margin to the Centre*, ed. Jamal Malik, 161–184. (Münster: LIT, 2004) (based on a paper presented in Erfurt in 2001), Alexandre Caeiro has published various papers on the Council based on rich fieldwork (cf. Caeiro, "Transnational 'Ulama', European Fatwas and Islamic Authority: A Case Study of the European Council for Fatwa and Research," in *Producing Islamic Knowledge: Transmission and Dissemination in Western Europe*, ed. Martin van Bruinessen and Stefano Allievi (London: Routledge, 2010), 121–141); his excellent thesis on the subject is not yet published (June 2015).

[75] The website is available at http://www.islamic-sharia.org/

[76] For details cf. Rohe, *Islamic Law in Past and Present*, 10f. with further references.

(e.g. Can a Muslim be punished for adultery in a Western country? Is a Muslim allowed to accept a secular non-Muslim government, etc.?).[77]

The answers given suggest four trends: First, Islamic legal sanctions which have to be implemented by state institutions are declared to be inapplicable in a non-Islamic state. Thus, there is no room for penal sanctions according to traditional shariʿa law. Other legal norms should be considered within the scope of the law of the land, but the legal institutions of the law of the land should be respected and used, for example, concerning marriage.

Second, Islamic religion, ethics, or morals should be maintained as much as possible. The traditional patriarchal view on gender and family issues is mostly maintained, but mitigated by appeals not to use violence or exercise pressure to implement the rules; this is also the main topic of religious literature offered in mosques and Islamic bookstores. Specifically, there is a trend to apply traditional Shariʿa norms in a way which is most favorable to women on the basis of new interpretations (*ijtihad*), but still within a patriarchal framework. Sometimes very traditional approaches are upheld. Regarding the shariʿa provisions of evidence, which exclude women from appearing as witnesses in some cases or demand two female witnesses as an equivalent for one male, the London Shariʿa Council does not shy away from explanations which were commonly held worldwide before the nineteenth century: women are supposed to be mainly emotional, whereas among men rationality prevails; men are able to concentrate fully on one single task, whereas women are able to multi-task (e.g. in the kitchen), and thus might be distracted from relevant observations, etc.[78]

Third, the *muftis* following the "moderate" direction would mostly search for viable solutions to reconcile economic and social needs with religious commands, for example, in the areas of labor and finance. This is usually explained by the Islamic principles of necessity (*darura*) and common interest (*maslaha*), which has to consider the particular circumstances Muslim minorities face. These are the most significant characteristics of the so-called *fiqh al-aqalliyyat* (Islamic law for Muslim minorities, minority *fiqh*). In contrast, many Salafis would propagate strict separation from the non-Muslim environment by establishing parallel (competitive) Islamic structures as far as possible.[79] The same is true for non-Salafi extremist movements like Hizb al-Tahrir or individuals like Muhammad Ahmad Rassoul,[80]

[77] Cf. Rohe, "Sharīʿa in Europe"; H.A. Hellyer, *Muslims of Europe: The "Other" Europeans* (Edinburgh: Edinburgh University Press, 2009), 79–99; Sarah Albrecht, *Yūsuf al-Qaraḍāwīs Konzept des fiqh al-aqallīyāt* (Würzburg: Ergon, 2010); Caeiro, "Transnational 'Ulama'"; Shavit, "Wasaṭī and Salafī Approaches."

[78] Cf. the relevant *fatwa* used to be available online at http://www.islamic-Sharia.org, but in fact has been removed at the time of writing.

[79] Cf. e.g. Shavit, "Wasaṭī and Salafī Approaches."

[80] Cf. Muhammad Ahmad Rassoul, *Das Deutsche Kalifat* (Cologne: Islamische Bibliothek, 1993).

who propagate the establishment of a worldwide caliphate according to traditional Islamic state law.[81]

Fourth, open and friendly relations with the non-Muslim environment are not only permissible, but required, while the religious commands of Islam should be preserved to the largest possible extent. Such *fatawa* might respond to challenges from Muslim majority countries such as Saudi Arabia, where prominent persons and institutions try to influence Muslims all over the world with their very intolerant interpretations of Islam, in opposition to different Muslim attitudes and other religions. For example harsh *fatawa* of the late Saudi *muftis* Ibn Baz and al-Uthaymin are distributed for free in mosques and other institutions, demanding that Muslims build their own institutions in opposition to the secular ones within the country, to refrain from congratulating Christians on their religious holidays, etc.[82] At the other end of the spectrum, the representatives of *fiqh al-aqalliyyat* are much more moderate and open to inter-religious communication. They usually take the view that living in a non-Muslim environment requires the adoption of friendly attitudes toward everyone, this being the only way to convince people of the values of Islam.

Since the idea of *fiqh al-aqalliyat* refrains from claiming legal validity, it reflects a broader trend among western Muslims toward a de-territorialization and de-legislation of shariʿa, interpreting it anew as a merely or primarily ethical/moral set of norms providing guidance rather than governance.[83] The debate has reached a global level, as Muslim scholars living in western countries interact and are received worldwide, and particularly in states where Muslims form minorities. Thus, while this chapter concentrates on Western Europe and authors based there, we must not forget the rich transnational and even global debate among Muslim scholars and laypersons, which influences internal developments irrespective of the place of residence of the participants. Indeed, it was a US-based scholar, Taha Jabir al-ʾAlwani, who invented the term *fiqh al-aqalliyyat*.[84]

Not all Muslim scholars would follow the idea of *fiqh al-aqalliyyat*, which in itself illustrates a broad range of approaches.[85] Others like Smail Balić,[86] Soheib

[81] Cf. Rohe, *Islamic Law in Past and Present*, 51ff. with further references.

[82] Cf. e.g. ʿAbdul Azeez Ibn Baz and Muhammad ibn Saalih al-Uthaymeen, *Muslim Minorities—Fatawa Regarding Muslims Living as Minorities* (Hounslow: Message of Islam, 1998).

[83] Cf. Abdullahi Ahmed An-Naʾim, *Islam and the Secular State: Negotiating the Future of Shariʿa* (Cambridge, MA: Harvard University Press, 2008), 28–44 in particular.

[84] Al-ʾAlwānī, Ṭaha Jābir, muqaddima fī fiqh al-aqalliyyāt, (sine loco) 1994.

[85] Cf. e.g. the works of Tareq Oubrou, "Introduction théorétique à la chariʿa de minorité," *Islam de France* 2 (1998): 27ff.; Tareq Oubrou, "La charia de minorité: contribution pour une integration légale de l'islam." February 21, 2003. The topic is dealt with in some detail in Sarah Albrecht's Ph.D. thesis, published in 2016.

[86] Cf. e.g. Smail Balić, *Der Islam im Spannungsfeld von Tradition und heutiger Zeit* (Würzburg: Echter, 1993) and *Islam für Europa* (Köln: Böhlau, 2001).

Bencheikh,[87] Tariq Ramadan,[88] Abderrahim Lamchichi,[89] Dilwar Hussain,[90] Lamya Kaddor,[91] Mouhanad Khorchide,[92] or Benjamin Idriz[93] argue from a broader religious or philosophical perspective, perceiving themselves to constitute simply one part of European society and being obliged to contribute to the common welfare. They implicitly or openly reject the concept of minority *fiqh*, since they would argue that Muslims should not perceive themselves as a (distinct) minority, but as an integral part of the societies in which they are living ("entrenchment approach").[94]

Within the broader Muslim debate on shari'a in the West, there are four major trends to be discerned: Some Muslim scholars and intellectuals try to remove the "ethnic-cultural layer" from "true Islam," aiming at reconciling Islam with human rights standards and democracy. Others, mostly Salafis, are doing the same for the opposite purpose: developing an imagined "original pure Islam" opposed to democracy and human rights, which are denounced to be western inventions. The latter ideas are promoted by some aggressive converts to Islam like the Jamaican-born preacher Bilal Philips, who does not shy away from demanding the death penalty for homosexuals.[95] The third trend might still be the dominant one: Preserving "moderate" ("middle-range" *wasati*)[96] Islamic religious and cultural traditions to avoid both harshness and leniency in interpreting shari'a norms. Very often its representatives still adhere more or less to the culture of their countries of origin, whereas the younger generations are defining themselves more and more as Muslims rather than with regard to the national origin of their families. Thus, the fourth trend can be described as adapting religious rules to local circumstances (e.g. prayer in schools; fasting, etc.), but also as creating a self-conscious Muslim identity as a part of western societies. Tariq Ramadan, one of the most influential Muslim thinkers in Western Europe, aims at a culture of entrenchment while preserving Muslim identity:

> [W]e are to feel at home and apply in a positive way the Islamic principle of integrating all that does not contradict the prohibitions and making it our own ... As citizens of states that recognize human rights, Muslims are no longer under the law of foreign states or former

[87] Cf. Soheib Bencheikh, *Marianne et le Prophète—L'Islam dans la France laïque* (Paris: Grasset, 1998).

[88] Cf. Tariq Ramadan, *Radical Reform: Islamic Ethics and Liberation* (Oxford: Oxford University Press, 2009) and e.g. his earlier works *To be a European Muslim* (Leicester: Islamic Foundation, 1999), *Musulmans d'Occident* (Lyon: Tawhid, 2002), and *Western Muslims and the Future of Islam* (Oxford: Oxford University Press, 2004).

[89] Cf. e.g. Abderrahim Lamchichi, *Islam et musulmans de France* (Paris: L'Harmattan, 1999).

[90] Cf. the essays on his weblog https://dilwarh.wordpress.com/ (last accessed June 14, 2015).

[91] Cf. e.g. Lamya Kaddor, *Muslimisch—weiblich—Deutsch! Mein Weg zu einem zeitgemäßen Islam* (Bonn: BPB, 2011).

[92] Cf. Mouhanad Khorchide, *Islam ist Barmherzigkeit* (Freiburg and Breisgau: Herder, 2012), 116ff, and *Scharia—der missverstandene Gott* (2nd edn. Freiburg and Breisgau: Herder, 2014).

[93] Cf. Benjamin Idriz, *Grüß Gott, Herr Imam* (München: Diedrichs, 2010).

[94] Cf. Rohe, *Islamic Law in Past and Present*, 515ff. with further references.

[95] Cf. the report "Islamprediger Philips wird ausgewiesen" from April 21, 2011, available at http://www.n24.de/news/newsitem_6828865.html. Philips was expelled from Germany in 2011.

[96] Cf. Shavit, "Wasaṭī and Salafī Approaches."

colonies and they should reject the status of subcitizens ... To regain confidence in oneself, one's values, one's role also means in practice, reclaiming one's rights and respect. Through involvement in education reform, social and political participation, economic resistance, interreligious dialogue, and contributions to culture.[97]

IV. Concluding Remarks

Islamic law in Western Europe is a new field of research, mostly based on migration developments in the twentieth century. Scholarly research on the impact of the legal aspects of Muslim life in Western European states has only emerged on a broader basis during the last three decades. Before that, it was mainly courts and administrations which dealt with the issue on a case-by-case basis. Until now, relatively few publications cover Southern Europe (Spain, Portugal, Italy) despite the fact that a considerable number of Muslims are citizens or permanent residents of these countries. In the field of law, two particular aspects deserve further consideration: How are (former) Islamic legal institutions treated under the respective provisions of domestic contract and family law? How do Muslims reinterpret Islamic legal institutions within the Western European legal environment (e.g. regarding inheritance)? More research is needed on Muslim self-perceptions and the development of a Muslim theology in Western Europe.

References

Ahdar, Rex and Aroney, Nicholas, eds., *Shariʿa in the West* (Oxford: Oxford University Press, 2010).

Al-'Alwānī, Ṭaha Jābir, muqaddima fī fiqh al-aqalliyyāt: (sine loco), 1994.

Albrecht, Sarah, *Yūsuf al-Qaraḍāwīs Konzept des fiqh al-aqallīyāt* (Würzburg: Ergon, 2010).

Aldeeb Abu-Sahlieh, Sami and Bonomi, Andrea, eds., *Le droit musulman de la famille et des successions à l'épreuve des ordres juridiques occidentaux* (Zürich: Schulthess, 1999).

Alidadi, Katajoun, "The Western Judicial Answer to Islamic Talaq." *UCLA Journal of Islamic & Near Eastern Law* 5 (2005): 1–80.

Alidadi, Katajoun, Foblets, Marie-Claire, and Vrielink, Jogchum, eds., *A Test of Faith? Religious Diversity and Accommodation in the European Workplace* (Farnham: Ashgate, 2012).

Allievi, Stefano and Dassetto, Felice, *Facettes de l'Islam belge* (Louvain-la-Neuve: Bruylant, 1997).

[97] Ramadan, *Radical Reform*, 224f.

Aluffi Beck-Peccoz, Roberta and Zincone, Giovanna, eds., *The Legal Treatment of Islamic Minorities in Europe* (Leuven: Peeters, 2004).

An-Na'im, Abdullahi Ahmed, *Islam and the Secular State: Negotiating the Future of Shari'a* (Cambridge, MA: Harvard University Press, 2008).

Balić, Smail, *Der Islam im Spannungsfeld von Tradition und heutiger Zeit* (Würzburg: Echter, 1993).

Balić, Smail, *Islam für Europa* (Köln: Böhlau, 2001).

Bälz, Kilian, "A Murabaha Transaction in an English Court." *Islamic Law and Society* 11 (2004): 117–134.

Bälz, Kilian, "Scharia Jet Set: Islamic Banking." *INAMO Berichte und Analysen* 57 (Spring 2009): 14–17.

Bano, Samia, *An Exploratory Study of Shariah Councils in England with Respect to Family Law.* (Reading: University of Reading, 2012). (Bano 2012a) http://www.reading.ac.uk/web/FILES/law/An_exploratory_study_of_Shariah_councils_in_England_with_respect_to_family_law_.pdf.

Bano, Samia, *Muslim Women and Shari'ah Councils: Transcending the Boundaries of Community and Law* (Basingstoke: Palgrave Macmillan, 2012). (Bano 2012b)

von Bar, Christian, ed., *Islamic Family Law and its Reception by the Courts in the West* (Köln: Heymann 1999).

Bencheikh, Soheib, *Marianne et le Prophète—L'Islam dans la France laïque* (Paris: Grasset, 1998).

Berger, Maurits, ed., *Applying Shari'a in the West* (Leiden: Leiden University Press, 2013).

Bernard-Maugiron, Nathalie and Dupret, Baudoin, eds., *Ordre public et droit musulman de la famille en Europe et en Afrique du Nord* (Bruxelles: Bruylant, 2010).

Bowen, John R., *Can Islam be French? Pluralism and Pragmatism in a Secularist State* (Princeton: Princeton University Press, 2009).

Bowen, John R., *Blaming Islam* (Cambridge, MA: Boston Review, 2012).

Büchler, Andrea, *Islamic Law in Europe? Legal Pluralism and its Limits in European Family Laws* (Farnham and Burlington: Ashgate, 2011).

Caeiro, Alexandre, "Transnational 'Ulama', European Fatwas and Islamic Authority: A Case Study of the European Council for Fatwa and Research" in Martin van Bruinessen and Stefano Allievi (eds.) *Producing Islamic Knowledge: Transmission and Dissemination in Western Europe* (London: Routledge, 2010) 121–141.

Cesari, Jocelyne, ed., *The Oxford Handbook of European Islam* (Oxford: Oxford University Press, 2015).

Charnay, Jean-Paul, *La Charia et l'Occident* (Paris: L'Herne, 2001).

Cilardo, Agostino, *Il diritto islamico e il sistema giuridico italiano* (Napoli: Edizioni Scientifice Italiane, 2002).

Conseil de la communauté marocaine à l'étranger, ed., *Le statut juridique de l'Islam en Europe.* Acte du colloque international organize par le Conseil de la communauté marocaine à l'étranger Fès, 14 et 15 Mars 2009 (Rabat: Marsam, 2010).

ad-Darsh, Syed Mutawalli, *Questions & Answers about Islam* (London: Ta-Ha Publishers, 1997).

Deutsche Islam Konferenz, ed., *Bessere Integration von Musliminnen und Muslimen in den Arbeitsmarkt* (2nd edn. Nürnberg, 2012). http://www.deutsche-islam-konferenz.de/SharedDocs/Anlagen/DIK/DE/Downloads/LenkungsausschussPlenum/dik-broschuere-pg-a-download.pdf?__blob=publicationFile.

Douglas, Gillian, Doe, Norman, Gilliat-Ray, Sophie, Sandberg, Russell, and Khan, Asma, *Social Cohesion and Civil Law: Marriage, Divorce and Religious Courts* (Cardiff: Cardiff University) June 1, 2011. http://papers.ssrn.com/sol3/papers.cfm?abstract_id=1940387.

European Parliament, Directorate General for Internal Policies of the Union, *Islam in the European Union: What's at Stake in the Future?*, May 2007 (PE 369.031).

Ferrari, Silvio and Bradney, Anthony, eds., *Islam and European Legal Systems* (Aldershot: Ashgate, 2010).

Ferrari, Silvio and Pastorelli, Sabrina, eds., *Religion in Public Spaces: A European Perspective* (Farnham and Burlington: Ashgate, 2012).

Foblets, Marie-Claire, Marechal, Brigitte, and Nielsen, Jorgen, eds., *Convergences musulmanes: Aspects contemporains de l'islam dans l'Europe élargie* (Louvain la-Neuve: Bruylant, 2001).

Foblets, Marie-Claire and Carlier, Jean-Yves, *Le code marocain de la famille: Incidences au regard du droit international privé en Europe* (Bruxelles: Bruylant, 2005).

Foblets, Marie-Claire, "The Admissibility of Repudiation: Recent Developments in Dutch, French and Belgian Private International Law." *Hawwa* 5 (2007): 10–32.

Foblets, Marie-Claire, Gaudreault-Desbiens, François, and Dundes Rentel, Alison, eds. *Cultural Diversity and the Law* (Bruxelles: Bruylant, 2010).

Foblets, Marie-Claire, Graziadei, Michele, and Vanderlinden, Jacques, eds., *Convictions Politiques et Religieuses et Droits Positifs* (Bruxelles: Bruylant, 2010).

Fournier, Pascale, *Muslim Marriage in Western Courts: Lost in Transition* (Farnham: Ashgate, 2010).

Gärtner, Verena, *Die Privatscheidung im deutschen und gemeinschaftsrechtlichen Internationalen Privat- und Verfahrensrecht: außergerichtliche Ehescheidung im Spannungsfeld von kultureller Diversität und Integration* (Tübingen: Mohr Siebeck, 2008).

Gassner, Michael and Wackerbeck, Philipp, *Islamic Finance* (2nd edn. Köln: Bank-Verlag, 2010).

Gaudreault-Desbiens, Jean-François, "Religious Courts' Recognition Claims: Two Qualitatively Distinct Narratives" in Rex Ahdar and Nicholas Aroney (eds.) *Shari'a in the West* (Oxford: Oxford University Press, 2010) 59–69.

Grillo, Ralph, Ballard, Roger, Ferrari, Alessandro, Hoekema, André, Maussen, Marcel, and Shah, Prakash, eds. *Legal Practice and Cultural Diversity* (Farnham and Burlington: Ashgate, 2009).

Hallaq, Wael, *An Introduction to Islamic Law* (New York: Cambridge University Press, 2009).

Hattenhauer, Hans, *Europäische Rechtsgeschichte* (3rd edn. Heidelberg: C.F. Müller, 1998).

Heinisch, Klaus, ed., *Kaiser Friedrich II. In Briefen und Berichten seiner Zeit* (Darmstadt: Wissenschaftliche Buchgesellschaft, 1970).

Hellyer, H.A., *Muslims of Europe: The "Other" Europeans* (Edinburgh: Edinburgh University Press, 2009).

Hoekema, André, "Does the Dutch Judiciary Pluralize Domestic Law?" in Ralph Grillo, Roger Ballard, Alessandro Ferrari, André Hoekema, Marcel Maussen, and Prakash Shah (eds.) *Legal Practice and Cultural Diversity* (Aldershot: Ashgate, 2009) 177–198.

Horst, Eberhard, *Der Sultan von Lucera: Freidrich II. und der Islam* (Freiburg in Breisgau: Herder, 1997).

Ibn Baz, ʿAbdul Azeez/al-ʿUthaymeen, Muhammad ibn Saalih, *Muslim Minorities—Fatawa Regarding Muslims Living as Minorities* (Hounslow: Message of Islam, 1998).

Idriz, Benjamin, *Grüß Gott, Herr Imam* (München: Diedrichs, 2010).

Kaddor, Lamya, *Muslimisch—weiblich—Deutsch! Mein Weg zu einem zeitgemäßen Islam* (Bonn: BPB, 2011).
Kahn, Philippe, ed., *L'étranger et le droit de la famille: pluralité ethnique, pluralisme juridique* (Paris: La Documentation française, 2001) [Mission "Droit et Justice"].
Khorchide, Mouhanad, *Islam ist Barmherzigkeit. Grundzüge einer modernen Religion* (Freiburg and Breisgau: Herder, 2012).
Khorchide, Mouhanad, *Scharia—der missverstandene Gott* (2nd edn. Freiburg and Breisgau: Herder, 2014).
King, Michael, ed., *God's Law versus State Law: The Construction of an Islamic Identity in Western Europe* (London: Grey Seal, 1995).
Klarmann, Reinhard, *Islamic Project Finance* (Zuerich, Bâle, and Genève: Schulthess, 2003).
Koch, Julia, *Die Anwendung islamischen Scheidungs- und Scheidungsfolgenrechts im Internationalen Privatrecht der EU-Mitgliedstaaten* (Frankfurt: Lang, 2012).
Lamchichi, Abderrahim, *Islam et musulmans de France* (Paris: L'Harmattan, 1999).
Malik, Jamal, ed., *Muslims in Europe* (Münster: LIT, 2004).
Malik, Maleiha, *Minority Legal Orders in the UK.* London: British Academy Policy Centre, 2012. http://www.britac.ac.uk/policy/Minority-legal-orders.cfm.
Mantecón Sancho, Joaquín, *L'Islam en Espagne*, in R. Potz and W. Wieshaider (eds.) *Islam and the European Union* (Leuven: Peeters, 2004) 109–142.
Meeusen, J., Pertegas, M., Straetmans, G., and Swennen, Fr., eds., *International Family Law for the European Union* (Antwerp and Oxford: Intersentia, 2007).
Mehdi, Rubya and Nielsen, Jørgen S., *Embedding Mahr (Islamic Mahr) in the European Legal System* (Copenhagen: DJ Ø F Publishing, 2011).
Milbank, John, "The Archbishop of Canterbury: The Man and the Theology Behind the Shari'a Lecture" in Rex Ahdar and Nicholas Aroney (eds.) *Shari'a in the West* (New York: Cambridge University Press, 2010) 43–57.
Mir-Hosseini, Ziba, "Islamic Family Law and Social Practice: Anthropological Reflections on the Terms of the Debate" in Siegfried Hass (ed.) *Family, Law and Religion. Debates in the Muslim World and their Implications for Co-operation and Dialogue* (Vienna: Austrian Association for the Middle East Hammer-Purgstall, 2009) 37–48.
Nichols, Joel A., ed., *Marriage and Divorce in a Multicultural Context* (Cambridge: Cambridge University Press, 2012).
Nielsen, Jørgen, *Muslims in Western Europe* (Edinburgh: Edinburgh University Press, 1995).
Nielsen, Jørgen and Christoffersen, Lisbeth, *Shari'a As Discourse: Legal Traditions and the Encounter with Europe* (Farnham: Ashgate, 2010).
Oubrou, Tareq, "Introduction théorétique à la chari'a de minorité." *Islam de France* 2 (1998): 27–41.
Oubrou, Tareq, "La charia de minorité: contribution pour une integration légale de l'islam." February 21, 2003. http://www.islamlaicite.org/article24.html (accessed December 10, 2014).
Pahud de Mortanges, René and Tanner, Erwin, eds. *Muslime und schweizerische Rechtsordnung: Les musulmans et l'ordre juridique suisse* (Freiburg: Universitätsverlag, 2002).
Panafit, Lionel, *Quand le droit écrit l'islam* (Bruxelles: Bruylant, 1999).
Pearl, David and Menski, Werner, *Muslim Family Law* (Lahore: Brite Books, 1998).
Potz, Richard and Wieshaider, Wolfgang, *Islam and the European Union* (Leuven: Peeters, 2004).
Poulter, Sebastian, *Ethnicity, Law and Human Rights* (Oxford: Clarendon Press, 1998).
Ramadan, Tariq, *To be a European Muslim* (Leicester: Islamic Foundation, 1999).

Ramadan, Tariq, *Musulmans d'Occident* (Lyon: Tawhid, 2002).
Ramadan, Tariq, *Western Muslims and the Future of Islam* (Oxford: Oxford University Press, 2004).
Ramadan, Tariq, *Radical Reform: Islamic Ethics and Liberation* (Oxford: Oxford University Press, 2009).
Rassoul, Muhammad Ahmad, *Das deutsche Kalifat* (Cologne: Islamische Bibliothek, 1993).
Rohe, Mathias, "Islamic Law in German Courts." *Hawwa* 1 (2003): 46–59.
Rohe, Mathias, guest ed. "Sharīʿa in Europe." *Die Welt des Islams Special Theme Issue* no 3 (2004): 44.
Rohe, Mathias, "The Formation of a European Sharīʿa" in Jamal Malik (ed.) *Muslims in Europe: From the Margin to the Centre* (Münster: LIT, 2004 (LIT)) 161–184.
Rohe, Mathias, "Alternative Dispute Resolution in Europe under the Auspices of Religious Norms." *RELIGARE working paper*. http://www.religareproject.eu/content/alternative-dispute-resolution-europe-under-auspices-religious-norms.
Rohe, Mathias, "Family and the Law in Europe: Bringing Together Secular Legal Orders and Religious Norms and Needs" in Prakash Shah, Marie-Claire Foblets, and Mathias Rohe (eds.) *Family, Religion and Law: Cultural Encounters in Europe* (Farnham: Ashgate, 2014) 49–78.
Rohe, Mathias, *Islamic Law in Past and Present* (Leiden and Boston: Brill, 2015) (translated by Gwendolyn Goldbloom).
Rohe, Mathias, "Shariʿa in Europe" in Jocelyne Cesari (ed.) *The Oxford Handbook of European Islam* (Oxford: Oxford University Press, 2015) 656–700.
Rohe, Mathias and Elster, Sebastian, "Zur öffentlich-rechtlichen Situation von Muslimen in ausgewählten europäischen Ländern" in Bundesministerium des Inneren Wien and Sicherheitsakademie (eds.) *Perspektiven und Herausforderungen in der Integration muslimischer MitbürgerInnen in Österreich* (Vienna, 2006).
Shadid, Wasif and Van Koningsveld, Pieter, eds., *Religious Freedom and the Neutrality of the State: The Position of Islam in the European Union* (Leuven: Peeters, 2002).
Shah, Prakash and Menski, Werner, eds., *Migration, Diasporas and Legal Systems in Europe* (London: Routledge Cavendish, 2007).
Shah, Prakash, Foblets, Marie-Claire, and Rohe, Mathias, eds., *Family, Religion and Law: Cultural Encounters in Europe* (Farnham: Ashgate, 2014).
Shah-Kazemi, S.N., *Untying the Knot: Muslim Women, Divorce and the Shariʿah* (London: Nuffield Foundation, 2001).
Shavit, Uriya, "The Wasaṭī and Salafī Approaches to the Religious Law of Muslim Minorities." *Islamic Law and Society* 19 (2012): 416–457.
Voorhoeve, Maaike, ed. *Family Law in Islam: Divorce, Marriage and Women in the Muslim World* (London: I.B. Tauris, 2012).
Waardenburg, Jacques, *Muslims and Others: Relations in Context* (Berlin: de Gruyter, 2003).
Williams, Rowan, "Civil and Religious Law in England: A Religious Perspective." Lecture, Royal Courts of Justice, 2008. http://www.archbishopofcanterbury.org/articles.php/1137/archbishops-lecture-civil-and-religious-law-in-england-a-religious-perspective.
Witte, John, "The Future of Muslim Family Law in Western Democracies" in Rex Ahdar and Nicholas Aroney (eds.) *Shariʿa in the West* (Oxford: Oxford University Press, 2010) 279–292.

Yassari, Nadjma, *Die Brautgabe im Vermögensrecht* (Tübingen: Mohr Siebeck, 2014).

Zakariyah, Luqman, "Legal Maxims and Islamic Financial Transactions: A Case Study of Mortgage Contracts and the Dilemma for Muslims in Britain." *Arab Law Quarterly* 26 (2012): 255–285.

Zucca, Lorenzo, *Law and Religion in the European Constitutional Landscape* (Oxford: Oxford University Press, 2012).

CHAPTER 30

SHARI'A IN AUSTRALIA

ABDULLAH SAEED

In a Muslim minority context such as Australia, the question of the place of Muslim ritual, ethical, and social practices and their relationship to a secular system of law is critical, and it is one that has received a great deal of attention from the media as well as from political leaders. For example in May 2011, the then Attorney General Robert McClelland unequivocally stated there was no place for "Sharia law" in Australian society, and that the government strongly rejected any proposal for its introduction.[1] The following year the then Attorney General Nicola Roxon again affirmed the government's position, stating "[t]here is no place for sharia law in Australian society and the government strongly rejects any proposal for its introduction, including in relation to wills and succession ..."[2]

The topic of shari'a is often treated pejoratively in the public arena, in a way that typically deploys overgeneralized definitions of the term and what it entails. This hinders any complex or nuanced discussion. However, as Black and Sadiq point out, not all aspects of shari'a have been framed in such a negative way. Islamic finance, which is seen as potentially attracting foreign investment, is strongly supported by the government.[3] This reveals an interesting paradox. While some aspects of shari'a are viewed positively, particularly those that have potential financial or

[1] Patricia Karvelas, "Imam Wants Sharia Law Here, But A-G Says No Way," *The Australian*, May 18, 2011.

[2] Patricia Karvelas, "Roxon Baulks at Role for Sharia by Australian Muslims," *The Australian*, March 17, 2012.

[3] Ann Black and Kerrie Sadiq, "Good and Bad Sharia: Australia's Mixed Response to Islamic Law," *UNSW Law Journal* 34, no. 1 (2011): 384.

economic benefits for Australia, other aspects of shari'a, such as the recognition of Islamic family law, are either ignored or outright rejected as incompatible with the Australian context.

The purpose of this chapter is to provide a historical perspective and overview of the development of the discourse on shari'a in the Muslim minority context of Australia. The chapter explores some of the key arguments and debates that are currently occurring, seeking to tease out the areas of controversy and common ground. It begins with a brief historical overview of the coming of Islam and shari'a to Australia and the emergence of Muslim communities, followed by a discussion of some key areas of shari'a. These include family law, Islamic finance, Islamic dress codes, and shari'a courts in Australia.

I. Islam and Shari'a in Australia: A Historical Perspective

Since at least the sixteenth century, when Muslim fishermen from the region known today as Indonesia used to travel to the northern parts of Australia, at least some Muslims seemed to observe the ritual and social requirements of their faith on Australian soil. While a few Muslims came to Australia when the first ships with European settlers arrived in Australia in the early 1800s, significant Muslim settlement only began in the mid-nineteenth century with the arrival of the "Afghan" cameleers, from the regions known today as Pakistan, India, and Afghanistan. They were brought to Australia from the 1860s by Australian entrepreneurs to provide camels for transport across the largely desert interior of central Australia.

The Afghan settlers were usually single men without families. They were brought to Australia as part of a temporary arrangement and it was believed that they would go back to their home countries once their initial term of work in the camel transport industry was over. By the end of the nineteenth century there were close to 3000 Afghan cameleers in the country who controlled large parts of the camel transport industry.

This small community of "Afghan" Muslims attempted to meet their religious requirements in various ways, focusing on the need for places of worship and meat slaughtered in the halal fashion. Expedition leaders like Saleh, who led the Giles Expedition of 1875–76 across the Nullabor Plain to Perth and back to South Australia, is said to have dutifully performed his prayers on his own, although he was "regularly teased by the others."[4] Given that Muslim communities were small and scattered across Australia's vast expanses, meeting such needs was a challenge. Their

[4] Bilal Cleland, *The Muslims in Australia* (Wembley: Islamic Human Rights Commission, 2000), 10.

needs were not prioritized by governments and the fact that these communities were largely transient[5] and socially and economically disadvantaged contributed to this lack of consideration. However, some positive gestures were made, including government acknowledgement of their right to freedom of religion and worship. The main Muslim congregation in Coolgardie established two mosques[6] and on average eighty people attended Friday prayers.[7] The community also established designated places of burial with the support of the authorities.

With the establishment of Australia as a federation in 1901, the presence of non-European Australians came into sharp focus. European settlers saw Australia as a white, European-dominated country and believed this should be maintained, principally by prioritizing European migration. These attitudes were enshrined in what came to be called the White Australia policy, which emphasized the need for Australia's population to remain white and European, framed as an attempt to maintain ethnic and racial harmony. The policy was implemented through various laws that restricted migration to Australia, particularly for non-whites or non-Europeans. Although the key issues post-federation involved race and ethnicity rather than religion the negative effect of this White Australia policy on non-white residents of Australia, including Muslims, must have been significant. Some "Afghan" Muslims left Australia to return home; although many remained, living on the margins of society.

As the Muslim community was largely transient, many Muslims early on probably did not intend to marry or settle. Some who came at the time had wives back in their home countries who were not brought to Australia. Despite this, there were some marriages that were held in mosques, suggesting that they were enacted according to shari'a, although this was not made explicit. In accordance with Islamic principles, there is evidence that Afghan Muslims paid the *mahr*. At a time when "a good weekly wage was two pounds, bride prices of one hundred and fifty and two hundred pounds have been documented."[8] Some Muslim men also married indigenous women,[9] who were even more marginalized than the "Afghans." These Afghan–Aboriginal families remained in Australia without many of the rights accorded white Australian citizens at the time. While many of these families probably had difficulty in following key aspects of shari'a, some continued to practice at least some Islamic legal requirements, particularly those related to dietary requirements;

[5] Ibid., 16.

[6] It is unclear when the mosques were established, however in 1898 the Acting Collector of Customs reported their presence and that men from Perth were leading the congregations in prayer. See The Islamic Council of Perth Western Australia, *The Muslim Community Before the Great War*. Available at http://www.islamiccouncilwa.com.au/after-the-second-world-war March 7, 2014.

[7] Ibid., 12. [8] Ibid., 18.

[9] Peta Stephenson, "Long History with Islam Gives Indigenous Australians Pride," *The Conversation*, December 14, 2011. Available at http://theconversation.com/long-history-with-islam-gives-indigenous-australians-pride-3521 August 31, 2013.

aspects of family law, such as the payment of the *mahr* upon marriage;[10] and rites of burial.[11] At this point in time there seems to have been little formal governmental support or recognition of Muslims' religious needs.

In the 1920s and 1930s significant numbers of Albanian Muslims, who were not affected by the White Australia policy (as they were white), migrated to Australia. The small amount of evidence available indicates that these Albanian Muslims were primarily concerned with the basic aspects of Islamic practices that applied to their personal lives, and were little concerned about many other aspects of shari'a.

By the late 1960s the White Australia policy was under severe strain. The value of different cultures gradually came to be recognized and in the early 1970s, under Labour Prime Minister Gough Whitlam, the policy was formally abolished. Later, under the conservative leadership of Malcolm Fraser, a policy of multiculturalism emerged. This adopted a more inclusive approach toward people of different cultures and backgrounds.

During the second half of the twentieth century, the Muslim community in Australia began to increase significantly in number and diversity. In the 1960s, with European migration slowing, Australia was in great need of labor to sustain its expanding economy.[12] The Australian government eventually came to an agreement with Turkey, resulting in 10,000 Turks being offered permanent residency and later citizenship in Australia. There are reports that some Turkish women sought and received permission to wear headscarves to work in this period.[13] The Turkish influx was followed by the migration of significant numbers of Lebanese Muslims during the Lebanese civil war, from the mid-1970s onwards. Newly arrived Muslims from Turkey, Lebanon, and elsewhere now found themselves in a more positive environment where, under the banner of multiculturalism, their cultures were recognized as legitimate. They could therefore maintain their cultural and religious identity while subscribing to the concept of Australian citizenship. By this time Australians comprised a broad range of different ethnic and cultural backgrounds and religious traditions. The commonly held belief was that all Australians should be able to subscribe to a common citizenship, while at the same time respecting each individual's cultural and religious traditions.

As Muslim numbers increased, basic community infrastructure was consolidated, leading to the development of a number of Islamic organizations,

[10] Cleland, *The Muslims in Australia*, 18.

[11] Dost Mahomet, a prominent Afghan camel driver, was buried three km from Menindee on the road to Broken Hill. He is thought to be the first Muslim to be buried on Australian soil. See http://www.migrationheritage.nsw.gov.au/exhibition/objectsthroughtime/broken-hill-mosque-collection

[12] Centre for Research on Social Inclusion, "Muslim-Australians & Local Government: Grassroots Strategies To Improve Relations Between Muslim And Non-Muslim-Australians" (2008), 4:2.

[13] Cleland, *The Muslims in Australia*, 33.

including the Australian Federation of Islamic Councils in 1976.[14] These developments encouraged new discussion about the nature of Muslim identity in Australia and the extent to which Islamic ethics, norms, and legal rules should play a part in this identity. Much of the focus was on meeting the needs of newly arriving migrants, establishing places of worship, and ensuring access to halal meat, with a view to the Muslim community ultimately becoming less reliant on overseas support.[15]

Questions about Islamic identity in a Muslim minority context were brought into some focus, and the place and authority of shariʿa in Australia also emerged as a topic of debate. However, as before, Muslims who migrated to Australia during this period (1960s to 1980s) seem to have considered that it was sufficient to maintain an Islamic identity by meeting the basic requirements of the religion.

While changes to the Australian Marriage Act in 1961 were difficult for Australian Muslims, disallowing "ministers" of the "Islamic religion" from solemnizing marriages,[16] the dominant message in broader society at that time was one of assimilation and integration, and most Muslims seem to have accepted this approach. Some, however, were not comfortable with the idea of assimilation, emphasizing instead the importance of maintaining, if not strengthening their religious and cultural identity.

As the Muslim community grew, by the 1990s, there came to be a greater demand for services that catered to an increased demand among Muslims for practices perceived as being in greater conformity with shariʿa. This included Islamic finance, but also greater recognition of the reality that elements of shariʿa based family law had already been practiced among Muslims for many years. Muslims also began to discuss the possibility of shariʿa-based "courts" or quasi-judicial bodies.

The development of the debate on shariʿa in Australia has been closely associated with the degree to which the community has consolidated and developed key institutions, such as Islamic societies, Islamic councils (at the state level), and the Australian Federation of Islamic Councils (at the national level), not to mention the large number of mosques that have been established in the country. On the education front, perhaps one of the most important developments at the community level occurred in the early 1980s when Muslim communities in Victoria and New South Wales decided to set up Islamic schools. The purpose of this project was to provide a base for second generation Muslims to acquire an Islamic education while adhering to the state-based curricula. This gave students religious grounding, and enabled them to seek higher education in any discipline. Thus the first Islamic school—King Khalid Islamic College—was established in Victoria in Coburg in 1983.

[14] The Islamic Council of Peth Western Australia, *After the Second World War*. Available at http://www.islamiccouncilwa.com.au/after-the-second-world-war January 29, 2014.

[15] Cleland, *The Muslims in Australia*, 34.

[16] Ibid., 18.

Outside basic day-to-day practices and fundamental religious rituals, there was probably little or no discussion about the application of shari'a as law in Muslim life in Australia in the 1980s. The first generation Muslims (of the second half of the twentieth century) came from diverse backgrounds, such as Pakistan, Iran, Bangladesh, Egypt, Turkey, and Lebanon. To these Australian Muslims, their religious life in a new and different country was not something to be governed by rules and regulations imposed by the state; rather they saw it as something to be managed and handled by individuals in the community. There was no understanding of state enforcement or control of one's religious life. This attitude to law, rules, and regulations seemed to have functioned reasonably well in Muslim societies across the world in terms of day-to-day life, so that any governance of shari'a was typically handled at the personal and family level. Community participation involved celebration of particular events, such as births, naming, circumcision of boys, marriage, and burial. This emphasis is a very different understanding of shari'a to what some Muslims have been calling for in recent years, and to what has been termed the Islamization of the legal system. In general, first generation Muslims in Australia adopted a view of shari'a that was highly personal and subject to the existing laws enforced in the country. Given that the legal system in Australia, by and large, had no major difficulties with the fundamental practices of Islam, it was relatively easy for Muslims to adopt a highly personal and community-based view of shari'a.

This emphasis on the "personal" aspects of shari'a began to change somewhat toward the later part of the twentieth century and early part of the twenty-first century. At a global level, a split seems to have emerged between Muslims in the west who have been able to integrate and live under secular systems of law and those Muslims (though relatively few in number) who claim that shari'a should not be subordinate to any other system. This latter position, particularly felt by some second and third generation Muslims, is perhaps a product of their desire to express their Muslim identity, which is felt to be under threat. It has led to the adoption of some "extreme" positions on Islamic law as a way of regulating Islamic identity.[17]

Such "extreme" positions have led to a widespread fear in Australia that Muslims in general do not integrate and are trying to create a second legal system that will challenge the liberal and democratic nature of the Australian state. The concern is that the views held by some elements of the Muslim community—regardless of how small the numbers actually are that hold these views—could potentially damage the foundations on which Australia is based, thus threatening the notion that all citizens must function under one law and one legal system. In the post-9/11 context there has been an increased emphasis by Australian governments on the need for all citizens—including Muslim citizens—to remain united under one legal system. Leaders from both major political parties have emphasized that

[17] See, e.g., Oliver Roy, *Globalised Islam: The Search for a New Ummah* (New York: Columbia University Press, 2004).

neither the Australian parliament nor Australian people in general would recognize a different legal system in any form. For example in May 2006, the then Treasurer Peter Costello stressed that, "Anyone who believes Islamic sharia law can co-exist with Australian law should move to a country where they feel more comfortable."[18]

II. Shari'a Based Family Law

Shari'a based family law is perhaps the part of Islamic law that represents the greatest concern for many Australians. This may be because family law "embodies the quintessential culture of a distinctive group,"[19] and thus is perhaps one of the most distinctive areas that distinguishes Muslim culture from mainstream Australian culture.[20] Shari'a based family law is also generally viewed as being out of date in contemporary Australia, and based on traditional gender roles deemed generally "out of step" with twenty-first-century values.[21]

A. Marriage

Although the Australian government formally denies a place for shari'a in the Australian legal system, an informal space already exists in the recognition of Islamic marriage and divorce. The Marriage Act 1961 (Cth) governs marriages in Australia, and allows marriages to be solemnized and registered by a minister of religion. The Marriage (Recognised Denominations) Proclamation 1999 (Cth) includes Islam. Thus, an authorized imam may perform a marriage according to shari'a and register it, and it will be recognized by the state.

However, as Black and Sadiq point out, some Muslims can and do choose to enter into Islamic marriages that are not formally solemnized and registered in Australia for many reasons, including maintaining autonomy over this important area of personal and religious life.[22] It may also be the case that young Muslims see

[18] "If You Want Shari'a Law, Move: Cogstello." *Sydney Morning Herald*, February 23, 2006.

[19] Black and Sadiq, "Good and Bad Sharia," citing Sebastian M. Poulter, "The Claim to a Separate Islamic System of Personal Law for British Muslims," in *Islamic Family Law*, eds. C. Mallat and J. Connors (London: Graham & Trotman, 1990), 247.

[20] Poulter, "The Claim to a Separate Islamic System of Personal Law for British Muslims," 147, cited in Black and Sadiq, "Good and Bad Sharia," 396.

[21] Black and Sadiq, "Good and Bad Sharia," 397.

[22] Ibid., 398.

Islamic marriage as a precursor to an intended civil marriage, which allows them to enter into a form of relationship that would otherwise be forbidden by traditional and religious mores. More controversially, unregistered Islamic marriages allow for situations where a marriage could not legally be registered under Australian law, such as polygynous marriages,[23] or in some cases marriages where one party is below the legal minimum age of 18.[24]

Although these are examples of where Australian law is more restrictive than shari'a, there are also circumstances where traditional understandings of shari'a are more restrictive than what is legally permissible in Australia. One example is the restriction on Muslim women marrying non-Muslim men.[25] There is no such restriction in Australian law. However, a problem is likely to arise if a Muslim woman wishes to marry outside the faith but her family tries to prevent her. In this case, while her actions are perfectly legal under Australian law, the civil marriage may not be recognized by her community, leading to, perhaps, distressing personal and social ramifications for the woman.

B. Divorce

Divorce in Australia is governed by the Family Law Act 1975 (Cth) (FLA). As Parashar points out, the FLA takes a hands-off approach, preferring to allow parties to negotiate and agree on their property relations themselves. It is only if they cannot do so that the Family Court will step in, and it then has a broad discretion to decide on a fair distribution.[26] In other words, the FLA allows for flexibility in divorce related property settlements, providing a space where shari'a principles can be applied if parties work through the framework of dispute resolution. Although Islamic divorce is not recognized under the FLA, concerns are often raised, however, about how gender equality can be maintained when applying shari'a principles in the context of divorce, specifically in relation to the legality of unilateral, no-fault divorce—a privilege reserved only for men under shari'a. That is, a man has the power to terminate the marriage contract and maintain certain rights over the wife and children, without a corresponding right being enjoyed by his wife.[27]

[23] A polygynous marriage (a marriage between a man and a woman where the man continues to be lawfully married to another woman) falls under the definition of the crime of bigamy under the Marriage Act 1961 (Cth), s 94.

[24] This is determined by the Marriage Act 1961 (Cth) s 11. A person aged between 16 and 18 can apply for special permission to a court.

[25] This is based on Qur'an 60:10 and 2:221.

[26] Archana Parashar, "Australian Muslims and Family Law: Diversity and Gender Justice," *Journal of Intercultural Studies* 33, no. 5 (2012): 575.

[27] M. Voyce and A. Possamai, "Legal Pluralism, Family Personal Laws and the Rejection of Shari'a in Australia: A Case of Multiple or 'clashing' Modernities?" *Democracy and Security* 7, no. 1 (2011): 342.

In addition, after such a unilateral divorce, the Qur'an prescribes an approximately three-month waiting period for the woman (unless the wife is pregnant, in which case the waiting period is extended: Qur'an 65: 4). This is much shorter than the Australian legal requirement of a separation period of twelve months (section 48 of Part VI of the Family Law Act 1975 (Cth)).[28] However, it is possible to meet the requirements of both shariʿa and Australian family law if a couple waits the twelve-month period of separation required under Australian law and then applies for divorce on the grounds of the irretrievable breakdown of marriage.[29]

A more significant issue is the lack of agency given to women in the instigation of divorce under shariʿa. A wife has more limited options for initiating divorce than a husband under shariʿa. Unless she is able to persuade her husband to pronounce *talaq* (unilateral divorce), she has three options:

- *Ta'liq* or *talaq tafwid*, when the husband has breached a term of the marriage contract. This may include a nonstandard term stipulated by the wife prior to marriage, such as agreement not to take a second wife or live in a certain city.
- *Faskh*, which occurs when the husband can be proven to be "at fault" according to certain recognized categories, such as extended absence, impotence, cruelty, and failure to maintain his wife and child.
- If none of these applies then the wife may apply for *khul'*, which often involves the return of her *mahr* (dowry). If the dowry is significant, as it is in many Muslim societies, this amounts to the wife "buying her way out of the marriage."[30]

Although these avenues are available to Muslim women, they all require a third party to act as an adjudicator, usually an imam, who determines whether or not the woman should be released from her marriage and can mediate in decisions about the division of property and care of any children. In Australia where there is no formally recognized shariʿa process, legal oversight of such adjudication does not occur. While in fact this may not be a significant problem for "empowered Muslim women," it is a different story "for those who lack the contacts, knowledge and confidence to proceed."[31] The requirement of an adjudicator can also expose women to "spousal, religious and community pressures to resolve the marital dispute in accordance with what is presented as the right version of Islamic law."[32] In some cases a woman may face reluctance from the imam to "grant" the divorce, especially if her husband is unwilling to participate in the dialogue or to agree to ending of the marriage.[33] The

[28] Black and Sadiq, "Good and Bad Sharia," 399.

[29] Ann Black, "Legal Recognition of Sharia law: Is this the Right Direction for Australian Family Matters?" *Family Matters* 84 (2010): 65.

[30] Black and Sadiq, "Good and Bad Sharia," 340.

[31] Ann Black, "Legal Recognition of Sharia Law," 65. [32] Ibid.

[33] ABC Radio, Mediation in the Mosque. October 21, 2008. Transcript available at http://www.abc.net.au/radionational/programs/lawreport/mediation-in-the-mosque/3192152#transcript

issue of "authority" of the imam to "grant" such a divorce is problematic as Australian law does not recognize such an authority. But within certain sections of Muslim communities, such a "religious" divorce may have a symbolic function.

Thus, a Muslim woman who is formally divorced from her husband in accordance with Australian law might still be considered married within the Muslim community, and re-marriage would be viewed as a form of adultery. If a Muslim woman divorced in this way were to travel to a country where shari'a had more weight in state law, her divorce might also not be recognized by that jurisdiction. This phenomenon is known as "limping marriage," a term which has had a long existence in western law, primarily referring to differences in annulling marriage between national jurisdictions. Its existence attests to the fact that differences in views about the lawful termination of marriage are not solely a phenomenon arising from shari'a based law.

An attempt to clarify various issues in Australian divorce law was made in the August 2001 report to the Attorney General prepared by the Family Law Council (FLC), entitled *Cultural-Community Divorce and the Family Law Act 1975: A Proposal to Clarify the Law*. The report highlighted problems in both the Australian Jewish and Muslim communities arising from differences between "cultural–community" divorce rules and the Australian family law system. Interestingly, the FLC concluded that "establishment of a Sharia court in Australia would alleviate many of the divorce difficulties experienced in the Islamic community." However, such an option was "clearly not a matter for the Australian Government" and rested in the hands of the community. This statement clearly contradicts those of senior government figures such as Attorney General McClelland and a series of prime ministers, who have repeatedly rejected the notion of a shari'a court.[34]

The Council did recommend the adoption of a proposal by the Executive Council of Australian Jewry and the Organisation of the Rabbis of Australasia (ECAJ/ORA) to order parties to attend a "recognised tribunal"—defined as a Beth Din for Jews—and also to order a party to remove any "barriers to ... re-marriage."[35] In the context of Australian Jews, this was an attempt to resolve the issue arising when a husband refuses to deliver the document known as the *get*, which is necessary to formalize a religious divorce. However, although the proposal would presumably apply equally to Australian Muslims, though the "tribunal" would not be a Beth Din, the Council noted that the submissions it received from the Muslim community were more diverse than those received from Australian Jews, and consequently there was very

[34] See, e.g., Barney Zwartz, "Australia's Muslims Cool on Change," *The Age*, February 9, 2008 or Karvelas, "Imam Wants Sharia Law Here, but A-G Says No Way."

[35] Family Law Council, "Cultural Community Divorce and the Family Law Act 1975: A Proposal to Clarify the Law," August 2001, 28. Available at http://www.ag.gov.au/FamiliesAndMarriage/FamilyLawCouncil/Documents/Cultural%20community%20Divorce%20and%20the%20Family%20Law%20Act%201975.pdf August 31, 2013.

little consensus on what legislative changes were desirable. It might be noted that in traditional understandings of shariʿa, a recognized judicial body is able to nullify a marriage if certain conditions are met, which may be different to the situation under Jewish law. In any case, according to the website of the Australian Law Reform Commission, the FLC report that incorporated and built on the recommendations of ALRC Report No. 57 on Multiculturalism and the Law, "has not been accepted" by the Australian government.[36] However, the issue of multiculturalism and the law remains an "ongoing issue," and one that the federal government has "pursued."[37]

c. Custody

Another area of divergence is custody law. Under Australian law arrangements for children are determined either by consent (which is ratified as Consent Orders by the Family Court), through family dispute resolution or, as a final measure, through an application for parenting orders that is heard by the Court.[38] The Family Law Reform Act 1995 (Cth) "implements ALRC recommendations, specifying that in considering the welfare of the child the court should consider the relationships that the child has with each parent or with other persons and the importance of maintaining links with their culture."[39] As distinct from Australian family law, shariʿa based family law places particular importance on the distinction between custody and guardianship: for children below a certain age (which differs according to the Islamic school of jurisprudence one follows) custody is granted to the mother, while guardianship remains with the father. Thus, an order that the Family Court might make for custody might be in conflict with a community expectation that a child stay with his or her mother, for example. However, it should be noted that the shariʿa requirements are not determined solely by the Qur'an but emerge from statements of the Prophet and the practice of the various legal schools.[40] Thus, there are different positions on this issue, and a mother's presumptive right of custody may be overruled if there is evidence she has mistreated the child, for example.[41]

[36] Australian Law Reform Commission, *Multiculturalism and the Law* (2012). Available at http://www.alrc.gov.au/inquiries/multiculturalism-and-law August 31, 2013.

[37] Ibid.

[38] Family Law Courts, *Parental Responsibility and Parenting Orders*. Available at http://www.familylawcourts.gov.au/wps/wcm/connect/FLC/Home/Children%27s+Matters/If+you+can%E2%80%99t+agree+on+arrangements/ March 7, 2014.

[39] Australian Law Reform Commission, *Multiculturalism and the Law*.

[40] Louay Safi, "The Maqasid Approach and Political Rights," *Intellectual Discourse* 18, no. 2 (2010): 215.

[41] Black and Sadiq, "Good and Bad Sharia," 400.

D. Polygyny

Another feature of shari'a based family law that is quite well-known is its permission of polygyny. In Muslim minority contexts such as Australia this issue generates heated debate. In mainstream discourse, polygyny (usually wrongly called polygamy) serves as one of the key examples of the perceived incompatibility of shari'a with Australian law. Quite simply, polygyny is seen as contrary to Australia's established values concerning marriage and gender equality and, as set out in the Marriage Act, is illegal, attracting a penalty of five years' imprisonment.[42] Nevertheless, valid Muslim polygynous marriages lawfully entered into overseas are recognized in Australia.[43]

A closer look at the debate reveals that only a small section of the Muslim community in Australia argues for the legalization of polygyny. This includes Keysar Trad, spokesperson for the Islamic Friendship Association, who has called for the legal recognition of polygyny, arguing that the Australian system should be more inclusive.[44] As Parashar suggests, "[t]he resilience of a liberal system to accommodate difference comes under severe stress at this point"[45] and thus is met with blanket refusals for its accommodation by Australian politicians.[46] Regardless of this, the reality in Australia, as in Muslim majority countries, is that the vast majority of Muslim marriages are monogamous. Nor does there appear to be a great push to have Australian marriage laws changed. This is made clear in Ghena Krayem's research on Islamic marriage in which 90 percent of Muslims interviewed stated that they did not want Australian marriage law to change; a position likewise promoted by the Australian National Imams Council.[47]

In some sections of the Muslim community, there seem to be concerns that the overriding jurisdiction of Australian courts limits the potential for a shari'a based family law to be applied in its totality, and that any attempt to incorporate shari'a law into the larger Australian system would lead to "the inevitable fragmentation of Sharia."[48] An alternative position here, as lawyer and academic Krayem argues, "is not recognition of sharia per se—whatever that means—but a dispute resolution process that is useful to the Muslim community and is sensitive to their needs."[49]

Essentially, two views emerge in the debate about whether and how shari'a based family law can be accommodated. For some there is an argument to be made for the Australian legal system accommodating certain aspects of shari'a based family

[42] Marriage Act 1961 (Cth) s 94 makes bigamy illegal. [43] Family Law Act 1975 (Cth) s 6.

[44] Black, "Legal Recognition of Sharia Law," 67.

[45] Parashar, "Australian Muslims and Family Law," 578.

[46] Black and Sadiq, "Good and Bad Sharia," 398.

[47] Ibid., 409. [48] Ibid., 406.

[49] Ghena Krayem, cited in Sally Neighbor, "The Way to the Watering Hole," *The Monthly* (December 2012–January 2011): 25.

law. The other possibility is for a dual system of law to be established. However, in reality, it is unlikely that the latter could actually materialize, due to the nature of the Australian legal setting. Parashar points out that "claims in the name of cultural difference" are deemed irrelevant if they are seen to threaten the ideals of liberalism.[50] However, liberalism may potentially be reconceptualized to accommodate difference that may at first seem incompatible.[51] The debate around shariʿa is therefore twofold, concerning the requirements for Muslims in Australia of certain aspects of shariʿa based law, but also broader questions about how shariʿa based family law could or should be integrated into the Australian legal system. Should only some aspects of shariʿa family law be integrated into the Australian legal system? Or should it be formally recognized as a separate system that complements Australia's existing legal code?

While not specifically addressing claims to implement aspects of shariʿa based family law, the Australian federal government did formally respond in 1995 to Australian Law Reform Commission (ALRC) Report No. 57,[52] which considered issues surrounding multiculturalism and the law, and specifically discussed the implementation of shariʿa based family law in the Australian context. The government indicated strong support for a majority of the report's recommendations and stated that it would develop, for example, a range of initiatives to improve access to justice for Aboriginal and Torres Strait Islander people and people of non-English speaking background. However, the recommendations related to cultural and religious divorce (including those related to shariʿa based family law) were not implemented, nor were those compiled in the ALRC's later (2001) report on the same matter.[53]

III. Islamic Finance

Islamic finance is about financial transactions that are in line with norms and practices that are approved by shariʿa. Although the most well-known element of Islamic finance is the ban on interest, there are in fact several other elements that are commonly understood as representing the essential requirements of shariʿa, particularly in regard to modern finance. Examples include a ban on financing certain

[50] Parashar, "Australian Muslims and Family Law," 578. [51] Ibid.

[52] Issued in association with the Attorney General's Justice Statement of May 1995, which outlined the Australian government's policy with respect to access to justice (in response to the recommendations of the Access to Justice Advisory Committee).

[53] See http://www.alrc.gov.au/inquiries/multiculturalism-and-law.

economic sectors such as the sex industry, alcohol, and gambling. On the other hand, regulation of the payment and distribution of *zakat* is also considered part of Islamic finance.

The development of Islamic finance in Australia has been strong over the last decade. It is quite clear that the Australian government has responded to the issue of Islamic finance significantly differently to its response to the calls for recognition of shari'a based family law. Paradoxically, while accommodation of shari'a based family law was openly rejected, there has been a surprisingly high level of support for accommodating Islamic finance. For example, in 2010, the then Assistant Treasurer Simon Crean acknowledged the growing value of worldwide Islamic finance assets, demonstrating "the enormous extent of the opportunities available for both business and government" in Australia.[54]

Despite Australia's relatively small Muslim population, a growing domestic market is evident with the development of a number of Islamic financial institutions. Among them is the Muslim Community Cooperative Australia (MCCA), which was established in 1989.[55] The MCCA is based in Sydney and Melbourne. Its membership is open to both Muslims and non-Muslims. The institution's acceptance by the broader Australian community was recognized in 2006 when it received the annual Australian Business Award for Small and Medium Enterprises.[56]

Two other Islamic financial institutions are the Islamic Cooperative Finance Australia (ICFA), established in 1998,[57] and Iskan Finance,[58] established in 2001.[59] More recently, Islamic superannuation funds have been established.

Australian banks have also shown interest in the development of Islamic financial products. For instance, the National Australia Bank (NAB) has been involved in the development of Islamic finance in Australia since 2006.[60] In 2007 the NAB introduced an A$25,000 scholarship in the area of Islamic finance with the aim of exploring ways in which the bank could broaden its understanding of Islamic finance.[61] It has also been working on developing a range of Islamic financial products, such as shari'a compliant bonds. Other international banks are also becoming involved in this sector, with HSBC and Citibank considering the introduction of some form of Islamic finance initiatives in Australia.[62]

[54] Simon Crean, "Landmark Islamic Finance Publication" (Media Release, February 12, 2010). Available at http://www.trademinister.gov.au/releases/2010/sc_100212.html.

[55] Abu Umar Faruq Ahmad and A.B. Rafique Ahmad, "Islamic Microfinance: A Case Study of Australia," *Journal of Islamic Economics, Banking and Finance* (2008): 68.

[56] MCCA Media Release, cited in Ahmad and Ahmad, "Islamic Microfinance," 69.

[57] Ahmad and Ahmad, "Islamic Microfinance," 71. [58] Ibid.

[59] Iskan Finance. Available at http://www.iskan.com.au/ August 31, 2013.

[60] Abu Umar Faruq Ahmad, Noor Mohammad Osmani, and Mohd Fazlul Karim, "Islamic Finance in Australia: The Potential Problems and Prospects," paper delivered at Seventh International Conference *The Tawhidi Epistemology: Zahat and Waqf Economy*, Bangi, 2010, 232.

[61] Ibid., 232. [62] Ibid., 233.

The Australian government has taken a strong interest in Islamic finance. Austrade, the government's trade and investment promotion agency which facilitates trade between Australia and overseas markets, has been at the forefront of organizing a range of seminars on this topic and it highlights the role of Islamic finance:

Islamic finance is one of the fastest growing areas of the financial services industry, with sharia-compliant assets held globally by financial institutions estimated to be worth US$822 billion in 2009 and projected to be US$1 trillion in 2010.[63]

A wide range of benefits for Australia are mentioned in the debate on Islamic finance: strengthening economic links with Muslim majority countries; flow of funds from cash-rich Gulf countries; and access to Islamic capital markets. A report by the Australian Financial Centre Forum, known as the *Johnson Report*, states that: "the greatest opportunity for Australia in terms of accessing offshore capital pools at competitive rates would appear to be in the area of developing sharia-compliant wholesale investment products."[64] This report recommends that the Australian legal system accommodate further the imperatives of Islamic financial law, and highlights the impediments that currently exist in taxation law, including the regulatory barriers to Islamic finance. The government responded in the 2010 federal budget by announcing the establishment of an "interdepartmental committee" to review these barriers and address the issue on the basis that "lack of regulatory support is what continues to hamper the rapid expansion and acceptance of Islamic finance in Australia."[65] The then Commonwealth government's commitment is made clear in the statement that, "Islamic financing is a crucial plank in the Government's strategy to make Australia a financial hub in the Asia Pacific region."[66]

The barriers in Australia to embrace Islamic finance until recently can perhaps also be attributed to a lack of uniformity in approaches to existing regulatory impediments.[67] On the one hand, some researchers argue for a separate regulatory framework on the basis that the principles of Islamic finance are fundamentally different from the financial status quo in Australia.[68] On the other hand, Black and

[63] Kerrie Sadiq and Ann Black, "Embracing Sharia-Compliant Products through Regulatory Amendment to Achieve Party of Treatment," *Sydney Law Review* 34 (2012): 194, citing Austrade, *Islamic Finance* (Australian Government, 2010).

[64] Sadiq and Black, "Embracing Sharia-Compliant Products," 190, citing Australian Financial Centre Forum, *Australia as a Financial Centre: Building on our Strengths* (November 2009), 70.

[65] Ibid., 71.

[66] Sadiq and Black, "Embracing Sharia-Compliant Products," 189–189, citing Australian Government, Austrade, "Landmark Islamic Finance Publication Ministerial" (Media Release, February 12, 2010). Available at http://www.austrade.gov.au/Landmark-Islamic-finance-publication-inisterial/default.aspx

[67] Ahmad, Osmani, and Karim, "Islamic Finance in Australia," 220.

[68] Ibid.

Sadiq suggest that the Australian Taxation Office could instead issue administrative guidance, which would mean that legislative reform could be avoided.[69] For example, the *Johnson Report* recommended "removal of any regulatory barriers to the development of Islamic financial products in Australia, guided by the principle that there should be a 'level playing field' for such products."[70] The report recommended that,

> the Treasurer refer to the Board of Taxation the question of whether any amendments to existing Commonwealth taxation provision are necessary in order to ensure that Islamic finance products have parity of treatment with conventional products, having regard to their economic substance.[71]

These moves were supported by Austrade, which in January 2010 stated that regulatory reform was "particularly important for countries that currently only have tax regulation for a conventional finance and banking system."[72] Similarly, as Black and Sadiq outline, companies such as Blake Dawson and Ernst & Young, and institutions such as CPA Australia, the Taxation Institute of Australia, and the Australian Financial Markets Association "all support the facilitation of a 'level playing field' for the provision of Islamic finance alongside conventional financing, via legislative amendment."[73]

In response, in 2010 the Board of Taxation announced that it would "undertake a comprehensive review of Australia's tax laws to ensure that, wherever possible, they do not inhibit the expansion of Islamic finance, banking and insurance products."[74] This review resulted in a discussion paper titled, "Review of the Taxation Treatment of Islamic Finance," which was released in October 2010.[75]

In general, these responses evince a broad willingness to think about ways to facilitate Islamic finance in Australia by broadening taxation policy, rather than through the establishment of a separate regulatory body.

[69] Sadiq and Black, "Embracing Sharia-Compliant Products," 199.

[70] Ibid., 201–202, citing *Australia as a Financial Centre*, 98.

[71] Sadiq and Black, "Embracing Sharia-Compliant Products," 202, citing Australian Financial Centre Forum, Australian Government, *Australia as a Financial Centre:Building on our Strengths* (November 2009), 71.

[72] Sadiq and Black, "Embracing Sharia-Compliant Products," 202–203, citing Austrade, *Islamic Finance* (Australian Government, 2010).

[73] Sadiq and Black, "Embracing Sharia-Compliant Products," 203.

[74] Sadiq and Black, "Embracing Sharia-Compliant Products," 202, citing Australian Government, The Treasury, "Board of Taxation to Review Australia's Tax Laws to Ensure Islamic Finance Market Can Expand" (Media Release, no. 076, April 26, 2010). Available at http://ministers.treasury.gov.au/DisplayDocs.aspx?doc=pressreleases/2010/076.htm&pageID=003&min=njsa&Year=&DocType=0

[75] Sadiq and Black, "Embracing Sharia-Compliant Products," 202, with reference to Australian Government, Review of the Taxation Treatment of Islamic Finance (Discussion Paper, Board of Taxation, October 2010).

It is interesting to note that Islamic finance plays a positive role in the broader debates surrounding shariʿa based law in terms of how this law is popularly imagined or perceived in Muslim minority settings like Australia. More importantly, the fact that Islamic finance, as an aspect of shariʿa, can be integrated into the Australian legal context is an example of how other aspects of shariʿa could likewise be integrated. That is to say, through the broad acceptance of Islamic finance, shariʿa based law may be framed as not *necessarily* incompatible with liberal legal systems. Thus, Islamic finance in Australia serves as an instrument to communicate to the broader public that shariʿa is not necessarily an archaic system of law.

IV. Islamic Dress

The debate that centers on Islamic dress is often publicized and highly emotive. In a Muslim minority context such as Australia, the veil is a case in point. The veil has come to signify the idea of the so-called Islamic "threat," and so, even though this aspect of Muslim practice is not incompatible with Australian law, it often generates extremely heated debate.[76] As Kolig and Kabir note:

> While female dress code does not usually constitute a problem insofar as the wearing of the *hijab* is not forbidden in any public sphere and discrimination on this basis is against the law, it can emerge at times as an issue.[77]

Mainstream politicians have explicitly entered into this debate; for example in 2005, with Liberal backbenchers Sophie Panopolous and Bronwyn Bishop calling for headscarves to be banned in public schools.[78] As Anne Aly and David Walker highlight, former Prime Minister John Howard also entered the debate when, in February 2006, he stated that "most Australians" would find the Islamic dress "confronting,"[79] apparently a reference to the face-covering veil. Indeed, in Australia, "the political and public debate surrounding the right of Muslims to wear

[76] Anne Aly and David Walker, "Veiled Threats: Recurrent Cultural Anxieties in Australia," *Journal of Muslim Minority Affairs* 27, no. 2 (2007): 210.

[77] Erich Kolig and Nahid Kabir, "Not Friend, Not Foe: The Rocky Road of Enfranchisement of Muslims into Multicultural Nationhood in Australia and New Zealand," *Immigrants & Minorities* 26, no. 3 (2008): 276.

[78] Aly and Walker, "Veiled Threats," 211, citing comments made by Sophie Panopoulos MP in Parliament on September 5, 2005. Available at http://www.aph.gov.au/hansard June 17, 2006.

[79] Aly and Walker, "Veiled Threats," 210, citing "Muslim Garb 'Confronting': PM," *The Age*, February 27, 2006.

the various forms of the veil: *hijab, chador* or *burqa* often masks a deeper concern with the Islamification of Australia."[80] Aly and Walker claim that in both the political and media arenas, the veil "represents both oppression and dissention," and, as such, "veiling spells the rejection of Australian society and the political values of liberal democracies."[81] So much so, that "the veil is inextricably linked to the cultural threat posed by Islam": a threat that was perceived to have expanded in the post-9/11 context.[82] This cultural threat was highlighted when, in September 2006, the Mufti of Australia at the time, Sheikh Taj al-Din al-Hilali, publicly commented that, in his view, non-Islamically dressed women could be compared to "uncovered meat," apparently blaming them for inciting men to rape.[83] These widely-covered comments were "taken by some mainstream politicians to reveal an incompatibility between Islamic values and the freedom enjoyed by Australians to dress as they liked."[84]

In contrast, another interesting case highlights how in an environment like Australia's, the issue of traditional forms of Islamic dress can be accommodated. The so-called *burqa* case in New Zealand illustrates a novel approach to the issue of Islamic dress, perhaps, as Kolig and Kabir note, giving "a hint of the complexities of multiculturalism."[85] The *burqa* case involved two Afghan women who were called as witnesses in a case before the Auckland district court "wearing *burqa*-type clothing."[86] Initially, the women "refused to publicly unveil [arguing] that under the Bill of Rights Act 1990 their religious right to adhere to Islamically prescribed clothing should be preserved."[87] The judge ruled that in this particular instance the women were required to unveil "but allowed them to remain behind a screen to shield them from the public gallery and most of the court staff."[88] This case, among others, serves as an example that "reveal[s] the prevalent reasoning that it is better to reach compromises in individual cases than risk a serious clash with human rights legislation and cherished concepts of freedom through regulative or restrictive measures."[89] In other words, the way this case was dealt with demonstrates one example of how conflicting cultural and religious norms can be temporarily accommodated within a liberal legal system.

80 Aly and Walker, "Veiled Threats," 210. 81 Ibid.

82 Ibid. 83 Kolig and Kabir, "Not Friend, Not Foe," 278.

84 Ibid., 279.

85 Ibid., 277. See E. Kolig, "Muslim Traditions and Islamic Law in New Zealand: The 'Burqa Case' and the Challenge of Multiculturalism," in *Asia in the Making of New Zealand*, eds. H. Johnson and B. Moloughney (Auckland: Auckland University Press, 2006), 204–233.

86 Kolig and Kabir, "Not Friend, Not Foe," 277.

87 Ibid. 88 Ibid. 89 Ibid.

V. Shariʿa courts

Shariʿa courts are not formally recognized in Australia. Muslims by and large do not call for establishing such courts in Australia. However, there is strong interest among certain sections of the Muslim community to have community-based bodies that can deal with some areas of shariʿa based family law. To address this, such bodies have been set up and do operate informally alongside, the country's legal system, although they are not recognized by the legal system. Several boards of imams based in different states of Australia follow shariʿa principles and selectively use Australian law to address family matters related to divorce, property, and children.[90] Voyce and Possamai suggest that these extra-judicial bodies are "hybridist": consisting of unofficial mediation and arbitration processes while in some cases handing down "judgments" and operating within existing secular law.[91] In this sense, "they are operating in the context of Australian family law and ... what they recommend might only be a first step in a longer legal process."[92] In other words, these bodies act in the place of formally recognized shariʿa courts in relative conjunction with Australian law, though not recognized officially.

A number of criticisms have been made of these bodies due to their unregulated and informal nature.[93] These criticisms include the structural disadvantage of women, "who may suffer intimidation or be unable to give full consent to processes applied";[94] and that they may encourage the phenomenon of "imam shopping" or "forum shopping," in which the parties in question seek out "legal" counsel that suits them best.[95] Arguments have also been made that, due to their ability to hand down shariʿa based "legal" rulings that may not be in line with Australian legislation, these boards negate the central ideology of the liberal state—one legal system for all. However, the Family Law Act 1975 does allow "a considerable amount of plurality in practice, and it has been argued that group differentiated rights ... are not antithetical to liberal democracy."[96]

If shariʿa courts were established in Australia, a whole new set of debates would emerge. The Muslim community is heavily divided ethnically, theologically, and religio-politically. There is no single body that collectively represents Muslims and similarly religious authority within the community is not one either. This "diversity of viewpoints and lack of consensus" was noted in 2001 by the Family Law Council

[90] Voyce and Possamai, "Legal Pluralism," 343. [91] Ibid.
[92] Ibid. [93] Ibid. [94] Ibid. [95] Ibid. [96] Ibid., 344.

of Australia, which discussed the divorce difficulties experienced by some Muslims in Australia.[97] In addition, there are differing legal schools within Islam, and thus the question must be asked: which of these would govern or oversee such a shari'a court? Furthermore, how would the various Islamic organizations and groups that operate in Australia be represented in the functioning of such a court or courts? Finally, how would such a court be funded?[98] In any case it is likely that over time Australian family law and shari'a based family law will continue to converge, as exemplified in the shared support for monogamy. Likewise, the global propagation of human rights norms will inevitably shape Islamic law, which has proven to be more flexible and context-sensitive than typically framed. In light of this it is relevant to ask: "If both systems of law converge, will there be any real need to establish Sharia courts?"[99]

VI. Community and Shari'a

Indeed, the majority of Muslims do not seem interested in a parallel or separate shari'a based legal system. Rather, for most Muslims in Australia, shari'a appears to be very much about ethical and moral norms that can be implemented largely in one's personal life and within the family. For them, shari'a entails practicing fundamental rituals such as prayer, fasting, *zakat*, and the *hajj* as well as Islamic ethical and moral norms. This form of shari'a also entails abstaining from things that are prohibited by shari'a, such as consumption of alcohol, pig meat and fat, gambling, prostitution, and sex outside marriage. These aspects of shari'a do not require any state intervention or a regulatory legal system.

In relation to western law and its impact on Muslims in countries like Australia, Kolig and Kabir argue that: "the notion of immutability of divinely prescribed laws and the flexibility of constant law changes in a Western legal and parliamentary system sit uneasily together."[100] Certain Australian politicians also exacerbate the debate. The perception of the inherent foreignness of shari'a based law and concern for its potential to change the Australian legal system was exemplified in Chris Bowen, the then Minister for Immigration's, statement: "[a]nybody who calls for

[97] Black, "Legal Recognition of Shari'a Law," 67.

[98] Abdullah Saeed, "Reflections on the Establishment of Shari'a Courts in Australia," in *Shari'a in the West*, eds. Rex Ahdar and Nicholas Aroney (Oxford: Oxford University Press, 2010), 236.

[99] Saeed, "Reflections on the Establishment of Shari'a Courts," 238.

[100] Kolig and Kabir, "Not Friend, Not Foe," 281.

Sharia law is not doing so in the name of multiculturalism. They are doing so as extremists and extremists need to be dealt with, whatever their creed."[101] The fear of the radicalization of Australian Muslims has been reflected in the discourse of senior politicians over the past decade. For example, in 2006 former Treasurer Peter Costello made the statement:

> [T]here is one law we are all expected to abide by. It is the law enacted by the Parliament under the Australian Constitution. If you can't accept that then you don't accept the fundamentals of what Australia is and what it stands for.[102]

In the same year former Prime Minister John Howard elaborated: "what Peter [Costello] was basically saying is that if people don't like what this country is then they shouldn't come here."[103]

Cory Bernardi, a Liberal Party senator from South Australia, added to the public debate: "[w]e should not entertain any thought of introducing any aspect of sharia law into Australia. Sharia law is wholly incompatible with the Australian way of life,"[104] and that, "[w]e need to stop the expansion of fundamentalist Islam in Australia lest we lose the foundation, the essence, the very culture of our great nation."[105] Similarly, in 2010 the then Labor Attorney General Robert McClelland commented that the "Rudd government is not considering and will not consider the introduction of any part of Sharia law into the Australian legal system."[106] Other politicians, though still in opposition, held less extreme positions, calling for "equality before the law," claiming that ' "mainstream" legal values [will] adjust "organically" to the growing cultural diversity within Australian society.[107]

These views and comments together function to create a discourse that supports a uniform Australian identity based on secular law that is "equally applied to everyone by a neutral state."[108] Anyone with views that differ from this discourse is seen as "un-Australian" and is publicly scrutinized.

[101] Black and Sadiq, "Good and Bad Shari'a," 398, citing Sabra Lane, "Multiculturalism is Back" *ABC News AM Program*, February 17, 2011 (Hon Chris Bowen). Available at http://www.abc.net.au/am/content/2011/s3141073.htm

[102] Black, "Legal Recognition of Shari'a Law," 64, citing P. Costello, *Worth Promoting, Worth Defending: Australian Citizenship. What it Means and How to Nurture it.* Address to the Sydney Institute, Sydney. Available at http://www.treasurer.gov.au/tsr/content/speeches/2006/004.asp para 44. July 3, 2009.

[103] Saeed, "Reflections on the Establishment of Shari'a Courts."

[104] Neighbor, "The Way to the Watering Hole," 22.

[105] Ibid.

[106] Black, "Legal Recognition of Sharia Law," 64, citing B. Zwartz, "Australia's Muslims Cool on Change," *The Age*, February 9, 2008. Available at http://www.theage.com.au/news/world/australias-muslims-cool-on-change/2008/02/08/1202234168549.html July 3, 2009.

[107] Voyce and Possamai, "Legal Pluralism," 349.

[108] Parashar, "Australian Muslims and Family Law," 578.

VII. Concluding Remarks

The debate about shariʿa in Australia is essentially about the place of Muslim ritual, ethical, and social practices and their relationship to a secular system of law. Shariʿa first came to Australia largely with the "Afghan" cameleers. Initially it was mostly an expression of private religious beliefs, but with time, as the Muslim community increased in number and consolidated, community expressions of shariʿa developed with the need for places of public worship and prayer, designated places of burial, halal meat, and institutions to support the community. By the 1980s, a clear demand for services or practices that conformed to shariʿa could be identified, while in parallel, the development of Islamic societies and councils provided a voice to give expression to these collective needs.

During the later part of the twentieth century and early part of the twenty-first century discussions among Muslims about the role and place of shariʿa in Australia have intensified. At the same time, the broader Australian public has shown discomfort with the notion of any explicit recognition of shariʿa law, fearing that Muslims do not integrate and are trying to create a second legal system to challenge the liberal and democratic nature of the Australian state. Shariʿa based family law is perhaps one area that represents the greatest concern for many Australians. It is generally perceived as being out of date with contemporary Australian values and based on traditional or stereotypical gender roles. In reality some aspects of shariʿa based family law are already in line with existing Australian legislation. Whether in future this informal "accommodation" will be given explicit recognition or greater accommodation remains to be seen, although so far law reform recommendations in the area of cultural and religious divorce have not been pursued by various Australian governments.

Islamic finance, on the other hand, has been given a markedly different reception, with the Australian government responding positively at both a rhetorical and legislative level. Indeed, responses from the government show a broad willingness to think about ways to facilitate Islamic finance in Australia by broadening taxation policy. The fact that this aspect of shariʿa law can be integrated into the Australian legal context perhaps establishes a precedent for how other aspects of shariʿa could likewise be incorporated. Future research could indeed consider how the informal accommodation of Islamic family law might be given greater accommodation or perhaps, at the very least, some positive recognition. In any case, the favorable reception of Islamic finance can contribute much to debates about how shariʿa law is popularly imagined or perceived in Australia.

References

ABC Radio, Mediation in the Mosque. October 21, 2008. Transcript available http://www.abc.net.au/radionational/programs/lawreport/mediation-in-the-mosque/3192152#transcript March 7, 2014.

Ahmad, Abu Umar Faruq and Ahmad, A.B. Rafique, "Islamic Microfinance: A Case Study of Australia." *Journal of Islamic Economics, Banking and Finance* (2008).

Ahmad, Abu Umar Faruq, Osmani, Noor Mohammad, and Karim, Mohd Fazlul, "Islamic Finance in Australia: The Potential Problems and Prospects." (2010) Paper delivered at Seventh International Conference *The Tawhidi Epistemology: Zahat and Waqf Economy*, Bangi.

Aly, Anne and Walker, David, "Veiled Threats: Recurrent Cultural Anxieties in Australia." *Journal of Muslim Minority Affairs* 27, no. 2 (2007): 203–214.

Austrade,"Landmark Islamic Finance Publication Ministerial." Media Release, February 12, 2010. Available at http://www.austrade.gov.au/Landmark-Islamic-finance-publication-ministerial/default.aspx August 31, 2013.

Australian Financial Centre Forum, Australian Government, *Australia as a Financial Centre: Building on our Strengths*. November 2009.

Australian Government, "Review of the taxation treatment of Islamic Finance." Discussion Paper, Board of Taxation, October 2010.

Australian Law Reform Commission, "Multiculturalism and the Law." (2012). Available at http://www.alrc.gov.au/inquiries/multiculturalism-and-law August 31, 2013.

Black, Ann, "Legal Recognition of Shari'a Law: Is this the Right Direction for Australian Family Matters?" *Family Matters* no. 84 (2010): 64–67.

Black, Ann and Sadiq, Kerrie, "Good and Bad Sharia: Australia's Mixed Response to Islamic Law." *UNSW Law Journal* 34, no. 1 (2011): 383–412.

Centre for Research on Social Inclusion. "Muslim-Australians & Local Government: Grassroots Strategies To Improve Relations Between Muslim And Non-Muslim-Australians." (2008).

Cleland, Bilal, *The Muslims in Australia: A Brief History* (Wembley: Islamic Human Rights Commission, 2000).

Costello, P., *Worth Promoting, Worth Defending: Australian Citizenship. What it Means and How to Nurture it.* Address to the Sydney Institute, Sydney. February 23, 2006. Available at http://www.treasurer.gov.au/tsr/content/speeches/2006/004.asp July 3, 2009.

Family Law Act 1975 (Cth).

Family Law Council, "Cultural Community Divorce and the Family Law Act 1975: A Proposal to Clarify the Law." August 2001, 28. Available at http://www.ag.gov.au/FamiliesAndMarriage/FamilyLawCouncil/Documents/Cultural%20community%20Divorce%20and%20the%20Family%20Law%20Act%201975.pdf August 31, 2013.

The Islamic Council of Perth Western Australia, *After the Second World War*. Available at http://www.islamiccouncilwa.com.au/after-the-second-world-war January 29, 2014.

The Islamic Council of Perth Western Australia, *The Muslim Community Before the Great War*. Available at http://www.islamiccouncilwa.com.au/after-the-second-world-war March 7, 2014.

Karvelas, Patricia, "Imam Wants Sharia Law Here, But A-G Says No Way." *The Australian*, May 18, 2011.

Karvelas, Patricia, "Roxon Baulks at Oole for Sharia by Australian Muslims." *The Australian*, March 17, 2012.
Kolig, Erich and Kabir, Nahid, "Not Friend, Not Foe: The Rocky Road of Enfranchisement of Muslims into Multicultural Nationhood in Australia and New Zealand." *Immigrants & Minorities* 26, no. 3 (2008): 266–300.
Neighbor, Sally, "The Way to the Watering Hole." *The Monthly* (December 2010): 22–27.
Parashar, Archana, "Australian Muslims and Family Law: Diversity and Gender Justice." *Journal of Intercultural Studies* 33, no. 5 (2012): 565–583.
Poulter, Sebastian M., "The Claim to a Separate Islamic System of Personal Law for British Muslims" in Chibli Mallat and Jane Connors (eds.) *Islamic Family Law* (London: Graham & Trotman, 1990) 147–166.
Roy, Oliver, *Globalised Islam: The Search for a New Ummah* (New York: Columbia University Press, 2004).
Sadiq, Kerrie and Black, Ann, "Embracing Sharia-Compliant Products through Regulatory Amendment to Achieve Parity of Treatment." *Sydney Law Review* 34 (2012): 189–211.
Safi, Louay, "The Maqasid Approach and Rethinking Political Rights in Modern Society." *Intellectual Discourse* 18, no. 2 (2010): 211–233.
Stephenson, Peta, "Long History with Islam Gives Indigenous Australians Pride." *The Conversation*, December 14, 2011. Available at http://theconversation.com/long-history-with-islam-gives-indigenous-australians-pride-3521 August 31, 2013.
Saeed, Abdullah, "Reflections on the Establishment of Shari'a Courts in Australia" in Rex Ahdar and Nicholas Aroney (eds.) *Shari'a in the West* (Oxford: Oxford University Press, 2010) 223–238.
The Treasury, "Board of Taxation to Review Australia's Tax Laws to Ensure Islamic Finance Market Can Expand." Media Release, no. 076, April 26, 2010. Available at http://ministers.treasury.gov.au/DisplayDocs.aspx?doc=pressreleases/2010/076.htm&pageID=003&min=njsa&Year=&DocType=0 August 31, 2013.
Voyce, M. and Possamai, A., "Legal Pluralism, Family Personal Laws and the Rejection of Shari'a in Australia: A Case of Multiple or 'clashing' Modernities?" *Democracy and Security* 7, no. 4 (2011): 338–353.
Zwartz, Barney, "Australia's Muslims Cool on Change." *The Age*, February 9, 2008.

PART V

SUBSTANTIVE LEGAL AREAS

A

CASE STUDIES

CHAPTER 31

ISLAMIC LAW AND CONSTITUTIONS

NATHAN J. BROWN AND MARA REVKIN

A constitutional text can be defined as a formal instrument "whose primary purpose is to order a political society."[1] Since a constitution is, among other things, a fundamental legal document, the relationship between written constitutions and the Islamic legal tradition is an obvious subject for scholarly attention. And it has become one, though perhaps more gradually than might have been expected. Indeed, scholars have largely followed practice in this regard. But if interest began slowly, it has picked up force and speed in recent years. Over the past century and a half, the relationship between Islamic law and constitutions has moved from a concern for specialists to a central political struggle in many Muslim societies; for scholars of Islam, the topic has similarly moved from a specialized concern to become a major topic of inquiry.

Alongside an interest in constitutional texts, scholars have also shown a growing interest in the related area of study encompassing Islamic forms of constitutionalism—with that term suggesting a range of practices and ideologies based on holding political authorities accountable and limiting government in accordance with clear (generally legal) standards and procedures. While constitutions and written constitutions can be distinct targets of inquiry, they are often intermeshed.

[1] Beau Breslin, *From Words to Worlds: Exploring Constitutional Functionality* (Baltimore: Johns Hopkins University Press, 2009), 8.

In this chapter we will begin by tracing the origins of the scholarly interest in the relationship between Islamic law and constitutions, coming as it did at a time when it attracted primarily specialists in religion and specifically those focussed on the classical Islamic heritage and a small number of countries. Until the last two decades, academic interest in the intersection of Islam and constitutionalism was expert and narrow. But pushed by changing political realities and pulled by their colleagues, we will show how a new generation of scholars from other disciplines have joined those older scholarly efforts, themselves hardly abandoned. In particular we will move to a consideration of how the focus of recent scholarship has shifted from heavily textual methodologies prioritizing specifically religious and intellectual questions to more contextualized lines of inquiry exploring the legal, institutional, historical, and policy implications of Islamic constitutional development. Much of this expansion has taken place since the 1990s. It has not simply coincided with a growing political interest in many predominantly Muslim societies in religion and constitutionalism; it has come about partly in response to that interest. That is, as religious, social, and political forces have focussed more on constitutions, and as constitutional arrangements for Islam specifically and religion generally have become more varied and contentious, scholars from a variety of disciplines have noticed and reacted. Of course older textual and interpretive scholarly concerns are still very much present, but are now part of a broader and more diverse set of academic fields. And we will show how these various approaches have sought to understand what the issues are, whose voices are authoritative, and where debates take place.

We will begin with a quick review of constitutional texts: what do they say about Islam? We will then move to a more abstract level, examining whether the Islamic religion generally, and the shari'a specifically, lend themselves to constitutionalism. The remainder of the chapter will focus on three scholarly debates (ones that have been connected to debates among Muslim political and legal thinkers): what is the relationship between Islam and constitutional texts; who has interpretive authority in such matters; and where do debates take place?

I. Textual Provisions

Scholars have shown increasing interest in the constitutional language used to refer to Islam in large part because that language has grown stronger and more detailed over time. Muslim-majority states have adopted a variety of constitutional frameworks defining the role of Islam with respect to political authority, sources of law, personal freedoms, and human rights. They have even defined themselves in a starkly different set of terms, ranging from Islamic republics based on divine sovereignty to secular republics to monarchies in varying religious garbs. Of those countries that have adopted religious language in their constitutions, scholarly analysis has focussed especially on clauses in two main areas: identity and structure of the state and law.

First, some clauses involve the basic identity of the state. In some constitutional texts, the state is defined as an Islamic one; more commonly, Islam is defined as the official religion or the religion of state. Some constitutions even seek to entrench the principles of Islamic governance and law as immutable and permanent. For example, Iran's constitution defines Islam as "the eternally immutable religion" of the state of Iran,[2] and Afghanistan's constitution states, "The provisions of adherence to the provisions of the sacred religion of Islam and the republican regime cannot be amended."[3] At the other extreme, Turkey has entrenched its secular nature. Article 4 of the Turkish constitution bars amendments to Articles 1 through 3, which define the Republic as secular.[4]

Scholars have noted that the practical implications of such clauses are often unclear, but they have therefore turned specific attention to some more detailed provisions that sometimes bar non-Muslims from the nation's highest office and occasionally extend to other high-level officials, as is the case in Tunisia, Syria, and Pakistan. Related clauses may also require the president and other officials to take an Islamic oath, for example in Yemen, where the constitution requires not only the president but also his ministers and all members of the legislative assembly to pledge fidelity to the Qur'an, in addition to respecting the constitution and safeguarding the Republican system of government.[5] Some Islamic constitutions go so far as to identify a particular sect of Islam as a prerequisite for public office. For example, only Sunni Muslims are eligible for the presidency in the Maldives,[6] while only Shafi'i Muslims can serve as prime minister in Brunei.[7]

Second, constitutions in Muslim societies have specific provisions governing law that reference Islamic sources; the variety of language has attracted an enormous amount of scholarly attention. For instance, so called "repugnancy clauses," pioneered by Pakistan, prohibit the introduction of any legislation "repugnant" to the injunctions of Islam. Authority for implementation of such clauses has varied—for instance in Pakistan, the regular courts have sometimes been specifically barred from reviewing legislation in light of this clause; however, Pakistan's constitution does include a justiciable shari'a clause providing for Islamic review of legislation by the Federal Shariat Court, which has the authority to decide whether or

[2] Article 12, Constitution of the Islamic Republic of Iran (1979, amended 1989).
[3] Article 149 (1), Constitution of Afghanistan (2004).
[4] Article 4, Constitution of the Republic of Turkey (1982).
[5] Article 161, Constitution of Yemen (1991, amended 2001).
[6] Article 109(b), Constitution of the Maldives (2008).
[7] Article 4(5) of the Constitution of Brunei (1959, amended 1984).

not a particular legal provision violates the injunctions of Islam.[8] Some texts give Islamic jurists the authority to review or invalidate laws deemed to be in conflict with the dictates of shari'a. For example, the constitution of Somaliland empowers the council of 'ulama to decide whether any particular law or policy is consistent with the shari'a.[9] Egypt's 2012 constitution required taking into account the opinion of senior scholars in al-Azhar on matters related to the shari'a[10]; its 2014 successor backed off but still guaranteed the institution state support, independence, and declared it the "main reference for religious sciences and Islamic affairs."[11] The constitution of Iran obligates judges to base their decisions on codified Islamic law, and in the absence of written jurisprudence, they may refer to "authentic fatawa" as supplementary sources.[12] Some countries (such as Iran and Saudi Arabia) impose limitations on the adoption of any treaties or human rights conventions that contradict the shari'a.[13]

More general and increasingly widespread provisions identify the shari'a as either "the" principal source of legislation or "a" principal source of law.[14] Eighteen of the twenty-two countries that define Islam as the official state religion have taken such a step of establishing a constitutional role for Islamic law and jurisprudence, though the precise phrase used and its implied meaning vary greatly. These "source of law" clauses can also be found in several predominately Muslim countries that have not established Islam as the state religion.[15] Some documents carve out a special area for personal status law (ironic in part because the term itself is not borrowed from the Islamic legal tradition), covering the rights and obligations of men and women in matters of marriage, divorce, child custody, and inheritance. Some constitutions—for example those of Egypt (in 1971, though the clause was

[8] Article 203D(1), Constitution of the Islamic Republic of Pakistan (1973, amended 2015). Article 203D(1) states, "The (Shari'a) Court may, either of its own motion or on the petition of a citizen of Pakistan or the Federal Government or a Provincial Government, examine and decided the question whether or not any law or provision of law is repugnant to the Injunctions of Islam, as laid down in the Holy Quran and the Sunnah of the Holy Prophet, hereinafter referred to as the Injunctions of Islam."

[9] Article 115(1B), Constitution of the Republic of Somaliland (2001).

[10] Article 4, Constitution of the Arab Republic of Egypt (2012).

[11] Article 7, Constitution of the Arab Republic of Egypt (2014).

[12] Article 167, Constitution of the Islamic Republic of Iran (1979, amended 1989).

[13] Article 77 of the Constitution of the Islamic Republic of Iran (1979, amended 1989) states that "international treaties, protocols, contracts, and agreements must be approved by the Islamic Consultative Assembly." Article 26 of the Basic Law of Saudi Arabia (1992) states, "The State shall protect human rights in accordance with the Sharia."

[14] e.g. Article 2 of Egypt's 2014 Constitution states, "The principles of Islamic Sharia are the main source of legislation."

[15] The four states that invoke Islamic principles, law, or jurisprudence in their constitutions without having declared Islam as the state religion are Comoros, Gambia, Sudan, and Syria. See Tad Stahnke and Robert C. Blitt, "The Religion–State Relationship and the Right to Freedom of Religion or Belief," United States Commission on Religious Freedom (March 2005), 9.

removed in 2012 and then restored in 2014 without qualification), Bahrain, Yemen, Saudi Arabia, and Iran—guarantee gender equality to the extent that it is consistent with Islamic jurisprudence.

In addition to the most common religious provisions outlined above, Islamic constitutions may also include language requiring that a range of state policies—in areas such as education, commerce, and national defense—comply with the injunctions of Islam. For example, Afghanistan's constitution compels the state to adopt measures to foster religious schools and improve the condition of mosques.[16] Saudi Arabia's Basic Law defines the armed forces as the guardian of Islam,[17] while Yemen's 1970 constitution required the enforcement of Islamic law in business transactions.[18]

There is thus a rich and varied set of experiences with bringing Islam into constitutions. How have scholars understood these efforts?

II. Does Islam Lend Itself to Constitutionalism?

The possible constitutionalist nature of the Islamic legal tradition and the way in which modern constitutional texts should therefore make reference to Islam and Islamic law has long been a topic of early interest among legal specialists and constitution writers in several places in the Islamic world working in the first three-quarters of the twentieth century. It was similarly an occasional topic of interest among scholars of Islamic law. But outside of a few locations (such as Iran), Muslims' discussions about the relationship tended to be both highly specialized and muted, and scholarship reflected a technical nature, often with a focus on religious texts and abstract debates about general principles much less than the historical and political context in which they were embedded. And this debate was often abstract, focusing on the compatibility of the shari'a with the emerging practice of writing constitutions. In this section we will present some of the early scholarly debate on the constitutionalist nature of the shari'a as well as a consideration of the scholarly effort to understand initial constitutional experiments in Muslim societies.

[16] Article 17, Constitution of the Islamic Republic of Afghanistan.

[17] Article 33, Basic Law of Saudi Arabia.

[18] Article 152, Constitution of Yemen (1970).

A. Growing Interest

Scholars of the classical Islamic legal heritage have gradually showed a growing interest in constitutional aspects of Islamic law. In the nineteenth century, some intellectuals in the Muslim world noted possible parallels between their Islamic legal heritage on the one hand, and emerging European ideas about constitutionalism on the other. This parallelism seeped occasionally into western scholarship on Islamic law as that field was emerging, though it was not a major concern until very recently.[19]

Two processes—one political and one scholarly—have contributed to more active scholarly engagement with Islamic law and constitutions over the past three decades.

First, political and legal struggles over fundamental structures and procedures in the postcolonial era have prompted reformers to envision new constitutional orders that increasingly draw inspiration from the shari'a. In the twentieth century, many predominantly Muslim societies have sought to define the place for Islam in general and the shari'a specifically in their constitutional texts, which has thereby occasioned scholarly attention.

Second, the increasing salience of issues of Islam and constitutionalism has attracted a steadily growing group of scholars from a widening range of disciplines (including political science, sociology, history, religious studies, and law). As new disciplines and perspectives have entered the arena, they have brought with them different concerns and methods, leaving the field intellectually enriched but far less coherent. Most of all, they have placed new questions on the scholarly agenda, moving beyond a focus on texts to probing the political context, implications for religious authority, and modes of enforcement and interpretation.

B. Was Islamic Law Constitutionalist?

Scholars interested in the classical Islamic legal heritage occasionally stepped back and reflected on the ways in which Islamic legal and political thought could provide intellectual justification for political constraints on rulers and protections for individual rights. They also noted how legal scholars in Islamic societies were carving out a powerful sphere of influence for themselves, from which they could either leverage their expertise to check the authority of temporal rulers or, conversely, find

[19] One example is the work of Ahmad Kamal Abu al-Majd, an influential Egyptian legal scholar trained in part in the United States. See his "Nazarat hawla al-Fiqh al-Dusturi fi al-Islam" [A View Concerning Constitutional Jurisprudence in Islam], lecture delivered January 9, 1962 (Cairo: Matba'at al-Azhar).

themselves subject to intense pressure to mold their interpretations of Islamic law to serve the will of the powerful.

Historians focusing on Islamic law have long noted the emergence of a distinct Islamic legal tradition, partially distinct from general religious and specifically theological inquiry, by the eighth century CE.[20] The derivation of law was distinct not only from other religious fields; it also had some autonomy from politics. Scholars interested in the development of *fiqh* quickly grasped that it was developed in a set of institutions and processes that lay at some distance from governance. But with the rise in Islamic thought and practice of what Marshall Hodgson has termed "shariʿa-mindedness"—consciousness of an Islamic moral code based on justice in the private as well as political realm—the possibility of a legal tradition that lay outside of—and could call to account—holders of political authority began to emerge.[21]

Yet scholars have differed on whether to emphasize the parallels with constitutionalism or the differences. Most earlier scholars, such as Joseph Schacht, G.E. Von Grunebaum, and Noel Coulson, evaluated Islamic law through the lens of European constitutional principles and Enlightenment philosophy but dismissed shariʿa as underdeveloped in that regard and ill-equipped to regulate or constrain political power.[22] Von Grunebaum found Islam to be incompatible with constitutionalism, describing the religion as "permeated by a sense of the autocracy of the Lord."[23] And "Islamic constitutional law never limited the power of the ruler."[24] Thus, Von Grunebaum described aspects of modern constitutionalism in the Muslim world as alien to Islam: "Ideas of popular representation, constitutional restriction of the executive power, separation of the judiciary and the executive, and the philosophy behind them are importations from the West."[25] But while arguing that constitutionalism is not indigenous to Muslim societies, Von Grunebaum allowed that that traditional Islamic reverence for egalitarianism and individualism provided a strong foundation for the development of a brand of democracy that could coexist with the shariʿa.[26]

[20] Baber Johansen, *Contingency in a Sacred Law: Legal and Ethical Norms in the Muslim Fiqh* (Leiden: Brill, 1999), 4–6 and 23–24.

[21] Marshall G.S. Hodgson, *The Venture of Islam, Volume 1: The Classical Age of Islam* (Chicago: University of Chicago Press, 1974), 317–318.

[22] Joseph Schacht, *Introduction of Islamic Law* (Oxford: Clarendon Press, 1964), 112 and Noel Coulson, *History of Islamic Law* (Edinburgh: University of Edinburgh Press, 1964), 120–121. See also John Strawson's discussion of Schacht and Coulson: John Strawson, "Islamic Law and English Texts," in *Laws of the Postcolonial*, eds. Eve Darian-Smith and Peter Fitzpatrick (Michigan: University of Michigan Press, 1999), 112–113.

[23] G.E. Von Grunebaum, *Islam: Essays in the Nature and Growth of a Cultural Tradition* (Menasha, Wisconsin: George Banta Publishing Company, 1955), 7.

[24] Von Grunebaum, *Islam*, 74.

[25] G.E. Von Grunebaum, *Islam: Essays in the Nature and Growth of a Cultural Tradition* (London: Kessinger Publishing, 1961), 75.

[26] Von Grunebaum, *Islam* (1961), 76.

But there have been other voices, and more recently their views have been more fully developed. Baber Johansen and other scholars have identified the emergence of a distinct community of jurists outside of the theological realm as the origin of an Islamic moral and legal framework that shared many of the characteristics of modern constitutionalism. Johansen has argued that the Islamic system of ethical and juristic norms known as *fiqh* historically functioned as an abstract social contract—long before the codification of written constitutions—by imposing a normative moral and legal framework on Muslim societies.[27] This system of rules "classifies and sanctions human acts, gives ethical and legal guidance to the believers and determines at the same time the rights and duties of the non-believers under an Islamic government," Johansen writes.[28] Bernard Weiss has similarly noted an emphasis in early Islamic scholarship on the rights of private individuals and their entitlement to protection from unjustified interference from governing authorities.[29] The use of Islamic scripture to justify limitations on the exercise of state power anticipated future debates on the rights of Muslim citizens and the infrastructure of democratic governance that would intensify centuries later with the codification of written constitutions.[30]

Scholars have not only tried to understand the Islamic legal tradition by reference to and comparison with categories of non-Islamic origin (like constitutionalism) but also to probe whether some strong features of the Islamic legal tradition might have constitutionalist overtones and implications. Three concepts have drawn particular interest—*maqasid, maslaha*, and *siyasa shar'iyya*.[31]

Maqasid refers to the general purposes of shari'a. The term, inherited from premodern jurists, has increasingly been appropriated by reformists seeking to adapt shari'a to modern contexts. Andrew March has documented efforts by reformist scholars to use the theory of *maqasid* to adapt shari'a to changing circumstances and to help adjudicate cases of indeterminacy or conflict between rulings, in a method he describes as "complex purposivism."[32] However, Anver Emon takes a different approach, arguing that the concept of *maqasid* was designed to limit the scope of deliberative reasoning.[33]

The concept of *maslaha*, best translated as "public interest," has been deployed by scholars to facilitate the derivation of legal rules in the absence of clear texts.

[27] Baber Johansen, *Contingency in a Sacred Law: Legal and Ethical Norms in the Muslim Fiqh* (Brill: Leiden, 1999), 61–62.

[28] Johansen, *Contingency in a Sacred Law*, 1.

[29] Bernard G. Weiss, *The Spirit of Islamic Law* (Athens, GA: University of Georgia Press, 2006), 182.

[30] See discussion of al-Ghazali's work in Halim Rane, *Islam and Contemporary Civilization: Evolving Ideas, Transforming Relations* (Melbourne: Melbourne University Press, 2010), 93–96.

[31] See Clark Lombardi, *State Law as Islamic Law in Modern Egypt: The Incorporation of Shari'a Into Egyptian Constitutional Law* (Leiden: Brill, 2006).

[32] Andrew March, "Theocrats Living under Secular Law: An External Engagement with Islamic Legal Theory," *Journal of Political Philosophy* 19, no. 1 (2009): 28–51.

[33] Anver Emon, *Islamic Natural Law Theories* (Oxford: Oxford University Press, 2008), 258–286.

Felicitas Opwis has traced the development of the concept from its origins in the classical philosophies of al-Ghazali, Fakhr al-Din al-Razi, and al-Qarafi to its increased usage and modern appropration by leading jurists in the nineteenth century.[34] Contemporary debates over the role of *maslaha* have become increasingly polarized between those who believe that *maslaha* should be used as a technique to make shari'a more relevant and practical, and those who fear that this practice will distort the shari'a to serve the interests of its interpreters.

Siyasa shar'iyya refers to the legal authority of Muslim theocracies to supplement the broad legal principles of the Qur'an and other legal texts of sacred origin on points of detail or ambiguity, and to make policy decisions in the public interest. Noah Feldman has explored the ways in which the doctrine of *siyasa shar'iyya* has been leveraged to justify positive law-making under an Islamic contract of governance.[35]

In all three areas, scholars have been led in some of their interest by recent Muslim attempts, explored later, to ground an Islamic form of constitutionalism in their Islamic legal heritage. Scholars have gravitated between two poles: one which is sympathetic to the attempt and those who see it as doing violence to the original concepts.

If scholars of Islamic law have differed in their willingness to read constitutionalist possibilities into the Islamic legal tradition, none has gone so far as to hold it up as a functional equivalent of modern constitutional texts. Even those who see constitutionalist possibilities in the Islamic legal tradition acknowledge that the actual practice of Islamic societies in the premodern era is unclear, and those scholars who have attempted to uncover how much the law in practice operated in accordance with that propounded by the *fuqaha'* have been forced to develop somewhat tentative conclusions. Further, the reluctance of many members of the premodern *ulama* to accept judicial positions has often been taken as a sign that Islamic legal scholarship viewed actual politics with distrust. Overall, when scholars have noted the existence of constitutionalist elements in the Islamic legal tradition, they have generally done so in a tangential manner; it was rarely a central concern and empirical evidence was rare. But where scholars are able to move from theory to practice, especially in some work on the Ottoman period—where documentation is richer—they sometimes suggest a more robust role for Islamic legal specialists in shaping the law in practice. The implication is that the *ulama* could deploy Islamic legal norms in a constitutionalist manner. Haim Gerber argues that the diverse practices of autonomous judges and jurists in the Ottoman Empire—operating to a large extent without oversight from state authorities—resulted in significant variation between the implementation of shari'a in different regions and communities, in a

[34] Felicitas Opwis, "Maslaha in Contemporary Islamic Legal Theory," *Islamic Law and Society* 2, no. 2 (2005): 182–223.

[35] Noah Feldman, *The Fall and Rise of the Islamic State* (Oxford: Oxford University Press, 2008).

phenomenon he describes as "law created by private experts."[36] Scholars have also suggested that rulers who used the regulatory and legal authority granted to them under sometimes permissive scholarly eyes still strove to do so in a manner completely consistent with shari'a-based norms.[37]

And for those focusing on the nineteenth century, the relationship of the Islamic legal tradition to constitutionalism in general and constitutional documents specifically became more pressing. This is in part because influential writers from various Muslim societies (notably Rif'at al-Tahtawi in Egypt and Khayr al-Din from Tunisia and the Ottoman Empire) showed some interest in European constitutionalist thought and its adaptability to their own domestic settings.[38]

c. The Impact of Early Constitutional Experiments

The innovation of constitutional texts, presenting themselves as such (or "basic laws")—in Tunisia, Egypt, the Ottoman Empire, and Iran—forced the issue of the relationship between Islamic law and constitutions on to the political (and thus the scholarly) agenda, drawing scholarly interest from historians and occasionally political scientists. Yet even this significant development initially attracted limited scholarly attention to the relationship between Islamic law and constitutions. First, in all four countries, the initial experiment with a constitutional text was shaky and short-lived. Second, the question of how and when the Islamic shari'a should be integrated into modern constitutional texts did not seem pressing. In one country (Egypt) issues of Islamic law did not arise in constitutional discussions; in another (Tunisia) the constitution itself was expressed in familiar Islamic terms and accompanied by the intellectual efforts of Khayr al-Din to steer Islamic legal and political thought in a constitutionalist (though hardly liberal or democratic) direction, but that example inspired few followers perhaps because the Tunisian constitution had such a short life.

The Ottoman Empire and Iran both experimented with constitutional texts in a more sustained and influential manner and have therefore attracted greater scholarly attention. In the Ottoman Empire in 1876, a fiscally strapped government resorted to adopting a constitution involving an elected parliament and an attempt by that parliament to use oversight tools the document seemed to give it.

[36] Haim Gerber, *Islamic Law and Culture, 1600–1840* (Boston: Brill, 1999), 24. See also Haim Gerber, "The Public Sphere and Civil Society in the Ottoman Empire," in *The Public Sphere in Muslim Societies*, eds. Miriam Hoexter, Shmuel N. Eisenstadt, and Nehemia Levtzion (Albany: SUNY Press, 2002), 66–67.

[37] Albert Hourani, *Arabic Thought in the Liberal Age 1798–1939* (Cambridge: Cambridge University Press, 1983), 69–76.

[38] See Carl Brown, "Introduction," in *The Surest Path: The Political Treatise of a Nineteenth-Century Muslim Statesman* (Cambridge, MA: Harvard University Press, 1967).

Suspended after a short period, the Ottoman Constitution of 1876 still had enormous impact on subsequent constitutional documents in much of the region. The Ottoman Constitution of 1876, which was the first self-described constitutional document promulgated in the Muslim world, did proclaim Islam to be the official religion and occasioned a brief but intense debate among leading religious officials about the appropriateness of writing a constitutional text in an Islamic political system.[39] Interestingly, however, the Ottoman experiment has drawn less attention from scholars, and those who have studied it have not focussed centrally on any relationship with the Islamic legal heritage.[40]

The early twentieth-century constitutional experiment in Iran, by contrast, has drawn very significant attention from scholars who focus on various angles—including the social, intellectual, political, and economic background. Indeed, the Iranian basic laws of 1905–06 initiated an uneven (and sometimes unhappy) but quite involved history of constitutional texts in that country that continues up to the present. While the Ottoman Constitution of 1876 was very much a product of the political elite, the Iranian experiment—coming also at a time of fiscal and political crisis—was a response as well to popular pressure. And the way in which Iranian struggles over the constitution pulled in Islamic intellectuals and legal specialists—often strongly in support of the Iranian constitutional experiment but with others skeptical and uninterested, and with an important strain actually hostile—has led subsequent generations of scholars of Iran and Islam to give significant attention to constitutionalism as an idea. And perhaps because of the multifaceted nature of the Iranian experiment—one which drew in popular participation and intensive intellectual debates—scholarly interest in the Iranian constitution and contemporary political struggle began to merge textual and intellectual analysis with social, political, and economic analysis from the beginning. Ervand Abrahamian and Said Amir Arjomand, for instance, have led such an interdisciplinary approach focusing on the economic and social infrastructure of Iranian politics and constitutional development.[41]

While the Iranian experiment of the early twentieth century has thus drawn interest from scholars in a wide variety of fields, outside of Iran, most of the initial scholarly interest focussed less on specific texts and more on the intellectual dimensions of constitutionalism in the Muslim world—unsurprisingly because

[39] Noah Feldman, *The Fall and Rise of the Islamic State* (Princeton: Princeton University Press, 2012), 71.

[40] Robert Devereux, *The First Ottoman Constitutional Period: A Study of the Midhat Constitution and Parliament* (Baltimore: Johns Hopkins University Press, 1964).

[41] Ervand Abrahamian, *Iran: Between Two Revolutions* (Princeton: Princeton University Press, 1982). See also Said Amir Arjomand's discussion of economic frustration and social stratification under the Shah's rule as contributing factors to the political awakening that preceded the 1905–11 Constitutional Revolution in *The Turban for the Crown: The Islamic Revolution in Iran* (Oxford: Oxford University Press, 1988), 34–35.

intellectuals gave great attention to the subject but constitutional texts tended to be fairly laconic on religious issues. And the debate among Muslim intellectuals has been wide-ranging. Beginning in the nineteenth century (and with full force in the twentieth century), the globalization of Islamic intellectual inquiry led to growing interest in the relationship and potential for compatibility between Islam and western liberal rationalism.[42] As Muslim-majority countries grappled with challenges of state- and nation-building in the postcolonial era, they turned to constitutions as a vehicle for codifying issues of sovereignty, identity, and independence. In the first half of the twentieth century, prominent intellectuals in the Arab world (including the Syrian intellectual Rashid Rida, the Egyptian scholar Muhammad 'Abduh, and the Egyptian jurist 'Abd al-Razzaq al-Sanhuri) became increasingly critical of orthodox Islamic legal scholarship as excessively rigid and evinced varying signs of exploring a syncretism between western principles of liberal constitutionalism and the Islamic legal heritage. This generation of thinkers sought to construct new legal and political frameworks in which modern constitutional principles could coexist symbiotically with the shari'a.[43]

These early experiments in constitution-writing—occurring before the mid-twentieth century, mainly in the Middle East—sparked formative national dialogues and debates on the role of Islam in the modern state and society, with a range of different outcomes. Over time, the debate over the appropriate role of religion in constitutions has intensified in Muslim-majority societies and scholarly attention has widened considerably; the topic has attracted attention of scholars from neighboring fields (such as political science and law); there has even been growing interest in broader public and policy debates.

And just as the field attracted widening attention, those steeped in the classical Islamic legal tradition—led by scholars like Muhammad Qasim Zaman, Wael Hallaq, and Baber Johansen—have taken a far stronger interest in the past decade in the intersection between classical Islamic scholarship and the modern phenomenon of constitutionalism.[44] Rather than abandon the field to legal scholars, political scientists, and specialists in public policy, scholars of Islamic religion have broadened the scope of their own scholarship to incorporate insights from and respond to questions first introduced by other disciplines. For example, Anver Emon's study of the secondary literature on the Constitution of Medina, a document allegedly drafted by the Prophet of which evidence is found exclusively in literary references

[42] Muhammad Qasim Zaman, *The 'Ulama in Contemporary Islam: Custodians of Change* (Princeton, New Jersey: Princeton University Press, 2001), 171.

[43] Nathan Brown, *Constitutions in a Non-Constitutional World: Arab Basic Laws and the Prospects for Accountable Government* (Albany: SUNY Press, 2002), 164. See also, "Introduction," in *Islamic Law and the Challenges of Modernity*, eds. Yvonne Yazbeck Haddad and Barbara Freyer Stowasser, 2–3.

[44] Muhammad Qasim Zaman, *The 'Ulama in Contemporary Islam*; Wael Hallaq, *The Origins and Evolution of Islamic Law* (Cambridge: Cambridge University Press, 2005); Baber Johansen, *Contingency in a Sacred Law: Legal and Ethical Norms in the Muslim Fiqh* (Leiden: Brill, 1999).

by historians living centuries after the time of the text's purported creation, explores the ways in which Muslim scholars have attempted to situate such texts in the political, social, economic contexts in which they were produced.[45] Nader Sohrabi has argued that two chronologically parallel constitutional revolutions in Iran and the Ottoman Empire in the early twentieth century were "historical products of their time" and must be understood not as isolated and purely local phenomena, but as part of a continuous wave of democratic movements that swept Russia, Mexico, China, Europe, and America in the short period between the French and Russian revolutions.[46] Wael Hallaq has studied the ways in which Orientalist and other scholarly paradigms have structured modern understandings of Islamic law, and has recently applied an epistemological methodology to the legal, moral, and constitutional history of premodern Islam to argue that the idea of a modern Islamic state is both impossible and fundamentally self-contradictory.[47]

A fairly new phenomenon, in which scholars combine a specialized legal training with a grounding in the classical tradition, has become notable in recent years.[48] This disciplinary intermingling has led scholarly interest to focus on three questions: *what* are textual provisions and what does Islamic law say; *who* has authority to decide such questions; and *where* does the debate take place within the breadth of the Muslim world.

III. What Role for the Shari'a?

As written constitutional documents have proliferated in various Muslim societies over the course of the past century and a half, several notable trends have increased the salience of the relationship between the shari'a and constitutionalism in scholarly eyes.

[45] Anver Emon, "Reflections on the Constitution of Medina," *UCLA Journal, of Islamic and Near Eastern Law* 1 (2001–02): 103–133.

[46] Nader Sohrabi, *Revolution and Constitutionalism in the Ottoman Empire and Iran* (Cambridge: Cambridge University Press, 2011), 2–3.

[47] Wael Hallaq, *The Impossible State: Islam, Politics, and Modernity's Moral Predicament* (New York: Columbia University Press, 2012).

[48] See Clark Lombardi, *State Law as Islamic Law in Modern Egypt: The Incorporation of Shari'a Into Egyptian Constitutional Law* (Leiden: Brill, 2006); Kristen Stilt, *Islamic Law in Action: Authority, Discretion, and Everyday Experiences in Mamluk Egypt* (Oxford: Oxford University Press, 2011); Haider Ala Hamoudi, "Thinking Beyond the Original Bargain: Post Ratification Constitution Making and the Case of Iraq," APSA 2012 Annual Meeting Paper, University of Pittsburgh Legal Studies Research Paper No. 2012-26 (2012); Khaled Abou El Fadl, *Islam and the Challenge of Democracy* (Princeton: Princeton University Press, 2004).

Most obviously, constitutional provisions for Islam have generally grown more extensive over time. Additionally, drafting processes have become more public and at least ritualistically participatory (that is, wider parts of the population have become nominally if not always more effectively involved). In the context of broad-based social movements seeking political reforms and human rights protections, Muslim publics have come to expect and demand that constitutional processes reflect the will of the people rather than the preferences of elites or foreign powers. For example, in the aftermath of the 2003 Iraq War, Ayatollah Ali Sistani issued a *fatwa* proclaiming that the members of the body tasked with drafting Iraq's post-war constitution should be democratically elected and that any draft constitution should be submitted to a popular referendum for ratification.[49] Finally, widening groups of intellectuals in the Muslim world have increasingly debated the relationship between the shariʿa and constitutions. The overall result is that discussions that were restricted to more specialized circles in the nineteenth century burst into full public view in the twentieth century.

Scholarship has reacted to these trends in Muslim societies in two ways. First, and most notably, constitutional provisions on Islam have been analyzed in both historical and comparative fashion. Second, the wide-ranging intellectual debates over shariʿa and constitutionalism have generated some cross-over between international scholarly debates and discussions among Muslim jurists, religious specialists, and intellectuals.

A. Exploring and Understanding Textual Provisions

Scholars have probed constitutional provisions for Islam in predominantly Muslim societies by seeking to understand the language used—they have worked historically, examining the origin of specific phrases and cross-nationally with broad comparative work that cuts across a broad swath of cases. More specifically, scholarly analysis on textual provisions has taken three forms.

First, the majority of such analysis has focussed on particular cases and probed the effect of such provisions on the legal and political order. By considering precise wording and its implementation by authoritative institutions, such writings have focussed on the ways in which Islamic provisions distribute interpretive authority between state, judicial, and religious authorities, and may induce conflict between these competing entities. For example, Saudi Arabia's Basic Law demands unconditional loyalty to the King but simultaneously constrains royal powers in accordance

[49] Fatwa of Grand Ayatollah Ali al-Sistani, June 26, 2003, as cited in Stefan Talmon, *The Official Documents of the Coalition Provisional Authority and the Iraqi Governing Council* (Bloomsbury Publishing, 2013), 582.

with the Qur'an, thus setting up a confrontation between what Frank Vogel terms "microcosmic judicial ijtihad" (defined as inner-directed instance-law linked to a concrete event) and "the macrocosmic ruler's siyasa" (meaning outer-directed rule-law, in the form of general, abstract rules issued by a worldly institution that has been delegated limited authority by God).[50] An example of microcosmic law would be a *fiqh* rule, which is technically a non-binding opinion, as opposed to binding instance-law that is unique to a particular event. In contrast, an example of a macrocosmic law would be a generally applicable law issued by the ruling authorities, such as legislation aimed at improving public welfare. The tension between these two forms of law is rooted in the question of whether an individual Islamic judge (*qadi*) is entitled to reject or invalidate a policy or decision made by the King if the latter is found to have violated injunctions of the Qur'an or the shari'a. Scholars have also looked to the evolving jurisprudence of Egypt's Supreme Constitutional Court (SCC) to explore the question of whether constitutions requiring adherence to shari'a are compatible with universal human rights principles and rule of law. In their study of the SCC's decision-making, Nathan Brown and Clark Lombardi concluded that the SCC has developed over many years a creative theory of Islamic law that interprets Islamic legal norms to be consistent with democracy, international human rights, and economic liberalism.[51]

Iran's constitutional development has been another area of focus for scholars concerned with the impact of shari'a provisions on the distribution of political authority and the relationship of citizens to the state. Chibli Mallat's analysis of the conceptual origins of the Iranian constitution describes a "dual emanation of sovereignty" from two conjoined legitimacies, religious and political, which were fused in the concept of *wilayat e-faqih* "rule by the jurists."[52] Asghar Schirazi notes that although the Iranian constitution was based on the universality and supremacy of shari'a, the infrastructure of the Islamic state it created borrowed heavily from western institutional models of parliament, the judiciary, and electoral systems.[53] Schirazi's work highlights the internal contradiction between the constitution's legalistic and democratic components, which are in tension with the paramount status of shari'a. Schirazi argues that growing recognition of the limitations of Islam as a legal and political basis for government has led to a gradual realignment of the political system in favor of pragmatism and the prioritization of the state's interests and policy agenda over shari'a.

[50] Frank Vogel, *Islamic Law and Legal System: Studies of Saudi Arabia* (Leiden: Brill, 2010), 297.

[51] Nathan Brown and Clark Lombardi, "Do Constitutions Requiring Adherence to Shari'a Threaten Human Rights? How Egypt's Constitutional Court Reconciles Islamic Law with the Liberal Rule of Law," *American University International Law Review* 21 (2006): 379–435.

[52] Chibli Mallat, *The Renewal of Islamic Law* (London: Cambridge University Press, 1993), 72.

[53] Asghar Schirazi, *The Constitution of Iran: Politics and the State in the Islamic Republic*, trans. John O'Kane (New York: I.B. Tauris, 1997), 17–18.

Second, some research has focussed on particular cases, but historically oriented—that is, they have explored how constitutional provisions have been products of a country's political history and socio-legal dynamics. Such attempts to understand how provisions related to Islam arose (and often expanded) has revealed that changes in text have not corresponded very directly to significant structural changes in the organization of state power; that is, wording has changed more significantly than structures of governance. Many scholars have cited Pakistan as an example of this trend.[54] Pakistan's 1956 constitution was forged out of heated negotiations between traditionalists (seeking a stronger role for Islam in the state) and secular modernists. In the end, the two sides agreed on the text of the document but their compromise hollowed out the Islamic provisions with ambiguity. As Afzal Iqbal described the gap between religious rhetoric and reality, "The constitution had an Islamic façade but the hard core was missing."[55] Other scholars have noted the disjuncture between text and reality in Egypt, where Tamir Moustafa notes that the foundations of the state were long considered to be secular in practice despite the introduction of a constitutional provision that explicitly defined shari'a as the principal source of legislation.[56] In the case of Indonesia, Arskal Salim notes that predominately secular aspects of the legal system—such as the laws governing marriage—have survived judicial review despite being inconsistent with Islamic marriage law because it is framed with reference to general principles of shari'a, such as the objective of reducing the frequency of divorce.[57]

More recently, some scholars have begun to look more extensively than intensively; that is, they have begun broader comparative work. The fact that the "source clauses" incorporated in modern constitutions show some striking similarities among countries has been cited by scholars as evidence that Islamic constitutionalism is a global as well as a domestically driven phenomenon.[58] Partly there is evidence of conscious borrowing, in which a provision citing shari'a as "the main source of legislation" in Syria's constitution of 1950[59] was later adopted by Egyptian drafters of the Kuwaiti constitution. A different version then passed into the Egyptian constitution of 1971. Awareness of these clauses has since set off

[54] See Rubya Mehdi, *The Islamization of the Law in Pakistan* (Richmond, Va.: Curzon Press, 1994); and John Esposito, "Pakistan: Quest for Islamic Identity," in *Islam and Development*, ed. John L. Esposito (Syracuse, NY: Syracuse University Press, 1980).

[55] See Afzal Iqbal, *Islamization of Pakistan* (Lahore: Vanguard, 1986), 65, quoted in Niaz A. Shah, *Women, the Koran and International Human Rights Law: The Experience of Pakistan* (Leiden: Martinus Nijhoff Publishers, 2006), 96.

[56] Tamir Moustafa, *The Struggle for Constitutional Power: Law, Politics, and Economic* (Cambridge: Cambridge University Press, 2007), 107.

[57] Arskal Salim, *Challenging the Secular State: The Islamization of Law in Modern Indonesia* (Honolulu: University of Hawaii Press, 2008), 13.

[58] Stilt, "Contextualizing constitutional Islam: The Malayan experience," *International Journal of Constitutional Law*, 13, no. 2, (2015): 407–433.

[59] Article 3.2, Syrian Constitution.

debates in various countries about whether to include such a provision and how it should be worded.

But even where there has been no conscious borrowing, some have argued that there are common processes at work. For instance, many have noted a significant increase in the number and strength of Islamic constitutional provisions since the 1950s, described by Nathan Brown as "Islamic inflation"—a phenomenon driven in large part by the nation-building efforts of governments seeking to construct cohesive political communities based on a shared religious identity and the more public processes by which constitutions have been written.[60] Academic analysis of this trend has focussed on Islamizing constitutional reforms in the Arab world, chiefly Egypt, Algeria, Kuwait and Yemen, Syria, and Saudi Arabia. Increasingly, constitutions have evolved beyond their original function as technical documents outlining the structure of governing institutions into ideologically charged manifestos aimed at engineering the fabric of Muslim societies to support the political objectives of modern authoritarian states.[61]

Third, the standardization of Islamic provisions has allowed some to make some initial forays into broad comparative analysis. This approach was adopted by Tad Stahnke and Robert C. Blitt in their comparative textual analysis of the constitutions of forty-four predominately Muslim countries.[62] Such work has only just begun, but it has been frequently used in both policy and purely scholarly circles as a way of understanding the variety of approaches used by Muslim societies.

But decontextualized comparative analysis, while useful for understanding the range of possibilities, has recently been supplemented by the far more labor-intensive task of developing a collection of more comparable but contextually and historically grounded studies of a large array of Muslim societies. Rainer Grote and Tilmann Röder have exhaustively mapped the defining features of Islamic constitutionalism in North Africa, the Middle East, and Central and South Asia in a comprehensive collection of country-specific case studies that draws on the methods of comparative constitutional law, Islamic law, international law, and legal history. Their research also examines the ways in which the key concepts of constitutionalism, including fundamental rights, separation of powers, democracy, and rule of law, may be adapted to an Islamic context, and the prospects for a constitutional "renaissance" in the aftermath of the Arab Spring.[63]

[60] Brown, "Islam and Constitutionalism in the Arab World: A Puzzling End to Islamic Inflation." Constitutional Transitions Colloquium, New York University, 2012, 6–7.

[61] Nathan Brown and Adel Omar Sherif, "Inscribing the Shari'a in Arab Constitutional Law," in *Islamic Law and the Challenges of Modernity*, eds. Yvonne Yazbeck Haddad and Barbara Freyer Stowasser, 62–63. See also Said Amir Arjomand, *Constitutionalism and Political Reconstruction* (Leiden: Brill, 2007).

[62] Stahnke and Blitt, "The Religion–State Relationship."

[63] Rainer Grote and Tilmann Röder, *Constitutionalism in Islamic Countries: Between Upheaval and Continuity* (New York: Oxford University Press, 2011).

B. Debates among Intellectuals

As recently as half a century ago, questions about the relationship between Islamic law and constitutionalism were explored by a limited number of specialists in Muslim societies and their debates drew only sporadic scholarly attention. But recent developments have not simply heightened interest in the subject matter but also increased its political centrality—both enriching but also complicating scholarly debate. First, publics have become more involved. The growing adoption of formal (though often merely ritualistic) mechanisms for popular participation in constitutional drafting has occasionally been deepened by truly inclusive processes (there were, for instance, elected assemblies that played very significant roles in the drafting process in Kuwait in 1963 and Iran in 1979). Second, the "Islamic inflation" noted by Brown, in which provisions for Islam have tended to grow more fulsome over time, has increased the degree to which actors taking stands on various religious issues—from Islamic institutions to social movements and political parties—have staked strong constitutional claims.[64] Third, the wave of political changes (independence; revolutionary upheaval in some countries; regime change in many more) has brought issues of constitutional design and redesign to the forefront of politics and raised fundamental questions about the sources of sovereignty.

The result has been not only a widening (and sometimes quite contentious) debate in Muslim societies but also a set of scholarly attempts to understand those debates. That scholarly interest has probed both the general and the specific: general arguments concerning the compatibility of the shari'a and constitutionalism; and more specific concerns about constitutional elements. In this section we will examine the general scholarly focus on the intellectual debates (and the parallels between discussions among Muslim intellectuals and scholars of Islam), the understanding of specific constitutional provisions, and the analysis of general discussions of sovereignty.

1. *Merging of internal and external debates*

The scholarly debate on shari'a and constitutionalism centers on the ways in which the classical Islamic legal heritage may be compatible with constitutional and governance principles, and to what extent Islamic law and constitutionalism can be combined. The origins of this discussion—in the nineteenth and early twentieth centuries—have already been noted. In recent decades, much of the agenda in many Muslim societies has been set by public intellectuals who have sought to anchor their claims very firmly both in the Islamic tradition and in constitutionalism. By arguing, for instance, that rule by consensus (*shura*) is not merely desirable and advisory for rulers, but obligatory and binding, these intellectuals explore ways of

[64] Brown, "Islam and Constitutionalism in the Arab World."

working simultaneously within both an Islamic and constitutionalist framework. Figures like Rashid al-Ghannushi of Tunisia, Tariq al-Bishri and Muhammad Salim al-'Awa of Egypt, 'Abd al-Karim Saroush of Iran, and Masykuri Abdillah of Indonesia have sought both to locate support in Islamic sources for constitutionalist institutions, principles and practices, and to ground constitutionalism in more recognizably Islamic garb. For instance, al-Ghannushi refutes the notion that the concept of "divine sovereignty" provides a basis for rule of law and government by the people.[65]

Such efforts at constructing what might be called an Islamic constitutionalism are anything but universally accepted. From the religious camp comes some sympathetic interest (Yusuf al-Qaradawi, for instance, has adopted many of their ideas and themes) but also strong concerns that Islamic concepts are being robbed of their content as part of this translation effort. From leftists and liberals also come some expressions of interest. Azmi Bishara, for instance, has written that "calls for the application of Shari'a may express a democratic tendency, or (at least) an opposition to despotism, simply because Shari'a rule implies restrictions on the exercise of political power over and above mere will of rulers."[66] At the same time, liberals and leftists worry that constitutionalist ideas lose their content as they are grafted onto religious roots. In studying different versions of constitutionalism in Egypt, Bruce Rutherford notes some degree of convergence between the separate philosophies of Islamic and liberal constitutionalism, but he also argues that the ideal state envisioned by Islamic constitutionalists would be "far more invasive than that found in Western liberal regimes."[67]

Efforts to develop an Islamic constitutionalism have drawn extensive scholarly interest, and, because they are themselves undertaken by scholars, there is even some cross-fertilization between scholars of Islam and Muslim intellectuals grounding themselves in part in the Islamic legal tradition. Some non-Muslim scholars have echoed the views of the Islamic constitutionalists. For instance, John Esposito and John Obert Voll have argued that the longstanding Islamic traditions of *shura, ijma'*, and *ijtihad* may not have precise equivalents in the vocabulary of western democracy, but they echo the principles of liberal constitutionalism.[68] Raymond Baker points to the formation of Egypt's moderate Islamist Wasat Party as a manifestation

[65] Rachid Ghannouchi, *Muqarabat fi al-'Ilmaniyya wa al-Mujatama' al-Madani* [Approaches to Secularism and Civil Society] (London: al-Markaz al-Magharibi lil-buhuth wa al-tarjamah, 1999), 155.

[66] 'Azmi Bishara, "Madkhal li-Mu'alajat al-Demoqratiyya wu-Anmat at-Tadayyun" [Introduction to Democracy and Modes of Religiosity] in *Hawla al-Khiyar al-Demoqrati* [On the Democratic Alternative], eds. Burhan Ghalyun et al. (Ramallah: Muwatin, 1993), 83. Cited in John Bunzl, *Islam, Judaism, and the Political Role of Religions in the Middle East* (Gainesville, FL: University of Florida Press, 2004), 108.

[67] Bruce K. Rutherford, *Egypt After Mubarak: Liberalism, Islam and Democracy in the Arab World* (Princeton: Princeton University Press, 2008), 126.

[68] John L. Esposito and John Obert Voll, *Islam and Democracy* (Oxford and New York: Oxford University Press, 1996), 27.

of an emerging reformist school of "New Islamists." And there are skeptics as well. Among non-Muslim scholars of Islamic law, Wael Hallaq has staked out a strongly skeptical position that the shari'a is not only in decline but is actually on the brink of extinction.[69] Hallaq argues that the advent of the modern nation-state ushered in "the demise of the shari'a" through the attempt to rigidify Islamic law in codified form, to separate the content of law from interpretative techniques formerly used to derive legal rules and norms, and to transfer legislative power from the *ulama* to predominately secular rulers. And some scholars of human rights have shown a corresponding skepticism that the efforts of Islamic constitutionalists can lead to restrictions on the rights of women and minorities. Citing the example of Saudi Arabia's Basic Law, Anne Mayer argues that Islamic constitutionalism tends to reinforce illiberal constraints on personal freedoms and theocratic authoritarianism.[70]

What is clear is that neither Islamic law nor constitutionalism remain unchanged by the effort to foster a syncretism between them. In that sense, those who seek to understand the relationship between them (even non-Muslim scholars) can easily find themselves as participants shaping the ways that both constitutional arrangements and the Islamic legal tradition are understood and implemented. Perhaps one of the most notable examples of this tendency is Abdullahi an-Na'im, a Muslim scholar at an American university. An-Na'im has argued for a form of Islamic constitutionalism that verges on secularism. Skeptical of the ability and effectiveness of the state to cultivate and enforce ethical behavior, An-Na'im nonetheless claims his approach recovers dormant understandings of the relationship between religion and politics in the Islamic tradition. An-Nai'im's self-proclaimed "retrieval project" aims to challenge the conventional historiographic narrative of Islamic constitutionalism by uncovering a "historical differentiation of state and religious institutions in Islamic societies."[71] Khaled Abou El Fadl has argued far less radically for a more ethically inspired reading of the shari'a, claiming that the meaning of the Qur'an "is not fixed simply by the literal meaning of its words, but depends, too, on the moral construction given to it by the reader."[72] Among scholars focussed on the nexus between constitutionalism and shari'a, Abou El Fadl remains far more anchored in the Islamic legal heritage and far less insistent on an effort to disentangle the shari'a from politics. Tariq Ramadan, whose work has explored the challenge of Muslim expatriate communities living in secular European societies, has argued that integration within western constitutional contexts is possible due to the inherent flexibility of Islamic principles and values. Rather than taking a literalist

[69] Wael Hallaq, "Can the Shari'a Be Restored?" in *Islamic Law and the Challenges of Modernity*, eds. Yvonne Yazbeck Haddad and Barbara Freyer Stowasser (New York: Altamira Press, 2004), 22.

[70] Ann E. Mayer, "Conundrums in Constitutionalism: Islamic Monarchies in an Era of Transition," 1 *UCLA Journal of Islamic & Near E.L.* 183 (Spring/ Summer, 2002), 183.

[71] Abdullahi Ahmed An-Na'im, *Islam and the Secular State: Negotiating the Future of Shari'a* (Cambridge, MA: Harvard University Press, 1998), 77.

[72] Khaled Abou El Fadl, *The Place of Tolerance in Islam* (Boston: Beacon Press, 2002), 15.

approach to the revealed texts, Ramadan argues that silences and ambiguities within classical Islamic jurisprudence allow "human analytic reason to stipulate inevitably diverse Islamic rules, through space and time, but ones which are still Islamic."[73] While Ramadan's work does not deal explicitly with Islamic constitutionalism, his focus on the compatibility of Muslim communities with European constitutional structures has been used by the political scientist Andrew March to support a theory of "overlapping consensus" between philosophical elements of political liberalism and Islam.[74]

2. *The shari'a in the constitutional text*

In addition to exploring (and joining) in the general debate about the relationship between the shari'a and constitutionalism, scholars have shown interest in far more specific issues involving constitutional texts. One such issue has been the effort to understand the motivation behind inscribing Islam or the shari'a in constitutions. Scholars, notably Noah Feldman, have focussed on the expansion of religious provisions to meet political demands for justice, rule of law, and anti-corruption measures.[75]

But just as striking has been the way some scholars have noted that blending constitutionalism with the Islamic legal heritage may actually empower state authority rather than limit or regularize it. The increasingly extensive provisions for Islam in the constitutions of some states carries the possibility that states will use them to shape religious understandings rather than the other way around. The phenomenon is not unique to Muslim societies. Ran Hirschl, a comparative politics scholar, makes this counterintuitive argument particularly strongly. Hirschl has claimed that the introduction of religious clauses is undertaken to curb what he terms "theocratic" politics: "Turning to constitutional law and courts to bring religiosity under check or defuse its potentially radical edge is a rational choice of action by secularists and moderates." [76]

More modestly—and in a manner that pays far more attention to local context—some have noted that the introduction of Islamic provisions in constitutions has been to promote the consolidation of a strong and cohesive national ideology as the basis for independent statehood. Many scholars have highlighted the functional role of Islamic constitutionalism in advancing nation-building projects in the post-colonial period. Kristen Stilt argues that states do not necessarily adopt Islamic constitutional clauses to institutionalize a particular brand of Islam, but rather to harness religious rhetoric in support of political or national goals; thus, decisions

[73] Tariq Ramadan, *To Be a European Muslim* (Leicester, UK: Islamic Foundation, 1999), 75.

[74] Andrew March, "Reading Tariq Ramadan: Political Liberalism, Islam, and 'Overlapping Consensus,'" *Ethics and International Affairs* 21, no. 4 (2007): 399–413.

[75] Noah Feldman, *The Fall and Rise of the Islamic State* (Oxford: Oxford University Press, 2008), 147.

[76] Hirschl, *Constitutional Theocracy* (Cambridge: Cambridge University Press, 2010), 19.

to integrate Islamic law within an overarching constitutional framework are often driven by economic, social, cultural, and even national security considerations.[77]

3. *Popular and divine sovereignty*

Another specific area of interest has been exploring the effect of the debate over the source of law engendered by constitutional drafting efforts. The tension between popular sovereignty and divine sovereignty, for instance, is a staple of efforts to understand the post-1979 Iranian constitutional order. Schirazi finds no room for popular sovereignty in the doctrine of *wilayat al-faqih* (rule by jurists). Because political power emanates "from God alone and is transferred from God to the Islamic jurists," Schirazi argues that the exercise of power "in no way depends upon the voice of the people for its legitimisation."[78] Arjomand points out that a number of Iranian religious scholars evinced discomfort with the strong version of *wilyat al-faqih* institutionalized in Iran, given its inconsistency with the doctrine of popular sovereignty, to which the Iranian constitution "pays lip service." However, these critics of Khomeini were largely suppressed through a campaign of intimidation and character assassination.[79]

In the Sunni world, while the introduction of clauses declaring the shariʿa as "a" or "the" source of law (as has been discussed already) has had uncertain practical effects, it has given traditionalists a constitutional foothold to advance their Islamizing agenda, as Nathan Brown and Adel Omar Sherif have argued.[80] Constitutional language authorizing Islamic judicial review of legislation for compliance with shariʿa has emboldened calls for the establishment or religious states and drawn Islamist movements into constitutional discussions.

Finally, legal scholars have addressed how Islamic provisions in constitutions may adversely affect the efficacy of international human rights instruments. Their interest stems from a concern for human rights when Muslim states attach reservations to their ratification of international human rights. International human rights standards allow states to recognize an official religion "if its followers comprise the majority of the population" as long as this arrangement does not violate the civil and political rights of non-believers and adherents of other faiths,[81] but scholars disagree

[77] Kristen Stilt, "Contextualizing constitutional Islam: The Malayan experience" *International Journal of Constitutional Law* 13 (2015): 407–433, 411.

[78] Asghar Shirazi, *The Constitution of Iran: Politics and the State in the Islamic Republic* (New York: I.B. Taurus, 1998), 14.

[79] Said Amir Arjomand, *Turban for the Crown: The Islamic Revolutionin Iran* (New York: Oxford University Press, 1998), 155–156.

[80] Nathan Brown and Adel Omar Sherif, "Inscribing the Shariʿa in Arab Constitutional Law," in *Islamic Law and the Challenges of Modernity*, eds. Yvonne Yazbeck Haddad and Barbara Freyer Stowasser, 62–63.

[81] UN Human Rights Committee's General Comment on Article 18 (freedom of thought, conscience, and religion) of the International Covenant on Civil and Political Rights (ICCPR) in Stahnke and Blitt, "The Religion–State Relationship," 8.

on whether or not women and religious minorities can be adequately protected from discrimination within an Islamic constitutional framework. Such concerns do not only come from nonspecialists. Human rights advocates have charged that Islamic constitutional and other legal provisions have undermined democratic development by obstructing the ratification of international human rights treaties on human rights in Islamic states such as Saudi Arabia, Pakistan, and Iran, where religious considerations have been invoked as "the determining factor in voting against or abstaining from human rights initiatives," according to Rüdiger Wolfrum.[82] Karima Bennoune has similarly raised concerns about the impact of Islamic fundamentalist movements on human rights law and practice, and criticizes the field of international legal scholarship for tolerating illiberal and even violent applications of shari'a as legitimate cultural or religious practices.[83]

IV. Who is Authoritative?

Scholarly interest in the intersection of constitutionalism with the Islamic legal tradition has taken on a markedly more practical focus in recent years. While previous scholarship focussed on constitutional text and intellectual context, the actual operation of constitutional provisions on Islam—and the realization that they are flexible and can be applied and avoided in many different ways—has begun to draw considerable focus to interpretative authority: who is empowered to speak for the shari'a in constitutional matters?

Some scholars have advanced what appears at first glance to be a sharp challenge to the question in this form. Hallaq, as described earlier, has argued that the shari'a, untethered from its anchoring in specific techniques and modes of transmission, is fluid and evolves new meanings in relation to changing historical contexts; the idea of enshrining Islamic law in constitutional texts and allowing the institutions of the modern state to interpret and implement it would thus seem to be alien to its nature. From a very different perspective, Lama Abu-Odeh has argued that the law in almost all Muslim societies is legislated, often based on civil law sources, so that the extreme interest in Islamic law in the western academy has fostered what she implies are distracting, antiquarian studies divorced from legal realities.[84] The

[82] Rüdiger Wolfrum, CIIC manuscript, 13.

[83] Karima Bennoune, "Remembering the Other's Others: Theorizing the Approach of International Law to Muslim Fundamentalism," *Columbia Human Rights Law Review* 41 (2010): 663–665.

[84] Lama Abu-Odeh, "The Politics of (Mis)recognition: Islamic Law Pedagogy in American Academia," *The American Journal of Comparative Law* 52, no. 4 (Autumn, 2004): 789–824.

implication of Abu-Odeh's view is that the question places far too much weight on the shari'a. Hallaq, on the other hand, emphasizes the role of Muslim jurists in shaping historical interpretations of shari'a and notes that "the particular legal norms to be derived from this moral domain are situational, subject to the never-ending *ijtihad*."[85] The implications of Hallaq's view is that the focus on the shari'a and constitutions overstates the degree to which the former informs or guides constitutional practice in a modern state.

While framed very strongly, these critiques serve as a useful corrective more than a cause for intellectual resignation. Hallaq's argument should serve as a reminder that when the shari'a is embodied, interpreted, or applied in the institutions of a modern state, some fundamental shifts take place from the Islamic legal heritage. And Abu-Odeh's practical concern with what the law actually is in practice should encourage scholars to anchor their understandings in current legal, political, and institutional realities. While very different in spirit, there is no logical contradiction between their views and that of Clark Lombardi who insists that scholars take what judges and legislators—employees of the modern state—describe as Islamic law very seriously; to the extent that Islamic law is practiced in many Muslim societies it is done precisely through the actions and interpretations of such individuals. Hussein Ali Agrama similarly views religion and state as intertwined in each other's ostensibly separate realms, and he argues that the shari'a is shaped by "the conditions of secular power and possibility established by a modern state."[86]

The differences among these approaches stand in stark relief with these recent scholarly contributions, but the basic issue underlying them is far older and indeed is intimately connected with the nature of political authority in a society that strives to be governed in accordance with God's will. A strong intellectual and popular consensus in support of this goal amounts to an acceptance that the shari'a—however defined—is binding for individuals and societies seeking to live in accordance with Islamic principles. And this consensus is the basis for the binding nature of the shari'a in Islamic constitutions, as all man-made laws and policies must comply with the injunctions of Islam.[87]

But the location of ultimate sovereignty with God presents a major dilemma for the construction of man-made political systems, and Islamic scholars have been confronted with the challenge of reconciling the principle of divine sovereignty with the necessity of delegating some interpretive and implementing authority to human institutions. As Sherman Jackson has noted, the process by which jurists traditionally acquired religious authority and transmitted it to their students took

[85] Hallaq, *The Impossible State*, 167. "Ijtihad" refers to scholarly attempts to derive legal rulings through independent interpretation of the Qur'an and hadith.

[86] Hussein Ali Agrama, *Questioning Secularism: Islam, Sovereignty, and the Rule of Law in Modern Egypt* (Chicago: University of Chicago Press, 2012), 5.

[87] Nathan Brown, *Constitutions in a Non-Constitutional World: Arab Basic Laws and the Prospects for Accountable Government* (Albany: SUNY Press, 2002), 174–175.

place "totally outside the apparatus of the state."[88] Thus, with the rise of Islamic constitutional states, the ruling authorities recognized that sources of religious authority operating outside of the government's jurisdiction posed a potential challenge to their sovereignty and legitimacy. Thus, states endeavored to draw away religious authority from non-state actors and obtain an influential role over the interpretation and application of Islamic law—a trend drawing frequent scholarly attention. Although modern states have attempted to transfer religious authority to elected parliaments and other government officials, their efforts have only been partially successful. State-sanctioned Islam continues to be challenged by entities that resist control by the ruling authorities: religious scholars, judges, and Muslim communities at large. The contestation of interpretative authority among these competing groups represents a serious issue for the sovereignty of modern Islamic states.

Modern states derive their legitimacy from maintaining a monopoly on the creation and enforcement of rules governing their citizens. For this reason, political authorities often view warily the existence of an autonomous Islamic legal realm beyond state control. Of course the autonomy was never complete—scholars of the Islamic legal tradition including Hallaq and Zaman have noted that as early as the Umayyads, rulers began patronizing these elites in an effort to co-opt their religious authority under state control.[89] The trend toward state encroachment into the religious realm seems to have intensified in many societies in the nineteenth century and continued into the postcolonial period. But it was met with significant resistance from non-state authorities—jurists, *ulama*, and religious communities—which challenged the ruling authorities' official interpretation of Islam and sought to promote their own understandings as authoritative.

States in which modern constitutions coexist with Islamic legal traditions have a strong incentive to co-opt or incorporate the latter, so that the state maintains a degree of control over official interpretations of the shari'a. Islamic constitutional states have, to varying degrees, delegated interpretative authority to one or more institutions and bodies: the judiciary, religious scholars (*ulama*), parliament and other state officials, or the broader community of citizens. Yet no entity has successfully monopolized the contested realm of interpretative authority; state institutions have competed for control over this domain with religious authorities in a relationship that is both symbiotic and at times antagonistic.

In this section we will explore how scholars have worked to understand how the constitutional structures of the modern state in predominantly Muslim societies empower (or limit) the authority of judges, *ulama*, parliamentarians and other

[88] Sherman Jackson, *Islamic Law and the State: The Constitutional Jurisprudence of Shihab Al-Din Al-Qarafi* (Leiden: Brill, 1996), xv.

[89] Hallaq, *The Origins and Evolution of Islamic Law*, 165.

state officials, and the community of Muslims to speak authoritatively on behalf of Islamic law.

A. Judges, Constitutional Interpretation, and the Shari'a

The insertion of Islamic provisions into constitutional texts has made judges potentially important actors in determining the ways in which Islamic principles and the shari'a inform, shape, or constrict political authorities. That potential has been realized in several influential countries, including Pakistan and Egypt, where judicial review has played a powerful role in shaping official interpretations of shari'a, and also functions as a preemptive constraint on law-makers, who have had to adapt to increasingly assertive judiciaries by tailoring new legislation to conform with their rulings.

Thus, scholars have examined the question of whether the expansion of judicial authority over time is more the result of textual changes in Islamic constitutions or the product of increasing activism and initiative on the part of judicial bodies. Martin Lau attributes the rise in the importance of Islam in Pakistan's legal and political realms to "judicial self-assertion" and innovative readings of the shari'a. Lau writes: "It is the flexibility of Islamic law in the hands of Pakistan's higher judiciary which has ensured and fostered the role of Islam in the legal system."[90] However, Lombardi attributes the expansion of judicial authority more to the introduction of specific justiciable shari'a clauses and the creation of new judicial institutions—such as Pakistan's Federal Shari'at Court—than to assertiveness by individual judges.[91]

The focus on judicial and institutional actors is unsurprising since explicit provisions are rare and are often very general on the specific matter of interpretive authority over the shari'a. Saudi Arabia is one of the few Muslim states that defines judges as the authoritative interpreters of the shari'a. In Iran as well, the constitution empowers the Council of Guardians to veto all laws deemed to be in violation of the shari'a, but the Council's status is complicated by the presence of parallel authorities with vaguely defined and often competing mandates: six members of the Council are appointed by the *rahbar* (Supreme Leader), who enjoys sole authority to resolve conflicts between the Council and the *Majles* (Parliament). Separate from the *Majles*, another clerically dominated body—the *Maslahat* Council—has undermined the authority of the Council of Guardians by exercising its independent law-making authority (enhanced by constitutional amendments in 1989) to amend legislation

[90] Martin Lau, *The Role of Islam in the Legal System of Pakistan* (Leiden: Brill Academic Publishers, 2006), 211–212.

[91] Clark Lombardi, "The Challenges and Opportunities of Islamic Review: Lessons for Afghanistan from the Experience of Other Muslim Countries," USIP Position Paper (2012), 4.

or enact entirely new laws that are not subject to appeal.[92] More typical, however, is Pakistan, where interpretative authority is vaguely defined and fiercely contested among judges, state institutions, and religious scholars.[93]

Yet however vaguely defined, the potential role for judges has been anchored in a large number of countries by provisions for the judicial review of the constitutionality of legislation (often through the construction of specialized constitutional courts or councils). Provisions for judicial review rarely mention the shari'a at all, but they effectively bring it within judicial purview. Indeed, the expansion of Islamic constitutional provisions has corresponded to an expansion in the political power of the judiciary. But although judicial bodies have increasingly asserted the right to judicial review and constitutional interpretation, judges are still subject to significant oversight and interference from the executive institutions they should be overseeing. Thus, Islamic constitutions have often enhanced the authority of judges more than their autonomy.

More recent scholarship has linked judicial opinions involving constitutional provisions to more general arguments about the compatibility of Islam with democratic and constitutional principles. Pointing to the cases of Egypt and Pakistan, Lombardi argues: "The courts have developed an interpretation of Islamic law (and of the restraints that Islamic law places on the ruler) that is consistent with many elements of liberal constitutionalism and, in some ways, reinforces it."[94]

B. *Ulama* and Religious Specialists

Scholarly interest in the sources of interpretive authority has prompted inquiry into the role of the *ulama* (Muslim religious specialists) in promoting or challenging the constitutionalization of Islamic law. In different historical contexts, the *ulama* have at times functioned as autonomous nodes of religious authority that challenge temporal rulers' efforts to maintain a monopoly on the interpretation and enforcement of shari'a; However, in other cases, the *ulama* have enjoyed symbiotic and mutually beneficial partnerships with political authorities. Scholars in the field have focussed on the interface between the *ulama* and the state to better understand how interpretive pluralism shapes the evolution of Islamic constitutions and their application.

The community of traditionally educated Muslim religious specialists has been active and influential in Muslim societies for over a millennium. Whereas the *ulama* once maintained a near-monopoly on authoritative religious knowledge,

[92] Said Amir Arjomand, *After Khomeini: Iran Under His Successors* (Oxford: Oxford University Press, 2009), 45.

[93] Lau, *The Role of Islam in the Legal System of Pakistan*, 211–212.

[94] Clark Lombardi, "The Challenges and Opportunities of Islamic Review: Lessons for Afghanistan from the Experiences of other Muslim Countries," USIP Paper (2011), 10.

their privileged status has been challenged, and, some scholars argue,[95] significantly eroded in the modern era.

The rise of print media, public education, and the expansion of bureaucratic institutions dedicated to regulating all aspects of political life and religious activity have contributed to what Zaman describes as a "fragmentation" of the authority of the *ulama*. According to Zaman, the determination of modern states not only to regulate religion but also to frame the relationship between religion and state in constitutional form has deepened the challenge to the traditional religious specialists, confronting them not only with rivals but also with more heavy-handed oversight by the state.

Two opposing camps of scholars offer divergent views on the extent to which the *ulama* have (or have not) adapted successfully to the legal challenges of the modern era. In the first camp are those who regard the *ulama* as antiquarians resisting change. The French sociologist Olivier Roy regards the *ulama* as bastions of traditionalism who have "endeavored to ignore or disqualify anything new."[96] In his study of the role of the *ulama* in India and Pakistan in the first half of the twentieth century, Syed Zaidi highlights the antagonistic relationship between a traditionalist class of *ulama* and the Pakistani Muslim revivalist leader Abul Ala Maududi, who viewed the change-averse *ulama* as an impediment to his ambitious legislative agenda envisioning sweeping social reforms.[97] John Obert Voll argues that the *ulama* voluntarily adopted a quietist, apolitical role during the Ottoman era, in which they were co-opted into submission through state patronage.[98]

However, a second camp argues that the *ulama* have successfully resisted stagnation by adapting to modern challenges. Zaman, a leading voice within this group, uses the case of Pakistan's Deobandi madrasas to argue that religious scholars have enhanced their influence in a number of Muslim-majority societies by responding to change with activism, flexibility, and innovation.[99] Asef Bayat chronicles the efforts of modernist *ulama* in Egypt to resist British colonial rule. The nationalist-minded *ulama* sought to leverage Islam as a platform for innovation and progress in Muslim societies that would enable them to compete economically and politically with their European rivals.[100] Supporting the view of *ulama* as agents of social and

[95] Hallaq, "Can the Shari'a Be Restored," 22.

[96] Olivier Roy, *The Failure of Political Islam*, translated by Carol Volk (Cambridge, MA: Harvard University Press, 1994), 20.

[97] Syed Zaidi, *The Emergence of Ulema in the Politics of India and Pakistan 1918–1949* (iUniverse, 2003), 67.

[98] John Obert Voll, *Islam: Continuity and Change in the Modern World* (New York: Syracuse University Press, 1994), 34.

[99] Muhammad Qasim Zaman, *The 'ulama in Contemporary Islam: Custodians of Change* (Princeton, NJ: Princeton University Press, 2001), 2.

[100] Asef Bayat, *Making Islam Democratic: Social Movements and the Post-Islamist Turn* (Stanford: Stanford University Press, 2007), 37.

political change, Mongol Bayat identifies the *ulama* as the primary intellectual catalyst that precipitated Iran's constitutional revolution of 1905–09.[101]

The scholarly debate over the *ulama* is directly tied to conceptions of their constitutional role. Both camps acknowledge that the collision of the traditional community of *ulama* with the machinery of the modern constitutional state has led to politically portentous struggles in some societies—sometimes replicated within the *ulama* themselves. This may have played out most dramatically in Iran. Hamid Algar refers to Iran's Constitutional Revolution (1905–09), which culminated in the formation of an elected parliament, as a case in which the conflict between the *ulama* and the bureaucratic state was particularly pronounced.[102] Although a number of prominent reformist *ulama* initially supported the revolution, seeing it as a likely tool for meeting public needs in accordance with Islamic principles, some became disillusioned a few years later when a second wave of constitutional reformers sought to disestablish Islam and introduce a secular educational system.[103] Said Arjomand argues that scholars have underestimated the significance of the *ulama*'s opposition to constitutionalism in Iran.[104] Division and debate among the ranks of the *ulama* inspired what is recognized as one of the first theories of Islamic constitutional government—without reference to European models—by the Iranian Shi'a religious scholar Muhammad Husayn Na'ini, who argued that in the absence of the Prophet/Imam, it was impossible to fully implement shari'a, thus necessitating the next best temporal alternative: a political system designed to constrain executive power and condition sovereignty on the "performance of duties for the public benefit." In Na'ini's view, this system of limited and responsible government required two features: a constitution and a consultative assembly.[105] A. Hairi is another scholar whose work has highlighted growing clerical opposition to constitutionalism in Iran. Hairi identifies a schism between two rival camps of *ulama*: "constitutionalist *ulama*" aligned with the bourgeois nationalists who believed that constitutions could be designed in ways consistent with the shari'a and "absolutist *ulama*" affiliated with the Royal Court and conservative middle class who rejected constitutionalism as fundamentally incompatible with Islam. This ideological conflict within the *ulama* gave rise "to a considerable volume of political literature, both for and against constitutionalism."[106]

[101] Mongol Bayat, *Iran's First Revolution: Shi'ism and the Constitutional Revolution of 1905–1909* (New York: Oxford University Press, 1991).

[102] Hamid Algar, *Religion and the State in Iran 1785–1906: The Role of the 'ulama in the Qajar Period* (Berkeley: University of California Press, 1969), 242.

[103] Ira Marvin Lapidus, *A History of Islamic Societies* (Cambridge: Cambridge University Press, 2002), 475.

[104] Said Amir Arjomand, "The 'ulama's Traditionalist Opposition to Parliamentarianism: 1907–1909" *Middle Eastern Studies* 17, no. 2 (April, 1981): 174–190.

[105] Muhammad Hussein Naini, *An Admonition to the Nation and an Exposition to the People* (Najaf, 1909), 6–15. Quoted in Esposito, *Islam and Politics*, 88–89.

[106] A. Hairi, *Shi'ism and Constitutionalism in Iran* (Leiden: Brill, 1977), 153.

The fragmentation of the *ulama* throughout the Islamic world has allowed specialists who are not products of a traditional religious training to participate in debates. In the early centuries of Islam, the *ulama* were less identifiable as a distinct group and that phenomenon might be returning in recent decades. There are, to be sure, numerous formally trained scholars, many of whom occupy positions in officially supported religious institutions. But they are joined as specialized participants in discussions about the relationship between the Islamic legal heritage and the appropriate legal and constitutional order with those from universities, research institutes, and even popular movements. Such specialists adopt a wide range of attitudes toward positive law. On the more permissive end of the spectrum are those such as Rashid al-Ghannushi and Kamal Abu al-Majd, who approach the shari'a as a body of general guidelines flexible enough to accommodate man-made laws, so long as they do not directly contravene the Qur'an or Sunna. Drawing on the work of moderate Islamist thinkers, Bruce Rutherford has suggested that a reform-minded wing within the Muslim Brotherhood is working to accommodate a concept of citizenship and universal civil rights independent of religion within the framework of shari'a.[107] The arguments of such thinkers—using older concepts such as the *maqasid* of the shari'a or *maslaha*—have now passed into general usage, and mainstream Islamist intellectuals often promote a shift away from literalism and specific rules and toward an interpretation of abstract principles in ways that advance the common good.[108] Felicitas Opwis explains the growing prominence of the concept of *maslaha* in Islamic scholarship in part as an adaptive intellectual response to the forces of social and political change that provides a mechanism for reforming and modernizing shari'a. While noting the different ways the concept was used in early centuries, she notes that it now "presents jurists with a framework to tackle the problem, inherent in a legal system that is based on a finite text, of bringing to bear the limited material foundation of the law (i.e., Quran and hadith) on everyday life in an ever-changing environment."[109] The effects of such arguments are not merely intellectual but can be constitutional and legal: proponents effectively demand a high threshold of "repugnancy" for invaliding legislation, perhaps reducing the authority of the *ulama* relative to temporal law-makers.

But these views are hardly uncontested. The rise of salafism and the increasing willingness of salafi legal specialists to engage in broader debates outside their own circles has introduced a far more textually oriented approach to such discussions, resistant to reading broad themes that might be seen as devices to trump particular

[107] Bruce K. Rutherford, *Egypt after Mubarak: Liberalism, Islam, and Democracy in the Arab World* (Princeton: Princeton University Press, 2008).

[108] Robert Hefner, *Sharia Politics: Islamic Law and Society in the Modern World* (Indiana: Indiana University Press, 2011), 30.

[109] Felicitas Opwis, "Maslaha in Contemporary Islamic Legal Theory," *Islamic Law and Society* 12, no. 2 (2005): 182–223.

shari'a-based rules. Describing the strict textualist mode of salafi thought, Bernard Haykel argues that salafi scholars reject alternative understandings of Islam, which they view as "corrupt deviations from the straight path of Islam."[110] And it is not only salafis who view the latitude given to positive legislation very skeptically. 'Abd al-Qadir 'Awda, for instance, a former judge who became active in Egypt's Muslim Brotherhood, tried to develop exacting shari'a-based standards for all laws originating outside of the shari'a; others continue to insist on leaning heavily on the *ulama* to articulate strict interpretations of Islamic law that limit expansive interpretations.[111]

c. Parliament and State Officials

In juxtaposition to the *ulama* and Muslim specialists who assert interpretations of shari'a outside of the state, parliament and government officials also play an active role in shaping Islamic constitutional doctrine. Scholars have focussed on the ways in which state officials and law-makers have strategically deployed the language of shari'a as well as Islamic constitutional reforms to bring about structural changes in political systems—either in an authoritarian or democratic direction. For example, Islamic constitutions have been leveraged to consolidate power in the executive branch through the assertion of divine legitimacy, but have also been deployed by proponents of Islamic democracy to support a redistribution of power in the direction of the legislature.

The effort to construct a constitution that is grounded in Islamic legal principles can be double-edged. On the one hand it can be seen as a way of limiting the authority of public officials and holding them accountable to standards that are not wholly of their own making. But it can also empower those same officials and encourage them to use constitutional provisions on Islam to augment rather than limit their authority. Individual leaders have attempted to bolster their personal Islamic credentials as a basis for advancing their legislative and policy agendas. The king of Morocco has leveraged his religious claims as "commander of the faithful" to promote codification of shari'a-based personal status laws and induce the parliament to accept the interpretations he has favored.[112] Whatever its original intent, *wilayat al-faqih* in Iran has had a similar effect of subordinating religious inquiry to political

[110] Bernard Haykel, *Revival and Reform in Islam: The Legacy of Muhammad al-Shawkani* (Cambridge: Cambridge University Press, 2003). See also Bernard Haykel, "On the Nature of Salafi Thought and Action," in *Global Salafism: Islam's New Religious Movement*, ed. Roel Meijer (London: Hurst, 2009).

[111] 'Abd al-Qadir 'Awda, *Al-islam wa-awda'na al-qanuniyya* [Islam and Our Legal Situation] (Beirut: Mu'assasat al-risala, 1985; originally published 1951), 14 and 17.

[112] Jan Michiel Otto, *Shari'a Incorporated: A Comparative Overview of the Legal Systems of Twelve Muslim Countries in Past and Present* (Leiden: Leiden University Press Academic: 2010), 27.

authority. States have attempted to regulate and maintain an official brand of Islam by bringing clerical activities and religious scholarship under the umbrella of state-sanctioned institutions. In post-Attaturk Turkey, the state has attempted to control the role of religion in public life and the legal realm through the official state office for religious affairs known as the Diyanet.[113]

Some Islamic constitutionalists have responded to this challenge by seeking to integrate democratic mechanisms into the understanding of an appropriate Islamic constitutional framework, such as those (like Egypt's al-Awwa and Tunisia's Ghannushi) who find divine sovereignty to be compatible with democratically elected legislative bodies. These elected assemblies, they argue, should have the authority to deliberate among multiple potential interpretations of shariʿa and apply the rule that best serves the public interest.[114] Some strains of recent Shiʿi thought can be used to point in a similar direction. Writing on the intellectual background to the Iranian revolution, Chibli Mallat identifies Muhammad Baqir al-Sadr's claim of "dual emanation of sovereignty" from both God and the people, giving rise to a "double-tier separation of powers" in which the people indirectly control the exercise of legislative and executive powers through direct election of their president and parliamentary representations.[115]

D. Popular Sovereignty

Indeed, the idea that an Islamic constitutional system can blend divine and popular sovereignty has drawn considerable attention among Muslim intellectuals. Some skeptics long maintained that there is no place for popular sovereignty in the Islamic state. Abdul A'la Mawdudi, the founder of Jamaat al-Islami in Pakistan, concluded that Islam is "the very antithesis of secular Western democracy" based solely on the sovereignty of the people.[116] However, beginning in the 1980s and 1990s many religious intellectuals in various Muslim societies became increasingly receptive to the possibility that divine sovereignty does not necessarily contradict popular sovereignty, and that the Islamic principle of *shura* (consultation) provides a basis for engaging the public at large in an inclusive dialogue with both the state and religious establishment. Modern Islamic thinkers have cited the principle of *shura* as evidence of the compatibility of Islam and democracy, suggesting a form of

[113] Otto, *Shariʿa Incorporated*, 27.

[114] Nathan Brown, *Constitutions in a Non-Constitutional World: Arab Basic Laws and the Prospects for Accountable Government* (Albany: SUNY Press, 2002), 189.

[115] Chibli Mallat, *The Renewal of Islamic Law: Muhammad Baqer al-Sadr, Najaf and the Shi'i International* (Cambridge: Cambridge University Press, 1993), 72.

[116] Ali Rez Abootalebi, *Islam and Democracy: State–Society Relations in Developing Countries, 1980–1994* (New York: Garland Publishing, 2000), 128.

popular sovereignty in which citizens are entitled to share or at least challenge the religious authority claimed by their leaders and elite jurists.

Academic interest in these debates has focussed on Pakistan, Egypt, and especially Iran, where the post-1979 constitutional order promised both divine and popular sovereignty; it also seemed to subordinate the state to Islamic law but also put officials in the position to speak authoritatively for Islamic law. Scholarship has focussed not only on these paradoxes but also on alternatives to the Iranian experiment that have been offered. Muhammad Baqir al-Sadr, an Islamic scholar executed by the Iraqi regime in 1980, showed far more comfort with democratic mechanisms than Khomeini, though he ultimately swung in support of Khomeini in the immediate wake of the Iranian Revolution. Al-Sadr proposed a unique interpretation of divine sovereignty in which authority is exercised by the people, who are in turn accountable to God.[117] A small minority of liberally minded Iranian *ulama*, including Mohsen Kadivar, pursued this line by challenging the Iranian constitution's delegation of religious and political authority to the scholarly elite, arguing instead for the supremacy of popular sovereignty over *wilayat al-faqih*.[118] The Iranian scholar Abdolkarim Soroush believed that Islam was fully consistent with participatory democracy, and argued for a reinterpretation of classical Islamic texts to provide a basis for guaranteeing individual sovereignty, rule of law, and a just system of government based on the obligations of rulers to rights-bearing citizens.[119] Soroush promoted a brand of Islamic constitutionalism inspired not by western models of political liberalism, but firmly anchored in and legitimized by classical Islamic jurisprudence. Soroush said in an interview: "An ideal religious society cannot have anything but a democratic government."[120]

V. Where Does Debate Take Place?

While scholarly interest in the relationship between Islamic law and constitutionalism has broadened and deepened, it still remains highly geographically focussed. There are scholars who have examined the issues in a wide range of settings,

[117] Chibli Mallat, *The Renewal of Islamic Law: Muhammad Baqer al-Sadr, Najaf and the Shi'i International* (Cambridge: Cambridge University Press, 1993), 72–73.

[118] Mohsen Kadivar, *A Study of People's Divergence from Ruling System* (2002) in Arjomand, *Constitutionalism and Political Reconstruction*, 136.

[119] Abdolkarim Saroush, *Essential Writings of Abdolkarim Sorouh*, Mahmoud Sadri and Ahmad Sadri eds. and trans. (New York: Oxford University Press, 2000), 63.

[120] Robin Wright, *Dreams and Shadows: The Future of the Middle East* (New York: Knopf, 2000), 40.

but (as the previous sections made clear) a very small number of countries have drawn the bulk of scholarly attention: Iran, Egypt, and Pakistan most particularly. Other countries—such as Afghanistan, Iraq, and Indonesia—have drawn sporadic attention as well, often in reaction to specific constitutional transitions. There is a combination of factors that has led to a special interest in these cases: a historically prolonged experience; international attention (and sometimes, as in the cases of Iraq and Afghanistan, direct international involvement); dramatic political contestation on a domestic level; and the scope of international influence (with debates in Pakistan and especially Egypt reverberating outside of the country).

This focus is thus understandable, but it leads to significant gaps. For instance, it passes over an attempt to understand why some predominately Muslim countries have not introduced any constitutional provisions concerning the Islamic nature of the state or official religion. In addition, the focus has been on political systems that are—at least on paper—highly centralized. However, in a number of countries—including Nigeria and Indonesia—constitutional silence on the role of Islam at the national level has given rise to a phenomenon described by Ran Hirschl as sub-national "religious jurisdictional enclaves," in which a permissive constitutional framework allows local governments to pass Islamic legislation with little resistance from federal authorities.[121] In the case of Indonesia, the province of Aceh was granted a "special autonomy" status that included the right to implement shari'a law as part of a peace agreement with the national government negotiated to end three decades of separatist fighting. In 2009, Aceh law-makers took advantage of this autonomous status to pass a law imposing death by stoning on Muslim adulterers, inspiring other local governments to introduce shari'a provisions and criminal penalties. At least sixty-six local shari'a ordinances have been promulgated and enforced between 2005 and 2010, prompting human rights activists to raise concerns that the federal government's tolerance of local religious laws outside of the constitutional framework is enabling the *de facto* implementation of shari'a-based norms at the national level, even thought the constitution makes no mention of it. But despite the increasing codification of shari'a law at the local level, R. Michael Feener has suggested that "the actual implementation of law in the province has been minimal," raising the possibility of a discrepancy between laws that exist on the books and their lax enforcement in practice.[122]

Nigeria is another case in which a nominally secular constitution has permitted the establishment of sub-national jurisdictional enclaves in which local shari'a ordinances have flourished. Nigeria's constitution, while secular and prohibiting the

[121] R. Hirschl, *Constitutional Theocracy* (Cambridge: Cambridge University Press), 32.

[122] R. Michael Feener, "Social Engineering through Shari'a: Islamic Law and State-Directed Da'wa in Contemporary Aceh," *Islamic Law and Society* 19 (2012): 275–311, 278. See also R. Michael Feener, *Shari'a and Social Engineering: The Implementation of Islamic Law in Contemporary Aceh, Indonesia* (Oxford: Oxford University Press, 2013).

establishment of a state religion, simultaneously allows sub-national units to grant additional jurisdiction to their local courts, leading to a significant expansion in the jurisdiction claimed by shari'a courts.[123] As a result, the shari'a has been instituted as a main body of civil and criminal law in nine Muslim-majority states and in some parts of three Muslim-plurality states since 1999.

VI. Conclusion

As constitutional texts have emerged as battlegrounds over the distribution of authority and the role of Islam in Muslim-majority societies, scholarly interest in the intellectual history and historical development of these documents has intensified. The study of the intersection of Islamic law and constitutionalism was initially richer in its focus on broad intellectual themes but is increasingly showing signs of focus on actual practice. This is the outcome of two processes: a growing tendency among scholars of Islamic law toward an extension of their analysis to political and social developments in Muslim-majority societies that were once considered beyond the scope of their field, and heightened interest in the subject from an increasingly wide array of disciplines and methodological approaches. And it might also be said that Lombardi's suggestion that scholars take non-*ulama* or "lay Islamist" actors seriously as interpreters and transmitters of Islamic law is gradually winning out.[124] Scholars concerned with the relationship between the shari'a and constitutions are increasingly expanding their focus to include a wide variety of institutions and actors—particularly Islamic legal professionals and lawyers[125]—whose understandings of Islamic law are competing with those of the clerical elite in an environment of unprecedented intellectual pluralism, in which historical monopolies on interpretive authority are gradually eroding.

The tasks for scholarship in the coming years will be threefold.

First, those writing from different disciplines will have to strive to draw on (and fertilize) each others' work; the time for textual analyses of laws that ignore political context and history or for political understandings that ignore debates among

[123] Feener, *Shari'a and Social Engineering*, 32.

[124] Clark Lombardi, "The Challenges and Opportunities of Islamic Review: Lessons for Afghanistan from the Experiences of other Muslim Countries," USIP Position Paper, Conference on the Afghan Constitution, September 2011 (Kabul, Afghanistan), 14. See also Clark Lombardi, "Can Islamizing a Legal System Ever Help Promote Liberal Democracy?: A View from Pakistan," *University of St. Thomas Law Journal* 7, no. 3 (2010): 649–691, 658.

[125] Clark Lombardi and Michael Feener, "Why Study Islamic Legal Professionals?" *Pacific Rim Law & Policy Journal* 21, no. 1 (January 2012): 1–12.

rival religious, ideological, and intellectual visions is past. Increasingly those from different disciplinary perspectives are asking similar questions, but they often seem to be carrying out their discussions in isolation from each other.

Second, the sharply limited geographical focus of past scholarship needs to be widened to encompass a far more varied array of experiences than has previously been noted in much work. Attention has focussed on a small number of cases, many of them centered broadly in the Middle East and neighboring regions. This is understandable, since these cases (Egypt, Iran, and Pakistan, for instance) have drawn a disproportionate share of the attention in the Muslim world. But very significant cases (such as Malaysia and Indonesia) as well as the influence of constitutional thought in Muslim-minority societies (such as India and Europe) needs to be more fully integrated within scholarly understandings.

Third, the increasingly transnational aspects of the issue—in which debates and even clauses migrate across national borders—should be a fruitful avenue of inquiry. Scholars of constitutional law more generally have noted a significant internationalization of what had appeared to earlier generations to be primarily a national experience. The same may be taking place within the Muslim world with the development of a transnational set of Islamic approaches to constitutional questions. In a sense, this trend has always been visible since the beginning of the experience with written constitutions in the nineteenth century, but it is only now beginning to receive full attention as a transnational phenomenon.

References

'Awda, 'Abd al-Qadir, *Al-islam wa-awda'na al-qanuniyya* [Islam and Our Legal Situation] (Beirut: Mu'assasat al-Risala, 1951, reprint 1985).

Abootalebi, Ali Rez, *Islam and Democracy: State–Society Relations in Developing Countries, 1980–1994* (New York: Garland Publishing, 2000).

Abou El Fadl, Khaled, *The Place of Tolerance in Islam* (Boston: Beacon Press, 2002).

Abou El Fadl, Khaled, *Islam and the Challenge of Democracy* (Princeton: Princeton University Press, 2004).

Abrahamian, Ervand, *Iran: Between Two Revolutions* (Princeton: Princeton University Press, 1982).

Abu al-Majd, Ahmad Kamal, "Nazarat hawla al-Fiqh al-Dusturi fi al-Islam" [A View Concerning Constitutional Jurisprudence in Islam], lecture delivered January 9, 1962 (Cairo: Matba'at al-Azhar).

Abu-Odeh, Lama, "The Politics of (Mis)recognition: Islamic Law Pedagogy in American Academia." *The American Journal of Comparative Law* 52, no. 4 (Autumn 2004): 789–824.

Agrama, Hussein Ali, *Questioning Secularism: Islam, Sovereignty, and the Rule of Law in Modern Egypt* (Chicago: University of Chicago Press, 2012).

Algar, Hamid, *Religion and the State in Iran 1785–1906: The Role of the 'Ulama in the Qajar Period* (Berkeley: University of California Press, 1969).

An-Na'im, Adullahi, *Islam and the Secular State: Negotiating the Future of Shari'a*, (Cambridge, MA: Harvard University Press, 1998).

Arjomand, Said, "The 'ulama's Traditionalist Opposition to Parliamentarianism: 1907–1909." *Middle Eastern Studies* 17, no. 2 (1981): 174–190.

Arjomand, Said, *The Turban for the Crown: The Islamic Revolution in Iran* (Oxford: Oxford University Press, 1988).

Arjomand, Said, *Constitutionalism and Political Reconstruction* (Leiden: Brill, 2007).

Arjomand, Said, *After Khomeini: Iran Under His Successors* (Oxford: Oxford University Press, 2009).

Bayat, Aasef, *Making Islam Democratic: Social Movements and the Post-Islamist Turn* (Stanford: Stanford University Press, 2007).

Bayat, Mongol, *Iran's First Revolution: Shi'ism and the Constitutional Revolution of 1905—1909* (New York: Oxford University Press, 1991).

Bennoune, Karima, "Remembering the Other's Others: Theorizing the Approach of International Law to Muslim Fundamentalism." *Columbia Human Rights Law Review* 41 (2010): 663–665.

Bishara, Azmi, "Madkhal li-Mu'alajat al-Demoqratiyya wu-Anmat at-Tadayyun" [Introduction to Democracy and Modes of Religiosity] in Burhan Ghalyun et al., (eds.) *Hawla al-Khiyar al-Demoqrati* [On the Democratic Alternative] (Ramallah: Muwatin, 1993).

Breslin, Beau, *From Words to Worlds: Exploring Constitutional Functionality* (Baltimore: Johns Hopkins University Press, 2009).

Brown, Carl, "Introduction." In *The Surest Path: The Political Treatise of a Nineteenth-Century Muslim Statesman* (Cambridge, MA: Harvard University Press, 1967).

Brown, Nathan, *Constitutions in a Non-Constitutional World: Arab Basic Laws and the Prospects for Accountable Government* (Albany: SUNY Press, 2002).

Brown, Nathan, "Islam and Constitutionalism in the Arab World: A Puzzling End to Islamic Inflation." Constitutional Transitions Colloquium, New York University, 2012.

Brown, Nathan and Lombardi, Clark, "Do Constitutions Requiring Adherence to Shari'a Threaten Human Rights? How Egypt's Constitutional Court Reconciles Islamic Law with the Liberal Rule of Law." *American University International Law Review* 21 (2006): 379–435.

Brown, Nathan and Sherif, Adel Omar, "Inscribing the Shari'a in Arab Constitutional Law" in Yvonne Yazbeck Haddad and Barbara Freyer Stowasser (eds.) *Islamic Law and the Challenges of Modernity* (Walnut Creek: AltaMira Press, 1994) 55–80.

Coulson, Noel, *History of Islamic Law* (Edinburgh: University of Edinburgh Press, 1964).

Devereux, Robert, *The First Ottoman Constitutional Period: A Study of the Midhat Constitution and Parliament* (Baltimore: Johns Hopkins University Press, 1964).

Emon, Anver, "Reflections on the Constitution of Medina." *UCLA Journal, of Islamic and Near Eastern Law* 1 (2001–02): 103–133.

Emon, Anver, *Islamic Natural Law Theories* (Oxford: Oxford University Press, 2008).

Esposito, John, "Pakistan: Quest for Islamic Identity" in John L. Esposito (ed.) *Islam and Development* (Syracuse, NY: Syracuse University Press, 1980) 139–162.

Esposito, John and Voll, John, *Islam and Democracy* (Oxford and New York: Oxford University Press, 1996).

Feener, R. Michael, "Social Engineering through Shari'a: Islamic Law and State-Directed Da'wa in Contemporary Aceh." *Islamic Law and Society* 19 (2012): 275–311.
Feldman, Noah, *The Fall and Rise of the Islamic State* (Oxford: Oxford University Press, 2008).
Feldman, Noah, *The Fall and Rise of the Islamic State* (Princeton: Princeton University Press, 2012).
Felicitas, Opwis, "Maslaha in Contemporary Islamic Legal Theory." *Islamic Law and Society* 2, no. 2 (2005): 182–223.
Gerber, Haim, *Islamic Law and Culture, 1600–1840* (Boston: Brill, 1999).
Gerber, Haim, "The Public Sphere and Civil Society in the Ottoman Empire" in Miriam Hoexter, Shmuel N. Eisenstadt, and Nehemia Levtzion (eds.) *The Public Sphere in Muslim Societies* (Albany: SUNY Press, 2002) 65–82.
Ghannouchi, Rachid, *Muqarabat fi al-'Ilmaniyya wa al-Mujatama' al-Madani* [Approaches to Secularism and Civil Society] (London: al-Markaz al-Magharibi lil-buhuth wa al-tarjamah, 1999).
Grote, Rainer and Röder, Tilmann, *Constitutionalism in Islamic Countries: Between Upheaval and Continuity* (New York: Oxford University Press, 2011).
Hairi, A., *Shi'ism and Constitutionalism in Iran* (Leiden: Brill, 1977).
Hallaq, Wael, "Can the Shari'a Be Restored?" in Yvonne Yazbeck Haddad and Barbara Freyer Stowasser (eds.) *Islamic Law and the Challenges of Modernity* (Walnut Creek: AltaMira Press, 1994) 21–54.
Hallaq, Wael, *The Origins and Evolution of Islamic Law* (Cambridge: Cambridge University Press, 2005).
Hallaq, Wael, *The Impossible State: Islam, Politics, and Modernity's Moral Predicament* (New York: Columbia University Press, 2012).
Hamoudi, Haider, "Thinking Beyond the Original Bargain: Post Ratification Constitution Making and the Case of Iraq." APSA 2012 Annual Meeting Paper, University of Pittsburgh Legal Studies Research Paper No. 2012–26, 2012.
Haykel, Bernard, *Revival and Reform in Islam: The Legacy of Muhammad al-Shawkani* (Cambridge: Cambridge University Press, 2003).
Haykel, Bernard, "On the Nature of Salafi Thought and Action" in Roel Meijer (ed.) *Global Salafism: Islam's New Religious Movement* (London: Hurst, 2009) 33–57.
Hefner, Robert, *Sharia Politics: Islamic Law and Society in the Modern World* (Indiana: Indiana University Press, 2011).
Hirschl, Ran, *Constitutional Theocracy* (Cambridge: Cambridge University Press, 2010).
Hodgson, Marshall, *The Venture of Islam, Volume 1: The Classical Age of Islam* (Chicago: University of Chicago Press, 1974).
Hourani, Albert, *Arabic Thought in the Liberal Age 1798–1939* (Cambridge: Cambridge University Press, 1983).
"Introduction" in Yvonne Yazbeck Haddad and Barbara Freyer Stowasser (eds.) *Islamic Law and the Challenges of Modernity* (Walnut Creek, CA: Altamira, 2004) 1–20.
Iqbal, Afzal, *Islamization of Pakistan* (Lahore: Vanguard, 1986).
Jackson, Sherman, *Islamic Law and the State: The Constitutional Jurisprudence of Shihab Al-Din Al-Qarafi* (Leiden: Brill, 1996).
Johansen, Baber, *Contingency in a Sacred Law: Legal and Ethical Norms in the Muslim Fiqh* (Leiden: Brill, 1999).
Lapidus, Ira, *A History of Islamic Societies* (Cambridge: Cambridge University Press, 2002).
Lau, Martin, *The Role of Islam in the Legal System of Pakistan* (Leiden: Brill, 2006).

Lombardi, Clark, *State Law as Islamic Law in Modern Egypt: The Incorporation of Shari'a Into Egyptian Constitutional Law* (Leiden: Brill, 2006).

Lombardi, Clark, "Can Islamizing a Legal System Ever Help Promote Liberal Democracy?: A View from Pakistan." *University of St. Thomas Law Journal* 7, no. 3 (2010): 649–691.

Lombardi, Clark, "The Challenges and Opportunities of Islamic Review: Lessons for Afghanistan from the Experiences of other Muslim Countries." USIP Position Paper, 2012.

Lombardi, Clark and Feener, R. Michael, "Why Study Islamic Legal Professionals?" *Pacific Rim Law & Policy Journal* 21, no. 1 (2012): 1–12.

Mallat, Chibli, *The Renewal of Islamic Law: Muahmmad Baqer al-Sadr, Najaf and the Shi'i International* (London: Cambridge University Press, 1993).

March, Andrew, "Reading Tariq Ramadan: Political Liberalism, Islam, and 'Overlapping Consensus.'" *Ethics and International Affairs* 21, no. 4 (2007): 399–413.

March, Andrew, "Theocrats Living under Secular Law: An External Engagement with Islamic Legal Theory." *Journal of Political Philosophy* 19, no. 1 (2009): 28–51.

Mayer, Andrew, "Conundrums in Constitutionalism: Islamic Monarchies in an Era of Transition." *UCLA Journal of Islamic & Near Eastern Law* 1 (Spring/Summer, 2002): 183–228.

Mehdi, Rubiya, *The Islamization of the Law in Pakistan* (Richmond, Va.: Curzon Press, 1994).

Moustafa, Tamir, *The Struggle for Constitutional Power: Law, Politics, and Economics* (Cambridge: Cambridge University Press, 2007).

Naini, Muhammad, *An Admonition to the Nation and an Exposition to the People* (Najaf, 1909).

Opwis, Felicitas, "Maslaha in Contemporary Islamic Legal Theory." *Islamic Law and Society* 12, no. 2 (2005): 182–223.

Otto, Jon, *Shari'a Incorporated: A Comparative Overview of the Legal Systems of Twelve Muslim Countries in Past and Present* (Leiden: Leiden University Press Academic, 2010).

Ramadan, Tariq, *To Be a European Muslim* (Leicester, UK: Islamic Foundation, 1999).

Rane, Halim, *Islam and Contemporary Civilization: Evolving Ideas, Transforming Relations* (Melbourne: Melbourne University Press, 2010).

Roy, Olivier, *The Failure of Political Islam* Translated by Carol Volk (Cambridge, MA: Harvard University Press, 1994).

Rutherford, Bruce, *Egypt After Mubarak: Liberalism, Islam and Democracy in the Arab World* (Princeton: Princeton University Press, 2008).

Salim, Arskal, *Challenging the Secular State: The Islamization of Law in Modern Indonesia* (Honolulu: University of Hawaii Press, 2008).

Saroush, Abdolkarim, *Essential Writings of Abdolkarim Sorouh.* Edited and translated by Mahmoud Sadri and Ahmad Sadri (New York: Oxford University Press, 2000).

Schacht, Joseph, *Introduction of Islamic Law* (Oxford: Clarendon Press, 1964).

Schirazi, Asghar, *The Constitution of Iran: Politics and the State in the Islamic Republic.* Translated by John O'Kane (New York: I.B. Tauris, 1997).

Shah, Niaz, *Women, the Koran and International Human Rights Law: The Experience of Pakistan* (Leiden: Martinus Nijhoff Publishers, 2006).

Shirazi, Asghar, *The Constitution of Iran: Politics and the State in the Islamic Republic* (New York: I.B. Taurus, 1998).

Sohrabi, Nader, *Revolution and Constitutionalism in the Ottoman Empire and Iran* (Cambridge: Cambridge University Press, 2011).

Stahnke, Tad and Blitt, Robert, "The Religion-State Relationship and the Right to Freedom of Religion or Belief." United States Commission on Religious Freedom (March 2005).

Stilt, Kristen, *Islamic Law in Action: Authority, Discretion, and Everyday Experiences in Mamluk Egypt* (Oxford: Oxford University Press, 2011).
Stilt, Kristen, "Contextualizing constitutional Islam: The Malayan experience." *International Journal of Constitutional Law* 13(2) (2015): 407–433.
Strawson, John, "Islamic Law and English Texts" in Eve Darian-Smith and Peter Fitzpatrick (eds.) *Laws of the Postcolonial* (Michigan: University of Michigan Press, 1999) 109–126.
Talmon, Stefan, *The Official Documents of the Coalition Provisional Authority and the Iraqi Governing Council* (London: Bloomsbury Publishing, 2013).
Vogel, Frank, *Islamic Law and Legal System: Studies of Saudi Arabia* (Leiden: Brill, 2010).
Von Grunebaum, G.E., *Islam: Essays in the Nature and Growth of a Cultural Tradition* (London: Routledge and Kegan Paul, 1955).
Weiss, Bernard, *The Spirit of Islamic Law* (Georgia: University of Georgia Press, 2006).
Wright, Robin, *Dreams and Shadows: The Future of the Middle East* (New York: Knopf, 2000).
Zaidi, Syed, *The Emergence of Ulema in the Politics of India and Pakistan 1918–1949* (Bloomington, IN: iUniverse, 2003).
Zaman, Muhammad, *The 'Ulama in Contemporary Islam: Custodians of Change* (Princeton: Princeton University Press, 2002).

CHAPTER 32

ISLAMIC LAW AND HUMAN RIGHTS

SHANNON DUNN

THE question of whether Islam and universal human rights are compatible has been posed frequently by scholars in the late twentieth and early twenty-first centuries.[1] Some scholars and political activists view these traditions as fundamentally incompatible, arguing that Islam represents a premodern legal framework, on the one hand, and universal human rights represents a modern legal framework, on the other. Other skeptics view "human rights" as a western colonial invention used to oppress Muslims by making them conform to certain western norms. Yet others esteem the Islamic tradition as the highest manifestation of human rights, and engage in apologetic explanations of the human rights components of the classical tradition.

In order to better comprehend the genesis and diversity of scholarship associated with this topic, this chapter examines post-Second World War human rights discourse and Muslim responses in a way that contextualizes the specific areas of conflict and agreement. Historically, many Muslims have adopted the human rights discourse of inviolability to advocate for religious freedom and gender equality, while others, particularly Muslim religious and political elites, have used the human rights discourse of dignity to argue for religious exclusivism and respect for patriarchal norms. These disagreements have illumined the legacy of the modern western rights tradition

[1] The number of scholars and written projects that address this topic is too numerous to list comprehensively here, although I will address several works over the course of this chapter.

for universal human rights discourse, and highlighted unresolved questions about western power and political influence in a postcolonial context. These tensions are reflected in particular declarations and treatises that address human rights from an Islamic perspective, and in scholarship that deals with this topic.

Throughout the chapter, I identify four basic paradigms in scholarship on Islam and human rights: (1) a model that privileges a secular (non-religious) paradigm for rights; (2) a Muslim apologist model, which privileges a purely "Islamic" conception of rights over secular models; (3) a Marxist/postcolonial critique of rights as a western imposition of power; and (4) a Muslim reformist paradigm of rights that highlights points of continuity between western legal and Muslim legal traditions. These four descriptions are not exhaustive, and some thinkers and groups may fit more than one description. Overall, these categories are useful ways of thinking about persistent trends in the discourse of human rights and Islam.

I. Human Rights

The economic and political international turmoil that culminated in two world wars led to the founding in 1945 of the United Nations (UN) in San Francisco and the ensuing Charter of the United Nations. The adoption of the Universal Declaration of Human Rights (UDHR) in 1948 responded to the need to articulate a set of moral and legal criteria that could affirm the dignity and inviolability of the human person. The atrocities of fascism and Nazism, specifically the Holocaust, provided the immediate context for such a document. Johannes Morsink explained how various articles of the Declaration were drafted specifically in reaction to Nazi practices and legal policies. For example, Articles 6 through 12 of the UDHR treated legal human rights, which recognized that leading up to and during the war, German law had been thoroughly Nazified. Some of the representatives, notably the delegate from Lebanon, worried that "law" could be distorted to justify any practice of the state.[2] The idea that law could be exploited as a legitimizing vehicle for power would continue to be a concern especially for postcolonial critics of western hegemony into the twenty-first century.

The need to protect individuals from racist discrimination, whether it was directly enforced or tacitly supported by the state, extended beyond the European context. Legalized racial segregation proliferated in both mid-twentieth-century

[2] Johannes Morsink, *The Universal Declaration of Human Rights: Origins, Drafting, and Intent* (Philadelphia: University of Pennsylvania Press, 1999).

Southern United States and South Africa, for example. Member parties of the United Nations shared a commitment to enumerating an individual's rights both within and, if necessary, against the state. The drafting process of the Declaration (1946–48) coincided with the breakup of colonial empires, and representatives from former colonies raised questions about how best to apply human rights to members of then-present or former colonial territories.

The creation of the UDHR stands out as a watershed moment in western conceptions of rights, mainly because of its international character as a response to atrocities carried out on a massive scale. The Declaration represents a departure from a European model of political rights held by persons by virtue of their citizenship in a specific territory or country. Anthony Pagden argued that this understanding of the rights of man, popular during European colonial expansion, "became increasingly useless as a notion in international or intercultural relations."[3] Thus, Pagden argued, John Stuart Mill could only speak with confidence of "rights" within a "civilization." The events of the Second World War, as well as the disintegration of European empires, led to the discrediting of this view of rights. A distinguishing feature of the UDHR was its emphasis on, and appeal to, individual agency independent from the individual's political community.

The political organization of the modern state has remained central to the protection of international human rights. The norm of state sovereignty meant that the state was not obligated to protect the same human rights of foreigners, for example. Donnelly explained that this view of human rights has strong roots in liberal social contract theory, and that the modern sovereign state paradoxically poses both the greatest threat to human rights as well as the greatest potential for the effective implementation of rights.[4] The question of how strongly to identify the UDHR as a product of the western rights tradition, and the implications of this identification for the inclusion of non-European and non-secular nations and other groups, is in many ways an unresolved one.

Prior to 1948, there were seven drafting stages to the document. The process of achieving an international consensus was important for the legitimacy of the UDHR. Scholars in the early twenty-first century have made an effort to better understand Islamic voices in the drafting of the Declaration. Delegates from Muslim majority states participated in, and actively supported the creation of the UDHR. As Irene Oh observed, however, this does not mean that the language of human rights in this document and in other related international treatises represented accurately the views of all Muslims.[5] The presence and geopolitical power of some

[3] Anthony Pagden, "Human Rights, Natural Rights, and Europe's Imperial Legacy," *Political Theory* 31, no. 2 (April 2003): 190.

[4] Jack Donnelly, *Universal Human Rights in Theory and Practice* (Ithaca, NY: Cornell University Press, 2003).

[5] Irene Oh, "Islamic Voices and the Definition of Human Rights," *Journal of Church and State* 53, no. 3 (2010): 376–400.

states over others undoubtedly had an influence on the drafting of the document. Representatives from Muslim majority states faced the difficult task of reconciling the idea that their former colonizers were now the "vanguards of an ideological revolution purporting to assert the equal dignity of all humans."[6]

Susan Waltz documented the participation of Muslim states in the creation of not only the UDHR, but all three entities comprising the International Bill of Human Rights.[7] (As a declaration, the UDHR does not have legally binding power, as opposed to a signed covenant.) In 1966, two covenants were adopted: the International Covenant on Civil and Political Rights (ICCPR) and the International Covenant on Economic, Social, and Cultural Rights (ICESCR). In her survey of UN records during the period from 1946–66, Waltz identified five central issues of focus for delegates who identified themselves and their countries with the Islamic tradition: religious freedom and the right to change religion; gender equality in marriage; social justice and the indivisibility of rights; the right to self-determination; and measures of implementation. Saudi Arabia's abstention from the UN General Assembly's vote to approve the UDHR is well-known. The Saudi delegate to the UN, Jamil Baroody, was actively involved in the twenty-year process which culminated in the passing of the two covenants. His refusal to vote in favor of the UDHR had more to do with disagreement on issues involving gender equality in marriage and religious freedom (the subjects of Articles 16 and 18, respectively) than with any disagreement about the project of human rights per se.

Article 16 of the Declaration states that marriage must be entered into with the full consent of both parties; that men and women must be of "full age"; and that men and women are entitled to equal rights during marriage and at its dissolution. Baroody submitted an amendment that had two concerns, related to the full age requirement and to the requirement of equal rights during marriage and at its end. In the end, however, "both elements of the Saudi amendment failed by a large majority, that necessarily included several delegations from Muslim states."[8] Regarding Article 18, which states that all persons have the right to freedom of thought, conscience, and religion, Baroody also raised an objection. Specifically, he did not accept the language regarding the right of persons to change religion or belief and wanted to omit it from the article.

The question of universal human rights and their relationship to Islamic principles and legal and moral traditions did not disappear after the adoption of the UDHR and the two covenants. Political leaders and visionaries from Muslim majority countries and from within minority contexts continued to think about the distinctive contributions of the Islamic tradition to human rights discourse. As

[6] Oh, "Islamic Voices," 381.

[7] Susan Waltz, "Universal Human Rights: The Contribution of Muslim States," *Human Rights Quarterly* 26 (2004): 799–844.

[8] Waltz, "Universal Human Rights," 821.

geopolitical conflicts unfolded in a postcolonial and globalized world, such leaders and visionaries had ample opportunity to articulate them.

II. Islamic Human Rights Declarations and Muslim Apologetics

The drafting and reception of international human rights documents should be placed in their respective geopolitical contexts. Ann Elizabeth Mayer argued that many majority Muslim countries viewed western legal systems and the enterprise of universal human rights with more skepticism after the Arab–Israeli war of 1967.[9] Prior to the war, many Muslim leaders were keenly aware of power imbalances between western countries and the Muslim majority. This event served as a major catalyst not only because it consolidated a critique of western military hegemony, but also insofar as it occasioned an internal critique of secular pan-Arab movements.

In the period following 1948, external human rights organizations such as Amnesty International were critical of the ways that some Muslim majority countries were not in compliance with certain provisions of the UDHR. As a declaration, the UDHR was not intended to have legally binding force, and many of its goals were understood as aspirational. This factor was significant for the appropriation and adaptation of human rights discourse in Muslim contexts for two reasons. First, non-compliance with certain provisions of the Declaration could not be legally punished. Second, the format of the Declaration provided room for Muslim states to engage in their own formulations of human rights—both as a form of resistance to western hegemony and as a constructive assertion of Islamic values. Thus it is useful to examine specific Islamic political bodies and human rights documents and their relation to the broader international human rights sphere, as well as some critical assessments of them.

The 1972 Charter of the Organization of the Islamic Conference (OIC) affirmed the legitimacy of international law and human rights. The OIC is comprised of fifty-seven member states, and in 1990 the organization signed the Cairo Declaration of Human Rights (CDHR). The Cairo Declaration bears some resemblance, in form and content, to the UDHR. The central difference is that it draws upon specific Islamic teachings and sources—for example, Qur'an, hadith—in its formulation of human rights. In contrast to the UDHR, the opening paragraph of the document

9 Ann Elizabeth Mayer, *Islam and Human Rights: Tradition and Politics* (Boulder, CO: Westview Press, 1999).

stipulates a different foundation for human rights: the narrative of the Islamic Umma as having a "civilizing and historical role" as a model for all of humanity. The document goes on to state that Islam is the basis for fundamental human rights and freedoms, because it is based upon teachings of justice and freedom found in the Qur'an and in the shari'a.

The Cairo Declaration reiterated some of the dissenting arguments given by some delegates of Muslim majority countries in the drafting of the UDHR. Specifically, the document expressed notable disagreements with the UDHR in articles dealing with gender, the family, religious freedom, and importantly, self-determination. Regarding gender and the family, Article 5 of the Cairo Declaration maintains that men and women have a right to marriage "with no restrictions stemming from race, color, or nationality." Absent from these categories is religion, which is included in UDHR Article 16. In Article 6 of the Cairo Declaration, it is stated that although women and men are equal in human dignity, each gender has distinct rights and duties to perform (consonant with the classical Islamic legal tradition).

The authors of the Cairo Declaration grounded their conception of human rights in the shari'a: shari'a is mentioned throughout the entire document as the most authoritative source of law, and Article 24 maintains that all enumerated rights and freedoms are subject to the shari'a. Article 25 states, "The Islamic Shari'a is the only source of reference for the explanation of clarification of any of the articles of this Declaration." This statement is interesting for several reasons. First, it presupposes agreement on what shari'a entails, as if it referred to a self-contained and coherent body of law that could be consulted and applied by anyone anywhere, without the help of a jurist or other legal specialist. Second, there is an assumption of legal relativism: every culture is allowed their own declaration of rights according to their traditions and sacred sources. Third, the framing of the document in this way serves as a cogent reminder that human rights frameworks, whether Islamic or secular, are hardly devoid of philosophical or theological arguments about the human person, her purpose, and her relationship with her community. This last point is not to suggest, however, that international consensus on rights is useless or meaningless. Rather it means that particular human rights documents come into being in different geopolitical conditions, drawing upon distinct theological and/or philosophical sources. The Cairo Declaration also addressed slavery in relation to colonialism, which the UDHR does not do. Both documents forbid slavery; but the Cairo Declaration, Article 11, elaborates: "Colonialism of all types being one of the worst forms of enslavement is totally prohibited." This matter comes under the umbrella of the right to self-determination, which was a part of the International Bill of Rights.[10] It is interesting, however, that under the influence of Islamist arguments,

[10] The conflict in Israel/Palestine likely influenced the development of this argument. It is notable that whereas Hamas initially was secular in framework, Israel's military, economic, and social oppression of Palestinians encouraged the organization to adopt a more religious (Islamist) ideology.

self-determination also became about the identification of Islam with a certain kind of political project involving the revival of a conservative and even reactionary form of Islamic governance.

The London-based Islamic Council issued the Universal Islamic Declaration of Human Rights in 1981. Islamist groups largely represented those at the Council, and many of the representatives were engaged in political opposition to repressive Muslim regimes. The document stressed the political rights of Islamic dissidents vis-à-vis the state, and it posited the shari'a as an alternative to the UDHR. Muhammad Khalid Masud argued that the Cairo Declaration was drafted in part as a response to the UDHR, although both documents differed substantially with the UDHR on matters of religious freedom, penal laws, marriage, and holding public office.[11]

The formulation of Islamic human rights documents, modeled on the design of the UDHR in the latter half of the twentieth century indicates a desire of Islamist leaders to participate in international human rights discourse, but to do so in a distinctive way that could give voice to what Falk (1997) called "serious grievances" within the global Islamic community. The areas of grievance pertain to European colonization of traditionally Muslim lands, and the ensuing imposition of European legal structures; the impact of European law on Muslim family law; and the European Christian missionaries who converted, or attempted to convert, Muslims. In the postcolonial period, the disenfranchisement of Muslims related to participation in the development of international human rights—a disenfranchisement resulting from western political and economic hegemony, combined with negative media portrayals of Islam in western countries. Falk argued that statist identity has failed many Muslims, and that an acceptable alternative would be a human rights discourse that recognized "civilizational identity," although it is not clear how this model would operate.

Both the Cairo Declaration and the UIDHR employed apologetic language, insofar as "Islam" was portrayed as the pinnacle of human civilization and as the originator of universal human rights discourse. Among exponents of the idea that Islam invented human rights is the twentieth-century Islamist thinker Abul A'la Mawdudi. Mawdudi was the founder of Jama'at-i-Islami and an influential voice in the articulation of twentieth-century political Islam. He conceived of the Islamic state's legitimacy as resting on the sovereignty of God instead of the will of the people, and this conception has been adapted by Islamist political ideologues ranging from Sayyid Qutb to Ayatollah Khomeini.

In his discussion of "Basic Human Rights," he asserted that Islam alone gave equal rights to all human beings, regardless of race or nation. The only basis for difference among human beings, Mawdudi argued, was piety or "God-consciousness."[12]

[11] Muhammad Khalid Masud, "Clearing Ground: Commentary to 'Shari'a and the Modern State,'" in *Islamic Law and International Human Rights Law: Searching for Common Ground?* ed. Emon et al. (New York: Oxford University Press, 2012), 104–114.

[12] Abu A'la Mawdudi, *Human Rights in Islam* (London: The Islamic Foundation, 1976).

Mawdudi saw fit to list contradictions that inhere in the western human rights tradition, such as the legality of the Atlantic slave trade that went on for several hundred years. He also discussed the difference between general international human rights, and the rights of citizens in an Islamic state, which he claimed were more extensive. In the chapter, "Human Rights in the Islamic State," Mawdudi advanced claims for the superiority of Islamic conceptions of certain rights, such as freedom of expression, over conceptions in the western tradition. Mawdudi argued that the qualitative difference lies in the refusal of Islam to "propagate evil and wickedness," which he ties to the Islamic duty of commanding right and forbidding wrong.[13] The government must not prevent people from performing this duty, which is distinct from the right to freedom of expression found in UDHR Article 19, for example. Mawdudi maintained, however, that in an Islamic state people should abide by the Qur'anic injunction in 2:256: "There should be no coercion in the matter of faith." Individual religious choices are to be respected, and Islam does not sanction abusive language toward people of other faiths. This claim for tolerance is important to consider, as Mawdudi made an interpretive choice with this verse over other Qur'anic verses that would limit the rights of non-Muslims in the area of religious freedom.[14]

III. Critics of Muslim Apologetics in Human Rights Discourse

Several scholars have found wanting the claims of Mawdudi and other Muslim apologists in the area of Islamic human rights. Mayer's *Islam and Human Rights: Tradition and Politics* addressed the way in which Islamic human rights schemes have been used to defend a particular conception of "Islam" against the corrupt and hegemonic "West." Islamist ideology that espouses this binary tends to contribute to the erasure of human rights rather than their maintenance. Mayer contended that the major difference between the two is that Islamic human rights schemes are formulated on the basis of revealed texts, the Qur'an and Prophetic hadith, while western human rights schemes are based on rationalism and individualism. Her normative claim was that Western Enlightenment philosophy is more coherent in terms of providing a foundation for human rights.

[13] Mawdudi, *Human Rights in Islam*, 31.

[14] e.g. some Islamist militant interpreters have drawn from Qur'an 9:1–35, a series of verses that enjoin Muslims to fight against "idolaters" and also the People of the Book, to legitimize their militant action against non-Muslims.

Mayer identified as a key issue the rights of the individual vis-à-vis the state. The ideal of an Islamic state, in which leaders govern by Islamic law and order public life to reflect that system, gained some popularity in the twentieth century among political Islamists and in a relative few cases, it led to the founding of religious states (the Islamic Republic of Iran serves as a prominent example). Much of the rhetoric around the conception of an Islamic state reflected a kind of utopian idealism, premised on a seamless harmony between the individual's rights and the community's rights, as characteristic of an Islamic system of governance. According to Mayer, most apologetic Muslim rights theorists who were invested in a conception of the Islamic state, such as Mawdudi, failed to grasp the potential of the state to violate individual human rights. Mayer attributed this failure to an inability to be critical of the deficiencies of religious belief.

On the one hand, Mayer's critique has been validated by the failure of many Muslim majority countries to protect their citizens equally, due to an unrealistic view of an Islamic system as a panacea to all types of political corruption and oppression. On the other hand, Mayer's account should be placed within the context of secular rights theories that dismiss "religion" as a source for ideas about human rights. Her targeting of religion as opposed to human rights may be misplaced, insofar as the issue is not the inherent deficiency of religious legal systems and ideas, but rather the dangers of political and religious authoritarianism.

Other criticisms of Islamist human rights schemes come from voices within the Islamic tradition. Some accounts focus on the way that apologists have used a separate scheme of Islamic human rights to disguise or perpetuate abuses. Regarding the implementation of the Cairo Declaration in Muslim majority countries, Abdullah al-Ahsan argues that some leaders using "Shari'a law" have ignored the high human rights standards that he thinks the shari'a imposes upon Muslim rulers, such as refraining from torturing political enemies.[15]

In order to address this problem, some Islamic legal scholars make a sharp distinction between shari'a as an ideal versus shari'a as a codified system of law. Abdullahi An-Na'im's work distinguishes between shari'a as (1) the basis for religious identity and spirituality and (2) as a program for social and moral reform enforced by the state. In *Islam and the Secular State* (2008), he maintained that the codification of shari'a by the modern state has often historically resulted in human rights violations. Muslims are bound by religious obligation to observe the shari'a, and they are best able to do so when the state remains neutral regarding religious doctrine. "The diversity of Shari'a principles means that whatever is enacted and enforced by the state is the political will of the ruling elite, not the normative system of Islam as such. Yet such policies and legislation are difficult to resist or

[15] Abdullah Ahsan, "Law, Religion, and Human Dignity in the Muslim World Today: An Examination of OIC's Cairo Declaration of Human Rights," *Journal of Law and Religion* 24, no. 2 (2008–09): 569–597.

even debate when presented as the will of God."[16] In order to support this argument, An-Na'im cites an example from early Islamic history of the failure of *al-Mihna* (the Inquisition), in which political leaders attempted to force a particular religious doctrine about the createdness of the Qur'an on the ulema and ultimately failed. This example provides a warning against the totalitarian aspirations of some Islamists for the complete unity of state power and Islamic belief.

Significantly, An-Na'im argued that there was no fundamental difference between western traditions of separation of church and state, on the one hand, and the separation of politics and shari'a, on the other. This idea might strike many Islamists, who understand the secular West's moral depravity to originate precisely from its marginalization of religion from politics and other aspects of public life, as "un-Islamic." His argument does not advocate for the privatization of religion as such, but rather for Muslims to understand their religious convictions in ways that are not automatically adversarial toward, or intolerant of other's beliefs and traditions. This argument carries important implications for the protection of religious minorities' human rights, a point about which these Islamic human rights documents are largely silent.

Some Muslim scholars attribute the underlying reasons for discord between human rights and Islam to specific historical dynamics involving western dominance and the destruction of traditional Muslim authorities in the colonial and postcolonial period. Khaled Abou El Fadl has argued that this has resulted in the "systematic undermining and devaluing of the humanistic tradition in Islam."[17] In an attempt to chart a different path for Islamic human rights discourse, Abou El Fadl encouraged the reform of Islamic doctrines and the rethinking of certain theological traditions, particularly theological–political traditions that place a conception of God's sovereignty as prior to human rights. He argued that the interpretive component in Islamic theological and legal traditions offered a way for Muslims to transition from adhering to premodern views that privilege God's rights to a modern paradigm that privileges human rights.

A. *Maslaha* and *Maqasid al-Shari'a*

Other Muslim legal scholars have charged scholars like Abou El Fadl and An-Na'im as being too conciliatory toward western normative legal traditions in their constructions of human rights. Mashood Baderin, in *International Human Rights and Islamic Law*, argued for the necessity of the Islamic principle of *maslaha* for

[16] Abdullahi An-Na'im, *Islam and the Secular State: Negotiating the Future of Shari'a* (Cambridge, MA: Harvard University Press, 2008) 29.

[17] Khaled Abou El Fadl, "The Human Rights Commitment in Modern Islam," in *Human Rights and Responsibilities in the World Religions*, ed. Runzo et al. (London: Oneworld, 2003), 301.

realizing human rights in the Islamic world. In this work he maintained that the sources and methods of Islamic law can be fruitfully employed in contemporary human rights discourse. As an interpretive strategy, *maslaha* refers to the idea of public interest in relation to the law (shariʿa): divine law should be understood as benefitting humanity. In relation to human rights, some Islamic scholars have invoked the principle of *maslaha* in the context of *maqasid al-Shariʿa* (goals and purposes of the law) in order to talk about human rights as a tradition that has strong compatibility with the Islamic tradition.

Baderin criticized scholars like Mayer and An-Naʾim of being too uncritical of international law as a western construct, and yet he also expressed skepticism of human rights violations in Muslim majority states that have been justified, however weakly, in the name of Islamic law. Baderin views the interpretive principle of *maslaha* as a way to avoid the pitfalls associated with each approach: "Through mutuality and accommodation, the legitimizing force of Islamic law in many Muslim States can be positively utilized for the enforcement of international human rights law in the Muslim world."[18]

In making the case for a *maslaha* approach to human rights, Baderin did not attempt to resolve long-standing disagreements between western and Islamic countries on matters concerning either gender and the family or the treatment of religious minorities. Regarding gender and the family, Baderin restated certain modern Islamic arguments by asserting ontological equality between women and men, found in the Qur'an, but differed in emphasizing their complementary roles in the family and wider society. As for the treatment of minorities, Baderin cited the Qur'anic injunction not to discriminate based on race or ethnicity, but not necessarily on religion. In Baderin's work, we can discern traces of Mawdudi's arguments, as well as the technique of turning to the Qur'an directly for guidance. Importantly, Baderin does not seem to share Mawdudi's conviction that the Islamic state is the best vehicle for the implementation of shariʿa principles. Rather, Baderin has endorsed a kind of legal pluralism wherein Muslims can draw from religious principles in shaping their legal and social arrangements.

Anver Emon offered important criticisms of the recourse to *maqasid al-Shariʿa* as a strategy employed by modern reformists. In *Islamic Natural Law Theories*, Emon showed that in the context of debates about the relationship between revelation and human reason, premodern jurists used the principle of *maqasid al-Shariʿa* to argue for restricting the use of human reason.[19] Moreover, Emon has maintained that modern Muslim reformers should take into account the original context of *maqasid al-Shariʿa*, which includes metaphysical presumptions about Islamic natural law theory. He argued, "To cover up and perpetuate those presumptions may

[18] Mashood Baderin, *International Human Rights and Islamic Law* (New York: Oxford University Press, 2005), 219.

[19] Anver M. Emon, *Islamic Natural Law Theories* (Oxford: Oxford University Press, 2010).

inadvertently limit the effective use of that model in a new historical moment when such presumptions are vulnerable to critique in light of prevailing theories of knowledge, philosophies of law, and theories of government."[20] It is thus important for Muslim reformers to consider the historical context in which *maqasid al-Shari'a* developed and the historically specific (premodern) problems to which the theory responded. Emon's critique implies that any modern appropriation of *maqasid al-Shari'a* must account for substantial differences in modern epistemology and politics.

IV. Freedom of Religion

As mentioned previously, the Saudi delegate Baroody contested the right to freedom of religion during the drafting and adoption of the UDHR, as did later Islamic organizations that drafted human rights treaties. An enduring question for many scholars in the Muslim world was whether freedom of religion meant the right to change belief. In the context of Islamic human rights discourse where the shari'a is assumed to be a complete basis for human rights, a conception of freedom of religion is construed as freedom to follow Islam. Article 9 of the Cairo Declaration stipulates that the state is required to allow for education (enumerated, albeit differently, in UDHR Article 26), specifically education in becoming acquainted with the religion of Islam. Article 10 of the Cairo Declaration states that: "It is prohibited to exercise any form of pressure on man or to exploit his poverty or ignorance in order to force him to change his religion to another religion or to atheism." The combined language from Articles 9 and 10 addresses the concern about missionary conversions of Muslims, but also shows the influence of Islamist arguments, initiated by thinkers like Sayyid Qutb, that people should have the freedom to follow Islam.[21]

Just as there is no one Islamic perspective on human rights, there is no singular Islamic perspective on religious freedom. In an essay on Islam, freedom of religion, and the UDHR, John Kelsay noted the pervasive influence of Wahhabism on Baroody's arguments as the Saudi delegate. Twentieth-century Wahhabi doctrinal beliefs assert the primacy of God's revelation and the state's role in propagating the

[20] Anver M. Emon, "Sharia and the (Em)brace of Difference: From Theology to Law to Identity Politics," in *The Kuyper Center Review vol. 2: Revelation and Common Grace*, ed. John Bowlin (Grand Rapids: Eerdmans, 2011), 185.

[21] For an interesting discussion of Qutb's and other Islamist views about the Islamic right to proselytize, see Andrew F. March and Naz K. Modirzadeh, "Ambivalent Universalism? Jus ad Bellum in Modern Islamic Legal Discourse," *The European Journal of International Law* 24, no. 1 (2013): 367–389.

truth of Islam.[22] Kelsay demonstrated that the association of true religious belief with state power made it difficult, if not impossible, for Baroody to assent to Article 18 as it had been drafted. (Baroody's objection may also have stemmed from a concern about the historical reality of colonial Christian missionaries in traditional Muslim lands.)[23] For other Muslim delegates, there were concerns about apostasy from Islam. There was diversity among Muslims on this point, however: another Pakistani delegate, Khan, argued that Islamic sources could support Article 18 as drafted.

Some scholars have identified a Protestant bias in American practices of church–state separation, which they argue has framed in normative and hegemonic terms the way that we understand rights as involving freedom of religion. Critical theorist Talal Asad argued that human rights discourse is emblematic of the modern western state's massive power. He maintains that because rights are, as a category, subject to conflicting interpretations, all discourse about them is "a matter of domination rather than negotiation."[24]

Following Asad, Peter Danchin questioned the neutrality of the modern democratic state vis-à-vis religion and criticized the conception of individual moral rights upon which practices of establishment and disestablishment rest.[25] The state promotes a normative view of freedom that, in Danchin's argument, is too bound up with bifurcating the secular public sphere and private religious sphere. Danchin, like other critics of secular human rights discourse, disagreed with argument that the current human rights framework is "neutral" enough to accommodate diverse expressions of religion.

Thus, the matter of religious freedom both in the Muslim world and elsewhere continues to be the subject of debate. Asad's and Danchin's respective works reflect a postcolonial critique of western hegemony in international human rights concepts, both in terms of the genesis of the discourse and what they perceive to be the thinly disguised interests of the modern state. But historical evidence demonstrates that not all Muslims are suspicious of a concept of religious freedom, and in fact, many support it as a human right. To return to An-Na'im's argument, the right to freedom of religion is not a trivial matter, insofar as ideally it protects the individual from the

[22] John Kelsay, "Saudi Arabia, Pakistan, and the Universal Declaration of Human Rights," in *Human Rights and the Conflict of Cultures: Western and Islamic Perspectives on Religious Liberty*, eds. David Little et al. (Columbia: University of South Carolina Press, 1988).

[23] John Stuart presents evidence that British Protestant missionaries in Egypt understood "religious liberty" to consist in a freedom to proselytize, so this worry is not unfounded. See Stuart, "Empire, Mission, Ecumenism, and Human Rights: 'Religious Liberty' in Egypt, 1919–1956," *Church History* 83, no. 1 (March 2014): 11–134.

[24] Talal Asad, *Formations of the Secular: Christianity, Islam, Modernity* (Stanford: Stanford University Press, 2003), 151.

[25] Peter G. Danchin, "The Politics of Religious Establishment: Recognition of Muslim Marriages in South Africa," in *Varieties of Religious Establishment*, eds. Winnifred F. Sullivan and Lori G. Beaman (New York: Ashgate, 2013), 165–186.

imposition of the state's religious or non-religious ideology and from the imposition of religious norms and practices of dominant groups within a society. A central focus of the UDHR and international covenants is the protection of the individual. Although the ideal of state neutrality vis-à-vis an individual's religious beliefs and practices may never be perfectly realized—as the state has an interest in creating a certain kind of subject—the constitutional separation of state power from institutional religious authority has historical credibility.

V. Gender, Human Rights, and Islamic Feminisms

The equality of women and men has been an important and also a contentious component of scholarly debate on Islam and human rights. As previously noted, this topic has served as a central point of departure for Islamist human rights frameworks. Although the focus of this section is primarily Muslim arguments about gender equality, several non-Muslim majority countries have expressed strong reservations about international treaties involving gender equality as well. For example, the United States has not ratified the Convention on the Elimination of All Forms of Discrimination against Women (CEDAW).[26] This section will address briefly the scholarship concerning: (1) the postcolonial critique of the rights discourse on gender equality; (2) Muslim women's engagement with feminist ideas and theories in arguments about human rights; and (3) formal international commitments to gender equality.

A. Critiques of Gender Equality Discourse

Authors writing from a postcolonial perspective have frequently been critical of western frameworks of universal rights that ignore the substantial differences in economic, political, and social power that characterize groups of people. Postcolonial critics have observed that colonial empires were content to violate human rights when it served their economic and political interests. Not all postcolonial critics have argued against the possibility of universally recognizable human rights, but

[26] For a rebuttal of American arguments against ratification, see Harold Hongju Koh, "Why America Should Ratify the Women's Rights Treaty," *Case Western Reserve Journal of International Law* (2002): 263–276.

they have consistently expressed a deep skepticism about how groups in power seek to preserve that power at the expense of other less powerful groups. Thus, despite the language of equal rights in the UDHR, the economic and social marginalization of Muslim-majority countries by western countries, as well as the social marginalization of Muslim minorities in some western countries, has indicated a persistent failure to recognize the equal rights of Muslims.

In terms of a postcolonial feminist critique, Chandra Mohanty questioned western feminist discourse around the subject of so-called "third world" women. She charged western feminists with defining their third world sisters in ways that make them "victims" of a "backward" civilization.[27] This argument built on Edward Said's work *Orientalism*, which was critical of the way that western scholarship on the East and Islam has reinforced a dichotomy of western superiority and Islamic inferiority.[28] Mohanty challenged western feminist claims to universality on the grounds that they often falsely assimilated the experiences of all women, in the process failing to acknowledge key differences in race, class, and religion. With regard to religion generally and Islam specifically, Mohanty asserted that feminist scholars who study other religious and cultural traditions should recognize a plurality of interpretations within a tradition.

Fatima Mernissi also examined gender, human rights, and Islamic culture through the lens of postcolonial politics. She observed that by signing the UDHR, Muslims were redefining themselves in "the eyes of their former colonizers" and in doing so, they undermined sexual hierarchy and the scale of values that constituted male identity.[29] In contrast to Mohanty, however, Mernissi examined patriarchal practices within the Islamic tradition, noting that the contradictions between Arab patriarchies in particular and gender equality politics of human rights discourse generated tensions for Muslims, especially Muslim men. While the concept of western individualism was a foreign cultural construct, the idea of the individual rights of women deeply unsettled cultural norms and practices.

Leila Ahmed's *Women, Gender, and Islam* addressed historically the complex treatment of women within the Islamic tradition, and how European colonialism shaped the trajectory of gender reform in Egypt. Ahmed argued that the "Muslim woman" as a social construct came to occupy an important symbol in the western colonial imagination after the eighteenth century. There is great irony in the Victorian colonizer who rejected the feminist movement in Europe, but who turned around and used "feminism" to make the case for rescuing the victimized Muslim woman from her backward culture. Ahmed explained, "Colonial feminism, or feminism as

[27] Chandra Talpade Mohanty, "Under Western Eyes: Feminist Scholarship and Colonial Discourses," *Feminist Review* 30 (1988): 61–88.

[28] Edward W. Said, *Orientalism* (New York: Vintage Books, 1994).

[29] Fatima Mernissi, *The Veil and the Male Elite*, trans. Mary Jo Lakeland (New York: Basic Books, 1992), 22.

used against other cultures in the service of colonialism, was shaped into a variety of similar constructs, each tailored to fit the particular culture that was the immediate target of domination."[30]

The idea that Islam was inherently inimical to women gained currency during the colonial period, but its effects have been far-reaching into the twentieth and twenty-first centuries. Feminist Islamic legal scholar Ziba Mir Hosseini maintained that this idea has influenced attitudes of westerners, and particularly Americans, in offering justification for the "war on terror" following the terrorist attacks of September 11, 2001.[31] But for Mir Hosseini and Ahmed, feminism as a set of tools for the liberation of women was not merely synonymous with the exercise of hegemonic power. In her 2006 article, Mir Hosseini traced the development of an indigenous Islamic feminism in post-revolutionary Iran, noting that the feminism embraced by a strong contingent of Iranians was not the same as the colonial feminism described above. This feminism came about as the result of women's oppression in the area of Islamist restrictions on women's marital rights and child custody rights, to name a few examples. Mir Hosseini was extremely critical of Islamist pretensions to an ahistorical and de-contextualized "Shari'a law" as a viable human rights framework, and her work has promoted human rights in Islamic contexts.

The respective works of Mohanty, Mernissi, Ahmed, and Mir Hosseini suggest that the idea of a fundamental Islamic hostility to women's rights was originally a product of colonialism. Mir Hosseini's work also shows that Islamist political and militant activists have employed this construct to undermine the rights of Muslim women, in the name of defending an "authentic" Islam. Islamists who argue against gender equality, both in public and in the home, often rely on a premodern vision of Islam. Mir Hosseini observed that as a result, the gap between notions of gender justice and rights in the Islamic legal tradition and international declarations addressing gender justice widened in the twentieth century.[32]

B. Engaging Feminist Ideas: Islamic Family Law

The relationship between western feminism and Muslim women's human rights is complicated by the history of colonialism, as well as the so-called "war on terror," but these factors do not ultimately limit the ways that Muslim women use feminist critique to argue for women's human rights within Islamic contexts. These women

[30] Leila Ahmed, *Women and Gender in Islam* (New Haven: Yale University Press, 1992), 151.

[31] Ziba Mir Hosseini, "Muslim Women's Quest for Equality: Between Islamic Law and Feminism," *Critical Inquiry* 32, no. 4 (Summer 2006): 629–645.

[32] Ziba Mir Hosseini, "Justice, Equality, and Muslim Family Laws: New Ideas, New Prospects," in *Gender and Equality in Muslim Family Law: Justice and Ethics in the Islamic Legal Tradition*, eds. Z. Mir Hosseini et al. (New York: Palgrave MacMillan, 2013), 7–34.

have rejected the idea that women's human rights are a strictly secular construct. While some Muslim women have embraced apologetic strategies—such as claiming that in the Qur'an and hadith, Islam granted human rights to women[33]—others have taken a more nuanced approach by examining the historical contexts and norms that influence ideas about gender and religion.

For example, Lynn Welchman examined women's rights and family law in Arab states, noting shifts in the codification of Muslim personal status law (family law).[34] The focus on such laws and debates surrounding them sheds light on the particular regional issues at stake. Ethnographic studies that take into account the lived experience of Muslim women and their interaction with Islamic law, cultural customs, and secular law, are important contributions to scholarship in the area of women's studies and Islam. Samia Bano's study of shari'a councils in Britain examined Muslim women's agency in their use of such councils in obtaining a divorce.[35] Bano's study dealt with Muslim women in a minority context, showing how Pakistani British Muslim women conceptualize rights within marriage, and how they understand "Islam" to grant them human rights, such as the right to divorce an abusive husband (based on some rudimentary knowledge of Islamic personal law). Bano concluded that the British shari'a courts had little effect on the promotion of rights of Muslim women within family law. However, her study reveals the significance of situating the analysis contextually. As Bano pointed out, Islamic jurisprudence is not the guiding framework for these shari'a councils. Rather the framework reflects a complex intersection of Islamic "law" as interpreted by council members (who are sometimes, but not always, religious scholars), agentive pious Muslim women, and members of ethnic/kin groups.

While this contextualized scholarship offers considerable insights into the operation of Islamic law in highly contested spaces of life, it nonetheless raises a moral general question about the relation between civil law and Muslim communities in countries where Muslims live as religious minorities. The state, while still the formal guarantor of rights, is not always in the position to enforce them (particularly when it gives latitude to religious groups to determine the content and enforcement of family law through alternative dispute resolution mechanisms). This can lead to problems when religious teachings—and in particular the practical effects of such teachings—conflict with civil law.

[33] Riffat Hassan called the Qur'an the *Magna Carta* of human rights in "Rights of Women within Islamic Countries," *Canadian Women's Studies* (1995).

[34] Lynn Welchman, *Women and Muslim Family Laws in Arab States: A Comparative Overview of Textual Development and Advocacy* (Amsterdam: Amsterdam University Press, 2007).

[35] Samia Bano, *Muslim Women and Shari'a Councils: Transcending the Boundaries of Community and Law* (New York: Palgrave Macmillan, 2012). This type of study affirms Kecia Ali's observation that women's studies in Islam, initially focussed on women's oppression, moved in the early twenty-first century toward a new focus on women's agency. See Ali, *Marriage and Slavery in Islam* (Cambridge, MA: Harvard University Press, 2010). For a prominent example of this kind of work, see Saba Mahmood, *Politics of Piety: The Islamic Revival and the Feminist Subject* (Princeton: Princeton University Press, 2006).

c. Muslim Feminist Interaction with Human Rights Discourses

One way to approach these interrelated questions and bring the conversation back to universal human rights discourse is to inquire about the effect of international human rights treaties on women's rights. The United Nations ratified the Convention for the Elimination of Discrimination against Women (CEDAW), in 1979. The signatories to CEDAW committed to eradicating discrimination against women in both public and private spheres, although some of the countries that agreed to the convention continued to discriminate against women. Several Muslim majority countries issued reservations to CEDAW based on a perceived conflict with the shari'a. Egypt's representative issued a reservation to CEDAW, for example, arguing that Islamic law had "already liberated women."[36] This argument is consonant with the Cairo Declaration's understanding of shari'a law as providing the ultimate reference point for human rights.

In terms of bridging the gap between statements of international human rights for women and the failure to guarantee such rights in practice, non-governmental organizations have played an important role. Musawah (Arabic for "equality") was founded in 2009 by Muslim women. An international organization, Musawah has drawn on the work of activists—both male and female—to reinterpret Islamic scriptures and reform legal practices so that they support the rights of women. Women's organizations like Musawah have worked to encourage Muslim majority countries to adopt international women's rights conventions like CEDAW. Welchman has observed the impact of Musawah's advocacy work in promoting gender justice in the area of family law reform. Musawah has notably influenced legal discussions of gender roles in marriage in several Arab states; one observable trend is the move from gender-complementary roles (stressing a husband's fairness and wifely obedience) to roles that involve more equality and mutuality.[37]

Musawah provides an example of how Muslim feminists have appropriated feminist ideas and adapted them specifically to fit the needs of their various contexts, in the forms of critical scholarship and activist bodies. Their work has demonstrated that "feminist" is not a monolithic term, but rather a fluid category that can encompass considerable variance in its cultural meanings and applications.

[36] Michele Brandt and Jeffrey A. Kaplan, "The Tension between Women's Rights and Religious Rights: Reservations to CEDAW by Egypt, Bangladesh, and Tunisia," *Journal of Law and Religion* 12, no. 1 (1995–96): 105–142.

[37] Lynn Welchman, "Musawah, CEDAW, and Muslim Family Laws in the 21st Century," *Islamic Law and International Human Rights Law: Searching for Common Ground?* eds. Emon et al. (New York: Oxford University Press, 2012), 309–319.

D. Critiques of the State: Islamists, Secularists, and Muslim Feminists

Since the ratification of the UDHR in 1948, a pattern of disagreement has manifested around religious freedom (and how to treat religious minorities) and gender equality between Muslim governments and Islamists, on the one hand, and western states, on the other. We may attribute this persistent tension in part to the political, religious, and economic realities occasioned by colonialism and its aftermath. In many respects, however, the modern state itself remains an important object of focus and inquiry in this disagreement. It is necessary to recognize the tremendous power of the modern state over the lives of its citizens and non-citizens (inclusive of persons that reside within its borders and those that do not). Given the reality of the state's power to confer or deny rights, any kind of international rights declaration or convention risks impotence if it runs counter to the political aims of the state's elite members.

By examining meta-critiques of the state, we may identify the various stakes involved for Islamists, Muslim feminists, and western secularists. In Muslim-majority contexts, Islamists have sought to bring the secular state into greater alignment with Islamic principles and values (often based on their interpretation of shariʿa) in order to confer legitimacy.[38] From this perspective, state or international law, if devoid of an Islamic foundation, is not a legitimate ground for human rights. Therefore a topic like religious freedom, vexed already as it is based on historical memory of unfavorable colonial encounters with missionaries, remains in tension with the Islamist belief that the only correct framework for governance is an Islamic system. For male elites within this system, gender equality as a measure imposed externally by an international system of law symbolized another attempt at colonial control. Lisa Hajjar identified this problem when she explained, "Women's rights, and the issue of gender relations more generally, have become the primary redoubts of anxieties about cultural and legal imperialism."[39]

Western secularists—and others who endorse some measure of separation of religion and government—have tended to avoid meta-critiques of the state insofar as they have imbued secular leaders and governmental processes with legitimacy and have trusted in the ability of state elites to either check their power or to respect the constitutional limits (where provided) on their power. An-Na'im endorsed a conception of secular government in order to emphasize the separation of religious authority from state authority and the right of people to make collective decisions about governance. Critical to secularism is a concept of freedom of religion—but

[38] In some cases, however, Islamist groups have pursued international military action without the affiliation of a sovereign state—e.g. al-Qaida.

[39] Lisa Hajjar, "Domestic Violence and Shari'a," in *Women's Rights and Islamic Family Law: Perspectives on Reform*, ed. Lynn Welchman (New York: Zed Books, 2004), 250.

whether that means protecting the freedom of religious actors to practice in public spaces or prohibiting establishment or dominance of a religion is an American debate that has continued into the twenty-first century.[40] Sometimes, secular ideology has entailed the outright rejection of religious frameworks for law and governance. Regarding gender, many western secular critiques, such as Mayer's, focussed on the way that the state ought to protect women's rights against inherently oppressive religious systems.[41] As Leila Ahmed has noted, however, the view that Islam in particular is oppressive to women is a colonial trope. And yet this view has had remarkable endurance due to the ideological war (in addition to the military conflicts of the twentieth and twenty-first centuries) between Islamism and secular nationalism.

Modern Muslim feminists have faced the challenge of negotiating their political and religious participation in light of the ideological dialectic of "secularism" and "Islam" in the context of the modern state. Their activism—which takes place within but also across national borders—proves the instability of the secular/religious dichotomy insofar as they work dynamically within spheres of religious and secular systems to achieve greater rights for women. Muslim feminists like Ziba Mir Hosseini have highlighted the way that powerful state ideologies—whether Islamist or secular—have functioned to oppress women. Her work has also demonstrated the way that Muslim feminist practitioners grant authority to, or resist, practices and social norms. Whereas antireligious secularist and Islamist discourses have tended to imperil Muslim women's agency, Muslim feminists have demonstrated that the modern political climate created novel opportunities for Muslim women to engage politically—and in ways that have criticized excessive state power and religious ideology that have both caused harm to women.[42]

VI. Conclusion

This chapter has identified four basic scholarly orientations to the topic of Islam and human rights since the end of the Second World War. First, some scholars rooted in the western rights tradition have privileged the secular and rational underpinnings

[40] This debate has a long history. For two discussions, each with a distinct perspective, of how these questions have affected discourse around the American constitutional separation of church and state, see W.F. Sullivan, *The Impossibility of Religious Freedom* (Princeton: Princeton University Press, 2007) and Martha Nussbaum, *The New Religious Intolerance: Overcoming the Politics of Fear in an Anxious Age* (Cambridge, MA: Belknap Press, 2012).

[41] Susan M. Okin, "Is Multiculturalism Bad for Women?" In *Is Multiculturalism Bad for Women?* eds. Joshua Cohen et al. (Princeton: Princeton University Press, 1999).

[42] See Ziba Mir Hosseini, "Beyond 'Islam' vs 'Feminism'," *IDS Bulletin* 42, no. 1 (2011): 67–77.

of human rights and eschew any religious foundation for rights. To some extent, Mayer's work fits into this category. The obvious bias in this view is that religious actors are understood as acting less rationally than secular actors, and that secular systems of law are perceived as more stable and conducive to human rights than religious ones. Such scholarship may be more likely to identify the whole of the Islamic position of human rights with Islamist political rhetoric and apology, failing to account for different positions among Muslim intellectuals and activists. This position, if asserted uncritically, may overlook the geopolitical context of colonialism and postcolonialism and the way that this history shapes human rights discourse.

Second, Muslim apologists like Mawdudi argued for the primacy of the shariʿa in their human rights frameworks, but neglected to distinguish between premodern systems of governance and law, on the one hand, and contemporary systems of governance and law, on the other. In doing so, they elided necessary questions of textual interpretation and application and relied on idealized conceptions of Islamic law. This seems to be at least in part a response to the modern bureaucratic separation of value spheres, and involves nostalgia for the integration of religion and law, a relationship which had been severed during the colonial period (with the exception of family law).

Third, there are postcolonial critics who, by way of Marxist or other ideological critique, argue that human rights have too often been defined and enforced by those with global privilege. This critique is not particular to the issue of Islam and human rights, although a number of scholars, like Falk and Mohanty, have applied the critique to Islamic cases. These critics are not invested, theologically or legally, in a revival of shariʿa, but instead are interested in allowing Muslim communities more freedom in defining their human rights commitments. They might endorse a kind of legal and/or moral pluralism.

Fourth, there are Muslim scholars who take up the task of universal human rights but who reject the ahistorical approach associated with both the first and the second camps, as well as the strict limitations that the first camp places on religious participants in human rights discourse. As a group, they tend to be more critical of the way that Islamic programs of legal reform, often at the state level, have led to human rights abuses (placing them in disagreement with the second and third camps). This group consists generally of reformist scholars, including Muslim feminists, who seek to bring into more harmony a conception of universal rights and Islamic thought, usually through the revision of Islamic teachings (although they approach this task in various ways—ranging as they do from scholars of law to historians and theologians). We may also include *maslaha* approaches to human rights in this category, insofar as such approaches involve making changes to Islamic teachings based on public interest.

In accounting for the diversity of views regarding Islam and human rights, recognizing these four views may help to identify and comprehend persistent areas of disagreement. Yet these classifications are limited. For example, some participants in this discussion, like members of Musawah, share the commitment of Muslim reformers to bring into harmony international human rights discourse with Islamic legal traditions, but also may sympathize more with Muslim apologetics than secular human rights advocates. Another example is that of Baderin, whose revival of *maqasid al-Shari'a* places him within the category of Muslim reformers who seek harmony with international rights concepts and Islam, but whose method of retrieval ignores some fundamental differences in context between premodern and modern epistemology and politics. There are also scholarly works that bring into direct comparison international law and Muslim law on the topic of rights, which affords an important opportunity for cross-cultural conversation without staking an ideological claim.[43]

As the relationship between Islam and human rights continues to be a topic of political discourse, it is important to be able to assess the relative strengths and shortcomings of these various positions, and to identify the areas for most productive consensus and progress toward implementing human rights commitments. While genuine moral disagreements continue about the content of particular rights, often issues of political ideology exert a significant influence on the way that rights claims are imagined. Moreover, while conceptions of international human rights rely on abstraction from specific contexts, their efficacy relies on the ability of participants to find legal, moral, and political relevance in applying them.

References

Abou El Fadl, Khaled, "The Human Rights Commitment in Modern Islam" in Runzo, Martin, and Sharma (eds.) *Human Rights and Responsibilities in the World Religions* (London: Oneworld, 2003) 301–364.

Ahmed, Leila, *Women and Gender in Islam* (New Haven: Yale University Press, 1992).

Ahsan, Abdullah, "Law, Religion, and Human Dignity in the Muslim World Today: An Examination of OIC's Cairo Declaration of Human Rights." *Journal of Law and Religion* 24, no. 2 (2008–09): 569–597.

A'la Mawdudi, Abul, *Human Rights in Islam* (London: The Islamic Foundation, 1976).

An-Na'im, Abdullahi, *Islam and the Secular State: Negotiating the Future of Shari'a* (Cambridge, MA: Harvard University Press, 2008).

Asad, Talal, *Formations of the Secular: Christianity, Islam, Modernity* (Stanford: Stanford University Press, 2003).

Baderin, Mashood, *International Human Rights and Islamic Law* (New York: Oxford University Press, 2005).

Bano, Samia, *Muslim Women and Shari'a Councils: Transcending the Boundaries of Community and Law* (New York: Palgrave Macmillan, 2012).

[43] See, e.g., Anver M. Emon, Mark Ellis, and Benjamin Glahn, eds., *Islamic Law and International Human Rights Law: Searching for Common Ground* (Oxford: Oxford University Press, 2012).

Brandt, Michele and Kaplan, Jeffrey A., "The Tension between Women's Rights and Religious Rights: Reservations to CEDAW by Egypt, Bangladesh, and Tunisia." *Journal of Law and Religion* 12, no. 1 (1995–96): 105–142.

Danchin, Peter G., "The Politics of Religious Establishment: Recognition of Muslim Marriages in South Africa" in Winnifred F. Sullivan and Lori G. Beaman (eds.) *Varieties of Religious Establishment* (New York: Ashgate, 2013) 165–186.

Donnelly, Jack, *Universal Human Rights in Theory and Practice* (Ithaca, NY: Cornell University Press, 2003).

Emon, Anver M., *Islamic Natural Law Theories* (Oxford: Oxford University Press, 2010).

Emon, Anver M., "Sharia and the (Em)brace of Difference: From Theology to Law to Identity Politics" in John Bowlin (ed.) *The Kuyper Center Review vol. 2: Revelation and Common Grace* (Grand Rapids: Eerdmans, 2011) 173–199.

Emon, Anver, Ellis, Mark, and Glahn, Benjamin, *Islamic Law and International Human Rights Law: Searching for Common Ground?* (Oxford: Oxford University Press, 2012).

Falk, Richard, "False Universalism and the Geopolitics of Exclusion: the Case of Islam." *Third World Quarterly* 18, no. 1 (1997): 7–23.

Hajjar, Lisa, "Domestic Violence and Shari'a" in Lynn Welchman (ed.) *Women's Rights and Islamic Family Law: Perspectives on Reform* (New York: Zed Books, 2004) 235–272.

Hassan, Riffat, "Rights of Women within Islamic Countries." *Canadian Women's Studies* 15, no. 2–3 (1995).

Kelsay, John, "Saudi Arabia, Pakistan, and the Universal Declaration of Human Rights" in David Little, John Kelsay, and Abdulaziz Sachedina (eds.) *Human Rights and the Conflict of Cultures: Western and Islamic Perspectives on Religious Liberty* (Columbia: University of South Carolina Press, 1988).

Koh, Harold Konju, "Why America Should Ratify the Women's Rights Treaty." *Case Western Reserve Journal of International Law* (2002): 263–276.

March, Andrew, and Modirzadeh, Naz K., "Ambivalent Universalism? *Jus ad Bellum* in Modern Islamic Legal Discourse." *The European Journal of International Law* 24, no. 1 (2013): 367–389.

Masud, Muhammad Khalid, "Clearing Ground: Commentary to 'Shari'a and the Modern State.'" In *Islamic Law and International Human Rights Law: Searching for Common Ground?* Edited by Emon, Ellis, and Glahn, 104–114 (New York: Oxford University Press, 2012).

Mayer, Ann Elizabeth, *Islam and Human Rights: Tradition and Politics* (Boulder, CO: Westview Press, 1999).

Mernissi, Fatima, *The Veil and the Male Elite*. Translated by Mary Jo Lakeland (New York: Basic Books, 1992).

Mir Hosseini, Ziba, "Muslim Women's Quest for Equality: Between Islamic Law and Feminism." *Critical Inquiry* 32, no. 4 (Summer 2006): 629–645.

Mir Hosseini, Ziba, "Beyond 'Islam' vs 'Feminism.'" *IDS Bulletin* 42, no. 1 (2011): 67–77.

Mir Hosseini, Ziba, "Justice, Equality, and Muslim Family Laws: New Ideas, New Prospects" in Mir Hosseini et al., (eds.) *Gender and Equality in Muslim Family Law: Justice and Ethics in the Islamic Legal Tradition* (New York: Palgrave MacMillan, 2013) 7–34.

Mohanty, Chandra, "Under Western Eyes: Feminist Scholarship and Colonial Discourses." *Feminist Review* 30 (1988): 61–88.

Morsink, Johannes, *The Universal Declaration of Human Rights: Origins, Drafting, and Intent* (Philadelphia: University of Pennsylvania Press, 1999).

Nussbaum, Martha, *The New Religious Intolerance: Overcoming the Politics of Fear in an Anxious Age* (Cambridge, MA: Belknap Press of Harvard University, 2012).
Oh, Irene, "Islamic Voices and the Definition of Human Rights." *Journal of Church and State* 53, no. 3 (2010): 376–400.
Okin, Susan Moller, Is Multiculturalism Bad for Women? Edited by Joshua Cohen et al. (Princeton: Princeton University Press, 1999).
Pagden, Anthony, "Human Rights, Natural Rights, and Europe's Imperial Legacy." *Political Theory* 31, no. 2 (April 2003): 171–199.
Said, Edward W., *Orientalism* (New York: Vintage Books, 1994).
Stuart, John, "Empire, Mission, Ecumenism, and Human Rights: 'Religious Liberty' in Egypt, 1919–1956." *Church History* 83, no. 1 (March 2014): 11–134.
Sullivan, Winifred F., *The Impossibility of Religious Freedom* (Princeton: Princeton University Press, 2007).
Waltz, Susan, "Universal Human Rights: The Contribution of Muslim States." *Human Rights Quarterly* 26 (2004): 799–844.
Welchman, Lynn, *Women and Muslim Family Laws in Arab States: A Comparative Overview of Textual Development and Advocacy* (Amsterdam: Amsterdam University Press, 2007).
Welchman, Lynn, "Musawah, CEDAW, and Muslim Family Laws in the 21st Century" in Emon, Ellis, and Glahn (eds.) *Islamic Law and International Human Rights Law: Searching for Common Ground?* (New York: Oxford University Press, 2012) 309–319.

CHAPTER 33

ISLAMIC LAW AND FINANCE

ANVER M. EMON

ISLAMIC finance is a field of economic activity that has, since the 1980s, informed a global industry that is variously valued in the billions, if not trillions, of dollars. Often framed in terms of a Qur'anic ban on charging interest on loans, Islamic finance is frequently promoted as a response to market demand by Muslims who wish to comply with Islamic strictures when participating in market transactions. Yet it is not so easily reducible to this simple proposition. As will be discussed in this chapter, this explanation is often a post-hoc justification for practices that arose when (1) Gulf states enjoyed financial surplus from the 1970s oil book, and (2) free-market ideologies informed government regulatory policies in areas such as banking and finance. The link between Islamic finance and Islamic law lies in the underlying contractual paradigm that informs the shape of different Islamic financial instruments. Consequently, Islamic finance offers a subject matter at the intersection of both law and economics in an increasingly globalized, transnational marketplace.

This chapter will review the literature on Islamic finance to inform the reader about what Islamic finance is, where and how it operates, its justifying logics, and the critiques of Islamic finance in both the academy and public policy sector. It will conclude with a set of questions to guide future inquiries into a field that has thus far been dominated by economists and finance specialists/practitioners.

I. The Law in Islamic Finance

A. *Riba* and *Gharar* as Conceptual Pillars

Two Qur'anic proscriptions inform the pantheon of Islamic financial thought and practice. The first concerns *gharar*, which is understood to prohibit transactions with a high degree of risk, if not fraud and deceit. *Gharar* includes within its scope of prohibition insurance contracts, as well as futures. For example, on *gharar*-based reasoning, insurance involves premiums paid for a possible payout in the event of an accident or injury covered by an insurance policy. Speculative contracts like these are presumptively banned by the *gharar* principle, because the insured is paying premiums for the possibility of a payout that may never occur.

The second, which is the most well-known feature of Islamic finance, is the ban on *riba*, which is often translated as "interest" albeit with considerable disagreement. Specialists in the field debate whether "interest" is a suitable translation or is too loaded with conventional economic thinking given its place in global banking and finance. Fazlur Rahman has sought to historicize the term, with the consequence of challenging its translatability from a premodern trade environment to a modern, transnational financial one.[1]

There are two verses in the Qur'an in which *riba* is identified as a proscribed practice.[2] Qur'an 3:130 states: "O those who believe, do not consume *riba* doubled and multiplied. Fear Allah so that perhaps you may prosper." This verse has been understood to refer to a situation where someone borrows money for a fixed period. At the end of the period, the borrower either pays off the entire loan, or opts for an extended loan period, in which case the creditor would "double or multiply," or substantially increase, the cost of lending the principal amount.[3] According to Ziaul Haque, this curious Qur'anic phrase should not be read narrowly or strictly; there may have been many forms of *riba* transactions. He states: "*riba* of the pre-Islamic times was of many forms which were widely extensive in loans and sales of money and commodities."[4]

The more general proscription that informs the presumptive ban on interest occurs in Qur'an 2:275 (emphasis added):

> Those who devour *riba* stand as he who the devil strikes by [his] touch. That is because they say that bay' [sales] is the same as *riba*. *But God permitted bay' and prohibited* riba. So

[1] Fazlur Rahman, "Riba and Interest," *Islamic Studies* 3, no. 1 (1964): 1–43.

[2] Though there are other instances in which the term is used, but not necessarily as a proscription against a certain practice. See for instance, Qur'an, 30:39.

[3] See e.g. Jalal al-Din Muhammad bin Ahmad al-Mahalla and Jalal al-Din al-Suyuti, *Tafsir al-Jalalayn* (Turkey: Maktaba Arslan, n.d.), 89; Abu Bakr al-Jassas, *Ahkam al-Qur'an* (Beirut: Dar al-Kutub al-'Ilmiya, 1994), 2:47.

[4] Ziaul Haque, *Islam and Feudalism: The Economics of Riba, Interest, and Profit* (Lahore: Vanguard Books, 1985), 6.

whoever receives a warning from God and then halts his conduct, then he is entitled to his past profits, and his affairs are for God [to judge]. Those who resume their conduct shall be companions in Hell Fire forever.

Premodern jurists articulated a legal framework to regulate transactions that could potentially violate the *riba* prohibition. As Nabil al-Saleh has helpfully explained, jurists articulated two different categories of *riba: riba al-fadl* and *riba al-nasi'a*.[5] *Riba al-nasi'a* is the category most often addressed by contemporary scholars on *riba*.[6] Here, an "increase" arises "by delaying completion of the exchange of countervalues ... with or without an increase or a profit."[7] This type of *riba* could occur in an exchange of dates for a delayed exchange of wheat, whether of the same weight or not. Or it could be a loan of gold currency for a later repayment of gold, whether there is an increase or not.[8] Today, *riba al-nasi'a* is often addressed in the context of bank loans, where a bank lends money for an extended period of time, after which the borrower repays the loan with interest. The interest is what falls under the rubric of *riba*, and is thereby unlawful.

The second category is *riba al-fadl*, which involves a surplus that might arise in a simultaneous, spot exchange, for instance, in a barter of dates for wheat. Notably, this category of *riba* poses limited relevance in contemporary scholarship on Islamic finance. This is not surprising given the advent of currency, which fixes an equivalent exchange value for two qualitatively different commodities. Currency operates as a mediating device to ensure a fair trade. But where there is no money, the rules of *riba al-fadl* regulated barter-based transactions to ensure a fair and just exchange. It is precisely because of such changes in economic practice that scholars such as Haque challenge the salience of *riba* as a concept in a contemporary setting. On his view, the categories of *riba* "correspond[ed] to the economic conditions of a medieval-feudal society, based on barter, an underdeveloped money economy and agriculture."[9]

B. Contract Law: Between Form and Substance in Islamic Finance

Taken by themselves, the terms *riba* and *gharar* are broad and general principles that enjoin risk and distribute equity across all parties to a transaction. This injunction stands in contrast to conventional mortgages, for instance, where the homeowner

[5] Nabil al-Saleh, *Unlawful Gains and Legitimate Profit in Islamic Law* (Cambridge: Cambridge University Press, 1986).

[6] Haque, *Islam and Feudalism*, 71–72.

[7] Al-Saleh, *Unlawful Gains*, 13.

[8] Ibid, 19–25.

[9] Haque, *Islam and Feudalism*, 93–94. See also Chibli Mallat, "The Debate on Riba and Interest in Twentieth Century Jurisprudence," in *Islamic Law and Finance*, ed. Chibli Mallat (London: Graham & Trotman, 1988), 81; Rahman, "Riba and Interest," 2, 8–12; al-Saleh, *Unlawful Gains*, 28–30.

enjoys equity, but also all the risk in case of disaster or non-payment. By contrast, the bank avoids risk by securing the property as collateral on the loan, giving it primacy over other potential creditors upon bankruptcy.

The distribution of equity and risk can take different forms depending on the transaction, thus informing the range of nominate contracts in Islamic law. These contractual forms set the boundaries within which premodern jurists evaluated the legality of different transactions, and in a sense, regulated commercial practices. The contract forms are varied and detailed. Since many books and articles on Islamic finance provide an overview of these contract forms, there is no need to repeat that exercise here. Nonetheless, some discussion of these contract forms is necessary in order to appreciate the historiography of this field.

Scholars in this field emphasize the importance of *musharaka* and *mudaraba* arrangements in maximally distributing both risk and equity among transacting parties. *Musharaka* is generally translated as "partnership," where partners in an enterprise share risk in relation to the equity they invest. *Mudaraba* is a type of partnership that most closely resembles traditional financing: one party provides the capital (*rabb al-mal*) while the other manages its use. According to Vogel, this model is an example of "pure finance, enabling the owner of capital to invest his capital without himself becoming involved in managing that capital and without exposing himself to liabilities in excess of that capital."[10] In other words, if the partnership fails, the laborer gains nothing from any expended labor, while the capital investor's loss is limited to the original investment.[11] Of course, it is not clear what would happen to creditors whose claims against the *mudaraba* partnership cannot be met by the initial capital investment. In contemporary legal systems, resolving the claims of creditors against a failing enterprise with a finite capital reserve is governed by bankruptcy law.

For many scholars and practitioners in the field, *musharaka* and *mudaraba* best represent the shared equity and risk approach that characterizes Islamic finance and economics. Yet the actual practice of Islamic finance across different jurisdictions does not generally employ these contractual forms. As Clement Henry suggests: "Islamic banks labour under a major disadvantage: long-term financing with *mudaraba* or *musharaka* seems far riskier than the medium- or long-term lending of conventional banks."[12] These Islamic instruments presuppose, as Henry argues, "a high degree of trust" between business partners, whereas conventional banks take a more "hands-off relationship," in part by collateralizing their investments to secure their position as a favored creditor. Consequently, it is perhaps not surprising that the Islamic financial market experiences what Tarik M. Yousef calls the "*murabaha* syndrome."[13]

[10] Vogel, 130. [11] Ibid.

[12] Clement M. Henry, "Financial Performances of Islamic Banks versus Conventional Banks," in *The Politics of Islamic Finance*, eds. Clement M. Henry and Rodney Wilson (Edinburgh: Edinburgh University Press, 2004), 104.

[13] Tarik M. Yousef, "The Murabaha Syndrome in Islamic Finance: Laws, Institutions and Politics," in *The Politics of Islamic Finance*, eds. Clement M. Henry and Rodney Wilson (Edinburgh: Edinburgh University Press, 2004), 64.

Murabaha is a type of sale contract that enables the seller to charge a mark-up on the item sold. *Murabaha* is more amenable for long-term, low-risk financing, such as mortgages for homes. On this model, the buyer asks a third party—usually a bank—to purchase an item from the seller. After taking legal title to the new property, the third party then sells it immediately to the buyer for an increased price, perhaps paid out in installments over a period of years. *Murabaha* deals insulate banks from excessive risk and protect their interests, especially if upon the marked-up sale they take a security interest in the underlying property to assume a preferred creditor status. Critics of Islamic finance often argue that the *murabaha* is a formalistic work-around that shrouds an interest charge in the language of a second, independent sale. As Yousef states: "[t]he predominance of *murabaha* represents a challenge to the very notion that Islamic finance would provide an alternative to interest-based conventional financial systems."

More recently, developments in Islamic finance showcase the importance of *sukuk*. The *sukuk* is a bond-like structure that facilitates, through a lease paradigm of an underlying asset, long-term investment with limited risk. The lease paradigm is informed by the nominate contract form of *ijara*. *Ijara* ensured the owner held an interest in the underlying asset while profiting from renting the usufruct rights to a tenant for a fee. The fact that there is an underlying asset-based interest in the *ijara* reflects the equity-orientation in Islamic finance. As El-Gamal writes: "[t]he increased popularity of lease-based financing and securitization stems from the existence of underlying physical assets, the usufruct of which is being transferred under various leases or subleases."[14] Moreover, once the rents on the usufruct can be securitized, the *sukuk* becomes a useful vehicle for developing security interests that can be traded on a secondary market.[15] In other words, the Islamic legal validity of the *sukuk* differs from a fixed-income bond because, at least for secondary market purposes, the *sukuk* does not involve trading in debt, which most Islamic schools of law prohibited.

II. The History of Islamic Finance in a Global Market

Islamic banking and finance, since the mid-twentieth century, have operated on the presumption of economic markets in which national currencies provide the medium of price setting across a range of products, markets, and jurisdictional

[14] El-Gamal, 97. [15] Ibid.

lines. While Islamic financial mechanisms draw upon a premodern legal tradition, the practice of Islamic financing is a modern invention. Consequently, this chapter considers Islamic banking and finance to be recent developments, taking shape starting in and around the 1960s, and expanding thereafter from the Muslim majority world onto the stock market floors of exchanges such as the FTSE and NYSE.

Monzer Kahf noted that while economists and others theorized about the possibility of Islamic banking and finance, no real attempt at it began till the late 1950s in Malaysia and Egypt. Shortly after Malaysia's independence, a special funding program, *Tabung Hajji*, was created to support Muslim Malays wishing to perform the annual pilgrimage (*hajj*). *Tabung Hajji* was a "government-sponsored and -supervised financial institution that collect[ed] savings for *hajj* and invest[ed] them in accordance with *shari'a*."[16] This experiment blended banking with investment finance to facilitate an Islamically defined objective, specifically supporting Muslim Malays wishing to go on the *hajj*.

The second experiment occurred in rural northern Egypt in 1963, where Ahmed al-Najjar created a series of savings and investment houses. His financial endeavor, *Mit Ghamr*, was named after the town where the initial investment house was created. *Mit Ghamr*, however, soon found itself embroiled in domestic politics over the place and role of Islamism in Egypt. As Islamic groups and their members became clients of *Mit Ghamr*'s branches, they transformed this financial institution into a political lightning rod. Kahf explains that "[t]he Egyptian experiment emerged at a time when the government and the ruling class were ultra-sensitive against any Islamic political activity," specifically the Muslim Brotherhood.[17] By 1967, *Mit Ghamr* was defunct and all assets liquidated. But *Mit Ghamr* nonetheless filled a void (or perhaps created one) that its liquidation left gaping wide. By 1971, the Egyptian government created a government-sponsored Islamic bank, Nasser Social Bank (NSB). As Kahf recounts, the NSB was government-financed and -owned, and premised upon "Islamic principles such as interest-free financing and distribution of *zakat* [alms tax]."[18]

Islamic banking and finance advanced considerably from the 1970s onward. Two factors in particular helped spur the growth of this market. The first was the incredible profit margins oil-producing Gulf states enjoyed during the 1970s.[19] These profit margins created surplus wealth that prompted governments in the region either to develop their own mechanisms for investment (e.g. Islamic banks),

[16] Monzer Kahf, "Islamic Banks: The Rise of a New Power Alliance of Wealth and *Shari'a* Scholarship," in *The Politics of Islamic Finance*, eds. Clement M. Henry and Rodney Wilson (Edinburgh: Edinburgh University Press, 2004), 18.

[17] Kahf, 19. [18] Ibid.

[19] Lena Rethel, "Whose Legitimacy? Islamic Finance and the Global Financial Order," *Review of International Political Economy* 18, no. 1 (2011): 75–98, 83.

or invest in the existing global financial market, which saw this new infusion of wealth as reason enough to consider creating Islamic vehicles for global investment purposes.[20] Ibrahim Warde writes that in 1974, the then-named Organization of Islamic Conference (OIC) created the inter-government Islamic Development Bank (IDB), "which was to become the cornerstone of a new banking system inspired by religious principles."[21] Other banks followed, and member states of the OIC soon declared their entire banking sector to be fully "Islamized."[22] But these newly created banks operated domestically only, and were not always the most effective in fostering an active investment environment, in comparison to the international financial market. Warde notes generally that the turn to international markets served various purposes. International markets had a knowledge base upon which new Muslim investors and Islamic investment houses drew. They also provided a wider range of investment products for the newly acquired surplus wealth.[23] In this global context, two figures were historically significant for situating Islamic finance in the international financial market. Prince Muhammad al-Faisal, the son of the late King Faisal, founded the financial institution Dar al-Mal al-Islami (DMI), which is based in Geneva but operates worldwide. Meanwhile, Saudi entrepreneur Sheikh Saleh Kamel founded the Dallah al-Baraka Group, a massive conglomerate with a financial services portfolio specializing in Islamic banking and investment. Banking groups such as DMI and Dallah al-Baraka operate Islamic banks with active Islamic investment streams and do much of their business in the financial centers of London, New York, and Geneva, thus embedding Islamic finance within the global conventional financial market.

The second factor that spurred the growth in Islamic finance was the deregulation of the banking and financial sectors in the 1980s and 1990s in countries such as the United Kingdom and the United States. As noted, the international financial regime offered greater financial products for Islamic investor groups and banks to invest their assets. This diversity of financial products, though, was not a mere accident or natural outcropping of the conventional financial industry. Writing about the United States and the repeal of the Glass-Steagall Act of 1933, Warde notes that the deregulation of the 1980s liberated financial institutions from "traditional commercial banking" and allowed them to develop more risk-oriented financial investment techniques.[24] Moreover, financial and banking deregulation created an investment environment in which capital could move without restriction, weaving together global financial markets.

[20] Clement Henry and Rodney Wilson, "Introduction," in *The Politics of Islamic Finance*, ed. Clement M. Henry and Rodney Wilson (Edinburgh: Edinburgh University Press, 2004), 9.

[21] Ibrahim Warde, "Global Politics, Islamic Finance and Islamist Politics Before and After 11 September 2001," in *The Politics of Islamic Finance*, eds. Clement M. Henry and Rodney Wilson (Edinburgh: Edinburgh University Press, 2004), 39.

[22] Ibid. [23] Ibid., 41. [24] Ibid., 45–46.

Today, Islamic finance is part of various banking regimes in the Muslim majority world, as well as international investment firms. Featured as part of a broader "values-based" offering, Islamic finance is a "screened" product that allows investors to couple rational profit maximizing goals with "non-rational" value-based commitments.[25] "A screen is defined as a specific investment criterion used to include or exclude firms based on lines of business or corporate behavior."[26] Islamic financial products sit alongside investment products that appeal to Catholics, Jews, and other faith-based groups. These sorts of value-based screens have populated the market since the 1990s in the United States,[27] which incidentally is also when regulatory frameworks freed up financial analysts to create innovative investment vehicles.

The "screening" of funds for what is called "shari'a-compliance" is one of the more important sites of controversy and critique. The screening function is played by shari'a boards, which consist of individuals who claim to have or are represented as having expertise in the field of Islamic law and finance. For instance, the Dow Jones Islamic Market Indices screen stocks to remove corporations involved in industries such as alcohol, pork-related products, conventional financial services, entertainment, tobacco, and weapons and defense production.[28] Its "Shari'ah supervisory board" consists of four "Shari'ah scholars from around the world," whose geographic diversity (namely, Bahrain, Malaysia, Saudi Arabia, and the United States) arguably provides a proxy for diversity of Islamic views on financial products.[29] Writers on Islamic finance describe these supervisory boards as characteristic of the Islamic financial market system.[30] They provide implicitly, if not explicitly, a form of economic regulation outside the formal state legal system. But they are also subject to intense analysis and critique. As Kahf explains, the shari'a boards of several banks and investment firms consist of "well-known names in *fiqh* in the circles of professional *shari'a* scholars."[31] For instance, US-based Yusuf Talal DeLorenzo serves on the shari'a board for the Dow Jones Sharia Market Index and Guidance Financial Group, among others.[32] These boards convince "the religious-minded public" to deposit or invest their funds with the bank or investment firm. They provide conventional, mainstream, global bankers and investment firms a cover of acceptability in order to reach a market of potential Muslim investors who would have presumably found these conventional firms objectionable, but for grounds broadly but

[25] Incidentally, as Lyn and Zychowicz have shown, faith-based investing does not, given the economic irrationality (and potential inefficiency) of introducing values-based investment, underperform in relation to the market overall. Esmeralda O. Lyn and Edward J. Zychowicz, "The Impact of Faith-Based Screens on Investment Performance," *Journal of Investing* 19, no. 3 (2010): 136–143.

[26] Ibid., 137. [27] Ibid., 136.

[28] See http://www.djindexes.com/islamicmarket/ (accessed September 29, 2016). [29] Ibid.

[30] Ibrahim Warde, *Islamic Finance in the Global Economy* (Edinburgh: Edinburgh University Press, 2000), 5.

[31] Kahf, "Islamic Banks," 24.

[32] For the list of board members at Guidance Financial, see http://www.guidancefinancial.com/principled-finance/assurance-process/shariah-supervisory-board/ (accessed September 29, 2016).

ambiguously identified as "Islamic."[33] Morever, these shariʿa advisors have potential conflicts of interest in serving on these boards, given that they are paid handsomely[34] and can (and do) serve on multiple boards of competing firms.

III. A Critical Appraisal of Islamic Finance

A. Theory, Practice, and Status Quo

Given the difference between the theory and practice of Islamic finance, it is hardly surprising to find critics of the Islamic finance regime. Mahmoud El-Gamal, for instance, argues that Islamic financing is not designed, in practice, to achieve fair pricing or efficiency in transactions. Rather, as he expressly argues: "Islamic finance has placed excessive emphasis on contract forms, thus becoming a primary target for rent-seeking legal arbitrageurs"[35] chasing the conventional financial market.[36] Timur Kuran draws on the neo-classical economics of F. Hayek to suggest that the telos of an Islamic economics as a just distribution of equity, risk or resources, is little more than a "false conceit."[37] The most common critique, however, is that the various techniques to facilitate an interest-free banking or financial regime do not, in fact, avoid interest. The *murabaha* contract is often singled out for this critique. Advocates of Islamic finance would call *murabaha* a contractually based sale with a price mark-up. But this is only possible because of the two contracts involved in the transaction. Recall that in the case of a home mortgage, the bank purchases a home from the seller for, say, $100,000. It then turns around and sells that same home to the buyer for $120,000 in monthly installments paid over the course of a set of years. Technically, each contract is valid on its own terms. But taken together, it is hard not to see the price-markup as equivalent to interest-based financing. While one can argue that the bank assumes the full risk of home ownership pursuant to the first contract, that equity interest may be illusory where the two contracts are formed within seconds of each other to facilitate the sale of the house by the seller to the buyer.

Advocates of Islamic economics in general, and financing in particular, claim that the Islamic perspective on money, distribution, and trade offers an antidote to capitalism—which they critique for its crass individualism and inequality—and to

[33] Kahf, "Islamic Banks," 25. [34] Ibid., 26. [35] El-Gamal, xi. [36] Ibid., 178.

[37] Timur Kuran, "The Economic Impact of Islamism," in *Islam & Mammon*, 1–37 (Princeton: Princeton University Press, 2004), 33.

socialism—which they critique for its failure to respect private property and ownership.[38] As Lena Rethel explains, Islamic economic philosophy:

> contains strong elements of redistribution (as through *zakat*, mandatory alms-giving by individuals and firms), the idea of participatory economic growth, and risk-sharing as the basis of a more equitable development ... Thus Islamic finance bases its claim to legitimacy on the greater social justice of the *outcomes* it intends to achieve.[39]

Moreover, advocates of Islamic finance situate this philosophical disposition within a broader conception of the purposes or aims of Islamic law, namely the *maqasid al-shariʿa*. This concept is drawn from premodern sources of legal theory (*usul al-fiqh*), and provides an interpretive vehicle for advocates to reconcile historical change with a legal tradition premised upon the expression of divine will. The *maqasid al-shariʿa* are often defined as the values that Islamic law seek to protect and enhance, of which the following five values are commonly proffered: life, lineage, property, mind, and religion.[40] The protection of property, these advocates argue, provides the foundation for erecting a market-based system of trade, commerce, and financial investing, subject to general prohibitions against undue risk-taking, waste, and other forms of excess. On a *maqasid* theory, as some argue, "Islam considers profit motive of entrepreneurship to be halal and moral so far as it is free of interest, hoarding, bribery, speculation, monopoly, exploitation, and it [e.g. profit] is not the ultimate goal."[41] Yet critics suggest that the same *maqasid al-shariʿa* objectives can be invoked as standards to show that in practice, Islamic finance and banking fails these internal-to-Islamic law metrics of social justice.[42] In other words, the *maqasid* protection of private property interests ultimately flattens the distinction between Islamic finance and the conventional free market.

Islamic finance in theory aims to distribute risk and equity in order to facilitate a more just economic distribution among parties to a transaction. However, this commitment to fair distribution of risk and equity does not play out in practice. The formal partnership structures addressed above (*mudaraba* and *musharaka*) do not constitute the primary share of Islamic financial products in the Islamic banking and financial sector. Instead, Tarek Yousef's examination of eighty-one Islamic banks and financial institutions from 1994 to 1995 shows that *murabaha* financing vehicles constitute a significant percentage of financing in the Muslim majority world. For

[38] Timur Kuran, "The Economic Impact of Islamism," 1–37.

[39] Rethel, "Whose Legitimacy?" 75–98, 79.

[40] On *maqasid al-shariʿa* generally, see Felicitas Opwis, *Maslaha and the Purpose of the Law: Islamic Discourse on Legal Change from the 4th/10th to the 8th/14th Century* (Leiden: Brill, 2010).

[41] Farida Mohammed Shehu, Nor Hayati Binti Ahmad, and Al-Hasan al-Aidaros, "Islamic Entrepreneurship in the Light of Maqasid al-shariʿa: A Critical Review," *Journal of Social and Development Sciences* 6, no. 4 (2015): 6–14, 12.

[42] Walid Mansour, Khoutem Ben Jadidia, and Jihed Majdoub, "How Ethical is Islamic Banking in the Light of the Objectives of Islamic Law?" *Journal of Religious Ethics* 43, no. 1 (2015): 51–77.

instance, in the Middle East and North Africa, *murabaha* accounted for 67 percent of total financing in the region's Islamic banks and financial institutions. In South Asia, the figure was 67.5 percent. East Asia had the lowest percentage share of *murabaha* financing, with only 44.7 percent of total financing.[43] "From the perspective of many Muslim scholars and outside observers, the figures presented ... are at odds with the predictions of an equity-based Islamic model that is predicated on the profit-and-loss sharing principle."[44] It would seem that Islamic banks that rely on *murabaha* are no less risk-averse than conventional financing institutions. In fact, as Rethel has suggested, "given the path currently taken, Islamic finance will actually largely serve to reproduce, to legitimate, and thus to further entrench current financial structures, instead of creating a more equitable economic order."[45] Rather than offering an alternative to conventional financing and economic analysis, Rethel doubts whether Islamic finance "can evolve into a mainstream-capable alternative to the existing international financial system, while still meeting its own ethical pretences."[46]

B. Islamic Finance, Criminal Finance, and Security

When viewed through a security and policing lens, many writers remark how the structure of Islamic finance resembles the financial techniques of criminal organizations. As El-Gamal writes, the use of underlying assets in Islamic finance derivatives (in contrast to trading on debt) echoes how criminal organizations launder their illicit finances by "[relying] on commodity and asset trades—with over- or underinvoicing—to achieve their illicit goals."[47]

It should be noted, though, that this crime-like quality to Islamic financing is not inherent to the transaction. Rather it is imputed to this mode of financing because of a confluence of factors that bring together Islamic financing, Islamist political groups, and the global concern about terrorism since September 11, 2001. The historical link between Islamic finance and Islamist political groups extends back to the beginnings of Islamic finance, in particular the *Mit Ghamr* experiment in Egypt in the 1960s. Writers differ on why that experiment failed. Some offer no explanation at all,[48] while others merely note that the bank inspired others to develop similar experiments elsewhere.[49] But many suggest that the failure of *Mit Ghamr* had to do with its appeal to Islamist ideals and parties to the chagrin of Gamal Abd al-Nasser,

[43] Yousef, "The *Murabaha* Syndrome," 65. [44] Ibid., 66.

[45] Rethel, "Whose Legitimacy?" 89. [46] Ibid., 95.

[47] El-Gamal, *Islamic Finance*, 176. [48] Rethel, "Whose Legitimacy?" 82.

[49] Mohammad Malley, "Jordan: A Case Study of the Relationship between Islamic Finance and Islamist Politics," in *The Politics of Islamic Finance*, eds. Clement M. Henry and Rodney Wilson (Edinburgh: Edinburgh University Press, 2004), 192.

who considered the Islamist parties a threat to his regime. El-Gamal asserts that the founder of *Mit Ghamr*, Ahmed al-Najjar, was "equally influenced by the social and economic thought of the Muslim Brotherhood in Egypt and the mutual banking institutions that Dr. Al-Najjar witnessed in West Germany during his years of study there."[50] Others, however, suggest that al-Najjar had no such commitment to Muslim Brotherhood values. Kahf claims that al-Najjar "and people close to him were in fact at a considerable distance from the Muslim Brotherhood. He himself was very far from being of any political affiliation or aspiration."[51] Even Kuran argues that the bank itself was not avowedly Islamic, except perhaps in its public relations ploy to attract customers: "Mit Ghamr was not modeled after some Islamic enterprise of the past. Although it assumed a religious identity as a public relations ploy, its essential features were transplanted from a non-Islamic source [e.g. German mutual savings banks], with no attempt to disguise this appropriation."[52] Kahf suggests that the real problem, for the Nasser government and thereby for *Mit Ghamr*'s future, was the predominance of Islamists and Muslim Brotherhood members as clients and even employees of the *Mit Ghamr* banks.[53] Warde summarizes the various views on *Mit Ghamr*'s demise: "[b]y certain accounts the bank had encountered severe financial problems. Others suggest that the bank was commercially successful but was closed for political reasons, which ranged from fear of Islamic fundamentalism to disagreements over how the bank should be regulated."[54]

The story of *Mit Ghamr* illuminates the political implications of *raison d'etat*, reason of state, in the fortunes of Islamic finance. Even when El-Gamal describes Islamic finance as echoing criminal financial techniques, he situates the comparison in the context of terrorism in a post-September 11, 2001 environment: the danger of criminality in Islamic finance seems particularly poignant "in today's post-9/11 legal and regulatory environments."[55]

The security concerns about Islamic finance as a criminal façade coincides with security concerns about financing terrorism by Islamist groups such as al-Qaida. Shortly after the attacks on the World Trade Center, US government officials aimed their sights not only on Bin Laden, but also on the financial networks that made his organization and terror activity possible. The anti-terror policies and legislation that arose in the wake of those attacks cast a dark shadow of suspicion on Islamic banking and finance. As Henry and Wilson write, "[a]t least one offshore Islamic bank was shut down, and American officials, ignorant about Islamic finance, viewed any 'Islamic' bank with heightened suspicion."[56] The implication is not merely that Islamic finance and banking have become securitized (in the policing fashion), but

[50] El-Gamal, *Islamic Finance*, 163.

[51] Kahf, "Islamic Banks," 19 (footnotes omitted).

[52] Kuran, *Islam and Mammon*, 14.

[53] Kahf, "Islamic Banks," 19. See also Kuran, *Islam and Mammon*, 14.

[54] Warde, *Islamic Finance*, 74.

[55] El-Gamal, *Islamic Finance*, 176.

[56] Henry and Wilson, "Introduction," 1. See also Rethel, "Whose Legitimacy?" 86; Warde, "Gobal Politics," 52–56.

that they have assumed the mantle of marginal, peripheral, and "other." "[I]n the wake of the war on terror, Islamic finance has been portrayed as shady activities outside the 'normal' spheres of financial practice, 'underground money.'"[57]

Rethel argues that this othering of Islamic finance in political discourse has created the incentives for the Islamic financial sector to create regulatory bodies that improve its financial credibility[58] in large part by creating an institutional regulatory framework that gives greater transparency and accountability to the Islamic financial market. These institutions, such as the International Islamic Financial Market (IIFM), the Liquidity Management Center (LMC), the Accounting and Auditing Organization for Islamic Financial Institutions (AAOIFI), and the Islamic Financial Services Board (IFSB), are designed to ensure quality, transparency, and accountability in the Islamic financial market. Importantly, these Islamic financial oversight organizations take their design and knowledge-base from the "existing international financial architecture,"[59] which ironically further informs critics of Islamic finance who accuse its adherents of failing to offer an alternative to the conventional approach to finance and banking.

IV. Future Directions of Research

There are various directions to consider when thinking about future research in the field of Islamic finance. How one approaches this subject will depend on whether the "Islamic" denotes an object of analysis, or whether the "Islamic" serves as a standpoint from which to critique. The suggestions in this Section see "Islamic finance" as a site of epistemic and material practices that are equally objects of critique, and vantage points from which to parochialize the assumptions behind "conventional" investment structures. By approaching Islamic finance as both object and standpoint of critique, we can better witness and appreciate the intersection between the rise and critique of "Islamic finance" and the rise and critique of "neoliberalism."

A. Economic Rationality and the Secular

So much ink has been spilled in recent years on addressing the relationship between the religious and the secular, and in particular how the religious—more

[57] Rethel, "Whose Legitimacy?" 86. [58] Ibid. [59] Ibid., 88–89.

often the "Islamic"—can best be understood by reference to the secular as a state project. These research endeavors have opened the door for considerable reflection about the politics of the secular, the politics of religion, and the place of religion in avowedly secular states. In these projects, one thing that has remained stable, a constant that ought to become a variable—the state. Hussein Agrama's study on secularism and Islamic law takes the Egyptian state and its institutional bureaucracy for granted as he ethnographizes how people engage *state* institutions like the judiciary and the *fatwa* council.[60] Saba Mahmood's important study on religious freedom also takes aim at religious freedom jurisprudence by juxtaposing the jurisprudence in the Muslim majority state of Egypt on the country's Coptic Christian minority, and the decisions of the European Court of Human Rights.[61] By situating "Islamic" in relation to its legal and institutional other, both Agrama and Mahmood use the "Islamic" methodologically as a standpoint from which to better appreciate the claims that animate the secularizing logic of state institutions and human rights norms.

One scholarly by-product of this reckoning with the "Islamic" has been an interrogation of the relationship between the religious and the secular, in particular whether and how the religious can only be understood by reference to *the secular as a state project*. These research endeavors have opened the door for considerable reflection about the politics of the secular, the politics of religion, and the place of religion in avowedly secular states. But they have also raised a fundamental challenge against the presumptively "secular" frame of "critique" in the academy.[62]

But even if critique is not necessarily secular, whether framed in Marxian or other terms, what would a non-secular critique look like? More specifically, what would an "Islamic" critique look like? Would it be an oppositional critique of the state, for instance, or an alternative critique of the state? Would it seek to subvert or alter the modes of production, the distribution of wealth, the exercise of power? Or perhaps, the competing ideas of a "secular" critique and an "Islamic" critique are themselves distortions of—or perhaps distractions from—the often painstaking work of critique.

Without taking a stand on critique as secular or something else, future scholars may find that Islamic finance provides an opportunity to examine how we construe "rational action" in the market amid a range of considerations that cannot be reduced to the descriptor of "secular."[63] Critics have suggested that rather than

[60] Hussein Ali Agrama, *Questioning Secularism: Islam, Sovereignty, and the Rule of Law in Modern Egypt* (Chicago: University of Chicago Press, 2012).

[61] Saba Mahmood, *Religious Difference in a Secular Age: A Minority Report* (Princeton: Princeton University Press, 2015).

[62] Talal Asad, Wendy Brown, Judith Butler, and Saba Mahmood, *Is Critique Secular? Blasphemy, Injury and Free Speech*, 2nd edn. (New York: Fordham University Press, 2013).

[63] In contrast, the Nobel laureate economist Douglas C. North consistently couched his approach to economic history as an "analysis of secular changes." Douglas C. North, *Structure and Change in*

offering an alternative to capitalism or socialism, Islamic finance is more often a formalistic attempt at chasing the returns of conventional financing products. If this criticism is right, then it allows others to interrogate whether and how the already existing (presumably secular) market becomes the measure of an avowedly "religious" set of financial practices that is no less concerned with maximizing profits.

B. Islamic Philanthropy as Mirror

The field of Islamic finance so emphasizes the legal architecture of capital investment, business, and entrepreneurship that it virtually excludes from its ambit the Islamic tradition of charity, which is no less financial, but aims at redistribution rather than profit maximization. Of interest, then, is not only that both coexisted historically and today, but also (and most intriguing) that they are nearly sequestered from each other in contemporary debates about Islamic finance and Islamic economics. Adam Sabra's *Poverty and Charity in Medieval Islam* offers a preliminary social history of poverty and its alleviation in Mamluk Egypt. His study examines the poor, who occupy a special religious status, and the implications of their status across different literary genres (e.g. law and Sufism) that address potential benefactors.[64] Examining "poverty and piety as conceptualized by Muslims,"[65] he reveals how poverty had both religious, intellectual, and social salience in premodern Muslim societies. In contrast to twentieth-century welfare reform that has criminalized the poor as "welfare queens,"[66] for instance, Sabra reveals how premodern Muslim literature cast poverty as an "indication of extreme piety," and a "sign of being chosen by God."[67]

Studies of Islamic charity across the *longue dureé*, in other words, reflect a very presentist concern about the fate of the welfare state in a context of increased privatization of government services. Amy Singer is explicit about the link between contemporary debates on welfare and premodern Islamic approaches to charity:

> To understand the history of charity means also to understand how notions of entitlement and obligation evolved in societies, creating the networks of responsibility and dependence in which we live today. Without an appreciation of the ways in which states and societies develop effective forms of relief for dependent individuals and groups, one can scarcely

Economic History (New York: W.W. Norton, 1981), 20. See also Albert O. Hirschman, *The Passions and the Interests* (Princeton: Princeton University Press, 2013), for a critical analysis of the history of what would become economic rationality.

[64] Adam Sabra, *Poverty and Charity in Medieval Islam: Mamluk Egypt, 1250–1517* (Cambridge: Cambridge University Press, 2000).

[65] Sabra, *Poverty and Charity*, 7.

[66] Julilly Kohler-Hausmann, "Welfare Crises, Penal Solutions and the Origins of the 'Welfare Queen,'" *Journal of Urban History* 41, no. 5 (2015): 756–771.

[67] Sabra, *Poverty and Charity*, 17.

comprehend much of contemporary political and economic discourse and culture. The same is true of the past.[68]

More provocatively, Mona Atia examines the relationship between piety, charity, and governmentality in her analysis of what she calls "pious neoliberalism." Pious neoliberalism, she explains, "connotes a transformation in both religious practice and modalities of capitalism. It represents a new compatibility between business and piety that is not specific to any religion, but rather is a result of the ways in which religion and economy interact in the contemporary moment."[69] Her examination of Islamic charity in modern Egypt serves as a case study that allows her to situate charity alongside Islamic finance in her broader critique of neoliberalism as policy, ideology, and governmentality. In her study, she recasts Islamic charity "as an economic act" and challenges the "scripting of the economy and charity as mutually exclusive."[70] Indeed, she explicitly links the formation of "Islamic finance" as knowledge and practice to Islamic charity and philanthropy:

> Much like the production of conventional finance, the production of Islamic finance required a drastic recalibration of the field to sever finance from charity. Divorcing the economy from social concerns by separating out charity from other aspects of Islamic economics allowed investment and development to occur unabated by rising inequality while perpetuating and accelerating the neoliberalization of the economy.[71]

Atia's study imaginatively brings together a critique of neoliberalism and a study of Islamic charitable practices in Egypt to gesture toward new scholarly inquiries that bring the field of Islamic finance into conversation with other fields deemed distinct or disparate. For instance, Jonathan Benthall and Jérôme Bellion-Jourdan offer a useful example that illustrates the relation between Islamic charity, Islamic finance, and the marketized rationality of individual piety. In an examination of the Muslim cleric Yusuf al-Qaradawi, Benthall juxtaposes Qaradawi's monumental study of the Islamic alms tax (*zakat*) and the relief of poverty with his recasting of *zakat* in more entrepreneurial terms in his capacity as a shari'a advisor to Islamic investment banks. As Benthall describes, "[a]ccording to Qaradawi and some other authorities, zakat funds may be used to help an individual set up his own business."[72] In other words, the operation of charity may be inserted into the very enterprise of Islamic finance, thus transforming the charitable act into an Islamic financial investment, where instead of focusing on the pious poor, philanthropy becomes a risk-averse investment procedure that rewards the enterprising and profit-maximizing entrepreneur.

[68] Amy Singer, *Charity in Islamic Societies* (Cambridge: Cambridge University Press, 2008), 3.

[69] Mona Atia, *Building a House in Heaven: Pious Neoliberalism and Islamic Charity in Egypt* (Minneapolis: University of Minnesota Press, 2013), xvi.

[70] Ibid., xvii. [71] Ibid.

[72] Jonathan Benthall and Jérôme Bellion-Jourdan, "Waqf and Islamic Finance: Two Resources for Charity," in *The Charitable Crescent: Politics of Aid in the Muslim World* (London: I.B. Tauris, 2003), 43.

References

Agrama, Hussein Ali, *Questioning Secularism: Islam, Sovereignty, and the Rule of Law in Modern Egypt* (Chicago: University of Chicago Press, 2012).

Al-Jassas, Abu Bakr, *Ahkam al-Qur'an* (Beirut: Dar al-Kutub al-'Ilmiyya, 1994).

Al-Mahalla, Jalal al-Din Muhammad bin Ahmad and al-Suyuti, Jalal al-Din, *Tafsir al-Jalalayn* (Maktaba Arslan: Turkey, n.d).

Asad, Talal, Brown, Wendy, Butler, Judith, and Mahmood, Saba, *Is Critique Secular? Blasphemy, Injury and Free Speech* (2nd edn. New York: Fordham University Press, 2013).

Atia, Mona, *Building a House in Heaven: Pious Neoliberalism and Islamic Charity in Egypt* (Minneapolis: University of Minnesota Press, 2013).

Benthall, Jonathan, and Bellion-Jourdan, Jérôme, "Waqf and Islamic Finance: Two Resources for Charity." In *The Charitable Crescent: Politics of Aid in the Muslim World*, 29–44 (London: I.B. Tauris, 2003).

Haque, Ziaul, *Islam and Feudalism: The Economics of Riba, Interest, and Profit* (Lahore: Vanguard Books, 1985).

Henry, Clement M., "Financial Performances of Islamic Banks *versus* Conventional Banks" in Clement M. Henry and Rodney Wilson (eds.) *The Politics of Islamic Finance* (Edinburgh: Edinburgh University Press, 2004) 104–128.

Henry, Clement, and Wilson, Rodney, "Introduction" in Clement M. Henry and Rodney Wilson (eds.) *The Politics of Islamic Finance* (Edinburgh: Edinburgh University Press, 2004) 1–16.

Hirschman, Albert O., *The Passions and the Interests* (Princeton: Princeton University Press, 2013).

Kahf, Monzer, "Islamic Banks: The Rise of a New Power Alliance of Wealth and *Shari'a* Scholarship" in Clement M. Henry and Rodney Wilson (eds.) *The Politics of Islamic Finance* (Edinburgh: Edinburgh University Press, 2004) 17–36.

Kohler-Hausmann, Julilly, "Welfare Crises, Penal Solutions and the Origins of the 'Welfare Queen.'" *Journal of Urban History* 41, no. 5 (2015): 756–771.

Kuran, Timur, "The Economic Impact of Islamism." In *Islam & Mammon*, 1–37 (Princeton: Princeton University Press, 2004).

Lyn, Esmeralda O., and Zychowicz, Edward J. "The Impact of Faith-Based Screens on Investment Performance." *Journal of Investing* 19, no. 3 (2010): 136–143.

Mahmood, Saba, *Religious Difference in a Secular Age: A Minority Report* (Princeton: Princeton University Press, 2015).

Mallat, Chibli, "The Debate on Riba and Interest in Twentieth Century Jurisprudence" in Chibli Mallat (ed.) *Islamic Law and Finance* (London: Graham & Trotman, 1988) 69–88.

Malley, Mohammad, "Jordan: A Case Study of the Relationship between Islamic Finance and Islamist Politics" in Clement M. Henry and Rodney Wilson (eds.) *The Politics of Islamic Finance* (Edinburgh: Edinburgh University Press, 2004) 191–215.

Mansour, Walid, Jadidia, Khoutem Ben, and Majdoub, Jihed, "How Ethical is Islamic Banking in the Light of the Objectives of Islamic Law?" *Journal of Religious Ethics* 43, no. 1 (2015): 51–77.

North, Douglas C., *Structure and Change in Economic History* (New York: W.W. Norton, 1981).

Opwis, Felicitas, *Maslaha and the Purpose of the Law: Islamic Discourse on Legal Change from the 4th/10th to the 8th/14th Century* (Leiden: Brill, 2010).

Rahman, Fazlur, "Riba and Interest." *Islamic Studies* 3, no. 1 (1964): 1–43.

Rethel, Lena, "Whose Legitimacy? Islamic Finance and the Global Financial Order." *Review of International Political Economy* 18, no. 1 (2011): 75–98.

Sabra, Adam, *Poverty and Charity in Medieval Islam: Mamluk Egypt, 1250–1517* (Cambridge: Cambridge University Press, 2000).

Saleh, Nabil al-, *Unlawful Gains and Legitimate Profit in Islamic Law* (Cambridge: Cambridge University Press, 1986).

Shehu, Farida Mohammed, Ahmad, Nor Hayati Binti, and Aidaros, Al-Hasan, "Islamic Entrepreneurship in the Light of Maqasid al-shari'a: A Critical Review." *Journal of Social and Development Sciences* 6, no. 4 (2015): 6–14.

Singer, Amy, *Charity in Islamic Societies* (Cambridge: Cambridge University Press, 2008).

Warde, Ibrahim, "Global Politics, Islamic Finance and Islamist Politics Before and After 11 September 2001" in Clement M. Henry and Rodney Wilson (eds.) *The Politics of Islamic Finance* (Edinburgh: Edinburgh University Press, 2004) 37–62.

Warde, Ibrahim, *Islamic Finance in the Global Economy* (Edinburgh: Edinburgh University Press, 2000).

Yousef, Tarik M., "The *Murabaha* Syndrome in Islamic Finance: Laws, Institutions and Politics" in Clement M. Henry and Rodney Wilson (eds.) *The Politics of Islamic Finance* (Edinburgh: Edinburgh University Press, 2004) 63–80.

CHAPTER 34

ANIMALS

KRISTEN STILT

I. DEFINING THE QUESTION

THIS chapter examines the new and growing field of study of Islamic animal law. Before determining what makes animal law Islamic, it is helpful first to define the term "animal law" and to consider the developments in the field of animal studies that have profoundly affected the way that we think about the relationship between human and nonhuman animals, and the role of law in that relationship. In its most general sense, animal law is understood to refer to laws that human animals have made to categorize, regulate, and control nonhuman animals, conceptually and physically.[1] In doing so, humans have drawn a stark and rigid divide between "us" and "them." The laws humans have made include rules on, for example, the sale of animals and how to treat animals, such as at the time of slaughter. Most typically, animals are objects under this broad definition of animal law, such as objects of a transaction or of a ritual.

The concept of animal law has recently shifted to accommodate a new animal-centered view, which was influenced by an increasing scholarly interest in animals and the relationship and connections between humans and animals. This growing interest in animals, often called the "animal turn," has resulted in the broader interdisciplinary movement of animal studies. Following other areas of critical studies, the field of animal studies seeks to "foreground the nonhumans with whom we

[1] For a discussion of the concept of "animal law," see Kristen Stilt, "Law," in *Critical Terms in Animal Studies*, ed. Lori Gruen (Chicago: Chicago University Press, 2018).

share this planet"[2] and to critically examine the interactions between human and nonhuman animals.[3] It boldly and simply calls upon scholars to view animals as subjects.

Within the field of law, the "animal turn" has involved the recognition that the sentience of nonhuman animals is legally relevant, leading to new types of scholarship as well as to calls for animals to be treated, and protected, as sentient beings in the physical world. The historical roots of this new approach in western legal systems can be found in Jeremy Bentham's call in 1780 to recognize the legal significance of animal sentience;[4] its first full expression came with Peter Singer's *Animal Liberation* and his assertion that "capacity for suffering and enjoyment" is the criterion for determining whose interests matter.[5] Alongside a traditional notion of animal law, then, an animal-centric animal law has developed and is now a significant part of legal scholarship. Animal-centric animal law is, in its most basic sense, "statutory and decisional law in which the nature—legal, social, or biological—of nonhuman animals is an important factor."[6] It is law in which the interests of nonhuman animals matter.

This brief overview of the field of animal law allows for a meaningful definition of Islamic animal law and for an understanding of the similarities and differences between animal law in non-Islamic and Islamic contexts. In the Islamic context, the same general evolution as outlined above applies, with some important additions and nuances. Premodern Muslim jurists dealt with animals in their legal doctrine (*fiqh*) in many ways, under headings as diverse as prayer, purity, zakat tax, contracts, slaughter, lost items, and permissible food. Some premodern Muslim scholars were, to varying degrees, concerned with animal subjectivities and not just with animals as an instrument of the desires and demands of humans. There are very few texts from the premodern period in which animal welfare is central, most notably, a short book by Muhammad b. ʿAbd al-Rahman al-Sakhawi (d. 1497) that includes hadith on topics such as the treatment of riding animals.[7] Modern works that reflect a broad conception of animal law—meaning any law that concerns nonhuman

[2] Paul Waldau, *Animal Studies: An Introduction* (New York: Oxford University Press, 2013), ix.

[3] Waldau, *Animal Studies*, 1.

[4] In *An Introduction to the Principles of Morals and Legislation* (Mineola, NY: Dover Publications, 2007), Bentham famously stated that "the question is not, Can they *reason*? Nor, Can they *talk*? But, Can they *suffer*?" (at 311).

[5] Peter Singer, *Animal Liberation: A New Ethics for Our Treatment of Animals* (New York: HarperCollins, 1975), 7.

[6] Sonia S. Waisman et al., eds., *Animal Law: Cases and Materials*, 5th edn. (Durham, NC: Carolina Academic Press, 2014), xxxi.

[7] Muhammad b. ʿAbd al-Rahman al-Sakhawi, *Juz' fi tahrir ʿan darb al-dawab* (Beirut: Dar al-Hazm, 1998). The editor, Muhammad Khayr Ramadan Yusuf, finds the title (which refers to the beating of animals) inexplicable. The first few pages of the book do cover the rules on the beating of animals and when it is permissible, but given that most of the book is about the protection of animals, Yusuf wrote in his preface that a better title, and one that he informally provided as subtitle, was *Min ahkam al-rifq bi-l-hayawan fi-l-sunna al-nabawiyya* (*The Rules of Kindness to Animals in the Prophetic Sunna*).

animals—are common. These modern publications, which merely summarize and restate rules from the schools of law, are typically titled *Ahkam al-hayawan fi-l-fiqh al-Islami* (*Rulings on Animals in Islamic Jurisprudence*) and are concerned with animals only insofar as they are part of the legal rules pertinent to humans.[8]

Recently, however, there has been a growing body of legal scholarship on the subject of animal protection in Islamic law, and scholars are asking questions of the sources to retrieve lines of thought that have been overlooked or obscured by traditional notions of animal law. Their scholarship directly or indirectly connects to the concerns generated by the broader field of animal studies introduced above, but their historical reference is not to Bentham or even to his time period, but rather to the earliest sources of Islamic law. From the formative period, there were strains of concern for animals themselves, leading to the oft-made claim, as noted later in this chapter, that Islamic law was concerned with the welfare of animals long before the West. The comparison between Islamic and non-Islamic notions of animal welfare is a prominent theme in the literature discussed in this chapter, which suggests that animal law is similar to other areas of law in which contestations have developed over which legal system, religion, or society treats a particular group or issue better, and which was the first to do so—contestations that have included women's rights and human rights, and now include the rights, welfare, and interests of animals.[9]

This chapter focuses on animal-centric law in the Islamic context—that is, scholarship in which concern with the subjectivity of animals is an important or the main factor. This relatively new field of study is rapidly growing, with several important projects currently in progress, and it is an area with significant potential for new scholarship. As with animal law in other religious traditions, or with other subject areas within Islamic law, current interest in Islamic views on animals also intersects with the concerns of advocates, and animal protection activists in Muslim contexts are searching for Islamic arguments to support their cause.[10] This chapter begins with a discussion of the historical development of this field, paying attention

[8] See, e.g., two publications with this title: one by Husam Sufayhi (Cairo, 2006) and the other by ʿAbd Allah b. Husayn Mawjan (Jedda, 2004).

[9] See, e.g., Farah b. Taha Farah Al Taha, *al-Rifq bi-l-hayawan fi-l-Islam* (Amman: Wa'il, 2003) for the assertion that Islam predated the concern of western civilization with animal welfare by more than twelve centuries. See also Mahfouz ʿAzzam, *Huquq al-insan wa-l-hayawan fi-l-Islam* ([Cairo]: Dar al-Hidaya li-l-Tibaʿa wa-l-Nashr wa-l-Tawziʿ, 2013).

[10] A prominent contemporary Egyptian activist, Amina Abaza, used the short publication by H.M. Makhluf, discussed in Section II, for many years in her advocacy efforts, before she commissioned a booklet on the same topic that spoke specifically to the current issues relating to animals and the Islamic rules for their treatment. Abaza carried hundreds of photocopies of Makhluf's book in her car, and passed them out to Egyptians whenever she had a conversation about animals. A short publication written in an advocacy context is *Animal's Rights in Islam* (Saarbrücken, Germany: VDM Verlag, 2009), by Fakhar-i-Abbas, a Pakistani biologist. He led a campaign in Pakistan on behalf of the organization World Society for the Protection of Animals (since renamed World Animal Protection) aimed at combatting abuses of the wild bears that are nearly extinct in the country, and subsequently wrote the booklet to "highlight the importance and treatment of wildlife according to Islamic injunctions" (at 7).

to two authors in particular. It then moves to an assessment of contemporary scholarship, organized according to four areas of scholarly focus: purity and the dog; the permissibility of killing animals; anthropocentricism; and slaughter and the category of *halal* as it applies to animals consumed as food. It concludes by highlighting promising areas of new scholarship.

II. Historical Development of the Field

The modern field of animal-centric law in the Islamic context has its origins in a brief publication from 1964 entitled *al-Rifq bi-l-hayawan fi-l-shari'a al-Islamiyya* (*Animal Welfare in Islamic Law*).[11] The author, Hasanayn Muhammad Makhluf (d. 1990), recognized the sentience of animals and was explicitly concerned with their welfare. He had served as the Grand Mufti of Egypt (1946–1950, 1952–1954), and this was his only publication about animals.[12] His preface reveals his reasons for writing: A conversation had taken place fifty years earlier between his father, Muhammad Hasanayn Makhluf al-'Adawi (d. 1936)[13] and an unnamed Egyptian elder on the topic of kindness to animals (*al-rifq bi-l-hayawan*). The distinguished elder noted that being kind to animals was something that foreign countries were concerned with and that societies dealing with kindness to animals had been established there. A similar kind of society had finally been set up in Egypt, the elder said, adding that the topic was not a significant one for his forefathers in Islamic countries, and that they had not even been aware of it. Al-'Adawi confirmed that kindness to animals was important, but corrected the elder by asserting that Islam had been concerned with it for fourteen centuries before the West. He pointed to Prophetic hadith that mention it, as well as to the position of controller of the public space (*muhtasib*) that existed in Islamic countries, implying that the *muhtasib* was responsible for animal welfare in the marketplace. The elder was surprised and pleased by this news, and asked al-'Adawi to provide him with some of the hadith texts to use in his lectures and to persuade foreigners concerned with kindness to animals that Islam predated their concerns, and that Islam was a religion of mercy and kindness.

[11] Hasanayn Muhammad Makhluf, *al-Rifq bi-l-hayawan fi-l-shari'a al-Islamiyya* (Cairo: Matba'at al-Madani, 1964). The book was reprinted in Cairo in 2011.

[12] See Jakob Skovgaard-Petersen, *Defining Islam for the Egyptian State: Muftis and Fatwas of the Dar al-Ifta* (Leiden: Brill, 1997), 170–181, for a biography of Makhluf.

[13] See Skovgaard-Petersen, *Defining Islam for the Egyptian State*, 170–171, for a short biography of al-'Adawi.

Makhluf then relates that his father instructed him to write a treatise on the topic of kindness to animals, and directed him to the sources he needed. Makhluf carried out the order and printed the treatise in Egypt in 1914 (of which there does not seem to be an extant copy). As reason for the 1964 publication, Makhluf wrote that it seemed appropriate, after such a long period, to revisit the topic and revise the original treatise. The father's conversation with the unnamed elder is significant for conveying that Makhluf's initial impetus for writing the treatise was to show foreigners that Islam predated their concerns, but there is no explanation for what made Makhluf want to turn his attention again to it in the early 1960s, after a long writing career when he did not once touch upon the topic. There is no discussion, in the preface or in the revised text itself, of the social context for the period in which he was writing, so we do not know if he was even aware of the most pressing problems for animals at that time. The hadith that make up the book are quoted with little commentary or other discussion that would help interpret the hadith in order to connect to Makhluf's contemporary situation or to be applied in a reader's personal life. Nevertheless, *al-Rifq bi-l-hayawan fi-l-shari'a al-Islamiyya* is the first modern effort at a publication focusing specifically on animal welfare in the sources of Islamic law, even though it limits itself to compiling those sources without any critical analysis.

Overall, Makhluf's short book indicates that there is strong support in Islamic legal jurisprudence for kindness to animals. He cites the many Prophetic hadith that urge kindness to animals in general, and then turns his attention to specific kinds of animals. Camels receive extensive treatment, reflecting their central role in the Arabian Peninsula at the time of Islam's revelation. Kindness to sheep is also highlighted, especially with respect to their treatment during slaughter. Makhluf does not question the permissibility of slaughter or ask whether slaughter is compatible with kindness to animals. The first hadith of the book, however, enjoins Muslims to be as merciful as possible when slaughtering an animal; it does not explain how this requirement should be understood in practice or what kinds of actions cause an animal pain, but Makhluf does cite the hadith that are concerned with the suffering of animals at the time of slaughter—for example, "Umar b. al-Khattab forbade slaughtering one sheep in front of the other because of the pain and fear it caused the second."[14] In another hadith cited, a butcher approached a sheep in order to slaughter her, but the sheep escaped and ran to the Prophet, with the butcher running behind. The butcher began to drag her by the leg, and the Prophet told him to herd her gently.[15] Although Makhluf does not say so specifically, these hadith seem intended to protect the interests of the animals. There is no explicit sense that there is a specific human benefit, although one could be construed regarding the quality of the meat of a terrified animal at time of death.

[14] Makhluf, *al-Rifq bi-l-hayawan fi-l-shari'a al-Islamiyya*, 27.

[15] Ibid.

The few hadith on dogs that were chosen by Makhluf are positive, providing examples of people who either received a heavenly reward for treating a dog with compassion or were punished for treating a dog cruelly. Significantly, however, the book does not try to address the many hadith that are negative toward dogs (as discussed below in the section on purity). Cats are left out completely, even though there are many hadith that view cats positively. Despite these limitations, especially those of bare quotation, the treatise marks an important moment in the development of the historiography of animal-centric Islamic law, a fuller expression of which emerges in the book that is discussed next.

III. Masri and the Turn to Animals

Scholarly attention to animal-centric Islamic law developed further with the 1987 publication in England of a short book entitled *Islamic Concern for Animals*.[16] The author, Basheer Ahmad Masri (d. 1992), was born in India and became the imam of the renowned Shah Jahan mosque in Woking, England. *Islamic Concern for Animals* is part scholarship, part sermon, and part advocacy, prompted by Masri's sense of "moral responsibility" to "express my views candidly on the current spate of cruelties to animals."[17] He drew upon many of the same primary sources as Makhluf, but used them in a way that is explicitly tied to his view of his contemporary world. As such, Masri was the first to connect classical Islamic law to contemporary questions about practices involving animals and he did so from the perspective that animal lives are worthy of respect and protection. He noted the general lack of awareness of the topic: "The learned theologians generally remain blissfully uninformed on this subject" and "the general Muslim public is not fully aware of the scale on which the human pecuniary, selfish and short-sighted interests have started exploiting the animal kingdom and making havoc of the ecological balance."[18]

Why did Masri devote attention to animals at this time, especially when he received comments that he "should be more concerned with other multifarious problems which Muslims are facing these days"?[19] By the time of its publication, 1987, concern for animals had started to become widespread, due in part to the publication of Singer's *Animal Liberation* in 1975. Singer's focus on factory farming and vivisection in particular brought these issues into the public spotlight in a new way. In 1987, Masri also spent considerable time on these two topics, although in contrast

[16] Basheer Ahmad Masri, *Islamic Concern for Animals* (Petersfield, UK: Athene Trust, 1987).
[17] Ibid., vii. [18] Ibid. [19] Ibid.

to a secular concern for animals, along the lines of Singer's utilitarian philosophy, he clearly voiced an Islamic concern.

Masri's message was even stronger than Makhluf's stated goal to show that Islam's concerns for animals came first by many centuries: "Our Islamic countries too have started treading in the footsteps of the West in the name of commerce and trade. No doubt we have a lot to learn from the Western technology and science, but surely animal welfare and environmental conservation is not one of these subjects."[20] He claimed that the Islamic concern for animals not only predated that in the West but was substantively superior, and that the development of factory farming and animal research in the West was not a model of emulation: "The Islamic instruction and guidance on animal rights and man's obligations concerning them are so comprehensive that we need not go elsewhere for any guidance."[21]

Masri used the term "animal rights" but he regarded humans as holding the collective position of "God's representative on earth" and recognized "Islam's corroboration of man's claim of superiority over the other species."[22] But this superiority does not give humans limitless powers, according to Masri; rather, the superiority is "circumscribed by mental, moral and physical limitations in the exercise of this power."[23] Substantively, Masri examined a series of topics from an Islamic vantage point, relying mainly on hadith, and he reached some strong conclusions. Although, like Singer, he was most interested in scientific testing on animals and factory farms, Masri went beyond those topics to many other areas of law. In the area of research, he noted that "there is no doubt that the Islamic prohibition against the cutting or injuring of live animals, especially when it results in pain and suffering, does apply to modern vivisection in science."[24] He asserted that "all life is sacrosanct" and advocated for an approach that would "set forth for ourselves the criterion that any kind of medical or scientific research that is unlawful on humans is unlawful on animals."[25] He condemned animal fighting by citing a hadith ("God's Messenger forbade inciting animals to fight each other")[26] and concluded that there is "no excuse for the Muslims to remain complaisant about the current killing of animals in their millions for their furs, tusks, oils, and various other commodities. The excuse that such things are essential for human needs is no longer valid."[27]

Some of his strongest language was directed at factory farming: "Man's exploitation of animals and the resources of nature is spreading like an epidemic. The contagious influence of the West has started affecting the character and destiny of the developing countries. Formerly, in those countries, cruelty to animals used to be inflicted mostly through individual ignorance and the lack of veterinary

20 Ibid. 21 Ibid.
22 Ibid., 2. This is a view that scholar Sarra Tlili challenges, as discussed in part B. Harming Animals.
23 Ibid., 2–3. 24 Ibid., 23. 25 Ibid., 18–19. 26 Ibid., 24. 27 Ibid., 20.

facilities. Now it is becoming a mammonish creed of rapacious grabbing by fair means or foul."[28] His depiction of the new form of the farm indicated concern with the conditions in which animals are raised, "tightly packed together in windowless houses of factory farms."[29] He noted the damage to rivers and streams from the runoff of these concentrated animal feeding operations (or CAFOs, a term—and acronym—that Masri did not use, but he certainly described the same type of operation). He criticized the treatment of dairy cows; the holding of male calves in restrictive crates and their slaughter at the age of sixteen weeks; the tightly restrained conditions of egg-laying hens; and the way in which modern farmers are taught to resist treating their animals as individuals.[30]

As for the slaughter of animals for food, Masri accepted that Islamic law permits it and he examined the rules of slaughter for concern with the welfare of the animals. Rather than focus on the technical requirements of what was permitted (*halal*), which is what the jurists typically did when discussing slaughter, Masri cited the many hadith that appear to be concerned with the animal's well-being, along the lines of the approach that Makhluf had taken, such as "when you must kill a living thing, do it in the best manner and, when you slaughter an animal, you should [use the best method and] sharpen your knife so as to cause the animal as little pain as possible."[31]

In 1989, Masri published *Animal Welfare in Islam*, an expanded version of his earlier book, which retained the original publication as its first chapter and added several new chapters, all dealing with animal consumption, in which he advocated bolder positions than in the earlier work.[32] While admitting that Islamic law allows for the killing of animals for food, he went beyond his earlier criticisms of factory farming to add new information about the environmental and economic unsustainability of meat-eating and the nutritional benefits of a vegetarian diet. Advocating for the latter, he asserted that Islam "has left the choice to the individual to be a vegetarian or a meatarian."[33] He addressed the issue of the sacrifice of animals, and in particular the sacrifice made during the pilgrimage (*hajj*) in Mina and replicated worldwide on the day of the Sacrificial Feast (*Eid al-Adha*). Masri was critical of Muslims who insist on sacrificing an animal at Mina on the pilgrimage, even when the amount of meat produced is far more than the pilgrims can consume. Masri also suggested that other means of making a charitable contribution might replace animal sacrifice at some point in the future, which would greatly reduce the number of animals killed.[34]

Masri presented Islamic law as providing support for animal welfare. In both *Islamic Concern for Animals* and the revised *Animal Welfare in Islam*, Masri did not

[28] Ibid., 24. [29] Ibid., 25. [30] Ibid., 25–27. [31] Ibid., 31.

[32] Basheer Ahmad Masri, *Animal Welfare in Islam* (Leicestershire: The Islamic Foundation, 1989).

[33] Ibid., 86. [34] Ibid., 116–127.

consider ways in which Islamic law has been understood to work to the detriment of animals or question how humans have interpreted Islamic law over the centuries in ways that were harmful for animals. Even without this critical lens, Masri's work is significant for opening up a new field of inquiry that examines the current state of the treatment of animals in light of Islamic law, going far beyond the work of Makhluf, which was limited to decontextualized hadith. Masri charted out many of the issues that scholars would later pick up and examine from an explicitly scholarly perspective. By firmly establishing a new field of inquiry, his work is important for taking a further step in the direction of animal-centered Islamic legal scholarship, which would develop more fully in the subsequent decades.

IV. Contemporary Scholarship

After these first steps, animal-centric Islamic legal scholarship fully emerged as a field of study in the twenty-first century. Richard Foltz's book, *Animals in Islamic Tradition and Muslim Cultures* (2006), deserves notice for its call for scholarship and for its recognition that the Islamic legal tradition is more complicated with respect to animals than has been previously acknowledged in modern scholarship. He states that he wrote the book "because there needs and deserves to be something available on the subject of animals in Islam, and for the present at least, no one else seemed prepared to do it."[35] Foltz's range of coverage in the book is broad—it includes animals in philosophy, science, literature, and art—but the section on animals in Islamic law is short, covering permissible food, wildlife, and domestic animals.

Foltz asserts that "the Islamic tradition does indeed offer much that can lend itself to respect for species other than our own, but it also contains much that is problematic from an animal rights activist point of view."[36] Commenting on the texts written on the subject of animals and Islamic law, he notes that they are typically merely collections of Qur'anic verses and hadith: "While such resources are no doubt valuable, today's conditions would seem to call for more than just reminders of forgotten premodern Islamic norms. What is largely missing now in the world of Islamic jurisprudence is any kind of deeper discourse that engages contemporary understandings of animal rights, factory farming, and species preservation."[37] While he only touches briefly on law and issues a general call for others to begin

[35] Richard Foltz, *Animals in Islamic Tradition and Muslim Cultures* (Oxford: Oneworld Publications, 2006), xii.

[36] Ibid., xii. [37] Ibid., 42–43.

working in this area rather than providing an in-depth analysis himself, Foltz is part of a new generation concerned with animal-centric legal scholarship.

A. Purity and the Dog

Purity is a concern of humans and the subjectivity of animals is irrelevant: animals are just one potential impurity among others. But purity issues do have significant implications for animals, and for dogs in particular. This can be seen in Marion Holmes Katz's *Body of Text* (2002), which, though it is a study of the development of Sunni ritual purity law, serves to highlight important issues and suggest paths for new scholarship related to animal welfare.[38] As Katz explains, Islamic law requires that a Muslim's body, clothing, and space for prayer be free of any impure substance (*najasa*) before performing acts of worship requiring purity. Thus, the body, clothing, or space must be washed before prayer if touched by a substance that is considered impure. "The main impure substances recognized by *most* schools of Islamic law are blood, bodily wastes (of humans and some animals), alcohol, carrion (that is, the dead bodies of animals that have not been ritually slaughtered), and the living or dead bodies of pigs and dogs."[39] For dogs, there are some important variations to this general rule of impurity. It is mainly the Hanbali and Shafi'i schools of law that hold that dogs are impure, so that touching a dog or being licked by a dog requires washing that portion of the body or clothing. The Maliki school does not consider dogs impure, and jurists of the Hanafi school generally consider only the saliva of dogs to be impure, so that only the part of the body or clothing that the dog's saliva touched needs to be washed.[40]

Khalid Abou El Fadl is particularly concerned with critically examining commonly understood Islamic legal views on dogs and their implications for animal welfare.[41] His essay on dogs in *Conference of the Books: The Search for Beauty in Islam* (2006) is the fullest published discussion of the status of the dog in Islamic law from a critical perspective. In *Conference of the Books*, a compilation of short essays, Abou El Fadl explains that "the essays were written in response to actual recurring problems in the Muslim community that are directly relevant to the moral

[38] Marion Holmes Katz, *Body of Text* (Albany: State University of New York Press, 2002).

[39] Holmes Katz, *Body of Text*, 2 (emphasis added).

[40] See the article on "Dog" (*kalb*), in *al-Mawsu'a al-fiqhiyya* (Kuwait: Ministry of Pious Endowments and Islamic Affairs, 1993), 35: 129.

[41] On the topic of the dog, see also Anver Emon, "Negotiating Between Utility and Purity in Medieval Islamic Law: A Case Study of the Dog in Early Islamic Legal Debates" (M.A. diss., The University of Texas, 1999).

and ethical definition of Islam in the contemporary world."[42] As well as dogs, topics include "censorship, political oppression, terrorism, the veil and the treatment of women, marriage, parental rights, the role of Islamic law, the dynamics between law and morality, and the character of the Prophet Muhammad."[43] Abou El Fadl's larger criticism is that "Muslims today are uprooted from their intellectual tradition, and the result has been that Muslims have lost the ethos of knowledge, as well as their moral and intellectual grounding."[44]

The essay on dogs is structured around a *fatwa* from Saudi Arabia that deals not just with purity but with the most significant legal rules concerning dogs generally. Abou El Fadl deconstructs the *fatwa* using the literary device of a study circle in Cairo that he participated in as a student:

> The gist of this *fatwa* was that a man told the Saudi shaykh that he once had a dog for a number of years. The man then heard that owning dogs is unlawful for Muslims and so he put his dog out in the streets. The dog, however, would not leave, and kept hanging around the front door of the man's house. Feeling sorry for the dog, the man and his children would put water and food outside the house for the dog to drink and eat. The problem the man said was that since the dog refuses to go away and the dog lives and is fed outside the house, is this situation lawful? May he continue to give the dog food and water outside the house although that necessarily means the dog will not go away? The Saudi shaykh responded that this situation is not acceptable because technically he still owns a dog, which is forbidden. The shaykh advised the man to stop supplying the dog with water and food, and if he stops feeding the dog, the Saudi shaykh claimed, it will only be a matter of time before the dog goes away.[45]

Through an examination of the *fatwa*, Abou El Fadl scrutinizes commonly held beliefs about the status of the dog. The first concerns the "black dog." One view is that "black dogs are devils in animal form," as reported in *Musnad Ahmad*.[46] In Abou El Fadl's narration, the study group leader, Shaykh Wadi, asks a student about the authenticity of the report, and praises her for responding that it is considered apocryphal by scholarly consensus. The Shaykh then moves to the question of impurity, and tells the students: "Assume that the dogs are indeed impure, why would the author of the *fatwa* suggest not only that the man put out the dog, but that he even stops feeding it so that it will go away?" One student's reply raises the issue of the many hadith that have a negative message about dogs: "Some of such hadith

[42] Khaled Abou El Fadl, *Conference of the Books: The Search for Beauty in Islam*, 2nd edn. (Lanham, MD: Rowman & Littlefield, 2006), xv.

[43] Ibid., xv. [44] Ibid., xvi. [45] Ibid., 319.

[46] Ibid., 320. Although Abou El Fadl often cites the names of texts, he does not provide full citations. This one refers to Ahmad b. Hanbal's *Musnad*. As noted earlier, the Hanbalis believed in the impurity of dogs.

state that angels will not enter the abode of a dog keeper [while] other hadith state the company of dogs voids a portion of a Muslim's good deeds. [Some] claim the Prophet commanded Muslims not to trade or deal in dogs, and even to slaughter all dogs, except those used in herding, farming, or hunting."[47] Although some of these "anti-dog" hadith are found in the canonical collections, Abou El Fadl reports that he "researched their authenticity and there is no consensus on the matter. All the traditions are of singular transmissions, most were declared weak or apocryphal—for instance, the tradition about the slaughtering of dogs, a number of scholars found that it was invented at a time of a rabies plague in Medina."[48]

The discussion then turns to an examination of these kinds of hadith from the perspective of reason and the principles of Islam. Regarding the hadith in which the Prophet ordered the killing of dogs, Abou El Fadl comments that "the vast majority of jurists rejected the traditions mandating the killing of dogs as pure fabrications because, they reasoned, such behavior would be wasteful of life."[49] Challenging them from a different perspective, he adds that "many of the commentaries on hadith have pointed out that these traditions conflict with stronger traditions; other sources argued that these traditions are inconsistent with the principles of Islam."[50] And putting rationality at the center, he added, "the rational question presented is how could God create these creatures and endow them with such qualities [of an inclination to domesticity and of loyalty] only to command us to hate them—why would God make them drawn to us by nature and yet command us to detest them."[51]

Shaykh Wadi directs the students to the issue of purity and asks: "What is the specific problem here?" Another student in the study circle replies that the focus is on the "Prophetic reports instructing that if a dog, regardless of the color, licks a container, the container must be washed seven times, with the sprinkling of dust in one of the washings. ... The essential point conveyed in these reports is that dogs are impure animals, or, at least, that their saliva is a contaminant that voids a Muslim's ritual purity."[52] Returning to the Saudi *fatwa* that sparked the discussion, the student adds that: "the authors of the *fatwa* could have warned the questioner that the saliva of dogs negates ritual purity, and leave it to the man to perform ritual cleansing when he comes into contact with the saliva. The issue of ritual impurity would definitely not call for the extreme measures recommended by the authors of the *fatwa*."[53] Shaykh Wadi comments that the issue about washing is actually just advice on an elementary point: "Do not eat and feed dogs from the same plates without first thoroughly cleaning them. Today this may seem to us a rather obvious point, but not back then."[54]

[47] Ibid., 321. [48] Ibid., 322. [49] Ibid. [50] Ibid.
[51] Ibid., 323. [52] Ibid. [53] Ibid., 324. [54] Ibid.

Abou El Fadl summons further evidence to show that the washing is just about cleaning for good health and not an obligatory act of ritual for worship. Sources indicate, for example, that the Prophet's cousins and some companions had puppies. Some reports show that the Prophet prayed with a dog nearby, and "there is considerable historical evidence that dogs roamed freely in Medina and even entered the Prophet's mosque";[55] others record that "a prostitute, and in some versions, a sinning man, secured their places in Heaven by saving the life of a dog dying of thirst in the desert. These various reports are in clear tension with reports prohibiting the ownership of dogs or reports that de-value the moral worth of dogs."[56] As a result, "the principles are not airtight and this frees considerable space to apply rational principles of analysis."[57]

Having dismissed all previous issues as insufficiently supported by evidence, two questions about the purity of the dog remain in Abou El Fadl's examination: "Is the saliva of dogs impure requiring the performance of ritual cleansing?" and "Are the bodies of dogs impure, similar for instance to the bodies of pigs, so that contact with the bodies of dogs requires the performance of ritual purity?"[58] Many jurists averred that there is no rational basis for dogs' impurity but that, like pigs, they must be considered impure due to religious texts. Other jurists, mainly belonging to the Maliki school, said that "everything found in nature is presumed to be pure unless proven otherwise, either through experience or text," which Abou El Fadl takes to mean that "all of the hadith we already discussed are not of sufficient reliability or authenticity so as to overcome the presumption of purity."[59] The conclusion that Abou El Fadl reaches is that "dogs and their saliva are pure."[60] The reason is that "unlike the case of pigs, the Qur'an does not contain a ruling about dogs. The Prophetic traditions are conflicting on this issue, and so returning to the legal presumption of the purity of everything in creation is correct."[61] Abou El Fadl does not stop there, but adds a caveat: "The exception, Shaykh, is if we have reason to believe a dog is filthy or consumes filth. I do agree that especially in the case of domesticated dogs, their consumption could be controlled and their cleanliness could be insured, and thus, their ownership is allowed."[62]

Abou El Fadl's chapter makes the important contribution of critically examining the Islamic legal rules concerning dogs, including but not limited to the issue of purity. His motivating concern is one of methodology and the importance of the use of reason to re-examine a position that purports to be supported by legal proof. In doing so, Abou El Fadl ends by marginalizing stray or street dogs and suggesting that they indeed might be literally dirty, and potentially also

[55] Ibid., 325. [56] Ibid. [57] Ibid., 326. [58] Ibid.
[59] Ibid., 327–328. [60] Ibid., 328. [61] Ibid. [62] Ibid.

ritually impure. He also does not raise any questions about the status of the pig; presumably the pig is out of bounds of critical reinterpretation for Abou El Fadl, although from the perspective of sentience, or intelligence, the dog and the pig are equals.

More scholarship on the origins of purity rules is needed in order to question the treatment of both the dog and the pig. A critical animal-centric approach would ask why some animals are considered impure, and what legal and social consequences result accordingly for those animals. Marion Katz provides some clues by noting that dogs and cocks were "the object of religious reverence among Zoroastrians"[63] and cites the influential orientalist Ignaz Goldziher (d. 1921) for the idea of "polemical reversals of Zoroastrian conceptions," including "the Muslim belief that dogs are impure (which contrasted sharply with Zoroastrian veneration of dogs)."[64] Investigating the social origins of these rules is a very promising area of future research and would help to explain why the dog, in particular, is the subject of so many hadith, many of which are negative. Such an examination would also reveal continuities and disruptions of views between Islam and other religions as well as the influence of law and social practice of these religious communities on the young Islamic community.

B. Harming Animals

Sarra Tlili has carefully looked for attention to the interests of animals in the classical sources of Islamic law in an effort to reread the tradition for animal-centric strains that have been overlooked or lost. She has made significant contributions to the literature in two areas: killing (and eating) animals and the issue of anthropocentrism.

In her chapter, "Animals Would Follow Shafi'ism: Legitimate and Illegitimate Violence to Animals in Medieval Islamic Thought," Tlili focuses her attention on the harming and killing of animals.[65] She investigates this issue in depth, beginning with the significant starting point that "nonhuman animals' sentiency is fully acknowledged in the mainstream tradition."[66] She supports this with the evidence of rules that prevented "*ilam al-hayawan* (inflicting pain on animals) and *ta'dhib al-hayawan* (causing animals to suffer)."[67]

[63] Katz, *Body of Text*, 4. [64] Ibid., 6.

[65] Sarra Tlili, "Animals Would Follow Shafi'ism: Legitimate and Illegitimate Violence to Animals in Medieval Islamic Thought," in *Violence in Islamic Thought from the Qur'an to the Mongols*, eds. Robert Gleave and István T. Kristó-Nagy (Edinburgh: Edinburgh University Press, 2015), 225–244.

[66] Ibid., 226. [67] Ibid.

Killing an animal for human consumption is acceptable because the "Qur'an pronounces an act that is generally considered violent—namely, killing—as legitimate" in the context of food.[68] In his revised edition of *Animal Welfare in Islam*, Masri stated that killing animals for food is permissible in Islamic law, but that Muslims are not obligated to eat meat.[69] Tlili expands further on this issue by stating that since the Qur'an permits (but does not require) meat consumption, exegetes concluded that Muslims may not prescribe meat-eating on the basis of Qur'an 5:87 ("Believers, do not prescribe the good things that God made permissible for you").[70] The permissibility of killing for food is constrained by the rule that it is wrong to cause additional pain—pain beyond that necessarily inflicted by the death—on the basis of the hadith seen in the writings of Makhluf and Masri.[71]

Why did God allow humans to harm some animals and even kill them for food? Tlili explains that while some scholars believed that animals were created for human use and did not probe the question any further, others sought an explanation for why innocent beings were used and even perished for the sake of humans.[72] One explanation is the idea of compensation, seen in the Muʿtazali theological school (fl. eighth to tenth centuries CE): "What allows the act of inflicting pain on animals to be acceptable is not the mere fact that God ordained it, but rather the assumption that He will compensate the victimised animals in the hereafter."[73] God has imposed obligations on both humans and nonhumans, and they will be rewarded for fulfilling them; in the case of animals consumed by humans, their obligation is to be slaughtered. All schools of law agreed that "gratuitous killing and mutilation are impermissible," with varying definitions of "gratuitous."[74]

Another example Tlili gives to show the value of animal life concerns animals as spoils of war captured by Muslims. Some schools of law allowed Muslims to kill the animals they captured if they were not able to take them away, for fear that leaving

[68] Ibid., 227. In addition, killing five types of animals (called *fawasiq*) outside the context of food is legitimate: "According to one report, these species are mice, kites, mottled crows, scorpions and ferocious dogs; whereas another mentions snakes instead of scorpions" (at 227). The Prophet may have instructed Muslims to kill the lizard and the Prophet is also "reported to have commanded the killing of the dogs of Medina, a command that he later reversed" (at 227–228). Aggressive beasts of prey also may be killed (at 228).

[69] This agrees with Kecia Ali's argument in an article on meat-eating that "secular feminist vegetarian insights can help Muslims concerned with gender justice to understand the intertwined nature of meat-eating and female subjection." Ali also asserts that "Muslim advocates for gender justice should be vegetarians." Kecia Ali, "Muslims and Meat-Eating: Vegetarianism, Gender and Identity," *Journal of Religious Ethics* 43, no. 2 (2015): 269.

[70] Tlili, "Animals Would Follow Shafiʿism," 227–228. Ali ("Muslims and Meat-Eating," 273 n. 2) notes that similar arguments are sometimes made against calls for the prohibition of polygamy and slavery.

[71] Tlili, "Animals Would Follow Shafiʿism," 228. [72] Ibid., 230.

[73] Ibid., 230–231. [74] Ibid., 233.

them behind would aid the enemy. The Shafiʿi view, in contrast, forbade the killing of animals other than the riding animals of soldiers engaged in warfare. The reason rests on the idea that animals have "two *hurmas* [inviolability] 'one belonging to their owners and the other to their Creator'."[75] On this reasoning, an owner of an animal is not allowed to neglect it, even though it is his property, because he is not allowed to neglect a right of God.[76] While this second *hurma* is a right of God, and not a right of the animal, Tlili argues that it should be seen not as a disregard of the animal but rather as the idea of *huquq* Allah, or God's rights, "imparting to their rights a degree of sanctity and accountability that is ultimately even more beneficial to them."[77] And yet some animals, such as a pig or even a "fierce dog," do not have a *hurma* and animals that do have *hurma* but can be slaughtered for food have a different calculation.[78]

Tlili concludes that the Shafiʿi school is the most protective on the issue of killing animals, or causing them harm, which does not mean that Shafiʿis have a particular interest in animals as animals—rather, it is at least in part a result of the school's methodology. Tlili also finds that the Hanbali school is more attentive overall to the interests of animals than the Malikis and Hanafis. Yet, since the Shafiʿis and Hanbalis share a methodological preference for texts, Tlili judges them more "Hadith champions than … animal champions."[79] As seen earlier in the discussion of Abou El Fadl's work, in the context of purity the textual preference means that the dog is in a less favorable position in the Shafiʿi and Hanbali schools than in the Maliki and Hanafi schools.

c. Anthropocentricism

Sarra Tlili's book, *Animals in the Qur'an*, has been recognized as the most significant monograph dealing with animals and Islamic law. She asks fundamental questions, focusing on the issues of anthropocentricism and theocentricism. The book is an "eco-centric reading of the Qur'an" that "seeks to challenge the assumption that only humans or the so-called rational beings are capable of engaging in meaningful relationships with God."[80] As she says in the preface, "I am totally persuaded that a non-anthropocentric reading of the Qur'an is not only warranted, but also much needed. This is the case not only because such reading deepens our understanding of the Islamic scripture, but also for its (interconnected) theological and ecological

[75] Ibid., 237. [76] Ibid. [77] Ibid., 238. [78] Ibid., 240. [79] Ibid., 244.
[80] Sarra Tlili, *Animals in the Qur'an* (New York: Cambridge University Press, 2012), ix.

implications."[81] Connecting her inquiry to the current treatment of animals, she comments that "in an Islamic context, there seems to be a correlation between the exaggeration of humans' status, which has peaked in modern Islamic thought, and Muslims' deteriorating attitudes toward nature in the last century or so."[82] Tlili uses the term "nature" but she is concerned specifically with animals.

Tlili explicitly positions herself in the growing field of animal studies, noting that in the past few decades the kind of questions that are asked about animals has changed dramatically.[83] She observes that the heightened interest in animals is related to the growing level and volume of abuse against animals in biomedical research and agribusiness in particular.[84] Her brief review of the practices in these two areas echoes concerns raised by Singer and Masri in their respective publications. She turns to Singer and his concerns about religion directly: "Although scientific inquisitiveness and financial gain are the main motivations for these practices, some thinkers maintain that they find their roots in old cultural and, more importantly, religious attitudes toward other animals."[85]

She notes that, in general, religion is seen as problematic for animals for two reasons: religions allow and sometimes even require that animals are killed for food and for religious sacrifice and religions promote anthropocentrism by placing humans at the top of a worldly hierarchy.[86] On the issue of anthropocentrism in particular, Tlili states that: "a number of modern ethicists and philosophers have challenged the notion of humans' superiority to other animals,"[87] including Peter Singer, with his approach of equal consideration for sentient beings, and the American philosopher Tom Regan, who advocates for rights for mammals of a certain maturity. While noting that scholars of Islam such as Georges-Henri Bousquet (d. 1978),[88] Masri, and Foltz assert that Islam recognizes the superiority of humans over animals, and conceding that these statements "do reflect the dominant views of Muslims concerning nonhuman animals," Tlili argues that "there are other plausible interpretations of Islamic, and more particularly, Qur'anic views of other animals."[89]

She attributes the loss, or the obscuration, of the non-anthropocentric aspects of the Qur'an to two factors. The first is that "some passages of the text seem to suggest the inferiority of other animals to humans," such as the permissibility of eating them, and the second concerns "anthropocentric ideas that have been (and

[81] Ibid., x. [82] Ibid., xi. [83] Ibid., 3–4. [84] Ibid., 4.
[85] Ibid., 5. [86] Ibid., 5–6. [87] Ibid., 6.
[88] Here, Tlili refers to his article "Des animaux et de leur traitement selon le Judaïsme, le Christianisme et l'Islam," *Studia Islamica* 9 (1958): 31–48.
[89] Tlili, *Animals in the Qur'an*, 7.

continue to be) projected on to the Qur'an."[90] Tlili explains why these ideas have been conceived and why they have endured for so long: "Challenges to anthropocentric attitudes cannot be expected to come from the parties that may have a personal interest in contesting them."[91] She compares this phenomenon to other interpretive issues in the Qur'an, especially issues of gender. Her goal is to "examine the status and nature of animals, human and nonhuman, mainly as portrayed in the Qur'an and to point to new possible ways of reading the Qur'an's animal themes."[92]

Tlili relies mainly on four Sunni exegetes: al-Tabari (d. 310/923), al-Razi (d. 606/1210), al-Qurtubi (d. 671/1273), and ibn Kathir (d. 774/1373) for their methodological diversity and because they are acknowledged as authoring major works of Qur'anic exegesis. Using them as her primary source, she asks the important question about nonhuman animals: "Are they inferior?"[93] She discusses the fact that "the Qur'an states that many animals are at the service of humans and goes into detail concerning how humans are entitled to use them" but argues that servility does not mean that their status is lower.[94] Instead, in Tlili's reading, "God does not delegate to humans any type of dominion over other animals; He only allows humans to derive a number of benefits from them."[95] She disputes the common idea that humans are God's representative, or vice-regent, on earth.

The most important Qur'anic verse for establishing "egalitarian tendencies" for species is 6:38 ("There is not an animal in the earth, nor a flying creature flying on two wings, but they are peoples like you. We have neglected nothing in the Book [of our decrees]. Then unto their Lord they will be gathered").[96] While this verse indicates that there are similarities between humans and other animals, it does not specify what these similarities are or what that implies for the treatment of animals. The exegetes found some similarities but more generally they had a "tendency to minimize the significance of this similarity, emphasize humans' distinction, or even interpret this verse in terms that are unflattering to nonhuman animals."[97]

Overall, based on the depiction of nonhuman animals in the Qur'an, Tlili concludes that they "come across as multidimensional beings with impressive depth" and "there is sufficient evidence in the Qur'an to suggest that nonhuman animals are considered moral, rational, and even accountable beings."[98] The Qur'an is theocentric, not anthropocentric, she argues, and while it spends much more time discussing humans than nonhumans, she attributes this to the simple fact that it is directed to humans. Her argument is that speaking about humans and to humans does not mean that the Qur'an "cherishes or values them more."[99] Rather, "privileged

[90] Ibid., 8. [91] Ibid., 9. [92] Ibid., 11.
[93] This is the title of Chapter 3 of *Animals in the Qur'an*.
[94] Tlili, *Animals in the Qur'an*, 136. [95] Ibid., 253.
[96] Ibid., 138. [97] Ibid., 139–140.
[98] Ibid., 138–139. [99] Ibid., 252.

status is contingent on moral and religious uprightness, not species membership."[100] The Qur'an also "lends itself to an eco-centric reading" in the sense that all that God has created is valued.[101]

Tlili's project goes far beyond previous scholarship to ask new questions that are theologically and legally very significant for animals. She reads the texts against the grain, looking for views that have not been fully articulated or have been lost over centuries of an anthropocentric culture. In doing so, she follows a similar research path to that which has been used for other areas of inequality, suggesting that the methodologies of recovering gender egalitarian readings are similar to those for recovering species egalitarianism.

D. Slaughter and the Designation of *Halal*

There is a tremendous amount of literature, mainly juridical, on the rules of *halal* slaughter, dating from the earliest writings of the jurists and continuing to the present.[102] Since an animal that is impermissible to eat is *haram*, or forbidden, ensuring that animals are slaughtered properly is a major issue in Muslim societies.[103] The requirements for *halal* are few and deal mainly with the act of killing. Interpretations of some *halal* matters vary among the legal schools, including, of the type of animal that is *halal*; of the invocation of the name of God at the time of slaughter; and of the religion of the person carrying out the slaughter.[104] There is also some disagreement as to the proper method—a widely held view is that at least one of the two jugular veins must be cut; some scholars require that both be cut, and some also require the trachea and esophagus to be cut as well.[105] A tool sharp enough to sever the veins must be used; it does not need to be a knife per se.[106] The slaughterer must pronounce the *basmala* (i.e. say "in the name of God") at the time of slaughter (according to some scholars, a forgetful omission is allowed). Finally, the person carrying out the slaughter must be a Muslim or a "person of the book"—a Jew or a Christian.[107]

As Sarra Tlili has shown, jurists were concerned about the animal's pain and suffering at the time of slaughter, although disregard for it does not, by itself, call

[100] Ibid., 252. [101] Ibid.

[102] For summaries of the rules, see Muhammad Taqi Usmani, *The Islamic Laws of Animal Slaughter*, trans. Amir Toft (Santa Barbara, CA: White Thread Press, 2006).

[103] On the relationship between the rules of slaughter and the rules regarding women, see the discussion at Section V.

[104] Usmani, *Islamic Laws of Animal Slaughter*, 26.

[105] Ibid., 9–30. [106] Ibid., 31.

[107] Ibid., 47.

the *halal* designation into question. New scholarship aims to look at these issues in even greater depth through a detailed study of the discussion of killing animals in Sunni *fiqh*, forthcoming from Nuri Friedlander.[108] This work will provide the first comprehensive review of how Sunni jurists understood the concept of killing for food and what limitations and requirements they placed on it. In the modern period, questions about the pain inflicted on animals in the process of slaughter include the significant issue of stunning. Stunning, such as by a blow to the head or by electric shock, is supposed to render the animal unconscious, both to reduce or prevent the sensation of pain and to allow the slaughterhouse workers to easily handle the animals. Modern Muslim scholars eventually had to address the issue of stunning, which was historically not part of *halal* slaughter, and determine whether it is permissible, which has led to significant debates among scholars and varying views. The legal history, and politics, surrounding these debates are also part of Friedlander's forthcoming work.

V. Areas for Future Research

As the discussion in this chapter has shown, the area of Islamic animal law is relatively new, with the most significant work written after the year 2000. It is also an area with substantial potential for growth, tracking the overall increasing attention to animal studies and animal law. Most scholarship to date has been doctrinally focussed, but there are still many areas of legal doctrine that need exploration and new legal questions about the treatment of animals and the human-animal relationship are constantly arising. Scholarship that examines the historical origins of legal doctrine concerning animals, and in particular the social context of the emergence of that doctrine, has significant potential. Also, the doctrinal work to date has been focussed on Sunni Islam, whereas significant differences between Sunni and Shiʿi Islam regarding some issues concerning animals, and purity in particular, merit careful attention to Shiʿism.

Scholarship that examines the relationship between animals and women in the Islamic context, following the work of Carol Adams (*The Sexual Politics of Meat: A Feminist Vegetarian Critical Theory*, 1990) outside of the Islamic context, is also very promising. Kecia Ali has taken preliminary steps in this direction, showing that further

[108] Harvard University, Ph.D. diss. (in progress).

work in this area could be very engaging. Drawing on her scholarship in the area of gender, Ali makes a connection between women and animals: "In a variety of Muslim contexts, female bodies (properly covered) and animal bodies (properly slaughtered) serve as potent signifiers. Not only are there parallels between women and animals, and between sex and food, but the conceptual utility of women and animals is linked: hierarchical cosmologies affirm male dominance in family and society and affirm human dominion over animals, legitimating their use, confinement, slaughter, and consumption." She argues that "patriarchal ideologies have come under fire by Muslim feminists" but "little attention has been paid to the related problem of animal subjection—indeed, there is typically no recognition that these issues are connected."[109] Ali has made that connection and charted a path for future work in this area.

Comparative work that looks for relationships between and among religions, both in doctrine and in practice, is another important direction for future scholarship. Recent work by Beth Berkowitz, Marion Katz, and Carol Bakhos has compared Islam, Judaism, and Christianity in several ways concerning animals.[110] More of this kind of work is needed, as is scholarship that considers the historical influences of other religious beliefs and practices on Islamic law and society, along the lines of the questions that Katz raised in *Body of Text* about the influence of Zoroastrianism on the early Muslim community's view on dogs.

There is also a great opportunity for future scholarship that takes a law-and-society approach to Islamic animal law. Advocates for change in animal law and in the treatment of animals in Muslim contexts are working to interpret and use Islamic law to their advantage, following the paths of advocates in other areas of Islamic law. There is, therefore, significant potential for new scholarship that uses the tools of the social sciences in particular to study Islamic law in these settings. For example, a forthcoming article by Kristen Stilt, "Constitutional Innovation and Animal Protection in Egypt," studies the animal protection movement in Egypt and examines the range of arguments that the Egyptian advocates used in an ultimately successful attempt to achieve a state obligation to provide for animal welfare, *al-rifq bi-l-hayawan*, in the 2014 Egyptian Constitution.[111] The advocates used Islamic arguments alongside appeals to international law and to the relationship between violence against animals and violence against humans. The drafters of the constitution also recognized the connection between protection of animals and protection

[109] Ali, "Muslims and Meat-Eating," 268–269.

[110] See Beth Berkowitz and Marion Katz, "The Cowering Calf and the Thirsty Dog: Narrating and Legislating Kindness to Animals in Jewish and Islamic Texts," in *Islamic and Jewish Legal Reasoning*, ed. Anver M. Emon (London: Oneworld Publications, 2016), 61–111; Carol Bakhos, "Jewish, Christian, and Muslim Attitudes Toward Animals," *Comparative Islamic Studies* 5(2) (2009): 117–219.

[111] Kristen Stilt, "Constitutional Innovation and Animal Protection in Egypt," *Law & Social Inquiry*, forthcoming 2018.

of the environment. There is a thriving animal protection movement throughout the Muslim world that deserves scholarly attention. Work that compares this relatively recent movement with other advocacy efforts, such as women's rights and human rights, could also be particularly effective.

References

Abou El Fadl, Khaled, *Conference of the Books: The Search for Beauty in Islam* (2nd edn. Lanham, MD: Rowman & Littlefield, 2006).

Adams, Carol, *The Sexual Politics of Meat* (New York: Continuum, 1990).

Al Taha, Farah b. Taha Farah, *Al-Rifq bi-l-hayawan fi-l-Islam: Dirasa haditha mawdu'iyya muqarana ma'a al-hadara al-gharbiyya* (Amman: Wa'il, 2003).

Ali, Kecia, "Muslims and Meat-Eating: Vegetarianism, Gender and Identity." *Journal of Religious Ethics* 43, no. 2 (2015): 268–288.

'Azzam, Mahfouz, *Huquq al-insan wa-l-hayawan fi-l-Islam* (Cairo: Dar al-Hidaya li-l-Tiba'a wa-l-Nashr wa-l-Tawzi', 2013).

Bakhos, Carol, "Jewish, Christian, and Muslim Attitudes Toward Animals." *Comparative Islamic Studies* 5, no. 2 (2009): 177–219.

Bentham, Jeremy, *An Introduction to the Principles of Morals and Legislation* (Mineola, NY: Dover Publications, 2007; repr. Oxford: Clarendon Press, 1907; first publ. 1789).

Berkowitz, Beth, and Marion Katz, "The Cowering Calf and the Thirsty Dog: Narrating and Legislating Kindness to Animals in Jewish and Islamic Texts" in Anver M. Emon (ed.) *Islamic and Jewish Legal Reasoning: Encountering Our Legal Other* (London: Oneworld, 2016) 61–111.

Bousquet, Georges-Henri, "Des animaux et de leur traitement selon le Judaïsme, le Christianisme et l'Islam." *Studia Islamica* 9 (1958): 31–48.

Emon, Anver, "Negotiating Between Utility and Purity in Medieval Islamic Law: A Case Study of the Dog in Early Islamic Legal Debates." M.A. diss., The University of Texas, 1999.

Foltz, Richard C., *Animals in Islamic Tradition and Muslim Cultures* (Oxford: Oneworld, 2006).

Katz, Marion Holmes, *Body of Text: The Emergence of the Sunni Law of Ritual Purity* (Albany: State University of New York Press, 2002).

Makhluf, Hasanayn Muhammad, *Al-Rifq bi-l-hayawan fi-l-shari'a al-Islamiyya* (Cairo: Matba'at al-Madani, 1964; repr. Cairo: Kashida li-l-Nashr wa-l-Tawzi', 2011).

Masri, Basheer Ahmad, *Islamic Concern for Animals* (Petersfield, UK: Athene Trust, 1987).

Masri, Basheer Ahmad, *Animal Welfare in Islam* (Leicestershire: The Islamic Foundation, 1989).

al-Mawsu'a al-fiqhiyya. 45 vols. (Kuwait: Ministry of Pious Endowments and Islamic Affairs, 1983–2006).

al-Sakhawi, Muhammad b. 'Abd al-Rahman, *Juz' fi tahrir 'an darb al-dawab* (Beirut: Dar al-Hazm, 1998).

Singer, Peter, *Animal Liberation: A New Ethics for Our Treatment of Animals* (New York: HarperCollins, 1975).

Stilt, Kristen, "Law" in Lori Gruen (ed.) *Critical Terms in Animal Studies* (Chicago: Chicago University Press, 2018).

Stilt, Kristen, "Constitutional Innovation and Animal Protection in Egypt." *Law & Social Inquiry*, forthcoming 2018.

Tlili, Sarra, *Animals in the Qur'an* (New York: Cambridge University Press, 2012).

Tlili, Sarra, "Animals Would Follow Shafi'ism: Legitimate and Illegitimate Violence to Animals in Medieval Islamic Thought" in Robert Gleave and István T. Kristó-Nagy (eds.) *Violence in Islamic Thought from the Qur'an to the Mongols* (Edinburgh: Edinburgh University Press, 2015) 225–244.

Usmani, Muhammad Taqi, *The Islamic Laws of Animal Slaughter: A Discussion on the Islamic Laws for Slaughtering Animals and a Survey of Modern-Day Slaughtering Methods.* Translated by Amir A. Toft (Santa Barbara, CA: White Thread Press, 2006).

Waisman, Sonia S., Pamela D. Frasch, and Bruce A. Wagman, eds., *Animal Law: Cases and Materials* (5th edn. Durham, NC: Carolina Academic Press, 2014).

Waldau, Paul, *Animal Studies: An Introduction* (New York: Oxford University Press, 2013).

CHAPTER 35

A HISTORIOGRAPHY OF ISLAMIC FAMILY LAW

LYNN WELCHMAN

THERE are many ways of going about a historiography of Islamic family law for the purposes of this volume. For manageability and access, this is a story of English-language scholarship and is mostly focussed on the Middle East and North Africa, although I also refer to scholarship on legal practice in Muslim majority states in South and Southeast Asia and Africa, and in Muslim communities in Western Europe and North America. For organizational purposes I approach the task with three questions in mind: What is Islamic family law? Who says so? And so what?

Two relatively recent historiographies of Islamic family law serve to orient my introduction. In 1999, Annelies Moors published a seminal reflection entitled "Debating Islamic Family Law: Legal Texts and Social Practices" in a collection reviewing the state of scholarship on women and gender in the Middle East.[1] Framed as a response to the 1968 claims of Anderson on "The Eclipse of the Patriarchal Family in Contemporary Islamic Law," Moors' review shows how the debates have been opened up by the entry into the field of differently placed scholars—notably women, and even more notably women from the region, and from disciplines other than law and what was then called Oriental Studies, such as those working in women's and gender studies, anthropology, and history. The debates she covers focus on challenges to the idea of the traditional Muslim family, monolithic, unchanging, patriarchal, governed by the text of Islamic family law as understood

[1] Moors in Meriwether and Tucker 1999. Anderson 1960.

from classical *fiqh* texts. The challenges are made through examination of different sources, including evidence of social practice as found in court records, *fatwas*, and oral narratives. They show women in history exercising agency within the given framework, going to court, mobilizing resources, negotiating, controlling property, and they seek to identify women's voices in the telling of this history.

Moors identifies this shift in perspectives to the late 1970s, and goes on to consider the role of the state, the relationship between the exigencies of postcolonial state-building, the construction of ideal family types as reflected in national codifications of Muslim "personal status law" (a term which Cuno shows to have entered Egyptian legal terminology via French colonial practice in Algeria)[2] and citizenship expectations and aspirations. She looks at the state's organization of its judiciary, the attitudes of the judiciary, at "Islamic modernity," the rise of political Islam and "Islamic feminism," women's activism and the impact of and on family law of all these, as debated in the scholarship she reviews. To these areas—all still attracting scholarly interest—I would add the burgeoning scholarship on international human rights law and Islamic family law. Moors' focus on gender as a lens through which to examine Islamic family law scholarship matches the development of gender as a theoretical construct more generally. Of particular significance here is historian Judith Tucker's *Women, Family and Gender in Islamic Law*, published as one of the "themes in Islamic law" series edited by Wael Hallaq and intended "to interpret the complexities of the subject for those entering the field for the first time."[3] The book is thus a landmark—and a considerable achievement—in applying feminist legal theories and gender analysis to the historical articulations and current narratives of Islamic family law in a monograph intended as an introductory account of the substance. Appropriately, Tucker joins the more recent pattern of scholars in entering the text in the first person.

The second historiography, this time from a law and society perspective, comes from Susan Hirsch in 2006. Although a broader overview in that it looks at scholarship in Islamic law more generally (i.e. not only family law and not only in the Middle East), the bulk of this review is on family law as "the substantive area of Islamic legal practice most prevalent in the world today."[4] Hirsch situates her review in the post-9/11 world, reflecting on the impact of those events on scholarship as well as on popular discourse and arguing that this scholarship "speaks to the thorny social and political challenges" post9/11.[5] She finds an emphasis on diversity in the practice of Islamic family law, and argues that the scholarship has as much value in its contribution to wider social theory as to the specific understandings of Islamic law. This stand against academic exceptionalism invokes the scholarship of Dupret and others reviewed here later. Hirsch begins with what she refers to as "source books," one edited by An-Na'im within the framework of a larger project looking at

[2] Cuno 2015. [3] Tucker 2008. [4] Hirsch 2006, 165. [5] Hirsch 2006, 166.

the application of Islamic family law (IFL) in different parts of "a changing world," and introduced by An-Na'im with a "plainly stated reformist agenda"; and the other by the network Women Living Under Muslim Laws with a specifically activist agenda, evaluating different applications and understandings of IFL with a view to suggesting which positions in state laws are more or less protective of women's rights.[6] Hirsch goes on to look *inter alia* at scholarship focusing on Islamic family law as one among other "competing normative orders," at gender identity construction and intersectionality, at ethnographic work looking at women's agency in and indeed beyond courts applying Islamic family law, at social movements advocating for law reform, and at scholarship on Islamic family law practices in non-Muslim majority states.

As should already be clear, then, English-language scholarship on Islamic family law currently includes a variety of academic disciplines and methodologies, geographical focuses, and substantive themes. Some of the scholarship focuses on family law issues to explore another primary theme—for example, in historical work, the early origins and development of *fiqh*; or in contemporary ethnographic work, the way women use courts. Outstanding examples of this in edited collections in the "Islamic law" discipline are the volumes on *Islamic Legal Interpretation* (on *muftis* and *fatwas*)[7] and *Dispensing Justice* (on judges and the courts).[8] Outputs focussed specifically on family law include monographs, articles (published in a range of journals beyond the field of Islamic studies or indeed comparative law), edited collections on themes and geographical regions, websites, manuals for practitioners, multi-party collaborations, and documentary films. Audiences, beyond academia, include policy makers and the wider public, Muslim and non-Muslim thinkers, activists and citizens. All of which brings us to the first question posed: what is Islamic family law?

I. What Is It?

Substantively, Islamic family law covers the heterosexual spousal relationship (marriage, its conduct, and its termination by death or divorce), the parental relationship (legal recognition of the parent–child relationship or affiliation or legitimacy of birth and rights and obligations arising therefrom, child custody, and

[6] Hirsch 2006, 172; An-Na'im 2002; WLUML 2003. See also Welchman 2004.

[7] Masud, Messick and Powers 1996. See in this volume Motski, Masud, Haeri, Vogel, Layish.

[8] Masud, Peters and Powers 2006, 2012. See in this volume Stiles, Bowen, Dupret, Johansen, Fierro, Masud, Powers.

guardianship), succession (although this is often treated separately and will not be included here), and other family relationships insofar as they give rise to legally regulated rights and obligations such as maintenance and responsibility for minors.

The classical jurists did not write of "family law" as a distinct category; indeed, as no doubt explained elsewhere in this volume, the lack of distinct categorizations of substantive areas of law such as "contract" and "family," setting out a body of law recognizable as such by imperial and colonial visitors from other (western, notably French and English) legal systems, was one of the reasons that *fiqh* was found to be, somehow, not quite "law." I discuss further later scholarship on the entanglement of Islamic family law with the modernity discourses of colonial and imperial powers and modernizing elites in different states, and implications for the state-endorsed structure of the Muslim family. To begin with doctrine, however, an appropriate place to start is with the family law section of *Issues in Islamic Law*, the second of a recent three-volume collection of "the best and most influential contributions" to the debates on Islamic law edited by Mashood Baderin and situated by the publishers in the context of increased attention to Islamic law after the events of 9/11.[9] The scholarship selected by Baderin in this volume presents the "classical" *fiqh* debates and positions—in some cases as background to a comment on a recent development or change—on the marriage contract, the wife's right to dower from her husband, the concept of *kafa'a* (equality) required of the husband, marriage guardianship, the marital relationship, polygyny, and divorce.[10] The scholarship thus mostly comprises doctrinal examination of the sources and the differences between the schools on particular issues in Islamic family law.

A. Marriage Contract Law and Doctrine

Baderin's selection includes some "classic" older pieces as well as more recent articles, and thus illustrates the ways in which doctrinal approaches have developed. The first piece in the collection, for example, is a very short overview of marriage in Islamic law with an update on twentieth-century reforms in Middle East and North African (MENA) states, and opens with an explanation of how pre-Islamic marriage law and practice (among Hijazi Arabs) was reformed by "the new law under Islam—the Shari'a," specifically looking at Qur'anic provisions on the family that became the basis for *fiqh* formulations of the family.[11] Khadduri's consideration of the limitation on polygyny in particular takes us to the debate as to whether these changes to pre-existing practice in the particular Hijazi context of the revelation

[9] Baderin 2014.

[10] Khadduri 1978, Anderson 1950, Ziadeh 1957, Siddiqui 1995, Carroll 1987, Hinchcliffe 1970, Kola 2010, Ahmad 2009, Khan 2009, and Welchman 2011.

[11] Khadduri 1978, 213.

were meant to coalesce into a fixed doctrine for all time and place, or whether, as he suggests, it was as far as it was possible to go at that time and place: "[t]he ultimate intent of Quranic marriage law, then, was to legitimate monogamy, rather than to endorse polygamy."[12] Reformist thinkers have focussed on the importance of context in reading these and other Qur'anic verses related to the family;[13] Leila Ahmed, in a highly significant text, makes a case for a different view of pre-Islamic history and argues that women's rights in general (and in the family in particular) were constrained (against the spirit of the Qur'an) during the first few centuries of Islam through the jurists working in their own context and time.[14] And to see how the task of setting out the basic rules on Muslim marriage is approached in twenty-first-century scholarship, look no further than the fine contribution by Kecia Ali to the excellent 2008 collection on *The Islamic Marriage Contract*; Ali does the field a great service in setting out the basic rules on marriage in classical *fiqh*, indicating main differences between the four Sunni schools and Ja'afari doctrine.[15]

Baderin's second choice is a classic article by J.N.D. Anderson, an in-depth presentation of "one of the most bewildering problems in Muslim law," i.e. "the classification and effect of various types of invalid marriage contract,"[16] focusing here on the differences within the Hanafi school on which type of contract belongs in which category (void or invalid/irregular), why, and with what legal effects. Anderson has already been mentioned in reference to Moors' critique of his article on the "eclipse of the patriarchal family." Of the relevant scholars of Islamic law writing in the West in the 1950s to 1970s and whose scholarship is often characterized as "Orientalist" in the Saidian sense,[17] it was J.N.D. Anderson who wrote most prolifically on Islamic family law. In particular, it was Anderson who followed the codifications of family law issued by independent Arab states in the 1950s in what I have called the second phase of Muslim family law reform.[18] This part of Anderson's body of work is still quoted in contemporary scholarship looking at text and court application;[19] and it is worth remembering that it was considerably more difficult then to physically get hold of new legislation from different parts of the world. In retrospect of course, this body of work presents as "looking for *shari'a* in the law," as compared to the traditional jurists "looking for law in the *shari'a*," and presumably falls foul of Dupret's admonition, discussed further in Section II, Who Says So?, with regard to scholars judging what is and is not "Islamic" in law and legal practice.[20]

Anderson's tone is distinctly of its time, but his much-quoted observation in regard to family law, that "Muslims have regarded that law as partaking most closely of

[12] Khadduri 1978, 217. [13] See Mir-Hosseini 2003, 11. [14] Ahmed 1992.

[15] Ali in Quraishi and Vogel 2008. For an older text on the contract see El Alami 1992.

[16] Anderson 1950, 357. [17] Said 1978.

[18] Welchman 2007; Anderson 1950, 1951 (a,b,c), 1952 (a,b,c), 1955, 1960. Jeppie, Moosa, and Roberts 2010 identify Anderson's *Islamic Law in Africa* as his first major publication and note that he "took the colonial context for granted" (at 21).

[19] See Van Eijk 2012. [20] Dupret 2006, 2007.

the very warp and weft of their religion,"[21] goes to the familiar and current assertion that family law is inextricably tied up with religion in Muslim communities. This assumption has recently been challenged by Cuno's historical examination of the development of the relationship between Muslim family law and the state in Egypt from the late nineteenth century, in particular judicial reorganization and the consequent reduction in jurisdiction of shari'a courts. Cuno finds that "the close association of the family with religion and religious law" was "a contingent development and neither inevitable nor an expression of 'the centrality of the family in Islam,' as often claimed.... Colonial scholarship produced the idea that family law is the 'heart' of the Sharia."[22] Neither the fact that public opinion surveys carried out in certain Muslim majority countries suggest a preference for "*shari'a*-based" law in family regulation, nor scholarship on the conduct of "Islamic marriages" in minority Muslim communities in the West, necessarily detract from Cuno's assertion that this is how colonial modernity has fixed the relationship.

Anderson's article commences with an examination of Abu Hanifa's views of contracts other than the contract of marriage, to show that the latter applied "exactly the same principles and method of reasoning" to the contract of marriage: Abu Hanifa was, according to Anderson, "relentlessly logical."[23] The issue of the validity of the contract is of enormous importance: "Marriage is a contract of civil law" according to Schacht, and "[t]his contract is the only legally relevant act in concluding marriage."[24] In other words, it is not a sacrament and no religious ceremony (alone) or the involvement of religious personnel constitutes or are required for the valid performance of this contract. Nevertheless, Mir-Hosseini notes that while the legal form of marriage is dealt with under the status of *mu'amalat* (social transactions), jurists "often speak of marriage as an act of worship (*'ibada*)," thus making marriage "one of the very few contracts in *fiqh* that crosses that boundary between *'ibadat* and *mu'amalat*."[25] For Mir-Hosseini, this is tied up with the social context in which the jurists were reading the revelation, and has consequences for the way in which rules regarding women and gender more generally—but particularly in the family—were and are constructed by jurists down the centuries, and how arguments against changes in these rules are framed now, how ideas of normativity develop among different communities. These angles were not of such interest to Anderson or his peers, although Fyzee insisted on this point (marriage being both *mu'amala* and *'ibada*) from the perspective of a practitioner.[26]

[21] Anderson 1976, 7.

[22] Cuno 2015, 183–184; citing (critiquing) Esposito with Delong Bas 2001, xiv.

[23] Anderson 1950, 358, 357. [24] Schacht 1964, 161.

[25] Mir-Hosseini 2003, 11. See also Kecia Ali 2008; Tucker 2008, 41; Sonbol 2008, 114; Shaheen Ali 1996, 162; Lindbekk 2014; Fyzee 1974, 89–90.

[26] Fyzee 1974, 89–90.

1. *The mahr: contract, property, and gender*

The wife's right to dower—arising at and from the contract, although also connected with consummation—is a matter that has drawn the attention of scholars interested beyond the law as narrowly interpreted as it illustrates women's access to property, the transfer of property through generations, and social practice in different times and places as evidenced by various forms of records. Thus Rapoport investigates extant early Islamic marriage and divorce deeds in Egypt from the eighth century CE onwards as well as the jurists' discussions on the validity of deferral of part of the dower,[27] comparing this Egyptian position to those taken by jurists elsewhere to establish a link with social practice. Rapoport argues that evidence of an increasingly common practice of recording deferred dower undermines arguments (here he cites Ahmed) that the second and third centuries of Islam were detrimental to the position of women.[28] At the same time, he examines matrimonial gifts more broadly, including among Jews and Copts in Egypt, to make a broader argument about "the interaction of nascent Islamic law and local marriage practices" which he finds to have "influenced and transformed both the views of Muslim jurists and the actual marriage settlements."[29]

Women's access to property through dower (as well as through inheritance) has also been investigated in depth since the 1990s. Moors traces dower patterns in Jabal Nablus in Palestine over the course of the twentieth century, tracing an increase in deferred dower over prompt and the rise of the token dower, an "innovation of the modernizing elite"[30] although accompanied by the increasing registration of household goods and gold. Attending to differences between women (social class and employment, as well as urban/rural differences) and drawing on oral narratives as well as court records and legal texts, Moors investigates discrepancies between the dower registered in contracts and that actually received by the bride. This involves not only the earlier practice of the bride's father retaining a proportion of the dower,[31] but the reasons why wives do not necessarily claim their full dower from their husbands or, in the case of widows, renounce their deferred dower in favor of their children (in cases where they have at least one son). Moors situates changes in dower patterns in "the context of changing property relations and changes in the meanings of gender,"[32] with increasing emphasis on the conjugal family and a growing emphasis on the husband as provider. In company with other scholars, Moors has shown how women from different classes use the institution of dower within informal strategies for the protection of their rights including protection against divorce from their husband, or in support of their own demand for divorce.[33] In Iran, where law requires that a cash amount of dower is to be adjusted to allow for inflation, Mir-Hosseini similarly observes the way the wife may exercise her right to

[27] Rapoport 2000. [28] Rapoport 2000, 21. [29] Rapoport 2000, 4.
[30] Moors 1995, 309. See by contrast Wynn 2008. [31] See also Stiles 2006.
[32] Moors 1995, 325. [33] Moors 1995; Wynn 1996; Hoodfar 1996; Mir-Hosseini 1993, 72–83.

demand payment of her dower in order to persuade a husband to divorce her, or to agree to other changes that she wishes to see in her marriage.[34]

The issue of dower has also been a focus of scholarship examining the way in which courts in non-Muslim majority countries deal with Islamic family law, a body of work that has grown as the case law grows. Pascale Fournier's *Muslim Marriage in Western Courts* lucidly examines the meanings of dower as it "travels" to courts in North America, France, and Germany.[35] Lau and Freeman trace the earliest leading case in English law to 1965 and note the preference of English courts to invoke principles of contract law rather than matrimonial law in such cases.[36] Quraishi and Syeed-Miller note that in Muslim marriage contracts in the United States, there seems to be "only one thing really important that would not otherwise be included in a standard civil marriage licence"—i.e. the dower.[37] Their examination includes the social debate as to whether dower should be rejected (or converted into a "token") because in effect it puts "a monetary value on the bride," or whether it should be seen rather, as in the case of deferred dower, as security for the eventuality of death or divorce and as a deterrent against unilateral divorce.[38] This discussion has also been common in the Middle East and North Africa; in Algeria, Lazreg notes that despite feminists holding dower to be "an antiquated custom that objectifies women" it remains a major feature of marriage.[39] Calls of different groups are recorded for dower to be reduced particularly in critical periods of national history, while scholarship maps ways of subverting officially decreed upper limits on dower.[40] While law may regulate what can be claimed in court from whom and when, scholarship increasingly confirms that social practice and strategic action provide the real meanings of dower.[41]

B. *Kafa'a*: Suitors, Suitability, and Stratification

Other requirements arising at the contract of marriage have also attracted scholarly attention that departs in its framing (and sometimes its findings) from earlier considerations of these areas of Islamic family law. Farhat Ziadeh opens his early piece on the concept of *kafa'a* (suitability, or equality as Ziadeh has it) by observing that perhaps "no criterion is more indicative of social stratification among a group than that of whom they consider equal to, and therefore worthy of, marrying their

[34] Mir-Hosseini 2007, 120. See also Longinotto and Mir-Hosseini 1998.

[35] Fournier 2010. See also Yassari 2013; Jones-Pauly 2008; Quraishi and Syeed-Miller 2004, 200–208.

[36] Freeland and Lau 2008.

[37] Quraishi and Syeed-Miller 2004, 188.

[38] Quraishi and Syeed-Miller 2004, 189.

[39] Lazreg 1994, 181–182. See also Dahlgren 2005, 137–140; and Mir-Hosseini 1993, 32.

[40] Badran 1995, 139–140; Wing 1994, 188–189; Wurth 2003, 13.

[41] See Moors 2008.

daughters."[42] This encapsulates two key points in regard to *kafa'a*: first, it is a measure that distinguishes between otherwise apparently equally situated Muslims, and secondly that it "requires the husband to 'measure up' to the wife and not vice versa."[43] *Kafa'a* is originally a Hanafi doctrine and attributed to the influences of the social environment in Iraq in which early Hanafi jurists were working. Looking into the early jurisprudential debates and the sources invoked for and against the doctrine, Ziadeh finds that "there can be no doubt that there is a preponderance of evidence to show that *kafa'ah* is contrary to the spirit of Islam."[44] This again invokes more recent scholarship arguing that many *fiqh* rules on marriage were developed as a result not of the substance of revelation but of the jurists' own living and working environments.

At the end of his piece Ziadeh provides two famous cases regarding *kafa'a* in the early twentieth century, one in Egypt and one from the Alawi community in Singapore. Although he finds (in 1957) that as a legal doctrine, *kafa'a* has waning force, it is included in reduced form in different formulations of family law codes in Arab states. *Kafa'a* applies at the time of the contract, and as Khalid al-Azri explains in a recent and in-depth study, it is closely connected with the authority of the guardian; in his view, "guardianship and *kafa'a* exist to control the aptitude of a woman in her marriage selection."[45] Al-Azri's examination of *kafa'a* includes jurisprudential analysis of diverse opinions on *kafa'a* between and among Sunni schools and Ibadi scholars (the Shi'a do not recognize it)[46] as well as social perceptions (including a lively internet discussion) and court practice in Oman. He sets his discussion clearly in the social and political context, traces cases through court records to show judges coming to different conclusions on how to apply the doctrine, considers the background and training of different judges, and the tensions between Ibadi doctrine, the Omani Personal Status Law, and the Basic Law's guarantee of non-discrimination on grounds of (*inter alia*) gender, origin, and social status. Another recent contribution to the scholarship on *kafa'a* comes from Malaysia, where Noor and Lee trace acrimonious debates in the early twentieth century between members of the Hadrami-origin Arabs divided into *sayyids* (claiming descent from the Prophet) and non-*sayyids*.[47] The former applied the principle of *kafa'a* to restrict *sayyid* women to marriage with *sayyid* men only, excluding other Arabs as well as everybody else; the non-*sayyid* community objected on the grounds of the general principle of equality in Islam, while in some reported cases objecting to women from their own community marrying non-Arabs.

42 Ziadeh 1957, 503. 43 Ziadeh 1957, 509. 44 Ziadeh 1957, 508.

45 Al-Azri 2012, 2013, 39. See also Siddiqui, "Law and the Desire for Social Control" 1996.

46 Al-Azri 2012, 2013, 38. 47 Noor and Lee 2013.

c. *Wilaya*: Guardianship, Agency, and Gender

The broader notion of male guardianship over women is seen by some Muslim feminist scholars as part of the "DNA of patriarchy" in *fiqh*.[48] Marriage guardianship over minors and in some cases over adult women was an issue much discussed among the classical jurists and is immediately connected with the issue of consent: whether the woman needs her guardian's consent to her marriage, and whether he needs her consent to marry her off.[49] The Hanafi and the Shiʿa traditionally allowed adult women to contract their own marriage without the guardian's consent, and this theoretical position has been substantiated by social historians who have found evidence of women exercising this right at different times and in different places—with the support of courts and *muftis* while in opposition to social practice and customary expectations.[50] Social norms in different Muslim communities may continue to expect a woman, particularly at her first marriage, to have the approval of her family guardian, whether or not this is required in law. Stiles' recent ethnographic work in and beyond a Zanzibari shariʿa court explores the increasing willingness of young women to take their fathers to court demanding the right to marry the man of their choice; Stiles' interest lies also in exploring the impact of a greater awareness of Islamic law on the part of young women in decisions both to challenge their elders and to refrain from so doing.[51] In Pakistan in the 1990s, considerations by Ali and Lau of a widely publicized case on a woman's right to marry without her guardian's consent situate the court's deliberations not only in terms of Hanafi law and statutory interventions but the ways in which judges' statements reflected the primacy of social expectations beyond the letter of the law.[52] The case involved the young woman fleeing to a women's refuge following her father's attempt to have her marriage contract cancelled; the case was raised by the father against the refuge for abduction. The challenge to familial and social expectations of the guardian's involvement in a woman's marriage, and a woman's "right to marry," thus entangle different bodies of law and different social actors, which scholarship now addresses also in terms of constitutional guarantees of equality and *habeas corpus* in a human rights perspective.[53]

On the other hand, the marriage of minors (where legal consent to the contract is given by the guardian) has been a continuing focus of historical scholarship, often examining the "option of puberty" which under Hanafi law could be exercised by a female married in her minority by a guardian other than her father or paternal grandfather to exit a marriage upon reaching puberty. Messick's account of a young woman doing precisely this in mid-twentieth-century Yemen, reconstructed from a series of court records, is an arresting account of how the rules and gendered assumptions of female behavior in this regard played out "in the last

[48] Mir-Hosseini 2015, 35. [49] Carroll 1987. [50] See Tucker 1998, 50–51.
[51] Stiles 2006. [52] Ali 1996, Lau 1996. [53] See e.g. Hossain 2011.

decades of Shari'a law application under an indigenous Islamic state."[54] Messick also observes that the young woman involved "must have had good legal advice," while Motzki suggests on the basis of evidence from seventeenth-century Palestine, to the effect that the option of puberty was commonly invoked, that there was widespread awareness of this rule.[55] Yazbek agrees, also working on the Palestine court records but in the nineteenth century, reflecting on the "weight of the male gaze" in the records, speculating as to what strategies were involved in bringing cases to court, and wondering at explicit descriptions by (only just) pubescent girls of sexual intercourse and menstruation.[56] Tucker considers the apparently straightforward position of Hanafi *muftis* supporting the need for an adult woman's consent to her marriage compared to court cases, in seventeenth- and eighteenth-century Ottoman Syria and Palestine, to wonder about the extent to which social norms of male control were actually accommodated in practice while the formalities of the woman's consent were attended to in the written record.[57] On the other hand, she has also noted that the "seemingly widespread practice of appointing mothers as guardians in the Ottoman period is one more instance of the society's view of women as appropriate and competent managers of private property."[58]

The marriage of minors is statutorily less countenanced now, but the twenty-first century witnessed a rise in scholarship (as well as advocacy) on "forced marriage," drawing on and contributing to wider concepts of choice, consent, and coercion.[59] While in the UK for example the scholarship insists on not making this a "Muslim issue," Bano uses the example of the role of the Muslim Arbitration Tribunal to consider the implications more broadly of "the increasing privatisation of disputes," feeding into a wider debate on the use of mediation mechanisms in situations of serious power imbalances.[60] The South Asian country studies in Hossain's 2014 handbook for lawyers include background on the statutory regulation of Muslim marriage (as well as Christian and Hindu marriage), including the position on minor marriage, as well as constitutional guarantees, and civil and criminal remedies for forced marriage.[61]

D. Polygyny, Divorce, and Pluri-legality

Similarly, Islamic family law rules on polygyny and divorce are increasingly addressed in scholarship invoking not only Islamic family law rules and statutory

[54] Messick 2008, 160. [55] Messick 2008, 175; Motzki 1996, 139.
[56] Yazbak 2002, 398. [57] Tucker 2008. [58] Tucker 2008, 157.
[59] See e.g. Gill and Anitha 2011; Siddiqui 2011. More broadly see Abu-Lughod and Rao 2011.
[60] Bano 2011, 177.
[61] Warraich 2014, Hossain 2014, Lawyers' Collective 2014. See also in the UK Arshad 2010, 64–87.

developments in different states but also international human rights law.[62] Twenty-first-century scholarship may focus on the fact that polygyny and unilateral divorce (*talaq*), as prerogatives of men, are easily framed as contradicting the norms of equality and non-discrimination. An example of earlier scholarship that did not refer to this frame is provided by Hinchcliffe (1970), while Mashhour's 2005 article illustrates the distance (and the direction) that scholarship in this area travelled in three and a half decades—not least the fact that the latter piece is published not in a journal focusing on Islamic law or Muslim matters more generally but in an established human rights journal and includes "gender equality" in its title.[63] A recent piece from Southeast Asia notes proposals for reform to Malaysian law and procedure by women's groups but focuses on controlling abuse of the institution, notably by men who engage in "forum-shopping" to avoid the involvement of their existing wife in the procedures to obtain permission for a polygynous marriage, or who cross national borders to conclude contracts under different rules, or who simply fail to register them.[64] Yamani's study of polygyny in Saudi Arabia includes legal analysis of both the classical Sunni law and Saudi regulations and beyond this provides an explicitly "insider" perspective on this debate, including an examination of the "nationalist, Islamic, political debate, which automatically labels any form of regulation of the practice and its management as a sign of heresy, a mark of joining in with the anti-Islamic Western conspiracy."[65]

Legal pluralism analyses address not only unregistered polygynous marriages in parts of the Muslim world but also polygynous unions among Muslim communities in western states; Shah for example examines English court cases in support of his broader argument that "a dominant legal system is ill-advised to attempt to impose a mono-cultural and ethno centric regime upon a legally pluralist social base."[66] Elsewhere in the Middle East and North Africa, polygyny has been treated through a consideration of the restrictions imposed by statute and the connected issue of registration requirements.[67] Najjar's discussion of the public and parliamentary debates on the 1979 Egyptian law's option of divorce for a first wife without having to prove harm, but rather from the bare fact of a polygynous marriage by her husband (a provision withdrawn in 1985) was a relatively early contemporary foray into documenting the environment surrounding particular legislative reforms; this kind of effort is of course facilitated in more recent times by social media, online records, and other electronic resources.[68]

Besides its highly gendered nature, Islamic family law regulation of polygyny is connected to the rules on divorce through the recurring issue of stipulations in

[62] See Rehman 2007. [63] Hinchcliffe 1970; Mashhour 2005. But see also Siraj 1964.
[64] Kamaruddin and Abdullah 2008. [65] Yamani 2008, 33.
[66] Shah 2007, 370. See Yilmaz 2005.
[67] Wurth 2003; Mitchell 1997; Welchman 2007, 77–87; Anderson 1976, 61–64.
[68] Najjar 1988. See Bernard-Maugiron 2008.

the marriage contract: and in particular, stipulations securing the wife a delegated power of *talaq* either in general terms or in the event that a husband contracts a polygynous union or other formulations seeking to prevent the husband from so doing. Some of the most interesting scholarship on the delegation to the wife of the husband's power of *talaq* relates to South Asian jurisdictions. The dominance of the Hanafi school, with its very restricted grounds on which women could petition the court for judicial divorce, is the context of Khan's consideration of a *fatwa* from a prominent Indian jurist in the early 1930s on the need for reform in divorce law.[69] The regional context included the validity of Muslim wives using apostasy from Islam as a "legal device" to dissolve their marriages in the absence of other options. This was a strategy encouraged by certain Christian missionaries, an issue discussed in depth by Masud who notes that "[i]t was this fatwa that triggered the movement for Islamic legal reform in India" leading eventually to the Dissolution of Muslim Marriage Act 1939.[70] Khan examines the part of the *fatwa* dealing with the husband's delegation of *talaq* to his wife, and includes an incisive and very twenty-first-century reading of Thanawi's "important counsel" on "women's intellectual deficiency."[71] Somewhat similar procedural rules were included in Fyzee's "Agreement for Dissolution of Marriage" which was drafted in the 1960s with his assistance by a Bombay solicitors' firm "at the instance of" a woman whom Fyzee describes as "a prominent worker in the cause of women's rights."[72] Recalling this in her own 1982 consideration of delegated divorce, Carroll notes the continuing utility of this approach to contract in India, Pakistan, and Bangladesh: "the grounds on which the wife is authorized to exercise her delegated right of divorce are so broad that the matrimonial power-balance in regard to dissolution of marriage is substantially equalized."[73] Carroll's article on stipulations in the marriage contract focuses mostly on stipulations against polygyny and for delegated divorce, but she also looks at other stipulations for example on post-divorce maintenance and the residence of the spouses, and her piece tracks how the different rights and obligations arising from the contract arise in interaction with special stipulations. She examines Indian cases from the early twentieth century and how the courts invoked the requirements of "public policy" to (often) uphold the wife's stipulations, coming up to date with more recent cases and concluding with the space provided in Pakistani and Bangladeshi marriage registration forms for such conditions to be included, noting a lack of information on whether and how such options have been exercised.[74] Her article has the advocate's engagement: she wonders "what, if any, efforts women's organizations are making to popularize the use" of Fyzee's model agreement.[75] Later in the following decade, Carroll worked with the network Women Living Under Muslim Laws (WLUML) to publish a "toolkit" on delegated divorce.[76] The

[69] Khan 2009. [70] Masud 1996, 196. [71] Khan 2009, 514–516. [72] Fyzee 1974.
[73] Carroll 1982, 303–305 at 304. [74] Carroll 1982, 308. [75] Carroll 1982, 305.
[76] Carroll 1996.

engagement of scholars and activists, in particular in regard to women's rights and options and with a view to a different constituency and audience for this scholarship, is discussed in Section III. So What?, but it is worth noting here that Carroll and WLUML also treated the complex issue of a wife's post-divorce maintenance in a collection issued on the tenth anniversary of the famous Indian case of Shah Bano.[77]

Another region-specific issue is that of triple *talaq*, by which a husband ends his marriage finally and irrevocably, and requiring an intervening marriage by the wife should the couple wish to re-marry. Ahmad's 2009 "critical appraisal" of this "abominable practice" by Muslim husbands in India investigates mainly the "Qur'anic philosophy" on divorce, sources from the *hadith* of the Prophet and the early caliphs and jurists.[78] The sources invoked, and the tone of insider outrage, distinguish this doctrinal piece for a more general audience. On the other hand, in the Middle East and North Africa, where codifications of family law have mostly dealt with the challenge of triple *talaq* by rendering such formulae as a single revocable divorce, Agmon has suggested from her reading of late Ottoman court records that "many marital disputes ... give us the impression that women sometimes found ways to provoke their husbands into making the *talaq* call, thus obtaining the divorce."[79] Moors similarly includes the abolishing of conditional and triple *talaq* as examples of reforms that "do not always work to women's benefit; in the past, women have made selective and strategic use of these in order to bring about a desired divorce."[80]

Historians have demonstrated that women's access to divorce was considerably wider in court practice than might have been assumed under ruling authorities that privileged Hanafi *fiqh*. Tucker's evidence shows that *muftis* would recommend that a Hanafi judge transfer the case to a deputy from another Sunni school who would grant a divorce on grounds not available from the Hanafi sources.[81] Abdal-Rehim's study of Egyptian court records from the late sixteenth century includes examples of *khul'* divorce, in traditional *fiqh* a form of divorce initiated by the wife who in return for the husband's *talaq* renounces her remaining financial rights (maintenance and deferred dower) and sometimes repays dower already received. Particularly noteworthy here is his finding that the judge would enforce a *khul'* petition from the wife "even when the husband was not willing to go through with it."[82] Other historians, examining evidence from different times and places, disagree.[83]

The issue of "judicial *khul'*," in the sense of a *khul'* divorce pronounced by the court in the absence of consent from the husband, has been addressed by doctrinal scholarship on the Middle East and North Africa since the Egyptian law of 2000 providing for this form of divorce; scholars of South Asian law had dealt previously

[77] WLUML 1998; and see Holden 2012.
[78] Ahmad 2009, 59, 54.
[79] Agmon 1996, 136.
[80] Moors 1999, 155–156. See also Layish 1975, 175.
[81] Tucker, 1998, 78–112.
[82] Abdal-Rehim 1996, 106. See also Ivanova 1996, 118–119.
[83] Tucker 2008, 110; Rapoport 2005, 74.

with the 1967 Pakistani precedent establishing judicial *khulʿ*.[84] Arabi provides an in-depth consideration of relevant Maliki rulings and the constitutional developments in Egypt that he argues led to the promulgation of this law;[85] others have noted the sheer length of time it took to press a claim for judicial divorce through the Egyptian court system.[86] The title of Arabi's piece indicates what he clearly considers the momentous nature of this legislative intervention as well as something of the tenor of public reaction ("women may divorce at will"); Sonneveld says that "the Egyptian nation was rocked" by the new law; El Alami calls it "nothing short of revolutionary."[87] Scholarship on *khulʿ* and indeed other forms of divorce in the Muslim world has deployed new methodologies and new theoretical frames that are discussed further in Section II.

E. Authority and the Marital Relationship

Male prerogative in traditional *fiqh* on divorce has been identified as a key part of the overall conception of male authority in marriage and the family (*qiwama* and *wilaya*);[88] for some, the press and public debates on *khulʿ* in the Middle East essentially revolve around the challenge to male authority raised by the idea of women being able to exit the marriage without proving fault on the part of the husband.[89] In the marital relationship, Kecia Ali establishes the husband's authority in classical *fiqh* as follows: "The husband's main right is to derive sexual enjoyment from his wife, and to that end he may exercise control over her mobility."[90] Compare this to Anderson's earlier presentation: "Broadly speaking, the marital relationship envisaged in the traditional law may be summed up in terms of a wife's duty to obey her husband in every lawful demand he may make—provided only that he has given her her 'prompt' dower—in consideration for his duty to provide her with suitable maintenance and support."[91] What Moors has termed the "gender contract" and Sonneveld the "maintenance-obedience relation" has been summed up by Tucker as "the marital bargain of *nafaqa* [maintenance] for absence of *nushuz* [disobedience]" which, together with guardianship, she finds to have been "constants in Islamic marriage," the great diversity in rules notwithstanding; despite the limitations on the husband's authority—upheld by the jurists—"*nushuz* could not but be a defining concept for marital relations."[92] This does not contradict Cuno's finding that the application of the "legal formulation" of obedience rules "in real life varied according to the economic and social status of the household."[93]

84 Hinchcliffe 1970; Carroll 1996; Holden 2013.
85 Arabi 2001, 170–188.
86 Bernard-Maugiron and Dupret 2008.
87 Sonneveld 2012a; El Alami 2000, 135.
88 Al-Sharmani 2013a.
89 Welchman 2007, 114.
90 Kecia Ali 2008, 12.
91 Anderson 1976, 114–115.
92 Tucker 2008, 82, 55. Moors 1995; Sonneveld 2012a, 17.
93 Cuno 2015, 6; and see 215.

Cuno's particular consideration of the "curious case of the house of obedience" focuses on the changes in Egyptian procedural rules and court system in the nineteenth century, accompanied by the emerging "new family ideology" on the part of the elite in Egypt: he finds, like Sonbol before him, that the enforcement of this concept, in the sense of the court being empowered to return a "disobedient" wife to her husband's house against her will, was an invention of the late nineteenth century.[94] Their scholarship from court records establishes that prior to this, the sanction of the court was to hold the wife no longer entitled to maintenance from her husband, which is similar to the situation pertaining now in those MENA states that maintain the concept of "obedience" in their laws. Cuno traces the coercive enforcement of "obedience" orders in Egypt to France, via Algeria: "French colonial knowledge of Muslim family law was the likely vector of its transmission to Egypt."[95] This scholarship explicitly challenges assumptions about what Cuno calls the "infamous legal regime" of the "house of obedience" and pins it clearly on "legal modernization."[96]

Scholarship carried out on the maintenance–obedience relationship in current or at least more recent practice includes examination of how the different claims of husband and wife are managed by courts and indeed—often strategically—by husbands, wives, families, and wider communities.[97] A feature of the scholarship discussed further later is the "growing disconnect" between the normative model of marriage with the husband as provider, and the implications this has for perceptions of law. But another area of academic—as well as activist—focus in recent years has been special stipulations inserted in marriage contracts, which have the potential of modifying the effects that otherwise flow from the fact of the contract and notably of clarifying the circumstances in which a wife would not be held to be in a state of *nushuz*. Anderson deals with this issue briefly in his monograph on law reform, while El Alami mentions it only in passing (in discussing polygyny).[98] Anderson's 1976 comment on practice (repeated from an earlier analysis of the then new Jordanian law of 1951) is illustrative of the way that attention to practice has changed in scholarship on MENA law: "I am told . . . that the insertion of such stipulations in marriage contracts is today the rule rather than the exception in upper class families in Jordan, and is becoming increasingly common in all classes."[99] Subsequent scholarship researched marriage contracts in court records in neighbouring Israel and Palestine with a view to ascertaining usage and scope.[100] Similarly, later doctrinal scholarship devotes more time to stipulations in the marriage contract,[101] and the 2008 edited volume on *The Islamic Marriage Contract* includes a number of articles

94 Cuno 2015, 185–191; Sonbol 2008, 115–116.
95 Cuno 2015, 185.
96 Cuno 2015, 15.
97 Shehada 2009; Al-Sharmani 2013a.
98 Anderson 1976, 114–117; El Alami 1992, 129.
99 Anderson 1976, 116; see also Anderson 1951 JLFR, 192 n 4.
100 Layish 1975, 31–32; Welchman 2000, 163–182.
101 Musa 1955, 252–263; Kecia Ali 2008, 21–27.

specifically focussed on stipulations.[102] Interestingly, two of the chapter authors indicate a change in position from their earlier (late 1990s) considerations of stipulations in the contract.[103]

But Anderson's 1976 comment on the motivation on the part of the legislators in expanding prospects for the enforcement of stipulations is perceptive: the intention was not only to provide relief in certain situations (i.e. divorce) but to give wives "a measure of control over their own circumstances and those of their children."[104] This comment provides context for historical scholarship that, from the 1990s, establishes that in certain places in past centuries, in the earliest Islamic centuries and indeed from pre-Islamic times, it was commonplace for the wife (or her guardian on her behalf) to insert conditions in the contract and that it was routine for courts to enforce them, in the sense of not holding her disobedient or in granting her a divorce should the circumstance stipulated against arise.[105] Hanna has explained part of the significance of this scholarship in relation to the "Oriental Despot model, developed with regard to the state," which she argues "has often been applied to the family in the premodern period, either in explicit or implicit terms."[106] Largueche's work on the "Kairouan marriage contract" (routinely stipulating monogamy) supports these efforts ("real history could be lived very differently to the ideals transmitted in doctrine").[107] Sonbol and Cuno argue that modernizing reforms to the Egyptian legal system in the nineteenth and early twentieth centuries essentially closed the space previously accorded to negotiations on the shape of the contract and gave women considerably less control over the terms of their marriage than they had had pre-reform. Cuno uses this as well as associated reforms such as the "Hanafization" of Egyptian legal practice in family law to dispute the "standard narrative" that family law remained untouched by legal reforms until the codes of the twentieth century.[108] Sonbol in particular insists that women's (and indeed men's) insertion of stipulations should not be viewed in the first instance as having conditions of divorce secured, but rather as revealing, for specific historical contexts, "the expectations of a broad range of people" in regard to how their marriage would be lived, as well as illustrating women's agency in exerting a certain degree of control.[109] Women largely stopped inserting stipulations in the newly issued marriage contract forms over the twentieth century, and even more recent research confirms that, in Egypt at least, judicial practice does not generally see stipulations as enforceable, with the exception of the delegation of *talaq*.[110] Still, at the end of the twentieth century, the

[102] Quraishi and Vogel (eds) 2008; see in this volume Sonbol, Zomeno, Shah, Wynn, Zulficar.

[103] Wynn 2008 and 1996; Mir-Hosseini 2008 and 2007.

[104] Anderson 1976, 117.

[105] Zomeno 2008; Sonbol 2008; Abdal-Rehim 1996, 98–103; Rapoport 2005, 74–76; Cuno 2015, 132–137; Hanna 1996.

[106] Hanna 1996, 143.

[107] Largueche 2010, 3.

[108] See also Agmon 2006, 54–55 challenging the "accepted wisdom" that in Ottoman lands family law was not affected by nineteenth-century reforms.

[109] Sonbol 2008, 96.

[110] Zulficar 2008, 234–235; Sonbol 2008; Lindbekk 2014, 95.

"New Marriage Contract" campaign in Egypt produced considerable scholarship from both observers and insiders: Zulficar, involved closely as the drafter of the document, notes in regard to the Egyptian women's movement that "we reclaimed our right to redefine our cultural heritage as Muslim women under the principles of *shari'a*."[111]

Zulficar's statement implicitly supports the more recent assertion by Sharafedin, who notes, in an article on Egyptian family law, that *fiqh* produced by the jurists was "sometimes different" from the practice of law in the shari'a courts in history: "[t]his is why we may have two interrelated but different manifestations of 'Islamic law.'"[112] In this, she follows Sonbol's earlier argument that, given the historical evidence of the disparities between *fiqh* manuals and court practice, "we should reconsider the idea that what *fiqh* has to say is synonymous with Shari'a."[113] The state comes next, with its codifications of Islamic family law and integration of the court system, and the colonial and postcolonial retention of "shari'a" jurisdiction, in one way or another, in Muslim family law matters led to the assertion that family law was indeed the "last bastion" or the "last stronghold" of the shari'a in many Muslim majority states: or, more accurately as Moors puts it, the "last stronghold of the *shar'i* establishment."[114] Cuno, following Messick, disputes that this was inevitable, arguing that "colonial-era scholars identified family law as the 'core' or the 'heart' of the *shari'a*."[115] Tucker has wondered "[w]hether Islamic law retains any central identity or rather has devolved into fragmented sets of rules deployed for various purposes of politics and power."[116] And for his part, Dupret challenges scholars on the assumption "that personal status is, in Egypt and in many other Arab countries, the last stronghold of Islamic law."[117] Dupret's challenge is methodological, disputing the way scholars frame their research into legal practice in Muslim majority states—in this work, personal status law in Egypt—arguing that "law is a practical accomplishment not an archaeological search for the Islamic pedigree of the norm."[118] All of which brings us to the second question: Who says what Islamic family law is?

II. Who Says So?

It is certainly a commonplace to assert the diversity of Islamic family law, whether in relation to the differences within and between the traditional schools of law

111 Zulficar 2008, 242. See also Shah 2008.
112 Sharafeldin 2015, 166, 223.
113 Sonbol 2008, 88.
114 Moors 2003, 2. See Coulson 1969, 115–116.
115 Cuno 2015, 159; Messick 1992.
116 Tucker 2008.
117 Dupret 2012, 145; and see 2007, 97; Dupret and Voorhoeve 2012, 2.
118 Dupret 2007, 97.

on different specific subjects, or in relation to practice in today's world of states, codified laws, courts applying them, and engaged citizens demanding change. Here, a useful distinction has been made between "discourses *on* the law" (public, political and religious debates) and "discourses *of* the law" (the practices of judges, lawyers, and litigants).[119] Some of the most interesting recent historical scholarship looks at Islamic family law in practice with a view to hearing voices (judges, litigants) other than those heard through the *fiqh* literature and particularly the manuals of the schools. But it is with the advent of the state (colonial and postcolonial) that we really see what Tucker has referred to as an "epistemological break in the legal system" and the concerted questioning of who gets to say what Islamic family law is.

The codification of Islamic family law in the modern period constitutes "an alteration far more consequential than the move to a new framework of numbered articles might seem to indicate," including the passing of "a key dimension of interpretive authority" from individual jurists "to the collective bodies of national legislatures."[120] Even if the state agrees that what it legislates is not the only valid expression of Islamic family law, its enforcement and recognition of certain rules and acts seek to construct "the family" under Islamic law in particular forms.[121] From the 1950s on, J.N.D. Anderson tracked the substance of details of the family law codifications in the Middle East and North Africa in detailed commentaries on the statutes and their origins in different *fiqh* sources, but without attempting to investigate their application himself. Anderson's scholarship is of its time, with a generally uncomplicated attitude to "reform" and a positivist approach to "law," legislation, and the state. Noel Coulson published less specifically on family law (apart from inheritance) and did occasionally express reservations as to the application of Arab state codifications beyond the urban elite, referring to particular cases or trends in courts in different countries that had been reported to him.[122] More broadly, however, in commenting on what he termed the "modern process of comparative law" employed by states to design family laws appropriate to their societies by drawing on the range of views available on different matters in *fiqh*, Coulson called this "a healthy process of social purpose" and noted that "[t]he status of women has been immeasurably improved."[123]

The assumptions behind such statements by earlier scholars have been challenged since the mid-1990s by historians on a number of levels. Both Tucker and Sonbol question whether reforms of the late nineteenth and early twentieth centuries

119 Dupret and Voorhoeve 2012, 7. 120 Masud, Messick and Powers 1996, 27.

121 See Cuno 2015, 1–2 and Sonbol 2008, 111, 117–118 on the modern introduction of the Arabic terminology of *al-usra* for "the family" and the accompanying focus on the nuclear family and the production of offspring as the object of marriage.

122 Coulson 1969, 114. 123 Coulson 1969, 39, 97.

under the Ottomans and in Egypt were an unadulterated good for women in particular.[124] Sonbol looks at cases before and after the Egyptian reforms and concludes they proved "a mixed bag for Egyptian women."[125] Tucker focuses on the range of opportunities in *fiqh* compared to the limitations imposed by the Ottoman Law of Family Rights (1917), and in her later book weighs the benefits of the substantive reforms as "offset by the loss of the leeway built into the traditional Islamic legal system."[126] The comparison between the "openness" of the premodern *fiqh* system and the "closed" nature of the code (often expressed as flexibility versus rigidity) is emphasized by other scholars working with historical material.[127] The way in which states selected particular *fiqh* rulings to construct their ideal-type Muslim family under their statutory interventions is described by Sonbol as a process of "state patriarchy," an interesting foil to Anderson's description of the "eclipse of the patriarchal family."[128] The extent of the difference between Islamic family law and practice before the reforms and after, she says, merits the current manifestation being called "a new *shariʿa*."[129] The crystallization of this "new" Islamic family law, under pressures of colonialism, imperialism, and state formation, and later in the twentieth century of the growth of political Islam and what are seen as increasingly conservative visions of society and with it the family, is challenged in more recent scholarship.

Key to the idea of pre-codification flexibility is the way in which the courts operated in premodern times. Coulson asserted that the new way that Islamic family law was being applied by states gave greater room for the recognition of social exigencies: "traditionally the *qadi* was hidebound" by rigid procedural and evidentiary rules as well as by substantive legal rules in his school's manuals, "which left him little or no room for personal initiative," while the current situation sees states explicitly giving wider discretion to the courts in applying Islamic family law "so that they now assume, to a much greater extent than hitherto, the responsibility of organs of real social purpose."[130] Historical scholarship on the workings of shariʿa courts in premodern and early modern times (in Egypt and under the Ottomans) has drawn a much more nuanced picture, with the court at different times and places being very much tied in to the community, serving a fundamental purpose as arbitrator and mediator in pursuit of what the *qadi* would then have considered "gender and social justice."[131] In addition, as already noted, questions are raised as to the extent to which the traditional doctrine as set out in the *fiqh* texts reflected social (and court) practice.[132] More recently still, as discussed further later, scholars discuss whether the script set for marital relations in codifications of Islamic family law across the Muslim world reflects the reality of marriage today in a variety of contexts: and if not, what the implications are.[133]

[124] Tucker 1998; Sonbol 1998. [125] Sonbol 1998, 285. [126] Tucker 2008, 22.
[127] Messick 1992; Cuno 2015, 204. [128] Anderson 1968; Sonbol 1998, 285.
[129] Sonbol 1998, 285. [130] Coulson 1969, 107–108.
[131] Agmon 2006, 45, 55–55, 128; Sonbol (ed) 1996. See also Semerdjian 2008, Peirce 2003.
[132] Moors 1999. Messick 1992.
[133] Mir-Hosseini 2015, 17–18; Al-Sharmani 2013a, 51; Shehada 2009, 44.

In a different kind of scholarship, from the 1970s, we see compilations (mostly translations by the authors) of different statutory interventions in different states. The first of these appears to have been Tahir Mahmood's extraordinary effort, ranging over multiple jurisdictions in the Middle East and North Africa, South and Southeast Asia and Africa (including in the final edition statutes of Islamic family law in non-Muslim majority states), and appending summaries of case law.[134] Mahmood presented his work as "essentially descriptive" and explicitly denied any evaluative purpose in his analysis.[135] He also assumed a certain "basic" familiarity with the principles of Islamic family law; this approach is not followed in subsequent compilations, with El Alami and Hinchcliffe in the 1990s presenting an introduction on "the uncodified law" before embarking on the substance of their work, translations of "Islamic marriage and divorce laws" in the Arab states.[136] Jamal Nasir, whose works include one text focusing on the Arab states and one including also South Asian material, aims his work primarily at practitioners in the non-Muslim West as well as Muslim communities in western states; he includes an introduction to Islamic jurisprudence and proceeds through the different areas of Islamic family law setting out the positions according to the different schools followed by a presentation of how those issues are dealt with in the different states under consideration.[137] Such "manual" type publications[138] refer mostly to primary and *fiqh* sources and do not refer to western scholarship around the issues discussed, nor do they problematize the notion of "*shari'a*" or "Islamic family law." They are vulnerable to being quickly overtaken by the promulgation of new or modified statutes, of course, necessitating revisions and updates; and more recently the change in accessibility of statutes notably through electronic resources (let alone, as yet, the imminent transformation of online translation capabilities for the individual practitioner or researcher).

In a sense what the last two examples of source books are doing is setting out what contemporary states have presented as Islamic family law in their codes compared with what the traditional jurists expounded as doctrine on the individual issues. Other types of scholarship have also to a certain extent tracked the codes, but with a focus on time and place-specific application in the courts. The first such effort appears to have been Layish's research into shari'a court practice with Palestinian Muslims from the establishment of the state of Israel to the late 1960s. This informative 1975 study can be situated in its time: it is intended among others for "the Orientalist" and explores how "the *sharia* has reacted" in light of the fact that "[t]he traditional equilibrium between the *shari'a* and Muslim society has been irrevocably upset, not by change from within, but as a result of direct contact with

134 Mahmood 1972, 1987, 1995.

135 Mahmood 1972, Preface, reproduced 1995, iii.

136 El Alami and Hinchcliffe 1996, 1998.

137 Nasir 1986, 1990, 2001, 2009; 1990, 1994, 2009. See also El Alami 1992.

138 See Nasir 1990, 5.

a modern Western society."[139] Subsequent studies provide the basis for the finding, in the twenty-first century, that a "distinctive feature of recent scholarship" is the focus on local practice, away from "an idealized model of Islamic law to its manifold instantiations in specific times and places."[140] While some of these focus on court practice as read from the court records, including considering the practical implementation through the courts of the state codifications,[141] others draw also on anthropological approaches to engage the material as observed in particular frames that do not take the "law" as the starting point.[142]

The processes of family law reform that began in what I have termed the "third phase" of Muslim family law reform in MENA has generated scholarship that shows the changed nature of interest in Muslim family law. Women's rights are a foregrounded issue, along with the advocacy positions of women's rights organizations in the national debates and also often involving international and diasporic women's rights organizations, and gender as an analytical framework. A collection of these "discourses on the law" were published in 2003 as a themed issue of *Islamic Law and Society* looking at public debates in these processes,[143] and another set were included in a 2009 edited collection, notably including Cole's exposition of the process in transitional Iraq.[144] The Egyptian law of 2000 (legislating for judicial *khulʿ*) has also given rise to a substantial scholarship, focusing on the text, the state's textual justification of it, and parliamentary and other debates.[145] Sonneveld's recent monograph combines an analysis of the texts, court practice, and out-of-court narratives with an examination of the public debate *inter alia* through the medium of films and cartoons.[146] Above all, the 2004 Family Code in Morocco gave rise to a veritable deluge of commentaries and analyses, some considerably better than others. The volume of scholarship can be at least partly attributed to the invocation of international human rights discourse (particularly the equality principle) in the debates and indeed in the law, and the engagement of the Moroccan authorities with the international human rights system. The availability of unofficial English translations of the law online quickly after its promulgation not only indicates interest from international women's rights activists but also facilitated the production of articles on this law. The best scholarship on the substance of this law goes beyond "assessments" of the text and its equality provision to include reflections on court practice with a view to future amendments to the law.[147] In line with recent scholarly interest in family law regulation among Muslim communities in the West, Foblets considers the implications of the new law for Moroccans living in Europe.[148]

139 Layish 1975, x.
140 Masud, Peters, and Powers 2012, 4.
141 Welchman 2000, Shaham 1997; and see the essays in Mallat and Connors' *Islamic Family Law* 1990.
142 Rosen 1989, 2000; Mir-Hosseini 1993; Hirsch 1998; Moors 1995.
143 Moors, Buskens, Schultz, Welchman, and Wurth 2003.
144 Cuno and Desai 2009. See also Abu-Odeh 2004.
145 Arabi 2001; Bernard-Maugiron 2008; Al-Sharmani "Egyptian Khul'," 2012.
146 Sonneveld 2012a.
147 El Hajjami 2013; Carlisle 2013; Rosen 2008.
148 Foblets 2008.

Away from court implementation of the codes, the influential study of the first codes of Algeria, Morocco, and Tunisia by Charrad, a comparative-historical sociologist, investigates the political circumstances of the adoption of the three laws with a view to situating how the different postcolonial states dealt with women's rights in their postcolonial family laws in light of "the relationship between state and tribe."[149] Tucker has since partly disputed Charrad's findings on the relative lack of impact of women's rights activism on the content of the codes, while other scholarship has also focussed on the mutual and dynamic relationship between state formation (and development) and Islamic family law substance and processes, with citizenship becoming a key frame.[150] Another angle from the 1990s was Mayer's 1995 suggestion that the spousal relationship in North African family law codifications might have more to do with "Mediterranean" than with Islamic law. Mayer's examination poses the prospect of higher courts taking positions such as that in Turkey on issues previously included in statutory law (in this case, the wife's need for her husband's consent to her work outside the home). But the scholarship on significant decisions on Islamic family law by higher courts in Arab countries is mostly concerned with Egypt's Supreme Constitutional Court.[151] This scholarship, insofar as it deals with family law, is less focussed on the substance of family law than on the way the Court handles the matter of its own interpretative authority—i.e. in the Court saying what Islamic family law is. This scholarship considers how the Court approaches the authority of the *fiqh* texts, Egyptian statutory law (being challenged by the petitioner), and the Court's own mandate in deciding whether or not a particular statutory intervention in family law was contrary to the principles of the shariʿa. Looking at a 1996 decision on post-divorce maintenance and a 2002 ruling on the constitutionality of the law on *khulʿ*, Johansen tells us that "[t]he authors who are empowered to rethink and reformulate Islamic law and Islamic normativity are clearly identified by the SCC: the legislature, political authorities, expert jurists and, of course, the judges of the SCC." The Court, he tell us, "relates norm production directly to political authority."[152] Classical *fiqh* norms—in our case, on family law issues—no longer bind the Court or indeed the legislature.[153]

In South Asia, English-language scholarship, starting under British colonial rule, focussed primarily on jurisprudence from the courts, first under British control with eventual authority to the Privy Council in London, and subsequently under independent states. Under colonial rule, principles of English law were invoked in the interpretation of the Hanafi manuals available to judges, and the common law system gave precedent a status not familiar in civil law systems (nor yet in the traditional

[149] Charrad 2001, 9. See also Hasso 2014.
[150] Tucker 2008, 115; Sevgin 2013; Maktabi 2013.
[151] Although see also Mitchell 1997 and Voorhoeve 2014.
[152] Johansen 2012, 192–193. See also Bernard-Maugiron 2008.
[153] Johansen 2012, 191. See also Arabi 2001, 169–188 and Bernard-Maugiron 2008.

Islamic law system), thus lending added authority to the courts' findings of what Islamic law is. There is a voluminous literature examining "Anglo-Muhammad Law" or Muhammad Law, a term for which Fyzee offers an apology: "this ugly term as well as its variants . . . are all open to serious objection."[154] Much of this literature concerns family law, with in-depth analysis and detailed examination of leading cases, and various authors have discussed the substantive impact of colonial-era scholarship and jurisprudence on Islamic family law. Michael Anderson however suggests in a 1990 collection that "it would be a mistake to ascribe too much importance to the effects of colonial law," noting that "indigenous processes" of scholarly study were also at work, with a resulting increase on "a scripturalist approach to the *shari'a*" in the late nineteenth and early twentieth centuries.[155] Post-independence textbooks on Islamic family law in South Asia, besides Fyzee's work on India, include a large 1998 textbook by Pearl and Menski, updating previous works by Pearl. The joint-authored text, which as Hirsch notes is not without its critics,[156] examines Islamic family law in India, Pakistan, and Bangladesh but also includes separate and systematic consideration of how the English courts have dealt with what the authors term *agrezi shariat*.[157]

The British colonial authorities issued certain piecemeal legislation particular to Muslim family law during their rule in India, some still in force, with amendments, in Pakistan and Bangladesh as well as India. And judges in the highest courts in British colonial rule in India set precedents in case law on substantive issues of Muslim family law. In Britain itself however, as cases began to come to court involving migrants from South Asia and British Muslims particularly of South Asian origin, the state's principle of a unified family law for all citizens allowed no such particularized statutory intervention. Over the last half century, and increasingly in common with other Western European and North American states, the courts have dealt with different claims, including those involving foreign law—the family laws of Muslim majority states—in issues of private international law (or conflict of laws), but also including claims between Muslim citizens. Scholarship on the treatment of dower in European and North American courts has already been noted, but there are also issues about the recognition of marriage and divorce processes: i.e. legislatures are asked to rule not whether a marriage or divorce is "Islamic" but rather whether it is a marriage or divorce under their domestic law. In the twenty-first century, scholarship has tracked these developments not only in regard to case law[158] but, increasingly, in regard to Muslim community-based mechanisms and their role in family law regulation in western states. Some of this can be squarely placed in Hirsch's consideration of post9/11 anxieties on the part of states and majority communities; the sub-title of Berger's 2013 timely collection

154 Fyzee 1974, 1–2. 155 Anderson 1990, 220. 156 Hirsch 2006, 176.
157 Pearl and Menski 1998, 58.
158 Foblets 2007; Fournier et al 2012; see Arshad 2010 for a handbook for UK practitioners.

("Facts, Fears and the Future of Islamic Rules on Family Relations in the West") points to this context of "moral panic"[159] and includes case studies from across Europe, North America, and Australia. Another recent collection focusing on "divorce in Islam" likewise includes a number of contributions from non-Muslim majority jurisdictions in Europe but also in South Africa, and includes similar references to anxiety on the part of non-Muslim states.[160] And another, *Managing Family Justice in Diverse Societies*, while not specific to Islamic family law, contains considerations of it in the UK, Iran, Bangladesh, and South Africa, with something of a shared theme of legal pluralism and the standing of constitutional norms, for example of gender equality.[161] The essays collected in Jeppie et al.'s excellent (2010) volume, *Muslim Family Law in Sub-Saharan Africa*, are attentive to constitutional dynamics in postcolonial states as well as to the "colonization" of Islamic family law under British and French colonial regimes.[162]

In the UK, initial proposals for a separate Muslim family law system came in the 1970s; the first two Shari'a Councils were set up in the 1980s and Nielsen (who was involved in a contemporary cross-country study) observes that the issue for many Muslims is the legitimacy of the judicial authority—"it is the authority under which a judicial process functions, rather than the substance of the law itself which becomes a key consideration." That is, it is not so much a question of "what is Islamic family law" as of "who says so"? More broadly Nielsen suggests that it "could be argued that the tensions regarding the wish for some form of *shari'a* family law principles to apply among Muslims living in Europe are—yet another—consequence of Europe's past imperial adventures."[163] The tensions to which Nielsen and others refer increased considerably in different contexts in the post 9/11 world. A burst of scholarship followed the public debates and government action following the announcement by a Muslim organization in Canada "that it was setting up a '*shari'a* court' in Ontario under the auspices of the Arbitration Act."[164] The authors detail the debates, the law, and potential legal ramifications of the proposal and the subsequent exclusion of binding faith-based arbitration on family law matters; human rights obligations and constitutional guarantees are evoked and the frame of citizenship is a focus, while the persistence of Muslim family law practice is also noted—"*shari'a* and *talaq* are alive and well."[165] A piece by Marion Boyd, a previous Attorney General who was charged by the authorities with providing recommendations for ways forward, details the interventions by those who were in opposition and gives a sense of the

[159] See Turner and Richardson 2013, 55; Razack 2008, 92.

[160] Mehdi, Menski, and Nielsen (eds) 2012.

[161] Maclean and Eekelaar (eds) 2013, in which see Bano, Ghanea, Chowdhury, and Amin.

[162] Jeppie, Moosa, and Roberts 2010: see especially the Introduction and chapters by Allie, Moosa, Hirsch, Lydon.

[163] Nielsen 2013, 90, 94. Compare Poulter 1990.

[164] Boyd 2013, 177–178.

[165] Fournier, Setrakian, and McDougall 2012, 237. See Bakht 2004, 2006; and Islam.

painful nature of some of the debates.[166] Sherene Razack provides an insightful and reflective analysis from a panel of Muslim feminists and the contradictions they found themselves facing: Muslims were presented as "pre-modern" in the debates and it is, she writes, "often through the language of human rights and gender equality that empire is accomplished today."[167]

Boyd's piece is included in a volume published a few years after a second major public controversy on Muslim family law in the West. This was the 2008 intervention, in a high profile practitioner–academic lecture series on "Islam and English law," by the then Archbishop of Canterbury, Rowan Williams. Williams proposed a "transformative accommodation" and was reported as referring to the "unavoidable adoption of *shari'a* law."[168] The "media storm" that ensued was followed, in due academic time, by scholarship that included a 2013 volume edited by the original convenor of the lecture series and including a particular focus on legal pluralism, particularly in relation to Muslim family law in the UK.[169] In this context, some scholars argue for greater recognition by state law and courts of Muslim marriage and divorce practice with a more pluralist approach to law;[170] others are more cautionary;[171] and others concentrate on the implications, mostly for women, of reliance on these non-state processes, particularly in regard to securing a divorce under Islamic law alongside a civil divorce—the so-called "limping marriage" where a marriage is held extant in one legal system but not in another or where a wife has obtained a civil divorce but is unable to obtain a religiously recognized divorce from her Muslim husband.[172] The frames of multiculturalism and citizenship and the paradoxes posed by attention to both individual and community rights are central to scholarship on mechanisms for Muslim family law regulation.[173] Scholars also investigate the motivations of those Muslims in the West who engage in "Islamic marriages" without reference to registration (and therefore "recognition") processes. In the Netherlands, Moors finds that unregistered marriage among Muslims provokes anxiety on the part of the state about this being "an indication and instrument of radicalization and an attempt to develop a parallel society based on the *shari'a*."[174] That is, the anxiety is provoked not by the fact that the couple is not concluding a civil marriage, but rather by the fact of its being an "Islamic" marriage. Moors found no evidence that ideology was producing a refusal of state procedures and registration on the part of young women involved in such marriages but rather a wide variety of reasons for concluding (first, at least) an Islamic marriage. On the other hand, in the mid-2000s, scholarly effort in the UK went into a collaborative community-based effort to draft model Muslim marriage contracts presented as

[166] Boyd 2013. [167] Razack 2008, 86.
[168] Williams 2013, 2008; Griffiths-Jones 2013b. [169] Griffiths-Jones 2013a.
[170] Shah 2013; Pearl and Menski 1998, 77–80 and 170–175. [171] Ali 2013.
[172] Bano 2012, Rutten 2013, 102–104. Liversage 2012.
[173] Bano 2013; Boyd 2013; Shah 2013; Foblets 2008. [174] Moors 2013, 159.

compliant with law in the UK,[175] while in the US scholars reported a growing interest in the Muslim population in drafting more "personalized" Muslim marriage contracts—documents that are "not a generic stamp of mere legal status conferred by some external authority, but rather, full, detailed expressions of the way each couple defines itself."[176]

At the same time, a deliberate lack of engagement with state registration procedures and requirements for marriage and divorce is also documented in Muslim majority states, sometimes presented as the normative pull of shariʿa in a contested socio-political environment. A considerable amount of scholarship has focussed on the legal and social motivations and implications of marriages (notably lack of judicial remedy) conducted outside the state system in different Arab states, and the reactions of the public and the judiciary to the statutes, particularly in Egypt but also in Morocco and more recently in Syria and the UAE.[177] In Indonesia, Bedner and Van Huis argue pragmatically against proposals that the state enforce more strictly its existing rules on marriage and divorce registration.[178] In regard to "unofficial" (unregistered) marriages in the Middle East and North Africa, public disquiet appears to have centered not so much around people marrying without the knowledge of the state, but at young family members (mostly females) marrying without the knowledge of their families. Hasso considers these "secret marriages" in Egypt and the UAE as "marital innovations" and notes that "customary relationships in the contemporary period are often interchangeably referred to as 'secret' marriages to stress their perceived violation of '*shariʿa*' and state law."[179] Her analysis of these marriages focuses on what the motivations are and how the courts deal with them when they are brought to their attention, often in cases where there is a child and the husband has disappeared or is denying the marriage, obstructing access to a birth certificate and therefore to other public resources.[180] Hasso goes on to consider "*misyar*" or "ambulant" marriage as "secret polygyny."[181] Arabi had earlier considered in the context of 1990s Saudi Arabia the arguments for and against this type of marriage, where the wife agrees at the time of the contract to waive her rights to the husband providing a marital home and to maintenance, and where the secrecy paradigmatically involves keeping the marriage secret from an existing wife; his treatment is in the framework of the way in which people's practice created pressure on Saudi authorities to recognize (albeit in restricted fashion) this institution, an example of what he calls "grass roots law-making."[182]

Carlisle's observation-based analysis of a Damascene court's consideration of a claimed out-of-court marriage focuses on the efforts by the Syrian judge to establish

175 See Muslim Marriage Contract 2008; for an earlier effort see Carroll and Kapoor 1996, 176–177.
176 Quraishi and Syeed-Miller 2004, 191.
177 Shaham 1995, Mir-Hosseini 1993, Carlisle 2008; Hasso 2011.
178 Bedner and Van Huis 2010. 179 Hasso 2011, 81–82. 180 Hasso 2011, 80–88.
181 Hasso 2011, 88–92. See also Yamani 2008, 106–111. 182 Arabi 2001, 147–167.

whether, according to the witnesses, "the events resulted in a valid marriage," and to this purpose investigating social practices as a part of his assessment.[183] The scholarly interest in "Islamic family law" as understood by judges (as well as jurists) and by lay people is a feature of the more recent scholarship.[184] We have already seen how historians have challenged previous accounts of Islamic family law by reviewing court records and other sources. This work also applies to more recent historical periods and indeed current times. Perhaps one of the most vivid debates on how to read court records comes in the disagreement between Islamic law historian Aharon Layish and anthropologist John Davis, published in the 1998 introduction to a collection of mid-twentieth-century Libyan shariʿa court records, over half of which concern family law. Davis had collected the facsimiles of the records during extensive field work and subsequently made them available to Layish. In his introduction, Layish insists *inter alia* that "the historian of Islamic law makes a clear distinction between *shariʿa* and tribal custom."[185] Davis disputes Layish's notion of a "process of sedentarization," arguing that "modern scholarship" contests "label-driven accounts" (such as nomads being ruled by custom and settled peoples by law). "Anthropologists and legal historians come to study law in different ways," he tells us, and the events that bring people to court are linked to different contextual elements that may be inferred from the "event-droppings" provided by documents. "That is quite different from an explanation in terms of a disembodied 'process'—of Islamisation, or civilisation—involving a struggle between two bodies of law assumed to be coherent, monolithic and incompatible."[186] In a 2005 reflection covering the English translation of the same documents, Layish concedes that it is "anthropologically significant" if the Bedouin in the records "identify their day-to-day legal practice indiscriminately with the *shariʿa*," but insists that "the historian of Islamic law cannot simply accept this assumption. A clear distinction exists between orthodox *shariʿa* and tribal customary law, and when the Bedouin are following custom, the scholar must point this out."[187] Who says what Islamic law is?

It is certainly the case that much twenty-first-century scholarship on Islamic family law unsettles the more orthodox narratives of both "what is Islamic family law" and "who says so." There is considerable work on contemporary court practice, often with insights drawn from court observation, following the routine procedural focus of judges in adjudication and mediation, the work of court-appointed arbiters, litigants, and their perception and conduct.[188] Some of this maps the discourses and procedures followed by the actors studied in order to discern, for example for Stiles, a cultural anthropologist, "when are certain cultural practices understood as 'properly Islamic' or 'religious' and by whom?"[189] Or, in the case of Guinchi, introducing

[183] Carlisle 2008. [184] See Tucker 2008, 19. [185] Layish 1998, 6.

[186] Davis 1998, 10–13. [187] Layish 2005, viii.

[188] Hassan and Cederroth 1997; Lindbekk 2014; van Eijk 2012, *Family Law in Syria* 2016; Carlisle 2007, 2013; Clarke 2014; Voorhoeve 2014; Sadiqi 2014; Bernard-Maugiron 2014; Vatuk, "The Application of Muslim Personal Law in India" 2014.

[189] Stiles 2012.

her court practice-focussed collection, the "religiously-inspired judicial activism" of judges.[190] In 2006, Masud, Peters, and Powers suggested that "in future scholars may want to focus greater attention on the work of the *qadi* and the process of judicial decision-making."[191] That same volume contained an article by Baudouin Dupret that has had significant influence on subsequent studies. Using an Egyptian family law case to illustrate his argument, Dupret states that:

> [t]here is no reason to assume that what people refer to as Islamic law is identical to a set of technical provisions that form the idealized model of Islamic law. Nor is there any reason to assume the contrary. To a certain extent, the question is not relevant.... To the question, What is Islamic law? we should substitute the question, What do people do when referring to Islamic law?[192]

His point is that by focusing on an assumed framework, research misses its aim. A later piece co-authored with Maaike Voorhoeve critiques the tendency, in scholarship on the legal systems of MENA, "to ascribe overarching importance to Islam in the inception and organisation of the law."[193] In this regard they very appositely remind us that family law is but one small part of the legal systems of MENA countries. They advocate "paying attention to practice as the only area where the law is seen to be at work" and that scholars must consider how Islam is invoked and referred to: "thus, 'Islamic law' corresponds to what people consider as specifically Islamic in the law, independent of any consideration about the truth of such a claim."[194] The articles in this collection illustrate this approach.[195] Following Dupret in 2014, Voorhoeve applies an "ethno-methodological study of behaviour" to take the statements of actors about their own behavior at face value in her study of family law practice at a Tunisian court and speaks of a "new wave" of scholarship in this vein, with scholars who acknowledge that their data are "messy" and do not assume *a priori* structural frames through which to view it.[196]

Thus, with no straightforward answers to the question "what is Islamic family law?" nor yet "who says so?" we move, relatively straightforwardly, to the question "Islamic Family Law: So What?"

III. So What?

In a situation where the authority of apparently agreed-upon substance, and the authority to pronounce thereon, are increasingly unsettled, a growing body of

190 Giunchi 2014, xiv.
191 Masud, Peters, and Powers 2006, 2012, 6.
192 Dupret 2006, 2012, 167.
193 Dupret and Voorhoeve 2012, 1.
194 Dupret and Voorhoeve 2012, 3.
195 Masud, Peters, and Powers 2006.
196 Voorhoeve 2014, 9, 18. She references the work of Dupret, Carlisle, and Shehada.

scholarship engages with what Islamic family law could/should/might be. Two recent and significant contributions in this regard are the collections edited by Mir-Hosseini with different colleagues in 2013 and 2015.[197] The nature of the scholarship, and the processes that gave rise to the publications, are as significant as the content. The volumes engage with Muslim family law (2013) and Muslim legal tradition (2015) and both focus particularly on male authority in the family (guardianship—*wilaya* and *qiwama*), notions of gender equality, and the "lived realities" or "social reality" of Muslim women in order to explore family law issues. The first collection was facilitated by the "Oslo Coalition on Freedom of Religion or Belief"; those involved are at pains to emphasize that "this was not an inter-religious dialogue, but a Muslim project, bringing together Muslim experts" from different disciplines and professions.[198] The 2015 collection is the first output of the Knowledge Building Initiative of Musawah (the Global Network for Justice and Equality in the Muslim Family), which was launched in 2009 in Kuala Lumpur.[199] Both are examples of engaged scholarship: an explicit aim is the "reform" of Muslim legal tradition and in particular that related to family law, as a basis for the reform of Muslim family law and relations. They include textual, philosophical, and jurisprudential reinterpretations and exegetical analyses[200] as well as situation-specific explorations of reform processes.[201] Women's and human rights are invoked as well as gender equality and feminist method and engagement.[202] The 2015 book wants to "develop feminist knowledge that is grounded in Muslim tradition while engaging critically with it."[203] The distinctive features of this scholarship include its emergence from collaborative processes, not only among but between scholars, scholar-activists, and activists. Not all scholars have welcomed this work; anthropologist Lila Abu-Lughod, in a critique of Musawah, is uneasy about "the new consensus in the international rights community and among many Muslim feminist activists and scholars that Islam and women's human rights must be reconciled and that internal reform is necessary."[204] There is also disquiet at the use of Muslim family law as a trope for constructing the (less than "civilized") nature of Muslim men in the context of the imperial adventures of western powers particularly since 9/11 and the complex alliances—or at least resonances—between these military and other exercises and certain feminist discourses in the West.[205]

[197] Mir-Hosseini, Vogt, Larsen, and Moe 2013; Mir-Hosseini, Al-Sharmani, and Rumminger 2015.

[198] Mir-Hosseini et al., Introduction 2013, 2.

[199] See Anwar 2013, 115, 2008; Mir-Hosseini 2012. Musawah's publications are available online.

[200] Masud 2013, Abu-Zayd 2013, Abdul Kodir 2013, Eshkevari 2013, Kadivar 2013 and Emon 2013; Mir-Hosseini 2015, Abou-Bakr 2015, Lamrabet 2015, Chaudhry 2015, Wadud 2015.

[201] Al-Sharmani 2013c, Sharafeldin 2013, El Hajjami 2013, Anwar 2013; Sharafeldin 2015, Welchman 2015, Larsen 2015.

[202] Sharafeldin 2013, 2015, Al-Sharmani and Rumminger 2015.

[203] Mir-Hosseini et al, Introduction 2015, 4.

[204] Abu-Lughod 2013, 185.

[205] See also Kapur 2012 on the right to gender equality; and Hirsch 2006.

Muslim feminist scholarly approaches to jurisprudence and equality arguments have been established since the 1990s,[206] but Zainah Anwar (a founder and former director of Sisters in Islam in Malaysia and a co-founder of Musawah) records increasing interest on the part of activists in exploring Islamic sources after the turn of the century.[207] The 1990s saw examples of engaged scholarship involving broader networks and not involved in seeking to rework Islamic jurisprudence—notably, Women Living Under Muslim Laws (WLUML), under whose auspices two valuable collections were published in 1996, both edited by established scholars. Thus in WLUML's first "Special Dossier" Hoodfar as editor refers to women "galvanizing for change" in different societies around the world and situates the publication as a contribution to these efforts by examining some of the strategies being used in different contexts.[208] The second publication was an "Information Kit" on delegated *talaq* ("the Muslim woman's contractual access to divorce") and pertains particularly to South Asia, with a range of documents including the forms of different marriage contracts as well as academic essays and practical advice on how to draft a marriage contract containing an effective delegation of *talaq* to the wife.[209] WLUML went on to produce several versions of an ambitious "action-research" resource book, *Knowing Our Rights*, looking across different Muslim communities and evaluating existing family law provisions and structure with a view to assessing the most "option-giving" for the greatest number of women affected by them "at the current historical moment."[210] North African scholars compiled the *Guide to Equality in the Family in the Maghreb* that in turn is cited as an inspiration for Musawah's work.[211] Another "global resource book," edited by Abdullahi An-Na'im, began life as an online project out of Emory University that subsequently produced two collections of materials aimed at "serving as a resource for internal initiatives aimed at expanding and protecting women's rights in the family as articulated in human rights norms."[212] An-Na'im insists on the "futility of adopting a reductive approach to the study of Shari'a-based family law" and that while the material presented in his collection will indeed serve as a "resource book," it is intended "also to encourage a more candid and thorough examination of the underlying issues." His own position, set out in greater detail in his later publications, is "admittedly controversial" as he calls for "a clear and categorical acknowledgement of the fact that family law in Islamic countries today is not, and indeed cannot and should not be, founded on Shari'a."[213]

206 See al-Hibri 1997 and "Muslim Women's Rights" 2000.
207 Anwar 2013; Emon 2013, 237.
208 Hoodfar 1996, 4. See in this collection especially WRAG 1996.
209 Carroll and Kapoor 1996.
210 WLUML 2003, 21. The last version 2006 is available online.
211 Collectif 95 Maghreb-Egalité 2005; Anwar 2013, 116.
212 See Welchman 2004, 1; this is the companion volume to An-Na'im 2002.
213 An-Na'im 2002, 20.

Thus since the 1990s we have activists working with scholars, and scholars identifying as "scholar-activists," with manuals and "toolkits" and more recently still websites and different forms of communication and dissemination that are used to elicit and spread ideas about the workings of Muslim family law in different contexts, strategies for making the greatest use of the law for the best protection of different areas of women's rights in the family, and the prospects for reform of the law and strategies to achieve it. Interestingly, Tucker links this kind of advocacy to previous centuries of women "waging law" by demanding their rights at court.[214] While noting considerable opposition to this work and the groups carrying it out, Tucker considers that "these are the people and groups to watch in the near future, in light of both their energy and commitment."[215]

Tucker's book also illustrates the extent to which human rights law and norms are now invoked or implicated in Islamic family law scholarship as well as advocacy.[216] Besides examining the advocacy campaigns, scholars may compare human rights norms (particularly the equality and non-discrimination norms) with institutions of Muslim family law and/or practice in particular postcolonial states, or consider similar issues arising in non-Muslim majority states in regard to their minority Muslim populations and proposals for a degree of legal pluralism.[217] And international human rights organizations also now publish lengthy reports on matters of Muslim family law and practice in particular Muslim states.[218]

We also see scholarship mapping and analyzing family law reform processes from a range of angles. Some look at state procedures and processes and responses to civil society demands;[219] some focus on women's activism, feminist activism, and women's movements—and indeed individual participants therein—and how and in what circumstances their discourses and demands change;[220] some start from a focus on citizenship to examine processes of Muslim family law reform or use family law as a lens through which to examine other subjects, such as feminism.[221] In much of such scholarship, "the law" and its discourses certainly lose ground to discourses "on" the law; often the issue of it being "Islamic" or "Muslim" family law is treated entirely matter-of-factly, almost incidentally. This appears entirely inevitable. If there is no longer a familiar body of jurisprudence from a recognized source of authority who may expound and indeed expand it, then others, from non-orthodox academic or disciplinary backgrounds may join the debate; and the debate may become not so

[214] Tucker 2008, 223–224; and see 124.

[215] Tucker 2008, 225. [216] Tucker 2008, 80–81.

[217] See e.g. Rehman 2007; Mir-Hosseini 2012; Ali 2000; Amin 2013; Foblets 2013; Weiss 2009.

[218] Human Rights Watch 2004, 2011, 2015. For a critique of this approach see Modirzadeh 2006.

[219] Cole 2009; Welchman 2009; Chowdhury 2013; Fawzy 2004.

[220] Anwar 2008, 2013; Dahlgren 2012, 2013; Shah 2008; Salime 2009; Sharafeldin 2015; Shehada 2013; al-Sharmani 2013c; Osanloo 2013; Nazneen 2013.

[221] Maktabi 2013; di Ricco 2012; Sadiqi 2008.

much about what the law is (normatively and descriptively) but what it could and perhaps should be. See for example the explicit attention given to "alternative forms and sources of knowledge" in Musawah's compilation of women's life stories as a way to understand the "meaning" of male guardianship and authority.[222] This research is carried out precisely to understand how this framing of the family works in daily realities, or rather whether it does: in these stories, as is noted in many other context-specific examinations, the maintenance part of the formula is failing as men are unwilling or unable to provide for their families.[223] There is a "disconnect" between the gendered roles and rights in the family recognized and endorsed by state law invoking *fiqh* authority and the realities of economic and social pressures on the family in different parts of the Muslim world.[224]

Another type of scholarship that may uncover such tensions administers and analyzes the results of opinion polls asking respondents about family law and revealing significant insights about what people think about the law and what they expect it to do.[225] In Palestine, polls have shown a strong emphasis on context—so for example revealing support among both men and women for divorced women to have some degree of access to assets acquired during the course of her marriage with her former husband. Hammami and Johnson consider this finding to be a result of "changes in the traditional male breadwinner/economically dependent wife model" and an increasing recognition of the wife's contribution to building marital assets, as well as her economic vulnerability in the case of the termination of her marriage.[226]

IV. Concluding Remarks

Such analyses clearly have meaning for the complex relationships of different Muslim constituencies with their perceptions of Muslim family law, perhaps in particular how different sectors and communities expect the law to produce justice, in their place and time, at least as much as where they expect to find its inspiration or its origin. More generally, English-language scholarship on Islamic (or Muslim family) law is expanding exponentially, within as well as beyond the disciplines with

[222] Al-Sharmani and Rumminger 2015, 226.

[223] Ibid., 233.

[224] Sonneveld 2012b; Shehada 2009; Al-Sharmani 2013; Bedner and Van Huis 2010, 184–185; Larsen 2015.

[225] Fawzi 2004; Hammami 2004; Hammami and Johnson 2013.

[226] Ibid., 2013, 11.

which it was traditionally associated. The state is no longer regarded uncritically, and approaches to Islamic family law have become—among other things—one lens among others through which to explore a number of different political and social relationships. A substantial scholarship continues to explore court practice in specific contexts, and to investigate the wider implications of particular concepts within Islamic family law and their meanings in lives lived beyond the court. The positionings of courts, and indeed of judges, are examined through frames beyond the substance (or text) of rulings. Increasing attention is paid to the way in which "lay" people—litigants, petitioners, their voices emerging from the historical record as well as from contemporaneous observation—act on their understandings of the law. Some of the most recent scholarship, nourished by and feeding into sustained dialogues and conversations, is purposively constructed to produce fundamentally new paradigms and ways of thinking about law, authority, and indeed the family. New voices and new critiques, as well as new challenges, are demanding attention; critiques of past frames, practice, and scholarship continue to inform and indeed to correct; but right now, most eyes are on those who can go some way to proposing how these challenges might be met.

References

Abdal-Rehim, Abdal-Rehim Abdal-Rahman, "The Family and Gender Laws in Egypt during the Ottoman Period" in Amira El Azhary Sonbol (ed.) *Women, the Family, and Divorce Laws in Islamic History* (Syracuse: Syracuse University Press, 1996) 96–111.

Abdul Kodir, Faqihuddin, "Gender Equality and the Hadith of the Prophet Muhammad. Reinterpreting the Concepts of Mahram and Qiwama" in Ziba Mir-Hosseini, Kari Vogt, Lena Larsen, and Christian Moe (eds.) *Gender and Equality in Muslim Family Law. Justice and Ethics in the Islamic Legal Tradition* (London: I.B. Tauris, 2013) 169–189.

Abou-Bakr, Omaima, "The Interpretive Legacy of Qiwama as an Exegetical Construct" in Ziba Mir-Hosseini, Mulki Al-Sharmani, and Jana Rumminger (eds.) *Men in Charge? Rethinking Authority in Muslim Legal Tradition* (London: Oneworld, 2015) 44–64.

Abu-Lughod, Lila, *Do Muslim Women Need Saving?* (Cambridge, MA: Harvard University Press, 2013).

Abu-Lughod, Lila and Anupuma Rao, eds., *Women's Rights, Muslim Family Law and the Politics of Consent*, socialdifference-online 1, 2011.

Abu-Odeh, Lama, "Modernizing Muslim Family Law: The Case of Egypt." *Vanderbilt Journal of Transnational Law* 37 (2004): 1043.

Abu-Zayd, Nasr, "The Status of Women between the Qur'an and *Fiqh*" in Ziba Mir-Hosseini, Kari Vogt, Lena Larsen, and Christian Moe (eds.) *Gender and Equality in Muslim Family Law. Justice and Ethics in the Islamic Legal Tradition* (London: I.B. Tauris, 2013) 153–168.

Agmon, Iris, "Muslim Women in Court According to the Sjill of Late Ottoman Jaffa and Haifa: some methodological notes" in Amira Sonbol (ed.) *Women, the Family and Divorce Laws in Islamic History* (Syracuse: Syracuse University Press, 1996) 112–125.

Agmon, Iris, *Family Court: Legal Culture and Modernity in Late Ottoman Palestine* (Syracuse: Syracuse University Press, 2006).

Ahmad, Nehaluddin, "A Critical Appraisal of 'Triple Divorce' in Islamic Law." *International Journal of Law, Policy and the Family* 23, no. 1 (2009): 53–61.

Ahmed, Leila, *Women and Gender in Islam* (New Haven: Yale University Press, 1992).

Al-Sharmani, Mulki, "Egyptian Khul: Legal Reform, Courtroom Practices, and Realities of Women" in Rubya Mehdi, Werner Menski, and Jorgen S. Nielsen (eds.) *Interpreting Divorce Laws in Islam* (Copenhagen: DJOF Publishing, 2012) 85–104.

Al-Sharmani, Mulki, "Qiwama in Egyptian Family Laws: 'Wifely Obedience' between Legal Texts, Courtroom Practices and Realities of Marriage" in Ziba Mir-Hosseini, Kari Vogt, Lena Larsen, and Christian Moe (eds.) *Gender and Equality in Muslim Family Law. Justice and Ethics in the Islamic Legal Tradition* (London: I.B. Tauris, 2013a) 37–55.

Al-Sharmani, Mulki, ed., *Feminist Activism, Women's Rights, and Legal Reform* (London: Zed Books, 2013b).

Al-Sharmani, Mulki, "Reforming Egyptian Family Laws: The Debate about a New Substantive Code" in Mulki Al-Sharmani (ed.) *Feminist Activism, Women's Rights, and Legal Reform* (London: Zed Books, 2013c) 73–100.

Al-Sharmani, Mulki, and Rumminger, Jana, "Understanding *Qiwamah* and *Wilayah* through Life Stories" in Ziba Mir-Hosseini, Mulki Al-Sharmani, and Jana Rumminger (eds.) *Men in Charge? Rethinking Authority in Muslim Legal Tradition* (London: Oneworld, 2015) 219–255.

Ali, Kecia, "Marriage in Classical Islamic Jurisprudence. A Survey of Doctrines" in Asifa Quraishi and Frank E. Vogel (eds.) *The Islamic Marriage Contract. Case Studies in Islamic Family Law* (Cambridge, MA: Harvard University Press, 2008) 11–45.

Ali, Shaheen Sardar, "From Muslim Migrants to Muslim Citizens" in Robin Griffiths-Jones (ed.) *Islam and English Law. Rights, Responsibilities and the Place of Shari'a* (Cambridge: Cambridge University Press, 2013) 157–175.

Ali, Shaheen Sardar, *Gender and Human Rights in Islam and International Law. Equal before Allah, Unequal before Man?* The Hague: Kluwer Law International, 2000.

Amin, Waheeda, "The Gendered Benefits and Costs of Legal Pluralism for Muslim Family Law in South Africa" in Mavis Maclean and John Eekelaar (eds.) *Managing Family Justice in Diverse Societies* (Oxford and Portland, Oregon: Hart Publishing, 2013) 107–123.

Anderson, James Norman Dalrymple, *Islamic Law in Africa* (London: HMSO, 1954).

Anderson, James Norman Dalrymple, "Invalid and Void Marriages in Hanafi Law." *BSOAS* 13, no. 2 (1950): 357–366.

Anderson, James Norman Dalrymple, "Recent Developments in *Shari'a* Law (III): The Contract of Marriage." *Muslim World* 41 (1951a): 35–48.

Anderson, James Norman Dalrymple, "Recent Developments in *Shari'a* Law (IV): Further Points Concerning Marriage." *Muslim World* 41 (1951b): 186–198.

Anderson, James Norman Dalrymple, "Recent Developments in *Shari'a* Law (V): The Dissolution of Marriage." *Muslim World* 41 (1951c): 271–288.

Anderson, James Norman Dalrymple, "Recent Developments in *Shari'a* Law (VI): The Testamentary Bequests." *Muslim World* 42 (1952a): 33–47.

Anderson, James Norman Dalrymple, "Recent Developments in *Shari'a Law* (VII): Intestate Succession." *Muslim World* 42 (1952b): 124–140.

Anderson, James Norman Dalrymple, "Recent Developments in *Shari'a* Law (VIII): The Jordanian Law of Family Rights." *Muslim World* 42 (1952c): 190–206.

Anderson, James Norman Dalrymple, “The Syrian Law of Personal Status.” *BSOAS* 17 (1955): 34–49.

Anderson, James Norman Dalrymple, “A Law of Personal Status for Iraq.” *ICLQ* 9 (1960): 542–563.

Anderson, James Norman Dalrymple, *Law Reform in the Muslim World* (London: The Athlone Press, 1976).

Anderson, Michael, “Islamic Law and the Colonial Encounter in British India” in Chibli Mallat and Jane Connors (eds.) *Islamic Family Law* (London: Graham and Trotman, 1990) 205–223.

An-Na'im, Abdullahi, ed., *Islamic Family Law in a Changing World: A Global Resource Book* (London and New York: Zed Books, 2002).

An-Na'im, Abdullahi, “Shari'a and Islamic Family Law: Transition and Transformation” in Abdullahi An-Na'im (ed.) *Islamic Family Law in a Changing World. A Global Resource Book* (London and New York: Zed Books) 1–22.

Anwar, Zainah, “From Local to Global: Sisters in Islam and the Making of Musawah: A Global Movement for Equality in the Muslim Family” in Ziba Mir-Hosseini, Mulki Al-Sharmani, and Jana Rumminger (eds.) *Men in Charge? Rethinking Authority in Muslim Legal Tradition* (London: Oneworld, 2015) 107–124.

Anwar, Zainah, “Advocacy for Reform in Islamic Family Law: The Experience of Sisters in Islam” in Asifa Quraishi and Frank E. Vogel (eds.) *The Islamic Marriage Contract. Case Studies in Islamic Family Law* (Cambridge, MA: Harvard University Press, 2008) 273–284.

Anwar, Zainah, “From Local to Global: Sisters in Islam and the Making of Musawah: A Global Movement for Equality in the Muslim Family” in Ziba Mir-Hosseini, Kari Vogt, Lena Larsen, and Christian Moe (eds.) *Gender and Equality in Muslim Family Law. Justice and Ethics in the Islamic Legal Tradition* (London: I.B. Tauris, 2013) 107–124.

Al-Azri, Khalid M., *Social and Gender Inequality in Oman: The Power of Religious and Political Tradition* (London: Routledge, 2012).

Al-Azri, Khalid M., *Social and Gender Inequality in Oman. The Power of Religious and Political Tradition* (Abingdon: Routledge, 2013).

Arabi, Oussama, *Studies in Modern Islamic Law and Jurisprudence* (The Hague: Kluwer Law International, 2001).

Arshad, Raffia, *Islamic Family Law* (London: Sweet and Maxwell, 2010).

Baderin, Mashood, ed., *Issues in Islamic Law* (Farnham, Surrey: Ashgate Publishing Limited, 2014).

Bakht, Natasha, “Family Arbitration Using Sharia Law: Examining Ontario's Arbitration Act and its Impact on women.” *Muslim World Journal of Human Rights* 1, no. 1, article 7 (2004).

Bakht, Natasha, “Were Muslim Barbarians Really Knocking on the Gates of Ontario: The Religious Arbitration Controversy—Another Perspective.” *40th Anniversary Edition Ottowa Law Review* 67 (2006): 67–82.

Bano, Samia, “The Practice of Law Making and the Problem of Forced Marriage: What is the Role of the Muslim Arbitration Tribunal?” in Aisha K. Gill and Sundari Anitha (eds.) *Forced Marriage. Introducing a Social Justice and Human Rights Perspective* (London: Zed Books, 2011) 177–199.

Bano, Samia, “Muslim Women, Divorce and *Shari'ah* Councils in Britain” in Rubya Mehdi, Werner Menski, and Jorgen S. Nielsen (eds.) *Interpreting Divorce Laws in Islam* (Copenhagen: DJOF Publishing, 2012) 259–288.

Bano, Samia, "Muslim Dispute Resolution in Britain: Towards a New Framework of Family Law Governance?" in Mavis Maclean and John Eekelaar (eds.) *Managing Family Justice in Diverse Societies* (Oxford and Portland, Oregon: Hart Publishing, 2013) 61–86.

Bedner, Adriaan, and van Huis, Stijn, "Plurality of Marriage Law and Marriage Registration for Muslims in Indonesia: A Plea for Pragmatism." *Utrecht Law Review* 6, no. 2 (2010): 175–191.

Berger, Maurits S., ed., *Applying Shari'a in the West. Facts, Fears and the Future of Islamic Rules on Family Relations in the West* (Leiden: Leiden University Press, 2013).

Bernard-Maugiron, Nathalie, "The Judicial Construction of the Facts and the Law. The Egyptian Supreme Constitutional Court and the Constitutionality of the Law on Khul'" in Baudouin Dupret, Barbara Drieskens, and Annelies Moors (eds.) *Narratives of Truth in Islamic Law* (London and New York: I.B. Tauris, 2008) 241–264.

Bernard-Maugiron, Nathalie and Dupret, Baudouin, "Breaking Up the Family: Divorce in Egyptian Law and Practice." *Hawwa* 6 (2008): 52–74.

Bernard-Maugiron, Nathalie, "Courts and the Reform of Personal Status Law in Egypt: Judicial Divorce for Injury and Polygamy" in Elisa Giunchi (ed.) *Adjudicating Family Law in Muslim Courts* (Abingdon: Routledge, 2014) 106–120.

Boyd, Marion, "Ontario's 'Shari'a Court': Law and Politics Intertwined" in Robin Griffiths-Jones (ed.) *Islam and English Law. Rights, Responsibilities and the Place of Shari'a* (Cambridge: Cambridge University Press, 2013) 176–186.

Carlisle, Jessica, "'Asbab al-darb ktir basita': The Legality of Claims of Violence during Judicial Divorce Cases in Syria." *Hawwa* 5, 2–3 (2007): 239–261.

Carlisle, Jessica, "Moroccan Divorce Law, Family Court Judges, and Spouses' Claims: Who Pays the Cost When a Marriage is Over?" in Mulki Al-Sharmani (ed.) *Feminist Activism, Women's Rights, and Legal Reform* (London: Zed Books, 2013) 151–176.

Carlisle, Jessica, "From Behind the Door: A Damascus Court Copes with an Alleged Out of Court Marriage." In *Les Metamorphoses du Mariage au Moyen-Orient*, 59–74 (Beirut: IFPO, 2008).

Carroll, Lucy, Talaq-i-tafwid and Stipulations in a Muslim Marriage Contract: Important Means of Protecting the Position of the South Asian Muslim Wife. *Modern Asian Studies* 16 (1982): 277–309.

Carroll, Lucy, "Marriage-Guardianship and Minor's Marriage at Islamic Law." *Islamic and Comparative Law Quarterly* 7 (1987): 249–260.

Carroll, Lucy, and Kapoor, Harsh, *Talaq-i-Tafwid: The Muslim Woman's Contractual Access to Divorce. An Information Kit.* WLUML 1996 (np).

Charrad, Mounira, *States and Women's Rights. The Making of Postcolonial Tunisia, Algeria and Morocco* (Berkeley: University of California Press, 2001).

Chaudhry, Ayesha S., "Producing Gender-Egalitarian Islamic Law: A Case Study of Guardianship (Wilayah) in Prophetic Practice" in Ziba Mir-Hosseini, Mulki Al-Sharmani, and Jana Rumminger (eds.) *Men in Charge? Rethinking Authority in Muslim Legal Tradition* (London: Oneworld, 2015) 88–105.

Chowdhury, Farah Deeba, "Muslim Family Law in Bangladesh: Resistance to Secularisation" in Mavis Maclean and John Eekelaar (eds.) *Managing Family Justice in Diverse Societies* (Oxford and Portland, Oregon: Hart Publishing, 2013) 263–269.

Clarke, Morgan, "Shari'a Courts and Muslim Family Law in Lebanon" in Elisa Giunchi (ed.) *Adjudicating Family Law in Muslim Courts* (Abingdon: Routledge, 2014) 32–47.

Cole, Juan, "Struggles over Personal Status and Family Law in Post-Baathist Iraq" in Kenneth M. Cuno and Manisha Desai (eds.) *Family, Gender and Law in a Globalizing Middle East and South Asia* (Syracuse: Syracuse University Press, 2009) 105–125.

Collectif 95 Maghreb-Egalité, *Guide to Equality in the Family in the Maghreb*, Women's Learning Partnership (nl) 2005.

Coulson, Noel J., *Conflicts and Tensions in Islamic Jurisprudence* (Chicago: University of Chicago Press, 1969).

Cuno, Kenneth M., *Modernizing Marriage. Family, Ideology, and Law in Nineteenth- and Early Twentieth-Century Egypt* (Syracuse: Syracuse University Press, 2015).

Cuno, Kenneth M. and Desai, Manisha, eds., *Family, Gender & Law in a Globalizing Middle East and South Asia* (Syracuse: Syracuse University Press, 2009).

Dahlgren, Suzanne, "Women's *Adah* versus 'Women's Law': the Contesting Issue of *Mahr* in Aden, Yemen" in Baudouin Dupret et Francois Burgat (eds.) Le Shaykh et Le Procurer. Systèmes Coutumiers et Pratiques Juridiques au Yémen et en Égypte (CEDEJ: Égypte/Monde Arabe no.1 - 3e série, 2005) 125–144.

Dahlgren, Suzanne, "'She Brings up Healthy Children for the Homeland': Morality Discourses in Yemeni Legal Debates" in Maaike Vooerhoeve (ed.) *Family Law in Islam. Divorce, Marriage and Women in the Muslim World* (London and New York: I.B. Tauris, 2012) 13–20.

Dahlgren, Suzanne, "Readjusting Women's Too Many Rights: The State, the Public Voice, and Women's Rights in South Yemen" in Mulki Al-Sharmani (ed.) *Feminist Activism, Women's Rights, and Legal Reform* (London: Zed Books, 2013) 48–72.

Davis, John, "A Social Perspective" in Aharon Layish (ed.) *Legal Documents on Libyan Tribal Society in Process of Sedentarization (Part I: Documents in Arabic)* (Wiesbadan: Harrassowitz, 1998) 7–13.

Dupret, Baudouin, *Le jugement en action: ethnométhodologie du droit, de la morale et de la justice en Egypte* (Paris: Librairie Droz, 2006).

Dupret, Baudouin, "What is Islamic Law? A Praxiological Answer and an Egyptian Case Study." *Theory, Culture and Society* 24, no. 2 (2007): 79–100.

Dupret, Baudouin, "The Practice of Judging: The Egyptian Judiciary at Work on a Personal Status Case" in Khalid Masud, Rudolph Peters, and David Powers (eds.) *Dispensing Justice in Islam. Qadis and their Judgements* (Leiden: Brill, 2012) 143–168.

Dupret, Baudouin, and Voorhoeve, Maaike, "Introduction" in Maaike Vooerhoeve (ed.) *Family Law in Islam. Divorce, Marriage and Women in the Muslim World* (London and New York: I.B. Tauris, 2012) 1–12.

Eijk, Esther van, "Divorce Practices in Muslim and Christian Courts in Syria" in Maaike Vooerhoeve (ed.) *Family Law in Islam. Divorce, Marriage and Women in the Muslim World* (London and New York: I.B. Tauris, 2012) 147–170.

Eijk, Esther van, *Family Law in Syria. Patriarchy, Pluralism and Personal Status Law* (London and New York: I.B. Tauris, 2016).

El Alami, Dawoud, *The Marriage Contract in Islamic Law, in the Shari'ah and Personal Status Laws of Egypt and Morocco* (London: Graham and Trotman, 1992).

El Alami, Dawoud, "Remedy or Device? The System of Khul' and the Effects of its Incorporation into Egyptian Personal Status Law." *Yearbook of Islamic and Middle Eastern Law* 9 (1999–2000): 134–135.

El Alami, Dawoud, and Doreen Hinchcliffe, *Islamic Marriage and Divorce Laws of the Arab World* (London: Kluwer Law International, 1996, reprinted 1998).

El Hajjami, Aicha, "The Religious Arguments in the Debate on the Reform of the Moroccan Family Code" in Ziba Mir-Hosseini, Kari Vogt, Lena Larsen, and Christian Moe (eds.) *Gender and Equality in Muslim Family Law. Justice and Ethics in the Islamic Legal Tradition* (London: I.B. Tauris, 2013) 81–105.

Emon, Anver, "The Paradox of Equality and the Politics of Difference. Gender Equality, Islamic Law and the Modern Muslim State" in Ziba Mir-Hosseini, Kari Vogt, Lena Larsen, and Christian Moe (eds.) *Gender and Equality in Muslim Family Law. Justice and Ethics in the Islamic Legal Tradition* (London: I.B. Tauris, 2013) 237–258.

Eshkevari, Hassan Yousefi, "Rethinking Men's Authority Over Women. *Qiwama, Wilaya* and their Underlying Assumptions" in Ziba Mir-Hosseini, Kari Vogt, Lena Larsen, and Christian Moe (eds.) *Gender and Equality in Muslim Family Law. Justice and Ethics in the Islamic Legal Tradition* (London: I.B. Tauris, 2013) 191–211.

Esposito, John L. and DeLong-Bas, Natana J., *Women in Muslim Family Law* (Syracuse: Syracuse University Press, 2001).

Fawzy, Essam, "Muslim Personal Status Law in Egypt: The Current Situation and Possibilities of Reform through Internal Initiatives" in Lynn Welchman (ed.) *Women's Rights and Islamic Family Law. Perspectives on Reform* (London and New York: Zed Books, 2004) 17–94.

Foblets, Marie-Claire, "The Admissibility of Repudiation: Recent Developments in Dutch, French and Belgian Private Law." *Hawwa* 5, no. 1 (2007): 10–32.

Foblets, Marie-Claire, "Marriage and Divorce in the New Moroccan Family Code: Implications for Moroccans Residing in Europe" in Rubya Mehdi, Hanne Petersen, Erik Reenberg Sand, and Gordon R. Woodman (eds.) *Law and Religion in Multicultural Societies* (Copenhagen: DJOF Publishing, 2008) 145–174.

Foblets, Marie-Claire, "Accommodating Islamic Family Law(s): A Critical Analysis of Some Recent Developments and Experiments in Europe" in Maurits S. Berger (ed.) *Applying Shari'a in the West. Facts, Fears and the Future of Islamic Rules on Family Relations in the West* (Leiden: Leiden University Press, 2013) 207–226.

Fournier, Pascale, *Muslim Marriage in Western Courts. Lost in Transplantation* (Farnham, Surrey: Ashgate, 2010).

Fournier, Pascale, Setrakian, Aida, and McDougall, Pascal, "No-Fault Talaq: Islamic Divorce in Canadian Immigration and Family Law" in Rubya Mehdi, Werner Menski, and Jorgen S. Nielsen (eds.) *Interpreting Divorce Laws in Islam* (Copenhagen: DJOF Publishing, 2012) 235–258.

Freeland, Richard and Lau, Martin, "The Shari'a and English Law: Identity and Justice for British Muslims" in Asifa Quraishi and Frank E. Vogel (eds.) *The Islamic Marriage Contract. Case Studies in Islamic Family Law* (Cambridge, MA: Harvard University Press, 2008) 331–348.

Fyzee, Asaf A.A., *Outlines of Muhammadan Law* (New Delhi: Oxford University Press India, 1949, 1955, 1964, 1974, 1999).

Gill, Aisha K. and Anitha, Sundari, eds., *Forced Marriage. Introducing a Social Justice and Human Rights Perspective* (London: Zed Books, 2011).

Giunchi, Elisa, ed. *Adjudicating Family Law in Muslim Courts* (Abingdon: Routledge, 2014).

Griffiths-Jones, Robin, ed., *Islam and English Law. Rights, Responsibilities and the Place of Shari'a* (Cambridge: Cambridge University Press, 2013a).

Griffiths-Jones, Robin, "The 'Unavoidable' Adoption Of *Shari'a* Law—The Generation of a Media Storm" in Robin Griffiths-Jones (ed.) *Islam and English Law. Rights, Responsibilities and the Place of Shari'a* (Cambridge: Cambridge University Press, 2013b) 9–19.

Haeri, Shahla, "Divorce in Contemporary Iran: A Male Prerogative in Self-Will" in Chibli Mallat and Jane Connors (eds.) *Islamic Family Law* (London: Graham and Trotman, 1990) 55–69.

Haeri, Shahla, "Mut'a: Regulating Sexuality and Gender Relations in Postrevolutionary Iran" in Muhammad Khalid Masud, Brinkley Messick, and David S. Powers (eds.) *Islamic Legal Interpretation. Muftis and their Fatwas* (Cambridge, MA: Harvard University Press, 1996) 251–261.

Hammami, Rema, "Attitudes Towards Legal Reform of Personal Status Law in Palestine" in Lynn Welchman (ed.) *Women's Rights and Islamic Family Law. Perspectives on Reform* (London and New York: Zed Books, 2004) 125–143.

Hammami, Rema, and Johnson, Penny, *Change and Conservation: Family Law Reform in Court Practice and Public Perceptions in the Occupied Palestinian Territory* (Birzeit: Institute of Women's Studies, December 2013).

Hanna, Nelly, "Marriage among Merchant Families in Seventeenth-Century Cairo" in Amira Sonbol (ed.) *Women, the Family and Divorce Laws in Islamic History* (Syracuse: Syracuse University Press, 1996) 143–154.

Hassan, Sharifah, Syed, Zaleha, and Cederroth, Sven, *Managing Marital Disputes in Malaysia. Islamic Mediators and Conflict Resolution in the Syariah Courts* (Richmond: Curzon, 1997).

Hasso, Frances, "Bargaining with the Devil. States and Intimate Life." *Journal of Middle East Women's Studies* 10, no. 2 (2014): 107–134.

Hasso, Frances, *Consuming Desires. Family Crisis and the State in the Middle East* (Stanford: Stanford University Press, 2011).

al-Hibri, Azizah, "Islam, Law and Custom. Redefining Muslim Women's Rights." *American University Journal of International Law and Policy* 12, no. 1 (1997): 1–44.

Hinchcliffe, Doreen, "Polygamy in Traditional and Contemporary Islamic Law." *Islam and the Modern Age* 1, no. 8 (1970): 13–38.

Hirsch, Susan, *Pronouncing and Persevering. Gender and the Discourses of Disputing in an African Islamic Court* (Chicago: University of Chicago Press, 1998).

Hirsch, Susan, "Islamic Law and Society Post-9/11." *Annu. Rev. Law Soc. Sci.* 2 (2006): 165–186.

Holden, Livia, "Divorce at the Woman's Initiative in India, in Pakistan and in the Diasporas" in Rubya Mehdi, Werner Menski, and Jorgen S. Nielsen (eds.) *Interpreting Divorce Laws in Islam* (Copenhagen: DJOF Publishing, 2012) 131–153.

Hoodfar, Homa, ed., *Shifting Boundaries in Marriage and Divorce in Muslim Communities.* WLUML, 1996 (np).

Hossain, Sara, "Remedies for Forced Marriage in Bangladesh" in Sara Hossain and Lynn Welchman (eds.) *Remedies for Forced Marriage: A Handbook for Lawyers* (London: INTERIGHTS, 2014) (available at http://www.interights.org/forced-marriage-handbook/index.html).

Hossain, Sara, "'Wayward Girls and Well-wisher Parents': Habeas Corpus, Women's Right to Personal Liberty, Consent to Marriage and the Bangladeshi Courts" in Aisha K. Gill and Sundari Anitha (eds.) *Forced Marriage. Introducing a Social Justice and Human Rights Perspective* (London: Zed Books, 2011) 221–240.

Human Rights Watch, "*Divorced from Justice: Women's Unequal Access to Divorce in Egypt.*" HRW, 2004.

Human Rights Watch, "'How Come You Allow Little Girls to Get Married?' Child Marriage in Yemen." HRW, 2011.

Human Rights Watch, "Unequal and Unprotected. Women's Rights Under Lebanese Personal Status Law." HRW, 2015.

Ivanova, Svetlana, "The Divorce Between Zubaida Hataun and Esseid Osman Aga: Women in the Eighteenth-Century Shari'a Court of Rumelia" in Amira Sonbol (ed.) *Women, the Family and Divorce Laws in Islamic History* (Syracuse: Syracuse University Press, 1996) 1126–1140.

Ivanova, Svetlana, Shamil, Jeppie, Moosa, Ebrahim, and Roberts, Richard, "Muslim Family Law in Sub-Saharan Africa. Colonial Legacies and Post-Colonial Challenges" in Shamil Jeppie, Ebrahim Moosa, and Richard Roberts (eds.) *Muslim Family Law in Sub-Saharan Africa: Colonial Legacies and Post-Colonial Challenges* (Amsterdam: Amsterdam University Press, 2010) 305–330. And "Introduction," 13–60.

Jeppie, Shamil, Moosa, Ebrahim, and Roberts, Richard, *Muslim Family Law in Sub-Saharan Africa: Colonial Legacies and Post-Colonial Challenges* (Amsterdam: Amsterdam University Press, 2010).

Johansen, Baber, "The Constitution and the Principles of Islamic Normativity Against the Rules of Fiqh" in Muhammad Khalid Masud, Rudolph Peters, and David Powers (eds.) *Dispensing Justice in Islam. Qadis and their Judgements* (Leiden: Brill, 2012) 169–193.

Jones-Pauly, Christina, "Marriage Contracts of Muslims in the Diaspora. Problems in the Recognition of *Mahr* Contracts in German Law" in Asifa Quraishi and Frank E. Vogel (eds.) *The Islamic Marriage Contract. Case Studies in Islamic Family Law* (Cambridge, MA: Harvard University Press, 2008) 299–330.

Kadivar, Mohsen, "Revisiting Women's Rights in Islam. 'Egalitarian Justice in Lieu of Desserts-based Justice'" in Ziba Mir-Hosseini, Kari Vogt, Lena Larsen, and Christian Moe (eds.) *Gender and Equality in Muslim Family Law. Justice and Ethics in the Islamic Legal Tradition* (London: I.B. Tauris, 2013) 213–234.

Kamaruddin, Zaleha and Abdullah, Raihanah, "Protecting Muslim Women against Abuse of Polygamy in Malaysia: Legal Perspective." *Hawwa* 6, no. 2 (2008): 176–201.

Kapur, Ratna, "Unveiling Equality: Disciplining the 'Other' Woman Through Human Rights Discourse" in Anver M. Emon, Mark S. Ellis, and Benjamin Glahn (eds.) *Islamic Law and International Human Rights Law. Searching for Common Ground?* (Oxford: Oxford University Press, 2012) 265–290.

Khadduri, Majid, "Marriage in Islamic Law: The Modernist Viewpoints." *American Journal of Comparative Law* 26 (1978): 213–218.

Khan, Fareeha, "Tafwid al-Talaq: Transferring the Right to Divorce to the Wife." *Muslim World* 99, no. 3 (2009): 502–520.

'Kola, Abdul-Fatah Makinde, "Women and Divorce: The Position of the Shari'ah." *Islamic Quarterly* 54, no. 3 (2010): 249–260.

Lamrabet, Asma, "An Egalitarian Reading of the Concepts of *Khilafah, Wilayah* and *Qiwamah*" in Ziba Mir-Hosseini, Mulki Al-Sharmani, and Jana Rumminger (eds.) *Men in Charge? Rethinking Authority in Muslim Legal Tradition* (London: Oneworld, 2015) 65–87.

Largueche, Dalenda, "Monogamy in Islam: The Case of a Tunisian Marriage Contract." Institute of Advanced Studies, School of Social Science Occasional Papers, 39 (September 2010) available at: http://www.sss.ias.edu/files/papers/paper39.pdf.

Larsen, Lena, "'Men are the Protectors and Maintainers of Women...' Three Fatwas on Spousal Roles and Rights" in Ziba Mir-Hosseini, Mulki Al-Sharmani, and Jana Rumminger (eds.) *Men in Charge? Rethinking Authority in Muslim Legal Tradition* (London: Oneworld, 2015) 197–218.

Lawyers Collective, Basu, Asmitu, and Kothari, Jayna, "Remedies for Forced Marriage in India" in Sara Hossain and Lynn Welchman (eds.) *Remedies for Forced Marriage: A Handbook for Lawyers* (London: INTERIGHTS, 2014) (available at http://www.interights.org/forced-marriage-handbook/index.html).
Layish, Aharon, *Women and Islamic Law in a Non-Muslim State. A Study Based on Decisions of the Shari'a Courts in Israel* (New York: John Wiley and Sons, Jerusalem: Israel Universities Press, 1975).
Layish, Aharon, *Legal Documents on Libyan Tribal Society in Process of Sedentarization (Part I: Documents in Arabic)* (Wiesbadan: Harrassowitz, 1998).
Layish, Aharon, *Shari'a and Custom in Libyan Tribal Society. An Annotated Translation of Decisions from the Shari'a Courts of Adjabiya and Kufra* (Leiden, Boston: Brill, 2005).
Lazreg, Marnia, *The Eloquence of Silence: Algerian Women in Question* (New York: Routledge, 1994).
Lindbekk, Monika, "The Enforcement of Personal Status Law by Egyptian Courts" in Elisa Giunchi (ed.) *Adjudicating Family Law in Muslim Courts* (Abingdon: Routledge, 2014) 87–105.
Liversage, Anika, "Muslim Divorces in Denmark—Findings from an Empirical Investigation" in Rubya Mehdi, Werner Menski, and Jorgen S. Nielsen (eds.) *Interpreting Divorce Laws in Islam* (Copenhagen: DJOF Publishing, 2012) 179–201.
Longinotto, Kim, and Mir-Hosseini, Ziba, *Divorce Iranian-Style* (New York: Women Make Movies, 1998).
Maclean, Mavis, and Eekelaar, John, *Managing Family Justice in Diverse Societies* (Oxford and Portland, Oregon: Hart Publishing, 2013).
Mahmood, Tahir, *Statutes of Personal Law in Islamic Countries. History, Texts and Analysis* (Delhi: ALR, 1987, 1995).
Mahmood, Tahir, *Family Law Reform in the Muslim World* (Delhi: Indian Law Institute, 1972).
Mallat, Chibli, and Connors, Jane, eds., *Islamic Family Law* (London: Graham and Trotman, 1990).
Maktabi, Rania, "Female Citizenship in the Middle East: Comparing Family Law Reform in Morocco, Syria and Lebanon." *Middle East Law and Governance* 5 (2013): 1–28.
Mashhour, Amira, "Islamic Law and Gender Equality. Could there be a Common Ground? A Study of Divorce and Polygamy in Sharia Law and Contemporary Legislation in Tunisia and Egypt." *Human Rights Quarterly* 27, no. 2 (2005): 562–596.
Masud, Khalid, "Apostasy and Judicial Separation" in Muhammad Khalid Masud, Brinkley Messick, and David Powers (eds.) *Islamic Legal Interpretation. Muftis and their Fatwas* (Cambridge, MA: Harvard University Press, 1996).
Masud, Khalid, "Gender Equality and the Doctrine of *Wilaya*" in Mir-Hosseini et al., (eds.) *Gender and Equality in Muslim Family Law. Justice and Ethics in the Islamic Legal Tradition* (London: I.B. Tauris, 2013) 127–152.
Masud, Muhammad Khalid, Messick, Brinkey, and Powers, David S., eds., *Islamic Legal Interpretation. Muftis and their Fatwas* (Cambridge, MA: Harvard University Press, 1996). And: "Muftis, Fatwas and Islamic Legal Interpretation."
Masud, Muhammad Khalid, Peters, Rudolph, and Powers, David, eds., *Dispensing Justice in Islam. Qadis and their Judgements* (Leiden: Brill, 2006, 2012).
Mayer, Ann Elizabeth, "Reform of Personal Status Laws in North Africa. A Problem of Islamic or Mediterranean Laws?" *Middle East Journal* 49, no. 3 (1995): 432–446.

Mehdi, Rubya, Menski, Werner, and Nielsen, Jorgen S., eds., *Interpreting Divorce Laws in Islam* (Copenhagen: DJOF Publishing, 2012).

Messick, Brinkley, *The Calligraphic State. Textual Domination and History in a Muslim Society* (Berkeley: University of California Press, 1992).

Messick, Brinkley, "Interpreting Tears: A Marriage Case from Islamic Yemen" in Asifa Quraishi and Frank E. Vogel (eds.) *The Islamic Marriage Contract. Case Studies in Islamic Family Law* (Cambridge, MA: Harvard University Press, 2008) 156–179.

Mir-Hosseini, Ziba, *Marriage on Trial. A Study of Islamic Family Law* (London: I.B. Tauris, 1993).

Mir-Hosseini, Ziba, "The Construction of Gender in Islamic Legal Thought: Strategies for Reform." *Hawwa: Journal of Women in the Middle East and the Islamic World* 1, no. 1 (2003): 1–28.

Mir-Hosseini, Ziba, "A Woman's Right to Terminate the Marriage Contract: The Case of Iran" in Asifa Quraishi and Frank E. Vogel (eds.) *The Islamic Marriage Contract. Case Studies in Islamic Family Law* (Cambridge, MA: Harvard University Press, 2008) 215–230.

Mir-Hosseini, Ziba, "How the Door of Ijtihad was Opened and Closed: A Comparative Analysis of Recent Family Law Reform in Iran and Morocco." *Washington & Lee Law Review* 64, no. 4 (Fall 2007): 1499–1511.

Mir-Hosseini, Ziba, "Women in Search of Common Ground: Between Islamic and International Human Rights Law" in Anver M. Emon, Mark S. Ellis, and Benjamin Glahn (eds.) *Islamic Law and International Human Rights Law. Searching for Common Ground?* (Oxford: Oxford University Press, 2012) 291–308.

Mir-Hosseini, Ziba, "Muslim Legal Tradition and the Challenge of Gender Equality" in Ziba Mir-Hosseini, Mulki Al-Sharmani, and Jana Rumminger (eds.) *Men in Charge? Rethinking Authority in Muslim Legal Tradition* (London: Oneworld, 2015) 13–43.

Mir-Hosseini, Ziba, Al-Sharmani, Mulki, and Rumminger, Jana, eds., *Men in Charge? Rethinking Authority in Muslim Legal Tradition* (London: Oneworld, 2015). And "Introduction," 1–12.

Mir-Hosseini, Ziba, Vogt, Kari, Larsen, Lena, and Moe, Christian, eds. *Gender and Equality in Muslim Family Law. Justice and Ethics in the Islamic Legal Tradition* (London: I.B. Tauris, 2013). And "Introduction: Muslim Family Law and the Question of Equality," 1–6.

Mitchell, Ruth, "Family Law in Algeria Before and After the 1404/1984 Family Code" in Robert Gleave (ed.) *Islamic Law, Theory and Practice* (London: I.B. Tauris, 1997) 194–204.

Modirzadeh, Naz K. "Taking Islamic Law Seriously: INGOs and the Battle for Muslim Hearts and Minds." *Harvard Human Rights Journal* 19 (2006): 193–235.

Moors, Annelies, *Women, Property and Islam. Palestinian Experiences 1920–1990* (Cambridge: Cambridge University Press, 1995).

Moors, Annelies, "Debating Islamic Family Law: Legal Texts and Social Practices" in M. Meriwether and Judith Tucker (eds.) *A Social History of Women and Gender in the Modern Middle East* (Boulder: Westview, 1999) 141–175.

Moors, Annelies, "Public Debates on Islamic Family Law Reform: Participants, Positions, and Styles of Argument in the 1990s." *Islamic Law and Society* 10, no. 1 (2003): 1–11.

Moors, Annelies, "Registering a Token Dower: the Multiple Meanings of a Legal Practice" in Baudouin Dupret, Barbara Drieskens, and Annelies Moors (eds.) *Narratives of Truth in Islamic Law* (London and New York: I.B. Tauris, 2008) 85–104.

Moors, Annelies, "Unregistered Islamic Marriages: Anxieties about Sexuality and Islam in the Netherlands" in Maurits S. Berger (ed.) *Applying Shari'a in the West. Facts, Fears and the Future of Islamic Rules on Family Relations in the West* (Leiden: Leiden University Press, 2013) 141–164.

Motzki, Harald, "Child Marriage in Seventeenth-Century Palestine" in Muhammad Khalid Masud, Brinkley Messick, and David Powers (eds.) *Islamic Legal Interpretation. Muftis and their Fatwas* (Cambridge, MA: Harvard University Press, 1996) 129–149.

Musa, Muhammad Yusuf, "The Liberty of the Individual in Contracts and Conditions according to Islamic Law." *Islamic Quarterly* 2, no. 4 (1955): 252–263.

Muslim Marriage Contract (2008) available at http://www.muslimparliament.org.uk/Documentation/Muslim%20Marriage%20Contract.pdf.

Najjar, F., "Egypt's Law of Persona Status." *Arab Studies Quarterly* 10, no. 3 (1988): 319–345.

Nasir, Jamal, *The Islamic Law of Personal Status* (1st and 2nd edns. London: Graham and Trotman, 1986, 1990). (3rd edn. The Hague, London: Kluwer Law International 2001 (reprinted Leiden: Brill, 2009)).

Nasir, Jamal, *The Status of Women under Islamic law and Modern Legislation* (1st and 2nd edns. London: Graham and Trotman 1990, 1994). (3rd edn. Leiden and Boston: Brill, 2009).

Nazneen, Sohela, "Men Aboard? Movement for a Uniform Family Code in Bangladesh" in Mulki Al-Sharmani (ed.) *Feminist Activism, Women's Rights, and Legal Reform* (London: Zed Books, 2013) 101–124.

Nielsen, Jorgen S., "An Early Discussion on Islamic Family Law in the English Jurisdiction" in Maurits S. Berger (ed.) *Applying Shari'a in the West. Facts, Fears and the Future of Islamic Rules on Family Relations in the West* (Leiden: Leiden University Press, 2013) 79–96.

Noor, Zanariah and Lee, Nazirah, "The Conflict among Hadrami Arab Community in Malaysia Regarding the Isues of Kafa'a in Muslim Marriage." *Journal of Women of the Middle East and the Islamic World* 11 (2013): 252–274.

Osanloo, Arzoo, "From Status to Rights: The Shifting Dimensions of Women's Activism in Iranian Family Law Reform" in Mulki Al-Sharmani (ed.) *Feminist Activism, Women's Rights, and Legal Reform* (London: Zed Books, 2013) 125–150.

Pearl, David and Menski, Werner, *Muslim Family Law* (3rd edn. London: Sweet & Maxwell, 1998).

Peirce, Leslie, *Morality Tales: Law and Gender in the Ottoman Court of Aintab* (Berkeley, CA: University of California Press, 2003).

Poulter, Sebastian, "The Claim to a Separate Islamic System of Personal Law for British Muslims" in Chibli Mallat and Jane Connors (eds.) *Islamic Family Law* (London: Graham and Trotman, 1990) 147–166.

Powers, David, "Four Cases Relating to Women and Divorce in al-Andalus and the Maghrib, 1100–1500" in Muhammad Khalid Masud, Rudolph Peters, and David Powers (eds.) *Dispensing Justice in Islam. Qadis and their Judgements* (Leiden: Brill, 2012) 383–409.

Quraishi, Asifa, and Vogel, Frank, eds. *The Islamic Marriage Contract. Case Studies in Islamic Family Law* (Cambridge, MA: Harvard University Press, 2008).

Quraishi, Asifa, and Syeed-Miller, Najeeba, "No Altars: a Survey of Islamic Family Law in the United States" in Lynn Welchman (ed.) *Women's Rights and Islamic Family Law. Perspectives on Reform* (London and New York: Zed Books, 2004) 177–229.

Rapoport, Yossef, "Matrimonial Gifts in Early Islamic Egypt." *Islamic Law and Society* 7, no. 1 (2000): 1–36.

Rapoport, Yossef, *Marriage, Money and Divorce in Medieval Islamic Society* (Cambridge: Cambridge University Press, 2005).

Razack, Sherene, *Casting Out: The Eviction of Muslims from Western Law and Politics* (Toronto: University of Toronto Press, 2008).

Rehman, Javaid, "The Sharia, Islamic Family Laws and International Human Rights Law: Examining the Theory and Practice of Polygamy and Talaq." *International Journal of Law, Policy and the Family* 21 (2007): 108–127.

di Ricco, Massimo, "Reclaiming Changes within the Community Public sphere: Druze Women's Activism, Personal Status Law and the Quest for Lebanese Multiple Citizenship" in Maaike Voorhoeve (ed.) *Family Law in Islam. Divorce, Marriage and Women in the Muslim World* (London and New York: I.B. Tauris, 2012) 31–49.

Rosen, Lawrence, *The Anthropology of Justice: Law as Culture in Islamic Society* (Cambridge: Cambridge University Press, 1989).

Rosen, Lawrence, "*The Justice of Islam: Comparative Perspectives on Islamic Law and Society*." In *Oxford Socio-Legal Studies* (Oxford: Oxford University Press, 2000).

Rosen, Lawrence, "Revision and Reality in the Family Law of Morocco" in Rubya Mehdi, Hanne Petersen, Erik Reenberg Sand, and Gordon R. Woodman (eds.) *Law and Religion in Multicultural Societies* (Copenhagen: DJOF Publishing, 2008) 131–144.

Rutten, Susan, "Applying Shari'a to Family Law Issues in the Netherlands" in Maurits S. Berger (ed.) *Applying Shari'a in the West. Facts, Fears and the Future of Islamic Rules on Family Relations in the West* (Leiden: Leiden University Press, 2013) 96–123.

Sadiqi, Fatima "The Central Role of the Family Law in the Moroccan Feminist Movement." *British Journal of Middle Eastern Studies* 35, no. 3 (2008): 325–337.

Sadiqi, Fatima, "The Potential Within: Adjudications on Shiqaq (Discord) Divorce by Moroccan Judges" in Elisa Giunchi (ed.) *Adjudicating Family Law in Muslim Courts* (Abingdon: Routledge, 2014) 121–135.

Said, Edward, *Orientalism* (London: Routledge & Kegan Paul Ltd, 1978).

Salime, Zakia, "Revisiting the Debate on Family Law in Morocco. Contexts, Actors and Discourses" in Kenneth M. Cuno and Manisha Desai (eds.) *Family, Gender and Law in a Globalizing Middle East and South Asia* (Syracuse: Syracuse University Press, 2009) 145–162.

Schacht, Joseph, "*An Introduction to Islamic Law.*" In *Clarendon Law Series* (Oxford: Oxford University Press, 1964).

Sevgin, Yuksel, *Human Rights under State-Enforced Religious Family Laws in Israel, Egypt and India* (Cambridge: Cambridge University Press, 2013).

Semerdjian, Elyse, *Off the Straight path. Illicit Sex, Law and Community in Ottoman Aleppo* (Syracuse: Syracuse University Press, 2008).

Shah, Nik Noriani Nik Badli, "Legislative Provisions and Judicial Mechanisms for the Enforcement and Termination of the Islamic Marriage Contract in Malaysia" in Asifa Quraishi and Frank E. Vogel (eds.) *The Islamic Marriage Contract. Case Studies in Islamic Family Law* (Cambridge, MA: Harvard University Press, 2008) 183–199.

Shah, Prakash, "Judging Muslims" in Robin Griffiths-Jones (ed.) *Islam and English Law. Rights, Responsibilities and the Place of Shari'a* (Cambridge: Cambridge University Press, 2013) 214–256.

Shah, Prakash A., "Attitues to Polygamy in English Law." *International and Comparative Law Quarterly* 52 (2003): 369–400.

Shaham, Ron, "Custom, Islamic Law and Statutory Legislation: Marriage Registration and Minimum Age at Marriage in the Egyptian Shari'a Courts." *Islamic Law and Society* 2, no. 3 (1995): 258–281.

Sharafeldin, Marwa, "Egyptian Women's rights NGOs: Personal Status Law Reform between Islamic and International Human Rights Law" in Ziba Mir-Hosseini, Kari Vogt, Lena Larsen, and Christian Moe (eds.) *Gender and Equality in Muslim Family Law. Justice and Ethics in the Islamic Legal Tradition* (London: I.B. Tauris, 2013) 57–80.

Sharafeldin, Marwa, "Islamic Law Meets Human Rights: Reformulating *Qiwamah* and *Wilayah* for Personal Status Law Advocacy in Egypt" in Ziba Mir-Hosseini, Mulki Al-Sharmani, and Jana Rumminger (eds.) *Men in Charge? Rethinking Authority in Muslim Legal Tradition* (London: Oneworld, 2015) 163–196.

Shehada, Nahda, "House of Obedience: Social Norms, Individual Agency and Historical Contingency." *Journal of Middle East Women's Studies* 5, no. 1 (2009): 24–49.

Shehada, Nahda, "Debating Islamic Family Law in Palestine: Citizenship, Gender and 'Islamic' Idioms" in Mulki Al-Sharmani (ed.) *Feminist Activism, Women's Rights, and Legal Reform* (London: Zed Books, 2013) 23–47.

Siddiqi, Dina, "Crime and Punishment: Laws of Seduction, Consent, and Rape in Bangladesh." *Social Difference-Online* 1 (2011): 46–53.

Siddiqi, Dina, "Of Consent and Contradiction: Forced Marriages in Bangladesh" in Lynn Welchman and Sara Hossain (eds.) *"Honour." Crimes, Paradigms and Violence Against Women* (London: Zed Books, 2005) 283–307.

Siddiqui, Mona, "Mahr: Legal Obligation or Rightful Demand?" *Journal of Islamic Studies* 1 (1995): 14–24.

Siddiqui, Mona, "Law and the Desire for Social Control: An Insight into the Hanafi Concept of Kafa'a with Reference to the Fatawa 'Alamgiri (*1664–1672*)" in Mai Yamani (ed.) *Feminism and Islam* (London: Ithaca, 1996) 49–68.

Siddiqui, Hannana, "Violence Against Women: Not in My Name." *Agenda: Race Equality in the Spotlight, Raceon the Agenda* 35 (2011): 22–24.

Siraj, Mehuen, "The Control of Polygamy." *Malaya Law Review* 6 (1964): 387–405.

Sonbol, Amira El Azhary, "Adults and Minors in Ottoman Shari'a Courts and Modern Law" in Amira Sonbol (ed.) *Women, the Family and Divorce Laws in Islamic History* (Syracuse: Syracuse University Press, 1996) 236–256.

Sonbol, Amira El Azhary, "Ta'a and Modern Legal Reform: A Re-reading," *Islam and Christian-Muslim Relations* 9, no. 3 (1998): 285–294.

Sonbol, Amira El Azhary, "A History of Marriage Contracts in Egypt" in Asifa Quraishi and Frank E. Vogel (eds.) *The Islamic Marriage Contract. Case Studies in Islamic Family Law* (Cambridge, MA: Harvard University Press, 2008) 87–122.

Sonneveld, Nadia, *Khul Divorce in Egypt. Public Debates, Judicial Practices, and Everyday Life* (Cairo: American University in Cairo Press, 2012a).

Sonneveld, Nadia, "Rethinking the Difference between Formal and Informal Marriages in Egypt" in Maaike Voorhoeve (ed.) *Family Law in Islam. Divorce, Marriage and Women in the Muslim World* (London and New York: I B. Tauris, 2012b) 77–107.

Stiles, Erin, "Broken Edda and Marital Mistakes: Two Recent Disputes from an Islamic Court in Zanzibar" in Khalid Masud, Rudolph Peters, and David Powers (eds.) *Dispensing Justice in Islam. Qadis and their Judgements* (Leiden: Brill, 2012) 95–115.

Tucker, Judith E., *In the House of the Law. Gender and Islamic Law in Ottoman Syria and Palestine* (Berkeley: University of California Press, 1998).

Tucker, Judith E., *Women, Family and Gender in Islamic Law* (Cambridge: Cambridge University Press, 2008).

Tucker, Judith E., "Questions of Consent: Contracting a Marriage in Ottoman Syria and Palestine" in Asifa Quraishi and Frank Vogel (eds.) *The Islamic Marriage Contract. Case Studies in Islamic Family Law* (Cambridge, MA: Harvard University Press, 2008) 123–135.

Turner, Bryan S., and Richardson, James T., "America: Islam and the Problems of Liberal democracy" in Maurits S. Berger (ed.) *Applying Shari'a in the West. Facts, Fears and the Future of Islamic Rules on Family Relations in the West* (Leiden: Leiden University Press, 2013) 47–64.

Vatuk, Sylvia, "The Application of Muslim Personal Law in India. A System of Legal Pluralism in Action" in Elisa Giunchi (ed.) *Adjudicating Family Law in Muslim Courts* (Abingdon: Routledge, 2014) 48–69.

Voorhoeve, Maaike, ed., *Family Law in Islam. Divorce, Marriage and Women in the Muslim World* (London and New York: I.B. Tauris, 2012). And "Judicial Discretion in Tunisian Personal Status Law," 199–229.

Voorhoeve, Maaike, *Gender and Divorce Law in North Africa. Sharia, Custom and the Personal Status Code in Tunisia* (London and New York: I.B. Tauris, 2014).

Wadud, Amina, "The Ethics of *Tawhid* over the Ethics of *Qiwamah*" in Ziba Mir-Hosseini, Mulki Al-Sharmani, and Jana Rumminger (eds.) *Men in Charge? Rethinking Authority in Muslim Legal Tradition* (London: Oneworld, 2015) 256–274.

Warraich, Sohail, "Remedies for Forced Marriage in Pakistan" in Sara Hossain and Lynn Welchman (eds.) *Remedies for Forced Marriage: A Handbook for Lawyers* (London: INTERIGHTS 2014) (available at http://www.interights.org/forced-marriage-handbook/index.html).

Weiss, Anita M., "Straddling CEDAW and the MMA. Conflicting Visions of Women's Rights in Contemporary Pakistan" in Kenneth M. Cuno and Manisha Desai (eds.) *Family, Gender and Law in a Globalizing Middle East and South Asia* (Syracuse: Syracuse University Press, 2009) 163–183.

Welchman, Lynn, *Beyond the Code. Muslim Family Law and the Shar'i Judiciary in the Palestinian West Bank* (The Hague: Kluwer Law International, 2000).

Welchman, Lynn, ed., *Women's Rights and Islamic Family Law. Perspectives on Reform* (London and New York: Zed Books, 2004). And "Introduction," 1–14.

Welchman, Lynn, *Women and Muslim Family Laws in Arab States. A Comparative Overview of Textual Development and Advocacy* (Amsterdam: Amsterdam University Press, 2007).

Welchman, Lynn, "Family, Gender and Law in Jordan and Palestine" in Kenneth M. Cuno and Manisha Desai (eds.) *Family, Gender and Law in a Globalizing Middle East and South Asia* (Syracuse: Syracuse University Press, 2009) 126–144.

Welchman, Lynn, "A Husband's Authority: Emerging Formulations in Muslim Family Laws." *International Journal of Law, Policy and the Family* 25, no. 1 (2011): 1–23.

Welchman, Lynn, "*Qiwamah* and *Wilayah* as Legal Postulates in Muslim Family Laws" in Ziba Mir-Hosseini, Mulki Al-Sharmani, and Jana Rumminger (eds.) *Men in Charge? Rethinking Authority in Muslim Legal Tradition* (London: Oneworld, 2015) 132–162.

Williams, Rowan, "Archbishop's lecture—Civil and Religious Law in England: a religious perspective." http://rowanwilliams.archbishopofcanterbury.org/articles.php/1137/archbishops-lecture-civil-and-religious-law-in-england-a-religious-perspective, 2008.

Williams, Rowan, "Civil and Religious Law in England: A Religious Perspective" in Robin Griffiths-Jones (ed.) *Islam and English Law. Rights, Responsibilities and the Place of Shari'a* (Cambridge: Cambridge University Press, 2013) 20–33.

Wing, Adrien Catherine, "Custom, Religion and Rights: the Future Legal Status of Palestinian Women." *Harvard International Law Journal* 35 (1994): 149–200.

Women Living Under Muslim Laws, *Knowing Our Rights. Women, family, laws and customs in the Muslim World* (London: WLUML 1st edn. 2003, 3rd edn. 2006).

Women Living Under Muslim Laws, *Shah Bano and the Muslim Women Act, A Decade On.* (ed. Lucy Carroll) (Grabels Cédex: WLUML, 1998).

Women's Research and Action Group, "Marriage and the Politics of Social Change in India's Muslim Communities" in Homa Hoodfar (ed.) *Shifting Boundaries in Marriage and Divorce in Muslim Communities* (WLUML, 1996 (np)) 168–187.

Wurth, Anna, "Stalled Reform: Family Law in Post-Unification Yemen." *Islamic Law and Society* 2, no. 3 (2003): 12–33.

Wynn, Lisa, "Marriage Contracts and Women's Rights in Saudi Arabia" in Homa Hoodfar (ed.) *Shifting Boundaries in Marriage and Divorce in Muslim Communities* (WLUML, 1996) 106–120.

Wynn, Lisa, "Marriage Contracts and Women's Rights in Saudi Arabia: Mahr, Shurut, and Knowledge Distribution" in Asifa Quraishi and Frank E. Vogel (eds.) *The Islamic Marriage Contract. Case Studies in Islamic Family Law* (Cambridge, MA: Harvard University Press, 2008) 200–214.

Yamani, Maha, *Polygamy and Law in Contemporary Saudi Arabia* (Reading: Ithaca Press, 2008).

Yassari, Nadjma, "Understanding and Use of Islamic Family Law Rules in German Courts: The Example of the Mahr" in Maurits S. Berger (ed.) *Applying Shari'a in the West. Facts, Fears and the Future of Islamic Rules on Family Relations in the West* (Leiden: Leiden University Press, 2013) 165–187.

Yazbak, Mahmoud, "Minor Marriages and Khiyar al-Bulugh in Ottoman Palestine: A Note on Women's Strategies in a Patriarchal Society." *Islamic Law and Society* 9, no. 3 (2002): 386–409.

Yilmaz, Ihsan, *Muslim Laws, Politics and Society in Modern Nation States. Dynamic Legal Pluralisms in England, Turkey and Pakistan* (Aldershot: Ashgate, 2005).

Ziadeh, Farhat, "Equality (Kafa'ah) in the Muslim Law of Marriage: Problem of Sources." *American Journal of Comparative Law* 6 (1957): 503–517.

Zomeno, Amalia, "The Islamic Marriage Contract in al-Andalus (10th–16th Centuries)" in Asifa Quraishi and Frank E. Vogel (eds.) *The Islamic Marriage Contract. Case Studies in Islamic Family Law* (Cambridge, MA: Harvard University Press, 2008) 136–155.

Zulficar, Mona, "The Islamic Marriage Contract in Egypt" in Asifa Quraishi and Frank E. Vogel (eds.) *The Islamic Marriage Contract. Case Studies in Islamic Family Law* (Cambridge, MA: Harvard University Press, 2008) 231–274.

Index

Please see individual main entries for countries/regions.